PENGUIN BOOKS

TOTAL WAR

Peter Calvocoressi was educated at Eton and Balliol, where he obtained a First in History. He was called to the Bar in 1935, and served in Intelligence during the war. He was seconded to the trial of major war criminals at Nuremberg in 1945–6. Peter Calvocoressi joined the staff of the Royal Institute of International Affairs in 1949, then in 1954 became a director of Chatto & Windus and The Hogarth Press. From 1965 to 1971 he was Reader in International Affairs at Sussex University, and from 1972 to 1976 Editorial Director and, later, Chief Executive of Penguin Books. He has written numerous books, including *The British Experience 1945–75*, published in Penguins in 1979. Peter Calvocoressi is Chairman of Open University Educational Enterprises Ltd.

Guy Wint was born in London in 1910 and educated at Dulwich College, Oriel College, Oxford, and Berlin University. In 1932 he went to China as a secretarial assistant of the League of Nations Technical Mission. From China he went to India and spent some years there studying the working of the Indian Constitution. He spent most of the war years in government service in India, Singapore, America and China, and in 1947 published *The British in Asia*. He then became a journalist and was for ten years a leader-writer for the *Manchester Guardian*.
Guy Wint died in early 1969.

PETER CALVOCORESSI AND GUY WINT

Total War

Causes and Courses of the Second World War

PENGUIN BOOKS

Penguin Books Ltd, Harmondsworth, Middlesex, England
Penguin Books, 625 Madison Avenue, New York, New York 10022, U.S.A.
Penguin Books Australia Ltd, Ringwood, Victoria, Australia
Penguin Books Canada Ltd, 2801 John Street, Markham, Ontario, Canada L3R 1B4
Penguin Books (N.Z.) Ltd, 182–190 Wairau Road, Auckland 10, New Zealand

—

First published in Great Britain by Allen Lane The Penguin Press 1972
First published in the United States of America with the subtitle
The Story of World War II by Pantheon Books 1972
Published in Pelican Books 1974
Reprinted 1979
Published in Penguin Books in the United States of America 1979

—

—

Made and printed in Great Britain by
Hazell Watson & Viney Ltd,
Aylesbury, Bucks
Set in Monotype Times

Contents

The Western Hemisphere

Part I
THE SOURCES OF WAR IN EUROPE

Part II
HITLER'S WARS: 1939–41

Part III
EUROPE UNDER THE NAZIS

Part IV
THE MIDDLE GAME

Part V
THE DEFEAT OF GERMANY: 1942–5

The War in Asia

Part I
ASIAN CONFLICT

Part II
OCEAN CLASH

Part III
THE HIGH TIDE OF WAR

Part IV
THE DEFEAT OF JAPAN

EPILOGUE

List of Illustrations

II HOME FRONTS

List of Maps

Acknowledgements

The author and publishers wish to thank the following for permission to reproduce photographs:

The Associated Press Ltd: 2, 22, 53 · Belgrade Military Museum: 68 · Black Star: 47, 60, 76, 78, 93 · BPC: 29, 30, 31, 39, 52 · Bundesarchiv: 66 · Camera Press: 5, 6, 11, 12, 13, 14, 15, 16, 17, 26, 32, 46, 48, 50, 51, 55, 61, 69, 71, 75, 77, 80, 81, 86, 88, 91, 92, 98 · Central Press Photos Ltd: Frontispiece (1), 21, 45, 64, 65, 82 · Editions Rencontre, Paris: 37 · Fox Photos Ltd: 3 · George Rodger: 59 · Imperial War Museum: 9, 10, 18, 19, 23, 24, 28, 34, 35, 38, 43, 44, 58, 63, 70, 79, 85 · John Hillelson Agency Ltd (Robert Capa): 56 · Keystone Press Agency Ltd: 72, 73, 74, 83, 90, 95, 96, 97 · Library of Congress, Washington: 84 · National Maritime Museum: 40 · Navy Department, National Archives, USA: 27 · Novosti Press: 4, 7, 8, 20, 33, 49, 54, 86, 89, 94 · Official US Air Force photo: 41 · Paul Pepper Ltd: 25 · Radio Times Hulton Picture Library: 57, 67 · Ullstein GmbH, Berlin: 29, 36, 62 · United Press International Ltd: 42

Acknowledgement is due to Martin Gilbert, of Merton College, Oxford, to Weidenfeld & Nicolson Limited, and to the Macmillan Company for their kind permission to use the maps on pages 102, 108, 120, 156, 167, 172, 181, 219, 223, 225, 233, 235, 339, 445, 448, 460, 473, 480, 522, 739, 869, and 884, which have been adapted from the following: *American History Atlas,* edited by Martin Gilbert, cartography by Peter Kingsland, copyright © Martin Gilbert, 1969; *Jewish History Atlas,* edited by Martin Gilbert, cartography by Peter Kingsland, copyright © Martin Gilbert, 1969; *Recent History Atlas,* edited by Martin Gilbert, cartography by John Flower, copyright © Martin Gilbert, 1966; *Russian History Atlas,* edited by Martin Gilbert, cartography by Arthur Banks, copyright © Martin Gilbert, 1972.

Foreword

THE idea for this book was Guy Wint's. He died before it was finished and the loss has been inestimable. He was a man who knew much, thought carefully, was insatiably curious and revelled in the unexpected. Rarely did I spend an hour in his company without being presented with a comparison or parallel which I would never have thought of for myself. History gave him immense satisfaction. He loved its grand sweeps and the business of disentangling these from the dense detritus of the past. History also provided him with entertainment, of a tolerant rather than a cynical kind, for with a strong belief in the effectiveness of the individual in public affairs – which he typically saw as drama – he combined an indulgent affection for the occasional human absurdities which the record bleakly reveals. In his writings therefore, and even more so in conversation which he specially enjoyed until his first stroke made it painful for him, he was a scholar with a difference which his friends recognized though might find hard to define.

One day he told me that he had come across a young person who was not only baffled by the role of Finland in the Second World War but could not make out which side Italy had been on. This conversation showed him that the war had become part of the past for our younger contemporaries and that it might be a good idea to write a book showing why it happened and how it went. We knew from the start that we did not want to write a military or campaign history and were not qualified to do so, but apart from that negative consideration we were at first uncertain about what the book ought to contain. We wished to give a substantial amount of space to the sources of war but it was more difficult to decide which aspects of the war in progress to treat at length. We felt that it was essential to tell enough about the actual fighting to enable the reader to know who was winning at any particular point, but we were not so much concerned to give a round-by-round account of the fighting as to show why particular campaigns were fought, when and where they were fought, and also what happened behind what used to be called 'the lines'.

The arrangement of the book was also a problem, about which a word here is in place. We began by planning a chronological treatment in which a section about one part of the world would be followed by a section covering much the same period in another part of the world, after which the story narrated in the first part would be taken up where it had been broken off, and so on several times over until we got to 1945. We agreed that I should be primarily responsible for the European, Atlantic, African and Middle-Eastern theatres, while he should take as his prime task the whole of the rest of Asia and the Pacific. But we soon abandoned the plan to march in alternating tandem from the beginning to the end of our story – for two main reasons. First, we concluded that it would be horribly confusing for our readers to have to do so much switching from one half of the world to the other; and second, we came to believe that the wars in the two hemispheres were much less closely interdependent than we had at first supposed. They were of course contemporaneous or nearly so, and they raised questions of priorities – specially on the Anglo-American side and specially in relation to the wars at sea – which were sometimes crucial. But in their origins and to a large extent even in their courses Hitler's wars on the one hand and the Sino–Japanese and American–Japanese wars on the other constitute distinctly intelligible stories which can, we thought, more conveniently be told in sequence (with the necessary cross-commenting) than in parallel.

When Guy Wint died he had covered his allotted sphere. (The whole of his work on this book was done between his first and second strokes.) But the latter sections of what he wrote were still on his death in a rudimentary stage. We have done our best to follow up all the traces of the material he has used, but if something has not been acknowledged we should like to hear. It was his habit to write and re-write many times over; his first drafts were always many times the length intended for their final form, which was achieved only after a series of refining revisions. Consequently there remained much work to be done, and this work was undertaken by Freda Wint. Besides her natural interest and talents Mrs Wint had the advantage of having discussed much of the book with her husband before his death. Nevertheless she has had to assume a significant responsibility as well as setting aside very many hours of labour in order to bring Guy Wint's last drafts into publishable shape. I myself and the readers of this book are greatly beholden to her. She was greatly helped by Dr Ian Nish who most kindly read all that Guy Wint had written and was generous with expert comment and advice.

For myself I have a special debt to record. I had always supposed that I could not work with a research assistant but only by myself. Yet my other commitments forced me to try the experiment. It has been from my point of view a triumphant success and I very happily acknowledge the great debt which I owe to Rosemary Righter for the work she did for me and the way she did it. I now believe that being a research assistant is more difficult than having one. Without Mrs Righter's stimulating help I should not only have taken twice as long over my task but would also have missed a number of telling points.

My wife read every word of various drafts of every chapter that I wrote and has very greatly helped me to clarify my mind and my text. In illustrating this text with his excellent maps Arthur Banks has wrought with an enthusiasm and a skill which are as gratifying to me as they must be helpful to the reader.

Finally, I wish – and I know too that Guy Wint shared this wish – to thank Dieter Pevsner and André Schiffrin, publishers and friends, for the interest they have shown in our work as it went along and notably for the extensive oral and written criticisms which they have made at various times. I happen to know that publishers have busy lives and so I appreciate all the more warmly the amount of time and thought that these two set aside for our benefit.

PETER CALVOCORESSI

The Western Hemisphere

Part I

THE SOURCES OF WAR IN EUROPE

THERE are two extreme views about the European origins of the Second World War. One is that it was all Hitler's fault. The other is that it was a war in which Hitler, along with a lot of other people, and for much the same reasons, got involved. Both views stand condemned by their very simplicity. This book supports neither but it has to start somewhere, and it starts with Hitler and the Nazis.

To begin with Hitler is not to endorse the view that the war was Hitler's war. No great upheaval can plausibly be ascribed to a single individual, however extraordinary. The war that occurred in 1739 is called after a certain Captain Jenkins and his ear, but it was not much of a war and Captain Jenkins may, if a little spuriously, have it. But the conflict of 1939–45 was a World War and not one man's war. It embraced a number of originally distinct wars which merged. Some of these were, in a formal sense, started by Hitler, but the causes of this six-year compendium of fighting in Europe have to be examined in terms of much more than Hitler, or the Nazis, or Germany, or even of Europe. A World War has necessarily complex origins.

But it does not follow that Hitler was a man or a politician like any other. He was not. On the contrary, he was decidedly outside the normal run of men and of statesmen, and the things that made him different contributed to war. He saw human affairs as a conflict; he portrayed this conflict as a moral one in which he had a role which justified every means; yet morally speaking he was, by any ordinary standards, himself a criminal who used murder openly and massively. Such beliefs and such behaviour cannot fail, if allied with power, to promote war.

Hitler, however, was not the demiurge. He could not create or even destroy in a vacuum, and there were, without him, the makings of war in the world and the makings of the sort of wars which were begun like a spreading fire in the years 1939–41.

To see how Hitler and the Nazis came to power in Germany in 1933 it is necessary to understand not only Hitler and the Nazis but also Germany in 1933, and in order to understand the Germany of that time it is necessary to ask questions about the Europe of which Germany had been geographically and culturally a part centuries before Hitler was heard of.

CHAPTER 1

The Background

Adolf Hitler was born in April 1889. In January 1933, at the age of forty-three, he became Chancellor of the German Reich. Six years later Germany invaded Poland and so began Europe's part of the Second World War. These are three facts among countless others which belong to the history of the sources of the Second World War. They are cardinal facts. Without them things would have been very different. But by themselves they explain nothing. The war was not the work of one man or one nation but a phenomenon which punctuated the course of Europe's history and the whole world's.

Adolf Hitler's father Alois was the illegitimate son of Maria Schicklgruber. Alois took the name of Hiedler or Hitler after Maria's husband, who may have fathered him before the marriage. Alois was a reasonably well-off minor official, inclined to be self-indulgent and quick tempered, something of a womanizer. He died in 1903 at the age of sixty-six after having married three times. His third wife bore him six children, of whom only Adolf and a sister Paula survived beyond childhood. Adolf did poorly at school and was difficult at home. From elementary school he went to a *Realschule* and not to a *Gymnasium* which was the goal of the cleverer children or of those with the more ambitious parents. He left school at sixteen and stayed at home, spending his time drawing and making plans for buildings. He dreamed of being asked to design a new municipal theatre for the city of Linz. When he was eighteen he went to Vienna with a competence which was supplemented shortly afterwards when his mother died and he got a small pension. He also sponged on a penurious aunt. He wanted to go to the Academy of Fine Arts but failed the examination. He lived at first quite well but as his money gave out he became not only idle but increasingly lonely, shabby and bitter. He earned a little money by copying pictures; a friend hawked them for him; he was a pavement artist without a pavement. He became a middle-class misfit in a lower-class environment. He was humiliated by this decline and also shocked by what he saw. Years later in *Mein Kampf* he referred to the 'economic misery' of the companions he had at this time and to the 'crudeness of their habits and morals and the low level of their cultural development'. He also noted the fear which grips a social group when it sees itself falling down the social scale and becoming classed with the lowest workers. He looked around for someone to blame.

Vienna, in its last years as an imperial city, a polyglot centre dominated by Germans who were nevertheless fearful of losing their dominant position, was overcrowded and short of housing. The poor and destitute congregated in homes and rest-rooms. Hitler was among them. Here he picked up the common grouse that things would be much better if only Jews and foreigners – especially Czechs – were not allowed to get all the jobs. When things were specially bad this grumbling turned to hatred. Some Austrian politicians played on it and Hitler may have learned in Vienna how potent a weapon racial prejudice can be, for the forerunners of the Austrian Nazis were already at work scaring German Gentiles with the prospect of a flood of undesirable aliens who would overwhelm them economically and besmirch the purity of their race. Statistics were invoked to increase repugnance and envy. Between the middle of the nineteenth century and the outbreak of the First World War the Jewish population of the city rose from 2 per cent to nearly 9 per cent, and in Hitler's time Jews gained more than a quarter of all the places in secondary schools and university. Financial or sexual scandals were exaggerated or invented. Hitler himself swallowed the story that the city's prostitutes were run by a Jewish ring, when it is very unlikely that they were run by a ring at all. Hitler's description of Jewry in *Mein Kampf* as the 'bacillus which destroys humankind', a pestilence like the Black Death, was probably formulated during his years in Vienna, and he specifically wrote of Vienna as the 'ancient nursery of German culture' battened on by 'promiscuous swarms of foreigners'.

In 1913 Hitler left Vienna, probably in order to evade military service. He went to Munich but was traced by the Austrian authorities and summoned back to Austria, where, however, he was pronounced unfit to serve. He returned to Munich. His circumstances were still wretched and he lived the life of an urban beachcomber until war broke out and he joined a Bavarian regiment. The army and the war provided him with activity and a social framework; he became a corporal and won the Iron Cross Second Class and – a rarity for an NCO – First Class. He was in hospital after a gas attack when the Germans collapsed on the western front in 1918. He never served on the eastern front.

After the war Hitler returned once more to Munich. Bavaria had ceased to be a kingdom within the German empire and had become a province within a German republic. This change increased rather than diminished the Bavarians' dislike for Prussia and for centralized government. Moreover, after a brief communist phase, initiated and extinguished by violence, authority in Munich passed to right-wing groups which were at odds with the more left-wing government in Berlin. They were also at odds with one another. There were monarchists who wanted to restore the independent Bavaria which had existed before Bismarck's time; separatists with vaguer but similar aspirations; protagonists of a south German union between Catholic Bavaria and Catholic Austria. Hitler, while sharing the general antipathy to the central government in Berlin, wanted neither the restoration of the Bavarian royal house nor union with the Austria which he despised. He was employed in the Press and News Section of the army headquarters in Munich, was appointed a *Bildungsoffizier* (a cultural instructor or ideological education officer) and was detailed to investigate, among other things, a new political party called the German Workers' Party – DAP. He joined the party, became its star platform performer, provided it with a programme and gave it a new name – the National Socialist German Workers' Party, NSDAP. His military superiors were not only happy to see a member of their staff, still not demobilized, engaging openly in politics in this way; later they also put up some money to enable the party to buy a newspaper, the *Völkischer Beobachter*. Hitler was put on his political feet by the army and when he left the army in April 1920 he was the leader of a party which was similar to a number of other parties except that it had a startling future before it. Post-war Munich saw many parties spring up, wilt and die. They appealed to those who were afraid of Bolshevism, afflicted by defeat in war or crippled by inflation, and they offered an escape into a nationalism which dilated on the glories of the German past and the wickedness of other nations with the implication that the glories could be revived and the wicked put down. Their programmes combined this nationalism with a sort of socialism in so far as they offered the little man protection against the communist commissar on the one hand and the capitalist banker on the other.

Munich provided Hitler with a second political novitiate. Vienna had taught him to hate Jews and had given him glimpses of how to play on popular prejudices and fears. Munich added hatred of Bolshevism, further training in the uses of propaganda, the conviction that the base of political power was mass support, and the further conviction that the way to win this support was not by reasoning but by stirring up emotions. He picked up the idea that Jews and bolsheviks were equally loathsome and so could be treated as essentially the same thing. His experiences showed him that an audience is better captured by a 'syste-

matically one-sided approach' than by a balanced evaluation of a problem which allows the audience to wonder whether the speaker is himself
really convinced of the truth of what he is preaching. This second novitiate closed with a bang and a valuable lesson. In 1923 Hitler staged a
putsch. He did so in alliance with General Erich Ludendorff, one of the
military heroes of the war, who suffered abnormally from the stings of
defeat because his own loss of nerve in 1918 had contributed to it. The
putsch was a farcical failure, but the association with Ludendorff gave
Hitler the attention of the whole nation. At his trial he announced that
he was a man 'born to be a dictator'. He was sentenced to prison for
two years, served nine months, did some thinking and wrote *Mein
Kampf*. The lesson he learned was that he should try to gain control of
the state by constitutional means and not by frontal assault and never
against the army.

Mein Kampf, a mixture of autobiography and political manifesto,
was an immensely successful book which sold so well that Hitler
eventually made a fortune out of it. It is a long book in bad German.
Its author remained largely unknown until 1930 and was not taken
seriously by many of those who did hear of him. This was a pity because
for all its hyperbole *Mein Kampf* proclaimed much of what Hitler
wanted to do and how. As a politician Hitler was an unnatural mixture
of the normal and the eccentric. After the 1923 putsch he superficially
adopted the normal forms of party organization, speech-making and
publicity, but he also adapted them up to and beyond the point of distortion. His conformity, so far as it went, reflected his caution and
shrewdness, but it was far from being a complete index to his character
for his grip on his party was autocratic and intolerant, his speech-
making took place in a setting of ostentatiously armed henchmen, party
meetings became hierophantic rallies quite unlike the meetings of normal political parties, he was uncommonly uninhibited by scruple and an
unrestrained liar (who may have believed what he said while he was saying it but who also believed that lying paid), and he was prepared to use
violence whenever and however it served his purpose. In the organization of his party he insisted from the first on his personal ascendancy
and refused to allow even his principal colleagues to have views of their
own; in his speech-making he was conspicuously violent in what he
said and how he said it; and in his propaganda, his mass meetings and
the dress and deportment of his followers he deliberately gave his party
the appearance, as he himself said, of 'a political fighting force and not a
debating society'. If on the one hand he was using the accepted imple-
ments of politics, he was also transforming them.

Hitler did not have the mind of a statesman but rather an impresario and improviser. Where a Bismarck imposed himself on events, Hitler imposed himself on people by the fervour of his personality. He was a leader of men first and a framer of policies only a poor second. He was not an original thinker or theorizer but he was adept at picking up ideas which suited him and at taking the opportunities given him by others; he knew how to wait for his chances and how to seize them, and he was guided by certain basic preconceptions. He had a view of history. He was a Manichee, a man who sees the world and its history in terms of black and white, good and evil, god and devil. He saw two powers face to face in 'a world of everlasting conflict where the one creature feeds on the other and the death of the weaker implies the life of the stronger'. For such people the problem is to identify the good and the evil. Hitler saw no difficulty here. He defined the party of the good as the Aryans – a 'race' or biological group which was superior and so had to be tended, preserved and improved by political leaders acting like farm bailiffs.

This definition of good and evil in terms of race stemmed from certain European philosophers and historians who had, during the nineteenth century, evolved the view that races and nations could be graded on a scale of merit and that those lower down the scale would for ever remain below their betters higher up. This way of thinking was fortified by Darwin's contributions to biological science which, taken up by social scientists, were thought to show that social groups, like natural species, evolved to higher stages by a process of conflict involving – and justifying – the extinction of some groups and the survival and expansion of others. Thus backwardness, an inferior culture, was seen as a natural phenomenon rather than as a social challenge, as something to be observed rather than something to be changed. Hitler imbibed these ideas. Conflict, he said, was 'the father of all things'. The German people had to be embattled and purified, preserved from the taint of mixed blood which had caused the downfall of the ancient civilizations; it had also to be trained in devoted obedience to its Leader, to whom had been vouchsafed a vision and a mission to save the world. But to save the world from what?

The party of evil was even more easily identifiable than the party of the good. It consisted of the Jews who, ever since the time of Moses, had been labouring with diabolical ingenuity to destroy nothing less than the human race itself. Hitler's anti-semitism was a genuine and potent hatred. It was sharpened by his ability to equate Jewry with communism. For him Lenin was the latest reincarnation of Moses, Bolshevism the latest device of Jewish malevolence and 'the most radical form of the genocide [plotted] by the Jews'. Through Marx and Lenin and Bolshevism the Jews were repeating what they had done through St Paul and Christianity: European civilization was to be destroyed by the one as Rome had been destroyed by the other. At one time or another Hitler conflated all his adversaries, all those who stood for values which he despised, with the loathed Jews, so that Jewry became a sort of cultural generic term embracing – because it had inseminated and poisoned – not only communism but also social democracy, liberalism, the intellectuals, aristocrats, international finance and Christianity. Either these would be extirpated or they would extirpate humanity. A Jewish triumph would be the 'funeral wreath of the human race' and would leave the planet diving through space 'once again without any human life on its surface'. It was as simple and as terrible as that. The simple view, when wrong, can be the worst because it removes doubt and justifies every means. Hitler did not recoil from slaughter; it was so obviously necessary that it probably never occurred to him to consider whether it was agreeable or disagreeable. Genocide was not a moral issue but the practical application of physical means to social ends. He did not enjoy indiscriminate killing in the way that many simpler Nazis did, although he savoured personal revenge (he revelled over the films of the hangings of the conspirators of July 1944). He enjoyed secondhand descriptions of living and dying in concentration camps but was a strong anti-vivisectionist and could not stomach a demonstration of slaughter when he saw one with his own eyes.

Between the Germans or Aryans on the one hand and the Jews on the other were peoples who were neither. These peoples, of whom the Slavs were the most prominent example, did not have to be exterminated. Their function was to serve the party of the good. Their chief characteristics were their inferiority and their number. These were related terms since it is the destiny of an élite to rule over inferior hordes and use them, as for example the British did in India (Hitler admired the British empire for reasons which would have horrified the Indian Civil Service).

Nazi contempt for the Slavs merged with a far more ancient German-Slav hostility. The conflict between Germans and Slavs is a thousand years old. After the period of the great barbarian invasions and migrations in Europe the Frankish king Charles created in an era of dawning stability an empire in western Europe to match the eastern empire of Byzantium. This empire reached tentatively to the Carpathians and extinguished the alien Avar power in central Europe, but it failed to embrace the rising Slavic state of Moravia; nor did it weld the western Franks of France, still less those in Spain, to its Germanic core. This empire was shortlived. What survived was the idea of a western empire blessed by the papacy – and so essentially Italian as well as German – and distinct from Byzantium. It was revived by Charlemagne's successors in the tenth century, the Saxon emperors. By this time the place of the Avars in central Europe had been taken by the no less alien Magyars or Hungarians, whom the Saxons checked but did not exterminate. The emperors also made war on the Slavs in what is now northern Germany and on the Poles – the first Germano-Polish conflict. They made no attempt to bring the western Franks back into the empire but were even more strongly pulled towards Italy and the papacy than Charlemagne had been. This 'renovation' of the empire was clearly to include Italy but exclude the lands west of the Rhine and Rhône. About the Slavs, however, there were doubts. Otto III (A.D. 983–1002) conceived a great western Christian empire in which other princes besides himself would have wide autonomous authority as kings. Such an empire could include non-Germans, and the Polish, Czech and Hungarian princes welcomed it and joined it. But Otto died young. His conception of the empire died with him. His successors reverted to fighting the Slavs and the Slavs, missing an opportunity to create a countervailing empire of their own, quarrelled among themselves: the Czechs remaining in the empire, which the Poles renounced. A pattern evolved which endured, with variations, for centuries and produced in more modern times a strong German power flanked to the east by separate and weaker Polish, Czech and Hungarian ones.

By the twentieth century the opportunities created by this pattern of power were combined with racial theories and economic appetites. In the eyes of German nationalists the Slavs were biologically inferior peoples destined to become a caste of slaves; they also occupied valuable space which was needed by the Germans who, by virtue of their superiority, had every right to take it. The notion of *Lebensraum*, the idea that Germany was too small for the German race, was not invented by Hitler. It was current during the First World War and was one of the pseudo-intellectual props of the policy of *Mitteleuropa* which aimed to establish a continental empire fit for Germans (and stretching in some versions from France into Asia Minor). Hitler appears to have been genuinely convinced of the need for *Lebensraum* which, with his racial fantasies, constituted the basis of his foreign political attitudes. In *Mein Kampf* he wrote that National Socialism 'must attempt to remove the disproportion between our population and our living space – the latter regarded both as a source of food and as the basis of political power – between our historic past and the hopelessness of our present impotence'.

Hitler belonged to 'the race of men who dream concretely – a very dangerous breed' (the words come from Ernst Jünger's parable *The Marble Cliffs*). Taken by itself his idea that one being waxes as another declines is neither original nor startling. Goethe wrote:

> *Du musst steigen oder sinken,*
> *Du musst herrschen und gewinnen*
> *Oder dienen und verlieren,*
> *Amboss oder Hammer sein.*
> (Man must rise or fall, He must win and rule Or
> lose and serve, Be the anvil or the hammer.)

But there is a world of difference, in practice and in intent, between the figurative speech of a poet and the concrete programme of a practical politician with a literal mind and power at his command. Hitler's concrete dream envisaged a German nucleus of some hundred million people, flanked by subordinate federations colonized by other Germans. He did not think that this re-ordering of Europe could be effected without war, nor did he think that war was at all agreeable. He said that the next war would be extremely horrible and enormously destructive, but like so many of his contemporaries he believed it would be short. He also believed that too much peace was bad for a people and he took pleasure in the thought that a greater and more beautiful Germany would rise from the devastation, inhabited by survivors welded into a nation by their experiences and guided by a messianic leadership which would last a thousand years: Hitler was a chiliast as well as a Manichee. Some people have been tempted to judge that Hitler did not mean what he said when he indulged in language of this kind, that he got carried away; but it is equally possible to believe that he never spoke truer to his own nature than at these moments. Although cautious, he was not moderate.

Hitler's principal instrument was the Nazi Party which, exploiting the circumstances of his day and age, he used to win power over the German people and the German state. Through the party he practised the violence, verbal and physical, whose effectiveness became increasingly contrasted with the ineffectiveness of his opponents and of the constitution. The Nazi Party was like the feudal system. In it a man was obligated to an immediate chief and also to the supreme Führer. There were Führers at every level but the supreme Führer was linked with all members of the movement by direct personal allegiance as well as through the hierarchy. The supreme Führer, besides being the apex of a pyramid, was also a unique being, infallible, prophetic, the incarnation of the general (Aryan) will: 'The will of the Führer is law.' His authority was not only absolute but he himself was irreplaceable: he could have no true successor. Successors of a sort – caliphs to Hitler's Mahomet – could be nominated, but this concession to human mortality did not detract from the urgency of fulfilling the Nazi mission in Hitler's own lifetime and while he was still in the prime of life.

This concept of the Führer was reflected in Hitler's relations both with his principal henchmen and with the generality of his followers. After the capture of power in 1933 the machinery of party and the machinery of state coexisted in a kind of semi-merger. The Weimar constitution was never abrogated – it was simply ignored – and the machinery of state was left largely intact, but power passed to numerous party agencies which were given overlapping functions with the result that many decisions could be made only by the Führer; the bureaucracy, reduced to a state of confusion and inefficiency, was eliminated as a barrier between Führer and *Volk,* ruler and ruled. Hitler's principal lieutenants were not men of conspicuous ability and they never constituted a team. Perhaps only Goebbels was more than ordinarily talented and even Goebbels was more marked by the extremity of his devotion to Hitler than by outstanding intellect. There was little trust or friendship in the party's higher reaches and not much cooperation. The Nazi leaders feared and intrigued against each other and, at the end, against Hitler too. Hitler seems to have been neither surprised nor dismayed by this lack of solidarity, so long as it did not affect relations with himself. A suspicious man, he expected others to be suspicious too, and he built their mutual mistrust and malice into his system of government. As a result the principal organs of the party and, after 1933, of the state, were run by feudatories and government at the top proceeded by a series of clashes. The heads of the government did not govern by talking and working together, and the supreme chief – whether as party Führer or Reich Chancellor – was a dictator conducting a wilfully discordant band which he was not particularly anxious to orchestrate. What mattered to Hitler was the obedience of his lieutenants to himself. They did not have to agree among themselves. The party was held together by the Leader's personal magnetism and not by fellowship or community of ideas. The *Führerprinzip* was hostile to ideas, since an ideologist might find himself in a conflict between his doctrine and his Führer. Alfred Rosenberg, the party's chief racial theorist, never became a figure of the first rank and was increasingly ignored by

Hitler, and the Strasser brothers, leaders of the more radical groups of the Nazi Party in northern Germany, were pressed out of the party when the Führer came to have no use for their quasi-socialist ideas.

With his remoter followers the Führer's relations were special in two ways. Without the Führer the followers were nothing, so that the Nazi Party dissolved in 1945 not merely because the Nazi Reich had been defeated but because the Nazi Führer was dead; and secondly, there was an intimacy between Führer and rank and file, a mutual dependence, which gave the movement a democratic force based, not on majorities or voting (a degrading exercise), but on the identification of the leader with the led, expressed by the former's unquestioned authority. The function of the party organization was to 'communicate a definite idea . . . to ensure its conversion from theory to reality' and to do these things with as little intervening 'machinery' as possible. This relationship between party leader and party members was repeated at second remove and transmitted from the movement to the even wider circle of the German people as a whole. While membership of the party was limited and pride (and profit) in membership preserved undiluted, the outer circle of sympathizers was progressively enlarged to create a wider mass movement which, like the party members but less intensively, was attached to Hitler personally and which, because of this emotional attachment, had a stake in his success. Hitler realized the importance of getting the masses to feel but not to think. The Führer divulged his inmost thoughts in a narrow circle whence they percolated to the Nazi élite, thence again into the party in general, beyond the party to the people and beyond the people to the outside world. At each stage they lost something in the telling and so became assimilable by people who would otherwise have rejected them as mad and bad. In such a system the élite and the leader himself could afford to propagate preposterous ideas and even to do so cynically, because the party followers and the people as a whole were blinded by their devotion and their distance from the centre. Hermann Rauschning, with whom Hitler had long and intimate talks until their breach in 1934, relates that Hitler once told him that he was well aware that there was no such thing as race, but that he needed it for his political and salvationist purposes. A saviour of the human race may well permit himself a touch of cynicism. Nor is it incompatible with fanaticism.

The Nazi party served two main purposes. Through its ideology it united the people with their leader and through its techniques it perfected the elimination of opposition. It was not a party in the ordinary sense of the word since it could never be satisfied with partial allegiance or partial dominance. It presented a comprehensive, total way of life, explaining everything, past and future, and regulating everything, public and private. Hitler did not achieve this purpose by catechizing or by arguing. He neither instructed his audiences nor explained things to them. He presented views which, half inarticulately, they were already disposed to welcome, and one reason for his success was his ability to appeal to a variety of different types of people – the disgruntled generation of the First World War, the middle classes downgraded by inflation, the deprived classes which had never played a part in German politics before, youth, the nationalism of the old order and the nationalism of the masses. But although he appealed to these classes, he did not appeal to them as classes. At a meeting addressed by Hitler the message went from Hitler to each listener separately. The audience was a crowd of distinct depersonalized objects. In the aggregate they formed not classes but a mass, 'uniform [as he said once at a marchpast] not only in ideas, but even the facial expression is almost the same . . . a hundred thousand men become a single type'. Each man and woman, whether marching past the Führer or standing in a packed crowd to listen to him, had his eyes and soul focused onto a man who had placed himself in a unique position in German political life: sufficiently remote from the normal political structure which was crumbling (Hitler never got himself elected to the Reichstag and so never operated as a party political leader in that restricted field) and at the same time intensely close to the magnetized individual who wanted a Leader rather than a choice between leaders.

Hitler used fear and persuasion to an unsurpassed degree. Physical terror was one of his principal political weapons. To quote *The Marble Cliffs* again: 'A cloud of fear preceded the Chief Ranger like the mountain mist that presages the storm. Fear enveloped him, and I am convinced that therein far more than in his own person lay his power.' The Nazis thought nothing of assaulting their opponents, torturing them and murdering them – frequently with fanatical brutality. Sadistic thugs were given a licence instead of being shut up, and this licence was accorded to them by Hitler not out of indifference to the finer standards of behaviour but with the positive intention of assuring his hold over Germany in this way. Overt opposition died and even individual thinking was stifled. The dominance of the party was rendered as nearly total as it could humanly be by fear. Education, controlled after 1933 by the certifiable Dr Rust, became a means for destroying the individual's capacity to form opinions and indoctrinating the young with Nazi versions of history and ethics (and even with German, as opposed to inferior, mathematics) through rewritten textbooks and politically reliable teachers. Teachers who did not toe the line were reported by the Hitler Youth which came virtually to control the schools. Boys and girls spent their leisure hours in uniformed youth associations where the process was continued. Books, plays, the press and broadcasting were brought under Nazi control and censorship. Justice became a farce. It was, said Hitler, 'a means of ruling'. The courts were used to complete the suppression of the individual; the legal profession was regimented, the Führer had the power to quash proceedings, his deputy the power to increase inadequate sentences in cases involving offences against the Führer, the state or the party; illegality was legalized by the invention of the principle of 'hidden right'; an advocate who got his client acquitted would see him being bundled into a police van as he left the court. The whole of life was subordinated to the Nazi purpose with the concentration camps, or the mere knowledge of their existence, in reserve to quell those who felt like protesting openly or, given the perfection of delation within the family, even in private.

This colossal subversion of civilized values was acquiesced in by the German people and to some extent by Europe too. Only the war put an end to it. What permitted this acquiescence?

Hitler joined an ancient practice with a modern force – ritual with the mass meeting, mumbo-jumbo focused on the microphone. In great squares and open spaces, which he converted into cathedrals of Nazism, he filled ordinary Germans with a sense of destiny, giving them a wonderful vision of unreality as an escape from the chanciness of life and also laying bare to them, with telling candour, how much he had already achieved by violence and how much more he was going to achieve the same way. His performances were brilliantly staged but they would have remained historically inconsequential if they had not fitted the time and place of their presentation.

GERMANY

Germany had been something of an anomaly in Europe for more than a century before Hitler came to power. The Germans did not form a compact group in Europe like the French or the English, nor did they create a nation state; and they failed to find adequate outlets beyond Europe for their power, talents and ambitions. For both these reasons they were the more disposed towards expansion and conquest in Europe.

Modern Europe is a patchwork of conscious nationalisms expressed or seeking expression in statehood. Some of these have been recogniz-

able entities for centuries but the bursting time of European nationalism came with the turn of the eighteenth into the nineteenth century.
At this period the dynast, an individual with hereditary right and a
personal demesne (his kingdom), came to seem old fashioned. Two
changes, the one domestic and the other international, were involved: a
shift of political power within the state and a redefinition of the boundaries of the state. The first of these favoured 'the people' at the expense of the dynast; the second was based on the idea of 'the nation',
as opposed to history or geography or power, as the criterion for
deciding where one state stopped and the next one should begin. The
new ideas were most effective in western Europe where the making of
Italy was their outstanding advertisement; they were least effective in
eastern Europe where polyglot autocracies continued until well into the
twentieth century. In the centre of Europe Germany looked as though
it had developed into a nation state but the appearance was deceptive.

German nationalism was promoted by reaction against French cultural and military hegemony. It asserted that Germans had a separate
identity and the right to mind their own affairs instead of being part of
Napoleon's empire and of a French-dominated cosmopolitan culture.
It aimed not only to liberate Germans but also to unite them and so
helped to produce a powerful and efficient state out of an agglomeration
of feeble ones. But if German nationalism looked at this stage very
much like other European nationalisms, it diverged as the Germans
both began to think of themselves as not only distinct but superior and
at the same time failed to achieve a nation state to focus and absorb
their national energies.

German writers and thinkers made much of the nation state and provided the most famous of the state's champions in the nineteenth century,
and the Reich created in 1870 was designed by Bismarck and regarded
by almost everybody as the German nation's state. But Bismarck's
Germany was incomplete. It was a federation of German-speaking
states dominated by Prussia and excluding not only Austria, which was
only partly German, but also numerous Germans scattered about eastern Europe; the Germans were too dispersed and too intermingled with
other peoples to constitute a nation state. Bismarck's Germany was not
a national gathering together, like Cavour's Italy. It was an extension of
Prussian power, achieved by defeating Austria and France, and a consolidation of class power, achieved by blanketing German liberalism
and passing enough social legislation to take the wind out of the German socialists' sails. It was therefore incomplete not only in the sense
that many Germans were left outside it but also because whole classes

of Germans within the state were excluded from effective political activity and remained subordinated to the socially superior ruling classes: it was a nation state neither in its geographical extent nor in its social cohesion. It was unstable and tense both within and at its borders. Unlike Italy, it was not even a geographical expression. If anything, it was a linguistic aspiration seeking political form and traversed by social rifts. Since it was also the most central of European states and became the most powerful, its malaise dominated European affairs for a century.

German nationalism foiled of what was, in nineteenth-century terms, its natural outcome turned to racialism. Germanism materialized as *Reich* and *Volk*, a pair of politically disruptive and often mystical concepts. A *Reich* is a claim to dominion; a *Volk* is a people linked not by habitat but by race. *Reich* and *Volk* combined imply racial dominion. (When, later, the Nazis chanted: *Ein Reich, ein Volk, ein Führer*, they were acclaiming the political activation of this dual concept.) At the same time the desire to establish a separate identity for Germans was replaced by the idea that Germans were not only distinct but superior. The line between pride and arrogance is a thin one and the assertion of an independent personality passes very easily into a claim to superiority. The Germans were neither alone nor unusual in thinking themselves better than other people, but from early in the nineteenth century Germans began to make extraordinary claims for Germanism as the embodiment of superior virtues deposited by God in people who spoke the German language. Racialists see history as a conflict between races – an alternative to Karl Marx's explanation of history as a conflict between classes – and racialists conscious of their own superiority see a world in which they are bound to do battle with other races and win. Nineteenth-century German racialist ideology postulated an Aryan race of purer, ideal human beings, the founders and custodians of all human culture. History and science were invoked to prove these unhistorical and unscientific postulates, and ancient racial gods were resuscitated to give spiritual support to this denial of the essential equality of man which had been preached for centuries in the tradition of Stoics and Christians. The pseudo-science of phrenology, which enjoyed a curious vogue in an age avid for anything which might be called scientific, measured the differences between Aryan and other skulls and when these outward signs of distinction proved disappointingly trivial, racialists fell back on inner measurements of souls which, though they were more difficult to demonstrate, were also more difficult to deny. Darwin's theories were also used. The world of men (*The Origin of Species* dealt with plants and animals) was divided into the fit and the unfit, and the survival of the fittest was taken to justify and even require the extermination of the unfit. Conflict, in any case inevitable, was the means for the improvement of the race and therefore also noble. There was no such thing as a right to live – let alone a right to liberty or the pursuit of happiness. Human rights were replaced by strife as the path of progress.

German racialism, having evolved from German nationalism, took a further step and became imperialist. Where a race and a state do not coincide the racialist may achieve his aims either by the migration of outlying members of the race into the fatherland or by the extension of the rule of the race to all parts of the world inhabited by the race or needed by it. German minorities in foreign countries were, by definition, superior people living under the rule of their inferiors. Either they must be repatriated or German rule must be extended to cover these areas. The second solution was the more appealing. Hence the notion of a Greater Germany, a German Reich extending to areas well beyond any normally accepted confines of Germany but where Germany ought to rule because some members of the German *Volk* lived there. Towards the end of the nineteenth century various Pan-German groups emerged, both in Vienna with its windows on the east and in Berlin with its consciousness of superabundant power, to advocate what was in effect a German empire in Europe. They were not inspired solely by ideology. Unlike the other great powers of Europe Germany had found no worlds to conquer outside Europe. While the western European nations conquered overseas and the Russians conquered in Asia, the Germans – partly because they were too late – conquered nowhere. Bismarck was indifferent to colonies and Germany's interest in Africa at the end of the nineteenth century was half-hearted as well as belated. So Germany's field of conquest became eastern or middle (*Mittel*) Europe. Bismarck himself preferred that Germany should live in a state of equilibrium with the Russian and Habsburg empires to the east of it, but the German-ness of the Habsburg empire was a standing invitation to all Germans to go east, to regard the Slavs as their Red Indians or 'fuzzy-wuzzies', to embark on one of the great movements of European expansion and colonization – only this time within Europe itself and at the expense of peoples whose systems were neither so alien nor so technically backward as the Asian and African societies which other Europeans subjugated. Like all imperialists the Germans easily convinced themselves that they were benefiting inferior peoples by interfering with them – until eventually the Nazis dispensed with the idea of benefiting anybody but themselves.

These racial and imperial strands in the modern German experience were picked up by the Nazis. Nazism was a product of elements in

German history and elements in European history. Its peculiarly evil character was a consequence of amalgamating the worst in German public life with the worst in European public life. It was the German version of European fascism, combining special German features with the general characteristics of the wider, European genus to which it belonged. Its outstanding special features were the demand for *Lebensraum*, which was a euphemism for imperial conquest, and its anti-semitism. Its special victims therefore were the Jews and the Slavs. These two elements were not unconnected, for the Pan-Germans of the late nineteenth century who pointed Germany towards an imperial destiny not in the sense of Bismarck's compact central European Reich but as a vast overlordship over Slav peoples and lands beyond the strictly German horizon, were also markedly anti-semitic.

During most of the nineteenth century Germans, with some reservations in regard to Austrian Germans, were not pre-eminently anti-semitic. Nor is anti-semitism a necessary ingredient of fascism, although it has been a common one; the Italian fascists, for example, were comparatively free of anti-semitism until they imported it by a process of reverse Lend-Lease from Germany in the closing phase of the *fascismo*. German anti-semitism seems to have been mainly an indigenous growth coinciding with the growth of German political consciousness. Pan-German anti-semitism was an expression of resentment against people who insisted on being different and who refused to be assimilated to Gentile society and full participation in the German dream. (Hitler's original contribution to anti-semitism was to abandon this demand that Jews become Germans, to insist on the contrary that they could never be Germans and to emphasize the unbridgeable gap by marking each Jew with the star of David.) Although many Jews – not least in Germany in the 1920s – were assimilated into Gentile society when they themselves wished to take this course and when the surrounding circumstances favoured it, they remained liable to be singled out and attacked whenever the Gentile society had a grievance to be vented somewhere. In the latter part of the nineteenth century they were used by conservatives to pin unpopular ideas on: liberal ideas feared by the privileged classes were characterized as Jewish in order to make these classes revile the Jews. This use of racial prejudice for political purposes was begun by Bismarck and adopted and magnified by Alexander III in Russia, where anti-semitism has continued to be exploited in this way ever since. The appearance of the Jews is often markedly recognizable (though it has been embarrassingly discovered that a number of Jews have blue eyes and fair hair). They have a religion and a language which they share with nobody else. In Europe they have performed a function as useful as it is often unpopular – that of the capitalist who provides money for other people's enterprises or follies – but in the nineteenth century they preserved more of their unpopularity than their usefulness as Europe's growing Gentile bourgeoisie began to supplant them as the providers of money. The state found them less useful as it turned to financing its needs more by taxation and less by loans. Moreover, the Jews lacked two characteristics which seemed natural to everybody else: the Jew had no state and, in the state in which he lived, counted as a Jew rather than as a member of an economic or social class. In a society of classes and in a polity of nation states he was a misfit; the fact of his belonging to something which was neither state nor class fostered suspiciousness of exclusive racial loyalties and the myth of machinations behind the scenes; and his exclusion from the class structure helped his defamers to represent him as an enemy of all social structures. In the heyday of his usefulness the Jew had often been close to power and when his usefulness declined his power was thought to have become covert rather than diminished.

Racism endangered the Jews because they were the pre-eminent example of a self-chosen race. Any other self-chosen race was bound to clash with them and hate them. The Germans did so more than most and ascribed to them all the vices which were the counterparts of Aryan virtues. The German master race arraigned the Jews and the Nazi party became the principal instrument for destroying them. Again, Hitler did not invent anti-semitism; he gave it a special twist and he provided the tools and the opportunities for satisfying it. And the Nazi state did not protect these people within its borders because in the Nazi scheme of things the state was not an instrument for preserving public order or securing the rights of men but an instrument for furthering the destiny of the German *Volk*. The SA sang:

> *Erst müssen Juden bluten,*
> *Erst dann sind wir befreit.*
> (First must Jewish blood be shed,
> Only then will we be free.)

EUROPE

The ending of the old European order, by the dissolution of its economic and social foundations and consequently of its political structures, was effected by a variety of forces which together can be called democratic. Their general direction was to extend, in the name of freedom, equality and fraternity, the narrow bases of élitist societies and exclusive policies. The history of this movement, which is the stuff of the modern world, cannot be resumed here even in the briefest compass, but it is relevant to point out that it has been both divided and opposed. The division created eventually the two broad and increasingly discordant streams called liberal democracy and totalitarian democracy (that is to say, communism) – both rooted in the eighteenth-century Enlightenment but diverging over two fundamental issues, the former regarding politics as a part of human activity where the latter regards politics as comprehending the totality of human activity, the former giving a higher value than the latter to individual choice and well-being in the inevitable conflict between the individual and the group. The opposition to democracy has been authoritarian, the rejection of the democratic principle of extension and the reassertion of the right of special men or special groups of men to lay down the law. Where democracy diffuses power, authoritarianism concentrates it once more.

This authoritarian opposition too has been divided. It has conservative and radical branches. The conservatives have tried to arrest democratic change, or to minimize and delay it; they have been ambivalent about democracy, usually accepting for pragmatic reasons a measure of what in principle they dislike. The radical authoritarians on the other hand have been frankly anti-democratic and have set out to destroy democracy and revert to a political and social order dominated by a special caste or individual, although not necessarily by the same castes or individuals who were invested with power under the *anciens régimes*. Fascism is the outcome of this active and radical, as opposed to the passive and conservative, opposition to democracy. Mussolini defined fascism as opposition to the principles of 1789, by which he meant opposition to what others have called the Rights of Man. It was also opposed to the Enlightenment, to reason. It preferred violence: fascists have been bent on destroying an existing democratic order and on doing so by deed and not by argument.

The politics of Europe in the last 200 years have revolved round the ideas summed up in the phrase 'the French Revolution', and the political terms in common use – such as right and left, progressive and reactionary – relate to attitudes towards those ideas. The Bolshevik Revolution of 1917 sharpened the conflict typified by 1789 and, with conservatives often passive or confused about their role, there developed in the twentieth century a triangle of forces and eventually war between the temporarily reunited streams of liberal and totalitarian democracy and their fascist foes who captured the power of the state in various parts of Europe where weak government by conservatives or democrats helped them to do so.

Modern Europe has had to digest industrial, demographic and technical revolutions and at the same time a questioning of accepted values which has amounted to a social and cultural mutation. These changes have been very unsettling. The fundamental change has been the growth of populations and the growth of towns, so that at one and the same time there were quite quickly many more people, many of them living in a completely new way. The change in the demographic and geographical patterns produced social changes. Old ties were loosened and aristocratic and paternalist structures, based mainly on land and caste, were eroded by the motor forces of the Enlightenment (emancipation from dogma and despot) and of the Revolution (power to the people). The new urban classes began to exert pressure and command sympathy. What they wanted was vague – less misery and poverty, more fairness, more self-respect – but it implied upheaval. The traditional givers of laws and *mores* (churches, kings and nobles), and the laws and *mores* themselves, lost authority under rational scrutiny and popular suspicion. It was not immediately clear what the new values were nor where they were to come from. New élites, professing a democratic instead of an aristocratic faith, emerged to take or share the power which was slipping from the exclusive grasp of the old régime and which, owing to technical revolutions in communications and manufacturing, was rapidly becoming much greater than ever before. For the most part power was shared, whether in concert or in a parliamentary system of alternating bouts between nostalgic conservatives and moderate progressives. The result was an orderly but slow development, too slow for those who maintained that no really radical social changes had yet occurred, too decided for the radical forces of the Right which were opposed, not so much to change, but to democracy. There was therefore an ever present possibility of a reversal of alliances in which the conservative opponents of change and the fascist opponents of democracy would join forces against the Left despite the fact that the one group was essentially passive and the other essentially revolutionary. The outstanding example of such a combination was the government in which the aristocratic Papen served as Vice-Chancellor under the fascist Hitler as Chancellor. As early as 1850 Palmerston, in the Don Pacifico debate in the House of Commons, recognized two varieties of radicalism, the reactionary as well as the Jacobin, but it was not until a century later that the fascist combination of reaction with violence was widely recognized as a potent and pernicious threat to European societies.

The fascist leader, like the democrat, had his ideological roots in the eighteenth century, but whereas the democrat put his faith in reason and debate the fascist believed in the power and virtue of the will. Traditionally the high road to right action has been knowledge discovered by reason; the function of reason was to uncover the knowable which, when revealed, was common property. Reason and knowledge assumed therefore universal values. The will, however, was personal. Whereas the individual impelled by reason was moving towards agreement with other individuals, the individual impelled by will was at least as likely to be moving towards a clash with other individuals. The will was subjective rather than communal, aggressive rather than irenic. The will was seen as a creative force in its own right operating in a world in which the objective reality sought by the reasonable man of the Enlightenment was an illusion. There were no external criteria of rightness, only inner promptings. Therefore the strong-willed had right on his side, and the stronger his will the more right he was. What was real was the product of each individual's inner self, and this product was *ipso facto* valid as well as real, so that the individual was entitled and indeed under some compulsion to make his will prevail. His destiny was that of a sovereign creator in a world of his own which impinged upon the personal worlds of other sovereign creators; it was not his lot, nor was it within a man's capability, to discover a single world in which all would participate, because such a world did not exist to be discovered. The world was not a semi-known and orderly system but an unknowable and anarchic non-system.

The consequences of this view were conflict and uncertainty. Both cried out for leadership. What sort of leadership? With knowledge and reason at a discount the emotions were promoted to a dominant role and the intensity of a man's feelings were rated above the soundness of his judgement: there was a deeper, inward truth in the soul by comparison with which the reason was superficial, and the leader was to be distinguished by the qualities of this ill-defined, unlocated, non-rational, even irrational soul. He was above all a doer, an activist, and whatever he wanted to do was right, including crushing weaker beings. He was unpredictable but he was to be trusted and followed none the less, since his unpredictability was only in the eye of the beholder; so long as his acts and commands issued from the dictates of his will they were not to be questioned—and it was as impossible to prove, as it was imprudent to suppose, that they issued from anywhere else. The Italian fascists summed up the position in the slogan: *Credere! Ubbedire! Combattere!* (Believe, Obey and Fight). The fascist leader was also a saviour and redeemer, more of a superman than a man, half-way between god and man, what the ancients called a hero. By dubbing him Duce and Führer – leader in Italian and German – the fascists usurped a term to which they had no exclusive right, for Churchill and de Gaulle were leaders too. What distinguishes the fascist chief is not leadership, but the role of hero. The hero disdains reason (Homer's heroes never engage in rational debate) and prevails by the weight of authority and by killing. His criteria are quantitative – the bigger the better, whether the subject matter is the length of a speech, the volume of sound at a concert or the number of deaths in a slaughter.

His antithesis is the representative leader who derives his authority from parliaments and elections and depends on a choate body of opinion as opposed to the inchoate mass following on which fascist power is based. In countries like France and Great Britain which have had strong rationalist or parliamentary traditions fascist leaders, although they existed, made little headway. These countries did not go fascist. But their right-wing leaders felt drawn to foreign fascists and praised Mussolini and Hitler and later Franco, who were regarded by conservatives as ready helps against the extreme Left and as performing the salutary task of getting their countries out of messes into which they had fallen. Afraid of rather than familiar with Marxism, they misinterpreted fascism. Fascist movements and fascist leaders were in truth revolutionary and dynamic, but because they had also certain characteristics which were conventionally dubbed right-wing, they were frequently mistaken for a rather uncouth kind of conservative. The characteristic British and French leaders of this period were capable rather than intelligent, well educated only in terms of an educational system designed to produce mere custodians, suspicious of and so ill equipped to understand new ideas and forces. They could see that communism aimed to subvert the existing order of which they were themselves a part – the communists themselves said so – but they failed to draw the same conclusion about the no less revolutionary fascists, whom they persisted in regarding as respectable. In some degree they were bemused by their own standards and their own democratic precepts. They could not believe that people who said such crazy things as the Nazis meant what they said; the British in particular took little account of theories which they considered to have little bearing on practical politics; they felt that a movement which attracted millions of votes could not be as bad as surface appearances sometimes suggested: thus were they able to turn a deaf ear to the very explicit statements of aims by Nazi and other fascist leaders. (In 1933 Hitler said publicly that the democracies had fortunately not understood what Nazism was about, for otherwise they could have stopped it.) In political circles Neville Chamberlain was a representative figure, hoping that Hitler and the bulk of his party were more sensible than the rowdies of the S A, hoping that they would be tamed by office and responsibility, regarding the Nazis as just another party in the twenties and then from 1930 as a necessary one for the working of government, gradually losing heart and at the end doing his best to avoid war in an impossible situation which had been created partly by his own incomprehension. Outside political circles many leaders, including in particular Roman Catholic hierarchs from the Pope downwards, were over-indulgent – to say the least – to fascism and to atheistic Nazism because they hated communism more. The propertied classes, underrating the threat of fascism because they compared it with communism, not expecting to be killed by fascists or even to have to surrender too much of their power and property, had no strong objection to helping fascists with their money. The march of the fascists on Rome in 1922 was a harmless parade compared with the Bolshevik Revolution of five years earlier and life in Mussolini's Italy was disagreeable only for socialists and liberals. Mussolini was appointed Prime Minister by the King in due constitutional form, as Hitler was appointed Chancellor by Hindenburg, and people who read of these appointments in newspapers without seeing for themselves what was going on in streets and prisons were confirmed in their prejudgements that these strange new groups were not revolutionaries in the accepted guillotine sense but champions of order and stability. If King Victor Emanuel of Italy and President von Hindenburg of Germany chose to act thus, what right had any foreigner to object or interfere? It was odd but not outrageous, and if socialists and Jews were having a rough time, they were probably getting no more, or not much more, than they deserved. The ruling classes of western Europe consisted on the whole of cultivated and humane men, but they were men who had also acquired a certain stolidity in the face of misfortune – their own or other people's – which could amount to callousness. They were used to ruling not only their own countries but large empires as well, populated by strange peoples to whom they owed justice and sound administration but over whom it was undesirable for practical reasons to sentimentalize. They were acquainted with 'inferior' races as well as 'inferior' classes, so that the social structure and the imperial experience of Europe combined to establish an order of values and a pragmatic indifference to inequalities which could sometimes be reconciled with ideals of justice and decency only by not inquiring too closely into what was going on. In sum the fascist attitude to socialists and Jews was not utterly different from the imperialist attitude to Blacks. The difference was one of degree, and differences of degree can be minimized or dismissed more easily than most. Hitler, in this respect as in many others, was the supremely disgusting example of something which was not so alien to the European mentality: the tendency to put different kinds of people into different sealed categories and then treat them differently. What his contemporaries, other than his victims, refused to see in time was that the degree of difference in the treatment was so extreme that it amounted to a difference in kind and went in any case far beyond the bounds of what Europe had learnt to call civilized.

CHAPTER 2

From Versailles to the Soldiers' Oath: 1919–34

THE First World War did not destroy German power. As in France after 1870 and Germany once more after 1945 recovery was swift. It was, however, punctuated by economic distress at the beginning and the end of the twenties which had profound political consequences, shaped by Germany's refusal to accept the verdict of 1918 and by resentment against the terms of the peace treaty. Nor did the war destroy much of Germany's pre-war social structure. The departure of the Hohenzollerns and other monarchs gave an appearance of political and social change which masked the fact that the rest of the ruling establishment remained in being and in power. Above all the army remained, until 1934, the arbiter of German politics.

Germany's military traditions were a legacy of its Prussian origins. The Prussian army made Prussia in the seventeenth and eighteenth centuries, and transmitted its traditions to the German Reich in the nineteenth. These traditions included the social exclusiveness of its officers as an aristocratic caste, the military virtues of rectitude and obedience, and a somewhat vague and unspecified position as the guardians of the state's wellbeing as well as its frontiers. The creation of the Reich in the nineteenth century reaffirmed the prestige of the army from the struggle against Napoleon I to the defeat of Napoleon III. The German officer was trained in the exercise of individual judgement on the grounds, elaborated by Clausewitz and other theorists, that the practice of war throws up a great variety of situations which cannot be foreseen and can best be handled by the officer who has learned to take decisions for himself. In addition the German officer had a wider education than his British or French counterpart in the sense that he was expected to concern himself with matters beyond the strictly professional. Yet, because freedom of speculation was not similarly encouraged, his actions in the wider political field were rigidly conditioned; politics were included in his province, but his political equipment was narrow. The German army was therefore significantly different from the British and French armies. The British army, from its beginnings in the time of Cromwell and his rule through Major-Generals, was more suspect as a threat to the civil power than respected as the guardian of the nation (a role reserved for the navy which had the special advantage of all navies that it guarded the nation from outside without being able to interfere in the streets or take part in politics as armies can). The British army had come to accept its place as subordinate and obedient to the civil government and was therefore denied some of the sources of esteem and self-esteem enjoyed by the German army. In France too the army was regarded since the Revolution as an instrument of civil government and not as properly a power in its own right. There was also a further difference between Great Britain and France on the one hand and Germany on the other. In all these countries the nineteenth century saw the *haute bourgeoisie* trying to get a share in political power. In Great Britain and France it did so by adopting liberal values but in Germany it opted instead for partnership with Bismarck and became a contented adjunct of a conservative oligarchy. The German *bourgeoisie*, having entered upon the political scene later than its French and British counterparts and – more important – at a stage in the evolution of Germany when military power was still actively forming the state, left power to the traditional classes and did not mediate between them and the deprived proletariat. Thus in Germany the power of the military aristocracy in affairs of state was not curbed by civilian, liberal, middle-class opinion. In Bismarck's time it was curbed by Bismarck himself who opposed and even snubbed the army when he felt so inclined, but he did so not because he incarnated the civil power but because he was Bismarck. After his retirement the army, confronting a series of weak Chancellors, achieved a pre-eminence which culminated in the First World War when Generals von Hindenburg and Ludendorff established a military régime which not only dictated to and dismissed civilian Ministers but also invaded the prerogatives of the Kaiser. In 1918 the Kaiser went too, and the army, contemplating even weaker governments than those of the last thirty years, claimed an autonomy which was not successfully challenged by the civil power until Hitler became Chancellor. Its first post-war chief, Hans von Seeckt, a general endowed with exceptional political acumen, devoted himself to preserving what was left of the German army and its traditions and to rebuilding it. He regarded the Weimar republic as something to be survived and he was prepared to wait and survive it.

The Weimar constitution provided a framework in which Germany might evolve from an oligarchical authoritarianism to a popular democracy, but the evolution was slow to start and then struck by adversity which it was too frail to survive. The middle classes, after being blanketed by the exigencies of war, were torpedoed by the post-war inflation. During the lifetime of the Weimar republic only the Roman Catholic

Centre Party maintained its strength (at about 15 per cent of votes
cast). Other centre groups declined steadily until they almost vanished.
Further to the Left the Social Democrats, who remained to defend the
republic with the Centre Party, also lost ground, unused to the political
game from which they had been excluded too long, obsessed by the
communist threat on their left, and puzzled by the adaptation of Marxism to a vigorous industrial society which falsified some of its premises
and drew part of its sting. They ruled Prussia, but whereas Prussia had
been the decisive element in Bismarck's and William II's Reich, in
Weimar Germany it was only the most important administrative unit.

Weimar Germany enjoyed a number of years of economic prosperity
and a remarkable cultural outburst, but politically it remained a promise
unfulfilled. It looked as though it might become a parliamentary democracy but it did not look as though it had. After the election of Field
Marshal von Beneckendorf und Hindenburg (who had retired from
active service in 1911) to succeed Ebert as Chancellor in 1925 it looked
more like the pre-war monarchy than anything else and so long as he
lived Hindenburg, himself an avowed monarchist, seemed more likely
to play General Monk than General Washington. Thus Weimar Germany, besides being smaller and weaker than the old Reich, was uncertain and disunited. At first it was also turbulent. Free Corps, formed out
of the disbanded army originally to guard Germany's eastern frontiers,
became autonomous units owing shadowy allegiance to senior army
officers but acknowledging none to the state. They assumed roving commissions to put down left-wing activities (1919 saw a rash of communist
risings in large cities) and where they thought fit they organized murders. They were a throw-back to the medieval Free Knights, freebooters
tricked out in romantic trappings. In 1920 the Kapp putsch in Berlin, a
right-wing and pro-monarchist attempt by one of these Free Corps to
overthrow the government with the open support of a part of the army,
demonstrated – the more so because it was a ludicrous failure – the
weakness of government and the instability of society. Kapp and his
associates failed to take over the government but the government, by
failing to punish them or to disband the Free Corps, showed that it was
not master in its own house. A similar coup in Munich succeeded and
all but withdrew southern Germany from Berlin's authority. There was
a continuing struggle for power in Germany in a vacuum in which
groups operating outside the law took things into their own hands by
virtue only of the fact that they had arms. The atmosphere of violence
was aggravated by the murder, by the Free Corps, of the moderate
political leaders Matthias Erzberger and Walther Rathenau and also by

the fascist march on Rome in 1922 and the Franco-Belgian occupation of the Ruhr in 1923. But the years 1924–9 (from the Dawes settlement to the great depression) were much less turbulent: under Stresemann's guidance Germany sought to satisfy its grievances by discussion and by entering into the comity of Europe: it joined the League of Nations in 1926 and saw the withdrawal of the victors' Military Control Commission in 1927; American loans and efficient administration combined to stabilize the currency, modernize communications, re-equip industry and reduce unemployment to (in 1928) 650,000. The army remained in the background. The more extreme parties made less noise. Germany began to look and to behave like the bourgeois politicians who were in charge of its affairs. By the end of this period it had the best roads, the fastest railways and the most modern merchant fleet in Europe. Real wages were back to what they had been before the war; industrial production was more than 20 per cent higher. But the republic was perpetually threatened by a possible alliance between the nationalist ruling classes and the nationalist masses and its governments were inevitably constricted by the aftermath of defeat.

The peace treaty had taken from Germany all its colonies, one eighth of its European territory and one tenth of its European population, and most of its iron and steel and shipping; it had placed the Rhineland and the Saar temporarily under foreign control, eliminated the German navy and air force and reduced the German army to a force of 100,000 men who were required to serve for at least twelve years in order to prevent the creation of reserves; it had extracted from Germany a written admission of war guilt and imposed an obligation to pay extensive but as yet unlimited reparations. These terms were harsh. This, however, was to be expected. They came also to be considered unjust, not only by Germans, on the pleas that the war guilt clause was a vindictive oversimplification of the causes of the war, that the reparations were excessive, that the plebiscitary principle was applied only to Germany's disadvantage and was excluded where it might have worked the other way, and that Germany had surrendered on the terms of Wilson's Fourteen Points which the peace treaty had then contravened. This last plea does not stand up to examination since no such bargain was struck, but the belief was independent of the facts – like the belief, fostered by the ruling classes, that Germany had not been defeated in the field at all but had been forced to surrender by the collapse of civilian morale.

There was nothing unusual about charging the cost of a war to the losers. Most of the war damage had been done to and not by the victors and they felt entitled to get back what they could in order to repair the damage done to their lands and buildings, their disabled soldiers and their widows and children. The obvious way to do this was to present a bill and demand payment in cash; a more sophisticated method, devised by British and French officials and welcomed by the Germans, whereby the damage in north-eastern France would have to be repaired by German labour using German materials, was blocked by French building interests. What was unusual about the bill presented to Germany after the First World War was the refusal of the victors to say how much would satisfy them. For twelve years the Germans did not know how much they might have to pay. In 1921 the Allied Reparations Commission produced the figure of 132 milliard gold marks (£6,850 million) but this amount might be increased later if the Commission decided that Germany could pay more. J. M. Keynes, whose own assessment of Germany's capacity to pay was £2,000 million, stigmatized this arrangement as morally detestable, politically foolish and economically nonsensical. Keynes also argued that all inter-allied war debts should be cancelled, since otherwise they would only be repudiated, in which prophecy only Finland proved him wrong.

This interim reparations settlement was almost immediately destroyed by the collapse of the mark which fell during 1922–3 from a par value of 4.20 to the dollar to 4,200 billion to the dollar. Germany could neither pay nor borrow. It defaulted at the end of 1922, whereupon France and Belgium exercised in January 1923 their right to reoccupy the Ruhr. Great Britain disapprovingly kept apart. A new mark, the Rentenmark, was called into existence by Hjalmar Schacht, President of the *Reichsbank*, to replace the old mark which had become a valueless string of noughts, and in 1924 a fresh attempt was made to quantify reparations. Under the Dawes Plan Germany undertook to resume payments at the rate of 1 billion new marks a year (about £50 million) rising to 2.5 billion in 1928–9. These sums were charged on the product of customs, railways and industry and were to be paid by the *Reichsbank* to Germany's creditors, who provided half the directors of the Reichsbank and also exercised control over the German railways. The money for the first payments was lent to Germany by the principal foreign national banks. There was still no limit fixed to Germany's total indebtedness, but Germany's more pressing worries were relieved by its creditors' willingness to lend and go on lending. In the next six years, 1924–30, they lent over 30 billion marks, enough not only to meet the Dawes outgoings but also to replace the capital destroyed by the great inflation of 1922–3, finance post-war reconstruction, pay annual deficits on foreign trade and create a gold reserve. These were good years for Germany. Then in 1930 the Young Plan reduced the Dawes payments, fixed a limit for German reparations, provided Germany with yet another loan of $300 million, removed foreign controls over the *Reichsbank* and the railways, and secured the evacuation of the Rhineland in 1930 instead of partly in 1930 and partly in 1935.

But the Young Plan still kept Germany under a heavy economic sentence. Reparations were to continue for fifty-nine years and, as *The Times* noted, Hitler was able to appeal to millions of Germans who could 'know nothing of the war but that the bill for it will outlast their lifetime'. Moreover the Young Plan, unlike the Dawes Plan, did not turn out to be a fresh start. The depression, which had started in the United States in 1928–9, was already spreading to Europe. Factories were closing, unemployment was growing and American loans were ceasing. Among the casualties was the Weimar republic and among those who gained was Hitler.

During the twenties Germany was put back on its feet by foreign governments, specially the United States, but the mere fact that Germany was once more an active competitor in the world economy revived international strains which had accompanied Germany's first advance to economic power at the end of the nineteenth century. The technically advanced countries were producing more than they themselves and the rest of the world could buy. The obvious remedy for this state of affairs – produce less – was not available since the industrial and technical revolutions which had increased the productivity of the strongest economies had also increased their need for capital accumulation and hence their appetite for higher profits and bigger markets. By the end of the twenties overproduction was creating unemployment, while in various parts of the world surplus stocks were lying unmoved and unconsumed. Germany, with its post-war neuroses and without colonial markets, was particularly vulnerable in this competition for the best slices of the international cake and its business community was looking for a government which would give priority to the requirements of its section of the nation and would secure by any means the revision of a post-war settlement which had cut down Germany's place in the world. Germany was thus predisposed to become increasingly authoritarian and revisionist.

The depression of the late twenties was virtually worldwide. It put twenty to thirty million people out of work, halved the volume of international trade, impoverished national banks and exchequers as well as families, baffled political leaders and helped men like Hitler to take power. It was dramatized, near its beginning, by the sensational collapse of the New York stock exchange in the last hour of business on 23 October 1929. On that day nearly 20 million shares were sold at lower and lower prices and by the end of that month investors were poorer by some $40 billion.

In the United States the late twenties were one of those periods of immense material optimism in which people stop thinking about limits. In a booming economy men of property believed, or acted as if they believed, that an era of richness for all had arrived and that stock prices would continue indefinitely their great leaps forward. As profits and savings satisfied and exceeded the demand for consumer goods and luxuries, they were used to create yet more monetary wealth and were re-consigned to the stock market, where they pushed stock prices up further still. Those who paused to think assumed that higher prices were being matched and justified by higher productivity. In fact, however, the great American boom had shown signs of slackening several months before the stock market's crash in October. Industrial production had taken a downward turn. This had happened before, temporarily, but in 1929 the setback was not followed by a quick recovery; it was not a pause but an about turn.

The effects of the collapse were felt over a vast area because the United States had failed to adjust to the post-war situation in the world at large. During the twenties countries all over the world were importing American goods and borrowing American money. The borrowing had two principal reasons. The first was the high tariffs which the United States maintained and which prevented its customers from selling in the United States enough goods to balance their purchases; they were forced to balance their trade either by payments in gold or by continuous American loans. The second reason was a consequence of the First World War which created vast inter-governmental debts, partly contracted by the victors in the course of fighting the war and paying for it and partly in the form of reparations. The bulk of the inter-allied debts was owed to the United States, Great Britain and France (although France was only a net creditor if Russian debts were taken at their face value) and the bulk of the reparations payments was owed by Germany to its near neighbours. The debtors borrowed from the United States in order to discharge their obligations. After 1929, however, American loans were no longer forthcoming and at the same time the United States raised its tariffs still further, notably by the inopportune Smoot-Hawley Act of 1930. Since American lending had been financing post-war reconstruction and development in Europe as well as debt settlements and international trade, the turning off of the American tap – first because private investors preferred to play the rising markets in the United States and then because of the collapse of those markets – throttled Europe's economies.

The economic interdependence of different parts of the world was largely a consequence of the industrial and technical revolutions which had begun and flourished in western Europe and northern America. These revolutions created both a demand for primary products in places where they did not exist and speedy means of getting them there. Western Europe, with its higher standards of living and advanced skills, consumed the food and the minerals which other continents produced for its kitchens and factories. But this pattern contained the seeds of its own transformation since international trade enriched the poorer countries as well as the richer and helped the poorer to improve their own standards of living and so eat more of the food they could grow. The First World War also affected the pattern. By concentrating man's needs on munitions it boosted the demand for minerals and their price, and by disrupting communications it boosted food production for local consumption and, likewise, the farmer's profits. In the United States and other prosperous societies agriculture expanded owing to the fear that the war would prevent food from distant countries from reaching its destination. When therefore the war ended, more food was being produced than could be disposed of. Prices began to fall and continued to do so throughout the twenties with only a brief pause in 1925–8. Instead of reducing production, governments, in particular the government of the United States, subsidized the farmer's prices and so encouraged him to keep under cultivation the land which he had worked so successfully under different circumstances. Moreover, since the wartime expansion of American agriculture had been financed by credit, the farmer in the post-war world was not merely an over-producer but an indebted over-producer. From 1929 the system took perforce the violent way to solution by numerous bankruptcies.

The end of the war also brought a drop in the prices of primary products other than food. Initially this change benefited the manu-facturing countries at the expense of the producers, but it soon damaged the industrial societies too by contracting their markets; the suppliers of raw materials were also the purchasers of manufactured goods, and when they no longer got good prices for their raw materials they ceased to be able to buy manufactured goods. Less was bought and sold throughout the world. There was less wealth.

By the end of the twenties there were therefore three interlocking problems: agricultural overproduction; the shrinkage of international trade which was leading nations to protect themselves by tariffs and other barriers; and reparations and inter-allied debts which, like the reconstruction of Germany and deficits on trade between the United States and Europe, were being financed by copious but not inexhaustible American loans. At the end of the twenties the politicians who were grappling with these economic problems became overwhelmed by them.

In Europe the acute phase of the crisis began in Austria in the spring of 1931. Austria, from having been the centre of a great empire, had become a small new state athwart the division between modern industrial western Europe and the relatively backward agricultural hinterlands of south-eastern Europe. It was prohibited by the treaty of St Germain – Austria's counterpart of Versailles – from uniting with Germany and this prohibition had been reinforced by the Geneva Protocol of 1922 when economic aid had been provided for Austria in return for renewed assurances that it would not unite with Germany. Equally Austria was prevented from combining with its other neighbours in a Danubian or central European federation, because these neighbours were determined to have nothing to do with anything which looked like a revival of the Austro-Hungarian empire. Austrian independence was a shibboleth of France as the foremost champion of the post-war settlement, of Czechoslovakia as the most vigorous of the new progeny of the settlement, and of Rumania and Yugoslavia as its beneficiaries, but independence in this case did not mean the defence of Austrian independence against an aggressor but insistence on Austrian independence against, if necessary, the interests of the Austrians themselves. Since Austria was poor as well as small, those who insisted on its independence had to pay to keep it solvent or see it become a dependency of some other power.

Austria's future became an active topic of discusssion and negotiation in 1930. Germany was afraid that Austria was looking to Italy for its salvation and regarded an Austro-German union as the only natural solution. Many Austrians would have preferred a wider solution in order not to become a mere province in a new German empire, but this way seemed to be blocked. France and Great Britain were at cross purposes. France was determined to prevent an Austro-German union but Great Britain was less alarmed by this prospect and wanted to patch up Franco-German differences rather than give France unequivocal support. Great Britain preferred the role of mediator to that of ally. In March 1931 Germany and Austria announced that they had agreed to form a customs union. France in particular regarded this projected union as a political scheme rather than an economic expedient. It was referred to the Permanent Court of International Justice at The Hague, which eventually declared it contrary to the Geneva Protocol but not contrary to the treaty of St Germain (in both cases by eight votes to seven). The plan was abandoned.

Meanwhile economic forces were gaining control. In May the principal Austrian bank, the *Credit-Anstalt für Handel und Gewerbe*, closed its doors. It was unable to meet its short term obligations because of the decline of Austrian industry and trade which had impoverished Austrian concerns to which the bank had lent its money. Its difficulties were accentuated by the withdrawal of French capital after the announcement of the customs union, and now France refused to help except on unacceptable terms. Although German banks and the Bank of England lent to the *Credit-Anstalt*, they were unable to save it and succeeded only in weakening themselves. Before the end of the month the German banks were in similar troubles from their own clients. By June the *Reichsbank* had lost over a billion marks and in July one of the leading German banks, the *Darmstadter National*, also closed its doors. American banks which had lent to German banks began to feel alarmed. The Bank of England too was in trouble and borrowed from the Bank of France – France was financially the strongest country in Europe. British industrial and commercial activities were in decline. Unemployment was growing, and in June it became known that under existing arrangements the British government could meet only half of the calls on it for unemployment relief. The Labour government decided that it must balance its budget as a precondition to getting loans from American finance houses, even if part of the cost had to be paid by the unemployed. A special cabinet committee recommended cuts in public expenditure amounting to £78.5 million. The full cabinet decided that cuts of £56 million would do but it then disagreed over one item, a proposal to reduce by one tenth the dole payable to the unemployed. At Invergordon there was a mutiny when it was discovered that cuts in the pay of the lower ranks in the Royal Navy were to exceed the 10 per cent deduction required of all employees of the Crown. The government broke up and the country went off the gold standard.

Some temporary relief, psychological rather than economic, was provided by President Hoover's offer to suspend for one year the payment of debts due to the United States if other inter-governmental debts were likewise suspended. Hoover's offer anticipated an inevitable

German default and shortly afterwards Germany declared that it would not resume payments after the end of the Hoover year. The Young Plan was scrapped and a conference at Lausanne in 1932 sanctioned, in camouflaged language, the abandonment of reparations. Another conference at Stresa later in the year tried to find a solution for economic ailments of Austria and south-eastern Europe but, failing, left the area open to Germany.

The great crash and the great depression shattered more than material things. They destroyed morale. They injected a great amount of fear into ordinary people (including the ordinary people who sat in cabinets) and so turned them to an intent concern for their own affairs, present and future. The sense of community narrowed. Nation protected itself against nation, class turned against class. The millions of victims of the mysterious workings of economics looked for somewhere to lay the blame for their sufferings, and for somebody to lead them out of the mess. And nowhere were the confusion and disruption worse than in Germany which had relied most completely on foreign loans. There too factories began to close, unemployment grew by leaps and bounds, and the cost of unemployment relief exceeded the capacity of the treasury to pay it. The resulting problem sundered the democratic parties. The Left wanted higher taxes, the Right higher unemployment contributions and lower relief; the Left, in other words wanted the economy as a whole to subsidize the unemployment fund, while the Right wanted the fund to balance itself at whatever level was dictated by circumstances. Although both sides were prepared to temper their claims, neither would go far enough to meet the other. For two years Heinrich Brüning, who had been appointed Chancellor in March 1930, tussled with diminishing success with these economic and political storms.

Brüning was an intelligent man in his mid-forties, socially of the middle class, politically of the centre-Right, well intentioned and determined to save the republic. It was his fate to preside over the collapse of German credit and German democracy. By 1929 the steady economic expansion of 1925–8 had come to a halt and in the three ensuing years – 1930–32, the worst of the crisis – the national income was almost halved and one in three of the working population was put out of work. The Austrian crisis having triggered off a German crisis and foreigners (to whom half of all German credits were owed) having hurried to demand repayment of their short-term loans, the credit system collapsed. At the same time the problem of how to relieve the unemployed created dissensions among the centre parties of the Reichstag. Brüning, whose instinctive loyalties went not so much to democratic

institutions as to the person of the chief of state, once his regimental
commander, failed to hold the coalition together, a failure for which
the Social Democrats share the blame. His policies were wrong enough
to aggravate political dissension among the moderates and then
belatedly right enough to give his ultimate successors, the Nazis, a
good start. His methods – government by decree in the last resort –
accustomed Germany to procedures which the Nazis turned into common form, and so accustomed foreigners to seeing Germany governed
that way.

He took office with the determination not to inflate. The post-war
inflation was remembered with such horror that any degree of inflation
was very difficult to contemplate. A moderate or controlled inflation
was not part of the German experience; inflation meant run-away
inflation, a situation in which the value of a house falls to that of a box
of matches between breakfast and lunch. Any inflation was a national
phobia. So Brüning took the traditional, but beyond certain limits
socially intolerable, course of deflation. His immediate problem was
the flight of capital from Germany. Having decided against devaluation
he resorted to import licensing and exchange controls (both of which
were later developed by the Nazis) and to deflation, but deflation failed
to boost German exports partly because the government deflated too
little and partly because Germany's customers had devalued their
currencies. The balance of payments grew worse and the reserves went
on falling. At home the attempt to balance the budget by cutting social
benefits and increasing taxes widened the rift between Right and Left.
Brüning's 1930 budget had to be enacted by decree. The Social Democrats moved in the Reichstag to annul the decrees. The President
dissolved the Reichstag. No parliamentary majority could be found. If
Brüning hoped to gain control of the Reichstag by new elections he was
disappointed, for at the elections of September 1930 the Nazis increased
their seats from twelve to 107 and the communists from fifty-four to
seventy-seven. The anti-parliamentary extremes were carried by the
votes of the unemployed to a dominant position in the parliament and
even with Social Democrat cooperation Brüning was now dependent
on the President and his power to legislate by decree. By the beginning
of 1931 unemployment was aproaching the 5 million mark (it continued
to rise until the latter part of 1932), production had declined by nearly
half of what it had been in 1928, and parliament and the constitution
were unworkable. Brüning's policy had failed and the failure, a product
of the unenlightened economics of the time in government in Washington, Berlin and other political capitals, visited on the German populace

economic hardships unparalleled in peacetime in an advanced industrial country. It also alienated an influential segment of the business class which had previously supported Brüning's Centre Party and so, indirectly, the Weimar republic. The economic crisis laid bare weaknesses in the German banking system which the government could not go on ignoring, but Brüning's attempts to correct these weaknesses – by the introduction of state supervision and inspection of banking practices – caused bankers and their associates in industry and commerce to look round for other parties to patronize. The developed world's economic ignorance and incompetence played a large part in making Germany choose Hitler.

Deflation was abandoned in 1932. It had done no good except to prove the need for something different. A new expansionist policy, based on expenditure on public works, was adopted. It was to be greatly expanded by the Nazis and to reduce unemployment – even before the impact of rearmament – from a peak of over 6 million to 2.6 million at the end of 1934. The Nazis, unafraid of state interference with private enterprise and unhampered by the trade-unions which they overpowered, pursued a policy of inflation controlled by tax increases and by wage, price and dividend restrictions. By 1937 Germany was short of labour. But a few years earlier inflation had seemed impossible. Because there had been so much of it in the early twenties, there was too little of it in the early thirties and too late. Deflation reduced Germany to something approaching despair and chaos at a time when powerful forces – the Nazis and the communists – could see that despair and chaos were what they needed.

The Nazi Party had made little impression during the years of prosperity (1924–9). It won only twelve seats in the Reichstag in 1928, but between 1929 and 1933 it grew into a mass party of the discontented. The Nazis attacked in the name of socialism the parties and policies which could produce nothing better than unemployment; they accused the entire political establishment of callousness and unimaginativeness. At the same time and in the name of nationalism they denounced the treaty of Versailles as an affront to Germany and a prime source of its economic ills. In the Reichstag elections of September 1930 they jumped from the category of a splinter party on the lunatic fringe into that of a political force which could be left out of no calculation. Six and a half million Germans voted Nazi and made the party the second biggest in the Reichstag. Newspapers abroad dug into their records to tell their readers something about its Austrian leader, Adolf Hitler, who now became world famous. Less than two years later this popular vote was more than doubled to give the Nazis 230 seats and make it the biggest in the Reichstag. But they never polled half the electorate in a free election. Even after Hitler won the chancellorship the Nazi vote in the election of March 1933 was only 43.9 per cent. But by then figures no longer meant much.

The rapid rise in Hitler's popular support created a problem for the other nationalist and right-wing parties. Either Hitler would come to power in alliance with them or he would be swept into power by the masses, with or without violence. Hitler could see this too and in the declining years of the Weimar republic he played politics in the knowledge that the German Right was in a dilemma. The Right had this much in common with the Nazis that both were anti-republican. The Right believed, or hoped, that Hitler's wilder strains were the sort of political moonshine which can be ignored by sensible men and which is forgotten by even the worst demagogue when he gets office; Hindenburg among others seemed more put off by Corporal Hitler's social inferiority than by his manic utterances. The Nationalist Party, led by the rich industrialist and newspaper owner Alfred Hugenberg, was the first to make an alliance with the Nazis. Others waited, but when Hitler stood against Hindenburg for the presidency in 1932 the Right voted for Hitler. There were four candidates for the presidency, none of them democrats. Only Hindenburg was strong enough to beat Hitler. So the Field Marshal, receiving substantial support from an unaccustomed quarter, was re-elected, after a second poll, by the votes of the Left – to which he was now useless from senility as well as conviction.

After his re-election Hindenburg discarded Brüning and replaced him by Franz von Papen, the nominee of the anti-parliamentary forces of the Right – the army, the big landowners and big business. Papen was a member of the lesser nobility who was sufficiently insensitive to political reality to imagine that he could outwit Hitler and run a right-wing government without him. Papen fell between two stools. First he destroyed what slight chance of a centre coalition still existed when, in violation of the constitution, he dismissed the Social Democrat government of Prussia and subordinated it to the central government of the Reich. Then he changed his mind about the Nazis and offered Hitler the Vice-Chancellorship. But he was too late. His offer was not good enough for Hitler who had meanwhile, in the elections of July 1932, become the leader of the biggest parliamentary party. Hitler asked for the Chancellorship. He was refused. Hindenburg declared that he would not give the Nazis full powers because 'they intended to use these powers to further their own ends'. Hitler was both checked and humiliated. Optimists grasped at any sign that somehow somebody was going to prevent Hitler from triumphing. But there was also a growing feeling that the Nazis would and should come to power. The more they spread chaos the more they gave the impression that they alone could allay it. Street violence was an everyday occurrence: public political murders, put at forty-two in 1929 and fifty in 1930, had quadrupled in the first half of 1931 and were still increasing. Terror and brutality, by communists as well as Nazis, sickened public opinion and alarmed the army which shrank from the prospect of having to fight Nazis and communists at once. Hitler deliberately raised the stakes by sending a telegram of sympathy and support to some Nazis who had broken into the house of a young communist called Hans Potempa and kicked him to death before his mother's eyes. At the same time the Nazis were saying – and demonstrating – that they alone had the energy and the willpower to restore order. The public became inured to the idea that the price of order was a Nazi government.

On the parliamentary front Nazis, communists and socialists combined to defeat Papen in the Reichstag in September and in the ensuing elections in November the Nazi tide receded slightly. But Papen still commanded no majority in the Reichstag and, having failed to contain the Nazis or come to terms with them, he was no longer any use. He had been made Chancellor because the army wanted him and the President commanded him and his failure forced the army to take the Chancellorship itself in the person of General Kurt von Schleicher. Papen had been a nominee of the army, Schleicher was its embodiment: seconds were out. Schleicher had been in favour of bringing Hitler into the government until he discovered that Hindenburg would not have Hitler. He still thought it necessary to bring Nazis into the cabinet and he proceeded to offer the Vice-Chancellorship to Gregor Strasser, the leader of the northern and more radical section of the party and the representative of what was left of socialism in National Socialism (a by-product of attempts in the twenties to woo the working classes and lesser *bourgeoisie*). Strasser was willing but stipulated that Hitler must first bless the union, which Hitler refused to do. It is difficult to understand how either Schleicher or Strasser ever imagined that he would, and Strasser merely destroyed himself by letting Schleicher use him in this way. Schleicher, who was a political neophyte, next tried an approach to the democratic Left, whereupon the financial and industrial establishment put pressure on Hindenburg to recall Papen and install a Papen–Hitler coalition. The army too failed to stand solid for its own Chancellor. Some officers, led by General von Blomberg, went over to the Nazis. Hitler now had enough backing from the conservatives, the moneyed interests and the army to make his own terms. This was the end of Schleicher, whose short period in office marked the end of the German army's exercise of political power. Out of deference to Hindenburg, who thus performed a last service by easing Hitler into power, Schleicher quietly relinquished his post. On 30 January 1933 Hitler was appointed Chancellor by Hindenburg with Papen as his Vice-Chancellor.

Hitler became Chancellor constitutionally. To say that he became Chancellor legally would be to ignore the activities of his party which, in the preceding years, had committed countless acts of criminal violence, including murder; but technically Hitler (like Mussolini) did not seize office, it was conferred upon him. There is a difference between seizing office and assuming power. Hitler assumed power between 1929 and 1933 by violent means but he forbore to lay hands on the institutions of the state which he proposed to manipulate. Ever since his abortive putsch in 1923 Hitler had been sagacious enough to sense and insist upon the advantages of observing prescribed constitutional processes. He was a better respecter of pieces of paper than pieces of humanity, because he realized the strength of formalities and the bemusing effect of a show of continuity. He had made no secret of his intentions. In 1931, for example, he had told a German editor, a political opponent, that although he intended to come to power by winning seats in the Reichstag, after he had done so the Reichstag might as well close its doors and be turned into a museum; and after his appointment as Chancellor it took him only a matter of months to master the whole apparatus of power and propaganda in Germany. The steps which he took were characteristic: legislation and murder.

Between 9 and 10 p.m. on 27 February 1933 the Reichstag was burnt to the ground. Hitler at once blamed the communists. He probably really thought they had done it. Others equally promptly assumed that the Nazis had burnt it with the intention of incriminating the communists and liquidating their party, and at the end of the war General Halder said that Goering had boasted in 1942 that the fire was his doing. The question remains obscure and there is much to be said for the view that the Dutch communist Marinus van der Lubbe did, as he himself claimed, conceive the conflagration and effect it on his own as a one-man protest. It is evident that the three Bulgarian communists tried with van der Lubbe (who was executed) had nothing to do with the deed. They were even acquitted. Whatever the truth the Nazis seized their opportunity with alacrity – proof either of their efficiency or their complicity. Arrests were made within a matter of hours, communist newspapers were suppressed, and an emergency decree was issued the next day overriding basic civil rights such as freedom of expression and assembly, permitting arbitrary searches and seizure of property, empowering the central government to assume the functions of local authorities and imposing severe penalties. This decree was never repealed. In March Hitler supplemented it by an Enabling Act which in effect converted him into a one-man legislature. This act, which required a two-thirds majority in the Reichstag, was passed only because the Centre Party (at the bidding of the Vatican) voted for it. A few Social Democrat voices were raised, for the last time, in courageous but futile protest. With the powers thus conferred upon him Hitler decreed all parties except his own out of existence, subordinated the federal states to the central government, and won 92 per cent of the vote in elections which he staged in November 1933. He abolished free trade-unions, intimidated the churches and virtually annexed the judiciary and the educational system, thus moulding a new society in which only Nazi ideas, ethical, social and political, might be expressed and protected.

Hitler also struck down a part of his own movement, the armed S A or *Sturmabteilungen*, led by Ernst Röhm, an even earlier member of the Nazi Party than Hitler himself and one of the few men with whom he used the intimate second person singular '*du*'. The S A had had a job to do on the streets in the days before the Nazis came to power. They provided the rough and tough arguments for supporting the Nazis or keeping out of their way. But Hitler had had trouble with them from the start. They regarded themselves as an independent force like the Free Corps from which many of them were initially drawn and they wished to be as autonomous *vis-à-vis* the party as the German army traditionally was *vis-à-vis* the state. Hitler had been obliged in 1930 to eliminate their leader Franz Pfeffer von Salomon, an ex-Free Corps man, because he proved too independent and opposed Hitler's policy of achieving power by constitutional means. He also had to suppress an open revolt by the Berlin S A in the same year and had further trouble in the next year. Moreover the S A were growing fast. At the beginning of 1931 they were 100,000 strong, the same size as the army; at the end of that year they were 300,000 strong. By the middle of 1934, their ranks swollen particularly by unemployment and by the march-fever which swept through Germany in these troubled years, they had reached a strength of 4.5 million and were scaring the army as well as Nazi Party chiefs. The S A were the most prominent of various Nazi organizations which duplicated the organizations of the state (like a shadow cabinet duplicates a cabinet) but which become irrelevant or embarrassing when their party becomes the state. Röhm saw the SA as replacing the regular army. Politically naïve and temperamentally unbalanced, he overplayed his hand fantastically. He thoroughly alarmed the officer caste by letting it be known that in his view the armed services should be reduced to being training organizations for the SA, and he failed to see that Hitler needed the army. His ambitions contributed to the alliance which both Hitler and the army desired and provided it with a sacrificial victim. The army began at this period to dismiss its Jewish officers to please Hitler and early in 1934 Hitler forced Röhm to agree, formally and in writing, to moderate his ambitions. But rumours of an SA putsch persisted and in June Blomberg, now Minister for Defence, warned Hitler that the army would turn him out, get Hindenburg to declare martial law, hand over the government to the military and probably restore the Hohenzollerns if the SA were allowed to usurp the functions of the army; if the SA were suppressed, the army would see that Hitler got the Presidency. Hitler thereupon organized a massacre. On 30 June Röhm and about fifty other SA leaders were murdered. The opportunity was taken to murder a great many other people too; they included Schleicher and also Gregor Strasser, although there are doubts whether Hitler wanted the latter's death. But the principal beneficiaries of the destruction of the SA were not the army but Heinrich Himmler and his SS or *Schutzstaffeln* which flourished on the ashes of the SA and became the rival military force which the army had sought to destroy with the SA.

A month later Hindenburg died. The office of President was merged with that of Chancellor. More important, the death of Hindenburg provided Hitler with the opportunity to annex the officer corps to his revolution. With some exceptions the officer corps disliked the Nazis but it shared some of Hitler's aims and was confident that its power was greater than his. From Hitler's point of view the army differed in two ways from every other institution in the state: it was too powerful to be destroyed and he needed it. Although within Germany it might challenge the power of the Nazis, externally it was essential to Hitler's purposes, especially for the conquest of *Lebensraum*. Therefore it had to be strengthened and at the same time rendered domestically harmless. On the day after Hindenburg's death every member of the armed services swore a new oath of obedience to Adolf Hitler in person as 'the Führer of the German Reich and people and Commander-in-Chief of the armed forces'. This oath was devised by General Walther von Reichenau, one of a group of officers who were at this time keenly pro-Nazi. It gave Hitler a moral authority over the officer corps which endured almost undented until the end of his life. The army which had virtually ordered the elimination of the SA had placed itself under the Führer's personal orders by the oath, the mystic force which bound the army together and determined its relation to the state. By this oath the army equated the guardianship of the German state with obedience to the command of Hitler who was henceforward not only Führer but also President and Supreme War Lord.

CHAPTER 3

The Futile Opposition: 1934–8

IN external affairs Hitler's first aim was to restore German power. He intended to recover for Germany the lands and the peoples lost in Europe after the First World War and to re-establish the armed services which had been destroyed or crippled by the peace settlement. These aims were not novel but they were accompanied by another which, though likewise not novel, was rationalized by Hitler in a new way. Hitler intended that Germany should expand into non-German lands and his reason was his conviction that a people must either wax or die. He did not believe that a people could remain static and survive. So safeguarding the German people meant increasing their number (a biological rather than a military necessity) and securing somewhere for them to live. In *Mein Kampf* he had written, with a mixture of conviction and guff, of securing

... the existence and increase of our race and nation, the sustenance of its children and the purity of its blood, the freedom and independence of the fatherland, and the nation's ability to fulfil the mission appointed to it by the creator of the universe.

The British, so far as they paid any attention to this sort of thing, thought it might be met by offering Hitler colonies, a partial acceptance of the German demand to revise Versailles and a sop to assuage or eliminate his more dangerous aims in Europe; they dangled colonial carrots before Hitler up to the last months of peace. But Hitler was not to be put off in Europe by presents in Africa. He intended to colonize in Europe, not Africa. He made this clear both privately and publicly. A few days after becoming Chancellor he told his service chiefs that the restoration of German power entailed the creation of a unified German nation by converting or breaking all opposing forces and by mastering youth, the struggle against Versailles, the colonization of parts of Europe in order to gain living space, and the reinforcement of the armed services. Publicly he was no less explicit. 'The foreign policy of a nation (*völkisch*) state', he wrote in *Mein Kampf*, 'must assure the existence on this planet of a race encompassed by the state; it must do this by creating a healthy, life-giving and natural balance between the present and future numbers of the *Volk* on the one hand and, on the

other, the quantity and quality of its territory.' In his next paragraph
Hitler made it clear that the prime aim of this foreign policy was to
make the *Volk* self-sufficient in food within the boundaries of its state
and by extending those boundaries if necessary. This passage comes
near the beginning of a chapter entitled Eastern Policy. It left therefore
no doubt where Hitler coveted land. It was included in the abbreviated
English translation of *Mein Kampf* which was published in 1933 – and
reissued in 1935 in a cheap, paperback edition which sold nearly
50,000 copies in three years.

In 1933 he did not know how or when he was going to achieve these
aims. In this sense he had no plans, but he had aims and the achievement of his aims for the German people included from the outset
measures which other peoples would never willingly accept. He himself was aware of this. He did not expect to win *Lebensraum* – that is to
say, other people's territories – without war.

Among the European powers Hitler distinguished between France
and the USSR on the one hand and Great Britain and Italy on the
other. France he regarded as an irreconcilable foe, the USSR as an
inevitable one. Thus the two chief traditional opponents of the extension of German power were opponents still (although the Franco-
Russian treaty of 1935 did not create so menacing a combination as the
old Dual Alliance). Hitler's attitudes to these two powers were, however, very different. The irreconcilability of Germany and France came
from the French side. In his view it was the French who were perpetuat-
ing the Franco-German feud; they were unbiddable, nothing could
abate their animosity. At the same time Hitler despised them, so that
although French hostility was a fact it was not a very serious one.
French power was enough to give Hitler pause but not to thwart him –
as he showed when he remilitarized the Rhineland in 1936 against the
advice of his generals.

Hitler's feelings about the USSR included hatred as well as contempt.
Although he despised Russians as Slavs and sub-men and lacked that
respect for their tenacity which was felt by many Germans who, unlike himself, had fought on the eastern front in the First World War,
the overmastering sentiment in his references to the USSR was a
passionate loathing for their communism which was for him one of the
principal contemporary expressions of the age-long Jewish conspiracy
against the human race. Ultimately too it was the USSR which
Germany would have to fight for *Lebensraum*.

Italy and Great Britain came into a different category. They were
potential allies or at least non-objectors. To begin with Hitler thought

of Italy as no more than a medium power which could prove useful by engaging and distracting France and Great Britain in the Mediterranean, but the course of international politics in the mid-thirties threw Mussolini into Hitler's arms. The two dictators, though personally loyal to one another, never established a close and confidential alliance between their countries like the wartime Anglo-American alliance. Still less did they coordinate their war efforts, but the Rome-Berlin axis justified Hitler in his judgement that Italy could be brought to serve his purposes by helping to demoralize France with multiple preoccupations in the central and western Mediterranean and to convince British governments that they could not face war with Germany unless Italy were first neutralized.

Hitler's feelings about Great Britain were complex and in the end wrong. The British were Aryan and they were successful imperialists. He could respect them. Hitler must have been aware of the view current in Germany that the challenge to Great Britain in 1914 by the invasion of Belgium had been a mistake, although by the end of 1939 – after war had begun – he said that the violation of Belgian (and Dutch) neutrality was a matter of no importance. *Mein Kampf* assumed no conflict with Great Britain and a decade after he wrote his book Hitler was still pursuing the same policy of appeasement when he sent Ribbentrop to be his Ambassador in London. The Nazis avoided the Kaiser's challenge to British sea power and Hitler never had any intention of rebuilding the German High Seas Fleet. But Hitler's admiration for the British was for what they had done in the past and he thought that they had had their day. He despised Neville Chamberlain when he met him although he admired Lloyd George. The question was whether Great Britain would stand in his way. On the whole he thought not. There was, he believed, a difference between Great Britain and France: whereas France wanted to prevent Germany from becoming powerful at all, Great Britain was only concerned to prevent Germany from becoming the sort of world power which would threaten British world power. But Hitler did not want to threaten this British position. He envisaged two world powers, the one based on dominion in Europe and the other based on dominion of the seas, and he hoped that if he made this plain Great Britain would not object to German hegemony in Europe. Subsequent events seemed to show that Hitler was wrong about Great Britain and failed to gauge its inevitable and implacable opposition to his plans. But his error was pardonable. His view of Anglo-German relations was not confined to Germans. When Halifax was about to visit Hitler in 1937 Sir Nevile Henderson, the British

Ambassador in Berlin, urged the Foreign Secretary to 'look facts in the face' and remember that 'the main point is that we are an *island* people and Germans a continental one. On that basis we can be friends and both go along the road of destiny without a clash of vital interests.' Further, as late as 1940, when France fell, some British political leaders gave thought and utterance to coming to terms with Hitler and letting him be. They did not prevail but their hesitations show that Hitler's error about Great Britain was only a marginal one, albeit one of those marginal errors which turn out to be fatal.

Hitler's problem in foreign affairs was to nullify international opposition to his international aims, until he was strong enough to dictate abroad as well as at home. He had to ensure that Germany's strength grew faster than fear of Germany, for if the fear grew faster then the forces which had opposed and beaten the Kaiser's Reich might together destroy the new Reich. Fortunately for Hitler this possibility was largely theoretical, for the victors of 1918 were no longer united. After that war two of them, France and the United States, had put forward entirely different solutions to the German problem and in the upshot neither scheme survived in working order. The twenties therefore had seen the elaboration of substitutes, so that when Hitler came to power the principal formalized constraints upon his freedom of action beyond his borders were, in the west, the Locarno treaties of 1925 and, in the east, a patchwork of alliances designed by France – systems which were scrappily deputizing for the treaty of Versailles and the Covenant of the League of Nations.

After victory Clemenceau's solution to the problem of what to do about a powerful Germany was to put such constraints upon it as to make it harmless for as long as possible. President Wilson's solution was to devise a system which would nullify the excesses of every state. Clemenceau was seeking a specific solution to a specific problem, Wilson a general solution to a universal ill. Clemenceau was by nature a pessimist, Wilson an optimist. Clemenceau was a Frenchman first and a European afterwards, Wilson was not a European at all.

The best that France could hope for at the Peace Conference was to dismember Germany (French policy since Richelieu), extend France and get Great Britain and the United States to promise to go to war as soon as Germany attacked France again, This programme failed completely. Great Britain and the United States offered to guarantee France's territory as part of a bargain which included, in the American case the acceptance of the Covenant of the League and, in the British case, the formalization of the American guarantee. When the US

Senate refused to endorse the Covenant the American guarantee to France lapsed and with it the British. Nor was France allowed to annex German territory west of the Rhine. It had to be content with the demilitarization of these Rhineland areas together with their occupation by the allies until (in different zones) 1925, 1930 and 1935 and with the possibility of acquiring the small Saar territory, economically rather than strategically valuable, by plebiscite. Germany was also to be and to remain substantially disarmed, and was, as we have already seen, subjected until shortly before Hitler's accession to paying reparations designed to keeping its economy trained upon the discharge of debt instead of the creation of military might.

The collapse of the American and British guarantees was not France's only diplomatic setback. In the east Russia itself had collapsed. To most Europeans the new USSR did not look like a useful (or respectable) ally at any time between 1917 and 1941. This was to be an immensely valuable aid to the revival of Germany as a major power. France tried to replace its eastern ally by new ones – by Poland, which was re-created in 1918 and with which France made a treaty in 1921, and by making friends with Czechoslovakia, Yugoslavia and Rumania, the so-called Little Entente, all of them beneficiaries of the break-up of the Austro-Hungarian empire and so, like France, supporters of the Versailles settlement. The weaknesses of France's eastern policies became clear in the thirties. Poland was no substitute for Russia as an ally against Germany except in the limited sense that it lay at Germany's back door. Poland did not feel committed to an anti-German policy as a first priority but developed a policy of keeping its balance between Germany and the USSR. Its population was only three-quarters Polish and it was on bad terms with its neighbours. It had barely re-emerged as a state when it was launched by Pilsudski on an ambitious attempt to recreate the ancient empire of Poles, Lithuanians, White Russians and Ukrainians. It had invaded the USSR in 1920 and, as a result of securing its old 1792 borders, contained within its frontiers six million Ukrainians and White Russians; it had seized Vilna from Lithuania in 1920 and it coveted Teschen which had been awarded to Czechoslovakia in the same year at a moment when its invasion of the USSR was going badly; it enjoyed special rights in Danzig, the port of the Vistula but demographically a German city with which it was linked by a corridor cut through Germany; and it gained much – Germans thought too much – of Upper Silesia in 1921 after a dubiously interpreted plebiscite. It was a Slav state at odds with other Slav states, a revived state with more than a touch of the intransigence

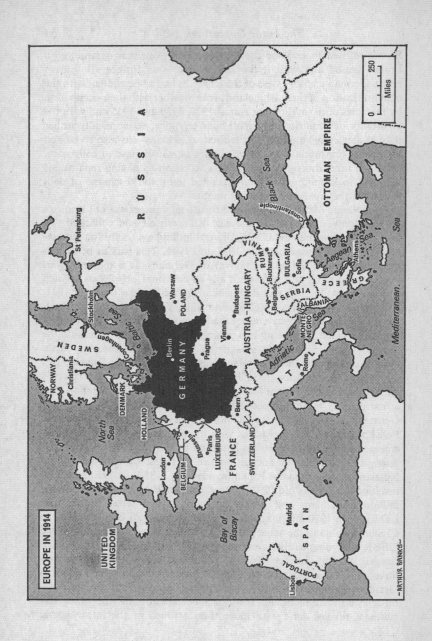

EUROPE IN 1914

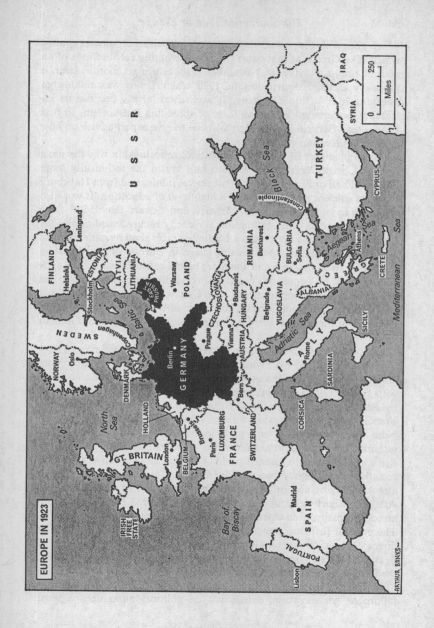

EUROPE IN 1923

0 ————— 250
Miles

IRAQ

SYRIA

TURKEY

CYPRUS

U S S R

Leningrad

Black Sea

Constantinople

Aegean Sea

Athens

CRETE

Mediterranean Sea

FINLAND

Helsinki

ESTONIA

LATVIA

LITHUANIA

EAST PRUSS.

Warsaw

POLAND

CZECHOSLOVAKIA

RUMANIA

Bucharest

BULGARIA

Sofia

GREECE

ALBANIA

YUGOSLAVIA

Belgrade

Budapest

AUSTRIA HUNGARY

Prague

Vienna

Adriatic Sea

I T A L Y

Rome

SICILY

Stockholm

S W E D E N

NORWAY

Oslo

Baltic Sea

Copenhagen

DENMARK

Berlin

G E R M A N Y

Bern

SWITZERLAND

Sea

SARDINIA

CORSICA

North Sea

HOLLAND

BELGIUM

Brussels

LUXEMBURG

Paris

F R A N C E

GT. BRITAIN

London

IRISH FREE STATE

Bay of Biscay

Madrid

SPAIN

PORTUGAL

Lisbon

ARTHUR BANKS

which goes with the proud reconquest of independence, a new republic which (like Greece at that date) cherished tempting recollections of an ancient empire. Revived in November 1918, at war six months later, it narrowly escaped destruction in 1920 when Lenin was talking of sweeping over it into Germany. It was saved largely because its instability exacerbated European fears of spreading Bolshevism, so that France sent General Weygand to Warsaw to give expert advice on how to stop the Russian counter-attack.

Of the members of the Little Entente Czechoslovakia was the most favoured, partly because its western half lay in the technically more advanced half of Europe and partly because it inherited from Habsburg times an efficient civil service and a high level of education. It was also fortunate in its founders, T. G. Masaryk and Edvard Beneš. But these advantages and its outstanding liberal record obscured weaknesses, for Czechoslovakia was even more a medley of races than its name implied and was also the principal meeting place in Europe of the thrusting industrialism of the west and the more placid conservatism of the agricultural east. In Yugoslavia racial and religious antagonisms made this new state even less homogeneous than Czechoslovakia, while Rumania had received the uncomfortable war prize of a large Hungarian population. And throughout eastern Europe there were significant German minorities.

Furthermore, Great Britain was never happy with the new eastern Europe reorganized on Wilsonian principles. These new states were children of the United States and soon orphaned. They were also allied with France but the alliances were brittle so long as they were disliked by France's greater ally, Great Britain. They were an ingredient in a French policy which was not France's only policy. This policy was to build up a pro-French and anti-German system in the east, while retaining the power to attack Germany directly in the west. The alternative was alliance with Great Britain. This was an alternative and not a complementary policy because Great Britain did not want France to attack Germany and did not want to be entangled in eastern Europe. After the abortive occupation of the Ruhr in 1923 France never did attack Germany, even when Hitler remilitarized the Rhineland in 1936. The price of British support was, first, the surrender of the policy of a direct French threat to Germany and, later, the abandonment of France's eastern system: the first was formalized at Locarno in 1925, the latter consummated at Munich in 1938.

Neither the instability of post-imperial eastern Europe nor France's failure to get territorial safeguards or political guarantees against

Germany would have mattered much if the system of collective security embodied in the Covenant of the League of Nations had been made to work. Before 1914 statesmen had tried by various means – diplomacy, conferences, the balance of power, arbitration – to prevent wars within the framework set by a multiplicity of nation states. The First World War not only signalized the failure of these techniques but was regarded as a condemnation of the multi-national system itself. A new comprehensive international system was required. President Wilson, who was among politicians the principal champion of this radical thinking, regarded a collective security system as an alternative to what had gone before, not as a supplement: the old system was bad in itself. He shared the belief that wars were caused by alliances, by armaments and by arms races; he saw the First World War as a logical consequence of the formation of the Triple Alliance and the Triple Entente and Anglo-German naval competition, and he wanted to create an international system which would make such things unnecessary and proscribe them. But the new system embodied in the League of Nations did not work in the Wilsonian way because too many important states remained outside it, because it was too new to be trusted, and ultimately because some of its more important members did not want it to work.

Between the French and American approaches to peace in Europe there emerged a distinctive British attitude which sought security by reconciling Germany with its former enemies and with the terms of the peace settlement, if necessary by modifying the latter. Champions of reconciliation argued that it was a surer safeguard of the peace than anti-German alliances, that the Germans were not after all the horde of savages portrayed by wartime propaganda but a Christian nation which had produced Goethe and Beethoven, that there was in Germany much to admire from standards of public behaviour and public administration to open air weekends of an unimpeachably healthy nature, that the reparations demanded by the peace treaty were unfairly discriminatory. This was a laudable attempt to bury hatchets, all the more laudable since the British public continued to harbour powerful anti-German emotions. It was also firmly grounded in political calculation. The alternative to reconciliation with Germany was the prospect of a second European war against Germany and the maintenance in peacetime of a military establishment, which however natural to a Frenchman, was anathema to the British: the Dominions too disliked a view of things in which the British empire was a reserve force to be used to redeem the imbalance of power in Europe. Both as an island and as an empire Great Britain was congenitally wedded to a view of the German question which was different from the French view. The principal achievement of the British view was the Locarno treaties of 1925, a local and limited settlement which, however, by-passed the Wilsonian general approach to security and also contradicted the essential bases of French policy.

The Franco-Belgian occupation of the Ruhr in 1923 had been a failure and the tough school in Paris was eclipsed when Raymond Poincaré was succeeded by Édouard Herriot and France accepted the Dawes Plan in 1924. A first attempt to reassure France focused on strengthening the League's machinery of collective security. The Covenant provided that a state must not carry a dispute to the point of war without first trying to settle it in one of a number of specified ways and accepting a cooling-off period of three months. If a signatory of the Covenant broke this rule, it was branded as an aggressor and other members would together apply sanctions against it. But the rule was a limited one. It did not apply if the Council of the League was not unanimous about the rights and wrongs of the dispute; it did not apply if the dispute was found to lie within the domestic jurisdiction of the state concerned; and it did not apply if that state observed the cooling-off rule and the dispute was still unresolved at the end of it. These exceptions were called the gaps in the Covenant and in 1924 the so-called Geneva Protocol sought to plug the gaps by providing for the compulsory arbitration of all disputes and the application of sanctions to every resort to war. The protocol was accepted by the British Labour government but the Conservatives, returning to power in 1924, refused to ratify it because Great Britain, strongly reinforced by the independent British Dominions, thought that the scope of the Covenant was already wide enough and ought not to be enlarged in such a way as to cumber members of the League with further commitments. The new British government then proposed something else – a system for keeping the peace in western Europe, based on the acceptance of Germany as a state like any other. This was the genesis of Locarno.

What France feared was a fresh German attack one day across the Rhine and through the Rhineland. Austen Chamberlain, the Foreign Secretary in Stanley Baldwin's new government, proposed that Great Britain and Italy should guarantee the Franco-German and Belgo-German frontiers without discrimination as to an aggressor; that is to say, Germany was guaranteed as much as France and Belgium. For Great Britain this reciprocity was more than a diplomatic nicety, since it ruled out a second Franco-Belgian occupation of the Ruhr, but for

France reciprocity meant the end of a special advantage and a fundamental review of French strategy. It was no longer possible to hope that
another war would begin beyond France's frontiers instead of with an
invasion across them. The best thing now was to take steps to keep the
Germans out. A few years later the Maginot Line was begun, a line of
fortifications which proved useless when the Germans invaded in 1940
but which meanwhile corroded the French spirit since the obvious thing
to do with a fortified line is to sit tight behind it. (The Maginot Line has
been chiefly derided for its psychological effects on French military
thinking and general French morale. Tactically it was defective even on
the premises of those who believed in it, since it did not cover the whole
of France's eastern front – Pétain having pronounced the Ardennes to
be impassable. Even had it been completed it was still an anachronism,
a defensive line performing essentially the same function as a trench but
ineffective in a war of movement in which no line could stop all the
enemy's armour or even most of it.)

The Locarno system was also defective from the French point of
view because Great Britain refused to extend it to eastern Europe. Germany did not accept its eastern frontiers. It was in fact Stresemann's
intention to alter these frontiers, as well as other features of the Versailles treaty which were obnoxious to Germany, and his acceptance of a
firm settlement in the west, including the demilitarization of the Rhineland which was freely reaffirmed at Locarno, was part of the price he
was willing to pay in order to separate western from eastern problems
and gain a greater freedom of manoeuvre in the east. With Poland and
Czechoslovakia he agreed to conclude arbitration treaties but no more.
France extended guarantees to these two countries but the British
refusal to do so was more significant. In the west Locarno confirmed
Versailles, in the east it questioned Versailles and it did so because Great
Britain, anxious to conciliate Germany, and Germany, anxious to keep
a free hand in the east, prevailed over France which would have preferred to strengthen the anti-German forces in that area. Locarno was
also a principal source of the mistaken notion that Italy was a Great
Power.

The Locarno settlement provided the formal basis for western European security for eleven years (1925–36). In 1926 Germany joined the
League of Nations. It also took part in the Disarmament Conference
which assembled at Geneva in February 1932 in a belated attempt to
fix and reduce arms levels as the Covenant of the League had envisaged
more than a decade earlier. But to Hitler treaties and conferences
represented limitations upon his freedom of action, preventing Germany

from getting strong in military muscle and breathing space. As he him-self later said he had to extricate Germany from the toils of the League and the Disarmament Conference. He left both in October 1933 and in the next year he concluded a non-aggression pact with Poland, a first stab at the French system in eastern Europe. For some years Hitler managed to persuade foreigners that the sum total of his ambitions was the rectification of legitimate German grievances by negotiation. There was some nervousness about his methods but a strong tendency to credit him with the same aims as Stresemann and Brüning. Hitler achieved this chiefly by alleging it to people who wished to believe it and were in the habit of treating statements as true until they were proved to be un-true: westerners were particularly influenced by his renunciation of claims to Alsace and Lorraine.

Within six months of Hitler's appointment as Chancellor the four principal European Powers concluded a pact among themselves. This Four Power Pact was more important for its signatories than for what it contained, which was vague and platitudinous. It was promoted by Mussolini who wanted to assert Italy's right to a place above the salt, welcomed by Great Britain because it accorded with the British policy of general reconciliation, accepted by Hitler because it gave him time and recognition, and signed by France because not to sign was to court isolation. It implied that the treaty of Versailles was no longer the basic factor in European affairs and that these would be regulated in future by a concert of the more powerful states, opponents of Versailles as well as its champions. The countries chiefly threatened by this prospect were the medium states of central and eastern Europe which owed their existence to Versailles and were allies of France. One of them, Poland, took the startling step of making a pact with Hitler.

But the lines were not yet drawn. An Anglo-French-Italian front against Germany seemed possible, until it was extinguished by the Ethiopian crisis which put Italy firmly on Hitler's side. Before that Ger-many and Italy were at arm's length because of Austria. Austria had a Nazi Party of its own, which was subordinate to the German party. It had also a militaristic right-wing organization, the *Heimwehr* (supported by Italian funds), and a reactionary clerical government under a Chancellor, Engelbert Dollfuss, who had become Chancellor in 1932 and was secretly in league with Mussolini to crush the socialist opposi-tion without having to ally himself either with the *Heimwehr* or, still less, the Austrian Nazis. Soon after Hitler became Chancellor in Ger-many Dollfuss banned the Austrian Nazi Party. Hitler had been encour-aging the Austrian Nazis to make a bid for power, but he realized that he would do himself more harm than good if, with Germany still less than semi-armed and more than semi-isolated, he were to stir up so much trouble in Austria that other states would unite against him. Mussolini was at least as anxious as France to keep Austria from being annexed by Germany and he entered into agreements with Austria and Hungary, whose leaders he received in Rome in March 1934. Hitler decided therefore to hold his hand for the time being, but the Austrian Nazis were less responsive to restraint than to encouragement and in July – with the connivance of some German Nazis but perhaps not Hitler himself – they attempted a coup and assassinated Dollfuss. Mussolini staged an armed display on his frontier with Austria. Hitler did nothing and the coup was a failure. This string of incidents is revealing. Hitler did not lack political courage but he combined courage with caution. He was inclined to attend upon circumstances with the result that the timing of his principal operations was often dictated by circumstance. The later history of Austria confirms the point. At the end of 1937 Hitler was still waiting with a wary eye on France, and although he actually went into Austria in March 1938 the timing was, as we shall see, still not of his own choosing. This readiness of Hitler to bide his time can produce the misleading conclusion that Hitler's aims were never formulated so precisely in his mind as events made them appear; but it was only his timetable and not his programme which was vague. He was like those persons who love to make lists of things to do but without any clear idea when they will get done. This does not mean that he did not intend to do them.

Austria was one of the two keys to Italian policy. The second was the Balkans. Italy looked nervously at its frontier with Austria on the Brenner and also at Albania where the eastern shore of the Adriatic comes closest to Italy. In the twenties Mussolini's policy was comparatively pacific – to secure Italian interests by treaties of mutual friendship. He wanted a government in Vienna which was neither too left-wing to make and keep bargains with fascist Italy nor too powerful to need to bother about them. In 1925 he was unenthusiastic about the Locarno plan because it created two categories of frontiers, the guaranteed and the unguaranteed, the Brenner frontier being one of the latter, and in 1934 he was alarmed by the prospect of a strong German government in Vienna in place of a more tractable Austrian one. In Albania he had rejected the policy of direct intervention advocated by nationalists like Luigi Federzoni in favour of reducing Albania to puppet status by economic domination and by marrying an Italian princess to King Zog (in the event she married another Balkan monarch, King Boris of

Bulgaria, instead). Here Italy's dominant concern was not Germany but France. Albania apart, the eastern shore of the Adriatic belonged to Yugoslavia which was an ally of France and suspected Italy of coveting the Dalmatian coast. Mussolini pursued an irregular policy; Italy was not strong enough to enable him to be anything but opportunistic, especially when his European concerns became linked with ambitions in Africa. He tried to secure his two soft spots in Europe by agreement with France in Laval's time but his attempt to include in the bargain the conquest of Ethiopia caused the collapse of the Franco-Italian rapprochement and propelled him into alliance with Hitler. Then, largely at Ciano's prompting, he reverted to the policy of direct intervention in Albania which he proceeded to conquer in April 1939.

Had Mussolini's ambitions been limited to Europe a Franco-Italian alliance might have come into being, but Mussolini wanted to cut a dash in the world, especially in the Mediterranean which he regarded as an Italian lake and in Africa where, to his chagrin, France and Great Britain had acquired more prestigious empires than Italy. With a sort of Disraelian rapture Mussolini decided to conquer Ethiopia and nominate the King of Italy as emperor. He anticipated no real objections from Paris or London which, as he correctly judged, were not really interested in Ethiopia. He had had his first encounter with Hitler in June 1934 just before the coup in Austria, but in January 1935 Pierre Laval visited Rome in an attempt to divert Mussolini to a pro-French attitude.

Laval became Foreign Minister in October 1934 in succession to Louis Barthou, who was murdered by a Croat in Marseilles along with King Alexander of Yugoslavia in what was probably an Italo-Hungarian plot to disrupt the Franco-Yugoslav alliance. Laval signed the pact with the USSR which had been negotiated by his predecessor but he did so only because this pact was in any case stillborn. France had a conservative government and the USSR a communist one. Ideological differences were not by themselves a bar to an alliance with a country which Richelieu had allied with Turks against Christians at the noontide of the Ottoman advance into Europe. But Richelieu had never feared what the Turks might do to France, whereas the politicians of the Third Republic feared very much what the USSR might do to France by means of the French Communist Party. Unlike the Sultan, Stalin had a political party inside France which was directed by the Communist International inside the USSR. Although Stalin had abandoned Trotsky's policy of permanent revolution, he had not gainsaid it and as a result an alliance between the USSR and the French Third Republic was all but impossible. For Laval the pact with the USSR which he inherited was distasteful but it was also a possible means to a different end: a rapprochement with Germany.

Laval, like a number of his contemporaries and like even more Frenchmen after the Second World War (including de Gaulle), sincerely desired to put an end to Franco-German hostility. He worked towards a rapprochement by using a Franco-Russian pact as a reserve threat and also by seeking an understanding with Italy which would still further isolate Germany. His Italian policy was dangerous because it disturbed the countries of the Little Entente. These wanted France to make an alliance with the USSR, but they distrusted Italy which was allied with Hungary – an anti-Versailles state which had lost territory to all three members of the Little Entente. So Laval risked losing his Little Entente allies unless he could reconcile them, especially Yugoslavia, with Italy. Moreover Mussolini had his price. It was a free hand for Italy in Africa. During his visit to Rome Laval at least implied that France would pay this price, although it is still open to doubt whether he was signalling to Mussolini that Italy might go ahead and attack Ethiopia or whether he meant no more than to concede to Italy an exclusive economic field in that country. The vagueness was not unintentional. Mussolini interpreted it in the most favourable light to his own ambitions and, at Stresa in April of the next year, he joined France and Great Britain in condemning breaches of the treaty of Versailles and subscribed a series of agreements whose general message was that these three powers were constituting an anti-German front. Again part of the bargain, in Mussolini's mind, was a free hand for Italy in Africa but again the understanding was so tacit that Ethiopia was not even mentioned. The Stresa front was a flimsy affair. In any case the front quickly obeyed its own nature and fell apart. In June the British government, still rather more intent on making friends with Germany than building an opposition to it, made a naval agreement with Germany in contravention not only of the treaty of Versailles but also of the declarations of the Stresa conference. France and Italy were not consulted, although France was informed at a late stage in the negotiations; its protests were ignored. This episode emphasized Great Britain's abandonment of the full letter of Versailles, but by conniving at a breach of Versailles Great Britain undermined its ability to protest against breaches of Locarno, which was its substitute for Versailles and was soon to be equally flouted by Hitler.

Although an Italian conquest of Ethiopia might endanger no vital French or British national interest, it could only be undertaken in breach of the Covenant of the League of Nations. It was therefore bound to weaken international stability by infringing the general principle of *pacta sunt servanda* as well as the precise terms of the Covenant, and a substantial body of opinion in France, Great Britain and elsewhere was not prepared to connive at Italian aggression for fear of encouraging aggression generally and weakening institutions which might be used to stop Hitler. Besides which the butchering of innocent Ethiopians to make a Roman empire was offensive on elementary human grounds. Consequently when war broke out in October, six months after the Stresa meeting, Mussolini discovered that his campaign was running up against more than a scandalized outcry. Laval discovered that his pro-Italian policy would not work so easily and he was forced to take a lead, jointly with Great Britain, in invoking sanctions against Italy.

But Great Britain and France did not persist. Torn between a policy of upholding the Covenant and the rule of law and, on the other hand, securing Italian friendship at the cost of letting Ethiopia down, they found that their zeal for sanctions stopped short of those measures which could have effectively checked Mussolini. Such measures, they feared, would force Mussolini to go to war with them. They were probably right, for Mussolini was too far committed in Africa and too vulnerable at home to refuse the challenge and survive. But by the same tokens he would not only have resorted to war; he would most probably have lost it. London and Paris were, however, not minded to bring the issue to the testing point. They preferred to bluff (a threat of British naval action which had no effect on the Italian government but persuaded the Italian people that Great Britain was an enemy) and they also entered into separate manoeuvres behind the scenes to give Mussolini satisfaction in Africa. In London the Foreign Secretary, Sir Samuel Hoare, resurrected a proposal for partitioning Ethiopia which had been put to Mussolini before the fighting began and took it to Paris where Laval improved on it – from the Italian point of view. The two governments were at this point closer in their foreign policies than at most times between the wars. But somehow or other this Hoare-Laval plan was then leaked to the press before it was presented to Mussolini. There was a public out-cry and the plan (and Hoare) had to be dropped. But Mussolini got what he wanted anyway with the result that France and Great Britain got the worst of both worlds. The failure of sanctions discredited the League and the mechanisms of collective security and created a mood of pessimism. The Stresa front dissolved and the Rome–Berlin Axis was created – although the phrase itself, invented by Mussolini, did not appear until shortly after the outbreak of the Spanish civil war. Mussolini used force with impunity. Hitler converted a potential enemy into an ally and had a free demonstration of how boldness pays. France, estranged from Great Britain by the collapse of the Hoare-Laval plan which confirmed all the worst French suspicions about the British, was left with no entente with Italy, only an empty pact with the USSR, no rapprochement with Germany, and damaged relations with Poland and the Little Entente.

In March 1935, just before the Stresa conference, Hitler had introduced compulsory military service in breach of the treaty of Versailles (his first breach of the treaty) and acknowledged the existence of the German air forces. In the same year he recovered the Saar by plebiscite, with nine tenths of the voters choosing reunion with Germany; concluded the Anglo-German naval treaty; promulgated the viciously anti-semitic Nuremberg decrees; recorded a 99 per cent victory in a referendum; and prepared Berlin for the oldest surviving festival of peace, the Olympic Games. In March 1936, he ordered his army to march into the Rhineland which was demilitarized not only by Versailles but also by Locarno which he had reaffirmed twelve months previously. He was copying Mussolini but was still not sure whether he could repeat in Europe the success which Mussolini had had in Africa. The French government of the day was a pre-election caretaker team, divided within itself, estranged from Great Britain by the collapse of the Laval-Hoare plan, filled with fear by the gloomy and timorous advice of its own generals, and deceived by a German cover plan which induced it to believe that Hitler was using 265,000 men instead of only a few battalions backed by four divisions. Hitler assured his own generals, who feared war and defeat, that no French soldier would stir and half way through the operation he refused a request from Blomberg for a partial withdrawal. He had the satisfaction of seeing his generals much more nervous than he was, and the success of the coup redoubled his ascendancy over them, his own self-assurance and his belief in the use of force. This was not Hitler's first challenge to the western powers – his withdrawal from the League and from the Disarmament Conference in October 1933 may be said to be the first and his acknowledgement of German rearmament the second – but it was the first in which he used his army. Yet the risks which he ran were not as great as they seemed, for three months earlier his Ambassador in Paris had passed on to him a strong hint from Laval that the French army would be used only to defend French soil and would not cross France's frontiers. Although the French Foreign Minister, Étienne Flandin, argued that a mere show of force would send the Germans scuttling back, only a minority of his cabinet supported him and it is unlikely that after the first few hours a show of force would have been enough.

By the remilitarization of the Rhineland Hitler challenged with impunity the two strongest powers in Europe, who had been also the principal champions of Versailles and were, since Locarno, Germany's allies in a comprehensive scheme for keeping the peace in western Europe. He broke France's system of alliances in the east no less than the settlement in the west by exposing the feebleness of France's will, and he implicitly asserted that Germany was a greater power in eastern Europe than either France or the USSR; thereafter nobody was prepared to put the assertion to the test. Against these gains there was only one feeble warning signal. The USSR had joined the League of Nations in 1934 and concluded a treaty of mutual assistance with France in May 1935. A similar treaty was made with Czechoslovakia and a British Minister, Anthony Eden, visited Moscow the same year. But the effectiveness of the USSR as an ally was discounted (Germany had beaten Russia in the First World War and seemed well able to do so again), the ratification of the Franco-Soviet pact was tellingly delayed for nine months and Great Britain was even further from considering such a reversal of alliances.

In July 1936 (the month in which sanctions against Italy were abandoned) a revolt broke out against the republican government of Spain. The ensuing civil war cemented the alliance between Hitler and Mussolini who recognized and helped the forces of revolutionary fascism under General Francisco Franco; it created a new threat to France's back door; it crystallized and embittered the ideological conflict in Europe between fascism and communism and added to the perplexities of democrats; it raised the level of violence and made it international, for in Spain battle was joined internationally as foreign volunteers and foreign governments took sides in a war which ended only six months before the beginning of the World War in Europe.

The sources and course of the Spanish civil war will not be related here but we have to consider its effects in Europe as a whole. All the principal European powers were faced with the question whether to intervene and, if so, how and how much. The insurgents appealed at once to Italy and Germany for aid. The government appealed to France. Italy and Germany responded promptly but with different motives. Mussolini, and even more so his son-in-law and Foreign Minister Galeazzo Ciano, were comparatively wholehearted in desiring Franco's victory. On the German side such a victory would bring advantages; in a future European war Germany would be entitled to expect Spanish help in the form of submarine bases and iron ore and even possibly co-belligerence, while active participation in the civil war would, as Goering pointed out and as the town of Guernica later discovered, give the Luftwaffe useful training. But Hitler did not want the civil war to turn into a general war for which he felt himself as yet unprepared and he therefore reacted with some caution and limited German aid to the insurgents until he came to feel that this risk was very small. German and Italian help to Franco were decisive on more than one occasion.

The British government was as determined as Hitler to prevent the extension of the war, and this determination overrode all other considerations. In France, Léon Blum wanted at first to help the legitimate Spanish government with arms but changed his mind owing to opposition in his cabinet and parliament: he feared civil war in France too, were he to persist in supporting a Spanish Popular Front which included communists. British opposition added to Blum's constraints. His more right-wing colleagues urged him not to get out of step with Great Britain. Thus the war in Spain intensified French dependence on Great Britain and its right-wing policies at the one moment in the thirties when France, under a socialist Prime Minister, might have been disposed to seek an opening to the Left in its foreign policy and an understanding with the USSR.

There was also a division of opinion in the United States administration where the anti-interventionists, led by the Secretary of State Cordell Hull, won the day, again partly influenced by the British decision. A Non-Intervention Committee, comprising two dozen states, was created and continued to function throughout a war in which intervention was unconcealed. The principal effects were three: first, that the continuance nonetheless of Italian and German help created profound cynicism; secondly, that the persistence of Great Britain and France nonetheless in the policy of non-intervention earned the one a reputation for hypocrisy and the other a reputation for feebleness which were equally deserved; and thirdly, that the Spanish government could get help from nowhere except the USSR which supplied it to the considerable benefit of the Spanish communists who were able greatly to enhance their initially modest position on the government side. Stalin's attitude to aid for Spain was much like Hitler's. He decided to give some aid but not too much. He too feared the extension of the war (if everybody had known of everybody else's fears, each might have been less afraid), but he also feared a Franco victory which, by further distracting and weakening France, might encourage Hitler to press his ambitions in eastern Europe.

In retrospect the Spanish civil war appears as the extreme example of a phenomenon of much wider extent in Europe. It has often been said that one of the most upsetting changes in twentieth-century Europe was the dismemberment of the Habsburg and Ottoman empires, but no less upsetting was the disintegration of apparently more coherent societies like France and Spain. In Spain, as the civil war revealed, the nation dissolved into groups which not only warred among themselves but looked beyond Spain for friends and helpers. Even in countries which did not disintegrate so spectacularly as Spain national bonds were so far enfeebled that ideological chieftains like Mussolini (a successful one) or Charles Maurras (a relatively unsuccessful one) were able to treat whole sections of their fellow-citizens – communists, socialists – as inferior parts of society, as outsiders within the walls. Social conflict was internationalized as these groups looked increasingly to their friends in other countries to help them against their own governments.

The war in Spain had a further consequence for European politics. The tactical and psychological successes of the German dive-bombers, the Stukas, created a false impression of the power of modern air forces, an impression which was immensely to Germany's advantage and played a substantial part in conditioning Anglo-French policies in the year of Munich. The Stukas in Spain spread fear far beyond it.

In November 1936 Germany and Japan signed the Anti-Comintern Pact, a short document by which the signatories undertook to exchange information and consult together about the international activities of communism and to concert counter-activities. Other countries were invited to adhere and Italy did so a year later, but the main point of the published agreement was to worry the USSR about its eastern frontiers and Great Britain about its position as an Asian power. By a secret protocol signed on the same day as the treaty Germany and Japan promised, in the event of an unprovoked attack or threat by the USSR against either of them, to do nothing which would make things easier for the USSR; each of them also promised to enter into no treaty with the USSR without the consent of the other. This secret part of the pact was not all that Hitler desired since Japan had declined to give positive help to Germany in the event of hostilities between Germany and the USSR. Japan was not to be drawn into a European war.

One of the most important pieces of evidence which we have concerning Hitler's intentions at this period is a document known as the Hossbach memorandum. This document was written by Colonel Hossbach five days after a meeting in Berlin on 5 November 1937 which he attended and at which he secretly took notes in spite of instructions by Hitler to the contrary. The meeting was attended by Hitler, his Ministers for War and Foreign Affairs (Blomberg and Neurath) and his three Commanders-in-Chief (Fritsch, Raeder and Goering), and lasted from 4.15 to 10.30 p.m. It consisted of a long statement on foreign affairs by Hitler, introduced with unusual solemnity as the fruit of four and a half years' reflection and as his political testament in the event of his death. Hitler stated, not for the first time, that the object of German policy was the security and multiplication of the German people. He repeated what he had said and written publicly on other occasions about *Lebensraum*. He rejected colonies as a solution; the necessary space had to be found in Europe, although later generations might have other problems which would force them to seek other solutions. There could be no solution without force, and this meant risks. Hitler then got nearer to details. He said that although nobody could tell what the situation would be in the years 1943–5, one thing was certain: Germany could not wait longer than that, partly because he himself would be past the peak of his powers and partly because Germany's advantages would begin to wane as its armament became obsolete and its enemies caught up. At that point he would in any event attack in order to resolve the space problem. Before it he would be guided by circumstances. He would watch his western and south-eastern flanks and he envisaged action against Austria and Czechoslovakia if France were weakened by trouble at home or by embroilments with Italy in the Mediterranean.

This document demonstrates once more Hitler's two main characteristics in external affairs: the fixity of his purpose, which was Germany's forcible territorial expansion in Europe, and the vagueness of his timing. Apart from setting an ultimate date – at least six years in the future and possibly eight – when he would definitely take the initiative, Hitler was leaving everything to opportunity, and in the event he attacked Austria and Czechoslovakia separately and not simultaneously, without the benefit of such a French crisis as he had envisaged or of a diversionary Mediterranean war. When he invaded Austria on 12 March 1938 and annexed it to the German Reich he did so because the Austrian Chancellor, Kurt von Schuschnigg, forced his hand. Schuschnigg decreed a plebiscite in order to strengthen his position in dealing with Austrian Nazi excesses – and Hitler feared Schuschnigg might succeed all too well. There were many stories at the time of the unreadiness of the German forces. Hitler had taken one of the risks which, as he had said in his lecture in the previous November, always attend the use of force. It was not a very big risk. Nobody did anything to stop him. Mussolini acquiesced. He had no choice, but Hitler's effusive thanks reflected his

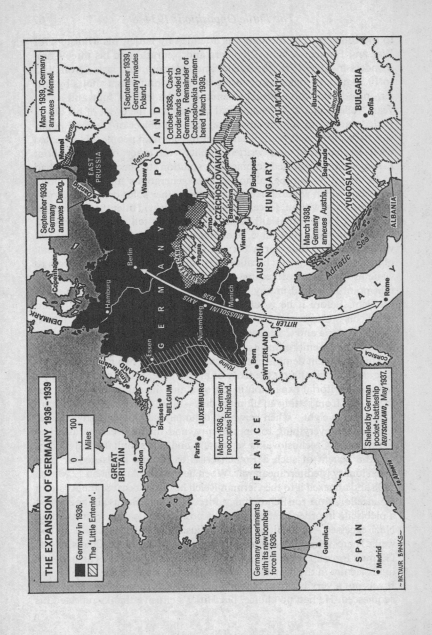

THE EXPANSION OF GERMANY 1936-1939

Germany in 1936.

The 'Little Entente'.

March 1939, Germany annexes Memel.

1 September 1939, Germany invades Poland.

October 1938, Czech borderlands ceded to Germany, Remainder of Czechoslovakia dismembered March 1939.

September 1939, Germany annexes Danzig.

March 1938, Germany annexes Austria.

March 1936, Germany reoccupies Rhineland.

Shelled by German pocket-battleship DEUTSCHLAND, May 1937.

Germany experiments with its new bomber force in 1936.

0   100
Miles

—ARTHUR BANKS—

concern about Mussolini's reaction to the flouting of a basic precept of Italian foreign policy. Hitler's relief on this occasion may explain his loyalty to Mussolini through the next seven years.

In the eighteen months following the *Anschluss* Hitler attacked two other states, Czechoslovakia and Poland. The difference between the Austrian case and these other two does not lie in the result: all three states were eliminated. Hitler reckoned that he could have his way with them because greater states than they did not want to fight for their sake. When an earlier land-grabber, Frederick the Great, had seized neighbouring territory, other European powers took up arms (whether successfully or unsuccessfully is not here the question). They did so, however, in circumstances different from those in which Hitler operated and his enemies agonized over what to do about it. Eighteenth-century monarchs had at their disposal special professional bodies maintained for the express purpose of performing or defeating such acts, but modern cabinets had to consider another kind of war. They could either call a whole nation to arms or do nothing, and so they greatly preferred to do nothing. Calling a nation to arms was a fearful and expensive way to prevent a rearrangement of the map, as Bismarck's enemies had discovered when they were beaten and as the Kaiser's enemies had discovered too, even though they won. But Hitler pressed his adversaries too far. Opposition to him stiffened with a slow desperation until, over Poland as it happened, it overbore their reluctance to go to war.

CHAPTER 4

Munich ... Prague ... Warsaw

CZECHOSLOVAKIA was a product of the disruption of the Austro-Hungarian monarchy. It was a sturdy democracy with natural resources, modern skills and – except on its southern or Austrian side – strong frontiers. But this promising offspring of the doctrine of self-determination was also a negation of that doctrine. It was, like Great Britain at the end of the Middle Ages, a mixture of peoples not yet congealed into a nation. It had a population of 14 to 15 million, of whom 10 million were Czechs or Slovaks, 3 million were Germans and the remainder consisted of small but self-conscious Hungarian, Ukrainian and Polish minorities. Most of the 3 million Germans lived scattered along the Bohemian and Moravian borderlands and in the principal cities. They came to be known as Sudeten Germans, but this was a deliberate misnomer. The Sudetenland, properly so called, lay north and east of their homes, but for propaganda purposes it was convenient to attach a name to them and so give the impression that they constituted a compact and detachable ethnic group.

By its nature and origins Czechoslovakia was anchored to the peace settlement which had created it, and was opposed to the reconstitution of a Danubian empire and to the resurgence of German power, especially a German power which would include Austria and so outflank it at its weakest point. Its founder and first president, T. G. Masaryk (resigned 1935, died 1937), and his successor Edvard Beneš based their policies for survival on the military strength and strategic importance of their country. They did not expect to be able to stand alone against a powerful German enemy but they aimed to make Czechoslovakia valuable and perhaps even essential to the vital interests of western states which would see to it that the Czechs and Slovaks were not once more subjected to Germans. They wanted to ensure that an armed attack on Czechoslovakia would never be a local affair; an aggressor would have to reckon with allied powers and so would think twice before beginning what was, if pledges meant anything, bound to become a general war. In 1938 Czechoslovakia had one of Europe's most noted armaments industries and an army which was almost the equal of the German army in men and equipment, though inferior in staying power because of Czechoslovakia's smaller population and human reserves. It had also an alliance with France to counter this weakness: by holding a proportion of the German army in the west the threat of a French attack would prevent a German victory.

But in 1938 the threat did not work. Hitler did not believe it. France no longer gave the Czechoslovak alliance top priority. The chink in Czechoslovakia's armour was Great Britain.

Great Britain had persistently refused to enter into commitments in eastern Europe, so that Masaryk and Beneš never succeeded in getting a British guarantee as well as a French one – until it was too late. Moreover, as the European situation got more menacing Great Britain began to work to demolish the French guarantee in the belief that it was not, as the French themselves had intended, a way of deterring Germany from going to war but had become a trap whereby a local war in central Europe would be expanded into a general European war. Great Britain hoped that the abrogation of the guarantee would remove this danger and provide a breathing space in which somehow war might be averted. The logic of British policy was to inflict the consequences of war and defeat on Czechoslovakia in the hope of saving everybody else. Czechoslovakia proved vulnerable because the French guarantee was not an Anglo-French guarantee and because, for France, the British alliance was more important than the French security system in central Europe of which the Czechoslovak alliance was a part. Since the evident revival of German power in Europe France had been on the defensive against Germany, and since the collapse of Franco-Italian relations in 1935–6 France had been left with no effective ally in the west except Great Britain. When therefore Great Britain required France to abandon Czechoslovakia, France did so.

British policy at this period has been summed up in the word appeasement. Appeasement describes a range of attitudes stretching from the desire to be fair and decent to a defeated foe to the policy of buying off a resurgent one. It covers the whole of the period between the wars, becoming more disreputable with time. The object of appeasement in the twenties was Weimar Germany, in the thirties Nazi Germany; its aim in the twenties was justice, in the thirties safety; the price in the twenties was the reduction of reparations (primarily to Great Britain) and equal rights for Germans, in the thirties the price was turning a blind eye to German ambitions and what these cost other people (primarily Czechoslovakia). Munich, where Czechoslovakia was sacrificed, became synonymous with betrayal, as Canossa with a similar kind of abasement.

Great Britain's rulers slid into this dishonour from a mixture of prejudices and half-truths. The British ruling class had a propensity for seeing what was least admirable in Frenchmen and what was best in Germans, so that a subliminal distrust and dislike of France nourished pro-German sentiments which were often expressed in kith-and-kin terms – though without the excessive racialism of complementary German thinking. (There was also a number of fervent Francophiles who understood the French dilemma, but they were a minority and an increasingly lukewarm one.) This Anglo-Saxon or Anglo-Prussian kinship was reinforced after 1919 by the radical Anglo-French disagreement about the right way to behave towards Germany. Where France felt cheated at not having secured the Rhine frontier, Great Britain felt that Germany was being cheated by the special restrictions imposed on German sovereignty in the Rhineland, by inordinate reparation claims and by the limitations on German armament. Great Britain's vision was of a purged Germany playing its due part in European affairs, and too many British politicians retained this vision even when, with the Nazis, the purging ceased to be a cleansing and became an abomination. They persisted in regarding the change of régime in Germany in 1933 as something like a normal change of government in Great Britain. They were not men who found it easy to recognize abnormality and they persisted in regarding Hitler as a responsible statesman because he occupied the position of one. Even though British Ambassadors (Sir Horace Rumbold and Sir Eric Phipps) and other observers reported what was happening to the German Jews as early as 1933, they clung to a way of thinking and a way of doing business which were tragically inappropriate, to say the least. The efforts of Chamberlain and the language of a later Ambassador, Sir Nevile Henderson, betrayed an inability to understand Hitler which was based on a determination not to: Hitler's ravings were passed over and he was regarded as a man who would make bargains and stick to them because it was difficult to see what to do if he was really a totally different kind of person.

In this way men who were pro-German before Hitler found too little difficulty in going on being pro-German with Hitler. Hence the extreme ludicrousness of their comments about Hitler, when they went to visit him or simply expressed themselves about him without that effort. They believed that there was a point at which Hitler, if given enough territory round his borders and some colonies, would become 'reasonable'. They persuaded themselves that they were giving Hitler pieces of territory which Germany ought to have on the basis of the principle of national self-determination or equal rights and that, having done so, they would have turned Hitler into a man of peace. They had no objection to the absorption of Austria by Germany, and little compunction about bundling a small *parvenu* state like Czechoslovakia into the new German Reich. What they wanted was a version of the Anti-Comintern Pact, an Anglo-German understanding for which they were willing to give Hitler other people's territory in central Europe and (in the mistaken belief that Hitler's quest for living space was a hankering for lost lands overseas), British colonies and even mandated territories entrusted to Great Britain by the League, if these readjustments of real estate would remove the obstacles to a *pax Anglo-Germanica*. In the last years of peace British Ministers discussed among themselves how France might be persuaded to give some of its African territories to Germany in return for British territory in West Africa; or how the whole of tropical Africa might be re-partitioned, a throw-back to the nineteenth century's method of allaying European rivalries by removing them into another continent and buying off the more dangerous and discontented Europeans with African coin.

In May 1937 Neville Chamberlain succeeded Stanley Baldwin as Prime Minister. Chamberlain had been a highly successful provincial politician who, after being Mayor of Birmingham, had moved rather late in life into national politics and had there enhanced his reputation by his work as Minister of Health and Chancellor of the Exchequer. He had the strength, manifested in cabinet before he became Prime Minister as well as afterwards, of the man who sees one side of a case only. He was never the cleverest man in any of the cabinets in which he sat, but it so chanced that his cleverer colleagues were weaker in debate and less effective when it came to taking a decision. As Chancellor he won applause by introducing the lowest defence estimates of the inter-war years. He had the virtues and the limitations of a prosperous middle-class conservative and he had the misfortune – which was also his country's misfortune – to display his virtues in the earlier part of his career and his faults during the last years of his life. He was a man of proved ability who suffered from the peculiarly English notion that there is nothing that a really intelligent man cannot tackle. In this spirit of gilded amateurism he tackled foreign affairs and Hitler. Since he was ignorant, naïve and stubborn he did not succeed.

He began by getting rid of his Foreign Secretary, Anthony Eden, who was pushed into resignation in February 1938 by the Prime Minister's manners and, to a lesser extent, his policies. Chamberlain was determined to come to terms with Mussolini in spite of the conquest of Ethiopia and Italy's continuing intervention in the Spanish civil war. There was something to be said for recognizing the conquest of Ethiopia once it was an accomplished fact. (Eden himself was in favour of recognizing Franco a year later.) There was also much to be said for repairing Anglo-Italian relations if a European war seemed likely: the Italian navy was a significant factor in world politics, especially before 1939 when Roosevelt, at British request, moved American naval forces from the Atlantic to the Pacific to counter possible Japanese designs against Australia and New Zealand, which the Royal Navy was pledged to protect. Eden, however, was in no hurry to seek Italian friendship so long as Mussolini went on helping Franco. Chamberlain on the other hand regarded the matter as urgent in order to keep Mussolini at least at arm's length from Hitler. This issue – the timing of Anglo-Italian conversations – was the immediate occasion of Eden's resignation. Behind it were both a larger issue and personal pique. Chamberlain was contemptuous of American statesmanship and, like many of his class, basically anti-American. Eden was neither so arrogant nor so blinkered. Roosevelt, like Eden but unlike Chamberlain, was opposed to *de jure* recognition of Italy's African conquests without a specific and simultaneous undertaking to take Italian forces out of Spain. Further, Roosevelt ventured to offer his services as a mediator in Europe's affairs. Chamberlain, without telling Eden or consulting the Foreign Office, brushed this offer aside. Unlike Baldwin, Chamberlain was determined to play a leading part in international affairs, as a British Prime Minister has every right to do, but Eden – more experienced in this field, if in general a less able man – was irked by this incursion into his special fief. Eden's assessment of the forces which shaped European politics included not only the four powers which Chamberlain treated as the only ones that mattered, but also to some degree the USSR, the League and the United States. Yet their policies were at this time so little apart that Eden's resignation was heard by some of his cabinet colleagues with astonished incredulity.

Chamberlain's attempt to create a concert of four was in any case pre-doomed to failure. Mussolini privately assured Hitler that Anglo-Italian conversations and agreements would never be allowed to harm the Italo-German accord and when Chamberlain renewed his wooing of Italy after the Munich crisis neither Mussolini nor Ciano took the proceedings seriously. Chamberlain was no less anxious to come to some arrangement with Hitler. During most of 1938 the immediate obstacle to the British policy of appeasement was the so-called Sudeten problem. The Nazi Party had in Czechoslovakia a counterpart called the Sudeten German Party and led by Konrad Henlein, who adopted German Nazi doctrines and behaviour and received funds and instructions from Germany. Henlein was agitating for local autonomy for the

German minority. His agitation was echoed by the lesser minorities. It created confusion and disorders calculated to call in question the authority of the central government in Prague at a time when this government was engaged in discussing the rights and status of minorities. At every turn in these discussions Henlein made increasingly unacceptable claims, backed by the undefined but inescapable menace of German military action. In April he demanded not only self-government for Germans in Czechoslovakia but also the subordination of Czechoslovakia's foreign policy to Germany's interests.

In the previous November, a few weeks after the Hossbach meeting in Berlin, British and French Ministers had conferred in London about whether and how to resist German moves in central Europe. They agreed that they should do nothing about a German annexation of Austria but, largely on the insistence of the French Foreign Minister Yvon Delbos, they accepted that a German attack on Czechoslovakia would involve France in war pursuant to its treaty obligations. Since Great Britain could not risk seeing France engaged in war with Germany and defeated, Great Britain too faced war over Czechoslovakia. The only escape lay in a German-Czech settlement acceptable to, or at any rate accepted by, both Hitler and Beneš, and this became the prime object of British policy. It entailed pressure on Prague rather than Berlin since Czechoslovakia was the weaker state, undoubtedly so if its allies could be eliminated from the equation, which Great Britain thought they could be: after the *Anschluss* France and the USSR had both reaffirmed their obligations to defend Czechoslovakia but the USSR was not judged to be in a position to do much and France was in no position to jeopardize Great Britain's friendship. In the summer of 1938 therefore Chamberlain decided to intensify British pressure on Czechoslovakia which, supplementing German pressures, Great Britain had been exerting since the previous year. After consulting the German government about his proposed intervention but without informing France, Chamberlain sent a special emissary (Lord Runciman) to Czechoslovakia to get Beneš, under the guise of mediation, to accept whatever might be necessary to keep the peace. Runciman arrived in Prague at the end of July. He subsequently reported to the cabinet that Beneš was insincere, stubborn and too clever by half.

Yet it was by this date sufficiently clear that the Sudeten problem was not the real danger to peace and that the excision of this problem would not remove the danger of war. To the accumulating evidence on Hitler's wider intentions there was added in June 1938 a specific warning. In that month Goering's adjutant, General Karl Bodenschatz, officially informed the French assistant air attaché in Berlin that Germany was preparing to build a line of defensive fortifications from the North Sea to the Swiss border, that Germany had no aggressive intentions against France or Great Britain but that, having first secured its southern flank against any threat from Czechoslovakia, it intended to eliminate the 'Soviet threat' and simultaneously secure the living space which was indispensable for Germany. Bodenschatz specifically mentioned the Ukraine and compared Germany's eastward expansion in Europe with the way in which France had secured its own needs by expanding into Africa. This was a clear enough indication of Hitler's intention to overpower Czechoslovakia, make war on the USSR and protect himself in the west by a series of fortifications which could not be completed before the middle of 1939 at the earliest. It presented France and Great Britain with a choice between keeping out of a war in eastern Europe or joining in such a war. It ruled out the possibility of preventing a war in eastern Europe by appeasement.

At the beginning of September Beneš declared himslf ready to accept all the demands of the Sudeten Germans for autonomy. On 12 September Chamberlain, under pressure from many sides – the French and American governments, the Vatican, the opposition in the House of Commons, Churchill – and in the hope of inducing Hitler to be less explosive than usual in the speech which he was due to make in Nuremberg on that day, decided to go to the lengths of reminding Hitler that France was bound to fight for Czechoslovakia and that Great Britain would fight with France, but from Berlin Henderson asked the cabinet to excuse him from passing this warning on. Henderson's role in these years negates the view that Ambassadors no longer count. Whereas Chamberlain's dominant aim was to keep Great Britain out of war, Henderson had a more positive policy. He did not want Great Britain to stand in Hitler's way. It is impossible to read his statements and despatches or observe his conduct without concluding that he endorsed Hitler's aims more than he deplored Hitler's character and behaviour. He wanted an Anglo-German entente which would preserve Great Britain's imperial position in the world and license Hitler to lay the USSR low, and he made no secret of his views, whether privately or publicly. He even discussed them with Goering, at which point he found that he had gone further than Chamberlain would countenance.

During the summer and autumn of 1938 a violent anti-Czech campaign was in progress in Germany. Press and radio were presenting, with the utmost emotional mendacity, a picture of persecution of Germans in Czechoslovakia and at Nuremberg on 12 September

Hitler spoke with such exceptional violence that his words provoked an abortive rising by Sudeten Germans and the imposition of martial law in parts of Czechoslovakia on the 13th. Henlein fled to Germany and with his departure the situation became more manageable. But this improvement at the storm centre was lost on observers further away and two days later Chamberlain unwittingly reversed it. He resolved to put into operation a plan which he had been preparing for some time. He would go and see Hitler. This plan had been discussed only with four Ministers separately (but not in cabinet), with Nevile Henderson and with two or three other close advisers. Like Eden nearly twenty years later in the Suez crisis Chamberlain kept his cabinet very much in the dark about his plans and policies. As with the Runciman mission France was not informed. Although he had hoped to influence Hitler's tone at Nuremberg, he was also resolved to go and talk with Hitler whatever he said at Nuremberg and however he said it. He flew to Berchtesgaden on 15 September and on the same day he agreed in principle that the Sudetenland, an area still undefined, ought to be detached from Czechoslovakia and given to Germany. At no point does the difference between these two men, now meeting *tête-à-tête* to settle the fate of Europe, appear in retrospect more glaring: Hitler humouring his distinguished guest but keeping up his preparations to use force; Chamberlain returning to London to affirm his belief that Hitler was the sort of man who would be 'rather better than his word'. The nearer the appeasers got to a settlement with Hitler the more they clung to this tattered premise – and the more they needed to still their consciences by working themselves up into a state of hatred against the Czechs as the people who might spoil the whole game.

Besides coercing the Czechs and coming to terms with Hitler, Chamberlain needed to cow France. His policy required him to scare France into dishonouring its treaty with Czechoslovakia. The British Ambassador in Paris, Sir Eric Phipps, had no great difficulty in scaring the French Foreign Minister, Georges Bonnet. He also fortified Chamberlain's views by refraining from reporting to London what Frenchmen of another stamp were saying, until ordered by the Foreign Office to do so. Yet during the September crisis of 1938 the French government and even the pessimistic General Gamelin seemed resigned to going to war for Czechoslovakia and advancing into Germany. After the robber synod at Berchtesgaden however, to which they had not been invited, French Ministers were confronted with an accomplished and perhaps not wholly unwelcome fact. After a conference in London on the 18th they accepted the Anglo-German compact and joined with Great

Britain in forcing the Czechs to agree to surrender all territories where half the inhabitants were German. Beneš, who had already conceded all reasonable German demands, at first refused but he had no real choice. He was told that France refused to fight without a promise of British backing and that Great Britain refused to back France in a war begun for Czechoslovakia. All he could get, with French help, was an Anglo-French guarantee of the independence and neutrality of the new Czechoslovakia in place of the discarded French guarantee for the old one. Great Britain reluctantly agreed to give this vulnerable and enfeebled state the promises which it had refused to give to a much more worthwhile ally.

But this was not the end. So far from removing an obstacle to peace the Czechoslovak surrender brought war nearer. Hitler, baulked of the military destruction of Czechoslovakia which he had been talking about, declared that the terms forced on Beneš by Great Britain and France no longer satisfied him. Chamberlain flew back to Germany where, at Godesberg on the 22nd, he discovered that Hitler now demanded even larger stretches of Czechoslovakia, a plebiscite in other areas and the entry of German troops into Czechoslovakia before the lines of partition had been settled. This second meeting was punctuated by a stream of reports of Czech outrages which Hitler caused to be concocted and brought to him while he and Chamberlain were conferring. Chamberlain, returning to London on the 24th, told his cabinet that he believed that he had established some influence over Hitler. He was for accepting Hitler's terms and getting Beneš to accept them but the opposition within the British cabinet was hardening and was temporarily joined by Halifax. Daladier too, once more in London, was firmer; he seemed resigned to war. The Czechs had mobilized on the 23rd. Chamberlain wavered. On the 26th a last attempt by British emissaries to get Hitler to see 'reason' produced a scene of such fury that they fled without saying what they had been told to say. On the 27th Chamberlain, after some hesitation, authorized the mobilization of the British fleet which the First Lord of the Admiralty, Alfred Duff Cooper, had been urging for some days. On the 28th Chamberlain, while speaking in the House of Commons, received an invitation to go to Munich, the outcome of a British appeal to Mussolini to do something.

At Munich on the 29th the substance of the Godesberg demands was conceded – on the basis of proposals which were advanced by Mussolini as a compromise but had been drafted for him by the German Foreign Office. In substance Chamberlain and Daladier let Hitler have practically all he wanted, Mussolini being in attendance. The Russians were treated as irrelevant and neither invited nor consulted. Czechoslovakia, whose representatves came to Munich but were confined to the vestibule, chose acquiescence rather than slaughter. Beneš resigned. On the day after the conference Chamberlain, while taking leave of Hitler, produced a piece of paper on which he had drafted an Anglo-German declaration of friendship and of the determination of the two peoples never to go to war with one another. Hitler, who had no desire to fight the British, was delighted and the two leaders signed then and there. In London Duff Cooper resigned but cabinet colleagues who had talked earlier of doing so too decided not to: Chamberlain's control over his cabinet and his large and still docile majority in the House of Commons was at this time more complete than that of any British Prime Minister since the eighteenth century. In France three Ministers who had resigned before Munich withdrew their resignations after it. In December a Franco-German declaration of friendship, similar to the Chamberlain-Hitler scrap of paper, was signed. Poland took the opportunity to seize in October the area of Teschen, dubiously Polish in character but undeniably a plum.

The Munich agreement was greeted with relief by everybody except the Czechs and Slovaks. So acute had been the fear of war that this relief burst out in scenes of enthusiasm which were particularly galling to the minority whose shame or apprehension overmastered their relief. For most British and French Ministers the surrender had at least staved off war. Chamberlain had enough faith in the piece of paper which he had got Hitler to sign to talk of having secured 'peace for our time'. But some were considerably less sanguine. Soon after Munich Halifax, now Foreign Secretary in place of Eden, wanted to introduce conscription and in the following January – when there was a scare over reports that Hitler was about to invade Holland – he advocated staff talks with France and Belgium, consultation with Washington and soundings about the acceptability of British guarantees to Poland, Rumania, Greece and Turkey. Two months later, in March 1939, all lingering delusions were finally blown away when Hitler, in defiance of the Munich agreement, completed his conquest of Czechoslovakia.

The mutilated Czechoslovakia created in 1938 consisted of three federated provinces: Bohemia-Moravia, Slovakia and Ruthenia. In October Hitler directed his armed services to be ready to deal with the rest of Czechoslovakia and to seize Memel. On 14 March 1939, on orders from Berlin, Slovakia declared itself independent of Prague and asked to become a German protectorate. Hitler had a minor piece of luck over

Slovakia. The union of the Slovaks with the much more numerous Czechs had not been a smooth one. When Czechoslovakia was created, Slovakia, formerly a dependency of Hungary, was much less developed than the Czech lands of Bohemia and Moravia which, under Austrian rule, had enjoyed considerable educational as well as industrial advancement. Consequently the Slovak parts of Czechoslovakia were largely administered by Czechs after independence and the Slovaks accused the Czechs with some degree of justice of being slow to remedy this imbalance. Although on nearly every occasion Slovaks gave more votes to Czechoslovak parties than to the specifically Slovak one, there was a significant autonomist movement led by Father Andrew Hlinka. In 1938 Hlinka died and his successor, Monsignor Tiso, abandoned autonomy in favour of separatism. This was a help to Hitler.

Besides turning Slovakia into a distinct German satellite Hitler completed the destruction of Czech independence. Beneš's successor, President Emil Hácha, and his Foreign Minister took the road to Berlin where both were subject to such verbal bludgeoning that Hácha fainted. German troops were already marching on Prague. Under threat of a bombing of their capital the Czech Ministers submitted and Bohemia-Moravia too was declared a German protectorate. Ruthenia was annexed by Hungary in two bites. In November 1938 Hitler, who was not particularly fond of the Hungarians but was pressed by the Italians and Poles, had allowed Hungary to seize part of Ruthenia by what was called the Vienna Award. In March 1939 Hungarian troops occupied the rest of it. Great Britain and France did nothing. Five days before Hitler seized Czechoslovakia Chamberlain told the House of Commons that Europe was settling down and the British Government was turning its attention to disarmament and to more trade with Germany. When the blow fell on Prague both its western guarantors defected on the plea that the severance of Slovakia from Czechoslovakia had nullified their guarantee: the country guaranteed had ceased to exist. A week later Hitler extorted Memel from Lithuania by an ultimatum containing false accusations of Lithuanian brutality. Memel had been renounced by Germany by the treaty of Versailles – like Danzig, which now reached the top of Hitler's agenda.

Danzig stood for different things. It was, in the first place, a largely German city to be recovered for the Reich. Secondly, as a bone of contention between Germany and Poland it was a possible cause of a German-Polish war. In that context it raised, thirdly, the two ultimate issues in Hitler's European policy – the attitude of the western democracies to a German attack on Poland and the attitude of the USSR.

Immediately after the final partition and subjugation of Czechoslovakia Hitler seems to have been in two minds over his next move. If
Danzig could have been acquired as easily as Memel Hitler's obvious
move was to proceed against Danzig. But Danzig could not safely be
isolated in this way. So it was more than ordinarily desirable for Hitler
to explore and exploit every possibility of securing Danzig, as he had
secured the Sudetenland, by threats and cajolement and without war.
He could, and in October 1938 did, push forward his planning for
aggression in the west. He needed to be prepared for every contingency.
But he also tried in the same month to do a deal with Poland: Danzig
and a road across the Polish corridor to be surrendered to Germany,
Poland to join the Anti-Comintern Pact. On these terms Poland could
be reprieved, but this settlement could hardly be more than an interim
one unless Poland were to be persuaded later, as Czechoslovakia had
been constrained in its second round, to cede Polish Silesia too (Hitler
had already talked of recovering the whole of Silesia) and to remain at
least benevolently passive when Hitler decided that the time had come
to seize his *Lebensraum* farther east.

Poland rejected the German offer and stood on its rights. It would
neither endorse the incorporation of Danzig in the Reich nor would it
join the Anti-Comintern Pact and so fatally embroil itself with the
USSR and render itself dependent on its other big neighbour, Germany.

Danzig, renounced by Germany by the treaty of Versailles but
peopled chiefly by Germans, was a Free City with a government of its
own under the protection of the League of Nations and with a resident
League Commissioner to supervise the maintenance of its status and
constitution and adjudicate disputes between the Free City and Poland.
It was within the Polish customs area and Poland had rights of access
to it along a route or corridor which traversed German territory. In
elections in 1933 the local Nazi Party won, partly by force and fraud,
just over half the votes. Thereafter it rapidly and illegally strengthened
its control, while the League abdicated its responsibilities. The city
was to all intents and purposes firmly under German and Nazi control
for at least two years before it was forcibly incorporated in the Reich on
the eve of war.

Polish foreign policy between the wars was a series of expedients
designed to preserve a relatively small country from attack by stronger
neighbours. It was based at first on the alliance with France. During the
twenties this alliance seemed to serve its purpose but with Germany and
Russia both recovering from their defeats in the First World War it was
not really tested: Poland's problem was postponed until the revival of

German and Russian power. When this took place the French alliance began to look undependable, which it was. Poland then adopted a policy of self-preservation by making defensive treaties with its two big neighbours (the non-aggression pacts of 1932 and 1934 with Stalin and Hitler respectively) and by refusing to be drawn into alliance with the one against the other. This policy too seemed to work for a while but although a number of Polish-German issues were resolved the intractable problem of Danzig remained and Poland was in danger as soon as Germany under Hitler became strong enough to attack the USSR. During the thirties Poland's strategic position was weakened by the declining efficacy of alliance with France and by the destruction of Austrian and Czechoslovak independence. Colonel Jozef Beck, Foreign Minister from 1932, clung to the policy of non-alignment between Germany and the USSR and also secured in 1939 a British alliance. He has been much criticized for failing to opt for the USSR against Germany. This refusal was influenced by his anti-communism, which was pronounced, and also by the fact that Poland had been at war with the USSR as recently as 1920, but alignment with the USSR would also have been a complete reversal of a policy which kept Poland reasonably safe so long as Germany and the USSR neither concluded between themselves any agreement overriding their several non-aggression pacts with Poland nor aimed to fight one another over Poland's dead body. In the end Poland was undone because Germany and the USSR did conclude such an agreement. In running the risk that they might Beck was blinded by his own over-estimate of Poland's importance and power.

According to Rauschning Hitler was thinking of partitioning Poland with the USSR even at the time of the German-Polish treaty of 1934 and regarded a German-Russian agreement as a way of safeguarding his eastern front during a war in the west which would be a necessary preliminary to a war against the USSR. Hitler's anti-communism was no bar to an ephemeral deal with Stalin. He himself said on another occasion that treaties were only meant to be kept so long as they served the purpose for which they had been made in the first place. On this thesis the German-Polish treaty could be succeeded by a German-Russian agreement for the partition of Poland, and a German-Russian agreement could be a prelude to a German attack on the USSR. These were problems in timing and tactics. But in relation to the western democracies Hitler had a problem of a different order: whether to attack them or not. He had no direct interest in doing so; there was no sense in making war on states which showed neither the will nor the capacity to

thwart his plans in eastern Europe. The risk of effective French interference was a declining one, and if necessary France could be defeated.
Great Britain too would probably not interfere, but if it did it could not
so easily be defeated. The Luftwaffe was not suited to an attack on
Great Britain and at sea Germany was a secondary power. When Hitler
thought about Great Britain he preferred to dwell on the reasons why it
should be willing to come to terms with him than on what he would do
if it did not. He aspired to appease Great Britain, not to defeat it.
Mein Kampf presupposed friendship with Great Britain; the dispatch
of Ribbentrop to London as Ambassador was a step, however misguided, to this end; the purpose of the Anglo-German naval agreement
of 1935 had been not so much to detach Great Britain from France and
Italy (although it had that welcome effect) or to sanctify breaches of the
naval clauses of the treaty of Versailles (which Hitler had hardly yet
begun), but to reassure Great Britain that Hitler intended no threat to
Great Britain's naval empire. But by 1939 it was doubtful whether
Great Britain could be neutralized. It was also becoming possible that
the western democracies might enter into an alliance with the USSR.

The disappearance of Czechoslovakia as an independent state automatically moved Poland and Rumania into the German firing line. Both
these states had frontiers with the USSR and so in a sense Hitler's
entry into Prague on 15 March 1939 brought Germany and the USSR
face to face. For five and a half months between that day and the signing of the Russo-German pact during the night of 23–24 August the
pattern of European politics was, on the surface at least, uncertain, as
the USSR, moving to escape from an isolation which had become
particularly dangerous since Munich, hesitated which side to take. At
first the western democracies and the USSR seemed to be trying to
overcome their mutual antipathies and draw together. Following a
scare in March of imminent German action against Rumania Great
Britain made an approach to the USSR. London was at this point
more worried about Rumania than Poland, but the Rumanian scare
subsided almost at once and when the USSR suggested a conference
between itself, the two leading western democracies and the two countries threatened by Hitler, the British took evasive action, being reluctant to rub shoulders so formally with the USSR. Poland was even more
reluctant. But it was also the main point of danger. It had partially
mobilized on 23 March, three days before rejecting Germany's proposals for a settlement, and Chamberlain, afraid that Danzig was about
to create a war at any moment, resolved to cast a British mantle over
Poland. He offered it a guarantee and on 6 April, after a visit by Beck to

London, the two governments publicly announced their intention to sign a treaty by which Great Britain would go to Poland's aid if it were attacked. France promised to do so too. At the beginning of May Hitler, already enraged by Beck's rejection of his proposals, secretly ordered his army to get ready to attack. Beck publicly proclaimed that peace was less precious than Poland's honour.

Great Britain and France, having committed themselves to succouring Poland, were gambling on a negotiated Danzig settlement which would once more remove a threat to peace, that is to say, give Hitler what he wanted. In default of such an agreement they would almost certainly be called upon to redeem in arms the promises which they had made. But by making these promises Great Britain in particular, which had not before been under any obligation to Poland, had forfeited the power which it had wielded in similar circumstances over Czechoslovakia. Beck was emboldened to continue to refuse to negotiate over Danzig. The guarantee given to him was a guarantee of Poland's national integrity, a guarantee therefore against attack by a dissident minority as well as from external aggression, and most exceptionally the Polish government was itself to judge if and when circumstances had called the guarantee into play. Thus Beck had a weapon which Beneš never had, although in the end it did him no good. The charge that can be made against Beck is that he did not see that the Anglo-French guarantee was worthless. Although aware of the unwillingness of his guarantors to fight for Poland, he did not believe that they would go so far as to dishonour their promises. But Great Britain and France did not mean to implement these promises. For them the guarantee was a means to gain time and to deter Hitler, while they continued to try to lever the Poles into concessions over Danzig: a military promise used as a diplomatic weapon. As such it was inept. The charge against Chamberlain, the principal author of the manoeuvre, is that by giving the guarantee he diminished the pressure that he was trying to exert on Poland over Danzig and at the same time improvidently and inopportunely deprived himself of his chance of an agreement with the USSR. Coupled with Great Britain's known determination on a peaceful settlement of the Danzig question, the guarantee was weak support for Poland and weak deterrence of Hitler.

Great Britain and France gave similar guarantees to Greece (in view of Mussolini's invasion of Albania on 7 April) and a little later to Rumania. Hitler eventually overran all these countries. The guarantees were little more than anti-German slogans shouted into the wind. They had no effect one way or the other on Hitler's attitudes to the countries guaranteed, although they may have had some effect on his attitude to Great Britain. Hitler was a man of moods and rage was one of them. He was in a state of rage between the Berchtesgaden and Godesberg meetings in September 1938 and it seems likely that Chamberlain's guarantee to Poland affected him the same way. He riposted by denouncing not only his recently reaffirmed non-aggression pact with Poland but also the Anglo-German naval treaty. He ordered his forces to be ready to attack Poland at the end of August, and he now envisaged – although he still hoped to avoid – a war on two fronts. The essential thing was to keep the USSR out of such a war.

The Russians, like the Germans, feared a war on two fronts. Germany and Japan were allies by the Anti-Comintern Pact and there was already an undeclared war going on in Manchuria between Russian and Japanese forces. Stalin found it difficult to believe that the British and French ruling classes preferred Russian communism to European right-wing fascism. This not implausible judgement had been strengthened by the Anglo-French failure to solicit Russian support for the defence of Czechoslovakia and the transience of the British interest in cooperation for the defence of Poland and Rumania. In any case, what Great Britain and France wanted was not what the USSR needed. Great Britain and France were concerned about the independence and integrity of Poland and Rumania and might in an emergency welcome Russian help to safeguard these states, but Stalin cared nothing for the integrity of Poland or Rumania. He was worrying about the USSR and its vulnerability to German attack. He might welcome British and French aid to avert such an attack but so long as Great Britain and France wanted to strengthen Poland and Rumania and preserve their sovereignty, Stalin saw little chance of turning these states into a defensive glacis which was the only useful function that they could perform for him. Stalin needed help against Hitler and a free hand in the debatable lands between the USSR and Germany; Great Britain and France were looking for help for Poland and Rumania not for the USSR, and were unwilling to blackmail Poland into giving Stalin what he wanted in the way in which they had blackmailed Czechoslovakia into giving way to Hitler.

Stalin had made a mistake about Hitler several years earlier. He had viewed with equanimity the coalition between German conservatives, the German army and the Nazis. The conservatives and the army had a tradition of alliance with Russia, and Stalin believed that these would prove the dominating forces in a post-Weimar Germany. He regarded the Nazis as no more than ephemeral auxiliaries in the overthrow of

Weimar and so instead of impeding Hitler's rise to power by directing the German communists to make common cause with the socialists he incited the communists against the socialists and so played a part in destroying Weimar and making Hitler its heir. Stalin quickly realized his mistake and tried to rectify it. In 1934 he joined the League of Nations and in 1935 he made his ineffective alliance with France. The failure of this alliance and the obvious weaknesses of collective security forced him a couple of years later to seek with Nazi Germany the sort of accord which he would have liked to make with a military-conservative Germany. In 1937 he began the process of appeasing Hitler by dissolving the Polish Communist Party. Poland re-killed would, if necessary, seal the new compact. Stalin knew that Hitler was his enemy as much as Great Britain and France, indeed more so and more menacingly. But he also saw the basis for a business deal with Germany which could give him what he needed – time. Moreover if, like western conservatives, he too saw a world divided into communists and non-communists, he could nevertheless draw some distinction between fascist anti-communists and democratic anti-communists. He despised and distrusted the latter and concluded in consequence that he would probably have to do a deal with the former, since the countries which had had no stomach to defend Czechoslovakia would be incapable of doing anything useful for the USSR even if they wanted to. But it is doubtful whether he finally made up his mind until August 1939. Until a few days before the signing of the Russo-German treaty he kept open the possibility of an agreement with Great Britain and France.

By their guarantees to Poland and Rumania Great Britain and France had undertaken to help two countries whose ability to withstand Germany was clearly nil. The British estimate of Poland's capacity to resist, measured in time, was two weeks – and Poland's forty divisions constituted an army twice as large as Rumania's. If Hitler invaded Poland, France and Great Britain could invade Germany, but unless the USSR were added to the alliance the Poles would fight alone and not for long. Thus east–west negotiations were dragged onto the political scene by the logic of events. The French government and, in London, the Foreign Office but not the Prime Minister were driven to seek an alliance with the USSR despite some well-founded doubts about its political value at this date. Political missions proceeded from Paris and London to Moscow in June. They did not give an impression of enthusiasm, but the real cause of their ultimate failure was not their attitude so much as the backlog of distrust between their countries and the impossibility of agreement on the crucial issue of a Russian right of entry into Poland. By the end of July a stalemate was reached when the western powers refused to give Stalin a free hand in the Baltic states. They felt that they were being asked to connive at the suppression of the independence of these countries, which was indeed so, but was not very different from what they had done at Munich. Stalin then reanimated the talks by suggesting the dispatch of military missions. These began discussions in Moscow on 12 August. The fact that they went by ship instead of by air has been the subject of some ridicule and again there was a display of an evident lack of enthusiasm (although Daladier at least wanted an agreement at almost any price), but there was a case for the chosen method of travel since it was only on board ship that the two missions got to know each other and were able to concert their plans.

It is impossible to say whether Stalin was by now merely playing with the western powers or was hoping to do a deal with them. He had been looking both ways since April when he initiated the first in a series of moves which eventually produced the Russo-German pact, and the replacement of Maxim Litvinov by Vyacheslav Molotov as Foreign Commissar on 3 May was regarded by the French Ambassador in Moscow as a step towards a Russo-German alliance. Hitler responded with further initiatives in June and then appeared to lose interest, but serious exchanges were renewed before the end of July, at which time the German Ambassador in Moscow was forecasting a Franco-British-Russian alliance. On 12 August, the day on which the military talks began in Moscow, Hitler was telling his Italian allies of his intention to make Stalin his ally, on 20 August he sent a personal telegram to Stalin to speed things up, and on the 22nd in an address to military and civilian chiefs he spoke as though the attack on Poland were imminent and the Russian pact assured. In the intervening week the military missions had been pressed by the chief Russian delegate, Marshal Voroshilov, to answer the question whether Russian troops would be allowed by Poland to advance into Poland to meet the German armies. The British and French missions could not give a straight answer, for although Poland (and Rumania) had withdrawn initial objections to a Franco-British-Russian alliance, the Polish government still refused to permit any entry by Russian forces except upon request to be made at the time and it assumed that the request would be for air support and not for ground units. At the last moment a member of the French mission was sent to Warsaw to press the Poles to give way, but the Poles refused and it is probable that Stalin knew on 19 August of this refusal from intercepted cipher traffic. On the 21st Daladier cabled the French mission to sign anything they could get, but on the same day a Russo-

German economic agreement was signed in Berlin. This agreement was regarded as portending something more spectacular and in Moscow a visit by Ribbentrop was openly spoken of. Stalin consented to a visit by the .Nazi Foreign Minister a week after the signing of the economic agreement but this was too late for Hitler. Ribbentrop arrived in the afternoon of the 23rd and a few hours later, to the amazement of the rest of the world, Germany and the USSR signed a treaty of friendship and non-aggression by which each of them abjured the use of force against the other and undertook not to help any third party in an attack on the other and not to join any group oriented directly or indirectly against the other. The treaty was to endure in the first instance for ten years. It was supplemented by a secret protocol defining spheres of interest: to the USSR, Finland, Estonia, Latvia; to Germany, Lithuania including Vilna; in Poland, the division to run along the line Narev–Vistula–San, the continuance of an independent Polish state to remain an open question; in the south-east the USSR stressed its interest, and Germany its *désinteressement*, in Bessarabia. These arrangements were later altered to give Lithuania to the USSR and the Polish provinces of Lublin and Warsaw to Germany.

Whether or not in August 1939 Stalin was still considering an alliance with the western democracies or was merely playing for time, using the Anglo-French missions to needle Hitler into a Russo-German pact and incidentally seeing how much useful intelligence he could worm out of the British and French negotiators, it is in retrospect clear that an Anglo-French-Russian pact was of interest to Stalin only upon terms which Great Britain and France could not fulfil. These powers, having lost Czechoslovakia and a possible Russian alliance, were forced back onto a third and much weaker policy. On 25 August, the day after the Russo-German pact was made known, an Anglo-Polish treaty, implementing the Chambêrlain-Beck declaration of April, was signed. It had been delayed by the Anglo-French-Russian conversations but by 22 August the British and French governments knew that the Russo-German entente was imminent. Chamberlain was still determined to avoid any provocation of Hitler and was hoping for a visit from Goering which would somehow prevent war, but he could no longer delay the formalization of his earlier undertaking, empty though it was. The treaty of August, like the declaration of April, was more an attempt to check Hitler than solid comfort for the Poles. The earlier pledge was embodied in a formal pact of mutual assistance against any act of aggression or any direct or indirect threat to the independence of the signatories. An indirect threat meant in fact a German seizure of Danzig. At the same time Great Britain both assured Hitler through diplomatic channels that British promises to Poland meant what they said, and intimated that Germany ought to have Danzig and Great Britain would like to see a peaceful cession of the city. France concluded a similar treaty with Poland, although it was not signed until 5 September, after Hitler's attack.

The only chance of averting war, so it seemed to those who wanted to do so, was to call in Mussolini again and arrange another Munich. Great Britain tried once more to use Mussolini as a lifebelt and a means of appeasing Hitler with Danzig, but the French government, unaware of what Great Britain was doing, was trying to detach Italy from Hitler by emphasizing the dangers ahead without realizing that the Italians knew from their contacts with London that Great Britain was hoping to remove the dangers by giving way to Hitler. Mussolini was unwilling to lose credit with Hitler and with himself by urging a peaceful settlement which Hitler did not want. On the other hand he was not ready for war and knew it, and Ciano was telling him that a German attack on Poland would begin a general war. He told Hitler that Italy could not join in a war which brought Poland's allies into the field unless Germany could supply the materials of war which Italy still lacked. Asked to specify Italy's needs he submitted a huge list. This was tantamount to asking for the impossible. Privately Hitler accepted the conclusion that Italy would not fight. Mussolini resigned himself to the fact that Hitler would make war on Poland.

Hitler's Japanese ally was also proving a disappointment. After Japan joined the Anti-Comintern Pact in November 1936 Hitler tried to get a promise of Japanese military assistance against any enemy of Germany and not merely against the communist USSR. By 1939 the Japanese army was keen on an alliance with Germany and Italy against Great Britain and France but the emperor, his Foreign Minister and the navy opposed such a commitment. Prolonged negotiations during the early months of 1939 ran into the sands and on 22 May Germany and Italy signed the Pact of Steel, which marked the end of hopes for a tripartite alliance against the western democracies. Six months later Japan was the more deeply aggrieved by Hitler's pact with Stalin because Japan was actually engaged in hostilities against the USSR. Japan complained that the Russo-German pact was a breach of the Anti-Comintern Pact. A few days later its government fell and its attitude became more uncertain, but temporarily the Japanese alliance had become irrelevant for Hitler who had just given the order for the war against Poland in which the USSR was his ally.

On 25 August Hitler gave the order for Poland to be attacked before dawn the next morning. At the last moment he revoked his order – so late that one unit could not be reached in time, advanced across the frontier and was destroyed. Hitler's change of plan may have been influenced by the behaviour of his Italian and Japanese allies or by the announcement – also on the 25th – of the Anglo-Polish treaty, but the guarantee to Poland was already an established fact and Hitler was more probably hoping that Chamberlain and Daladier, if given a few extra days to reflect upon the Russo-German pact, would either coerce Poland as they had coerced Czechoslovakia or abandon it. On the 25th he assured the British and French Ambassadors that he had no designs on the British empire and was not hankering after Alsace-Lorraine, and in the days which followed he tried to get Great Britain and France to force Poland to send a plenipotentiary to Berlin to negotiate the reversion of Danzig to Germany and a plebiscite in the Polish corridor. Given the fate which had attended other plenipotentiaries who had visited Berlin Beck (who had already agreed in principle to negotiate with Germany) refused and his allies felt unable to press him to accept.

Germany invaded Poland on 1 September. The first act in the war was a grisly stroke. In order to put the blame on Poland a party of Germans from a concentration camp, dressed in Polish uniforms, was given lethal injections, taken to the German radio station at Gleiwitz, deposited in front of it with bullets in their bodies and left there as exhibits in a propaganda game. A few hours later Danzig's Nazi Gauleiter declared the city to be a part of the German Reich; there was some fighting (there is an exciting account of the fight for the Post Office in Günther Grass's novel *The Tin Drum*) but Danzig was not now what mattered. Hitler had taken a risk. He calculated, correctly, that he could dispose of Poland without fear of British or French intervention, and he was happy to know that his generals who feared a war on two fronts would again be proved wrong. But he also calculated, wrongly, that Great Britain and France would either not declare war or not fight if they did. The British and French governments hesitated, but in the House of Commons Chamberlain's reluctance to declare war in response to Great Britain's pledges and Poland's plea for action against Germany in the west, produced tense and angry scenes. Chamberlain's government, it was said, would fall if it did not declare war. On 3 September Chamberlain spoke the necessary words, but it was the Commons of England rather than the government which had taken the plunge. France followed suit.

*

The outbreak of war in September 1939 marked the failure of policies, for which British and French politicians have been amply criticized. The French recipe for peace and security in Europe had already broken down because it rested on incompatibles – a system of continental alliances plus an alliance with Great Britain to whom the continental alliances were obnoxious. As a result of the failure of the French recipe Great Britain came to be in a position to call the tune. It called it wrong. But why? The obtuseness of British politicans in the face of the fascist phenomenon is only a part of the answer.

It is a commonplace of history that France, denied the British and American guarantees which were its first requirement in 1919, had to fall back on second best policies which were adequate in the twenties only because France was not then seriously threatened. The significance of Barthou and, in his different fashion, Laval was that these two Ministers tried a second time in the thirties to create an alliance system strong enough to contain Germany and that when this attempt too failed France's isolation was manifest to foe, friend and itself. Thereafter France accepted the consequences of this isolation – inability to conduct an independent foreign policy.

It is no less a commonplace that the United States kept itself aloof from European affairs between the wars. How far the United States was truly isolationist and why will be discussed in a later chapter. American isolationism, unlike the French abnegation, was a matter of choice. But it too involved withdrawal.

What has been little, if at all, noticed is that Great Britain too was isolated. The difference in the British case was that, unlike France and the United States, Great Britain refused to abnegate and continued to try to play an active role. It was, however, reduced to playing the only role possible for a state with commitments but without allies – the role of a man who gives way on one thing after another until he finds he has his back to a wall. Great Britain's commitments remained heavy and worldwide. In particular it had obligations to its imperial partners, obligations which even as late as the Imperial Conference of 1937 it reaffirmed on its own initiative; although these partners had become fully independent by the Statute of Westminster of 1931, they continued to look to Great Britain and the Royal Navy for their defence. Meanwhile Great Britain's alliances had dissolved or wilted. At the turn of the century Great Britain had been committed to that search for allies which eventuated in the agreements with Japan, Russia and France on the basis of which the First World War was fought. After that war the Japanese alliance was abandoned under American pressure, the Russian alliance disappeared with the ancient Russian state itself, and the French alliance became more of a problem than a support because of disagreements over German policy, the growing deficiencies of France as a military partner and the element of contempt and distrust in the British ruling class's attitude to France. In this situation British governments, no less than French, would have liked to believe that the new system of collective security embodied in the League of Nations was the answer to their problems and they consistently gave a high priority to support for the League for this reason, but they also knew that the collective security of their day would not work.

They were not unaware of their dilemma but in the first post-war decade it did not seem a pressing one. Then, just as the world came to look more menacing, they were struck by a catastrophe of a different kind which they did not understand and which they consequently greatly exaggerated. The economic crisis of 1931 terrified the governing class, reduced Ministers to a state of helplessness and convinced them that Great Britain had been permanently and irreparably weakened. This misjudgement was a major cause of the refusal to spend money on arms in the thirties, and this failure in turn reinforced the feeling of weakness. By the mid-thirties a combination of diplomatic isolation, economic nightmare and military unpreparedness had produced political and intellectual paralysis. And this paralysis produced wrong decisions. Munich was a wrong decision.

The betrayal of Czechoslovakia at Munich has been justified on the grounds that the only alternative was to fight Hitler and be defeated. This is a plea of *force majeure*. It is a bad plea. In the event France was beaten anyway. Great Britain won the Battle of Britain but the correct conclusion to draw about Munich is not that Chamberlain there gained time to build up the RAF and so save his country but rather that Munich brought upon Great Britain a battle which it would not otherwise have had to fight.

In 1938 Czechoslovakia was the one country among the possible combatants which was ready for battle. Great Britain and France were not ready, nor was the USSR. More significantly, Germany was not ready. Nor of course was Italy. So any alliance with Czechoslovakia in it would have started with a peculiar advantage over its enemy. Czechoslovakia was not only ready but strong, as strong as Germany in all important departments except manpower. The Czechoslovak army of thirty-five divisions faced a German army which was about the same size or slightly larger but which, if the aggressor, needed to be twice as large as its defending antagonist. In 1938 Germany could just about match Czechoslovakia division for division with four or five regular (but imperfectly trained and incompletely officered) divisions over to guard its western front – where Czechoslovakia's ally, France, mustered seventy-six divisions. The Czechs were better equipped than the Germans in a number of ways, notably in artillery and armoured fighting vehicles. The German amoured divisions which scattered and destroyed the French army and its allies in 1940 hardly existed in 1938; even in September 1939 Hitler had only six armoured divisions in place of the ten with which he made war in the west; four of these ten had Czech tanks.

Czechoslovakia was the sixth industrial power in Europe, possessed one of Europe's most famous, extensive and efficient armaments industries and had made plans to remove it from the west to the comparative safety of Slovakia. After 1939 its output, which was roughly equivalent to Great Britain's arms output, was added to Germany's own capacity – not the least of Germany's gains at Munich. Germany also secured the existing equipment of the Czechoslovak armed forces, including 1,500 aircraft. Czechoslovak mobilization plans were excellent. The government was ready to evacuate half the population of Prague. Morale was high. All Czechoslovakia asked in return for these substantial contributions was a declaration of war by France. Confident of its ability to hold the Germans for a matter of months, it did not even depend on an immediate French offensive in strength – unlike the Poles who required, and secured from France in the following year, a promise that the French army would commit the bulk of its forces against Germany within fifteen days of French mobilization.

But there was no equivalent confidence in France or Great Britain. The pessimism of French and British staffs and politicians arose largely out of the view held in the west that, since the *Anschluss*, Czechoslovakia's soft underbelly had been exposed and its capital lay at the mercy of a German pincer attack. In fact Czechoslovakia's southern defences were far from soft and the Germans did not plan a pincer movement. Hitler and his generals had decided that an attack on Prague from the south and the north-west would be held up for too long by the Czechoslovak army and fortifications and they therefore planned a thrust from the west. When, as bloodless victors, they were able to inspect the Czech defences they were awed by the strength and depth of a system which stretched back from the frontiers almost as far as Prague. Addressing 400 journalists a few weeks after Munich Hitler told them of his feelings when he inspected these fortifications and enthused over his success in getting hold of them without firing a shot.

What Stalin would have done in the event of war in 1938 still remains an enigma. The fact that the Russian obligation to act was dependent on French action provides no clue, since this clause in the Russo-Czecho-slovak treaty of 1935 was inserted not by the Russians in order to provide a let-out but by the Czechs, on French insistence, in order to discourage the Russians from acting on their own. During 1938 and before Munich the USSR delivered aircraft to the Czechs (who were short of bombers). Moscow also warned Poland not to take action against Czechoslovakia, threatening to denounce the Russo-Polish treaty if Poland attacked Czechoslovakia. Two weeks before the Munich conference Rumania lifted its embargo on Russian aircraft flying over its territory and one Russian aircraft which made a forced landing in Rumania on its way from the USSR to Czechoslovakia was not only given emergency repairs but was allowed to fly on. An airfield in Slo-vakia was stocked with fuel and spare parts for various types of Russian aircraft. The French Ambassador in Moscow believed that the Russians intended to go to the help of Czechoslovakia. Russian ground and air forces were moved westward in considerable numbers, although for what purpose is uncertain. They could have been used as a contribution to collective action on behalf of Czechoslovakia, or their deployment may have been no more than a defensive precaution, or Stalin may have been keeping both his options open. Furthermore the possibility of Russian action was in itself a factor since it gave Hitler not merely two fronts to worry about but three. He was risking an attack on East Prussia and had no means of meeting it. When war came a year later over Poland this threat had been eliminated. From the Anglo-French point of view Stalin was a far from certain ally in the event of war over Czechoslovakia, but he was an all but certain non-ally in a war begun anywhere else in central Europe.

Hitler's aggression against Czechoslovakia was based on a political calculation, not a military one. On a military calculation it was the lunacy which his generals held it to be. They, seeing only the military equation, were scared out of their wits and even conspired to overthrow him. Hjalmar Schacht too, the coolest of men – the financial genius who served many masters, financed German rearmament, mocked Hitler as he mocked everybody with his merciless drawing-room wit, but who did not leave the Nazi government until he was dismissed from it in January 1938 – bemoaned Chamberlain's visit to Godesberg no less than the generals: Schacht said that Chamberlain could do nothing to prevent war and that Germany was therefore lost. It follows that Czechoslovakia's allies' own calculations were, militarily, wrong. Hitler's political gamble came off not because France and Great Britain were militarily incapable but because they were strategically inept. The French army would have had little more on its hands than a *promenade militaire*, the one military performance which an out-of-date army can execute as well as an up-to-date one. In 1940 the French forces were destroyed in a few weeks by a weight of armour which in 1938 the Germans did not possess. It is moreover implausible to suppose that in 1938, with the Germans engaged in Czechoslovakia, with only five German regular divisions and seven others in the west, with the entire Luftwaffe committed in the east, with incomplete German defences described by General Jodl as a building site, and with the spur of a treaty obligation, the French army would have remained futilely static. However poor its leadership and equipment it could hardly have failed to do better than it did when war came; at least it could not have done worse.

The British case was different. The British army was irrelevant both in 1938 and 1940. Although its role in Europe's wars in the twentieth century was to send troops and not, as in the past, find the money to subsidize the armies of other countries, Great Britain did not in fact equip itself with troops to send. It was therefore unable to contribute much more than a token to continental land warfare until it had raised a wartime army in wartime, fighting meanwhile defensive battles to gain the time to do this. Consequently the crucial issue was the defence of Great Britain itself and the crucial battle was the air battle of 1940. The case for Munich from the British point of view is that Great Britain was too defenceless against air attack in 1938 to risk war with Germany. The Air Staff was telling the cabinet that Great Britain could not be defended against the Luftwaffe's bombers. This was true: Great Britain lacked the aircraft, guns and searchlights. The cabinet was so alarmed by this state of affairs that, unlike Hitler, it failed to put the larger question which – in the British case – was whether the kind of attack which the Air Staff said would be fatal could in fact take place. The cabinet was too overpowered by the answer to the narrower military calculation to pose the wider strategic one whether, in the event of Great Britain and France declaring war to help Czechoslovakia, the Luftwaffe would be able to send its bombers over England. (This was a repetition of the mistake made by the cabinet when it allowed itself to be swayed in the mid-thirties by the Admiralty's fears of the Italian fleet. The Admiralty may have been right to be scared of the Italian fleet, but the cabinet should have asked itself whether the Italian state was, regardless of the strength of its navy, in a position to fight a war – which it was not. The cabinet is not to be blamed for getting the answer to this question wrong. It is to be blamed for not asking it.)

The British case for Munich has to be tested at two points – in 1939 when war in fact came and in 1940 when the crucial battle was fought. Rearmament was accelerated after Munich, although without much intensity until the fall of France (and Chamberlain) in 1940. Between Munich, when battle was refused, and September 1939, when it was accepted, Great Britain's expenditure on armaments was one fifth of Germany's. British fighter production was about half Germany's. There was therefore no improvement in the British position relative to the German during these twelve months; in these respects the British position actually got worse. At the time of Munich the vital radar screen was incomplete; so it was a year later. The supplementary screen against low-flying aircraft, wholly non-existent in 1938, was still wholly non-existent in 1939. If the British government feared defeat in 1938 it had even more reason to fear it a year later when the country's defences were still ineffective against air raids and its aircraft, though more numerous and more modern, had declined in proportion to the German air force.

By the spring of 1940, on the eve of the Battle of Britain, British aircraft production had begun to overtake Germany's, so that the gap between the two forces had stopped growing and was beginning to close. In 1938 Great Britain had 600 fighter aircraft, of which 360 were immediately available for operations, but only one in five of these was modern. In 1940 all Fighter Command's forty-three squadrons had Hurricanes or Spitfires (but the squadrons overseas had not). It is therefore plausible to argue that had the Battle of Britain been fought in 1938 the result would have gone the other way. But it is implausible to assume that anything like the Battle of Britain would have been fought in a war begun in 1938 with Czechoslovakia as an ally, for the essential prerequisite to the Luftwaffe's attack on Great Britain was the possession of airfields in France and Belgium – airfields which had first to be captured by the German army which, on the 1938 hypothesis, would have been fully occupied in Czechoslovakia. Great Britain was woefully ill equipped in 1938 but it does not follow that it would have fought Germany at a greater disadvantage in that year than it did when, with Germany also better armed and above all unencumbered to the east, Great Britain was forced into war for Poland in 1939 and so forced to defend its own shores in 1940. On the contrary, there is reason to calculate that the avoidance of war in 1938 was not only a shameful act but an inexpedient and foolish one. The surrender at Munich, by postponing war, shaped its future course, ensured the defeat of France and, so far from buying time for rearmament, committed Great Britain to a battle which it nearly lost.

Part II
HITLER'S WARS: 1939–41

THE European war began when the Germans invaded Poland on 1 September 1939. On 17 September the Russians did so too and Poland ceased once more to exist as an independent state. Successful in the east Hitler paused, but Stalin in November made demands on Finland which led to a war which the Russians at first bungled but eventually won in March 1940. In April Hitler conquered Denmark and Norway and in May–June the Netherlands, Belgium and France. In July–September he failed, in the Battle of Britain, to win the air superiority necessary for an invasion. Great Britain remained at war, not only in the west, but also with naval, ground and air forces in the eastern Mediterranean. Hitler toyed with the idea of a descent into the western Mediterranean through France and Spain, but the war was resumed in the eastern Mediterranean when Mussolini attacked Greece unsuccessfully in October and the British attacked the Italians successfully in North Africa in December. In 1941 Hitler consolidated his control of south-eastern Europe, including Greece, and went to the help of the Italians in Africa. On 22 June he attacked the USSR which, besides strengthening its defences in the north by the peace imposed on Finland, had annexed the three Baltic states of Estonia, Latvia and Lithuania and the Rumanian provinces of Bessarabia and northern Bukovina. There were therefore at the end of 1941 three separate theatres of war: first, the USSR where Leningrad was invested, German forces had come within sight of Moscow, and the Ukraine had been overrun by German armies on their way into the Crimea and the Caucasus; secondly, the remnant of a war in the west maintained by the Royal Air Force in Great Britain but pushed out into the Atlantic and waged chiefly by German U-boats and their pursuers; and thirdly, the Mediterranean where the Germans and Italians were trying to win North Africa – and thence the Middle East – against the opposition of the British Mediterranean fleet and British land and air forces based in Egypt and Malta. At the end of the year this European war, begun in 1939, ceased to be purely European and merged with the wars begun before and after it by Japan – against China in 1937 and against the United States in 1941.

CHAPTER 5

From Poland to the North Cape

THE German attack on Poland was a combination of a straight punch and a pincer movement. The central German blow was delivered from Pomerania, Silesia and Moravia and was accompanied by simultaneous attacks from eastern Pomerania in the north and Slovakia in the south. All attacks were made with withering material and technical superiority, Hitler having taken the risk of committing the whole of his armoured and mechanized forces in Poland and of denuding his western fronts. The Polish forces fell back rapidly, taking the civilian authorities with them and leaving the German inhabitants exposed to the harsh vengefulness of their Polish neighbours. Fantastic rumours about the activities of a German fifth column – rumours which were to be repeated all over Europe and which were almost totally groundless – produced a panic-struck wave of summary injustice in which as many as 7,000 Germans may have been killed.

No help came to Poland from its guarantors. The French army put a symbolic toe across the German frontier but otherwise France composed itself to await the arrival of the British (that year or the next) and, when pressed by the Polish Ambassador in Paris, hedged over the promise given in May to launch an immediate major offensive. General Gamelin did not disown the promise but said, evasively and incorrectly, that French forces were engaging the enemy on the ground and in the air. Great Britain sent twenty-nine aircraft to attack German shipping (and lost seven of them) but for six months dropped nothing more serious than leaflets on German soil. The cabinet feared massive air reprisals and in parliament the Secretary of State for Air went so far as to defend this inactivity by reminding his more bellicose critics, who wanted the RAF to attack the Ruhr which was within its bombing range, that the targets proposed were private property. The Germans in the west uneasily occupied the incomplete West Wall. They deployed thirty-three divisions, twenty-five of which were of the second grade or lower. They had no tanks, no aircraft and three days' supply of ammunition. Opposite them was the French army with over seventy divisions on the border, nearly 3,000 tanks and command of the air.

The Poles, whether from misplaced hopes or through temperamental impetuosity or sheer desperation, had placed their forces in forward positions where they were quickly overwhelmed by an enemy who was superior in every way. Their mobilization was slow, their leadership poor, their communications flimsy, their reserves thin, their aircraft obsolete and their tactics – cavalry charging tanks with the aim of dashing into Germany – hopeless. On the ground they were thrown back at all points by the German armour and dive-bombers. In the air the rest of the Luftwaffe, although hampered by fog on the morning and evening of the first day, quickly forced the Poles to battle by attacking Warsaw. The Polish air force was crippled in two days and extinguished in two weeks as a result of air combats and the overrunning of its airfields by the German army. The Polish army scored one noteworthy success by a night attack southwards across the river Bzura on 9–10 September, but this stroke was held in check by the Luftwaffe and although one German army was temporarily disorganized a second, which was already to the east on its way to Warsaw, turned about and, together with a third army north of the Polish force, encircled the Poles and inflicted fatal casualties on them. On 25 September Warsaw was bombed all day. German command of the air was so complete that even Ju. (Junkers) 52 transports joined in the bombing, and the city surrendered the next day. Hitler arrived to see it on 5 October.

The German victory disconcerted the Russians both for what it was and by its speed, and on 17 September Russian forces moved into what the Russians called Western Belorussia and Western Ukraine on the plea that the Polish state had disintegrated. At the cost of 734 dead the Russians occupied half Poland (admittedly the half where Poles were in a minority). They also, in October, took control of Estonia, Latvia and Lithuania by exacting from their governments treaties of mutual assistance which permitted the entry of Russian troops and meant in effect that the Russians would take over if the Germans looked like doing so. Upon Finland the Russians had even more serious demands to make because of the vulnerability of Leningrad, situated no more than fifteen miles from the Finnish frontier on the Karelian isthmus and close to Lake Ladoga whose shores were partly Finnish territory. The Russians wanted to protect Leningrad against land and sea attack by obtaining Finnish territory in the immediate neighbourhood of the city and control of the Gulf of Finland.

The issue was one between Russian security and Finnish rights. During October and early November Finnish delegations went three times to Moscow. On each occasion the Russians made small concessions but they refused to abate the substance of their demands: a lease

The destruction of Poland was primarily a German action, 1,700,000 German troops soon defeated the 600,000 Polish soldiers. German air attacks destroyed the centres of the main Polish cities. The Poles hoped to make a final stand in the Pripet Marshes, but the U S S R advances destroyed all chance of further Polish resistance against either Germany or the U S S R.

THE GERMAN AND RUSSIAN INVASIONS OF POLAND 1939

LATVIA

LITHUANIA

Baltic Sea

Memel

Danzig

EAST PRUSSIA

Polish corridor

Vilna

Suvalki

Minsk

Augustov

Grodno

Bialystok

Pinsk

Pripet Marshes

Poznan

Modlin

WARSAW

Brest–Litovsk

Lodz

P O L A N D

Lublin

Lutsk

GREATER

Sokal

Rovno

GERMANY

Tarnov

Cracow

Yaroslav

Lvov

Przemysl

Stanislavov

SLOVAKIA

HUNGARY

RUMANIA

Dividing line between the German and U.S.S.R zones of occupation, agreed between Germany and the U.S.S.R in August 1939.

Miles

Annexed to the U S S R October 1939.

Annexed to Germany.

Annexed to Lithuania.

0   100

German advances commencing 1 September 1939.

Russian advances commencing 17 September 1939.

~ARTHUR BANKS~

of Hangö in south-western Finland at the entrance to the Gulf of Finland, the cession of a number of islands in the Gulf, a slice of territory in the Karelian isthmus (including the town of Viipuri) to the north-west of Leningrad and – in the far north – the Finnish half of the peninsula guarding the approaches to the Russian port of Murmansk. In exchange the Russians offered a piece of Russian Karelia twice as large as the areas demanded. They also asked for a treaty debarring each signatory from entering into agreements directed at the other. Finnish opinion was overwhelmingly against making any large cessions to an hereditary enemy, although one or two leaders argued that the Russians were not bluffing and could not in the end be denied. When the Russians saw that they could not get what they wanted by negotiation they set up a puppet Finnish government and attacked on the last day of November – for which the USSR was expelled from the League of Nations. Four Russian armies, comprising forty-five divisions, went into action, one on either side of Lake Ladoga, one directed across the waist of Finland and the fourth in the far north. The Finnish armies of 200,000 men offered magnificent resistance. They were much better clad and better shod than the ill-prepared Russians and they operated in small ski groups against inappropriately large Russian formations, but in the long term they lacked practically everything except courage and discipline. Within a short time of the opening of the campaign they were relying on teenagers to fill their fighting ranks.

The Russians began by mismanaging the campaign so thoroughly that their attacks in the south were brought to a standstill before the end of the year and they were decisively defeated in the centre in January. The Russian troops had been led to believe that they would win without serious fighting. They found themselves instead fighting unsuccessfully in a particularly cold winter in which the temperature fell below -50 degrees C. They suffered commensurately. The Finns on the other hand were so buoyed up by their initial successes that they believed that they had secured the necessary breathing space to allow foreign friends to come to their aid and complete the defeat of their enemy. (The Americans had a special regard for Finland as the only country in Europe which went on paying interest on its foreign debts in spite of the economic collapse of 1931.) But no help came. Hitler stuck to his bargain with Stalin and urged the Finns to come to terms. Sweden, Finland's nearest neighbour, was prepared to offer all aid short of war, but not fighting men. In Great Britain and France there was fervent sympathy and admiration for the Finns. Volunteers scented a cause in which they could worthily engage themselves instead of staying inactively at home watching other weak nations being bullied by Germany.

The British and French governments had more complicated reactions. Going to the help of Finland was part of a scheme for strangling Germany without having to fight it. If Germany's supplies from the USSR and Scandinavia could be stopped, Hitler would be forced to negotiate. So General Weygand, who was in Syria, would march on Baku (the Caucasian oil port) and might even link up with an Anglo-French expeditionary force starting from Finland 2,000 miles away – which would in any case meanwhile get into Scandinavia ahead of the Germans, stop Germany's supply of Swedish iron ore and, even if it could not bring the war to a halt, possibly force Hitler into a war in a northern theatre instead of the threatened attack in the west. This plan, one of the wildest surmises of the war, entailed either the cooperation of Norway and Sweden or the violation of their neutrality. Both countries refused to allow the passage of British and French troops through their territory. Plans were therefore made – or, more correctly, discussed, for nothing like a coherent plan emerged – to send four divisions to fight the Russian armies in Scandinavia. As a first step they were to invade Norway in order to prevent the Germans from getting there first, but while these measures were being discussed by cabinets and staffs in London and Paris (which had however no adequate information about the terrain or the road and rail systems which they hoped to use) the situation at the front changed. The Russians recovered themselves and launched in February a new and overwhelming attack under Marshal Timoshenko in the Karelian isthmus. The Finnish air force was reduced to one hundred aircraft against eight times that number. The Finnish line was broken. The government came to the conclusion that foreign help would be too little and too late. It decided to make peace in spite of Anglo-French – particularly French – attempts to keep Finland in the war and on 12 March Finland capitulated. At a cost of 68,000 dead the Russians secured all their original demands and a few more. Two hundred thousand Finns had to pack up and leave their homes and cross a new frontier in order to remain in their own country. Leningrad was a few degrees safer. The relations between the Soviet Union and Great Britain and France – and the United States – were several degrees colder. But Great Britain and France had been saved by the Finnish collapse from making war on the USSR while they were still at war with Germany. When, a few weeks after the end of the Russo-Finnish war, they entered Scandinavia they did so to fight the Germans and not the Russians. One consequence of this episode was the fall of Daladier. He was succeeded by Paul Reynaud who concluded with Great Britain an agreement that neither country would make a separate peace with Germany.

In February there had occurred one of those incidents which catch the imagination and help perhaps to precipitate events. The German supply ship *Altmark* was threading her way through the Leads along the coast of Norway, homeward bound from the south Atlantic. Aboard were 299 British captives, taken off ships which had been caught by the German battleship *Graf Spee*.

Graf Spee was by this time on the bottom of the sea. Like her sister ships *Scheer* and *Deutschland* (the latter renamed *Lützow* in 1940), *Graf Spee* was a pocket battleship designed to comply with the provisions of the treaty of Versailles which forbade Germany to have warships of more than 10,000 tons. In fact she slightly exceeded that limit. The pocket battleships were faster than anything which could outgun them and outgunned in range and weight of shell anything which could catch them. On the eve of war *Graf Spee* and *Deutschland* were dispatched into the Atlantic and from October to December they harried the commerce of Germany's enemies in the southern Atlantic and Indian Oceans. Their success was moderate. *Graf Spee* claimed nine victims before the end of her career – roughly one a week. Eight groups from the British and French navies were formed to hunt the German raiders and soon after dawn on 13 December one of these – a British and New Zealand cruiser force consisting of *Exeter*, *Ajax* and *Achilles* under Commodore Henry Harwood – opened battle. *Exeter* was soon very badly damaged and after an hour and a half *Ajax* and *Achilles* were forced to break off the engagement and limit themselves to shadowing. The damage and casualties which they had managed to inflict on *Graf Spee* were slight, but her commander, Captain Hans Langsdorff, decided to make for harbour and shortly after nightfall she dropped anchor in Montevideo Roads in the estuary of the River Plate. The British representatives in the capital of neutral Uruguay used every device of international law to prevent her from sailing again before Commodore Harwood, waiting off shore with *Ajax* and *Achilles*, could be reinforced. During the night of the 14th–15th, the cruiser *Cumberland* joined him. On the 17th *Graf Spee* was seen to be disembarking her crew. In the afternoon she set course for the open sea, accompanied by a German merchant ship. A few miles out the remainder of her crew left her. At sunset she blew up. Captain Langsdorff had been authorized to destroy his ship if he saw no way of bringing her back home. Nevertheless two days later he shot himself.

A sea chase and a sea victory have for centuries given a special delight to the British people. The sinking of *Graf Spee* was a timely tonic during a period of mixed disaster and inactivity. It was an item in the stiffening resolve of Great Britain which was to be put to the test when France fell and the decision to fight on against Hitler rested more upon spirit than reason. More immediately there was the question of *Graf Spee*'s victims whom she had transferred to *Altmark* before being engaged by Commodore Harwood's cruisers. Two months after *Graf Spee* sank, *Altmark* and her prisoners entered Norwegian waters homeward bound. She raised a question of international law. Norway was a neutral and it was argued on the British side that it was a breach of neutrality for Norway to permit the passage of prisoners of war through neutral territorial waters. Moreover the Norwegian authorities, upon being assured by *Altmark*'s captain that she carried no prisoners, had failed to carry out an effective search. A light British force thereupon sailed into Norwegian waters on 17 February, boarded the German vessel and rescued the captives. This dashing episode was another boost to British morale, greatly irritated Hitler and brought an incidental compliment from Ciano who told the British Ambassador that it reminded him of the boldest traditions of the British navy in the time of Francis Drake. (The Italians were already annoyed with Hitler's Scandinavian policies. Hitler had refused to allow Italian aircraft, ordered by Finland before the Russian attack, to be sent via Germany. Pro-Finnish demonstrations in Rome had had a clear anti-German tone.)

The Finnish war and the *Altmark* episode showed that Norway's hopes of keeping out of the Second World War as it had kept out of the First were tenuous. Norway was too important. Its main geographical feature is its coastline of a thousand miles, guarded and punctured by islands and inlets. This coast could provide valuable bases either for a British blockade of Germany or for a German offensive against shipping in the Atlantic. It had also a second importance as an outlet for Swedish iron ore. Northern Sweden is one of Europe's principal sources of iron ore, and early in the war exaggerated hopes were attached to preventing this ore from reaching Germany. The Swedish orefields lie midway between the Swedish port of Luleå in the Gulf of Bothnia, which freezes over in winter, and the Norwegian port of Narvik, which does not. By the beginning of 1940 both sides had their eyes on Norway and when the Finnish war ended in March Churchill wanted nonetheless to proceed to secure a foothold in northern Norway. But he failed to carry the cabinet with him and it was decided instead to mine the Leads and to make preparations to land in Norway if the Germans landed or seemed clearly about to do so.

On the other side Hitler had been pressed for some time by Grand Admiral Raeder to take action against Norway before Great Britain did. By December 1939 he had made up his mind to do this and in that month Raeder introduced to him Vidkun Quisling, the only personage of the Second World War who was destined to give his name to a human type. Quisling, two years older than Hitler, was a well educated, romantic racialist, who had had the beginnings of a brilliant army career before 1914, had helped his great compatriot Fridtjof Nansen with his humanitarian work for the League of Nations in the twenties, had gone to work and found a wife in the Ukraine, and had then turned to politics as something between a socialist and a communist. Tactless and unpopular, as well as talented, he did not fit into party life and after holding office briefly as Minister of Defence in 1931–3 he founded his own party and newspaper, both of which were complete failures. He was taken up by the Nazi ideologist and eastern specialist, Arthur Rosenberg, and a few years later was passed on to Hitler by Raeder as a useful instrument of German policy. His rewards were the post of Prime Minister during the German occupation and execution by his countrymen after the end of the war.

Hitler issued a formal directive for an invasion of Norway (plus Denmark because it was on the way) on 1 March 1940. Operations were placed under the control of the OKW – *Oberkommando der Wehrmacht*, the inter-service planning headquarters of which Hitler himself was chief with the pliant Keitel to do his bidding. The plan was a daring one. Resistance by Danes and Norwegians could not be a serious obstacle but Great Britain held command of the seas and Germany might therefore be expected – and was expected in Great Britain – to proceed by land (much as the Anglo-American armies proceeded up Italy by land three years later). Hitler chose, however, to confront British naval superiority and to seize points along the Norwegian coast as far north as Narvik, while at the same time seizing airfields by airborne troops – the first such enterprise ever attempted. The attack on Norway, from Oslo to Narvik, was launched on 9 April. In gales and snowstorms it was successful at most points, although a number of ships were lost, including the battleship *Blücher* sunk by gunnery while trying to force the passage up the Oslo fjord, and the admiral and general in command of operations were both captured. So was a Gestapo party on its way to arrest the king. The Norwegian parliament conferred full powers on the king who refused to surrender and, after

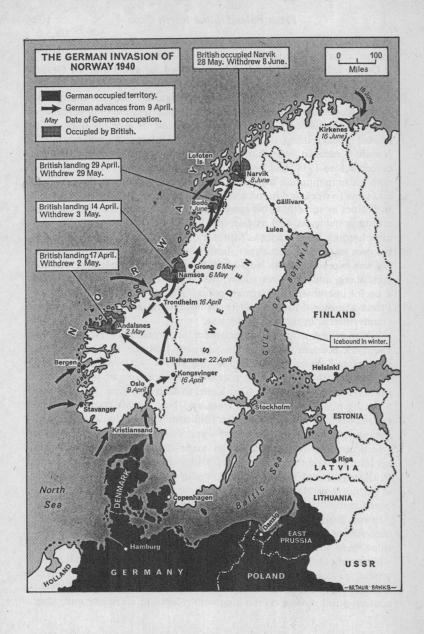

THE GERMAN INVASION OF NORWAY 1940

British occupied Narvik 28 May. Withdrew 8 June.

0   100
Miles

German occupied territory.
German advances from 9 April.
May Date of German occupation.
Occupied by British.

British landing 29 April. Withdrew 29 May.

British landing 14 April. Withdrew 3 May.

British landing 17 April. Withdrew 2 May.

Lofoten Is.

Kirkenes *16 June*

16 June

Narvik *8 June*

Bodö *1 June*

Gällivare

Lulea

Grong *6 May*
Namsos *6 May*

Trondheim *16 April*

Andalsnes *2 May*

Bergen

Lillehammer *22 April*

Kongsvinger *16 April*

Oslo *9 April*

Stavanger

Kristiansand

N O R W A Y

S W E D E N

G U L F   O F   B O T H N I A

FINLAND

Icebound in winter.

Helsinki

Stockholm

ESTONIA

Riga
L A T V I A

LITHUANIA

North Sea

DENMARK

Copenhagen

Baltic Sea

Hamburg

Danzig

EAST PRUSSIA

USSR

G E R M A N Y

POLAND

HOLLAND

~ARTHUR BANKS~

escaping death in an air attack on a village where he had been located, held out in the hope of British and French help.

In London reports that the Germans had landed as far north as Narvik seemed so incredible that they were for a time believed to be a mistake for Larvik, which is near the Oslo fjord. Although Swedish sources had given warnings of the assembly of the invading forces in north German harbours, it was believed in London that these were being held ready to counter an Anglo-French invasion and not to make the first move. The British cabinet was taken by surprise, the British staffs found themselves equipped with inadequate information about harbours and airfields, plans were made and unmade in confused succession even after operations had been set in motion. With the Germans in occupation of all ports and airfields the British and French were faced with the necessity of making hazardous landings from the sea or air. They proposed at first to go ashore near Narvik but then switched to Trondhjem fjord in central Norway, where the Norwegians wanted to concert a combined campaign. Next it was decided to attempt both the northern and the central ventures but later still a direct attack up Trondhjem fjord was abandoned in favour of two separate landings at Namsos and Andalsnes 125 and 190 miles away. In this confusion, made worse by notably inefficient cooperation between the army and the navy, British, French and Polish forces went into action against heavy odds and were worsted. In Scotland troops which had been embarked for Norway were disembarked when news of the German attacks arrived, in order to get the ships to sea as quickly as possible, but were then not used. At Namsos French forces were put ashore but were without even skis or snowshoes, let alone guns and tanks, since the ship carrying their equipment found on arrival that it was too big to enter the harbour. For a week these men were immobile and defenceless against air attacks. Inferior in numbers and ill supported from the air, Anglo-French forces in the centre were withdrawn in the first week of May, giving their Norwegian allies lamentably short notice of the necessity to capitulate. In the north evacuation was delayed until the beginning of June when it was harassed by the German fleet. The Royal Navy lost the aircraft-carrier *Glorious* with two squadrons of aircraft and failed to discover the intentions or the whereabouts of German heavy units which were at sea in the area. The retreating transports nevertheless escaped and reached Great Britain with the survivors of the expedition and also the Norwegian king. The Germans were left in possession of bases from which to operate against Atlantic traffic and, later, convoys bound for the USSR. There would in future be no difficulties about the transport of Swedish iron ore to Germany. Hitler's victory was won by the imaginative use of air transport, skilful handling of naval forces, good inter-service cooperation and a superior meteorological service – helped by the bungling of his adversaries. The cost was borne by the German navy which (like the German glider and parachute arms in the battle for Crete) suffered crippling losses at the hands of the defenders in the first phase of the operation.

The sorry Norwegian campaign was debated in the House of Commons on 7 and 8 May. The Chamberlain government was deserted by one hundred and one of its supporters, and although the Prime Minister still commanded a majority of eighty-one in that solid, stolid House he no longer had the backing needed to carry on the war. He tried to convince himself and others that mounting disaster made it desirable for him to remain at the helm, but this argument did not work. He was deposed by the Commons as a result of disorder within its Conservative ranks. There was also growing a feeling that the country needed an all-party government and the Labour Party would not serve under Chamberlain. The obvious successor in political terms was Halifax. Chamberlain himself, the Conservative Party and the king all wanted Halifax and the Labour leaders were willing to join a Halifax administration. But at a meeting between Chamberlain, Halifax and Churchill on 9 May the lot fell on Churchill. Chamberlain proposed Halifax, expecting Churchill to express his agreement, but Churchill, acting on advice given him by Brendan Bracken, stayed silent. In breaking an awkward pause to say something about the difficulties of leading a government from the House of Lords Halifax threw away his chances, and shortly afterwards Chamberlain was on his way to Buckingham Palace to tell the king that it must be Churchill, who thus assumed office and the responsibility for victory or defeat on 10 May.

When he took office in 1940 Churchill was sixty-five years old. He had been a prominent political figure for forty years and famous for most of that time. He had sat in the House of Commons since 1900 (with only a brief exclusion in 1922–4) and in cabinet on and off since 1908. He had held office as President of the Board of Trade, Home Secretary, First Lord of the Admiralty, Minister of Munitions, Secretary of State for War, Secretary of State for Air, Colonial Secretary and Chancellor of the Exchequer. He was unusually versatile. He had written over a dozen books, including a history of the First World War in five volumes, an excellent biography of his father and another in four volumes of his remoter ancestor the first Duke of Marlborough. He was a competent amateur painter and an addict of English and European history. He had been a war correspondent in Africa and India. In the variety of his aptitudes and his achievements he was matched by two only of his predecessors in the premiership, Disraeli and Balfour; he was closer to the colourful talents of the former than the philosophical intellect of the latter. He had also the vigorous and independent spirit of Palmerston, manifested in longevity and the ability to appeal to the masses. Churchill and Palmerston are the only British Prime Ministers who have been popularly referred to by friendly nicknames. As a war leader Churchill has inevitably been compared with Lloyd George but the similarities between the two men lie in their circumstances rather than their characters or tastes.

Yet in 1940 Churchill had held no office for over ten years. First a Conservative, then a Liberal and once more a Conservative after the First World War his political career was tinged with an inconstancy which is rare in British politics and is regarded with distrust. Even after the war, when his standing was unique in British political history, he was suffered to become the leader of the Conservative Party because of his enormous popularity and not because he was regarded by Conservative leaders as one of them, and during the thirties he was to all intents and purposes a man without a party, an eccentric without an accepted place in political life. In these years he was chiefly prominent for his opposition to the Conservative government's India Bill and for his campaign in favour of rearmament. He had spent three years of his early life in India and had formed a romantic attachment to the idea of the British-in-India which penetrated his prose style and ever afterwards provided him with some of the most effective embellishments of his oratory. But he was neither much interested in the real India nor well informed about it, so that his opposition to the Bill was romantic rather than sensible and his long but ineffectual crusade against it had no effect on the history of India. It did, however, widen the gap between him and the leaders of his party, and it strengthened the view held by many in political circles that, however great his abilities, his judgement was erratic. He was more liked than listened to. This element in his reputation was not new. As against Baldwin he had been on the side of toughness in dealing with the General Strike in 1926 and he had come in for criticism because as Chancellor of the Exchequer he had accepted, against his better judgement, the arguments for a return to the gold standard in 1925 at the pre-war parity. In 1936 he made no concealment of his sympathies with King Edward VIII during the abdication crisis – a generous attitude which may have been applauded by the people at large but greatly irritated the Baldwin government and the rest of the establishment in state and church. His campaign for rearmament won him few friends: while the left dubbed him a warmonger, Conservatives resented his opposition to their policy of appeasement and feared – especially in the light of the by-election in Fulham in 1933 where the Conservative candidate was defeated by, it was thought, pacifist sentiment – that his agitation was costing them votes.

But when war came there was an almost universal feeling that Churchill must have a big share, perhaps the biggest, in conducting it. It is easier to record this judgement than to identify its sources. There was first of all the fact that Churchill, however often he had been wrong in the past on this issue or that, had been right about Hitler's Germany. His knowledge of history was here crucial, for it was as a historian and not as a moralist that he took his stand. He had not only absorbed European history but had understood it thoroughly and acquired insights which equally well read and more intellectual observers missed. He became certain that war was coming and that Great Britain could not avoid it, for he saw the rise of Nazi Germany in terms of the classic British doctrine that no single power must be allowed to dominate the European continent. He did not suffer from the delusion that Great Britain was not a part of the continent and so could sidestep the catastrophe. Although he sensed the strategic challenge to Great Britain before the moral one to civilized behaviour – he was no quicker than most of his countrymen to react to the moral issue, commended Mussolini's rule on a number of occasions and was for a time ambivalent about Hitler – he developed also a deep and genuine loathing of Nazi brutishness and had the power to express it with peculiar sting.

This was the second source of his special position when war came. The challenge once seen, Churchill was exceptionally well equipped to expose and meet it. He was combative and patriotic in the best sense of these words and he gave the most reassuring appearance of being firm in purpose and unhesitating in action. He was not in fact a man who knew no doubts – only a singularly stupid or vain man could have avoided them and he was often fearfully worried – but he had the courage and the skill to hide his anxieties and to give the impression that he was certain of his course and applying himself undividedly to the business of doing what had to be done. He was able to communicate his attitudes to the British people and to evoke from them their latent determination to resist danger and conquer evil. The essence of his famous oratory was his ability to give voice to elemental sentiments in big words and simple phrases. He was moreover the kind of leader who suited the British people. He was both an aristocrat and a democrat, a combination which the British like and which does not strike them as a paradox. Churchill had the assurance, even something of the arrogance, of the born aristocrat, but he combined this superiority with a capacity for feeling himself a part of the people and not apart from them. For him the people meant all the people and not, as so often in British parlance, the working-class bottom half.

He possessed, finally, an abundant mental energy. This worked both ways. His habits of work sometimes irritated and exhausted his advisers who were required to consider a stream of ideas, some of which were inevitably bad ideas, and to do so at unconventional hours of the day or night. But the gain was great, for with Churchill in command there could never be any doubt about whether things were happening or not. Churchill was a leader who had no intention of allowing anybody inferior to give directions, but he was also a respecter of the people and of their principal institution, the House of Commons. Undoubted head of the executive and of the armed services, master of the bureaucracy and sometimes a rough master, he was at the same time the servant of the legislature and the electorate. He showed, because he believed, that one does not have to be a dictator to be a leader.

On the day that he became Prime Minister Hitler invaded France and the Low Countries. The so-called phoney war had come to an end. The phoney war was a period in which nothing very warlike happened (except locally, sporadically and briefly) and, more than that, in which it was possible for people who were so disposed to go on hoping that nothing very warlike would happen. It was the time in which the era of appeasement and the years of war overlapped. In May 1940 Hitler made war on the western democracies. Less obviously but no less significantly Churchill's government did something which Chamberlain's government had never done: it dropped a bomb on Germany.

CHAPTER 6

The Fall of France

HITLER had won Poland almost as easily as Austria and Czecho-slovakia. Although force had to be used instead of being merely bran-dished and the Russians had to be allowed their share, the operation was swift and was concluded without the intervention of any other power. It might be just the latest in the series of Hitlerian conquests, more ex-pensive and more brutal but essentially not very different. Or it might be the beginning of something much more serious. Hitherto all Hitler's victories had been in central Europe – in Germany itself (the Rhineland) and then in Austria, Czechoslovakia, Danzig, Memel and Poland. Should he now attack France, even though France had acquiesced in the Polish *fait accompli*? Hitler was for action now. In the past he had disagreed with his advisers, especially his military advisers, about the reactions and the capacities of the western powers and he had always proved his advisers wrong.

The Polish collapse could be exploited in different ways. There were those who hoped that the reluctance of the western democracies to help Poland would finally eliminate western opposition to German ambitions in central and eastern Europe without the need for a show-down; that the defeat of Poland would be accepted in the west as a defeat for the west too. On the other hand the glittering successes of the Polish campaign were an incitement to a similar campaign in the west, and so long as there was any doubt whether a war against France would have to be fought one day there was also the argument that from the German point of view the sooner it were fought the better. Before the end of September Hitler, without consulting General von Brauch-itsch, the Commander-in-Chief of the army, gave the order to prepare for an attack on France that autumn and a directive was issued by OKW on 9 October. Brauchitsch swallowed this usurpation of his functions and got to work, while continuing to argue that a spring offensive would be more prudent because the army needed to train fresh units and because the autumn weather might bog down the tanks and ground the aircraft. In the event an autumn campaign was washed out by the weather and after several postponements it was cancelled. In addressing his service chiefs at the end of November, Hitler, prefer-ring to lay the blame for his disappointment on the human factor, was so abusive about the army that Brauchitsch offered to resign. He was not allowed to – yet. The postponement of the attack had a most important consequence since it gave army leaders the time to urge changes in the German plan of campaign.

The fundamental factors in German planning were the experiences of their forerunners in 1914 and the Maginot Line. The latter was a string of fortified positions, begun in 1929 and guarding the western approaches to France between its Swiss and Belgian frontiers. This line had an awesome reputation but owing to Belgium's neutrality it stopped short at a geographical point which had little strategic significance. Its existence, however, virtually dictated a German attack through Belgium to the north of it and the question which remained open was the main objective of such an attack. Too much pondering of the campaigns of 1914 had led the German General Staff to plan an attack on a broad front stretching all the way from Luxembourg northwards, with the main weight in the north and the main objective the Channel ports which they had failed to win in the race with which the First World War had opened. This attempt to repeat and improve on the performance of August 1914 reflected a preoccupation with this failure and a special concern with Great Britain rather than France, since the principal value of the ports was their use for submarine warfare against the British Isles. This plan did not aim, primarily at any rate, to knock out the French army as the Polish army had been knocked out and it therefore admitted the prospect of a long and possibly static war. Even if the plan succeeded, the war in France would not be over; and its success was dubious since it involved a direct attack on French and British forces which, if not defeated outright, might stand on prepared lines in northern France and keep themselves supplied through the ports.

General von Manstein, the plan's most effective critic, had other ideas. He proposed that the main weight of an attack in the north should be on its left wing rather than its right and that the prime object should be the annihilation of the French capacity to resist and not the conquest of the Channel coast or any other terrain; the enemy's territory in its entirety would become a prize of war as a consequence of the defeat of his armies. Manstein proposed that German forces attacking through the Ardennes should turn southwards as well as northwards and envelop the French to the west of the Maginot Line. Manstein was Chief of Staff to Field Marshal von Rundstedt, whose Army Group A would win the chief role in the campaign if the Manstein concept were accepted. They together urged Brauchitsch, who agreed with them but did not enjoy arguments with the Führer, to press their views on Hitler; and they had a stroke of luck early in January. An officer taking the plans to a headquarters in the west fell in with some air force friends, celebrated the meeting so well that he missed his train, got his friends to fly him on his way but took a wrong course and crashed in Belgium. With the plans in enemy hands there were special grounds for changing them. (The western staffs, however, concluded that the crash had been a fake and the plans planted on them.)

Hitler was prepared to listen. A serious student of military affairs, he liked discussing military problems with those of his generals whom he respected, and Manstein was one of these for the time being. Hitler was not, as he himself imagined, a military genius, but neither was he the ignoramus and bungler that surviving generals subsequently tried to make out. From the career point of view he was an amateur and not a professional military man, but then so were Stalin and Churchill and, for good or ill, Hitler had studied the science of war at least as carefully as the first and possibly with more application than either. But his talents and inclinations were the reverse of what was needed in a supreme commander. He was strongest on detail. He knew the names of bits and pieces of military equipment and what they were for, just as he was also exceptionally well versed in the details of the architect's craft. He had the mind of a fascinated and perhaps even an inventive quarter-master, but this gift did not make him a strategist and, as a strategist, he was handicapped because his cast of mind was basically political and not military. He put political aims before military sense. His catastrophic fault as a war lord lay even more in attempting the impossible than in his strategy. On this occasion he saw the force of Manstein's arguments (he may have been thinking independently along similar lines) and accepted his plan with some modifications.

Hitler did not begin his attack in the west with any marked material superiority. The battle of France was won by superior skill and not by the crushing weight of numbers. In the vital department of tanks the Germans were numerically the weaker with some 2,700 against nearly 3,000 French and 200 British. The quality of the tanks on the two sides was about the same. But in tactics and leadership the French and British were outclassed. For many French and British officers the tank was a horseless carriage to be used in the role of a horse rather than a carriage, a mechanized charger, more expensive and less lovable than a horse but performing essentially the same function as the cavalry of a bygone age which had fought closely with the infantry arm along a defined front. But defeat in the First World War and the restrictions imposed by the treaty of Versailles had made the German army more receptive to new ideas. Under General von Seeckt, himself somewhat old-fashioned in his views but willing to encourage novel thinking in others, the German army of 100,000 was re-created on the principles, first, that compensation for small numbers lay in mobility; secondly, that armoured vehicles could provide this mobility in place of the horse; thirdly, that the armour of a tank, unlike that of a medieval knight, was even more valuable in offence than for protection; fourthly, that tanks should be used in massed cohorts – divisions, corps and even tank armies – distinct from the other arms of the service; and finally that, with this combination of speed, weight and numbers, their prime purpose was to penetrate the enemy's lines and destroy his communications.

This was the Blitzkrieg and it revolutionized not only the handling of armoured forces but also the whole concept of war as a face-to-face contest between rival fronts. The basic ideas were not German. They were developed in the first place by British theorists like Captain B. H. Liddell Hart, Major-General J. F. C. Fuller and Major-General G. le Q. Martel. In Germany the doctrines of these men and later the similar teaching of Charles de Gaulle, published in 1937 and better known in Germany than in France, were studied by Heinz Guderian and other young officers. Before 1933 they were tried out in practice in the USSR under arrangements made clandestinely by Seeckt with the Russian army and government, and although Hitler stopped this collaboration his special interest in armoured warfare encouraged the progressives in the German army and contributed to the formation of the first two Panzer divisions soon after the Nazis took power. In May 1940 the Germans had ten Panzer divisions. (Rather more than half of their tanks were Pkw. Is and IIs, the rest the Pkw. IIIs and IVs which were to become the mainstay of the German armour until the Panther and Tiger began to arrive at the front in 1943. Three divisions with the heaviest punch were equipped with tanks made in Czechoslovakia's captured factories.)

The Blitzkrieg had also a special place for airborne troops whose task was to seize key points ahead of the advancing armour. Germany's parachutists so captured the imagination by their novelty that extraordinary steps were taken to defeat them: policemen were armed and trained to deal with them, in Great Britain church bells were to be rung to give warning of their descent and the most fanciful accounts, some of them official, circulated about the guise in which they were likely to do so. But there were far fewer of them than was commonly believed. Hitler had envisaged a war of the future as a 'sky black with bombers and, leaping from them into the smoke, parachute storm troops, each grasping a machine gun', but the Germans never had more than one division of parachutists and in their most notable operation – Crete – most of them jumped with pistols or knives and had to search around afterwards for the machine guns which were dropped separately and sometimes far away.

The German attack in the west opened on 10 May simultaneously against the Netherlands, Belgium, Luxembourg and France. In the Netherlands the weight of the attack was directed against Rotterdam. Its airfield, Waalhaven, was seized by parachute troops who also captured the intervening bridges over the Maas. The main bridge in the centre of the city was seized by units which landed by it in seaplanes. A subsidiary attack on airfields near The Hague was unsuccessful. On the 14th Rotterdam was still holding out. The Germans summoned it to surrender and parleys ensued. At this point the heart of the city was heavily bombed; within a few minutes great destruction was caused and 980 were killed. Nothing like this had been seen in the war so far. Two hours later the city capitulated and on the 15th the Dutch laid down their arms everywhere. The bombing of Rotterdam has been regarded as a piece of unprincipled savagery and vandalism, but there were extenuating circumstances. The air attack seems to have been made in ignorance of the parleys which were in train and in spite of German attempts to cancel it, and when the bombers appeared German commanders on the spot tried to signal to them to desist and did succeed in making a part of the force sheer off. Whether Goering and Kesselring can also be absolved remains open to doubt.

In Belgium the attack began with one of the most original strokes of the war. The conquest of Belgium involved crossing a series of waterways, notably the Meuse (or Maas) and the Albert Canal which branches off the Meuse just south of Maastricht on a north-westerly course towards Antwerp. Maastricht, which is on the Dutch side of the frontier between Belgium and Holland, is only twelve miles from the German border. Just south of it and in Belgium lay the great fortress of Eben Emael, a wedge-shaped hill unassailable except from the sky and commanding the end of the Albert Canal and three vital bridges over it. In the early hours of 10 May forty-one gliders took off from German airfields with 363 men for an operation which they had rehearsed many times. Two of the gliders came to grief on the way but the rest arrived silently over Eben Emael and in the first glider-borne attack in history captured the fort and its 1,200 defenders and two of the three bridges with the loss (to the attackers) of only five lives.

As soon as the German attack in the west was known, French and British forces began to move forward to make contact with the Belgian army on the line of the river Dyle and so create an unbroken line of resistance to the Germans from the English Channel to the borders of Switzerland. Owing to Belgium's neutrality advance planning had been dangerously meagre, so much so that positions which French forces were to occupy had not been prepared for them. Almost immediately the allied line was punctured farther south. German armour under General Erwin Rommel proved that the Ardennes were not the obstacle to tanks which had been supposed and on 12 May German units, having broken through a sector which was lightly held by second-class divisions, found themselves on French soil north of Sedan. The next day they were across the Meuse at a number of points and after only one more day they had prised open a fateful gap fifty miles wide between two French armies. General Georges, commanding the north-eastern fronts under a cumbrous arrangement as a semi-independent subordinate of the Commander-in-Chief, General Maurice Gamelin, ordered a redisposition on the basis of a false report that French forces were in flight: the general who sent the report shot himself the next day, Georges suffered a nervous collapse (he had been ill for years) and two days later a third general was dismissed for losing his nerve.

In three days the RAF lost half of the 200 bombers which it was operating in France – the highest loss percentage which it ever suffered – and the French air force was extinguished. The French First Army, the British Expeditionary Force to its left and the Seventh French Army further north still were cut off from the rest of the French armies, and French and British reinforcements moving up to the Dyle line were ordered to suspend their advance. On the following day, 16 May, with the Dutch already out of the war, the plan for Belgium having miscarried and the Germans racing into France, Gamelin disclosed to an Anglo-French council of war in Paris that he had no reserves left. His predicament was of his own making. He had neglected to create a reserve before war began, even though one of the main objects of building a defensive position like the Maginot Line was to avoid having to string men out along a long static line and so be able to hold them in a mobile reserve instead. Gamelin had done the opposite, committing his troops to fixed positions from which he could not easily switch them when the need arose. He had compounded this basic mistake by allowing men to go on leave from 7 May in spite of accurate warnings from reliable sources of the date and place of the German attack. Three days later French soldiers hurrying to rejoin their units failed to find them

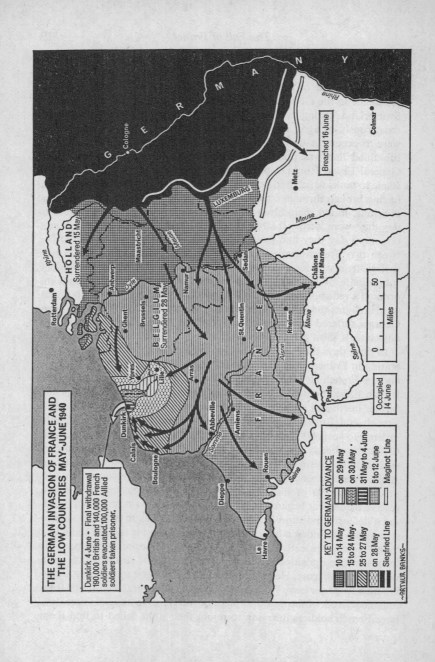

THE GERMAN INVASION OF FRANCE AND
THE LOW COUNTRIES MAY–JUNE 1940

Dunkirk 4 June – Final withdrawal
190,000 British and 140,000 French
soldiers evacuated,100,000 Allied
soldiers taken prisoner.

KEY TO GERMAN ADVANCE

10 to 14 May   on 29 May
15 to 24 May   on 30 May
25 to 27 May   31 May to 4 June
on 28 May   5 to 12 June
Siegfried Line   Maginot Line

Breached 16 June

Occupied
14 June

Colmar

Metz

Châlons
sur Marne

Rheims

Sedan

Namur

St.Quentin

LUXEMBURG

Maastricht

Antwerp

Ghent

Brussels

B E L G I U M
Surrendered 28 May

Ypres

Lille

Arras

Abbeville

Amiens

Somme

Rouen

Paris

Dieppe

Le
Havre

Boulogne

Calais

Dunkirk

Rotterdam

H O L L A N D
Surrendered 15 May

Rhine

Cologne

G E R M A N Y

Rhine

Meuse

Meuse

Marne

Aisne

Seine

Seine

F R A N C E

0   50
Miles

~ARTHUR BANKS~

before they were overwhelmed. Yet Gamelin had all the same a small reserve of eight infantry divisions; but it was behind the Lorraine and Rhine fronts.

From the Meuse the German armour pushed on for the coast with powerful and efficient air support. They reached it on 20 May. Instead of a Franco-Anglo-Belgian line containing the Germans there was a German line stretching from Germany to the sea and cutting the allied forces in two. This German line was a thin one, for the German forces which had made it were comparatively small and had advanced far ahead of their supporting formations. The problem for the German high command was to consolidate the line and produce plans for dealing with the two distinct allied forces to the north and the south of it. The problem for the allies was to try to break the line and re-establish contact between their disrupted armies.

Reynaud, who had never had confidence in Gamelin and had been on the point of dismissing him when news of the German invasion arrived, replaced him on 19 May by General Maxime Weygand, a soldier full of honour but also of years (72). Reynaud also appointed another and even older hero, Marshal Philippe Pétain (85), to be Deputy Prime Minister. Weygand's fame and barely diminished sprightlyness infused some hope into headquarters staffs but he was powerless to rectify Gamelin's cardinal error. He could not in the midst of a battle create a reserve. He inherited from Gamelin a plan to attack the German corridor simultaneously from north and south but postponed its execution while he made a tour of headquarters. This tour wasted precious days (whether telephone communications were destroyed or overlooked is not clear) and largely failed to achieve its aim, since of the two principal commanders north of the corridor, one, Lord Gort, failed by accident to keep his appointment with Weygand and the other, General Billotte, was killed – also accidentally – immediately after it. But in any case Gort, acting on Gamelin's earlier orders and apparently unaware of Weygand's cancellation of them, shot his bolt prematurely and was checked by the Germans, so that by the time Weygand put the plan in motion again there was no response from the north. The effect therefore of supplanting Gamelin at this late stage was added confusion: an attack from the north at a time when the complementary attack in the south had been stayed, and consequently no possibility of an attack from the north when the new Commander-in-Chief was ready to give the signal for attack in the south. The German line became unpierceable (if it was not so already) and the Germans were able to consider in comparative leisure how they would complete the campaign. If on 20 May, when they reached the sea, there had been some doubt about whether their victories so far had been decisive, the next few days showed that no effective counter-attack could be launched against them and that, whichever way they turned first, they could outnumber the allied divisions on either front by at least two to one.

Yet they were undecided about how to proceed. The allied armies, although disrupted and disjointed, had fought well. The German generals hardly perceived the extent of their triumph. They were anxious to reinforce their forward units and nervous about the large French armies on their southern flank. The first thing to do was to mass their own forces once more. To the south there was need for caution. To the north there was no need for speed since the allied armies were surrounded and the idea that any great number of them could escape by sea entered nobody's head. So after covering 300 miles to reach the Channel in three days the Germans took over three weeks to go another thirty miles up the coast. Rundstedt, although delighted by the dashing successes of his younger subordinates, was taken aback by the speed of his victory, decided not to press his luck too far and ordered his Army Group to halt and regroup.

But Brauchitsch was ready to let the Panzers push on without delay and round up the allied forces to the north, while plans for the subjugation of the rest of France were being worked out. He was angered by Rundstedt's order. On the day of the order, 24 May, Hitler arrived at Rundstedt's headquarters. The plan which, at Manstein's urging, Hitler had adopted early in the year, had emphasized the prior importance of a southward rather than a northward sweep after a break-through. Presumably Hitler still had Manstein's basic reasoning in mind. He endorsed Rundstedt's order and as a result the German armour halted for three days, facing north but motionless. These days were an invaluable respite for the allied armies trapped between the Germans on the Somme and other German armies in Belgium – and the main cause of the salvation of so many men from Dunkirk.

Hitler's motives in blunting his attack on them have been one of the principal enigmas of the war. Among his motives were two different, even contradictory, considerations. Faced with a force which was now mainly British his ambivalence about Great Britain may have reasserted itself. He had no plan for continuing the war against Great Britain and expected it to make peace after France had been beaten. There was nothing to be gained by pounding the British forces on the continent and then incarcerating what was left of them. On the other hand he was under pressure from Goering to leave the rest of this battle to the Luftwaffe. Goering had taken little part in the Battle of France. The Luftwaffe was engaged in close support of the armies; the independent role of Commander-in-Chief of the Luftwaffe had, with the exception of the few days' operations against Holland, been eclipsed. Moreover Goering himself had been suffering from one of his recurrent bouts of drug-taking (to which he had become addicted since drugs had been prescribed for a painful leg wound sustained in the 1923 putsch) and upon emerging from this enforced retreat he was all the more eager for action and distinction. Like Mussolini, he figured that the time was now or never. Although Goering's pleas to leave it to the Luftwaffe and Hitler's political preoccupations with Great Britain could hardly be reconciled, they did have one thing in common: halt the Panzers.

The allied forces were in a bag round Dunkirk. Boulogne had been lost on 25 May and Calais the next day after a whole day's pounding by artillery, Stukas and tanks. At Dunkirk the evacuation and the Luftwaffe's attacks both began on 27 May. The first results were very discouraging for the beaten troops, who were fiercely battered in the town and on the beaches and bitterly reproached the RAF for not protecting them. Then the weather came to their help. With rain half the day on the 29th and fog and rain all day on the 30th the Luftwaffe's onslaughts were restrained and the evacuation rate rose to eight times what it had been on the first day. But on 1 June it turned fine and evacuation by day had to be suspended. By this time the men waiting on the beaches were suffering extreme physical and nervous exhaustion and many of those who got off were sunk in the sea before they reached the other side of the Channel. But in an astonishing rescue operation by large and small craft of every description, by which the British Admiralty had hoped at the outset to save perhaps 100,000 men, more than three times that number – 338,226 – were brought away from Dunkirk.

The Belgian army was forced to lay down its arms soon after the operation began, but many French and other allied combatants escaped with the British (one third of those rescued were not British). The last British troops were taken off on 2 June but the British flotillas returned to collect Frenchmen for two more nights. The Germans were left with 40,000 prisoners. In France a further 190,000, mostly belonging to rear formations, were later evacuated from Normandy and Bordeaux, but an attempt to withdraw the British 51st Division from St Valéry failed, partly because of fog. Altogether over 558,000 (again one third non-British) were evacuated from different parts of the continent into Great Britain. This was a triumph for the British navy and a corresponding defeat for Goering, although the result might have been different if the

Luftwaffe had been able to operate at full strength in the Dunkirk area on more days than the weather permitted. Significantly for the future the RAF lost over Dunkirk fewer aircraft than the Luftwaffe. British fighters, flying from bases nearer to the battle area than the German bases, took heavy toll of the Luftwaffe's bombers and Stukas.

On 5 June, the day after the close of the Dunkirk operation, the Germans launched from the Somme–Aisne line a series of attacks to the south which (together with a secondary attack through Alsace) destroyed the French army. They had spent the interval since 20 May debating whether to bring the weight of their armour to the west or east of Paris. The debate serves only to show how unsure the Germans still were about the hard facts of the situation, for in truth it did not much matter which they did. They reached the Seine at various points in three days, entered Paris on 14 June and spread rapidly into the farthest corners of France. The French army fought them – up to the bitter end French units continued to put up tough resistance in spite of the physical and psychological shocks which they had suffered – but was incapable of stopping them. The only conceivable hope of avoiding complete defeat lay with Great Britain. France, defeated and despairing, could no longer rely on itself. It turned to its ally. On the ground the British contribution had always been conceived as ancillary. The British Expeditionary Force might help the French army but could neither be a substitute for it nor rescue it. In the air, however, the British had more to offer. When the campaign opened the RAF committed thirty-nine squadrons to the battle. Ten of these were obsolescent medium bombers which were so badly mauled in daylight operations that they had to be regrouped as six squadrons within a week. The remainder were fighters (including ten Hurricane squadrons) and reconnaissance. The Hurricane force was almost doubled in the next few days but the French government appealed for still more. A first request for ten squadrons was refused. Instead heavy bombers were ordered to attack the Ruhr and then the advancing German armies. On 16 May six more fighter squadrons were detailed to the battle in France, although these aircraft had to operate from bases in Kent. Thenceforward the British squadrons engaged in France were progressively withdrawn to English bases as airfields in France were overrun. By 20 May only a token force remained. On 2 June Reynaud asked for twenty more squadrons, an impossible request. The British government provided a modest reinforcement but as the days passed and it became increasingly clear that Weygand could not turn the tide of battle, the British cabinet had to harden its heart against sending aircraft to France simply to be lost. By 11 June Weygand was himself

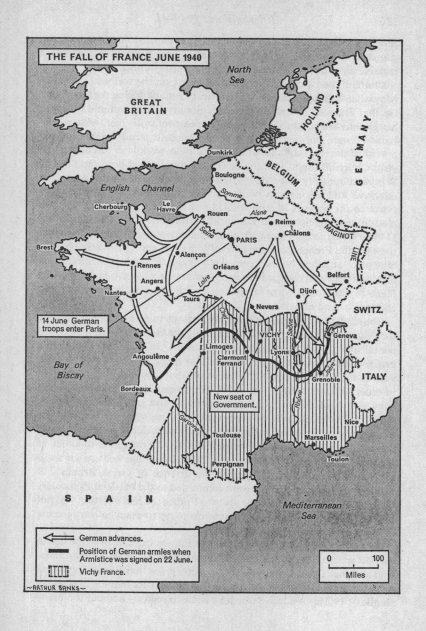

THE FALL OF FRANCE JUNE 1940

North Sea

GREAT BRITAIN

HOLLAND

GERMANY

Dunkirk

BELGIUM

Boulogne

English Channel

Somme

MAGINOT LINE

Cherbourg

Le Havre

Rouen

Aisne

Reims

Châlons

Brest

Seine

PARIS

Alençon

Orléans

Belfort

Rennes

Angers

Loire

Dijon

SWITZ.

Nantes

Tours

Nevers

14 June German troops enter Paris.

Cher

VICHY

Geneva

Bay of Biscay

Angoulême

Limoges

Clermont Ferrand

Lyons

Saône

Grenoble

ITALY

Bordeaux

New seat of Government.

Garonne

Rhône

Isère

Nice

Toulouse

Marseilles

S P A I N

Perpignan

Toulon

Mediterranean Sea

⟵ German advances.

▬ Position of German armies when Armistice was signed on 22 June.

▥ Vichy France.

0   100

Miles

~ARTHUR BANKS~

prophesying the end at any moment. His exhausted divisions were engaged at all points, he had no reserves, and Reynaud's plea for a massive air attack to save the day was painfully unrealistic.

Churchill had seen for himself the writing on the wall as early as 16 May when he made the first of five visits to France during the campaign. On that first visit he heard Gamelin's gloomy assessment and observed his gloomy mien. Outside the conference room old men with wheelbarrows were burning secret papers. Churchill faced the unexpected horror of the total collapse of his only ally. A week later, on his second visit, Churchill found that the dejected Gamelin had been replaced by Weygand but only a few days later Gort abandoned all thought of an offensive and decided to withdraw the entire British Expeditionary Force to the coast; Churchill's third visit on the last day of May took place during the fighting at Dunkirk. By the time he returned again on 11 June Great Britain had no troops on the continent, Italy had entered the war, the French government had left Paris and the meeting had to take place at Briare on the Loire. Two days later the last of these meetings was held at Tours, where the government was bivouacking on its flight to the south with Ministries and Embassies dispersed in old châteaux round about.

Churchill was throughout fervently anxious to do everything possible for France and keep it in the war. Fighting the Germans without a continental ally would pose huge new problems. In addition, Churchill's generous impulses urged him now, as they urged him later on over convoys to the USSR, to go to the brink of what was wise and practicable in order to help an ally. But other voices counselled otherwise. During May and June the Air Staff became more and more alarmed about losses in France. Scarce and precious Hurricanes were being lost at the rate of twenty-five a day when the factories were delivering new ones at the rate of four a day. At one moment the Commander-in-Chief of Fighter Command, Air Marshal Sir Hugh Dowding, went so far as to say that he could not answer for the defence of Great Britain and would resign if more fighters were committed to the battle in France. By the time of Churchill's last two visits to France the real question was not how to help in that battle but what terms to try to exact before agreeing to France's inevitable surrender.

At Tours Churchill refused to release France from its promise not to make a separate peace. He promised that there would be no recrimination and that Great Britain would, in victory, see that France recovered its full dignity and greatness if it fought on. But Reynaud's cabinet reshuffle of 19 May – a move which he came to regret – had put too many doves among the hawks. Pétain, supported by Weygand and some of the civilian members of the cabinet, was in favour of giving up the fight. They had no hope for themselves and no belief that Great Britain could do anything to help them. On 15 June, with the Germans now in Paris and the French government in Bordeaux, Reynaud proposed that the French army should lay down its arms (as the Dutch had done) but that the government should remain at war and move, with the fleet and air force, to North Africa. The generals and their supporters expressed horror at this idea which would cast the whole odium of defeat on the army. Besides, the losses suffered at the beginning of the campaign made it possible to argue that there was nothing left to carry on with. The Under Secretary for War, Charles de Gaulle, supported Reynaud and those civilian members of the cabinet still anxious to fight on. De Gaulle had earlier urged Reynaud to move his government to Quimper in Brittany rather than Bordeaux in the hope that this could be a first step to a further move overseas and a refusal to surrender. Reynaud's proposal was approved by a majority of the cabinet but the Prime Minister hesitated, unwilling to insist on a course disapproved by the generals. He hoped that by the next day Pétain could be persuaded to talk Weygand round. Instead Pétain resigned.

When the cabinet met again on the 16th Reynaud had received from Churchill Great Britain's consent to Franco-German armistice negotiations on condition that the French fleet should first sail to British ports; Churchill also urged safe passage for Polish and Czechoslovak troops to Africa. But at the last moment de Gaulle telephoned to Reynaud a new proposal from Churchill for the continuation of the war on the basis of a Franco-British political union and common citizenship after the war and a pledge of total British support. This strange plan, which would have revived the abortive union effected by Henry V by the treaty of Troyes in 1420, seems to have been devised by French and British officials, notably Jean Monnet and Arnold Toynbee with the support of Lord Vansittart. It was regarded by most of the French cabinet as irrelevant to France's plight. Perhaps the British cabinet, in endorsing the plan, anticipated the French reaction, for had it been otherwise Great Britain might have found itself committed to military actions which would have lost the war as well as to a political course which would have baffled the British people. Reynaud, upon seeing that the argument among his colleagues was going against the idea, resigned that day (the 16th). Pétain took his place, formed a new government during the ensuing night and immediately sued through Spain for an armistice. But the fighting went on for another six days and so did the talk about moving to Africa. Preparations were made to transport Ministers, members of parliament and others, but nobody actually gave the word to go and so in the end nobody went – except as refugees. The opponents of the idea kept the Germans informed about what was going on and urged them to produce acceptable armistice terms as quickly as possible. After a preliminary meeting between Hitler and Mussolini at Munich terms were presented. They were accepted after what was virtually an ultimatum requiring unconditional French acceptance and on 22 June at Compiègne, surrounded by the memories and even part of the furniture of the armistice scene of 1918, France signed. Two days later a separate agreement was signed with Italy which, in one of the cheapest and least exhilarating conquests of modern times, acquired Nice and part of Savoy.

Ten days after the signing of the armistice at Compiègne Great Britain took drastic action against the French fleet. The fall of France threatened the naval balance in the Mediterranean. Together the French and British fleets had dominated that sea. Without a French ally, and with other seas to command as well, Great Britain faced a serious Italian challenge. Although marginally superior in battleships (seven against six) and possessing two aircraft carriers against none, the British Mediterranean fleet was significantly outnumbered in cruisers and destroyers. Italy had the largest submarine fleet in the world and ten land-based aircraft for every one which the RAF could spare for the Mediterranean theatre. If, in addition, the French fleet actively joined the war on the Axis side Great Britain might well be swept from the Mediterranean.

The armistice terms originally provided for the recall of all French ships to French metropolitan ports where they were to be demobilized under German or Italian supervision – Germany undertaking not to use them except for coastal defence and mine-sweeping. The French negotiators wished to secure the right to demobilize their vessels in colonial ports and on this issue the Germans proved not unrelenting – presumably because their control over ships in distant ports was in any event limited. The armistice terms were amended to provide for demobilization in any port outside that part of France which the Germans proposed to occupy. But the fate of the French fleet was of such cardinal importance to Great Britain that the British government decided that it must be placed permanently beyond German clutches or be destroyed.

Admiral Darlan had ordered his captains on 24 June to ensure that their vessels should in no circumstances fall into German hands, but the British did not grasp the full significance of this signal, which was made available to them only in abbreviated form. Some French ships were in

British ports and these were painlessly disarmed; others were in French waters; but most were in African harbours – Alexandria, Bizerta, Mers-el-Kebir (Oran), Algiers, Casablanca, Dakar. At Alexandria diplomatic interchanges between the British and French admirals resulted in the disarming of the ships by the French themselves, but in the western Mediterranean the issue was decided by gunfire. Admiral Gensoul's force at Mers-el-Kebir included two of the most powerful capital ships afloat, *Strasbourg* and *Dunquerque*. On 3 July Admiral Somerville delivered to Gensoul an ultimatum giving him four choices: to join Great Britain in the war, to sail with reduced crews and under British control to internment in a British port, to sail under British escort for demilitarization in a French Caribbean port or to United States custody, or to scuttle within six hours. Somerville told Gensoul that if he refused all four courses the British would use whatever force might be necessary to prevent the French ships from falling into German hands. Somerville was empowered to accept a French proposal, if it were made to him, to demilitarize the ships where they were provided this could be done in six hours and under his supervision and in such a way as to keep them out of service for at least a year even at a fully equipped dockyard. This last proposition was not known to Gensoul.

When Gensoul received these terms his fleet was already almost under British fire and, affronted by this manoeuvre, he told the French Admiralty only about the fourth choice put to him. The Admiralty promised to send help. Some hours later Gensoul proposed to Somerville to demilitarize his ships at Mers-el-Kebir and, if threatened by the Germans or Italians, to sail for Martinique or the United States; he said that the disembarkation of crews had already begun. But the day was wearing on and Somerville, who had been instructed to bring matters to a conclusion before nightfall, shortly afterwards opened fire. Action was broken off but then renewed when *Strasbourg* put to sea. *Strasbourg* and twelve other vessels made good their escape to Toulon. *Dunquerque* went aground. Two other battleships were disabled. Nearly 1,300 Frenchmen were killed.

In the Caribbean French ships were damaged and put out of action for the rest of the war. At Dakar in West Africa the battleship *Richelieu* was slightly damaged but played a part in thwarting an expedition by British and gaullist forces in September. This venture, based on faulty intelligence about the inclinations of the local French authorities who had opted for Vichy, began with an attempt by a few gaullists who were landed in two light aircraft and one motorboat to talk the authorities into changing sides. When this mission failed the supporting British naval force began a two-day bombardment which was then abandoned because the French did not give in at once. They were, as it happened, about to do so when the attack was stopped and the attackers sailed away.

These episodes, although minor ones in the retrospect of the history of the war, planted a sting in Anglo-French relations which was to endure for a generation. Great Britain, so it seemed to many Frenchmen, acted at the time of France's abasement to take away from France all that the Germans had left to be taken – its navy and its colonies. But for Great Britain the immobilization of the French fleet was as necessary as the evacuation from Dunkirk to enable the war to be carried on from the British Isles themselves and in the Mediterranean.

The collapse of France in 1940 was first and foremost a military defeat although, as we shall see in a later chapter, there was more to it than that. The French forces were badly equipped, badly trained and badly led. They had not been modernized after the First World War because the military and political chiefs of the Third Republic had based their policies more on hope than on preparation. They had hoped after 1919 that Germany had been as much sickened by war as France and would not start another one, and later they had postponed rearmament and re-equipment because post-depression economics gave them an added reason for doing so. In the vital sectors of tanks and aircraft, industry was producing too many types and too few machines. French tanks were too lightly armoured to survive and their tactics were obsolete. The air force had adopted a modernization plan in 1934 but four years later, when the Czech crisis came, its first line strength was below 1,400 (half the size of the Luftwaffe) and only one in ten of these aircraft belonged to the 1934 programme. Transport, clothing and light weapons were all in short supply, although nobody could say exactly how short. Commanders from Gamelin downwards were paralysed by a well founded pessimism. In the circumstances the French forces fought surprisingly well.

The defeat of France was the high-water mark of the German army – and something more. The Germans had beaten the French as easily as they had beaten the Poles. From one angle these were two separate examples of the superiority of German arms. But the two events did not strike contemporaries that way. The defeat of Poland was no surprise. Nobody expected the Poles to hold the German army for long. Theirs was a much smaller, much less up to date and much less skilful force. But the French army was one of the great armies of the world and France itself stood – if any single country could be said so to stand – as the embodiment of western civilization. The fall of France was much more than a military decision. It was a portentous distortion of history, all the more shattering because its completeness led nearly everybody to suppose that it was final and irreversible: the post-war resurrection of France and its re-emergence as one of the few countries in the world capable of conducting an independent foreign policy and as a nuclear power were in 1940 all but inconceivable. Whereas the defeat of Poland had been a tragedy which further shifted the balance of power in Europe Hitler's way, the fall of France opened an abyss of uncertainty for the whole continent and shook the imagination as perhaps nothing had shaken it since the victory of the Turks at Mohacs in 1526.

CHAPTER 7

The Battle of Britain

THE defeat of France reduced hostilities in Europe to a single point, the Anglo-German fight. In Great Britain some people felt that the war was over, though not many cared to say so. Churchill's character and temperament told against a compromise peace and his gifts infused the British spirit and confirmed a latent feeling that, although the fighting had so far been disastrous, Hitler was so wicked an enemy that peace with him would be dishonourable. Disgust with the barbarities of Nazism kept the British at war under a new leader who was himself pugnacious enough in spirit to shoulder the miseries and scent the triumphs to come.

Hitler more than half hoped that Great Britain would make peace. On 19 July he made a speech which, in his eyes at least, amounted to a peace offer, but its tone and tenor were very ill adapted to any such purpose and it was brushed off by Churchill. As after the defeat of Poland Hitler had ready no precise plan of what to do next. He was half-hearted about attacking Great Britain. He wanted not to conquer it but to ensure that it would let him have his way on the continent. Moreover Great Britain was not only an island fortress but also a Mediterranean power, so that a continuing war could oblige Hitler to campaign against British bases and routes in the Mediterranean, to occupy or at least control the whole of France and Spain, and to put German forces into North Africa. War on this scale would be something very different from the *Blumenkriege* and *Blitzkriege* which he had fought so successfully on the continent. Great Britain was the wrong kind of enemy for the German armed forces, and Hitler, who liked short sharp operations with discernible ends, could not see where such a war might take him. On the other hand Great Britain unsubdued was a thorn in the German side, and so long as the British Isles remained in the war there was a danger that they might become a base for a new war between Germany and the United States. Although the German army could not march into England as it had marched into other countries, the German navy might blockade and starve the British, or the German air force might pound them into submission or destroy their defences and so let the army in.

A naval strategy entailed submarine warfare supplemented by commerce raiding by surface vessels and the mining of coastal waters. But Hitler had neglected his navy, partly because he was not much interested in it and partly because he never wholeheartedly faced up to the possibility of a fight to the finish with Great Britain. At the outbreak of war the German surface fleet consisted of two antiquated and Baltic-bound battleships, three 'pocket' battleships, two battle cruisers, eight cruisers, twenty-two destroyers and as many torpedo-boats and E-boats. In the Norwegian expedition three cruisers and nine destroyers were sunk and two cruisers and one destroyer were damaged. These losses were never made good, although two new battleships and a cruiser – *Bismarck*, *Tirpitz* and *Prinz Eugen* – were commissioned in 1941. The submarine fleet was quite inadequate. On the outbreak of war Admiral Doenitz, the supreme U-boat commander, had only fifty-seven ocean-going boats and, although he made good use of what he had, no prospect whatever of fulfilling his hope of having 300 boats at sea at a time; normally the striking force would consist of one in three – or, at best and for short periods, one in two – of the total force. The British navy, although hardly less antiquated, was much larger.

The alternative to a naval blockade was an air offensive designed either to make Great Britain capitulate under the sheer weight and terror of bombing or to clear the way for an invasion by destroying the air defences of Great Britain, especially its fighter squadrons. This was what Hitler and Goering tried to do and, in the two months from mid-July to mid-September 1940, failed to achieve.

The renown of the Luftwaffe after the campaigns of 1939 and the first half of 1940 was prodigious and its morale was excellent. Officially it was only five years old since the treaty of Versailles had denied Germany an air force and none had been acknowledged until 1935. But the reality was different. The prohibition was evaded in a number of ways. Aircraft designers were sent to work in other countries and German aircraft types were developed in the USSR, Sweden and elsewhere. The commercial airline *Lufthansa* was used to train men, to test machines and above all to keep alive the experience and the spirit of airmanship built up during the First World War.

The principal fashioners of the Luftwaffe were Erhard Milch and Ernst Udet – together with Walter Wever, whose early death in 1936 deprived the Luftwaffe of the heavy bomber force which he alone among the three believed in. Milch was the organization man who created an aircraft industry behind the scenes, supervised the development of new types of aircraft, and used *Lufthansa* (of which he was chairman), weekend flying clubs and foreign factories and bases to make Germany a first-class air power. He became a friend of Goering, who appointed him to take charge of the Air Ministry in March 1935 when the Luftwaffe's existence was officially revealed. It was largely thanks to Milch that the Luftwaffe sprang into existence with over 1,000 aircraft, 20,000 men and the not implausible ambition of achieving parity with the Russians by growing to 4,000 aircraft by 1939–40.

But Milch and Goering fell out; probably Milch became jealous of Goering, while Goering found Milch a bore. The result was a rise in the influence of Udet and a shift in policy. Udet was lively to the point of instability – he committed suicide in 1941 – but he was no organizer and lacked Milch's capacity to get things done. He was interested in fighters and dive-bombers rather than bombers and can claim some of the credit for the appearance in 1938 of the single-seater Messerschmitt (Me.) 109E, an excellent aircraft with good manoeuvrability and an armament of four machine guns or, alternatively, two machine guns and two cannon. Udet also set his faith in the Junkers (Ju.) 87 Stuka or dive-bomber, a fearsome aircraft which dived on its target at 200 m.p.h. in order to drop its two bombs with special precision and with the added psychological effect to be derived from fitting screaming devices and painting sharks' faces on the nose of the aircraft: but it was slow and had a low ceiling and so was better at attacking refugees in open country than at surviving anti-aircraft fire or enemy fighter attacks. It was successful against shipping so long as ships' anti-aircraft guns were poor, as they tended to be at the beginning of the war, but after its successes in the continental land battles the Ju. 87 suffered severely at the hands of British ground and air defences and had to be virtually withdrawn from the battle. Udet, finally, neglected the heavy bomber. Plans for two four-engined bombers like the British Stirlings, Halifaxes and Lancasters were dropped in the mid-thirties and a third – the Heinkel (He.) 177, originally designed as a long-range reconnaissance aircraft – failed to hold Udet's interest when he discovered that this huge machine could not be made to dive. Thus Germany entered the war and fought it with fast, lightly protected medium bombers – the He. 111 and Dornier (Do.) 217, supplemented from 1940 by the Ju. 88 – which were very vulnerable in daylight unless heavily escorted by fighters. But the Me. 109E was not right for this work and had not been designed for it. It was short in range and endurance – its range was 100–125 miles and its endurance about one and a half hours – and the combination of a fighter of this kind with medium bombers was the wrong recipe for the Battle of Britain. The Luftwaffe's long-range fighter, the Me. 110, was something of a disappointment and had to be relegated to night fighting and light bombing; its failure meant that German bombers operating beyond the south-east corner of England had to do so unescorted.

In the Spanish civil war a force of 400 German aircraft – the Kondor Legion – practised bombing and mobility under war conditions and tested new types, all with gratifying results. At the time of Munich the Luftwaffe had a front line strength of 2,800 (it was believed to be stronger) and a year later, on the outbreak of the World War, its front line strength had passed the 4,000 mark. Its reserves, however, were low because the war was expected to be short. The RAF's front line strength in September 1939 was 1,660 but its reserves were proportionately more than twice as large as the Luftwaffe's and, more significant, British aircraft production was rising the faster. It did not, however, overtake German production until it passed the thousand a month mark in the spring of 1940 and so began at that point to close the gap. The French air force had, on paper, a first line strength slightly above Great Britain's but poor reserves and an even more alarming degree of obsolescence.

In the Polish campaign the Luftwaffe committed less than half its front line strength: 700 long-range bombers, 400 fighters, 150 Stukas and 350 reconnaissance aircraft. Besides bombing Warsaw, they were used chiefly to attack Polish airfields and army communications and they met little effective opposition from an enemy who had out-of-date fighters and no radar or other early warning system. The force used in Norway was less than half that used in Poland. Its tasks were to attack enemy shipping, patrol and protect German units at sea, and convey small parachute detachments to seize Norwegian airfields. These tasks were performed efficiently and, as in Poland, with very little loss in spite of atrocious weather. For the Luftwaffe the Norwegian campaign was a cross between a real war and a training exercise, and an opportunity to introduce the Ju. 88 bomber into active service for the first time. The attack on the Low Countries and France was much more serious and varied work. Practically the whole of the Luftwaffe's front line strength was involved and for six weeks it averaged 1,500 sorties a day. In Holland parachutists were used in large numbers for the first time, capturing Rotterdam airport in the face of tough Dutch opposition. After the surrender of the Dutch the weight of the German air effort went into the support of the German army against the French army and against the British in Belgium. Airfields and factories were also attacked but the role of the Luftwaffe was first and foremost army cooperation. Only after the disintegration of the French ground forces was certain did the German bombers operate seriously against French railways, harbours and towns. The sole check to the Luftwaffe's easy superiority was in its encounters with the RAF over Dunkirk. This was symptomatic.

There was at this time still no way of measuring the effects of the heavy air bombardment of a defended target. The Germans had wiped out Guernica in Spain and had bombed Warsaw and Rotterdam, but against virtually no opposition. It appeared that the real test would come in Great Britain. In the event German bombing never came near to the point of winning the war by destroying the British economy or morale. The Second World War showed that this could not be done before the development of nuclear weapons. But air forces continued to believe that it might be. So did civilian defenders. In London committees had been set up many years before the war to estimate the probable weight and effects of bombing. They came to the conclusion that Great Britain must expect 3,500 tons of bombs in the first twenty-four hours of war, followed by a further 700 tons a day, each ton causing fifty or more casualties – that is to say nearly two million casualties in the first two months. The material damage, which commercial insurance companies refused to underwrite on any terms, was put at £550 million in the first three weeks, and this apocalyptic vision of the triumph of Belial included the need to evacuate three quarters of the population of London and bury corpses in their thousands in quick-lime, and to witness the complete collapse of communications and other public services, panic, epidemics and three to four million cases of mental breakdown in six months. These forebodings, so unlike the contents of the usual government paper, were carefully concealed from the public. They were also very wide of the mark, for over the whole course of the war casualties per ton of bombs dropped in Great Britain were under twenty and totalled 60,000 dead and 86,000 seriously and 149,000 slightly injured.

Even had it been technically possible for an air force to inflict in 1940 the sort of damage which the planners of the thirties feared, the German air force had not been designed primarily for that function. Its heavy bombing arm was, as we have seen, the least developed and the Luftwaffe – paradoxically, in view of its status as an independent service – was built up as a partner of the army rather than as an independent force which was going to win wars on its own. The bombing of British military or civilian targets in order to wreck production or break morale was therefore only one way of approaching the problem of how to defeat Great Britain, and not the obvious way. The alternative – assuming that the slow process of blockade and starvation were rejected – was a combined operation in which the Luftwaffe would begin by nullifying the RAF and would then, with the navy, cover the transport of the German army into England. What actually happened was something between the two: a projected invasion in force preceded by an independent onslaught by the Luftwaffe which oscillated between the attempt to destroy Great Britain's Fighter Command and heavy assaults on centres of production and population. Since the Luftwaffe's attack failed, the invasion never took place.

The idea of an invasion was popular in army circles but nowhere else. The navy regarded an invasion as almost impossibly risky. Raeder's conditions were control of the air, the right weather and an attempt no later than the autumnal equinox. The navy regarded the army's requests for naval protection for its vast and lumbering armadas against the Royal Navy as grotesquely unreal, although the naval staff was not very successful in conveying this appreciation to the army staff. The Luftwaffe was not so much hostile as uninterested. Goering and his principal lieutenants hardly troubled to reply to memoranda or attend conferences about it. Hitler himself was half involved, half aloof. He so far responded to the enthusiasm generated by the army staff as to order plans and preparations and he may have hoped that the navy's precondition would be met by the Luftwaffe's separate operations. Men were assigned and trained; barges, tugs and other craft were assembled. There was a great deal of exercising and (often contradictory) paper work. Hitler kept all the options open, including retreat. He was sceptical but also serious. He would have been delighted to finish off the war in the west this way but never confident that he could do so and therefore prepared both to give it a try and to abandon it if it did not work.

The first plan for a landing, produced by the army staff in December 1939, aimed at the east coast. After cutting naval criticism this idea was abandoned in favour of landings at a series of points along almost the entire south coast. The navy consistently argued that the only feasible operation, if any, was one concentrated in the south-east where the waters were narrowest. The first directive to prepare an invasion was issued by Hitler on 17 July 1940. It prescribed that the RAF must first be reduced to insignificance, that all minefields be cleared and that the Royal Navy be kept at a distance in northern waters or the Mediterranean. If these circumstances were met the army proposed to put ashore 260,000 men in three days, assemble a force of eleven divisions in two weeks and bring Great Britain to surrender in a month. Landings would take place along three stretches of coast between Folkestone and Brighton to the accompaniment of feints against Scotland and Iceland to distract the Royal Navy. The SS would follow with a list of 2,700 persons to be incarcerated, and a special booklet was prepared for the use of the six SS commanders and their staffs who were to extinguish opposition (including the Boy Scouts who were thought to be an arm of British Intelligence). The invasion fleets moved from their assembly points to their departure stations in the first days of September, but in these same days the RAF was thwarting the Luftwaffe in what Churchill had already christened the Battle of Britain.

In July 1940 Generals Kesselring and Sperrle, commanding *Luftflotten* 2 and 3 in Belgium and northern France, and General Stumpf, commanding *Luftflotte* 5 in Denmark and Norway, had a front line strength of around 3,000 aircraft, including some 1,400 long-range bombers, 300 dive-bombers, 800 single-engined fighters and 280 twin-engined fighters or fighter bombers. Of this force 2,500 aircraft at most were serviceable and ready for action at the beginning of the battle. In the engagements which followed, Kesselring and Sperrle could on a normal day put up 800 long-range bombers and 820 fighters. On the other side the Royal Air Force had emerged from the Battle of France with less damage than might have been the case if Dowding and Churchill had not hardened their hearts against sending more fighters to help the French. (Half of those sent were lost. The RAF's losses between 10 May and 20 June were 944. They were made good by mid-July but pilot losses were not. Milch wanted to invade Great Britain on the tail of the Dunkirk retreat.) Morale was undented by the fall of France and leadership from Dowding downwards excellent. The RAF's front line strength on the eve of the Battle of Britain was 1,200. It included 800 Hurricane and Spitfire single-seater fighters, of which 660 were operational, and in this sphere the British were roughly equal in numbers to the units opposed to them. Reserves were healthy, production good and expanding but there was only a narrow margin of trained pilots. This weakness was a worrying one, for although one new aircraft was as good as the machine it replaced, a new pilot was not the equal of an experienced one. On the other hand the RAF saved many more of its pilots than did the Luftwaffe since the former could bale out over their own territory and return to the fight, whereas most of the German pilots in the like case became prisoners of war.

The Hurricane and Spitfire, with their eight guns apiece, had the best single-engined fighter armament in the world – thanks largely to Squadron Leader R. S. Sorley and to Dowding. They could destroy an enemy bomber with a two-second burst. Sorley had been so impressed by the mock-up of the Hurricane that he tried, unsuccessfully, to get it put into production before it had flown. The prototype of the Hurricane first flew in 1935 and by the outbreak of war Fighter Command had 400 of them. A year later a total of 2,000 had left the factories. The Spitfire, which first flew a year later than the Hurricane, began to reach the service three months before Munich and nine squadrons had been formed by the outbreak of war. At one point during the Battle of Britain reserves of Spitfires fell to thirty-eight but at no time did the Command ask in vain for replacements of this or any other type of aircraft. On the eve of the battle fighter production was verging on 500 a month, which was considerably higher than German fighter production or some German estimates of British production. (Goering thought that British production of all types was only 300.)

Besides this force Great Britain relied for its defence on an early warning system of revolutionary and decisive importance. It was based on radar or, as it was at first called in Great Britain, RDF – Radio Direction Finding – a method for detecting the position of distant objects by the reflection of radio rays. Without radar too many bombers would have got through. After the First World War the problem of how to stop the bomber was acute. Some despaired of solving it. Others examined desperate remedies like the death ray, an attempt to find ways of killing enemy aircrews by (for example) suddenly raising their blood to boiling point, or ways of stopping their engines by radio transmissions. No death ray was ever invented but from 1934 radar was developed by a number of men, including in particular Professors Henry Tizard, A. V. Hill and P. M. S. Blackett; H. E. Wimperis, a civilian engineer who was given a post at the Air Ministry; and Robert Watson-Watt of the Radio Research Laboratory. (Considerable discord was introduced into the research and its application when Professor F. A. Lindemann, later Lord Cherwell, was injected into the work on the insistence of Churchill who, although not in the government, had been made privy to these and other secret matters. Lindemann was neither liked nor highly regarded by many of his fellow scientists. He was wholeheartedly anxious to give of his best for the defence of the country but he tended to treat research as a branch of politics. His day came when Churchill became Prime Minister. He was one of Churchill's closest advisers.) A chain of fifty-one radar stations was built round the coast. Although still incomplete, it was brought into continuous operation in the spring of 1939 and it was later supplemented by a second chain specially designed to detect low-flying aircraft. As early as 1936 Tizard suggested that very small radar sets could be made to go into aircraft and help fighter pilots to find and destroy enemy bombers at night.

Supplementing the radar system was the Observer Corps which, armed with binoculars, manned a network of posts which spotted aircraft as soon as they came within sight or hearing. There were a thousand of these posts. They and the radar stations were connected by telephone with an operations room, to which they transmitted their estimates of the positions, speeds, heights, numbers and directions of all aircraft within their ken, and this information was plotted on large tables by counters which were moved across the table as the information came in. Orders to aircraft, whether waiting on the ground or airborne in search of the enemy, were given by Controllers watching these tables day and night. Radar and the Observer Corps relieved Fighter Command of the need to keep forces on permanent patrol in the air in order to be able to engage the enemy and avoid destruction on the ground. The Controller in the operations room, watching the plots coming in every few seconds and knowing that the aircraft represented were no more than 12–20 miles ahead of the position shown, could order his aircraft off the ground in time and direct them on the right course at the right height until the pilots could see the enemy with their own eyes (or, in later battles, with the radar devices in their cockpits). In the operations room hours of watchful, almost motionless routine would be suddenly broken when a girl in uniform placed a small arrow on the edge of the table which, if it did not turn out to be an atmospheric freak or a flock of geese, was the prelude to action – down below the drama of tenseness combined with the efficiency of techniques mastered by familiarity; up above the more fearful drama of the duel as the pilots cast around them for the enemy and then pitted against him their flying skills and their marksmanship. The Germans knew about radar but underrated its value to the defence of Great Britain.

The preliminary phase of the Battle of Britain was an attempt by the Luftwaffe, beginning on 10 July, to establish local air supremacy over the straits of Dover. Attacks on shipping still using this passage were used as a dress rehearsal to test the tactics and capacities of Fighter Command before proceeding to the main purposes of enticing it into a major battle in order to destroy it. By the end of the month the advantage lay with the RAF which had lost 150 aircraft (promptly replaced) to 286 lost by the Luftwaffe. On the other hand this initial success gave little indication of the ultimate result since the RAF had to husband its strength after its losses in France and could not afford a steady drain of aircraft, whether or not German losses were higher. In the second week of August the Luftwaffe began to attack Fighter Command's airfields and operations rooms with the intention of crippling it on the ground or provoking it into a major battle in which it would be destroyed in the air. Owing to bad weather the Luftwaffe was unable to keep up its attacks on consecutive days and again in this phase the Luftwaffe's losses were the greater – 290 aircraft to 114. In the main battle of this phase, on 15 August, the losses on the German and British sides were 75 and 34. Attacks on shipping continued, chiefly with Ju. 87s which suffered so severely that they virtually disappeared from front-line operations. After a pause between 19 and 23 August the attack on Fighter Command was resumed in combination with secondary night attacks on cities. This phase, which lasted until 6 September, opened well for the Luftwaffe but was not decisive. The British suffered heavy damage on the ground. Fighter Command's No. 11 Group, covering London and south-east England, had six of its seven sector (or main control) airfields seriously damaged and five of its forward stations put out of action. One sector headquarters, Biggin Hill, had its operations room and all its communications wrecked. Further blows of this kind would have exposed London to great danger and would have forced upon Fighter Command a change in tactics (owing to the disruption of ground control) which might have overstrained its resources. But except on one day German losses of aircraft of all types exceeded British losses and by the end of this phase German losses were approaching 1,000 while Great Britain's were 550. On the other hand, in fighters alone the RAF's losses were greater and although by the end of the month the RAF was making more sorties per day than the Luftwaffe, fighter losses were beginning to exceed current production and the pilot situation was becoming a grave worry.

Although Great Britain's defences were severely tested during this phase the Luftwaffe failed to take a step which could have strained them even more severely. On direct orders from Goering it gave up attacking radar stations. Goering may have underrated the vital significance of these stations. He certainly underrated the possibility of putting them out of action. Their slim masts were not an ideal target for aircraft and nobody on the German side noticed that one of them – at Ventnor on the Isle of Wight – had been knocked out by a raid which left delayed-action bombs lying on the site. This was one of the more notable failures of Intelligence during the whole war. The radar screen continued to function almost without interruption throughout the Battle of Britain. German attempts to jam it were too primitive to impair it to any significant degree.

A second major error on the German side occurred at the beginning of September when the mounting attack on Fighter Command was abandoned in favour of attacks on London and other cities. It is impossible to be sure of the chief reason for this switch. Both sides enormously exaggerated enemy losses and on the German side the inflated figures were taken to mean that Fighter Command and fighter production had been virtually eliminated from the battle. Kesselring, though not Sperrle, shared the view of the Air Staff that the battle was won. In addition both Hitler and Goering had been stung by British bombing raids into retaliating against British cities. On 25 August, and thereafter on a number of nights, Bomber Command raided Berlin. The first of these raids was itself a retaliation for the first German raid on London which was itself a mistake – so that the German bomber offensive which began on 7 September was in a sense a consequence of a German error. (The first raid by either side on a town had taken place on 10–11 May when the British attacked München Gladbach, a few miles west of Düsseldorf.) The British raids on Berlin did little material damage but they had enormous psychological effect. They were a great surprise. Neither the Nazi leaders nor the people of Berlin thought that Great Britain was in a position to do anything of the kind, and the former had expressly assured the latter that they could not. The answer was to attack London. An afternoon attack on 7 September was followed by another raid that night. The damage was very heavy and a thousand people were killed. This daylight raid was not repeated and the next night raid did not come until four nights later, but the attack was then renewed.

In Germany hopes rose high. The invasion craft moved to their action stations. On 11 September Churchill broadcast an invasion warning. But the day before Hitler had – for the second time – postponed the day for taking the decision whether to order the invasion or not. He would decide on the 14th. When the 14th came he postponed the date again and on the 15th the final major engagement of the Battle of Britain took place. In the course of two battles in the morning and afternoon the German bombers suffered heavily (they lost sixty aircraft that day, the RAF lost twenty-six fighters) and the German fighters again failed to win the clear victory that they had been seeking for so many weeks. Two days later, on 17 September, Hitler called off the invasion by postponing the day of decision indefinitely. In October, when the Italians arrived to take part in the air battle, it was over. By the middle of that month the barges and other transports had all melted away. The Luftwaffe turned to night bombing of London and other cities. The famous raid on Coventry took place on 14 November. With radar not yet developed for night defence the Luftwaffe was able to cause serious damage at comparatively small cost to itself until the preparations for Barbarossa took the bulk of the bombers to the east, but once more Great Britain was able to fend off part of the attack by its technological skill. The German bombers were directed on to their targets by radio beams, flying along one beam until an intersecting beam told them that they were over the target, but British scientists quickly discovered how to deflect the beams and so cause many German bombs to be dropped in the wrong place – preferably of course in open country but sometimes on an unintended target, as for instance when Dublin was bombed by a German force which had been making for Belfast.

Losses can be computed in different ways. No precise figure is un-challengeable. But, taking the Battle of Britain to have lasted from 12 August to the last day of September, the Luftwaffe may be said to have lost in operations over 1,100 aircraft of all types (not 2,698 as the British claimed at the time). The defence of Great Britain cost Fighter Command about 650 aircraft (not 3,058 as the Germans believed).

The reasons for the Luftwaffe's failure were various. Its previous triumphs were to some extent delusive. They had been won in the role of army support and not in combat with an enemy air force, and the handling of the Luftwaffe in this role had necessarily been governed in practice by the strategy of the army command. Having taken little or no part in the battles in France Goering took charge during the Battle of Britain with the enthusiasm of one who feels that his moment has come. It might have gone better for the Luftwaffe if he had not, for he must take the greater part of the blame for the Luftwaffe's ill considered switching from one strategy and one set of targets to another. To some extent this mistake may be ascribed to bad Intelligence. The gross overestimates of casualties made by both sides were more damaging to the attackers than the defenders. The German higher command, ignorant of the continuing powers of resistance of Fighter Command, made wrong decisions. Similar mistakes by the British were of less consequence, since the RAF's role was to go on resisting in any case. But there were two other and more important reasons for the Luft-waffe's loss of the battle. The first was that it did not have enough fighters. Of 1,050 fighters stationed in France and Belgium 800 were Me. 109s, excellent aircraft but not ideal for close escort work and not numerous enough to provide adequate cover for bombers on daylight missions which, ideally, required at least two fighters for every bomber. The bomber squadrons in Norway and Denmark had no single-engined fighter escort and only a small protecting force of twin-engined

Me. 110s. This secondary force in Scandinavia was intended by the German Air Staff to split Fighter Command's effort by attacks on north-eastern England, but only one such attack was made during the Battle of Britain and the Me. 110s proved in general insufficiently manoeuvrable for the role of bomber protection. Consequently the German commanders found themselves in a constant dilemma, since every strengthening of the fighter escort which they provided for their bombers reduced the number of fighters available to engage the British fighters. In the event the bombers failed to wreck Fighter Command on the ground and the fighters failed to destroy it in the air.

The second principal reason for the defeat of the Luftwaffe was Fighter Command itself – the spirit of its pilots and the quality of its machines, the ceaseless toil in the factories where production kept ahead of losses, the efficiency of the repair services which put damaged aircraft back into service in the shortest possible time, and finally the higher strategy adopted by Dowding and his principal lieutenant Air Marshal Park and persisted in against mounting criticism which, after the battle, ensured the replacement and semi-disgrace of these two steadfast and wise commanders. The greatest danger to Great Britain during these two months was the erosion of its fighter force. The reserves were never exhausted but they were never plentiful. Dowding and Park had therefore to minimize losses by cautious handling of their men and machines without thereby courting defeat or lowering morale. They could not afford to indulge in unnecessarily dashing tactics. They had to count the cost every day. In the end the sum came out right.

The Battle of Britain was lost by Germany; the invasion of Great Britain was never attempted; the blockade went on. But much was changed that summer. Great Britain's prestige was raised high by the RAF and Hitler was tempted into a blunder. Having failed to end the war with Great Britain before attacking the USSR, he now proceeded to attack the USSR none the less. He had always meant to attack the USSR at some time in order to get *Lebensraum*. The fact that he now deluded himself into attacking the USSR on the grounds that this was a way to defeat Great Britain is an example of how disappointment can impair judgement. Moreover, the failure in the Battle of Britain prevented Hitler from concentrating all his strength against the USSR and eventually transformed a cloud in the west no bigger than a man's hand into the Anglo-American hurricane which, in concert with the blast from the east, was finally to devastate the Third Reich. The Battle of Britain was therefore one of the decisive events of the war.

CHAPTER 8

The Mediterranean, North Africa and the Middle East

FOR Hitler the failure to defeat Great Britain, following the fall of France and the entry of Italy into the war, created a new range of diplomatic and strategic problems. His hopes of peace in the west had been dashed first by Great Britain's determination to fight on and then by its success in doing so. He told those round him that Great Britain was sustained by the prospect of Germany embroiled with the Soviet Union, and this misreading of the British mood gave him a new reason – besides the quest for *Lebensraum* – to deal with the USSR. He faced a complex situation in the Mediterranean which was a theatre of war so long as Great Britain refused to make peace and where the interests of Italy, France and Spain – an ally, a vassal and a coy courtesan – collided. And thirdly, the war at sea, which became once more the chief means of reducing Great Britain, involved some risk of war with the United States.

On 27 September 1940, before the invasion of Great Britain had been officially abandoned, Hitler revived a project for a Tripartite Pact between Germany, Italy and Japan. Each of the signatories undertook to come to the aid of another in the event of an attack by any state not yet at war. The Japanese Foreign Minister, Matsuoka Yosuke, was becoming alarmed about the possibility of Japan finding itself at war with the USSR, the United States and Great Britain all at once. He was therefore willing to fall in with Hitler's plans in order to deter Washington from joining Great Britain in a war against a two-continent coalition, and in order also to put pressure on Stalin to come to terms with Japan in Manchuria. (Matsuoka's manoeuvres were stultified when Hitler abandoned his pact with Stalin and invaded the USSR.) Hitler's aims were similar. He too needed to deter the United States and intimidate Stalin – although he professed to be anxious to improve relations with the USSR and even to get it to join the pact, which would then have become an anti-American four-power club whose members divided the world into spheres of influence among themselves and collectively dared the United States not to move out of its allotted sphere in the New World. But Molotov, who visited Berlin in November, asked awkward questions about the presence of German troops in Finland and the German guarantee of Rumania and observed that so long as discussion had to be conducted in an air raid shelter, there was something unrealistic about a plan for partitioning a world in which the British Empire was presumed to have ceased to exist.

Hitler's most immediate problem was the Mediterranean. This theatre was bisected by his ally Italy. At the western end were Vichy France and Spain, at the eastern end the Balkans. In France Hitler had established an occupational régime in the north and along the Atlantic coast and a satellite régime for the rest of the country. But this satellite was a satellite with a difference. Pétain had a certain number of cards in his hand – the not inconsiderable remnants of an important fleet, territories and strategic positions in North and West Africa and the Middle East, a degree of American benevolence, and a willingness to run France on lines broadly acceptable to Hitler and so relieve the Germans of administrative problems so long as they did not try to push Vichy too far. The Nazi leaders disliked the French but they could not treat France in the same way as Czechoslovakia or Poland. Therefore they could not give Italy the satisfaction, nor Spain the bribes, which these other Latin countries wanted at France's expense.

Hitler regarded Franco's Spain as a natural ally and as a debtor. A republican Spain he might have invaded without more ado but Franco's Spain he sought to bargain with. His aim was to allure Franco into active alliance in order to secure control of the western gateway into the Mediterranean and possession of one of the Canary islands as a base for the Battle of the Atlantic. The bait for Franco was Gibraltar. On his side Franco had allied Spain with the Axis by a Treaty of Friendship with Germany in March 1939 and by joining the Anti-Comintern Pact, and in June 1940 he had seemed on the verge of joining the war a few days after Mussolini did so. But there were arguments against as well as for. Hitler's attack on Roman Catholic Poland in partnership with Stalin had disconcerted the profoundly anti-communist Spanish dictator, and his innate wiliness and caution were accentuated by the need to keep Spain out of further trouble after the civil war and particularly by the need to import food. Franco, whose Ambassador in London was being cajoled by Churchill and was even given to understand that Spain might help itself to part of French North Africa, did not rise to the German bait of a joint German-Spanish attack on Gibraltar and at a long meeting with Hitler and Ribbentrop at Hendaye on 23 October he frustrated the German leaders in a bout of arguing in the course of which, besides pitching Spanish claims very high – Oran, the whole of French Morocco, large quantities of food, fuel and military equipment – he left Hitler in two minds about whether he intended to join in such an adventure at a date which he would not yet disclose or whether the securing of the western end of the Mediterranean would have to be undertaken not with him but against him. Further meetings at the end of the year between Hitler and Franco's Foreign Minister Ramón Serrano Suñer at Berchtesgaden and between Franco and Hitler's military intelligence chief Admiral Wilhelm Canaris in Madrid only increased the uncertainty. Mussolini was equally unsuccessful and Hitler toyed with the idea of a direct parachute attack on Gibraltar, which his advisers however had already considered and rejected. The German invasion of the USSR altered the atmosphere since this was something which Franco could wholeheartedly support and he sent 18,000 men to share in the anti-communist crusade of his fellow dictators. He was shocked by Churchill's prompt support for Stalin and even more by the Anglo-Russian alliance, which, Eden had assured his Ambassador in London, was unthinkable. But he continued to prevaricate over active operations in his own part of the world, so that Hitler was driven at one time to making inquiries about the chances of a coup to replace him by another general and considered as late as 1943 plans for an invasion of Spain.

If Hitler's dealings with Franco were a disappointment to the Führer, his relations with Mussolini went more seriously wrong. Mussolini's ideas were large, impracticable and not always consonant with German policy: if Hitler was to rule from the Atlantic to the Urals, Mussolini was going to rule the Mediterranean and all its circumambient lands (except presumably Spain). For Mussolini the rise of Hitler had offered a means not only of settling scores with Great Britain and France but also of winning an empire beyond Europe while Hitler kept him inviolable in Europe. The symbol of this vision was the Pact of Steel of May 1939. But at that date Mussolini was not ready for war. Like Hitler, but with more reason, he planned not to go to war until 1942 and the defeat of France in 1940 therefore upset his timetable. It did not, however, moderate his visions. At a meeting in October 1940 at the Brenner the Italian leaders made clear to their German partners that their first shopping list included not only a piece of southern France but also Corsica, Malta, Tunisia, part of Algeria, an Atlantic port in Morocco, French Somaliland and the British position in Egypt and the Sudan. Besides running counter to Hitler's plan to operate a limited accord with France, the creation of an Italian empire of this size, straddling the Mediterranean from the Atlantic to the Red Sea and marching with an equally vast German empire to the north of it, threatened to raise questions about the Middle East which Hitler was, vaguely, proposing to approach via the Caucasus and Mussolini, much more purposefully, via Suez.

Hitler had been generally content to leave Europe south of the Alps to Mussolini. He had expected Mussolini to attack Malta in the summer of 1940 but Mussolini made no move; he was still intent on keeping out of serious wars. The Italian air force was obsolescent and the fleet, though large and in some respects first-class, was lightly armed by comparison with the British and French fleets and untrained in night operations. The army was gravely ill equipped and, although Mussolini did not know it at the time, its morale was poor: shouting fascist slogans proved a bad way of inspiring troops and the Italians were to fight badly until they were pressed back into Tunisia in 1943 and then changed sides later that year to fight the Germans on Italian soil. Mussolini's decision to go to war in 1940 was therefore the beginning of a series of disasters for Italy. Moreover, his opening of a campaign in Greece which he could not finish was seriously to distort Hitler's overall strategy.

Hitler had already in July decided to attack the USSR in the following spring and on 18 December he issued his first Barbarossa directive. In it he stated that the USSR might be invaded 'even before' the war with Great Britain was over. Since he assumed, correctly, that Great Britain could not help the USSR by opening a second front for at least eighteen months, he was not risking a war on two fronts unless the Russians held out that long. He expected to dispatch the Russians within six months and then revert to the problem of the British. But at the end of 1940 he was forced by the Italians, who attacked in Greece, and by the British, who counter-attacked the Italians in Africa, to undertake far more than he had intended in south-east Europe and eventually in Africa too. The Balkans, instead of being a flank to be secured before Barbarossa, became an independent theatre of war with extensions leading German troops and air squadrons away from the USSR into waters and sands beyond Europe's southern confines.

The Balkans and Hungary were already dominated by Germany before the war began. Annexed, by economic power, in the thirties they were to be lost in the military clash of the forties. These states had emerged as exemplars of the principle of national self-determination – which, however, they exemplified imperfectly since none of them was nationally homogeneous, although each was sufficiently a nation to have national quarrels with its neighbours. To other states they were chiefly of interest in the light of an older theory: the balance of power. Between the wars France made friends with Rumania and Yugoslavia because they stood for the maintenance of the Versailles settlement of 1919 and opposed any signs of a revival of German hegemony, but the waning of French influence in the thirties and its eclipse at Munich in 1938 forced France's friends to look elsewhere for salvation. Economically adrift and fearful of their Bulgarian and Hungarian neighbours (both of them hurt by the post-war settlement and waiting to alter the map once more), they were forced to turn to Germany. By 1939 all the states of the region, pro-Versailles or anti-Versailles, were wooing Germany with what they had – which was raw materials – in the hope either of protection or redress. To Germany they were important, as they had once been to France, not for any reasons connected with the politics of the area itself but for extrinsic reasons.

The Russo-German pact of 1939 recognized a Russian interest in the Balkans by assigning Bessarabia to the USSR. A year later Stalin, by annexing northern Bukovina as well, signalled that his interest was not limited to Bessarabia. Rumania thought of going to war but was restrained by Hitler who had other plans. Although in 1939 he had declared himself disinterested in this part of the world, he was not. Rumania's natural resources and its strategic position on the southern border of the USSR made it very important for him. In the autumn of 1940 he further partitioned Rumania by giving a piece to Hungary (the second Vienna Award, in August) and a piece to Bulgaria (the treaty of Craiova, in September). By this time King Carol was ready to throw in his hand. He had tried unsuccessfully to rule through a minor party and then through the Patriarch as Prime Minister, but after the humiliating territorial losses exacted by Hitler he abdicated and what remained of Rumania was controlled by Germany through Marshal Ion Antonescu with the title of Conducator. In November Rumania, Hungary and Slovakia – a Balkan northern tier along the Russian southern flank – all adhered to the Tripartite Pact. German troops appeared. Hitler was peacefully strengthening his control of the Balkans. He did not want it otherwise. He had no wish for a war in what was to him a storehouse and a waiting area. But on 28 October Mussolini had invaded Greece, and Hitler gradually found himself forced to make new plans and to interpose a military campaign in the Balkans before his invasion of the USSR.

Mussolini had given Hitler no proper notice of his attack on Greece. He sent a letter at the last moment and ante-dated it by five days. This was his way of retaliating against Hitler's habit of invading other countries without telling his ally in advance. In any case he knew that Hitler would object to his plans, because Hitler had been urging him to bide his time. This silly failure in cooperation was characteristic of the partnership between the Axis allies. Neither of the dictators was by nature a cooperator. They lacked – indeed despised – the habits of intercourse and interchange which are the everyday experience of democratic politicians. Moreover, by the time that their alliance had become formal on the eve of war, their relationship had begun to lose some of its strength. This was more Mussolini's fault than Hitler's, for while Hitler entertained a genuine admiration for Mussolini as his forerunner among men of iron will and retained a feeling of obligation to him, Mussolini had from the start been attracted to Hitler partly in spite of himself. He gravitated to the Axis more through repulsion from the western democracies than through any love of Hitler or of Germany, and he quickly allowed congenital jealousy to corrode an alliance which, although it had become essential for his policies, cast him as a manifestly junior, increasingly uncomfortable partner.

Jealousy and suspiciousness were strong features in Mussolini's character. He was a solitary. He had neither friends nor intimates. He had the singlemindedness and determination of the man who cares little for money or the other ordinary comforts of life (except sex), but he too often failed to relate his purposes to his resources. He was energetic without being industrious, so that his achievements were those of the gambler who leaves even the calculable to chance. His working-class origins, his poverty in early life and his consciousness of defective education and social poise made him aloof, secretive and assertive; he had neither the training nor the character to rectify his shortcomings by methodical hard work or by arguing (as Hitler sometimes did) with people who had ideas or knowledge to offer. He remained sketchily informed about public affairs and averse to listening to advisers who might be cleverer or better informed than he was; his energies, which were considerable until the last years of his life, went into posturing and rhetoric. He believed in the regenerative virtue of violence but much of the violence was, unlike Hitler's quests for *Lebensraum* and racial purity, pointless. There is something symbolic about the fact that the prelude to his rule was a spectacular event – the March on Rome – which never took place. Mussolini was appointed Prime Minister not because he advanced on the capital like a conqueror but because he outwitted rival politicians by devious scheming which he conducted at a distance in Milan and which made a grand coup unnecessary. He arrived in Rome by train.

Mussolini was a shrewd and stubborn politician who used the apparatus of tyranny because he was also a bully. Being ruthless and unprincipled he liked the short cuts which the strong arm of lawlessness provides, and very soon after becoming Prime Minister he discovered how well these methods can work in both international and domestic affairs. In 1923 General Enrico Tellini and other Italians who were members of a commission engaged in surveying the unsettled Greco-Albanian frontier were murdered on Greek soil. Mussolini bombarded and seized Corfu, berated the Greek government in extravagant style and had the satisfaction of seeing the British and French governments pressing Greece to accept Italy's humiliating and unjustifiable demands. In the following year Italy scored a substantial victory against Yugoslavia over Fiume because Yugoslavia could muster no outside support for its case. Foreign politicians were beginning to show respect for Mussolini as a statesman of consequence and were therefore contriving to turn a blind eye to such aspects of Fascism as the murder of the socialist leader Giacomo Matteotti (to which Mussolini's language certainly contributed, even though he may have given no precise order for the deed) and the suppression of personal and civil liberties in the name of efficiency and good order: they noted improvements in the public services but ignored the deterioration in manners and morals. By the time that Hitler came to power Mussolini had had a decade of experience in the techniques and fruits of brutality. He was secure at home and respected (by governments) abroad. He was ready to impress Hitler as he had impressed other leaders, but he had not bargained with the possibility that both he himself in relation to Hitler, and Italy in relation to Germany, might have to play a subordinate role in world politics. For the rest of his career he kicked ineffectually against these pricks. The invasion of Greece in the autumn of 1940 was the uncoordinated reflex of an ally who was not a good partner, of a secondary power seeking to establish parity with a first-class power by attacking a third-class one.

Mussolini wanted Italy to be a Balkan power as well as an African one. Greeks were well aware of this and Venizelos had begun in 1928 to mend Greece's relations with Yugoslavia and Turkey. He made a treaty with Italy in the same year but it became a dead letter. Venizelos wanted to end the old feud with Bulgaria too but in 1930 King Boris married an Italian princess. A Balkan pact concluded (without Bulgaria) in 1934 was mainly an anti-Italian mutual defence measure, but it lacked coherence and strength. By the summer of 1940, after Mussolini had won a little territory from France but not much glory, an Italian offensive in the Balkans seemed more than probable, the more so when the Greek cruiser *Helle* was torpedoed by an Italian submarine in the Aegean in August. The British guarantee could not be rated very high. The only hope was that Hitler would restrain his ally.

This hope was destroyed when Mussolini's Ambassador delivered an ultimatum in the middle of the night of 27–8 October. Italian troops had already crossed the Greek frontier with Albania. But the attack was a complete failure. It was undertaken against the advice of all three Italian Chiefs of Staff, who gave Mussolini accurate estimates of Greek resistance. The Duce preferred, however, to listen to his Commander-in-Chief in Albania who promised to overrun the whole of Epirus in ten to fifteen days and secure the capitulation of the Greek army. He assured Mussolini that everything had been prepared down to the smallest detail which, since the attack had been envisaged nearly four months earlier, should have been the case. But there had in fact been little planning and the operation launched on 28 October was more like a whim than a campaign. The invading force of three divisions was totally inadequate and within a week the Greeks were counter-attacking and advancing into Albania. The Italians had attacked in three prongs. Their central prong was cut off, and the two prongs on either side had to be withdrawn. Italian casualties were heavy. Prisoners were taken by the thousand. By the third week in November there were no Italians left on Greek soil. In addition the British Fleet Air Arm damaged three Italian battleships in a night attack at Taranto on 11–12 November, as a result of which Taranto was abandoned and all Italian vessels of war were moved to harbours on the west coast. The British also moved forward into Crete and the Aegean – whence the RAF could threaten the Rumanian oilfields.

Things were also going badly for Italy on the other side of the Mediterranean. There Marshal Graziani had an army of 215,000 men in Libya. So long as France was in the war Graziani had a good case for lying low, since he was sandwiched between the French in Tunisia and Algeria and the British in Egypt, but as soon as France collapsed Mussolini began to urge him into action. Graziani was reluctant but in September, after having been ordered to fight, he began the first of the series of attacks and counter-attacks which were to constitute the battle for North Africa which lasted until May 1943. In the first week of December, in a daring offensive of great political moment, the British retaliated. This move, by a force of little more than 30,000 men, was designed to show that Great Britain was still very much in the war. With remarkable daring, Churchill had sent reinforcements to the

Middle East in the middle of the Battle of Britain. He hoped that a show of spirit far away from home might even get France back into the war, and although in this the desert campaign failed, it did make Hitler nervous about a rising in France and finally turned Franco against the Gibraltar plan and the entry of German troops into Spain.

Militarily the British offensive was an astonishing success. Throughout December and January the small British force under General Sir Archibald Wavell advanced from Sidi Barrani inside Egypt to Tobruk (which was captured in twenty-four hours) and then, both along the coast and across the desert, to Benghazi in the north-western corner of Cyrenaica. What had begun as a demonstration turned into a major victory. Wavell's mixed force of British, Indian, Australian, New Zealand, French and Polish units covered 500 miles in two months and destroyed an Italian army six times its own size. This success also had wider repercussions. It forced Hitler to send help to the Italians, to revise and enlarge the scope of his contingency plans for a move into the Balkans on the basis that the British too might move into Greece in strength, and to make arrangements despite Russian objections for the entry of German troops into Bulgaria and that country's adherence to the Tripartite Pact.

But at Benghazi, which was captured on 7 February, the British advance stopped. The British cabinet had decided that it must be limited. Wavell had already been required to send four squadrons of aircraft (Blenheims and Gladiators) to help the Greeks on the Albanian front and anti-aircraft units to defend Athens; he had another war to fight in East Africa; he was responsible for the safety of Palestine and the Suez Canal, which could be threatened by an anti-British government in Iraq or by the Vichy French in Syria; and five days after the fall of Benghazi Rommel arrived in Tripoli, followed a couple of days later by the first of the German tanks which were destined to transform a desert war which now ceased to be an Anglo-Italian affair.

German intervention in North Africa had first been mooted and then dropped in October 1940. In November, during a not very amicable conference at Salzburg between Hitler and Ciano, Hitler began giving instructions and making promises. He urged the Italians to push on into Egypt and he promised air support. During that winter some 400 German aircraft operated in the Mediterranean protecting supply routes to Africa and attacking British shipping and air bases. Malta, which had been inadequately equipped to defend itself against air attack, was besieged by the German and Italian air forces which succeeded in interdicting it to the British navy and making the

Mediterranean impassable by British convoys. The British continued their attacks on Italy, bombarding Genoa from the sea and bombing Spezia and Leghorn from the air in February. The Italians retaliated with hazardous but often successful attacks by small torpedo boats on British heavy units in harbour, but on 28 March British naval superiority was massively affirmed in a battle off Cape Matapan in which three Italian cruisers and two destroyers were sunk. Although the main target, the battleship *Vittorio Veneto*, got away, the Italian navy ceased to be a major factor in the war. (Italy also lost East Africa at this time. In August 1940 the Italians had forced Great Britain to leave British Somaliland and were threatening the Sudan and Kenya but the British returned in February 1941 and with the help of South African, Nigerian, Indian and French troops proceeded to invade Ethiopia and Eritrea. Addis Ababa was abandoned at the beginning of April. Resistance continued in the north and the final, inevitable surrender did not come until November. The campaign was remarkable for the extraordinary exploits of Gideon Force which consisted of Ethiopian and Sudanese men under Lieutenant Colonel Orde Wingate and other British officers and took over 15,000 prisoners in three months.)

In the spring of 1941 the Germans attacked on the Balkan and North African fronts in campaigns which were subordinate to the attack on the USSR to come in June. Hitler had already left one front unsettled when he desisted from his attack on Great Britain in the autumn of 1940. Now, in the south, if he failed to conclude either his Balkan or his North African operations before beginning Barbarossa, he would again have multiplied his commitments. He concluded the one but not the other.

The immediate cause of Hitler's descent on the Balkans was a coup in Yugoslavia. The Regent Paul had hesitated about following the Rumanian and Bulgarian example and joining the Tripartite Pact (thus isolating Greece). He was urged by Great Britain and the United States to resist German pressure and attack the Italians in Albania, but neither London nor Washington was able to offer any practical help. The Regent, impressed by the fall of France and hoping to get Salonica as his reward, took the plunge and signed on 25 March. Two days later his government was overthrown by General Simovic, the leader of a group hostile to the Regent and supported by the Serb Orthodox Church. Simovic wanted to steer a neutral course by keeping clear of pacts and wars, and he continued to refuse to attack the Italians. But this was not good enough for Hitler, who was worried about a possible British advance into the Aegean and Greece and had already made plans to forestall it, using Yugloslav bases among others. He now resolved to invade both Greece and Yugoslavia. The latter was attacked on 6 April by a force which included seven Panzer divisions and 1,000 aircraft. After heavy bombing and grievous casualties Belgrade fell on the 13th. The government capitulated four days later. Yugoslavia disintegrated. On the heels of the German conquerors Hungary, Bulgaria and Italy helped themselves to pieces of what they, wrongly, took to be a corpse; the Croat leader Anté Pavelic arrived from Rome to establish a separate Croat state; Serbia became a German puppet.

Greece was attacked simultaneously and defeated only slightly less abruptly, but whereas Yugloslavia fought and fell alone, the British were involved in the fate of Greece. The modest help given by the R A F to Greece against the Italians in Albania had been increased in February in an attempt to eliminate the Italians before a German invasion. At the same time Great Britain embarked on discussions about more substantial aid against Germany. Although Greek resistance to the Italians had created powerful philhellene feeling in Great Britain, Churchill's motives were mainly political. In the first place there was the British guarantee of 1939; it was time a British guarantee was honoured. Then there was Turkey to be considered and the United States. Churchill hoped to get Turkey into the war against Germany; successful support for the Greeks would weigh with the rulers of Turkey. (Lack of success did too. Turkey decided to stay neutral.) The United States was more important. Great Britain had shown that it could win battles against Hitler but Churchill knew that Great Britain alone could never defeat Hitler on the continent. From the time he took office as Prime Minister Churchill kept his mind firmly on the big central issue of forming a coalition powerful enough to destroy Hitler and the Nazis, and the United States was the essential element in this design. A failure to help the Greeks, whose cause had been very popular in the United States ever since their brave and successful resistance to the Italian invasion the previous year, might discredit Great Britain; help for the Greeks, even if it did not succeed, would be accounted to Great Britain for virtue. These were political arguments.

But before allowing them to prevail Churchill had to assess the military arguments and weigh them against the political. In doing so he was influenced by the over-optimistic views of the military possibilities which were relayed to him from Athens by Eden, now once more Foreign Secretary, who was visiting the Near East with the CIGS, Sir John Dill. On this basis Churchill who, like Wavell, was reluctant to prejudice the campaign in North Africa by deflecting ground and air forces to

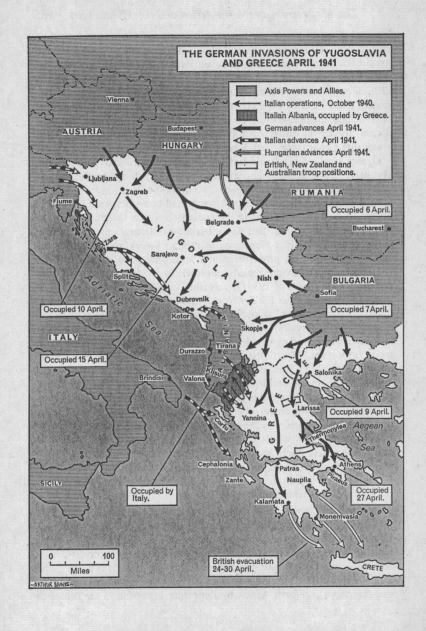

THE GERMAN INVASIONS OF YUGOSLAVIA
AND GREECE APRIL 1941

Axis Powers and Allies.
Italian operations, October 1940.
Italian Albania, occupied by Greece.
German advances April 1941.
Italian advances April 1941.
Hungarian advances April 1941.
British, New Zealand and
Australian troop positions.

AUSTRIA

Vienna

Budapest

HUNGARY

Ljubljana

Zagreb

Fiume

RUMANIA

Belgrade

Occupied 6 April.

Bucharest

Y U G O S L A V I A

Zara

Sarajevo

Split

Nish

BULGARIA

Occupied 10 April.

Dubrovnik

Kotor

Sofia

Occupied 7 April.

Adriatic Sea

ITALY

Durazzo

Tirana

Skopje

Occupied 15 April.

Brindisi

Valona

Klisura

Salonika

Corfu

Yannina

Larissa

Occupied 9 April.

G R E E C E

Thermopylea

Aegean Sea

Cephalonia

Patras

Athens

Piraeus

Zante

Nauplia

Occupied
27 April.

SICILY

Kalamata

Occupied by
Italy.

Monemvasia

0   100
Miles

British evacuation
24-30 April.

CRETE

~ARTHUR BANKS~

Greece, decided in favour of helping Greece and told Wavell that in the event of a German attack he would have to go to Greece's help. The Australian and New Zealand governments were also reluctant but they too agreed. The Greek government was dubious on the grounds that the arrival of a small British force – the only kind available – would provoke the Germans without being able to stop them; but it agreed too at the end of February, and the discussion moved from the general issue of cooperation to the practical planning of it.

At this point there was a muddle. An attack through Bulgaria, Greece's traditional enemy, was taken for granted. But Yugoslavia's attitude was uncertain. In the vortex of Balkan politics Yugoslavia and Greece had been over the years more friendly than unfriendly, and if this friendship held – indeed, until it was obvious that it would not hold – the Greeks wanted to keep their communications with Yugoslavia open. In order to do this, they must plan to meet the German-Bulgarian attack on a line north and east of Salonica, even though this line was unfavourable for natural reasons and harder for the British to reach. The British favoured the more southerly line along the river Aliakmon and even this position was likely to prove untenable if Yugoslavia allowed the Germans to invade through Yugoslavia as well as Bulgaria – or, as in fact happened, was unable to stop them. The situation was further complicated by the unfinished war with the Italians in the west, since a withdrawal south of the Aliakmon, without a matching retreat in the west, would expose the Greek forces facing the Italians to encircle-ment by the Germans – which is what happened. The Greek govern-ment hoped and expected Eden, who arrived in Athens at the end of February, to clarify Yugoslavia's position and believed Eden to have agreed that there should be no Greek withdrawal to the Aliakmon line until this had been done. This was the first of a series of muddles for which the blame is still not clear. While the British imagined the Greeks to be regrouping on the Aliakmon line, they were in fact wait-ing in the north, where they were eventually caught.

The German attack on 6 April was preceded by a fresh Italian offen-sive in mid-March. Hopeful and ill-informed, Mussolini crossed to Albania, but had to go back again when his attack failed. The German attack followed. Fifty thousand British, Australian and New Zealand troops, supported by only one squadron of modern aircraft, could do little to succour the Greeks. Seven thousand Greeks were made prisoner and much valuable British material was captured. By the end of April resistance on the Greek mainland was over. Survivors from the Greek and Commonwealth forces were transported to Crete, which had been in British occupation for six months. Unfortunately for them little had been done to defend Crete in the mistaken belief that Great Britain's command of the sea made it impossible for an airborne invasion to be sustained. Churchill had urged that it be turned into a fortress bristling with everything from tanks to road blocks and defended by armed Cretans as well as British and other Commonwealth troops. He did not know that the requisite defences had not been constructed or that essential reconnaissance of the terrain had been neglected. Nor did he discover until afterwards that Intelligence about the enemy's intentions and dispositions was disbelieved by commanders in the field who could not imagine, and were not told, how such information could possibly be obtained. The 3,500 Greek troops in the island had only one rifle per six men and three rounds of ammunition each; existing airstrips were not mined and proposals to build hidden airstrips in the hills not carried out; in spite of a plentiful supply of Italian prisoners of war landing stages were not constructed on the south shore nor roads to link north and south, with the result that supply ships from Egypt had to circle dangerously round the island and unload under intense enemy air attack; there were hardly any tanks and a fatal lack of radio and telegraph equipment.

The attack began on 20 May with glider and parachute landings from a fleet of 500 transport aircraft. These operations were very costly. Although air cover had been withdrawn from the defences before the invasion began, so that the approach of the air armada was unopposed, the reception was very hot and whole units were wiped out on landing or soon afterwards, many of them before they could reach the weapons which were dropped for them separately. Reinforcements were delayed because the airfields which the Germans were using in Greece were inadequately prepared dust bowls. But during the ensuing night Maleme airfield at the western end of the island was abandoned by the New Zealanders and the Germans started using it the next day. All efforts to dislodge them failed. This was a vital turn in events since, contrary to British belief, the German airborne forces were largely dependent on airfields and could not mount a concentrated attack with units dropped at random over the countryside.

A supplementary sea-borne invasion on the second night was baulked by the British navy, which suffered, however, seriously from air attacks. The defenders, believing that the main weight of the attack was bound to come from the sea, paid more attention to shore defence than to the recapture of Maleme, from which the Germans pressed eastward gradually and in increasing force. A week after the beginning of the attack it was clear that the main issues were the timing of the evacuation of the defenders and the number who would be saved. Withdrawal began on 1 June. Only half the defenders got away. The British Mediterranean fleet suffered seriously (three cruisers and six destroyers sunk, two battleships, three cruisers and an aircraft carrier damaged) in the attempt to thwart the invasion and the subsequent rescue operations and had to suspend the latter for fear of incurring further losses which would jeopardize its control of the eastern Mediterranean.

The capture from the air of an island defended by superior naval forces was a spectacular achievement but a freak. The defenders had failed to make good use of their six months' occupation of the island, failed to interpret correctly or to act upon the intelligence which forewarned them of what was to come, denuded the island of its air fighter defences, failed with a force of 32,000 men to hold all of the three vital airfields and, having unnecessarily abandoned Maleme, failed to recapture it or to appreciate the full significance of its loss. The Germans tacitly drew the conclusion that they should not have captured Crete. Over a third of their airborne invaders were killed or wounded, the Luftwaffe lost 220 aircraft and no parachute operation of this kind was ever again attempted. Hitler, having won an extra base for helping Rommel and having driven the British beyond air range of Ploesti's oilfields, scrapped plans for a similar attack on Malta and turned his parachute units into infantry regiments.

It has been suggested that the Cretan operation delayed Barbarossa and so saved Moscow and even possibly the USSR itself in 1941. The Simovic coup in Belgrade occurred on the day, 27 March, for which Hitler had convoked a conference to discuss Barbarossa. The conference discussed Yugoslavia instead, Hitler decided to invade it as soon as possible and he postponed Barbarossa from mid-May to 22 June. Since the thaw came late that year there would have been some postponement anyway. The decision to interpose a Balkan war was chiefly important because the tanks used in it (800 of them) would need a breathing space for refitting between campaigns. This they were able to have. The further decision to take Crete caused some confusion (but nothing more serious) as the forces designated for Crete were moved south while the forces being shifted from Greece to the Russian fronts moved the other way, but the air squadrons left in Greece to cover the Cretan operation could move to their Barbarossa stations at shorter notice and the parachute troops were not intended for use in the USSR at all. Moscow was not saved by a mere alteration to the timetable of a week or two, and although the proposition cannot be incontestably proved or refuted it is very hard to see that the campaigns in Yugoslavia and Greece or the attack on Crete had any significant effect on Barbarossa. What might have helped the USSR would have been a successful defence of Crete and a prolongation of the battle there. At one time it looked to Halder as though Barbarossa would have to be further postponed but on 30 May Hitler confirmed the 22 June date.

The seizure of Crete was at the time more apparent than the cost and Cyprus seemed a possible next step. This was all the more alarming for Great Britain because the French in Syria and Lebanon recognized Vichy, in Iraq Great Britain's enemies had raised their heads and taken power, in Palestine the Mufti Haj Amin was strongly anti-British, and in Egypt King Faruq was not much less so. Consequently the whole British position in the Middle East was in jeopardy and might be scattered by a German attack.

The British position in the Middle East was anomalous. It rested on force, although with the lone exception of Aden no part of the area was constitutionally within the British Empire. During the nineteenth century the rivalries of the European powers had prevented any one of them from annexing portions of the Ottoman empire in Asia as they had annexed parts of Africa, but Great Britain had established *de facto* control over Egypt (and Cyprus). It also controlled the Persian Gulf and the lesser principalities along its western shores. The First World War produced the long-awaited withering away of the Ottoman empire and in anticipation the allied powers struck bargains for its partition in order to avoid fighting among themselves. The Russians, however, dropped out owing to the revolution of 1917 and the Italians withdrew when they scented the emergence of a Turkish national state out of the Ottoman imperial debris. Great Britain and France were left in control but the temper of the times required control to be veiled. France in Syria and Lebanon, and Great Britain in Palestine, Transjordan and Iraq established their rule under mandates. These mandates gave Great Britain a solid block of territory in the Middle East all the way from Egypt to the Persian Gulf. British forces dominated the area more effectively than Ottoman forces had ever done and this domination was practically unaffected by the grant of formal independence to Egypt in 1922 or the termination of the Iraqi mandate ten years later. Special treaties ensured the continued presence of British naval, military and air forces (although the treaty with Egypt took over ten years to negotiate) and the development of road, rail and air communications made assurance double sure. There was no Arab power to gainsay the British but there were Arab nationalists who, observing European politics in the thirties and remembering the interest of an earlier generation of Germans in the Middle East, hoped that Germany might come in useful to put an end to British rule over them. The German campaigns in the Balkans in the spring of 1941 stimulated these hopes, especially in Iraq.

The Arabs had also a second reason for being anti-British besides their nationalist resentment against the British imperialism which (with French imperialism) had frustrated their hopes of ruling themselves as soon as the Turks had been got rid of. In Palestine the British administration allowed a Jewish immigration which, given the background of the Zionist demand for a Jewish state, was a threat to Arab aspirations. During the First World War Great Britain endorsed the Zionist claim to a national home in Palestine (a camouflaged way of referring to the Jewish state which most Zionists wanted and which their founder Theodore Herzl had envisaged at the end of the previous century when he wrote his book *The Jewish State*). Under British rule the Jews in Palestine increased from less than 10 per cent of the population to nearly 30 per cent and the Arabs, who regarded the Jews as alien colonizers of Arab soil, began to look for foreign friends. The Nazis with their anti-Jewish tirades were an obvious choice for an anti-British flirtation. The Arabs were also impressed by the failure of Great Britain and France to check Mussolini in Ethiopia and encouraged by the extensive Arab revolt in Palestine in 1936. Upon the approach of war Great Britain tried to safeguard its position in the Middle East by dropping attempts, which were in any case futile, to find a way of pleasing both Arabs and Jews in Palestine and adopted instead a pro-Arab policy. In 1938 the BBC started broadcasting in Arabic, the first of its foreign language programmes. In May 1939 a British White Paper proposed severe limits on Jewish immigration (at the very moment when the case for it had been enormously enhanced by Hitler's concentration camps) and assured the Arabs that beyond these limits further immigration would be subject to Arab acquiescence. The White Paper saved Anglo-Arab relations and the British Empire in the Middle East for the war years – but not beyond.

One of the Arab politicians who wished to play the Germans off against the British and use the war to extract concessions from Great Britain about post-war Palestine was Rashid Ali el-Gailani, who became Prime Minister of Iraq in March 1940. A year later he was briefly ousted but returned with increased power. He was supported by four colonels picturesquely known as the Golden Square who were the principal spokesmen and pressure group for politically-minded army officers. The immediate question for Rashid Ali's government was whether to honour Iraq's treaty obligations to Great Britain and allow British troops to use the port of Basra at the head of the Persian Gulf on their way to reinforce the British position in Egypt. Rashid Ali and his friends, besides wanting to take a firm line with Great Britain, were afraid that the pro-British party led by Nuri es-Said would lead Iraq into the war in spite of the fact, as it seemed to them, that Great Britain was losing it. Rashid Ali therefore wanted to find out how much German help he would get if he resisted the British, but he found the Germans disappointingly vague. On the one hand Hitler was reluctant to give the Arabs what they wanted because Mussolini, who was still regarded as having at least an equal say in Middle Eastern affairs, had reservations. An Axis declaration endorsing Arab nationalistic aspirations did not square with Mussolini's intention to assume overlordship of Egypt and the Sudan in place of the British. Consequently Hitler hesitated over his Arab policy and eventually agreed to a declaration which fell short of Arab nationalist hopes. On the other hand Hitler did not want Great Britain to score a success in Iraq because such a success could swing Turkey (which had so far fallen down on obligations to Great Britain and France undertaken in a treaty of October 1939) into the British camp with embarrassing results for Germany's drive into the Caucasus and beyond. So in the end Hitler promised to give air support to Rashid Ali and to try to get Vichy to send him arms from their stores in Syria.

The British, fearful for their communications with India via Basra and their supplies of Iraqi oil, forced the pace by bringing what forces they wanted to Basra; they ignored Iraqi conditions limiting the numbers of British troops to be allowed on Iraqi soil at any one time and the length of stay of each unit in transit. On 2 May they attacked Iraq. A force from Palestine and another under Brigadier Glubb from the Arab Legion in Transjordan struck north towards Baghdad which surrendered on the last day of the month. Rashid Ali, having expected too much from the Germans, found himself a refugee in Teheran. The Germans, having expected too much from Rashid Ali and done too little for him, lost such chance as they had of taking the Middle East by frontal assault. Great Britain lost no time in making sure of Syria and Lebanon, and Iran too.

One consequence of the Rashid Ali episode had been a temporary intensification of German-French cooperation. The dominant figure at Vichy at this time was the acidly anti-British Admiral Darlan, with whom the Germans were engaged in negotiating the Paris Protocols which provided for extensive and active cooperation in the Middle East and Africa. In the Middle East Darlan agreed to give the Germans transit and landing rights for aircraft on their way to Iraq and to provide Rashid Ali with French arms, but this policy of resurrecting France through a working partnership with the Nazis was too much for Pétain who brought Weygand over from North Africa early in June in a manoeuvre to resist Darlan. The Paris Protocols thereupon lapsed but not before they had caused the British, with the Free French, to invade Syria and Lebanon.

The local French commander, General Dentz, proposed to resist with German help, but Vichy prevaricated partly through fear of British retaliation in Morocco and partly through fear of offending the Americans and so forfeiting the food and other materials which the Americans were sending to France. So Vichy attached conditions to the acceptance of German air support in Syria which caused the Germans to decline to give any help at all. They were in any case doubtful about the wisdom of helping a mandatory power which the Arabs, whom they were courting, wanted to see evicted. The British put pressure on Turkey to refuse facilities for French reinforcements and supplies (except oil which was covered by an existing agreement); Turkey refused, however, a British invitation to enter Syria from the north. General Dentz, strong in spirit and comparatively strong in numbers but weak in everything else, was forced to capitulate on 14 July after five weeks of fighting.

This British success not only extinguished Vichy's authority in Syria and Lebanon but also constrained de Gaulle to grant these two countries their independence – which was endorsed by Great Britain. But the gaullists were not happy with the idea of recovering French territory from Vichy and then letting it go from the French empire at British behest, and no further steps were taken until 1943 when elections were held and governments installed with something less than sovereign status. In Lebanon a quarrel between the government and the French led to the arrest of the newly elected President and the dissolution of the newly elected parliament, but Anglo-American intervention forced the French to retreat and to concede real powers to the governments of both countries. Arab countries under British rule took note, waiting their turn. The United States and the USSR recognized independent Syria and Lebanon and although France tried at the end of the war to exact special privileges for itself like those enjoyed by Great Britain in Egypt, Iraq and Transjordan, and even bombed Damascus, it was frustrated by British action and forced to recognize that its defeat in 1940 had cost it its empire in the Levant.

A few weeks after the capitulation of General Dentz in July 1941 Great Britain made doubly sure of its Middle Eastern position by occupying Iran in concert with the Russians. The Shah was bundled off to an island in the Indian Ocean and later to South Africa where he died.

Thus at mid-summer 1941 Germany had appropriated the Balkans and Great Britain had replied by dominating the whole of the Middle East. The first of these positions was not to be contested until the general German retreat at the end of the war, which liberated the Balkans. In the Mediterranean and North Africa the war went on. The battle for Cape Matapan in March and the withdrawal of the Luftwaffe for the Russian campaign in June eased the British position, and in July Malta welcomed the first convoy to reach port since January. Another followed in September and for a few weeks Malta became once more a naval base, but the loss of the aircraft carrier *Ark Royal* in the western Mediterranean and the battleship *Barham* in the east, and damage to Great Britain's two remaining battleships by Italian mines fixed to them in harbour at Alexandria, reasserted the challenge to British naval power.

On land Rommel advanced, retreated and survived. His first offensive, launched at the end of March 1941, carried him from Tripolitania through Cyrenaica and into Egypt. Benghazi fell but Tobruk was held by an Australian, New Zealand and Polish garrison. (The Australians were replaced by British troops during the siege, when the Australian government felt compelled to withdraw its forces in view of the growing Japanese threat. The New Zealand troops remained. New Zealand was the only nation besides Great Britain to send fighting troops to every theatre of war.) Rommel's success offered tantalizing prospects of a German advance to Suez, Iraq and the Persian Gulf, but Hitler decided that all this must wait. The Balkans must come first because they were essential for the launching of Barbarossa before mid-summer. So Rommel had to pause. In May and June he and Wavell engaged in a series of dingdong battles for the Halfaya Pass on the borders of Egypt, and Wavell then made an attempt to relieve Tobruk which failed. In a trial of skill in armoured warfare Rommel came off best, the British suffered serious losses of newly arrived tanks, and Wavell was relieved of his command on the day of the German invasion of the USSR. He was replaced by General Auchinleck with General Cunningham in command on the desert front.

Until November Rommel remained on the Egyptian frontier, experiencing increasing difficulties with his supply lines across the Mediterranean. In that month Hitler sent Field Marshal Kesselring to Rome with the title of Supreme Commander South, reinforced the Luftwaffe's meagre strength in the Mediterranean and switched half his U-boats from the Atlantic to the Mediterranean. Generals Auchinleck and Cunningham attacked in mid-November. At the southern end of the front they defeated an Italian armoured division but in the north confused fighting, in which British and German tank formations often found themselves behind what would have been the enemy's lines if any lines had existed, produced no decisive result. At one moment the defenders of Tobruk attempted a break-out which failed. At another, Rommel, encouraged by British losses, made a dash for Egypt which also failed. Rommel's two armoured divisions were superior to the British in fire power but inferior in numbers, and in the first week of December he decided to retreat to avoid encirclement. Thus the siege of Tobruk was at last raised, but as Rommel withdrew once more into Tripolitania (his skill in withdrawal was as great as his dash in attack) leaving the British in control of Cyrenaica an acrimonious debate broke out on the British side. The main object of the campaign had not been achieved; the German Panzer army had not been destroyed. During the battle Auchinleck had dismissed Cunningham and summoned General Ritchie from Cairo to take his place. Since the battle and until the present day there has been controversy about the events of these weeks. It has been argued that if the British had waited for Rommel to attack they would have had a better chance of annihilating his forces, and it has also been argued that the retention of forces in the Middle East for this indecisive action contributed to the fall of Singapore in the following February. By this time Rommel had received new tanks via Tripoli and was planning a second eastward advance. The war in Africa was not concluded until eighteen months later and after the second front in north-west Africa, closed by the fall of France in 1940, had been reopened by the Anglo-American invasion of November 1942.

CHAPTER 9

Barbarossa

THE Russo-German treaty of August 1939 served its German purpose for almost two years. During that period Hitler made himself virtual master of the whole of continental Europe outside the borders of the USSR. A few neutrals existed on the fringes and one – Switzerland – in the middle, but nowhere was there opposition to Germany. These conquests had not been achieved without alarming Stalin. He had shared in the spoliation of Poland, annexed the three Baltic states after the fall of France and taken Bessarabia and northern Bukovina from Rumania. Hitler then carved up Rumania and forced it, together with Hungary and Slovakia, to adhere to the Tripartite Pact. After Mussolini's unsuccessful invasion of Greece he added Bulgaria and Yugoslavia to the Tripartite Pact and moved into Bulgaria. Stalin protested – he had protested the previous year that the partition of Rumania was a breach of the Russo-German treaty of 1939 only to be met with the obvious retort that he himself had already broken it by helping himself to northern Bukovina. When the Simovic government in Belgrade repudiated the Tripartite Pact Stalin made a formal declaration of friendship with it but did not commit the USSR to go to its aid against a German attack. The two pseudo-allies were manoeuvring for positions in the one sizable undistributed area in Europe and the Germans were getting the better of the game because they did not mind provoking the Russians, whereas the Russians were still anxious not to provoke the Germans.

Stalin's agents abroad were reporting that Hitler was about to attack the USSR, the British and American governments were repeating the warnings, and German troop movements told the same tale. Most tellingly of all, German deserters were crossing what had become a Russo-German front line in Poland to give warning of the German attack. A week after the opening of the German campaign in the Balkans and on the day when Belgrade fell, Stalin concluded a neutrality pact with Japan. But he did not trust Japan to keep it and even after Hitler's attack he hesitated for some time before moving troops from his Asian to his European fronts. On 5 June he became President of the Council of Commissars or, as we would say, Prime Minister, in place of Molotov who became Deputy Prime Minister as well as Foreign Minister. (Stalin had hitherto held only the post of Secretary General of the Communist

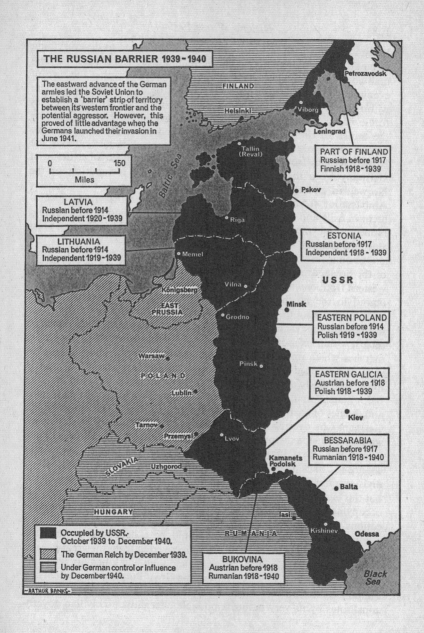

THE RUSSIAN BARRIER 1939-1940

The eastward advance of the German armies led the Soviet Union to establish a 'barrier' strip of territory between its western frontier and the potential aggressor. However, this proved of little advantage when the Germans launched their invasion in June 1941.

0 _____ 150
Miles

FINLAND

Helsinki

Viborg

Petrozavodsk

Leningrad

Tallin (Reval)

Pskov

PART OF FINLAND
Russian before 1917
Finnish 1918-1939

LATVIA
Russian before 1914
Independent 1920-1939

Baltic Sea

Riga

ESTONIA
Russian before 1917
Independent 1918 - 1939

LITHUANIA
Russian before 1914
Independent 1919-1939

Memel

Vilna

USSR

Königsberg

EAST PRUSSIA

Grodno

Minsk

EASTERN POLAND
Russian before 1914
Polish 1919 -1939

Warsaw

POLAND

Pinsk

Lublin

EASTERN GALICIA
Austrian before 1918
Polish 1918-1939

Tarnov

Przemysl

Lvov

Kiev

SLOVAKIA

Uzhgorod

Kamanets Podolsk

BESSARABIA
Russian before 1917
Rumanian 1918-1940

Balta

HUNGARY

Iasi

RUMANIA

Kishinev

Odessa

■ Occupied by USSR.
October 1939 to December 1940.

▨ The German Reich by December 1939.

▤ Under German control or influence
by December 1940.

—ARTHUR BANKS—

BUKOVINA
Austrian before 1918
Rumanian 1918-1940

Black Sea

Party.) But during these last months Stalin continued to do everything he could to avoid or postpone the German attack. The ease of the German conquest of Yugoslavia and Greece showed him that the turn of events in south-eastern Europe would do little or nothing to interfere with Hitler's plans to attack the USSR. He increased Russian supplies to Germany, promising and punctually providing special facilities for the transit of rubber from the Far East and making other economic agreements favourable to Germany; he stopped arguing about the Russo-German frontier in the Baltic area; he expunged all criticism of Germany from the Russian press; he withdrew recognition of the Norwegian and Belgian governments in exile, expelled the Yugoslav Ambassador from Moscow, refused to recognize the Greek government in exile and recognized Rashid Ali's pro-German régime in Iraq. None of these things had been asked for by Hitler and the German press was told to make no mention of them.

At home Stalin had two paramount problems. The first was the state of the Soviet armed forces and the second was strategic. The USSR's western frontier was a long one. At no great distance behind it lay Leningrad in the north and the mineral and agricultural riches of the Ukraine in the south. In the centre Moscow, although more distant, was not beyond the reach of a powerful, mechanized enemy determined to seize it within six months. This central front was bisected by the Pripet marshes which impeded switches between one sector and another. In spite of the misgivings of his professional advisers Stalin had moved forces into newly occupied territories – Bessarabia, Poland, Finland, the Baltic states – and out of the so-called Stalin Line (whose powerful guns and tangles of barbed wire in difficult forest country later impressed the Germans who overran it), until by May 1941 170 Russian divisions were stationed outside the pre-1939 frontiers of the USSR. Stalin may have been hoping that Hitler's adventures in the west would give him a chance to attack again on the Finnish front (where he had twenty-seven divisions, including five armoured) or win further ground in the Balkans but this is surmise. The fact is that well over half the Russian army was occupying new positions whose fortifications and rearward communications were incomplete.

Furthermore, the forces which would be called upon to take the shock of the German attack were still recovering from the great purges. Where Hitler had tamed his officer caste, Stalin had killed his. The purges of the armed forces were a part of the Great Purge of the civilian and military establishments which Stalin began in 1936. An officer corps constitutes by its very nature a possible alternative to civilian government and Stalin was afraid of it. The Russian army had no tradition of revolution; its sole attempt to usurp the civil power – the Decembrist coup of 1825 – had collapsed after a day; but Stalin was obsessed with the example of Bonapartism and he proceeded in the thirties to emasculate the civil war generation whose leaders, military or civilian, might conspire against him. Because of his fears he was quick to lend an ear to accusations that his officers were plotting against him. One of his agents in Paris provided false evidence against Marshal Tukhachevski, the Chief of Staff of the Army, who was alleged to be in treasonable correspondence with German officers. This evidence was planted on Beneš who guilelessly passed it on to Moscow where it was used as reliable confirmation from an untainted source of prefabricated charges. In addition Russian agents persuaded German Intelligence to forge supporting documents which were likewise sent to Moscow to build up the case against Tukhachevski even further. Tukhachevski was arrested and executed after a trial lasting one day. Six of the eight officers who constituted the court martial were also executed. The further victims of the purge embraced three of the five Marshals of the Soviet Union, all eleven deputy Commissars for Defence (that is to say, deputy Ministers), seventy-five of the eighty members of the Military Soviet, all the commanders of the military districts into which the country was divided in peacetime, thirteen of fifteen Army commanders, over half the corps commanders and 20–40 per cent of all officers below brigade. They were replaced by retired stalwarts or young party enthusiasts who were either too out of touch or too unprofessional to inspire confidence or to understand the new equipment which the army was beginning to receive.

This stupendous amputation of head and members, which affected the political as much as the military side of the Soviet army's dual control, disorganized and dispirited the services more than enough to prevent them from being a threat to the régime but also almost enough to prevent them from being a threat to an enemy. The invasion of Poland in September 1939 posed no fighting problem since the Poles had already been beaten by the Germans (it did, however, disclose organizational and logistic inefficiency) but the Finnish war was an inglorious shock, forcing the Russians to employ one and a half million men and to take three months over the sort of operation to which Hitler would have allotted a week or two. But this shock was also perhaps a boon. It forced Stalin to accelerate the reorganization of his defences. In May 1940 S. K. Timoshenko was made a Marshal and Defence Commissar at the age of forty-five, replacing the veteran Bolshevik K. E. Voroshilov. New training programmes were introduced. So were professional

titles for ranks. Military commissars were abolished (they were reintroduced in 1941 and abolished again in 1942) and steps were taken to
boost the prestige of the armed services. In February 1941 G. K.
Zhukov, who had recently concluded a successful campaign against the
Japanese in contrast to the deplorable performance of some of his
colleagues on the Finnish front, was promoted full general and Chief of
Staff of the Army; he became the pre-eminent figure among Stalin's
Marshals but, like Marshal Soult whom he in some ways resembled
(including the possession of a political temperament), was as heartily
disliked by some of his fellows as he was lauded by others.

In the field, however, only a few of the army's new leaders had
emerged, its divisions were below strength and its preparations –
especially in frontier districts – had been impeded up to the last moment
by Stalin's continuing obsession with avoiding provoking the Germans
and so prolonging the respite. By ill chance the Russian forces were
caught in the process of changing over to the T 34 tank which was only
beginning to emerge from the factories. In addition they were, not for
the first time, changing their tank tactics. In earlier years the Russians,
like the Germans, had imbibed some of the new ideas about tank warfare propounded by Liddell Hart, Fuller and Martel, but in the thirties
Stalin had changed his mind. The defeat of the Italians at the battle of
Guadalajara in the Spanish civil war, perhaps also Marshal Tukhachevski's support for the new doctrine, and Russian experience in Mongolia
and Finland, all undermined Stalin's faith in large tank formations and
he decided that tanks should not be concentrated in tank corps and tank
armies but should be spread through other formations in accordance
with an older doctrine. Then the German successes in France made him
change his mind again, although not in time to enable the Russian
forces to be regrouped before suffering severe defeats.

Hitler's attack was launched on 22 June, two days earlier than the
date on which Napoleon had led the Grand Army across the Niemen in
1812. It was the biggest military operation ever mounted. Although Hitler believed that the USSR would collapse, he was taking no chances
and in any case he loved sheer size. His hosts, which included contingents
of a dozen nationalities, attacked in three directions. Northern and
Central Army Groups under Field Marshals von Leeb and von Bock
headed towards the cities of Leningrad and Moscow, Southern Army
Group under Field Marshal von Rundstedt for the Ukraine, the Don
basin, the Crimea and the Caucasus with their wealth of grain, coal and
oil. Their main objective was to surround and destroy the Russian
forces in western Russia and prevent any 'battleworthy elements' from

escaping into the interior: the capture of cities and provinces would then follow automatically. Surprise was complete: psychological surprise, because the Russian public had been allowed no hint of what was in store; tactical surprise, because the Russian forces in western areas were not forewarned.

The Russian front was broken in several places within hours of the opening of the attack on the first day. The main weight of the German attack was in the centre. The striking power of each Army Group was concentrated in Panzer Groups. Army Group Centre had two of these; each of its neighbours one. The Panzer Groups struck swiftly and directly, disrupting the enemy front and outdistancing the rest of the German forces which advanced as a second wave in encircling movements to trap the Russian forces which had been severed from each other by the slicing Panzers. In this way the Russians were cut up into sections and surrounded in pockets, and the speed and success of the German Panzer Groups were so great that the pockets were very large. Some of them contained up to fifteen Russian divisions. Huge numbers of prisoners were taken. On the Russian side there was almost total disorganization. Roads and railways were made unusable by the Luftwaffe. Every kind of communication failed. Frantic reports from the front and appeals for instructions, sent *en clair* for want of time to encipher them, dismayed incredulous staffs at higher echelons which retorted that the reports must be wrong and reprimanded the senders for not using their codes. But amid this confusion the Russians faced forward and even counterattacked, driving their tanks suicidally into German artillery fire and pouring uncoordinated masses of men into the path of the unstoppable Germans. Others retreated or fled, destroying such installations and livestock as they could, often themselves destroyed either by the Luftwaffe or by the machine guns of the NKVD. Their officers were summoned back to Moscow to be shot there. The Germans, advancing up to fifty miles a day, were equally amazed by their own success and by the violent, valiant and often ferocious resistance of men who should have been totally demoralized. They began from the start to perceive that the war in the east was going to be different from the other campaigns of the past two years.

In mere numbers the Russians could match the Germans at many points. They had more men and more tanks, field artillery and aircraft. They had about 20,000 tanks, of which some 7,000 were in forward areas, but most of them were obsolescent and according to Marshal Konev, writing after the war was over, losses were so heavy that by September there were only forty-five serviceable modern tanks between the

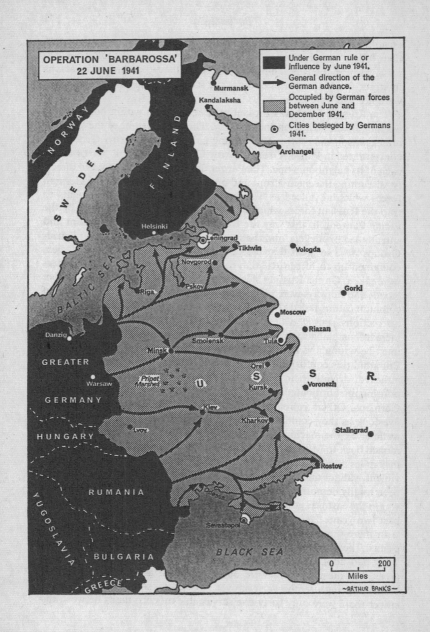

OPERATION 'BARBAROSSA'
22 JUNE 1941

■ Under German rule or influence by June 1941.
→ General direction of the German advance.
▨ Occupied by German forces between June and December 1941.
◉ Cities besieged by Germans 1941.

NORWAY

SWEDEN

FINLAND

Murmansk
Kandalaksha

Archangel

Helsinki

BALTIC SEA

Leningrad
Tikhvin
Vologda

Novgorod

Riga
Pskov

Gorki

Danzig

Moscow
Smolensk
Riazan

GREATER

Minsk
Tula

Warsaw

Pripet
Marshes
U

Orel
S
R.
Kursk
Voronezh

GERMANY

HUNGARY

Kiev

Lvov

Kharkov

Stalingrad

Rostov

YUGOSLAVIA

RUMANIA

Sevastopol

BLACK SEA

BULGARIA

GREECE

0   200
Miles

~ARTHUR BANKS~

Germans and Moscow. Konev, one of Stalin's outstanding tank commanders, regarded the Russian T 34 as the best tank in any army during the entire war, but it did not become the mainstay of the Russian forces until 1943. Russian manpower was immense but infantry divisions were still not motorized and shortages ranging from radio equipment to medical supplies were crippling. Large areas of the USSR passed into German hands. Goebbels proclaimed on 10 July: 'The eastern continent lies like a limp virgin in the mighty arms of the German Mars.' As whole armies surrendered and cities fell (Minsk 28 June, Smolensk 16 July) the German victory in the field seemed complete. But the Russians were not quite overwhelmed. Their armies were not destroyed. Nor were their air forces.

The Russian air forces (the largest in the world) and Russian aircraft production were, like the Russian army, in a stage of re-equipment and expansion in the years immediately before war came. Although markedly inferior to the German and British air forces – in machines, output, design, technical equipment, training, maintenance, ground organization and airfield construction – the Russian air forces had reached a point where improvement in all these departments could be rapid. The most important feature of the air war in the east after 1941 was that this improvement was not only astonishingly rapid but far more so than the Germans or anybody else had believed possible. In the first half of the war the Russians were able to offset their all-round inferiority by superiority in one thing – numbers. In the second half of the war they had air forces which were not only bigger but better than the Luftwaffe.

Russian aircraft production passed German production about the end of 1937, that is to say, before Munich. It then rose steadily from around 800 a month to 900 in 1939 and 1,000 by the time of Barbarossa. The first deliveries from new factories built in the Urals in the early thirties began to reach units in 1939, but when production and assembly plants in the west were overrun by the German armies total output was halved. It recovered by the middle of 1942 and then rose remorselessly to a peak of 3,000 a month. First line strength was 3,000–3,500 at the beginning of 1938, 4,000–5,000 a year later; after surmounting the crisis of 1941–2 it reached 10,000 by mid-1943, 15,000 by mid-1944 and over 20,000 before the war ended. But when war began reserves were poor. There was no pool of aircraft on which operational units could draw in order to replace their losses; new aircraft had to go straight from factory to units, so that the operational strength of units depended directly on the irregular factory flow and was sometimes down to half the prescribed establishment – with depressing effects on morale as well as on strengths.

There were acute shortages of high-octane fuel at the front and essential raw materials for the factories. The Russian air forces had no radar, no ground control, not enough fighters and very few night fighters. Such fighters as could be spared from the fighting at the front were concentrated on airfields round Moscow for the defence of the capital. Strategic bombing of targets in the enemy's rear was impossible in 1941 and hardly developed at any time. Russian long-range bombers, unequipped with radar, engaged in dangerous and largely ineffective missions in which a half to three quarters of modest forces of about one hundred aircraft failed to find their targets. Bomb loads never exceeded two tons, a light load compared with the ten tons carried by the British Lancaster. Finally, the Russian air forces were still divided in 1941 between a western front against the Germans and an eastern front against the Japanese, and in spite of Stalin's growing assurance that he had nothing to fear in the east he hesitated to denude his eastern front until the threat to Moscow forced him to transfer 1,000 fighters and fighter bombers westward in the autumn of 1941.

The first three months of the campaigns of 1941 were catastrophic but just not fatal. The Russian air forces, attacked by an enemy who was technically much superior, were caught by surprise, inadequately camouflaged, undispersed, unsure of their supplies and communications: Russian fighters, 20–100 m.p.h. slower than the German Me. 109s, were outfought, frequently in the course of retreating from one airfield to another further back. Great numbers were destroyed on the ground, either by surprise attack or because they had to be left behind owing to shortages of fuel or spare parts. The Luftwaffe claimed to have destroyed 1,489 aircraft on the ground on the first day; a first attempt to retaliate by bombing German targets cost the Russians 500 aircraft. On the day after the battle opened one commander of a Russian bomber group committed suicide after losing 600 aircraft against only twelve German. Russian losses by the end of August probably amounted to more than 5,000 aircraft. A month later their front line strength in the west had been halved and the Germans believed that the Russian air force had ceased to exist. Significantly, they were puzzled by the continued arrival of reinforcements. They were handicapped by their inability to reach and bomb the factories in the east where many of these aircraft were being turned out. They continued to shoot down the new aircraft which were thrown by the Russians desperately into the battle as soon as they arrived, but the flow never ceased and the Luftwaffe itself began to feel the strain.

German front line strengths shrank too, sometimes to half establishment. Space and snow came to the help of the Russians. The Luftwaffe, however excellent, was too small for a 2,000-mile front. As units were switched from Leningrad in the far north to the Ukrainian or central front, operational efficiency declined. The Luftwaffe could not keep up its initial effort of 1,500–2,000 sorties a day. It was farther away from its bases at home than it had ever been, its communications longer and more precarious, its flying conditions more testing. Once again it was short of fighters, and although the Stukas made their final onslaught of the war they too were too few to deliver along this huge front the series of packed punches which had drilled holes in the armies on the western fronts. When the snow came and the airfields froze, the High Command of the Luftwaffe failed to provide its men with the right clothing or its machines with anti-freeze. Its difficulties were accentuated by the make-shift nature of some of the airstrips which it was obliged to use and which were inferior to the airfields round Moscow being used by the Russians. By the end of the year German operational strength along the whole front had fallen to 1,500 and in the Moscow sector the Russians had assembled twice as many aircraft as the Luftwaffe.

But this capacity of the Russian air forces to survive was secondary. The decisive fact was the survival of the Russian ground forces. At the end of the first four weeks of the campaign the Germans paused for breath – and for argument. The Panzer units were farther ahead of the infantry than had been expected and some of them were 200 miles from their depots in eastern Poland; spare parts had to be flown to them since many roads were only unsurfaced tracks and there were hundreds of thousands of armed Russians behind the German lines. How many it is impossible to say: certainly 250,000, perhaps twice that number, whole armies cut up and disoriented but not eliminated. Guderian and other tank commanders wanted to resume their advances as soon and as fast as possible in order to keep on hammering the Russians, prevent the consolidation of a new line of Russian defence, exterminate the enemy's fighting capacity and capture Moscow. Hitler on the other hand wanted to hold in the centre, strengthen his northern and southern Army Groups, bypass and isolate Leningrad with the one, and push south with the other until he was in a position to sweep round behind Moscow and the Russian armies to the west of it. Besides this strategic problem Hitler and his generals were worried by the gap which had already developed between the Panzers and the rest of the army and would be yet further increased if the Panzers were given their head, and they were worried because their advance not only extended their lines from west to east but also, fanwise, on a north–south axis – owing to the fact that the starting line of June had been considerably shorter than the line along which they were forced by geography to operate by the end of July.

The German forces were becoming stretched in all directions and it was not impossible to envisage the Russians inserting unused reinforcements between the Panzers and their supporting units, while at the same time breaking out of one or two pockets farther west and starting effective guerilla action against the German lines of communication. To give point to their fears several thousand Russian troops did break out of the Smolensk pocket. So from mid-July to mid-August the debate went on; the Germans failed to make the best of some of the most favourable weather of the summer or to exploit the chaos reigning in western Russia where local commanders and local party officials tussled with problems of discipline and administration and no firm directives reached them from the top (except simply to attack Germans whenever they were seen); the battered Russians had time to breathe, to re-group and to rush reserve divisions into the gaps. These divisions were half-trained, poorly equipped, sometimes still in civilian clothes, but they arrived and played their part; the Germans had not thought that they could be brought into the line so quickly. So great was the urgency on the Russian side that when trains reached their destinations the locomotives were uncoupled and sent back post haste without waiting for the rolling stock.

During these weeks Stalin's authority became assured. It is not certain that it was so in the first disastrous weeks of war, or that he believed it to be so. A few days after the German invasion a defence committee to run the war was established under his chairmanship. The other members were Molotov, Voroshilov, Malenkov and Beria. Below this committee was the *Stavka*, a supreme planning staff which controlled the Fronts – the Russian term for Army Groups. The *Stavka* consisted originally of a dozen senior officers but Stalin, Molotov and Voroshilov were added to it soon after the outbreak of war. In July Stalin became, like Churchill, Defence Minister as well as Prime Minister; in August, like Hitler, Commander-in-Chief too. But during the first two weeks of war nothing was heard from him. He may have been, as some suppose, too badly rattled to speak, or he may have been weighing things up and waiting to see whether the German attack would be followed by a Japanese attack or a popular revolt against his rule or a military take-over by his generals. When on 3 July he made his first wartime broadcast, what he had to say struck many of his listeners as flat and uninspiring. His plight, as he himself saw it in this month, is revealed by his avowal to Harry Hopkins, Roosevelt's special emissary, that he would welcome American troops on any part of Russian soil under unrestricted American command. But by the autumn, he, like Russia, had weathered the first storm and was ready to face the next. He reorganized the higher commands and imposed his will on his commanders. The system of dual military and party control in the armed services, abolished shortly before the war began, had been reintroduced a few weeks after the German attack and command of three Fronts entrusted to Voroshilov and Zhdanov in the north, Timoshenko and Bulganin in the centre and Budyenny and Kruschchev in the south. Budyenny, a dashing hero with a big moustache but a little brain, was later relieved and succeeded by Timoshenko, who was replaced in the vital central sector first by Konev and then by Zhukov who was recalled from Leningrad after only a month in that city and put in charge of the defence of the capital.

On 23 August the pause on the German side ended. The attack was resumed – in the south Guderian's armour was switched from Bock's Army Group Centre to Rundstedt's Army Group South. Two days later Dnepropetrovsk fell and the Russians blew up the great dam at Zaporozhe which supplied the power for the mass of industries in the Dnieper bend, a self-mutilation which proclaimed that they had little hope of recapturing lost territory in the near future. Kiev was now at the western tip of a Russian salient, half encircled and urgently threatened. To Budyenny and Kruschchev its loss seemed certain and its abandonment a strategic necessity, but Stalin insisted on a fight to the finish. This was not pure stubbornness. Stalin may have reasoned that Budyenny, whose forces were larger than those facing him, ought to be able to hold Kiev; that in any case any delay was worth while in order to check an advance which threatened to envelop Moscow; and that the retreat of so large a force at this juncture would be psychologically disastrous. Kiev had to pay the price, which turned out to be very high. Four Russian armies were surrounded and when they surrendered on 17 September the number of prisoners who fell into the German bag (even if they were fewer than the German claim of 665,000) was immense. Here, as elsewhere in this savage war, the prisoners were worse off than the dead, for the Germans frequently failed to give them medical assistance or to feed them properly. From Kiev the Germans swept on to conquer the whole of the Ukraine and most of the Crimea before the end of the year. The only Russian successes were the recapture of Rostov at the end of November and the resistance of Sebastopol.

Guderian's armour, switched back to the central sector after only a couple of weeks in the Ukraine, prepared for its last thrust of the year, the drive for Moscow. It was launched at the end of October. Again the

Russians were taken by surprise – their air reconnaissance and their wireless Intelligence were poor – and they suffered enormous losses. Something like panic developed in Moscow, accentuated by reports of how the Germans were treating prisoners and civilians and the NKVD shooting deserters. Some two million Muscovites were evacuated in due order and others simply fled. But Stalin and his principal military advisers and civilian subordinates remained. Reinforcements were rushed up from Mongolia – a switch which was less of a gamble than it appeared on the surface because Stalin had been told by the spy Richard Sorge in Tokyo that Japan had decided to attack in the Pacific and not in north Asia.

After the first week of the German October offensive the weather broke and converted the battlefields into mud swamps so thick that tanks and vehicles struggled in them in vain. The Germans slithered and stuck and prayed for frost to harden the going again. But they were unlucky once more. The mud was late in freezing over, and when it did in November the temperature fell not only late but sharply, causing them terrible suffering. In December came blizzards which reduced visibility to fifty yards. Clothing was inadequate. A request by Guderian for winter supplies had earned him a rebuke for implying that they might be needed. The men stuffed their clothes with paper to keep warm, often with leaflets sent to the front to be showered upon the enemy and tell him that surrender was his only sane course. By Christmas the Germans had 100,000 cases of frostbite. Dysentery was rife. Like their comrades in the Luftwaffe the army had no anti-freeze. Their guns would not fire. Yet they were constantly harassed, usually by small parties of Russians at night. The intense cold and snow also prevented supplies of food from reaching them. What food they had often had to be cut with axes or saws. Soup froze if a man paused for a minute in getting it into his mouth. The medal earned by these afflicted men was nicknamed the Order of Frozen Flesh. Some committed suicide. Looking back over the war when he came to write about this time Guderian recalled 'the endless expanse of Russian snow during this winter of our misery . . . the icy wind that blew across it . . . too thin shelter . . . insufficiently clothed, half-starved men'.

At the beginning of December the attempt to reach Moscow, only twenty miles away, was abandoned and three days later the Russians counter-attacked, recovered some ground and eased the pressure on the capital. Although their success was less than had been hoped, it was enough to keep Hitler from emulating Napoleon's feat – in 1941 or ever. Inhibited by caution and by a multiplicity of objectives, Hitler had failed to take Moscow. Perhaps if he had taken Guderian's advice and tried the direct punch before the right hook, he might have succeeded; and perhaps he would then have won his war in the east. But neither of these propositions is certain. What is certain is that in the first week of December 1941 one of the most precarious moments of the war was reached and passed.

Leningrad too survived. The siege of Leningrad was one of the epic events of the war. The magnificent capital of Peter the Great, built on either side of the Neva and on the islands in its estuary, contained three million inhabitants, of whom close on one million died in the siege. When the German invasion was launched desperate but belated preparations were made to withstand an assault and the Russian forces renewed their attack on the Finns, who, despite protestations of neutrality, were expected to make common cause with the Germans. Finnish forces re-occupied territory lost in the war of 1939–40 but Field Marshal Mannerheim was unwilling to overstep the 1939 frontiers (which his troops reached in August) and, partly in response to American pressure, refused persistent German requests for an alliance and joint operations against Leningrad.

The northern group of German armies advanced rapidly. It reached the river Drina in four days, pressed on to Pskov after a short pause and might perhaps have captured Leningrad before the end of July. Its leading units, which had covered 470 miles in three weeks, were only sixty miles from the city but at this point they halted and did not resume the advance until 8 August. Hitler – in a mood not unlike the one which had allowed the British to escape from Dunkirk – wanted to nurse his armour and reduce the city by siege and air attack, after which it was to be razed to the ground as a symbolic extirpation of its eponymous guardian, the founder of the bolshevist state. He seems always to have been in two minds about Leningrad. On the one hand he willed its obliteration, but when he was thinking in broad strategic terms he did not want to waste before it large forces which should be advancing into the heart of Russia. The first shells fell on it in the first days of September. Zhukov arrived to direct the defences on the 11th. The city had been all but completely invested a few days earlier.

Leningrad had been the scene of the most celebrated episodes in the overthrow of the Tsars (whose capital it had been) and the jealous defender ever since that date of all that was purest in communist tradition and doctrine. Inside this city men, women and children now laboured ceaselessly on civil defence and emergency fortifications; to seaward the Russian Baltic fleet, whether riding the waters or imprisoned in the ice, provided an extra ring of guns; even the guns of the ancient cruiser *Aurora* which had been turned into a museum were removed and put into the first line; industries and population were evacuated to the east; patriotic enthusiasm was fanned by propaganda lectures. Leningrad was besieged from September 1941 to January 1944. It had at the outset only one to two months' supply of basic foods, much of which was then destroyed by air attack. Unlikely substitutes were turned into eatables. Uneatables were eaten. Equally catastrophic was the shortage of water for elementary cleansing and of medicines. Deaths from hunger began to occur before the end of 1941 and the monthly rate soon reached the annual average; deaths from privation ran at the rate of several thousands a day and created a serious threat to the morale as well as the health of the survivors, who were already exhausted by extreme cold, hard work, hunger, disease, and the collapse of public services. On Christmas Day 1941 about 4,000 died. The most serious threat came in November 1941 when Tikhvin was taken by the Germans. This town, due east of Leningrad, was on the railway by which the Russians hoped to keep the city supplied, and when it was lost the Russians were compelled to begin the construction of a road from a point safely east of Tikhvin to the eastern shore of Lake Ladoga, whence supplies would be taken across the water or the ice to the south-western corner of the lake thirty-five miles from the city. The first plan was to build a railway line across the ice but a large frozen lake is far from being a flat surface and the first train left its rails near the beginning of its journey. Next came a plan to tear up the city's tramlines and re-lay them on the lake but this scheme was abandoned almost as soon as it was thought of. Finally, the Russians began to build a road and collect lorries – from Moscow and from the American and British vehicles arriving in the far north – to make the passage by night, in the bitter cold of an exceptionally bitter winter (the temperature averaged twenty degrees below freezing over a whole month) and against the fierce north-east winds which constantly swept the surface of the lake. Some supplies got in this way but it was a desperate expedient which could hardly have saved the city. Fortunately the Russians recaptured Tikhvin in December. The encirclement of Leningrad was never complete because the Russians kept possession of the south-western corner of Lake Ladoga. Nevertheless starvation was sometimes only one or two days off during this first and most exacting winter of the war. In Berlin invitations to a reception in Leningrad to be attended by Hitler were printed but never sent out.

Leningrad won a further reprieve in 1942 owing to the resistance of Sebastopol where the German 11 Army, which was designated to switch

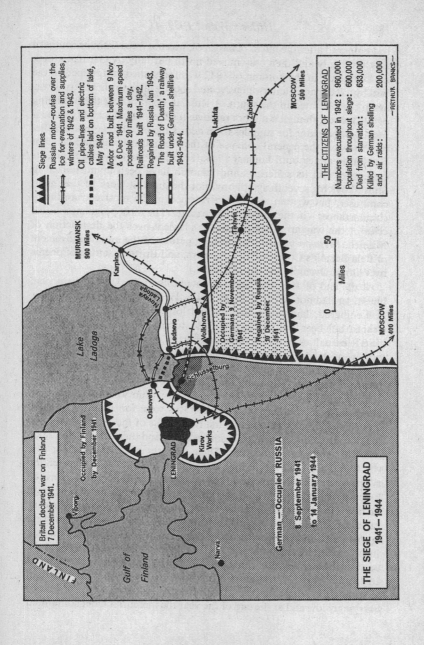

THE SIEGE OF LENINGRAD
1941—1944

FINLAND

Gulf of Finland

Narva

Viborg

Occupied by Finland by December 1941

LENINGRAD

Kirov Works

Osinovets

Lake Ladoga

Novaya Ladoga

Karpino

MURMANSK 900 Miles

Schlusselburg

Lednevo

Volkhova

Occupied by Germans 9 November 1941

Regained by Russia 10 December 1941

TIKVIN

Lakhta

Zaborie

MOSCOW 500 Miles

MOSCOW 400 Miles

German — Occupied RUSSIA

8 September 1941 to 14 January 1944

Britain declared war on Finland 7 December 1941.

Siege lines.

Russian motor-routes over the ice for evacuation and supplies, winters of 1942 & 1943.

Oil pipe-lines and electric cables laid on bottom of lake, May 1942.

Motor road built between 9 Nov & 6 Dec 1941. Maximum speed possible 20 miles a day.

Railroads built 1941–1942.

Regained by Russia Jan 1943.

"The Road of Death", a railway built under German shellfire 1943–1944.

THE CITIZENS OF LENINGRAD

Numbers evacuated in 1942 : 960,000.
Population throughout siege: 600,000
Died from starvation : 633,000
Killed by German shelling and air raids: 200,000

Miles

0   50

—ARTHUR BANKS—

to Leningrad after the fall of Sebastopol, was not freed from its southern task until July and then only moved north partially. A German attack on Leningrad in the autumn of 1942 was forestalled and nipped in the bud by a Russian counter-offensive and shortly afterwards 11 Army was again concentrated in the south. A Russian operation at the beginning of 1943 eased, though it did not remove, the German blockade by opening a new corridor for supplies from across the lake but complete relief had to await the general collapse of the Germans. Leningrad was not freed from attack until January 1944. It received the Order of Lenin. Its endurance and its sufferings and triumph have been immortalized in Shostakovich's seventh symphony, not the greatest work of that great composer, but written and first performed in the most extraordinary circumstances – in the city during the siege. (The most poignant musical cries of the war are Richard Strauss's lament over the destruction of Munich, *Metamorphosen*, the thrilling pathos of the middle movement of Béla Bartók's Concerto for Orchestra, and Britten's setting of poems by Wilfred Owen in his *War Requiem*.)

At the end of 1941 the German conquests in the USSR were vast, but Hitler had not defeated the Russians. He had failed to take Moscow or Leningrad, had taken Rostov and lost it again, had overrun the Crimea but been baulked before Sebastopol, and had suffered in the USSR casualties of about three quarters of a million, of whom one in four were dead. The very arguments about priorities – Moscow or Leningrad, Leningrad or the Ukraine, Sebastopol or Leningrad – prove that from the very beginning the German forces were stretched. Once Russian resistance was not wholly broken within weeks, the German command faced choices because the tasks were too many. The same applied to the Luftwaffe. In the first four weeks of the campaign a force of 3,000 aircraft averaged 2,500 sorties a day and thereafter 1,500–2,000 a day for the rest of the year. Their performance was excellent (the Me. 109F, faster but less heavily armed than the Me. 109E, was making its first operational appearance) but in spite of this remarkable effort the force was too thinly spread for its commitments and again switches told the tale – to Leningrad at one moment and then back again to the central front for the main assault on Moscow. Air raids on Moscow were hardly more than token gestures. The city was attacked seventy-six times between the beginning of the campaign and the end of 1941 but the weight of the attack was often trivial. The largest force employed in a single night was 127 and in far more cases than not the bombers could be counted in single figures. The Luftwaffe's reserves were sometimes worryingly low and at the end of the year the mercurial Udet committed suicide. Thus the startling achievements of 1941 on the ground and in the air had by December essentially failed, and a fresh advance in 1942 was to culminate in the disaster of Stalingrad, whereafter the two great land powers of Europe were measured against one another until the Germans were utterly repulsed.

On the Russian side crippling casualties – at least three million men and probably 18,000 tanks in the first disastrous three months – were offset by patriotic determination and furious despair which mounted as the Germans resorted to monstrous cruelties. Sadistic and debauched proconsuls and their henchmen were invested with authority in the rear of the advancing armies (whose commanders preferred to turn a blind eye to proceedings which disgusted them – within limits). Mass executions and the deliberate burying alive of half killed victims united and fired all Russians who escaped this appalling demonstration of the dark side of human nature. At the top Stalin's nerve held, a new layer of brilliant field commanders was moving into the crucial positions and Soviet Intelligence from agents in Switzerland and Germany itself as well as Tokyo was providing a reliable basis for the conduct of the war. One of these agents was Richard Sorge in Tokyo, a handsome and talented German in Russian pay who had become a personal friend and confidant of the German Ambassador and had the almost incredible experience of discovering the answer to one of Stalin's most vital questions on the very eve of Barbarossa and on the day before the Japanese police arrested him as a spy. From his contacts with the Japanese cabinet Sorge was able to tell Stalin that the Japanese were not going to attack the Russians in Mongolia, but the Americans in the Pacific. When Sorge's information was confirmed by Japanese inactivity, Stalin began to nerve himself to denude his eastern frontiers. He did so just in time, although he still hesitated until he was within sight of the end of the short Siberian campaigning season. Reinforcements from the east, including 1,700 tanks and 1,500 aircraft, reached Zhukov on the Moscow front at the beginning of November at the point when the Russians had drained the last reserves from their training schools and the Germans thought that the Russians were finished.

The German failure to defeat the Russians in 1941 was the second and greatest turning point in the war in Europe. If Hitler could not beat the Russians in six months he could not beat them at all. He had prepared for a short war. He had not prepared for and he could not win a long one. Nor could his relations with his generals survive a long one. At the end of 1941 he took over command of the army himself from Brauchitsch and nine months later he would dismiss Halder, his Chief of Staff.

More important perhaps, the handling of the 1941 campaign had produced quarrels with more highly respected field commanders and had deepened the mutual distrust between Hitler and the officer corps. By the end of the year Guderian, Rundstedt and Hoepner had all been dismissed. Others would follow later. In assuming personal command in the war in the east Hitler jettisoned his ablest generals.

It was at this point – the end of 1941 – that the European war begun in Poland in September 1939 was converted into a world war. On 7 December the Japanese attack on the American fleet at Pearl Harbor opened the war in the Pacific and made the United States a belligerent in that theatre. With one of the most startling gestures of the whole war Hitler immediately made the Americans belligerents in the Atlantic and Europe as well by a declaration of war. Germany was thenceforward engaged in a war that had spread right round the world.

CHAPTER 10

War with America

On 11 December 1941 Hitler declared war on the United States of America. In retrospect the actual participation of the United States in the war in Europe and the hugeness of its contribution to victory obscure the fact that, all through 1941, the United States was still a largely unwilling and uncertain belligerent. Many Americans felt that the war was not theirs, in the sense that it could affect no vital American interest; and those who nevertheless felt emotionally involved hoped that they could contribute to the defeat of the dictators without having to send their own sons to be killed.

Europeans have become used, during the twentieth century, to describing their wars as World wars, the implication being that everybody of any consequence automatically gets involved once Europeans start fighting. To many Europeans in both World Wars American participation took the form of a belated recognition of the obvious. But it was not obvious that a European war must become a World war or that the United States must send fighting men to Europe. Even after the United States became a belligerent Americans regarded their country's intervention as assistance to friends in need rather than as the defence of essential American interests. There was a lot to be said for this view. The American continent was a long way from Europe. It could not be hit or invaded by German air or land forces and could only be marginally harassed by naval ones. Hitler showed in any case no desire to do any of these things. There was (save possibly from Japan) no external threat to the United States, no enemy within sight. Moreover this commonsensical geographical view of the matter fitted comfortably into American history and mythology – the creation of the United States as a society detached from Europe and its ills, a community which had better things to do than get involved in the deceits and squabbles which constituted European politics.

Not that the United States had in fact been as isolationist as it believed itself, and was believed by others, to be. In the famous debates in the Senate after the end of the First World War about adopting the Treaty of Versailles and joining the League of Nations there had at no time been a majority against the new internationalism. Debate had been about the conditions to be attached to ratifying the treaty, and the combined forces of those who wanted unconditional acceptance and those who wanted conditional acceptance decisively outnumbered the isolationists who wanted no acceptance at all. The entry of the United States into the League was vetoed by the Senate only because the compact body of Wilsonian internationalist Senators joined forces with the small band of isolationists to defeat the amendments proposed by Republican internationalists. The event was decided by Wilson's determination to have all or nothing. The Senate's action was nevertheless interpreted as a signal of American withdrawal. Nor was this interpretation altogether wrong, for the League became the principal outward and visible sign and the principal organ of international involvement, and it never had the United States among its members. Yet the United States was willy-nilly enmeshed in European affairs because of the war debts owed to it by its recent allies, debts which these allies could not pay unless they in their turn were paid the war reparations owed to them by Germany. Consequently the United States took an active part in the attempts to sort out these problems, so much so that the two main plans for settling the German debt – the Dawes Plan and the Young Plan – were named after the American members of the teams which produced them. But this special kind of involvement, backward looking to the last war, was no pointer to a wider international involvement. On the contrary, it kept alive memories of the unpleasantness of war and added to them resentments about allies who, after the war, defaulted on their financial engagements.

Further than that, there grew up in the United States a suspicion that the American declaration of war in April 1917 had been engineered by chicanery. Catastrophic events tend to breed, a generation later, a critique which probes for hidden, and perhaps disreputable, motives. Americans were perturbed by the notion that the arms industry – the merchants of death as they were more picturesquely called before the invention of the sterner term military-industrial complex – had promoted belligerence for the profits to be made out of it, while yet other Americans blamed Wilson for feebly succumbing to cunning allied propaganda about the wickedness of U-boats. Criticisms of this nature became so strong that they were investigated, and given added circulation, by a committee of the Senate – the Nye Committee – between 1934 and 1936. This scrutiny contributed to the mood which induced Congress to pass the Neutrality Acts of 1935, 1936 and 1937. These Acts were intended to make clear the American resolve to keep out of another war and to prevent a President from leading the nation into one. Neutrality, a posture usually adopted by small states to avoid getting hurt in the quarrels of the great, became paradoxically the statutory refuge of the greatest power on earth. In order to give body to this general policy the Congress decreed that American arms were not to be delivered to belligerents or to be carried in American ships (but belligerents might buy non-military goods provided they paid cash for them and carried them away in non-American vessels); further, the President was empowered to take other precautionary measures by, for example, forbidding American citizens to travel in belligerent ships. It was in implementation of these Acts that Roosevelt issued in September 1939 a declaration of American neutrality.

There has been much debate over the attitudes of the American people towards external affairs, and even more about President Roosevelt's role in leading his country towards war. American isolationism was, as already noted, rooted in history and plausibility. The United States came into existence as a result of war against a European power and was peopled by migrants who left Europe out of distaste or discomfort. With an enormous and comparatively empty country to explore and exploit they concluded, as well they might, that other people's affairs were of no account and that they themselves had no vital interests beyond their own bounds (with the exception of the central American and Caribbean lands to the south which were not so distant as not to matter). The threat to the Union in the 1860s and the problems of reconstruction after the Civil War intensified the tendency to introspection, but two forces in particular were working against it. The first was the diversification of American economic interests and their consequent expansion overseas, coupled with a growth in American power which both tempted and enabled the United States to scan larger horizons. These material considerations were reinforced by the moralistic ingredient in American society, a factor in the American make-up which derived partly from the puritan origins of many of its communities and partly from that remoteness from events which allowed Americans to think of external politics in general terms of right and wrong instead of the more pragmatic categories of expediency and prudence to which Europeans, with their eyes on close neighbours and sensitive frontiers, were more prone.

This moralistic trend found expression, in political affairs, in a self-dedication to freedom and democracy, and this dedication made nonsense of isolationism. The isolationist attitude had found expression in neutrality, which is the formal expression of the emotion of isolationism. Covertly, however, neutrality negated isolationism, for whereas isolationism asserted that other people's conflicts could be overlooked, neutrality could mean that they were looked at and found to be equally lacking in merit on both sides. Thus neutrality was a Trojan horse in the isolationist camp, since Europe between the wars proved on inspection not to be an arena where unregenerate Europeans were simply tangling over issues of no significance. On the contrary, Fascism threatened democracy, Nazism threatened even more basic human norms; there were fights abroad in which all good men must join to put down brutality and faithlessness and uphold democracy and civilized manners. So a conflict developed within the United States. As the troubles of Europe and Asia became more troubled (by, for example, the Japanese attacks on Manchuria and China and the Spanish civil war), there was an atavistic and very powerful resolve to keep all the clearer of them, but at the same time a minority which concerned itself with foreign affairs developed a strong reprobation of the aggressive and fascist powers. Being neutral turned out to be more difficult than it used to be. To most Americans neutrality meant keeping out of wars, but to some Americans it began to appear that neutrality in Hitler's wars meant keeping out of a just war. Keeping out of wars was self-evidently sensible, but keeping out of a just war was not so clearly right.

The debate over Roosevelt's personal responsibility in bringing the United States into war has been not untinged by the emotions roused by Roosevelt in issues which have nothing to do with the war. Roosevelt was one of those men who can instil passionate enthusiasms and also intense hostility, even hatred. By his keenest admirers he has been credited with the foresight of genius; to his bitter enemies he was little better than a charlatan. The only common ground here is the acknowledgement that he had uncommon influence over the course of events. This is not the place for a complete assessment of Roosevelt as President, but we have to inquire into the nature of his influence, the use he made of it and the evolution of his policy in relation to international crises and to war.

Roosevelt was elected President in 1932 in the wake of exceptional turmoil in the United States. Although Americans had no external enemy to fear, they had experienced another kind of fear and disaster. The economic collapse which began so dramatically on Wall Street on 23 October 1929 took away from millions the basic material conditions of their lives and left them feeling helpless, bewildered and scared. The shock to morale was all the greater because, unlike the soldier who in some sense covenants with death, the brusquely impoverished father of a family had not contemplated this material bereavement, had done nothing to deserve it and scarcely understood it. There was more panic in the face of this economic blast than in the face of rifle fire or bombs. It was up to Roosevelt to do something about it and he did do, and was seen to do, lots of things. Not all these things were useful or even sensible but all of them, the failures as well as the successes, were activities and activity was a large part of what was needed. One can argue about the value of planting thousands of trees or of creating new government agencies, but it is impossible to doubt that the sum total of sheer activity by government became transmuted into a bank of popular confidence on which Roosevelt was ever afterwards able to draw. He became at once a strong president, capable of weathering storms and of giving a lead, the more so because the strength of his political position was buttressed by exceptional (though not infallible) political skill, superior intelligence and eloquence. But Roosevelt was no revolutionary or visionary innovator, either domestically or in foreign affairs. At home he was a compassionate, managerial conservative whose New Deal meant some change in the distribution of power, little change in the direction of policy. In external affairs his attitudes were at first no different from those of millions of Americans. He was an isolationist in the sense of wanting to keep out of foreign affairs on the assumption that these spelt trouble, but he was not opposed to playing a part where no trouble seemed to brew. Thus, he proposed in 1935 that the United States join the Permanent Court of International Justice, but was defeated by the Senate. He not only took an interest in disarmament but offered to join a European collective security system if the Europeans would first disarm. He was riled by the failure of the Disarmament Conference in 1933 and blamed Germany, which was seeking to increase its armament, rather than France or Great Britain, which were simply declining to reduce theirs. On the other hand he allowed Hitler's introduction of conscription in 1935 to pass without protest even though it was a breach of the American-German peace treaty of 1921 (the treaty concluded by the United States in place of the Treaty of Versailles). Again like millions of Americans, Roosevelt, disposed though he was to criticize the fumbling policies and imperial philosophies of France and Great Britain, was coming to regard Nazi Germany as nastier and more dangerous – though not in the same devilish category as the USSR. The remilitarization of the Rhineland in 1936 added to the general uneasiness and to the share of blame to be attributed to Germany. Nazi anti-semitism also began to have its effect. It offended decent Gentiles as well as American Jewry (which counted for more than something in Roosevelt's own state of New York), but on the other hand there was good business to be done with Germany and it entered nobody's head in Washington that government could or should interfere with business. Roosevelt and the American people, like European leaders and peoples, were divided and unclear about trends in Europe during the thirties and about what initiatives, if any, to take in respect of them. But they were becoming increasingly anti-Nazi and so anti-German, and this trend was fed by the association of Japan with Germany. Both countries came to be seen as cruel and power-hungry, associated moreover not only by their domestic oppressiveness and external aggressiveness but also in their economic policies which were imposing a blatant economic hegemony in their respective spheres of influence in place of the American ethos of the Open Door which was not only more subtle and more amiable but also calculated to serve American commercial interests.

In November 1936 Roosevelt was re-elected President by a margin of 11 million votes (as against 7 million in 1932). Foreign affairs played little part in the electioneering and what Roosevelt had to say was along conventional keep-out-of-trouble lines. During his second term Roosevelt suffered a decline in popularity which was to be marked by the reduction of his majority to 5 million votes in 1940. The New Deal was not wholly successful and very far from being universally popular. The President's tussle with the Supreme Court and the manoeuvres by which he tried to pack it lost him the support and respect of many who had been among his warmest admirers. Moreover, if tradition was anything to go by, he would cease to be President in 1940 because no President had ever tried to serve more than two terms. He was still a strong President and an intelligent and eloquent one, but his strength was flecked by failures and by the running out of his time. He was not well placed to innovate in foreign affairs, especially if innovation meant running a risk of war. But foreign affairs imposed themselves on his attention. The Japanese attack on China in 1937 with its reminder of the growth of Japanese power and the consequent threat to American power in the Pacific posed for Americans a problem of a special kind. In Great Britain, where it was axiomatic that a war against Germany, Italy and Japan at once would be suicidal, the question debated was whom to conciliate: many people's first choice, notably in the Foreign Office, was Italy, but others, notably in the Treasury and in the services (the pledge that Australia and New Zealand would be protected from Japan by the Royal Navy was a constant consideration and was re-affirmed at the Imperial Conference of 1937) argued that the growth of Japanese power meant that Great Britain should revert to the alliance with Japan which had been abandoned after the First World War under

American pressure. But Americans did not see Japan that way. An American-Japanese alliance was an impossibility and so American-Japanese rivalry created an external threat such as Hitler never posed. It was in the context of the Pacific and East Asia that the United States began to evolve a policy of meeting a threat by extending to an ally – in this case China – all aid short of war and within the Neutrality Act. Moreover, Japanese aggression affected American public opinion owing to the extent of pro-Chinese feeling in the United States.

Partly in response to these worries on his eastern flank and partly because he wanted to be useful, Roosevelt tried in the last two years of peace to mediate in European affairs. He thought of meeting Hitler (as, later, he would hope to resolve other problems by personal contact with Stalin). He proposed a conference of neutrals to discuss modes of international behaviour, disarmament and access to raw materials. Although offended by the manners and behaviour of the dictators, he thought of himself at this time as one of the neutrals rather than as one of the democrats. Nor did the leading democrats do much to swing him to their side. Chamberlain, deep in his ineffective attempts to make friends with Italy and Germany, did his best to head off the American President. He wanted no joint Anglo-American initiative and preferably no American initiative at all – at this point; for it is only fair to add that, under some pressure from cabinet colleagues and the British Ambassador in Washington, he kept up his correspondence with Roosevelt and left a way open for an American initiative later on. Roosevelt might have overridden these obstacles if he had had any clear idea of what to do, but beyond offering his good offices in a vague and general way he was essentially without a European policy. It was hardly possible for him to have such a policy so long as the precondition of all American activity in Europe was to minimize involvement. He did not intend to fight the dictators and there was at this time no government in Europe which wanted him to. He was reduced to following events – in both senses of that phrase. He had little faith in Chamberlain's manoeuvring to avoid war over Czechoslovakia, but privately supported Chamberlain in the absence of anything else to do and publicly stated that the United States would not fight if France and Great Britain went to war for Czechoslovakia. Like most people he was relieved when war was avoided at Munich; like many people he was shocked by Hitler's breach of the Munich agreement and the annihilation of Czechoslovakia in March 1939. By this time his ineffectiveness in European affairs had strengthened Hitler's view that he did not have to worry about the United States, but round about this same time Roosevelt was becoming convinced that war was certain and American involvement at least a possibility. Within six months war had started.

Whereas Churchill was temperamentally a man of action upon whom full responsibility fell after war had begun, Roosevelt was an intellectual in a situation of half-peace half -war. His country was not equipped for war militarily or industrially and his fellow citizens were not ready for it psychologically. His nature and his circumstances alike made him gingerly in pace, and it was only as circumstances developed that he was able to resolve his hesitations about what American opinion would endorse and what he himself ought to do. To Americans the war in Europe presented itself as a contest between Germany on the one hand and Great Britain and France on the other. The question was who would win. A second question was whether it mattered to the United States who won. At the outset Roosevelt established a distinction: the United States was formally a neutral but it cared about the result of the war and, since it cared, it should use 'all methods short of war' to help Great Britain and France to defeat Hitler. This position did not go unchallenged. A not inconsiderable part of the American press and a number of influential public figures were either hostile to Great Britain or entranced with Nazi ideas or genuinely indifferent. Anti-British and anti-imperial groups were, if limited, vocal. There was no surge of pro-British feeling until the Battle of Britain (in which a number of American volunteers took part in defiance of the laws of their country), and even the Battle of Britain had only moderate effect in the western United States and less still in the psychologically more remote Middle West. On the other hand pro-German propaganda was an almost complete failure. The German-American Bund never had more than 6,000 members and could not efface the image of the Nazi as a bully.

But however partisan Americans might become it still did not follow that they could see the war as one which affected American national interests. It was difficult to believe that the United States, bounded by the Atlantic and Pacific Oceans, was not also protected by them. To the ordinary American it appeared that, although there might be a moral case for helping the democracies to defeat Nazism, there were no strategic issues of self-interest which required the United States to make war. The argument, a familiar commonplace in Great Britain, that no state must be allowed to become all powerful in Europe did not make sense to a people separated from Europe by the Atlantic Ocean and not merely by the English Channel. In the thirties the speeds which were to be reached within a generation and the weapons which were to annihilate distances as well as cities were undreamt of by all save a few.

If there was a danger it seemed more likely to emerge from Latin America. Recollecting perhaps German attempts in the First World War to get Mexico, in alliance with Japan, to make war on the United States, and greatly exaggerating the potential threat from the Germans settled in the southern parts of the American continent, the United States turned immediately on the outbreak of war to the problem of immunizing the New World from it. In October 1939 the American states met at Panama in an inter-American conference and agreed to quarantine the New World by proscribing transfers of territory within it from one European power to another and by designating a security zone extending 300–1,000 miles seaward from its eastern shores. Belligerents were required to abjure naval operations in this area. Great Britain, France and Germany contested the legality of this declaration but the British soon ceased to complain when they discovered that the United States was prepared to connive at infractions of the ban, even to the extent of helping to detect and locate German vessels.

The dangers from the German population of Latin America were largely a product of war nerves. There were 300,000 German nationals (*Reichsdeutsche*) and 1.75 million persons of German extraction (*Volksdeutsche*) in the sub-continent, and Nazi propaganda and German trade had both been intensified in the thirties, but the likelihood and consequences of pro-German coups were alike exaggerated. Here, as in other parts of the world, the *Reichsdeutsche* in particular were regarded as a disciplined fifth column which had been prepared by the External Affairs Department of the Nazi Party to play an active role in war. But out of about three million *Reichsdeutsche* living outside the Reich only 30,000 had been enrolled by the party by 1939, and the belief in the sinister efficiency of these people was a myth, a projection of the German reputation for thoroughness coupled with the glamorous novelty of the idea of the fifth column, a term coined during the Spanish civil war. (Absurd stories were spread with hysterical waywardness in many countries, particularly in Europe; these stories were reported by most of the world's leading newspapers and treated as undeniable by parliamentarians and others who raised a patriotic clamour for indiscriminate arrests; nobody was allowed to be what he seemed to be; thousands of innocent persons, including Jewish refugees from Germany, were seized and many of them were shot.)

In the two years and a bit which elapsed between Munich and the American elections of 1940 Roosevelt rearmed, tried to restore peace by diplomacy and gave what aid he could to the western allies. He had asked Congress in January 1938 for a 20 per cent increase in the navy allocations; his request had created an uproar but been granted. The same thing happened a year later when he asked for more money for the army and air forces. Early in 1940 he sent Under Secretary Sumner Welles on a tour of European capitals, sent a special emissary to the Vatican to initiate American-Papal mediation and tried to keep Italy out of the war. All these efforts were failures. The war went on and Ribbentrop, visiting Rome on the heels of Welles, extracted from Mussolini a promise to enter it at some unspecified date. The fall of France shifted American opinion, official and unofficial. After that catastrophe there was no significant opposition to huge and rapid rearmament, and a Selective Service Act was passed in September. The elimination of French power and the probable elimination (as it seemed) of British power too forced Americans to think about the consequences to themselves of the disappearance of two great friendly navies and the emergence of a new German-Italian naval power which had also annexed the French fleet. The United States made unconventionally strong representations to Pétain and his Navy Minister, Admiral Darlan, in order to prevent the French government from surrendering its fleet to Germany in the armistice negotiations. Here was a visible external threat similar to the growth of Japanese power in the Pacific. Roosevelt strengthened his cabinet by inviting two eminent Republicans, Henry L. Stimson (a former Secretary of State) and Frank Knox to become his Secretaries of War and the Navy: unlike Churchill Roosevelt looked to the Right rather than the Left in constructing a war coalition.

When in 1940 it seemed that Hitler was winning the war rather easily Roosevelt still could do little to stop him. He had refused a request from the French government to send troops to Europe. But it was becoming plainer than ever that if Hitler was to be denied a complete victory more would be required of the United States than methods short of war. Helping the western allies meant ensuring the flow of traffic across the Atlantic against U-boats and German surface raiders. It meant supplies and protection; later it was to mean credit too. A first attempt to amend the Neutrality Act failed but Congress soon relented so far as to permit belligerents to buy military as well as non-military goods on a cash-and-carry basis. For the moment cash was not an immediate problem, but carrying was. Then, if the United States was to help protect the carriage, it would have to risk its own vessels and invite German retaliation, engaging in unneutral activities which might lead to war. Non-belligerence, which was essentially an attempt to get the best of two incompatible worlds – those of neutrality and partisanship –

would be put at risk and would prove to be no more than the transitional stage from the one world to a full role in the other.

Roosevelt both saw and accepted the risks rather sooner than most people. Since the American people later proved by their actions that they accepted the consequences, Roosevelt might justly claim that his leadership had been endorsed and any deviousness which might have been involved condoned. But to some extent too his leadership determined the course. His simple presentation of the issues, his patience in unfolding his policies, his readiness to accept responsibility, and his calm handling of critical national decisions – for all the superficial detachment which he sometimes displayed as he turned from affairs of state to his stamp collection – these qualities inevitably led him to form and not merely observe the popular will. In which exercise of power he was giving an example of democratic leadership.

During 1940 Roosevelt resolved to seek a third term in the presidency, an event not only unprecedented in American history but so obnoxious to American instincts that after the war it was prohibited by constitutional amendment. The war was not the only reason for this decision. He was deeply concerned to preserve the social innovations of the New Deal and he saw among leading figures in his own party no liberal Democrat upon whom he could rely to do this. But the conviction that the United States was going to become more deeply involved in war and that he should guide it also played a major part in his decision. At this stage Roosevelt developed the idea that the United States was in substance, if not formally, already under attack. He was a master of the art of democratic communication, and his regular fireside chats – one of the adroitest political uses of radio, which had at this period only been used effectively by politicians of a different stamp, Hitler and Mussolini – gave him the ear and the confidence of the people. They trusted him and when in 1940 they were asked to give him a third term 27 million of them decided to do so : his attractively unusual Republican opponent Wendell Wilkie (with whom in later years Roosevelt thought of making a progressive alliance and a new party) received 22 million votes, a big gap in a modern American presidential election. But it would be wrong to conclude that the 27 million who voted for Roosevelt did so because they were ready to fight against Hitler. They were with Roosevelt in wanting Hitler to be beaten – as were the great bulk of the 22 million who voted for Wilkie – but they wanted Hitler to be beaten by the British and were not yet convinced that the British could not do this without the United States as a fighting ally. Roosevelt himself still clung to the hope that the American role need not be a fighting one or that, if it came to fighting, the American share could be limited to sea and air and would not involve sending army conscripts overseas. During his campaign he promised again and again not to send Americans to fight in foreign lands 'except in case of attack' (on one occasion, subsequently much quoted against him, he left out the proviso) and there must have been many who voted for Roosevelt because he had kept the country out of war and who would have refused him a third term had they supposed that he would not continue to find ways of doing so. No opinion poll during the year before Pearl Harbor showed more than one in five Americans opting for war.

If in 1940 the defeat of France had been offset by the British success in the Battle of Britain, in 1941 the defeat of Great Britain became once more a possibility to be reckoned with. The threat to Great Britain at sea, which had come near to success in the First World War, was manifested on the first day of the second when the German U-30 sank the British passenger ship *Athenia* (the victims included twenty-eight Americans). The threat at sea was posed by mines (laid by surface vessels, submarines or aircraft), surface raiders and U-boats. At the beginning of the war the magnetic mine did much damage to British shipping in coastal waters, but it was quickly mastered by technical countermeasures. Surface raiders, such as the pocket battleships *Graf Spee* and *Deutschland* whose exploits have already been narrated, caused much concern but comparatively little damage. The enduring enemy was the U-boat. Fortunately for the British, Doenitz's fleet was a small one. He divided his boats between Atlantic and North Sea raiding and minelaying and in 1939, his operations were not too alarmingly successful: 114 merchantmen sunk, but at a cost of nine U-boats. (U-boats also sank the aircraft carrier *Courageous* in September and the battleship *Royal Oak* in Scapa Flow in October.) In 1940, however, the U-boat fleet, reinforced by a production drive, began to score abundantly. One convoy lost thirty-two ships in an attack which continued through four consecutive nights, and Hitler's new conquests gave him bases in Norway for U-boats and armed merchant raiders, bases for E-boats along the entire length of the English Channel, and bases for long-range aircraft – the F.W. 200 or Condor – which flew from Bordeaux over wide spaces of the western Atlantic and landed at Trondhjem in Norway, flying back the next day. Great Britain occupied the Faroes and Iceland when Denmark was overrun, but losses in this year mounted at an intolerable rate and Doenitz lost only twenty-two of his rapidly growing force.

Churchill turned to Roosevelt. A week after the British declaration of war in 1939 Churchill had began, as First Lord of the Admiralty, an intimate correspondence with the President. He continued it when he became Prime Minister. The two men developed a very special relationship which was of incalculable benefit to Great Britain. This personal partnership, and its post-war institutionalization in the continuing Anglo-American alliance, appear so solid a part of the international scene that they have come to be regarded as a natural by-product of a common language and common traditions. In fact, however, Anglo-American relations were bad throughout the twenties and despite an improvement at the time of the London Conference in 1930 politicians on both sides continued to refer to each other privately in scathing, sometimes almost scurrilous, terms. There was neither trust nor liking between them. Their two countries were in the process of exchanging roles, particularly on the high seas where Great Britain's cherished naval supremacy was passing away, and against this background politicians sparred with conscious and unconscious jealousy. In constructing their alliance Churchill and Roosevelt had to work with a mixed legacy.

One of the first fruits of their special relationship was the destroyer-bases deal of September 1940 which placed in British hands fifty extra ships with which to prosecute the war against the U-boats. At this time Churchill was at least as worried about the war at sea as he was elated by victory in the Battle of Britain. Roosevelt, after lengthy study and intricate legal argument, agreed to transfer these fifty old but serviceable American destroyers to Great Britain in return for a promise never to surrender the British fleet and for the lease to the United States for ninety-nine years of six bases in the western Atlantic. (Two other bases were accepted as a gift. Churchill had wanted the two deals to be wholly distinct gifts but Roosevelt's advisers, already in difficulties about deciding whether the President could effect the exchange without recourse to Congress, insisted that there must be a substantial, related *quid pro quo*.) But by the end of 1940 British shipping losses were running at the rate of 300,000 tons a month and were destined to rise in February, March and April 1941 to 400,000, 500,000 and 600,000 tons. Great Britain was running out of cash too. The timing of American aid had become vital.

Roosevelt's policy was to aid Great Britain by all means short of war. So much was clear. What was unclear was how and how quickly aid could be made available and, more distantly, whether aid short of war was going to be enough. Soon after his re-election Roosevelt received an urgent plea from Churchill. In reply he moved to depart from all semblance of neutrality in order to ensure that Great Britain should receive the tools it needed to survive. The device was Lend-Lease. He told the American people that if a neighbour's house was on fire it was only common sense and self-protection to lend him a hosepipe. The necessary Bill, which the President always referred to as the Aid to Democracies Bill, was introduced early in January 1941 and signed by the President on 11 March. Thereafter Great Britain placed orders for American materials with the American government which purchased what was required from American firms and paid them. The materials were then lent or leased to the British in return for a promise of payment after the war: the United States agreed to accept post-dated cheques in lieu of cash when there was no cash left.

Lend-Lease was a gesture of very great moral significance. It buoyed Great Britain up by promising to bring nearer the day when it would no longer be fighting virtually alone. Churchill wanted American belligerence even more than he wanted American aid, and to him, as to most people in Great Britain, financial aid was the prelude to co-belligerence, not an alternative. The material benefits of Lend-Lease were at first limited. Until some months after Pearl Harbor and Hitler had forced the United States into war on two fronts American industry was largely on a peace-time basis, the main exception being the Liberty ship programme which launched its first ship in September 1941; Great Britain's own war production was greater than that of the United States. During 1941 Great Britain got little more from the United States than it had imported in 1940 and continued to pay cash for most of it. But what did come was important: for example, in 1941 a million tons of food (a fifteenth of British imports of food) and enough fuel oil to raise stocks from a danger point of 4.5 million tons to 7 million tons, which was maximum storage capacity.

The Lend-Lease Act was followed a few months later by an equally significant act, drawing the United States closer to war. When Hitler attacked the USSR, Roosevelt, following Churchill, promised aid to Stalin. The attack was no surprise to Roosevelt and his advisers who had known from secret sources from early in 1941 that Hitler had signed his first directive for the campaign. Roosevelt and his Secretary of State, Cordell Hull, had been doing their best to keep on reasonably good terms with the USSR, but the anti-Soviet voices in the United States were much more numerous than the anti-British ones had been. Anti-communism was a powerful emotion, especially among Roman Catholics. Stalin's seizure of half Poland, his war on Finland and his annexation of Estonia, Latvia and Lithuania caused bitter anger, which was not confined to the émigré communities from these countries. The time would come when admiration for Russian resistance to Hitler, especially during the battles for Stalingrad, would raise a tide of pro-Russian feeling, while at other levels and later in the war Churchill was to be criticized for being too anti-Russian, but American sympathy for the Russians never sufficed to efface underlying emotions of an opposite order and even at the fearful juncture of Stalingrad's agony – when Americans watched with genuinely bated breath and, perhaps, with less mixed emotions about the Russians than for many years before or after – there was (as too in the Battle of Britain) no plan to do anything to save the city if the last hour should strike. Roosevelt's promise of aid in 1941, therefore, was an act of leadership from which another President, heeding the cross-currents within his country, might have refrained.

Whatever the value of this act in time to come, when it was translated into $11.3 billions' worth of supplies, the immediate effect was slight and could not be otherwise. Even in relation to Great Britain Roosevelt was still treading warily. The Lend-Lease Act itself underlined the peculiar posture of the United States by once more expressly prohibiting the entry of American vessels into combat areas and the use of the US navy for convoy duties. But less than four weeks later the sinking in a single night of ten ships in a British convoy of twenty-one showed that further steps were necessary if the United States set more store by the defeat of Hitler than keeping out of a shooting war. Roosevelt ordered the occupation of Greenland and contemplated occupying the Azores. A force of three battleships with an aircraft carrier, cruisers and destroyers was transferred in May from the Pacific to the Atlantic. In the same month Roosevelt declared an unlimited national emergency. American shipyards were opened to British ships in need of repair. American ocean patrols were extended, shadowed Axis vessels and reported their positions to British units every few hours. A number of coastal cutters were transferred to the British flag. Roosevelt adopted and popularized a phrase of Jean Monnet dubbing the United States 'the arsenal of democracy'. But the United States remained officially non-belligerent and even the sinking of the *Robin Moor* by the Germans provoked no declaration of war.

In May the British scored a ringing success at sea. Raeder, who had more faith in capital ships than Doenitz and was continuously frustrated by Hitler's refusal to allow the indiscriminate use of submarines, renewed his surface challenge. Attempts to do this in 1940 had proved abortive, but in 1941 two new ships, the battleship *Bismarck* and the cruiser *Prinz Eugen*, were ready. Raeder planned a great offensive with them in conjunction with *Scharnhorst* and *Gneisenau*, which had been at Brest since March. But these two battle cruisers had suffered damage and had not recovered by the time that *Bismarck* and *Prinz Eugen* were ready to sail from Gdynia on 18 May: they never sailed the high seas again.

Bismarck was sighted by a Swedish ship soon after she left her German berth, and London was quickly informed. From Bergen she proceeded with *Prinz Eugen* north-westward, passing north of Iceland and thence into the Denmark Strait between Iceland and Greenland. Emerging from the Strait into the Atlantic the two ships were spotted and shadowed. Battle was joined west of Iceland soon after dawn on 24 May by the battleship *Prince of Wales*, also newly commissioned, and the 20-year-old battle-cruiser *Hood*. *Hood* was sunk within minutes by a shell which pierced her decks, and all but three of her complement of 1,419 died. Half an hour later *Prince of Wales*, also hit, was forced to break away, but the aircraft carrier *Victorious* came up and delivered a first attack before the end of the day. *Bismarck* managed to shake off her pursuers but then, incomprehensibly, gave away her position by breaking wireless silence with a long message to the German Admiralty. Even then she might have escaped – as her instructions required her to do – for the British Admiralty got its calculations wrong and misdirected the searchers. But early on the 26th the RAF came into the picture. An aircraft of Coastal Command sighted *Bismarck* and the aircraft carrier *Ark Royal* chased her. *Ark Royal*'s aircraft, having first attacked but missed one of their own attendant cruisers, so wounded *Bismarck* that she became a sitting target for the British ships converging on her from all quarters. Encircled and doomed, she was sunk by torpedoes early in the morning of the 27th. One hundred and fifteen of her complement of about 2,400 were saved.

This German challenge on the surface was never to be renewed (although – with *Scharnhorst* and *Gneisenau* only damaged and *Tirpitz* about to come into service – the British Admiralty could not know this) and the Battle of the Atlantic was once more left to Doenitz, who built up his U-boat force to 120 during 1941 and was contriving to keep as many as half of them at sea at once. Although the pressure from the U-boats was relaxed when half of them were diverted to the Mediterranean at the end of the year, the newer boats were operating at longer ranges and the Atlantic crossing was as hazardous as ever. On the other side Roosevelt took yet further measures. The second half of 1941 was the period in which the Russians were now fighting but the Americans were not. In July Roosevelt nevertheless sent US marines to Iceland to join the British troops who had been stationed there since May 1940. This extension of American arms entailed supply and escort duties by the US navy in an operational zone. In August British and allied shipping was allowed to join American convoys and sail in them. American vessels of war were, without the knowledge of the public or the Congress, fighting an undeclared war farther and farther away from the shores of the American continent. Inevitably the German navy was in fact retaliating, although Hitler kept up the appearance and even the substance of restraint. He authorized in July attacks on American merchantmen but only in a restricted zone in the eastern Atlantic and not on the approach routes to Iceland.

In August, at Placentia Bay in Newfoundland, Roosevelt and Churchill held their first wartime meeting. It had been planned as early as January when Roosevelt's unconventional personal emissary, Harry Hopkins, paid his first wartime visit to London. Attended as it was by the Chiefs of Staff of both countries, the Placentia Bay conference looked like a joint council of war and many on the British side hoped that it was the curtain-raiser for an American declaration of war. Stalin too wanted such a declaration and had made his wishes and his plight clear to Hopkins in Moscow a week earlier. But Roosevelt was not yet ready to take that plunge, perhaps not convinced that he would have to, and the conference's main product was the Atlantic Charter, which many of the British participants regarded as a gust of high-sounding irrelevance. But the Atlantic Charter was more important than that. If the Americans were to go to war they must know why and wherefore, and the Charter set out war aims which would be worth fighting for. Merely contemplating war aims is a step towards war, while in the absence of war aims a democratic leader can hardly ask a people not under attack to start fighting. The Atlantic Charter was a part of the preparation of the American people for war, even though it turned out not to be strictly necessary since the issue of war or peace was decided by Hitler's act and not by the choice of Americans. The Placentia Bay conference was also a prelude to war in another sense, for after it the President ordered an inquiry into what the United States would require if war should come – a pre-war war plan. And thirdly, the conference inaugurated the personal acquaintance between service chiefs which was to grow much closer and be formalized by the creation of the Anglo-American Combined Chiefs of Staff Committee.

At sea the war continued to suck at the American resolve to avoid it. In September, following an astutely publicized encounter between a U-boat and the USS *Greer* – an inconclusive engagement described by

Roosevelt as an attack on an American vessel – the President announced that the United States would protect non-American as well as American shipping in the Atlantic security zone and would fire at sight on all German and Italian warships seen there. Incidents multiplied. American opinion was growing more anti-German than anti-war. In October and November 1941 the neutrality legislation was being progressively eroded by Congress. American merchantmen were armed and the President was empowered to send American ships into British ports. The United States was virtually making war in defiance of the rules. But it showed no sign of actually declaring war: undeclared war was serving the dual purpose of helping the democracies and keeping the bulk of Americans out of the firing line (those who wanted to go and fight were tacitly allowed to join the British or Canadian forces). When the United States was attacked at Pearl Harbor the President only asked Congress to declare war on Japan. Then, four days later, Germany declared war on the United States.

This act by Hitler has been described as one of gratuitous folly. It is certain that, by adding the United States to his overt enemies at a time when Germany was fighting both the British Empire and the USSR, Hitler sealed his doom. But the die was cast before December 1941. By the time Hitler declared war the United States was already an active ally of the British and the Russians. Up to the middle of 1941 Hitler had every reason to keep the United States out of the war at almost any cost and he did, as we shall see, set himself firmly not only to avoid provoking Roosevelt but also to ignore Roosevelt's provocations of him. After the turn of the year, however, the situation changed. With the launching of Barbarossa, Hitler was involved in the dreaded war on two fronts, while the United States was, though neutral in name, already decreasingly so in substance. Hitler therefore embarked on the policy of goading the Japanese into war partly in order to distract the Americans from Europe and the Atlantic and partly also because, obsessed with the British, whose survival forced him to fight the USSR with half a hand tied behind his back, he wanted Japan to deal Great Britain a knock-out blow in Singapore and India. In pursuance of this complicated aim he was forced, in November 1941, to promise Japan that Germany would declare war on the United States if Japan did. This policy failed because the Japanese blows at Pearl Harbor and Singapore were not knock-outs and because of the unforeseen capacity of the Americans to fight, uniquely, a war in every quarter of the world.

Hitler badly misjudged the Americans, partly because of his preconceptions and partly because he was badly served. He entertained fantastically wrong notions of American society and politics. He believed that the masses of decent Americans (whose ancestors, he incorrectly recalled, had failed by only one congressional vote to adopt German as their national language) were on the verge of revolt against a dominant Jewish ruling class and that the United States, so far from being a bastion of democracy, was a corrupt and demoralized country fit and eager for the reception of Nazi ideas. To Hitler, Roosevelt, especially in his 1940 election campaign, was a desperate trickster clutching at any opportunity to win votes and retain power in defiance of a groundswell of popular enlightenment. On this view the United States was not nearly such a formidable enemy as its material power might make it appear. Besides being blinded by his prejudices Hitler was misled by exceptionally inept reporting by his emissaries in Washington, especially his service attachés who, pandering to these prejudices, devoted more ink to political nonsense than to technical reports. He overrated and misjudged the pro-Nazi German-American Bund; failed to appreciate the distaste of Americans for his racialism; overestimated the addiction of Americans to a comfortable neutrality; and mistook the prominence of men like Colonels Charles Lindbergh and Robert R. MacCormick, Senators Burton K. Wheeler and Gerald P. Nye and the 'radio priest' Father Charles E. Coughlin for real political influence.

He was also, and more pardonably, misled by the American record in the thirties. The economic crisis and isolationism prevented the United States from playing an effective role in world affairs in that decade. Hitler understood this, but he did not understand how far war would change American attitudes and policies. When Japan invaded Manchuria in 1931 (partly to forestall a possible Russian move which could precipitate a new Russo-Japanese war) the Secretary of State, Henry L. Stimson, had toyed with the idea of intervention. He was well aware of the force of isolationism in the United States but he hoped that by a show of determination he might influence the political balance in Tokyo where a civilian cabinet was at odds with the army factions which had provoked the fighting in Manchuria. This cabinet had no desire to begin a war with China in order to stave off a war with the USSR, but it fell. Stimson thereupon proposed economic sanctions against Japan but President Herbert Hoover did not like the idea (nor did the British government). Stimson pressed his interventionist policy again a few months later when Japanese troops were landed at Shanghai, but the President remained opposed to it and Stimson knew that American opinion would not tolerate it: he was using the prospect of sanctions as a counter, but in the knowledge that he could not play it. In the Ethiopian crisis Stimson's successor, Cordell Hull, instituted voluntary sanctions against Italy but there was little cooperation between the United States and the leading members of the League and Hull's initiative merely associated the United States with a failure. The remilitarization of the Rhineland, the Spanish civil war, the conclusion of the Axis and Anti-Comintern Pacts, the extension of the war in the east to China itself in the summer of 1937, the sinking of the American gunboat *Panay* and three tankers on the Yangtse in December all reinforced the American desire to keep clear of wars; and were seen to. Moreover, Roosevelt's unhappy attempts to intervene diplomatically in European politics in the late thirties, revealing his own hesitations and the hiatus between the American and British governments, roused only Hitler's scorn, and his attempts to avert war at the last moment were brushed off by Hitler. The war was going to be short. Either Great Britain and France would do nothing to help Poland or they would intervene and be quickly subdued. On this basis there was no American problem. But the basis was wrong. The war was not short and the Americans soon began to take a menacing hand in it.

The six months which embraced Hitler's invasion of the USSR and his declaration of war against the United States marked also the destruction, by his own acts, of his power of initiative in world affairs. The failure of Barbarossa was crucial, for had he defeated the USSR before the end of the year he would have been supreme in the European continent and either he would have issued no declaration of war against the United States or he could have done so without involving himself in the pincer movement which finally crushed him. It was the burden of Barbarossa which led him from a European to a world strategy, from a league in which he could certainly play and possibly win to a league in which he must lose.

But, secondly, the survival of Great Britain was also crucial because, without it, it is unlikely that the United States would have joined the war as an ally of the USSR against Germany.

Hitler's failures in Barbarossa and the Battle of Britain were both narrow ones. Something has already been said about both these engagements and more will be said later in this book about the sources of Russian endurance and victory. If Hitler had lived (as Napoleon did) to ponder his mistakes and failures in tranquillity, he would no doubt have fought the battles of the autumn of 1940 and the autumn of 1941 over and over again. He might also have puzzled no less over the incomprehensibility of the Americans and the British, who behaved in these critical years 1939–41 with what, to an outsider, could only seem perverse inconsequence. If Hitler made mistakes about the Anglo-Saxon peoples, whom in some moods he judged to be not much inferior to the German, he could claim that he was to some degree misled by their illogicality as well as by his own preconceptions and advisers.

He could hark back to the British declaration of war at the very beginning. This declaration, which was a formal consequence of the German attack on Poland two days earlier, had no discernible practical results at the time. If it was anything more than an empty formality it implied a determination to attack Germany. But neither Great Britain nor France had forces or plans for doing so, nor did they do so. (The only plans extant were for air operations in response to full-scale German action in the west.) In the event it was Hitler who attacked them and not the other way round. Seven months later he defeated France and prepared to defeat Great Britain. His plans posed a threat to American security which the Americans could, by the use of naval and air forces, have helped to defeat. Yet they too declined, as the British had declined in 1939, to take any direct action, and if they abstained at this critical point they might be counted most unlikely to intervene in a European war at any other. On this premise Hitler's own declaration of war at the end of 1941 was a formal act without practical consequences – like the British declaration in 1939; the practical consequences, if any, would be in the Pacific where the Americans were already embroiled with the Japanese. But the Americans, who had abstained from direct action in the face of the threat in 1940, were ready by 1941 to throw themselves into the European war and even give it priority over a Pacific war. The intervention which had seemed politically impossible in 1940 became automatic in 1941. To Hitler it might have appeared that the British and Americans had leaders who did not understand power. The British had ostensibly engaged themselves in 1939 to do something which they had not the power to do; the Americans in 1940 had the power to intervene in a situation of critical importance to themselves but abstained from doing so. But in this assessment of the seeming political ineptitude of his adversaries Hitler failed to take account of Aristotle's diagnosis of the nature of the commercial state, slow to action but rich in the capacity to procrastinate and then triumph – not to mention Bernard Shaw's analysis of the Englishman's genius for triumphing through an insensitivity to the dangers of his own position amounting to a kind of sublime arrogance.

Hitler had for years intended to make war on the USSR but he never wanted a war against either Great Britain or the United States. These

wars he merely accepted when they came. He tried to come to terms with
Great Britain and then to defeat it, and when both these efforts failed he
turned away. He tried for a time to avoid war with the United States. On
the outbreak of war in 1939 he forbade attacks on passenger ships, and
when the *Athenia* was sunk with its twenty-eight American passengers
he had the crew of U-30 sworn to secrecy on their return to port and
tried to persuade the world that the sinking was a British stunt to drag
the United States into war. In October he permitted attacks on enemy
merchant ships without warning and on enemy passenger ships after
warning (the need for this warning was lifted at the beginning of
November), but he still refused to sanction attacks on neutrals. He
allowed the *City of Flint*, which had been captrued, taken to Norway
and there released by the Norwegians (who interned the German
boarders), to proceed without further molestation and he kept to this
reticent policy despite the insistent pleas of his naval advisers. If Roosevelt's only concern had been to avoid incidents in the Atlantic he would
have had no great problem, for Hitler wanted to avoid such incidents
too. As late as the summer of 1941 Hitler was still turning a deaf ear to
Raeder's pleas to sanction indiscriminate retaliation in the undeclared
war which the Americans were waging in the Atlantic.

Thus Hitler had pursued in the Atlantic a policy of avoiding conflict
with the United States up to the last months before he declared war. But
in the Pacific, where he operated at second remove through his Japanese
allies, he had the choice between restraining Japan in order to prolong
American non-belligerency and, alternatively, egging Japan on. He
chose the latter course. Engaged in a war on two fronts in which the
Americans were becoming unofficially or even formally involved, he
wanted to create a second front for the Americans too. Japan could
open this front and at the same time attack the British Empire which
had so sadly failed to respond to Hitler's offer of an honourable place in
a world partitioned on Hitlerian lines. Hitler knew from his agents that
Japan had decided not to attack the USSR, and, by relaying to Tokyo
his own version of Great Britain's helpless plight and his contemptuous
estimate of American valour, he encouraged the more bellicose members of the Japanese cabinet. Discussions in Washington between the
Americans and the Japanese during the autumn puzzled and worried
Ribbentrop and his Ambassador in Tokyo, who could not make out
whether they represented a genuine attempt to avoid war. Even after the
fall of the comparatively moderate Konoye cabinet and the appointment of General Tojo as Prime Minister on 18 October the Germans
were afraid that the Japanese might fail them, and so in November

Ribbentrop went so far as to promise to help Japan in a war against the United States and not to make a separate peace. On 11 December Hitler fulfilled this promise. Italy declared war too.

After 1941 Hitler started no more wars. He gradually lost those he had started.

Part III

EUROPE UNDER THE NAZIS

CHAPTER 11

The New Order

FOR four years Germany dominated the greater part of Europe more completely than it had ever been dominated before. How far was this domination also purposeful? Every conqueror sets out with a complex of aims. On the one hand he has ideas, more or less precise, about what he wants to do with the lands he intends to conquer. On the other hand his attitude will be to conquer first and leave the rest till afterwards. Among the Nazis there were some who regarded the conquests of 1939–41 as a prelude and an opportunity: they had a Grand Design, even though this design was more of a vision than a plan and even though they could not always agree among themselves about what they wanted or how to achieve it. There were also others, more pragmatic, who treated the gains of these years as assets to be exploited in the war that was still going on: in so far as they had a Grand Design, it was one with a low priority for the time being. Hitler himself belonged rather to the pragmatic school. He was concerned first and foremost with winning the war and one of his keenest interests – perhaps his main interest – was in military equipment and military tactics. But he was hardly less preoccupied with the two great questions of *Lebensraum* and race, and his ideas and writing were the stuff out of which men like Alfred Rosenberg and Heinrich Himmler, although often with different interpretations and opposing aims, began to create a New Order for Europe during the war years.

Politically the New Order was simple. German hegemony was to be extended by German arms and accepted by everybody else. Nazi values were to be exported from their German centre and the pattern of Nazi revolution and Nazi life repeated in other lands. The first pre-condition of the New Order was conquest: land had to be got. How much land was left vague. It adapted itself to circumstances. At the high tide of German successes the concept of the *Grossraum*, or Greater Germanic Estate, embraced Europe from the Atlantic to the Urals, although a little earlier it had seemed to make do with rather less of Russia. The determining features of the *Grossraum* were not its borders but its nature. Instead of finding where people lived and then drawing permanent or semi-permanent frontiers to fit the ethnic facts, the Nazis began by designating an area and then moved people around in order to make demography fit the facts of power. The *Grossraum* therefore might be any size and in 1942 one writer envisaged it as covering one sixth of the globe. It was not a fixed area but a biological habitat like a nature reserve. It was where the German family lived.

The Germans themselves were to be the proprietors and directors of the *Grossraum* but not its only inhabitants. It would also contain the other Nordic races, who were only a little inferior to the Germans but would have no effective political or economic power; and non-Nordic peoples who, suitably regrouped and assigned to their economic functions, would be the helots of the *Grossraum*. (Hitler liked reading history books and admired Sparta.) These sub-human varieties would be kept in subjection by, among other devices, depriving them of education. As Hitler himself put it, they were to 'know just enough to understand road signs, so as not to get themselves run over by our vehicles. For them the word "liberty" must mean the right to wash on holidays'. His aim in the USSR was to 'Germanize the country by the settlement of Germans and treat the natives as redskins'. An even more inferior variety of human being, too vicious to be allowed any place however menial, would be eliminated. Thus re-ordered, the *Grossraum* would be made economically self-sufficient, independent of the other major areas in the world although specially linked, in some versions, with Africa in a Eurafrican super *Grossraum* which was partly just an even more grandiose vision, partly an extension designed to furnish Europe with the raw materials of which it had not got enough, and partly a way of finding an exciting but peripheral role for the Italians, whose position in a purely European *Grossraum* was, for obvious reasons, never spelled out.

Given these imaginings there were two main fields for action, the demographic and the economic. People had to be moved or removed; the work they did had to be reorganized to fit the plan for a Germano-centric autarkic Europe. During the war quite a lot was undertaken demographically, but the economic planning of the New Order was overshadowed by the exigencies of war economics.

The economic aspects of the New Order were never condensed into a single document or plan and it is to some extent misleading to propound any such plan by piecing together what was said about it by different people at different times. Nevertheless a general outline existed.

The Nazis were centralizers, but half-hearted ones. At one level they believed in the concentration of power. They converted federal Weimar Germany into a unitary state and they would have carried this centralizing process beyond Germany into Europe, making Berlin the political, economic and cultural – in sum, the totalitarian – capital of a super-state. But although they focused power on a single central capital, they also diffused it among the departments and agencies which were centred in the capital. This fragmentation was partly a reflection of Hitler's policy and his character: he was not an administrator and he ruled by dividing. It was also a consequence of lack of foresight. Especially during the war new problems thrust themselves upon Germany's rulers and the Nazi way of dealing with them was to create new agencies. In this respect they acted more like the Americans with their similar propensity for bureaucratic proliferation than like the British or French, who have characteristically preferred to accommodate new problems and new functions within the settled framework of the existing civil service and the existing machinery of government. The New Order, had it come into being, would have been controlled by a single but fissiparous and philoprogenitive machine.

This machine would have existed to serve Germany's interests but it would have claimed incidentally to serve other interests too. The core of the *Grossraum* – a Germany which had engulfed Alsace-Lorraine, Luxembourg, parts of Belgium, and Silesia – would be to Europe what the Ruhr was to Germany. Here would be most of Europe's heavy industry and all its arms industries. Beyond it industries would exist on sufferance only and their primary purpose would be the production of consumer goods for Germans. Each conquered area would be a tributary, judged and regulated in terms of the needs of Germany. Besides consumer goods these areas would produce food, and their agriculture would be re-planned to suit Germany: more arable in Denmark, for example, and less dairy farming. In return Germany would provide a guaranteed market for all Europe's food production and abolish unemployment. The countries beyond the central core would, by virtue of centralized planning, become specialized producers knowing what they could export, how much credit they could have and how much labour they would need; an international labour pool would enable the planners to operate an effective international division of labour. This picture was neither entirely unfamiliar nor entirely unattractive to Europe. The notion of an economic entity larger than any existing political unity, and of the need for Europe to organize economically on a wider scale, had been propagated by various champions of European unity ranging from men in official positions like Aristide Briand in France and Paul van Zeeland in Belgium to the League of Nation's Inquiry for European Union and private enthusiasts like Count Richard Coudenhove-Kalergi. Europe moreover had had more than its fair share of economic instability between the wars and might therefore be persuaded that it was worth forgoing the freedom to choose for itself what it would make or grow, if it could buy stability in exchange for economic sovereignty.

The German New Order was in this sense an attempt to construct an economy broader than a national economy and it suffered from the basic defect of most such schemes attempted in a nationalist world. Its scope was international but its purpose was national. Long range planning, long term agreements, guaranteed markets, fixed exchange rates, a European clearing system – plans to link the Baltic and the Black Seas by an Oder–Danube canal, the Rhine and the Po by another, plans to dam the Straits of Gibraltar in order to endow all Europe with cheap power – all these things could not conceal the fact that the basis of the New Order was German power and German requirements and not a European cooperative. The benefits to everybody else would be the crumbs from the rich man's table. It could hardly look otherwise during a war.

Ideas of this kind were peace aims rather than war aims and when the war turned into a long war and a losing war they were inevitably submerged. Up to 1942 the New Order was proffered with a kind of openhanded exultation and in the belief that it would strike some response, but from 1942 onwards the voice of Germany turned from allurements to warnings, prophesying communist horrors to come rather than a new Eden. At the same time the New Order, such as it was, had to be applied to keeping Germany going in a painfully immediate present. Instead of enlarging and fertilizing Europe's economy, it had to nourish Germany's war effort.

The lengthening war also held up the demographic planning of the New Order but it did not do so entirely. Some movements of population were undertaken and horribly much was achieved in the war of extermination. Both these aspects of the matter fell primarily, though not entirely, within the province of the SS and they acquired from the SS their overriding characteristic of ferocious brutality.

The SS grew out of a small blackshirted bodyguard originally called the *Stosstrupp Hitler* and renamed *Schutzstaffeln* (SS) in 1925. Even more than the Nazi Party itself they were the instrument of Hitler's personal will. They were drenched in Nazi ideology and they enjoyed a life of special licence which was nowhere better illustrated than on the very slopes of Hitler's own Bavarian eyrie where they could revel offduty in an efficiently organized orgiastic hedonism calculatingly and cynically proffered to them by their non-alcoholic and near-chaste Führer. They were the principal beneficiaries of the destruction of the

SA in 1934 and from that time their power expanded as they absorbed the police forces of Germany, built up a well equipped private army of thirty divisions, became an economic force in control of a large part of the Reich's labour and of extensive factories, and duplicated their German functions and powers in occupied Europe. The SS became the rulers of Germany, the effective core within the amorphous mass of the Nazi Party. Their chief from 1929 (when their strength was under 300 men) was Heinrich Himmler, a man pre-eminent among the senior Nazi leaders for his mediocrity, a quality which ensured Hitler's confidence almost – but not quite – to the end. He was said to be so obsessed by blondness that he could not bear to have dark-haired people around. He had a little knowledge of Germanic origins and runic inscriptions which he pursued with the unintelligent concentration of a man whose hobby is his life, but paradoxically he was also a visionary with ambition who throve in the struggle for power because of his enthusiasm for a purer Germanic world on Nazi principles – which he accepted wholesale and uncritically without any of the cynical reservations of the sharper-minded Hitler or the softer-living Goering. Himmler was also acute enough and lucky enough to rise to the top in the Nazi jungle and stay there. Before the war ended he was not only *Reichsführer SS*, Chief of the German Police and Minister of the Interior but also Commander-in-Chief of the Home Army and he had twice – on each occasion briefly, ineptly and for the most part at a distance – held command of an Army Group in the field. He had become a contender for supreme power in succession to Hitler, although Hitler himself said in 1945 that Himmler would not do as his successor because he had no culture.

The annexation of the police by the SS was the vital step in the transformation of the SS from its modest beginnings within the Nazi machine into the power which ruled Germany and terrorized a continent. In Weimar Germany each province had its own government and its own police force. The most important of these forces was the Prussian police controlled by the Prussian Minister of the Interior, who was a more influential personage than the shadowy Reich Minister of the Interior. As Minister of the Interior and then Prime Minister in Prussia, Goering was, before he exchanged cruelty for easefulness, the most powerful policeman in Germany. Himmler was chief of the Bavarian police in Munich. But Himmler also got himself a subordinate post in the Prussian system.

The Prussian police was a rambling system whose branches included the Schupo (traffic police and men on the beat), the Orpo (*gendarmerie* living in barracks), the Kripo or criminal detectives, the Gestapo or secret state-security service, and special services like the fire brigades and

railway police. Himmler became deputy head of the Prussian Gestapo
and he also became Chief of Police in various other provinces besides
Bavaria. In 1936 a unified German police force was created with Himm-
ler at its head, and in 1943 he became also Reich Minister of the
Interior, an office which, with the centralizing tendencies of the Third
Reich, had by then outstripped its Prussian counterpart in importance.

After 1936 the next step was to incorporate the detective and intelligence functions of the police into the SS. The new German police was
divided into two main branches, the Orpo on the one hand and on the
other the Sipo or Security Police embracing the Kripo and the Gestapo.
As head of the Sipo Himmler appointed Reinhardt Heydrich who was
already head of the *Sicherheitsdienst* (SD) or security services of the
SS. For a short time the Sipo under Heydrich remained with the rest of
the police within the Ministry of the Interior, but shortly before the outbreak of war it was transferred to one of the main branches of the SS,
the newly created R S H A – *Reichssicherheitshauptamt* or Reich Security
Division. Departments III and VI of the R S H A were the S D (Home)
and S D (Foreign); Department IV was the Gestapo and its sub-depart-
ment IV 4b meant Jews. In personal terms the R S H A was Heydrich
until his assassination in Prague in May 1942, when he was succeeded by
Ernst Kaltenbrunner; Department IV was Heinrich Müller; IV 4b was
Karl Adolf Eichmann.

The chain of command Heydrich–Müller–Eichmann exhibits the
variety of the SS. Müller, the head of the Gestapo, was the type of the
faceless professional policeman who knew his job and did it; he was for
a long time not a member of the Nazi Party; his origins were obscure
and probably lowly and he had a chip on his shoulder. It was in a sense
fitting that in April 1945 he simply vanished after walking out of Hitler's
bunker to go back to his office and has never been heard of since. He has
been suspected of being in Russian pay and of taking refuge in Moscow
at the end of the war, where he is said to have died in 1948. Heydrich
and Eichmann, his immediate superior and subordinate, were very
different. Both had goals rather than jobs. Heydrich's driving force
came from ambition, Eichmann's from obsession. Both were virulent
anti-semites. Eichmann became in practice the principal agent in the
destruction of the Jews, supervising and directing the application of
Nazi racial policies first in Bohemia and Moravia and then in Poland
and ultimately in Hungary. After the war he escaped to South America
but in 1960 he was traced and kidnapped by a Jewish organization and
delivered to Israel where he was tried, condemned and executed.
Heydrich, a failed naval officer, was Hitler's right-hand man in the

massacre of June 1934 and it was he rather than Himmler who ensured that the victors should be the SS and not the army. He pursued his course by vigour harnessed to ability and by intrigue served by his intimate knowledge of the personal weaknesses of the senior Nazi chiefs and the skeletons in their cupboards. As head of the RSHA he was one of the most powerful men in Germany, although not in the top rank, and it has been conjectured that when he took the office of Protector of Bohemia and Moravia in 1941 he did so with an eye to climbing higher by this circuitous route. He was as ruthless and violent as any of his colleagues and much more intelligent. (He also played the violin and at his funeral the cultivated, anti-Nazi Admiral Canaris wept.) His death removed Himmler's most formidable rival.

Heydrich was still a little-known figure in the thirties. Müller and Eichmann were even less well known, and comparatively few members of the general public would have recognized them. But the SS itself was not difficult to recognize. First in Germany and then throughout Europe its members strode along the streets or hurtled along the roads in cars in the special costumes designed to make them look as terrifying as possible – the sinister uniformity of the black shirt, no jacket to impede the swing of the arm, the expensive breeches and the hard shiny boots, and on every cap the head of death as a *memento mori* to every living citizen. The complexity of the German SS and police added to the terror. In occupied Europe the men of the Orpo were the visible intimation of police rule and police brutality. They were the men who could be seen rounding up one's neighbours and who might at any time of day or night come for oneself, while behind them in the recesses of buildings whose whispered addresses became household fears were the men of the Gestapo and the SD.

Himmler's long-term plans for the re-ordering of Europe were based on reducing the Slavs by 30 million and planting a German upper crust in selected parts of Poland, the Baltic states and the USSR. In 1942 the SS produced a blueprint or Eastern Plan covering the next twenty-five years. It involved the establishment of temporary German strongpoints, partly garrisons and partly colonies, peopled by peasants under arms. These settlements would be at central points. At the same time permanent settlements were to be planted at the extreme edge of the *Grossraum*, where, at first under SS control, they would shield the *Grossraum* like the marcher principalities of feudal times. This Germanic population would reach 3.5 million at the end of twenty-five years. Among them would be a local population of landless poor. The plan was revised and re-issued but at the beginning of 1943 Hitler decreed that all these schemes must await the end of the war and so stopped Himmler from putting it into operation. At about the same time some Americans, including the Secretary of the Treasury Henry Morgenthau, were evolving a similar plan for turning Germany into an agricultural zone after the war.

Himmler was concerned not only to dispatch Reich Germans out into the *Grossraum* but also – and not without a degree of contradiction – to gather *Volksdeutsche* back into the Reich. (Hitler was more interested in the latter than the former programme.) As a first step *Volksdeutsche* in occupied territories were treated as a privileged class, given positions of minor authority where possible, allowed to use special shops and so on, but this policy, first adopted in Czechoslovakia and Poland, sharpened the Russians' natural distrust of *Volksdeutsche* and led to large numbers of them being deported to the east before the Germans could reach them. Himmler's plans were further confounded by disputes among the Germans themselves. While the SS started registering the *Volksdeutsche* whom they found round the Black Sea and elsewhere with a view to resettlement, for diverse reasons the army commanders, Rosenberg and Goering all wanted them left where they were. It also transpired that fewer of them still spoke German than had been expected. The only transfer of any consequence effected by the SS in the USSR was the eviction of a number of Ukrainians from the neighbourhood of Zhitomir and Kalinovka to make way for Volhynian Germans who did not want to go there. Significantly perhaps this single practical example had not been envisaged by the Eastern Plan. It created trouble in the German administration of the Ukraine and squabbling in Berlin and had no sensible purpose. Apart from this there was no considerable displacement of the *Volksdeutsche* of the USSR until the tide of war turned and about 300,000 of them were swept westward not as settlers but as refugees.

In other areas Himmler was less obstructed by rival authorities. One hundred and thirty-two thousand *Volksdeutsche* from Bessarabia and Northern Bukovina and another 32,000 from southern Bukovina and the Dobrudja were earmarked for Germany and about 46,000 of them were settled in annexed territories; the rest probably spent the war in transit camps. Another 9,000 Germans from Warsaw and 14,000 from Slovenia had a similar fate. Poland was to be sorted out by moving 164,000 Germans westward from what had been the Russian zone in 1939 and an equivalent number of Ukrainians and White Russians from the original German zone eastwards. In addition 80,000 Baltic Germans were to find new homes in Poland. In the west Alsace-Lorraine and

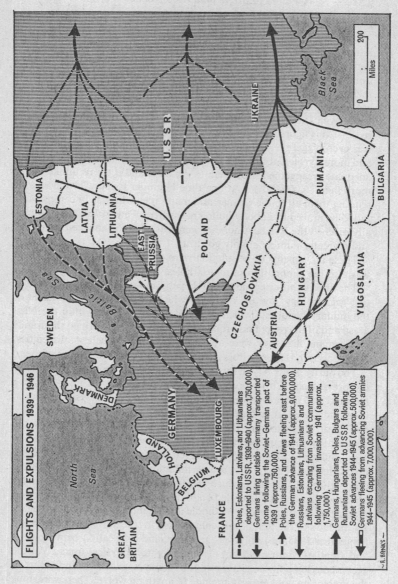

FLIGHTS AND EXPULSIONS 1939-1946

Poles, Estonians, Latvians, and Lithuanians deported to U.S.S.R, 1939-1940 (approx.1,750,000).

Germans living outside Germany transported home following the Soviet–German pact of 1939 (approx.750,000).

Poles, Russians, and Jews fleeing east before the German advance of 1941 (approx.9,000,000).

Russians, Estonians, Lithuanians and Latvians escaping from Soviet communism following German invasion 1941 (approx. 1,750,000).

Germans, Hungarians, Poles, Bulgars and Rumanians deported to U.S.S.R following Soviet advances 1944-1945 (approx.500,000).

Germans fleeing from advancing Soviet armies 1944-1945 (approx.7,000,000).

~R. BANKS ~

Luxembourg were prepared for Germanization by removing 105,000 inhabitants ('foreign elements') from the former and 7,000 from the latter. In practice these schemes produced chaos and a degree of incidental economic disruption which led to complaints about the damage done to the war effort by the SS. Some of the Baltic Germans found themselves moved back to where they had come from after only a few months, while the fate of the German-speaking Tyrolese was like a scene from Dante. In a plebiscite in 1939, 185,365 opted for the Reich; by 1941 this figure had somehow grown to 220,000 and the next year it was even bigger; but while somebody was apparently persuading more and more Tyrolese to ask to be moved to the Reich, nobody was making adequate arrangements for them to get there and it seems unlikely that more than 80,000 did so. At one time Himmler toyed with the idea of sending them all to the Crimea and many spent the war in camps waiting to be moved to nobody quite knew where. Few *Volksdeutsche* actually reached the Reich. A number were settled in the annexed territories and a greater number simply got lost.

These movements of population were only a part of the plan. There was also the elimination of undesirables, notably Jews and Slavs.

The attempt to exterminate whole peoples was a logical consequence of Nazi ideology, and the degree to which it succeeded was a result of the military conquests which placed millions of Jews within the Nazi grasp and of the reiterated propaganda which so transformed thousands of Germans that they were able to perform the cruellest obscenities. Many thousands more witnessed them or were otherwise aware of them.

The purity of the Aryan race did not require mass murder. It required the prevention of inter-breeding, but the prevention of inter-breeding required also the prevention of all human contact since even the strictest laws and the most intense propaganda cannot guarantee correct responses of the heart and the flesh. Moreover, in Nazi mythology the purity of the Aryan race was linked with the salvation of the human race, and since both doctrines posited a Jewish enemy, they together bred a hatred of Jewry and a determination to exterminate it. The discrimination against Jews, which was first prescribed by law immediately after the Nazis took power, led on to degradation, outlawry, pillage and murder; mass murder was methodically organized after the war began. By the laws of the first phase, culminating in the Nuremberg decrees of September 1935, not only were marriage and fornication between Jews and Gentiles condemned but also the slightest physical touch. Yet the accompanying pathological ravings of some Nazi zealots and a part of the press were not seen as a prelude to anything worse. There was some emigration and a few suicides, but even when a special Jewish Bureau was established without any concealment in 1936 (Eichmann was its chief) hope and incredulity were still allowed to prevail over desperation. Emigration moreover was baulked by prohibitions on the export of property and by the inaccessibility of the obvious haven, Palestine, where the British, caught between the irreconcilable promises given to Jews and Arabs in the First World War, refused to admit more than 1,500 Jews a month unless they brought £1,000 apiece with them.

But persecution was already grievous and in November 1938 a young seventeen-year-old Jew called Herschel Grynszpan decided to force it upon the attention of an unwilling world by a desperate deed. He murdered a German diplomat in the Paris embassy, Ernst vom Rath (whom he mistook for the Ambassador). Retaliation took the form of a pogrom which the Nazis were able to organize in advance because von Rath lingered in hospital before dying. News of his death reached Hitler in Munich where he had gone to celebrate the fifteenth anniversary of his 1923 putsch. Local party and SS authorities had already been warned of what was coming and of the need to conceal the fact that it was pre-arranged. Traffic in selected areas was diverted, the telephone lines of Jewish subscribers were cut and at 2 a.m. organized squads wrecked 200 synagogues and other Jewish property (including a Jewish sanatorium), murdered seventy Jews in the Buchenwald concentration camp and arrested 20,000 Jews. So much plate glass was broken that the outburst of this one night was given the name of the *Kristallnacht*. In addition the Jewish community was collectively condemned to pay twenty-five million marks for the repair of damaged property and also a fine of one billion marks – which practically dispossessed it of the goods and enterprises which had not already been taken from it. Jews were expelled from hospitals, old folks' homes and schools, and public places were put out of bounds to them. A proposal to take away their driving licences was discussed but dropped. No foreign government protested. The British Foreign Secretary, Lord Halifax, ruled that a protest would constitute unjustifiable interference in the internal affairs of another state and warned his subordinates against giving unnecessary offence to Hitler. In this last year before the war the German Jews began to flee their fate, but the acquisition of Austria and Bohemia and Moravia added to the Reich as many Jews as left it. From the Nazi point of view the problem remained the same size – about 357,000. Then the conquest of Poland enormously increased that number, multiplying it by ten.

In 1938 Hitler discussed with Himmler the killing of whole sections of the population of Czechoslovakia ånd a year later similar discussions took place as a prelude to the Polish campaign. SS chiefs conferred with army chiefs about the modalities of this first instalment of the New Order. The ruling class, the intelligentsia, the Jews were to be collected and killed. The German Jews were not thrown into the programme at this stage partly because the Nazis had not finally made up their minds between deportation and extermination, and partly for logistical reasons: there was so much to be done first in Poland and later in the USSR that the mills of destruction could not grind fast enough.

The last serious attempt to purge Germany of Jews without killing them was the Madagascar plan. This plan had been adumbrated before the war and was revived after the fall of France, whose colony Madagascar was. The plan was to send all European Jews to this island in the Indian Ocean where they could be autonomous under German sovereignty and would, as Hitler put it, be hostages against the 'good behaviour of their co-racialists in America'. Problems of transport and the like were examined in some detail but the war did not end with the fall of France and so the Germans could not get hold of Madagascar or send Jews there. Instead they kept the German Jews in Germany until they could be sent to Poland to be killed along with Jews from other parts of Europe.

In the interval between the defeat of Poland and the attack on the USSR, Hitler set up a new agency, Operations Staff Rosenberg, which began as a research body for the collection of material about Jews, communists and Freemasons and the formulation of a policy for combating these pests. With a hideous simulation of scholarly application it assembled a huge library and, by combining pillage with study, amassed incidentally a fabulous art collection. It was expanded into a Ministry for the East, in which thousands of industrious, ingenious and even learned Germans worked away at schemes which had no relevance to the war going on around them; their activities were viewed with irritated scorn by the professional staff of the German Foreign Ministry and with even more irritated jealousy by Ribbentrop who considered that Rosenberg was being allowed to poach on his own preserves as Foreign Minister. Since the East meant the Baltic states and the USSR, Rosenberg became on paper the potential disposer of the Russian empire. His aim was to destroy the Russian state in perpetuity by fragmenting and pastoralizing it and by creating new separatist states out of the debris. Hitler had decided to give Leningrad to Finland and Bessarabia and Odessa to Rumania. From what remained Rosenberg intended to fashion at least four states: a Russian rump, renamed Muscovy, stretching from the Arctic to Turkestan and containing 60 million

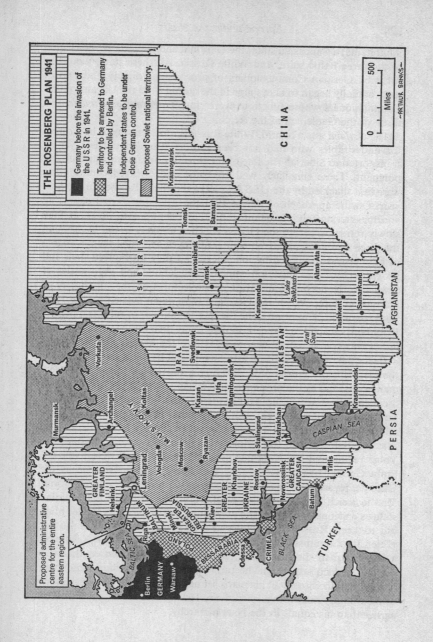

THE ROSENBERG PLAN 1941

- ■ Germany before the invasion of the U.S.S.R. in 1941.
- ▨ Territory to be annexed to Germany and controlled by Berlin.
- ▤ Independent states to be under close German control.
- ▨ Proposed Soviet national territory.

Proposed administrative centre for the entire eastern region.

0   500
Miles

~ARTHUR BANKS~

CHINA

SIBERIA

Krasnoyarsk

Tomsk
Barnaul

Novosibirsk
Omsk

Alma Ata

Lake Balkhash

Karaganda

Samarkand

Tashkent
Aral Sea

TURKESTAN

U R A L
Sverdlovsk

Vorkuta

Magnitogorsk
Ufa
Kazan

Krasnovodsk

AFGHANISTAN

Murmansk
Archangel
Kotlas

CASPIAN SEA

R U S S I A
Vologda
Leningrad
Moscow
Ryazan
Stalingrad
Astrakhan

PERSIA

GREATER FINLAND
Helsinki

Kharkhov
Kiev
Rostov
Novorossisk
GREATER CAUCASIA
Tiflis
Batum

Riga
BALTIKUM
MINSK
GREATER BIELORUSSIA
POLAND
GREATER UKRAINE

BALTIC SEA

Berlin
GERMANY
Warsaw

BESSARABIA
Odessa
CRIMEA

BLACK SEA

TURKEY

inhabitants; a Caucasian state; the Ukraine; and the *Ostland*, consisting of the three Baltic states and White Russia. All these states would be ruled by German Commissioners of proconsular dignity and two of them actually began to take shape in the *Ostland* and the Ukraine under Commissioners whose functions were similar *in partibus infidelium* to those of the Gauleiters of the Reich.

The *Ostland* was a hybrid. White Russia's function was to be a dump for undesirables who had not been murdered and could not yet be transported to Siberia. The fate of the three Baltic states was peculiarly poignant. These singularly well governed and civilized communities were first shackled by the USSR in 1939 and then absorbed in the next year. On the approach of war in 1941 the Russians started deporting and massacring the inhabitants, and they continued to do so as they slowly retreated before the Germans. The Germans began by treating the three states comparatively lightly and even accorded them a degree of administrative autonomy, but in 1942–3 they introduced their full programme of concentration camps, slave labour and the murder of Jews – to the accompaniment of public lectures on the superiority of German culture. (When the Germans were again evicted by the Russians, the killings went on none the less. A number of refugees, mainly Estonians, escaped to Sweden, though many died on the way. Depopulation was completed by deportations into the USSR after the war.)

In the Ukraine Rosenberg was encouraged by signs of welcome for the Germans (an autonomist, anti-Soviet movement raised false German hopes) and by the surrenders of Russian troops in the first weeks of the campaign (which he exaggeratedly ascribed solely to political rather than military causes). But his schemes never came to anything. Hitler was not interested in separatist vassal states. He told Rosenberg that the Baltic states, the Crimea, Baku and its neighbourhood, the Volga region and the Kola peninsula in the far north were to be entirely German. Erich Koch too, Rosenberg's Commissioner in the Ukraine, regarded his bailiwick simply as a source of food and labour for the Reich and derided his chief's political vision of a Ukrainian state as a stepping stone on the way to the Caucasus and a fender hung out to keep Russians and Poles at a safe remove. For Koch, as for Hitler, the Commissariat was a prelude to colonization. But Koch was a cleverer man than his chief Rosenberg. He soon sensed that this prelude had no sequel and he rarely visited the Ukraine. Rosenberg himself had to witness all his plans set on one side even before the turn of the military tide extinguished them. He experienced complete failure earlier than his equals in the Nazi hierarchy.

GERMAN RULE IN THE EAST 1941-1944

Six million Jews were murdered in the concentration camps and cities plus an equal number of non-Jewish Russians and Poles, two million of whom were children. Two million Soviet prisoners of war also were starved or beaten to death, and this policy of mass-murder led to partisan activity behind the German front line.

Baltic Sea

Reval
Novgorod
Pskov
Riga
Dvinsk
Volokolamsk
OSTLAND
Kovno
Vitebsk
Danzig
STUTTHOF
Vilna
UNOCCUPIED
TERRITORY
GREATER
GERMANY
TREBLINKA
Minsk
Bialystok
Orel
Kalisz
CHELMNO
Warsaw
Gomel
Kursk
Lublin
SOBIBOR
Chernigov
MAJDANEK
BELZEC
Rovno
SLOVAKIA
Cracow
Kiev
AUSCHWITZ
Zhitomir
Lvov

HUNGARY
UKRAINE
RUMANIAN MILITARY GOVERNMENT
Nikopol
Rostov
Melitopol
Stavropol
RUMANIA
Odessa
Krasnodar

Sevastopol
Yalta

Black Sea

	Areas ruled by the German military.
	Administered by the General-Government of Poland.
	Administered by the Ostland and Ukraine Reichskommissariats.
	Annexed by Germany.
□	Main concentration camps.
★	Partisans active in these areas.

0   200
Miles

~ARTHUR BANKS~

Rosenberg's activities provided a cloak for the operations of the SS. Although Rosenberg's Ministry, like the government of Hans Frank in Poland, was regarded by the SS as a nuisance and there was a good deal of friction between these different authorities, they became in effect collaborators in measures designed to kill even more people than the regular armed forces. They dealt death in the open and death in the camp.

Death on a grand scale by one or other of these methods was resolved upon in 1941 before the invasion of the USSR. A massacre programme was discussed between SS and army chiefs in May and four special squads or *Einsatzgruppen* were formed by the SS to round up and kill ideological opponents such as communist officials, political commissars and Jews. A special order for the murder of political commissars was issued by Hitler and transmitted through army channels at the beginning of June. A commissar was not defined, and, whether or not the vagueness was intentional, its effect was to license indiscriminate killing. Not only were suspected commissars shot out of hand or delivered by the army to the SD (which came to much the same thing): in addition recalcitrant or awkwardly sick prisoners could be dubbed commissars and summarily disposed of. The trigger-happiness of army officers and other ranks was encouraged by a further order, issued on the eve of the invasion, which did away with judicial proceedings in the military area and empowered battalion commanders and upwards to hear cases and impose penalties (including death) without the formality of assembling a court.

The four *Einsatzgruppen* were quite small – each was 500–800 strong – but their importance was shown by the choice of their commanders, who included the heads of Departments III, V and VIa of the RSHA. These men expected to end up in the four principal cities of the USSR where they would blossom into the local tsars of the New Order. Meanwhile their business was simply to kill. They began by inciting pogroms but were disappointed by the unenthusiastic response and were obliged to set to work more systematically. Leading Jews were required to assemble their fellows at given points, whereupon all were driven off to a nearby open space, stripped and shot. The dead and half dead were tumbled into trenches. Others were drowned or burned alive wholesale. No concealment was attempted or possible. The razzias were witnessed by thousands, talked about and even photographed. The executioners had to be kept up to their task by being made half drunk (which did not improve their aim), by treble pay and long holidays. A typical operation involved several hundred victims and took several hours. The largest single operation was the killing of over 33,000 Kievan Jews in two days in September 1941 as a reprisal for the blowing up of a hotel – the fearful inspiration of Yevtushenko's poem *Babi Yar* and the basis for Anatoly Kuznetsov's novel of the same name; the mass grave of these dead and dying Jews continued to be used as a dump for what the Nazis regarded as human refuse until it contained at least 100,000 corpses. A year later about 16,000 Jews were killed in a single day at Pinsk with the help of grenades, axes, dogs and SS cavalry. On the only occasion on which Himmler attended a massacre, it turned his stomach and made him order a change in technique: there was to be less shooting and more gassing.

Each of the *Einsatzgruppen* tended to magnify its achievements, so that it is impossible to take at its face value the boast by one commander, Erich Ohlendorf, that he had been personally responsible for the death of 90,000 people, most of them Jews, before he relinquished his command in June 1942, but it is probable that the number of Jews killed by Germans in the east was about two million. The disposal of the bodies was so rudimentary that the gases generated by decomposition betrayed the places of burial by a continuous barrage of small explosions, and a special squad had to be formed to open the graves and lay this ghastly evidence by chemical action, bonfires or mechanical pulverization.

The Jews of the rest of Europe were meanwhile being driven to their principal graveyard, the extermination camps of Poland. These camps were a specialized variety of the concentration camps which the Nazis had established in Germany immediately after coming to power.

A concentration camp is essentially a guarded area where people are sent and kept against their will, as though in prison. But a concentration camp is something different from a prison. A camp may be established because the prisons are full, but this is not why the Nazi camps were established. A man is sent to prison because he has been accused and convicted of a crime, and he is sent by a court. The men and women who were sent to the concentration camps were not accused or convicted of crimes; they were simply obnoxious to the régime, either because they were opposed to it or because they were – like the Jews – obnoxious by definition. And they were not committed to the camps by a court. They were sent there by party functionaries exercising a whim like an absolute monarch signing *lettres de cachet*. Further, the men and women in the camps were not meant to come out again. They were meant to rot and die there, and usually they did. Finally, the concentration camps were not created, like prisons, to hold men in durance and no more. They were also intended to intimidate those who remained outside them, and they did so by the cruelty of those who ran them and whose behaviour was no secret, and by the doubts which were allowed to circulate about citizens who abruptly disappeared from normal life.

The first concentration camp was established in March 1933, within a few weeks of the Nazis taking power. It was at Dachau, near Munich. Others were established in the years that followed, and the camp business received a boost when the *Anschluss* with Austria and the subjection of Bohemia-Moravia opened up new areas for the Nazi press gangs. With the beginning of the war the nature of the camps as well as their scale changed, for they became the scene of the Nazi policy of mass extermination. In the next few years millions were killed in them, perhaps seven millions – by hard labour, privation, epidemics, medical experiments on their bodies, fusillade, bastinado or asphyxiation.

During this period the camps were divided into two main categories. Most of them were labour camps, in which people from all over Europe toiled for Germany for a certain number of months until they dropped dead or were killed off because they had become useless. Some of these camps were near important factories and were run by the captains of big industry. In a different category were the death camps, whose business was extermination. There were five of these, all of them in Poland. The first was established at Auschwitz (Oswiecim), near Katowice in Silesia, soon after the defeat of Poland in 1939. Auschwitz developed into a complex of camps, one of which was the showpiece of modern technical killing by means of the gas called Cyclon B (guaranteed to kill within ten minutes) and of modern technical disposal in the ovens of its crematorium. After the invasion of the USSR four more extermination camps were established in Poland at Chelmno, Treblinka, Sobibor and Belsec (not to be confused with Bergen-Belsen which was partly a Wehrmacht hospital camp and partly an SS internment camp near Hanover in Germany).

The Polish Jews had priority because they were on the spot. There were in Poland in 1939 over three million Jews. Their numbers made them a special case. Nowhere except in Palestine did Jews constitute so large a proportion of the population. Nowhere except in the United States were so many Jews to be found. Nowhere at all, probably, was anti-semitism so potent or the extermination of Jews so readily acceptable to Gentiles. The first German plan was to concentrate all Jews from the German zone of Poland in an area in the east of the zone, but the attempt to do this created such chaos on the railways that the plan had to be abandoned. Instead ghettos were established in the principal towns. A Jew found outside a ghetto could be executed. Those inside were starved and overcrowded. Epidemics developed fast. Jew-baiting was encouraged with the inevitable results of torture and private-enterprise murder. The Warsaw ghetto, whose sealing walls were completed in October 1940, contained about half a million Jews. The extermination camps began functioning at the end of 1941 with Chelmno destroying about a thousand human beings a day, and during 1942 the Polish ghettos were gradually emptied into them. At one time Treblinka alone was taking 6,000 a day, and Auschwitz, which killed well over one million people in less than three years, could take twice as many in its stride. The disposal of the Warsaw ghetto began in July 1942 when there were probably still about 380,000 Jews in it. By the beginning of October there remained only 70,000 hiding in cellars and sewers, and in April 1943 an enfeebled residue of 14,000 rose. They fought alone. Yet their struggle lasted a month before all were either killed or taken and shipped to the gas chambers. Their enduring memorial is Schoenberg's threnody for speaker, chorus and orchestra, *A Survivor from Warsaw*.

By this time the stench of the camps had become so horrible and the danger of epidemics so great that mass burials and mass pyres had been largely superseded by cremation in specially designed ovens which would take half a dozen bodies at a time. The congestion in the extermination camps (sometimes aggravated by technical breakdowns which obliged trainloads of living victims to wait unloaded in sidings for several days) was caused by the international character of the Polish camps. Deportations from Germany itself and occupied countries swelled the traffic from the end of 1941.

In this year the Nazis finally decided to rid Germany of all its Jews. A plan to deposit them in the USSR having been frustrated by transport difficulties, they were routed instead to Auschwitz and eastern Poland for extermination. A conference in January 1942 decided also to kill all Croat, Slovak and Rumanian Jews in occupied territory and to inform the governments of Croatia, Slovakia, Hungary and Bulgaria that the Germans were ready to deal with their Jews too. Jews from Austria and Bohemia-Moravia were treated as German Jews. The same conference came up against the problem which had been worrying Nazi racists for years: what to do about Germany's half-Jews and quarter-Jews. Heydrich proposed that the former should be sterilized instead of being deported, but Hitler objected, mainly because at bottom he opposed any solution except their removal from German soil. The problem of the half-Jew continued to be debated but was never settled one way or another. Quarter-Jews, who were exempt from the Nuremberg laws, were to remain unmolested unless they were too obviously Jewish in appearance or – sinister opening for blackmail – there were special circumstances. There was a special category of privileged Jews. These included war veterans, Jews over sixty-five, holders of the Iron Cross First Class, senior civil servants, Jews with foreign connections or an international reputation, and others who still had the means to bribe the police. Their fate depended very much on the personal whims of the local Gauleiter and other officials. Privileged Jews remained subject to blackmail, often crudely expressed in such terms as 'going up the chimney' or 'making compost'. They had no legal status or redress and might suddenly find themselves dispatched to a concentration camp for talking in a tram or smoking in the street or receiving a food parcel. The camp at Theresienstadt (Terezin) in Czechoslovakia was reserved for them and was from time to time opened to representatives of the Red Cross. Privileged Jews died in Theresienstadt instead of in other camps, until the confusion of the last stages of the war caused them to be dispersed for extermination. When the war ended Theresienstadt had a residue of 20,000 inmates, one third of them not Jews.

The Greater German Reich was declared purged of Jews in November 1943. This was not strictly true. Many Jews who had married Gentiles, as well as half-Jews and quarter-Jews, survived. There were about 33,000 of them in Germany at the end of the war.

In western occupied countries Jews were removed immediately from public office and subjected to petty inhumanities such as being forbidden to eat in cafés or restaurants, use public transport or (in Holland) ride a bicycle. Next a census would be taken, property confiscated, segregation enforced. During 1942 many western Jews were driven into labour camps in their own countries and in the following year deportation began. It was substantially completed before the end of 1943. At first certain categories were exempted – for example, childless Jews married to Gentiles were given the alternative of sterilization – but these were administrative measures designed to ease the logistics of mass transport and mass murder and keep sections of Jewry quiet until their turn came. In 1943 Auschwitz was so busy that Jews from Holland and Luxembourg had to be sent all the way to Sobibor and Treblinka respectively. French Jews on the other hand went mainly to Auschwitz. Preparations for their deportation began in March 1942 and were extended in June to include the unoccupied zone: 100,000 Jews were to be collected and sent east. After the biggest single round-up – in July when 13,000 men, women and children were crammed into the concentration camp at Drancy and the Vélodrome d'Hiver in hideous conditions – French Jews were being transported to Poland at the rate of a thousand a day. By a curious twist, however, a number of French Jews were saved by French anti-semitism. France had an anti-semitic strain of its own hardly less pronounced than Germany's. Even today, after the Nazi holocaust, no Jew has replaced the French Jew Alfred Dreyfus as the principal symbol of European anti-semitism. French anti-semites were given their heads by Vichy and at Laval's direction the French police helped the SD to round up the Jews in France, but Laval's perverted nationalism insisted that French Jews, as opposed to Jews of different nationality who had fled to France, should be dealt with by the French authorities instead of being sent to Germany or Poland. Some of them survived and after the extension of the German occupation to the whole country in November many escaped to the Italian zone and Monaco. Thus the Germans contrived to kill only about a quarter of French Jewry as compared with half the Belgian Jews and over three quarters of the Dutch. (The last were specially vulnerable in a small country in which it was difficult to hide. They had nowhere like the Ardennes, where many Belgian Jews and other refugees congregated, and as a community they had had little contact with the Gentiles who alone could have concealed large numbers of them.) In the west as a whole the 7,500 Danish Jews fared least badly. An attempt was made to round them up after the Germans took over in 1943, but all save a few hundred were saved. A German official leaked a warning of the plan and practically the entire Jewish community was first hidden and then transported in small vessels to Sweden, where they were looked after until the end of the war. When the Germans came to round up their victims, they found that the birds had flown. Of Norway's small Jewish community of about 2,000 some 750 were caught. Italian Jews were deported to Auschwitz and other camps by the Germans after the fall of Mussolini.

South-eastern Europe also provided its share of victims – about one million. In Rumania, with its large Jewish community of nearly three quarters of a million, pogroms were initiated without German encouragement and two thirds of Rumanian Jewry perished during the war in one way or another. In Bulgaria on the other hand the government's agreement to fall in with German plans by surrendering its Jews for deportation was thwarted by demonstrations of public disgust. In Serbia and Croatia most Jews were killed without being deported. (In Croatia Serbs were killed too.) A number of Croatian Jews escaped from the German to the Italian zone of occupation and thence later to the partisans. Of the 75,000 Greek Jews in Salonica at least two thirds were sent to Auschwitz in 1943.

In Slovakia the work of deportation and extermination was begun in 1942 with the cooperation of the puppet government but then suspended; it was resumed and completed after the Slovak rising of 1944. Hungary's Jews survived for the most part until 1944 when Eichmann arrived in Budapest to conduct a special operation which, despite opposition from the Regent Horthy until the removal of his régime in October and despite outside protests from the Pope, the king of Sweden and other quarters, succeeded in reducing the Hungarian Jews from 800,000 to 100,000. This operation was punctuated by a curious proposal from the German side to barter one million European Jews for 10,000 heavy lorries, to be used on the eastern front only, and for quantities of tea, coffee, cocoa and soap. Although Jewish leaders realized that the western belligerents would never agree to help the German effort against the Russians, some of them hoped that the negotiations might be spun out in such a way as to stave off the killing of the survivors of their race or to organize their ransom for money instead of lorries. But the offer was not taken seriously by the outside world and the chief emissary of the Hungarian Jews, Joel Brand, was even put in prison by the British authorities in the Middle East with whom he was trying to negotiate. Those Nazis, Himmler perhaps included, who hoped in this way to make contact with the west and negotiate a peace which would leave them at least their lives and perhaps some of their power, were outflanked by other Nazis, Eichmann included, who were riled by this interruption to the work of genocide.

The separateness of the Jews militated against their survival. Cut off and marked out by their history and their circumstances, they were exposed to separate destruction in a way in which no other groups were exposed. Their alternatives were to resist in isolation or just wait. They did both: many waited but others, belying the passivity which had marked their people between their risings against the Romans and the outrages of the twentieth century, rebelled in arms as well as in spirit. Flight from the community was inhibited by family loyalties. It tended to be postponed from month to month in the desperate hope that, as in the past, the Jew would be saved because he was useful: in the *Ostland* a Jew's most precious document was his work certificate. In Germany a number of Jews passed themselves off as bombed-out refugees, resorting to every kind of disguise and desperate expedient to save themselves and their families; in Vienna this was called 'doing a U-boat',

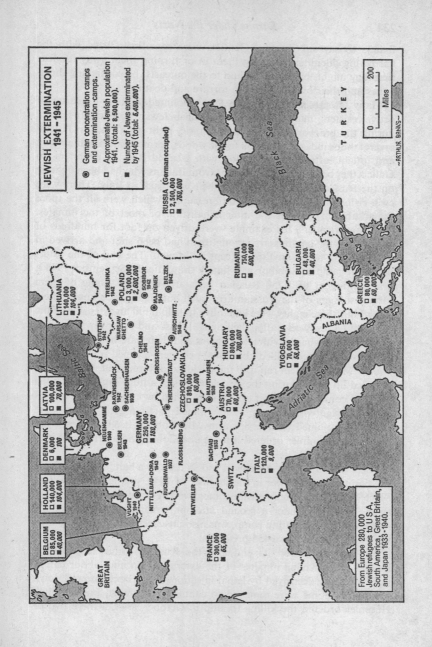

JEWISH EXTERMINATION 1941 – 1945

- ◉ German concentration camps and extermination-camps.
- ◻ Approximate Jewish population 1941. (total: 8,500,000).
- ◼ Number of Jews exterminated by 1945 (total: 6,400,000).

—ARTHUR BANKS—

0   200
Miles

RUSSIA (German occupied)
◻ 2,500,000
◼ 760,000

Black Sea

T U R K E Y

RUMANIA
◻ 750,000
◼ 500,000

BULGARIA
◻ 48,000
◼ 40,000

GREECE
◻ 80,000
◼ 60,000

ALBANIA

Adriatic Sea

YUGOSLAVIA
◻ 70,000
◼ 58,000

HUNGARY
◻ 800,000
◼ 700,000

LITHUANIA
◻ 140,000
◼ 104,000

◉ TREBLINKA 1942

POLAND
◻ 3,000,000
◼ 2,600,000

◉ SOBIBOR 1942

◉ BELZEC 1942

◉ MAJDENEK 1943

◉ AUSCHWITZ

◉ STUTTHOF 1942

WARSAW GHETTO

◉ CHELMO 1941

◉ GROSSROSEN

THERESIENSTADT

CZECHOSLOVAKIA
◻ 810,000
◼ 60,000

◉ MAUTHAUSEN 1938

AUSTRIA
◻ 70,000
◼ 60,000

LATVIA
◻ 100,000
◼ 70,000

Baltic Sea

◉ RAVENSBRÜCK 1942

◉ SACHSENHAUSEN 1936

◉ NEUENGAMME 1940

◉ BELSEN 1943

GERMANY
◻ 250,000
◼ 180,000

◉ MITTLEBAU-DORA

◉ BUCHENWALD 1937

◉ FLOSSENBERG

DENMARK
◻ 6,000
◼ 100

HOLLAND
◻ 140,000
◼ 104,000

BELGIUM
◻ 85,000
◼ 40,000

◉ VUGHT 1940

◉ NATWEILER

SWITZ.

◉ DACHAU 1933

ITALY
◻ 120,000
◼ 9,000

FRANCE
◻ 300,000
◼ 65,000

GREAT BRITAIN

From Europe 280,000 Jewish refugees to U.S.A., South America, Great Britain, and Japan 1933 - 1940.

that is to say submerging. Gentiles were sometimes faced with the harrowing dilemma of taking them in or turning them away for fear that they might, by giving asylum to the outcasts, be consigning themselves and their own children to torture and death.

Many Jews resisted. In France Jews amounted to about a quarter of active resisters, many of them being Polish Jews who had left Poland during the pre-war period of anti-semitic, right-wing rule. In Poland several thousands of Jews took to the woods, formed bands of their own and fought, often in cooperation with escaped Russian prisoners. In Galicia they bought or took weapons from Italians who had been fighting on the Russian front but were on their way back to Italy. There were even risings inside the concentration camps, which were all the more remarkable in view of the utter exhaustion of most of the inmates. (Russian prisoners, for example, were driven on foot for hundreds of miles after the commissars among them had been shot and arrived in no condition to do anything except fall down.) The end of the extermination camp at Sobibor was highly dramatic. In September 1943 a first contingent of 1,750 Russian Jews arrived there, some of them former soldiers of the Russian army. All but eighty were immediately gassed but these eighty were kept alive to help build an extension of the camp and a few weeks after their arrival these and other Jews rose and attacked their guards with axes, knives and their bare hands. After ten SS guards had been killed about 400 prisoners escaped from the compound. Many of them ran into minefields and were killed. Others were rounded up again during the next few days in a hunt organized by the local SS command and yet others were killed by anti-semitic members of Polish right-wing bands. A few joined partisan groups and some eventually rejoined the Russian army. But Sobibor itself was destroyed by this act. Himmler ordered it to be abandoned and all traces of it to be expunged.

There were risings at Auschwitz too. A first, by a handful of surviving Russian prisoners of war in the summer of 1942, was largely a failure. Some were shot trying to escape, others were recaptured later; a few got away. Two years later a second attempt, organized by Jews in the Auschwitz extermination camp, was also unsuccessful. Four SS guards were killed but so were 455 prisoners.

As the war neared its end and the Russian armies approached Poland the surviving inmates of the extermination and labour camps were hurriedly destroyed by lethal injections or by being mowed down by gunfire. Some were removed to camps farther west, but although Himmler ordered the killing to stop in October 1944, a mere two or

JEWISH RESISTANCE 1940–1944

Baltic Sea

Gulf of Riga

Riga

LATVIA

LITHUANIA

Niemen

1942–1944 The 'Vilna Avengers.'

Vilna

1943–1944 The 'Tobias Bielski' Division.

EAST PRUSSIA

Lida

Minsk

Mir

Bialystok

"Jerusalem"

WHITE

Treblinka

WARSAW

Bug

RUSSIA

Vistula

Sobibor

1943–1944 Jewish sanctuary in the woods.

P O L A N D

Vistula

Lublin

Lutzk

UKRAINE

Czestochowa

Koniecpol

Zhitomir

Sosnowica

Bendzin

Sielce

Brody

Auschwitz

Cracow

Tarnow

Lvov

Tarnopol

Stryzow

■ Ghettoes in which the Jews organized risings against German rule.

▨ Areas of Jewish partisan group activity.

◉ Concentration camps in which Jewish risings occurred.

0   50
Miles

~ARTHUR BANKS~

three per cent of all the Jews abducted during the war survived it. The number of deaths is incalculable. It lies somewhere between four and six million. The gypsies, who were also marked down for total destruction, lost perhaps 200,000 lives; the evidence about their sufferings is vague, but on one occasion at Auschwitz 4,000 of them seem to have been gassed in a single, if prolonged, operation. Gentiles too were killed in droves, including Germans for whom the first concentration camps were originally instituted: at least half a million men and women died in the German concentration camps during the war from illness and ill treatment. Himmler's aim of reducing the world's Slav population by 30 million was not attained, although the losses suffered by the Russians in battle and at the hands of the SS went some way towards realizing this abominable ambition. The apostles of the New Order showed that, given time, their destructive plans were not beyond the compass of human techniques and human will.

The massacre of millions of European Jews was a culminating act in the history of the relations between Jew and Gentile. Hitler did not invent anti-semitism. It was wrapped up in Europe's inheritance from Christendom. It lay ready to Hitler's hand and he used it with a pitiless thoroughness which made him a special kind of anti-semite. The myth of a Jewish conspiracy to pervert the world is a Christian myth which has been propagated by Christian writers of eminence and authority almost as far back as the origins of their religion and right up to the present century, and the same writers have also been responsible for the odious slanders against the character and practices of the Jews which Hitler and other modern anti-semites were able to cite and endorse. (One of the commonest of these myths is the charge that Jews murdered non-Jewish children for ritual purposes. The first child alleged to have been killed in this way, William of Norwich, who died in 1144, is still officially venerated by Roman Catholics as a saint and martyr although there is no particle of evidence about the manner of his death. Nor is there any better evidence about any of the other cases of this kind.)

In the eighteenth century opponents of Christianity, such as the leaders of the Enlightenment, who might have been expected to defend the Jews, had their own kind of anti-semitism since they reprobated Jewry as the forerunner of Christianity, while in the nineteenth century racist theories sharpened the persecution of the Jews by making their offence inexpiable. So long as the Jew was persecuted on account of his religion he might escape its worst consequences by baptism, but when he was persecuted on account of his race he had no way out except death. Whether Hitler, who called himself a Roman Catholic, believed Christianity's anti-semitic inventions or those of the racists is a question which he himself would have regarded as senseless. The point was not whether they were true but whether they were useful, and, as he once said to Rauschning, anti-semitism was an essential tool for spreading Nazism in Germany and beyond. On this issue his political cynicism fitted nicely with his deeper emotions, since besides using anti-semitism he hated Jews.

The enormity of what was done in the forties has led to a search for an explanation: what are the origins of this conflict and its Hitlerian solution? This is one of the most complex problems in the history of Europe, to which much learning and ingenuity have been devoted. Certain general factors appear at first sight: the religious differences, accentuated by Christendom's condemnation of the Jewish race for deicide; the recognizable physical features of many Jews; their own insistence on their religious and national identity, accentuated by their dispersal; the special functions which, historically, they filled in European societies, often unpopular ones such as money lending. At a deeper level theories about the vulnerability of the Jews have been advanced. One of the more interesting of these attaches importance to the fact that the special services which they once provided came to be no longer needed; for example, their function as the financiers of the state was essential so long as the state was financed through personal borrowing by monarchs but became otiose when this method was replaced by government taxation of the whole community. But the more that Jewish-Gentile relations are probed the more dangerous does it appear to generalize beyond a certain point, for it becomes clear that the position of the Jews in Christendom has varied greatly from time to time and from place to place, so that an explanation of the plight of the Jews in Poland in the twentieth century, for example, will not – except superficially – fit their circumstances in France at the same or any other date.

The premeditated execution of four to six million people by methods of singular barbarity should, one hopes, be difficult to explain. Part of the explanation is to be found in the fact that anti-semitism is ancient, widespread and irrational; yet this is no explanation, since it merely shifts the question back into the past and, by raising it again in a remoter historical context, makes it even more difficult to answer. The emotions which anti-semitism produces are fierce, and the ends which these emotions have compassed have been tacitly approved by thousands or millions of people who would themselves recoil from the methods used. Schemes for saving Jews from Nazi Germany were half-hearted at best. Before the war the Nazis would promise only a small annual exodus of workers without families or capital and tried to link this exodus with a boost to German exports by getting the receiving countries to undertake to increase their purchases of German goods. No country could be found willing to take substantial numbers of Jews; the British barred Palestine to them except in small numbers and on stringent terms; the Americans were so unimaginative as to require certificates of birth which few German Jews possessed and none could ask for from a German official (but a number of Christian priests forged baptismal certificates for them); a Bill to permit 20,000 Jewish children to enter the United States was killed by a 'patriotic' lobby in the Congress on the grounds that it offended against the sanctity of family ties and in spite of the fact that the immigration quotas from Germany were regularly underfilled. Even after Hitler's decision to exterminate the Jews became known through official sources during 1942 and was confirmed by the preparations for its practical implementation, this information was received in the west with a *sang-froid* akin to complicity. Hitler was able to exult that nobody wanted the Jews and so, since there was nowhere for them to go, he had no option but to destroy them.

The Roman Catholic church had, it may be thought, a special obligation to do something for the Jews both because of its special contribution to anti-semitism over nearly 2,000 years and because of its own teaching on brotherly love. Very many churchmen were compassionate men horrified by Nazi crimes but the church as a body was caught in the toils of its own propaganda, old and new. In modern times Jewry, besides being collectively charged with the judicial murder of Jesus, was associated with a special kind of ungodliness. The French Revolution and the Bolshevik Revolution were both blamed, again by professed Christian writers, on the Jews, who were made the scapegoats for whatever was alarming to the established order, and specially to the established ecclesiastical order, in a world which had begun to change faster than seemed desirable to those who were used to running it. Again, Hitler did not invent the equation of communism with Jewry; but he was able to profit from it. The more sophisticated and honest enemies of communism knew that the government of the USSR was very far from being run by Jews, but, because they detested and feared communism, they hesitated to speak out against Nazism for fear of undermining the German state and so helping Russian communism to advance into the centre of Europe and join hands with powerful communist parties in the west. The Jews – and the Christian conscience – were sacrificed to this dilemma.

The Roman Catholic church in Germany was persecuted by Hitler. It also came to terms with him and in 1933, on orders from the Vatican, the Centre Party, which was the political face of the church, voted for the Enabling Act which gave Hitler full authority to destroy the German constitution and society. Most of the Roman Catholic bishops then made haste to take back all that they had been saying about the beastliness of the Nazis, Roman Catholic theologians set themselves the task of demonstrating the essential compatibility of Christian and Nazi doctrine, and pulpits which had been used to denounce the latter emitted a new view of the Führer as a man of God. The church so far attuned itself to Nazism as to overlook the concentration camps and endorse Hitler's foreign policy. When war came the German Roman Catholic clergy broadly supported it and continued to do so in spite of the murder of their Polish colleagues, officially reported, and in spite of Hitler's unwarranted attacks on small, helpless neutrals; his attack on the USSR evoked a crusading enthusiasm. But many Christians, priests and laymen, exerted themselves and risked their lives to succour Jews. The Dominican and Jesuit orders were specially mindful of their Christian duty.

In the Vatican two Popes, Pius XI and Pius XII, had to contend with the spiritual and practical crises occasioned by the rise of Fascism and Nazism. Pius XI, who became Pope in 1922, was faced with the problem of the relations between the Vatican and first Italy and then Germany. Pius VIII had faced a similar problem in his dealings with Napoleon. Mussolini and Hitler, like Napoleon, wished to establish treaty relations with the Vatican and both succeeded. In the case of Hitler, Pius XI and his nuncio in Berlin and eventual successor, Eugenio Pacelli, believed that a concordat with Hitler would do more good than harm because it would give the Vatican a stronger claim to interfere on behalf of persecuted priests. A concordat was concluded in July 1933. Its effects were disappointing since Hitler persecuted the German clergy more than ever once he had got it, but the motives of Pius and Pacelli were sincere and their reasoning could not be definitely condemned before the event. Both men were disgusted by the Nazis and by anti-semitism. In March 1937 Pius XI issued, in German, the encyclical *Mit brennender Sorge* which was read from all Roman Catholic pulpits in Germany and, although it contained no explicit reference to anti-semitism, was understood as a clear and sharp attack on Nazi policies; but again the effects were very limited. Pacelli, who was consulted by the Pope before the encyclical was issued, toned up its language. He was himself more anti-Nazi than many western conservatives and diplomats, delivered in the same year an openly anti-Nazi speech at Lisieux and upon his accession to the Papacy was condemned by the Nazis as even worse than his predecessor.

Despite the ritual mystery surrounding the election of a Pope the elevation of Pacelli to the Papal see on the death of Pius XI in 1939 was a foregone conclusion. Pius XI, departing from all precedent, had practically designated Pacelli as his successor, and one of the shortest conclaves on record sufficed to fill the vacancy. Pius XII, as the new Pope called himself, had served as nuncio in Munich and then in Berlin and had other special connections with Germany, but he was also the most widely travelled Cardinal in Europe and beyond ever to become Pope. The breadth of his experience and of his intelligence were alike unusual. His opposition to inhumanity and aggression were beyond question. Yet he has been assailed for failing in his human and Christian duty. This supreme accusation against a supreme pontiff relates to his conduct in relation to both Christians and Jews. It was made soon after he became Pope. Cardinal Tisserant chided the Pope for unbecoming reticence when the Ustachi (Roman Catholic Croats) were giving Orthodox Serbs the choice between re-baptism and death and were in the process of killing half a million of them. Similarly the Pope, although copiously informed about the Germans' treatment of the Poles, kept silent. Directly and by his example he did much for thousands of Jews who were saved from death and given money, food, clothing and even employment in Roman Catholic institutions. But he made no public protest against the murders of Jews, did not use his awful weapon of excommunication against the murderers, refused to speak out against Vichy's anti-semitic laws (even when the French bishops did) and refused to intervene when, in October 1943, the Germans carried off over a thousand Jews from Rome itself to be gassed.

Pius XII could have argued, and perhaps did, that he must avoid the charge levelled against Benedict XV in the First World War of taking sides against Germany, that excommunication was no longer an incisive weapon (though he used it against communists after the war) and that public protest could do the victims more harm than good, but his posture in his dilemma was an unheroic one and contrasted unfavourably with that of some of his own nuncios and other Roman Catholic notabilities who were stirred to an open opposition which was often effective. He was in the uncomfortable dilemma of occupying an office whose pretensions were greater than its capacities and, in preferring the cautious to the outspoken course, he seemed to neglect his obligation to re-state the violated canons of human behaviour. Although he might not be able to save the victims, he could have pointed the finger of divine anger against the criminals. By keeping silent, he sanctioned the unheroic frailty of all those lesser men who prefer, unless exhorted and inspired, to pass by on the other side. He invited the charge of failing to keep the Christian conscience sharp and clean. That charge has since been laid. The record is mixed.

CHAPTER 12

Exploitation

THE pattern of German power in Europe was a patchwork. Very little territory was formally annexed to the Reich: Danzig, large slices of Poland and smaller ones of Belgium. Other areas were intended and prepared for annexation although not formally annexed and even formally assured of their continuing integrity and independence: Alsace and Lorraine, Luxembourg, parts of Slovenia. In these areas compulsory military service was introduced and the Reich Ministry of the Interior set about imposing German law and the German legal system, integrating postal, railway and customs services, changing place names and even personal names, adjusting citizenship rights and constraining the population to speak German. Formal annexation was only a matter of time. These were, from the practical point of view, districts which were contiguous with the Reich and had special strategic or economic value; from another point of view they were districts which had once been part of a medieval Germanic empire or were peopled by kinsmen of the German race.

Three other territories which were distinct from the Reich were never-theless completely subordinated to it through a Governor General, a Protector and a Reich Minister. These territories, all of which lay to the east of Germany, were brought within the German customs area; their separate existence in international law was barely conceded; and various overlords within the Reich such as Goering as Commissioner for the Five Year Plan and Sauckel as Plenipotentiary for Labour were entitled to direct demands to their rulers. They were the Government General of Poland, ruled by Hans Frank with the status of a head of government but not a head of state; the Protectorate of Bohemia and Moravia, in which parts of the administration (justice, for example) were placed under Reich Ministries in Berlin but which had also a nomi-nally autonomous administration in pseudo-diplomatic relations with Berlin and a Protector (first Neurath, then Heydrich and ultimately Frick) who advised this administration what to do and saw that it did it; and the Baltic and Russian territories which came under Rosenberg, who had theoretically the same executive and legislative powers as Hans Frank in Poland and exercised them through his Ministry for the East

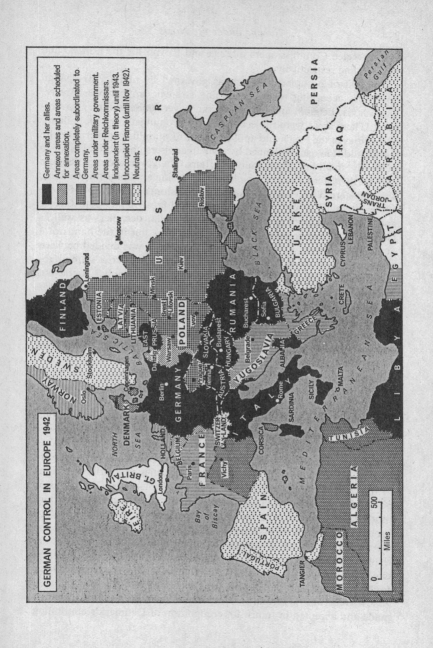

GERMAN CONTROL IN EUROPE 1942

Germany and her allies.

Annexed areas and areas scheduled for annexation.

Areas completely subordinated to Germany.

Areas under military government.

Areas under Reichkommissars.

Independent (in theory) until 1943.

Unoccupied France (until Nov 1942).

Neutrals.

and its Reich Commissioners in Riga and Rovno for the *Ostland* and the Ukraine respectively.

The rest of occupied Europe was governed by military or civilian governors according to its continuing strategic importance. Greece, Yugoslavia, Belgium and occupied France were under military government. These areas were subject to decrees promulgated by the military authorities of the Reich and applied by the local military governor, who was in addition usually helped by civilian advisers posted to his staff to guide him in all but purely military affairs. The government of Belgium and north-eastern France, which formed a single administrative zone, was transferred to a civilian Reich Commissioner in July 1944 for the better supervision and regimentation of the local population. Greece and Yugoslavia both saw Italian and Bulgarian occupiers as well as German. The native government of Greece was put in the hands of a puppet government in Athens, that of Yugoslavia was divided between a puppet government in Belgrade and the separatist Croat state established under Ante Pavelič. This state comprised not only Croatia but also Bosnia and Herzegovina and part of the Dalmatian coast and was roughly co-terminous with the eleventh-century kingdom of the same name. Pavelič was a rabidly anti-Serb Croat who had curried favour with the Italians before the war as an enemy of the Yugoslav state and was then pressed on an unenthusiastic Hitler by Mussolini. After May 1941 Pavelič, who had had to cede most of the Adriatic islands and Dalmatian coast to Italy and accept a prince of the Italian royal house as king in Croatia, turned against the Italians. The king never visited his kingdom.

Norway and the Netherlands were placed under civilian Reich Commissioners – Josef Terboven and Artur Seyss-Inquart – who were directly responsible to Hitler and were empowered to legislate by decree and review all existing laws. The powers of crown and government were transferred to them, and each appointed deputies to overlord sections of the central administration and its regional offshoots. Obnoxious or potentially subversive elements in public life, such as parliaments and other elective bodies, the press and broadcasting, were abolished or brought under control, and the national police was subordinated to the German police and SS. Denmark was exceptional in that its head of state, the king, remained in the country throughout the war and in the exercise of his functions for most of it; the Danish cabinet continued to look to the sovereign and the Danish army remained in being in designated zones. There was no formal agreement but the military capitulation was made and accepted in return for recognition of Denmark's continuing independence and neutrality. Until 1943 relations between Germany and Denmark were conducted through diplomatic channels, although German officials had to be reminded from time to time that they must not treat Denmark as just another occupied country. In 1943 the Germans took over the country, the king was closely confined, the army was disbanded, the navy scuttled itself, and the government and parliament were dissolved. Thereafter Denmark was run by the SS.

If Germany had won the war Denmark and the Netherlands would probably have been annexed despite explicit assurances to the contrary. In both countries, although earlier in the Netherlands than in Denmark, political forms and economic activities were adjusted to German patterns and needs. Political parties – other than the local Nazi variant – were extinguished, Nazi laws introduced, production and labour treated as segments of the German economy. In the Netherlands trade-union leaders began by cooperating with the Germans in the hope of preserving their various auxiliary institutions and activities, but membership of unions dropped sharply and the creation of a labour front in 1942 caused union officials to resign too. Some unions were dissolved by decree when their officials resigned in protest against the appointment of pro-German overseers; one Roman Catholic union was dissolved when the Roman Catholic hierarchy ordered members to leave it on pain of being denied the sacraments. Dutch SS were formed as early as the autumn of 1940 (from candidates with untarnished ancestry back to 1800), took a personal oath to Hitler as the Greater German Führer and provided fighting units for the eastern front. Himmler planned to plant Nordic settlers from these countries in various parts of the USSR, whether they wanted to go there or not.

France, unlike every other defeated country, was run from two different capitals, Paris and Vichy. From Vichy Marshal Pétain's government exercised authority over the whole country except Alsace-Lorraine, virtually annexed to the Reich, and the zone in the south-east ceded to Italy by the armistice. From Paris Hitler's plenipotentiary, Otto Abetz, also exercised functions which covered occupied and unoccupied France: he was a career diplomat whose tasks were to advise the military commander in the occupied zone on political matters, to maintain permanent contact with the French government in Vichy and its representatives in the occupied zone, and generally to influence French politicians, the press and broadcasting. He straddled France, advising the German rulers in the north and bringing pressure to bear on Pétain and his ministers in the south. But in practice France was partitioned. As a defeated country waiting for a peace settlement it was subject to the interim arrangements accepted with the armistice. The Germans exacted the right to occupy the north with military and police forces, detached the north-east which, in terms of military government but not of civil administration, was controlled with Belgium from Brussels, and created a prohibited zone running along the north and west coasts under strict military control. Abetz ruled indirectly in the unoccupied zone by addressing representations to Vichy, and Vichy's subservience to German power was never in doubt; although there was no outward German presence in the unoccupied zone until it too was occupied in November 1942 the SD operated there on a restricted scale from the beginning (for example, in tracking down wireless transmitters and operators).

In all these countries the pattern of German control at the top was invisible to most people who never had or were never given any clear picture of what role the Germans had assumed. What people saw was not a new pattern imposed by the conqueror but a series of random consequences of the impact of German rule on local administration. At the centre the Germans kept and even enlarged the powers of civil servants whom they converted from administrators into ministers-to-the-Germans with power to issue decrees, a form of indirect rule in which the Germans directed the civil service and the civil service directed everybody else. Local government bodies also remained in being, often with familiar faces in the same offices, but this reassuring continuity was contradicted by uncharacteristic behaviour on the part of mayors and other office-holders. Disturbingly, these no longer did what they were expected to do. Nor did one mayor behave like the next one, for each reacted differently, the one more obediently, the other more defiantly or more slyly, to the directions of his superiors. Mayors whom the Germans regarded as satisfactory remained in office and were given enhanced authority, but since unsatisfactory mayors were replaced, those who survived became in effect appointees holding office during good behaviour. German observers were inserted into the machinery of government at the centre and also to some extent lower down, for example, on the governing boards of French *lycées*; Labour Offices were put under undisguised German control, so that an unemployed worker coming in to register even in a comparatively small town would find himself face to face with a German official who might direct him to work in Germany or in some occupied country other than his own. But for the most part the general public continued to deal with local authorities whom it knew, and was unaware of the extent to which or the methods by which they were subjected to German regulation. In fact German control, even where it was not obtrusive, was thorough and pervasive. Courts, like the administration, continued to function outwardly much as before, but the German police kept a watch on the sentences given in criminal courts and might override them, with the result that criminal justice became something of a lottery in which sentences differed widely from court to court and the accused did not know whether his sentence would stand. He even had reason to fear a light sentence since the Germans were more likely to step in and increase it.

In all occupied countries, whether under military or civilian rule, a great deal went on which did not meet the eye and was not meant to, and in particular Himmler's Higher SS and Police Führers were a law unto themselves. They normally held SS rank equivalent to that of the military governor or local troop commander and, *de jure* or *de facto*, circumvented the German military and civil power in implementing policies determined by Himmler. In the inevitable quarrels with local governors the SS had the advantage of knowing exactly where they stood, since the SS and police authorities in conquered areas were replicas by extension of the system familiar in the Reich. Most other offices were *ad hoc* creations in which a good deal of confusion prevailed.

The Germans turned out to be much less fond of local Nazis and pro-German parties than vice versa. They used such parties but felt no call to support them. In Belgium, for example, they made use of various collaborationist groups until these cancelled each other out by their competitive jealousies. In the Netherlands Seyss-Inquart paid very little attention to Adrian Mussert and the Dutch Nazis although some individuals were given minor administrative office. The Danish Nazi Party also proved valueless. In Norway a rather different situation arose because the German Commissioner Terboven was determined to retain power in his own hands, governing through a council in Oslo and regional deputies appointed by himself until ordered by Hitler to acknowledge Quisling and make him Prime Minister; Quisling's original role had been to subvert Norway in the German interest but this plan had been abandoned in favour of the military conquest of the country with the result that it was not clear to the new rulers sent by Hitler whether Quisling still counted or not. Only in France, under the aegis of Vichy, did native fascists flourish for a while. For day-to-day administration the Germans relied, where they could, on the existing machinery of government and its existing staff, supplemented by an injection of German officials at key points with the title but more than the status of observers. In the east, where the machinery was less good, the reliance impracticable and Slav sub-men by definition unemployable, they had to take over themselves except at levels or in matters which did not interest them.

One country escaped: Switzerland. In 1940 the general Swiss view was that Germany had won the war. The question was whether it would pay the Swiss better to be tough in this situation or pliant. They knew before the war that the Nazis treated Switzerland in their training manuals as part of the Reich and showed it as such in official maps, and they also knew that the German army had plans for an attack on Switzerland. These plans were never put into operation but they nearly were on more than one occasion. One of the main reasons why they were not was the appointment and conduct of General Henri Guisan.

The Swiss constitution provides for the appointment of a military, as opposed to a civilian, commander-in-chief in times of emergency. On 30 August 1939 the Swiss parliament gave the cabinet emergency powers and on the same day Guisan was named commander-in-chief. The appointment was controversial and contested and Guisan had to be on his guard throughout the war against the intrigues of civilian and military personages who held that Switzerland's only chance of escaping a German invasion lay in a scrupulous emphasis on the Swiss tradition of neutrality: they believed that Switzerland must aim above all at avoiding any provocation of Hitler. General Guisan argued otherwise. He said that independence was even more important than neutrality, since without independence there would be no neutrality to protect; that the only threat to independence came from Germany; and that preparations must be made to meet this threat. On his orders a thousand factories, public works and public services, and Switzerland's numerous tunnels were prepared for demolition. In a dramatic scene on the historic Rütli the officers of the army took an oath to resist. A mountain redoubt was fortified where fighting would go on even if Switzerland's borders were forced and its frontier cities taken. Justified by results, Guisan lived to receive the acclaim of even the most timorous of his fellow citizens.

Germany's European allies complete the picture. They were Italy, Slovakia, Hungary, Rumania and Bulgaria. Slovakia was a puppet from the moment of its creation in 1939. In south-east Europe Hitler was prepared to let Rumania down as much and as often as it suited him, give Hungary most of what it wanted, enlarge Bulgaria to the dimensions tantalizingly glimpsed at San Stefano in 1877, and let Greece become an Italian province. If Hitler anticipated squabbles between Italians and Slavs he did so without distaste. Thus Bulgaria and Hungary were uneasy allies who made hay while the sun shone – Bulgaria at the expense of Rumania, Yugoslavia and Greece, and Hungary at the expense of the first two of these. When the sun stopped shining for the Germans in the middle of the war all these countries began to try to change sides. Rumania, which had tried to avoid taking sides between Germany and the western democracies, slid into alliance with Germany through fear of the Soviet Union but not without being forced by Hitler to yield territory to its neighbours and, indirectly, to evict its king. After being forced to cede Bessarabia and Northern Bukovina to the USSR King Carol sought territorial guarantees for the rest of his state from Hitler, but Hitler refused. The king, whose weak position was threatened not only by the loss of national territory but also by the hostility of the fascist Iron Guard (whose temper had not been improved by the murder in 1938 of its leader Corneliu Codreanu), tried to save himself by inviting the army leader Marshal Ion Antonescu and the Iron Guard to join his government, but they were advised by Germany not to. The loss of more territory by the second Vienna Award and the Treaty of Craiova (by which Hitler allotted parts of Rumania to Hungary and Bulgaria) made Carol's position impossible and he abdicated. Antonescu, a stupid rather than a sinister man, with a pushing wife, joined the government of the new King Michael and so too did the Iron Guard, but the mutual antipathy of the army and the Iron Guard produced a threat of civil war. The Iron Guard attempted a coup but Hitler, who wanted no trouble in Rumania and who had formed a favourable impression of Antonescu in the course of two visits by the Marshal to the Führer, decided to back the army which, with the help of German tanks, smashed the Iron Guard. Its leaders were lodged in internment camps until 1944 when, Antonescu having been overthrown by the tides of war, they were extracted to form a phantom Rumanian government in Vienna.

Italy was an ally of a different sort and its collapse in 1943 caused the biggest alteration to the pattern of German occupation before the retreat of the Germans themselves. The Germans were obliged to occupy those areas in south-eastern Europe which had been left to the Italians and to worry about the quantities of Italian arms which passed into the hands of Yugoslav and Greek partisans. Even more serious was the problem of Italy itself. Hitler was ill-informed about Italy. He had forbidden secret service activities there and the reporting of his civilian and service emissaries was deplorably poor. His belief in Mussolini made him reject warnings of the coming collapse. He helped Mussolini, rescued from captivity on the Gran Sasso by a spectacular piece of kidnapping in a small aircraft, to create a new Italian republic in the north, whose unreality and incapacity merely confused the picture but were not allowed by the German military and police commanders in the field to interfere with their respective businesses. Italy north of the allied line of advance became German occupied territory under military rule.

This patchwork of alliance and domination arose out of the needs and fortunes of war. It was not meant to endure. While it did, its function was to secure obedience to German wishes and, increasingly, to supply the German war machine with materials, goods, food and labour. As German needs became more urgent, German methods became harsher and resistance grew.

The German armies were accompanied in their invasions by special economic squads, whose first tasks were to seize what Germany wanted by way of pillage – raw materials and manufactured goods, gold and foreign currencies, machinery and rolling stock – and to protect valuable installations and essential factories, which were to be exploited as going concerns. Once these immediate aims had been achieved, the Germans began to look further ahead, but because they looked to an early peace and not to a long war they made mistakes. In either event the industries of non-German lands were to supplement the German economy, but expectations of an easy war led the economic planners to plan initially in terms of the New Order and, particularly in the east, to neglect or dismantle heavy industry: for over a year no attempt was made to repair factories and plants damaged by the retreating Russians, so that these were back in working order only shortly before the retreating Germans had to blow them up again.

The German economy had not been prepared for a long war. Hitler expected the war to be short and the German economy to take it in its stride. Production was adapted to the needs of the moment but not at first expanded. Thus in 1940 aircraft production was reduced (by 40 per cent) because the army needed more tanks and the navy more submarines, while in the next year factories which had made this switch were required to revert to aircraft because the Luftwaffe regained priority over the army and the navy in the light of its need to repair before Barbarossa the damage it had suffered in the Battle of Britain. But with the failure of Barbarossa to achieve its objectives by the end of the year it became inescapably clear that Germany needed a greatly expanded arms base and must also exploit the industrial potential of conquered countries both to contribute to Germany's arms production and to manufacture those other goods which Germany was ceasing to make for itself as its industry was converted to materials of war.

In areas formally or virtually annexed to the Reich, where there was no collision between short-term and long-term aims, industries were incorporated into German industry in order to enlarge its capacity. In Silesia, for example, coal production was very greatly expanded, synthetic oil refineries were built, and heavy engineering and arms production were developed. To the east of the areas which were treated as part of the Reich Goering ordered the transfer to Germany of all enterprises 'not absolutely essential for the maintenance of the bare existence of the inhabitants at a low level', unless transport difficulties made it more practicable to keep them at work on German orders where they were. In general, industry in the east was limited to producing goods and services required by Germany's armed forces and administrators, satisfying what Goering considered to be the bare needs of the local population and processing raw materials. In the west, after an initial few months of looting stocks and equipment, the policy was to exploit industrial capacity by nurturing and milking useful enterprises and to close down the rest by depriving them of raw materials. Factories which went on working had to deliver a high proportion of their output to the Germans; in some cases these levies reached 100 per cent (for example, of magnesium, heavy castings, industrial precision parts). The equipment of factories which closed was either taken to Germany or left to rot, while their labour was transferred to war work in Germany or occupied countries or assigned to the Todt Organization, which constructed the defences, installations and buildings needed by the armed forces outside Germany. Production of non-military goods was increased as German industry became more exclusively concentrated on war production, and towards the end of the war there was some dispersal of war production from Germany as a result of bombing.

The German apparatus of control was very powerful. Allocations of fuel and raw materials were regulated by licences issued by special agencies which were either German or under close German supervision. German specialists were often attached to industrial concerns. All contracts above a certain value had to be reported to the authorities and any firm attempting to do business without such notification lost its allocations. This relatively negative kind of control was supplemented by the active desire of collaborationist governments to keep their industries going and to maintain employment and the capital resources of the country. They therefore welcomed German orders. In some cases the German authorities placed orders with particular firms for goods which went straight to Germany and were paid for either through a clearing system or by being set against the occupation costs which the Germans charged for their presence and sustenance in occupied countries. (These occupation costs were far higher than the real costs of occupation. They were in fact huge, continuing fines.) In other cases general agreements were made covering whole industries, for example textiles, automobiles. In these cases the type of the product was fixed to suit the Germans, who took what they needed but set aside a proportion for the producing country: the Germans were also able to fix prices since they were the principal purchasers. Thus subordinate governments and foreign industrialists were largely in German hands. Either they worked for the Germans or they were forced to close, and if they were forced to close their employees would probably be sent to do forced labour in Germany. By August 1942 it was estimated that firms could only survive if at least three quarters of their output was for the Germans. The firms which remained in operation lost their independence. If the directors collaborated they had to allow German observers into their plants; if they refused, they were evicted and replaced by German managers and technicians.

Besides this subjection of industry by official processes businesses in occupied countries were taken over either by confiscation or by purchase. Jewish property was confiscated without compensation. So, later, was the property of enemies of the Reich, a category which was interpreted by Seyss-Inquart to include those who had assisted, were assisting or might be expected to assist anti-German activities. In the USSR, where the German state was declared to be the successor in title of the Soviet state, property of the Communist Party or any political association was, together with state property strictly so called, transferred into German state ownership. The same rules were applied to the Baltic states even though property had only been transferred to state ownership in 1939 and the population was markedly pro-German. In Poland an organization was established to confiscate land without compensation and re-sell it to Germans at nominal rates. The German banks extended German control by buying shares in foreign enterprises or in foreign banks which themselves had substantial holdings in such enterprises. In these ways the commanding heights of the economies of conquered countries were captured at practically no cost either by the German state or by major German industrial and financial groups. If this dual approach to expropriation contained within it the seeds of a conflict in Germany between state control and private control, the conflict itself was averted, or postponed, by the loss of the war.

Control was likewise imposed on agriculture. Again, the annexed areas were integrated with the Reich. In western and south-eastern Europe the Germans preferred to exercise control indirectly by strengthening the powers of local Ministries of Agriculture and forcing them to use their powers to implement the requirements of the Reich's Food Office, which prescribed production and delivery quotas, prices, subsidies, and feeding and seeding rates. Germany looked to these territories for much of its food and so kept them at first well equipped with farm machinery and fertilizers – many eastern districts were better supplied than before the war – but from 1941–2 the exigencies of the Russian campaign disrupted this policy. Before the war ended food production in occupied Europe fell by about a quarter and much of it was requisitioned. The requisitions were generally addressed to the individual farmer, who was required to deliver up his produce in return for a claim slip with which he was left to get what compensation he could from his government. Other materials, such as coal, were requisitioned in the same way.

The food left over for civilian consumption became increasingly hard to move as the transport system failed. As a result of shortages of fuel, rubber and rolling stock, food was either not distributed at all or went bad during interminable waits at sidings. The use of canals and barges, where these existed, provided a partial alleviation, but shortages and distribution bottlenecks operating upon each other caused prices to rise steeply. Black markets flourished. Some governments tried to beat them by fixing prices and buying in essential products in order to regulate supply. They were unsuccessful: at one time it was estimated that nine out of every ten eggs marketed in the *département* of the Seine were being sold on the black market. Rations, which were introduced all over occupied Europe at a lower level (Denmark alone excepted) than in Germany, were frequently not honoured. Diets became increasingly vegetarian, and while country people often managed to live well enough half the population was required to exist on two thirds or a half of the pre-war normal.

Epidemics developed – tuberculosis, diphtheria, polio – and were made worse by a shortage of medicines. One of the by-products of undernourishment was an increase in industrial accidents which probably damaged production more than sabotage did. In particular areas at particular times the daily diet sank catastrophically. The worst examples were Athens and some of the Greek islands where it was 600–800 calories in the winter of 1941–2 and some Dutch cities where it fell to 500 calories in the winter of 1944–5. Hunger was made all the more insupportable by cold. Clothing and fuel both became desperately hard to get and – between the drop in real wages and the black market – impossibly expensive. Dutch city-dwellers were reduced to cutting down trees in parks and stealing any scrap which they could find to burn to keep their enfeebled bodies warm. In the east the situation became a tragic farce. The produce of the great granary of the Ukraine was garnered for the Reich but then left to rot because there were not enough trains to move it, until the Reich Commissar, Erich Koch, hit on the idea of doling out surplus stocks to service men going on leave in the form of 'Führer food parcels'. Germany got less out of the USSR after invading it than before. But occupied Europe was forced to yield 25 million tons of food to Germany, most of it requisitioned. During 1941–3 these supplies increased Germany's civilian ration by something between a fifth and a quarter.

It is difficult to give a picture of life in occupied Europe in terms of individuals as opposed to statistics because conditions varied enormously from place to place and from month to month. The constant factor was uncertainty – uncertainty about what could be got and, if it could, what it would cost. Necessities were frequently unobtainable and then suddenly on the market – the black market – at impossible prices. In France, for which reliable figures are easier to come by, the official cost of a kilo of butter rose from forty to sixty-one francs during 1941–3 but this price was entirely unreal, for when butter was available in, say, Paris it fetched by 1943 600–800 francs. Tobacco and wine were rationed to a packet of the one and a litre of the other per adult per week but the rations were notional and black market prices were ten to twelve times the official price. Meat was frequently unobtainable for a month at a time. Meals could be got in subsidized works canteens or restaurants, but each lunch might cost a fifth of a weekly wage, so that a lunch a day more than consumed an entire pay packet. Shoes and clothes were already scarce and expensive by the winter of 1940 when a yard of woollen fabric or a pair of shoes cost the equivalent of half a weekly wage; by 1943 a pair of shoes absorbed six weeks' wages, a suit four to five months'. Coal and electricity were so rigorously restricted that the fuel ration was not enough to cook with, especially as the inferior food available could only be made edible by slow cooking. In Paris a ton of coal rose to the equivalent of two to four months' wages.

The most important of all the commodities which the Germans had to regulate was labour. Germany was short of labour before the war, while in a number of European countries there was appreciable unemployment. This imbalance was accentuated by the call-up of men for the German armed services and by the dislocations of war which put men and women out of work in conquered countries. The *Anschluss* with Austria and the annexation of the Sudetenland had automatically increased the Reich's labour force and there were in addition about

300,000 foreign workers in Germany in 1939 as a result of the operation of the law of supply and demand. During the war this force was enormously increased by three main methods: encouragement of more or less voluntary migration, the use of prisoners of war, and forcible recruitment.

In western and southern countries the Germans advertised the advantages of going to Germany for jobs: sure employment, good conditions, good pay, good holidays. Germany also made agreements with a number of satellite and allied governments, including Italy and Spain, for the supply of permanent and seasonal workers. The response was, however, inadequate, especially when reports of actual conditions in Germany filtered through and showed up the fraudulence of German enticements. Although a foreign worker from the west or south (as distinct from an eastern worker whose wage was derisory) was entitled to the same wage as a German worker, he was often put to less skilled work than he had been doing and so found himself earning less than he had expected. He had to pay German taxes and contribute to social insurance schemes from which he was not likely to benefit, since he did not expect to remain in Germany; and when inflation took hold of his home country without any corresponding increase in his German wage, he and his family found that the real return for his labours was drastically cut.

The Germans had therefore to stimulate volunteering by making work in occupied countries more difficult to come by and more unpleasant. Men who were physically fit but who declined to volunteer to go to Germany lost unemployment pay; men in prison for civil offences were released if they promised to go; managements were forced to dismiss entire categories of workers needed in Germany; factories were closed; normal working hours were extended to a seventy-two-hour week or a thirteen-hour day; ration cards were withheld. These measures were the bridge between voluntary recruitment and the use of physical force. Between May 1940 and May 1941 the foreign labour force in the Reich rose by almost two million, the percentage of foreign labour from 3.2 to 8.4. By mid-1944 the percentage was 19.7. The voluntary element became very thin, the more so after allied bombing added to the discomforts of working in Germany. Sauckel estimated in 1944 that out of five million foreigners working in Germany fewer than 200,000 had come voluntarily.

The first prisoners put to work were some two to three hundred thousand Poles captured in the 1939 campaign and this number was greatly increased by the German victories in west and east in 1940 and 1941.

Thereafter there were close on two million prisoners working for Germany until the war ended. The rules of war which Germany had accepted permitted the employment of prisoners other than officers, but the conditions which Germany's prisoners – most of them captured in the east – were forced to put up with during the Second World War contravened all the rules of war and of human decency. By 1944 about 40 per cent of them were, according to Albert Speer at Nuremberg, being used directly or indirectly in arms production. Non-commissioned officers were generally required to work and so too were Russian commissioned officers: the Nazis in effect did not recognize the validity of a Russian commission. Russian prisoners were paid half wages.

The German attitude to Russian combatants was one of calculated callousness. Since they regarded Slavs and communists as hardly better than Jews, the Germans killed them or allowed them to die with similar cruelty and, likewise, in millions. The total number of prisoners taken by the German armies in the USSR was in the region of 5.5 million. Of these the astounding number of 3.5 million or more had been lost by the middle of 1944 and the assumption must be that they were either deliberately killed or done to death by criminal negligence. Nearly two million of them died in camps and close on another million disappeared while in military custody either in the USSR or in rear areas; a further quarter of a million disappeared or died in transit between the front and destinations in the rear; another 473,000 died or were killed in military custody in Germany or Poland. (About 800,000 were released either on the grounds that they were not Russians or for volunteering to serve against the Russians, leaving therefore about one million, of whom 875,000 were, by German standards, fit for work.) This slaughter of prisoners cannot be accounted for by the peculiar chaos of the war in the east. In such a war some prisoners will die through insufficient attention, but not millions of them. The true cause was the inhuman policy of the Nazis towards the Russians as a people and the acquiescence of army commanders in attitudes and conditions which amounted to a sentence of death on their prisoners. The Nazis encouraged barbarity against Russians by warning German troops to expect barbarity from them. The Russians were portrayed as uncivilized hordes. In addition the Germans made play with the fact that the USSR had not adhered to the Geneva Convention of 1929 on the treatment of prisoners of war, although it was known in Germany that the Russian armies had been ordered to observe the Geneva rules and the USSR had formally through Sweden requested reciprocal observance. In practice the Germans refused. Goering told Ciano that Russian prisoners of war, having eaten everything possible including the soles of their boots, had begun to eat each other and, 'which is more serious, had also eaten a German sentry . . . some nations must be decimated . . . there is nothing to be done about it'.

As the war went on forced labour became the only possible answer to Germany's problems. It was in addition sanctioned by ideology. On the day of the inauguration of Hans Frank's régime in Poland all Jews were formally condemned to forced labour and all other Poles were equally formally deprived of any right to leisure. The obligation to work included the liability to be sent to work in Germany. These regulations were copied by Rosenberg in 1941 for the Baltic states and the USSR. They were enforced by terror. Any person resisting recruitment was likely to see his house burned down and his family seized as hostages and sent to a labour camp. One of Rosenberg's principal officials compared the proceedings to the blackest days of the slave trade. He recorded that people were rounded up and shipped to Germany without any regard to health or age and that by 1942 over 100,000 had had to be sent back because they were utterly useless. Many of them died on the way and the next contingent of westbound workers would have to wait until the dead bodies of their rejected compatriots had been thrown out of the windows in order to make room for them in the disgusting trains (which incidentally were badly needed by the army). Women gave birth in the trains and the babies were thrown out onto the embankment. One German official charged with the provision of skilled Ukrainian labour for the Reich complained that his trains were held up by returning transports filled with discarded persons packed fifty or sixty to a truck and that eastward and westward bound trains stood motionless alongside each other for long periods; he added that his recruits often went hungry in these circumstances and that even the German Red Cross refused to feed them on the grounds that they were Russian swine. Another official complained of the propaganda effects when 400,000 Ukrainian domestic helps were being sent to Germany and before they arrived the German press announced that they would have no free time, would not be allowed to go to cinemas, theatres or restaurants, and might only be absent from the house where they worked for three hours a week at the most. His memorandum denounced the political ineptitude of treating eastern Europeans as second class whites in the sight of the whole coloured world and reminded his colleagues that the Russians were fighting 'with exceptional bravery and sacrifice for nothing more nor less than the recognition of their human dignity'. But the mixture of incompetence and callousness went on. By the end of the war the age limit for labour recruitment in the east had been lowered to ten.

The influx of foreign workers enabled Germany to shift labour from civilian to military employment – nearly six million by May 1941, nearly eight million a year later – without introducing compulsory service for women. In 1942 the number of women in civilian employment in Germany was lower by 189,000 than in 1939. But in 1942 the situation was radically altered by the failure to defeat the Russian armies in the field. In 1941 the German army had suffered heavy casualties for the first time and became a competitor with industry for men. In the autumn of 1942 Himmler concluded formal agreements with the Minister of Justice, Otto Thierack, and the Minister for Armaments, Albert Speer, by which the inmates of concentration camps and prisoners of war were released for work in factories in return for the allocation to the SS of a percentage of their output of weapons. The hours of work of the concentration camp victims were unlimited and the Himmler–Thierack agreement provided that 'anti-social' persons might be worked to death.

Forcible recruitment of labour was introduced in the west and south-east as well as in the east. Stricter controls were imposed in the Reich and in March 1942 Fritz Sauckel was appointed Plenipotentiary for the Deployment of Labour with extensive powers over the recruitment, use and distribution of German and foreign labour. Sauckel, whose appointment was part of no plan but a reaction to external events, collected over two million more foreign workers by May 1943 and increased the total labour force in Germany by just under two million in one year in spite of the drain caused by the demands of the fighting services. But his field for recruitment was narrowing. Poland had already been forced to contribute to the limit of its capacity. South-eastern Europe could not be denuded without imperilling the supplies of food which it provided for the Reich. In the USSR skilled labour had retreated eastward with the Russian armies and unskilled labour was largely required by the military and civilian authorities in the German occupied zones. In western Europe unemployment had been eliminated by earlier labour drives and by the demands of factories which were working for the Reich. From 1943 the difficulties became even acuter in both east and west – in the east because the advancing Russian armies reduced the area from which labour might be drawn, and in the west because labour was needed locally to make good the shortfall in German factories occasioned by bottlenecks and bombing. Moreover the machinery of German control was breaking down. Even in the west the

Germans ceased to operate through local governments and began to round up labour in the streets of big cities – in one operation in Marseilles they kidnapped 1,000 French police by forcing them into lorries while they were on an exercise – and to seize the fathers of men who took to the woods and hills. Yet in Belgium 23,000 men evaded compulsory labour service by escaping to the Ardennes and in one area of France 95 per cent of those called for labour service during the winter of 1943–4 got away. Metaphorically Sauckel was being required to squeeze blood from a stone. In practice his minions squeezed it from human beings as they combed Europe for workers. Until the last year of the war Sauckel produced enough manpower to keep war production going and even to increase it, but after the middle of 1944 the economy began to crumble and not even the appointment of yet another plenipotentiary – this time Goebbels as Plenipotentiary for Total War – could keep the factories going.

The conditions of the millions of foreigners who worked for Nazi Germany varied according to their skills and racial ratings, but even the most favoured were shockingly treated. Jews as a rule were exterminated even if capable of working. Eastern workers fared worse than western or southern ones, Russians worse than Poles, Poles worse than the Baltic nations. The best treated were the skilled Danes, Flemings, Swiss and Hungarians, after them the French and Dutch, further down the scale the less skilled and racially inferior Balkan and Mediterranean peoples, including Italians and Spaniards, for whom the Germans had little respect even though they did not inspire the loathing directed against Slavs. For all of them Sauckel decreed that they should be fed, housed and treated in such a way as to ensure maximum production at minimum cost, and eastern workers in particular were kept in conditions which, besides being horridly inhumane, were also inefficient since they made them unfit for work and so reduced their output unnecessarily quickly. Agricultural workers were mostly housed and fed by their employers, but factory workers lived in barracks or in camps where they were segregated in huts by nationality. The camps, which were for western workers, were guarded by men and barbed wire; the inmates were not allowed out except to work. The huts were badly built, scantily furnished and scandalously lacking in sanitation. They were overcrowded, unheated and, as the war went on, unrepaired. Rations were in theory the same as those of German civilians, although in the case of eastern workers there was not even a pretence that they were: Goering ordered Russians to be fed lightly and without seriously interfering with German rations. In the camps ration cards were surrendered to the commandant who was free to provide what he thought fit in exchange. The diet of an eastern worker in a German labour camp was never within 1,000 calories of the lowest German ration, and the quality of the food was so poor that disease and mortality rates were preternaturally high. Concentration-camp workers received a diet roughly equivalent to the 1941–2 Athens famine rate.

But from the German point of view these miserable victims served their purpose. They constituted a fifth of Germany's wartime labour force; in 1944 there were seven million of them in the Reich. According to Albert Speer the western and Italian workers among them were at this date responsible for 25–30 per cent of the German effort. In addition Europe made, over the whole period of Germany's dominion from 1940 to 1944, contributions in kind equivalent to 14 per cent of Germany's own gross product and so increased by rather more than 50 per cent the resources available to Germany for the purchase of arms and equipment. No slavedriver could have hoped for more.

CHAPTER 13

Resistance

CONSCRIPTED labourers, prisoners of war, Jews, communists and gypsies were all minority groups. Even together they were still a minority of the peoples who came under German rule. The great majority stayed where they were or returned to their homes after having been temporarily scattered by the German advances. Some experienced life in a battle zone and in an army rear area; most of them a much longer spell under some form of occupational régime while the great bulk of Germany's front-line fighting forces was engaged on Russian soil. Only in the east, and to a lesser degree in Italy, did civilian populations live through protracted fighting.

The first shock left little room for anything except the sheer facts of defeat and abandonment. Those in the path of the *Blitzkrieg* were left dazed as the Germans swept away the familiar things of daily life from goods and houses to the governments and officials to whom a settled people is wont to turn for guidance or instruction in a crisis. Communities were atomized. The individual's first thought was to find his family, recover his belongings and get himself a job and a livelihood. The job became all important, first as a means for securing the necessities of life in a strange world and later in order to qualify for exemption from forced labour; a job meant also a renewal of contact with familiar routines, an assurance that some things remained the same. But jobs were scarce and in the immediate wake of defeat there was widespread unemployment. Many factories were reduced to a ten-hour week and earnings sagged until labour began to be required again for reconstruction and the occupiers' needs (building airfields, for example). Some employers paid reduced wages to help and keep their workers during temporary stoppages caused by lack of materials or power, but poverty spread alarmingly as the gap between earnings and prices widened at both ends and large quantities of food, clothing and other necessities disappeared into expensive black markets. Poverty caused neglect of children, social divisions and crime. The towns became resentful of the comparatively better-fed countryside; the law-abiding resented the profits made by black marketeers who, since they sold mostly to Germans, were beyond the reach of the law; the poor looked with rising anger at the advantages of the rich (in Paris, to take an extreme case, the six most famous restaurants were exempt from all restrictions until 1943). Crimes such as theft, whether committed by adults or juveniles, multiplied and became respectable; in the Netherlands the crime rate almost trebled; stealing was both a symptom of poverty and a form of protest. Scruples of all kinds wilted in the face of need, and the hostility of the have-nots against the haves quickened. Prostitution increased by as much as tenfold as a result of financial hardship and the break-up of family life; women with no previous police records traded themselves to German soldiers in spite of the hostility which their conduct provoked among their more forbearing compatriots.

As a general rule everybody over fifteen had to have an identity card, observe a curfew and expect to have his movements restricted. The police state arrived on the heels of the German army. Jews had to produce baptismal certificates of grandparents or lose their citizenship. Few people possessed such documents but a number were forged by Christian clergymen. Freedom of movement was curtailed by the virtual elimination of private transport and severe limitations on public transport. Bicycle-taxis appeared in towns. Mail was censored and in some cases prohibited: between the zones of France the only kind of mail allowed was printed postcards with simple messages of the 'we are well/ill . . .' type, from which the sender could choose one by crossing out the rest. Newspapers either became pro-German and sparse of news or disappeared; about half of the national and local press ceased publication and the circulation of the survivors dropped sharply. Radio programmes continued under German control. The Germans offered good pay to well-known broadcasters, kept favourite programmes on the air and tried to use radio to propagate their views, but the nature of radio prevented them from securing a monopoly, and although they penalized listeners to enemy broadcasts they could not proscribe transmissions from neutral Switzerland, whose broadcasts became an important item in preserving for the conquered a window on the world. But life narrowed and this spiritual retrenchment was reflected in swelling attendances at cinemas and sporting events – even when, later, the Resistance admonished people to stay away. It also threw families together and sharpened the demand for books, including serious books about national history and culture.

Immediately after the end of the fighting there was a marked difference between those parts of a country which had seen the war at first hand in the form either of enemy armies or of refugees, and other parts which had learned of it by hearsay. Soon, however, all parts faced the same question: attitudes to the victors; to which was added the secondary question of attitudes to collaborators, which were often more bitterly intense. As people recovered they tended to divide into two groups, those who on the whole accepted the new world in which they had woken up again and those who felt too angry or too ashamed to do so. Although ultimately the Germans earned widespread hate, at first their coming raised more questioning than clear-cut emotions. The behaviour of the occupying forces in the west was for the most part correct and even affable and it was some time before their habit of strolling around singly in villages and towns was replaced by more circumspect promenading in pairs or groups and the abandonment of attempts at social intercourse with the natives; even where there was from the beginning a wall of silence, there was also that mutual respect which has been most tellingly portrayed in Vercors' *Le Silence de la mer*. Some countries had an anti-German tradition but others – Greece, for example, which was anti-Italian but not initially anti-German – had not. The Germans were given the benefit of the doubt. Attitudes crystallized slowly in societies which had been atomized and people were thrown back on local or personal motives in deciding what to think and how to conduct themselves. There was something of a psychological vacuum in which the Germans had, and lost, their chances. There was no overall pattern. In a country like France, where the Third Republic had failed to command wide enough allegiance, the new order benefited at the start from adventitious aids such as the countervailing respect for Pétain (especially in the lower reaches of the social scale), an intensification of anti-British feelings among the bourgeoisie and a reinforcement of anti-radicalism. But these were not inherently pro-German feelings. They only gave a conditioned blessing to the German presence and perpetuated for a while after the armistice the confusion created by war. Only in the east did it swiftly become clear that the German occupation was a threat to the entire population and that the choice lay between resistance and extermination.

In most places there was a case for collaboration, for lying low for the time being. Moreover the disruptions of war and the contradictions of the occupation made it difficult for ordinary people to get a lead from their traditional mentors. In Belgium the king had declared himself a prisoner while his government had fled to London to continue the fight. In Denmark the king and government were undisguisedly anti-German. The king ignored German salutations on his daily rides through his capital, sent telegrams of sympathy to police wounded in a fight in which 300 Danish Nazis were arrested, gave an audience to a well-known historian just before he was arrested for spreading anti-German propaganda, and eventually threatened to abdicate if anti-semitic legislation was introduced, but he and his government also officially discouraged anti-German activities and recommended a policy of acquiescence for a considerable time.

Two things in particular resolved this ambivalence: the course of the war and the behaviour of the Germans. A numb acceptance of Germany's victories sprang not only from the shock of defeat but also from the conviction that defeat was complete and final. Men like de Gaulle who never accepted defeat at any moment were rare and had the logic of events against them. But even before the end of 1940 doubt began to spread. The failure of the Luftwaffe in the Battle of Britain and the British initiative in Africa at the end of the year showed that the war was not over. The entry of the Russians and then the Americans into the war in 1941 showed that the Germans were going to lose it. These events became well-known throughout occupied Europe through broadcasting and a clandestine press which became amazingly extensive. One of the most important facts about occupied Europe was that people in it knew what was going on. This knowledge was due to radio which prevented Europe from being totally cut off. The BBC's news services were widely heard and believed; Swiss radio, with its built-in reputation for neutral impartiality, played a similar role; communists, who took after June 1941 an exceptionally important part in Resistance, listened to broadcasts from the USSR, which possessed the most powerful transmitter in the world and the longest experience in broadcasting propaganda; governments-in-exile in London reached their compatriots with news and exhortation and gave them a factual and legal basis for opposing the Germans and their satellite régimes.

Foreign broadcasts nourished indigenous clandestine newspapers. The clandestine press became an industry of great potency in forming the will to resist. In Belgium about 12,000 persons came to be engaged in it and published 300 papers; in France underground presses produced books in fine editions as well as over 1,000 papers and pamphlets (this figure included regional editions of the same paper); in Denmark the number of papers published rose from 222 in the whole of 1943 to 315 in the first four months of 1945 and by the end of 1944 over 10 million copies of these papers and pamphlets had been printed and distributed; in the Netherlands some papers appeared three times a week after the confiscation of radio sets in 1943 and the five principal left-wing papers attained a combined circulation of 450,000. The distribution of this quantity of material was a well organized and yet highly risky business, handled by members of small local groups who took their lives in their hands with every sheet which they delivered to a neighbour. These groups and their newspapers recall the secret societies which carried on the revolution in France underground after the restoration of the *ancien régime* in 1814. Through their efforts the underground in Europe was in general better informed about the war than the regular combatants were about the underground. The flow of information was an essential factor in rebuilding the societies which had been smitten by the German victories and in stimulating opposition to a no longer invincible victor. It restored to the defeated a sense of coherence and a sense of purpose, and the clandestine press which raised the morale of Resisters likewise demoralized an enemy who, having thought that he had finished off the opposition, was presented with evidence of its persistence and even began to exaggerate it. The activities of the clandestine press led to other forms of resistance, as the confidence of these groups expanded and with their confidence their aims. Many active Resisters served an apprenticeship by helping to run a clandestine paper.

The German contribution to anti-Germanism was no less substantial. The natural nationalist opposition to the presence of Germans was swollen by opposition to their behaviour. Besides being aliens, they showed themselves inhumane: Jews were segregated, deported and killed – the round-up of Jews in the Vélodrome d'Hiver shocked Parisian opinion even more than the taking of hostages; human rights and freedoms were trampled on far beyond the necessities of war and occupation; the new rulers pillaged the material resources of the defeated, failed to provide them with enough food and conscripted them for labour in appalling conditions; prisoners of war did not come back; all in all the non-German individual was degraded body and soul. This inhumanity converted the resentment of the subject populations into hatred – which in Norway was given an edge of a very special kind, for in the First World War Norwegians had looked after German children, and they were filled with disgust at the thought that the invading armies of 1940 probably contained some of these very children grown to be violators of the charity shown to them twenty-five years earlier. Hatred of the Germans fostered various forms of opposition such as networks for helping fugitive allied servicemen who had been shot down or had escaped from prison camps; the collection and forwarding of military intelligence; the clandestine press; industrial sabotage, go-slows and strikes; and eventually the beginnings of organized and active armed resistance.

But the Germans went even further. Confronted with this opposition they took the iron fist right out of its velvet glove and began to use terror as a principal means of government. Hostages were taken and shot, concentration camps established, stunning reprisals exacted and picked areas devastated. Although the details varied in practice from country to country the overall pattern was uniform because it reflected not individual initiative or local eccentricity but a policy devised and commanded at the highest level in the German state, the Nazi Party and the armed services. Thus in December 1941 Keitel, as Chief of Staff of the Armed Forces, issued the *Nacht und Nebel* (Night and Fog) order which was designed to strike fear into whole populations. Hitler, he said, was interested in no penalty except death; no other deterrent seemed to him effective; even a sentence of hard labour for life struck him as a sign of weakness. Consequently the *Nacht und Nebel* order decreed that in cases where the death penalty was unlikely to be imposed by a court in an occupied country, offences against the Reich were to be visited with a substitute death. The offender was to be secretly spirited away to the Reich without trial, leaving friends and relations to tremble in suspense for his fate – and theirs.

The distinction between guilt and innocence had already been virtually abolished, for as early as September 1941 Keitel had instructed commanders on all fronts to ascribe all acts of resistance to communists and to execute batches of so-called communists for every German soldier killed: fifty to a hundred communists was the number recommended. A few weeks later fifty hostages were executed in France as a reprisal for the death of a German officer, and a further fifty a few days later when another officer was killed; the executions would have been twice as many but for strenuous intervention by Vichy. By the end of the war about 30,000 French hostages had been shot and the toll was comparable all over occupied Europe. In the Netherlands Seyss-Inquart revealed in May 1942 that 480 prominent Dutch personages were being held and that many had already been shot in retaliation for breaches of public order; on another occasion the village of Putten was burned down and all its males deported (very few ever returned) after a German motorcar had been attacked in the neighbourhood and one German wounded. In Poland a tally was established of one hundred Resisters to be killed for the death of every one German, and at Palmiry, a village near Warsaw, several thousand deaths were in fact exacted in revenge for a single attack. At Televaag in Norway 300 houses were burned down, 76 persons deported and a further 260 interned in April 1942 in an attempt to intimidate and quell Norwegian resistance. The first case of devastation and mass executions in Italy occurred at Boves in Piedmont in September 1943, while in Rome 330 people picked at random were executed in March 1944 after thirty-two German soldiers had been killed by a bomb. At Oradour-sur-Glane, selected by a mistake instead of a place of the same name a few kilometres away, only ten persons out of a population of 652 survived the calculated fury of the Germans, the men being shot and the women and children being locked into the church and burned to death. This last enormity occurred in July 1944.

The most famous of these razzias befell the village of Lidice in Czechoslovakia where the entire population was killed or sent to concentration camps with a horrifying sort of nonchalance in revenge for the assassination of Heydrich. At the end of 1941 two men from the Czechoslovak army in England, one a Czech and the other a Slovak, had arrived by parachute, with British assistance, in order to do this deed, which was undertaken in the belief that Heydrich and his police chief, Karl Hans Frank, were planning to destroy the entire Czech people. It was achieved in the following May when the two executioners threw a bomb into Heydrich's open car. He took a week to die. About 1,500 Czechs were immediately killed, including the executioners and another 120 members of the Resistance who had escaped into a church. In addition, 3,000 Jews were removed from the concentration camp at Terezin (Theresienstadt) and sent to Poland to be killed. But this was not the end. A few days after Heydrich's death, Lidice, apparently selected at random, was sealed off by the SD. That day nothing much happened, although a woman and a small boy were shot and killed for trying to escape. The next day the entire male population over sixteen years of age was shot in batches – 172 of them in a leisurely massacre which took ten hours; the women were sent to Ravensbrueck concentration camp and the children to a different camp; pregnant women were first allowed to give birth to their children in hospital and then joined their friends in Ravensbrueck, their babies having been killed. Lidice itself was razed to the ground. Lezaky, another small village near Prague, was treated in the same way a few days later. These savage reprisals were supplemented by some 10,000 arrests. The Czech composer Martinů, who had fled from Paris to the United States in 1940, composed an orchestral 'Memorial to Lidice'.

As things got worse for the Germans, so did their behaviour. In July 1944 Hitler ordered all saboteurs to be executed on the spot and all suspects to be handed over to the SD (which was worse). This decree, called the *Kugelerlass* or Bullet Decree, was a form of words for transferring wide categories of prisoners to the SD for execution. It did not apply to British or American combatants unless they were commandos (in which case they were already covered by the Commando Order of 1942 requiring them to be summarily slaughtered to the last man, even if they surrendered). The *Kugelerlass* was extended two months after its promulgation to prisoners under sentence and to those whose cases were still pending. Keitel explained that there was to be no compunction about innocent persons who might accidentally get killed in the course of the measures needed to eliminate what he called dissidents. The response to these foul and frantic measures was active armed resistance on a militarily significant scale and, complementarily, a dwindling of the numbers of collaborators and *attentistes* as the complicity involved in siding with the Germans or even doing nothing amounted to condoning the unforgivable.

Such were the cumulative sources of Resistance. The word itself did not make its appearance at once. In France it does not seem to have been in general use before 1943, although Gaullism had by that time become a well-known term. The phenomenon of Resistance, however, appeared immediately after defeat, if only in modest, disconnected and often unsuccessful forms, spontaneous expressions of spirit by disbanded officers and men of the fighting forces which the Germans were usually able to master without much difficulty. Most people remained, then and for some time thereafter, very vague about their neighbours' activities and about Resistance movements, and also ignorant (as they were meant to be) about the separate intelligence and escapers' networks. People heard that something was going on without knowing what it was. The development of Resistance was to some extent dependent on growing awareness of its existence and endorsement of its aims and methods, and this interacting process took time. It was not until the butcher, the baker and the candlestick maker felt moved to join active Resistance groups that there could be active Resistance groups for them to join. The process was one of awareness leading to complicity, and complicity leading to activity. Movements grew as householders sheltered Resisters, fed them, lent rooms for radio transmissions, failed to report raids on their farms by gangs who might be Resisters (though sometimes they were not), and so gradually became more deeply and sometimes more actively involved.

In point of time the earliest forms of opposition were intelligence networks which had in some cases been formed before the war began – in Czechoslovakia, for instance, in 1938. Some of these became so extensive that they were able to shadow and report on the entirety of the official administrative machine. Besides spying on German activities and installations they recruited their own agents and helped agents who arrived from outside (mostly by parachute). Belgium, partly because of its proximity to England, was specially active in this work, providing some 5,000 agents, supported by another 13,000 helpers. Czechoslovakia, to which aircraft from England could safely make the return flight only on moonless nights, was less closely linked but provided valuable information both to Great Britain and, before Barbarossa, to the Russians, to whom it supplied detailed warnings of the impending German attack, including the names of the airfields which the Luftwaffe intended to attack; Czech Intelligence also unmasked a German sabotage group working beyond the Urals. In Poland an underground organization operated throughout the country, reporting on German troop movements, following the Germans as far as the Volga and the Caucasus and dispatching in 1942–4 some 300 reports to the west by radio or by courier via Hungary, Sweden and Switzerland. In Greece, to take a further example from another quarter, 1,072 agents – Greek, British, American and Polish – were dropped during 1941–4 and stayed in the country for varying lengths of time, usually a few months.

Similar to the intelligence networks were the escape routes along which escaped prisoners or airmen who had been shot down (and who, especially in England in 1940, were urgently needed back with their units) or Europeans seeking a way to re-enter the fight by getting to England were passed from hand to hand, sometimes by men and women who had performed the same service in the First World War or by their children. These routes were often long and intricate, running from Belgium or northern France or Germany itself through Switzerland and unoccupied France to Spain, Portugal or Africa; or from Poland through Czechoslovakia, Hungary, Yugoslavia and Italy; or northwards to Sweden. In Belgium alone some thirty-five groups were engaged in this work at one time or another, employing 10,000 persons and using their own teleprinter communications.

These were examples of the more obviously useful services which Resisters could render. They were of their nature clandestine. But resistance was also effective in more open, if less concrete, ways. People came to realize that it was worth showing how they felt, and that strong feelings did not have to find vent in such dangerous activities as spying or such violent ones as guerrilla warfare. They used symbols and badges, like the red, white and blue knitted caps with which Danish students paraded their affinity with the RAF; or the Dutch habit of raising their hats when the traffic lights turned to the symbolic orange colour; or the Parisian students' mimicry of Germans, especially German whose dress they copied by sporting their biros in the way that the Luftwaffe wore daggers. They even used silence, abruptly terminating all conversation if a German entered a shop or, again in Paris, rising and leaving university lectures if Germans came in to attend them. (The Germans closed the Sorbonne after a demonstration at the tomb of the unknown soldier at the Arc de Triomphe in November 1940.) Anti-German leaflets were slipped into licensed newspapers before distribution, a simple way of getting a large circulation. University laboratories were used to make bombs for the Resistance. Post-office workers intercepted denunciatory letters addressed to the SD by opening all SD mail and significantly impeded the activities of the SD which depended on a network of correspondents – amounting in Paris alone to eight to ten thousand persons. Police went into the business of forging false identity papers, a contribution which they were specially equipped to make owing to their familiarity with the genuine articles and their possession of genuine official stamps. Administrators turned their talents to losing dossiers and protracting discussions with the occupiers. A peculiar form of patriotic self-denial practised in France was hoarding instead of spending coins containing nickel and bronze in order to deny the metals to the Germans; this ingenious tactic not only created an embarrassing shortage of small change but also represented a considerable sacrifice by the poor, who had to go without the things which their coins could have bought.

From these non-violent declarations of hostility Resisters passed to equally non-violent but more positive protests, such as the resignation of the Norwegian bishops and nearly all the judges of the Norwegian High Court and the almost unanimous refusal of Norwegian teachers to sign an undertaking to teach in accordance with Quisling's party line, a protest which was backed up by hundreds of thousands of signed letters from parents. But moral resistance of this kind was possible only in countries where the Germans were, at least comparatively, lenient. In the east spiritual resistance could not be overt, but it occurred none the less, as witness the clandestine education of two to three thousand students in Poland and the continuance of scientific work and the secret publication of its results.

Economic resistance occurred everywhere. The methods were sometimes almost trivial but the results were vast. Germany was denied the fruits of European labour and skill which, in an atmosphere less poisoned by hate, could have contributed extensively to Germany's war effort and home comforts. The means included going to work regularly a quarter of an hour late, mixing labels on packages so that they went to the wrong destination, more serious sabotage in factories and on railways, and strikes. Polish economic sabotage affected the delivery of Russian goods to Germany before Barbarossa and the supplying of the German armies on the eastern fronts after it, in both cases on a large scale. Sabotage in Czechoslovakia had become a serious worry to Heydrich before his assassination, and Czechs conscripted into the German army also engaged in sabotage. Strikes in Italy were the precursors of the fall of Mussolini and were repeated against the Germans when they occupied the northern half of the country. There were a number of extensive strikes in the Netherlands. But the strike was a dangerous weapon, which many workers were unwilling to use. It entailed not only loss of job and pay but, consequently, liability for deportation to compulsory labour service in Germany; and the leaders of the Dutch strikes were executed.

The more spectacular operations included two Anglo-Norwegian raids on the Lofoten Islands in 1941, when several thousand tons of shipping and eighteen cod-liver-oil factories were destroyed. These raids were a good example of the hazards of Resistance. Besides the material damage inflicted, they gave a boost to British and perhaps to Norwegian morale and kept Hitler guessing about his enemies' intentions, but they also provoked heavy reprisals and, when the British withdrew without warning on the second occasion after a week's stay which the local inhabitants had expected to be permanent, bitter resentment among the Norwegians left behind and an official protest from the Norwegian government in London. The reprisals severely damaged the Resistance movement in the same way, although not quite to the same extent, as the Czech Resistance movement which was virtually destroyed by the reprisals exacted after the death of Heydrich.

Limited operations could, however, be extremely valuable as well as less costly. The British were worried about German nuclear research. They wished to destroy the plant at Vemork in Ryukan in Norway where heavy water was being produced by electrolysis, and early in 1942 a first group of Norwegians from England was dropped in the region to spy out the land. In November a first attempt, by glider attack, to destroy the plant failed but in the following February a party of Norwegians succeeded in putting it out of action for five months. Later in 1943 it was bombed and partially destroyed by the Americans. The allies also wished to destroy the entire stock of heavy water. This involved the sinking of a ferry on which innocent Norwegians would be bound to be travelling. The Norwegian government in London was asked to decide whether this should be done. The government hardened its heart and gave the order to proceed. In similar limited operations valuable stocks of pyrites, iron ore and ball bearings were destroyed. Towards the end of the war sabotage groups were converted into anti-sabotage groups. One of their most notable achievements was the pre-servation by the Belgians of the port of Antwerp which was placed intact into the hands of the allies immediately they entered the city.

A large part of the Danish Resistance effort was directed to sabotaging Germany's exploitation of Denmark's food and strategic position. The Danish government refrained at first from encouraging sabotage for fear of reprisals, but the British pressed for more activity and got their way towards the end of 1942. The anomalies in the Danish situation were largely removed by the German take-over in 1943, when the official government ceased to function and a less inhibited, undercover government was formed under the name of the Freedom Council. From 1943 sabotage, and especially railway sabotage, increased: there were nearly 2,000 separate incidents in the first four months of 1945. At the other end of Europe the Greek Resistance, by blowing up the Gorgopotamos viaduct in November 1942, interrupted for six weeks the main route by which German supplies were going to Rommel in Africa and brought the port of Piraeus to a standstill. Subsequently Greek sabotage parties derailed 117 trains, destroyed 209 locomotives and 1,544 wagons, cut telephone wires and wrecked various tunnels, bridges and motor vehicles. Similar damage was inflicted on communi-cations all over Europe. Much of it was quickly repaired by the Ger-mans.

Economic sabotage merged into military action. The essential requirements were suitable terrain and climate and the support of the population. Without places to hide and people to help the dice were too heavily loaded in favour of the regular military and police forces of the occupiers. The Netherlands and Denmark, flat and bare, could not support a powerful militant movement, even with massive popular sympathy (in Denmark in elections in 1943 97 per cent of the votes cast were given to democratic parties and the Danish Nazis won only one seat out of 150); in the USSR partisan activity was impossible in the north and difficult in the Ukraine. Next, the Resistance forces needed training and organization which were to some extent of an orthodox military nature but also markedly unorthodox; and they needed arms. Secret armies had to operate on a cut-and-run basis until their German enemies were demoralized and themselves on the run. Attempts by partisans to fight pitched battles often led to disaster (as for example in

the Vercors and at Montmouchet, as will be related in a later chapter).
Active Resistance groups tended to form in the first place round regular
officers adrift from defeated armies, but these first leaders were as a
general rule superseded by new men who rose to command by proving
their aptitude for the new kinds of warfare prescribed by circumstances.
These leaders had to strike a balance between the need for caution in
the face of a superior enemy – the need to score points but also to survive to carry on the fight – and on the other hand the need to engage
the enemy frequently and effectively enough to satisfy their followers.
Arms were not less important than tactics and there was a constant tug
of war between the accumulation of arms (by raids or by parachute
drops from outside) and the loss of arms through discovery of dumps
by German Intelligence: this last danger put pressure on Resistance
leaders to use arms when they had them instead of waiting for a more
propitious moment.

Active Resistance contributed to the tribulations and ultimately to the
defeat of the Germans by tying down units or preventing their orderly
transfer from one front to another and by engaging them in battle. The
threat of an armed rising in Norway by the Resistance movement
called Milorg in cooperation with allied forces constrained Hitler to
detail thirteen army divisions, 90,000 naval personnel, 6,000 SS men
and 12,000 para-military troops to watch and control a country with a
total population of only three million, and at the end of the war Milorg
received the surrender of 400,000 Germans (ten times Milorg's own
strength) and liberated over 90,000 prisoners of war, nearly all of them
Russians. When the Anglo-American armies landed in Normandy in
July 1944 French Resistance forces delayed the reinforcement of the
crucial sector: the SS division *Das Reich* took nine days to get from
south-western France to the battle area. In September the Dutch paralysed the railways at the time of the allied advance towards Nijmwegen
and Arnhem. The Danes harassed and impeded the withdrawal of
German forces from Norway to the defence of Germany itself. National
armies were reborn and rejoined the war: 120,000 Belgians were
fighting as regular units by the end of the war, the Danish secret army
was 45,000 strong, 60,000 Czechs fought with the Russian army in
addition to the units which had been serving with British forces since
the beginning. In France the Alpine departments and the Massif
Central were liberated by the French Resistance, whose total contribution at the time of the re-invasion of Europe was put by Eisenhower at
the equivalent of fifteen divisions.

This impressive resurgence of European nationalism in arms helped to salve the humiliation of the defeats in 1940–41 and by doing so contributed more to the spiritual rehabilitation of Europe, which was in the balance, than to the defeat of Germany, which was assured by other forces. It also emphasized the national character of European policies since the Resistance movements were nationalist not only in the sense of being anti-German but also in the almost complete absence of any contacts among themselves. At one point Resistance leaders met at a conference in Switzerland and discussed a new and less nationally divided Europe, harking back to Mazzinian ideas of a confraternity of nationalisms, looking forward to a *Europe des patries*, echoing ideas which were being discussed at the same time by anti-Nazi conspirators inside Germany; but so long as the war continued there was little opportunity for common action. Attempts to concert French and Belgian, Yugoslav and Italian Resistance came to little. A Resistance movement had to be ultra careful about its security and it was often suspicious of its neighbour's politics or ideology. So the international character of the external attack on Germany by the Anglo-American-Russian coalition could not be matched by any corresponding internationalism on the continent. Communism, which might have served as a link between Resistance movements, did not do so during the war because communist resisters were no more able than non-communist resisters to make effective contacts beyond the bounds of their local field of operations. Thirdly, the patriotic aims of Resistance were yoked with objectives of national regeneration and revolution which will be more closely examined in the next chapters. Although Resistance movements began without any definite political purpose and were often anti-political in the sense that they distrusted the political parties and institutions which had failed them before the war, yet at the same time these movements were obliged to be political in another sense. They responded to prevailing popular emotions and aspirations which were of a political nature and, because they were constructive and not merely hostile to occupiers or pre-war régimes, imposed on the Resistance movements a distinctive blend of moral-political programme which was characteristically left-wing.

As Resistance developed it involved not only the Resistance movements themselves inside occupied countries but also governments in exile (all of them in London except the Greek government which was in Cairo) and the organizations established with similar aims by the British and American governments. The first of these in point of time, and for some time the most active, was the British Special Operations Executive (SOE) which was created in July 1940 as a department in the Ministry of Economic Warfare. The date indicated the need: to preserve or renew contacts with a continent from which Great Britain had been expelled and cut off. The Ministry indicated the prime aim: to injure Germany's war-making capacity by sabotage. The two together prescribed the method: to find, train and dispatch small groups of technically equipped demolitionists. At the beginning of the war the British government had made plans for interfering with Germany's supplies of iron ore from Sweden and oil from Rumania and although these had been attended by no success the notion of economic warfare had been embodied in a Department of State, and after Dunkirk Great Britain's inability to do much else in Europe, combined with the emergence of Resistance in the following year and Churchill's decision to foster it, focused attention on the possibilities of sabotage. SOE set to work to find saboteurs with the right aptitudes and languages (they were recruited in French-speaking Canada and polyglot South America as well as among the refugees from Hitler's Europe) and it eventually established sixty training schools for operations in Europe besides others for Asia. These schools sent 7,500 agents, mostly nationals of the countries concerned, to western Europe and 4,000, mostly British agents and military liaison parties, to Italy and south-eastern Europe.

Almost at the outset these operations were extended from sabotage to intelligence. Many intelligence contacts had been broken by the retreat from the continent. In addition, military intelligence networks had been penetrated by the Germans before the war: in Holland, for example, the British headquarters, which was next door to the house made famous in the First World War by Mata Hari, had been under surveillance since 1935 and all visitors to it had been regularly photographed as they went in and out. There was therefore something of an intelligence vacuum and it seemed natural to ask SOE, which was organizing sabotage trips, to get its agents to do some intelligence work too. Unfortunately agents of the one kind are not necessarily the right people for work of the other kind, nor had they been trained for it, and the confusion of the two functions endangered SOE's work. It also endangered Resistance groups, since there were more agents around who had contacts with these groups and were at the same time liable to be picked up by German counter-intelligence or to become unsuspectingly involved with double agents.

A further extension of SOE's work occurred when subversion and insurrection were added to its brief. Churchill told Hugh Dalton, the Minister of Economic Warfare, that it was his business to 'set Europe ablaze'. Prizing variety and unconventionality for their own sake, and stirred perhaps by the historical recollections of chouans, carbonari and klephts, Churchill welcomed the chance to revive the fighting spirit and fighting forces of Europe's nations. He wanted to summon them to make life hell for the Germans and, ultimately, to cooperate with the allies' regular armies when the time should come to return to the continent. But this part of the programme raised unforeseen political complications. SOE's emissaries became charged with diplomatic tasks: persuading Resistance groups to adopt certain policies or tactics, reconciling them with one another for the good of the common cause, reporting on them and advising which were more worthy of support than others. Supplying one organization with arms in preference to another was a political act. The British tried to operate on the principle that the only thing that mattered was harassing the Germans and the only touchstone for deciding between competing groups was this anti-German fervour. But this simple rule of thumb ignored the facts. The Resistance movements were not simply, sometimes not primarily, anti-German. They represented for the time being the domestic politics of their countries. Some of them were fighting against the pre-war order and distrusted or opposed their governments in exile with which the British government was in alliance; and they became more definitely left-wing after Hitler's invasion of the USSR unshackled the communists and set them free to join and try to dominate the Resistance.

To a man with Churchill's uncomplicated sense of purpose these were secondary matters so long as the Germans had to be beaten. He knew that war and politics could not be separated but he also knew which he was going to subordinate to the other. The political issues would have to be dealt with later, by which time they would doubtless present themselves in a new context and a new light. Meanwhile he pledged Great Britain to the restoration of the independence of Europe. He became a European leader. The V sign for victory which he coined and its aural equivalent · · · —, tapped out in Morse or played by the BBC to all Europe in the familiar phrase from Beethoven's fifth symphony, were symbols of an intimate link between Great Britain and the subject peoples of the continent without distinction between political creeds. Although a conservative and a monarchist, Churchill discarded all tests except that of anti-Germanism. Only when the war was manifestly won but not concluded did he turn from battling to politics and set himself, unsuccessfully in the one case, successfully in the other, to baulk the republicans in Italy and Greece.

The Americans saw things otherwise. They were quicker to see the communists than the klephts in the Resistance ranks. They were even inclined to suspect all Resistance movements, including Gaullism, of being either communist or stalking horses for communism. They appreciated the political implications of helping the Resistance. They fell into a different kind of unreality from the British. Traditionally wary of European politics and less well versed in them because of their distance from the scene, they sought to separate strategic from political issues, to avoid giving blank cheques to exiles and to get on with the war in the expectation that victory would produce a return to stability in Europe, a withdrawal of American intervention and a settlement of political problems by Europeans through the magic of free elections. But this expectation was wishful thinking. It is almost true to say of Roosevelt that he substituted a talisman for political analysis and had no political aim in Europe during these years other than getting agreement, particularly from Stalin but also from everybody else, on the holding of free elections all over Europe (except in Germany) as quickly as possible after the end of the war. On this basis it might be safe to help the Resistance. The Office of Strategic Services (OSS) was created to emulate and in many instances surpass SOE. American aid was lavish. It was given without acknowledging that this kind of intervention had political as well as military implications: whereas the British, in helping Tito for example, gave aid on the deliberate basis that military considerations overrode all others and that the obvious political implications must of necessity be subordinated, the Americans tended wishfully to believe that military and political considerations were so far distinct that military aid had insignificant political consequences.

Resistance created difficulties between the allied governments – in this case mainly the British – and governments in exile. The latter suspected the British of trying to dominate and direct a part of their national activity. They also protested on behalf of their nationals against what they regarded as foolish British tactics or serious British mistakes. There was an acrimonious feud between French and British authorities over which of them should employ French citizens as agents. The Norwegians and the British tussled ill-naturedly for control of Milorg and, as already mentioned, the Norwegian government protested sharply against experimental British coastal raids in 1940 which seemed to the unfortunate Norwegians in the places raided to achieve nothing beyond provoking frightful German reprisals. Relations with the Dutch were even worse and led to allegations that the British wanted to destroy the Resistance and that a senior SOE officer was a German agent. These accusations were the outcome of the

so-called *Englandspiel*, the penetration by German Intelligence of
SOE's networks in the Netherlands. An SOE agent was captured. He
sent a pre-arranged coded signal to warn his headquarters in London
of his capture and the vulnerability of his communications but London,
in breach of its own rules, decided to ignore this warning and assume
that the agent had made a mistake and could still be treated as secure.
This basic error was repeated and was observed by the Germans who
confirmed the illusion by staging bogus acts of sabotage to persuade
SOE that its plans were working as intended. As a result all but two of
sixty agents sent to the Netherlands were caught and sent to die in
concentration camps, enough British equipment to train and arm
10,000 men was intercepted by the Germans, and many arms dumps and
agents' networks were uncovered not only in the Netherlands but also
in France where brave men and women fell into the hands of the SD.

Disgruntlement arose also from lack of communication and so lack of
understanding on both sides. Resistance leaders did not realize that
SOE and OSS were the poor relations of the traditional armed services,
which tended to regard Resistance movements as amateur sideshows,
a drain on their material and planning resources, an impediment to the
more serious business of conventional campaigning and a distasteful
adulteration of honest fighting with dubious politics. Resistance commanders complained of being undervalued and undersupplied. They
asked in vain to be given the jobs which Bomber Command thought it
could do better, felt bitter when innocent civilians were killed because a
factory which could have been more easily and more cheaply disrupted
by sabotage was attacked by hundreds of bombers, and blamed the
allied organizations with which they were in touch. They did not know
that SOE and OSS frequently shared their views, nor did they know
how limited resources were (for a year SOE had only two aircraft) nor
perhaps how difficult they themselves were to reach. To take an extreme case: at the beginning of the war Great Britain had no aircraft
with the range necessary to fly to Poland and back without landing and
but for the invention of wireless the Poles' feeling of abandonment
would have been complete. The situation improved with the arrival in
service of the Lancaster and Liberator and the conquest of air bases in
Italy, but even then not many of the latest types of four-engined
bomber could be spared for liaison with the Polish underground,
eastern Poland remained out of reach of the western allies throughout
the war, and Poles never felt satisfied that the British were doing enough
to sustain what they regarded as a substantial arm of the general allied
war effort. Of the operations attempted – 858 in all – only a little over

half were successful. Polish complaints about the scale and purpose-fulness of British aid have to be judged against the Poles' own uniquely dangerous position. Caught in the German-Russian crossfire – and not for the first time in their history – they witnessed the fearful German onslaught on the Polish intelligentsia, were vaguely aware of a Nazi plan to deport 16–20 million Poles to Siberia after the war and judged from their experiences in 1939–41 that their treatment at Russian hands would be little less painful. Their appeals were attuned to their despera-tion.

Yet despite the mistakes and misunderstandings great and small, and despite the activities of double agents who were more numerous and more successful in their special brand of perfidy than the romantic would like to believe, the combination of Resistance and allied govern-ments was a considerable factor in winning the war. Men and women of many nations worked together with thrilling trust and courage even during the periods when the organizations to which they belonged happened to be quarrelling. SOE and OSS provided arms, wireless sets and a great range of ingenious equipment, invented new weapons and new gadgets, found, trained and dispatched thousands of remark-able men and women. The contribution to Europe's morale was also great. The BBC in particular not only linked the Resistance with Great Britain by providing news, encouragement and coded instructions but also created an *esprit de corps*. The Resistance could have become a separate war, but it did not. It has a special history and a special pride but they are part of the shared experience of the Second World War.

Sharing and cooperating imply communication. By the mid-twentieth century radio had put millions of people in direct touch with one an-other. In spite of prohibitions on listening, confiscations of radio receivers and jamming, a government could not prevent its people or its conquered subjects from hearing something of what other govern-ments had to say. Radio propaganda became one of the most effective subsidiary weapons of the war. It was used for communicating with friends, keeping their spirits up and concerting active operations against the enemy. It created a sense of presence, or impending presence, which was invaluable between Great Britain and the continent after other normal links had been broken. It also enabled belligerent govern-ments to address each other's peoples in attempts to shake their stead-fastness, undermine their morale and generally sow doubt and unease. It was a difficult weapon to use because it was relatively untried and two-edged. On the one hand it provided, like the activities of SOE and OSS, an extra means to attack the enemy's military efficiency. From this point of view any statement which upset the combatants on the other side was useful and it did not essentially matter whether the statement was true or false. Lies, forgeries and rumours were all used in the course of what came to be called black propaganda. Radio programmes supposed to emanate from secret stations in enemy territory – the most famous was *Soldatensender Calais* – spread stories about, for example, how top Nazi bosses were enjoying themselves with blondes and plenty of food and spending more time in specially safe air raid shelters than in visits to the front. Leaflets and forged copies of well-known German newspapers were used in the same way. But the basis of black propaganda was nevertheless credibility, and credibility required a substantial degree of truth. Therefore black propaganda, however much it might embroider the facts, could not do without them. Its basic technique was to retail facts and insert among them one or two tendentious and alarming items.

For white propaganda on the other hand truth was all important. White propaganda was directed against the enemy's civilian morale rather than his military efficacy. The distinction could on occasions be a fine one, but even in modern warfare there is a dividing line between the civilian and the military factors in the total war effort: white propaganda, like the mass bombing of civilian housing to which we shall come in a later chapter, was an attempt to destroy the enemy's will to fight as opposed to destroying his fighting forces. White propaganda also aimed to swing opinion in occupied Europe.

Neither side was very effective when it tried to subvert the other. German broadcasts to Great Britain were almost entirely ineffectual. British broadcasts to Germany, although much better informed and more imaginative, did not achieve their main object and Goebbels was able, as we shall see, to maintain German morale right to the end and against fearful odds. Suffice it to say here that the BBC's broadcasts to Germany, in which there was an almost dogmatic addiction to truth, were hampered because Goebbels could argue that they were not true. He repeated British bombing claims which the Germans themselves and neutrals could see to be greatly exaggerated and he was able for a time to decry BBC statements by recalling discredited accounts of German atrocities in the First World War and saying that the British were at it again. The BBC was also hampered by mass bombing which, although it had the same aim, proved to be counter-productive in the sphere of morale.

In their propaganda to occupied Europe the British and the Germans had opposite problems. The Germans, who were in occupation, cajoled, impressed and bullied. Their principal advantage was their monopoly of public entertainment and their principal instrument was the film. The British and the Americans, physically at a distance, exploited radio. Their principal advantage was that their audience wanted to believe what they were saying. Fostering and satisfying this desire required them to tell the truth and as the war progressed allied propagandists were in the happy position of having the truth working for them. It remains an open question, debated by psychologists, how far one man can make another act contrary to his basic wishes or instincts. Anti-German propaganda during the war had little effect on Germans for, although it may have penetrated their minds, it did not stir them to action against their leaders. But anti-German propaganda to non-Germans proved its worth.

CHAPTER 14

Revolution in the South-East

NONE of Hitler's European victims fought the war solely with the idea of defeating Germany and getting back to their pre-war circumstances. Even Great Britain, the most conservative of the countries involved, by turning massively to the Labour Party at the end of the war in spite of the risk of seeming ungrateful to an extremely popular national leader, recorded its dissatisfaction with the past. On the continent similar feelings were universal, but they differed greatly from place to place. Broadly speaking there were peoples who wanted to change the institutions under which they lived, if need be by force, and peoples who were content to retain their institutions but wanted to improve what went on within them. Again broadly speaking, it was in eastern Europe that the revolutionary current was strongest, while western Europeans aimed rather at reform – excepting perhaps the French (a case specially difficult to categorize and best considered separately). Thus the war against the Germans and Italians was crossed with civil wars, actual or incipient, whose roots lay in the pre-war past but which developed during the war because wars make men look more critically at their state and accustom them to action in pursuit of political goals.

Norway, Denmark and the Netherlands were relatively stable and united countries. They looked forward to the full restoration of their monarchies and parliamentary institutions. They participated in the war beyond their borders as well as by resistance at home. The Norwegian government had commandeered the Norwegian merchant fleet, 85 per cent of which was outside Norwegian waters at the time of the German invasion; it thus became the largest merchant shipping concern in the world. It was very much in the fight and also comfortably in funds. Contact with Norway was maintained by the so-called Shetland bus which conveyed persons to and from Norway and also several hundred tons of war supplies. Of the smaller but nevertheless appreciable Danish merchant navy over 60 per cent served with the allies. The Dutch also provided fighting men for the allied forces, and the Queen of the Netherlands, who escaped like the King of Norway to London, contributed to the unity and steadfastness of her occupied country by her broadcasts to them.

Belgium's case was superficially different because of its linguistic and racial divisions and because the king became an object of controversy. He was criticized for surrendering himself into captivity instead of accompanying his government to London, he was suspected (unfairly) of undue partiality for the Germans, and his re-marriage during the war was unpopular. The Germans exploited the differences between Flemings and Walloons (as they had done in the First World War) and exacerbated the social tensions in a country in which the monarchy had become a reflection of division instead of a symbol of unity. After the war the king obtained a popular vote of confidence but by so narrow a margin that he found himself obliged to abdicate within a few days of the resumption of his full functions. Yet here too there was no serious challenge to the country's political institutions, other than the monarchy. There was, however, in all four of these countries an intensified concern with social questions. The discussion of such questions was a long-established feature of western European political life, but during the war they became more real when different sorts and conditions of men shared their experiences – in fighting the enemy and helping one another, in receiving the same food rations and facing the same firing squads. War made Europe more egalitarian and more leftward inclined.

In eastern Europe this shift to the left occurred in situations in which social reform was barely conceivable, or at any rate not at all likely, without political revolution. Hence the special importance of the communists with their uninhibited attitude to violent revolution, an importance which is in the first instance distinct from the proximity of these countries to the Soviet Union. In the countries which were allied with Germany – the central strip comprising Hungary, Rumania and Bulgaria – opportunity did not present itself until the Germans and the governments under their protection began to fail, and when the opportunity came it came not to reformist or revolutionary groups but to the Russian conquerors and the account of what happened belongs to the story of the defeat of Germany and not of European Resistance. In Poland and Czechoslovakia too the decisive factor proved to be not an indigenous Resistance movement but Russian power. Czechoslovakia, less in need of reform than Poland and the other countries of eastern Europe, had a moderate government under Beneš which aimed to pursue a broadly based, middle-of-the-road policy in post-war Czechoslovakia and to maintain friendly relations with both Moscow and the western democracies; it succeeded only up to 1948.

The Polish government, established in exile in London, was a right-wing government which feared popular revolution and had every reason to fear the Russians as much as it hated the Germans. Its policy was to wait. It hoped, not unnaturally from its point of view, that the Russians and the Germans would exhaust and maim one another. It aimed therefore to build up a secret army in Poland but not to use it until German and Russian strength had been sapped and the pre-war régime could be restored with British and American help. Still less did it wish to provoke a national rising which would develop on similar lines to Tito's and leave the London government in exile for ever. Resistance to the Germans was therefore discouraged and until mid-point in the war was conducted almost entirely by Polish Jews and escaped Russian prisoners of war.

The secret army, or Home Army (AK), built up by the London government, was an amalgam of remnants of the old Polish army with bands which came into existence under German rule. Some of these bands were socialist, others consisted of right-wing Nationalists, yet others were affiliated to the Peasant Party. The socialists agreed in 1942 to become part of the AK, and the Peasant Party groups, although on the whole more hostile to the AK than friendly to it, accepted its authority the next year. Not all the Nationalist bands joined the AK. Some did so in 1944 after prolonged negotiation; others collaborated with the Germans. There were also left-wing groups which remained separate from the AK. Most of them were socialist and they created a small army of their own in 1944. The Communist Party, which had been harried by pre-war Polish governments and dissolved by Stalin before the war began, was being re-formed by Wladislaw Gomulka but it remained weak until the Russians began to send it arms at the end of 1943. In that year the London government's waiting policy was upset by the military successes of the Russian armies which destroyed the prospect of a long Russo-German bloodletting and also by a peasant rising in eastern Poland where Himmler, having discovered here the homeland of the ancient Burgundians, was creating a pure German colony – with Volksdeutsche from Rumania who had forgotten the German language. Owing to the AK's disinclination for risings the credit for supporting this rising against the SS went to the Peasant battalions and also to the communists who were able to score some anti-German successes in one or two areas including the country round Lublin. (Hitler's idea of reviving a Burgundian kingdom for Himmler was a typical piece of Nazi medievalism. Such schemes, although they may be dismissed as ridiculous extravaganzas, testify also to the hold of the romantic past on the German imagination. Historians – specially Treitschke who was as eloquent as he was eminent – had written excitingly about the way the Teutonic Knights had colonized and controlled eastern lands and had fired a new generation with the zeal to go out and do likewise. But Hitler was not unique in his historical romanticism. Roosevelt toyed with the idea of creating 'Wallonia' by putting together parts of Belgium and northern France, Luxembourg, Alsace and Lorraine.)

In south-eastern Europe revolution had freer play. In Greece and Yugoslavia civil war in fact occurred, in Greece hesitantly and ultimately unsuccessfully for the insurgents, in Yugoslavia on a full scale and successfully; in neither with Russian help. Albania, where various Resistance groups united against the Italians but then fell out and started a civil war from which the communists ultimately profited, was shifted from the Italian to the Yugoslav sphere of influence.

In Greece General Ioannis Metaxas, who had been appointed Prime Minister by the king in 1936 and quickly converted his power into a dictatorship, had been placed in a dilemma by the unsolicited British guarantee of 1939. This guarantee, a promise of aid against Italo-German aggressiveness, ran counter to Metaxas' policy of relying on Hitler to keep Mussolini away. This policy failed when Mussolini attacked without telling Hitler and so forced Metaxas into a fight which he had neither wanted nor foreseen. By responding stoutly to Mussolini's ultimatum he made himself a national hero and temporarily united Greek monarchists and republicans, whose feud was the mainspring of Greek politics. But he was slow to accept British aid, which he did not relish, and his sudden death in January 1941 did not entirely remove the obstacles to British collaboration first against the Italians and subsequently against the Germans.

When the brief German campaigns against Greece and Crete ended, the king and his government had disappeared to Egypt leaving behind a political void which was filled by a pro-Axis puppet government, consisting mostly of generals who not implausibly believed that the war was over and won by the Germans. This government had little authority. The country was divided and roughly, sometimes very roughly, administered by German, Italian and Bulgarian occupiers. Away from the towns guerrilla bands began to form in the hills which constitute so much of Greece and make it unattractive to regular military formations. These bands were all predominantly left-wing and republican. Their members were largely uninterested in or contemptuous of the old struggle between royalists and Venizelist republicans and saw in the exile of its protagonists an opportunity to refashion Greek politics on less sterile lines. Few of them were communists, and at first they gave communism little thought, for it seemed hardly conceivable that the Greek Communist Party could play a leading part in Greek affairs.

Founded shortly after the First World War the Communist Party had had a difficult row to hoe. It could make little appeal to the peasants, who formed the bulk of the population, because Venizelos had broken up big estates and given the peasants land of their own. Its anti-clericalism was equally lacking in appeal. Even more damning was its advocacy of separate Macedonian and Thracian states, which it had been forced to adopt by the international communist movement and which was regarded by practically all Greeks as the purest treason. After 1936 it was virtually destroyed by one of the few intelligent and sophisticated policemen to be produced by twentieth-century authoritarianism, Constantine Maniadakis, Minister of the Interior under Metaxas. Maniadakis' devices included the creation of a bogus Communist Party under his own wing and the publication of his own edition of the communist newspaper *Rizospastis* to the confusion of all concerned, especially communists. When the war came the party's principal leaders were either in prison or exile. But in the next three years they prepared to take over the country and came within measurable distance of success.

They did this in disguise. They created the National Liberation Front (EAM) which, with its armed bands (ELAS), became the principal symbol of Greek resistance to the occupiers and, carefully suppressing regular communist propaganda, provided the communist leaders with broad popular support on a basis of patriotic nationalism, calls for unity against the enemy and hopes of social reform after the war. Their aim was to establish their organization as the natural successor to the occupiers and the government of post-liberation Greece. There were three threats to this programme: the legitimate government which would try to return from exile; other patriotic Resistance movements which might thrive sufficiently to challenge EAM; and the British who appeared on the scene unexpectedly in order to organize sabotage of Axis lines of supply to North Africa.

The British military mission (it later became Anglo-American) was both an embarrassment and an opportunity. The leaders of EAM and other Resistance groups were ambivalent about waging war on the occupiers. Many of their followers were filled with a patriotic fury which they wanted to vent in action, but harrying the occupiers meant bringing down reprisals on the innocent country people upon whose goodwill the bands relied for sustenance and who were in any case their compatriots. Reprisals were exceedingly fierce. Hostages were taken and executed and whole villages were wiped out; 1,000 people were killed in a single incident at Kalavryta, 250 women and children were burned to death at Klisura. The total number of hostages executed in Greece has been put at 45,000. In addition the Germans, Italians and Bulgarians executed another 68,000. (But the greatest killer in Greece was famine. Nearly half of the Greeks who died in the war starved.)

The bands had moreover a further reason for avoiding engagements with the occupiers. Each band was suspicious of its neighbours, usually rightly, and did not want to waste its energies and endanger its survival before the day of reckoning which would come when the occupiers withdrew. On the other hand the British mission had arms and golden sovereigns to give away and these precious supplies had to be earned. The price was cooperation with the British against the occupiers. The principal military result was the destruction of the Gorgopotamos railway viaduct, already mentioned – a feat of diplomacy as well as daring, since ELAS and its chief rival EDES were persuaded to work together for the first, and last, time. A joint band of 150 Greeks engaged and destroyed an Italian force while British saboteurs blew up the bridge. The bands also cooperated with the mission in 1943 in an extensive railway sabotage programme which was part of a cover plan to make the Germans expect an allied landing in Greece instead of Sicily and which caused the diversion to Greece of a Panzer division and hampered its return.

This dependence of the bands on the allies was profoundly altered by the Italian surrender in September 1943. So too was the relationship between the bands. The surrender gave ELAS all the arms it needed. It so happened that ELAS predominated in the areas of Italian occupation, and although captured Italian arms were meant to be allocated between all the bands, ELAS was able – as a result of this piece of luck and of some high-paced intrigue – to keep the lot. It became an armed force of about 19,000 effectives, ten times the size of EDES. It had already attacked and destroyed some smaller bands and earlier in 1943 it had captured Colonel Stephanos Saraphis, one of the ablest non-communist leaders, and had persuaded him to become commander-in-chief of ELAS. Saraphis' ready acceptance, which surprised the communists, showed how far ELAS had established itself as the only band worth belonging to. Its most serious rival was EDES, a group formed by the republican Colonel Napoleon Zervas (its repute was later tarnished when it was joined by some shady right-wing characters seeking to escape the stigma of collaboration with the occupiers, and Zervas himself modified his republicanism partly to please Churchill);

but EDES was confined to a small region in the west. When in July 1943 the allied mission persuaded the bands to sign an agreement establishing a joint headquarters, this was located at ELAS headquarters. From this year onwards the communists were less concerned with their rivals inside Greece than with the Greek government in exile and its army and navy.

The leaders of EAM aimed to sow division in the military and political ranks of the exiles and above all to delay the king's return until they could make it impossible. First mutinies in the Greek army occurred in February 1943. The king broadened his government to the Left, whereupon a number of royalist officers resigned their commissions in protest. In order to assert its authority the Greek government asked the British to arrest these officers. The net result was a diminution of right-wing influence in the army. The king agreed in July to submit the issue of the monarchy to a referendum after the war but, when pressed also to undertake not to return to Greece before the question had been put to the vote, he refused. In this he was strongly supported by Churchill and Roosevelt. Churchill further advised him to refuse a request from EAM for seats in the government. EAM, influenced perhaps by the news that Great Britain had decided to back Tito and his communists in Yugoslavia and by the false hope that the Italian surrender heralded a general Axis collapse, made its first bid for power and opened operations against rival bands. But EDES survived, the war went on and this premature bid contributed to the ultimate defeat of ELAS by sowing dissension in its own ranks and stimulating the puppet government in Athens to recruit anti-communist security forces.

In March 1944 EAM established a provisional government inside Greece and so formally set up a challenge to the government in exile. In April more mutinies – this time in the navy as well as the army in Egypt – occurred and the conservative Prime Minister, Emmanuel Tsouderos, resigned under pressure from his left-wing colleagues. But his successors were no more able than he had been to control the situation and the British had to intervene again. Thus the government in exile disintegrated at the same time as EAM had set up a rival to it. But EAM now changed its tactics and instead of insisting on its own creation as the only legitimate government it entered into negotiations for a share in the government in exile which had again been reconstituted under a new Prime Minister, George Papandreou, the political heir of Eleutherios Venizelos. After murdering Colonel Psaros, the leader of a smaller but not inconsiderable band, EAM sent representatives to a conference in Lebanon convoked by Papandreou in order to form a coalition between the exiles and the Resistance organizations. The upshot was a new government which included communists, but some of these feared that Papandreou had outsmarted them and reduced them to a subordinate role instead of the dominant one which they might attain by steering clear of all the politicians in exile. They were, however, under pressure from the Russians to put national and anti-fascist unity before communist power and they even agreed in September that all the bands should be subordinated to the new government and placed under the command of a British general. A few weeks later, in October, when Papandreou and his colleagues moved to Athens on the heels of the retreating Germans, it looked as though he and the British had pre-empted a communist take-over. A small British force followed in December.

But EAM controlled most of Greece outside the capital and in December, very probably on Tito's advice, it reversed its policy and made a second bid for power. (An alternative but less easily acceptable version is that EAM was provoked into hostilities by the British, so that it might be destroyed. There is evidence for the proposition that the shooting in the main square of Athens which opened the fighting was not begun by EAM.) EAM was without outside help. A Russian mission had gone to Greece in 1944 but reported that the Greek communists were not worth helping. In any case Stalin, as he told the Yugoslav communist Edvard Kardelj at the time, was convinced that the Americans would not allow Greece to be taken over by communists. Accordingly he had agreed to allot Greece to Churchill in return for a free hand in Rumania, a bargain which was sealed when the two of them drew up spheres of influence at Moscow in October 1944. EAM was therefore trying to emulate Tito's success in winning power for communists without external aid. It began by attacking EDES, whose forces had to be evacuated by the British to Corfu, and openly assumed control of all Greece except a few islands and a small area in the centre of Athens from which the British could not be dislodged. The British, with tacit Russian support (evinced by the appointment of an Ambassador to the Papandreou government) and in spite of fierce criticism in the United States and in Great Britain itself, sent reinforcements and defeated the insurrection after six weeks' fighting. ELAS was not trained for regular as opposed to guerrilla fighting and its political leaders were probably divided: in some parts of Greece ELAS did not go over to the offensive and there were still those who preferred the tactics of coalition to a coup. The failure of the insurrection was accompanied by communist atrocities which left an indelible mark on a whole generation of Greeks.

In the face of these events Churchill compelled the king to delay his return until it could be legitimated *de novo* by a plebiscite. The archbishop of Athens was appointed regent while the British defeated EAM and negotiated a truce. A year later, in March 1946, the royalists scored heavily in elections and six months afterwards King George II was summoned back by a popular vote of more than two to one in his favour. The communists then renewed their insurrection with help from Yugoslavia, Bulgaria and Albania. They were not defeated until 1949 when the re-equipment and training of the Greek army by the Americans and the defection of Yugoslavia from the communist block sealed their fate. The communist domination of EAM and ELAS, the bitterness engendered by the atrocities of 1944 and the subsequent onset of the Cold War altered the nature of the political and social struggle which many Greeks had taken to the hills to prosecute in the early days of the war. For Greece the Second World War was an opportunity for change which came and went. Greeks who wanted social change but not communism discovered that they could have both or neither.

One of the many differences between the Greek and Yugoslav Resistance movements was the appearance in Yugoslavia of a commanding figure, Josip Broz, later known to all the world as Tito. No national Resistance fighter inside occupied Europe achieved anything approaching his eminence; outside it only de Gaulle surpassed him. He possessed courage, tenacity, intelligence, personal authority, and organizing experience gained in Moscow and the Spanish civil war (though he did not actually go to Spain). He created the independent communist state of Yugoslavia. He was helped by the divisions and weaknesses of his political adversaries at home, by the disorders of the times, by the terrain of his country and by outsiders – notably the British and Americans and to a small extent the Russians – but of all the elements in his victory his own personality was the outstanding one.

A second major difference between Yugoslavia and Greece was the fact that Tito fought his enemies during the war instead of waiting. This policy brought him into conflict with the other principal Resistance figure, Draza Mihailovič, and eventually earned him the support of the western allies who had begun by backing Mihailovič.

Mihailovič was the accredited representative in Yugoslavia of the government in exile, which conferred on him the rank of general and the titles of Commander-in-Chief and Minister for War. He was also early in the field. But he failed to become a national leader for two main reasons: he was not truly national and he refused to lead. He was an impassioned Serb rather than a Yugoslav, as compared with Tito who, although a Croat, insisted on Serb-Croat cooperation and a federated Yugoslav state. Mihailovič too was reluctant to court disaster for his movement and reprisals for his compatriots by embarking on large-scale operations before the Germans were weakened by outside events. He and his followers, who were called *četniks* and were mainly former Serb army officers, were ready to undertake limited daring exploits but they had no thought of starting a national rising such as was in the minds and in the teaching of communist leaders. Mihailovič aimed to re-create a regular army against the day of German withdrawal and meanwhile, isolated exploits apart, to wait. In the course of waiting his hostility to Tito and to communism developed to the point where he opted for collaboration with Yugoslavia's national enemies in order to save it from communism. And in so adjusting his priorities, he destroyed himself.

The beginnings of the communist Resistance movement were small but professional and immediate. Tito began to organize resistance as soon as the Germans invaded Yugoslavia and in spite of the fact that Stalin was at that time still one of Hitler's allies. He himself moved from Zagreb to Belgrade in May 1941 and was ready with a call for action by the end of June when the German armies attacked the USSR. He had the beginnings of regional organizations, sabotage plans and groups of followers who, although critically short of arms, included some three hundred veterans of the war in Spain. They inherited the traditions of the *hajduks*, heroes like the pig-breeder Karadjordje who had become the leader of the Serb revolt of 1804 against the Turks and the founder of the modern Serbian state. Although the Communist Party was small (it had about 12,000 full members in 1941) it had non-communist contacts and sympathizers as a result of following the Popular Front policy adopted by the Comintern in 1935. By the autumn of 1941 these partisan groups had grown strong enough to undertake operations in Serbia and establish a headquarters at Užice where they ran an arms factory and a printing press. These successes led to discussions for joint operations with the *četniks* (some of whom were being attracted to the communist side), and until attacked by the *četniks* the partisans supplied the *četniks* with arms from their Užice factory. Mihailovič, however, had been directed by the government in exile, whose grasp of the situation was naturally imperfect, to assume command over the communist partisans. This Tito was neither prepared nor obliged to accept in spite of chidings from Moscow whence Stalin, anxious above all for allied cooperation, was urging him to forget about communist revolution for the time being and concentrate on a common anti-Axis front with all friends of the western allies. Fighting broke out between *četniks* and partisans. The *četniks* tried but failed to evict the partisans from Užice and suffered a series of defeats. These events eliminated all possibility of cooperation and induced Mihailovič to accept arms from the Italians to continue the struggle. The immediate gain went to the Germans who took the opportunity to clear Serbia of all Resistance groups.

In the following year the partisans were hard pressed by the Germans and Italians. Hitler had become aware of their potential danger, and they were forced to suspend operations and seek refuge in the mountains of Bosnia and Montenegro. A number defected. But thanks to Tito's leadership, reinforced by the professionalism of the Spanish war veterans and of former officers of the Yugoslav army who joined the partisans, the movement survived, recuperated and re-emerged as a well-ordered army of four brigades. It also began to assume the functions of a civil administration in the areas which it controlled, fixing prices and decreeing social changes as well as keeping order. In November 1942 an Assembly at Bihac foreshadowed the partisans' claim to become the government of Yugoslavia.

In 1943, when their strength had risen to about 20,000, they were attacked by forces about six times as large, lost half their equipment and a quarter of their men killed in battle or massacred afterwards, but they escaped once more from Bosnia to Montenegro in the spring and back from Montenegro to Bosnia in the summer. Their losses were all the more grievous because the wounded either died or had to be shot until this grim and tragic burden was relieved by British medical supplies and a medical airlift to British hospitals in Italy. Their enemies in these operations were a combination of Germans, Italians, Bulgarians, *četniks* and *ustachi*. (The last were organized brigades of toughs who clustered round Pavelič's court in Croatia in an atmosphere described by Ciano as 'cowboy'. They massacred Serbs and Jews on a scale which horrified most other Croats; hated the Orthodox Church and the Cyrillic alphabet with pathological intensity; and became so corrupt that even Pavelič felt constrained to have two of their leaders shot.)

A few months after their defeat in Montenegro the fortunes of the partisans were transformed by the general Italian collapse. They gained control of most of Croatia including the Dalmatian coast and islands, seized large quantities of Italian arms and were able to recruit and equip an army of 250,000. They were now a formidable force, a nation in arms, and at the end of the year Tito was proclaimed Marshal of Yugoslavia and President of the Council for the Liberation, which was in effect an interim government. The king's return was to be conditional on a plebiscite in his favour.

For much of this time the outside world had known little about what was going on in Yugoslavia. The British sent a first mission in 1941 to discover what the guerrilla activities amounted to, with a view to giving some help. This mission revealed something of the rivalry between Tito and Mihailovič. Towards the end of the year a British officer who visited both headquarters advised that no help should be given to Mihailovič pending the outcome of talks which were then going on between the two groups, but this advice was not followed and Great Britain, partly out of loyalty to the Yugoslav government in London which was an ally, decided to build up Mihailovič by broadcast propaganda and military aid. Then for a year all communication between the British government and its emissary in the field was cut off by Mihailovič who confiscated the British officer's wireless set. Mihailovič's increasing reliance on the Axis occupiers in his struggle against Tito was unknown to London until further missions were dispatched to Yugoslavia at the end of 1942. These missions, which were prompted by the growing importance of the Balkans in overall strategy, reported the existence of civil war in Yugoslavia and raised the question which side to back. A reconciliation, such as the British and the Russians both desired, was by now plainly impossible. Great Britain decided to drop Mihailovič and his friends in London (who did not disown him until August 1944) and support Tito. This reversal of policy was influenced by the delayed discovery that Tito could be much more useful than Mihailovič (thus confirming simultaneous Russian arguments that Mihailovič had become no better than a collaborationist) and by the coincidence that a British mission to Tito in May 1943 arrived during a great battle in which 20,000 partisans, although defeated, proved that they were a disciplined army under skilled command and not a random collection of guerrilla bands. This engagement also provided first hand proof of the *četniks'* collaboration with the Germans as well as the Italians.

From this point aid to Tito became the largest item in the Anglo-American aid programme. A naval and air base was established on the island of Vis with a small naval detachment and a squadron of Hurricanes. Another air base was opened at Bari for operations in the Balkans. Yugoslav pilots and tank crews were trained in Egypt, and

Yugoslav prisoners in Italy were collected and formed into a Yugoslav legion. Yugoslav wounded were flown to hospitals in Italy. Great quantities of equipment were sent to Tito, mainly by the Americans – 100,000 rifles, 50,000 machine and sub-machine guns, 1,380 mortars, 630,000 grenades, 700 wireless sets, 175,000 uniforms, 260,000 pairs of shoes. (The first Russian supplies did not arrive until April 1944.) When the Germans launched another major offensive against the partisans in May 1944, allied air forces came to their support, flying 1,000 sorties a day. Later in the year these air forces cooperated with the partisans in attacks on the Germans' lines of communication and harassed their retreat – in spite of Tito's suspicions that this coopera-tion was intended to pave the way for an allied occupation of the Balkans. In London King Peter dismissed Mihailovič and instructed the *četniks* to put themselves under Tito's command, but Tito made it clear to Churchill that the king could not return unless recalled by a plebiscite. Mihailovič made a final bid to retrieve his fortunes by an understanding with Pavelič, but the partisans engulfed all opposition and on 20 October 1944 they entered Belgrade. The Russians who had entered the country as allies from the north-east departed again (in accordance with a prior agreement between Stalin and Tito) and Tito ruled unchallenged. For nearly four years the Germans had been obliged to hold down Yugoslavia by force of arms instead of ruling it indirectly through complacent nominees. After the Italian collapse this necessity had cost them a standing force of fifteen divisions. Most of these were German, although they had some help from Bulgarians, *četniks* and the puppet régime in Belgrade. As the Russians advanced in central Europe the main concern of the Germans was the Russian front bearing down on Yugoslavia from the north-east but their troubles were increased and their forces distracted by the guerrilla fighters who had engineered a national uprising. The human cost to Yugoslavia was a population almost precisely decimated.

The final stage in the transfer of power to the communists was accompanied by some transient formalities. In an attempt to save the monarchy Great Britain forced King Peter to appoint a new Prime Minister, Dr Ivan Subasič, who went to Yugoslavia and concluded in December 1944 an agreement with Tito which provided for an interim regency and a parliament containing pre-1941 parliamentarians (provided they had not collaborated with the enemy) as well as members of the wartime communist assembly. A provisional government, formed in March with Tito at its head, included leaders of other parties, but they did not last long and before the end of the year the monarchy too was formally abolished after elections which the communists could hardly fail to win and did win. Yugoslavia had become a communist state and an independent one, the first since 1917. In this its war fortunes were unique, although the establishment of other communist states in eastern Europe at this time led many people to confound Yugoslavia with these under the generic name of satellites.

CHAPTER 15

France

FRANCE suffered during the decade which ended in 1940 two collapses which opened two debates. The spectacular collapse of France as
a fighting force in 1940 was preceded by the collapse of the Republic
itself, a collapse as complete as the collapse of the Weimar republic but
unperceived; for although the symptoms of political and social disintegration were apparent and discussed, their full import did not
become clear until the catastrophe of 1940 tore away the veil of illusion
and showed that the Third Republic was no longer there. At this point
Vichy took, temporarily, the place of the Republic. In the years before,
France had become a vacuum governed by a *vis inertiae* deputizing for
political institutions.

The failure of these institutions in the thirties was marked by parliamentary instability, by the growth of anti-parliamentary forces and by
one significant but abortive attempt to arrest the drift of governmental
incapacity. The political parties in the Third Republic were numerous,
weak, young (none was as old as the republic itself or could even boast
a foundation date earlier than the twentieth century) and usually unable to combine to produce positive programmes or policies. They
combined in narcissistic and unproductive unions whose main effect
was to keep Ministers in Ministries. This vacuity brought parliamentary
democracy into contempt and encouraged the anti-parliamentarianism
of those still unreconciled to the revolution of 1789 and of a more
modern fascist brand, so that the republic was assailed from without
at the same time as it was decomposing within. Both menaces were laid
bare by a scandal which began, within a year of Hitler's seizure of
power, with the suicide of a financial crook called Stavisky in January
1934. It continued with accusations against Ministers of complicity in
Stavisky's swindles and against the police of hushing up the scandals
and murdering witnesses, and it culminated in anti-government
demonstrations which turned into drilled fascist riots. At this time
various fascist and other right-wing leagues had a combined enrolled
membership of about half a million and the sympathies of many times
that number. At the centre of the storm was the Radical Socialist Party
which was the pivot about which French politics turned.

The destruction of the Radicals would mean the destruction of the parliamentary system because the Radicals, as the centre party, were a *sine qua non* of any parliamentary coalition and because the party had personified the Third Republic almost from its inception. The Radicals were now, in the 1930s, the chief targets for charges of corruption and incompetence. Their lack of competence was partly a result of their position. They never won enough seats to form a stable one-party government and they found it difficult to make up their minds between alliance with socialists or conservatives. They had inherited a left-wing tradition of which they remained conscious and proud, but they had been moving steadily to the Right in their social outlook and their political programmes. Their inclination was to prefer the socialists, but the socialists were reluctant to join in government for fear of being outbid in the constituencies by the communists, from whom they had split off as a minority group in 1919. The socialists therefore resorted to the common but pernicious device of French parties of pledging support to another party but refusing to share office and responsibility – and then withdrawing their support, often sooner rather than later. These tactics, which the communists were to use against the socialists and Radicals in 1936, exposed all Left-inclined Radical governments to impermanence and eventually split the socialists themselves between those who wanted to give more support to the Radicals or less. The Radicals too were split between left- and right-wing groups, each hankering after a different kind of coalition. Further to the Right were a number of conservative parties, some more parliamentary and others more authoritarian.

The riots of 1934 had some cathartic effect and after an interlude of emergency 'national' government under Gaston Doumergue the socialist leader Léon Blum succeeded in creating a Popular Front stretching from communists to Radicals which, after an electoral victory in May 1935, took over the government with the hope of achieving parliamentary stability and social and economic reform. But the communists refused to join the government and displayed a chequered loyalty to it. A number of social reforms were introduced but Blum's administration was never able to concentrate attention, as its chief would have liked, on these overdue matters. The need to rearm absorbed funds required for social improvement and in 1936 the outbreak of civil war in Spain placed Blum in a dilemma from which he was unable to escape.

The Spanish government, also a Popular Front, appealed for help and Blum at first promised to give it, but his Radical colleagues represented middle-class Frenchmen who were afraid of the communist element on the government side in Spain and did not want to help it. Blum also feared that he could not count on the civil service or the armed forces and that, at the worst, he might even be risking civil war in France if he took sides actively in the civil war in Spain. Furthermore, the British government wanted to keep out and so Blum was forced by the balance of political power within France and by his principal ally to refuse help to the Spanish Popular Front. In June 1937, after little more than a year in office, his government was ousted by the Senate which had little liking for the Prime Minister's reforms and what they would cost the bourgeoisie. A second Popular Front government was formed under a Radical Prime Minister with Blum as his deputy and the communists in undisguised opposition. This government was a Popular Front only in name. In substance it was a return to the old Radical-dominated merry-go-round and it was not long before the socialists quitted it. Blum did not so much fail to give France government and reform as demonstrate the impossibility of doing so. Long before 1936 the opposition to reform had become too strong to beat. His administration also gave a sharper edge to the danger of civil war in France as people gathered in the streets to shout: Better Hitler than Blum; and meant it. For Blum, personally an exceptionally generous as well as an exceptionally clear-minded man, was hated for what he stood for – social justice – and for what he was – a Jew.

The collapse of the political fabric of the Third Republic was not unwelcome to many Frenchmen but the collapse of its armies was a shock to all. There had been a feeling of weakness in France for a decade, but few had realized the closeness of the connection between social malaise and military impotence. The weakness of France was in any case puzzling. It was not the natural weakness of a small country like Denmark, but weakness embedded in strength. France continued to manifest, throughout the period between the wars, a vigorous artistic, scientific and cultural life, nationally and internationally renowned, and possessed not only one of the largest armies in the world but also one of the largest bank balances. Yet France was uneasy and pessimistic. The pessimism went deep. It came from the feeling that there were not enough Frenchmen. Between Waterloo (1815) and Sedan (1870) the population of France had risen from 30 to 36 million, while that of the hereditary enemy, Great Britain, had doubled from 13 to 26 million and the Prussia of 11 million had become the Germany of 41 million. During the 1930s the marriage rate in France was halved and the death rate overtook the birth rate. The annual call-up, which had produced 600,000 men in 1914, produced only 240,000 in 1936 and was then again halved in the next four years. The economic scene was as dismal as the demographic. The French theory of government required the National Assembly, as the embodiment of the sovereignty of the people, to be master of the executive, and the French political system contributed to the relative weakness of the executive power by pro-liferating numerous and undisciplined parties, none of which was capable of forming a government on its own. The resulting coalitions did not dare to affront the voters and since France was still a country of small farmers and small businessmen the voters to whom govern-ments kowtowed were principally this section of the community. The kowtowing took the form of not imposing unpopular taxes and trying to find alternative sources of money for state expenditure. French insistence on war reparations from Germany was partly a consequence of this search, and when the reparations did not materialize govern-ments resorted instead to unbalanced budgets and borrowing, devices which undermined confidence at home and abroad in the French economy and the capacity of the politicians to run it. In universities and schools the prevailing tone of the twenties and thirties was cynical – and the influence of intellectuals was in France pronounced. No less pervasive was the attitude of the lesser bourgeoisie, which noted with alarm the fact that production was static. In external affairs the blood-iest war ever fought on French soil had been followed by disenchant-ment and disillusion. The attitudes represented in the massive figure of Clemenceau and the forceful policy of the Ruhr occupation of 1923 passed away. They were succeeded by disinvolvement and pacifism, especially among ex-combatants and those who might be expected to continue the warrior caste, with the result that the Munich settlement of 1938 was greeted with relief and the mobilization of 1939 accepted with reluctance. But the ignominious collapse of 1940 was nevertheless an unforeseen humiliation.

Hence arose the two questions which occupied Frenchmen during the next few years. Who was to blame for these collapses, and what was to take the place of what had collapsed?

The first answers were provided by Vichy because Vichy was, at first, a fact in a country where most facts seemed to have vanished. Vichy answered that it was all the fault of the parliamentarians of the Third Republic, especially the left wing, and that their place was now filled by Vichy. The history of France in the next few years is the story of the rejection of these answers.

The Vichy régime was the parent and the child of the armistice. The armistice was demanded by the generals, Weygand and Pétain, who dominated the last days and the last cabinets of the Third Republic and who showed themselves less stout than some of their civilian colleagues. The last President of the Republic, Albert Lebrun, appointed Pétain Prime Minister on the advice of his predecessor Paul Reynaud, who resigned because there was nothing else he could do. Pétain and Weygand, who notoriously had never agreed about anything else in the course of their long lives, insisted on an armistice for political as well as military reasons, and Vichy was therefore from the start a politically defined and not a national régime. The military reasons were no doubt compelling, for the army had been defeated, but the defeat of the army was something more than a military event. It raised also the spectre of revolution, and the generals felt it their duty to preserve the army to prevent revolution. Nor were they eccentric in taking this view. Vichy · may not have represented the broadest national consensus but its aims were widely sensed as sound preservative medicine : to retain the French empire by abandoning the fight, to gain for France an independent place in the German New Order, to mitigate and survive enemy occupation by judicious collaboration and to safeguard the traditions of France by firmly suppressing the degenerative forces of internal change. In order to achieve these aims the generals capitulated and agreed to set up a new government covering in effect only one third of France and to pay German occupation costs (which initially were nine times as much as the sums required of Germany under the Dawes Plan). Vichy left vague for the time being the extent of military, economic and political collaboration which would be needed in order to secure these aims. Like Hitler, Vichy did not foresee a long war or the demands that such a war would make.

The head of the new régime, and its symbol, was Pétain. Born during the Crimean War and taught his catechism by a veteran of Napoleon's *Grande Armée*, Pétain had been on the verge of retirement with the rank of colonel after a career that had been neither distinguished nor undistinguished, when the outbreak of the First World War opened the doors of immortality to him. At the end of that war he was one of half a dozen Marshals of France who were world famous – all of whom he then proceeded comfortably to outlive. His particular fame rested on two things: he had saved France at Verdun in 1916 and he had shown an unaccustomed humanity in the face of mutiny, preferring to decorate soldiers who had done well than shoot those who had failed. In person he was dignified, calm, unpretentious; in politics, so far as was known, he was detached, so much so that the Left trusted him as the sort of general who would not lend himself to coups; in religion he was a

Roman Catholic but not a pronounced one like Weygand, a poor church-goer and married (at sixty-five) to a divorcée. He seemed the type of figure who could be relied on to do the right thing in a crisis.

From 1921 to 1931 he was vice-chairman of the Council of War and so Commander-in-Chief designate if war came, and he remained a member of the Council after 1931 because in France, as elsewhere, old Marshals never died professionally so long as there was breath in their bodies. Although succeeded in the vice-chairmanship by Weygand and, after 1935, by Gamelin he remained a potent figure and his continuing availability was emphasized when, after the fascist riots in Paris in 1934, he was made Minister of War in the Doumergue government at the age of seventy-eight – a military dug-out called in to support a political back number. After a brief spell as Ambassador in Madrid, to which post he was appointed at the age of eighty-one, he returned to the centre of things in time to be present at the culminating crisis of 1940. In retrospect there is an element of slyness in the way he managed to be half a spectator and half a participant in the fall of France, observing in private conversation that Gamelin was incapable but refusing to give his opinion to the Prime Minister who, for all Pétain cared, might find out for himself. When the crash came he was stationed somewhere between the centre of the stage and the wings, so that only half a step was needed to carry him to the leadership of the nation.

At first the nation was on the whole relieved to have him. He was old but he had extraordinary physical fitness. He carried round with him a part of the glory of France at a time when this commodity was in short supply, especially in political circles. He was respected, if not vociferously popular; he was liked by the poorer people because he had been a soldiers' soldier as well as a Marshal of France. He had stood firm once before – *ils ne passeront pas* – and standing firm was again the vital need. He had never done anything blatantly wrong. What was wrong was concealed. He was vain as well as old and his physical fitness was beginning to be offset by declining mental powers. He was a narrow-minded, authoritarian reactionary and although his inertia created the impression that the sins of Vichy should be attributed to his entourage rather than to himself the pattern of Vichy was a reflection and emanation of his own ideas.

Vichy did not regard itself as a merely passive régime guarding France from its external enemies so long as the war lasted. No less than the Resistance movements, which opposed and eventually defeated it, Vichy had positive and revolutionary policies which were intended to transform France lastingly. The only thing that Vichy regarded as

temporary about itself was its capital, which it had chosen in preference
to Paris in order to keep a certain distance between itself and German
headquarters (and possibly the Parisians too). This spa of 25,000 inhabitants in the Auvergne, famous for repairing the stomachs and
livers of those who had lived too long or too hard in the colonies, could
serve as a capital because the government would soon move back to
Paris. But the government's work need not wait upon its move. Laws
and decrees poured out. Besides dealing with the immediate post-
defeat problems of refugees, unemployment and rationing, Vichy
charted what it called a National Revolution. Full powers to govern by
decree – powers more ample than those possessed by Louis XIV but,
in the eyes of reactionaries, none the worse for that – were bestowed on
Pétain as head of state, and the sufferings and humiliations of France
were declared to be the essential pre-condition for national regeneration
through the cultivation of the basic virtues and values of labour, family
life and patriotism. This, the conservative in contradistinction to the
radical way to salvation, was the core of Vichy's ideology. (But Vichy
did not succeed in monopolizing it. Gaullism heeded it too: after the
liberation a film by Marcel Pagnol, *La Fille du Puisatier*, made to extol
Pétain and Vichy's cultural revolution, continued to be shown with
little alteration to extol the spirit of Gaullism.)

Vichy's constitutional revolution was the work chiefly of Pierre
Laval who was ultimately to be the principal scapegoat for the Vichy
régime. Laval was an ex-socialist, an ex-parliamentarian, many times
a Minister of the Third Republic, a man of humble origins and markedly
unaristocratic appearance, a decidedly clever man but not a broadly
intelligent one, a political manipulator of the first rank but one inclined to mistake his own astuteness for achievement. When Pétain,
Weygand and their supporters in Reynaud's cabinet brought the war to
a stop, Laval appeared to talk deputies into giving the new government
legitimacy and plenary powers and so changed the nature of the state
which Pétain was to guide. By assiduous and insidious lobbying among
the flotsam and jetsam of the Third Republic which accumulated at
Bordeaux and then at Vichy, Laval got these representatives of legitimacy to turn Pétain, whom he mistook for a mere figurehead, into an
autocrat. The state still contained a Senate and a Chamber of Deputies
but they could only meet upon being summoned by Pétain and Pétain
had no intention of convoking them. The Vichy government operated
through a series of committees whose activities contrasted with the
impassivity of the Marshal and so gave the erroneous impression that
Pétain reigned but did not rule and ought therefore not to be blamed

for all the enormities committed in his name. Thus arose the Vichy myth of the martyr Pétain, beset by the conquerors of France on the one side and its political riffraff on the other, but preserving its dignity and its honour by his personal bearing.

Democracy and civil liberties were quickly abolished. Besides suppressing parliamentary rule at the centre Vichy decreed that local councils should be appointed and not elected except in communes with fewer than 2,000 inhabitants. Trade unions were disbanded and political parties forbidden. The judiciary lost its independence. Public officials became liable to arbitrary dismissal by the head of state and 2,000 were purged in Vichy's first six months. Those who remained in office had to take an oath of personal loyalty to Pétain. New laws were given retroactive effect so that people could be tried and condemned for doing things which had been lawful when done. They could also be tried and condemned for their opinions or for merely associating with persons who had fallen foul of the authorities. Prefects were empowered to arrest, without charge, anybody whom they judged to be imperilling the security of the state. By 1942 there were 80,000 in prisons or concentration camps. Their conditions were so appalling that some prisoners were reduced to eating the straw in their palliasses and in some prisons there were a hundred deaths for every one that had occurred before the war. Certain categories of person were deprived of the protection of the law. Vichy was profoundly anti-semitic and defined a Jew more strictly even than the Nuremberg decrees of the Third Reich: a woman with only two Jewish grandparents became a Jew if she married a Jew. Vichy's anti-semitism was more national and religious and less racial than Hitler's. It asserted the unassimilability of the Jew to French society and regarded him therefore as a threat to the coherence of that society, but it admitted that French-born Jews who had fought for France had become, by the baptism of blood, French rather than Jewish. The first anti-semitic laws were promulgated in October 1940. All Jews were excluded from the public service, from teaching and from positions of authority in industry and the press, radio and cinema. Foreign Jews – including Algerian Jews who were deprived of their French nationality – became liable to internment. Existing laws against libelling racial and religious minorities were repealed. A second batch of anti-semitic laws in June 1941 aryanized Jewish businesses. The owners, who had been promised in 1940 that they would not be deprived of their possessions, received inadequate compensation or none.

Vichy's national mystique did not stop at Jews. All foreigners and all persons with foreign fathers were made ineligible for the public service, and all naturalizations since 1927 became subject to review. This cleansing of the nation was reinforced by educational reform. Pétain was almost obsessively interested in education and had aspired at one time to become Minister of Education. He regarded education as a branch of morals rather than learning and he regarded physical exercises as the basis of sound morality. The body took precedence over the mind; sound thinking, as opposed to dangerous thinking, could be induced by setting all French children on the road to that physical fitness which characterized the Marshal himself; loose thinking meant morally faulty rather than intellectually untidy thinking. Therefore every child in a primary school had to do ten hours of physical training a week and this quota was reduced by only one hour in the secondary school. The rest of education consisted preponderantly of instruction about God and patriotic duties and Greek and Latin. In line with conventional Roman Catholic teaching Pétain, like Hitler, believed that woman's place was in the home and her purpose childbearing. Divorce was made more difficult, large families were encouraged, women could only get marriage grants upon undertaking not to go out to work, and abortion became not only a criminal but a capital offence. The family was the elemental institution in a collectivist scheme of things which denied the value of the individual. Pétain himself said that there was 'no creative virtue' in individualism and he regarded French society as a large family to be ruled firmly by himself and to some extent by God.

Pétain's Vichy was a reactionary, authoritarian, Roman Catholic, chauvinist corporatist state, but it was other things as well. Pétain was both a comfort to conservatives of all kinds in need of a father figure and a gift to an assortment of extremists who were looking for a stalking horse. Consequently Vichy became an *omnium gatherum* of antirepublican and anti-progressive forces which attracted pro-German and pro-Nazi Frenchmen and uncommitted opportunists. It gave scope to the most diverse personages. There was Jacques Doriot, the ex-communist bully who had been in German pay for a number of years before the war; Joseph Darnand, whose followers were required to swear an oath to fight 'democracy, Gaullist dissidence and the leprosy of Jewry', whose *milice* was merged with the *Waffen SS*, who commanded a French SS expeditionary force on the Russian front in 1943 and who returned as Secretary-General for the Maintenance of Order, in which capacity he made the *milice* even more feared and hated than the SD; the anti-German, monarchist publicist Charles Maurras who set up as a sort of ideologist for Vichy; and, from 1943, the Bourbon claimant, the Comte de Paris, who went to Vichy with an eye perhaps to Pétain's job but was fobbed off by Laval with an offer of a minor post and later declared himself a Gaullist. The most pro-German of French right-wing leaders, Marcel Déat, preferred Paris to Vichy, against which he kept up a steady flow of criticism. Many French fascists disliked Pétain.

In external affairs Vichy had no choice. It was compelled to collaborate with Germany. Its options were limited to the degree and manner of collaboration, and within this narrow field the most important person was Laval. On 11 June 1940, Pétain issued the first of his Constitutional Acts which, with the disdain of grammar characteristic of monarchs, opened with the words '*Nous, Philippe Pétain . . .*' and appointed him Chief of State. The office of President was by implication abolished. By succeeding Constitutional Acts, issued on the same day, Pétain gave himself plenary powers in the appointment of Ministers and civil servants, in legislation, budgeting and finance, in the control of the armed forces, and in the making of treaties. He might also declare a state of emergency but he might not declare war. The Senate and Chamber remained in being but were prorogued and might be recalled only by Pétain. By a further Act on the next day Pétain nominated Laval as his successor. Laval became therefore the Caliph to Pétain's Mahomet, and since Pétain was much older than Mahomet had ever been, Laval might regard himself as the real manipulator of the totalitarian powers with which, largely by his own efforts, Pétain was invested.

To Laval there was nothing shocking about the idea of collaborating with Germany. He had long been a champion of a Franco-German entente. He had been in politics since before the First World War, had been Prime Minister of France before Hitler came to power in Germany, and like many Frenchmen of his generation he saw European politics in terms of Franco-German conflict or agreement; and he preferred the latter. He observed the American disengagement from Europe after 1919 and he regarded the British with their extra-European empire as but dubious partners in Europe. He was not pro-German in the enthusiastic way in which some Frenchmen admired German achievements in the arts and politics, but as a political realist he desired a Franco-German understanding and wished to promote it sooner rather than later because he accepted the general view that, in relation to Germany, France would continue to become demographically and industrially the weaker. Italy he regarded as a natural and useful third member of the entente. As Prime Minister in 1931 he wished to settle the issues of reparations and disarmament in order to clear the way for a triple entente which, had he achieved it, would have anticipated the post-war cooperation of Robert Schuman, Konrad Adenauer and Alcide de Gasperi.

He was out of office from the beginning of 1932 until October 1934 when he succeeded Barthou as Foreign Minister. During this interval Hitler had become Chancellor in Germany. Laval had therefore a choice between persevering with his German policy or dropping it and reverting to the classical French policy of alliance with Russia against Germany which Barthou had been pursuing. Laval chose to persevere because his Franco-German vision of Europe still made sense to him – as it still did after 1940. His anti-communism, which was pronounced, pointed in the same direction and although he continued his predecessor's negotiations with Moscow he did so only in order to have an alternative policy to fall back on – and he even told the German Ambassador in Paris that this was his reason. The Ethiopian crisis wrecked his policy but did nothing to alter his belief in it.

In the summer of 1940 France, although decisively and humiliatingly defeated, still counted in the European balance, the more so because of its overseas colonies. Hitler had a vague plan for an anti-British, continental block which would include France as well as Italy and Spain; in such a block the French colonies could be strategically more useful to him than anything which Mussolini or Franco had to offer. German and French military chiefs seriously debated joint operations in Africa for the recovery of colonies which defected to de Gaulle and the transfer of British colonies to France. But Hitler was indecisive and half-hearted about cooperation with France. He himself and a number of his principal colleagues disliked the French and distrusted Laval personally. At Vichy the men round Pétain were also divided and uncertain; some agreed with Laval's policy of making the best obtainable bargain with a securely dominant Germany, while others cherished a lingering hope that Germany might fail to defeat Great Britain and believed that a British victory was not only possible but also better for France. Laval moreover discovered that Pétain was no mere puppet. This was not only a surprise and a disappointment but also a severe handicap since the two men had very little in common. There was life in the old Marshal yet and in December 1940 he showed it by dismissing Laval.

Laval's fall did not mean an end to the collaborationist policy. Pétain disliked Laval's pretensions rather than his policies. The

Marshal's distrust of his deputy was also exploited by some of Laval's colleagues who were afraid that Laval might worm his way into the Marshal's confidence to their own discomfiture. For a couple of months it was not clear who was Laval's successor. It might be Pierre-Étienne Flandin, another leading politician of the Third Republic and a sincere admirer of much that Germany had produced through the ages, or it might be Jean Darlan, the anti-British admiral who was moved less by respect for Germany than by anger over the British attack on his ships at Mers-el-Kebir. In February Darlan was appointed Deputy Prime Minister and Foreign Minister and, the next day, Pétain's successor; a few days later he was Minister of the Interior too, and a week later still a cabinet reshuffle which excluded Flandin and other Vichy notables confirmed Darlan's pre-eminence. But Darlan's collaboration soon went too far for Pétain who, having got France out of the war on one side, was determined not to re-enter it on the other. In May 1941 Darlan negotiated with the Germans a series of protocols by which France would provide extensive facilities and war material in the Middle East in connection with the revolt of Rashid Ali in Iraq and would give the Germans free harbour and railways facilities in Tunisia and permit the harbour and airfield at Dakar to become German bases. Since the routes between Bizerta and Europe were to be protected by the French navy, Darlan was not only sanctioning active military cooperation in the Middle East but also upsetting the most delicate and contentious element in the French surrender: the undertaking to Great Britain not to allow the French fleet to join the Axis. Pétain refused to endorse Darlan's policy and demoted the admiral from his high position in the state.

Equally, however, Pétain refused to be lured back into the war on the allied side. From January 1941 Roosevelt had in Vichy as his Ambassador and personal representative Admiral William D. Leahy, whose task was at first to keep French aid to Germany down to a minimum by arguing that the war was far from over and that Hitler was going to lose it, and by supplying France with food and other necessaries. In 1942 Roosevelt went further and sent a secret emissary to entice Weygand into bringing the French in North Africa over to the allies in conjunction with the planned Anglo-American invasion. Weygand was not to be drawn and reported the conversations to Pétain whence they were conveyed to Berlin; and Pétain instructed Weygand to reply that an Anglo-American landing would be opposed by the (very numerous) French forces in Algeria and Morocco. In April Leahy's recall marked the end of this abortive American attempt to deal with Vichy.

A few weeks later Great Britain's seizure of the French colony of Madagascar to prevent it from falling into Japanese hands embittered Vichy and during the rest of the year the possibility of Vichy making common cause with the Germans was again mooted. When the Anglo-American invasion took place in November Hitler asked Vichy to declare war. Pétain refused but broke off diplomatic relations with the United States. The Germans occupied the whole of France and seized the use of French ports in eastern Algeria and Tunisia. At this point some Vichy leaders revolted: Darlan ordered French naval vessels in metropolitan France to sail for Africa and the French Commander-in-Chief in North Africa, General Alphonse Juin, ordered resistance to the Germans and Italians who were occupying Tunisia. Pétain himself, at the head of a government becoming increasingly irrelevant to the practical course of events, began to play a less effective part in it. He retained the allegiance of some of his compatriots and when dispatched to Paris by the Germans in April 1944 to attend a memorial service for victims of allied bombing he was so warmly received that the Germans themselves felt that their attempt to make use of the Marshal in this way had been a mistake. For the most part he lived secluded at Vichy or near Rambouillet. The composition of his cabinet was increasingly determined by the Germans and after he had been forced to accept Déat as a member in 1944 he ceased to attend its meetings. Four years earlier he had been the strong silent soldier who had sat in Reynaud's government until he undermined it. At the beginning of the occupation his *silences* were taken to be a guarantee of the honour of France. They were found to be a guarantee of nothing.

Laval had been restored to power in April 1942 with the title of Prime Minister which he kept until August 1944 along with the posts of Foreign Minister and Minister of the Interior. He still thought that France could bargain with Hitler and when the Germans sought French cooperation against the allies in North Africa he tried to get a German-Italian guarantee of the French empire. But Hitler, who had less than no use for Laval personally and was no longer as interested as he had been two years earlier in France's colonial assets, saw no reason to bargain with France. Germany was now more interested in French labour and Laval was caught up in the satisfaction of German economic demands. He became in the process so identified with the machinery of German exploitation that he was, by the end of the war, the principal scapegoat for all the crimes of Vichy and was subjected to a disgracefully unfair trial before a singularly ugly execution.

By the armistice agreement France was required to pay 300 million francs for every day that the occupation lasted. This sum was supposed to represent the cost to Germany of occupying the northern zone and when therefore the occupation was extended the daily price was raised to 500 million in token of Germany's new obligation to defend southern France and Tunisia. After the allied landings in Normandy in July 1944 the price went up to 700 million, the surcharge representing France's contribution to the general defence of Europe. All these sums greatly exceeded the cost of occupation and were used by Germany for general purposes, including the purchase of French natural resources and industrial enterprises. (The Germans kept the value of the franc high, since they were being paid in francs and were using them to buy up valuable properties.) Thus the armistice payments went much further than reparations, for which in any case the Germans, having suffered practically no damage, had no claim. The payments were a levy fixed by a victor who was using this method to appropriate the capital assets of the vanquished. In addition the Germans requisitioned, and Vichy ceded, supplies of food and other raw materials to which the former were not entitled under the armistice agreement, while even in the southern zone French factories worked for the German war effort, producing aircraft engines and other indubitably military equipment.

These exactions, which began immediately after the capitulation in 1940, were compounded and transformed in 1942 when the Germans began to press for labour. Laval hoped to satisfy the Germans and pacify his compatriots by a deal by which France would supply labour in exchange for the release of prisoners of war (the *relève*). At the same time, in June 1942, he revealed the depth of the anti-communism which was absorbing him more and more as the German campaigns in the east went wrong, by exclaiming that he desired a German victory since otherwise Bolshevism would triumph everywhere. Fulfilling Germany's need for labour became the measure of his commitment to Germany's victory, but at the time when he was coming to see the Germans exclusively as a defence against communism, his compatriots were increasingly concerned with their reprisals against the Resistance and their drive for forced labour. A first labour plan, negotiated between Laval and Sauckel and covering the second half of 1942, provided for the delivery of 250,000 men. It was almost precisely fulfilled. So was a second plan covering the first quarter of 1943. Thereafter Laval tried to apply a brake, offering to transfer French labour to German war work in France but objecting to sending Frenchmen to Germany. Frenchmen themselves took to the woods to avoid compulsory labour service, but a total of 641,000 workers was sent to Germany under the

Sauckel programmes and in 1943 the French forced labourers in Germany outnumbered even the Russian conscripted and prisoner labour force – 1.7 million against 1.3 million. The French contingent included prisoners of war, workers enticed to Germany before the Sauckel programmes began and workers from Alsace-Lorraine and north-eastern France which were outside the Laval-Sauckel agreements. Vichy also shipped off to Germany thousands of Spanish refugees from the lost civil war. (Others, escaping Vichy's net and Hitler's camps, fought in various parts of Europe and some, flying their own flag, marched into Paris with Leclercq in August 1944.) France's sacrifice in labour lost to Germany during the war has been computed as the equivalent of the total output of the French labour force in a normal year. It was as if no work was done in France for a whole year. The value to Germany of the work done by French workers, including prisoners of war, has been estimated at 200 billion (1938) francs.

Laval's attempts to reconcile his countrymen to Sauckel's demands by securing the repatriation of prisoners of war failed. Between two and three million Frenchmen had been taken prisoner in 1940. Vichy's efforts to secure the return of these men were neither effective nor, in the eyes of many, wholehearted: returning prisoners might include obstreperous critics of pre-war and Vichyite policies and too high a percentage of communists. (To some extent the return of prisoners was feared by ordinary Frenchmen too because there were not enough jobs or food to go round.) During the Sauckel programmes prisoners were repatriated at the rate of about one prisoner for every six forced labourers. They returned to a country where production had been cut by a third since 1938, most foods had to be bought in a black market where they cost anything from twice to five times the official price, coal could only be had at ten to twenty or even thirty times the official price, rations were providing 1,200 calories a day or less than half the normal needs of an adult, and mortality was rising rapidly – especially among infants.

These conditions showed that at the most elementary level of material life Vichy had failed. It had also failed in three other respects. It had failed to lay the blame for the collapse of 1940 on its political enemies; it had failed to protect its own citizens; and it had failed to preserve the decencies of public behaviour upon which a conservative régime is wont to insist with special eloquence. Accordingly, even though no alternative French government was in the making, Vichy forfeited its own title to rule France.

The centrepiece of the attempt to lay the blame for France's disasters on the republican régime was the trial at Riom of Daladier, Blum and Gamelin. This trial, which opened on 19 February 1942, was meant to be a demonstration of treason in high places but became instead a counter-attack by the accused civilians on the criminal negligence of the French military establishment – which included Pétain himself, who had been Minister for War in the Doumergue government of 1934 and had stated, among other things, that it was impossible for an enemy to cross the Meuse at Sedan. (Because of Pétain's embarrassing involvement in the story of French inefficiency the scope of the trial was limited to the events of 1936 and later.) The principal issues were the extent of French unpreparedness for war, the failure of the army to use the credits allocated to it, and its inefficiency in the use of such weapons as it did have. In a welter of widely differing statistics the prosecution alleged material deficiencies of scandalous proportions while the accused (other than Gamelin who remained silent throughout) produced figures to show that the weapons had been made available in reasonable numbers but had then either been stored away by the military or so ineptly distributed that some formations had too much and others too little, while large stocks fell unused into German hands. The Riom trial was as unedifying a national *post mortem* as could be conceived and although the Vichy government was able to show that France had been materially ill-prepared for a war against the modern German armies – a fact well known to everybody – it was unable to prevent the accused from retorting that the defeat must also be attributed to bad military planning and coordination before and after the outbreak of war. Since Vichy represented the military establishment which was the target of this counter-attack, the trial was a failure – all the more important in that it left in possession of the field the rival view that Vichy, so far from being the high road to national salvation, was but the last refuge of those responsible for the republic's military ineptitude, political defeatism and moral unpreparedness, a cul-de-sac containing surviving specimens of the *deux cents familles* who were supposed, however exaggeratedly, to have dominated French industrial and social life for their own selfish ends. The trial was abruptly suspended after two months and was never resumed.

The authority of Vichy as a government was further eroded by the fact that on the one hand it lacked the power to protect French citizens against the Germans, while on the other it abetted German excesses. Some 30,000 French hostages were shot during the occupation, while countless other French men and women suffered transportation or mental anguish through the operation of *Nacht und Nebel*. France became a police state as well as an occupied country; Vichy's police assisted the German police and Vichy's administration and courts were progressively adapted to the requirements of the occupiers. Vichy's first anti-semitic law was passed in 1940, Darlan established a special Jewish office in 1941 and deportation of Jews began in 1942. With the increasing strength of Resistance movements all male relatives over eighteen of any Resister were made liable to the death penalty, his female relatives to forced labour and his younger relatives to detention in reformatories. Vichy fell back, in company with the Germans, on intimidation as a means of government, coupled with a proliferation of petty regulations enforceable by heavy fines (for example, the offence of carrying chickens to market with their legs tied together). But gradually, and without destroying the appearances of administrative propriety, local authorities, the police and the magistrature ceased to comply. Local officials either delayed or sabotaged instructions. The police, who frequently became covert allies of the Resistance, gave opportune warnings. Sentences passed by magistrates for breaches of occupation laws revealed so consistent a pattern of extreme lenience that the Germans protested to Vichy.

Public opinion began to manifest itself against Vichy at an early stage. Newspapers protested against increasing concessions to the Germans, applauded the Yugoslav revolution of 1941 and promoted a dialogue with their readers on such questions as censorship and the thinness of public information. Officials considered too zealous in their cooperation received miniature coffins as a warning. When Vichy broke off relations with the USSR in June 1941 popular reaction was so outspoken that Pétain felt obliged to broadcast – *c'est de vous-mêmes que je veux vous sauver* – and to double the police.

The ultimate condemnation of Vichy lies in the fact that for each Frenchman killed in the fighting in 1940 another died later as a civilian victim of the war. Vichy functioned as a satellite in Germany's New Order and was doomed to become nothing else, to sterility and transience. Neither its own roots in French society nor the shortcomings of previous governments were adequate to give it the credentials or the lifeblood of an independent French régime. Movements formed to sustain it showed by their wilting that it could not be sustained. *Les Amis du Maréchal* and, still more so, *Les Jeunes du Maréchal* were exposures of the barrenness of their own titles, while *Le Francisme* failed entirely in its functions as an anti-Resistance movement. Under Vichy the unity of France was a slogan which was belied not only by the physical disunity of the country but also by moral disunity. At the very best Vichy exercised a limited control over a minority; one third of the population lived in the non-occupied zone, while two thirds of France's home-grown food was produced in the north and so laid Vichy under the necessity to bargain with the Germans in order to secure fair shares for the south.

And Vichy was resisted from the start. Men demobilized from the defeated French forces did not cease to regard Germany as the enemy. Laying the blame for France's defeat on Great Britain – as Vichy tried to do but with only moderate effect – did not alter this fact, and Vichy was obviously Germany's creature: the hectic note of treason appeared from the first in the rejection of Vichy. Although there was at first little that they could do about the situation, the attitude of Resisters was clear to themselves and their friends and they took what opportunities they had of proclaiming and spreading it by such acts as scribbling slogans on walls or defacing propaganda posters. More purposeful sabotage was already in evidence by the autumn of that year. Personal and local protests of this kind provided the basis from which a mood might develop into a movement with nation-wide organization and purpose. This development occurred along two lines which had, at a point, to be merged. Within France local groups formed and came into touch with nearby local groups. Beyond France de Gaulle used the remnants of an army, the undecided loyalties of the French overseas empire and the force of his own personality and his own faith to create a new French régime whose authority would be accepted by all who were fighting against Germany – by French Resistance groups of all kinds and by the British, American and Russian governments.

When de Gaulle made his first broadcast to the French people from London on 18 June 1940 he was almost unknown. He was a general and he had been a junior Minister in Reynaud's last government owing to the accident of personal acquaintance with the Prime Minister. Within his profession he was noted for his intelligence and clarity of thought and for unorthodox ideas on tank warfare; he had also a reputation for incommunicativeness and intractability (he learned later how to communicate). Beyond the profession he was barely known, even by name. Among parliamentarians, for example, most of the members of the Committee on National Defence would have known something of him, but perhaps only a dozen other members of the Senate and the Chamber could have said who he was. When he began to be talked about, it was only with difficulty that a photograph could be found and for some months the face and figure which were to be so well known were only to be picked out in the back row of a formal photograph of Reynaud's last administration. There was no very strong reason why anybody listening to him on 18 June should imagine that this was a saviour and future President of France. He said that the war was not over and France not finished. Unlike many other Frenchmen at this time he did not argue about Great Britain's powers of resistance but about France itself: not about whether Great Britain could fight on but whether France could. And he did not so much argue as affirm. To argue about the fate of France at this point was almost certain to lead to a pessimistic conclusion. De Gaulle's resistance rested therefore on faith and action and he relied on these two forces to change the argument. He was able to do this because, besides being a patriot, he had in his bearing and his intelligence an authority which gave substance to his call for faith and action.

He was in this respect very like Churchill without Churchill's extraversion. Both men appealed dramatically to a people for sacrifices and in both cases the success of the appeal lay in the personality of the appealer, but whereas Churchill used words to make personal contact with his compatriots, de Gaulle used them in order to make himself not so much their leader as their symbol. To some extent the distinction was one of circumstances, for Churchill was among his people and was clothed with the legitimacy of office whereas de Gaulle was an exile without official standing of any kind (later in life he was to prove that he too knew how to move about among crowds); but the difference was even more a difference in character. De Gaulle's strength was that of the strong silent man of the English stereotype. His passions were under powerful control and during the early years of exile his natural reticence was reinforced by the fact that he was playing his hand from weakness. The poverty of his resources imposed on him the need to say as little as possible in order to reveal as little as possible. He was not interested in becoming a platoon commander in the Anglo-American host, for by doing so he might perhaps contribute to the defeat of Germany but without displacing Vichy and all it stood for. If as a Frenchman he was concerned to defeat the Germans, he was no less concerned, as a republican, to overthrow Vichy and restore and refine the post-revolutionary tradition of French republicanism. As a soldier from within this tradition he accepted the subordination of the military to the civil power but equally he wanted the wielders of civil power to behave better in future than they had behaved in the past. He was impatient of excessive parliamentary interference in the business of government and contemptuous of the past performance of political parties, but he wished to curb rather than abolish parliament and parties.

Consequently the simple solutions of the military dictator were not open to him. He wished neither to destroy the institutions of the republic nor to ignore the people, to whom on the contrary he appealed. But his respect for these institutions derived at least as much from his conservative temper as from any democratic conviction and his attachment to republic and people was long suspect in Resistance circles, especially on the Left where his sympathy and support for the Russians were as much a surprise as Churchill's. Like Churchill he envisaged a partnership between the populace and himself, but unlike Churchill he cultivated this union not only to win the war but also to restore and purge and to some extent refashion the republic. Unlike Churchill again, he was not a democrat in the Anglo-Saxon sense: he never used the word democracy and when he spoke of the republic he did so in the old Roman sense of the common weal. With regard to the war the movement which he set out to build was a military one, but with regard to *l'après-guerre* it was a civil movement which required the unification of all Resistance groups inside France with, and under, his own group in London and the empire. Gaullism was therefore *la France combattante* and also the next French republic. Since the Americans and, to a lesser extent, the British underrated the value of the first and refused for a long time to acknowledge the second, de Gaulle's role in exile became one of stubborn self-inflation.

De Gaulle's first task was to command the allegiance of as much as possible of the French empire, his second to command the attention of everybody else. Indo-China, the Middle East and North Africa had declared for Vichy, while in West Africa the attempt to acquire a foothold at Dakar was a failure. In general too little was known about the Gaullist group in London and its prospects to tempt distant proconsuls into rejecting the armistice and Vichy's claim to legitimacy. De Gaulle had first to build up his own forces, create a following in France itself and show that Hitler's principal enemies accepted him as an ally. However, Félix Eboué, the governor of Chad in French Equatorial Africa, chose the Gaullist side and was followed by other African colonies, by Tahiti, the Marquesas Islands and New Caledonia, and by the French colonies in India. One other colony, the oldest, was seized by de Gaulle, who thereby earned lasting hostility in Washington.

St Pierre et Miquelon had been divided since the fall of France between a Vichyite minority which was in control and a Gaullist majority. The colony consisted of a group of islands a dozen miles off the south coast of Newfoundland. It had some strategic importance, for it lay off the mouth of the St Lawrence and could be used against convoys by harbouring U-boats and reporting the movements of shipping. Atlantic cables passed through its waters and after these had been cut the colony remained in close contact with Vichy by means of a radio station which, besides transmitting weather reports and Vichyite propaganda, reported on shipping and gave instructions to agents. Both Newfoundland (then a British Crown Colony) and Canada were suspected of designs against the islands, and the United States warmly advocated Canadian annexation. Great Britain, however, and also Canada after some wavering, preferred a Gaullist coup and were embarrassed by American schemes. The Canadian cabinet settled on a compromise whereby Canada would, by threats of economic sanctions and in the last resort by force, seize the radio station but not remove the Vichyite governor or overthrow his régime.

In October 1941 de Gaulle broached with Eden the question of a Gaullist coup. Eden, although sympathetic, felt obliged to refer to Ottawa and Washington. De Gaulle dispatched Admiral Émile Muselier to end the discussions by taking the islands; the coup was not difficult since the population was largely pro-Gaullist. But Muselier decided to go to Ottawa first. There he found the government undecided between its own plan to seize the radio station and the Gaullist plan to seize the colony. The Canadian government consulted Washington which objected strongly to a Gaullist coup, largely because it had just negotiated a general agreement about all the French possessions in the western hemisphere with Vichy's representative, Admiral Robert. Roosevelt was ill informed and badly advised on French affairs; he refused to regard Vichy as fascist or de Gaulle as a democrat, he was partly right in both cases, but he was wrong in imagining that this simple categorization was all that mattered; he exaggerated American influence at Vichy and tended to be combatively uneasy about his pro-Vichy policy which he knew to be regarded with scepticism by his British allies and with distaste by his own press and public. Roosevelt was therefore all the more hostile to de Gaulle who represented an additional challenge to his Vichy policy and whom he in return represented as no more than a fringe military figure. His objections to the St Pierre adventure prevailed. The British and Canadian governments gave way with reluctance and so did de Gaulle and Muselier. But in almost the same breath de Gaulle ordered Muselier to go ahead and take the islands.

This Muselier, with three corvettes, a submarine and grave misgivings about the probity of his undertaking, did. Great Britain and Canada were privately pleased but officially reticent; the American press and public were enthusiastically in favour of this first stroke against European dictatorship in the American continent; but in Washington Roosevelt and his Secretary of State Cordell Hull, who was more convinced than the President that Gaullism was insignificant, were so infuriated that they issued unnecessarily offensive statements about the Gaullists and tried to get the Canadians to mount an expedition to recapture the colony – a project which only incensed Ottawa against Washington. The rights and wrongs of this episode are still not entirely clear. The overthrow of Vichy's authority in the colony was in the allied interest. Roosevelt and Hull were wrong in their estimates of Vichy and de Gaulle and their reactions to the event were out of proportion to its significance. Roosevelt would probably have been glad to treat the affair as an irritating episode and forget it – he called it a 'teapot tempest', which is presumably something not much bigger than a storm in a tea-cup – but Hull took it to heart to such a degree that he lost his judgement, nourished a personal animosity against de Gaulle and accused Great Britain of conspiring with de Gaulle against the United States. On the French side de Gaulle's action, of which Muselier disapproved, is less easy to assess. It is at least possible that, after accepting Washington's veto on his plan, he learned for the first time of the Canadian plan and thereupon, imagining himself deceived, reversed his decision. The most important consequence of the coup was to give de Gaulle and Gaullism great prestige throughout the French empire and in France.

For about a year the Gaullists were ill informed about happenings inside France itself. Resistance groups seemed to be small and uncoordinated. They might one day be useful adjuncts of a Gaullist army. For the time being their sabotage activities were good for French morale and good practice for the day when sabotage would help an invading force. Activities on a larger scale raised problems. They were for the moment premature; they might do more harm than good; they might tend towards the emergence of a separate centre of authority in competition with the Gaullists and, after 1941, increasingly under communist control. Guerrilla operations did not seem to be a good idea. De Gaulle's headquarters, predominantly military and right wing, discounted the value of large-scale populist resistance and viewed it without enthusiasm. But this attitude changed during 1942, by which time Gaullism as a whole had edged leftward in reaction to Vichyite positions and in sympathy with the Russian stand against Germany, and had learned more about the Resistance movements inside France.

The main concern of the Resistance was the revival and consolidation of all that was best in the French spirit as a necessary precondition to action against the enemy. It was therefore at least as much concerned with Frenchmen as with Germans, for the defeat of the Germans was to be only an intermediate operation between a revolution in French public feeling and – the ultimate end – a revolution in the structure of French society and politics. When the Germans first entered Paris and other French cities their reception was far from universally hostile. Fraternization was common not only in shops and restaurants but in casual encounters on streets and squares where crowds gathered to listen to news broadcasts or concerts and rubbed shoulders with Germans, whom they were ready to treat as ordinary human beings. Resistance-minded Frenchmen regarded all this as a dangerous, even disgusting, self-deception. They were also concerned to combat Vichy's implicit claim to provide the right answers for France, and to demonstrate that Vichy, so far from serving France, was putting German interests before French ones. Vichy started with a major advantage since there was widespread acceptance of the view that France's disasters should all be blamed on the parliamentarians whom Vichy was attacking and displacing, so that the Resistance, which also accepted this view, was forced into the awkward position of damning political parties but at the same time advocating a restored, if regenerated, political system. Essentially, as post-war events proved, this was an illogical position, for the system demanded parties by whatever name they might be called (movements, rallies and so on became in fact parties as soon as they moved into action). But the Resistance contrived to evade the illogicality. It was joined by men of different parties and different social backgrounds. It did not at first look to de Gaulle nor know much about his movement except that it was a long way away in London and possibly under British control. In the south men of right-wing temperament often dropped out in the early days and accepted Vichy, so that southern Resistance movements had begun to wear a left-wing air even before they were joined by communists after the German invasion of the USSR. This ideological colouring of the Resistance was increased by the hostility or ambivalence of the ecclesiastical establishment: in general the Roman Catholic episcopacy had an outstandingly poor Resistance record, redeemed only partially by the heroism of a minority of the lesser clergy. Political parties continued throughout the war to be regarded in the Resistance with some distaste and there was a vague hope (except among the communists) that the unity forged during the Resistance would somehow dispense with the need to resuscitate the old parties after liberation. Post-war problems were, however, subordinated to the needs of the present, and old political leaders worked alongside new non-political chieftains to create forces which would cause real embarrassment and damage to the German occupiers.

Their efforts were aided by the revulsion against Vichy. This was at first gradual and patchy. Its principal sources were Vichy's own actions, the behaviour of the Germans coupled with Vichy's failure to take even a moral stand against it, and the recovery of courage effected by time, nationalism and the growth of the clandestine press from amateurish hand-outs to real newspapers. Particular events accelerated the general trend: the introduction of forced labour, which transformed the scale of the Resistance by hitting the middle classes as well as the working classes (comparatively well represented in the Resistance from the start); and the raids on the continent at St Nazaire and Dieppe which confirmed what people were hearing on the radio about the progress of the war (although the Germans decreed the confiscation of private radios, they were unable to confiscate enough of them to stop people knowing about the war).

The rejection of Vichy automatically turned attention to de Gaulle as an alternative government and by the beginning of 1942 a number of Resistance groups had decided to accept de Gaulle's leadership. In the south the principal Resistance movements were the *Francs-Tireurs et Partisans* (FTP), *Combat* and *Libération*, all of them active by the end of 1941 and all in contact with de Gaulle. In the occupied zone, where Resistance was in the nature of things more difficult and dangerous, *Libération-Nord* and *Organisation Civile et Militaire* (OCM) played the leading part, became effective in 1942 and also established contacts with the Gaullists in London. Although the Communist Party denounced the war until Hitler invaded the USSR, many individual communists joined Resistance movements before that date. After June 1941 the *Front National*, which covered the whole country and embraced diverse opinions under communist leadership, pursued a policy of cooperation between all Resistance movements and advocated extensive and immediate action, even courting reprisals in order to intensify anti-German feeling. Its object was to harass and kill the occupiers in order not only to end the occupation but also to transform French politics. To the rank and file of Resisters, and even to their regional leaders, the politics of the movement to which they belonged were very often unknown.

At the end of 1941 de Gaulle sent one of his principal lieutenants, Jean Moulin, to France. Moulin began by uniting the movements in the south, thus completing the elimination of Vichy as a force for the future. The further work of combining Resistance movements in northern and southern France, and uniting the Resistance with Gaullism, was facilitated by the German occupation of the whole country in November 1942 and by the consolidation of de Gaulle's position as the unrivalled chief of French forces overseas in spite of American attempts to prefer Giraud or Darlan. The communists accepted de Gaulle's leadership at the end of 1942. In March 1943 Resistance movements from all parts of the country combined in the *Mouvements Unis de la Résistance*, which gave birth to the *Comité National de la Résistance* (CNR) which first met in Paris in May under Moulin's chairmanship and recognized de Gaulle as the national leader of France. A few weeks after this meeting Moulin and other French leaders were picked up by the Gestapo, tortured and killed, but during his last months in his native country Moulin had created the organs with which France would re-enter the war. (The CNR did not meet again until after the liberation. Owing to the activities of the German police it was forced to operate regionally.) The recognition extended to de Gaulle by the entire Resistance put him for the first time in command of considerable forces and greatly increased his political standing with his western and eastern allies.

Relations between the French Resistance and the western allies were uneven. Resistance leaders inside France (as elsewhere) suspected the British and American governments of not taking them seriously enough, of regarding them as a sideshow, and of sending fewer arms and other supplies than they could afford. They protested against the bombing of targets in France which they themselves could sabotage with much less loss of innocent civilian lives – although not, owing to the nature of sabotage, with lasting effect. Being in a position to observe the inaccuracy of strategic bombing they continually urged, without carrying conviction, that they had a better way of doing the job. Raids on Nantes from 16 to 23 September 1943 were a particularly grave example of the futility of the policy of total air warfare which the British and the Americans had uncritically taken over from the Germans. Senseless destruction threatened to alienate the population not only from the perpetrators but also from the Resistance which was in a sense allied with them. On the other side the British and American governments, besides underestimating the effectiveness of the Resistance, exaggerated the tensions within it and, the Americans especially, were afraid that a civil war would break out in France before the Germans were defeated and that the communists would win it. With more justice they regarded the Resistance movements as insecure and not to be trusted with information of value. In fact Anglo-American assistance to France was very great but it was of a kind not always visible to Resistance leaders. While these anxiously awaited parachute drops which never came or seemed (until the eve of invasion) disappointingly meagre, Great Britain lent France £30 million and the United States gave de Gaulle all the facilities of Lend–Lease from November 1941 and helped to equip and maintain large French forces in Africa from the time of the Casablanca conference and in France itself in 1944, particularly after the Ardennes offensive at the end of that year when eight new divisions were formed out of Resistance units. But politically Roosevelt continued to drag his feet. In July 1944, when the CNL declared itself the provisional government of France, Washington recognized it as a *de facto* government, delaying until October the further step of recognizing it as the *de jure*, though provisional, government; and Roosevelt opposed de Gaulle's presence at Yalta.

Within France Resistance of a quasi-military kind was intensified from 1943 and organized in regions under the aegis of a three-man directorate which was established by the CNR and coordinated the efforts of the various military bodies in the field. Bands were mostly fifty to a hundred strong, although some were as large as 500–1,000. Nearly all their arms came from the Americans and British who supplied 1,000 tons of equipment by March 1944 (of which the Germans seized a third) and 8,000 tons in the next six months, the period spanning the invasion of France. Early in 1944 the movements joined forces as the *Forces Françaises de l'Intérieur* (FFI), by which time their combined field strength had reached about 30,000 and it was commonly assumed that an allied return to the continent was not far distant. Increasing strength meant increasing temptation to use it and sometimes action was premature and tragic.

At Glières for example, in Haute Savoie, a band of 500 men organized during 1943 by a former lieutenant in the *Chasseurs Alpins* attacked a considerable force of heavily armed Germans in February 1944 and lost half its men. Such incidents became more frequent as the great moment of liberation approached and misunderstandings over the role of the FFI and cooperation with the invading forces took their toll. Thus at Montmouchet the Resistance, mistakenly believing that allied troops would arrive to join forces in an attack on the Germans simultaneously with the landings in the north, assembled a strength of 3,000–4,000 men and opened battle. Fighting went on for a week. The Germans suffered to begin with ten casualties for every one among their enemies but in the end they won a complete victory. A similar misunderstanding produced a similar tragedy in the Vercors. The Vercors, a natural fortress south-west of Grenoble, was occupied by Resistance units in the winter of 1942–3. From small beginnings – a group of local men in a small way of business, most of them socialists – the Vercors redoubt grew into an assembly centre and refuge of considerable importance, but it was not meant to be a stronghold to be defended in battle against regular German forces. Nevertheless such a battle took place. Again there were false expectations of outside help. Resistance leaders believed that plans for a joint operation had been endorsed by the French and allied authorities in London and Algiers when in fact these plans were, owing to administrative incompetence, not even known to many of the people who would have been involved. A few days before the landings in Normandy the Vercors Resistance mobilized and serious fighting began on 13 June. It continued for forty-one days, the Resistance force of 3,500 men holding an area where they expected allied reinforcements to land by air and so condemning themselves to static defence against two German divisions which eventually surrounded and liquidated most of them. This episode produced the sharpest disagreement between de Gaulle and his communist associates in the Provisional Government; the communists, who held among other posts the air portfolio, pressed for air support for the rising (which was rejected as impracticable) and accused de Gaulle of betraying the Resistance, in return for which de Gaulle dismissed the air member of his government.

But these episodes were not typical. Elsewhere the Resistance played a successful part in the defeat of the Germans. On a signal from the BBC the FFI mobilized 200,000 (lightly) armed troops and as many ancillaries in support. According to Eisenhower they were worth fifteen divisions and shortened the campaign by two months. They denied the French rail system to the Germans; disrupted road communications by felling trees and other devices; destroyed German minefields; cut down hedges in order to help the operations of allied tactical air squadrons; spread rumours of parachute landings which distracted the German command; obstructed the transfer of the German SS division *Das Reich* from the south-west so that it took nine days to reach the battle area in Normandy; forced 20,000 Germans to surrender to the Americans at Issoudun (and were very annoyed when the Americans gave their captives oranges, which no Frenchman had seen for years); successfully blocked off Brittany and then cleared it after the Americans had broken out of their Normandy beach-heads; took thousands of prisoners; protected works of art.

De Gaulle arrived in Paris on 25 August, the day after the surrender of the German military governor to General Jacques Leclercq of the revived French army and Colonel Rol-Tanguy of the Resistance as representatives of the French republic (the rising of the Parisians is narrated below in the context of the allied victories in France). He had already made careful preparations to assume the government of the country. The adherence of the Resistance to the Gaullist movement enabled him to do so by general consent. He was, however, apprehensive lest the communists might make a bid for power, using the local Liberation Committees which had been set up in each *département* and were mostly under communist control. Further, Roosevelt's hostility to him and the United States' continued refusal to recognize the CNR as a government or to come out against Vichy made him fear that the allies intended to impose a military government on France as they had on Sicily. He therefore chose and appointed *préfets* who were to be ready to assume authority as soon as invasion or Resistance had swept away Vichy's local government officials.

De Gaulle was also greatly concerned about the unity of the French people. He opposed the view, strongly held in the Resistance, that French society could be made healthy by a surgical purge of malign elements. The conflict between the Resistance and Vichy had generated much bitterness, which found vent during the occupation in the publication of lists of collaborators, the marking of their houses, summary executions (possibly 5,000 instances, plus another 5,000 in the throes and immediate aftermath of liberation) and an increasingly vocal determination to bring to trial and exact retribution from men and women of all ranks who had helped the enemy or served Vichy. In March 1944 a first Vichy Minister, Pierre Pucheu, was tried for treason and executed and a few months later another, Philippe Henriot, was assassinated in public and in daylight. Judicial and extra-judicial punishment of this kind was regarded by many in the Resistance and in de Gaulle's entourage as both inevitable and excusable, but de Gaulle himself deplored vengeance and regarded a purge, however conducted, as impracticable and likely to poison rather than heal French society. Some retribution was, however, inevitable and a special High Court was created to hear the principal cases. Fifty-eight cases were brought before this court, which passed eighteen death sentences (ten of them *in absentia*); three of the eighteen were executed. Altogether nearly 125,000 cases were heard by other courts and nearly 7,000 death sentences pronounced, of which 767 were carried out. Pétain was among those sentenced to death by the High Court. De Gaulle had hoped that

Pétain would not be captured by French troops, nor return, and he was relieved when the death sentence on the Marshal was accompanied by a recommendation to mercy which he accepted. Pétain was consigned to a fortress on the Île d'Yeu off the west coast of France where he read de Gaulle's memoirs and remained until a few weeks before his death in 1951, when he was removed from the fortress but not from the island.

As Head of the Provisional Government of France de Gaulle saw his task in the same terms as he had seen it in 1940 as a junior minister and then as a refugee: to ensure and assert France's position as a major power. Although he might and did toy with the idea of presenting France as the champion of smaller powers or medium powers (the latter was a category which was recognized by the practice of the League of Nations and which France tried unsuccessfully to introduce into the structure of the United Nations), his basic aim was to range France unequivocally with the Big Three. He rejected the idea that France was a western equivalent of Poland or a power of the same consequence as Yugoslavia. This aim was formally achieved when France was accorded equal status with the Big Three in the administration of Germany and a permanent seat in the UN Security Council, but France still needed a special role to sustain this equal status. De Gaulle hoped that France might mediate between Anglo-Saxons and Russians and at the same time create and lead a western European group embracing the Low Countries, Spain, Italy and part of Germany as well as France itself – the countries touched by the Rhine, the Alps or the Pyrenees. In both these notions he was echoing Resistance aspirations for Great Power harmony and a European federation. But the harmony of the Resistance itself began to disintegrate under the pressures of peacetime politics and when the communists tried to refashion the post-war all-party government by forming an alliance and excluding the new Roman Catholic party, the MRP, de Gaulle decided to retire and leave the parties to conduct their despised manoeuvres without him. He announced his decision in January 1946. By the end of the next year the communists too were out of office. For a decade the government of France reverted to the political forces of the Third Republic until revolt in Algeria and a threat of a military coup in Paris itself drove them in 1958 to abdicate in favour of de Gaulle, who returned to save France once more and to pursue his interrupted task.

Part IV

THE MIDDLE GAME

CHAPTER 16

The Muster against the Axis

THE alliance which confronted Hitler in 1939 was a Franco-British one. When France fell Great Britain had to consider whether to carry on the fight. In retrospect it is easy to conclude that there was never any doubt about the answer to this question. It was never directly put, but there was a question all the same and there was a case for answering it in the negative. The defeat of France seemed to put Great Britain in a hopeless position, safe perhaps from military invasion but incapable of beating Germany and doubtfully capable of warding off intolerable air attacks. To the staid man of cool mind who was trained to assess a situation and then ask what was the most sensible thing to do about it – to the typical British statesman – the conclusion could well be that a government's job was to make the best of a bad business or, in other words, come to terms with fate in the person of Hitler. Some members of the British government reasoned this way. The historical importance of Churchill is that he did not. Having assessed the situation he refused to deduce his own course from it; he determined rather to alter it. He treated the concept of peace offers from Hitler as a contradiction in terms and ignored them. Moreover his famous speech on 4 June – 'we shall fight on the beaches, we shall fight on the landing-grounds, we shall fight in the fields and in the streets, we shall fight in the hills; we shall never surrender . . .' – gave the lead that the country wanted. Its reception showed how far the British mood had cleared since 1938. Then the question had been whether the British should fight, but now it was whether they should fight on. It was an easier question to answer.

But Churchill had been Prime Minister for only a few weeks. He was not the entire master of his cabinet, still less so of the Conservative Party, and both were substantially what they had been in the last years of appeasement. Official as well as popular feeling had changed since Munich, but it had not changed out of all recognition. Two weeks after Churchill's no-surrender speech his Under-Secretary of State at the Foreign office, R. A. Butler, was telling the Swedish Minister that the Prime Minister's voice was not necessarily decisive, that the war might not have to be fought to a finish and that an opportunity to make a reasonable compromise peace would not be missed in spite of the 'die-hards' in the cabinet. The Foreign Secretary, Halifax, himself reinforced this appraisal by telling the same Minister that commonsense would prevail over bravado. (The Swedish government thereupon gave in to German pressure and allowed German soldiers going home on leave from Norway to travel through Sweden.) Another member of the old team, Hoare, who had wavered in the late thirties into toying with the idea of a Russian alliance and had then been relegated to the right wing as Ambassador in Madrid, was being similarly propitiatory. It was as a result of consorting too exclusively with people of this kind that the United States Ambassador in London, Joseph P. Kennedy, reported that Great Britain was finished – a judgement at variance not only with the facts but also with that of the Russian Ambassador, Ivan Maisky, who was assuring Stalin that the British would fight on despite the fall of France. (A year later Maisky found an ingenious solution to the reverse problem of persuading the British that the Russians would fight on and win in spite of Hitler's first victories in the USSR: he persuaded a British publishing firm to issue a cheap edition of Tolstoy's *War and Peace*.)

But wars are not won by spirit alone. The British determination embodied in Churchill could hardly have prevailed against Hitler but for Great Britain's insular geography and its imperial past. As an island state Great Britain could parry and gain time. But this was only a negative advantage. It might enable Great Britain to get left out of Europe's catastrophic affairs but it could not directly affect them. As an island Great Britain was an anti-German perch, but there was in 1940 nobody to perch on it, for the Americans were unlikely to join a war which had dwindled to a formal state of belligerence and no more. But Great Britain was also an empire and it was the combination of British Empire and British Isles which kept the war alive: the American armies first joined this war not in Europe but in Africa.

Great Britain's imperial past had two major consequences. First, it provided a base in the Middle East to serve as an alternative point for accumulating forces and launching them against the European continent and, secondly, it provided the men and materials which India, the Dominions and the colonies contributed to the war. When Great Britain declared war in 1939 the Dominions did so too – in the case of South Africa by a vote of eighty to sixty-seven in Parliament, in the other cases wholeheartedly. This response was not the automatic reaction which it had been in 1914 but a freely formed resolve based on the close links of kinship and imperial solidarity and on revulsion against Nazi enormities. In India the Viceroy, acting with complete constitutional propriety but almost equally complete obtuseness, declared war without consulting any Indian leader. In spite of this tactless insensitivity Indians fought once more in Europe's wars at Great Britain's behest – to such good measure that Wavell felt bound to complain to Churchill in 1942 that the Indian army had the equivalent of seven divisions in the Middle East (more than it had in India) at a time when the country was dangerously threatened by the Japanese. Throughout the war there was never any shortage of volunteers for the Indian armed services. The Indian princes also pledged all their resources to the British cause and the independent kingdom of Nepal, the home of the Gurkhas, maintained its distinctive fighting reputation.

By mid-1941 the British Chiefs of Staff were making plans for the following year on the basis that they would be able to deploy about sixty divisions, of which slightly over one third would come from India and the Dominions (India eight, Australia five and a third, Canada four and a third, South Africa two, New Zealand one). The bulk of the armour, the equivalent of twelve divisions out of fifteen, would be British, but otherwise the imperial contribution was striking. Some Canadian units reached Great Britain as early as 1939 and took part in the battle for France next year; Australia and New Zealand agreed in January 1940 to the dispatch of a division each to the Middle East. Similar contributions were made to naval and air forces. The Commonwealth Air Training Scheme, established by the British, Canadian, Australian and New Zealand governments, trained tens of thousands of pilots, radio operators, gunners and observers annually at elementary and advanced schools in the various countries, and South Africa and Rhodesia set up schemes of their own, the latter with British instructors and aircraft. All this help was given with little restriction. South Africa did not allow service outside the African continent and restricted service outside the Union itself to volunteers: they served in North and East Africa. Australia and New Zealand were concerned to ensure that operations overseas should not endanger their immediate security and Australia felt obliged to withdraw its units from Tobruk at a moment which was critical both for Tobruk and the defence of Australia against the Japanese. All the Dominion governments tried, as they were bound to do, to secure some say in broad strategic decisions and the right to be consulted on operational decisions of special moment to themselves. Australia and New Zealand complained about the dispatch of their units to Greece without adequate consultation, Canada showed concern about plans to commit Canadians to an assault on Trondhjem without express Canadian consent. But in general the Commonwealth commitment was unfettered as well as generous.

Thus, whether he fully realized it or not, Hitler was already in 1940 threatened from many quarters and by many peoples. The focus for this threat was the Middle East and it is conceivable that the threat to Hitler would not have materialized if Mussolini had not stirred it up by urging Graziani to attack in the desert and by invading Greece towards the end of 1940. By doing these things Mussolini opened a second front within range of British imperial power. He unshackled the British strategic initiative which had been neutralized when Great Britain lost in France its only fighting ally.

Churchill's problem after the defeat of France was how and with whom to get back to the continent. There were two possible ways of doing this. The one was to bring France back into the fight and the other was to make the journey back to within striking distance of Germany by way of the Balkans. A view of Europe from the south-east had been familiar to Englishmen since Egypt became to all intents and purposes a part of the British Empire and the Mediterranean, if not a British lake, at least a British highway signposted by Gibraltar, Malta, Alexandria and Suez.

Until the spring of 1941 the Balkans were debatable ground. Churchill built up British forces across the water in Egypt. But then Hitler conquered south-east Europe too, and the British in Egypt, their forces (mostly Australians and New Zealanders) thrown out of Greece and Crete, had to give up thinking of engaging the Germans anywhere on the continent; they were confined to the subsidiary problems of Libya and the Horn of Africa. At this point Hitler himself again re-opened the war in Europe and created for the German army an enemy who was to engage it until it was destroyed. His attack on the USSR in June 1941 transformed the war by carrying the bulk of Germany's ground forces to the east and out of occupied Europe, thereby making Resistance a serious practical possibility and opening for the British the prospect of returning to the continent either by assault on its weakened western defences or through ports captured by a French Resistance movement. Six months later Hitler's declaration of war against the United States ensured that this re-entry would be immensely massive. Hitler had dissolved the Anglo-French alliance only to create a convergence of British, Indian, Dominion, Russian and American forces against him. From 1942 onwards, the muster of these diverse enemies, joined by contingents from Hitler's victims, were on their several ways into Germany. But these ways had to be concerted.

The principal allies – the United States, the USSR and Great Britain – were united in their primary war aim but often divided about how best to achieve it. Between the Americans and the British there was an accumulation of trust and fellowship which produced, for all its occasional rubs, an exceptionally efficient and harmonious alliance, but between them and the Russians there stood a generation of mistrust, thousands of miles and ineradicable divergences on post-war aims.

The Grand Alliance which defeated Germany was fashioned by circumstances rather than by men. In the thirties the western European democracies had shunned the USSR because in a number of ways their rulers preferred Hitler to communism: either the USSR was weak, in which case it was no use as an ally, or it was strong, in which case it might dominate central Europe – an eventuality to be avoided at almost any cost. Stalin had no more liking for them than they for him and, concerned about how to keep out of trouble for as long as possible, he too had opted for Hitler in 1939: the victor in the ensuing war between Germany and the west would confront the USSR and probably be happy to attack it. But when in 1941, with that war still undecided, Germany invaded the USSR, an alliance between the west and the USSR became a natural sequel which imposed itself, or interposed itself, on the current of history. Although there was some surprise at the immediacy and wholeheartedness of Churchill's and Roosevelt's response, there was nothing surprising about the event itself. Hitler's decision to attack the USSR while he was still at war with Great Britain meant that an east–west alliance against him would precede the east–west conflict which he in effect postponed to 1945.

So long as the war lasted the maintenance of this anti-German alliance was a cardinal aim of the leaders on both sides of Germany. The war on two fronts was the war which Hitler could not win. A separate peace in west or east spelt danger for the other half of the alliance. For Great Britain the German attack on the USSR, because it came before Churchill had achieved his aim of seeing the Americans join the fighting, was an immense relief in a year of critical strain, and even after Hitler's declaration of war against the United States, six months after Barbarossa was launched, the maintenance of the Russian capacity and will to fight was essential to a western victory. Not until 1943 at the earliest were the German armies so mauled by the Russians that the western allies might hope to put their own great armies onto the continent without intolerable losses. Yet these forces must make their invasion not long after 1943 in order to be certain that new German weapons, such as chemical weapons, would not render it impossible. As late as the autumn of 1944 they were sharply reminded in the Ardennes that the Germans, even in a war on two fronts which they were clearly losing, remained dangerous foes.

On the Russian side Stalin, by his appeals for material aid and for the re-opening of a front in France, proved his urgent fear of defeat in single combat with the Germans, and although this fear was greatly relieved by the endurance of Stalingrad at the end of 1942 and all but completely removed by the Russian victories in the summer of 1943, the preservation of 'anti-fascist, solidarity' remained a cardinal principle of Stalin's war policy, even to the extent of discouraging sectarian communist ambitions; he dissolved the Comintern in May 1943 and restrained communists like Tito and Togliatti, lecturing the one on the need to conciliate and collaborate with anti-fascists of all kinds and telling the other to mute anti-monarchism until the war was over. It is arguable that, if forced to a choice, Stalin might have put the control over eastern Europe above the preservation of the alliance once the USSR's moment of vital danger had passed, and that he never regarded eastern Europe as negotiable during the last two years of war; but he was never called upon to make that choice, an escape for which he could claim some personal credit since it was partly due to his refusal to confabulate with Roosevelt and Churchill until the end of 1943.

But although the overriding needs of the partners ensured its maintenance, the alliance was neither deep nor harmonious. Evidence to the contrary is to be found only in communiqués, notoriously misleading, and in descriptions of banquet scenes, traditionally unbuttoned. The persistent reality was a background of mistrustful manoeuvre and speculation. Although anti-Germanism was strong enough to hold the alliance together, it was – apart from a certain mutual martial admiration – just about the allies' only bond. Churchill and Stalin might admire as well as need one another but Stalin could remember the Churchill who had advocated the overthrow of the new Bolshevik régime not only by backing Russian Whites and enlisting British volunteers but also by using German troops, while Churchill could remember that one of the first acts of the first Bolshevik government had been to desert the allied cause and make a separate peace with Germany. Difficulties appeared at once and were thereafter never absent. Churchill's declaration of sympathy and solidarity, made within hours of Hitler's attack, was followed by negotiations for an Anglo-Russian treaty which laid bare one of the problems which was never resolved until the Russians were strong enough completely to override their allies' views – the problem of Poland.

From Stalin's point of view the problem of Poland was the problem of the USSR's western frontiers. By agreement with Hitler he had acquired half Poland and he did not intend to surrender, in the moment of victory over Hitler, what he had won from Hitler when the Nazi leader was at the height of his power. Great Britain had gone to war for Poland, but Stalin had gone to war against it to recover lands and peoples which no Russian regarded as rightfully under Polish rule. Therefore he pressed Churchill to include in the Anglo-Russian treaty provisions about the post-war frontiers of the USSR. Churchill's policy was in general to mollify Stalin without entering into specific undertakings governing the shape of post-war Europe; in particular he could not concede Stalin's claims against Poland without flagrantly violating the Anglo-Polish treaty of 1939. (Bessarabia presented no such problem since Rumania had joined in the attack on the USSR, but the extinction of the three Baltic states raised political and moral principles which Great Britain could not flout in a formal diplomatic document.)

In August 1941, on a battleship off the coast of Newfoundland, Roosevelt and Churchill had signed the document which became known as the Atlantic Charter and which was intended as a declaration of general war aims. For Roosevelt the Atlantic Charter was the equivalent of Wilson's Fourteen Points, a working paper setting out the basis on which a new and fairer world would be constructed. For Churchill it was less a document than a call or proclamation to stir the world. For Americans it was the equivalent of the Constitution, for the British of the Magna Carta – the one a document with continuing practical effects, the other a piece of secular religion. By the Atlantic Charter Roosevelt and Churchill renounced territorial aggrandizement, asserted the right of all peoples to choose how they should be governed, condemned territorial changes contrary to the wishes of the inhabitants of the territory and looked forward to an equitable distribution of raw materials, fair trading practices, freedom of the seas, disarmament and an international security system. They hoped to get Stalin to endorse this declaration but they got no further than a vague statement of approval from the Russian Ambassador in London, Ivan Maisky. Early in 1942 a British mission to Moscow discovered that Stalin's post-war aims included, not only the recognition of the fruits of his pact with Hitler, but also fragments of Germany and the transfer to Turkey of the Dodecanese (which Great Britain's other ally, Greece, was expecting to be given as soon as Italy was defeated). But Stalin was not at this stage in a position to insist. The Anglo-Russian treaty, eventually concluded in May 1942, contained no undertakings about post-war frontiers and Stalin let the matter rest until the Teheran conference in November 1943, by which time his military position had greatly changed.

As important as Poland and more urgent was the question of a second front. Stalin pressed for one in July 1941 and again in September. Churchill's desire to help was genuine but he and many of his advisers were for a time sceptical about the value of the new ally which looked like being defeated and bundled out of the war almost as easily as France had been – in which event aid would have been wasted and Great Britain, once more alone, that much worse off. Churchill's spirit responded to the Russian needs but his strategic senses were more alert to the battles in the Middle East, the defence of the British Empire and the fear of a junction between the Germans and the Japanese. He had to count the cost of promises very carefully. Great Britain was a fighting ally of the USSR for six months before the United States too came into the war and the brunt of military aid to the USSR and the delivery of war material by the Arctic route must fall on Great Britain.

Roosevelt was less cautious. When, after the American entry into the war, Molotov visited London and Washington in the hope of getting more and quicker western aid, Roosevelt allowed himself to be less guarded than Churchill about the prospects for a second front and Churchill felt obliged to record his reservations in writing. From that moment the Russians regarded Great Britain as a drag on more purposeful and generous American policies. Early in 1942 Roosevelt implied publicly that there might be a second front in Europe before the end of the year, and in April the American planners produced, and the Chiefs of Staff adopted, proposals for an invasion of France by a million American troops in the spring of 1943 and for a smaller attack in the autumn of 1942 if either the Russians or the Germans showed signs of collapsing. The British did not object to this programme although they were convinced that any invasion in 1942 was out of the question. Churchill did not believe that so huge an American force could be assembled in England in time for a major invasion in 1943, especially if the war in the Atlantic had not first been won. Great Britain moreover was committed to the North African campaign, which could not on the most favourable estimates be completed in time to permit the opening of a new campaign thousands of miles away before the end of 1942; it was in fearful difficulties in the Far East, exemplified by the fall of Singapore and the Australian government's insistence on recalling troops from abroad for the defence of their homeland; and Churchill and his advisers were ceaselessly aware of their limited resources in men and materials.

In Great Britain Churchill's views prevailed, if not without question, yet without serious challenge. On the issue of the second front Lord Beaverbrook alone raised a voice of eminence and influence in favour of an immediate landing in France. Early in 1942 Beaverbrook had resigned from the government, which he believed to be crumbling, and had gone to the United States where he made a public appeal for the opening of a second front, recklessly if necessary, On his return to London he established an organization to campaign for a second front and lent himself for a while to anti-Churchill manoeuvres, but these came to nothing in spite of a certain amount of intrigue and gossip on the political fringes in which Beaverbrook's name was freely used. Beaverbrook then rallied to his old and loyal friend and found himself back in the government before the year was out.

Despite the loss of Singapore in February and Tobruk in June, Churchill's position was never threatened as Asquith had been threatened by the reverses of 1916. Public opinion saw no alternative to Churchill and wished for none. The Conservative Party, as a whole, having made Churchill its leader in 1940, knew that it could not prosper without him, while the Labour Party never aspired to the leading place. Churchill was master of his cabinet and of parliament as neither Asquith nor Lloyd George (the latter dependent in 1917–18 on the votes of a party not his own) had ever been. He was also in undoubted control of his service chiefs whom he could dismiss if he chose – again unlike Lloyd George, who distrusted Haig but dared not dismiss him. As Minister of Defence and chairman of the Chiefs of Staff Committee Churchill was a civilian warlord who had no cause to fear military intrigues against him; no British general in the Second World War complained to the king about civilian incompetence and interference as Haig did in the first war; in his relations with the military Churchill had an authority which no British Prime Minister – and, in France, only Clemenceau – had ever had before. Churchill's conduct of the war remained therefore remarkably uninhibited until it was curtailed by Great Britain's declining share in the total allied war effort. But this did not happen until there were more Americans than British under arms in the European theatre and up to 1943 it was still difficult to ship American forces to Europe owing to U-boats, shortage of transports and the competing claims of the war in the Pacific. At the end of 1942 there were only 170,000 American troops in Europe (and 140,000 in North Africa) out of 500,000 planned earlier in the year.

Roosevelt, as Commander-in-Chief as well as President, was confronted throughout the war with two series of strategic problems: the claims of the Pacific theatre against the European, and the alternative uses to which American power could be put within a theatre. Until

Munich the United States had no plans for fighting Germany. It had plans of a vague and general kind for a war against Japan. Munich stimulated thinking about new problems and new theatres and in April 1939 the Chiefs of Staff, faced with the possibility of a war on two fronts, provisionally recommended that Europe should come first. At the end of 1940, with war palpably nearer, the Chief of Naval Operations, Admiral Harold R. Stark, recommended a policy of attack in the Atlantic and defence in the Pacific, which he was prepared to subordinate to the war against Germany and the Anglo-American alliance. This policy had been affirmed at a joint Anglo-American staff conference in March 1941 which hoped that war in the Pacific might be avoided but recommended that, if it came, it be subordinated to the war in Europe; but there were always dissentients on the American side. In his State of the Union address to Congress at the beginning of 1942 Roosevelt said that Hitler came first. By this time the United States was actively involved in hostilities in the Atlantic, and Hitler's declaration of war three days after Pearl Harbor had removed any need to reconsider, in the light of Pearl Harbor, the priorities which had governed American planning for the past few years: Hitler made the Americans' war a war on two fronts from its first week.

But although American priorities were never reversed, they were inevitably questioned from time to time. At the beginning of 1942 American strategy in the Pacific was largely dictated by the requirements of the defensive, but the United States recovered from the blow at Pearl Harbor with astonishing rapidity and was able after the naval victories of the Coral Sea and Midway in May and June to go over to the offensive sooner than had been expected. This turn of fortune lent strength to the pleas of the Pacific commanders, Admiral Chester W. Nimitz and General Douglas MacArthur, who were authorized to take the offensive and who therefore succeeded in altering to some extent the division of forces between the theatres. At the end of 1942 there were more Americans in the Pacific than in Europe.

In the European theatre Churchill dominated the strategic debate on the western side during 1942. Although he did not convince the American, or British, Chiefs of Staff he won a wavering Roosevelt over to his plan for a major Anglo-American landing in North-west Africa (Torch) which would join forces with the British army in the Western Desert, bring the North African campaign to a close and make the Mediterranean safe for the allies. Roosevelt was the more easily won over because he saw action in North Africa in 1942 as a partial redemption of the half-promise which he had given to Molotov of action in France in

1942, and in August Churchill set out for Moscow for his first meeting with Stalin in order to explain and justify this strategy. The meeting was decisive in forming Stalin's view of Churchill: he liked the man but not his plans. Torch, more a British than an American plan, was not the second front that he was looking for.

When the Grand Alliance came into being in 1941 the war in Africa was for the British, the senior combatants, nearly the whole of the war, but both the Americans and the Russians were dubious about it and regarded it as a sideshow. The Americans regarded battles in the eastern Mediterranean as battles to salvage the British Empire, battles in the western Mediterranean as battles to salvage the French Empire; and they had not entered the war to save or restore empires. The Americans, and the Russians too, thought of battles as much bigger affairs than anything that had occurred in Africa and could conceive of no vitally significant operation except the biggest possible battle in Europe at the earliest possible moment. Again, the Americans and Russians looked to a victory to be achieved preponderantly by ground forces, whereas Churchill clung to the belief in victory by air bombardments. (If he had been right, Great Britain would not have become so junior a partner in the Anglo-American effort.) In the final analysis Churchill and the British Chiefs of Staff did not question the paramount importance of an invasion of France and they agreed that other operations had to be justified by their contribution to the re-opening of a western front. Where they disagreed was in their assessment of the relevance of operations in the Mediterranean to this overriding aim. They were also more impressed than the Russians by the difficulties of landing in France (they seem to have given up the notion that the French Resistance would capture French harbours for them) and their hesitations on this score were increased in August 1942 by the costliness of the experimental raid on Dieppe.

In this atmosphere every British argument in favour of exploiting success in Africa by expanding the campaign in the Mediterranean was interpreted by the Americans as an attempt to turn this campaign into an alternative way of defeating the Germans without the necessity for a frontal assault in the west, and American suspiciousness was increased by the realization that Torch would rule out an invasion of France not only in 1942 but in 1943 too. On the American side there was a feeling of having been tricked by crafty British with ulterior motives. Churchill's strategic agility – his addiction to a strategy of ingenious pinpricks at spots as remote from a decisive theatre as northern Norway or Rhodes, which were the products of his lively sense of opportunity and often disconcerted his own advisers as much as his allies – was interpreted, wrongly, as unwillingness to face up to the serious business and daunting casualties of a landing in France.

Torch developed into an open-ended temptation. While the fighting in North-west Africa was still going on Roosevelt and Churchill met in January 1943 at Casablanca. They accepted the premise that for the time being their primary weapon against Germany was not direct invasion but air bombardment, and they sanctioned an invasion of Sicily as soon as possible after the defeat of the Germans and Italians in Africa, which was not completed until May. In that month they met again in Washington and decided to do something more in the western Mediterranean after taking Sicily, but what this was to be – an attack on Sardinia and Corsica or in Calabria or somewhere else – was left undecided and was still undecided when Sicily was invaded in July. This invasion, which caused the fall of Mussolini, led the allies on to an invasion of the Italian mainland but did not deliver Italy into their hands, effectively removed all prospect of a landing in France (Overlord) before 1944.

For twelve months therefore – from the end in Tunisia to Overlord – the three allies went their separate and barely coordinated ways towards Germany. The Russians won in July 1943 the battles in the Kursk salient which, even more than Stalingrad, spelt the end of Hitler's bid to subjugate the USSR. The western allies conquered Sicily in the same month, and then, landing at Salerno, set out in September for Rome, which, however, they did not reach for nine months because Hitler, after some hesitation, reinforced his armies in Italy and built them up by the end of the year to twenty-five divisions by withdrawals from both the Russian and western fronts. These latter operations involved the western allies in further disputes which were not without interest to Stalin both for their bearing on Overlord and their wider political import.

In the year before Overlord the western allies had in mind three principal operations. They could not, however, attempt all three because all of them required landing craft and there were not enough landing craft to go round. The first of the three possibilities was a second landing on the Italian coast to supplement the landing at Salerno and expedite the capture of Rome; this was effected in January 1944 at Anzio. The second was a landing in the Andaman Islands in the Bay of Bengal intended to lead to the recovery of Sumatra and Malaya; this was promised to Chiang Kai-Shek by Roosevelt in Cairo in December 1943 but subsequently cancelled. The reason for the cancellation was the third operation – a landing in the Dodecanese. This was one of Chur-

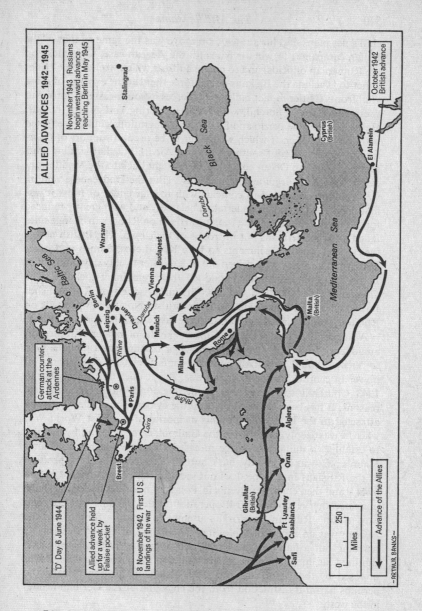

ALLIED ADVANCES 1942–1945

November 1943 Russians begin westward advance reaching Berlin in May 1945

October 1942 British advance

German counterattack at the Ardennes

'D' Day 6 June 1944

Allied advance held up for a week by Falaise pocket

8 November 1942, First U.S. landings of the war

Advance of the Allies

0   250
Miles

~ARTHUR BANKS~

Stalingrad

Black Sea

Cyprus (British)

El Alamein

Danube

Mediterranean Sea

Warsaw

Budapest

Vienna

Berlin

Leipzig

Dresden

Danube

Munich

Milan

Rome

Malta (British)

Baltic Sea

Rhine

Paris

Rhône

Loire

Brest

Algiers

Oran

Gibraltar (British)

Ft Lyautey
Casablanca

Safi

chill's pet plans and his strategic objective was the same as that of the Italian campaign: to win air bases (in the Aegean case, for attacks on the Rumanian oilfields) and to create a threat which would force Hitler either to evacuate the Balkans or reinforce them at the expense of more vital fronts (Hitler in fact built up his forces in south-eastern Europe to twenty divisions). Churchill was also keen to bring Turkey into the war. He argued that the Anzio and Dodecanese operations could be effected with the landing craft which were later to be used in support of Overlord by an invasion of southern France (Anvil), but that landing craft sent to the Indian Ocean could not be brought back to the Mediterranean in time. This argument won the day. (But the Dodecanese venture was a failure. Designed to coincide with the surrender of Italy, it was first postponed and then undertaken belatedly and with greatly reduced forces. An attempt to get the Italian garrison on Rhodes to change sides failed and the Germans put in troops of their own. The British nevertheless sent small detachments to take Kos, Leros, Samos and other nearby points. They were driven out of Kos after twenty days and out of Leros a month later and abandoned their remaining toeholds. The Germans made 900 allied and 3,000 Italian prisoners on Kos and shot Italian officers who had sided with the British. No attack was made on Rhodes. Turkey stayed neutral until the last week of February 1945.)

A successful British return to Greece, like the plan later proposed for an advance from Italy over the Brenner or through the Ljubljana Gap to Vienna, could have had political implications for the balance of power in central Europe after the war. But it does not follow that in 1943 Churchill sponsored his Dodecanese adventure for political reasons. It has been assumed on too little evidence that Churchill was attracted to the Dodecanese by his memories of the First World War when he was deeply enmeshed in the Gallipoli campaign and by a desire to establish a military presence in eastern Europe which would limit Stalin's post-war hegemony, but Churchill's concern about the position of the Russians in Europe does not seem to have been aroused before 1944 – and then chiefly by events in Poland – nor does he seem to have imagined that a minor British operation in the Balkans was the right way to limit Russian power. His attempt to regain a foothold in the Aegean was an aspect of exploiting the collapse of Italian Fascism by reaching out a hand to the Greek and Yugoslav partisans who had captured his imagination as doughty allies in the common cause. It was opposed by the Americans and the Russians as an unnecessary and perhaps harmful distraction from the engaging of the German armies in the west.

Nevertheless Churchill's strategies did acquire a political element which became increasingly evident as the war went on. He was proud of British achievements in Africa and the Mediterranean, aware that the victories to come in western Europe would be more American than British, subconsciously anxious to make the most of what was, in Italy, still at least as much a British as an American show. Like every great patriot he was a bit of a chauvinist. He was also a European, whereas Roosevelt, like Woodrow Wilson before him, was not a European and did not have the European's sensitivity to the balance of power in Europe. Churchill, largely because of his special interest in history, had this sensitivity to an unusual degree. In the last year of the war the coming domination of Europe by the Russians worried him quite apart from the fact that the government of the USSR was a communist autocracy, and he was also worried by his inability to get Roosevelt worried too. Roosevelt, again like Wilson, looked askance at power political issues and attached more importance to the creation of a new world organization which would impose universal harmony upon particular disharmonies. For this purpose Russo-American cordiality was all important and Roosevelt seized on the chance of wartime cooperation as a means to establishing a more enduring entente. Everybody else's salvation would flow from such an entente – a view of international order which died with Roosevelt and the Cold War but revived with mutual nuclear deterrence, the thaw of the 1960s and the fear of China to take the place of fear of Germany. But Churchill, like Clemenceau *vis-à-vis* Wilson in 1919, was more sceptical. In the heat of war Stalin might be pictured as the benevolent Uncle Joe projected by wartime emotions; with the approach of peace he could be looked at more coldly.

The first meeting of the three leaders of the Grand Alliance did not take place until the Russian victory in the east had been assured and the preponderance of American over British might in the west had been made manifest. There were only two such meetings during the war in Europe: the first, which lasted four days, at Teheran in November 1943 and a second, which lasted eight days, at Yalta in February 1945.

Before Teheran Roosevelt and Churchill had had a series of meetings as well as a continuous and intimate correspondence. Churchill had met Stalin once, and Roosevelt and Stalin had met not at all. During 1943 distrust within the alliance had become serious. In the United States the view that Stalin was no better than Hitler was being freely expressed in the press and elsewhere; it was reinforced by the revelation of the Katyn massacre in Poland and by the constitution in Moscow in July of a Free German Committee which was taken as evidence of Russian flirting with Germany. From Stockholm came reports of Russian feelers, designed either to end the war in the east by a separate peace or to scare the western allies into thinking that Stalin was about to do so. The western allies feared that Stalin might be content to push the Germans back into Germany and then leave the Nazi régime intact. On his side Stalin, besides being embarrassed and angered by the publicity given to Katyn, feared that the Americans might divert most of their strength to the Pacific and resented the suspension of the Arctic convoys for three months after disasters suffered in June 1942. Above all Stalin was trying to hold his allies to their promises to open a second front in 1943. By a second front he meant a landing in strength on the continent which would draw off great numbers of German divisions from the east. In the crisis of 1941 he had specified thirty to forty divisions. He accepted as adequate neither the western air offensive which engaged the best of the Luftwaffe's aircraft and aircrews (to the considerable advantage of the Russian armies) nor the operations in the Mediterranean which tied down a number of German divisions in the Balkans and diverted twenty-five to Italy. Although Churchill had given no promise of a cross-Channel invasion in 1943 he seems to have felt that, when in Moscow in August 1942, he had given Stalin grounds for expecting one; and Roosevelt had been much more explicit. Both western leaders had a feeling of unease about postponing the big assault to 1944.

Roosevelt and Churchill liked meeting for the sake of meeting. They believed in the value of man-to-man talks of a general nature, informal and on an assumption of shared aims and proved comradeship. Such meetings must, they felt, generate understanding and trust, eliminate the rubs in the alliance and so accelerate victory and lay a sure basis for post-war harmony. They envisaged not so much a diplomatic conference as a council of war. Stalin took a more professional view of summit meetings. He wanted a regular conference or nothing. He had exercised power and responsibility unremittingly for twenty years, during which he had got his way by always doing his homework more thoroughly than his adversaries, by never taking decisions in anybody's time but his own, by knowing how far to go at any given moment (unlike Hitler but not unlike Bismarck) – in short by arming an unusually clear mind and unusually ruthless character with the most rigorous professional techniques of the statesman and negotiator. Whereas Roosevelt and Churchill looked to their subordinates to supply these technical assets as required, Stalin embodied them in himself. He had neither the gifts nor the weaknesses of the amateur. He may have been a repulsive man but he was an exceptionally gifted and experienced master of his craft.

Roosevelt and Churchill, desiring a meeting on general grounds, thought that the sooner it took place the better. They pressed for it on and off throughout 1943. Stalin on the other hand had no use for a conference which was unlikely to further specific or particular objectives and he therefore blew hot and cold, favouring a conference when his fortunes and his bargaining power were in the ascendant, putting it off when they waned or when he was vexed. Early in 1943 he seemed willing to meet his associates. By this time the three great crises of the war, from the Russian point of view, were behind him: Moscow had been saved in 1941, Japan had not attacked when Germany did, Stalingrad had not fallen. Yet he still prevaricated, probably on account of the Anglo-American conference of May which resolved on further operations against Italy, and it was not until after the spectacular Russian victories on his central front in the summer which finally eliminated all prospect of a German victory over the USSR that he again reversed his position and agreed to a meeting in Teheran at the end of the year. The second front was no longer a condition of Russian survival. Rather the failure to open a second front could be used as a lever politically against the western allies. And the Polish problem had also been transformed by the certainty that Russian armies would soon be on Polish soil once more.

During 1943 Stalin broke with the provisional Polish government which had its headquarters in London. Relations with this government had been established after Hitler invaded the USSR by an agreement signed in London by General Wladislaw Sikorski, the head of the government, and Ivan Maisky; the agreement provided for an 'amnesty' for all Poles in the USSR and the raising of a Polish army on Russian soil. This was the season of Stalin's direst need. He was prepared not only to see American troops in the USSR but a Polish army too and General Anders, captured in the war of 1939, was disinterred from the Lubianka prison in Moscow to command it. The Poles in the USSR, however, were not enthusiastic about fighting alongside their hereditary and recent Russian enemies. Trouble soon came. The Russians accused the Poles of breaking the Sikorski-Maisky agreement by not committing their divisions to the front as quickly as they were formed. The Poles were probably reluctant to use up their fighting power in the defence of the USSR against the Germans, and as the pressure on the Russians eased, Stalin's priorities changed and he became more wary about a scheme which would take a Polish army, commanded by anti-Russian and anti-communist officers, into territories which he had recently seized from Poland and intended to keep.

Eventually, on Churchill's suggestion and with Stalin's consent, Anders's divisions left for Italy via Iran, thus incidentally ensuring that the liberation of Poland from the Germans would be accomplished by the Russians alone. Churchill, who established a personal friendship with Sikorski, hoped to be able to resolve the differences between his Polish and Russian allies by persuading Sikorski, who was in turn to persuade his compatriots, to cede territory in eastern Poland to the USSR in return for equivalent territory in the west to be taken from Germany: Poland was to be shifted westward. The Poles did not want to be shifted; they wanted the cancellation of the Russo-German deal of 1939 and the restoration of Poland's 1939 frontiers. But Stalin was determined not to give up what he had won in 1939 and talked of a new 'ethnic' Poland to the west of the Russo-German partition line which, for diplomatic reasons, he called – incorrectly – the Curzon line. Furthermore he did not intend that the new Poland should have its old government, and in 1943 events enabled him to begin the process of displacing it.

During the short war of 1939 a great many Polish officers disappeared. They were believed to be in Russian captivity but 4,000 of them failed to re-appear after the amnesty proclaimed in accordance with the Sikorski–Maisky agreement of 1941. They were in fact dead and in April 1943 the bodies of 1,700 of them were found in pits in the forest of Katyn. They had been murdered. The temper of the times inclined western opinion to the belief that they had been murdered by the Germans and when Goebbels proclaimed that they had been murdered by the Russians few people in the west believed him. Yet it gradually became obvious that this was the case. The Polish government in London asked for an investigation by the Red Cross, whereupon Stalin seized the occasion to sever relations in preparation for the creation of a separate Polish government amenable to Russian control. A few months later, in September 1943, the death of Sikorski in an aircraft accident at Gibraltar removed from the scene the one Polish leader who, because he enjoyed the friendship of Churchill and had some personal credit with Stalin, might have been able to repair the breach between Moscow and the London Poles and implement Churchill's policy of making territorial but not political concessions to the USSR.

After Sikorski's death Churchill was virtually without any cards to play against Stalin on the Polish question. Sikorski's successor as head of the government in exile, Stanislaw Mikolajczyk, saw the need for an understanding with the Russians but he lacked Sikorski's authority and both his Minister of War, General Kasimierz Sosnkowski, and General

Tadeusz Bor-Komarowski who succeeded to the command of the Polish Home Army (AK) when its first commander fell into German hands, were strongly anti-Russian. (They were also anti-semitic.) But Stalin, following his military successes of the summer, was about to take possession of the contested field, having turned Katyn to good account by divesting himself of the commitments in the Sikorski–Maisky agreement. At Teheran he was in a position to urge Churchill to acknowledge that Poland was his to dispose of, and Churchill, being already sufficiently in agreement with Stalin on the question of frontiers, went far towards doing so. He even took the lead in the discussions on Poland, leaving Stalin to concur. It was agreed that the Poles should be left out of the discussions until later. (About the three Baltic states nothing was said; the silence proclaimed their coming fate.)

Stalin had at Teheran other demands too: half East Prussia, a third of the Italian fleet (to be delivered in January 1944), the Kuriles, the southern half of Sakhalin and a free port at Dairen. In return he accepted an abortive plan propounded by Roosevelt for emasculating Germany by dividing it into five segments and putting the Ruhr, the Saar, Hamburg and the Kiel Canal under international control; agreed to join a world organization and to collaborate in a European Advisory Commission for the discussion of German problems; and repeated the promise already made by Molotov a few weeks earlier to join in the war against Japan as soon as Germany was defeated.

All these matters were dealt with in a single day. The other three days were devoted to military rather than political business. The principal outcome was a promise by the western allies to invade France in May 1944.

The comparatively long list of matters agreed at Teheran can be accounted for less by supposing a basic identity of views than by the fact that both Roosevelt and Stalin attached comparatively little importance to what the other most desired. Roosevelt was chiefly interested in establishing a personal relationship with Stalin, ensuring his entry into the war against Japan and enlisting his participation in the new organization which was to replace the League of Nations. Stalin had no objection to any of these things. For him the real importance of the conference lay in the territorial and political settlements which it might help to ensure in eastern and central Europe and to a lesser extent in the Far East: he intended to keep what he had won before Hitler's invasion from Finland, the Baltic states, Poland and Rumania and to round off these acquisitions by establishing a primary Russian influence in Bulgaria and the Straits. These were matters to which Roosevelt was much less alert than Churchill. How Roosevelt would have reacted to Russian meddling in western Europe it is impossible to say because Stalin showed no interest in western Europe. Beyond his immediate sphere of interest he postulated only the restoration of an independent Czechoslovakia and Austria and he talked vaguely about partitioning Italy. Churchill continued to have forebodings, but his objections carried in 1943 less weight than they would have done if the conference had been held at an earlier date, partly because of the turn of the military tide in the USSR and partly because the preponderant voice in the western alliance was no longer British but American. Stalin even allowed himself to make during the conference half bantering, half barbed attacks on Churchill which he would hardly have been likely to make a year earlier; he treated Roosevelt with immaculate respect and condescension. Roosevelt responded with what his detractors have called naïvety.

The charge is in part valid not because Roosevelt was a foolishly vain man, as lesser men have argued, but in the sense that Roosevelt seems to have overestimated his superabundant political gifts. He had wanted to meet Stalin without Churchill being present and had sent a personal emissary, Joseph E. Davies, a former Ambassador in Moscow, to prepare a *tête-à-tête*. He argued against the British that it was impolitic to engage in a conference at which Stalin might feel himself outmatched by two to one, but Roosevelt's deepest motive was his determination to talk Stalin into a personal friendship which would be the counterpart of his special relationship with Churchill. His own career had been based on his special gifts as a manager of men, and he seems to have thought that he could manage Stalin too in much the same way as he had managed American politicians of varying degree and varying views. It is said that old and sick men fall into the error of exaggerating their principal talents. Roosevelt, long a cripple, had held one of the most arduous offices in the world for an unprecedented number of years of unparalleled domestic complexity and external stress. Although at Teheran he seemed still to retain his extraordinary powers, at Yalta only fifteen months later he was dying. His mistake at the end of his life – if one can speak of a mistake in the case of a man whose faculties are deserting him – was to imagine that he could captivate a man like Stalin, a man of a kind uncommon even in American politics and placed in circumstances utterly remote from the imagination of any person raised in the American tradition. Roosevelt was the youngest of the three leaders – three years younger than Stalin, eight years younger than Churchill – but at Teheran and Yalta Stalin was the fittest of the three, not only fitter than Roosevelt but probably also fitter than Churchill who succumbed to pneumonia after Teheran, for the second time that year. It is not unnatural that Stalin had the best reason to be pleased with the way the conference went.

On the immediate strategic issue the Teheran conference agreed that the Anglo-American armies in Italy should advance to Hitler's Gothic Line (which ran from Pisa to Rimini). If necessary, Overlord might be postponed for a month, but once the Gothic Line was reached further operations in Italy would be entirely subordinated to the requirements of Overlord. This proviso meant in practice that the Supreme Commander in the Mediterranean, now Field Marshal Sir Harold Alexander, would have to relinquish a number of divisions for Anvil which was to take place simultaneously with Overlord. No thought was given to what would be done if the Gothic Line was not reached before the Anvil divisions had to leave the theatre to keep to the Overlord timetable. Yet this is what happened. The Anglo-American advance was so retarded by the Germans that Alexander had to request the cancellation of Anvil. The British Chiefs of Staff supported him; the American Chiefs were very angry but agreed to let him keep his divisions until after the capture of Rome. But Rome was not taken until two days before D-day for Overlord on 6 June with the result that Anvil, postponed until the middle of August, contributed nothing to Overlord and was proved by Overlord's success to be unnecessary before it took place. Alexander was denied the chance to press forward to the Danube, a plan of his which was warmly espoused by Churchill although regarded as over-optimistic by his military advisers, and the Mediterranean strategy petered out in the autumn rains of the Po valley.

On the eastern fronts the Russians gained in 1944 a series of military victories over the Germans and their allies which they were able to convert without impediment into political advantage. In the west the immense accumulation of American men and material for the invasion of France was accomplished without serious opposition from the German U-boats, and the invasion itself was successfully effected in June and equally successfully exploited until the German counter-attack in the Ardennes in November temporarily delayed the last stages of the overthrow of German power. These operations in east and west were affected by Germany's continuing need to defend itself on more than one front but otherwise the campaigns of the eastern and western allies owed little to one another. They were independent operations, usefully coincidental but only very loosely coordinated. In these circumstances allied cooperation became even more political and less military, more concerned with the post-war settlement and less with the conduct of the war.

In October 1944 Churchill went again to Moscow for his third meeting with Stalin (the second without Roosevelt who was campaigning for election for a fourth term as President). Churchill had now become much more worried about the fate of eastern and central Europe and the inability of the western allies to prevent the Russians from imposing communist rule in the countries which their armies were overrunning. He tried to strike a bargain with Stalin but since he was bargaining only about eastern territories, without being willing or indeed entitled to concede anything in the west in return, his position was not a strong one except in relation to Greece which, as a Mediterranean country, was more accessible to Anglo-American sea power than to Russian land power.

Stalin and Churchill agreed that all countries would be subject to the joint control of all three allies but that the degrees of interest of each of the three might be unequal and would vary from state to state. In a curiously offhand way in the course of one of their conversations they attempted to represent this idea arithmetically: the Russian interest in Rumania was put at ninety, the western at ten; the same interests in Hungary and Bulgaria were defined as eighty and twenty respectively, in Yugoslavia as fifty–fifty; Greece was rated 90 per cent a western sphere, 10 per cent Russian. This somewhat crude calculation gave offence to the Americans in particular who regarded it as a reversion to the worst practices of spheres of influence. It represented, however, certain realities, whether it was wise or not to put them down on paper. A mark of ninety or seventy-five to the one side acknowledged the impossibility of thwarting that side's wishes in that area; a fifty-fifty mark recorded uncertainty or a desire not to come to grips there for the time being.

Poland was not in the list. Both leaders probably thought that, so far as frontiers were concerned, the Polish question had been settled at Teheran, and before Churchill arrived in Moscow Stalin recognized the Polish National Liberation Committee, a group of communist and pro-communist Poles with headquarters in Lublin, as the provisional Polish government in opposition to the government in London. When Mikolajczyk, still apparently ignorant of what had passed at Teheran, flew to Moscow to try to get Stalin to accept Poland's pre-war frontiers, he failed and the Warsaw rising and its defeat by the Germans (described in a later chapter) eliminated the armed forces in Poland on which the London Poles were relying. Poland's fate had become settled, and both in Moscow and in London Mikolajczyk found himself treated as a wrecker whose inconvenient demands were imperilling the peace of Europe. He was even upbraided by Churchill in much the same terms as the Czechs had been chided by the appeasers of 1938.

The three leaders met again at Yalta on 4 February 1945. As at Teheran there was no formal agenda; each was free to raise or try to keep out whatever topic he wished to air or to pigeonhole. Poland was discussed briefly. Its frontier with the USSR was fixed and the city of Lvov was decreed to fall on the Russian side of it, but the western and northern frontiers were not agreed. Stalin, having discovered that there were two Neisses, tried to get his allies to agree to the western one but Churchill refused and Stalin had to wait for his armies to do the job. The government of Poland was to be reorganized under the direction of Molotov and the American and British Ambassadors in Moscow; it was to have an infusion of Poles from London to leaven the Lublin Committee and after the reorganization free elections were to be held with universal suffrage and a secret ballot. Thus what was left of the Polish issue was shifted out of the conference and onto a committee of three which was to meet later – in Moscow.

The conference was no more precise about the rest of liberated Europe. It adopted a general declaration promising free elections. Stalin agreed that France should have a zone of occupation in Germany and (after much argument) a place on the Allied Control Commission which was to administer Germany. He also conceded everything that Roosevelt wanted in relation to the United Nations: having asked for sixteen seats he accepted three without any fuss and even agreed to support an American demand for three seats if Roosevelt should consider that American public opinion demanded them. In separate Russo-American discussion on the Far East he sought and obtained reaffirmation of the promises already made to him together with an American undertaking to force Chiang Kai-shek to accept them and a further American undertaking not to tell Chiang what was afoot until Stalin was ready for this disclosure. Stalin succeeded in other words in making Roosevelt his accomplice in imposing, at a moment of his own choosing, conditions on Chiang which included recognition of the independence of Outer Mongolia (and its virtual dependence on the USSR), a Russian share in the running of the Manchurian railways, and a Russian naval base in China. A vague notion of sweetening this large pill by getting Great Britain to transfer Hong Kong to China never came to anything. At first sight Stalin's gains over Roosevelt at Teheran and Yalta over the Far East are surprising, but they have to be seen against Roosevelt's growing awareness of the uselessness of Chiang as an ally against Japan and his need therefore for Russian help at a time when the coming nuclear weapon was still too mysterious to be relied upon.

With Poland on the way to the solution desired by Stalin and with these considerable Far Eastern advantages underwritten by the United States the only remaining item of real interest to Stalin was reparations. On this issue Stalin got much of what he wanted but not all. Roosevelt took comparatively little part in the reparations discussions. Although the American position was virtually the same as the British, the arguing was left to the latter. Whereas the Russians wished to impose reparations as a penalty, the Americans and British regarded them as restitution only for civilian damage. They considered that reparations should be paid only out of current German production and only after securing to the German people a minimum standard of living. They were opposed to the removal of capital assets and to the pauperization of Germany. Stalin on the other hand hoped to secure, besides regular reparations, payments spread over ten years, a German labour force to work in Russian devastated areas for ten years and something like 80 per cent of Germany's surviving heavy industrial plant. He proposed that the USSR's share of reparations payments in cash should be $10 billion and that the apportionment of the total sum should be made on the basis of the contribution which each of Germany's victims had made to the German defeat and not on the basis of its losses – a method which could have operated to give very little to countries which had been quickly defeated, however much they had suffered afterwards. Although the conference reached no final decisions on reparations Stalin succeeded in stamping the figure of $10 billion on future discussions. Most tellingly, Stalin abandoned at Yalta the policy of dismembering Germany. The simplest explanation of this change is that, confident of the departure of American troops from Europe, he thought he had a chance to dominate all Germany.

When the Yalta conference broke up, the Russian armies were on the Oder and the Danube and the western armies on the Rhine. The Grand Alliance had won the war in Europe. One of its leaders did not live to see the end: Roosevelt died on 12 April. His successor Harry S. Truman, joined Churchill and Stalin at one more conference, at Potsdam in July. Its discussions were about war in Asia, but peace in Europe.

CHAPTER 17

The Clearing of North Africa

THERE is at first sight no obvious reason why a European war should be fought in Africa. The short reason why the Second World War spread from Europe to Africa was that the British and Italians were already there. The British had been the overlords of Egypt for sixty years and kept considerable military forces and military installations in Egypt. The Italians had begun to acquire an empire in East Africa at about the same time as the British occupation of Egypt in the 1880s and had extended it by taking Libya and Cyrenaica from the Turks on the eve of the First World War and by the conquest of Ethiopia in the 1930s. The campaigns of the Second World War in Africa were a consequence of these imperial positions, and the failures of the Italians in 1940–41 brought, as we have seen, the Germans into this field too. Nor was this all. France too had an empire in North Africa, exercising direct rule in Algeria which was juridically a part of France and indirect rule in the two flanking monarchies of Morocco and Tunisia which had been reduced to protectorates and where the French had steadily encroached on the authority of the native administration. This empire was preserved after the French collapse of 1940 so that the whole of North Africa from the Atlantic to the Red Sea was under European dominion throughout the Second World War. It was treated by Europeans as a campaign ground in their essentially European conflicts.

But these were not the only conflicts. North Africa was not a sand table. The military campaigns of 1940–43 were superimposed upon a further conflict between rulers and ruled, between imperial power and nationalist aspirations. The war provided nationalists with new opportunities in an old cause. The Americans, whom the war brought into the western end of this increasingly crowded scene in 1942, sympathized with the nationalists' hope of turning the evils of war to some good by accelerating the liberation of their homelands from foreign domination. To Europeans therefore Africa was one of the places where they vied among themselves, but to non-Europeans – whether African or American – one European was in this context much the same as another and none of them belonged there.

The system of government in Egypt was a three-cornered game

between the British, the king and the Wafd. The British had been the real rulers of Egypt since 1882 and still had the ultimate power since, in spite of conceding formal independence after the First World War, they retained by treaty the right to station considerable forces in the country. King Faruq, the last descendant of the Albanian line of Mehemet Ali, wished to rule as well as reign but was hedged in by the British on one side and the Wafd on the other. The Wafd, founded by Zaghlul Pasha and led since 1927 by Nahas Pasha, was an upper-class nationalist movement which wanted to be rid of the British and the king. On coming of age Faruq had dismissed a Wafd government but kept the apparatus of parliament in spite of the fact that there was no political party of consequence except the Wafd; every other party was no more than the *clientela* of notabilities, incapable of giving the king enough backing against the Wafd or the British, let alone both. The Wafd, smarting under its treatment by the king, was inclined to ally itself with the British against the king and justify this policy *ex post facto* by getting true independence for Egypt by agreement with the British, but it was on delicate ground since too much friendliness between it and the British caused some nationalists to defect, Egyptians being divided among themselves about whether to get independence from the British by helping them to win the war in the expectation of later reward or by siding with their enemies.

When the war began, Egypt had at once broken off diplomatic relations with Germany and taken further pro-British steps such as handing over control of Egyptian ports and imposing a censorship, but the German victories in Europe in 1940 and the entry into the war of Italy, which had a much larger army in North Africa than the British, raised the question whether a more ambiguous policy would not be wiser. Egypt severed diplomatic relations with Italy but declared that it would not go to war unless the Italians invaded Egypt or bombed towns or military targets in it; Egyptian troops were withdrawn from the western frontiers to avoid incidents; and the Egyptian government refused to act as severely against the large Italian population (60,000) as the British authorities would have liked.

But the British were still powerful on the spot and were not willing to tolerate a government which hedged in this way. It was forced to resign and was replaced by a more pro-British one. The British also obtained other changes, including the retirement of the Chief of Staff of the Egyptian army, at the price of promising to buy considerable quantities of Egyptian cotton which they did not want. When the Italian advance into Egypt was repulsed by Wavell at the end of 1940 the pro-British

policy was hailed as a success, but in April of the following year the
Italians, now accompanied by the Germans, re-crossed the frontier
and the champions of a stricter non-belligerence raised their voices once
more. There were demands for the withdrawal of British troops and
stores from Cairo and Alexandria. The Egyptian government was also
beset by the economic problems created by its inability to buy and sell
in foreign markets, by inflation and by the refusal of parties outside the
government to join in forming a national coalition. In February 1942,
following popular demonstrations in Cairo and a tiff with the king, it
resigned.

The British Ambassador had already tried to persuade Faruq to
retain his pro-British government. When it fell the Ambassador returned
to the palace to demand the appointment of Nahas – by six o'clock
that evening. The king refused. Three hours later British tanks and
infantry entered the palace grounds. The king gave way. Afraid of
retaining a mildly pro-British government when Rommel's star was in
the ascendant, he was forced to accept Nahas, who was both more
pro-British and a personal enemy, because that star was still at a distance. The drama at the palace when Faruq was forced to yield was a
re-enactment of similar scenes in the past: not long after the British
bombardment of Alexandria and the occupation of Egypt in 1882, Sir
Evelyn Baring (later Lord Cromer) initiated the full British raj in Egypt
by conveying to the Khedive Tawfiq (Faruq's uncle) the British
cabinet's decision that the Khedive's government must either toe the
British line or be evicted; and Tawfiq's son Abbas had been forced on
his accession in 1892 to dismiss his chosen Prime Minister. Faruq in his
turn was obliged to keep Nahas in office until nearly the end of the war,
although Nahas was then dismissed as he was preparing to present to
Great Britain his account for services rendered. After the war the Wafd
blocked British attempts to re-negotiate the Anglo-Egyptian alliance
with a non-Wafd government along lines which would have preserved
some of Great Britain's favoured status, but its triumph was shortlived for after 1952 the more radical nationalist movement of Naguib
and Nasser extinguished the Wafd as well as getting rid of both the
king and the British.

By its show of power at the beginning of 1942 Great Britain had
secured its base for the campaigns of the coming year. The first to move
was Rommel. He entered Cyrenaica from Tripolitania in the first days
of the year and so opened a series of campaigns in the North African
deserts which took him almost to the Nile and the Suez Canal before
the German and Italian forces were thrown back all the way to Tunisia

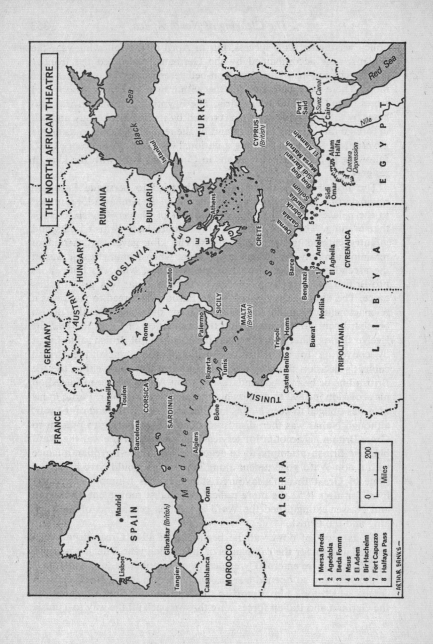

THE NORTH AFRICAN THEATRE

1 Mersa Breda
2 Agedabia
3 Beda Fomm
4 Msus
5 El Adem
6 Bir Hacheim
7 Fort Capuzzo
8 Halfaya Pass

~ ARTHUR BANKS ~

and he himself, ill and defeated, laid down his command and returned to Germany to rest, to recover, to resume great responsibilities, to rebel against Hitler's judgement and ultimately to kill himself on Hitler's orders.

Rommel was the dominating figure in the desert war. There were exceptional commanders on the British side too – Wavell, Auchinleck, Alexander, Montgomery – but they were many and on the Axis side there was only one such figure of fame. Rommel, unlike most German officers, had been not merely an acquiescent Nazi but a keen one and his unconcealed enthusiasm for the new régime probably played some part in furthering his career in the years immediately before the war. But it was by his talents rather than his opportunities that he became famous. He was a first-class divisional commander and he proved his worth in the campaign in France in 1940 when he led an armoured division from the Meuse to the English Channel with all the personal dash and professional skill expected of the new wave of German tank commanders. When the time came for his promotion to a different type of command he was fortunate in finding, in North Africa, the one higher command of the whole war which required many of the aptitudes of the divisional commander. On the British side Wavell, Auchinleck and Alexander all at one time or another exercised tactical control of their forces to a degree unusual in a supreme commander. Rommel did so continuously and his fame as a desert general rests not so much on his exercise of his higher army command as on the flexibility, improvisation and quickness of judgement which he displayed in battle. Later in the war he was to command army groups, but never with that outstanding success which, as commander of the German Afrika Corps and the German–Italian Panzer Army, singled him out from his brother generals and field marshals.

The distinctive character of the desert war derived from the terrain as well as the personalities involved. The distances were great, the forces small. At Alamein the opposed armies deployed between them only 1,500 tanks and 1,500 aircraft, and in that battle the full tally of men on the Axis side was no more than a fifth of the German casualties in the battles in the Kursk salient the next year. The desert war was a war of movement and supply. The men on the ground were tormented by the heat and by the sandstorms which were the mechanics' worst enemies, while the men at sea, hazarding the passage in the Mediterranean, lived in instant expectation of a submarine or air torpedo. Each time the British advanced westward the Royal Navy was set a hard task in maintaining the supply route along the coast against Axis submarine and air attacks. The Axis armies were dependent on supplies from Europe which were intercepted in crippling quantities by British naval and air patrols acting on increasingly full and precise intelligence – uncanny to those who did not know how it was done – about the sailing of tankers and other vessels from Greek and Italian ports.

After Rommel re-entered the lists at the beginning of 1942 both sides were preparing for a major effort. Churchill was urging Auchinleck to attack first. Great Britain needed a victory to offset disasters in the Far East. Singapore had fallen in February; the Japanese were occupying Burma; the War Cabinet ordered preparations for the destruction of the oil refinery at Abadan in western Iran and sent an expedition to take Madagascar before the Japanese did. The position of Great Britain again seemed critical. No American divisions could be expected to reach European or African theatres of war before the end of the year, while the Russians, although they had saved Moscow in 1941, could well lose the Caucasus in 1942. If they did, the British forces in the Middle East might have to face three ways: against Rommel advancing on Egypt, against new German armies descending from the north through Iran, and against the Japanese to the east. India too might be threatened from two sides – through Burma and through Afghanistan and Iran – in which event the Middle East command would lose its Indian divisions and all hope of further reinforcement from the Indian army. Hitler, who still regarded the Russians as mincemeat in the making, was not only dreaming of conquests of this kind but planning them. A special unit under General Helmuth Felmy (an exceptionally able army officer who had risen to the command of an Air Fleet but had been sacked after the episode of the crashed aircraft which gave away Hitler's plans for invading the Low Countries) had been formed with agreeable headquarters at Cape Sunion near Athens where it collected intelligence about the Middle East and trained Arabs for subversion. In 1942 it was moved to the Caucasus and began to take an interest in India too (although by the autumn it was back at Sunion with waning prospects).

Churchill's anxiety for an early victory in the desert was therefore not just a piece of impetuosity but a consequence of the disquieting view of the war seen as a whole from London. In the event Rommel attacked first and scored a great victory which carried him over the Egyptian border and produced the only occasion during the war on which Churchill is known to have allowed the strains to get the better of his emotions.

General Ritchie's Eighth Army was holding a series of positions stretching from Gazala, some thirty-five miles west of Tobruk, southward into the desert as far as Bir Hacheim which was garrisoned by a French force under General Pierre Koenig. These positions consisted of a number of strongpoints or boxes (not unlike the mile castles on a Roman wall) linked by minefields. They were meant to serve both as a shield for Tobruk and as a springboard for a British offensive. For this reason – and also because the longer the British line the farther would Rommel have to extend his supply lines if he planned to circumvent it – the British armour was dispersed, whereas Rommel's was concentrated for the attack which he launched on 26 May. Rommel moreover attacked in the south, whereas Ritchie had stationed the bulk of his forces at the northern or coastal end of the line. While the Eighth Army had the advantage in manpower and in tanks, the Luftwaffe was more than a match for the Desert Air Force.

Rommel's attack began with a feint in the north to distract attention from his main thrust which was made in the ensuing night by German and Italian armour in the south. Bir Hacheim held firm and Rommel fell into a dangerous trap which made his position desperate, exposed one Panzer division to air attack as it lay stranded for want of fuel, and brought a substantial part of his forces to within a few hours of surrender from thirst; but he was saved by his own resourcefulness and by the tentativeness of his opponent who failed to seize his opportunities. Bir Hacheim continued to hold out for two valuable weeks, at the end of which Koenig made good his escape with two thirds of his men. By this time the southern half of the Eighth Army's positions had been dissolved and Ritchie and Auchinleck were faced with the alternatives of a bold total withdrawal to the Egyptian frontier or a qualified withdrawal leaving a substantial force in Tobruk which, besides its considerable strategic importance, had acquired emotional and symbolic significance.

Neither British commander had intended Tobruk to stand a second siege and its defences were in no fit state to do so. There was a severe shortage of anti-tank weapons. Nevertheless Auchinleck decided to try to hold it and left a garrison of 35,000 in it. Rommel attacked on 20 June. Tobruk fell to him in a day. Practically the entire garrison was taken prisoner, including one third of all South Africans on active fighting service. Rommel captured invaluable supplies, fuel, vehicles and other provisions without which he would not have been able to remain on the offensive. Churchill, who received the news at the White House in Washington, gave way under his emotions. He called the loss of Tobruk a disgrace second only to the loss of Singapore. Less than a month after launching his attack, Rommel, promoted Field Marshal, entered Egypt on the heels of the Eighth Army. Cairo and Alexandria were seized with panic. Mussolini went to Africa where a white horse was waiting to carry him into the Egyptian capital.

Auchinleck took personal command of the Eighth Army in place of its defeated and dismissed commander and in a limited but nevertheless decisive duel in the first week of July, known as the First Battle of Alamein, he defeated the German and Italian forces opposing him so severely that the Axis command had to commit parachute troops (as ground troops) in order to save Rommel from having to retreat once more.

The appearance on the borders of Egypt of these troops, which could more appropriately have been used in an attack on Malta, symbolized a strategic choice which the German and Italian staffs had to make in the first half of 1942. They lacked the resources to take Cairo and Malta at once. Voices were raised in favour of reducing Malta first in order to secure complete control of the supply routes through and across the Mediterranean. From the narrowness of their lucky victory in Crete the Germans had concluded that Malta could not be taken by airborne landing alone, but it might be battered and starved until ripe for capture by combined seaborne and airborne assaults: a force of 1,000 aircraft (mostly from the Russian front) was assembled at the beginning of the year under the supreme command of Field Marshal Albert Kesselring, who set up his headquarters in Rome.

Great Britain's position in the Mediterranean had been endangered by serious naval losses inflicted at the end of the previous year by U-boats in both the western and eastern basins, by minefields and by the 'human torpedoes' with which the Italians penetrated the defences of Alexandria in order to fix explosives to the hulls of warships. During the short period at the turn of the year when Rommel had been driven out of Cyrenaica five supply ships reached Malta, but with Rommel's first forward moves at the beginning of 1942 the Luftwaffe was able to re-occupy North African airfields which, together with its bases in Crete, were used to interdict the passage of east–west convoys. In February an entire convoy, attempting to make this passage, was destroyed; its last surviving ship was scuttled in desperation. In March a convoy of four vessels, attacked from the air and by the Italian surface fleet, managed to get two ships through, but in the ensuing months this attack on Malta's lifelines was redoubled by fierce air attacks on the island itself. These occurred several times every day. In the harbour repair soon ceased to keep pace with destruction. All ships which could be removed sailed away and the rest were scuttled. Without shipping and without labour – the population took to living underground during daylight – the docks became a silent testimony to the triumph of air power. The air defences were too feeble to interrupt the work of destruction. Reinforcements of Spitfires, flown in from an American aircraft carrier in April, were destroyed on their airfields before they had had time to engage the enemy. Further reinforcements in May fared better owing to the frantic efficiency of the ground crews which serviced them and got them into the air again within a few minutes of their arrival, but by the middle of May Malta was holding out with little hope of survival against the bombing and the blockade. At this point Hitler, hesitatingly, agreed to divert the Luftwaffe and give priority to the attack on Egypt which Rommel and Mussolini were urging upon him – Rommel because he wanted to attack Ritchie before Ritchie attacked him, Mussolini because he was enticed by the prospect of entering Cairo and adding Egypt to the Italian empire.

The blockade of Malta continued while Rommel fought his battles with Ritchie and Auchinleck. In June an attempt was made to run convoys simultaneously from east and west. Of the eastern convoy no ship reached the island but from the west two out of seventeen merchantmen made port. In August a further convoy of fourteen merchantmen sailed from the west. Five of its ships reached Malta; one of them, the American tanker *Ohio*, torpedoed on two successive days, arrived lashed between two destroyers. In both these operations the escort fleets suffered very heavily. The losses included the British aircraft carrier *Eagle* which went down with a squadron of Spitfires on board. Over Malta itself the air fighting became fiercer both in intensity and in temper. The chivalry of the desert war was notably absent. With the arrival of another convoy in November the situation of the defenders was eased. The siege was raised by events in Africa.

These events were the final defeat of the German-Italian Panzer Army, of which the battle of El Alamein was the centrepiece. Before that battle Churchill had drastically changed the structure of command in the Middle East.

After Auchinleck's victory in July Churchill urged a further attack to destroy the Axis forces in North Africa once and for all, thereby eliminating the possibility of a war in the Middle East on two or three fronts and setting the Eighth Army in motion to the west before the Anglo-American invasion of North-west Africa which was in preparation for the late autumn. From the purely local point of view the better strategy was to wait and then launch an attack with far better prospects of success – which was what Auchinleck preferred to do and his successors in fact did. But Auchinleck, yielding to superior orders and wider arguments, attacked again in the summer and failed. This failure confronted Churchill at a time of peculiar stress, for he was about to go to Moscow to tell Stalin that there would be no Anglo-American invasion of Europe in 1942 since the western allies had concluded that the African campaign must be finished off first. Churchill knew that an invasion of North-west Africa would be a poor substitute for an invasion of Europe in the eyes of the hard pressed Russians, and he knew too that however sound his strategic reasoning his political good faith was bound to be distrusted by Stalin. But he had made up his mind, and had persuaded Roosevelt, that the sensible thing to do was to concentrate force in Africa before Europe and persuade Stalin that this strategic plan was conceived in the general allied interest and not in disregard of the Russian predicament. It would help him if he were able to show that success in North Africa was assured and likely to be prompt. He therefore decided to visit the African front on his way to his difficult assignment in Moscow and he arrived there in no halcyon mood.

It was clear that Auchinleck could not remain personally in command of the Eighth Army but Churchill was not satisfied that he should merely revert to his supreme command in Cairo. He had decided that Auchinleck's inability to pick the right commanders and the breakdown of morale in the Eighth Army after its defeats in the desert and the last failure in Egypt required dramatic changes, including the replacement of Auchinleck himself. He proposed to divide the cumbersome Middle East command, putting Auchinleck in charge of Iraq and Iran, and the Chief of the Imperial General Staff, General Sir Alan Brooke, in Cairo. For the Eighth Army Churchill wanted General Gott, one of its corps commanders, as opposed to General Montgomery, the choice of the C.I.G.S. Auchinleck and Brooke both refused the proffered appointments. Churchill got his way over Gott but a few days later Gott was killed in an aircraft accident and the army command went to Montgomery after all. The higher appointments in Cairo and Baghdad went to Generals Harold Alexander and Henry Maitland Wilson. Auchinleck returned to India where he was re-appointed to his old post of Commander-in-Chief when Wavell became Viceroy in the following year. Both these men were great soldiers whose careers became tinged with sadness instead of the glory which their gifts might so easily have commanded.

At the end of August Rommel made a last and desperate bid to reach the Nile but was checked by Montgomery in two days of fighting in the battle of Alam el Halfa. Rommel's supplies were now down to about

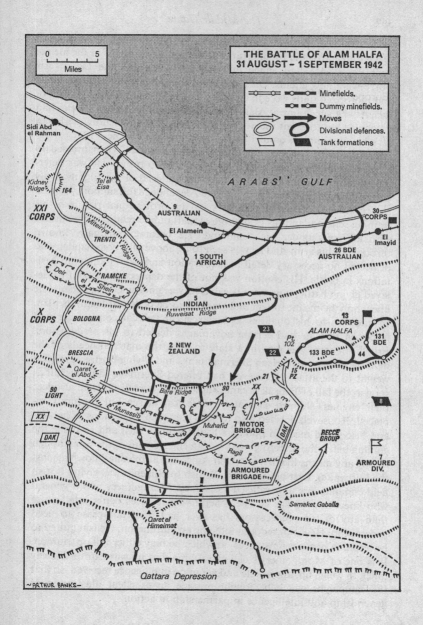

THE BATTLE OF ALAM HALFA
31 AUGUST – 1 SEPTEMBER 1942

Minefields.
Dummy minefields.
Moves
Divisional defences.
Tank formations

Sidi Abd
el Rahman

A R A B S ' '   G U L F

Kidney
Ridge
164
Tel el
Eisa
9
AUSTRALIAN
El Alamein
30
CORPS
El
Imayid
26 BDE
AUSTRALIAN
XXI
CORPS
Miteiriya Ridge
TRENTO
1 SOUTH
AFRICAN
Deir
el Shein
RAMCKE
5
INDIAN
Ruweisat Ridge
13
CORPS
ALAM HALFA
131
BDE
X
CORPS
BOLOGNA
2 NEW
ZEALAND
23
22
Pt
102
133 BDE
44
BRESCIA
Qaret
el Abd
Bare Ridge
90
XX
21
15
PZ
8
90
LIGHT
Munassib
Muhafid
7 MOTOR
BRIGADE
DAK
RECCE
GROUP
7
ARMOURED
DIV.
XX
DAK
Ragil
4   ARMOURED
BRIGADE
Samaket Gaballa
Qaret el
Himeimat
Qattara Depression

~ARTHUR BANKS~

6,000 tons a month and only a quarter of the shipping attempting to reach him across the Mediterranean was getting through. In the air the Axis dominance had ended and the Luftwaffe and the Desert Air Force were now equals. On the ground the German and Italian tanks and motorized units were in constant danger of being halted by lack of fuel. After their failure at Alam el Halfa the German-Italian armies had no choice but to await the attack of a stronger enemy who was able to pick his own time. Rommel himself was invalided home.

Montgomery had no intention of being hustled. When pressed to advance the date of his attack he threatened to resign. He was determined fully to repair the morale and the material of the Eighth Army before engaging the enemy and he had Alexander's full support. He won the confidence of his subordinates by the professional rigour of his training schemes and his (less professional) public relations encounters with all units under his command. He became personally known throughout his army and he was seen to be above all a commander who neglected no necessary detail in preparation and would know no hesitations in battle. His caution was not of the depressing kind: if he delayed giving battle, it was not because he was undecided but because he knew how he meant to win and was not to be deflected from his plan. In addition to his qualities as an excellent tactical commander and leader of men he had certain advantages denied to his predecessors. British industry was now in a state to meet the material needs of the fighting services. American Sherman tanks and Flying Fortresses added weight to the attack. Roosevelt had offered Shermans to Churchill as soon as the fall of Tobruk became known; 300 were dispatched at once; their engines, shipped separately, were lost at sea but promptly replaced. Roosevelt decided also to send complete formations of fighters and heavy and medium bombers to the Middle East and so made the coming battle the first Anglo-American engagement of the war (though not by any means the first in which American airmen had flown against the Luftwaffe). Last but not least, British Intelligence was giving British field commanders unparalleled assistance. Montgomery was a general who knew how to use it. The general who receives better intelligence than any of his predecessors has ever had does not cease to need generalship. He is not reduced to being an automaton. He is required to be tested in new circumstances, in which he may either fail or triumph. It is one of Montgomery's claims to fame that he was extraordinarily quick to weigh up, appreciate and act upon intelligence received, so that the campaigns which he fought provide an excellent illustration of generalship and intelligence in partnership in action.

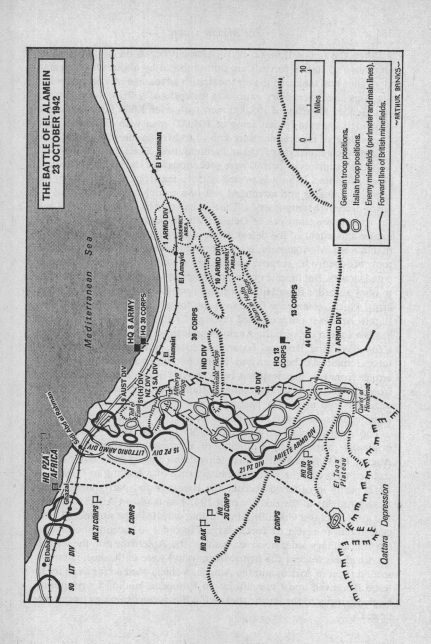

THE BATTLE OF EL ALAMEIN
23 OCTOBER 1942

German troop positions.
Italian troop positions.
Enemy minefields (perimeter and main lines).
Forward line of British minefields.

Miles
0   10

~ARTHUR BANKS~

Mediterranean Sea

El Hamman

1 ARMD DIV
ASSEMBLY AREA

El Amayid

10 ARMD DIV
ASSEMBLY AREA

Kidney Ridge

Kidney Ridge

13 CORPS

HQ 8 ARMY
HQ 30 CORPS

30 CORPS

El Alamein

4 IND DIV

Tell el Miteirya Ridge

Ruweisat Ridge

44 DIV

HQ 13 CORPS

7 ARMD DIV

9 AUST DIV
51 (H) DIV
NZ DIV

50 DIV

5 SA DIV

Tell el Eisa

HQ PZA AFRICA

Ghazal

LITTORIO ARMD DIV

15 PZ DIV

Sidi Abd el Rahman

ARIETÉ ARMD DIV

Qaret el Himeimat

21 PZ DIV

HQ 10 CORPS

El Daba

HQ 21 CORPS

21 CORPS

HQ 20 CORPS

HQ DAK

10 CORPS

El Taqa Plateau

90 LIT DIV

Qattara Depression

When the (second) battle of El Alamein began on 24 October the German and Italian forces were outnumbered by about two to one in men, guns and tanks. In the air the British advantage was narrower but the Axis unserviceability ratio was exceptionally high. Montgomery commanded an army of 195,000 men with over 1,000 tanks against a combined German-Italian army of 104,000 men with 500 tanks. The dispositions of his enemies were known to Montgomery in great detail. So were their shortages of fuel and ammunition. Their supplies, particularly their supplies of petrol, were precarious and the intelligence available to Rommel (who was posted back to the front at once) about his enemy's strengths and intentions was of a completely different and inferior order to Montgomery's. The tide had turned against Rommel and the issue in the last week of October was not defeat or victory but the nature and extent of the defeat. Both issues were decided in little more than a week. Montgomery, using a brilliantly elaborate deception plan, took his enemy by surprise and scored a skilfully designed and executed victory. But in spite of fuel shortages and in spite of a final attempt to obey an order from Hitler to stand firm, Rommel got away with an army which remained a force in being for several months more. The Eighth Army set out westward through Cyrenaica and Tripolitania to Tunisia to join up with the Anglo-American armies which landed there a few days after Rommel began his retreat, but Rommel's retreating forces remained in between and the first junction was not between allied armies from east and west but between Axis ones – Rommel retreating from Egypt and fresh German and Italian forces put into Tunisia in order to hold at least a part of Africa and prevent the British and Americans from closing this theatre of war.

The Anglo-American invasion of North-west Africa (Torch) was originally proposed by Churchill to Roosevelt at their meeting in August 1941. Roosevelt at first fell in with the scheme, but he later inclined to prefer the unrealistic alternative of a landing in Europe in 1942, partly in order to succour the Russians and partly because the British retreats in the early part of 1942 had made an African venture less attractive. But Great Britain's further defeats in the summer of 1942 caused him to revert to Torch, largely in order to succour the British. On the military side, however, neither the American nor the British service chiefs (except the British Admiralty) were enthusiastic about a second front in Africa, and the American chiefs went so far as to try to force Roosevelt and Churchill into a European landing by proposing to give priority to the Pacific theatre if a European campaign were postponed.

The strategy of the invasion of North-west Africa, which was finally accepted by all concerned in July 1942, was British and naval. The idea was to clear the Mediterranean. To the British naval staff the need to do this was self-evident. The other services were slow to respond, especially the air staff which was concentrating on how to smash Germany on its own by air bombardment. The American staffs were largely unaware of what was going on until the early summer when they woke up to it and precipitately concluded that it was all a ruse to forestall an invasion of France in the near future. This was a misinterpretation, for the British regarded an early invasion of France as impossible anyway and never intended operations in northern Africa or southern Europe to supplant that ultimately essential operation. The naval strategy of clearing the Mediterranean did not necessarily imply a campaign in Italy or even Sicily, and the naval staff in fact preferred the occupation of Sardinia, Corsica and the Dodecanese as threats to the Germans in southern Europe, threats to be posed by occupying these islands without using them as springboards for more ambitious land operations. There were no long term plans or even blueprints, no conferences to take the big decisions about the future which, if books about strategy and policies are to be believed, have to be taken by identifiable groups of decision-makers. Subsequent events – the invasion of Sicily and then the landings on the Italian mainland – followed pragmatically, each born out of the success of its predecessor, links in a chain which grew but was never preconceived.

The invasion of North-west Africa was an essay in military cooperation with political complications. The political complications were provided by the existence of rival French authorities and American misreading of their comparative values. France's North African possessions had been made safe for Vichy by Weygand, the first High Commissioner appointed by Pétain, and by General Alphonse Juin who was made Commander-in-Chief in North Africa in 1941 after being released from German imprisonment. For both these generals and many of their colleagues the task of a patriotic Frenchman was to preserve French territory from Germany and also from any other aggressor – which, after the affairs at Mers-el-Kebir and Dakar in 1940, meant for the time being Great Britain. Gaullism, owing to de Gaulle's links with Great Britain, was therefore not much in evidence and was thought to be even weaker than it was, especially in the United States where Roosevelt's dislike of de Gaulle encouraged underestimates of both the man and his movement.

In April 1942 General Henri Giraud escaped from the prison in

Germany where he had been kept for two years. He was sixty-three years old and his escape created a sensation which led the western allies to ascribe to him virtues which he never possessed. The Americans saw in Giraud an instrument for undoing de Gaulle. They smuggled him out of France to serve as an anti-Gaullist as much as an anti-Vichy rallying point but Giraud had neither the political sense, the intelligence nor the appeal of de Gaulle and he was a failure in the role for which the Americans cast him on the too slender grounds of being a senior general and a brave escaper. It was not long before the Americans wrote him off and reverted to their pro-Vichy stance. On the eve of the landings in Morocco and Algeria – whose precise date was not imparted to him – Giraud was taken by submarine and flying boat from France to Gibraltar and Roosevelt entered into an agreement with him placing all French forces in Morocco and Algeria under his command – apparently without properly informing Eisenhower, who believed that he had been given supreme authority over all forces, French as well as American and British. Meanwhile Eisenhower's deputy, General Mark Clark, had already been dispatched to Algeria by submarine to persuade the French political and military chiefs to collaborate with the coming invasion. Since the French forces in North-west Africa (about 120,000) outnumbered the Anglo-American assault forces, it was important to secure at least the neutrality of the French if the landings were to be successful and promptly followed by an eastward advance along the coast into Tunisia. Roosevelt was so apprehensive about the French reaction that he asked Churchill to keep the British fighting component out of action for at least a week. His policy was to win over Vichy's representatives in Algeria by keeping the British temporarily in the background and the Gaullists permanently out of the picture (a manoeuvre which de Gaulle never forgot).

Clark found that the senior French commanders, with the exception of Juin, were willing to accept Giraud as Commander-in-Chief but his limited time and limited instructions prevented him from probing the relative strengths of Vichyite and Gaullist sentiment. Had he done so, he would have found that the American partiality for Vichy did not correspond with the flow of French patriotism which Roosevelt and Churchill were seeking to re-engage in hostilities. Nor could he or anybody else on the allied side foresee that Darlan would be in Algiers on the day of the landings. This chance – Darlan had flown to Algiers to see his son, who was ill – capped all the existing confusions and misconceptions, since it gave the Americans the opportunity to do a deal with a senior representative of Vichy and so to outrage anti-Vichy feeling more completely.

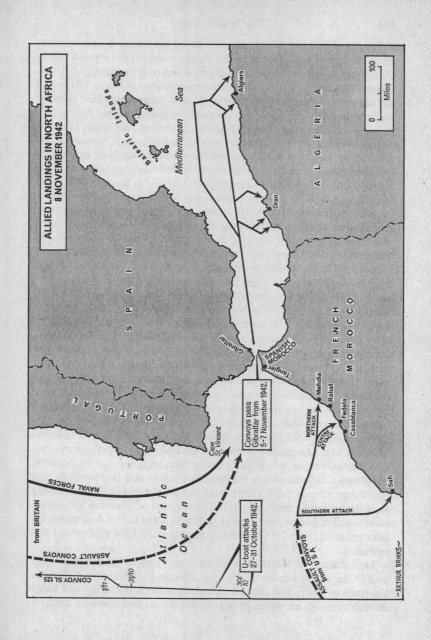

ALLIED LANDINGS IN NORTH AFRICA
8 NOVEMBER 1942

Balearic Islands

Mediterranean Sea

SPAIN

PORTUGAL

Cape St Vincent

Atlantic Ocean

from BRITAIN

NAVAL FORCES

ASSAULT CONVOYS

CONVOY SL125

1/11

-3/10

U-boat attacks
27-31 October 1942.

30/
10

ASSAULT CONVOYS
from U.S.A.

Gibraltar

Tangier

SPANISH MOROCCO

Convoys pass
Gibraltar from
5-7 November 1942.

Mehdia

Rabat

Fedela

Casablanca

NORTHERN
ATTACK

CENTRE
ATTACK

SOUTHERN ATTACK

Safi

FRENCH MOROCCO

Algiers

Oran

ALGERIA

0   100
Miles

~ARTHUR BANKS~

The American and British armadas sailed from their home countries direct to their landing places on the Atlantic and Mediterranean coasts of Morocco and in Algeria. Their most easterly landing point was fifteen miles east of Algiers. The advantages and the hazards of landing farther east in order to make sure of Tunisia as well had been debated and the hazards were held to outweigh the advantages. Roosevelt's political representative, Robert Murphy, informed Juin of the landings on the evening before, but when they took place on 8 November the chosen date had been revealed to no other Frenchman. This precaution precluded assistance by well-disposed French commanders and occasioned some resistance, but surprise was justified in military terms and opposition was soon rendered manifestly pointless. On the 9th Darlan ordered a cease-fire. The political confusion was, however, ludicrously complete and in the course of the day almost every senior Frenchman was arrested by one or other of his compatriots. Darlan's readiness to change sides was at first suspect to the Americans and British, the more so since the depth of his anti-British feelings was well known, but he was a more useful counter than the disappointing Giraud since, unlike Giraud, he was in a position to give orders to Vichy's proconsuls – Juin, the Commander-in-Chief in North Africa and Noguès and Estéva, the Residents-General in Morocco and Tunisia – who were showing regrettably little disposition to depart from their allegiance. The Americans – though not the British – had no basic objection to dealing with a Vichy Minister and were as willing to work with Darlan on this occasion as they – and the British – were willing to accept Badoglio as an ally against the Germans in the next year. Aware that they were giving serious offence to anti-Vichy feeling they tried to limit their commitment to Darlan but only succeeded in offending him as well. This tangle was only resolved on Christmas Eve when Darlan was assassinated by a fanatical Gaullist. The Americans fell back on Giraud who stepped temporarily into Darlan's shoes, which had already been adjudged too big for him, but Giraud had meanwhile displayed a considerable ineptitude for the role thrust upon him. At Casablanca in January de Gaulle and Giraud were persuaded to cooperate in the Committee of National Liberation established in Algiers, but Giraud gradually faded out of the picture. He later resigned from the Committee, leaving de Gaulle triumphant and resentful.

The invasion of North-west Africa introduced to the general public one of the major figures of the war, Dwight D. Eisenhower. General Eisenhower has too often been written down as a man who was lucky enough to rise to an eminence beyond his talents and there to contrive to make no disastrous mistakes. This judgement is wrong on both counts, for Eisenhower did make mistakes and yet he was bigger than this grudging estimate makes out. He is not among the great captains, but he was an exceptionally well-trained, methodical and unself-centred commander with in addition a humanity, perhaps unexciting but on occasions crucial, which enabled him to get on well with other people and also to help them get on well with each other. Few in 1943 expected him to go on from his North African command to even higher things, but his military and human competence so recommended him to his superiors that he was chosen to lead the allied invasion of France in the next year.

The German reaction to the invasion of North-west Africa was to occupy southern France and Tunisia and try to seize the French fleet at Toulon. This last endeavour failed. The fleet disregarded an order from Darlan to sail for Africa but it scuttled itself rather than fall into German hands. In Tunisia the Germans seized the opportunities presented to them by Anglo-American caution in making no landing east of Algiers. German and Italian troops occupied Tunisia and when the German commander, General Jürgen von Arnim, sent Kesselring pessimistic appreciations of the situation, Kesselring told him that he was not interested in appreciations and ordered him to hang on – an outstanding contravention of the Tolstoyan norm that supreme commanders are not the masters of events in battle. American and British forces occupied Bône in Algeria, near the Tunisian border, on 12 November and crossed the border four days later, but by the end of the year the Anglo-American attempt to secure Tunis had petered out and the Germans were pouring troops in by sea and air. In the east the Eighth Army had recovered Tobruk on 13 November and reached Benghazi on the 20th, while Rommel was retreating comparatively unmolested to join Arnim. Together their forces would outnumber their American, British and French adversaries and thwart them for six months.

In February 1943 Rommel crossed the frontier between Tripolitania and Tunisia, still followed at a discreet distance by Montgomery's advance guard and at a greater distance by the rest of the Eighth Army. Montgomery's advance guard established itself in the Mareth Line, a fortified position on the Tunisian side of the border built by the French in the thirties to keep the Italians out. Rommel was now between two fires but he had a plan for extinguishing both. He struck first at the Americans to the north of him and inflicted on them a sharp and humiliating defeat in the Kasserine Pass – the origin of the myth that the

Americans did not know how to fight. Rommel then turned about. He planned to take the Eighth Army's advanced positions by surprise and inflict on them such a defeat that Montgomery, whose supply lines and communications were stretched out along half North Africa, would be thrown all the way back to Cyrenaica or even Egypt, his army out of the battle and his reputation out of the history books. Rommel issued his orders. A few hours later they were in Montgomery's hands. (This was not a chance intelligence stroke; intelligence does not work like that in real life; it was almost a routine matter.) Montgomery, dropping all security precautions, drove his main forces through the night with headlights full on. They arrived in time and defeated Rommel's attack. Rommel was invalided home again. This battle did not end the war in North Africa but it decided the issue. The junction between the allied forces from east and west was made and two months later, on 12 May, the Tunisian bridgehead, which the Germans and Italians had held for six months, was eliminated by a final capitulation. Almost three years after Mussolini had goaded the reluctant Graziani into action against a British Empire lying naked in the Middle East after the fall of France the last Italian and German combatants – 150,000 of them – were prisoners of war.

The end of the fighting left a more complex pattern in North-west Africa than in the territories farther east. The former Italian colonies were under British military occupation and Egypt was for the time being under British politico-military control, but in North-west Africa there were, first, French authority; secondly, the American and British military commands and their civilian representatives; and, thirdly, the Sultan of Morocco and Bey of Tunis and the nationalist movements in their countries and in Algeria as well.

French authority had been unbroken, even by the collapse of 1940. Allowed by the armistice agreements with Germany and Italy to keep 120,000 troops in North Africa, the French had no difficulty in maintaining their control, particularly since nationalist leaders still at large had been picked up and put away just before the war began (the principal Moroccan leaders had been in prison since 1937). The humiliation of France was not unequivocally welcome to Arab opinion. The French empire had been a mixed experiment. On the one hand it represented the domination of one nation over another, a degradation and a denial of political rights and human values, but on the other hand it was a relationship between two cultures, a developing association which was prized so long as its fruits counterbalanced the thorns of unequal political dualism. Between the wars this balance had swung more and more the wrong way. The cultural association needed by its very nature to be an expanding one, but in France conservative views predominated, there was little awareness that the empire might be coming to a dead end and no willingness to grant more than minimal reforms. When the Popular Front produced a plan to extend the franchise and citizenship rights in Algeria – the *projet Violette*, so called after the Governor-General of Algeria – it was first blocked and then destroyed by the politically dominant and economically favoured white settlers or *colons* who threatened to disrupt the entire administration of Algeria if the plan were brought to the floor of the National Assembly. This rigidity sharpened nationalist animosities, and French governments were trapped between two increasingly hostile forces. But the nationalist movements were still weak. It took time for people at large to conclude that the nationalists might achieve more than abortive demonstrations and neither the bulk of the population nor, in Morocco and Tunisia, the sovereigns considered that conditions were ripe for a challenge to the power of France.

The defeat of France in 1940 changed this attitude only fractionally. That defeat was a shock which pained the Arab élite in spite of their quarrels with the French state. It also had unpleasant possibilities: Tunisia, for example, was immediately exposed to Italian covetousness and feared attack by land and sea. The Tunisian nationalist leader Habib Bourguiba, imprisoned at Marseilles, insisted that Tunisian nationalism must be anti-Axis. From the Vichy régime nationalists had nothing to hope for (Vichy's reaction was to apprehend any prominent nationalists still at large) and Bourguiba declared himself for de Gaulle and for the western allies. In Morocco, where General Noguès had established good relations with the Sultan after considerable disturbances in the early thirties, the Sultan had promised in 1939 to support the French war effort and the nationalists had promised not to impede it. The collapse of 1940 did not at first disturb these tolerances.

The year 1942 had profounder consequences, for in that year France suffered a second defeat when the Americans and the British landed in Morocco and Algeria without prior agreement with the French and opened fire on them. Moreover this second defeat was inflicted on France within the sight and hearing of the Arabs, it was followed by the quarrels between de Gaulle and Giraud which greatly harmed French prestige and it was accompanied by overt and covert American support for independence movements. In Tunisia, occupied by the Germans, there was the additional coincidence that a new Bey, more sympathetic to the nationalists than his predecessor, had just succeeded to the throne.

With the allied armies arrived thousands of copies of the Atlantic Charter which the Arabs had heard about and could now read for themselves. They concluded that the whole power of the invincible United States was now behind the independence movements. In Algeria Murphy, Roosevelt's political representative, encouraged nationalists to make claims designed to secure American and British pledges about the post-war government of Algeria. Algerian leaders offered their cooperation during the war in return for the immediate convening of a conference at which Algerians would draw up a new constitution for Algeria. The aims were unexceptionable but the tactics were dubious, since the French authorities were incensed by what they regarded as undercover blackmail and reacted indignantly not only against American interference but also against Algerian demands which otherwise they were not far from accepting – and went some way towards accepting once de Gaulle had established his authority over Vichy's minions and Washington's protégés.

In Morocco Roosevelt intervened personally. He had never made any secret of his detestation of imperialism in principle and his condemnation of the niggardliness of the French, British and other European empires in relation to their dependants, and during his stay at Casablanca in January 1943 he had a meeting with Sultan Mohammed V ben Yusuf, who came away from it with the belief that the United States would provide the political pressures and the economic aid needed to restore full Moroccan independence. The Sultan was already half way inclined to make common cause with the Moroccan nationalists and his encounters with Americans encouraged him to lean still further that way. A year later the Istiqlal or Independence Party, formed by the merger in this climate of separate existing bodies, issued a declaration of independence which sought unilaterally to abrogate the treaty upon which Franco-Moroccan relations rested. It was followed by demonstrations which showed how the populace as well as the sovereign rated the French connection and France's ability to maintain it. Towards the end of the war the French arrested – but never charged or tried – nationalist leaders whom they accused of complicity in German plotting. There were more riots and Frenchmen were massacred. The French reacted with too much counter-violence and talk of too little reform. The war boosted nationalist hopes and activity and at the same time set an example of violence which was to be followed on both sides as the nationalists proceeded to their goals after the war was over.

In Tunisia the new ruler, Bey Moncef, was more than half a nationalist. He succeeded unexpectedly in 1942 and decided that his best policy was to take the leadership of the nationalist forces. Since the principal nationalist leaders were in French prisons this was not too difficult but it led to strained relations and ugly scenes with Vichy's Resident-General, Admiral Jean-Pierre Estéva. Before the conflict could be resolved the Germans arrived in order to stop the Anglo-Americans from seizing Tunisia as well as Algeria and Morocco. For six uneasy months the German command and the French administration coexisted (Estéva was later condemned to life imprisonment for this collaboration), while Tunisian towns and villages were bombed in a war which Tunisians could not by any stretch of the imagination regard as their own. Some Tunisians collaborated with the Germans and some with the allies; most, including the Bey, waited as equivocally as possible.

A few weeks before the final defeat of the Germans, Bourguiba was released from prison, sent to Rome to be brainwashed with Axis seducements and then forwarded to Tunis. His policy was unchanged: independence and a treaty with France. But too many Frenchmen had come to regard him as an enemy of France and in addition Giraud, whom the allies had elevated to High Commissioner in North Africa, needlessly affronted Tunisians by deposing Moncef as soon as the Germans had been ousted. This tactless and illegal action – the Franco-Tunisian treaty gave the French government no power to appoint or depose a Bey – compromised the French at the moment when they were trying to re-establish their authority. Giraud shortly afterwards disappeared from the scene and the Gaullist régime in Algeria proposed some cautious reforms which, though they might have been acceptable before the war, no longer sufficed after the French setbacks of 1940–42. In March 1945 Bourguiba, concluding that discussions in Tunis would get nowhere, left secretly for Cairo where he established a Committee for the Liberation of the Maghrib with himself as secretary-general and the veteran Moroccan rebel Abd el-Krim as president. He did not return to Tunis for over four years.

In both Morocco and Tunisia the conflict was about the distribution of power between the French and native governments. Under the protectorate treaties the French had gradually assumed more power and more responsibilities and the nationalists were seeking to reverse the process by securing elected central and local councils with native majorities, freer access for Arabs to the upper reaches of the public services, equal pay for Arab and French employees and a strict application of the treaty provisions governing the role of French officials in the administration of the protectorates. These were questions of adjustment. What transpired during the war and immediately after it was that the adjustments would not be made. Each side calculated its position in such a way as to make it refuse to go near enough to the other side's position to effect agreement. The French calculation was a miscalculation, since in the end France had to concede complete independence and the ending of the protectorate status. The main source of this miscalculation was the blindness of pre-war and post-war French conservative governments which first failed to see the need for changes and then failed to see that changes which might have sufficed before the war did not meet the case after it. The brief Gaullist interlude of 1942–6 might have set a more generous course and so have reached the inevitable dénouement more quickly and less painfully, but it was constricted by American intervention and was impelled into an anti-Americanism which tainted its attitudes towards the nationalists, who were in turn tempted into believing that what they could not extract from France by themselves they could get by playing the American card. Gaullism, moreover, was a strange mixture of radicalism and conservatism. At Brazzaville in 1941 de Gaulle promised the Africans of France's sub-Saharan empire a bigger share in government, a wider franchise and more decentralization of public business, and in Algeria in 1943 de Gaulle and his chosen Governor, General Georges Catroux (who had been born in Algiers), showed that they appreciated the need for a new start. Yet the changes which were then proposed turned out to be disappointingly meagre and in Algeria, as in Tunis, the opportunity for an amicable and progressive re-ordering of relations passed sourly away.

On the last day of the war in Europe the inhabitants of the Algerian town of Sétif proposed to hold a procession distinct from the official one. They were given permission to do so provided no banners were displayed. The provision was ignored. Somebody started shooting. Twenty-one Frenchmen were killed. The affair developed into a revolt involving troops, air bombing and naval gunnery. Thousands more people were killed, mostly Algerians. Violence begot bestial ferocity on the one side which begot excessive reprisals and summary executions on the other. The established authorities prevailed but a number of the malcontents fled to the hills to carry on the fight. Although one war had ended in North Africa in 1943, two years later another and longer one had grown out of it, not to be ended until de Gaulle was brought back to power in 1958 to do so.

CHAPTER 18

The End of Fascism

THE allied victory in North Africa was only the half close of the Mediterranean campaign. Africa was not an end in itself but a part of a struggle for control of the Mediterranean and one way of getting back onto European soil. An invasion of Sicily was a logical sequel, for it could be argued that without Sicily and its airfields the free passage of the Mediterranean had not been unquestionably secured. At Casablanca in January 1943 Roosevelt and Churchill had agreed that the forces which they had assembled in North Africa should be used to invade Sicily. They had not, however, taken any further decision. Whether Sicily, besides being a sequel to Africa, was also to be a prelude to mainland Italy was as yet unresolved, although studies were put in hand for crossing the Straits of Messina, landing in the heel of Italy as well as the toe, and taking Sardinia and Corsica. Sicily was a hinge on a door which could be made to open either way.

The invasion of Sicily was launched on 10 July. The small island of Pantellaria had been easily captured a month earlier, but in spite of this pointer the Germans were preoccupied by a cover plan designed to make them fear a landing in Greece and wholly taken in by a piece of deception indicating an attack on Sardinia: a dead body with bogus plans was put in the sea in such a way that it would be washed up in Spain and in the justified belief that the Spanish authorities would hand the papers to the Germans.

Mussolini had no faith in the Sicilians. He did not dare to arm them and he had long since ordered all Sicilian-born officials to be transferred from the island to the mainland. The allies had command of the air. They landed at half a dozen points along the eastern half of the southern coast and along the east coast below Syracuse. An American plan for additional landings at Palermo and Catania was abandoned, largely at the instance of Montgomery, who had been impressed by the quality of German and Italian resistance in Tunisia and did not in any case want to see the allied forces spread too widely. The allied force, which sailed from American and British ports as well as North Africa and Egypt, consisted of a modest invasion force with very powerful naval and air cover. One hundred and sixty thousand men were put ashore in the first wave, with 600 tanks and 14,000 vehicles. They were supported by a fleet of 750 vessels and by over 4,000 aircraft. The British landings were completely unopposed and the Americans almost so, although there were 230,000 Italian and 40,000 German troops in the island. The first counter-attacks, which were directed against the Americans and almost dislodged them, were broken with the help of naval gunfire, and thereafter victory was swift. General George Patton's Third US Army, which had landed on the left flank of the combined force, reached Messina on 17 August by a round-about route which took his men swiftly across the centre of the island to the north coast and then eastward. They arrived just ahead of the British coming up by the shorter but more difficult east coast route. This was the end of the operation.

A military government was established in Sicily. In practice the island fell once more into the clutches of the Mafia. Mussolini, who understood gangsterism, had been the one ruler of Italy to get the better of the Mafia. His disappearance was the signal for its revival. *Mafiosi* from the United States, where they had been keeping their hands in, got themselves attached to the American forces because they could speak Italian and soon, partly by graft and partly from the need to fill local posts vacated by refugees, occupied most of the positions that mattered. Within a few months they were the government of Sicily. Later on, after toying briefly with Sicilian separatism, they entered into an alliance with right-wing politicians in Rome to defeat the Left and keep Sicily corrupt and miserable.

The conquest of Sicily spelt defeat for Italy but did not give the allies victory over the Germans in Italy. So far as it represented a way of defeating the Germans it left open the question whether a campaign in Italy was a worthwhile adjunct of the campaign in northern France which, everybody agreed, was to be the main blow. Italy itself, as a fighting force and as an independent sovereign state, was finished for the duration. It had undertaken a war for which it was neither equipped to fight nor willing to fight. Mussolini's Italy was hardly ready for any war in 1940, certainly not for a long one in two continents, but after attacking France and Greece it had become involved in wars in North Africa and East Africa and in the USSR. By the beginning of 1943 the Italians were not only dismayed and angered by the consequences of these gigantic miscalculations but were saying so. Strikes, beginning at the Fiat works in Turin, protested against rising prices and harsh working conditions and disclosed the workers' basic demand for peace. These strikes succeeded the defeats of the Italian armies on the Stalingrad front and were followed by the defeats in Sicily. Mussolini had already realized in 1942 that the war could only be won by negotiating a peace in the east but Hitler refused to consider such a thing. In February 1943 Mussolini in a general re-shuffle hedged his bets by demoting Ciano and Grandi, who were anti-German (and credibly rumoured to be plotting against him); he also appointed a new Army Chief of Staff who was suspected by Kesselring and Hitler of being ready to switch sides at the first opportunity. Ten days before the Sicilian landings Mussolini received Mihai Antonescu, who had come to suggest that Italy, Rumania and Hungary should all leave the war together and hoped that Mussolini would give the lead. After the Sicilian invasion he found himself compelled to fight on Italian soil with a million Italian servicemen engaged outside the country – 580,000 in the Balkans, 217,000 on the Russian front and 200,000 in France, not to mention those killed or taken prisoner in the Western Desert and Tunisia, who numbered at least 200,000 more. The defence of Italy required not only the recall of the Italian troops in the USSR (for which the landings in Sicily provided a welcome excuse) but also German reinforcements which would turn Italy into an occupied country.

Mussolini had no doubt what he ought to do but he did not dare to do it. In order to spur him on to ask for an armistice his advisers grossly exaggerated the size of the invading armies, which they represented as initially twenty-five divisions when they knew it to be eight. On 19 July Hitler and Mussolini met at Feltre, but Hitler did not allow Mussolini to get a word in and Mussolini's nerve, none too good by now even when Hitler was not around, failed him. After listening to one of Hitler's long disquisitions on the way the war was going, which included some very rude remarks about the Italians, he took refuge in silence. This failure sealed his fate.

The fascist chieftains or *gerarchi* feared for themselves and their régime. Mussolini's alliance with Hitler had proved a disaster. It had led to war, humiliation and defeat which, by 1942, were threatening the survival of Fascism. To save Fascism the alliance had to be broken. But Mussolini, who had made the alliance, was incapable of unmaking it. Moreover Italy was in no position simply to back out of the alliance unaided. It must change sides and make a new alliance in order to be rid of the old. There was no reason to think that this could not be done, although there was a question whether Mussolini himself might not have to be jettisoned in the process. The king might, if pressed by the anti-fascist members of the royal family, demand in a crisis the Duce's removal but he was very unlikely to insist on forming a government without any fascists at all. Similarly the allies would probably accept a partly fascist government. During the war they had made statements about the total overthrow of Fascism, but Churchill had also said that Mussolini was personally to blame for everything and until 1940 neither he nor Roosevelt had been notably anti-fascist. Both Great Britain and the United States had lived with Fascism for twenty years, for much of that time amicably enough.

The *gerarchi* therefore wanted a reversal of alliances, by and with Mussolini if possible, without and against him if necessary. After the Feltre meeting they knew that they must proceed the second way. On 24 July the Fascist Grand Council met for the first time since the outbreak of war. Twenty-eight men attended. Grandi proposed that the king should be restored to his post (taken from him in 1940) as Commander-in-Chief. He delivered a strong attack on Mussolini's conduct of the war. He spoke for over an hour and so impressed wavering members of the Council that when a pro-Mussolini resolution to adjourn was moved it was lost. There was a short pause during which Grandi and others moved around taking soundings. Mussolini himself seemed listless. Upon the resumption Grandi's proposal was approved by nineteen votes to nine. It was a vote of no confidence in the Duce. It was now two o'clock in the morning. The members of the Council dispersed without any very clear notion of what their vote portended. During the morning of the 25th Mussolini worked as usual in his office. In the afternoon he went to the Villa Savoia for a private talk with the king. Here he received a second knock. The king and his closest advisers had become as dissatisfied with Mussolini as the fascist *gerarchi* and when Mussolini arrived the king dismissed him from the office to which he had appointed him over twenty years earlier. It is not known whether Mussolini argued in his own defence. The interview lasted only twenty minutes. As the ex-Prime Minister emerged he was politely arrested and driven away in an ambulance. He showed no fight and seemed to have no stomach for the stirring events which lay ahead.

Mussolini was succeeded as Prime Minister by Marshal Pietro Badoglio, who had been a stalwart of the fascist régime but felt in this crisis a deeper loyalty to the monarchy. The king and his new Prime Minister wanted to get out of the war but they did not see how to do it without turning Italy into one more German-occupied country, unless the allies could be persuaded to cut off and overwhelm the Germans. Badoglio was willing to capitulate to the allies but he wanted to make conditions: he would capitulate if the allies landed on the mainland, the farther north the better. He tried to persuade them to land at Genoa. If they would not venture so far he argued for a parachute operation to seize Rome; all the airfields round Rome were held by the one Italian division indubitably loyal to the House of Savoy, the Piedmontese Grenadiers. In addition Badoglio, while publicly professing loyalty to the German alliance, had circulated instructions for action against an assumed communist plot which he intended to put into operation by a pre-arranged code word, accompanied by the simple instruction to substitute 'Germans' where the original plan said 'communists'.

The discussions between Badoglio and the allies were protracted. They were conducted in secrecy in Lisbon and then Madrid and were complicated by the fact that the allies conceived themselves to be negotiating a surrender whereas the Italian emissaries considered that they were discussing joint action against the Germans in Italy. The Casablanca declaration had expressly committed the allies to demanding the unconditional surrender of Italy as well as Germany with the result that much time was spent in negotiating the conditions of a surrender which was none the less to be made to appear unconditional. Moreover the allies were divided about undertaking a major campaign on the mainland. They were tempted by the ease of their conquest of Sicily and by Mussolini's fall. An occupation of southern Italy would give them air bases for bombing Germany and would force Hitler to choose between abandoning Italy altogether or reinforcing it at the expense of the western front which the allies were about to attack. Naples, with its prestige and its capacious port, was a prize worth having and, unlike Rome or Genoa, was within the range of allied air cover. The Americans, in accordance with their broader strategy, had been reluctant to lodge large armies in a new Italian theatre but an attack towards Naples could be represented as no more than a variation on the operations which were in the planning stage and so half way to being acceptable. They overcame their hesitations. The allies decided to cross from Sicily into Calabria, to land in the heel as well as the toe of Italy and to mount a third operation to land at Salerno, thirty-five miles short of Naples. From there, in some as yet undefined way, a road to Rome would be opened.

As the first troops were crossing into Calabria the negotiations with Badoglio were finally concluded. An act of surrender was signed on 3 September. It was to be disclosed on the 8th but Badoglio asked that publication should be delayed for a few days to enable him to redispose his forces. Eisenhower, who distrusted Badoglio, refused and had the news of the surrender broadcast on the appointed day. Badoglio was obliged to follow suit. The Italians were caught unprepared, the Germans immediately occupied Rome and its airfields, and a promised allied airborne coup against these airfields had to be cancelled. The king and his government fled to Brindisi. The Italian fleet, which put to sea and made for Malta, lost the battleship *Roma* – sunk by a new kind of bomb, controlled after release by radio by the pilot who dropped it. The formal Italian surrender was completed at Malta on 29 September and a month later, on 13 October, Italy declared war on Germany.

The Germans had expected an allied landing from the sea near Rome combined with a parachute operation and they proposed to withdraw all their forces south of Rome. This strategy was that of Rommel, who had been put in command in northern Italy. But Kesselring, who commanded in Rome and southwards, had other ideas. Decisive as ever, he believed that more of Italy could be held than the Lombard plain and circumstances helped him to wean Hitler away from Rommel's plan. For a time Rommel's plan prevailed and the Eighth Army was unopposed when it began to cross from Sicily into Calabria on 3 September. Montgomery proceeded sedately northward, the Germans withdrawing with equal circumspection. A separate landing at Taranto was similarly unopposed. In the early hours of 9 September the main assault on the Italian mainland was made at Salerno by an Anglo-American force of three divisions under the command of General Mark Clark which had sailed from ports in Algeria, Tunisia and Tripolitania. This landing was not unopposed. The defences, which had been manned by Italians, were in the process of being taken over by the Germans, who had just learnt of the Italian capitulation, and as they moved into their new positions they found themselves immediately in the path of the allied invasion. Their commander had no instructions covering this situation and he took it upon himself to resist. He was aware that the Eighth Army was advancing up the coast from Messina and he planned to throw the main invading force back into the sea before the Eighth Army could arrive. He nearly succeeded. After initial successes in getting ashore the invading force was thrown onto the defensive and Clark took preliminary steps for an evacuation. But the allied units held their ground and by skilful use of parachute units Clark was able to check his antagonist, who broke off the engagement and withdrew northwards upon the approach of the Eighth Army.

While the invaders were struggling to keep their grip on the beaches at Salerno the people of Naples rose against the Germans and fought them savagely for three days, suffering terrible reprisals before the allies reached Naples on 1 October, their first staging point in a long slog to the north.

Hitler was now converted to the strategy of holding central Italy as well as the north. A new German line was formed along the Volturno

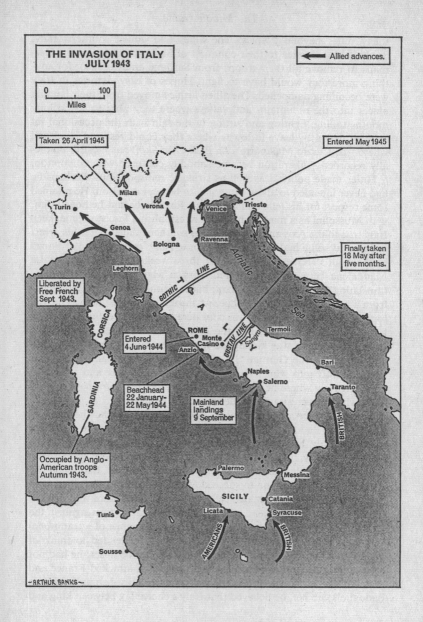

THE INVASION OF ITALY
JULY 1943

⟵ Allied advances.

0   100
Miles

Taken 26 April 1945

Entered May 1945

Milan

Turin

Verona

Venice

Trieste

Genoa

Bologna

Ravenna

Adriatic

Leghorn

GOTHIC LINE

Finally taken 18 May after five months.

Liberated by Free French Sept. 1943.

CORSICA

I T A L Y

ROME

Monte Casino

Anzio

GUSTAV LINE

Sangro

Termoli

Sea

Entered 4 June 1944

SARDINIA

Beachhead 22 January–22 May1944

Naples

Salerno

Bari

Mainland landings 9 September

Taranto

BRITISH

Occupied by Anglo-American troops Autumn 1943.

Palermo

Messina

SICILY

Catania

Tunis

Licata

Syracuse

BRITISH

Sousse

AMERICANS

~ ARTHUR BANKS ~

thirty miles beyond Naples. The allies had added southern Italy, Sardinia and Corsica to their conquest of Sicily (but allowed the Germans to remove all their troops from Sardinia and Corsica); for anything more they would have to fight. Hopes of easy victories in Italy were becoming dampened. The allied armies moved from their landing places into the mountains and valleys where they were to spend long months toiling, fighting and sitting in the rain with the occasional respite provided by leave in towns where they could rest and revel and where – as Curzio Malaparte's *La Pelle* (*The Skin*) has most dramatically recorded – liberation became shoddily confused with corruption.

Hitler made political as well as strategic redispositions. Perhaps he had never intended to allow Mussolini to be kept in prison. He retained some respect for his fellow dictator and forerunner and he hoped that, with Mussolini as a mascot, he could re-establish a fascist régime, keep Italy true to the Axis and so protect his southern flank. After his arrest in July Mussolini had first been held for ten days on the island of Ponza in the Gulf of Gaeta and then for three weeks on the island of La Maddalena between Sardinia and Corsica where he passed the time translating Carducci into German; but in neither was he judged secure from a possible attempt at rescue. At the end of August he was moved to the Gran Sasso, where he was considered entirely safe. But two weeks later, on 12 September when the battle on the Salerno beaches was still undecided, he was kidnapped in an operation of uncommon skill and daring by the German SS officer Otto Skorzeny and flown in a small aircraft into which he barely fitted to Germany and thence to northern Italy where he was established as the head of a new government which never attained either power or dignity.

The restoration of Mussolini to the political stage and the flight of the king and Badoglio to Brindisi were minor episodes in the campaign joined in Italy between the western allies and Germany, but in the history of Italy they had greater significance for there were many Italians who wanted neither Mussolini nor the king and Badoglio. The appointment of Badoglio to succeed Mussolini sufficed the allies, who had no particular animus against the monarchy and were well enough suited by any government which was prepared to turn against the Germans. Churchill was by temperament a monarchist of a traditional and sentimental kind; like most conservatives he tended to think of society as a number of applecarts which must not be upset; he had not been among Mussolini's enemies until Mussolini attacked France and declared war on Great Britain, he was prepared to see some fascists in Badoglio's cabinet, he believed that Italy's choice lay between king and

Communism, and he feared a second ELAS in Italy if anti-fascist elements forced the pace of political and social change. But Italians wanted change, more change than was involved in a palace revolution effected by the Fascist Grand Council and the king and his entourage. If and so far as Italy in 1943 could be likened to an applecart, the apples in it were rotten. Italians were not concerned, as Churchill was, simply to undo what had happened since 1940 and chase the Germans out of Italy; they wanted to undo everything that had happened since 1922 and destroy Fascism. Anti-fascists had existed in Italy before Nazis had been heard of. To them Mussolini's dismissal was no more than a cabinet re-shuffle, an acknowledgement that his foreign policy had failed and been discarded. But they were more concerned with internal than external affairs.

The anti-fascists were the inheritors from the Risorgimento of a successful tradition of resistance and conspiracy within the country and by exiles. Both the exodus and internal resistance had begun immediately after the March on Rome, exiles and anti-fascists in Italy regarding themselves as true Italians whose mission it was to destroy Fascism in the same way as their grandfathers had been dedicated to the destruc- tion of Austrian, Papal and Bourbon tyranny. Inside Italy anti-fascist groups formed, notably in universities. A clandestine press flourished as it had in the days of the *carbonari*. So did mural graffiti – slogans on walls played a prominent part in the struggle between fascists and anti- fascists. The Communist Party, well organized, covering the whole country and driven underground, managed to preserve some of the structure of the banned trade unions, organized strikes and other demonstrations (on May Day for example), displayed red flags and maintained active contacts with Italians and other sympathizers beyond the frontiers. Outside Italy the exiles spread over many countries from France, Switzerland and Belgium to Latin America and the United States. Many of them were comparatively humble people who were used to seeking seasonal work in other parts of Europe or who maybe had relatives more permanently settled in the New World, but they included also men who had made names for themselves in politics or the literary world. They too formed groups, issued newspapers and kept resistance alive.

In 1929 Carlo Rosselli made a dramatic escape from prison on the Lipari Islands and formed in Paris a movement called Justice and Liberty (with a paper of the same name) which brought anti-fascists of different political persuasions together and gave the anti-fascist crusade a distinctive flavour. For Rosselli and his friends it was not enough to be anti-fascist or to put the clock back to 1922. There must be a positive programme for putting the clock forward. These men not only hated Mussolini for his brutalities, especially after the murder of the socialist leader Giacomo Matteotti in 1924; they also regarded the Risorgimento as unfinished business and proclaimed once more the Mazzinian aims of democracy and a republic which had been submerged in Cavour's monarchist, bourgeois and capitalist Italy; and they added socialism to democracy and republicanism. They did not win the adherence of all anti-fascists. The more conservative of these formed a National Alliance which hoped to persuade the monarchy and the papacy to turn against Mussolini – but the Duce kept the king securely by his side and negotiated in 1929 a concordat with the Pope. The National Alliance issued pamphlets and disseminated them by getting each recipient to make six copies, of which at least two were to be sent to fascists. Its most famous exploit occurred in 1931 when the young poet Lauro De Bosis, taking off in an aircraft from the south of France, circled Rome for half an hour at dusk on an October evening and scattered 400,000 leaflets from 1,000 feet over the centre of the city before setting course for the sea, where, having run out of petrol or lost control of the aircraft which he had only just learnt to fly, he died.

Repression became severer as opposition persisted. Something like a small war developed between the fascist police and their enemies. Police agents followed the exiles abroad and this Italian civil war spilled over into foreign territory, particularly France and then Spain, where another civil war gave the anti-fascist exiles a chance to fight against Mussolini's fascist troops. In France consulates and other public buildings belonging to the Italian state were attacked. Men were killed on both sides. In 1937, on the thirteenth anniversary of Matteotti's murder, Carlo Rosselli and his brother Nello were murdered near Paris at Mussolini's bidding. When war came in 1940 the struggle, nearly twenty years old but still alive, was intensified. Mussolini now had fresh enemies and was beginning to lose some of his friends. The German alliance was unpopular; the Roman Catholic church was shifting away from Fascism. In August 1942 a conference of free Italians at Montevideo, presided over by the pre-fascist statesman Count Carlo Sforza, drew up a programme for a democratic and social republic of Italy. The next year the allied invasion of Sicily was regarded not as a conquest but as the beginning of liberation.

For thousands of Italians therefore, with all this behind them and within them, the Badoglio government was unacceptable. The government itself realized the precarious nature of its authority. It equivocated.

It freed political prisoners and banned the Fascist Party, but it retained the censorship and the black-shirted fascist militia. Party politics were not resumed and all party politicians were kept out of the government. The war went on. Ordinary people were confused and then became angry. German troops began to pour in – and were resisted by Italians at three or four points along the frontier. Rome was hit by the allies from the air and suffered 1,000 casualties and the king's car was stoned when he visited the scene. Outside Italy local commanders and troops did not know whom to fight, if anybody; some of them turned against the Germans and on Cephallonia in the Ionian Islands 8,400 Italians were killed. By September when the king and Badoglio fled from the capital and Mussolini was carried off by the Germans to create a second fascist state in the north and two thirds of the country was under German occupation, the new government had disappointed the hopes and forfeited the respect of a great part of the population and was only sustained by the allies, particularly the British.

This period of uncertainty and disenchantment between July and September 1943 was followed by a second period, stretching from the events of the latter month to the German evacuation of Rome in June 1944. After its declaration of war against Germany in October 1943 the Badoglio government devoted much of its constricted energies to re-orienting the Italian army; by the end of the year regular Italian units were fighting in the Anglo-American forces, which also included French, Polish, Greek, Indian and New Zealand contingents and even Japanese from California. Allied generals were not enthusiastic about Italian help, but after Montgomery's departure the Eighth Army helped to train and equip a number of volunteer brigades which showed that Italians could fight as well as anybody when they wanted to. The Americans refused to copy the Eighth Army's example and the war ended before it got very far. Had the war gone on longer the Eighth Army would have fathered a first-class Italian army – composed chiefly of communists.

Owing to the slowness of the allied advance up Italy most Italians found themselves in German-occupied territory. They could not join Badoglio's forces even if they wanted to. Disbanded soldiers and released prisoners-of-war – impelled by anti-German patriotism or fearful of being put to work or thrown into prison by the Germans or of being transported to forced labour in Germany – took to the hills. These men had not for the most part been anti-fascist but their defeats had caused a revulsion of feeling against Mussolini's senseless policies and a certain sympathy therefore for Mussolini's domestic enemies.

These groups were at first small and basically anti-German; they were aware of the existence of other similar groups but not coordinated with them; they had no doctrine or political aims. But they grew. Where Germans were present in ordered strength and fixed positions they were obliged to coordinate their ventures in order to survive (many of them did not) and be effective. They needed the support and cooperation of the settled population and gradually became an adjunct of something quite different, the anti-fascist popular movement which had a political, as opposed to a merely anti-German, purpose and was planning a national uprising.

The term Resistance was not used in Italy during the war. (It was adopted after the war by extension from other parts of Europe.) This is indicative, because Resistance implied resistance to the occupier; the Italian movement which developed from 1943 was not primarily concerned with the occupation. It was an attempt, which ultimately failed, to make a revolution and take over the government of the country. It included republicans, socialists, communists, liberals and those left-wing Roman Catholics who looked backwards to pre-fascist Christian Populism and subsequently became a section of the Democratic Christian Party. Their common watchword was Renewal. They created a joint committee – the Committee of National Liberation (CLN) – which they regarded as the future government of Italy and, like Charles Albert of Savoy one hundred years earlier, they relied on themselves and not on foreigners: *l'Italia farà da se.* Two groups were particularly prominent: the communists with their Garibaldi brigades and the Action Party, the heir of Justice and Liberty, with similar brigades.

On the political front old parties reappeared and new ones were formed. Exiles returned. Barred from the government by the king and Churchill, they held a congress at Bari in January 1944 which demanded the immediate abdication of the king. Publicly and privately Churchill resisted them, speaking in the House of Commons against any change in the Italian government and instructing his representatives in Italy to support the king and Badoglio; but the British on the spot, more alive than Churchill to the trend of events, fostered the revival of democratic politics. Ironically the monarchy owed its reprieve not to the British but to the communists against whom Churchill was trying to protect it. The communist leader Palmiro Togliatti, returning from eighteen years in the USSR, joined in the demand for a new government but argued, on Stalin's instructions, that the fate of the monarchy should be deferred until the end of the war. The upshot was the withdrawal of the king from public life with a promise to instal his son Umberto as

Lieutenant-Governor of the realm as soon as Rome was recovered. Badoglio remained Prime Minister but took representatives of six anti-fascist parties into his government. For the first time in history socialists and communists joined an Italian government.

When Rome fell the king transferred his powers to his son and Badoglio resigned. (The king still did not abdicate. He did so, belatedly, in 1946 when Umberto became king for a month. A plebiscite then abolished the monarchy by 12 million votes to 10 million.) The new Prime Minister was Ivanoe Bonomi, the penultimate pre-fascist Prime Minister and a respected figure acceptable to all anti-fascists in the short run. His government lasted until the end of the year when it was replaced by a narrower coalition, still under Bonomi. Another transient anti-fascist coalition was formed before the end of the war and lasted a few months after it. It was followed over the next twenty years by an unbroken series of Right-Centre governments. It is, however, tempting to see some consequences of the partisan movement in the post-war politics of north central Italy where much of the partisan activity took place. This part of the country has a tradition of opposition dating from at least the anti-Papalism of the Risorgimento; it has also a significant proportion of landless rural labourers. Since the war Emilia at its northern and Umbria at its southern end have given the communists their strongest base and their only popular majorities over the Christian Democrats, and between these two extremes the area, if less 'red', has still been consistently red with the exception only of a dent in Romagna where the radical but anti-communist Republican Party has been traditionally strong.

The attitude of the allies to the partisans was mixed. Churchill was in favour of guerrillas who harassed Germans. Most professional generals were hardly even that and all of them – generals, Churchill and other political leaders – were opposed to a national rising amounting to a civil war. Even in the midst of a Great War the idea of civil war was peculiarly repugnant with its moral implications of fratricidal strife and the special degree of unregulated cruelty which civil wars have evoked from early times down to the war in Spain still vivid in many minds. The allies looked with a favour which was exceptional on the national rising in Yugoslavia because it was successful and directed against their enemies and because they themselves were not there; but in Italy it was not so clear to the allies that the partisans were fighting against a common enemy and, besides, their activities might get in the way of allied military operations. The allies also, perhaps consequently, underrated the Italian effort. They were used to thinking of the Italian army as bad fighters and could hardly imagine that guerrilla forces might fight better than regular ones. Nevertheless allied aid, mainly British, was bountiful. It included 3,000 tons of supplies dropped by parachute – about half the partisans' total requirements.

After the fall of Rome partisan warfare in the countryside was intensified. So was sabotage by special action groups in towns. A series of strikes in northern cities in 1943 was capped in March 1944 by a general strike called by the CLN throughout the north. A million men and women responded and the strike lasted eight days. The Italian partisans became as numerous as any Resistance movement in Europe. By mid-1944 they numbered about 100,000 and were on their way to double or treble that strength before the war ended. Partisans killed, wounded or captured at least 50,000 Germans. Their own losses were heavy, particularly in areas where they assembled in large numbers and exposed themselves to organized German attack and also when the allied pressure was taken off the Germans and their northward advance blocked after the withdrawal of forces to France. Thirty-five thousand partisans lost their lives and another 20,000 were wounded. Another 10,000 civilians were killed in fights with the Germans or in reprisals. In addition 9,000 Italians were deported during the two years of direct German occupation, very few of whom were ever seen again.

As the winter of 1944 approached it became clear that the war would last into 1945. When General Alexander decided in November that he could undertake no further operations that year he advised the partisans too to suspend operations and go home. His message was broadcast *en clair*, so that it was received and read by German commanders who happened to be engaged at the time by substantial bodies of partisans. The partisans were infuriated by the message for many reasons. In the first place they could hardly go home without being arrested and shot. Further, they suspected that the allies wanted to deprive them of any share in the ultimate German collapse and make sure that the Germans should surrender to the Anglo-American command and not to any representatives of democratic Italy; they regarded the allied command as covert allies of the Right and knew that the popular rising with which they were preparing to end the war and inaugurate the new Italy was feared by the allies as a bloody communist revolution. They also resented the tone of the advice, which seemed to them too close to an order, and they had occasion to rue its consequences when the Germans, relieved of the necessity to bother about the allied armies, concentrated on the partisans and succeeded in killing thousands of them. Even Mussolini took heart and appeared in Milan and made a speech there.

The weather added to the stock of partisan troubles. The winter of 1944-5 was severe and the partisans suffered from it more than the German regular troops. But they were determined not to cease from their operations or to forgo their claim to be the liberators of Italy. They survived and, as the overall position of the Germans became more and more hopeless, they were able to renew the offensive in the spring. In April, when the Fifth and Eighth Armies launched their final attack, the northern cities rose; in Genoa 9,000 Germans surrendered to Italians and other great cities were captured by partisans. So was Mussolini who, politically, had survived the king after all and was trying in these last days to come to terms with the allies behind the backs of the Germans and through Cardinal Ildefonso Schuster, the Archbishop of Milan. At a meeting in the archiepiscopal palace of Milan on 25 April Mussolini learned that the Germans in Italy were negotiating with the allies behind his back and he thereupon dropped his own negotiations and set off for the Swiss border. He was captured and then recognized by partisans on 27 April and was shot the next day with his mistress Clara Petacci outside a small village. Their bodies with those of other fascists were displayed a day later upside down in front of a filling station in a square in Milan. They were suspended by meat hooks.

CHAPTER 19

Hitler's German Enemies

HITLER was hated by many Germans before the war began and, like Mussolini, he acquired fresh enemies when his wars turned to failures. There were plots against him before the war and more plots during the war. At first the conspirators aimed to displace him; later they came to believe that assassination was the only way to get rid of him. At first they were anti-Nazis of one kind or another; later they included Nazis who wanted to take his place or simply to save their own skins. The plots usually involved the army, since only the army had the organized power needed for a successful coup, but towards the end they involved also the SS which had grown into a separate and considerable armed force (the Waffen SS). Others, anti-Nazis or Nazis, might intrigue but only the leaders of the army or the SS had any hope of overthrowing Hitler's régime and taking control of the state.

Hitler's alliance with the army was crucial to his capture of power and to the prosecution of his external policies. He devoted a great deal of his political skill and his personal charm to this alliance. He was successful in the short run but even before war broke out he had become disappointed with the officer corps and distrustful of it; the build-up of the Waffen SS was a consequence of this disappointment and distrust. In its early days the Nazi Party had appealed to a number of German officers because they despised the civilian Weimar republic or were bored by it and were attracted by Hitler's promises of a better place for the army in a Nazi Germany and by Hitler's genuine personal interest in military matters. Hitler took care to moderate the radical strains in the Nazi Party which were likely to antagonize the preponderantly conservative officer corps and he traded on the political simplicity of a class which saw politics in black and white terms and was looking only for the most suitable partners with whom to fight socialism and Communism. Field Marshal Werner von Blomberg, who became Minister for War when Hitler became Chancellor, had deluded himself into thinking that the Nazi Party was based on military virtues and military values and he saw no danger in letting Hitler gradually extend his influence by indoctrinating the services with Nazi propaganda. A handful of officers, notably Generals von Reichenau and Rommel, were openly enthusiastic about the party and its leader, although this enthusiasm began very soon to turn to disenchantment and then hostility. Others, like the Commander-in-Chief, Werner Freiherr von Fritsch, had reservations. Fritsch was appointed Commander-in-Chief by Hindenburg in 1934. He came from a civilian, not an army, background, but he had proved to be a brilliant officer. In character he was extremely reserved, inclined to self-doubt and – adopting the army tradition – non-political in the sense of not wanting to have anything to do with politics and not understanding much about it. He was not Hitler's choice for the post and he made Hitler uneasy.

Hitler's alliance with the army had been cemented in 1934 by the destruction of the SA and by the Soldiers' Oath but it was not followed by the wholehearted partnership which Hitler had hoped for. The army played along with Hitler without letting him feel that he was one of them. Hitler explained his aims and attitudes to selected groups of officers on more than one occasion and at great length, but their response was not enthusiastic. The more he made it clear to them that the army's role was to conquer *Lebensraum* in the east, the more sceptical and chilling did they become. Hitler did not understand that, like most professionals, the generals were conservative and cautious, nor did he appreciate the persistence of pro-Russian feeling inculcated by Seeckt's post-war policy of collaboration and by the respect learned on the eastern front in the First World War. By 1938, having sacrificed the SA to the army, he was finding the army an unsatisfactory tool. He decided to change its leadership and an outlook which seemed to him altogether too defensive and spiritless.

Two years earlier the SS had tried to tempt him into a plot against the army but he had refused to be drawn. Now, tempted a second time, he accepted the bait. Blomberg had just married a second wife. Hitler himself attended the wedding although the new Marschallin had been only a secretary. After the marriage the SS informed him that she had a police record as a prostitute. Hitler, who was easily shocked about some things as well as easily angered, agreed that Blomberg must go. He resigned, recommending Goering (as Commander-in-Chief of the Luftwaffe) as his successor, but Hitler dismissed the idea with the offhand remark that Goering was too lazy and abolished Blomberg's post. In its place he created a new Combined Services Staff (OKW) under General Keitel, weak in character and not particularly strong in intellect, through whom he proposed to exercise closer personal control over the services. This step was unpopular with the army.

Hitler also got rid of Fritsch. Fritsch was framed by the SS. He was accused of being a homosexual, which he was not. The SS dug out some police files concerning a certain Frisch who was. Fritsch resigned but his brother officers insisted that he should be given a trial. The case collapsed; the SS had to spirit away the now inconvenient Frisch who would have given the game away under cross-examination; and Fritsch was acquitted. He was, however, only partially rehabilitated. In September 1939 he was wounded in the course of a patrol near Warsaw and died, apparently not unwillingly. The army was perturbed by the Blomberg episode and revolted by the Fritsch case but it did nothing beyond presenting a memorandum to Hitler against the creation of the OKW. Fritsch was succeeded by General Walther von Brauchitsch, an officer with a high professional reputation but only moderate strength of character: his wife, who nagged him, was a fervent Nazi.

By this time the officer corps as a whole had seen more of Hitler and the Nazis and come to like them much less. The army had acquiesced in and to some extent welcomed Hitler's rise to power because it was right-wing and anti-communist and looked forward to certain professional advantages from the new régime. It was also anti-semitic, though not so obscenely so as the Nazis; it wanted to be decently anti-semitic. But Nazi behaviour in power and the Nazi programme, especially Hitler's readiness to risk wars which the generals thought they could not win, disgusted and alarmed many officers who had not thought overmuch about the sort of people the Nazis were. By 1938 this was clear to all but the most determinedly blind. But it was not clear what should be done about it. The German army had no tradition of coups and did not know how to set about them. Its officers had exacting moral standards and a high sense of their duty to their country and they had come to believe that Hitler was a disaster. But they were by temperament neither political activists nor conspirators and they continued to serve Hitler while hating him. Hitler had every reason to distrust them but equally he had much reason not to fear them. They abhorred treason, particularly the graver form of treason which action against the head of state entailed. (Treason had two forms in Germany: the lesser *Landesverrat*, the betrayal of state secrets, and high treason or *Hochverrat*, involving action against an individual or a group.) Given their training and upper-class origins it is not surprising that few of them reached the conviction that treason was right; or that those who did so reached it only with extreme difficulty. They hated Hitler for being a murderer but did not want to be murderers themselves.

There were, however, exceptions and one of them was the Chief of Staff of the army, General Ludwig Beck. Beck was a quiet and industrious officer, a man with a wider culture than most of his fellows, much respected, perceptive and high-principled. He lacked, however, the talents of the successful man of action. In August 1938 he was retired by Hitler who may or may not have known that Beck was plotting against him. Beck had concluded that Hitler's foreign policies were insane and were leading to a war for which Germany was unprepared. Hitler must therefore be removed. As Chief of Staff Beck had ready access to all senior officers and he was also in touch with a number of civilians who thought like he did – including Ulrich von Hassell, an aristocrat and former Ambassador in Rome who was dismissed by Ribbentrop in 1937, and Carl Goerdeler, a former mayor of Leipzig. Admiral Wilhelm Canaris, the chief of the Armed Forces Intelligence Service (the Abwehr), Major-General Hans Oster, one of Canaris' principal subordinates, and other members of his department were also in the plot. This group tried in the summer of 1938 to get the British government to make an outspoken attack on Hitler whereupon army officers would arrest him on the grounds that he was leading his country into a suicidal war. But the British government did not speak out and Chamberlain's policies seemed to show that Hitler was running no risk of war and was far from insanely endangering Germany. Beck and his friends, appalled by Chamberlain's visit to the Führer at Berchtesgaden and conscious that German opinion after Munich was more likely to support Hitler than a group of conservative generals and diplomats, half of them retired, relapsed into impotence. This episode is characteristic. The British government believed that the foreign policies of the Beck group would not be very different from Hitler's (a judgement with some degree of truth in it) and concluded that there was therefore little to choose between it and Hitler (a wildly false conclusion). The conspirator's argument was that a British move would make all the difference, while the British response was to ask why the conspirators could not get on with the job without it. Even the more resolute army officers such as Beck looked for a first move by somebody else.

This military–civilian conservative opposition to Hitler was not the only one. There was intense and sometimes vocal opposition by students and among the clergy: many hundreds of priests, Roman Catholic and Protestant, were sent to concentration camps and killed. There was also opposition among former politicians from the middle-class world of the Weimar republic and among socialists from its dissolved trade-unions. Communist opposition was mostly of a different kind and consisted of spying for the USSR. The Rote Kapelle, a widespread, if overrated, communist network which penetrated even the Foreign Ministry in Berlin, succeeded in circulating an anti-Nazi periodical in six languages among foreign workers in Germany and later operated throughout much of occupied and neutral Europe. But the value of the information which it provided was not great, and it was destroyed in 1942 by the combined resources of the Abwehr, the SD, the Gestapo and the Chi-Stelle (the German code and cipher establishment at Potsdam).

Finally, there were groups of younger men, mostly belonging to the upper classes but radical or socialist rather than conservative and actively inspired by Christianity. They too objected to assassination on principle and toyed at first with schemes for arresting Hitler and putting him on trial. But they were more adept in conference than in conspiracy and their scruples complemented the efficiency of the secret police. Their interests were diffuse. They discussed plans for a post-war federation of European unions under an elective, revolving European presidency, as well as debating the removal or murder of Hitler. They took enormous personal risks which led many of them to the torture chamber and the scaffold. Although they shared the primary aim of the Beck group – getting rid of Hitler – they did not want the same kind of post-Nazi Germany. They distrusted Goerdeler, who was the conservatives' first choice for Chancellor but who appeared to them reactionary, incautious and over sanguine, and they proposed instead Martin Niemöller, an eminent Protestant divine and ex-naval officer who was in a concentration camp. Prominent in this set were Count Helmuth von Moltke, the pivot of the Kreisau circle, which was a small discussion and action group; Count Claus Schenk von Stauffenberg, an exuberant, widely travelled and widely read young Roman Catholic; Fabian von Schlabrendorff, a mildly conservative Prussian lawyer serving in a staff post in the army; and Adam von Trott zu Solz, a man of unusual physical and intellectual distinction, a socialist and a Christian with special links with Great Britain from his years at Oxford as a Rhodes Scholar. Trott's dilemma and fate were characteristic of his time. Deeply troubled about the right course for a patriotic and democratic German he decided, upon leaving Oxford, to temporize and postpone a decision between self-exile and returning to Germany to fight tyranny. After a spell as a lawyer in Germany he obtained, with the help of the chairman of the Rhodes Trustees, Lord Lothian, a semi-academic post in China. In order to secure the chance to return to Germany and enter the public service (which he ultimately did) he sent a number of reports containing anti-British judgements, but in the course of reinsuring his position on the German side he forfeited the trust of many of his British friends, who concluded that they had been duped. When therefore, after the outbreak of war, Trott tried to use his British and American connections in order to get allied support for anti-Nazi plots inside Germany he failed; so strong was the prejudice against him that even Sir Stafford Cripps, a friend who knew his true worth and had become a senior Minister in the British government, was forced by Eden (relying on reports in the Foreign Office about Trott's activities and on statements by some of his erstwhile friends) to desist from attempts to get his colleagues to take the German opposition groups seriously.

These groups were in truth relatively ineffective, although they were not, as many people in London believed, spurious, more German than anti-Nazi and so not to be trusted. Within Germany the Gestapo probably knew a great deal about their various activities but did not think it necessary to do much more than keep an eye on them, at any rate until after the attempted assassination of Hitler on 20 July 1944. In 1941 General von Witzleben, one of the more determined anti-Nazis, was dismissed from his post as Commander-in-Chief in the west on the eve of Barbarossa – possibly a precautionary move. In November 1939 two British Intelligence officers in Holland who believed that they were in touch with plotters in the German army were lured across the German border and seized. These officers, Captain S. Payne Best and Major R. H. Stevens, had been outwitted by the SD and had been having interviews with an SD officer, Walter Schellenberg, who was posing as an emissary of a group of disgruntled German officers. Schellenberg had had four meetings with Best and Stevens in Holland and had established a regular radio link with them and he was preparing to go to London to pursue his game there when he was ordered, much to his annoyance, to go instead back to Holland and kidnap Best and Stevens. On 8 November, the anniversary of the 1923 putsch, there had been a bomb incident in Munich and Hitler may have believed that this incident, although probably arranged by the Gestapo in order to enable it to spring a few traps, was a genuine attempt on his life in which British Intelligence was involved.

With the outbreak of hostilities plotting within the army became more difficult. The army officer's congenital reluctance to plot was greatly strengthened by war, which made treason peculiarly heinous, and the worse the war went – the nearer the dreaded Russians came – the more untimely did revolt seem. In addition war scattered the officers who might have concerted effective action. Brauchitsch and Beck's successor as Chief of Staff, Franz Halder, a capable but stolid Bavarian, listened to plotters, swayed this way and that, but could not bring themselves to do more than not give them away. The plotters hoped for a military reverse which would serve as a prelude to overthrowing Hitler. The Abwehr tipped off the Danes and the Dutch about the impending invasions of their countries, and others hoped that something would go wrong with the campaign in France. There were attempts to suborn senior commanders – Bock, Rundstedt, Kluge, Manstein, Guderian – who showed where their sympathies lay by not reporting these moves and showed also their own temper and perplexities by doing nothing else. Goerdeler displayed his lack of judgement by persisting in his belief that the generals could be made to act, and the Beck group discussed whether to try to rope some senior Nazis into an anti-Hitler conspiracy. Goerdeler was prepared to accept Goering as an interim Chancellor but Beck did not like the idea. At this time the group's aim was to get rid of Hitler, open negotiations with Great Britain and France and end the war. The emphasis was on the restoration of peace and Christian morality – but without the restoration of Czechoslovakia; parts of Hitler's conquests in Czechoslovakia and Poland were to be retained and the *Anschluss* was to be undisturbed.

The war made cracks in the Nazi Party. The first to show were in the troubled mind of Rudolf Hess who, on 10 May 1941, arrived in Scotland out of the blue. He had flown from Munich in a Me. 110 fitted with extra tanks and after failing to find the landing ground he was looking for had parachuted to earth and twisted his ankle. He was rescued by a farmer to whom he gave a false name and he asked to be taken to the Duke of Hamilton, whom he had met when the Olympic Games were held in Germany in 1936 and whom he knew to be commanding a Fighter Command sector in southern Scotland. Hess was, like a number of Nazi leaders from Hitler downwards, an *Auslandsdeutscher* or expatriate German. He had been born in Alexandria, where he lived until he was fourteen. He had taken part in Hitler's Munich putsch and had shared Hitler's cell after that fiasco. Shortly after becoming Chancellor Hitler nominated Hess as his deputy in the Nazi Party and in March 1939 he was declared second in line of succession to the chancellorship (Goering came first). He was therefore a very elevated Nazi, very close to Hitler and intimately involved over many years in the enormities of the Nazis within Germany. He was also a hypochondriac and a devotee of astrology and his wife was a member of the mis-called Oxford Group – later renamed Moral Rearmament – founded and led by Dr Frank Buchman, who had on one occasion thanked God for Adolf Hitler.

Like too many of the senior Nazis Hess liked to try his hand at foreign policy, a pastime which provoked angry scenes with Ribbentrop (whom later he had to sit next to in the dock at Nuremberg), and in 1941 he evolved a plan for getting Great Britain to make common cause with Germany against the USSR. He tried to get in touch with Hoare in Madrid and with the Governor of Gibraltar, and after failing in these endeavours he decided to go himself to Great Britain, where he imagined there to be an alternative anti-communist and anti-Churchill government waiting to come into existence. Since he left a letter explaining his motives to Hitler it is reasonable to assume that Hitler, though presumably aware of Hess's notions, had no foreknowledge of his flight. In Great Britain his arrival was treated as a bizarre phenomenon and a propagandist opportunity (reduced, however, by Goebbels' promptness in giving the news of the flight before the British did) but not as a serious political event. His position as deputy to the Führer was filled by Martin Bormann, a protégé of Hitler who made himself indispensable by being always around, a mean-spirited man who came to be specially feared and disliked by the other party chiefs. Hess remained in detention in Great Britain until he was taken to Nuremberg at the end of the war to stand his trial on charges of complicity in murder and other crimes. There was some doubt about his sanity, but doctors in Great Britain and at Nuremberg declared him to be sane enough to stand trial (although an amnesiac) and he was sentenced to life imprisonment. The doubts about his mental state saved him from being hanged.

More significant was the discontent of Himmler, who began to see the writing on the wall after the failure of the Russian campaigns of 1941. Goering's star had fallen with the defeat of the Luftwaffe in the Battle of Britain and the bombing of German cities, but Himmler's was rising with the wartime expansion of the Waffen SS into a considerable pretorian army. This expansion got under way in 1942 as Hitler's distrust of the regular army grew. The Waffen SS, so named in 1940, had grown out of the small but independent SS *Verfügungstruppe* which Hitler had created as a military (not a police) force as early as 1935. He had shown his affection for it by donning its uniform when he appeared before the Reichstag in 1939 to tell Germany and the world that Germany and Poland were at war and he had given it special tasks and opportunities in one campaign after another. He also gave it the best equipment, but its expansion from 1942 onwards perforce diluted its ethnic and ideological purity and even its prized standards of physical aptness and it became a mixed force which included even Slavs and Indians. Himmler, who thus found himself at the head of a personal army of eventually thirty divisions and so a power in his own right, began about 1942 to weigh the advantages of negotiating with the western powers instead of pursuing a war on two fronts which was coming to look more and more like defeat on two fronts. (Later on Himmler's doubts were greatly stiffened by the disclosures of Cicero, a German spy who, for £20,000, stole secret documents from a safe in the bedroom of the British Ambassador in Ankara. At the time of the Teheran conference these documents showed, among many other things, that Hitler's and Ribbentrop's reliance on the collapse of the East–West alliance was unfounded.)

In May 1942 the Bishop of Chichester, Dr George Bell, who happened to be in Stockholm on ecumenical business, was approached by German Christians who asked him to impress on the British government the reality of German resistance to Hitler. Their plans envisaged the overthrow of Hitler by the SS, followed by the overthrow of the SS by the army. The Bishop reported these matters to Eden at the Foreign Office but without effect. The approaches in Stockholm coincided with other feelers put out in Spain and Turkey and the British government suspected that, wittingly or unwittingly, the Bishop's Christian friends were being used by the Nazis to initiate discussions designed to lead to a compromise peace which would leave the Nazis in power in Germany and in possession of much of their ill-gotten gains – or at least designed to sow discord between the western allies and the USSR.

In January 1943 at Casablanca Roosevelt suggested and Churchill hesitantly agreed that they should declare that the only acceptable conclusion of the war was the unconditional surrender of Germany, Italy and Japan. Roosevelt got this idea from the State Department (which later became lukewarm or cooler towards it). He wanted at first to leave out Italy but it seemed simpler to include it. The phrase 'unconditional surrender', with its echoes of General Grant's ultimatum to General Buckner in 1862, sprang readily to the mind of every American but there were also more immediate reasons for adopting it: memories of the end of the First World War and of Germany's later claim that it had never really been defeated; the need of the two western leaders to find something ringing to proclaim at a moment when they could not foresee any very powerful military action against Germany for the immediate future; and their need to assure Stalin that they would negotiate no separate peace with Germany and to prevent him from doing so.

The most pressing aim of the declaration was to hold the Grand Alliance together at a time when Stalin was disappointed and angry and when both Japan and Italy were working for a separate peace between Germany and the USSR – a policy which Ribbentrop was known to favour. In retrospect the overriding importance of this aim still cannot be gainsaid. To risk letting the alliance fall apart implied either that the western allies could win on their own or that they could find another ally. Neither during the war nor since has it been seriously argued that the western allies could defeat Germany if the German armies were released from their commitments in the east. The only alternative ally that has been suggested is the anti-Nazi Germans. But there was too little reason to suppose that Hitler was going to be overthrown by an internal revolt or that Nazism would be eliminated if Hitler were murdered. The anti-Nazi Germans were no substitute for the USSR. Nor would a victory over the Nazis with the help of the German army cut down the disturbing power of the German state and the German threat to European stability and freedom which had been among the causes of the war.

The declaration on unconditional surrender, whatever its strategic necessities, may nonetheless have done something to consolidate German opinion and discourage Hitler's enemies at home. Although it was intended to proclaim an uncompromising opposition to Nazism, Fascism and Japanese militarism and not any intention to eliminate the German, Italian or Japanese states, still less their peoples, it inevitably acquired wider and fiercer connotation. Yet in fact the declaration did not quench German opposition to Hitler. The army plotters were becoming convinced of the necessity for Hitler's assassination rather than a coup aimed at no more than his removal from office. First in a senior staff post at army headquarters and then as Chief of Staff at Army Group Centre on the Russian front General Henning von Tresckow was working to put conspirators in key positions. He also tried to win the active support of the Commander-in-Chief of the Army Group, Field Marshal von Kluge, but Kluge could not make up his mind and consequently a plan to shoot Hitler when he visited the headquarters in March 1943 had to be abandoned. Instead a bomb, secreted in a bottle of Cointreau, was put on board the aircraft carrying Hitler back from Smolensk to Germany. But the bomb failed to go off. At least five more attempts on Hitler's life were made in the latter months of 1943, all of them equally unsuccessful because the determination and daring of the conspirators were not matched by technical efficiency.

There was then a pause before the famous and nearly successful attempt on 20 July 1944, when Stauffenberg carried a bomb in a briefcase into the Führer's conference room in his headquarters in East Prussia, placed it beneath the table and left to fly to Berlin where Beck,

Witzleben and other officers were waiting to take over the capital and the government. But Hitler had not been killed – he was only slightly hurt and was able to show Mussolini the workings of Providence a few hours later – and the group in Berlin, who might have achieved something all the same, did nothing for the two hours during which Stauffenberg's aircraft was in the air and out of contact. On landing, Stauffenberg announced that Hitler was dead but a few telephone calls proved that he was not. The telephone lines between Berlin and East Prussia had not been cut – a vital slip on the part of the conspirators. There was confusion in Berlin, arrests and counter-arrests, with the established order quickly coming out on top. Beck shot himself. Stauffenberg and three others were executed at once. Then the shootings stopped and a longer and more comprehensive hunt began. In the east Tresckow committed suicide by walking east into no-man's land. In Germany the principal result of this ill-fated scheme was the slaughter by the SD over the next six months of many fine men whom post-war Germany could ill afford to lose.

From 1938 to 1944 the conspirators against Hitler had sought outside help, especially from Great Britain, because they believed that without it they must fail. Denied it in 1938 they desisted for a while. Later, driven by a desperate patriotism, they acted without it and failed. By 1944 the worst horrors of the war had been perpetrated and, had they succeeded then, they would have done no more to it than shorten its final phase. Some uneasy questions remain. Were they right in their belief that outside help was essential? Probably they were, for they were never more than a small band attacking the centres of power of an exceptionally well-armed, well-disciplined and well-informed organization – the Nazi party and police at the controls of the German state. Potentially the conspirators represented a powerful counterforce, for they had brains and devotion and the concurrence of some men in positions of power. But they failed to make the all-important step from conspiracy to success in action and there is something to be said for the argument that the missing additive could have been supplied by the British. This is a very serious argument, for it amounts to saying that the British missed a chance, first, of averting war and then of shortening it. To this argument there is no certain conclusion. What is certain is that the conspirators failed to impress the outside allies whom they needed. For this they were, partly and negatively, themselves to blame. They were a diverse group, at times a number of groups, and their schemes seemed imprecise and variable, their effectiveness doubtful. It was not always clear what sort of help they wanted. But there was failure on the other side too. Plotters start at a disadvantage because most governments, even governments which share their aims, are congenitally opposed to plotting. The characteristic members of a British or American government have some difficulty in making mentally common cause with conspirators of any kind and are inclined to underrate them. There was a lack of imagination, a failure to understand the drive which animated the conspirators, the counterpart of the failure of conservative ruling classes to understand Fascism.

And finally there was an aversion not only to plotters but also to Germans. Many of those caught up in the war fought it with good spirit and a clear conscience because they hated Nazism and wanted to destroy it, but anti-Nazism would never have started the war. In order for there to be a war for the destruction of Nazism there had to be a war about something else. The signal to start a war, or to accept a war challenge by an enemy, is given by governments and no government in the thirties asked itself whether it should go to war to destroy Nazism. What governments did ask themselves was whether they would have to go to war to stop Hitler – by which they meant stopping the territorial expansion of the German state. So the war, when it came, was a war against Germany. The part of Hitler's programme which provoked it was not the beliefs and practices of Nazism but the infringement of frontiers by Germany. The German conspirators against Hitler were the natural allies of anybody fighting Nazism but they were not the natural allies of a state at war with – or contemplating having to fight – Germany. The common ground between the German anti-Nazis and the enemies of the German state was not as large or as open as it seemed to those for whom the struggle was about righteousness rather than territory. In the last analysis the conspirators failed to find outside allies because, besides being anti-Nazi, they were also German. They were therefore doomed to be the bravest but the least effective of Hitler's serious enemies.

Hitler died in the end by nobody's hand but his own. From 1943 all his principal subordinates were thinking of how to end a war which could not be won. He himself was not. Once he had lost all chance of ending it on his own terms he gave little thought to ending it at all. He became obsessed with continuing it and, regardless of the true state of affairs, conducted increasingly hopeless operations by issuing nonsensical orders to armies which were shrinking to the size of divisions. His principal associates did not share his monomaniacal delusions. They tried, first by persuasion and then by conspiracy, to make peace with one part of the Grand Alliance or another. To a man like Ribbentrop who had signed the Russo-German treaty of 1939 a second essay in *Realpolitik* on these lines was tempting; he was supported by professional diplomats who had favoured such an alignment since the early 1920s and by the Japanese who tried in September 1943 (on the eve of the fall of Mussolini) and again in the spring and autumn of 1944 to end the Russo-German conflict. (But Ribbentrop later became disenchanted with the Russians and offered to arrange a conference with Stalin at which he would shoot Stalin with a specially designed fountain pen.) From the German point of view a peace or truce on the eastern front would release all Germany's forces for new victories in the west and re-open the flow of food and other materials with which the (then unravaged) USSR had supplied Germany before Barbarossa. During the winter of 1943–4 German emissaries were taking soundings in Stockholm, probably with the knowledge but not necessarily with the endorsement of Himmler, but such prospects as they might have had were eliminated by the German belief that Germany was still successful enough to lay down conditions, such as the establishment of an independent Ukraine.

But if Ribbentrop wanted to make peace with the USSR Goebbels, who neglected no opportunity to denigrate Ribbentrop, took the opposite view and developed a lively concern for the preservation of western civilization against the barbarous east – at the same time equating the Nazi with the Anglo-American view of what that civilization stood for. The invasion of Normandy strengthened the ranks of those who wanted a separate peace in the west, since they saw the impossibility of fighting on two fronts and the certainty of defeat in the east unless they surrendered in the west. The success of Overlord meant that Germany no longer had the slightest hope, without western help, of preventing the Russians from doing to Germany what the Germans had done to them. To prevent this retribution even Hitler should be discarded. Himmler, who had been fully informed about anti-Nazi plotting from 1943 at the latest but preferred not to take action, was toying with the idea of an alliance between the army and the SS for the removal of Hitler and the installation of himself as Chancellor in a new government consisting of a few Nazis and representatives of the military and the civilian oppositions to Hitler. His Waffen SS had grown to a force of a million men with the best equipment. (The other irregular army, Goering's twenty-two Luftwaffe Field Divisions, was of poor quality; its failures hastened Goering's decline.) Himmler wrongly supposed that the western allies would accept the substitution of himself for Hitler as an adequate consummation of the war in the face of the Russian menace and he entered into clandestine correspondence with the western allies through intermediaries in Sweden, Switzerland and Italy. These schemings played a minor part in the surrender of the German forces in Italy and in Hitler's barren last-minute switches of posts in the Third Reich.

CHAPTER 20

Great Britain at War

THE British experience of war between 1939 and 1945 was unique in that Great Britain was assailed and blockaded without having any of its home territory overrun and that its war effort was accompanied by changes in society and in the scope and structure of government which were presided over and directed by an established and virtually un-challenged government. In meeting their emergency the British were not able to superimpose a war economy on their existing peacetime economy, as the Americans did in the comparatively unruffled circum-stances vouchsafed to them by physical inviolability and economic elbow room; nor could they, as the Russians did, fall back on the vast-ness of space and the rigours of autocratic rule to get the most in human labour and human endurance out of a patriotic people fighting against an enemy within the gates; nor, finally, were they left, as many continen-tal Europeans were left, to face the present and shape a post-war future in the absence of a native government or in defiance of it.

To the question why Great Britain fought on in 1940 only an im-pressionistic answer can be given. It would take in an accumulation of factors, of which the most important are these. The Munich agreement of 1938 was a relief to a great many people who sensed the onset of a war which was never represented to them as a national or patriotic necessity. But Munich was also felt as a disgrace, and the sense of shame was compounded six months later when Hitler tore up the Munich agreement and completed his annexation of Czechoslovakia. That action finally revealed to the British that they had had enough of Hitler. The full story of the concentration camps was still to come but revulsion was now pressing hard against the dam of incomprehension. Moreover when war came, it came with a weird slowness, so that for nearly a year the British watched the approach of the storm; and all they saw nerved them for a fight where others had been unnerved. When prognostications of an unimaginable rain of death proved ill founded, the British found themselves spectators in a phoney, unnatural and yet humiliating war: no help was given to the Poles; no help reached the Finns, whose gallantry was at least equal to that of the Poles and more effective; Norway, a much respected country, was occupied by the Germans under the British nose. When the campaign in the west opened, the bombing of Rotterdam revived the German reputation for Hunnish atrocities in the First World War. France collapsed – a shock but in a sense also a release, since the British as a nation had no great opinion of the French and were as happy to fight, if need be, without a French ally as with one. Whereas Munich and the occupation of Prague and the growing evidence of Nazi barbarity had braced the younger generation for a fight, the bombing of Rotterdam stirred an older stratum of anti-German patriotism which, inclined also to be contemptuous of France, was undismayed by the prospect of single combat. And old and young were equally fortified by the retreat from Dunkirk which with a glorious perversity they regarded as a victory.

Something must be said too about British society. Although socially stratified to an extraordinary degree, this society was ideologically more coherent than most in Europe, less distraught by fascist or communist fissures, readier to respond unitedly to the generous humanity, the aristocratic chauvinism and the courage of a Winston Churchill. Furthermore, Great Britain was a singularly law-abiding, government-conscious and well-governed country. It was well governed not in the sense that the government was good for the people as a whole, but in the sense that government worked well within the limits set for it by the people who did the governing. Great Britain between the wars was not an agreeable place to live in. It was crowded with misery and injustice: estimates of the underfed in the worst years in the thirties go as high as twenty million. Little was done by government to help this large section of the nation and much of what was done was silly, for the governors were for the most part men of limited awareness and only moderate intelligence. Yet the temper of Great Britain did not become revolutionary. Rather did it become resigned in the face of chronic unemployment, killing poverty and the obscene slums which were among the most frightful places in which Europeans had ever been expected to live; and one of the main reasons for this resignation may be found in the fact that Great Britain had strong government. Strong government does not in this case mean repressive government but a government which never looked like breaking down or running down and which remained fully competent to perform its allotted tasks and preserve the formal framework of the nation's life. Although government was bad in the sense that it was inadequate in conception and in performance, it worked. It accepted a deplorably narrow view of its functions, but this view was traditional and excited little rebellion (except of the intellectual kind) with the result that the machinery of government did not become discredited. There was in 1940 in Great Britain neither a feeling of disintegration nor a movement to take the opportunity to alter the system of government. The British did not rebel against inequality and injustice because on the whole they did not believe in equality or expect justice. These things were too abstract or remote to be pursued or regarded as ingredients in real life: real life in Great Britain was steeply graded, material goods and opportunities were seen to be unfairly distributed, and even the law was accepted as one thing for the rich and another for the poor. But this did not mean that the British were supine. It meant that their demands were peculiar. What they did require of their rulers was freedom for themselves – the note which was struck in the seventeenth century and has dominated all others ever since in English history – and financial honesty at the top, and because they got these things in large measure Great Britain was, despite blatant social inadequacies, law-abiding. Freedom and incorruption were the secular religion of Great Britain (religion in its essential Latin sense of something that binds together), and *in hoc signo* the British engaged the enemy as a united people. At Mons in 1914 desperate men had seen angels in the sky; at Dunkirk in 1940 they saw German aircraft; but what mattered on both occasions was not in the sky but in tradition.

For the British the crisis of the war came with the fall of France. This event left Great Britain alone, exposed to direct attack, committed to a vast industrial effort to re-equip its armed forces, and uncertain about its food supplies. Alongside the military problems of survival and riposte was a twofold problem of government. First, the direction of the war consisted in a series of choices. Great Britain could not simply do what it had not done earlier. Doing some things meant not doing others. Men, women and materials were needed in more places and for more purposes than they could fill and somebody had to decide which came first. Only the government could take such decisions and so the government found itself involved in a range of activities which it had not undertaken in peacetime. Secondly, the direction of the war had to command popular approval. This was to some extent assured by the very nature of the emergency and by the confidence inspired by Churchill personally, but British society was sufficiently sophisticated and emancipated to require to feel in broad terms that the conduct of the war was efficient and to see that it was fair. The military front was left by the public and also by Ministers themselves very much to Churchill and his professional advisers, but on the home front the government acknowledged the need to assume new responsibilities for an equitable distribution of the burdens of war and for post-war reforms. Churchill promised blood, toil, tears and sweat. But his government had to do more than promise what Clemenceau had called the grandeurs and miseries of war.

Social awareness and a social conscience were not a product of the Second World War. They can be glimpsed in British history in the earlier part of the century and indeed much earlier than that. In the thirties unemployment had thrust itself, with the help of the press, on public attention. Most people knew that slums existed, even if they had no idea what they were like. But the depression between the wars frightened members of the ruling class even more than it touched their consciences. They feared for their own standard of living (which they were apt to confuse with the wealth of the nation) and they were as much afraid of the poor as sorry for them. So they nailed their slogans to the mast of orthodox economics, demanded reduced expenditure even if it meant wage cuts, imposed heavy imports duties to keep prices up and opposed schemes for the relief of poverty as utopian and a threat to the value of sterling – which, by inverting their priorities, they regarded as more vital than finding work for the unemployed. The war, like previous wars, affected this emotional muddle in two ways. By throwing people together, whether in the armed forces or in fire-watching posts or in civilian billets or in the reception areas where urban evacuees migrated, it forced people to become rather less ignorant of each other's circumstances than they had been, or had preferred to be, before. Shock, shame and comradeship created a positive desire for reform for idealistic reasons. Secondly, by creating an emergency which required the mobilization of the whole nation, war forced government to take note of the whole nation, to make it fit for the fight in body and spirit and to cater for its basic needs. The health and morale of the entire population became, in the Second World War, a matter of the first concern in the same way as the stamina of professional armies and their loyalty to their princes had been the essence of warmaking in earlier times. Looking after the whole population, in and out of uniform, became a function of government for practical reasons. On the material side it included the provision of food, accommodation, medical services, adequate working conditions, fair wages; on the spiritual side it involved justifying the war morally (not difficult with the Nazis as enemies), making people feel that their hardships were being equitably shared and assuring them a better society when the war was over and not merely a return to things as they had been.

The relief of poverty, however poverty may be defined, had long been regarded as a proper function of government, as witness a series of acts from the Elizabethan poor law to industrial insurance. During the war government came to provide for people for other reasons too: because they were pregnant or because they were old (even if they were not necessitous) or because they were very young. Therefore the war became a stepping stone in the slow and piecemeal progress from the concept of relief to the concept of welfare. Further, attitudes to poverty itself changed too. The old poor law had been administered locally; the right to relief existed only within the parish. But many people no longer lived all their lives in the places where they were born, and the increased mobility of the population in wartime finally destroyed a basis for poor relief which had long been out of date as well as inhuman. The poor became a charge on the nation instead of a charge on the parish, and local authorities ceased to have an interest in chasing away poor people who might by tarrying acquire claims on the local budget.

The immediate need in the early summer of 1940 was to re-equip the armed forces and survive the air bombardment which was bound to come. This meant specially hard work in specially difficult conditions. Many basic pre-requisites were missing. British industry was short of equipment, notably machine tools, and of certain raw materials, notably steel, rubber and aluminium. It was also short of factory space and of statistics about factory space: neither industry itself nor government knew how much space there was or how it was being used or how it might be adapted for war. Much effort was put into new building when it could more economically have been employed in conversion. There was not a serious overall shortage of manpower but there was a shortage of some special skills. There was also a ludicrous and throttling lack of statistical information about manpower – information about how many people were doing what where, for example, how many people were employed in the building industry. The first wartime government had done little to remedy these deficiencies and the second, taking office on the day when Hitler attacked in the west, still did not know what was scarce and what was not: it assumed, for example, that there could be no shortage of coal or shipping. Its difficulties were compounded by the losses of men and material in France, by the primitive inefficiency of much of British industrial management, and by unforeseen shortages of foreign currency. Required to build and equip new factories, to replace lost weapons and design and produce new ones, to feed the population, ensure a bearable standard of living and bearable working conditions, and to import essential minima of overseas raw materials, it was forced to plan in a time of unprecedented stringencies and turmoil.

There were three principal domestic upheavals during the war. They were caused by evacuations, the blitz and the break-up of families through the direction of men into the armed forces or to industrial work away from home and the flow of women into factories, agriculture and the services. The government assumed the task of regulating these changes and mitigating their unwelcome consequences. The complex series of measures introduced for these purposes covered the provision and rationing of food and other goods, the control of manpower and the regulation of working conditions, the control of prices, the provision of new social services for all classes of the population and the preparation of social reforms for post-war Great Britain.

Because the damage which the Luftwaffe would do to London and other big cities had been greatly exaggerated, the government had prepared, among other things, a plan for moving several million people out of the main target areas. The general principles, adopted in 1938, were: the designation of evacuation, reception and neutral areas; no compulsory removal, except from special areas where national security rather than personal security so required; schoolchildren to be moved *en masse* with their teachers; and the government to take compulsory billeting powers. When war came, close on 1.75 million people were moved by train and boat under the government's scheme. They included very young children with their mothers, pregnant women, the blind and crippled, inmates of hospitals and prisons, and government departments. In addition two million people moved themselves (and over 8,000 went to the United States and Canada, one quarter of them with government aid). This migration of close on four million persons was smaller than had been expected, but the private enterprise element was larger: in some specially attractive areas official immigrants were outnumbered by eight to one. In general the arrangements at the points of departure were fair to good, the arrangements in the reception areas fair to bad. Owing partly to official parsimony and partly to the filling of prospective billets by unofficial, and usually more welcome, refugees the accommodation of the government's charges sometimes verged on the chaotic, and the refugees were made to perceive the distaste of country people for what were called, and sometimes were, urban dregs. Elsewhere their reception was all that generosity could desire. But everywhere there was a bit of a shock. Town children were not only put out by the change of scene, they were also disturbed by being separated from their families and became the more prone to obstreperousness by day and bed-wetting at night. The hosts looked with horror and for the first time at children whose clothes were thin and dirty and torn and whose hair had lice in it; some of them began to feel that much was being asked of them, even if there was a war on, others that not enough had been asked of them in peacetime to remedy the social ills of slum life which had never before been brought home to them. Such encounters may be salutary but they are hardly ever easy for either side. By the end of the year a million of the evacuees had decided that they would rather go back to the cities again. The discomforts of social adjustment, and the false sense of security engendered by the phoney war, repopulated the target areas. In 1940 a second evacuation took place when, after the fall of France, 200,000 schoolchildren were moved from London and other cities and some of the more exposed coastal zones were redesignated evacuation areas, but the partial failure of the first wave of evacuation caused a number of people to opt for bombing and death.

A secondary consequence of evacuation was an enormous increase in the mobility of the population. Military service and compulsory direction of labour had the same effect, and over the whole period of the war the number of moves made from one home to another inside Great Britain exceeded the total number of the population.

The London blitz, which began on 7 September 1940 and continued for seventy-six consecutive nights with only one intermission, caused great dislocation and some discontent, which were countered by solidarity and comradeship in adversity, by the efficiency of voluntary bodies and by the active sympathy and interest of superior beings like Churchill and the king and queen. Although the weight of the attack had been so far over-estimated that the tonnage of bombs dropped on London in the whole war was less than what had been expected in the first two weeks, the damage per ton was higher and the trouble and danger caused by unexploded bombs (5–10 per cent of the total) unforeseen. Casualties per ton on the other hand were lighter – fifteen to twenty per ton in place of the estimated fifty to seventy, a reflection not only of happily inaccurate forecasting but also of the effectiveness of precautions ranging from shelters in basements, gardens and subways to rescue, ambulance and hospital services. On the other hand victims often did not know what relief services existed or where they were to be found. There was much improvisation, for the homeless turned out to be a bigger problem than the dead, and the raids came by night instead of by day. Sleeping facilities had to be provided in underground railways and other public places, and rest centres – mostly provided at this stage by private effort – were initially too few, underequipped and overcrowded. At one point in 1940 there were about

25,000 homeless people in London and, in addition to death and destruction, human beings had to contend with lack of sleep, more dirt and more broken glass than most people had thought about, the blackout, sirens (reduced on Churchill's command from a two-minute to a one-minute wail), an increase in the accident rate especially among children, queues, and a continuous strain which was not totally lifted until the war ended. Outside London air raids were less concentrated. In the attacks on cities and ports which began at Coventry on 14 November 1940, when 554 people were killed and much of the city including its cathedral destroyed, the dispersion of the effort over two dozen major targets lessened the impact on each. The renewed attack in 1942 – the so-called Baedeker raids – was a tip-and-run operation which did comparatively little damage and the V weapons, arriving only in the summer of 1944, were too late to be a prolonged menace. Air raids killed 60,000 people, seriously injured 86,000 and slightly injured 149,000. Half these casualties occurred in London and two thirds of them while Great Britain was fighting alone.

The evacuation and the blitz were the two sides of a single coin depicting the parrying and withstanding of the enemy's attack. In this attack the family, the basic unit in British society, was buffeted in its two vital parts: the link between the spouses and the care of the children within the family group. The British family had become smaller since the First World War, more compact perhaps but also more vulnerable. It no longer had so many older children to look after the babies; the older children were fewer and not enough older. With the father away and the mother perhaps doing part-time work there was no reserve for emergencies. Older relatives and friends, who might have been expected to lend a hand, were also more likely to be out at work and when the bombing began there were soon many houses with a room or two damaged and so without the extra space for taking somebody in for a night or a week. People who had moved might not have got to know their neighbours well enough to ask for the little services of neighbourliness. Looking after a family with these traditional longstops gone became a constant worry.

The separation of the spouses was another worry. Husbands and wives do not normally want to live apart. During the war one or both of the separated spouses was often in danger. Sometimes neither knew for certain where the other was. Letters took a long time and in any case not everybody was used to conveying feelings by letter; many letters were awkward, stilted compositions which said nothing of consequence except that the writer was alive and well, or alive and recovering from something or other; they were, as Wilfred Owen wrote in the earlier war,

... the sighs of men, that have no skill.
To speak of their distress ...

Many separations began on the morrow of marriage, and many of the married were unusually young. Although the marriage rate fell during 1942–4 (it had been abnormally high in 1939–40), there was an increase in the proportion of marriages contracted by persons between twenty and twenty-four and a very notable increase in the number of persons marrying under twenty-one – nearly one third of the women who married for the first time during the war were under twenty-one. The birth rate, which fell in 1941 to its lowest recorded level, rose sharply from 1942 onward.

The number of illegitimate births rose dramatically – from 26,574 in 1940 to 64,743 in 1945; the percentage of single and widowed women bearing children rose from a pre-war average of 0.55 per cent to 1.04 per cent. Separation was one cause: the number of husbands separated from their wives by military service may have reached 2.5 million at its peak, about a quarter of a million men served overseas continuously for the full five years of war, and very many more were absent long enough to promote the conception of bastards on one side of the family or the other. Civilian husbands too were separated from their families when they were sent to work in distant factories or their offices were moved wholesale from one place to another. Although attempts were made to keep families together, it was impossible in wartime to provide the necessary accommodation. The number of foreign servicemen in Great Britain varied between a quarter and half a million and rose to 1.5 million before the invasion of Normandy. Many of them contributed to the illegitimate birth rate along with the relaxation of moral conventions occasioned by war, separation and the shortened expectation of life.

But although the number of illegitimate births rose so that something like 100,000 children were born illegitimate during the war who would otherwise have been born in wedlock, there is no evidence of an increase in extra-marital sexual intercourse and the proportion of extra-marital conceptions in fact fell. One seventh of all children born in the last year before the war had been conceived extra-maritally, and nearly 30 per cent of mothers had conceived their first child out of wedlock. During the years 1940–47 one eighth of children were so conceived. The war affected what happened after conception. Whereas before the war 70 per cent of the parents who procreated before marriage got married before the child was born, during the war they did so less and less until in 1945 only 37 per cent married in these circumstances. In sum, the rise in the number of illegitimate births in wartime betokens no change in sexual behaviour but a decline in the opportunities available to couples to regularize the status of their misconceived offspring. The result was a magnified social problem, often misinterpreted as a moral one. The percentage of unmarried mothers under twenty-five dropped during the war, although in the higher age groups it increased. The biggest increase (41 per cent) occurred among the thirty to thirty-fives.

There were more divorces. The grounds for divorce had been extended by statute in 1937 and a number of men and women found in the services advice about divorce and a cheaper way of getting one, but the increase from 10,000 petitions a year just before the war to nearly 25,000 in 1945 reflected also a general loosening of family ties, Juvenile delinquency also increased, although it still concerned only a small proportion (between 1 and 2 per cent) of the young. Cruelty to children and neglect increased. So did truancy from school. But drunkenness was halved.

The government had to take cognizance of these social trends. The armed services adopted a liberal attitude towards applications for compassionate leave or compassionate postings by anxious husbands or fathers. By the end of the war requests in these categories were being made at the rate of 200–300 a day and about half of them were being granted. At home the government established and paid for services for pregnant women, young children, old people and even, with some reluctance and a good deal of secrecy, unmarried mothers. State care for pregnant women was a new idea. Before the war local authorities had been empowered – but not, except in the case of midwives, obliged – to provide services, but where they did so the quality varied extensively, some were very bad and the death rate was shockingly high. There was little comprehensive care embracing pre-natal, midwifery and hospital services because these services often came under different authorities. The war exacerbated the problem since displaced mothers were seldom able to have their babies in billets and there was an acute shortage of maternity beds in hospitals. The government therefore established emergency maternity homes, which had high standards and a low death rate and which proved to be one of the most successful of the government's wartime incursions into the field of social welfare.

The unmarried mother remained a being apart. Practically her only recourse was to the old poor law and the workhouse; when she left the workhouse, even to go to work, she had to carry her baby with her in order to satisfy the authorities that she was not running away and abandoning it. She could get no public assistance outside the area to which she belonged owing to the rigid administration of the poor law by districts and the determination of each district to guard its territory against trouble and expense from beyond its borders; she was, for these as well as other reasons, unwelcome as an evacuee in a reception area. Apart from the workhouses there were in 1939 only four publicly assisted homes for unmarried mothers in the whole of England and Wales and further accommodation provided by voluntary organizations for 3,000–4,000 mothers per year – against a total of illegitimate births which, as already mentioned, passed 25,000 before the war began and then rose steeply. The death rate for illegitimate babies was twice the normal. The armed services assumed during the war some responsibility for the illegitimate children and so-called unmarried wives of servicemen and the government, with a similar eye on morale, gave some niggardly assistance to those similarly situated in war industries, but for moral and financial reasons the government's scheme was run in such a hole-and-corner way that many possible beneficiaries never got to hear about it. The war dented attitudes to the livelier consequences of adultery and fornication, but not much.

The government was bolder in grasping the nettle of venereal diseases, whose incidence roughly doubled during the war. New centres for treatment were established (some existed before the war) and considerable publicity was given to the dangers, causes and cures. Some newspapers, putting prudery before health, refused to accept the government's advertisements. Doctors were given power to order patients to submit to treatment for venereal disease, as also for scabies, which, according to the Ministry of Health, was developing into a threat to the war effort. At one point the Rubber Control stopped the manufacture of contraceptives but this particular exercise of administrative discrimination in relation to a scarce commodity had to be reversed as a result of representations by interested parties – an example of the power of the consumer.

The care of children under five presented special problems since they were not evacuated with their schools like their older brothers and sisters and many of the mothers who had been expected to stay at home and mind them went out to work. The call-up of women was one of the more contested and controversial decisions of the war on the home front. It was foreshadowed early in 1941 when women were required to register on a limited scale. This step was partly a precaution and partly an appeal. It was hoped that women who had neither jobs nor household duties would go to work, but the number of such women turned out to be small and when industry, notably the aircraft industry, began to run into serious labour shortages the net was extended and the power to direct women to work was used. The lower age limit was eighteen and a half and the upper, fixed in October 1942 at forty-five and a half, was raised by steps to fifty. Women with husbands at home or children under fourteen were exempt, but they were nevertheless asked to work and 13 per cent of those with young children did so. Older women also volunteered for work. By the end of 1943 the female labour force had increased by over two million, half of whom were working voluntarily and for no pay. The consequences, during the war and afterwards, were considerable. Women undertook work which they had not done before and persisted in it after the war: the diversity of female labour was greatly increased (the main cause, together with higher taxation, of the decline in domestic service – from 5 per cent of households to 1 per cent). Women also became more accustomed to working after marriage, another change which stuck. It was discovered, to the surprise of some men, that in most jobs undertaken by women a woman was the equal of a man – except when she came to be paid.

Day nurseries for very young children had first been established in 1880. They were expanded during the First World War but allowed to dwindle and in 1938 there were only 104 in existence. In addition there were nursery schools and classes, mostly in very poor districts, taking about 185,000 children, that is to say, one in ten of all children under five. There were also a number of children in workhouses. Voluntary and official bodies supported welfare centres, health visitors, medical attention and free meals. These services were cut when war began owing to a complete failure to foresee the problems which would arise when labour became scarce and even women with young children would be exhorted to go to work. Despite anxious prodding by the Ministry of Labour little was done for two years but thereafter the exigencies of the situation – and demonstrations in London and elsewhere – caused the government to pay more attention to this section of the population and before the war ended there were over 200,000 children in day nurseries or nursery schools. They were mostly run by voluntary organizations and paid for by the state. A small number of residential nurseries was also established, largely through American and Canadian generosity although the government ultimately agreed to foot the bill; they accommodated about 20,000 children. Finding premises, equipment and toys for all these establishments proved difficult; it so happened that the makers of cots had been specially unlucky in the blitz and at one point there was a shortage of rubber teats which had to be imported from the United States owing to a shortsighted prohibition on their manufacture in Great Britain; toys were made by air raid wardens waiting for raids and by prisoners, as well as being sent by sympathetic foreigners. Finding staff was also difficult and the number of mothers released for industry was not very much greater than the number of women employed to mind their babies, although it does not follow that the scheme was of minimal value since many of the child-minders could not have been usefully employed in anything except child-minding. The standards prevailing in the nurseries were high, epidemics very few and the idea of nursery schools caught on and survived the war.

In making provision for young children and pregnant mothers the government was extending to whole categories services which it had previously supplied only to the indigent, thus removing the stigma of poverty which had inhibited people from asking for what they needed. It had also to provide certain necessities for the whole population without distinction of class or category. The most important of these necessities was food.

Much of Great Britain's food came from overseas. Enemy action and shortage of shipping endangered the nation's food supply and created a corresponding need to produce more food at home. But Great Britain had very little surplus land to bring into cultivation. Therefore more food involved changes in uses of existing agricultural land and greater productivity per acre. This in turn meant more machinery, especially more tractors, and the modernization of agriculture which had been neglected during the pre-war years. Imports could be cut by increasing arable farming at the expense of livestock since feeding stuffs were largely imported. At the beginning of the Second World War Great Britain's arable acreage was smaller than it had been in 1914 by 2.75 million acres. The government therefore gave generous grants for ploughing up unploughed land and for improvements such as drainage. It also helped marginal farmers – a policy which was continued after the war. In the course of the war ploughland expanded from under 13 million acres to over 19 million and tillage from nearly 9 million to 14.5 million. The number of tractors rose from 52,000 just before the war to around 200,000 at the end. Cereal crops increased by 50 per cent and so did potatoes. Milk production was maintained but the country's population of pigs, poultry and sheep contracted sharply as imports of feeding stuffs fell from 8.75 million tons to 1.25 million. Yet the food value of this diminished animal population was considerably increased by more intelligent farming and its money value rose by 30 per cent at constant prices.

The needs of war changed both the structure of farming and even the landscape itself. In some areas small farmers retreated before the economics of a machine age until the average size of a farm was ten times what it had been. Much ploughed land did not return to pasture after the war. The Wiltshire downs, for example, which had been pasture land since neolithic times, were ploughed and have continued to be ploughed.

Local War Agricultural Committees were established to give advice (which was not always well received) on such comparatively new subjects as chemical weed control and soil analysis, to chide and if necessary evict bad farmers and to reclaim and work any derelict land that could be found. They had considerable powers and they used them. They also owned and hired out machinery. These committees consisted of unpaid local people assisted by paid officials, one of many examples of the blending of the voluntary system with the new expertise and the new concept of central direction. Although they were regarded by a conservative countryside as a regrettable and temporary necessity, their effects were salutary: output per acre was increased by 10–15 per cent, total production rose by 35 per cent with only a comparatively small increase in the labour force, neglected land was restored, finance became available and profits were made. The farmers with the most and best land did best, but all did better than before. After the war the powers of the wartime committees were perpetuated by statute (in more circumspect language) but the new committees used their powers much less.

Hardly less important than the production of food was its equitable distribution. Great Britain's wartime rationing system was almost a work of art. The simplest form of rationing is to assign to every individual a given quantity of a limited number of specified substances. This system becomes somewhat less simple when the quantities assigned vary according to categories of consumers – infants, pensioners, heavy industrial workers, diabetics, etc. Furthermore even a comparatively simple system of this kind will not work unless the authorities can ensure the continuous provision of adequate stocks of the rationed goods at all places and times, a task which was particularly difficult in Great Britain's case owing to the uncertainties of imports. But the British system was far more extensive and flexible than specific rationing of this kind. It embraced foods beyond the basic necessities and gave the consumer a certain range of choice. The system was tripartite: first, it specified precise rations of some foods, for example, butter. Secondly, it rationed meat by price instead of by quantity, so that a family might either pool its rations to buy a good joint once in a way or choose to have less good stewing meat more often. (Offal, rabbit and chickens were off ration.) Thirdly, the system imposed a general limit on purchases in a wider area – biscuits, jam, oranges, sweets were examples – within which, however, the purchaser was free to choose. This was achieved by a brilliant, if simple, device called the points system. Every individual was allotted a certain number of points, represented in his ration book by tokens of varying point-value which he could exchange for rationed foods at any time in a prescribed period. The goods which fell within this scheme were graded so that, for example, a packet of biscuits or a tin of sardines cost so many points. The gradings were altered from time to time, upwards or downwards, in accordance with the availability of stocks, and the individual's aggregate number of points in a quarter was also varied in order to increase or restrain his overall demand on rationed goods (other than specifically rationed ones). The points system introduced administrative difficulties since the consumer's freedom of choice made it impossible precisely to predict the demands which were likely to be made in a given period in different parts of the country – people in the south-west might develop a marked taste for biscuits while people in the north-east were making a run on sardines – but the flexibility in demand and consequent alleviation of the monotony of wartime diet were worth the extra effort, and the scheme as a whole was a major success for government planning as well as a triumph for fairness. The opulent could not (in theory – though appearances sometimes seemed otherwise) get unfair advantages by eating large meals in restaurants because for any meal costing more than 5s. (25p) coupons had to be surrendered. No coupons were required in works canteens but these meals were limited to a value of 5s. – and usually to baked beans and a mass-produced wartime invention called, after the Minister of Food, a Woolton pie. There was little cheating or black marketeering. Besides food, clothes and household goods were similarly rationed. Each individual had a separate book of coupons for these goods. Overall purchasing power was restricted but within this general limitation the purchaser could choose whether to buy half a dozen yards of cloth or a pair of sheets or a new dress.

Food and household goods were also cheap. The government's policy was to keep people healthy and vigorous by keeping the price of food down. Price controls were introduced in stages until by the end of 1942 they covered all goods in general demand. Special attention was paid to children, who, in this and other respects, were exceptionally well looked after during the war. They had different ration books and were provided gratis with milk, orange juice and cod liver oil (for vitamins) and meals in school. Standard – 'utility' – clothing and furniture were introduced, and utility clothing was exempted from purchase tax. These controls brought the cost of living down and, since wages were not brought down too, many people were financially better off during the war than they had been before it – a particularly grim commentary on the social outlook of pre-war governments. Average personal expenditure on food rose from 10s. 8d. (53p) to 14s. 6d. (72½p): that is to say, people continued to spend roughly between a quarter and a third of their net income on food, although by the end of the war they were buying at 14s. 6d. slightly less than they could have got for their 10s. 8d. at the beginning of the war. This stability was remarkable in view of the great increase in the cost of food. Home-produced food doubled in cost; imports, although reduced in volume (by 25 per cent), also doubled their cost. All in all the annual cost of food rose by £726 million, of which £472 million was paid directly by the consumer and £254 million was met by government subsidies. The extent of government intervention is shown by comparing this last figure with the pre-war cost of food subsidies – £72 million.

By this combination of measures – food production, rationing and price control – the government succeeded in ensuring an adequate, if monotonous, diet and an adequate, if uninspiring, supply of other basic goods. The first two years of war, with meat severely rationed and all imports of fruit discontinued, were a period of shortage but no danger to health. Civilian consumption was rather restricted by the shortage of steel, timber and aluminium, of which there was little left over for such things as kitchen utensils, furniture or sports goods. Textiles were also reduced by the transfer of labour from the textile industry to more urgent war production; part of the textile industry never recovered the labour and the markets which they lost. These were the years of the biggest cuts in civilian standards, personal expenditure on food dropping by 20 per cent during 1941, on other household goods by more than 40 per cent and on clothes by 38 per cent. There was, however, a compensating gain. The quality of what was available improved. The government imposed minimum standards on such goods as 'utility' furniture and fabrics, so that although richer people had to make do with goods inferior to what they had been used to, most people were getting a better buy than before the war. Design too, as well as the material itself and the workmanship, improved over a whole range of goods which had previously been turned out tastelessly for a public which was supposed not to care. Cheapness was no longer synonymous with shoddiness.

From 1942 life continued on a reduced plateau, which people at large accepted and the government maintained with such variations as it might introduce when supplies could be improved and the balance between military requirements and the demands of civilian morale could be adjusted. Housing began to present a bigger problem than food or goods. By the end of 1941 300,000 families were living in sub-standard houses and no fewer than 2.5 million persons in houses which had suffered bomb damage of varying degree. There was overcrowding and discontent, but the building industry was using the bulk of its depleted labour force (reduced by two thirds by July 1944) to build airfields and camps and to repair factories, railways and docks. From 1943, however, some of this labour had to be diverted to repairing domestic housing and converting large houses to accommodate more families. This work was given a high priority and in 1944 nearly 3.5 million men were engaged in repairing houses and maintaining and renewing industrial plant. They themselves created a lodging problem when they were drafted into cities in large numbers and their work was offset by the arrival of the V weapons but by the end of the war 40,000 houses were being repaired per week. Nevertheless the war left a massive housing problem which was only partially and temporarily eased by spending £150 million on 'pre-fabs'.

Although enough food of the right sort is the basis of fitness, diet is not the answer to everything. People still get sick or tired or bored. The government was therefore obliged to assume responsibility for hospital services, to intervene in the regulation of working conditions and even to provide entertainment and other resources for filling in time.

Great Britain's pre-war hospital services were an uncoordinated muddle, partially masked by the excellent and devoted work which went on in some sections of what could hardly be called a system. Hospitals included over a thousand voluntary hospitals which were unrelated to each other, many of them in shocking condition, short of equipment, antiquated and bankrupt. The War Office had its own hospitals; local authorities, of whom the independent voluntary hospitals were inherently suspicious, ran others. Apart from London and a few other rich areas there was a serious shortage of doctors and nurses. Plans had been discussed before the war for a comprehensive state hospital service but they made little headway against the rivalries of the different hospital bodies. Estimates of likely civilian casualties produced an irremediable problem: about 250,000 beds could be made available by cramping patients and staff and lowering standards of care and hygiene as against an anticipated need for 1 million to 2.8 million beds. Fortunately the problem never materialized and the government was granted the right combination of breathing space and exigency to impose (against the protests of the War Office and by overriding the independence of local authorities) a regional system in which new hospital boards, covering wide areas, allotted varying functions to hospitals of all kinds in their areas. The coming of war was an accelerator which forced a highly unsatisfactory state of affairs on the attention of government, provided an excuse for the beginnings of action and laid the basis for a new system in which the distinctions between the different kinds of hospital would be eliminated by overall state control, and a more sensible area of management – the region – would replace both the single voluntary hospital and the variety of local authorities which were often too small or too poor to do the job properly.

Hospitals clearly existed to perform a public service. In 1939 this was not true of the railways, which were generally considered to exist to make a profit. They were also unprepared for war and barely fulfilled their function in it. Before the war it was assumed that there would be no lack of carrying capacity on the railways and that they could cope with twice the amount of normal goods traffic provided the turn-around of wagons was accelerated and passenger travel drastically curtailed. But curtailing passenger facilities has psychological, not merely statistical, consequences and there were in any case no solid statistical grounds for this optimism, the main effect of which was to absolve the government from making any overall plans for war transport. The first winter of war exposed the fallacy. The distribution of coal was held up to such an extent that a quantity had to be diverted to coastal shipping and for several weeks coal was given absolute priority on the railways in order to prevent a national outcry. This was only the foretaste of a crisis which was compounded by the strains of a population on the move, by bombing and by the closure of ports, which forced traffic away from the coastal and into the inland system. During 1940 deliveries of coal to London, to take a single example, were all but halved and the points of intersection of the main railway lines nearly quivered to a standstill; cooperation between the different railway companies was far from good. In the next two years with less bombing and more planning, more coordination between the Ministries of Transport, Supply, Food and Mines, the institution of central control over rolling stock and road transport, and the loan of 400 locomotives from the United States and the War Department, things improved. By 1943 the government had established effective control over inland transport but it could not in wartime remedy the capital depreciation and mismanagement of the pre-war years and even as late as the penultimate winter of war about a hundred factories stopped work because they were short of coal. At this time the railways had increased by 50 per cent their capacity in terms of tons of goods carried per mile but they were also on the verge of collapse: government intervention and regulation were a salvage operation which averted disaster but could do no more.

Few things so frustrate industrial effort and fray tempers as traffic failures, and the railway failure during the war not only hampered production but also exasperated individuals who were kept waiting for trains (and buses) after long stints of overtime. Workers who had been moved some distance from their homes became specially disgruntled. Train fares were higher than corresponding bus fares with the result that trains were not used to full effect until fares were reduced and travel allowances given to the less well-paid workers. Transport was beginning to be regarded, at least in wartime, as a public service run for people and not as a commercial enterprise run for profit.

The government greatly extended its supervision of industrial life. Ernest Bevin secured the transfer of the Factory Inspectorate and the administration of the Factory Acts from the Home Office to the Ministry of Labour and expanded the whole concept of government intervention from safety in factories to welfare in industry. One of his first steps as Minister of Labour was the creation of a Factory and Welfare Division in his Department. All factories employing 250 people or more could be directed to instal amenities such as canteens and to appoint welfare officers. Bevin considered that adequate transport for workers, day nurseries for their infants and the rehabilitation of the disabled all fell within the scope of government responsibility. The numbers of factory doctors and industrial nurses were increased; when the war began there were only thirty-five whole-time and seventy part-time factory doctors in the whole country but by the time it ended there were 181 and 890. On the lighter side the BBC introduced 'music while you work' and outside working hours the government encouraged entertainers to make life as normal as possible. On the outbreak of war places of entertainment had been closed, but it was soon perceived that this mood was unhelpful and dance halls, cinemas, theatres and dog tracks were quickly reopened and football matches resumed. Museums too reopened although their most precious possessions were removed from danger and stored in caves, country houses and other refuges.

The main tool for the regulation of the pre-war economy, in so far as it had been regulated and not left to sort itself out, was monetary – the budget. The main tool in wartime was, however, not monetary but human – the allocation of manpower. The armed services, which employed fewer than 500,000 men and women before the war, topped 5 million before it ended. If civil defence and munitions workers are added to the armed services the total number required in these occupations of first importance was 8 million in 1941 and 10 million by the middle of 1942. The civilian labour force remained roughly static but had to be considerably redeployed. On the one hand a manpower budget was introduced. All users of manpower, military and civilian, were required to assess their future needs. These assessments were always excessive, sometimes falsified, and they always added up to a total that was not available. The reconciling of these competing claims was a cabinet matter. Secondly, in the civilian sector sweeping powers were given to the Minister of Labour and National Service (Ernest Bevin from May 1940 to July 1945) to direct labour from one occupation and one place to another and to forbid workers to leave specified kinds of employment. Bevin was at first slow to use the powers given to him because he was so short of accurate statistics that he did not know what directions he ought to give. He was also careful not to introduce compulsion until the need for it had become evident to those who were to be compelled. He himself gave much thought and personal energy to explaining the needs, thereby creating a sense of participation and comprehension without which direction of labour would have been exceedingly unpalatable. There was virtually no hostility to the idea that certain categories of persons having special manual or intellectual skills should be exempted from military service if they could make a better contribution to the war effort in some other way. The basic criterion was no longer the equal exposure of all to the dangers of the enemy's bullets but the graded contribution of each to a complicated mesh of national services. In one much debated instance Bevin directed young men away from military service not because they were specially skilful or specially clever but because a civilian service, coal getting, was desperately short of labour. At the beginning of the war, when there was unemployment in the coalfields, miners had been allowed to join the forces and the labour force had declined by 10 per cent before the government began to suspect that it might face a shortage of miners. Shortages of coal in the winter of 1940–41 were due to transport difficulties and not to supply. Coal was not rationed, but consumption was kept down by restricting the supplies allocated to coal merchants, and steps were taken to ensure that householders with storage space might not build up stocks in cellars at the expense of their less favoured neighbours. By 1942 it was clear that a serious crisis was at hand. With an ageing labour force, ailing machinery, incompetent planning or none, and a heritage of exceptionally bad labour relations the industry was unable to deliver the coal and the government created a new Ministry as a way of asserting central control. It also expedited and paid for the installation of modern machinery and decreed a national minimum wage – an important step in view of the low scale of pre-war wages in an industry noted for its insecurity and risks to health and life. In October 1943 Bevin directed that a proportion of the young men being called up for national service should be selected by lot for work in the mines instead of joining the armed forces – a direction which was popular neither with the recruits nor with the miners but which was necessitated by the decline of the industry and worked well enough to stem a further drop in the labour force and production in the mines. In the last eighteen months of war 21,800 'Bevin Boys' were directed into the mines. In 1945 175 million tons of coal were mined, 56 million less than in 1939.

Control over labour was matched by control of industrial materials (through a Production Executive established in 1942 and later expanded into a Department of State) for the purpose of keeping a just balance between production for the armed forces and production for civilian consumption and morale. By these two main instruments the government indirectly controlled British industry and sought to make the wisest allocation of the nation's resources in men and materials. Until the last year of war British industry produced 60 per cent of the munitions and weapons of war needed by British and Commonwealth forces, the United States contributing 25 per cent and the Commonwealth the remaining 15 per cent.

The manufacture and purchase of all these war materials and of essential civilian requirements had to be paid for. In financing a war a government has few options in the area of military supplies. It must buy or make all it can and pay for them by taxation and borrowing. Its choice is restricted to adjusting the balance between taxation and borrowing (when it does not have to do both to the hilt) and to spreading the burden of taxation in one way rather than another. In the area of civilian supplies, however, a government may feel less constrained. Subject to the obvious limitation of not calamitously underfeeding or overstraining its own people it may control the volume of goods supplied and their price with some regard to the financial implications. In other words it may screw down the level of privation more or less, and the less it does so – the more, that is, it eases the living and working conditions of the population – the more financial problems it creates for itself. In particular, a policy of cheap food and cheap household goods unaccompanied by wage control produces inflation. Great Britain did not abandon during the war the principle that wage rates ought to be fixed by bargaining and not by edict, the government accepted the principle that wages ought to be increased where they were particularly low or where productivity was boosted, and a steep rise in the cost of living early in the war produced inevitable wage claims. When these claims were met the working population had more money with which to buy cheapened goods. Wage rates were kept in check by voluntary restraint and a readiness to accept sacrifices, but nevertheless they rose substantially: between 1939 and 1945 money earnings increased overall by 81 per cent from a variety of causes, including wage increases (32 per cent) and overtime (20 per cent). Earnings rose faster than the cost of living index. (The figures were as follows. The rise in the cost of living index in 1939–41 was 26 per cent. Thereafter it rose only 3 per cent more. Since the index was an antiquated one it did not accurately reflect the real rise, which was somewhat greater. Given a pre-war base of 100, wage rates rose by the end of the war to 150, earnings to 180. The size of the civilian working population remained static.) But the gains of the working classes did not greatly disturb the economic gradation of British society. The rich and the very rich, although hard hit by direct taxation, found their compensations – the rich recovering after the war their ease and affluence through expense accounts and capital gains, and the middling and professional classes finding, somewhat to their surprise, that they were the principal beneficiaries of new social services such as subsidized further education of which the poor were often still too poor to avail themselves. Within the working classes the average wage of the unskilled worker rose from 70 per cent to 80 per cent of the basic wage of the skilled worker.

To contain inflation and keep borrowing within manageable proportions the government relied primarily on big increases in direct taxation: income tax, which stood at 7s. 6d. (37½p) when war began, was up to 10s. (50p) less than two years later. Purchase tax was introduced in 1940 – in two grades, 16.6 per cent and 33.3 per cent. An excess profits tax, designed to forestall complaints of war profiteering, was introduced at 60 per cent in 1939 and raised in 1940 to 100 per cent. The government laid down how much profit was too much – excess meant any increase over a specified pre-war standard – and this incursion into the operation of a market economy was accepted as not only inevitable but, in the circumstances, proper. But purchase tax was to a large extent a concession to popular feelings against war profiteering and economically a disincentive to production, and in 1941 the government tried to resolve this dilemma between social and fiscal policy by promising to repay 20 per cent of the tax after the war. Revenue from direct taxation was trebled. Indirect taxation rose by 160 per cent. But the government still had to borrow. Half of all national expenditure during the war (other than purchases covered by Lend-Lease and similar credits) was met by borrowing, at home or abroad. The government introduced a variety of savings certificates and defence bonds to attract the pennies and the pounds of different classes of person. The bulk of the national deficit was met by home borrowing.

The country's external debt rose by £3,500 million and a quarter of its overseas assets were sold. The United States government supplied Great Britain with materials to the value of $27,025 million under the terms of Lend-Lease (the pound sterling being at that time worth $5.00); taking into account goods and services rendered to the United States to the value of $5,667 million (in, for example, building camps and airfields for American forces in Great Britain) the net British debt to the United States was $21,358 million. Canada made a loan of $700 million free of interest in 1942 when Great Britain's liquid resources in Canada ran out. This loan was followed by a gift of $1,000 million and by further loans totalling $1,800 million. Great Britain's total bill for Canadian goods and services was $7,441 million, of which rather more than half was paid in cash. The United States and Canada were much the most important of Great Britain's suppliers and creditors, but non-dollar aid from various other sources amounted to £4,000 million, that is to say an addition of nearly half the total of North American aid.

American Lend-Lease was a blessing but a mixed one. It became available when Great Britain was left with no other way to pay for American goods, and all British dollar holdings and other assets in the United States had first to be sold, sometimes at considerable loss. For more than two years after the passing of the Lend-Lease Act the value of the goods paid for in the United States in cash exceeded the value of the goods acquired on deferred credit under Lend-Lease. The conditions attached to the loans were stringent. No British goods manufactured even in part with raw materials supplied under Lend-Lease might be exported; goods for civilian consumption were excluded, so that Great Britain had to use gold or hard currencies to buy such things as tobacco, thus depleting its dollar reserves, which the United States had (privately) resolved ought to be allowed to stand no higher than $1,000 million; and Great Britain had to undertake to eliminate discrimination from its post-war trading system and therefore to abolish imperial preferences. Reverse Lend-Lease was given to the United States without any strings. In 1944 Lord Keynes led a mission to Washington to salvage Great Britain's export business by persuading the American administration that exports were so vital to Great Britain that some conversion of industry to exports must be permitted during the war. Predicting a complete British collapse after the war, he was largely successful in his mission but in August 1945 Lend-Lease stopped in peculiarly damaging circumstances: goods to the value of $650 million which had either arrived in Great Britain or were on their way had to be paid for in cash. Great Britain, being completely incapable of earning dollars in this quantity immediately after the end of the war, had to borrow $3,750 million from the United States and accept burdensome conditions including a promise to make the pound convertible within a year of the rectification of the agreement by Congress. Until the end of the war Great Britain, like the United States, was in favour of free trade on the basis of the international post-war economy and had expressed this view in the Atlantic Charter (which declared that all states should have access on equal terms to the world's trade and raw materials) and at the Bretton Woods conference which evolved the International Monetary Fund. The convertibility of currencies was an important element in this scheme of things and the British government was sufficiently optimistic to imagine that the pound could be made convertible within five years of the end of the war. It was shocked by the American demand for convertibility within one year and unable to persuade the United States that this was impossible – as it proved to be when the free convertibility of sterling in July 1947 caused such a rush for Great Britain's reserves that it had to be discontinued after five weeks.

The purchase of war equipment in the United States was forced on the British government by the inadequacy of its own resources. American industry was not only bigger than British industry and immune from war damage but also more efficient technically and managerially and so quicker. By buying in the United States instead of at home the British government forfeited a measure of control over the nature of the product. It had, especially after Pearl Harbor, to persuade the Americans to part with materials and weapons which they needed for themselves and it had also to argue for designs which, although they were to be produced in the United States, were to be used by British troops and had to be as nearly as possible what British commanders wanted. These matters were handled through joint boards in Washington and by constant coming and going between the two capitals. Inevitably there were disagreements about weapon design and for the most part American rather than British designs were put into production. When placing orders with industry the American administration would order more than it needed for itself in order to cover possible, but not yet precisely ascertained, British requirements. What the British did not eventually want was sold on Lend-Lease terms to the Free French.

It remains to consider the post-war measures adopted in Great Britain while the war was still being fought, and here a *caveat* is needed. It is temptingly easy to see in the conduct of the war on the home front a compact in which people agreed to work and endure, to postpone attempts to better themselves and even forego some hard-won gains in return for promises of post-war reform. This is, however, a misleading analysis if it implies that the work and endurance were conditional on the promises. Post-war reforms were not needed as a bait nor were they offered as a reward. They were worked out – in the exceptionally difficult circumstances of war – as an instalment of something due, to which the accident of war and the ferment created by it in Great Britain contributed.

The impulse came from the Labour Party, which was the more insistent on wartime action because it did not expect to win the first post-war election. It was supported by Liberals and Tory reformers with similar aims and ideals, but opposed by the larger part of the Conservative Party and press which denounced social inquiry as a diversion from the war effort and, in extreme cases, as opening the door to Communism. Churchill himself was hostile but consented under pressure to the setting-up of an inter-departmental committee of civil servants with Sir William Beveridge as chairman to consider Social Insurance and Allied Services. The first initiative had come from the TUC, and the appointment of the Beveridge committee was partly a way of fending it off. But the committee came to life in an unusual way. Beveridge was not only an exceptionally well-equipped civil servant but a much less retiring one than most with a keen desire for radical reform and a no less keen political sense. He perceived that a report of the usual kind signed by the whole committee would be too tame and he got everybody concerned to agree that it should carry his own signature alone. The report, published in November 1942, was a closely reasoned and numerate technical document but its main lines were clear enough and radical enough to evoke great enthusiasm and great hostility. Beveridge proposed the extension of social insurance to the entire population on a compulsory contributory basis by which the cost would be shared between employers, employed and the Exchequer. He also declared that social insurance required new policies in relation to health, education, housing and unemployment. The opponents of welfare on this scale, reading the signs rightly, had begun attacking the report even before it was published. Alarmed by the spectre of continuing high taxation, which they regarded as a temporary war phenomenon not to be sanctioned for fighting any evils save those of Nazism, they denounced Beveridge's proposals as sapping the spirit and health of the nation. They were at the same time heatedly opposing Bevin's Catering Wages Bill which was designed to prevent employers from taking advantage of employees in a notably disorganized and therefore ill-paid industry. This opposition ultimately failed but Conservative hostility to Beveridge succeeded in preventing him from being invited to pursue his work. He thereupon produced on his own a second report on Full Employment in a Free Society which placed the prevention of mass unemployment at the centre of politics, argued that a return to mass unemployment after the war was immoral, uneconomic and avoidable, and attacked the view that government intervention in social policy must lead to an unacceptable destruction of freedom. The government so far accepted the paramount duty of maintaining employment as to issue its own White Paper on Employment Policy. These documents ensured that post-war governments for at least a generation would at the very least pay lip service to the doctrine that a government should plan to prevent unemployment instead of hoping not to be plagued by it; they asserted, even though without gaining universal assent for it, the proposition that a high level of employment (rather misleadingly called full employment) might be a prior aim to the maintenance of a particular ruling exchange value for the pound.

In 1943 a Ministry of Reconstruction was set up to think about post-war problems. These included the control of the environment and land use, about which three reports were issued during the war; a Town and Country Planning Act was passed in 1944. New Education Acts were also passed for England and Wales (1944) and Scotland (1945). They extended free education to children beyond the elementary stage. They also introduced a test to be taken at the age of '11 plus' in order, by dividing children into a clever minority and an ordinary majority, to enable the grammar schools to survive as separate and superior establishments. In terms of Great Britain's past achievements in providing education for all these Acts were a definite step forward. They were comparatively uncontroversial since the need for better education was evident on material as well as social grounds; the country needed more and better education in order to prosper and it had been shocked by the degree of ignorance and illiteracy revealed by the call-up of the nation to the armed forces. More controversial was the question of health and who should pay for it. A White Paper in 1944 on a National Health Service, raising the issue of a free and full medical (not merely hospital) service, was vague. It was welcomed by doctors as well as the general public but there was significant opposition to the idea of a salaried service and to the extinction of a private medical sector. It was, however, the precursor of the National Health Act which was introduced after the war by the Labour government along with a Family Allowance Act, a New Towns Act and a National Insurance Act.

The extension of the scope of government, whether to fight a war or to undertake a social transformation, affected the structure of government. Early in the war the Chamberlain government took sweeping powers by a series of legislative enactments, but it made sparing use of these powers and remained fundamentally a peacetime administration grappling with war problems rather than a war directorate prepared to accept and use the huge concentration of power foisted upon it by the nature of its responsibilities. The British system was government by the executive tempered by the executive's own distrust of power; the executive could do pretty much what it wanted but was traditionally shy of straying far outside the tracks delineated by *laissez-faire* dogma. This reluctance to take and use power was fortified by British belief in the value of voluntary effort, a belief grounded in experience and justified in war when voluntary organizations old and new played a highly important role in conjunction with officialdom. Nevertheless the business of war required the creation of nearly a dozen new Ministries, an expansion of the central government and a complication of the machinery of coordination in Whitehall which accustomed Ministers, civil servants and the public to think of government in widening terms. War also raised questions about government away from the centre. During 1937–9 the country was divided into a number of regions under Regional Commissioners, appointed, not elected – prefects, in the continental vocabulary – whose functions extended beyond the strict problems of civil defence. The Regional Commissioners were general factotums of the central government. As such they could be expected to be suspect, but they became in fact popular owing to the manifest inadequacy of the existing patchwork of elected local governments, which were very uneven in size, financially weak and endowed with only partial authority in a number of fields. There developed a popular demand for increasing the powers of the Regional Commissioners and so an opportunity to reform the geography and structure of local government by combining the old elective principle with the new pattern, but this opportunity was missed and the regions were allowed to expire. A unified fire service and regional hospital boards were the principal survivors of a reorganization which was otherwise expunged because, war being regarded as an ephemeral and malevolent phenomenon, most of its products were so regarded too.

More specialized but more enduring was the acclimatization of science and scientists in the machinery of government and the processes of decision making. This was another pre-war trend accelerated by war. It belied the view often expressed that modern science had become a world unto itself inaccessible to non-scientists, however clever they might be. The Second World War saw – not of course in Great Britain alone – a revival of the term military science in the broad sense in which it had once been used to designate a partnership between the field commander-staff officer and the inventor-designer, of whom Archimedes and Leonardo da Vinci were the archetypes. This partnership had been broken in the post-Clausewitz age when war became a profession for professional soldiers (notwithstanding that many nineteenth-century commanders were very amateurish indeed), but it was reconstituted in the twentieth century for two main reasons. First, new weapons became increasingly complicated. The tank, the aircraft and the submarine were already very different from the rifle even before radio and radar made them more different still. Designing them, and thinking of defences against them, were highly technical matters. The purely professional soldier could no longer tell the expert what he wanted because he did not know. He had to rely on the expert to diagnose his problem and find an answer to it. This was how the scientists came to present the air force with radar as the answer to the problem of how to stop the bomber. The scientist, tackling problems instead of waiting to be given specifications, acquired an initiative in war, which however he could only exercise in close consultation with the non-scientist. Secondly, scientists developed a new role called operational research. In cooperation with the fighting services they watched the battle and evaluated results with their analytical tools. Having invented new weapons they did not merely hand them over but took part in a continuing debate about the most effective way to use them. Thus hard tests of the effects of bombing during the German-Italian retreat in North Africa and in the capture of the island of Pantellaria before the invasion of Sicily served to build up the case for using bombs in tactical attacks on rail and road communications rather than in the mass bombing of civilians, housing and factories. The debate on this particular issue was protracted and bitter, but the significant thing is not that this was so but that scientists took part in it at the highest and most intimate levels.

These activities – together with the less ferocious aspects of science such as the uses of penicillin, the development of sulphonamides, skin-graft surgery and shock therapy – altered the popular conception of the scientist as a special kind of being who resided somewhere in the wings. Science acquired a place at the heart of the machinery of government, in the practical business of the conduct of war and, by analogy and under the name of technology, in the development of industry. In addition people began to recall that science simply meant knowledge. They felt that they ought to have more of it, even if its arcaner specialities were beyond them. Hence the debate on Two Cultures in which educated people lamented their inability to understand what other educated people were talking about and deplored the division of their culture into parts. They raised their voices against this estrangement partly because it was intellectually unhealthy and partly, whether they perceived it or not, because the war had shown that the gap was not unbridgeable. Hence too the growing suspicion that a system of government by men and women versed in only half a culture might not suffice to keep the country abreast of the times.

When the war ended the cost had to be counted. There had been much death and destruction. Damage to life and property had been less than anticipated and less than in the First World War; deaths in action, including the merchant navy, were 380,000, half the total for the earlier war, to which had to be added another 60,000 who lost their lives as civilians. But the blitz had been short as well as sharp, the V weapons had arrived mercifully late and the battles which were specially British – the Battle of Britain, the Battle of the Atlantic and the North African campaigns – were all fought by quite small bodies of men. Industrially there had been overstrain in some places. Inferior labour and materials had had to be used. The retail and distributive trades, the textile and clothing industries, building and pottery had all lost 50 per cent or more of their labour. Timber had been over felled. There was a permanent loss of some craft skills. Some overseas investments had been sold and the reserves had been depleted; Great Britain parted with a third in value of its foreign investments and a third of its gold reserve. But the investments were recovered or replaced within a few years of the end of the war and exports, cut by more than 60 per cent during the war, were restored to their pre-war level by the end of 1946. Here was vigour. The government was itself spending three quarters of the country's gross national product in place of one quarter before the war. It was doing so because its military expenditure had been doubled and it had undertaken expensive social obligations. The latter held promise for the future. It had constructed buildings and plant, much of it transferred to private industry when the war ended. It had trained more skilled workers than the country had ever had before and spent more in scientific research and development. All major industries except the clothing industry were producing more than before the war despite bombing and other tribulations, and Great Britain emerged from the war as a pioneer in nuclear technology and with an electronics industry stimulated by wartime investment. It had the makings of a more sensible control of economic policy in the practice, initiated during the war, of making estimates of the national income and expenditure – a practice which was unheard of in pre-war Great Britain and which amounted to a revolution in budgeting. The foundations had been laid for radical reform after a generation and more of economic and social failures. Even the arts were recognized as something more than a peripheral eccentricity; a Council for the Encouragement of Music and the Arts, created in 1939 with the help of the Pilgrim Trust, was later given a government subsidy and was preserved after the war under the name of the Arts Council. The strain and the achievement had been tremendous; there had been irreparable pain; the prospect was inspiriting.

War intensifies and simplifies emotions. Because of the pressures of an enemy at the gates the British people experienced a sense of community which loosened its class structure. Before the war the rulers saw their main enemy in Bolshevism, which was a threat to their class rather than to the state. During the war the threat was Nazism, which was hateful to all, and Germany, which was challenging the existence of the European nation state. Nazism enslaved human beings, Germany enslaved states and both reminded the British of all classes that they were determined never to be slaves. The enemy therefore stimulated national unity – as Napoleon and other conquerors had done. In Great Britain this national unity was further fed by a new richness of communication between governors and governed. On the military side Churchill's personality and talents not only inspired confidence but gave people the feeling that they were all in it together. On the social side – and it became more accurate to refer to non-military affairs as social rather than civilian – wartime planning and post-war planning added to the sense that the nation was one and that post-war Great Britain would be a better place then pre-war Great Britain had been. In terms of institutions war menaces democracy by requiring the suspension of democratic safeguards and processes, but in terms of popular participation and involvement in affairs war may – and in Great Britain did – nourish the substance of democracy even when it was temporarily dismantling some of its trappings. It gave more of the people more concern for and knowledge of affairs of state. They became, if not insiders, at any rate less outside than they had been. There was an enlargement of the body politic to something nearer the bounds of British society as a whole. The governors who had to look to the safety of the state and to the welfare of society were to that extent distracted from their pre-war preoccupations with the class interests and the imperial interests which had seemed to be their natural and proper business but which had either alienated or failed to stir the mass of their fellow citizens. The war made the British state more national and less imperial, more democratic and less oligarchic. It produced more social change than had ever been compassed anywhere in so few years, save only by revolution – and not often then. The ruling class abandoned the resistance of a generation to reform and therewith its own integrity. Society was no longer the same and the ruling class was no longer the same. The question for the future was whether, how far and for how long this impetus would be maintained; or how soon an enlarged ruling class would revert to the traditional role of ruling classes to keep things pretty much as they are, to institutionalize, to put a brake on change for fear of putting the skids under themselves. In July 1945 the British people manifested in a general election an uncommon seriousness and optimism about their common future. The main source of these feelings, and the main condition of their survival, was not simply the baneful fact of war but the clearing by war of the channels of communication within the nation. Soon after the end of the war these channels began to silt up again.

Part V

THE DEFEAT OF GERMANY: 1942–5

CHAPTER 21

The Battle of the Seas

GREAT BRITAIN'S survival in 1940 did not remove the danger of defeat. The U-boat might still succeed where the Luftwaffe had failed. The crisis of 1940 was followed by the crises of 1941 and 1942, when Great Britain's imports of food, weapons and materials for industry dropped to within sight of a war-losing level.

The essence of the crisis was shortage of shipping. Ships were needed for many purposes and all over the world. Supplies had to be brought to Great Britain across the Atlantic and from many distant sources of vital raw materials; troops and their equipment had to be moved to different battlefronts, including the Middle East, East Africa and the Far East; the blockade of Germany had to be maintained around the coasts of Europe, a task which was magnified every time the Germans won control of a fresh country; and there were special obligations like the dispatch of aid to the Russians by convoys which gathered in Scotland and Iceland to make the passage to Murmansk or Archangel. The fulfilling of these tasks against the U-boats, the German high seas fleet and the Luftwaffe entailed a battle which lasted several years and cost many lives.

The idea of a shipping shortage did not come naturally to the British. It seemed almost as absurd to suppose that Great Britain would lack ships as to suppose that it might run short of coal. In fact it did both and the reasons were similar. The neglect and mismanagement of the coalfields by their owners had become proverbial and had created so much ill will that it smouldered on and produced strikes even in the all-forgiving and all-compelling atmosphere of war. The shipyards were in not much better case. They were antiquated and inefficient, but such is the force of habit that the government did not wake up to the consequent dangers until some time after the war began. The provision of ships seemed to be one thing that Great Britain did not need to worry about. This complacency was fostered by the months of phoney war which were nowhere more deceptive than at sea. Great Britain lost 150 dry cargo ships in the first nine months of war and made good the loss by new building or capture. But this simple sum told only part of the story. Imports were affected by many factors: few foreign ships ventured to British ports; British ships had to take roundabout routes which delayed them (carrying capacity cannot be measured simply in numbers of vessels); at home, when the east coast ports had to be closed, unloading facilities elsewhere became overburdened; there was a shortage of hard currency to buy goods with; the fall of France increased voyage times by 30–40 per cent; the convoy system reduced the speed of all but the slower ships.

Imports began to sink rapidly. In 1941 they were 30.5 million tons of dry cargo against a peacetime norm of about 50 million. This was only very slightly more than in 1917 when population and industry were appreciably smaller, and yet the ports which were still working had difficulty in handling even this limited volume. 1942 was worse again – 22.9 million tons. Throughout this period cargo space declined. But in 1942 consumption at home was exceeding imports by the alarming amount of 2.45 million tons and half the imported raw materials consumed by industry had had to be drawn from stocks. Running down stocks at this rate was potentially catastrophic because stocks had not been built up before the war (wheat stocks at the beginning of the war were for three weeks, for example) owing to a facile and false view in the Admiralty that the invention of radar had put paid to the U-boat. The exploding of this view turned complacency into something like panic, aggravated by gross exaggerations of needs by the Ministries of Supply and Food and by the absence of any reliable statistics. Consumption was screwed down so that, until 1942, it was even lower than imports, but the corollary of this rigour was that rations could hardly be further reduced, or imported raw materials economized, without direct danger to the war effort, the creation of unemployment and a possibly lethal blow to morale.

In 1943 the decline was checked and stocks were replenished as imports topped consumption by 2.8 million tons. The balance swung into deficit once more in 1944 when imports fell by 1.3 million tons and consumption rose by 3.4 million, but by this date the U-boat had been beaten, the pattern of imports had been altered by Lend–Lease which enabled goods to be imported manufactured or semi-manufactured instead of in bulkier raw forms, and the government had learned by experience at what point it need get alarmed. But these figures tell the gravity of a situation which gave Germany its one chance of a substantial victory after the failure of its air forces over Great Britain and its armies before Moscow. For three years Great Britain was closely beleaguered and Hitler could entertain some hope of reconverting the war to a war on one front. Great Britain's survival at sea, which could never be confidently predicted in these years, saved the United States from the predicament posed for Great Britain by the collapse of France in 1940: whether to carry on or call it defeat.

There were two critical phases in this battle. The first followed the conquest of western Europe by Hitler and the second followed Pearl Harbor. Both events made Great Britain's position worse. The first cut Great Britain off from sources of supply, especially food. It put the Germans in possession of bases for submarines and long-range reconnaissance aircraft on the Atlantic coasts of Norway and France; U-boats took up new stations in concrete pens in Atlantic harbours and the long-range F.W. 200s began making wide sweeps over the ocean, flying from Bordeaux to Trondhjem one day and back another. From this time all traffic to London had to go north of Scotland (the trip round Scotland to London and back took more than half the time required to cross the Atlantic) and many ships were routed into ports unaccustomed to handling the cargoes they were carrying; there was much confusion in these ports. Finally, by closing the Mediterranean, Hitler's continental victories doubled the distance between Great Britain and Bombay and more than quadrupled the distance to Suez. Great Britain obtained some compensation in the muster of European shipping which took refuge in British ports and took service alongside the British merchant navy as one European country after another was overrun. Largely as a result of appeals – and veiled threats – put out by the BBC no ship at sea at the time of the conquest of its home port returned there, although not all of them went to British ports. Neutral shipping too carried goods for Great Britain. More than four fifths of Sweden's dry cargo shipping outside the Baltic did so. Not all of this can be ascribed to sentiment. Great Britain invented a warrant scheme and refused to issue warrants to ships sailing in conditions or under contracts which were damaging to the allies. Ships sailing without such warrants were denied facilities in ports under British control and in American and some other neutral ports, and found it almost impossible to get insurance.

Pearl Harbor inaugurated a second crisis by multiplying the calls on American shipping and unleashing a successful U-boat campaign against it. South African ports became so crowded with ships in search of asylum or in need of repair or on their way to the Middle East that by mid-1942 nearly eighty vessels at a time could be found waiting to berth or go into dry dock. The advance of the Japanese overland and at sea disrupted the economies of southern Asia by stopping the export of Burma's rice, oil and rubber and Bengal's coal: India's east coast ports were closed, the feeding of India, Ceylon and parts of east Africa became an allied responsibility, and countries round the Indian Ocean faced starvation and a general breakdown of public services. In Bengal in the summer of 1943 1.5 million people died of hunger. Thus commitments increased as carrying capacity was once more drastically reduced. It was at sea, much more than on land, that the several wars which together made a world war interacted.

The British government, besides welcoming the merchant fleets of its continental friends, bought second-hand vessels in any part of the world where they could be found, but this source was exhausted by the end of 1940. There remained the United States. But the American shipbuilding industry was in no better shape than the British. It had been allowed to atrophy after the First World War and in the years 1921–36 it constructed, tankers apart, only two ocean-going freighters. In 1941 total construction was under 1 million tons (lower than Great Britain's) as against an assessed need of 8 million tons for the war in Europe, excluding tankers and troopships and quite apart from whatever the United States might want for itself elsewhere. In May Roosevelt ordered 2 million dry weight tons, including tankers, to be found for Great Britain and other democracies at war. The British had hoped that it would be two million gross tons, excluding tankers, and all of it for Great Britain alone. (Two million d.w. tons equal 1.3 million gross tons.) So there was some disappointment as well as relief. Later in the year Roosevelt gave more help by sanctioning American escorts for allied vessels, by opening American ports to allied ships in need of repair and by Lend–Lease; but substantially Great Britain had to get through 1941 on its own. Rations were severely cut and some foods, including fresh vegetables and fruit, were deleted from overseas cargoes. The government budgeted on imports of 30 million tons, half in food and half in arms and industrial raw materials, and Churchill ruled that any reduction below 30 million tons must be borne by the Ministries of Supply and Food in the proportion of two to one. In the same year shipping was also needed to move an average of 29,000 men by sea per month, and it was estimated that the figure would rise to 70,000 a month in 1942. (The latter figure was almost reached. It included the transport of 16,500 men a month to the Far East in January–March 1942. The situation was eased by commandeering six large passenger liners which sailed fast enough to dispense with escorts and were refashioned to carry up to 15,000 men at a time.)

At the end of 1941 Pearl Harbor dashed hopes of increased American assistance. American construction was immensely increased in 1942 – to the 8 million tons prescribed a year earlier and then to 13.5 million in the following year, tankers and naval construction excluded –

but these astonishing achievements hardly sufficed to keep pace with the American need. The ships sunk by the Japanese at Pearl Harbor had to be replaced, while on the east coast the German U-boats, whose successes against British shipping were doubled in the first months of the new year, sailed zestfully into American territorial waters where the Americans, disdaining Great Britain's experiences in two wars, refused for several months to introduce a convoy system and lost in consequence a disabling number of vessels. In response to the crisis in the Pacific the great bulk of civil shipping requisitioned by the Administration after Pearl Harbor was committed to the Pacific theatre and when the Anglo-American invasion of North Africa took place at the end of the year Great Britain had to lend the United States troopships, dry cargo ships and practically all the tankers used in that operation.

Moreover, the estimates of the number of ships needed, and the time for which they would be needed, were both misjudged. For four months North Africa absorbed 106 ships a month in place of an anticipated sixty-six, and instead of going over to a maintenance basis in February 1943 the armies had to be kept supplied on a fully operational basis until May – the most serious consequence of the decision not to attempt any landing east of Algiers. These operations coincided with the U-boats' record month – 729,160 tons sunk in November 1942. In the second half of 1942 the United States was lending shipping to Great Britain but only on a modest scale, on a short-term basis and in smaller quantity than reverse British lendings to the United States: each American vessel was made available for a single voyage at a time. American aid increased Great Britain's carrying capacity by 7.5 per cent to 10 per cent in the second half of 1942, but British loans to the United States over the period of the North African campaign ran at the rate of 17 per cent of all the dry cargo tonnage sailing on British account (net of American loaned shipping) during the seven months October 1942 to April 1943. Great Britain's total dry tonnage cargo committed wholly or primarily to the needs of the armed services was greater than the total of American shipping committed in the same way – 8.5 million tons against 6 million. British requirements were at this time also greater since British troops overseas were more than twice as many as American troops overseas, British theatres of war were about twice as distant from their principal bases as American theatres, and the concurrent British civilian needs had no American counterpart since the United States did not have to import food or, to the same extent, raw materials. During 1942 Great Britain lost on balance 1.4 million gross tons while the United States merchant fleet rose by 2.7 million gross tons. By and large Great Britain's basic problem was its inability to match sinkings with new building. The United States built in most periods more than it lost, but the net increase in its fleet did not keep pace with the increase in its needs, so that there was a continuing conflict between satisfying the expanding needs of the US armed services and helping Great Britain and other allies.

The turning point in the Battle of the Seas came in the winter of 1942–3. In that period the U-boat was defeated. The Luftwaffe had been eliminated from this battle in 1942. Its anti-shipping force, though skilled, was always small. Its torpedo-carriers were a neglected and minor branch of the service; its long-range F.W. 200s were reduced by bombing of the Bremen factory where they were made; it was too deeply absorbed by prior commitments on the eastern front and in the Mediterranean. The U-boat was the weapon which threatened to turn the allied shipping shortage into an allied defeat, for the U-boat accounted for two thirds of all British, allied and neutral shipping losses during the war – 14.7 million gross tons out of a total of 21.6 million. Aircraft accounted for 13.4 per cent. Surface raiders came third. Of the tonnage sunk by U-boats nearly half – 6.3 million tons – went to the bottom in the year 1942. Over half of all these sinkings were in the North Atlantic.

The U-boats of the First World War had come so close to victory that Great Britain tried after the war to get submarines abolished by international agreement. Yet Germany began the second war with very few. Admiral Karl Doenitz, the commander of the U-boats, had argued in the thirties against the building of capital ships on the grounds that they would not be ready in time and that the space and effort could more profitably be used to build the fleet of 300 submarines with which he reckoned that he could starve Great Britain into surrender. Essentially Doenitz's argument was the same as that used by the champions of strategic bombing (whom we shall come to in a later chapter): he said that his weapon was a war-winning one on its own. It is not clear whether the verdict of history is that no single weapon can ever do the trick or that no government can ever be persuaded that it will. In any case Doenitz failed to convince Hitler and Germany began the war with fifty-seven submarines, of which thirty-nine were operational when war broke out but only twenty-three were capable of ocean-going operations. With such small numbers Doenitz could not essay the pack tactics which he had been elaborating and the first months of the war produced, as we saw in Part II of this book, no sensational results at sea. Then for eighteen months Germany's operational submarine force declined and it was not until the summer of 1941 that new construction so far outpaced losses as to give the force a real boost.

The task of defeating Doenitz and assuring Great Britain's sea-borne supplies fell first and foremost on the Royal Navy. But this was not its only task. It had also to secure its own bases, not one of which at home or overseas – even Scapa Flow – was adequately defended against air and submarine attack at the outbreak of war. It had, until 1940, to be ready to foil an invasion of the British Isles and it had to maintain – and, when lost, re-establish – important strategic routes in the Mediterranean. It had to nullify the German surface fleet. It possessed an impressive number of battleships: *Iron Duke*, a solitary survivor of the days before the First World War which spent the second war at anchor; ten survivors of the First World War of the *Queen Elizabeth* and *Royal Sovereign* classes; and *Nelson* and *Rodney*, both launched in 1925. The tally of capital ships was raised to sixteen by three battle cruisers, also survivors of the First World War. In addition a new class of battleships – *King George V* and her four sister-ships – had been laid down and the first of these were about to be commissioned. The decision to build these ships has been criticized as an obtuse failure to see that the battleship had had its day and that the money could more profitably have been spent on aircraft carriers, but it has also been pertinently argued that it was impossible in the radarless mid-thirties to foresee that an aircraft carrier and its aircraft could be any use except by day and when there was no fog.

From cruisers downwards the Royal Navy was uncomfortably short of modern vessels. It had sixty-one cruisers, but a third of them had been launched in 1919 or earlier. It had to obtain fifty old destroyers from the United States. Six of its ten aircraft carriers were old or converted, and it lost three soon after the war began. It was primarily designed to fight big fleet actions in which heavy capital ships would be ranged against each other and would prevail through the weight and accuracy of their gunnery; but so far as fleet actions were fought at all in the Second World War they were won by aircraft. It had paid too little attention to the design of aircraft suited for operations at sea – partly because it did not secure full control of its own air arm until 1937 – and it could call on very few long-range reconnaissance aircraft. The weakness in both these categories was not cured until the Americans remedied it. Between the wars it had, unlike the German navy, neglected the magnetic mine which both sides had used successfully in the First World War. It found that the Germans could lay mines faster than it could sweep them. During the crucial years to 1943 it was short of torpedoes, although the torpedo was the most destructive of all the weapons used at sea in the second war. But in spite of this backlog of deficiencies it prevailed because it was a highly professional and valiant force, because its adversaries had even more serious deficiencies and because it was seconded in its tasks by the RAF.

The lesson of the First World War on the protection of merchant shipping was clear: convoys and close escorts. This lesson had, however, been learned late in the war and after Churchill had left the cabinet. The problem was debated again intermittently during the thirties and the convoy system was adopted, hesitantly and conditionally, shortly before the second war broke out. But Churchill did not like close escort work. His conception of the war at sea was a series of sweeps, which he likened to cavalry sweeps. He believed that the emphasis should be at least as much on seeking out and destroying the enemy as on guarding the merchant ships. So the escort vessels available were split between close escort and wide forays. These tactics consumed fuel and wasted bombs and depth charges for comparatively little return, while the merchantmen plied their course at unnecessary risk. They were based on two false assumptions: first, that a convoy was more easily spotted by enemy forces and so more vulnerable than single ships and, secondly, that single ships could fight back successfully, if attacked. Not until 1942 did the figures and arguments of operational research convince Churchill that he was wrong, as the British cabinet had been wrong at the beginning of the first war and the Americans continued to be wrong in the second even later than the British.

The risks run by the merchant ships were accentuated by two other factors. Up to mid-1943 the Germans were able to read British naval ciphers which gave them the positions of British surface and submarine vessels and convoys. Secondly, the Royal Navy had been unable before the war to come to any arrangement with the RAF for operational control over the squadrons of Coastal Command, and even when it did so in 1941 that Command was still kept short of modern long-range aircraft which were allotted in priority to Bomber Command. Bomber Command undertook (among its many missions) bombing raids on U-boat bases and building-yards but the effects of these raids were disappointing and some of the aircraft employed in them could have been used to better purpose on Atlantic patrol.

The Battle of the Seas began in earnest after the fall of France. To defend their precious merchantmen the allies had insufficient escort vessels, insufficient reconnaissance aircraft, inadequate intelligence and inadequate gear for detecting submarines and destroying them. The

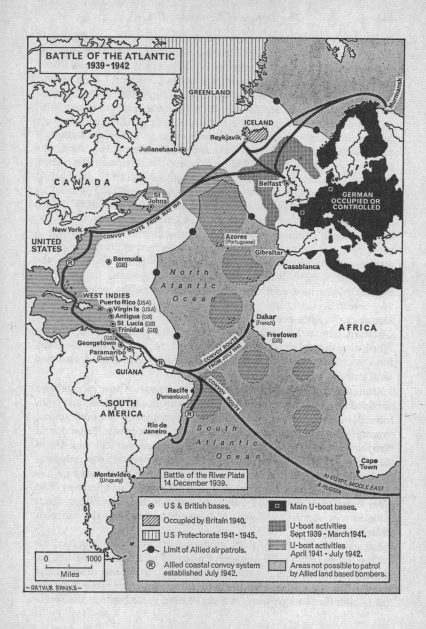

BATTLE OF THE ATLANTIC 1939-1942

GREENLAND

ICELAND

Reykjavik

Julianehaab

CANADA

St Johns

New York

UNITED STATES

CONVOY ROUTE FROM MAY 1941

Belfast

Murmansk

GERMAN OCCUPIED OR CONTROLLED

(R) Bermuda (GB)

North Atlantic Ocean

Azores (Portuguese)

Gibraltar

Casablanca

WEST INDIES
Puerto Rico (USA)
(R) Virgin Is (USA)
(R) Antigua (GB)
(R) St Lucia (GB)
(R) Trinidad (GB)

Georgetown (GB)
Paramaribo (Dutch)

GUIANA

Dakar (French)

Freetown (GB)

AFRICA

CONVOY ROUTE FROM JULY 1942

CONVOY ROUTE

(R) Recife (Pernambuco)

SOUTH AMERICA

Rio de Janeiro

South Atlantic Ocean

Cape Town

Montevideo (Uruguay)

to EGYPT, MIDDLE EAST & RUSSIA

Battle of the River Plate 14 December 1939.

~ARTHUR BANKS~

◉ US & British bases.	▢ Main U-boat bases.
▨ Occupied by Britain 1940.	U-boat activities Sept 1939 - March 1941.
▥ US Protectorate 1941-1945.	U-boat activities April 1941 - July 1942.
● Limit of Allied air patrols.	Areas not possible to patrol
(R) Allied coastal convoy system established July 1942.	by Allied land based bombers.

0   1000
Miles

German occupation of French and Norwegian Atlantic ports laid shipping under an aerial surveillance which forced it to take long and devious routes: an average crossing of the north Atlantic took fifteen days, a southerly crossing by way of Freetown in Sierra Leone twenty-one days. Great Britain lacked not only enough escorts to cover the convoys constantly at sea for this length of time but also escorts with enough range to accompany the merchantmen the whole way. At first close escorts accompanied convoys only as far as 15° west longitude – about 200 miles beyond the west coast of Ireland. This limit was gradually extended during 1940 to 19° west. At this point the escorts halted and made rendezvous with an eastbound convoy, which had been escorted by Canadian destroyers for the first 300–400 miles of its journey. But there was a gap in the middle and after the fall of France even short-range German surface forces could operate as far as 25° west. This gap could only be closed by providing escort vessels with a wider radius of action and by routing convoys farther north and giving air cover from Iceland and refuelling facilities there. The sloop, the only escort vessel which could go all the way across the Atlantic, eventually provided continuous protection but sloops were few when war began. Iceland, although occupied in 1940 when Hitler invaded Denmark, was not brought into the Battle of the Atlantic until 1941. Coastal Command was kept busy looking for invasion barges in the North Sea throughout most of 1940, and a request by the Admiralty for a reconnaissance squadron to be stationed in Iceland was not granted until early the next year.

From this date, however, things began to improve. Close escorts were provided up to 35° west, more than halfway from east to west, and from July 1941 convoys were given continuous protection in three stages, covered by groups based in the Western Approaches, Iceland and Newfoundland. But the cover, though continuous, was still thin. Up to the end of 1941 the average number of escorts per convoy was only two. At the same time the continuing lack of long-range reconnaissance aircraft enabled U-boats to patrol on the surface with fair immunity. The older boats took the risk of being spotted, and the newer ones which came into service in 1941 were able to operate beyond the range of British aircraft.

Losses at sea in 1941 of ships sailing on British account totalled 4.3 million gross tons (1,299 vessels). Losses of this order were not replaceable. In 1942 they were much worse: 7.8 million tons (1,664 vessels). The share of the U-boats in the latter year rose to four fifths and the U-boat fleet was growing. A force of ninety-one boats at the beginning of 1942 had grown to 212 by the end of the year despite the loss of eighty-seven boats during the year. In one battle in March 1942 U-boats caught two convoys at once and sank twenty-one out of ninety-eight vessels with the loss of only one U-boat. An action of this kind, which sent over 140,000 tons of shipping to the bottom, went a long way towards giving Doenitz the 800,000 tons a month which he was aiming at. A few months later, when American escort vessels were almost completely withdrawn from the regular Atlantic convoy service for tasks in the Pacific or to support the coming landings in North Africa, the U-boats scored heavily and consistently. They developed new tactics whereby one boat acted as a tracker which signalled the position of a convoy to other boats which then assembled for a surface attack by night. The weakness of these tactics was the need to break wireless silence and so reveal the position of the tracker to the allied listening services, but the risks proved worthwhile and Doenitz was not far wrong when he concluded that he was achieving his monthly target and his Führer's aim. But the sinkings of March 1942 – 273 ships totalling 834,164 tons – were only once exceeded – in June when 173 ships totalling 834,196 tons were lost. These were sinkings from all causes. In November exceptional successes by U-boats pushed the total above 800,000 once more and for the last time.

In London an anti-U-boat committee was formed, consisting of British and American brass and boffins under the chairmanship of Churchill himself, and early in 1943 the strategic bombers of both nations were directed to attack, as their first priority, U-boat construction yards in Germany and U-boat bases in France. The effects of these raids were at best marginal but on the high seas the balance of advantage was beginning to turn as more escort vessels, longer-range aircraft and new detection devices began to be deployed against the U-boat. There was also a dramatic and decisive turn in the war of codes and ciphers. While some escorts provided the close protection needed by the convoys, others could now be detached in groups, attended by aircraft carriers, to hunt down the U-boats before they attacked or after they were forced to break off an action. New radar detectors and new offensive weapons, such as new kinds of depth charge, tilted the balance against the U-boat, whose whereabouts and intentions came to be regularly known to allied Intelligence. The U-boats were now at the peak of their strength with over one hundred at sea at a time, and in March 1943 they had another exceptional month when they sank thirty-two vessels for the loss of only one U-boat. But this was their last major achievement. A few weeks later they broke off an engagement

BATTLE OF THE ATLANTIC
1942-1945

0 — 1000
Miles

SUBMARINE WAR 1939-1945
1,200 U-boats involved
700 U-boats sunk
32,000 German sailors drowned
2,700 Allied ships sunk.
30,000 British merchant seamen
drowned.
36% of the total British merchant
Fleet was sunk between June 1940-
December 1945.

GREENLAND

Reykjavik
ICELAND
Julianehaab

CANADA

Belfast

GERMAN
OCCUPIED OR
CONTROLLED

St
Johns
Halifax

Azores from
Oct 1943

Gibraltar
Casablanca

UNITED
STATES

New York

North

Bermuda
(GB)

Atlantic

Key
West
USA

Exuma (GB)
Guatanamo

Ocean

Dakar from Nov 1942

AFRICA

Jamaica

Puerto Rico (USA)
Virgin Is (USA)
Antigua
St Lucia (GB)
Trinidad

Freetown (GB)
Monrovia (Liberia)
Takoradi
(GB)

Panama
Canal

(GB)
Georgetown
Paramaribo (Dutch)
Cayenne
(French)

Belem

Ascension Is
(GB)

EXTRA CONVOY ROUTE

Recife
(Pernambuco)
Salvador
(Bahia)

SOUTH
AMERICA

Rio de
Janeiro

South

FROM

Atlantic

Cape
Town

Montevideo
(Uruguay)

1943

Ocean

⊙ US & British bases.

█▌ U-boat activities
August 1942 - May 1943

●— Limit of Allied air patrols.

▓ U-boat activities
June 1943 - April 1945

▫ Main U-boat bases.

Areas not possible to patrol
by Allied land-based bombers.

~ARTHUR BANKS~

in which they had lost six boats, and after further defeats of this kind they completely withdrew for a time from the Atlantic. New boats continued to be commissioned, but the rate of sinkings began to catch up with the rate of production and by 1944, when the Atlantic became a highway crowded with men and munitions making for France and Germany itself, U-boat sinkings exceeded in tonnage the allies' losses in merchant shipping. Altogether 1,162 U-boats were built and commissioned during the war and 941 of them were sunk or surrendered in the course of it. One of these was captured by an aircraft.

The latter phase of the war against the U-boats was waged simultaneously with the battle in Arctic waters in which the German surface fleet and the Luftwaffe joined to prevent the dispatch of allied aid to the Russians and to sink the allied vessels carrying it. After the loss of *Bismarck* in 1941 Hitler had little use for his capital ships but during 1942 he concentrated them in Norway, chiefly because he was afraid that the allies intended to invade that country. *Bismarck*'s sister-ship *Tirpitz* was moved to Trondhjem in January. The battle cruisers *Scharnhorst* and *Gneisenau* and the cruiser *Prinz Eugen* were recalled in February from Brest on Hitler's direct order (once again he had to override his professional advisers, Raeder considering the order so crazy that he refused to take responsibility for it). They succeeded in running the gauntlet of the English Channel by day to reach home ports, whence *Prinz Eugen* was directed to Norway. She was damaged by a torpedo on her way and had to turn back but Germany's strength in northern waters was further increased by the dispatch of the cruiser *Admiral Hipper* and the two battleships *Scheer* and *Lützow* and, in the following winter, two more cruisers and *Scharnhorst* and – once again – *Prinz Eugen*. Although *Lützow* ran aground and was out of action for several months, this build-up was alarming for the British Admiralty, the more so since attempts to cripple ships by air attack in harbour had proved disappointing. *Scharnhorst*, *Gneisenau* and *Prinz Eugen* had survived a winter's battering in Brest before making their successful dash up the Channel and it was proving impossible to do any real damage to *Tirpitz* in her narrow anchorage up the Trondhjem fjord.

Tirpitz, like *Bismarck* before her, was the most powerful vessel on either side in the Atlantic war. Yet she took part in no battle. Launched in April 1939, she did her trials in the Baltic during 1941 and was dispatched to Norwegian waters at the beginning of 1942. The British Admiralty feared another sortie into the Atlantic, like *Bismarck*'s the year before, and these fears gave rise to one of the most brilliantly daring ventures of the war. If *Tirpitz* made for the Atlantic, she would probably sooner or later need to put in at St Nazaire. An old American destroyer, *Campbeltown*, disguised as a German ship and filled with explosives, was sailed up the Loire estuary to St Nazaire, deceiving the German gunners defending the harbour until the last few minutes. Her captain and crew sailed her straight at the dock gates and rammed them, while commandos landed to destroy other selected installations. The next day *Campbeltown* blew up. The dock at St Nazaire was never repaired by the Germans.

But although *Tirpitz* never attempted a foray like *Bismarck*'s she indirectly inflicted grievous losses on allied shipping in Arctic waters. Churchill's response to Stalin's request for help in 1941 had been not merely generous in spirit but incautious in degree. He promised a convoy every ten days, to the dismay of the Admiralty which was thinking in terms of one every forty days – if it had to run any at all against such suicidal odds. The run of 1,500–2,000 miles lay through seas made dangerous by icebergs, tempests, fogs and interference to radar by natural causes. It was almost entirely within the range of the Luftwaffe, to which the interminable daylight of the summer months was an extra boon. The convoys could not sail eastward beyond a certain point without courting the risks of attack by shore-based German bombers and of a major fleet action, should German capital ships put to sea. It was therefore necessary to consider in advance which mattered more, the merchantmen or the escorts. If the merchantmen, then the escorts must be committed to the risk of heavy losses. If the escorts, then the merchantmen must in a crisis be abandoned. The Admiralty, faced with this predicament by Churchill's insistence on the overriding need to get supplies to the USSR by this route, decided that if and when a choice had to be made the merchantmen would be abandoned.

The first convoy sailed from Íceland in September 1941 and was followed by others at the rate of one about every two weeks. Their destination was Archangel or Murmansk, the former being seasonally, and the latter permanently, ice free. Murmansk's more temperate clime was offset by the fact that in 1941 it was only thirty miles from the front, and the Russians therefore preferred Archangel and undertook to keep it open with eight to ten icebreakers. But only two of these materialized and after one had been hit by a bomb in January 1942 five British ships were frozen into the ice for the rest of the winter. The principal problems of these early convoys were the shortage of escort vessels, the natural hazards of the journey, the inadequacy of ice-breaking and unloading facilities at the Russian end and the failure of the Russians to provide coal, ballast, stores or fresh water for the return

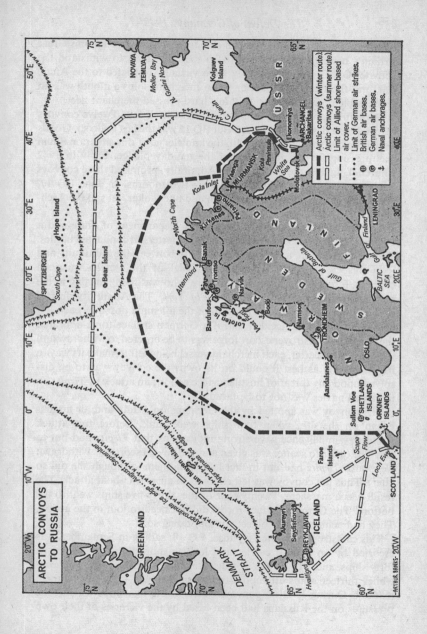

ARCTIC CONVOYS
TO RUSSIA

Arctic convoys (winter route).
Arctic convoys (summer route).
Limit of Allied shore-based
air cover.
Limit of German air strikes.
British air bases.
German air bases.
Naval anchorages.

GREENLAND

DENMARK
STRAIT

Akureyri
Seydisfjord
REYKJAVIK
Hvalfiord
ICELAND

Jan Mayen Island

Approximate Ice edge... August-September
Approximate Ice edge... July

Faroe
Islands

Scapa
Flow

ORKNEY
ISLANDS

Sullom Voe
SHETLAND
ISLANDS

Loch Ewe

SCOTLAND

Aandalsnes

Ramsøy
Namsos
TRONDHEIM
Bodø
Vest Fiord
Lofoten Is.
Bardufoss
Tromsø
Banak
Altenfiord

OSLO

Gulf of Bothnia

BALTIC
SEA

LENINGRAD

Finland
Gulf

FINLAND

SWEDEN

NORWAY

North Cape
Kirkenes
Petsamo
Kola Inlet
MURMANSK
Kola
Peninsula

White
Sea

Molotovsk

ARCHANGEL
Bakaritsa
Ekonomiya

U S S R

Kanin

C. Kanin N.
N. Gusini Nos
Moller Bay
NOVAYA
ZEMLYA

Kolguev
Island

Bear Island

Hope Island

South Cape

SPITZBERGEN

ARTHUR BANKS

journeys. The ships employed on this task, which were among Great Britain's newest and best, had to be specially fitted to withstand the climate. Once so equipped they were virtually restricted to the Arctic run, and the tying up of six or seven merchant ships a month was an appreciable drain on Great Britain's hard-pressed merchant fleet.

German opposition did not at first make itself felt. Twelve convoys reached their destinations intact. But PQ 12 was the last to do so. Goods were piling up in Iceland and with the knowledge of this situation Stalin was pressing for the fulfilment of the ten-day pledge. Early in 1942 Churchill, against the advice of the Admiralty, promised three convoys of twenty-five to thirty-five ships every two months. In June PQ 17, consisting of thirty-five merchantmen and one tanker, set sail for Archangel.

The British Admiralty was not only a Department of State and a General Staff but also an operational headquarters. It conducted battles. There was therefore a division of authority between the Admiralty and – in this case – the Commander-in-Chief of the Anglo-American covering force, Admiral Sir John Tovey, who was flying his flag in the newly commissioned battleship *Duke of York*. The Admiralty, fearful of the powers of *Tirpitz* and mindful of the dilemma posed by each PQ convoy in turn, had decided that if a German surface force appeared the cruiser and destroyer escort force was to be ordered to withdraw and the convoy to scatter, each merchant vessel being left to make its way to its destination as best it could on its own; the convoy was to be dissolved upon any threat of hostile surface action; an attack by *Tirpitz* on the allied navies was not to be faced.

The convoy was spotted by the Germans on 1 July and air attacks began on the 4th, when four ships were sunk. Before this attack Admiralty intelligence gave strong indications that *Tirpitz* had put to sea. The order to scatter was given and the naval escort was withdrawn westward. *Tirpitz* had not in fact left Trondhjem (although she did so later). Thus the convoy was left exposed to air and U-boat attack. The result was a massacre. Twenty-four of the thirty-five ships went to the bottom. The German surface forces did not need to join in the action. They had achieved their object without doing so.

This catastrophe dictated a pause. PQ 18, sailing in September, was escorted by an aircraft carrier and lost no more than thirteen of its forty ships, and PQ 19 was not dispatched until December. Betweenwhiles thirteen ships attempted the passage singly. Only five of them made it. During 1943 no convoys sailed in the light months. But the pressures on the Russians had been eased by the victories of their own

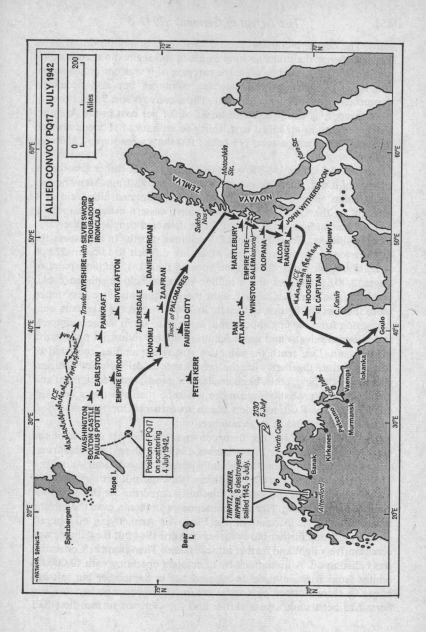

ALLIED CONVOY PQ17 JULY 1942

~ARTHUR BANKS~

Spitzbergen

Bear I.

Hope I.

ICE

WASHINGTON
BOLTON CASTLE
PAULUS POTTER

EMPIRE BYRON

EARLSTON

PANKRAFT

RIVER AFTON

Trawler AYRSHIRE with SILVER SWORD
TROUBADOUR
IRONCLAD

ALDERSDALE

HONOMU

DANIEL MORGAN

ZAAFRAN

Track of PALOMARES

FAIRFIELD CITY

PETER KERR

Position of PQ17
on scattering
4 July 1942.

TIRPITZ, SCHEER,
HIPPER, 8 destroyers,
sailed 1145, 5 July.

North Cape

2130
5 July

Altenfiord

Banak

Kirkenes

Petsamo

Murmansk

Lotta R.

Tuloma R.

Vaenga

Iokanka

Goulo

C. Kanin

Kolguev I.

EL CAPITAN

HOOSIER

ICE

WINSTON SALEM(ashore)

OLOPANA

EMPIRE TIDE

HARTLEBURY

PAN
ATLANTIC

Sukhoi
Nos

NOVAYA

ZEMLYA

Matochkin
Str.

Kara Str.

ALCOA
RANGER

JOHN WITHERSPOON

0   200

Miles

75 N

70 N

60°E

50°E

40°E

30°E

20°E

78°
N

70°
N

20°E

30°E

40°E

50°E

60°E

arms. The northern convoys caused hard feelings and produced bitter words between the allies so long as allied aid seemed a matter of life and death to the Russians, while the carrying of it was not only a severe strain on specially strained shipping resources but also peculiarly dangerous to the men engaged in it. These convoys lost 7.5 per cent of their cargoes, as compared with losses of 0.7 per cent in the Atlantic. Forty convoys in all sailed east, thirty-seven back; 811 merchantmen set out on the passage east, 715 back; 100 ships were sunk, 2,800 men died.

Not all aid to the USSR went this way. In fact rather less than a quarter of it did, the principal route being through Iran. After the war the Russian economist N. A. Voznesenski estimated allied aid at 4 per cent of the USSR's own production; western estimates range a little higher. In figures the United States delivered supplies to the value of $11.3 billion, Great Britain £428 millions' worth. In retrospect the lists are long, dry sets of figures which are difficult to take in: 22,000 aircraft, 13,000 tanks, 2.7 million tons of petrol, 15 million pairs of boots, 2,000 telephones and a million miles of field telephone cable; but while the war was being fought these shipments were very much more than sets of figures, especially in 1941–2 when the Russians were recovering from the first shocks and, as we shall see in the next chapter, struggling to salvage and move factories and get industrial production going again. One tenth (in value) of American supplies consisted of food and this, together with the miscellaneous deliveries of vehicles, chemicals, clothing, tents, blankets, leather goods, radio equipment and medicine were probably even more welcome than the tanks and aircraft which the Russians soon began to turn out for themselves, of excellent quality and in huge numbers.

The harassing of the northern convoys was the last exploit of the German high seas fleet. In September 1943 British midget submarines – craft of fifty feet manned by specially intrepid crews of four – attacked *Tirpitz* at her anchorage up Trondhjem fjord and put her out of action for six months. But the British Admiralty dared not let this powerful vessel remain in being. Her very existence was a threat, even though she remained inactive. Aircraft of the Fleet Air Arm, flying off aircraft carriers, inflicted further blows on her in April 1944 but the damage was comparatively light and further attacks failed. Then Bomber Command was called upon. A first attack by Lancasters operating with 12,000 lb. bombs from Russian airfields crippled her in September but left her afloat. A second attack by Lancasters in November sank her. *Scharnhorst* had been sunk a year earlier and the German surface fleet had long since ceased to play the role which Grand Admiral Raeder had looked forward to. He had resigned his command at the beginning of 1943 when his fleet was already crippled by fuel shortages and the loss of the Führer's confidence. Hitler felt that the men could be better used in other ways and talked of de-commissioning all capital ships. Above and below the waters the command of the seas was no longer disputed anywhere except between the Americans and the Japanese in the Pacific.

The high seas and the ships sailing upon them had been used to ensure or interdict supplies, not to stage major naval battles. There was nothing like the Battle of Jutland, let alone Trafalgar. The vital issues in the Battle of the Seas were, first, whether the British people should get enough to eat, British factories get enough to keep going and the British armed services get enough to fight on; and secondly, the movement of troops across the seas. The worst months of the blockade were also the months in which command of the seas was in issue all over the world – in the Pacific and Indian Oceans as well as the Atlantic – and all the active theatres of war depended on the movement of tens of thousands of men and their equipment every month. The Americans, unaided, were fully committed in the Pacific, so that the armies which they had promised to send eastward in fulfilment of their pledge to put Europe first, had to be transported largely in non-American vessels. The major role in keeping the routes open was played by the British with material help from some of their European allies. The British merchant service was maintained throughout the war at a strength of about 145,000 men. Volunteers could and did enter it at the age of sixteen. Employment was traditionally by the voyage, that is to say, any seaman could leave his ship upon his return from any voyage; but none did so. After March 1941 the government had the power to prevent seamen from leaving the service and to direct former seamen back to it, but the flow of volunteers was such that it never had to worry about the manning of the ships. Thirty-two thousand died directly or indirectly through enemy action and many more were disabled.

The defeat of the U-boat was, like the Battle of Waterloo, a 'damned nice thing – the nearest run thing'. The Germans came closer to victory at sea than anywhere else after 1941, and at the time of their defeat in 1943 they had not exhausted their capabilities. They lost, not because they had no more cards to play, but because they played them just too late. They had a new long-range torpedo which could be fired from ranges outside the scanning range of the victim's detecting apparatus; with this torpedo they could strike before being seen. They also had a faster U-boat equipped with the new device called Schnorkel. Thanks to its speed this boat could overtake and then outdistance vessels previously immune and thanks to its Schnorkel, a tube which just broke surface and enabled it to breathe without surfacing, it could remain virtually concealed from sight and from radar. These innovations did not have the chance to take effect in the battle because allied science had beaten the U-boat back to a position of no recovery.

The U-boat had started the war in a theoretically winning position because it was too difficult to detect and destroy. Sailing faster and deeper than the submarines of the First World War and more strongly built it was almost out of sight and, except when directly hit, it was impervious to depth charges which had improved little over twenty years. Yet, fortunately for Great Britain, it was still essentially what it had been in the First World War – a submersible surface craft and not one which could live permanently beneath the waters. It had to surface to live and it was therefore still vulnerable to detection and destruction by an enemy who knew where it was and had good enough weapons. Its main weaknesses were its inescapable need to surface to recharge its batteries and the practice, enforced by the German High Command, of maintaining contact with home and so betraying its position from time to time by breaking wireless silence. These weaknesses, coupled with the small number of available U-boats in the first two years of war, enabled the allies to turn the tables. As in the air, Great Britain's lead in radar was crucial. Radar was used to find the U-boats when they were forced to surface and a variant of radar – asdic or sonar, developed in both Great Britain and the United States – probed beneath the seas to find submerged boats. The Intelligence breakthrough robbed the unwitting U-boat of its invisibility, and as Coastal Command acquired aircraft which could fly farther, detect at great ranges and with greater accuracy and carry more lethal weapons than the pre-war depth charges, so the U-boat was forced from the offensive to the defensive. It did not recover in time to stage another round. Its reverses in 1943 added up to final defeat.

CHAPTER 22

The Victory of the USSR

THE USSR presented Hitler with a problem which was not only different in scale from his British problem but, militarily, diametrically opposite to it. Stalin had resources – of manpower, raw materials and space – which were greatly superior to Germany's. Against them Hitler had to pit superior skill and superior organization in a bid to win a quick victory. He had to break the USSR, not wear it down. In the west he could lose the Battle of Britain but still hope to win the long drawn out Battle of the Seas. In the east time was not on his side. He not only hoped to win in six months but needed to win in not much more. He threw the immensely efficient armed forces of a thoroughly modern industrial power against a colossus which had not reached the same stage of industrial sophistication and was, in addition, weakened both materially and psychologically by a generation of turmoil: revolution and civil war, followed by ostracism, the destruction of the peasantry, political and military purges, and a police tyranny and an inquisitorial system of government extremely ill calculated to elicit loyalty. Hitler relied on his military engine to destroy the enemy's power to resist and, at second remove, to encourage the peoples of the USSR to turn against their own government. Although at the end of 1941 he had failed to achieve the decisive victory which he had hoped for, the successes of German arms had been so great that the USSR was like a man who has had his weapon dashed from his hand and does not know where to turn to get himself another. A third of the USSR's industrial capacity had been overrun and another third was under fire from the German armies and air forces, its output gravely cut. The next three years produced fighting more ferocious and devastating than any experienced by man. Both in scale and temper – and therefore in its consequences – the war in the USSR was altogether different from any of the other campaigns embraced by the Second World War.

Although Stalin had played every available political card in order to fend off a war with Germany and although his military dispositions could be criticized for unpreparedness, he had taken a number of steps to prepare the USSR for war on the industrial front. He introduced measures at the end of 1938 to curb absenteeism in factories and restrict the excessive movement of labour which were a debilitating feature of the Soviet economy: absenteeism became grounds for dismissal and eleven months' employment in one job a prerequisite for two weeks' holiday. In 1940 new measures punished slacking and forbade certain changes of job without permission. In the same year the government took power to direct workers from one place to another. The costs of transporting and re-housing the worker and his family were to be paid by the state; he was to receive six days' pay on arrival at his destination; and he was promised that his wages would not fall. The government also tackled the problem of training. It had an alarming shortage of technicians, especially below the top ranges. It established vocational schools to take nearly a million trainees a year who were then assigned to jobs and were required, military service apart, to stay in them for four years. Young people who were not exceptionally clever or exceptionally privileged were diverted into these schools and away from high schools and universities, where fees were introduced for all but the favoured few; in the face of the emergency created by the threat of war higher education was denied to all but a small élite.

With the advent of war the armed services made big demands on manpower and their losses were so heavy that they continued to do so to the end. The population of the USSR in 1941 was about 200 million but at least one in ten of these died, in uniform or out of it, before the war was over. The territories annexed by the USSR in 1939–40 – an area larger than the United Kingdom – added to its population a million Poles and perhaps half a million Balts, but the total labour force fell from a pre-war total of 28 million to below 20 million by 1943. Half the workers in war industry were women and the proportion of women in agriculture was much higher. Something like half the male peasantry was conscripted into the army, leaving the fields to be worked by women, children and old men, or not worked at all. Millions of these peasants never returned to the countryside, for when the war ended the survivors among them were needed in the towns and factories and for many years after 1945 women continued to provide two thirds of agricultural labour.

The labour available for war industries was not only reduced by the needs of the fighting services and, by western standards, inadequately trained; it was also in the wrong places because industry itself was to a very large extent in the wrong places for a war which began with a German invasion. The removal of industry from threatened areas under the stress of war and the expansion of production in eastern regions of the USSR became a crucial factor in the USSR's victory – the most crucial factor after the Soviet armies had survived the first six months of war. This effect has been presented as nearly a miracle. Like all miracles it had a basis in hard fact.

The USSR was not in 1941 an industrial power like Germany or Great Britain or, least of all, the United States, but it was in process of becoming one. The industrialization of Russia had begun in the nineteenth century, albeit patchily, later than in western Europe and under the heavy disabilities of an ailing political and social system. The revolutionary régime which came to power in 1917 had ambitious ideas about modernizing and urbanizing the USSR and making it self-sufficient but the government's plans were severely hampered by the destruction caused by the First World War and the ensuing civil war and by its own political and economic isolation. The conditions were harsh and the base low. Capital was scarce; communications were poor; technical skills, even secondary education, were thinly spread; the USSR was rich in natural resources but they had never been properly surveyed. But a poor beginning makes for (statistically) impressive achievements, and during the first Five Year Plan (1928–32) and again during the second Plan capital investment, industrial output and gross national product were all doubled and transport facilities increased in even greater proportion. Education was extended and the shift of the population from the country to the towns was accelerated: while the population as a whole rose by a third between 1914 and 1940, the urban population was multiplied by 2.4. There was therefore a considerable alteration not only in the number of people at work but even more so in what they were doing.

The main industrial effort remained where it had been – in the areas round Moscow and Leningrad, in the Ukraine and the Don basin. The development of existing facilities had first priority. Nowhere else was there an adequate supply of skilled labour. But the development of other areas – the Urals, western Siberia and Kazakhstan – was a theme which appealed to communist propagandists as well as to the romantic imagination. These areas were known to be rich in minerals. The pre-revolutionary régime could be blamed for doing too little about them. Lenin had said that the right thing to do was to create industries where raw materials were to be got. Consequently the repair and extension of industry in the traditional centres in European Russia was to be matched by exciting new schemes farther east. This eastward trend was gradually intensified. Up to 1930 the traditional centres absorbed the bulk of the effort. During the thirties they still retained their primacy but at the same time vast sums began to be lavished on other areas, particularly

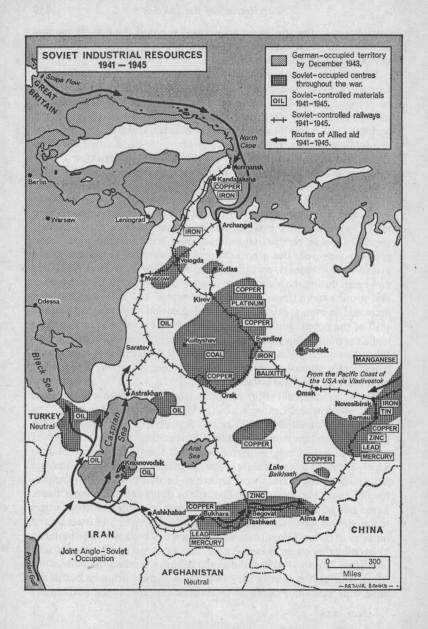

SOVIET INDUSTRIAL RESOURCES
1941 – 1945

German-occupied territory
by December 1943.

Soviet-occupied centres
throughout the war.

OIL   Soviet-controlled materials
1941–1945.

Soviet-controlled railways
1941–1945.

Routes of Allied aid
1941–1945.

Scapa Flow

GREAT BRITAIN

North Cape

Berlin

Murmansk

Kandalaksha
COPPER
IRON

IRON

Archangel

Warsaw

Leningrad

Vologda

Kotlas

COPPER

Moscow

Kirov

PLATINUM

Odessa

COPPER

OIL

Kuibyshev

Sverdlovsk

Tobolsk

COAL

IRON

MANGANESE

Black Sea

Saratov

COPPER

BAUXITE

From the Pacific Coast of
the USA via Vladivostok

Astrakhan

Orsk

Omsk

Novosibirsk
IRON
TIN

TURKEY
Neutral

OIL

OIL

Barnaul

Caspian Sea

COPPER

COPPER

ZINC
LEAD
MERCURY

OIL

Aral Sea

Lake
Balkhash

COPPER

Krasnovodsk

OIL

ZINC

Ashkhabad

COPPER
Bukhara

Begovat
Tashkent

Alma Ata

IRAN

LEAD
MERCURY

CHINA

Joint Anglo-Soviet
Occupation

Persian Gulf

AFGHANISTAN
Neutral

0   300
Miles

~ARTHUR BANKS~

the Urals and the Siberian district round Kuznetsk (the Kuzbas), and under the third Five Year Plan, which began in 1939, other areas in western Siberia and central Asia were promised increased attention of the same kind. Railways were built, electric power provided, resources surveyed and populations moved to where labour was required. In the new development areas there was not only a total lack of skilled labour but a considerable shortage of any labour at all, to remedy which the government compelled migrations and used convicts and political prisoners ruthlessly. (In 1941 the NKVD was responsible for a sixth of all new construction in the USSR.)

This relocation of industry, which was to prove strategically vital, was at first economically irrational. Thus coal was mined in the Kuzbas in Siberia and iron ore round Magnitogorsk in the Urals, but there was no iron ore near Kuznetsk or coal near Magnitogorsk and the two centres were well over a thousand miles apart. This situation was, however, later redeemed by supplying Magnitogorsk with coal by rail from Karaganda in Kazakhstan (half the distance away) and by opening up the new ironfields of Gornaya Shoriya in Siberia to be fed with Kuzbas coal. Thus nature justified the huge expenditure of capital and labour and the USSR found itself endowed with two new industrial complexes in place of one barely cohesive one. (The development of the Kuzbas illustrates the pace of expansion. In the decade 1928–38 its production of coal rose from 2 million to 16 million tons a year.) As the production of iron and coal rose upon the basis of improved communications and technology, more power and more labour, so the USSR began to be supplied with the quantities and the varieties of steel to sustain its expanding industries and, an increasingly more urgent preoccupation, its armament as well.

This wider distribution of the steel industry was the most important single element in the development of the eastern regions, but not the only one. Western Russia is poor in non-ferrous metals, which Tsarist Russia had imported on a significant scale. But copper had been mined in the Urals and the Caucasus since the seventeenth century, and the USSR planned to exploit the copper, lead and zinc of Kazakhstan. This work was put in hand before the war and greatly developed during it, so that Kazakhstan became second only to the Urals in sustaining the Russian war effort. The chemical industry was also diffused, although it remained preponderantly European and was so severely damaged that American, British and Canadian imports were required to make good the losses. The radio industry was also expanded. Besides 120 large broadcasting stations the USSR was operating 2,000 local stations before the war and had begun a public television service in 1938 (discontinued during the war).

In sum, the Ural, Siberian and central Asian areas, which had been opened up as ancillary industrial enterprises primarily in order to modernize the USSR and make it economically independent of capitalist countries, had become in addition an alternative arms base. Without this alternative the USSR might well have collapsed at the beginning of 1942. The German victories of the previous year had eliminated much of the fruits of the Russian industrial effort of the thirties: between a half and two thirds of its productive capacity in coal, pig iron, steel and aluminium, a quarter of its engineering output. Over 300 ammunition factories had been put out of action. By November 1941 the USSR's overall industrial output had been halved, and during November and December no coal whatever was delivered from the Moscow or the Donets minefields. Industry in the Urals and eastward could not immediately fill the gap but it supplied a base.

A gigantic movement of people and plants took place. The number of people involved may have been as high as 12 million. From Leningrad more than two thirds of the city's capital equipment, building excepted, were conveyed away. According to N. A. Voznesenski, the head of Gosplan (the State Planning Commission), these movements involved 'millions of people . . . hundreds of enterprises, tens of thousands of machine tools, rolling mills, presses, hammers, turbines and motors . . . 1,360 large enterprises – mostly war enterprises – were evacuated to the eastern regions of the USSR.' The impressive aspect of this undertaking was its hugeness, not its organization. The railways, although they had been singled out for improvement under the third Five Year Plan, were reduced to chaos as west-bound trains carried men to the armies at the front while east-bound trains, loaded with machinery, workers and deported Volga Germans and Polish prisoners of war, were pushed into sidings where some of the equipment stayed to rot and men and women to die. At the new sites wooden structures were thrown up to house machinery, but there was often neither time nor materials to build houses for the workers. They sometimes set to work, in temperatures below zero, before the roof was on their makeshift factory and they slept on the floor among the machines. Their privations were terrible. Food was scarce, hospitals (and schools) non-existent. They just worked as long as they could. Mortality was high, output per head poor. The wonder was that they were not worse. By their efforts war industry kept going. But the early months of 1942 were critical. Thereafter production in these regions expanded dramatically until their aggregate war production reached 2.5 times the total pre-war production of the entire USSR. Labour, while it declined overall, rose in 1940–43 from 1 million to 1.5 million in the Urals and by similar degrees in western Siberia and Kazakhstan, each of which had employed nearly half a million in industry on the eve of war.

The principal features of this victory on the home front were two: the rigours which an authoritarian government (aided by the appeal to patriotism) could impose on the people, and the adaptability of the Soviet economy, which partly made up for its technical weaknesses by its ready response to central planning and direction. Once the corner was turned and production resumed, expansion was astonishingly rapid. By the middle of 1942 arms production exceeded its pre-war level. In the next years output in the east continued to rise, while industry in the occupied western areas was rehabilitated with amazing vigour as fast as they were liberated. The Moscow coalfields, for example, whose pre-war production was 35,000 tons a day, resumed output in January 1942 at the rate of 590 tons a day, increased it to 22,000 tons by May and were back to normal by October 1942. Electrical generating capacity, nearly half of which was physically destroyed by the Germans, was also back to its pre-war volume before the war ended. Russian production of tanks and aircraft surpassed German production in 1943. At their peak they reached 40,000 aircraft and 30,000 tanks and other armoured fighting vehicles a year – alongside an output of 150,000 pieces of artillery, 500,000 machine guns and at least 2 million sub-machine guns and 3 million rifles. Stalin had won, by however narrow a margin, the fight for the material resources of war; but there was also the question of human responses.

The response of the people of the USSR depended not only on how they were treated during the war but also on how they had been treated before it. Wartime privations, however severe, were expected and attributable to the enemy, but the history of pre-war relations between government and governed gave rise on the German side to hopes of rebellion and, one may suppose, to equivalent fears on the Russian side.

The intensive industrialization of the thirties was Stalin's special contribution to the evolution of Soviet society. Through it he established his totalitarian authority and because of it he waged a savage fight against the peasantry which had been one of the protagonists in the revolution of 1917. The question of the peasants is the question of food. The food which peasants produce can either be bought or seized. During the confused years of revolution and civil war after 1917 it was most frequently seized but seized with some justification and consent, since the struggling revolution – to which the peasants adhered – had no money to pay for it and no means to produce the goods which the peasants might have taken in exchange for their produce. The peasants understood this, but they also learned the strength of their position and when the civil war ended they in effect bargained with the central government and forced it to reward them for their labours instead of merely appropriating its fruits.

For the next six years (1921–7) the New Economic Policy sought to provide goods to satisfy and stimulate the peasants, but some of the richer peasants continued to demonstrate their power by keeping food off the market when they were dissatisfied with the returns offered to them. A series of good harvests increased their power and the temptation to hold back supplies for the towns and play the markets, so much so that the government had to import grain to save the towns from starvation. The New Economic Policy not only derogated from the basic principles of the Bolshevik Party by making concessions to private operators and to the profit motive, so that bolsheviks like Stalin came increasingly to resent the power of the peasants and to determine to destroy it, even at the cost of another revolution; it also made the peasantry a rising power opposed to the party and opposed to the towns. So instead of running consumer industries to pay for peasant produce the government would force the peasants to pay for heavy industry by reverting once more to the civil war practices of exploiting their labour and taking their produce on the state's own terms. There was in fact no other way of paying for industrialization, since the USSR was neither forming the needful capital within its borders nor able to borrow it abroad. Peasants had paid for industrialization before – for example, in the Industrial Revolution in western Europe – but not nearly so harshly or so fast as Stalin made the Russian peasants pay.

They paid for internal reasons, but the way they were forced to pay was largely dictated by failures in foreign policy, in particular the rupture with Great Britain and the collapse of the attempt to foster Communism in China. These failures were all the more dangerous, given the failure to promote Communism in Europe a decade earlier. Industrialization could no longer wait and so with the first Five Year Plan the peasants were brigaded into collectives in order the better to be coerced. In the course of his war on the peasantry Stalin sharpened the totalitarian machinery and police terror of the state and converted the Bolshevik Party from a policy-making organization, which to some extent it still was in the twenties, into an apparatus of arbitrary power to be used not only against the peasants but also against townspeople and enemies or imagined enemies of all kinds. The more prosperous peasants were ruined, great numbers of peasants were killed and agricultural production was disastrously reduced. The horrors of these years made their contribution to the industrialization which Stalin had resolved to effect, but at a price which raised the question of how far the peoples of the USSR could be counted loyal to it in war. Unable to pay the Russians to work harder or inspire them to do so as perhaps Lenin or Trotsky might have done, Stalin had been left with only the modern equivalent of flogging them – a police régime in which the workers, trapped by informers and false accusations, were consigned wholesale to hard labour camps. Stalin was not blind to the risks inherent in this ferocity. His first wartime speech on 3 July 1941 appealed, in terms unwontedly similar to the appeals to patriotism made by democratic leaders, for sacrifices, ruthlessness and unity, for a scorched earth policy and guerrilla warfare to help the desperately struggling armed forces.

The sacrifices which the peoples of the USSR may have braced themselves to make in 1941 can hardly have been as gruelling as they turned out to be in fact. Life in the USSR during the war became not only grim but so difficult to sustain that about a million people died of starvation. The armed services and workers in war industry got enough to eat. By and large other people did not. The total amount of food provided and purchased was almost halved. Personal consumption fell below that of the frightful famine year in 1932. The sugar ration, to take an extreme example, was reduced to half a pound a year. The supply of vegetables was cut by nearly two thirds, of meat by more than half, of flour by nearly half. There was no attempt to keep up tobacco stocks, which fell by three quarters, nor the flow of vodka, which was halved. Production of consumer goods was not much more than adequate for the needs of the armed services. Real earnings were cut by a half or more. Compulsory saving was increased by contributions to war bonds which were to be redeemed after the war – but lost nine tenths of their value when the currency was reformed in 1947. Prices had begun to rise with fear of war in 1939 and rose sharply during 1940. After the outbreak of war in 1941 prices of rationed foods and goods were pegged at their, already enhanced, pre-war levels, but they were scarce in the state shops which sold rationed and price-controlled commodities, while in other shops prices rocketed upwards and reached by 1943 about fourteen times their 1940 levels. (After the war the prices of price-controlled commodities were re-adjusted, in a number of cases by trebling them. When rationing ended in 1947 basic prices were about three times what they had been in 1940. But vodka had gone up ten times.)

Hours of work were lengthened. Holidays, other than the weekly day of rest, were cancelled. The seven day week was reintroduced in 1940 – that is to say, one rest day in seven instead of one in six or (before 1929) one in five. The normal working day was extended from seven hours to eight, but plant managers could extend it up to eleven hours, for extra pay at higher rates. The state offered some palliatives. The USSR had a well-established, comprehensive social insurance scheme which worked on a non-contributory basis, was financed by central and local government authorities and the state's business enterprises, provided sickness and other benefits graded according to wages and length of service, and gave pensions to men at sixty and women at fifty-five: pensions ranged from 50 per cent to 100 per cent of the basic wage (the latter for the lower paid), but there was a ceiling which, although not ungenerous in the thirties, became niggardly with wartime inflation. The state also recognized the need for solace of a different kind. From the outbreak of war, churches became packed with people praying that their country would be saved from its enemies and that they themselves would have the fortitude to bear their increasingly intolerable burdens of mental anguish and physical pain. In 1943 Stalin re-established the Holy Synod of the Russian Orthodox church and allowed it to elect a patriarch and re-open seminaries.

A large proportion of the population of the USSR lived outside big towns and their attitudes were specially difficult to control or predict. While Stalin appealed to them from the one side, the Germans were hoping to find among them a substantial number of disaffected who would take the first opportunity to turn against their government. Both sides wanted them to take an active part in the war, the one as guerrilla partisans against the invaders, the other as auxiliaries on the German side.

Stalin seems to have envisaged guerrilla resistance before the German invasion took place, for instructions for it were issued within a few days. The civil wars after 1917, still a living memory in the USSR, had made partisan warfare less esoteric than it was in the west, and communist doctrine tended to blur the sharper distinction made in more traditionalist societies between professional and popular campaigning. The rapid advances made by the Germans in 1941 placed them in control of large areas from which the inhabitants had not had time to flee. German control was unevenly spread and Stalin could have ordered the civilian population to escape eastward; broad corridors, more or less unpoliced by the Germans, could be traversed without much danger. But no such withdrawals were made. Many of the inhabitants may have been unwilling to leave their homes, even though they were in enemy occupied territory, in order to be drafted into Stalin's armies, but it seems that Stalin did not in any case want to use them that way. They could be more useful as guerrilla fighters within the enemy's lines.

Bands were quickly formed to harass German units and communications, to collect intelligence and to exact vengeance upon anybody who collaborated with the enemy. From these beginnings a considerable force grew, although not without some initial setbacks. Moscow's first plan was to provide a core of organizers, with some elementary training in partisan warfare and of indubitable party loyalty, who would be reinforced by local anti-German patriotism and enthusiasm. This plan was not at first very successful. Local enthusiasm was not as marked as had been hoped and the first groups had to contend with some pro-German attitudes as well as the attentions of the SD. Problems of supply and communication were extremely severe during 1941 and these first groups achieved little beyond a few hit-and-run raids and enough reprisals against collaborationists to make people think twice before helping the Germans. A number of these bands were completely eliminated. In the same period other bands came spontaneously and haphazardly into existence. Out of the flotsam and jetsam of the defeated Russian armies, groups 300–1,000 strong formed, but their first aim was survival rather than further action against the Germans who, until the end of 1942, still looked like the winning side. During 1942, however, the government was able to impose a degree of organization and direction on the bands and began to draft the local peasantry into an effective, if subordinate and ancillary, fighting force.

The Germans employed around 250,000 security troops (usually substandard or foreign conscripts) in the USSR, partly in response to this activity, but shortages of men and materials limited their anti-partisan operations. The partisans harassed German communications and retarded reinforcements, notably in conjunction with the Kursk offensive in 1943 and before the Russian attacks in White Russia in the summer of 1944; they also inflicted about 35,000 casualties. They were helped from the start by the Germans themselves. The horrors, already related, perpetrated by the SD and the *Einsatzkommandos*, the destruction of over three million prisoners of war, the deportations to extermination camps and forced labour, the killing of a further million partisans and civilians in the USSR, the burning of villages and shooting of villagers by way of reprisal – on one occasion 158 villages were burned down as a single act of reprisal – all these things inflamed anti-German hatred and made villagers think that they might as well join the partisans instead of waiting to be killed or enslaved by the Germans. Thus although the Germans sent agents (operation Zeppelin) to infiltrate the bands and the *Volksdeutsche*; although the Ukraine contained the seeds of a separatist and anti-Soviet movement; although the Germans appointed a Russian civilian governor of Bryansk as an experiment; and although they captured a potential anti-Soviet leader in General A. A. Vlasov, their excesses (like those of the Poles in the same parts in 1920) ruined whatever chances they may have had of subverting any appreciable number of Soviet citizens and swelled the active ranks of their adversaries.

By mid-1942 the partisans probably numbered about 150,000. Their strongest ground was White Russia, where wooded country provided the best terrain; Bryansk became a principal base and from it they extended their operations into the Ukraine. But the government still could not spare them much in the way of up-to-date equipment. A year later the Germans put their strength at 200,000 and eventually they may have reached half a million. From 1943 they received new equipment from the USSR's reorganized factories, including mortars and artillery, special anti-tank guns for attacking locomotives, radios which kept them in touch with one another and with the Russian High Command, and medical supplies which had been almost totally lacking. They were supplied by air and constructed and maintained airfields for this purpose. Most of them were between seventeen and thirty-five years old, conscripted peasants with a sprinkling of army officers and other ranks and party officials. Whereas in the early days the emphasis was on reliable party members, the proportion of these inevitably fell as the movement became bigger; the consciously and actively political element may have been around one tenth in the later years. Towards the end of the war partisan brigades moved into other countries as an advance guard of Russian retribution and in order to help form local committees of reliable residents. In Poland they fought some minor engagements against the Polish Home Army and in Slovakia some 3,000 of them joined with Slovaks parachuted from the USSR in the Slovak rising against the Germans at the end of 1944, but in Rumania and Hungary their activities were insignificant and in Latvia they were driven out again.

The partisan movement had also a political purpose. The Germans occupied areas of the USSR containing a population of 70 million. These areas included large tracts, with a population of 20 million, which had only very recently come under Russian rule, and where anti-Russian feeling was intense. In all these areas, temporarily lost, Stalin was concerned to preserve some vestiges of the presence of the Soviet state. He had no reason to assume that the peasantry of the USSR would remain loyal to his régime and even less reason to suppose that the population of the Baltic states and eastern Poland would not jump at any chance, even a chance presented to them by the Germans, to repudiate it. The destruction by the Germans of the apparatus of government was a threat to the communist system, especially in areas where local separatism – political as in the Ukraine or religious as among the USSR's Muslim peoples – reinforced dislike of Stalin's communist autocracy and police rule, dislike of forced collectivization and dislike of war. The partisan movement was a reminder, if necessary a forcible one, that the government of the USSR was still in being and still in the fight. The partisans actively combated German attempts to subvert local leaders. Village elders appointed by the Germans were killed, so that fear of the German conqueror was more than offset by fear of the continuing capacity and omniscience of the central government of the USSR and its servants.

Yet a number of Soviet citizens did collaborate with the Germans or take service with them. There is more than a suggestion of severe disaffection in the fate of the Tartars, Kalmucks, Chechens and other minorities, about a million of whom were deported from the Caucasus in the winter of 1943–4, charged with collaborating with the Germans. The brutality with which they were treated (later acknowledged by Khrushchev), the thoroughness with which all traces of their homes and even their cemeteries were obliterated, and above all the date, betray a grim punitive intent persisting after all need for precautions had disappeared. In more lastingly occupied territories perhaps half a million or a million Russians, the so-called *Osttruppen*, took German pay. Their main reason was not a desire to serve against their own country but the appalling way in which the Germans behaved in the areas which they occupied. Joining the *Osttruppen* was a way out. Most of the *Osttruppen* were used as rear units in various parts of Europe but the Germans also made some attempts to form more active Russian fighting forces. In 1941 they established a Russian National Liberation Army (RONA) for anti-partisan warfare. It was later converted into the SS Division Kaminsky. In 1944 it participated in the suppression of the Warsaw rising where, even by current SS standards, its barbarous behaviour was outstanding and caused Guderian to protest to Hitler himself; its commander, Kaminsky, was killed by the SS themselves. There were one or two other formations of this nature, such as the XX SS Cossack Cavalry Corps. The SS overcame their prejudices against Slav sub-men by dubbing any Slavs who came over to their side Cossacks and pretending that Cossacks were not Slavs.

Another Russian formation on the German side was the Russian Liberation Army (ROA), which is connected with the name of General A. A. Vlasov. Vlasov began the war by deserving well of his country. Like Zhukov he had seen service in the Far East. After commanding a corps on the southern front in 1941 he was posted to the Moscow front as commander of the Twentieth Army at the age of forty-one and had a share with Zhukov in saving the capital. In the following summer he was captured by the Germans on the Leningrad front and by the autumn he had been transformed into an anti-communist leader.

The ROA was more of a scheme than an army. Hitler was afraid of creating a substantial all-Russian force and he refused to incorporate the *Osttruppen* in the ROA. He preferred to use it in non-combatant, paramilitary roles; it was a piece of window-dressing which was meant to imply massive Russian disaffection within the USSR, serving Goebbels's anti-Russian propaganda and helping to keep up the morale of the *Osttruppen* who might begin to wonder how prudent it was to go on working for the Germans. Late in 1944, however, Hitler toyed with the idea of assembling all his Russian bits and pieces into an army under Vlasov and recognizing Vlasov as the head of a Russian government in exile. As a result Vlasov found himself in 1945 in command of two divisions totalling about 50,000 men. A part of this force was sent into action on the eastern front in March. Whether designedly or not, it suffered very heavy casualties. In May further units under Vlasov himself went to the Prague front where they joined the Czechs and turned against the Germans. The commander of a Russian force moving south from Berlin towards Prague proposed joint action with a neighbouring American force, but the American commander refused, and when it became clear that Prague was about to fall to the Russians alone, Vlasov tried to escape to the west. He was caught and hanged by the Russians with nine of his associates. Several thousand of his army were turned over to the Russians by the Americans.

Vlasov was one of those Russians who had imagined that nothing could be worse than Stalin's rule. Before the Germans undeceived him on this point by their own bestialities he and others who thought like him had welcomed and incited desertions from the Russian forces to the German side. His supreme aim was another Russian revolution, to be achieved if necessary with the help of the Germans (he was never interested in cooperation with the Americans or British who were Stalin's allies). His crime and ultimately his fate lay in continuing to hold to this course after the Germans had displayed their own beastliness and had moreover become the losing side. He regarded Stalingrad as a defeat. He was therefore a traitor in the strict sense of the word. He was moreover a traitor who found in the end that he had misplaced his trust, so that he had doomed himself to a death without compensations. Like a number of traitors with a cause he is entitled to be remembered as a tragic figure. He was a premature anti-Stalinist whose anti-Stalinism involved aiding the invaders of his country.

*

In the field the decisive events, after Hitler's failure to score a knockout victory in 1941, were the bitter, yard by yard struggle for Stalingrad in the following winter and then the huge tank battles of the Kursk salient in July 1943.

At the beginning of 1942 Hitler, in spite of his disappointments the year before, still held the initiative. His plan was to clean up the Crimea, capture Leningrad and Stalingrad and occupy the Caucasus up to the Turkish border. Thus the main weight of the renewed German attack was to be in the north and, even more so, in the south while the centre remained relatively static. In the south the programme – the Crimea, Stalingrad, the Caucasus – entailed a number of differing and ultimately diverging operations. The whole of the Crimea was overrun by May except Sebastopol which, having heroically sustained a siege of 250 days, did not fall until July. Manstein's Eleventh Army, which had won these victories, was then switched to the Leningrad front although Manstein himself would have preferred to cross the straits of Kerch (which run along the eastern shore of the Crimea), strike northward with the sea of Azov on his left, make contact with the forces designated for the capture of Stalingrad and preserve the contacts between these forces (Army Group B) and others (Army Group A) which were heading south-eastward into the Caucasus.

In July 1942 Hitler moved his headquarters to Vinnitsa in the Ukraine, whence he had the satisfaction of seeing his armies advance without serious check across the Don to the Volga and to the Caucasus mountains. But these favourable beginnings were the end of Hitler's joy. Very unwisely Hitler had succumbed to the temptation to attempt simultaneously two operations which he had originally planned to put in motion one after the other and which, the more either of them succeeded, were bound to open a gap between Army Groups B and A, the one making for Stalingrad and the other disappearing right-handed into the Caucasus.

In the air the Luftwaffe was still supreme. Although the Russians had two or three times as many aircraft as the Germans (and four or five times as many fighters), and although they were also receiving American Tomahawks and British Hurricanes, and although the Germans had relinquished some squadrons for the Mediterranean, the Luftwaffe was able, when called on to make a maximum effort, to fly as many as 3,000 sorties a day – ten times as many as the larger Russian forces. But on the ground the Russian armies, reorganized, backed by reorganized industries and enjoined by Stalin in an order of the day of 1 July to yield no more ground, met their enemies with a new effectiveness and a new confidence. The German advances slowed down. Army Group A failed to reach the Caucasian oilfields before it had to turn round and fight its way back again. Army Group B crossed the Don, won a series of engagements in the narrow zone between the easternmost sweep of the Don and the Volga, and reached the Volga in the last days of August. But the capture of Stalingrad, which would put Hitler in command of one of the most important points in the rail and waterways system of the USSR, proved just too much for it.

The battle for Stalingrad has become one of the most celebrated episodes of the war. Its importance was realized at the time. In the summer, as the Germans approached, Stalin relieved Timoshenko who commanded what had become the South-west Front and appointed General V. N. Gordov in his place. In August Zhukov was dispatched to the Front with special powers – which caused, among other things, jealousies and disputes which had to be referred to Stalin. Stalin may have recalled how he had himself been a commissar on this front in 1919 and had attached to himself a group of officers and commissars antagonistic to the supreme warlord, Trotsky: Kruschchev was now unwittingly building a similar group of loyal friends who would stand by him in the decade after Stalin's death. As German pressure increased the South-west Front was divided into two, confusingly named, new Fronts: the Stalingrad Front, subsequently renamed the Don Front, and the Southeast Front, subsequently Stalingrad Front, the latter commanded in turn by Generals A. I. Eremenko and K. K. Rokossovski. But the most famous name on the Russian side was to be that of General V. I. Chuikov, second in command of the Sixty-fourth Army and then picked by Khrushchev on 12 September to command the Sixty-second Army. Chuikov had been an army commander before the war began. He was relegated early in the war but was soon reinstated. He was still an army commander when the war ended. He was ready in criticism of his superiors and sometimes unfair, and like a number of Stalingrad heroes

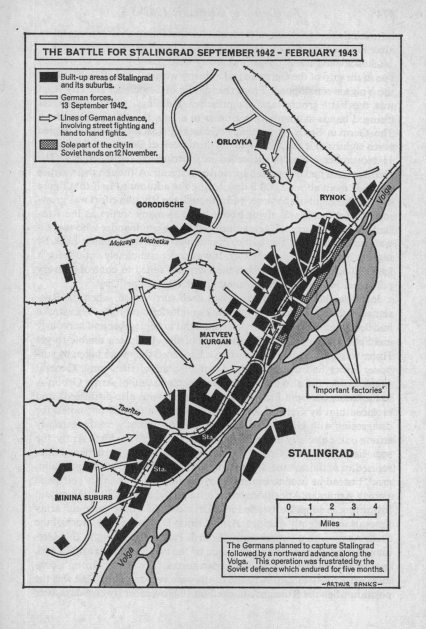

THE BATTLE FOR STALINGRAD SEPTEMBER 1942 – FEBRUARY 1943

- Built-up areas of Stalingrad and its suburbs.
- German forces, 13 September 1942.
- Lines of German advance, involving street fighting and hand to hand fights.
- Sole part of the city in Soviet hands on 12 November.

ORLOVKA

Orlovka

RYNOK

Volga

GORODISCHE

Mokraya Mechetka

MATVEEV KURGAN

'Important factories'

Tsaritsa

Sta.

Sta.

STALINGRAD

MININA SUBURB

Volga

0   1   2   3   4
Miles

The Germans planned to capture Stalingrad followed by a northward advance along the Volga. This operation was frustrated by the Soviet defence which endured for five months.

~ARTHUR BANKS~

he fancied that too much of the credit for that famous victory was taken after the event by Stalin, Zhukov and to a lesser extent Rokossovski.

Chuikov and the Sixty-second Army were penned into a city which was in the grip of the Germans; all industry within it and all traffic along the Volga were stopped. From the middle of September the city itself was the battleground and its principal buildings, which sometimes changed hands as many as five times in a day, the tactical objectives. The German Sixth Army under General Friedrich Paulus occupied seven eighths of it and twice – in the third week of October and again on 11 November – almost succeeded in overrunning the defenders. The Germans still had a definite superiority in the air. Although their sorties dropped from about 2,000 a day during the autumn to half that figure during the height of the siege, and although the Russian effort was growing, the Luftwaffe was flying about twice as many sorties as the Russians. The Sixty-second Army, inspired by its commander who was always in the thick of the battle, maintained itself by winning back by night ground lost during the day. It was never completely cut off, for it had its back to the river which the Germans failed to control at every point and beyond which was sited all the Russian artillery.

In November the Sixth Army was itself surrounded, when the Russians attacked and defeated the armies on its left and right. This stroke had been planned by the Russian command in September and nervously anticipated by the German generals, but they had been unable to get Hitler to guard against it and when it happened they were taken by surprise. Hitler had dismissed the Chief of Staff of the Army, General Franz Halder (he also took over personal command of Army Group A in the Caucasus from Field Marshal List, who was also dismissed), and replaced him by General Kurt Zeitzler who – although not noted for disagreeing with Hitler – warned him that his forces were dangerously strung out, especially in the Stalingrad sector where the Sixth Army, the spearhead of Army Group B, was worried about its flanks. Hitler refused to withdraw the Sixth Army and abandon the attack in Stalingrad. Instead he tried to buttress it by sending the Rumanian Third and Fourth Armies into positions to the left and right of the Sixth Army and by putting in some Luftwaffe Field Divisions, of whose value the army generals were rightly dubious. Army Group B consisted therefore of the Sixth Army with a Panzer army (Fourth Panzer) on its right, this German core being flanked on either side by the two Rumanian armies and, on the left, by Italian and Hungarian forces. The Army Group's contacts with Army Group A to the south were very tenuous. This was the position when the Russians attacked on 19 November (twelve days after

1 The First Day

I Battle Fronts

4 Snipers on the Finnish front, 1939

Russian War

5 A Russian girl rescues a soldier
6 Russian troops attack in Stalingrad, October 1942

7 Russians preparing rocket launchers

8 German retreat from before Moscow, December 1941

16 Normandy, 1944: first landings
17 Normandy, 1944: first landings

18 Rommel's seventh Panzers in France
19 . . . and British troops in Italy

22 Burma: Chinese troops
23 Burma: British troops

24 US aircraft flying to bomb Japan
25 US Marines establishing a beachhead on Guam

26 Guadalcanal
27 Iwojima: US Marines begin to attack, February 1945

28 Gurkha soldier crosses the Irrawaddy, 1945
29 Japanese boys hail Pacific victory

32 Italian partisans near Ravenna
33 Soviet partisans returning from an operation in the Pinsk bogs

34 German press corps at work in the forest of Compiègne
35 Commander-in-Chief, Western Approaches in his operations room

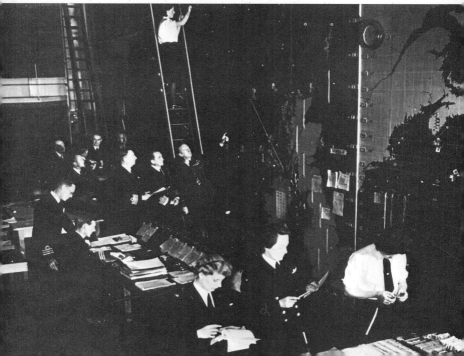

36 German fighter aircrews: after a sortie
37 German fighter aircrews: waiting

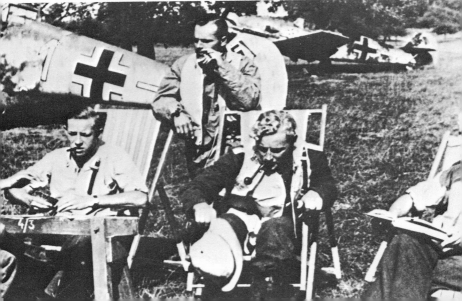

38 Dutch civilians calmly watching a low-level British attack on Rotterdam harbour

39 A bomber's view of an enemy fighter
40 A Fleet Air Arm Martlett taking off from HMS *Furious*
41 Incendiary bombs from B29 Super Fortresses falling on Japan

The War at Sea

42 A British destroyer making smoke during an engagement with a German warship in the North Sea

43 Ice in a Russian port and the British corvette *Honeysuckle*
44 Kamikaze: a Japanese suicide attack

45 The 'Anderson' shelter on display at a factory, February 1939
46 A rehearsal for dealing with gas casualties
47 Interned aliens lining up for accommodation on a
   housing estate in a northern town

50 The voice of the people

JUDEN RAUS!

D.R.G.M. 1446399

Das zeitgemäße und überaus lustige Gesellschaftss
für Erwachsene und Kinder

An diesem außerordentlich heiteren und zeitgemäßen Gesellschaftsspiel können sich 2–6 Personen be
gehören 1 Würfel, ████████ 6 Figuren und 36 Hütchen ████████ Jeder Spieler erhält eine Figur, die ∙

Für das Spiel gilt folgende Spielregel:

Jeder Spieler hat einen Wurf; nach der Höhe der geworfenen Augen werden die Startstraßen mit einer Spielfigur besetzt. Wer die Straße Nr. 1 besetzt hat ist Spielleiter und beginnt das Spiel. Jeder Spieler hat einen Wurf; so viel Augen er wirft, so viel Felder rückt er mit seiner Figur nach dem Mittelplatze zu vor. Überschreitet er die Stadtmauer, und kommt er auf ein besonders gekennzeichnetes Judenhaus zu stehen, so erhält seine Figur vom Spielleiter ein Judenhütchen aufgesetzt. Kommt er dann wieder zum Wurf, so geht er mit seiner Figur nach Maßgabe der geworfenen Augen nach dem Sammelplatz zurück und setzt das Hütchen dort ab. Hat ein Spieler z. B. sechs Augen geworfen und steht er nur drei Felder vor dem Sammelplatz, so setzt er den Hut im Sammelplatz ab und rückt wieder drei Felder vor. Das Hin- und Herlaufen zwischen der Stadtmauer und dem Mittelplatz wiederholt sich so lange, bis einer der Spieler sechs Judenhütchen auf den Sammelplatz gebracht hat. Hat er die sechsten Hut abgesetzt, so rückt er ohne Rücksicht auf die gekennzeichneten Felder nach dem Mittelplatze vor. Erreicht er ihn als Erster, dann bekommt er den ersten Preis. Die übrigen Spieler um die weiteren Preise fort, oder sie verteilen sie nach der Zahl der Hütchen, die sie auf ihren Sammelplätzen haben.

Eine zweite Spielregel:

Hat eine Spielfigur ein Hütchen bekommen, weiteren Würfen nach Maßgabe der geworfene erst auf dem Mittelplatz. Trifft er dort berei kann er dieser das oder die Hütchen abnehm platz bringen. Bei der Anwendung dieser Spi Spieler auf dem Wege zum Mittelplatz oder zeichnete Felder zu stehen kommt und demn sammen auf den Sammelplatz bringt. Hat er so muß er auf den Mittelplatz. Erreicht er ersten Preis gewonnen.

Herausgeber: Günther & (

51 Rules for playing the merry new game of Out with the Jews! For 2–6 players with one die, 6 men and 36 pawns

abandonnées,

faites confiance
AU SOLDAT ALLEMAND!

52 Trust the German soldier!

53 British factory workers making anti-aircraft guns
54 Russian women making bombs

56 Danger or routine?

63 Lieutenant General Sakai heads Japanese entry into Hong Kong

67 Smithfield, London
68 Belgrade

69 Budapest
70 Malta

71 Berlin after the capitulation
72 Tokyo after the capitulation

74 China: Japanese soldiers bayoneting prisoners
75 Malmedy, Belgium: attempting to identify civilian victims of the German offensive, December 1944

77 Dresden: immolating the thousands of victims of the Anglo-American air attack,
February 1945
78 Warsaw: hostages hanged after the rising
79 Grenoble: youthful members of Darnand's fascist militia executed after the liberation

III Men and Moments

Stirring the Pot in Central Europe

81 Hitler addressing a rally

82 Foreign Minister Beck announcing Czechoslovak acceptance of Poland's demands, October 1938

83 The Germans enter the Sudetenland

84 Pearl Harbor, December 1941
85 American might assembled in Italy for the
   invasion of southern France, August 1944

86 Goering and his staff gaze across the English Channel
87 Russians reach the Pacific, 1945

Victory and Defeat 88 Marshals Rokossovsky and Montgomery after the meeting of East and West: Cossacks salute the British Field Marshal with their battle cry

89 The Soviet flag raised over the Reichstag

90 Emperor Hirohito in his capital surveying bomb damage

91 Laval taken into American custody at Linz

92 Von Papen prisoner

Peace and After

93 Berlin, 1945
94 Stalingrad, 1945
95 In Saarbrücken 1,000 survivors of a population of 135,000 salvage their belongings

97 Citizens of Tokyo exhorted to sign a petition for the reprieve of General Yamashita from death

98 The war becomes history: picture postcards on sale twenty years later

the Anglo-American landings in Morocco and Algeria). The Rumanian Third Army was routed at once. So was the Rumanian Fourth Army the next day. There was now a gap between the Sixth Army and the Italians and Hungarians further to the left and a wider gap than ever between Army Groups B and A. And the Sixth Army, which consisted of twenty-two divisions and 220,000 men, had to be supplied by air or extricated.

The strains of the autumn months of 1942 made Hitler singularly moody and intractable. He stayed at his headquarters conducting the war on paper, refusing to allow his plans and his hopes to be upset by reports of what was actually happening in the field. The German staffs had good intelligence about the Russian forces and their dispositions; their intentions were not difficult to guess. But Hitler, pitting his will against the Russians' resources, continued to believe that he could prevail by insisting that that was how it was to be. The arguments of his generals failed to persuade him that he must give up the idea of taking Stalingrad and concentrate on saving the Sixth Army. By November the generals, now deeply pessimistic, were reduced to hoping that something would happen to change Hitler's mind before it was too late, but even after Paulus had been surrounded Hitler found arguments for sticking to his guns: the new Tiger tank would do the trick and meanwhile the Luftwaffe would keep the Sixth Army supplied.

But the Tiger was not yet in service and the Luftwaffe could do nothing of the sort. Goering, confronted with the question whether he could deliver 700 tons a day to the Sixth Army, declared that he could. This irresponsible pledge was partly the result of a successful supply operation earlier in the year to other forces surrounded on the Russian front. This operation, however, had been conducted in much better weather and before the Luftwaffe had had to send squadrons (including Ju. 52 squadrons) from Russia to Africa; and it had cost crippling losses. But Goering preferred to undertake, however vainly, to save the Sixth Army than to incur reproaches for not stepping forward to say he could. The generals at Hitler's headquarters knew that Goering's promise was absurd but their protests, muted by fear of the Führer, were passed over. The daily target of 700 tons was reduced to 300, but the Luftwaffe never came anywhere near it. It had no adequate landing grounds near the Sixth Army or within its shrinking perimeter and the cold, which set in early in November and was accompanied by thick fogs from the middle of the month, made flying extremely hazardous when at all possible and the servicing of aircraft on the ground a torture for frozen mechanics. The lift began on 25 November. On that day and the next sixty-five tons were delivered, on the third nothing. A big effort was made in mid-December but the fog came down again and although a few F.W. 200s continued to drop a few tons on most days until the end, the Luftwaffe's contribution was wholly ineffectual. The total supplied by drops and landings was 3,295 tons. The Luftwaffe lost 488 machines and 1,000 men.

At the end of November Manstein was given command of Army Group B (renamed Army Group Don) but it was still not clear whether he was to save the Sixth Army by opening an escape route for it to the west or by breaking the Russian ring round it and so enabling it to remain on the Volga. Hitler equivocated. Manstein's own plan was twofold: an eastward offensive by the Fourth Panzer Army and a simultaneous westward attack by a part of the Sixth Army, leaving however the rest of the Sixth Army still on the Volga; and, at a later stage, a breakout by the whole of the Sixth Army to the west. The operation began on 12 December and the German armour advancing from the west got to within forty miles of the Sixth Army's position, but nine days later it was halted. Neither Manstein nor – still less, since he was Manstein's subordinate – Paulus was willing to give the order to the Sixth Army to break out without Hitler's approval, which they could not get. Without it the first part of Manstein's plan was pointless and, as the events showed, also impracticable. By mid-December therefore the fate of the Sixth Army was sealed. The Russians, after inflicting further defeats on Italian, Hungarian and German armies north-west of Stalingrad, offered Paulus on 8 January honourable terms of surrender. Hitler made Paulus a Field Marshal and told him to stand his ground.

By this time the city had been turned into something which none of those who fought there had ever imagined and none who survived could ever forget. The closest and bloodiest battle of the war was fought among the stumps of buildings burnt or burning. From afar Stalingrad looked like a furnace and yet inside it men froze. Dogs rushed into the Volga to drown rather than endure any longer the perils of the shore. The no less desperate men were reduced to automatons, obeying orders until it came to their turn to die, human only in their suffering. The Germans were on half rations from the end of November. By the middle of January the German zone, which had measured twenty-five miles by twelve when Paulus was first surrounded in November, had been halved. A little later it was cut in two. Again the Russians called for surrender and again Hitler refused to permit it. The final capitulation came on 2 February. Ninety-one thousand survivors, including a Field Marshal and twenty-four generals, were taken captive. The Russians had already taken 16,700 prisoners during the last weeks of the fighting. Some

70,000 Germans died during the siege, many of them from exposure or starvation, some by suicide.

At Stalingrad the Russians first demonstrated the material strength which was to overwhelm the German armies in 1943 and 1944. They concentrated over a million men against German armies which were numerically slightly stronger and, although still inferior in aircraft, they had the measure of the Germans in tanks and guns. Even in aircraft the balance was shifting. A new Russian fighter, the La. 5, made (like the British Mosquito) of wood, came into service and helped the Russians to achieve local air superiority. Although at Stalingrad the Luftwaffe committed 1,000 aircraft – about half its strength in the Russian theatre but diminished in October when Hitler ordered some squadrons to Leningrad – its numerical superiority was beginning to be offset by growing experience, skill and morale on the Russian side and by anxieties about repairs, reserves and replacements on its own. From 1943 onwards the Germans continued to keep between a half and two thirds of the Luftwaffe in the east, but some of its best pilots, newest aircraft and latest equipment were reserved for the defence of the Reich and for other theatres, and the shortage of pilots and aircraft gradually increased to the point where at times new aircraft, even new types, were given to the Rumanian and Hungarian air forces, which had pilots to fly them, while at other times German squadrons were obliged to make do with obsolescent machines. The Russian air force on the other hand was not only growing in quantity and quality but, since it undertook very little strategic long-range bombing, was able to devote almost its entire strength to attacking the German armies and their installations and communications.

There was after Stalingrad also a qualitative change in the war in the USSR. The importance of Stalingrad was much more than statistical. This battle destroyed the idea that the German army could not be beaten: here, on the contrary, was defeat unmistakable. The surrender of the Sixth Army was a tremendous psychological as well as military blow to the Germans and an equally powerful boost to Russian morale and to Stalin's campaign to show that Russia's great patriotic war could be won. The effect on Hitler was to accelerate his physical and mental decline. In 1942 his speech and handwriting began to show the effects of Parkinson's disease, a general decay of the nervous system which destroys a man's coordination and eventually his understanding. A year later he had become a shambling, shaking wreck, pathologically suspicious of his generals, contemptuous of the qualities of his fighting men, driven increasingly to substitute his personal stubbornness for the divisions which he pretended to direct but which were often not really there. He showed at Stalingrad, in catastrophic degree, his inability to accept even the concept of defeat. His astonishing memory and grasp of detail, his energy and quickness, his serious application to the art of war and the way with men which he sometimes displayed – all these things were destroyed, first, by the distortions induced by failure in a mind of terrifying rigidity and irrationality, and then by disease. The nemesis of will was upon him and his people.

The defeats of Army Group B in the winter of 1942–3 exposed Army Group A to the risk of being bottled up entire in the Caucasus. The Russians planned to advance from the Don to the Donets and then turn about and capture Rostov at the mouth of the Don from the west. This manoeuvre would have established a Russian line from Stalingrad to Rostov, cutting off Army Group A's line of retreat. The Russian plan was, however, frustrated and the Fourth Panzer Army succeeded in making contact with Army Group A and opened an escape for it, thereby enabling its forces to survive and fight another day. The thaw in March eased the pressure on the Germans who recaptured Kharkov which they had lost a few weeks earlier. Thus the Russian victories, although massive, were not decisive and the Germans were able to regain the initiative and hold much of the Donets basin. This, if anything, was the Sixth Army's posthumous reward. But the losses of the German armies could not be replaced; after the middle of 1943 the eastern fronts had even to surrender units for Italy, the Balkans and the west, and by the end of that year thirty divisions – 15 per cent of those on the Russian fronts – had been disbanded for want of replacements to fill the gaps in their ranks.

As a result of the fighting in February and March 1943 the Russians held Kursk, a hundred miles south of Orel and a hundred miles north of Kharkov, both of which cities remained in German hands. The Russian position was therefore a huge bulge which Hitler proposed to attack from both sides as soon as the weather permitted. The attack was launched on 5 July by Kluge in the north and Manstein in the south with a combined force of a million men and 2,700 tanks. The Luftwaffe, despite its commitments in other theatres, was able to fly 3,000 sorties a day and Hitler hoped that after cutting off the Russian armies in the bulge he would be able to turn about and dash for Moscow, 200 miles north-east of Orel. The Russians were ready and equipped for the attack. Two fronts, commanded by Rokossovski and Vatutin, were backed by a reserve front under Konev which had been constituted in their rear. The Russian armies were plentifully supplied by Russian industry, and although the Russian Marshals had somewhat fewer tanks than their opponents, the Russian air forces were for the first time able to put many more aircraft into the air than the Luftwaffe. Russian intelligence was detailed and accurate.

The two ensuing battles in the Kursk salient were the main encounter of the war between the Russian and German armies and they were astonishingly short. The German attack in the north was held from the beginning and by 10 July Kluge was forced onto the defensive, partly by the weight of Rokossovski's artillery and the effectiveness of his anti-tank weapons, and partly in anticipation of a Russian counter-attack on his left flank. The Russians also used air to ground rockets which, although not much more destructive than other weapons, were more demoralizing. In the south Manstein was initially more successful and Konev's reserves had to be called upon to help Vatutin. The result was the biggest tank battle of the war. By 12 July it was a clear Russian victory. The German offensive had failed. It was in fact the last significant offensive in the campaign which had opened two years earlier. The Russians counter-attacked, took Orel and Kharkov and extended the fighting along the whole front from the Baltic to the Black Sea. Their gains included Kiev which fell to them in November.

The battles for the Kursk salient cost Hitler half a million men and when they failed all possibility of avoiding total defeat had gone. The rest was retreat. The Russian armies, under the meticulously competent overall direction of Stalin (who achieved a more effective relationship with his generals than Hitler did) now outnumbered the Germans. The German Tiger tank, which had appeared in the previous autumn, and the Panther, which made its first appearance in these battles, failed to give Hitler the decisive superiority in the tank war which he had hoped for and which had been eluding him ever since 1941. His Tiger II, first used in 1944, was too late to affect the issue. The Russians with the heavy Joseph Stalin tank, the medium T 34 (which had reached units just in time in 1941) and the light T 70 proved themselves at least the equals of the Germans in quality, and in 1942 Russian production out-stripped German. The Russians were great war builders, the peers – given the circumstances – of the Americans. From 1943 their annual production of armoured fighting vehicles (that is to say, tanks, armoured vehicles and assault guns) was around 30,000. In Germany, where after Stalingrad Hitler had charged Guderian and Speer jointly to overhaul and increase the output of armoured fighting vehicles, production reached a peak of 19,000 in 1944.

Despite defeat Hitler maintained his refusal to sanction any with-

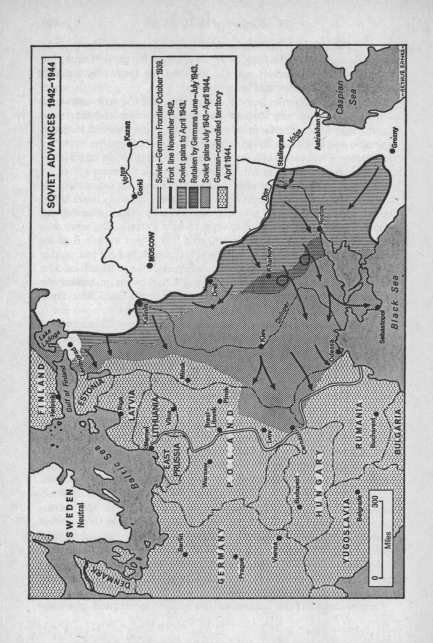

SOVIET ADVANCES 1942–1944

Soviet–German Frontier October 1939.
Front line November 1942,
Soviet gains to April 1943,
Retaken by Germans June–July 1943.
Soviet gains July 1943–April 1944.
German-controlled territory
April 1944.

— ARTHUR BANKS

Caspian Sea

Kazan

Volga

Gorki

Astrakhan

Grozny

MOSCOW

Stalingrad

Volga

Don

Rostov

Orel

Kharkov

Dnieper

Kiev

Black Sea

Kalinin

Sebastopol

Odessa

Lake Ladoga

Leningrad

Gulf of Finland

FINLAND

Helsinki

ESTONIA

LATVIA

Riga

LITHUANIA

Memel

Vilna

Minsk

Pinsk

Brest-Litovsk

Baltic Sea

SWEDEN
Neutral

EAST PRUSSIA

POLAND

Warsaw

Lublin

Lwów

HUNGARY

RUMANIA

Bucharest

BULGARIA

GERMANY

Berlin

Prague

Vienna

Budapest

YUGOSLAVIA

Belgrade

DENMARK

0   300
Miles

drawal, rationalizing his stubborn strategy by his need to keep Rumania, Bulgaria and Hungary in the war and Turkey from joining his enemies – none of which he succeeded in doing as he was pushed back from the Dnieper to the Bug to the Dniester. A fresh Russian winter offensive, beginning in December, relieved Leningrad early in 1944, cut off a Germany army in the Crimea and brought the Russians to the Carpathians and into Rumania in March. Hitler dismissed Manstein and other senior commanders.

The Russians paused before beginning a new series of attacks in the summer. These began on 23 June (just over two weeks after Overlord) in White Russia where the German Army Group Centre had been instructed to hold and protect Lithuania, East Prussia and northern Poland. The main Russian attack had been expected in the Ukraine and Army Group Centre was destroyed in a couple of weeks. North of it Army Group North, defending Latvia and Estonia, was cut off as the Russians advanced to the sea west of Riga. In the autumn it was pressed back into the Courland peninsula where it survived until the general capitulation. In Finland a Russian attack in June led to an attempt by the Finns to negotiate peace and a visit by Ribbentrop to Helsinki to stop them. President Ryti gave Ribbentrop his personal promise not to make peace but this was a trick to enable Finland to get German aid for a few more weeks and then come to terms with the Russians, as occasion served, by changing president. In August President Ryti was replaced by Field Marshal Mannerheim and an armistice was signed in September. Finland had to pay an indemnity, lease the naval base of Porkkala, ten miles from Helsinki, to the USSR for fifty years, and provide the Russians with other military facilities so long as the war against Germany lasted. In the farthest north the Russians forced back German troops until they crossed into Norway and operations were suspended by the weather.

In the Ukraine the winter offensive of 1943–4 had left the Germans with a huge salient bounded by a long, irregular line 450 miles long which was held by only thirty-two divisions, many of them depleted. Against this salient the Russians concentrated 179 divisions in four Army Groups under the supreme command of Marshals Zhukov and Vasilevski. The battle began on the third anniversary of the launching of Barbarossa. Its object was to complete the reconquest of the Ukraine and continue the advance westward into Poland. Within three weeks the German Army Group virtually disintegrated. One German army was encircled in the area of Bobruisk, another in the area of Minsk. The Germans lost 350,000 men. The Russians crossed the 1939

Russo-German boundary line in Poland (they had entered pre-war Poland in January). As the Germans retreated from the USSR into Poland the commander of the Polish Home Army (AK), General Tadeusz Bor-Komorowski, first instructed his men to harass the Germans and neither attack the Russians nor be drawn into the Russian army. He later ordered them to occupy towns abandoned by the Germans and, if absolutely necessary, to defend themselves against the Russians rather than allow themselves to be evicted from their positions. These later instructions amounted to a recognition of the fact that the Polish army might be required to fight the Russian army in order to assert the Polishness of Poland's eastern territories. The Russians for their part declared these territories to be Russian, refused to recognize the AK as a regular combatant force (as the United States and Great Britain did), arrested AK commanders in their westward progress and sponsored in July the Polish Committee of National Liberation (the Lublin Committee) which they recognized in August as the provisional government of Poland. In this situation the London government decided to play a major card. In order to gain control of the Polish capital before the Russians, and to prevent its rivals within Poland from taking the lead in opposing the enemy, it ordered Warsaw to rise.

This decision, which was a political one, was taken without notice to the American or British government and without notice to the AK that American and British help was unlikely to be forthcoming. But the Poles in Warsaw, though capable of putting up a stiff fight, could not defeat the German garrison without outside help. The rising took place on 1 August. By this date the Russians were within sight of Warsaw. They had reached the Vistula on 28 July and they established three bridgeheads south of the city during the first ten days of August. But their losses during July had been serious, their men were exhausted and they were able to hold their bridgeheads only with the greatest difficulty; German counter-attacks drove them back in some sectors as much as sixty miles.

Stalin has been accused of deliberately abstaining from helping the people of Warsaw when he could have done so. There is nothing implausible in the charge, since the Russians and the Polish government in London were already virtually at war with one another and Stalin's only reason for maintaining otherwise was the need to preserve good relations with his western allies. He was determined not to trust the Poles or treat them as allies but to conquer them, and his problem was how to do this without causing a breach in his grand alliance with the United States and Great Britain. He succeeded because the latter were no less anxious than he was to preserve the alliance and because geography was on his side. He was in Poland and they were not.

Yet it may also be true that, whatever Stalin's attitude to the Poles of the AK and Warsaw, he was not in a position to succour them in August and September, even had he wished to. General Chuikov, the hero of Stalingrad who was still in command of the Sixty-second Army (honorifically renamed the Eighth Guards Army), has recorded that German air attacks were intense in the Warsaw area, that the Russians lacked bridging equipment which was vital for forcing the passage of the Vistula and exploiting the bridgeheads, and that his superior officer, Marshal Rokossovski, believed (erroneously, as it happened) that the Germans had an armoured force east of the Vistula which could be used to attack southwards and endanger the Russian positions across the river.

The Warsaw rising lasted from 1 August to 2 October. The Poles seized half the city, fragmented the German garrison but could not annihilate it. The Germans consolidated their hold over the sectors left to them and then gradually expanded until they recaptured the whole city. On the Polish side 20,000 men took part, armed at the outset with rifles and sub-machine guns and ammunition for seven days. Of these 20,000, 10,000 were killed and 7,000 wounded before Bor-Komorowski ordered surrender. The total casualties in the rising on the Polish side were close on 200,000. Nine tenths of Warsaw were destroyed.

The western allies were at first reluctant to help because of the practical difficulties. From Italy Air Marshal Sir John Slessor reported that, in the absence of permission to land in Russian-held territory and refuel (which was not granted), operations to Poland were so impossibly dangerous and comparatively useless that he would not undertake them unless ordered to. He made, however, an exception in favour of a Polish squadron under his command. It suffered very heavy losses. The RAF and South African Air Force later joined in a desperate attempt to supply the insurgents and, with the Poles, dropped 233 tons. The US Air Force undertook a single operation with 110 Flying Fortresses on 18 September but most of their supplies fell wide of the mark and were in any case too late. This operation, which took place in daylight, was made with the consent of the Russians to landing on Russian airfields, but it took the Americans a month to get this permission. At one point Churchill suggested to Roosevelt that aircraft should land on Russian airfields without Russian permission and see what happened, but Roosevelt was not willing to go as far as that. On 13 September, by which time Rokossovski was ready to renew his advance and take advantage of the Germans' preoccupation with the rising, the Russians began dropping food and ammunition to Warsaw. At least fifty tons – perhaps considerably more – were dropped, most of it accurately but in damaged condition because parachutes were not used. Russian ground forces had successfully attacked the suburb of Praga on 10 September and a few days later they began an attempt to cross the Vistula and established a number of bridgeheads, but they were forced to retreat in the face of German opposition.

The recapture of Warsaw was one of Nazi Germany's last military successes. The city remained in German hands, demolished and depopulated, until the first day of 1945 when the Russians at last entered the capital before which they had been repulsed in 1920. The AK was dissolved by the Russian winter offensive and in March seventeen non-communist Polish leaders, proceeding under safe conduct and at Russian invitation to meet a Russian general, were dispatched to Moscow where all were imprisoned and some died. For Stalin the conquests of these years were a sequel to the unfinished business of 1917–20, the export of revolution, called by its champions liberation and by its victims conquest.

Upon recovering the Ukraine the Russians entered Rumania as well as Poland and posed an increasingly awkward problem for Germany's other allies: Bulgaria, Slovakia and Hungary. These allies had already seen the writing on the wall. The German defeats in 1943 and the capitulation of Italy in the same year had set them thinking about how to secure their future in a Europe which was going to be dominated by the USSR in place of Germany.

In Rumania Ion Antonescu's attempt to concert action with Mussolini in 1943 was fruitless. He was then recaptivated by Hitler and his talk of secret weapons but in August 1944 he was dismissed by King Michael after a stormy interview. Attempts to secure western help against the Russian wrath to come were fruitless, for there was nothing the western allies could do for the Rumanians and they were left to make the best terms they could. The king broke off relations with Germany and made contact with the Communist Party (which had been outlawed before the war). After a short period of confusion, during which Bucharest was bombed by the Germans and the German Ambassador committed suicide and his colleagues disappeared for good into the Soviet Union, a new and essentially communist government was installed under Petru Groza. Rumania was required to ratify its territorial losses to the USSR in 1940 but was promised the return of what it had lost to Hungary (but not what it had lost to Bulgaria); it was also required to pay an indemnity to the USSR and fight against Germany.

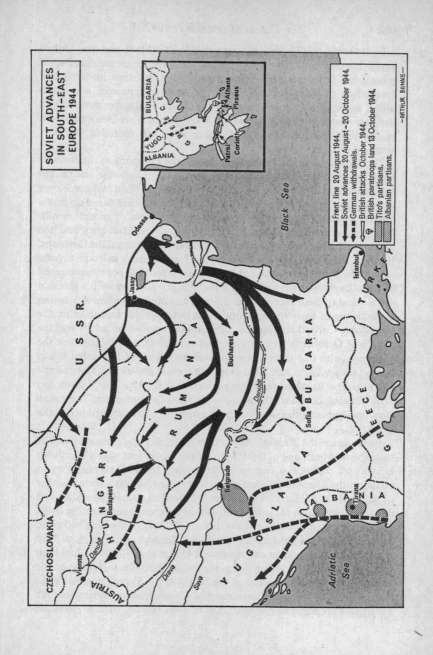

SOVIET ADVANCES
IN SOUTH-EAST
EUROPE 1944

Front line 20 August 1944.
Soviet advances 20 August – 20 October 1944.
German withdrawals.
British attacks October 1944.
British paratroops land 13 October 1944.
Tito's partisans.
Albanian partisans.

—ARTHUR BANKS—

Black Sea

Odessa

Jassy

U S S R.

R U M A N I A

Bucharest

Danube

Istanbul

TURKEY

B U L G A R I A

Sofia

Danube

Belgrade

CZECHOSLOVAKIA

Vienna

Budapest

H U N G A R Y

Danube

Drava

Sava

AUSTRIA

Y U G O S L A V I A

G R E E C E

Adriatic
Sea

A L B A N I A

Tirana

BULGARIA

YUGO.

ALBANIA

G R E E C E

Athens
Piraeus

Patras
Corinth

In Bulgaria, which was at war with Great Britain and the United States but not with the Soviet Union, the government declared itself neutral but failed none the less to stave off a Russian invasion and declaration of war. Bulgaria, under a new government, was compelled in September to declare war on Germany. In the same month Russian troops entered Yugoslavia. They shared with Tito's partisans in the capture of Belgrade in October and then retired a few days later.

The Slovaks, like the Poles, rose against the Germans as the Russian armies approached. Slovakia was an ally of Germany and a co-belligerent but in October 1943 an entire Slovak division had come over to the Russians and in the same period partisan warfare flared up inside eastern Slovakia. In 1944 the country was in a state of general revolt. National committees emerged and commandeered factories and the property of collaborators. An army 65,000 strong engaged the Germans. It hoped to be joined by the Russian army and there is still controversy about why it was not. Marshal Konev seems to have been approached by Slovak officers with a plan for a rising in conjunction with a Russian attack, and to have recommended Stalin to adopt this plan. A Russian advance began early in September. But the Russians had to cross the formidable Carpathians against stiff German opposition and it was the middle of October before they set foot on Slovak soil. By this time the Germans, who had been forewarned of the rising, had defeated it and burned sixty villages and filled at least 200 mass graves with slaughtered Slovaks. The Russians later complained that they had been given too little advance notice of the actual date fixed for the rising. They may also have been sceptical about Slovak estimates of the importance of the operation.

In Hungary the Regent, Admiral Horthy, Europe's senior head of state (he had been one of the leaders of the movement which overthrew Bela Kun's communist régime in 1919), was forced by events to try to abandon the German alliance which had served him well for a number of years. He had joined it because he belonged to a small, nostalgic and illiberal ruling caste for whom anti-Bolshevism was an overriding issue. He had benefited from the two awards of 1939 and 1940 which had given him chunks of his neighbours' territories, he had been happy to help Hitler invade Yugoslavia and the Soviet Union in 1941 and he had been gratified to find that Hitler did not want to oust him in favour of the leader of the local equivalent of the Nazi Party – Ferenc Szalasi of the Arrow Cross (who wanted even more of his neighbours' territories than Hitler was prepared to concede). Up to 1944 Horthy tried to persuade himself that Hitler, after abandoning the Balkans, might succeed in holding the Carpathians and Transylvania and so keep the Russians away from central Europe, but the impending collapse of Rumania showed him that he had no choice and he prepared – too late – to make his escape from the war, even at the price of turning to the communist USSR.

For Hitler, however, Hungary had exceptional strategic significance. He had to hold it so long as he had troops in south-eastern Europe and even if these were safely withdrawn the loss of Hungary would set the Russians well on the way into Vienna. He therefore took over Hungary (thereby initiating anti-Jewish razzias) and sent Otto Skorzeny, the saviour of Mussolini, to kidnap Horthy. Skorzeny first kidnapped the Regent's son and then, in a singularly bold escapade, seized the citadel of Budapest with one car and four tanks. The Regent escaped but immediately afterwards resigned and was taken to Germany under guard. The Germans installed an Arrow Cross government under Szalasi, who was however an incompetent visionary and was hated by the Hungarian army. At the end of 1944 Budapest was beleaguered by Marshal Malinovski. The Germans tried to relieve it but failed, and the city surrendered on 12 February 1945. In this case the Russians made no effort to restrain their troops, who proceeded to eliminate the *ancien régime* in the most direct and gruesome manner. Horthy's long reign ended, as it had begun, with terror and bloodshed, and Hungary virtually lost its independence too.

The Russo-German campaigns were the most terrible war that has ever been waged. The numbers of the dead were huge. The great sieges of Leningrad, Stalingrad and Sebastopol recalled the war-making of other times but the field campaigns were something new. They were the acme of (pre-nuclear) industrial warfare. The mechanized armies of tanks and workshops were industrial plants in motion attended by hundreds of thousands of technicians. These ponderous devastators, made of steel and moved by oil, churned up the countryside and at intervals blazed away at each other, leaving the land covered with warped steel, stinking oil and corpses. In between these armadas men in various kinds of armoured or unarmoured transport, and sometimes still on foot, covered great distances because they were winning or losing or simply because they were required to shift themselves laterally from one part of the front to another. Sometimes there were long lulls, passages of normalcy embedded in senselessness and horror, and if the weather was fine, men might go through the motions of ordinary life and, with their singing and their horseplay, behave as though they were on an excursion rather than a highly organized killing. But then for many months there would be slush and mud and clothes never really dry, or the intense cold which made it dangerous to take off a glove. The most remarkable thing about this war was that, on both sides, men went on fighting it for nearly four years.

CHAPTER 23

Mass Bombing

FRIGHTENING your enemy is the fundamental and presumably the oldest weapon of war. Starving him – hitting him where it hurts most – cannot be much less old. Mass bombing is the most modern way of trying to destroy both his morale and his economy at one and the same time. Where earlier warriors rushed upon their foes with painted bodies and hideous screams, or poisoned wells and beleaguered towns, their more sophisticated though hardly more civilized successors rain high explosives on factories and homes and set fire to whole cities. Only the techniques and the scale are new.

Perhaps the hallowed antiquity of the aim explains the fact that these new and fearful means were generally accepted in the Second World War. Air raids involving the indiscriminate killing of enormous numbers of civilians were the current step in the natural evolution of the art of war. The very concept of the civilian hardly remained valid. The traditional distinction between men setting forth to risk their lives and those who stayed behind out of range of death disappeared in the first half of the twentieth century. All were now combatants in their several ways. A civilian was a combatant who did not happen to be enrolled in the traditionally recognized fighting services; he was constantly proclaimed to be in the front line, a description implying that he was risking his life as much as anybody and would not think to complain about staking it. Even the deaths of children were accepted as, if not legitimate, yet logical consequences of war, occasioning special grief no doubt but relatively little indignation: that was the way things were.

At the beginning of the war Great Britain and France had promised, in response to a plea by Roosevelt, to confine bombing to strictly military targets provided the Germans did so too, but what was a military target was unclear and changeable. Yet there seemed to be one rule which still survived. There was still a sense of proportion and a feeling of uneasiness if it were disregarded, an acceptance of the ancient Greek tag that means must bear some relation to ends. To destroy factories or the people who worked in them, or the homes of people who worked in them, was perhaps legitimate; but to do these things – as for instance in the bombing of Dresden – without being able to point to a commensurate strategic advantage was not just a sad necessity but also uncomfortably hard to justify.

But if a majority acquiesced in what seemed to be the inevitability of the deplorable, a minority clung to an older teaching. This minority, trying to bend modern capabilities to the Christian faith instead of adapting the latter to the former, said that since all killing was wrong in the absence of special justifying circumstances, indiscriminate mass killing needed to be very meticulously justified indeed – and was not. Champions of this tradition such as Dr George Bell, Bishop of Chichester, accepted that the nature and context of war had so changed that many deaths, hitherto regarded as unjustifiable, must be accepted, but they alleged that there was still a line to be drawn somewhere and that the destruction of closely packed residential areas, because they were closely packed residential areas, was a sin and – even in the absence of any international convention on air warfare – a crime. Even if it was permissible to kill men and women at work in factories, it was not permissible to kill men, women and children in their homes. For keeping these Christian ideas before men's minds in spite of the clatter of arms the Bishop of Chichester was not elevated to the highest Christian office in England when the see of Canterbury, for which many inside the church and out considered him pre-eminently qualified, fell vacant at the end of 1944. He was even denied the lesser see of York many years after the war was over and after it had virtually been promised to him.

The advent of air power had brought with it a school of theorists who alleged that this new weapon could contribute to war-making by doing something that had never been done before, and could do this independently and without the help of the older sea and land forces. The Second World War put this theory to the test and (with air power as it was before the introduction of nuclear weapons) found it wanting. The prime aim of assailing industry, communications and morale was to compel the surrender of the enemy even though his armed forces had suffered no irreversible defeat in the field. Defeat in workshop and homestead was to take the place of defeat in the field as the first aim of strategy. This had been the aim of naval blockade, but no navy had ever succeeded in making a blockade more than an ancillary element in war-making. It had neither broken morale nor brought the machinery of war to a halt. If air power could succeed in these tasks, then the bomber aircraft would prove a truly revolutionary weapon, more revolutionary than either the submarine which upset a number of military concepts in the First World War or the tank which did the same in the Second.

Although aircraft had appeared in time to take part in the First World War, their role had been too limited and tentative for any settled conclusions to be drawn about the nature of air power. Consequently the question was much debated, *a priori* and often acrimoniously, between the wars. The importance of air power was conceded, but the best way to use an air force was hotly contested between those who thought of aircraft as a sort of extended artillery operating in conjunction with and under the control of army commanders and, on the other hand, those who held that air power had superseded land power. There were no even approximately accepted estimates of the amount of damage which a bomber force could inflict and most estimates were wildly excessive, largely owing to the unjustified assumption that if a bomber could reach its target, it would have relatively little difficulty in hitting it.

In 1917 Churchill, then Minister of Munitions, said:

> It is improbable that any terrorization of the civil population which could be achieved by air attack would compel ... surrender ... we have seen the combative spirit of the people roused, and not quelled, by the German air raids. Nothing that we have learned of the capacity of the German population to endure suffering justifies us in assuming that they could be cowed into submission by such methods, or ... not be rendered more desperately resolved by them.

But in 1940 he thought that 'only the Air Force' could win the war. It is not clear what changed his mind, but it is probable that the champions of bombing had succeeded between the wars in implanting in many minds the belief that precision bombing could win a war. This involved considerable loss of life in the factories hit, but it did not envisage the mass bombing of civilians in their homes as well as their factories. But when it came to the test, precision bombing failed to be precise and area bombing was substituted for it as a means whereby an air force could live up to its claim to win a war.

The weightiest of the early champions of the independent role of the bomber were to be found in Italy and the United States – in particular General Giulio Douhet and General William Mitchell – but its most effective protagonist between the wars was the Royal Air Force under Air Marshal Sir Hugh Trenchard. The US Air Force was the most powerful of all bomber forces before the war ended, but the RAF was the first to acquire and operate a heavily armoured four-engined bomber; the Luftwaffe never had one in any number which counted. In spite of the urgent need to equip Fighter Command with modern fighters, the Air Council decided simultaneously to provide Bomber

Command with four-engined bombers, ordered prototypes of the Stirling, Halifax and Manchester (later re-designed as the Lancaster) in 1937 and placed an order for 3,500 heavy bombers in October 1938 for delivery in the spring of 1942. Although these aircraft were not available as early as the Hurricane and Spitfire (with the result that Bomber Command's best crews had to fly antiquated Blenheims and die in them) they were brought into service in 1940–41. This decision by the Air Council, like the decision to build the eight-gun fighter, was undoubtedly justified, although it was partly the outcome of a conflict of views which was resolved by adopting both – by allowing Dowding to have his eight-gun fighter while at the same time going part of the way with the opposition to Dowding which decried the fighter arm and wanted to concentrate on a smashing bomber force, the symbol and justification of an independent air force.

In Germany a similar conflict was resolved in a different way. The accidental death of the protagonist of the heavy bomber, General Walther Wever, led to the cancellation of plans for such an aircraft, to a decision to rely on speed rather than armour, and to a disproportionate concentration on fighters, dive bombers and the role of army cooperation. The bomber became the Cinderella of the Luftwaffe. The Battle of Britain showed how ill judged this policy was. The Luftwaffe's relatively fast but lightly armed and lightly armoured medium bombers were defeated – as the RAF's obsolescent Blenheims had been over France a year earlier. For a time both sides were restricted to operations under the cover of darkness which were clearly not a war-winning effort. But although both sides were thus reduced to similar tactics, their circumstances were very different. The RAF's Bomber Command was conserving its strength, making few sorties in mass, keeping its losses down to about 3 per cent and awaiting the early delivery of the four-engined aircraft which were to take over from the two-engined Wellington, Witley and Hampden; between the outbreak of war and the end of 1941 it increased its strength from 200 to 500 and the latter figure included the first few dozen Stirlings and Halifaxes. The Luftwaffe had nothing of the kind in view.

On the British side a further consequence was the evolution of a singularly independent Bomber Command under a Commander-in-Chief less amenable than his fellows to the overall strategic control of the Chief of the Air Staff and dedicated to proving the proposition that his force could win the war independently and was doing so and ought not to be impeded by diverting new bombers to Coastal Command's war against the U-boats. This position was further enhanced when the heavy bombers reached the Command in strength in 1943, their radar aids became increasingly precise and the invasion of France was postponed to 1944. Moreover by this time Bomber Command's pertinacious activity had won for it a position of independence from the Americans which the British army, preparing for the role of minor partner in Overlord, could never claim. British independence, which had been saved by Fighter Command in 1940, was symbolized thereafter by Bomber Command.

The failure of daylight bombing by the two-engined bomber which could neither find its target nor hit it – at the beginning of the war even fair-sized towns were missed by two thirds of the then inexperienced crews – could be interpreted so as to lead to opposite conclusions. Either daylight bombing must be pursued in some other way, or it could be abandoned and the main bomber effort be put forth at night. The British opted for the latter alternative. The Americans believed in the former. In the British view it was not enough simply to get a bigger and better bomber to do what its predecessors had failed to do. It must also be used to do something different. This decision lay partly in the nature of things – the sheer difficulty of unescorted daylight bombing of any kind so long as the enemy had fighter defences – and partly in the need to employ the RAF's existing bombers pending the delivery of new ones. Great Britain, as a country at war, could not rest its bomber force; it was inconceivable that the force should not be used somehow, the more so as Great Britain had no other way of taking the offensive in Europe. Consequently the two-engined bombers were set from 1940 to attack the continent by night and in doing so they developed tactics and instruments which, with their crews, were inherited by the four-engined bomber. Bomber Command became a night-time and not a daylight predator.

Daylight bombing had failed. Then in the winter of 1940–41 photographic reconnaissance and other Intelligence sources revealed that the bomber could not hit the target even at night when the enemy's fighters (not yet equipped for night fighting) were virtually impotent. Bomber Command's claims, advanced with partisan fervour and, some thought, with a degree of partisan recklessness were shown to be very wide of the mark. One solution was to choose larger targets. Attacks on oil refineries were abandoned but attacks on rail centres continued, because these could be significantly damaged even if the bombs fell as much as 1,000 yards wide of the aiming point. But even rail targets could not be usefully attacked without the help of the moon and rather than do nothing on moonless nights Bomber Command began raiding areas of population and hoping for the best. Intelligence continued to report a significant number of misses by miles. This combination of operational imprecision and reliable intelligence drove the Command, under the forceful leadership of Air Marshal Sir Arthur Harris, increasingly to area bombing. It was powerfully supported by Churchill's fiercely singleminded Principal Scientific Adviser, Professor Frederick Lindemann (Lord Cherwell), who believed that it was both possible and legitimate to destroy half the working-class houses in all the larger German cities, but was strongly contested by other eminent scientists, notably Professors Henry Tizard and P. M. S. Blackett, who alleged (correctly, as it turned out) that expectations were greatly exaggerated and argued for more selective operations such as the war against the U-boats. The policy in action cost the lives of over 55,000 aircrew in Bomber Command – and twice as many in the American air forces in Europe.

When Harris assumed command in February 1942 his force was ready to make massive attacks within a restricted radius and in March Bomber Command's main campaign of the war opened with a raid on the ancient and inflammable city of Lübeck which was chosen because it was lightly defended and easily accessible from the sea. This was the first operational appearance of the Lancaster. Four raids on Rostock, east of Lübeck and also on the Baltic, followed in April. These raids were experiments and demonstrations. They provoked a German counter-attack on cities in England which were also lightly defended and historically and artistically noteworthy – the so-called Baedeker raids on places like Bristol and Exeter. In May Bomber Command hit back with the 1,000-bomber raid on Cologne, for which training machines and crews were pressed into temporary service. The material damage was not great, but the boost to morale in the force and among civilians, the shock to the Germans and the impression made on allies, Resistance movements and neutrals may be thought to have justified the effort and the cost. German retaliation was ineffective.

In the latter part of this same year Bomber Command's effectiveness was increased by the formation of a corps of specially equipped and trained Pathfinders, which preceded the main body of aircraft to locate and mark their targets. Other technical aids to navigation and aiming followed. The ground operated Gee was supplemented by Oboe, which helped pilots to keep to the right course but had limited range and was subject to jamming, and from 1943 by the airborne radar H 2 S which enabled the bomb aimer to 'see' his target in spite of poor weather and the heights to which he might be forced by anti-aircraft guns and searchlights. Nevertheless precision bombing remained impossible except at ruinous cost. When in May 1943 the Möhne, Eder and Sorpe Dams were breached in an attempt to immobilize industry in the Ruhr, the attack was made from the perilous height of sixty feet by a select band of nineteen Lancasters carrying a specially designed mine and crews which had been trained for months over replicas of the target area. Eight of these aircraft were lost, fifty-four men killed. This extremely heroic operation achieved the immediate purpose of breaching the dams but not the basic purpose of seriously impeding production in the Ruhr. Operations of this kind could never be more than exceptional and in fact no comparable raid was ever carried out. The bombing of cities remained Bomber Command's main way of proving the claim of air power to be a war-winner, the civilian population being the principal target with factories as, in the words of a Bomber Command directive, a bonus.

In this context the Ruhr was marked out as the Command's main target. But it was very heavily defended. Essen and Düsseldorf were both attacked in the summer of 1942. In retrospect these raids underline how far Bomber Command was and remained an élite force. Essen was attacked by 1,000 aircraft but this was the last time that Bomber Command put 1,000 aircraft into the air for a single raid before 1944. During 1943 it gradually intensified its campaign against the Ruhr and extended it to more distant targets such as Hamburg and Berlin. Its strength in aircraft was not much greater at the beginning of 1943 than it had been a year earlier, but half of these were four-engined aircraft. In addition the Mosquito, one of the outstanding aircraft of the war, designed in the mid-thirties but comparatively unnoticed until now, had the range and speed to enable it to brave the German defences all the way to Berlin with a 4,000 lb. bomb. On the other hand the Luftwaffe's early warning system, ground controls and night fighter tactics were being greatly improved. When the war began Germany had radar which was more accurate than British radar but of shorter range and not linked with a ground control system of the same complexity and sophistication. As a result the bombing operations of 1942 defeated the German night defences, but in 1943 the tables were turned and the German night fighters began to strike almost as freely as though they were operating by day. Bomber losses rose to over 5 per cent of the attacking force. For several months it was not clear who was winning. Nerves were taut on both sides and in August 1943 the Chief of Staff of the Luftwaffe, General Hans Jeschonnek, committed suicide.

In Berlin, which suffered sixteen major night raids spread over four months in the winter of 1942–3 as well as additional American daylight raids in the latter part of this period, the damage was severe enough to cause a considerable exodus and close all schools, but even in the immediate aftermath of the raids less than half of the city's industries stopped work and many of the stoppages were brief. Hamburg on the other hand, which was attacked by night and day seven times in nine days in July and August 1942, was savagely and to some degree permanently wrecked with the assistance of two new techniques: the dropping of strips of tinfoil called Window which so confused the defence's radar scanners that bomber losses on the first night were only twelve out of 800; and the raising of fire storms by incendiary bombs which created fierce currents of flame rushing at temperatures of 1,000° centigrade to the centre of the storm at speeds of 100–150 m.p.h. and incinerating people above and below ground. At least 50,000 were killed in this way and a million more fled from the city: half the houses were destroyed and more than half the remainder damaged.

Yet morale broke in neither city. Bomber Command failed to bring German industry to a halt and the German defences pushed bomber losses up beyond 5 per cent and, early in 1944, even to 10 per cent. A new German airborne radar called Lichtenstein gave the night fighters longer range and a wider angle of vision and also enabled them to overcome Window. In an attack on Nuremberg in March the Command lost ninety-four aircraft out of 791 (12.5 per cent). In four and a half months 1,000 aircraft were totally lost and 1,682 more seriously damaged. Such losses were not tolerable. The Command's onslaught had been parried. No other arm suffered such casualties during the Second World War. The cost and the results were horribly reminiscent of Passchendaele. The only consolation was that German counter-attacks on London and elsewhere in the early months of 1944 had been thwarted by the defences and the Luftwaffe could no longer even carry out reconnaissance flights over Great Britain.

The American strategic bombing offensive was showing the same pattern of destruction at great cost and without commensurate results. At the Casablanca conference of January 1943 Roosevelt and Churchill had agreed that strategic bombing was for the time being their principal weapon against Hitler and their principal way of helping Stalin. At that time, however, the US air forces were comparatively small and stretched over many theatres (the Pacific and Atlantic, North Africa and the Middle East), and it was not until the second half of that year that the US Eighth and Fifteenth Air Forces were able to add significantly to the British effort: the first American raid on Germany was

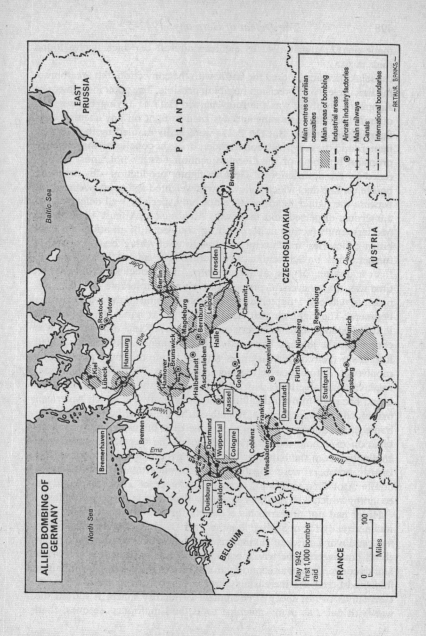

ALLIED BOMBING OF GERMANY

Legend:
☐ Main centres of civilian casualties
▨ Main areas of bombing
▨ Industrial areas
⊙ Aircraft industry factories
╫ Main railways
‒‒‒ Canals
‒·‒ International boundaries

~ARTHUR BANKS~

May 1942
First 1,000 bomber
raid

Miles
0   100

North Sea
Baltic Sea
EAST PRUSSIA
POLAND
CZECHOSLOVAKIA
AUSTRIA
HOLLAND
BELGIUM
LUX.
FRANCE

Rostock
Tutow
Kiel
Lübeck
Hamburg
Bremerhaven
Bremen
Hannover
Brunswick
Berlin
Magdeburg
Bernburg
Halberstadt
Aschersleben
Halle
Leipzig
Dresden
Breslau
Chemnitz
Gotha
Kassel
Darmstadt
Frankfurt
Wiesbaden
Coblenz
Cologne
Wuppertal
Düsseldorf
Duisburg
Dortmund
Schweinfurt
Nürnberg
Fürth
Regensburg
Munich
Augsburg
Stuttgart

Elbe
Oder
Weser
Ems
Rhine
Danube

made on 17 August 1942 by eighteen aircraft of which twelve found their target.

The Americans entered the battle with the conviction that area bombing was useless and precision bombing possible. The main instrument of American bombing was the four-engined B 17 or Flying Fortress, an aircraft bristling with guns and designed to fight off any enemy's daylight fighter attacks. But the B 17s were badly mauled by the German fighters and the American commanders drew the conclusion that effective precision bombing of the German economy as a whole must be preceded by the destruction of German fighter production – by precision bombing. The duel which followed was weighted against the Americans because the fighter factories were not only specially well defended but numerous, dispersed and far away. An attack in August 1943 on the Messerschmitt factory at Regensburg coupled with an attack on ball-bearing factories in Schweinfurt came to grief with excessive losses. A further attack on Schweinfurt two months later caused the loss of more than a quarter of the attacking force. The conclusion drawn this time was that successful precision bombing at tolerable cost was impossible without a fighter escort capable of going all the way with the bombers. The right aircraft happened to be at hand. The American P 51 (Mustang), already in service with the RAF in a modest way, was chosen for the job and equipped with long range tanks which enabled it to cover the required distances without losing too much speed or its capacity to outmanoeuvre the German fighters. This aircraft played a role as remarkable in its way as the Spitfire or the Mosquito, for after it had been put into production with the intensity for which American manufacturers were famous, it enabled the B 17s, withdrawn from the battle in the autumn of 1943, to resume their offensive, and this combination overcame the German defences. The German fighters were eliminated from the battle by their fighter foes and the American and British bombers were together able to undertake round-the-clock bombing of Germany and, from the summer of 1944, to pound an economy which had abruptly begun to disintegrate irretrievably fast.

Hitler had not prepared his economy for a long war and Germany was not ready for one when it came. In 1939–41 Germany was able to fight and win a series of campaigns on a half-stretched economy, but it could not overrun the whole continent on this basis, and after 1941 it had to convert to a war economy in the face of the crippling campaigns in the east and the increasingly severe bombardment from the west. Germany was not short of equipment or factory space; it started the war with twice as many machine tools, and multipurpose ones, than

Great Britain and probably still had more than the United States half way through the war. Its vital industries were as efficient as any in Great Britain or France and its ouput of coal and steel was greater than the combined British and French output; but it was economically inferior to the United States and the USSR, it was short of practically all minerals, and its steel and aluminium industries were dependent on imported iron ore and bauxite until sources had been overrun by the German armies. Stocks of some raw materials were low when the war began but they were replenished for a time by the bonuses of conquest. Germany's greatest economic weakness was the inefficiency of its administrative machine. Hitler's government was ill adapted to make the huge adjustments required in order to fight and beat the Russians and the Americans at one and the same time. Nazi Germany had no single central administrative authority; it was run by discordant authorities dominated by potentates more attuned to mutual in-fighting than to working together against outside enemies; its industries as well as its administration were a tangle. Hitler himself was in no sense a planner or an organizer. He seems to have regarded talk as a substitute for planning and, from the records that have been left behind of his sessions with his favourite associates, it would appear that the talk, which was of a miserably low intellectual order, was intended less for use than for ostentation. Nevertheless Germany was astonishingly successful for two years in sustaining an enormous war effort and expanding its war production.

The conquests of 1939–41 were regarded, from the economic point of view, as bonuses which enabled the government to fight wars and increase the German standard of living at the same time. Domestic consumption in Germany rose to the end of 1941. More significant, however, in the longer run were the failures of 1939–41: the failure to finish off Great Britain and, more serious still, the failure to defeat the Russians before the first winter of the war in the east. These failures forced Hitler to expand his arms base, his labour force and also his armed forces. The latter, which stood at 5.6 million in May 1940, expanded voraciously and, at the same date in the next three years, reached 7.2, 8.6 and 9.5 million; the rise of nearly a million in 1942–3 was achieved despite losses of the same extent in the same period, and with further losses of 1.6 million in 1943–4 the total armed manpower began to fall. In October 1944 all available males between sixteen and sixty were mobilized in the *Volkssturm*, to fight and not to labour.

During these same years the German labour force had dwindled steadily, until by the end of the war it had been reduced by a quarter.

This decline was not made good by the conscription of women (as was done in the much more tightly regimented British war economy), and although the proportion of German women at work in wartime Germany rose, their numbers did not, partly because of the Nazi doctrine that woman's place was in the home and partly owing to the afflux of foreign labour which obscured the need for a more extensive conscription of German labour. During the war the numbers of Germans at work increased by no more than the natural increase of the population, whereas in Great Britain and the United States the number of workers rose by 15 per cent over and above natural increase. (If, on the other hand, the significant manpower figures should embrace the armed services as well as industry, then Germany was using in these joint occupations a smaller proportion of its population than Great Britain.) As we have seen in an earlier part of this book, the German labour shortage was met by putting prisoners of war onto war production and raiding conquered countries for slavelike labour, but although the labour so acquired ran into millions of men (three million by May 1941, over four million a year later and over six million from May 1943), foreign labour was no substitute for German labour, especially in skilled jobs.

The re-orientation of German industry was begun by Fritz Todt, a brilliant technician who created at short notice an organization which stood up to unparalleled enemy bombardment for nearly three years after his death in an aircraft accident in February 1942. He was succeeded by Albert Speer, an indifferent architect with an aesthetic taste akin to Hitler's but also a gifted and versatile amateur with a flair for organization and an excellent sense for capturing and retaining Hitler's trust and friendship. Like Schacht, Speer has been judged, not without equivocation, to have been a non-Nazi technocrat who served the Nazi government in spite of his better nature and his better intelligence. Again like Schacht, he escaped the death penalty at the Nuremberg trial, where he was sentenced to twenty years' imprisonment for crimes against humanity (Schacht was acquitted on all counts) and he has since been treated by historians with some leniency, partly owing to his courage in refusing at the end to obey the (now decrepit) Führer's orders to lay Germany waste and partly because he survived the Nazi era to talk and write about it with some intelligence and show himself decent after the event. Speer's wartime achievement was considerable but not perhaps as remarkable as has been made out. He kept the German aircraft industry going in spite of crippling shortages and furious bombing, but what he and it produced was quantity rather than quality and the last aircraft of the Third Reich were inferior replicas of finer models. He believed in centralized capitalist control with the emphasis on the large leading industrial concerns as opposed to the Nazi partiality for the little man and the regionalism embodied in the local boss-rule of the Gauleiters. He kept the conveyor belts moving. Hitler backed him for three years, made him Minister for Armaments and Munitions (later Minister for Armaments and War Production) and defended him against satraps like Goering (as head of the Four Year Plan) and Funk (at the Ministry of Economics) and also against the army's own Office of War Production in his efforts to rationalize the German economy in terms of the overriding need for weapons. But Speer never won a completely dominant position. Goering and Milch managed to exclude aircraft production from his empire (except partially in 1944–5), and the odious and jealous Sauckel retained the control and procurement of labour to the end. Nevertheless Speer succeeded in more than doubling Germany's war production by the middle of 1943 and more than trebling it by the middle of 1944. Under his direction Germany produced arms in great quantities; in the latter part of the period it produced more weapons than the available divisions could use.

The areas of principal concern in the defence of Germany's war machine against air attack were the aircraft industry, the synthetic fuel plants, the Ruhr's coal and steel production and the rail, road and water services which linked these activities and distributed their output. In the end the interdependence of the different parts of the German economy proved to be its Achilles' heel. This was shown most clearly by the experiences of the aircraft and fuel industries.

Aircraft production, which reached a first wartime peak in the middle of 1943 and then fell back, rose again in 1944 and surpassed all previous records in the autumn of that year. But the squadrons had by then no fuel for their aircraft, because for a time there had been too few aircraft to defend the fuel plants. The pre-war target for the German aircraft industry was 2,000 a month, increased to 2,300 shortly after the war began. Actual production was 700–800 a month from 1935 to 1940. During the first part of this period the types which played the biggest part in the war were being evolved. During the first two years of war Hitler, still planning on a short war, was not worried about production or interested in the development of further new types since he believed that the war would be over before they could be brought into service. In 1941 there was a modest increase in production and in 1942 a well organized expansion in Germany and occupied Europe which raised production from 1,000 to 1,600 a month. In the summer of 1943 the damage inflicted by allied bombing – although it was repaired before the end of the year – forced the German Air Ministry, which still had more than thirty different types in production, to streamline the industry. Production, which had risen by June 1943 to 2,316 and had been set a new target of 3,000, was cut back by the raids to below 1,900.

In 1944 the industry was put under new management. Speer and Milch severely cut back the production of bombers, introduced a seventy-two hour week with high wages and improved working conditions, created new factories underground and provided the older ones with better defences, improved the repair services and raised the target first to 6,400 a month and then to 7,400. As a result production, which had again fallen at the beginning of the year to 1,369, rose in September to 3,538 new aircraft, while damaged aircraft returning to squadrons provided another 776, almost twice as many as in January; the production of single-engined fighters was more than doubled between February and June. Of a total of 113,514 aircraft produced during the war 40,593 were produced in 1944. The annual production of fighter aircraft in 1939–44 inclusive was 605: 2,746: 3,744: 5,515: 10,898: 25,285. Even in 1945 production of fighters almost reached a total of 5,000 for the four months before the war stopped. But this astonishing riposte to the bombing of the aircraft industry was in vain.

Until the end of 1943 Speer had been able to answer the allied bombing offensive. Reconstruction kept pace with destruction, stocks of vital materials (mostly large at the beginning of the war) were not dangerously run down and essential imports were maintained in spite of damage to railways and rolling stock. In 1944 the allied air forces were required to combine their attack on Germany with preliminary operations in aid of Overlord, but their own resources in the production of aircraft and the training of pilots enabled them, ominously for Germany, to fulfil both roles; the weight of the American attack was enormously increased, so much so that in one month in 1944 more American bombs were dropped than during the whole of 1942. Bomber Command similarly dropped in the last quarter of 1944 a bomb load four times as heavy as in the same part of 1943 and twenty times as heavy as in the same part of 1942. The synthetic oil industry, which was singled out for special attention in 1943–4, began to falter. Although the damage inflicted by a first series of raids was repaired, Speer's miraculous reconstruction services did not manage to cope so fully with a second series, stocks began to be drawn down alarmingly and production fell below demand. During nine consecutive days in September 1944 no aviation fuel whatever was produced except on one day, and production for the month was the hopelessly inadequate total of 9,400 tons. A pause in the bombing owing to bad weather gave some respite, but Germany's air defences were, if not totally eliminated, at least rendered negligible for the last six months of the war. When Dresden was bombed in February 1945, there was no defence of the city. Yet the aircraft industry was still producing 1,000–2,000 aircraft a month when the war ended.

This critical interdependence of aircraft and fuel production was made the more acute by the concentration of German heavy industry in the Ruhr and the dependence of industry outside the Ruhr on coal from the Ruhr. Germany was never short of coal but the damage done to communications in and around the Ruhr prevented Ruhr coal (80 per cent of Germany's output) from being moved to where it was needed. At the end of 1944 coal was being transported out of the Ruhr at one quarter of the normal rate and a few months later, after the winter's respite, this traffic was again halved. This dislocation of the Ruhr, combined with the conquest of Silesia and Lorraine by the Russians and Americans, strangled the steel industry which produced in the last quarter of 1944 less than 4 million tons in place of a projected 37.2 million. Other sectors of the economy collapsed with equal or greater suddenness in a chain reaction. At the end all fronts, except one, collapsed together – the fronts where the armies were still fighting and the economic front which finally succumbed under air attack.

The one front which held out with incredible tenacity was morale at home. This was the achievement of Joseph Goebbels, Minister of Propaganda and one of the few masters of his craft among the Nazi chieftains. What Speer did for Germany's war industry Goebbels did for its morale. Ultimately Hitler's greatest debt was to Goebbels whom he had once described – in an interview with a right-wing editor as early as 1931 – as his Field Marshal on the spiritual front, the man whom he would make Minister of Propaganda when he came to power and who would occupy a post as important as that of Foreign Minister or Chief of the General Staff.

Propaganda – the attempt to make an impact on large numbers of people in order to affect their mood and their actions, to get them to change their minds or not to change their minds, to get them to act in a certain way or not to – is an ancient instrument. It was modernized and immensely extended in the twentieth century by the invention of radio, and Goebbels was one of its master practitioners. He was not universally successful. In addressing himself to foreigners he was less adept than some British propagandists who had a better understanding of the society – and the language – of their enemy than Goebbels ever had. Also, like all propagandists, he found there was a limit to the extent to which he could affect people who basically did not want to believe what he had to say. But with German audiences he was very successful not only before the war but even in the face of the horrors of the Russian campaigns and mass bombing. He was appointed to his post a few weeks after Hitler became Chancellor and he held it until he and his entire family died with Hitler in Berlin.

He staffed the executive side of his Ministry with bright young men, half of them with a university education, and he taught them how to appeal to the emotions and the reason of the masses at one and the same time, so that an audience which had had its feelings roused would be captured not merely for the moment but also enduringly because a message had lodged in their minds. There were no limits to Goebbels's emotive appeals. He set out to intoxicate audiences and throw them into hysteria. The most rabble-rousing speeches of western politicians were by his standards sedate. In the years before and after the Nazi capture of power in 1933 Germany was in a state of crisis and Goebbels's techniques were designed to benefit from this feeling of crisis and to perpetuate it. People were screwed up, perils and evils were emphasized, the situation was presented as one which called above all for action – and for a man who could lead into action and must therefore be followed. From 1933 to 1939 German opinion was never allowed to let up, still less when war came. Goebbels could not make the Germans want war – there was a wild outburst of joyful relief in Berlin in October 1939 upon a false report that the British government had fallen and the war was over – but he created a mentality of endeavour and was able during the war to foster, against the odds, a solid mood of endurance. A crucial element in his technique was simplicity. Even in the most febrile and far-ranging tirades Nazi orators pinpointed and repeated one or two essential facts or arguments, eschewing generalization, representing issues as conflicts between good and evil, making them concrete and personal. While hammering away at favourite themes like the wickedness of Jews, the ill treatment of the Sudeten Germans, the need for *Lebensraum*, the western democracies' sinister but feeble attempts to encircle Germany, atrocity stories from the republican side in the civil war in Spain or, after the war began, successes in the field, Goebbels and his disciples held their audiences by the actuality of specific illustrations, true or false, which went home.

Goebbels made great use of shows: sporting events, funerals, festivals of every kind. Using entertainment to capture the public was not new – Thomas Cromwell had subsidized plays which were performed in town squares and on village greens throughout England in order to rub in Henry VIII's case against the papacy – but Goebbels made the most of its vastly increased scope. The Olympic Games of 1936 were turned into a propaganda event of the first magnitude. Goebbels also realized the importance of films, commissioning documentaries and newsreels and bringing pressure to bear on the film industry (which was not brought wholly under government control until it was nationalized in 1943) to make the sort of films he wanted. War films were used to impress neutrals as well as to fortify morale at home, where newsreels were compulsorily shown in all cinemas. These films, like Nazi oratory, were simple and repetitive. The press was not only regimented and bullied but overwhelmed by official hand-outs, press conferences and special briefings. The number of newspapers in Germany sank during the Nazi period from 4,700 to fewer than 1,000. Uniformity, imposed by decree and by fear, produced dullness but once again it simplified the issues. The reader did not get the impression that one paper was saying one thing and another another, so that it was impossible to know what to think.

In the first years of war Goebbels's task was made comparatively easy by the turn of events. He extolled Hitler as the infallible leader who told his people what he was going to do and did it. A cheap radio set (with a limited range) had been marketed just before the war and about 70 per cent of German households had a radio. Goebbels made play with the taunt that the British were fighting to the last Frenchman and ascribed the collapse of France to racial miscegenation, but by July he was restraining over-confidence about the collapse of Great Britain and was soon advising editors not to tell their readers that London was a heap of ruins: British resistance was futile but it might go on for a time.

The invasion of the USSR gave him a new line. He represented the German attack as pre-emptive, alleging that Hitler had certain intelligence of a Russian attack, and he plugged the theme of the brutal and subhuman Slav. He did not minimize the rigours of the new war. After a calculated pause of a week came twelve special announcements (*Sondermeldungen*), all issued on the same day – a Sunday – and taking up practically the whole of the day. This battery of victory communiqués created an overwhelming effect commensurate with the scale of operations in the east and gave anxious Germans, who had been struggling to make sense of unfamiliar names scattered about their maps, the assurance that details did not matter. But Goebbels was careful not to commit himself to the statement that the war was won and he was therefore all the more horrified when Hitler and his press chief, Otto Dietrich, declared in October with premature exuberance that it was. Goebbels had already foreseen that his theme was as likely to be the preaching of total war as the proclaiming of total victory, and as winter came on he reverted to his sober warnings, started a campaign to collect clothes for the men freezing at the front and made regular reports on the response to this appeal. On the more optimistic side he could at least claim that Hitler had done better than Napoleon in spite of General Winter and the brutish tenacity of the Russian soldier, and that the gains in oil, grain, iron ore and other materials were considerable. Rommel's victories also provided good cheer.

From 1942 Goebbels, as the chief upholder of the home front, had to counter the general decline in Germany's fortunes and two major catastrophes in the defeats of the German armies in Russia and the heavy bombing of German cities. At first the army's communiqués about Stalingrad had been optimistic, the strategic importance of the city was underlined and its capture was to be the climax of the war in the east. The capitulation of the Sixth Army was a tremendous blow and Goebbels, not without courage, took the unique step of issuing a *Sondermeldung* about a defeat instead of a victory. It was accompanied by muffled drums, the national anthem and a three-minute silence, and all places of entertainment were closed for three days. Two weeks later a vast – and picked – audienc was assembled in the *Sportpalast* in Berlin. Ten questions were put and answered to counter enemy propaganda that Germany had had enough and to pledge total war. In the shadow of Stalingrad this demonstration probably stiffened morale but it also made people think that total catastrophe might be on the way.

The tenth anniversary of Hitler's coming to power was marked by the first assertion that capitulation was out of the question: it was also the first mention of capitulation. The eastern battles in 1943 and 1944 increased the foreboding. There were only three *Sondermeldungen* in 1943; there had been sixty-five in 1941. The fall of Mussolini did not help. Hitler himself became remote, seldom appearing or speaking. Allied propaganda suggested that he had been driven to silence by his own mistakes; he had no words to explain what had gone wrong. Goebbels countered with a new image of Hitler as the supreme sufferer, stoically enduring like Frederick the Great in adversity, shunning the limelight unlike his flashy and temporarily successful opponents. At the same time, as disaster threatened, Goebbels worked to inculcate the feeling that the only way to avert it was to stick by Hitler.

Mass bombing was Goebbels's biggest problem. When bombing first began, Goebbels had repeated with sarcastic comment the exaggerated claims made by the British Air Ministry on the basis of aircrews' instant reports, but these tactics no longer sufficed when the destruction became heavy. Goebbels did not seek to deny it. He used it to stir up hatred against the enemy. He also showed himself all over Berlin, inspecting raid damage, showing that a Minister cared and was in control, and so forestalling panic and a break in morale. He initiated an anti-defeatist campaign (strengthened by a few death sentences) and although he could not prevent the German mood from drooping he succeeded in preventing it from turning into action against the government. His plea that this was the time for government and people to hang together was sufficiently widely accepted. Appointed Plenipotentiary for Total War in 1944 he extended normal working hours, conscripted women up to the age of fifty, cut entertainment, schooling and university courses and by these and other means ensured that Germans should go on fighting not just because they were afraid of the Gestapo but also because they were persuaded that this was the right thing to do. With a part of their minds they knew that they were defeated and that fighting on meant postponing the end without altering the outcome. But because Goebbels spoke to them straight, they took what he said as straight. By telling them, as one adult to another, that things were bad, he dissuaded them from facing the fact that they were hopeless. They behaved like a man who knows that he is condemned to death with cancer but prefers to believe the doctor who tells him that he has appendicitis. At the same time Goebbels piled on the horror of Slavic hordes about to sweep over Germany devastating the land and debauching its maidens. The nearer it came, the worse did Goebbels make fate sound, so that there seemed to be no purpose in doing anything except go through the motions of warding off the inescapable.

In the final assessment the bombers' contribution to the defeat of Germany must be judged a weighty one in the final stages of the war. In the light of the pretensions of the Douhet–Mitchell school of air strategists two questions arise: Did the bombers win the war? If they did not, could they have done? The answer to the first question is no. The German armies were fatally defeated by the Russians in July 1943 and at that point the bomber onslaught had barely begun and had caused no decisive damage; it did not do so for another year. The second question is hypothetical. Air power equipped with nuclear weapons may be a war-winning weapon in the sense that it can compel the surrender of an enemy whose armed forces in the field are undefeated. There was, however, no such air power in the European theatre in the Second World War. On the other hand it can be plausibly argued that the surrender of Japan after two nuclear bombs was a consequence of the overwhelming superiority of American air power over Japan's total defences. It is all a question of degree and there is nothing to prove that the fatal imbalance between attack and defence could be achieved by nuclear weapons alone. If the allied air forces had been even stronger than they were, and if allied air policy had not wavered between general attacks on population and morale and selective attacks on economic nerve centres and bottlenecks, then Germany might have been brought to surrender without the necessity for a major invasion and the hard-fought campaigns from Normandy to the heart of Europe. Such a possibility cannot be disproved, but the experiences of the American and British air commands show that this strategy would have been exceptionally costly in lives. It is moreover all but certain that, in a war in which Germany was being attacked by the USSR as well as by themselves, the western allies would never willingly have confined themselves to strategic bombing or have delayed their invasion in such a way as to allow the Russians to occupy the whole of Germany.

Leaving aside the inadmissible claim that bombing did win, or could have won, the war on its own, there emerges a different question: how far bombing, judged as a contributory instead of an independent factor, shortened the war. No precise answer to such a question is possible, but in general it is pertinent to recall that allied bombing diverted German air power from the offensive fronts to the defence of the Reich and diverted German labour – 1–1.5 million men, many of them skilled – to repair and reconstruction works. Perhaps these contributions should be adjudged significant subsidiary sources of Germany's defeat. They cannot be held to be decisive but they must have made the allied victory somewhat easier and somewhat quicker. Both area bombing and precision bombing made this kind of contribution, for even if a government at war is more intent on protecting its factories than its industrial proletariat, there is nevertheless a point beyond which it cannot leave its people undefended and unhoused. Speer's evidence after the war was that precision bombing could do crucial damage; but until the last phase the allies were not able to carry out effective precision bombing operations. Area bombing, to which they resorted instead, paid only a small dividend and one which those who bring ethics into the equation may well regard as too small.

CHAPTER 24

The Western Fronts

AMERICAN and British armies set foot on the mainland of Europe in
Italy in September 1943 and in France in the following June. The armies
in Italy reached Rome two days before the invasion of France. They
had spent over eight months fighting their way up the peninsula
against tough German opposition in harsh mountain country and
horrible weather.

When they landed in Italy the allies hoped to be in Rome before the
end of that year. Hopes in the Italian theatre were apt to be exaggerated.
Churchill in particular had got into the habit of regarding anything to
do with Italy as soft. The Americans were more sceptical. The opposition was German, not Italian, and it was commanded by Kesselring,
who had prepared three defensive positions south of Rome – the first
of these, the Gustav line, following the rivers Garigliano, Rapido and
Sangro which flow west and east off the sharp ridge of the Apennines
and are deep and strong in the winter months. The allies' best hope
was to strike rapidly northward with Clark's US Fifth Army, while
Montgomery supported his advance on the eastern side of the peninsula.
But both Clark and Montgomery made slow progress. Heavy rains
helped the defenders. Both armies gained ground but no road to
Rome was opened, there was no serious threat to the Gustav line,
and for the Germans the worst consequence of the landings in Italy
was the establishment of the US Fifteenth Air Force on Italian airfields whence it could attack targets in Germany, northern Italy,
Austria and Rumania.

At the beginning of 1944 the attack towards Rome was renewed with
a frontal attack on the Gustav line and a simultaneous landing at
Anzio seventy miles up the west coast from the mouth of the Garigliano
and forty miles from Rome. (The Germans, again crediting the allies
with an adventurousness which they did not display, believed that they
would have done better to land north of Rome at some place like
Leghorn.) The first part of this dual operation began on 12 January
when a British corps under Clark's command crossed the Garigliano.
French troops under Juin (campaigning with Chateaubriand in his
pocket) crossed the Rapido and made a strike towards Monte Cassino,
a craggy nodal point at the centre of the Gustav line and incidentally
the site of Saint Benedict's most famous monastery and its no less

famous library; but American forces trying to cross the Rapido above and below Monte Cassino were thrown back with such heavy losses that their attempts might have been called off but for the related operation towards Anzio. In the east the Eighth Army (now commanded by General Sir Oliver Leese in place of Montgomery who had been recalled to Great Britain to lead the coming invasion of Normandy) made no significant progress.

The landings at Anzio, the place where Nero had been born and the Apollo Belvedere found, were an attempt to break this immobility but the operation was hurriedly planned and timidly directed. The initial landings on 22 January were practically unopposed and a daring commander might have made a dash for Rome and got there, but General Lucas, the commander of the expedition and a man of basically pessimistic temperament, on discovering that there were no Germans in his path behaved as though there were. Kesselring was given time to organize a defence and seized it. By the end of a week the expedition was in trouble and when the Anglo-American force made a bid to advance from its carefully consolidated beachhead on 30 January, it incurred savage losses (one unit lost 761 men out of 767). Caution had not paid. The Germans counter-attacked in the first week in February; allied losses mounted, morale and confidence sank; the allies were all but evicted; the German attack was renewed in mid-February and after four days of heavy fighting the allies were again on the brink of total defeat when they saw to their surprise that the Germans, unaware how close they were to victory, were drawing off. The Anzio venture had failed to achieve its purpose but the Germans had failed to eliminate the beachhead.

In these same days the allies, baulked on the Gustav line, had undertaken one of the more questionable actions of the war – the bombing of the monastery on Monte Cassino, the hearth of western monasticism, though no longer the resting place of its founder St Benedict, whose body had been removed to the banks of the Loire thirteen centuries earlier to save it when other destroyers, the Lombards, were about to wreck the monastery. In the last week of January Juin's forces, supported by American units which had finally stormed their way across the Rapido in spite of stiff German opposition, were within striking distance of the town and monastery, but they could not cover the last thousand yards. In a final attempt to give aid to the units at Anzio New Zealand and Indian troops made a final assault against superior German forces. It failed and was called off on 11 February. Four days later the monastery was bombed.

It is still not entirely clear how this useless piece of destruction came about – useless because at the end of it the monastery was still not taken, the whole operation was temporarily abandoned and no German forces were deflected from Anzio. The allies believed the monastery to be a German strongpoint, but German officers said later that there were no Germans in or near it. (Nor were there any monks. The Germans sent them to Rome.) Allied commanders were aware of the criticism which they might incur and the order to bomb was only given after discussion at all levels and a personal air reconnaissance by the theatre Commander-in-Chief, Maitland Wilson, and his deputy, General Jacob L. Devers.

The allied attack was resumed on 15 March with a heavy air and artillery bombardment which reduced the town of Monte Cassino to a shambles. The New Zealanders went in again, only to be checked by German resistance and uncleared rubble. They failed to reach the heart of the town. A complementary attack by the Indians on the monastery likewise failed after getting within 400 yards. A week later both town and monastery were still in German hands and the attack was called off after a final New Zealand attempt to dislodge the defenders. The road to Rome remained blocked. The Gustav line was holding and there were two further lines between it and Rome. The best that the allies could claim was that they were holding twenty-two German divisions out of some other battle. The strategy of the Italian campaign had postulated the surrender of Italy and the creation of fresh options leading the allies to the Balkans or the Danube or into Germany itself. The collapse of Italian resistance had, however, produced a German resistance stout enough to bar all these routes, and the longer the campaign lasted the more pointless it became. Its object had been to give the allies useful victories in the interval between the re-conquest of the Mediterranean and the re-conquest of France, but the nearer the French invasion approached the more the Italian campaign became a sideshow producing nothing important which could not be obtained by invasion in the west.

But Kesselring's position was never more than a defensive one in a theatre of secondary importance. He could expect little in the way of reinforcements and in May he was finally forced to abandon all his positions south of Rome. British and Polish units of the Eighth Army opened a new attack which was at first held but French forces then executed a spectacular turning movement in almost impossibly difficult mountain country and forced the Germans to evacuate Monte Cassino at last on 17 May. On the next day the Poles entered the ruined abbey and the British the town, and the Germans began to retreat all along the line. The forces in the Anzio bridgehead broke out but were too slow to cut off the Germans who retired north of Rome in good order. Kesselring abandoned the Italian capital after declaring it an open city and established a fresh holding line through Lake Trasimene and a stronger one, the Gothic line, in Tuscany.

Clark entered Rome two days before Overlord, not six months as Churchill had hoped. General Sir Harold Alexander, the overall commander of the Fifth and Eighth Armies, was now in a position to exploit their successes, but the timing was wrong. Alexander's dual purpose was to entice German divisions into the Italian theatre and then keep them there or cut them off. He wanted to maintain both his armies at full strength, force the Gothic line and then move either left into France or right into Austria, sucking more German troops into the theatre as he intensified the threat to Germany itself. Although the soft underbelly of the Axis had proved less soft than Churchill had imagined, it was now pierced and the Italian campaign was on the verge of justification. On the last day of May Churchill promised Alexander his full support for keeping his armies up to strength, but Churchill's was no longer the deciding voice and Alexander was obliged to relinquish part of his forces for an invasion of southern France (operation Anvil or Dragoon) complementary to Overlord. The Americans, supported at first by Maitland Wilson and believing that Kesselring was more likely to be milked than reinforced, wanted to make a bigger thrust up the Rhône valley than up Italy, and after bitter argument they prevailed. Anvil turned out to be an unnecessary reinforcement of Overlord but Alexander lost seven divisions and part of his air strength and was told to go ahead with this reduced force; Kesselring on the other hand got four extra divisions.

Retreating in his own time, Kesselring reached the Gothic line in August and then held up the allies long enough for the autumn rains and mud to come to his assistance. Churchill and Alexander were still hoping to make for Vienna, but the Americans refused to reinforce a theatre which had become decidedly secondary and after a limited German counter-attack in the last week of the year operations were suspended and more allied troops were withdrawn from Italy. The last hope of staking a claim to be heard in the post-war settlement of central Europe by effecting a junction with the Russians in Vienna had gone.

It had never been a realistic one. Victory in Italy in 1943 was beyond the allies' grasp and victory in 1944 was pointless because there was never any thought of making the winning thrust anywhere but in France.

By 1944 no other front could hope for the men and material needed for so decisive a role.

*

In November 1943 Rommel was sent from a semi-active command in northern Italy to inspect the coastal defences of the western front from Dunkirk to Brittany. He found them rusty, uncoordinated and manned by second- or third-rate divisions which were well below strength. By this date the allies had already chosen the general area in which they would land but their decision was not known to the Germans. The alternatives were obvious. Either they might cross the Channel at its narrowest point and make their landings east of the Somme, or they might land in Normandy west of the Somme. The principal argument in favour of this latter plan was the unsuitability of south-east England for the accumulation of the vast quantities of men and stores which were to be put into the invasion and above all the meagre capacity of the Kentish ports compared with the Portsmouth–Southampton area. In addition the latter was less vulnerable to attack and less open to reconnaissance; and on the other side the strongest German defences were in the Pas de Calais. These considerations outweighed the disadvantages of the longer sea passage and the opening of the new front further away from the frontiers of Germany and the allies settled without much debate on the bay of the Seine.

When Rommel arrived in France he found that the Commander-in-Chief West, Field Marshal von Rundstedt, inclined to the view that the invasion would come in the Pas de Calais. O K W took the same view. Rommel, however, queried it and as the months went by the pattern of allied air activities and the absence of mining in the bay of the Seine strongly supported him. By the spring the Germans were nine tenths convinced that the main attack would be delivered in Normandy but some of them, Hitler in particular, expected either diversionary or follow-up operations in the Pas de Calais: they were deceived by spoof radio activity simulating the presence of large forces in south-east England and their inferiority in the air was by now so marked that they could not survey even Kent accurately enough to establish that there were no armies there.

More important than this initial divergence about where the invasion was to be expected was the dispute about how to meet it. Rundstedt saw no hope of preventing a landing. His strategy was to accept it and then throw the enemy back into the sea by a counter-attack. Rommel on the other hand believed that, in France as in North Africa, Sicily and

Italy, once the allies had gained a foothold they could not be forced off it again. He proposed therefore to deny rather than repel the invasion, by mining the shore and the beaches and by engaging the enemy before he could cross the vital hundreds of yards between the water's edge and the first natural cover beyond the open sands and rocks. Hitler decided in favour of Rommel and appointed him to command, under Rundstedt, the group of armies deployed from Holland to Brittany, but insisted with characteristic caution on retaining large forces east of the Somme after as well as before the invasion and with characteristic indecision on holding much of the armour in reserve outside Rommel's immediate command and immediate operational area. These prevarications proved specially perilous because allied air supremacy, and the extensive destruction of communications in the weeks before the battle began, immobilized German forces caught in the wrong place. On the eve of the invasion Rundstedt had sixty divisions, of which forty-three were available to Rommel (the remaining seventeen were south of the Loire), but of these forty-three only eighteen were in Normandy; five were in Holland, one in the Channel Islands and no fewer than nineteen in Belgium and France east of the Somme.

The preparations on the allied side were of the utmost thoroughness and ingenuity. There had been disputes about the timing of this operation but none about whether or not to launch it. Preliminary planning had been put formally in hand after the Casablanca conference of January 1943 and before that raids on the continent – at St Nazaire, for example, in March 1942 and at Dieppe in August – had been undertaken with an eye to gaining information and experience which would be valuable for a full scale invasion. Detailed and daring reconnaissances of the landing beaches were carried out in order to establish the lie of the land, the obstacles below and above the water line, the state of the going for tracked and other vehicles and a thousand and one other pieces of information. Elaborate feints were devised to keep the defenders guessing and dispersed. Entirely new accessories of war were designed and constructed, from the two artificial harbours (Mulberries) as large as medium sized ports which were towed across the Channel in sections (beginning on D-day) and the oil pipelines (Pluto – eventually twenty came into use) which were laid under it, to a variety of strange adaptations of tracked vehicles for carrying prefabricated bridges, laying carpets on the sand and destroying land mines.

The principal commanders had been designated in 1943 and had been working together and training their subordinates for much longer than is usually possible in war: General Dwight D. Eisenhower in supreme command with Air Marshal Sir Arthur Tedder as his deputy and General Walter Bedell Smith as Chief of Staff; Vice-Admiral Bertram Ramsay, General Bernard Montgomery and Air Vice-Marshal Trafford Leigh-Mallory in command of the three services in the assault phase; Generals Omar N. Bradley and Miles Dempsey commanding the two invading armies, the former destined to command an Army Group after the build-up. One and a half million Americans were transported across the Atlantic with all their own equipment and food and crammed into southern England. Unprecedented and often very irritating new security measures were introduced, affecting even the embassies of neutrals and allies. A fleet of over 5,000 vessels was assembled for the initial phase: 1,200 naval vessels, including seven battleships, to bombard the coastal defences, sweep mines, escort the invaders and tackle enemy sea- and air-craft; and 4,000 transports, barges, tugs and other sea-going and amphibious craft for the conveyance of the armies with their tanks, armoured cars, guns, vehicles, ammunition and the lavish variety of modern fighting gear. In the air the allies mustered 7,500 aircraft in direct support of the invasion and 3,500 bombers which could be and were used in this battle as well as for the continued strategic bombing of Germany. These air forces destroyed German communications to the battle area in accordance with a plan worked out in great detail by a civilian professor of anatomy. Naval and air supremacy assured the passage of the thirty-seven divisions assembled to strike the decisive blow in the west.

At two o'clock in the morning of 6 June the first invaders crossed the Channel by air and were dropped some miles behind the invasion beaches, and at dawn five separate groups approached these five beaches from the sea. These men – 20,000 airborne and 70,000 seaborne – were the advance guard of a force of two million drawn from a dozen nations which was to be set ashore in France within the next two months. Their first objectives lay along a line which stretched for forty miles from the eastern base of the Cotentin peninsula eastward to the mouth of the river Orne which flows into the sea eight miles north east of the town of Caen. The task of the first invaders was to get onto the beaches and then get off them again as quickly as possible.

The first day's objectives included Caen. Fortunes were mixed. At the westernmost beach the Americans secured their first objectives with the loss of only twelve men before the end of the day. At the next beach, however, the second American landing was an almost complete disaster and, after suffering 3,000 casualties, was saved only by the successes in neighbouring sectors. At the remaining three beaches British and

THE PRE-INVASION SCENE MAY - JUNE 1944

ALLIED PRE-INVASION CONSIDERATIONS

The longer route across Channel, but further from German aircraft. Also, German defences weaker in Normandy than in the Pas de Calais.

The shorter route across Channel, but German forces heaviest in Pas de Calais. Also Kentish ports unsuitable for large ship and troop concentrations.

ENGLAND

Weymouth
Southampton
Portsmouth
Dover
Strait of Dover
Calais
PAS DE CALAIS
Boulogne

ENGLISH CHANNEL

Cherbourg
Dieppe
Rouen
Caen
St. Malo
NORMANDY
Seine
Paris

0   50
Miles

GERMAN PRE-INVASION CONSIDERATIONS

ENGLAND   Allied bogus radio activity

KENT
Southampton   Dover
Weymouth   Strait of Dover   Calais
Portsmouth   PAS DE CALAIS
Boulogne

ENGLISH CHANNEL

Cherbourg   Dieppe
Rouen
Caen   Seine
NORMANDY   Paris

Rommel (and later, Hitler) believes the invasion will occur here and, thus he strengthens beach defences. He is anxious that the Allies do not achieve a foothold.

Von Rundstedt and OKW expect invasion to occur here. German strategy accepts the initial landings but envisages a counter-attack will dislodge the invaders.

0   50
Miles

ALLIED PRE-INVASION BOMBING

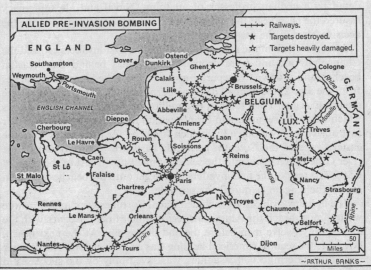

+--+--+ Railways.
★ Targets destroyed.
☆ Targets heavily damaged.

ENGLAND

Southampton   Dover   Ostend
Weymouth   Dunkirk   Ghent
Portsmouth   Calais   Cologne
ENGLISH CHANNEL   Lille   Brussels   Rhine
Dieppe   BELGIUM   GERMANY
Cherbourg   Abbeville   Moselle
Le Havre   Amiens   LUX.
Rouen   Laon   Trèves
Caen   Soissons
St Lô   Seine   Reims   Metz
St Malo   Falaise   Meuse   Nancy
Chartres   Paris   Strasbourg
Rennes   F R A N C E   Troyes
Le Mans   Orleans   Chaumont   Belfort
Nantes   Loire   Tours   Dijon   Rhine

0   50
Miles

~ARTHUR BANKS~

THE ALLIED INVASION OF EUROPE 6 JUNE 1944

THE ALLIED ATTACK

ALLIED DISPOSITIONS AND MOVEMENTS

BRITISH SECOND ARMY
- British and Canadian assault formations.
- 'Follow-up' units.

FIRST U S. ARMY
- United States assault formations.
- 'Follow-up' units.

THE NORMANDY BEACHES
- A Utah
- B Omaha
- C Gold
- D Juno
- E Sword
- ● Allied airborne dropping zones.

GERMAN DISPOSITIONS
- --- Army boundary
- GHQ
- Army Group
- Army
- Corps
- Division
- •••• Reserve
- Forming

3 U.S. ARMY

CHANNEL

ENGLISH

CONCENTRATION AREA

Guernsey

Jersey

NORMANDY

Paris

0   50
Miles

THE ALLIED LANDINGS

- Areas held by Allies at 2400 hrs on D-Day.
- Areas held by Germans at 2400 hrs on D-Day.
- Line of planned Allied beach-head at 2400 hrs on D-Day.
- ← First Allied assault waves.
- ← XXI Panzer Division counterattacks.
- ↑↑ Assault areas.

- Roads.
- +++ Railways.
- Flooded areas.

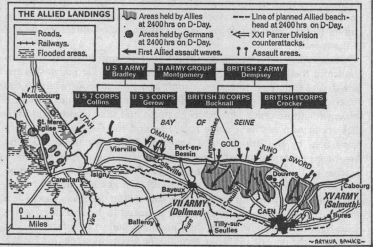

| U S 1 ARMY Bradley | 21 ARMY GROUP Montgomery | BRITISH 2 ARMY Dempsey |

| U S 7 CORPS Collins | U S 5 CORPS Gerow | BRITISH 30 CORPS Bucknall | BRITISH 1 CORPS Crocker |

Montebourg

St. Mere Eglise

UTAH

BAY   OF   SEINE

OMAHA

Vierville

Port-en-Bessin

Arromanches

GOLD

JUNO

SWORD

Douvres

Carentan

Isigny

Colleville

Bayeux

Cabourg

VII ARMY (Dollman)

CAEN

XV ARMY (Salmuth)

Bures

Balleroy

Tilly-sur-Seulles

Vire

Aure

0   5
Miles

~ARTHUR BANKS~

Canadian troops fought their way onto and beyond the shore against German opposition which stiffened uncomfortably after noon. At the end of the day the fate of the paratroopers was still uncertain and some of the Americans were in serious trouble, but the seaborne invaders had made their lodgement. At the eastern end of the line the British had got to within four miles of Caen but had failed to enter it and in general results were a little short of hopes, but on the German side Rommel's forces had proved unequal to the task of preventing the invasion and the Luftwaffe had completely failed in the crucial contest for command of the skies.

The next stage comprised, for the allies, the two tasks of build-up and penetration into France. The first of these ran into bad luck. By 18 June 629,000 men had been put ashore and the Mulberries, although not yet completed, were handling 6,000 tons a day. But on the next day a strong and unseasonable gale blew up and lasted for five days. It wrecked one Mulberry, damaged the other and blew about 800 craft onto the shore. Supplies directed onto the beaches and through the Mulberries, which had reached an average of 22,570 tons a day, were drastically cut and when the gale abated the armies had 20,000 vehicles and over 100,000 tons of stores less than they had been counting on. This shortfall was not made good for a month. Moreover Cherbourg, at the tip of the Cotentin, was only belatedly captured on 26 June with its port facilities wrecked and the harbour blocked; it could not be used at all for weeks, not fully for months. Nevertheless a million men were in France at the end of the first week in July and over a million and a half before the end of the month.

Montgomery, who was in command of all ground forces in northern France in the initial phases, planned to engage the Germans with the British and Canadian forces on his left and simultaneously launch the Americans on his right southward from the base of the Cotentin (except for those units detailed to go north and take Cherbourg) until they could turn east and come round behind the Germans who were being held by the British and Canadians. This plan succeeded. The Americans advanced at first slowly in the difficult country between their beaches and St Lô, which they did not take until 18 July. At the same time the British and Canadians were being held at Caen, and although they entered the town on the 8th they were not in complete possession until the 19th. A week later the allies attacked in both sectors. After fierce fighting and heavy losses the Canadians had to admit defeat, but to the west the Americans broke through the German opposition (which could have been stronger but for the battle fought by the Canadians) and Patton, splitting his Third Army, sent five divisions westwards into Brittany and the rest eastwards in a long hook which reached round and behind the main German forces to Rouen.

The task of retrieving this situation for the Germans fell on Kluge who succeeded to both Rundstedt's and Rommel's commands. Hitler had dismissed Rundstedt on 1 July and shortly afterwards Rommel was put out of action when his car was attacked by an aircraft. On Hitler's orders Kluge launched on 7 August an attack on Mortain which was designed to cut across the base of the Cotentin peninsula to Avranches (at its base on the west side) and so cut Patton's communications. The attack was, however, held by the US First Army under General Hodges and after five days' fighting the Germans fell back on Falaise. Here they were trapped. A corps from Patton's army moved northwards towards Argentan, almost due south of Falaise; Hodges moved southwards from Vire to confront them from the west; the British moved down from the north-west and the Canadians attacked from the north. On 17 August the Canadians took Falaise and the Americans Argentan and Kluge was dismissed. The Germans struggled to withdraw through the gap between Falaise and Argentan but on the 20th the gap closed and their troops in the pocket – about 60,000 of them – were nearly all captured or killed. The battle for Normandy was over and the allied armies were spreading all over France with little to stop them. Kluge committed suicide, probably because he knew that Hitler knew that he had been cognizant of the plot to kill Hitler on 20 July. For the same reason the convalescent Rommel was forced by the SD, acting on Hitler's orders, to kill himself.

The new Commander-in-Chief, Field Marshal Model, managed to extract some of the encircled troops in Normandy, but two days before his appointment fresh American and French armies under General Devers landed in the south of France (15 August) and two days after it Patton reached the Seine north-west and south-east of Paris. On that day Paris rose. Within the Paris Liberation Committee there were differences about whether to wait for the nearer approach of the regular armies or not, the communists being for action now, the non-communists for delay. The pressures for action became irresistible and the order was given for the liberation of the capital by its own people. There was fighting in the streets between the Germans and the Resistance. A truce was arranged but Hitler would have none of it and ordered the destruction of the city, if necessary by bombing. The truce degenerated into confusion and fighting started again. At one time the bells were ringing for victory while the guns were still firing as the last of

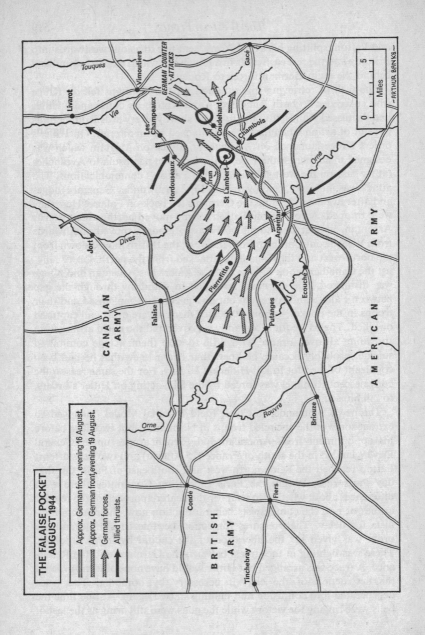

THE FALAISE POCKET
AUGUST 1944

Approx. German front, evening 16 August.
Approx. German front, evening 19 August.
German forces.
Allied thrusts.

0 — 5 Miles

~ARTHUR BANKS~

GERMAN COUNTER ATTACKS

Touques
Vimoutiers
Gace
Livarot
Vie
Les Champeaux
Coudehard
Chambois
Hordouseaux
Trun
St Lambert
Orne
Argentan
Jort
Dives
Pierrefitte
Ecouche
Falaise
Putanges
Orne
Rouvre
Briouze
Conde
Flers
Tinchebray

CANADIAN ARMY

AMERICAN ARMY

BRITISH ARMY

the SS and their French accomplices defended all that remained to them: their lives. De Gaulle urged that General Jacques Leclercq's Second French Division be sent forward since, left to themselves, the Parisians could be overwhelmed by the Germans and their city destroyed: 1,500 of them were killed in the rising and twice as many were wounded. After some hesitation de Gaulle's request was granted and Leclercq entered Paris on 24 August (the British tactfully declining an American suggestion that a token British contingent with a Union Jack should accompany Leclercq). On that day the German military governor, General Dietrich von Choltitz, who had disregarded and defeated Hitler's orders, surrendered to Leclercq and to Colonel Rol, alias Tanguy, one of the military leaders of the Resistance and a communist veteran of the Spanish civil war. Choltitz surrendered to the French Republic and not to the allied command, an action which the Americans, though riled, took in good part. The allies had already discovered that they could not get away with their facile assumption that upon the defeat of the Germans France would be provisionally administered by them. (They had prepared an occupation currency but de Gaulle's indignation on learning of its existence had blown it away.) On 25 August de Gaulle arrived in Paris to take over the government of France at the Hôtel de Ville.

After the end of August the allied advance slowed down. Hitler had ordered the German garrisons which still held a string of ports to resist to the last man in the hope that the allies would divert forces to invest these places and so be delayed. For the most part the allies ignored the garrisons which were therefore simply isolated and kept out of battles farther east until they were obliged by events to surrender, but in one or two cases German stubbornness paid off, notably at Brest which did not surrender until 18 September and so could not be used to supply the increasingly large and increasingly distant allied armies. On 1 September, the initial phase being completed, Eisenhower assumed command in the field in northern France and thenceforward exercised it to the end through his two Army Group Commanders, Bradley and Montgomery. Eisenhower's principal concern was the supply of his large and rapidly moving armies. He himself, underrating the Germans' capacity to pull themselves together for a last round, seems to have thought that he could keep up the pace along his whole front with the resources available to him. Montgomery was the most eloquent of those who said that this was impossible. He argued that the logistical problems produced by the unexpectedly swift advances after the break-out at Caen had made it essential to concentrate a punch either on the left or the right, and

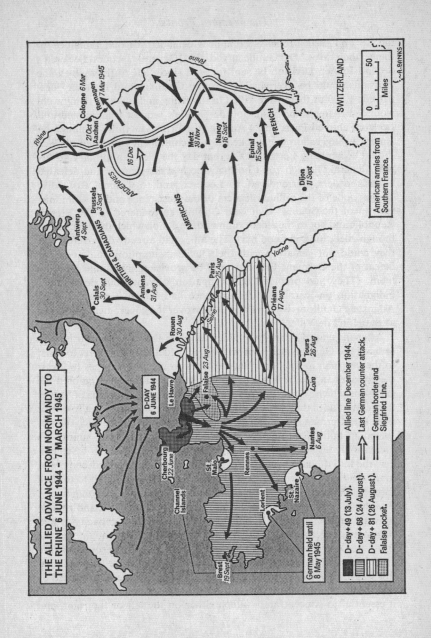

THE ALLIED ADVANCE FROM NORMANDY TO
THE RHINE 6 JUNE 1944 – 7 MARCH 1945

D-DAY
6 JUNE 1944

SWITZERLAND

0   50
Miles

American armies from
Southern France.

Allied line December 1944.

Last German counter attack.

German border and
Siegfried Line.

Falaise pocket.

D-day + 49 (13 July).

D-day + 68 (24 August).

D-day + 81 (26 August).

German held until
8 May 1945.

Rhine
Cologne 6 Mar
Remagen
7 Mar 1945
21 Oct Aachen
16 Dec
ARDENNES
Brussels
3 Sept
Antwerp
4 Sept
Calais
30 Sept
Amiens
31 Aug
BRITISH & CANADIANS
Rouen
30 Aug
Le Havre
Falaise 23 Aug
Seine
Paris
25 Aug
Yonne
Orleans
17 Aug
Tours
26 Aug
Loire
Nantes
6 Aug
St. Nazaire
Lorient
Rennes
St. Malo
Cherbourg
22 June
Channel Islands
Brest
19 Sept
Metz
28 Nov
Nancy
16 Sept
Epinal
15 Sept
Dijon
11 Sept
FRENCH
AMERICANS
Rhine
Rhine

A. 86 INKS

he naturally made the most of the case in favour of the left. He wanted all the support that the Supreme Commander could give him for a drive across the Somme, through Belgium, into the Ruhr and on to Berlin. This way he believed he could finish the war before the end of the year.

Eisenhower was sceptical. He was an exceptionally honest and fair man but he could hardly help being swayed, whether more or less powerfully, by a political problem. He was an American general in command of a preponderantly American force, and giving a preference to Montgomery meant favouring a British general whom the American public and many American senior officers disliked. Not only Eisenhower himself but also Marshall felt that the voice of Congress and the voice of the American press had to have some weight in these strategic decisions. Their sensitivity on this score was the more acute because the commanders on the American side included in Patton a soldier who was no less colourful than Montgomery and readier to resort to insubordination if he did not get the orders he wanted. Holding back Patton's drive from the Seine to the Saar in order to enable Montgomery to knock out the German army somewhere else was something that Eisenhower was not prepared to attempt.

On the last day of August Montgomery took Amiens, due north of Paris, and crossed the Somme and less than a week later he had taken Brussels and Antwerp and developed a bold plan for a further advance. The obstacles to continuing eastward into the Ruhr, apart from his difficulty in getting the undivided support of the Supreme Commander, were stiffening German resistance and the prepared defences of the Siegfried line (the West Wall) which guarded the German frontier from Switzerland up to and including Belgium – but excluding Holland. Montgomery proposed to strike north instead of east, advancing from Belgium into Holland instead of the Ruhr. By doing this he would cut across the German supply lines in Holland, isolate and surround the remaining German forces in Belgium and western Holland by extending his own lines to the coast at the Zuider Zee, get beyond the northern end of the Siegfried line and then turn east into the north German plain. He might also catch the Germans where they would least expect a major blow.

The operation was to be a dual one. Airborne troops would seize a series of bridges over the principal waterways in Holland and so gain control of key points along the north–south line Arnhem–Nijmwegen–Eindhoven. At the same time ground troops would advance from the south to Eindhoven, thence to Nijmwegen and finally – the crucial link – to Arnhem. Eisenhower approved the plan and gave Montgomery the Hundred-and-first and the Eighty-second US Airborne Divisions for the Eindhoven and Nijmwegen drops. The bridge over the Lower Rhine at Arnhem was to be captured by the British Airborne Division. But there remained some misunderstanding about how far Eisenhower had decided to give Montgomery all the material support he needed, even at the cost of staying Pattons's advance.

This operation, which was launched on 17 September and came to grief after a week's bitter fighting, was one of those failures which nearly succeed. The two American divisions accomplished their tasks, the Hundred-and-first Division comparatively smoothly and the Eighty-second Division on the fourth day after one of the most dashing exploits of the war in the west. The British ground forces (XXX Corps under General Horrocks) made punctual contact with the Hundred-and-first Division and then sent forward armoured units in time to follow up and consolidate the Eighty-second Division's successful capture of the bridge over the Waal at Nijmwegen. But XXX Corps' further advance towards Arnhem was impeded by mines and the skilful and vigorous recovery of the Germans, and meanwhile the British Airborne Division had got into trouble.

The airborne drops were spread over three days and the defences of the bridge at Arnhem were reputedly so fierce that it had been decided to drop the British division about eight miles from the bridge. In this way the division could expect to find itself on Dutch soil more or less intact and would then proceed to attack the bridge like an ordinary ground formation. In other words the defences at the bridge had persuaded the British, before a shot was fired, not to attempt a direct airborne *coup de main* but to mount a hybrid attack which was part airborne and, in the second and decisive part, a straight fight through fields and villages. Given these tactics it was peculiarly unfortunate that German strength in the area had been seriously underestimated. Although the anti-aircraft defences at the bridge itself may have been over-estimated, allied Intelligence had failed to locate two SS Panzer divisions which had arrived in the area for refitting, had been excellently equipped and turned out to be very ably commanded. In addition the British orders for the entire operation were captured on the first day off an American soldier whose glider crashed.

Nevertheless the first day's operations were everywhere successful and on the Arnhem sector the British units began their advance towards the town through a friendly population anxious to show their delight by hospitality of every kind. On the second day, however,

German opposition surprised the British and the situation began to get confused. Poor weather intervened and airborne supplies to the units which had already been dropped miscarried to such an extent that most of them were collected by the Germans. Aircraft losses were heavy. From the third day the British were being forced to make local withdrawals and it soon became clear that the fate of the Airborne Division depended on what speed XXX Corps could make to its relief. As hope faded, the story became one of endurance, heroism and the gradual strangulation of the perimeter, while the prematurely exuberant Dutch awaited the return of the Germans in the cellars of houses where they had been dispensing good cheer to the British but which were now being wrecked above their heads. The attackers' losses were 1,200 dead and over 3,000 taken prisoner. The Arnhem bridge remained in German hands until the middle of April 1945. The Arnhem operation, the last major parachute operation of the war, summed up the experiences of four years which had begun with the successful German operation which opened the campaign in the Low Countries in May 1940. There experiences showed that parachutists could play an important role as the advance guard of a main force which was not too far away and was advancing rapidly, but that they could not yet take an independent giant stride ahead on their own.

The failure at Arnhem gave the Germans a last chance to consolidate a line beyond Germany's own borders. On 5 September – the day after Antwerp had fallen in the north and Lyons to the Americans advancing from Toulon in the south, and two weeks before the Arnhem operation – Hitler had recalled Rundstedt once more and had given him the task of holding what was left of Belgium, Holland and the Siegfried line. But Hitler also intended Rundstedt to do more than that. He would take advantage of a lull on the eastern front to switch troops to the west for an offensive in the Ardennes at the end of November from the Meuse to Antwerp and the sea. He did not, however, tell his principal commanders in the west of the plans which they were to execute and it was not until the end of October that they were informed. Rundstedt, Model and their senior commanders and staff officers immediately objected that the plans were too ambitious. They proposed a watered-down version designed to encircle a part of the American forces west of Aachen with the option, in the event of speedy success, of going on to Antwerp at a second stage, but Hitler refused to consider any alterations to the plans which his own staff had already worked out in detail. All he would grant, under pressure of circumstances, was the postponement of D-day to 16 December.

The last German offensive of the war of any note was accordingly launched on that day. It achieved complete surprise. Thanks to rigorous wireless silence and providential covering mists and fog the Germans had assembled an entire Army Group with all its paraphernalia, including 1,000 tanks, undetected; and the allies, so used by now to full and accurate intelligence, were all the more disconcerted when it failed them. They were thrown into considerable disarray. Eisenhower placed all troops north of the German thrust – including two American armies – under Montgomery's command, a redisposition of some courage in view of the prevalent American animus against Montgomery and the contrary advice of Bradley who underrated the gravity of the situation. The Germans were lucky with the weather at the outset, for fog in England for the first three days, followed by fog on the continent, prevented the allied air force from taking part in the battle. Yet the German advances were not as great as had been planned and an order by Patton (who feared that the Germans might break left rather than right and so cut across his rear) to withdraw was not executed, so that the town of Bastogne was held and became an American strongpoint, brilliantly defended by the US Tenth Armoured and the Hundred-and-first Airborne Divisions and supplied by air. By the 22nd Rundstedt, under pressure on both flanks, was counselling the abandonment of the attack. The Fifth Panzer Division under General Hasso von Manteuffel continued to advance until Christmas Eve but was then diverted to Bastogne. From this point the Germans were forced onto the defensive and began to suffer increasing casualties. The battle of the Ardennes was substantially an American victory under a British commander. The German thrust failed, but it was a nasty shock to the allied commanders and publics because of the surprise which cast doubt on allied intelligence, its initial successes, and Eisenhower's alteration in the command which stirred up national animosities.

In January Hitler abandoned his offensive in the west. He had hoped for a quick victory, to be followed by a massive counter-attack on the Russians in the east. He had been defeated by allied air superiority, by the defenders of Bastogne, by poor cooperation among his own forces (especially between the Fifth and Sixth Panzer Divisions) and by a new weapon, the proximity fuse. This fuse contained a tiny radio device which, reacting to noise, made a shell go off at a distance from its target. It was estimated to increase the effectiveness of artillery tenfold. Although used against Japanese aircraft in 1943 it was not used in the European theatre before the emergencies of the V 1 and Ardennes offensives.

The end of the attack in the Ardennes coincided with a lesser attack in Alsace begun on the last day of the year, although originally conceived as a move to cover the left flank of the Ardennes offensive. This operation gave rise to a major row between Eisenhower and de Gaulle, about which there are many accounts, including accounts by Eisenhower, de Gaulle and Churchill. These accounts cannot be reconciled and so it is still impossible to produce an unassailable version. By the time the attack in Alsace came it was – whatever the original German plan – distinct from the flagging Ardennes offensive and a comparatively minor affair. But Eisenhower may not have seen it that way. Rundstedt's attack had forced him to contemplate a major switch of Patton's forces northward and a consequent re-deployment of his southern Army Group which, under Devers, had come up into the line from the south of France: Devers's forces might have to take over part of Patton's front and perhaps even withdraw from the Rhine to the Vosges. Such a withdrawal meant abandoning Strasbourg.

Devers' Army Group included a French army under General de Lattre de Tassigny, but Devers did not tell de Lattre, and Eisenhower did not tell de Gaulle, that a withdrawal was anything but a hypothetical contingency. Their reticence was no doubt due to their knowledge that a withdrawal, exposing Strasbourg to recapture and reprisals by the Germans, would be strenuously resisted by the French. De Gaulle meanwhile had instructed de Lattre to defend Strasbourg, the arch-symbol of Franco-German rivalry ever since 1870. In doing so he was ignorant of Eisenhower's instructions to Devers and convinced, correctly as it happened, that a withdrawal was unnecessary. The upshot was that Eisenhower and Devers got themselves into a position where they were trying to outwit de Gaulle and de Lattre by putting into execution a plan which had been represented as something less than a plan, while the French commanders were taking decisions into their own hands to the extent of denying the superior command powers of the American commanders. Upon discovering what was afoot de Gaulle sent Juin to Eisenhower's headquarters where a battle of threats developed between him and Bedell Smith, and sent a signal to Churchill who flew at once to France to smooth over the controversy. Strasbourg was not evacuated.

On 12 January a new Russian offensive opened. Hitler had already begun to switch part of his armour in the west back to the east in order to meet it. Since 6 June the Germans had lost three quarters of a million men in France. They were now defending the Rhine.

CHAPTER 25

Disintegration

By the beginning of 1945 the accumulation of Germany's reverses had produced disintegration. It is surprising that the war lasted into May. Even in the previous summer Montgomery had believed that Berlin could be reached before the end of 1944 and on the other front Chuikov, the defender of Stalingrad and ultimately the conqueror of Berlin, chafed at his superiors for not allowing him to make straight for the city at the beginning of the new year. Hitler no longer had an army capable of sustaining the fight, he had so little fuel that his soldiers had standing orders to siphon off the fuel in a disabled tank before abandoning it, he scarcely had an air force at all, his anti-aircraft units were manned by a mixture of regulars, prisoners of war and teenagers down to sixteen, and his secret weapons had not worked the miracles that were expected of them.

After 1942 the Luftwaffe had performed one function brilliantly at the cost of relinquishing all others. It had created a fighter defence of Germany which defeated American and British strategic bombing until the final phase of cumulative disintegration was reached. But otherwise – apart from limited local successes, as when it drove the British out of the Dodecanese in 1943 – it ceased to count in one theatre after another. Its formations were outnumbered, its airfields bombed and its new types and new weapons failed it. In 1943 the Do. 217 was equipped with a 1,000 lb. radio-controlled, glider bomb (Hs. 293 – first used against the Italian fleet as it escaped from Italy to Malta upon the Italian surrender) and also with a 3,000 lb. radio-controlled anti-personnel bomb (F X), but these were primitive prototypes of things to come and neither was successful. The He. 177 four-engined bomber appeared in 1943, but in small numbers only and after Germany's chance to affect the issue by heavy bombing had passed; the Luftwaffe was never able to drop the super-bombs which were dropped by its enemies on German cities (the heaviest bomb used against Germany was 22,000 lbs.).

The Me. 262 jet fighter and the Me. 163 rocket-propelled fighter appeared towards the end of 1944, but by then it was too late. Both these aircraft were the successors of earlier models which had flown before the war began and in both Germany was the pioneer, but their champions had been unable to persuade Hitler or Goering to adopt them because it was assumed that the war would be finished and won without them. The Me. 262 was, however, put into series production half way through the war (1,294 were made) because Hitler mistakenly supposed that this 500 m.p.h. fighter could be usefully converted into a bomber.

During 1942–3 the Luftwaffe had been called upon to fight on four fronts. It was not strong enough to do so. Its own bomber offensive was defeated, it failed to succour the German armies in the east or in the Mediterranean, and it was squeezed out of the Battle of the High Seas. The Russian campaigns acted like a magnet and a churn. Great numbers of aircraft were drawn into battles in which the Luftwaffe was gradually ground out of existence. In 1944 a new front was added in the west. This was the last straw. The destruction of the Luftwaffe was accelerated by a training crisis, a fuel crisis and a breakdown in its intelligence. By 1945 it was out of the fight.

Germany did not manage to produce the Second World War's most startling new weapon – the nuclear bomb. In the aftermath of defeat some German writers and scientists sought to ascribe this failure to the reluctance of German science to place so terrifying a weapon in the hands of so terrifying a man as Hitler, but the truth seems to be that the Germans failed to produce nuclear weapons because they took a wrong turning. They did, however, produce at the end of the war special weapons which, had they been brought into service earlier, might have had a considerable effect. These were the V weapons, V standing for *Vergeltung* or retribution.

There were three V weapons. The V 1 was a jet-propelled pilotless aircraft twenty-five feet long with a ceiling of 2,000–3,000 feet, a range of 200–250 miles, a speed of 470 m.p.h. and a one-ton warhead. It cost only £125 and consumed in flight only 150 gallons of low-grade fuel. Beginning in June 1944 2,448 of these weapons hit Antwerp, 2,419 London (out of 10,492 aimed at it) and 3,132 hit other parts of England. The V 2 was a rocket. It was fifty feet long and six feet in circumference and carried a one-ton warhead. It rose into the air for fifty to seventy-five miles and could reach a speed of 3,600 m.p.h. Its range was 220 miles. Its motor, controlled from the ground, was cut at the crucial moment, thus setting it on course. It was impossible to intercept and arrived without warning since it travelled faster than sound. The V 2 was therefore a more terrifying weapon than the V 1, but each V 2 cost about £6,000, exclusive of research and development costs. Again Antwerp was the chief sufferer, receiving 1,265 hits. London received 517 and other parts of England 537.

The V 3 was a long-range gun. One weapon of this kind – originally there were to be two – was installed at Mimoyecques, near Calais. It had twenty-five barrels, each of them 416 feet long, entirely embedded in limestone and concrete, and the whole weapon was serviced and controlled by an extremely elaborate underground network. Its construction absorbed 1,000 tons of steel. It was to fire one shell on London every twelve seconds, but although the site was well prepared the components did not start arriving until early in June 1944. Allied bombing first severed its electricity supply and then scored a direct hit with a heavy bomb. In any case trials in the Baltic had not been completed when the site at Mimoyecques was overrun by the allied armies.

Hitler hoped to begin the V 1 and V 2 attacks against England in 1942 but development and production were held up by rivalries between the army, which was in charge of the V 2, and the Luftwaffe, which was responsible for the V 1. These jealousies were accentuated when the SS tried to get control of the whole programme and at one point in March 1944 arrested the brilliant young researcher Werner von Braun and other key scientists. Allied Intelligence had wind of these inventions from the first days of the war but there was considerable doubt about their capabilities, particularly about the size of the warheads which they carried. These doubts arose from ignorance about the fuel used, there being a correlation between bulk of fuel, range, and size of warhead. In London these differences caused some of the bitterest quarrelling of the war because Lord Cherwell – who was not only an exceptionally stubborn and often ill-mannered man who allowed scientific disagreement to invade personal relations, but who also resented the fact that the coordination of intelligence about Hitler's secret weapons had been assigned to a committee under Duncan Sandys, Churchill's son-in-law, whom he did not like – began by disbelieving in the existence of any rocket threat at all.

The first V 2 was launched at the experimental station on Peenemünde in the Baltic in October 1942 after three earlier failures, and a first V 1 a few weeks later. Attempts were made to cripple the programme by bombing Peenemünde and other places where parts of the apparatus were being manufactured but most of these targets were at long range. On the night of 17–18 August 1943 600 bombers of Bomber Command attacked Peenemünde in three waves in the hope of interrupting research and killing key scientists. As a result of a successful feint towards Berlin the first and second waves suffered only slight losses in spite of a full moon, but fighter attacks on the third wave brought the total loss to forty-one aircraft. At Peenemünde 732 people, mostly non-

Germans, were killed, some projects were abandoned or moved elsewhere, but work on the V 1 and V 2 was only interrupted for a short
time. The attack on Peenemünde itself and related industrial targets
was supplemented from December 1943 by attacks on sites along the
north coast of France which had been identified by photographic and
other intelligence as launching sites for the V 1. There were about a
hundred of these sites known, from their appearance, as ski sites. These
attacks were moderately successful but they were countered by swift
repair and then by a German ruse. The Germans pretended to be repairing the sites when they were in fact abandoning them, using them
as dummies and constructing new sites by a new method which enabled
them to build a site in a matter of days. This deception was not discovered until May 1944 and during the first half of the year the allies
wasted more bombs on these abandoned sites than the Germans had
aimed at London during the eight months of the 1940–41 blitz.

The German failure to bring the V 1 and V 2 into operation before the
summer and autumn of 1944 respectively, by which time allied armies
were approaching, was largely due to teething troubles. British estimates
of the production and effects of these new weapons were unduly pessimistic. Plans were made to evacuate the population and the government from London on the assumption that V 1s would arrive at the
rate of 45,000 a month, and that the V 2s, arriving at the rate of one an
hour and carrying a ten-ton warhead, would cause 108,000 casualties
a month. At the beginning of the war the German production targets
for the V 1 and the V 2 were 3,000 and 900 a month. In 1944 the former
target was raised to 8,000. This figure was never reached but the earlier
one was passed in 1945. Altogether 32,000 V 1s were produced. Production of the V 2 rose from fifty in January 1944 to 253 in April when
it fell back because priority was given to the V 1. It picked up again
later in the year, was steady at around 630–60 in the last four months
and reached 690 in January 1945. Nearly 6,000 were produced in all.
These figures were creditable to the Germans and would, timing apart,
have been alarming for the British.

Hitler's plan of attack on England was to fire a salvo of V 1s at dawn
and dusk every day with intermediate single launchings every twenty to
thirty minutes, but when the attack began on 12 June from fifty-five
sites it was a rushed fiasco. On the first day ten V 1s were launched,
of which four arrived. Appreciable damage was caused to rail traffic,
factories, hospitals and housing, mostly south of the Thames. There
was then a pause of three days but in the ensuing two weeks 2,000 were
launched. At first spotter aircraft gave warnings but the number of

V 1s destroyed was small. Anti-aircraft guns in the London area had to cease firing after the first two days because they were bringing the V 1s down in the city. Batteries were re-deployed along the south coast and, with the help of radar and proximity fuses, gradually succeeded in hitting half and then three quarters of their incoming targets. Some V 1s were destroyed by jet aircraft. The attack on London was suspended in September (Antwerp and Brussels came under fire a few weeks later) but it was followed by the V 2 attack.

There was still much doubt about the potency of this weapon. In June parts of a V 2 fired from Peenemünde had come down in Sweden and valuable information about it had come into allied possession. Another came down in Poland without exploding; it was hidden, dismantled and secretly conveyed to England. But there were still controversies about the size of the warhead; estimates varied between ten tons and one ton (the latter being correct). On 6 September two V 2s were aimed at Paris but the firings were a failure. On that day Duncan Sandys announced in London that 'except possibly for a few last shots, the Battle of London is over'. Two days later the first V 2s struck London. They were fired from Holland. The worst aspect of the attack was the number of men, women and children who were blinded by flying glass before they knew that anything had struck. In spite of doctors working round the clock on delicate eye operations many lost their sight for life. There was also severe material damage, but the firing sites were already threatened and had to be removed as the British armies approached them. The weight of the attack was diverted to Antwerp which was more seriously damaged than London and did not get relief until March 1945.

There has been a tendency to laugh at Hitler's V weapons. This is partly because it seemed in 1944 the best thing to do. But the weapons were not negligible and would have been extremely dangerous if they had been available earlier. In the first two weeks the V 1s killed 1,600 people, seriously injured another 4,500 and damaged 200,000 houses; the casualty rate in England in June 1944 was as heavy as it had been in September 1940, although the weight of attack measured in tons of explosives was much lighter. Over the whole period of the V 1 and V 2 attacks 29,400 houses were completely destroyed in London and over a quarter of a million damaged. It may be argued that Hitler could have used to better purpose the 200,000 persons engaged in the development and production of the V 2 – he might, for example, have got more from their brains and their labour if they had worked on defensive projects – but against this must be set not only the chance that the V weapons might have been ready sooner, but also the hard facts that the British had to increase their fighter, anti-aircraft and balloon defences, suffer appreciable material damage and divert a significant air effort to Peenemünde and the launching sites. The V weapons failed but their failure does not prove that they were ridiculous. They were the forerunners of much that has been developed since the war. They may not have been the weapons that Hitler hoped for to settle the result of the war, but if their appearance had not been delayed by allied bombing by a few months, they could hardly have failed to affect its course.

The V weapons were Hitler's last offensive expedients. After their failure he continued to produce expedients but they were defensive. In October 1944 he called into existence a new force, the *Volkssturm*, a Home Guard of last resort under Himmler's command and consisting of all available men between the ages of sixteen and sixty. The Werewolves, another desperate expedient, were to constitute armed bands operating like marauding partisans after the defeat of Germany. The Alpine redoubt, where Hitler said he would make his last stand, was even more phantasmal. It never existed, it had no men in it or prepared defences, and the Führer himself did not go there.

The first front to go was the Italian. Early in 1945 senior SS figures in Italy made approaches to Swiss contacts and indirectly to the head of the American intelligence services in Switzerland, Allen W. Dulles. These SS officers wanted to negotiate a separate surrender to the western allies of the entire Italian front. Dulles was not interested in a partial surrender, but he was concerned to keep the discussions alive in the hope that they would contribute to a total and unconditional surrender on all fronts. In March the German Supreme Commander in Italy, Kesselring, the Luftwaffe commander, Pohl, and Hitler's Ambassador in Italy, Rudolf Rahn who was in command of Mussolini and his government, were all brought into the discussions. Although they thought at first that they were discussing a negotiated and partial surrender, they quickly came to realize that what was in train was capitulation on all fronts and that the western allies would neither accept any vestige of Nazism in a new German government nor envisage any split between themselves and the Russians. The Russians, however, who knew that Himmler was trying to do a deal with the west via Stockholm, not unnaturally assumed (as for a while did some in the west) that the talks initiated by the SS in Switzerland were part of an anti-Russian venture. After a delay caused by the transfer of Kesselring to the western front and the need to initiate his successor, Vietinghoff, a surrender of all the German forces in Italy was made on

1 May by the army and air commanders acting on their own authority. It was botched by a farcical succession of arrests and counter-arrests among the Germans themselves but clinched when the news of Hitler's suicide reached Italy on the next day.

On the main fronts the German armies were overwhelmed by superior numbers and material. After the retreats of 1944 Hitler hoped to hold the line of the Vistula in the east (where Himmler was appointed to command an Army Group) and the Rhine in the west. The Russians, opening a new campaign in mid-January, crossed the Vistula, turned northwards to the sea to envelop the German forces in East Prussia and overran Pomerania and Silesia up to the Oder and Neisse rivers which they reached at the beginning of February. In the south they captured Budapest on the 12th. In the west German commanders tried vainly to obey Hitler's orders to give no ground and transport neither men nor material eastward across the Rhine. They were weakened by the transfer of a whole Panzer division to Hungary after the failure of the Ardennes offensive, a transfer which gave rise to one of the allies' most misguided operations of the war – the bombing of Dresden by British and American air forces on 13 and 14 February in the belief that the German armour was passing through the rail junction at Dresden and could be hit there. This view was in fact wrong. The mistake was pointed out to both the bomber headquarters concerned, but although one of them was willing to call off the attack if the other was too, the other was unwilling to refer it to higher authority in the light of the information supplied. So the raids took place and one of Europe's most splendid cities was recklessly destroyed. Industrial targets were barely hit and the rail services were only put out of action for four days. The number of people purposelessly killed has been estimated at 135,000, although the true figure seems to have been about a fifth of this huge total. The slaughter was in any case immense. All this destruction was done in two night raids lasting half an hour each and a third raid of ten minutes at midday on the next day. One thousand two hundred and twenty-three aircraft dropped bombs. There was no opposition.

On 7 March an American unit, seeing to its surprise that a bridge at Remagen, south of Bonn, had not been destroyed, crossed the Rhine and in the next weeks large forces followed at several points. Three of the western armies hoped and believed that they were on their way to Berlin. In addition there existed a plan for airborne attacks on key points in Berlin by a force of 20,000 paratroopers. But in the event the western allies made no attempt to reach the German capital. The reasons for this abnegation were two: Eisenhower's strategic decisions and the existence of an agreed division of Germany into separate administrative zones, with Berlin inside the Russian zone.

The zonal agreement grew out of administrative planning which had not been intended to have – but did have – political consequences. At their conference in Teheran in November 1943 Roosevelt, Churchill and Stalin agreed to create a European Advisory Commission which, sitting in London, would produce preliminary plans for the occupation of Germany. This Commission inherited a plan prepared in London by the Anglo-American planning staff which subsequently became part of Eisenhower's headquarters. This plan divided Germany into three zones – a British one in the north-west, an American in the south-west and a Russian in the east: Berlin was inside the Russian zone. Roosevelt had indicated to his own officials before Teheran that he did not like the arrangements proposed for the American and British zones and wanted them the other way round. But the dispositions had evolved logically from the planning for Overlord which always put the American armies on the right of the allied forces and the British (and Canadian) armies on the left, and in addition Roosevelt's reservations and objections got lost in Washington and were not conveyed to the American member of the European Advisory Commission until too late. A separate American proposal for a corridor linking Berlin with the north-western zone also got overlooked. The Russians were well satisfied with an arrangement which gave them 40 per cent of Germany and its capital (subject though the capital would itself be to tripartite division and control), while the western allies, who continued to be afraid that Stalin might run out of the European war or refuse to join the war against Japan, were loath to suggest amendments of any kind. The plan was therefore adopted by the Commission in March 1944 and confirmed at Yalta in February 1945.

It did not, however, follow that western forces were not to advance to Berlin or anywhere else so long as the war lasted. The plan only bound them to observe fixed lines of demarcation when the war was over and the occupation had begun. Stalin expected the Americans and British to race him for Berlin and the western allies had strong motives for doing so as they speculated about the future of an alliance which was about to pass from military cooperation to political manoeuvre.

Montgomery's and Bradley's Army Groups both crossed the Rhine in the third week of March. Montgomery, commanding Canadian, British and American armies – the last was the Ninth US Army under General William H. Simpson which had been subordinated to him during the Ardennes offensive – was heading across northern Germany for Berlin; Bradley with three US armies under command was heading across central Germany. Further south the American–French Army Group under Devers was making equally rapid progress. A few days earlier Hitler had signed the first of a number of orders for the total destruction of everything. On the 28th the Russians made their first air attacks on Berlin. At this time Eisenhower, to the dismay of his subordinates and still more of Churchill, took his eyes off Berlin. Although there were no longer any meaningful German forces in the field Eisenhower clung to the view that his task was to seek out and destroy the enemy. In the pursuit of this aim he reinforced Bradley's central group of armies at the expense of Montgomery by re-allocating Simpson's Ninth US Army to Bradley, and he ordered Bradley to push eastward towards Erfurt, Leipzig and Dresden – on a line, that is, running well south of Berlin, which he declared to be irrelevant, and through Saxony, which was. He now adopted the policy of the concentrated thrust which Montgomery had urged upon him in the previous summer but he had chosen the wrong thrust. Further, in an unprecedented message to Stalin, which was probably dictated by anxiety to avoid an unpleasant clash between American and Russian forces, he disclosed his intention not to go for Berlin and gave Stalin a detailed account of the allied order of battle. Stalin was so surprised that he thought the message was a trick, did not send the equivalent information on Russian plans and dispositions which Eisenhower had asked for, and immediately accelerated his own measures to take Berlin. Churchill was not only surprised but appalled at this assumption of politico-strategic authority and by the revelation that the Supreme Commander had so little notion of the political importance of Berlin. To his own Army Group commanders Eisenhower remained for a time vague, so that when the first Anglo–American crossings of the Elbe were made the troops were still under the impression that they were on the last lap to Berlin. On 15 April, however, Simpson received a precise order to go no further. He was expecting to be in Berlin two days later. Thus it was at Torgau on the Elbe, on 25 April, that Americans and Russians first exchanged salutations.

Farther south too the Americans, spurting across Germany to Czechoslovakia, were reined back by punctilio. A line of demarcation had been agreed on 30 April. On 4 May, with German resistance vanishing, Eisenhower asked Moscow to let him keep up his momentum. He was only fifty miles from Prague and in a position to reach it before the Russians. Stalin, who had conceded to Eisenhower the right to advance as far as Pilsen, was not prepared to see him advance farther, and when

Bradley offered at a meeting with Konev on the 5th to cooperate in the taking of Prague Konev declined. On that day Prague rose against the Germans. But the Americans neither advanced to their assistance nor felt able to send supplies by air. Eisenhower and Truman felt that they had done their best; Truman had already told Eisenhower at the end of April that he was 'loath to hazard American lives' for what he described as 'political purposes', and neither leader saw much point in taking a city which would then be immediately turned over to the Russians. Konev began to move towards Prague from Saxony to the north-west on the 6th and Malinovski and Eremenko from the south-east and east respectively a day later. The first Russians entered Prague on the 9th. But by then the 30,000 insurgents had been overpowered by the Germans and 8,000 of them killed.

For his main central thrust in 1945 Stalin had grouped his armies in three fronts under the overall direction of his Supreme Headquarters in Moscow. These fronts were commanded, from north to south, by Rokossovski, Zhukov and Konev. D-day, originally fixed at 20 January, was advanced to the 12th at the request of the western leaders when hard pressed in the Ardennes. Rokossovski was directed north of Warsaw to Danzig and then westward. Zhukov, who relinquished his senior staff appointment in Moscow in order to become the captor of Berlin, struck straight towards the German capital from south of Warsaw. Konev, moving further south through Silesia, also had Berlin in his sights. The last barrier of any consequence was the river Oder, especially the fortress of Küstrin (which, bypassed, did not surrender until the end of March) at the junction of the Oder with the Warthe due east of Berlin. Chuikov's Eighth Guards Army reached the Oder on 1 February and began to cross the next day. Chuikov wanted to press on despite logistic difficulties and the risks, which he rightly discounted, of a last German stand. But Stalin, like Eisenhower, was wary. He ordered Zhukov to consolidate on the Oder and turn northwards into Pomerania and clean it up. Stalin overestimated German strength in Pomerania as well as the opposition lying between Zhukov and Konev and Berlin. Chuikov fumed against the restraints imposed on him and after the war he complained that Zhukov had failed in his duty by not urging a more adventurous strategy on the over cautious Stalin. He was probably right since Guderian had already expressed the opinion at the end of January that Berlin would fall in a few days and Hitler was sending such reinforcements as he could muster not to eastern Germany but to Hungary. But Stalin may have had a political motive when he reined Zhukov in. By doing so he enabled Konev to draw up. The two

Marshals were rivals and it suited Stalin to promote competition between them and let them both share the glory of taking Berlin rather than let one of them garner too many laurels singlehanded.

Stalin's delaying has also been explained in other terms. It can be argued that in the opening weeks of 1945 he was anxious not to take Berlin too soon. The city was doomed, its fate only a matter of time, and it was more important for him to safeguard the ravaged USSR against western hostility than to deliver the *coup de grâce* to Germany in one week rather than another. So long as Roosevelt lived Stalin probably felt that the American President's determination to remain on good terms with the USSR was a cardinal factor in his own foreign policies, but Stalin knew enough about western democracy to understand that Roosevelt was not the sole maker of policy and that there were significant anti-communist and anti-Russian forces in the United States and Great Britain. To take Berlin, assuming that he could have done so, while his western allies were still on the wrong side of the Rhine involved ending the war in a way which would have given him so dominant a position in Germany as to alarm the western powers and even revive visions of an anti-Russian alliance between them and the still not totally inconsiderable remnants of German military power. A dominant position in Germany could be more of a hazard than an asset so long as the war-weary USSR had not the strength to sustain it against a western coalition, and although Stalin banked on Roosevelt's determination to withdraw from Europe, he must also have recalled that Churchill had in 1919 not only supported western intervention in the USSR but had advocated the use of the German army to effect it. Whether such fanciful calculations did or did not pass through Stalin's mind remains unknown. The final onslaught was in fact delayed until April.

It was then mounted at short notice and, in the belief of Stalin's Marshals, under the impression that Montgomery had been ordered to get to Berlin before them. At a conference on 3 April Zhukov and Konev told Stalin that they could beat Montgomery and were told to produce their plans in forty-eight hours. Stalin drew a line on a map from east to west, dividing their zones of operations but stopping fifty miles east of Berlin with the implication that beyond that point the leading Marshal might be free to move on the German capital by any route he chose. The attack was launched on 16 April with 2.5 million men, 6,250 tanks and 7,500 aircraft against one million men, 1,500 tanks and 3,300 aircraft. Prolonged resistance by the Germans was impossible and by the 22nd the Russians were fighting in the streets of the capital. Konev's men had a slight lead over Zhukov's and there was

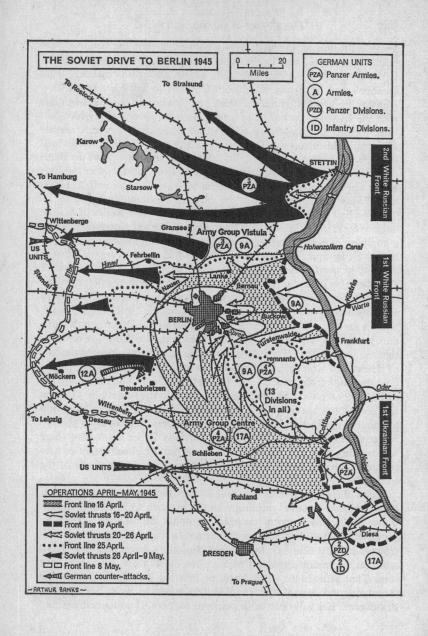

THE SOVIET DRIVE TO BERLIN 1945

Scale: 0 — 20 Miles

GERMAN UNITS
- (PZA) Panzer Armies.
- (A) Armies.
- (PZD) Panzer Divisions.
- (ID) Infantry Divisions.

To Rostock
To Stralsund
Karow
Starsow
To Hamburg
STETTIN
2nd White Russian Front
3 PZA
Wittenberge
Gransee
Army Group Vistula
Hohenzollern Canal
US UNITS
Fehrbellin
Havel
Lanke
Bernau
Köstrin
Warte
1st White Russian Front
3 PZA   9 A
Stendal
Elbe
Neuen
BERLIN
Spree
Buckow
9 A
Frankfurt
Möckern
12 A
Treuenbrietzen
9 A   4 PZA
remnants
Fürstenwalde
Oder
1st Ukrainian Front
Wittenberg
(13 Divisions in all)
To Leipzig
Dessau
Army Group Centre
4 PZA   17 A
Cottbus
Schlieben
US UNITS
Torgau
Ruhland
Diesa
DRESDEN
Elbe
2 PZD
2 ID   17 A
To Prague

OPERATIONS APRIL–MAY, 1945
- Front line 16 April.
- Soviet thrusts 16–20 April.
- Front line 19 April.
- Soviet thrusts 20–26 April.
- Front line 25 April.
- Soviet thrusts 26 April–9 May.
- Front line 8 May.
- German counter–attacks.

~ ARTHUR BANKS ~

some confusion as the two Fronts converged, but the suburbs were gradually reduced and in the early hours of 1 May General Krebs, Hitler's last Army Chief of Staff, acting under instructions from Goebbels and Bormann, sought out Chuikov to ask for an armistice. He told Chuikov that Hitler was dead and that he had come to negotiate with the Russians on behalf of a new German government which had been formed in compliance with Hitler's will and in which neither Goering, Ribbentrop nor Himmler had any part. Chuikov telephoned Zhukov. He was told that Stalin refused to negotiate. The Germans must surrender unconditionally on all fronts. Shortly after midday Krebs went back to the centre of Berlin where he shot himself. The next day, 2 May, the commander of the garrison capitulated.

Hitler had been dead two days. He spent the last weeks of his life underground in Berlin. By the Chancellery in the middle of the city was a complex of heavily protected underground shelters arranged in two floors. Hitler and his mistress Eva Braun had a set of rooms in what was called the Führer's Bunker at the deeper level. With them were Goebbels, his wife and five children, a doctor, a cook, a valet, a couple of secretaries and an Alsatian bitch which had just pupped. Nearby, in similar shelters, were Bormann, Artur Axmann, the Hitler Youth leader, and an assortment of adjutants, guards and so on. Other people came and went. Ten days before his end Hitler emerged from his delusion that the war could still be won and told Keitel that he accepted the fact of defeat and would shoot himself. He told Speer the same thing the next day. But from time to time hope still flickered and every day the increasingly senseless conferences took place in the war room. Goering had gone south but he quickly learned of Hitler's decision and sent him a signal proposing that he should immediately take over as though Hitler were dead. Since Goering was officially Hitler's successor there was nothing very odd about this proposal but it infuriated Hitler who ordered Goering's arrest and dismissed him from his command of the Luftwaffe.

A few days later Hitler was still further incensed on learning that Himmler, at a personal meeting with the Swedish Count Folke Berna-dotte, had taken it upon himself to propose capitulation. (Since he proposed to capitulate in the west but not in the east the western allies rejected his advances.) Hitler ordered Himmler's arrest and had his SS adjutant, Hermann Fegelein, who was in the Bunker, shot there and then. That same night, 28–9 April, he married Eva Braun. After the ceremony and a wedding meal Hitler retired to write his two last documents. His will dealt with personal matters. It contained nothing particularly unusual except the gift of his pictures to found a picture gallery in Linz. His political testament, a much longer document, rehearsed all his old attacks on the Jewish race and reaffirmed his belief in the German need for *Lebensraum* in the east. Next to the Jews he blamed the German officer corps for all that had gone wrong. Having dismissed Goering and Himmler, he appointed Doenitz President and Commander-in-Chief of the Armed Forces and Goebbels Chancellor. He also appointed a number of other Ministers and a new Commander-in-Chief of the Army to succeed himself. On the afternoon of the 30th Hitler said his good-byes. He then poisoned the dog and Eva and shot (or possibly poisoned) himself. Their bodies were burned outside in accordance with instructions which had already been given. That night the surviving inhabitants of the Bunker made their escapes, but not the Goebbels family. After the failure of the Krebs mission to Chuikov Goebbels gave poison to his children and either shot or poisoned his wife and himself – the second Chancellor of the Third Reich.

Doenitz, its President for a week, was also its undertaker. On 2 May he sent Admiral Wilhelm Friedeburg to Montgomery to negotiate a surrender in the west. Montgomery refused to negotiate. On 7 May representatives of all three of the Reich's fighting services arrived at Eisenhower's headquarters at Reims and there, in the presence of senior American, Russian, British and French officers (but not of Eisenhower himself) surrendered unconditionally to the western and Russian commands. After the formal act there was a brief encounter between Jodl and Eisenhower at which Eisenhower asked Jodl whether he fully comprehended what had been done and Jodl said he had. On the next day, towards midnight, and again in the presence of senior officers of the four principal victors, the act of surrender was ratified at Russian headquarters in the German capital, Berlin.

Epilogue

THE Second World War was fought to a finish in Europe and had to be. Hitler could have ended it by negotiation because he was fighting for material things and might have decided at some moment or other that he had won enough of them. He wished to do so after the defeat of Poland and again after the defeat of France, although with the reservation that making peace on either occasion was only a prelude to a fresh bid for *Lebensraum* in the east. There was no lack of peace-makers: the Pope, Mussolini, the massed sovereigns of the Low Countries and Scandinavia, the King of Rumania, all tried to mediate in various ways and at various dates in the closing months of 1939. The inactivity of France and Great Britain during the obliteration of Poland gave Hitler and others grounds for believing that their declarations of war had been retractable formalities. Hitler could hardly conceive how, although they had been silly enough to go to war on behalf of Poland, they would continue at war on behalf of what had become non-Poland. With the Right preponderantly and the communists wholly for peace and with the knowledge, leaked by German counter-intelligence, that Hitler had given orders for an attack in the west in November, France and Great Britain could logically be expected to give up. But 1939 brought neither peace nor war. Hitler had to postpone his attack in the west and the peace offensive continued in 1940 up to and again after the German campaigns in Scandinavia and the west. Roosevelt sent his Under-Secretary of State, Sumner Welles, on a long exploration in European capitals in February and March, and the Pope and Mussolini kept up their feelers. After the fall of France Hitler tried again to secure his gains and close the account but Churchill refused.

The hesitations in London about whether to seek terms or not in 1940 reveal the differences between Hitler's war aims and those of his enemies. Great Britain, the sole effective combatant at this point, was fighting for no specific or material gain. It was fighting against Hitler and Nazi Germany. On the British side therefore negotiation meant not compromise but the abandonment of British war aims, which, in so far as they could be rationalized at all, were the surrender of Germany and the collapse of Nazism. Unconditional surrender was implicit in the nature of the war long before it was proclaimed at Casablanca. The alternative, for Great Britain, was to acknowledge that it had no war aims and had got into war by a mistake; but, once in, it could get out in this way only with the utmost difficulty, for a declaration of war is so weighty a pronouncement that it is intolerable to regard it as meaningless. To retire from a war with nothing accomplished and without being beaten requires a very unusual psychological effort. In this particular case it entailed also a sense of shame, for the evils of Nazi Germany had sunk in and making peace with Hitler seemed iniquitous. Although fearful of war in 1938 and glad to be spared it, the British were by 1940 determined to see it through.

So the war went on and the aim of surrender was achieved, although at great cost. Fighting on had not only a certain inevitability nor was it only the fulfilment of a praiseworthy obligation. It involved the deaths of millions of people, including victims of Nazism – like the Jews – who might have been killed anyway but might not, and countless other civilians who certainly would not have died the premature and often horrible deaths which came to them. To ask whether the frightful cost was worth it is to ask an exceptionally painful question, but Hitler's régime was as horrible as any that Europe had ever seen and more horribly well equipped to pursue its fearful ends, and it may be thought that hardly any price could have been too high to pay for the elimination of the German Nazis. The tragedy was that the price had to be paid by so many people and so innocent.

As the Nazis recede into history they become objects of interest to historians, sociologists and psychologists, but they were in their own generation objects of pure horror. This horror can be expressed by saying that they represented a threat to civilized values and standards of behaviour; it can only be conveyed by recalling, with increasing effort over receding time, the things which they did to individual human beings. The battered but living skeletons found in the stinking degradation of the torture camps in 1945 are Hitler's truest memorial.

Hitler was many things, including an archcriminal, a criminal over and above criminals. His principal surviving accomplices were arraigned and tried in a series of trials in which they were charged with violations of the laws or customs of war, with 'crimes against humanity' and with 'crimes against peace'. The first of these categories includes offences such as the refusal to give quarter, the use of certain proscribed weapons (for example gas, expanding bullets) and the execution of prisoners of war, that is to say, acts which have become illegal by custom or have been declared illegal by international conventions. The most flagrant violations of these agreements during the Second World War were the execution of commandos after they had surrendered and the execution of commissars, or anybody said to be a commissar, among captured Russian soldiers. The expression 'crimes against humanity' was coined to designate acts which, although not explicitly proscribed by international pronouncement, are clearly contrary to law in civilized states, such as the killing of men and women simply because they belong in certain categories and without any allegation of criminal acts committed by them; or forced labour. 'Crimes against peace' denoted the preparation and waging of aggressive war in contravention of international law.

War crimes trials are not new. The notion that wars have rules which must be observed is at least as old as classical antiquity. It was reasserted by such eminent Renaissance jurists as Vitoria, Suarez and Grotius and the first adequately recorded war crimes trial in Europe took place nearly 500 years ago. During the Second World War Germany's enemies and victims gave early warning of their intention to bring war criminals to justice. At the beginning of 1942 nine countries jointly declared that the punishment of war criminals by judicial process was one of their war aims, and shortly afterwards a War Crimes Commission was established to collect and sift evidence and consider what should be done about it. In November 1943 Germany's three principal enemies declared that when the war was over criminals would be handed over to the governments of the countries where their crimes had been committed and that major criminals, whose crimes could not be attached to specific areas, would be tried by an international tribunal.

This tribunal, the International Military Tribunal, was formally constituted by an agreement signed in London in August 1945 on behalf of the American, British, Russian and (provisional) French governments and it subsequently conducted the most famous of all war crimes trials at Nuremberg in 1946. In addition the American authorities conducted twelve trials in their zone of Germany during 1946–9 under the provisions of a four-power ordinance (Control Council Law No. Ten) and the French held a smaller number of similar trials. The British, more tardily, put Manstein on trial on seventeen charges on nine of which he was found guilty, but dropped a plan to try Rundstedt, who had issued the commando order, on the grounds that he had become too old and feeble. The Russians held no trial under Control Council Law No. Ten. In Italy Kesselring was among the accused in trials held by the British. He was sentenced to death but this sentence was commuted to imprisonment, first for life and then for twenty-one years; and he was released on medical grounds in 1952. All over the rest of what had been occupied Europe, Germans from the SS, the armed services and the civilian administration had to face charges of murder, plunder and offences against the person of varying magnitude. Finally, the Germans themselves instituted similar proceedings when they recovered their juridical independence. Such trials were still occurring over twenty-five years after the end of the war as fresh facts came to light and criminals who had successfully lain low for years were discovered.

The first protests against war crimes in the Second World War and the first enunciation of a determination to prosecute the criminals were attempts to put a curb on the atrocities which were being perpetrated in Europe, by reminding people at all levels that even in war certain things were not permitted and that those who ignored the law might be brought to account. Further, there developed during the war a desire to assert both the existence of international penal law and the practicability of enforcing it by judicial process. And if the perpetrators of local crimes were to be indicted and perhaps executed, it seemed right and necessary to indict also those at the top who had either inspired or commanded these crimes. Hence the trial at Nuremberg in which twenty-two men who had wielded exceptional power and authority were put in the dock. (The indictment named twenty-four but one, Robert Ley, committed suicide in prison and a second, the industrialist Gustav Krupp von Bohlen, was found unfit to plead because of age and infirmity.) The Nuremberg defendants included the principal surviving political figures of the Third Reich but this and later trials were not confined to Nazi Party leaders since the prosecutors wanted to establish also the accountability of all, irrespective of party affiliation, who had wielded and abused power: service chiefs, police chiefs, industrial chiefs, holders of high judicial office, scientists and doctors who had used human bodies for inhumane experiments, etc. Twelve of the twenty-two accused were sentenced to death, three to life imprisonment, four to terms of ten to twenty years and three were acquitted. All the death sentences were carried out except that on Goering, who committed suicide after he had been sentenced, and Bormann who was either dead or in hiding and was convicted and sentenced *in absentia*. In the next most important trials – the twelve American trials under Control Council Law No. Ten – 185 defendants were indicted. Of these 177 stood trial, twenty-six were sentenced to death (but two of these sentences were remitted), thirty-five were acquitted and the remainder received sentences ranging from life to small terms which in fact resulted in their immediate release.

These proceedings commanded something less than universal approval among the general public and in the legal profession. The general public was worried by the appearance of unfairness resulting from the fact that the defeated were tried by their conquerors. Even though the trials were not unfairly conducted they were, from this point of view, not unassailable. Alternatives had been considered but rejected as impracticable. A trial by Germans was ruled out by the farcical outcome of the attempt to get the Germans to do the same job after the First World War, and a trial or trials by selected neutrals offered complications of procedure and language even more daunting than those involved in the solution adopted – quite apart from the fact that there were few neutrals and they did not want to assume the required role. (There was, however, at least one trial in the French zone of Germany at which French judges were joined by one Belgian and one Dutch judge.)

From the legal point of view the principal objection to the trials was the argument that, since there existed no international legislature to make international law, there was no offence of which the accused could be guilty or with which they could be charged. This argument raises a fundamental question about the nature of law: is it made by enactment, so that without enactment it does not exist; or can it evolve from some other source, so that it may be valid without enactment, in which case the enactment is not creative but declaratory? Murder, to take a simple example, has been regarded as a crime and punished in certain states before any legislative act declaring it to be a crime and saying how it would be punished. War crimes, properly so called, have been held by many authorities to be crimes quite apart from the Hague and Geneva conventions which declared them. Neither in the case of crimes against humanity nor in the case of war crimes could the criminals of the Third Reich claim that they did not know that the actions which were subsequently held against them were criminal. Nor, given the warnings issued by their adversaries from 1940 onwards, could they claim that they had not been warned that they would be tried. Many of the offences laid to their charge were committed after this date.

The category of crimes against peace is not so clear cut, but the International Military Tribunal, presided over by a Lord Justice of Appeal from Great Britain sitting with eminent judges and jurists from other countries, held that preparing and waging aggressive war had been a crime at least since the conclusion of the Kellogg–Briand Pact of 1928; that it was a crime which could be committed by an individual;

that although it might be difficult to define aggression in general it was possible to recognize it in particular cases; and that eight of the accused had committed this crime.

Some of the Tribunal's negative decisions were as striking as its positive conclusions. It refused to make any pronouncement on genocide in peacetime within a state's legitimate boundaries. After the war a convention banning genocide was adopted by the United Nations and ratified by a number of states but this convention contains no adequate provisions for enforcement. The Tribunal also refused belligerent rights to non-uniformed partisans and held that there is nothing in international law to prohibit in all circumstances the execution of hostages. Finally, the Tribunal did nothing – because it was not asked to – to adapt the laws of war to the age of mass bombing. Since the international code of war had not been revised since the Hague Convention of 1907, throwing a bomb from a balloon was expressly prohibited but dropping one from an aircraft was not (unless the target were totally undefended) and it appeared that, although gassing people was clearly unlawful in the same way as poisoning wells was clearly unlawful, the unlawfulness of indiscriminate bombing remained open to debate.

As a normative body the International Military Tribunal had serious limitations. It was an international body created by agreement among only a few nations. Even though the laws which it applied were not new, their codification was *ad hoc* and *post hoc*; its Charter was devised for the specific purpose of trying individuals who, however much they deserved to be tried and condemned, were in everybody's mind before the Charter or the indictment was drawn up. None but losers were tried. The judges, however fairly they discharged their judicial office, were provided by the victorious prosecutors from among their own nationals. There was therefore a risk that the principles enunciated at Nuremberg would lack moral backing and legal endorsement and that the trial itself would become a piece of history without contributing to international law.

In order to give them a wider sanction the General Assembly of the United Nations in 1946 unanimously affirmed the principles recognized by the Charter and by the Tribunal's judgement and asked the International Law Commission to re-formulate them. The Commission formulated in 1950 seven principles which have therefore, as a result of the war, become part of the corpus of international law. They proclaim: that a person who commits an act which is a crime under international law may be punished for it; that this liability is not avoided merely because the internal law of the accused's country provides no penalty for the criminal act, or because the accused was acting as a head of state or government official, or because he was following an order from his government or a superior (provided, in this last case, that he had a moral choice); that any person charged with a crime under international law has the right to a fair trial on the facts and the law. The principles also defined three kinds of crime: crimes against peace, war crimes and crimes against humanity; and stated that complicity in any such crime was itself a crime under international law.

Crimes against peace are defined as planning, preparing, initiating or waging a war of aggression or a war in violation of international compacts, or participating in a conspiracy to do any of these things. War crimes consist (as they have done since ancient times) of violations of the laws or customs of war: examples given include the murder, ill treatment or deportation – for slave labour or any other purpose – of civilians, the murder or ill-treatment of prisoners of war or persons on the seas, the killing of hostages, plunder of public or private property, wanton destruction of cities, towns or villages, or devastation not justified by military necessity. These definitions leave a lot of things open to argument, but they assert that it is proper to open the argument, to bring it before a judicial tribunal and to demand punishment. Finally, crimes against humanity are defined as certain acts against the civilian population when these acts are done in connection with any crime against peace or war crime. The acts are: murder, extermination, enslavement, deportation and other inhuman acts, and persecution on political, racial or religious grounds.

The Nuremberg trial and its aftermath were an attempt to establish that war is not so much a visitation like a plague or an act of state like a treaty of alliance, nor even a duty like a just war, but pre-eminently a crime and a punishable one.

*

The prime cost of war is measured in death and destruction. By this reckoning the cost fell most heavily on the USSR. Perhaps 20 million died – more than all the dead of all nations in the First World War and a staggering death roll for the short period of four years. Another twenty-eight million were made homeless. In the territories which they had occupied the Germans (whose scorched earth policy in retreat was much more efficient than the Russians' own destructiveness in 1941) destroyed half the living quarters in the towns and three quarters of it in the countryside. Two thirds of the wealth of these areas was extinguished.

Over thousands of square miles the land was bared, neglected and almost uninhabited: no towns, no villages, no buildings to shelter man or even beast, hardly any beasts, hardly any people. There was one cow where there had been ten, one sheep or one goat where there had been four, one pig in place of two. Crops had to be sown by hand. Such machinery as could be seen was unusable – rusting monuments to war but no longer aids to livelihood. The unoccupied areas had suffered too from neglect: in the oil industry, for example, technicians had had to go away and fight, leaving their machinery and installations to fall into shocking condition. Recovery was at first slow. Communications had been wrecked or worn out – 40,000 miles of rail track and a vast quantity of rolling stock destroyed. Production of many peacetime necessities had been all but abandoned – the output of tractors reduced from 116,000 a year to 8,000. Political conditions prohibited a quick reconversion of the economy – the American nuclear bomb had to be countered by a Russian one. So when in 1946 two thirds of the inhabitants of Stalingrad had returned to the city, only one sixth of its buildings had been patched up. Many of the rigours of war continued. There was little real improvement in living conditions for a decade. The memories of war were ineradicable and its consequences were prolonged with deep, if incalculable, effects on post-war domestic and international politics.

The next heaviest burden fell on the Germans. At least four and a half million of them died, including about a million civilians; their military dead were twice as numerous as in the first war. In Germany as well as the USSR material damage was very heavy. These two peoples – the Russian and the German – were the chief victims not only in the European war but also in the World War, since Japanese casualties were around two million. The one possible exception is the Chinese whose death roll, peculiarly difficult to assess, has been put as low as 2.5 million and as high as 13.5 million. Great Britain, France and Italy all suffered fewer deaths than in the first war. British fatal casualties, including civilians, were 450,000 with another 120,000 from the British Empire; in the first war the imperial total was nearly a million. France lost 200,000–250,000 in action and about as many civilians, as against nearly a million and a half in 1914–18. Italy, whose loss of life was greater than the French and not far short of the British, sacrificed 410,000 (one in every five a civilian) as against its earlier total of 615,000. Belgium's military casualties were approximately the same in both wars but in the second it lost more civilians than servicemen. Norway, Denmark and Holland had been spared the first war. Their losses in the second were small by comparison with the figures already quoted but sizable in relation to their own populations and Holland had the highest number of civilian deaths (200,000 or more) of any country in western Europe other than Germany itself. In central and eastern Europe the civilian deaths were very heavy indeed, since they included 5 million Jews, another 4 million non-Jewish civilians and a further million Yugoslav Resisters. In their regular armies the chief sufferers were Yugoslavia and Hungary, which lost some 400,000 each, and Poland and Rumania, which lost 300,000 each. The price paid by Austria was also around 300,000. Bulgaria escaped comparatively lightly with 20,000 deaths, half of them civilians, but in Greece the dead exceeded 250,000, two thirds of them civilians. American casualties on all fronts, Pacific as well as European, were 290,000, nearly six times as many as in the First World War. These casualties would have been higher if the Americans had not had the best medical services among the combatants. All these figures are, in the nature of the case, not only approximate but disputable. They add up to something like 50 million.

*

No great European war since the Seven Years War has so little changed the map of Europe or so much changed the map of the rest of the world. If Hitler had won, his New Order would have transformed Europe, but since he did not win states and frontiers were more restored than altered. Estonia, Latvia and Lithuania were the principal victims, engulfed in the USSR, their populations removed wholesale. Parts of Finland, Czechoslovakia and Rumania (and Afghanistan) were also annexed to the USSR. Poland had to submit to being shifted, partly because the boundaries which it had won after the First World War were not ethnically easy to justify. In eastern Europe a few provinces changed hands. But there was no post-war conference to allocate real estate, as after the defeat of Napoleon. The reason was not merely the fact that territorial annexation was out of favour (although this was so) but also the fact that real estate was ceasing to be an index of power. Stalin, who was an expansionist and was in a position to incorporate large areas in the USSR, did not do so because he did not need to. Communists believed that new Soviet Republics would be created; that Yugoslavia, for example, would become one of the Republics of the USSR. But Stalin decreed otherwise. He told Tito that Yugoslavia and other nearby countries were to become People's Democracies, juridically outside the USSR. He may have been deterred by the fear that the Americans would not tolerate the territorial expansion of the USSR but he did not need to put the issue to the test because Russian power sufficed to establish a new kind of Russian empire in central and eastern Europe – extending over much of the old Habsburg and Ottoman lands in Europe as well as those of the Tsars. Its authority could be assured by indirect rule through obedient communist cliques. It did not work in Yugoslavia but it worked everywhere else for the rest of Stalin's life and many years beyond. Where the First World War had dissolved Europe's empires, the Second resuscitated one of them and vastly enlarged it – in modern dress. The main thing for Stalin was to implant a particular social system where he could: annexation was not necessary for this purpose, occupation sufficed and occupation could be vicarious. He said to Djilas in 1944: 'This war is not as in the past: whoever occupies a territory also imposes on it his own social system. Everyone imposes his own system as far as his armies can reach. It cannot be otherwise . . .' But the determining factor was the radius of power of the army and not the legally established frontiers of states.

This new Russian empire was the product of circumstances and not of compact. The western leaders have been accused of handing over half Europe at Yalta to Stalin – as they have likewise been accused of cheating China at Teheran of its rightful claims in Asia. But Stalin would have established his empire even if there had been no Yalta conference. In the war on Hitler's eastern front, which was largely independent of the land, sea and air campaigns in the west, the Russian armies beat the German armies. Power in central Europe passed therefore by conquest from Germany to the USSR. What Roosevelt and Churchill tried to do at Yalta was to prescribe limits within which Russian power would be exercised. They have been criticized for not doing more to shackle that power. It is conceivable that, at Teheran fourteen months earlier, they could have driven a different bargain but it is unrealistic to forget that the circumstances of 1943 were inappropriate for driving post-war bargains at all. The Teheran conference was a war conference between partners intent on keeping each other in the war. Post-war problems – which is a euphemism for foreseeable and foreseen post-war disagreements – could only be raised at Teheran at some risk to the common war effort. Yalta was a different kind of conference, but by February 1945 Stalin's local power in eastern Europe could not be gainsaid. Roosevelt and Churchill extracted from him the declaration on liberated territories which was intended to assure basic democratic rights and procedures, but when Stalin disregarded this declaration there was nothing that any western power could do in the Russian sphere of influence created by Russian arms. All they could do was retaliate elsewhere. The creation in 1949 of the German Federal Republic and of Nato was a kind of retaliation against Stalin's exclusive and authoritarian hold over eastern Europe.

The biggest changes occurred in Germany. Since Hitler was not displaced by his army or his people, the surrender of Germany and the collapse of Nazism occurred simultaneously. They were a single event. Germany therefore was laid completely low. This had been envisaged: German power would disappear at the end of the war, in some versions for ever. There would of course be Germans and they would inhabit a place called Germany but this Germany would not exist as an independent unit in the power political structure. It was easy to see that this would be a fact immediately after the war. Less thought was given to how it would be perpetuated. Germany might be deprived of its industry, pastoralized, occupied, but the essential requirement for its indefinite subordination was the maintenance of an invincible alliance against its resurrection. This was assumed, if only superficially, and did not turn out to be so.

One of the main reasons why it did not turn out to be so was that Germany ceased to exist as such. Instead of persisting as a unit reduced to insignificance, it became divided into two units which rapidly became politically and militarily significant. This consequence of the war was entirely unforeseen and by removing Germany as a unit from the political scene it removed also the allies' main incentive to maintain their alliance. There was no Germany for them to keep down. There were instead two Germanies to be kept up, each appropriated by the one side or the other. The Cold War might have developed in any case. Probably it would, but the division of Germany fundamentally impelled and shaped it. To some extent a consequence of the Cold War, this division was also – more perhaps than has been appreciated – a major formative factor. Moreover the division of Germany, besides dividing the allies, did more than anything else to keep the Americans in Europe. They stayed, first, to administer Germany and argue about its future; later to defend Western Germany and their own positions in it. When the anti-Nazi alliance was converted into a duel between the victors, the Americans were still in Europe and acquired new reasons for staying there.

*

The Nazis and their fascist like had been defeated by the combined forces of liberal democracy and totalitarian democracy. In the exuberance of victory there were those who hoped that the alliance of the anti-fascists would endure, but soon these two traditional streams – the sources, as noted earlier in this book, of the collapse of Europe's *anciens régimes* – found themselves no longer side by side but face to face. Europe's triangle of forces resolved itself into the duel called the Cold War.

In terms of Europe the Cold War was an ideological contest between liberal democracy and totalitarian democracy; the simpler description of it as a contest between communists and anti-communists is misleading since not all anti-communists are liberal democrats. The Cold War was at the same time a power struggle between the United States and the USSR. Had this contest remained European the principal issue would have been the possible revival of Fascism, the reconstitution of the triangle of forces, and the manoeuvres of its three elements to make a pattern of two against one either in the same way as during the war or in some other way. War, being by its nature dual, had forced the triangle to conform for a few years (1941–5) to its law which says that there can be only two sides. After the war and the elimination of the one side the surviving forces moved from identity to opposition and so formed a new pattern, rigid until the appearance of some third element to give it mobility.

In the late forties and fifties this third element was neither European nor fascist. The Second World War, as has already been said, changed the map of the rest of the world as markedly as it left the outlines of the map of Europe recognizably familiar. The Seven Years War had decided that Great Britain and not France should have the lion's share of the dark continents in which Europeans had been seeking profit and adventure. North America and much of southern Asia were secured for Great Britain. France, the Netherlands and Portugal retained positions in Asia and, with Belgium, Germany and Italy, also shared in the later partition of Africa. The nineteenth and early twentieth centuries were the heyday of these European empires. The Second World War was the centrepiece of the last act of the story; the generation after the war was kept busy with the epilogue. As a result the nature of world conflict changed. This conflict had been a dispute centred in Europe, a dispute over political forms coupled with a struggle for power. It became a worldwide contest, still ideological and strategic, but one in which the third element was the – significantly dubbed – Third World which ceased on decolonization to be part of the Western World.

The new states which emerged from the dissolution of Europe's overseas empires, in far greater number than those which had emerged from the dissolution of its continental empires after the First World

War, decided for the most part not to attach themselves to either side in the Cold War but to take up a distinct, non-aligned position. So far as the Cold War was ideological they sensed, correctly, that the ideological issue was a European one and had little to do with their immediate needs. Further, they diagnosed the Cold War as essentially a struggle for power which was bound to hurt them and which they must therefore try to stop. They rejected neutrality – opting out – as neither possible nor desirable. The Second World War had shown how little a neutral could rely on having his neutrality respected; the changes in the nature of war suggested that neutrality was a thing of the past. The neutral's claim to stay out of a war required certain conditions which were disappearing. It rested upon the assumptions that a state of war was clearly distinguishable from peace and that a given war could be restricted to certain areas and prevented from leaking through the frontiers of the neutral state. But the very expression Cold War showed that the concept of war as something overtly declared and conducted with lethal weapons against proclaimed opponents no longer sufficed; guerrilla and subversive wars, whose techniques had been expanded in many parts of the world during the Second World War, also increased the uncertainty about what was a war and who was a belligerent. Air warfare eroded the significance of frontiers; nuclear fall-out abolished it.

For all these reasons attempts to keep out of war by choosing the classic posture of neutrality seemed to make little sense. Keeping out was no longer a guarantee of safety. Those who wanted to fend off war could no longer seek to barricade themselves against it; they must actively try to prevent or extinguish it. Thus third parties came to believe that they must in their own interests – to which it was easy to add the moral imperatives of the peace-keeper – play a part in international affairs rather than abstract themselves from the scene. Leaders of new states were in any case inclined towards a negative non-alignment: their consuming preoccupation with independence made them eschew alliance with a dominant power, their pressing economic needs made them seek trade and aid in all quarters, their concern for the cohesion of their new and often divided societies counselled them against a foreign alliance which would offend a particular domestic faction of the Left or the Right. But their non-alignment was not merely negative. Despite their weaknesses, of which they were only too well aware, they adopted a policy of positive non-alignment, that is to say intervention, in order to ensure the survival and independence which other states had tried in the past to safeguard by going into political purdah. And because they mattered to the protagonists in the Cold War, at least to the extent that each of these wanted to stand no less well than the other with the non-aligned, their emergence from European dominion into statehood after the war altered the terms and area of international politics.

*

Yet important though they were this widening of the scene and multiplication of the cast were almost trivial beside the irrefragable involvement of the United States in the world's proceedings. This involvement after the Second World War has become as much a commonplace as American isolationism after the First, and at times pushed to equally questionable limits. It was the war which marked the change.

The American experience of war was different from all others. First, the United States had war aims, in the sense of purposes to be accomplished by going to war as opposed to the bare winning of a war that had happened. Taking part in a European war which they did not feel obliged to fight in response to an external threat, the Americans needed war aims. A people which is not forced to fight must have a reason for doing so. A people which has no choice needs no aims, but a people which has a choice must have aims. To Europeans the American preoccupation with war aims seemed either unreal or hypocritical. Europeans had no war aims except the aim first to survive and then to win, and these were not aims freely considered and adopted but simply a formulation of the force of circumstances. (The Resistance did develop war aims, but these were adopted in the course of the war and not as a reason for going to war; and they touched only a proportion of Resisters and a very small proportion of the whole people, which is one reason why they were so thinly attained.) But Americans, who had not been attacked and were not fighting for survival, could not be led into war without some explanation of why they should do any such thing, and the simplest way of satisfying this natural requirement was to present a statement of what the war was about and how the world could be made better by helping the right side to win it. Such statements are necessarily vague and often grandiose. Therefore they are easy to contemn. But for a people not under compulsion they are a necessity.

They also colour that people's outlook after the war is over. If a war is fought and suffered for certain purposes, there is a duty – not least to the dead – to see that the purposes are achieved. Where victory is the end of war, the war ends with the victory. But Americans believed that there were other ends and that the war had been fought to rescue and restore values such as freedom and justice, which Nazis and fascists had scorned and destroyed (and imperialists, in their less brutal ways, were also ignoring). Americans were not more devoted to these values than good men elsewhere but they were more committed to doing something to secure them. The sins of communist governments could not be overlooked. Therefore the war spirit which had animated the United States in the war was not assuaged when the fighting – against the dictators – ceased but oppression and injustice did not; and Americans carried into the more complicated world of peace politics the guiding principles which had sufficed in the simpler world of war. They remained campaign-minded.

Secondly, the American homeland remained inviolate. Although the American contribution in manpower and materials was enormous, the men and women with their equipment went out of the United States to battle and never imagined doing battle in it. Nor did those left behind know, at first hand, anything of bombardment or the fear of bombs, resistance, evacuation or privation. At second hand, through press and radio, they knew more about distant events than a people at war had ever known before, but the events themselves remained distant. It was the kind of war which had once been familiar to Europeans but had ceased to be so. Although in material terms the American war effort was the most up-to-date imaginable, in social terms it belonged still to an era in which combatants set sail while non-combatants stayed safely behind. War fosters and sanctifies material effort: in the United States the materialism promoted by military exigencies was not countered, as in Europe, by the social emollients produced by shared dangers. In this respect the American experience of war brought changes which were comparatively less abrupt during the war but, as with the effects of war aims, comparatively more potent after it. The United States took the war in its giant stride but did not afterwards look nearly as much the same as Europe did ten to twenty years after the war ended.

Thirdly, there was the sheer size of the achievement. Over 15 million men and women were summoned to do services of one kind or another – as compared with 22 million mobilized by the USSR, 17 million by Germany and 12 million by Great Britain, the Dominions and colonies. Gross national product was nearly doubled, rising from $91 billion to $166 billion. Overall industrial output was doubled, while at the same time agricultural output also increased by more than a fifth. New industries were created (synthetic rubber) or given an enormous boost (electronics). The expansion of American shipbuilding from one to 19 million tons a year has already been mentioned. Such efforts were common. Aircraft production rose from below 6,000 a year on the eve of war to more than 96,000, the numbers employed in the aircraft industry from 46,000 to more than 2 million. Altogether the Americans made 275,000 aircraft, of which 40,000 went to their allies. American aircraft provided the RAF with an increment of 20–25 per cent over and above what it obtained from the British aircraft industry.

So too with tanks. American tank production, negligible in 1941, rose to 14,000 and 21,000 in the next two years. The American Sherman became the mainstay of the western allies. The British army possessed 3,300 Shermans on the day when it returned to France in 1944. The Sherman did not give the western allies the superiority over German models which they were looking for, but the Pershing, which came into service in 1944, proved a match for the last German tanks, the Tiger and Panther. British industry, obliged after Dunkirk to replace losses as quickly as possible, began by supplying current obsolescent models and the newer Churchill and then developed the Cromwell and the Comet which reached fighting units towards the end of 1942 and 1944 respectively, but tank design and production were, by agreement, primarily an American commitment and the resulting models were American designs with the incorporation of as many British ideas as fitted them. In addition to the first essentials of aircraft, tanks and shipping the United States produced a total of 64,000 landing craft (to Great Britain's 4,300) and equipped its allies as well as itself with practically all the transport aircraft, self-propelled artillery, amphibian vehicles and heavy trucks which they required. That remarkable vehicle the jeep was produced in such quantities that the Americans were able to spare 86,000 for the British. (The Germans had a jeep too, which was water and sand proof.) As a result of this war effort the United States, uniquely among the combatants, began the next phase of its history materially better equipped than before.

Fourthly, the war altered the distribution of power in the United States geographically and politically. It accelerated the shift of money and people from the east to the west coast and gave the south the boost which it had never had since the Civil War. Industry invaded the west where it had been relatively inconspicuous and the south where – outside Texas, already well supplied with capital from oil – it had hardly been at home at all. As the aircraft and telecommunications industries expanded into the south, employment and communications boomed. Atlanta, for example – designed by geography to be as much a natural centre in the age of aircraft as in the age of rail – a city where the complete devastation of the Civil War had opened the way for a *post bellum* entrepreneurial class to supplant the old upper class which had remained sufficiently dominant elsewhere (in Mississippi for example) to impede rejuvenation – had at last the opportunity to join the mainstream of American modernization and prosperity. The demands of war gave a new mobility both to southern whites who moved to the nearest city and to Negroes who, whether through the calls of economic expansion or through conscription, moved to all parts of the country, including parts where they had been little seen before. These shifts and needs helped the anti-discrimination cause. Roosevelt gave a pledge of no discrimination in industry, wrote non-discrimination clauses into the government contracts upon which industry increasingly lived during the war and created a Fair Employment Practices Commission. (But the pledge was widely evaded and the Commission harassed. In the armed services Negroes continued to be relegated to subordinate positions. Secretary Stimson debarred them from equal opportunities on the grounds that they were incapable of learning the necessary skills. Secretary Knox was even firmer. The Negro was not integrated in the armed services until the Korean War.) Thus the primacy of the old centres of wealth (and liberalism) in the north-east was eroded and movements of population, begun in the First World War but arrested by the great depression, were resumed. The consequences of these economic and social movements began to become apparent only in the generation which followed the war years.

The balance of political power was affected by more than geographical shifts. As the British and the Germans both discovered, war is a mighty centralizer. For the United States too the same proposition held good. War necessitated an immense increase in federal budgets and federal spending. The proportion of federal to other taxes grew. This centralization of authority accelerated a constitutional trend, as between the federal government and the states, but did not inaugurate any economic or social revolution, as between government and private interests. Roosevelt had to combat the marked reluctance of American society to entrust the government with regulating powers. His administration had at first no adequate control either over the estimates made by the armed services of their requirements and so of their demands on industry, or of industry itself, and it was not until 1943 that Roosevelt succeeded in imposing centralized government control over activities traditionally jealous of government interference. American capitalism produced the goods but it wanted also to remain sovereign in its own house, and resisted government direction until complaints of the monopolization of government contracts by the bigger corporations and rumours of scandals gave Roosevelt the opportunity and the necessary backing to create new government agencies to fix priorities, allocate orders and at the same time check inflation by price, wage and rent control. The Congress mistrusted the vast increase in the government's powers which accompanied the vast increase in the nation's efforts. It was only with difficulty persuaded that the one required the other. The unions too bridled against the shift which the war imposed on the balance of power between government and unions, and at one point Roosevelt was forced to nationalize the coal mines in the face of strike threats from John L. Lewis, the leader of the mineworkers. Roosevelt eventually secured control over the economy through the Office of Economic Stabilization, the Office of Price Control and his annual Finance Acts. The latter raised the income tax and extended it to whole classes which had never had to pay it before; federal income tax rose, at the top level, to 94 per cent. A corporation tax rising to 50 per cent was imposed and an excess profits tax was introduced which rose by stages to 95 per cent of the excess. Yet government expenditure on the war grew so fast that during the four war years only 41 per cent of it was covered by taxation. For the rest the government had to borrow and to control the consequent inflation by the statutory regulation of wages and prices.

The war finally brought the great depression to an end, but at the same time the semi-socialist New Deal gave way to a fully capitalist war economy. This war economy performed prodigies of productive valour in the service of the military. The achievements of the partnership were miraculous, so much so that they stamped a pattern on the further development of the American economy and American society in the nuclear age.

Fifthly and finally, the United States was not only transformed domestically but also was seen to have become to an unprecedented degree the world's most mighty power. This power, however reluctantly acknowledged, had played some part in propelling the United States into war. Even before the mobilization of its resources in manpower and production the United States possessed enormous industrial and military might. Its low posture in the twenties and thirties was out of line with its capacities and Americans were perhaps readier than appeared at first sight to be up and doing – preferably with a good cause – because the sense of power possessed is itself an incentive to the use of power. The war destroyed reticence. Victory destroyed bashfulness, since victory was seen as a triumphant use of power for good ends. Then the power itself was vastly accentuated by the American monopoly of the nuclear bomb, but neither victory nor the bomb was the source of American power. They were on the contrary among its consequences. Yet the bomb created a new situation since it made the United States more powerful than all other states put together, not merely more powerful than any other state or any conceivable coalition of states. It could impose its will universally, should it be prepared to threaten and resort to nuclear war. And, so it seemed in 1945, it might maintain this position indefinitely since it was widely, if wrongly, assumed that no other state would be able to make nuclear weapons for a long time to come.

The appearance of nuclear power as a military factor coincided with the disappearance of a system of international politics in which several states of roughly equal strength predominated. Although this system left its mark on the nascent United Nations, where five states were held to be superior and were given a permanent place and a veto in the Security Council, the new reality was a bipolar system in which predominant power belonged to the United States and the USSR, each of whom was accepted as markedly superior to everybody else. Since these two powers were presented and accepted as the protagonists of two opposed ways of life, the bipolarity was also inherently an actively hostile confrontation. Europe was the chief object of this ideological and power conflict.

Yet the universality of American power was, despite first appearances, limited. The Americans recoiled from the use of nuclear weapons. The novelty of these weapons made them more awful than anything that had gone before, even though the two occasions on which they had been used (described in the ensuing part of this book) had not caused as many deaths as some more conventional instances of slaughter. Their continuing toxic effect, vaguely apprehended, added to the revulsion. There was widespread feeling in the United States that nuclear weapons should not be used again. But if this were so, the threat to use them was not a threat but a bluff. Thus, even before the USSR itself constructed a nuclear bomb, the American monopoly had been negated and the American omnipotence converted into a predominance paralleled by Russian power. The American monopoly was both a fact and a myth.

In Europe in particular, American power was countered by Russian power. The Russians occupied half Europe and maintained very large armed forces within and beyond their borders after the war ended; Stalin, with a ruthlessness reminiscent of his war on the peasants in the thirties, gave an absolute priority to war industries and war research, in particular to discovering the scientific and technological secrets of nuclear power which Russian experts were already close to mastering. By postponing for a generation the amelioration of the quality of life in the USSR Stalin ensured that power in Europe should be shared.

The Cold War, which is the name for the rather novel way by which this contest for power was initiated and then conducted, was something that Roosevelt certainly, and Stalin probably, would have wished to avoid. It represented Europe's continuing claim on the attentions of the world's two super-powers and it was the principal outward and visible sign of the post-war involvement of the United States in international affairs. This involvement would probably have come about in any case, but historically it followed from the recognition of the facts of power and geopolitics, brought about by war and Roosevelt. The direction of the involvement, on the other hand, was determined by pre-war concepts and Truman. Shortly after Hitler's invasion of the USSR Truman, then a Senator, said that the United States ought to help the Russians so long as they were being beaten by the Germans but that, if the Russians began to win, then the United States should help the Germans, so that as many as possible of both might be killed. This was a denial of the thesis that the war was a war against Fascism and a re-assertion of the thesis that liberal democrats and communists could not live together amicably. Truman, like Stalin, belonged emphatically to the pre-war generation. He was also, unlike Roosevelt, relatively inexperienced in international affairs and so more dependent on the State Department and more receptive to an official line on the USSR which was harder than Roosevelt's had been. Those who believe that men make history will say that two men in particular, Truman and Stalin, made the Cold War. Those who believe that men operate only on the surface of deeper currents will point to Truman and Stalin as examples of the strength and direction of those forces which, having been driven underground for a space like the fountain of Arethusa, re-emerged after the defeat of Fascism to take control once more of men's conflicting destinies and destinations.

How events were shaped is a matter for debate. The events themselves are clearer. In June 1948 the United States formally abjured isolationism by the Vandenberg resolution adopted by the Senate, and ten months later it signed the North Atlantic Treaty in company with Canada and ten European states. These two events marked the end of isolationism – with a particular intent.

*

The cost of a war in men and materials, and the redistribution of territory and power which it brings about, are only two parts of the consequences of war. There is a third, less tangible but at least as important.

Wars intensify simple emotions and they also create opportunities and heighten expectations. Wars are horrible and bearing them is only made possible by hating one's enemy and by believing in a better future for one's self.

The hatred cannot be switched off. It may abate, though slowly, but since the Second World War the hatred felt for Germans in those years among Russians, Jews and others who suffered terribly has remained a factor in European affairs. It may be exaggerated for purposes of propaganda but it exists to be exaggerated and is easily rekindled. One of the war's many causes was the madness which took hold of Germany and one of the war's effects was to spread this madness and fill all Europe with violence and with the toleration, even the applause, of violence. There was in this respect a difference between the war in eastern Europe and the war in the west, and this difference has affected post-war emotions and therefore post-war political attitudes. The German onslaught in the west was less savage than in the east and German barbarity in western occupied territories was episodic whereas in the east it was planned and persistent. Consequently the western response was less vicious too. It is difficult to gauge the feelings of those who rejoiced, in Great Britain for example, at the news of the destruction of German cities. There was a certain grim Old Testament satisfaction, but there was little exultation and the dominant feeling was probably the thought that such blows must hasten the end of the war. There was much bitterness but little of the sheer hatred which disfigured the First World War, and although the two catastrophes were only a quarter of a century apart the generation of the second war would have considered it absurd to boo dachshunds in the London streets as their fathers had done. There was a certain sobriety.

There were also expectations and, after the war ended, a balance to be struck between satisfied and unsatisfied expectations. Making the world a better place to live in meant, in Europe, political, economic and social changes, a further instalment of the long-drawn-out revolution promising freedom, equality and brotherhood; outside Europe it meant, in the first place, the end of foreign and colonial rule. Of these twin aspirations the second was substantially satisfied in less than a generation after the end of the war and in some places within a few years. The British, French, Dutch and Belgian empires in Africa and Asia (but not the Portuguese) dissolved. They were doubtless already dissolving but the war accelerated the process by weakening the resources and the nerve of the metropolitan powers and by a revolution in thought which made empire seem in 1945 much more old-fashioned and dubious, as well as impermanent, than it had seemed six years earlier. By 1960 these empires were extinct or vestigial. Their demise constituted the greatest change ever made in a short space to the map of the world and to the mechanisms of international relations.

Within Europe the revolutionary current stimulated by the war was less successful. The old order proved remarkably tenacious, perhaps because the economic stringencies of the aftermath of war, on top of the strains of the war itself, drained the life out of reform movements. There were gains. In Great Britain, for example, the creation of a free public health service transformed the lives of millions of people not only by relieving or preventing sickness but also by removing the hideous worries of those who had had to endure illness or watch it in their children without being able to pay to do anything about it. In other countries too social services and social experiment received a fillip and even right-wing parties and governments took to thinking and acting in terms which they would have abhorred before the war. In eastern Europe civil liberties were obliterated by the political repression and economic obscurantism, worthy of Tsar Nicholas I, which Stalin, Khrushchev and the succeeding collective leadership in Moscow felt impelled to adopt, but in the USSR itself the government was the legatee of its own wartime promises of a better life and of wartime measures of toleration – such as the toleration of religion, the reappearance of priests, more freedom for writers, the appeal to popular sentiments in place of the use of disciplinary threats. Post-war stringencies produced a retreat from this tentative liberalization but did not altogether kill its seeds. War, it has been said, is the midwife of revolution. But nobody has said what is the period of gestation. The revolutions of 1848 occurred thirty-three years after the end of Napoleon's wars.

Finally there is the Middle East. Hitler's climax to Gentile persecution of the Jews – a drama unequalled for shame in the history of European civilization except by the slave trade – sharpened the desire of the survivors to depart to Zion. It probably also sharpened the desire of guilt-laden Europeans to see them go and it certainly accentuated the sympathies of some Gentiles for a people whom they had too often and now too fatally reviled. But Zion was no empty haven waiting to receive them. For half a century Zionists had been resolved to find a home in Palestine for the Jews and to create a Jewish state there. Some of them had imagined a state under Ottoman suzerainty and later some of their successors thought of an autonomous dominion within the British Empire, but most Zionist leaders realized from the first that what they sought must be an independent sovereign state. They also realized that it would be impolitic to say so, since the creation of this new state would entail the dispossession, or at least the subjection, of the existing Arab inhabitants of the lands for which Zionists yearned as a refuge and a religious fulfilment.

When the war ended the Zionists, who had refrained from harassing the British in Palestine so long as the war lasted, resorted to violence in their turn. They took up arms and terrorism and drove the British out. They then defeated the Arabs who came against them, jointly but hardly unitedly, and so won their state. It was a state whose doors were, as a matter of principle, open to all Jews whencesoever, and the Jews of Europe hurried to it – except those in the west who were too comfortable to move and some in the east who were not allowed to. This migration, which was supplemented by similar migrations of non-European Jews, opened a new chapter in the history of the Middle East by implanting the state of Israel in a part of the world which Arabs regarded as theirs, which they had hoped to inherit from the Turks with British help in 1919, which they had seen the British take for themselves, and from which they were now not only debarred but actually – by arms or by fear – evicted. The Jewish problem had been off-loaded by Christendom onto Islam. But it did not cease to concern Europe: for the Middle East remained what it had been for centuries – one of the world's most convenient highways – and what it had become in the twentieth century – one of the world's primary sources of mineral wealth – so that the world's Great Powers could not ignore it.

But their continued intervention took new shapes. The Second World War destroyed the pattern imposed after the first. Then the British and French had established a post-Ottoman condominium, in despite of the Arabs and to the exclusion of the Russians. But the Second World War eliminated first the French and then, more gradually, the British and so created new opportunities for Arabs – and Russians. These new opportunities coincided with swelling revolutionary and nationalist currents in the Arab world which foreshadowed a new Arab–Russian alliance in place of the Arab–British association which had governed Middle Eastern politics during the First World War and after it. Against this new Arab–Russian entente Israel and the United States constituted, however loosely, a counter-system and in 1967 the two Super-Powers of the post-war world found themselves on opposite sides in a shooting war from which they might have found it difficult to stay out if the war had not ended after six days.

*

It has been said that wars settle nothing. This is too caustic a dismissal of human endurance and human striving. At the end of this great war in Europe the Nazis and their fascist allies were beaten. Things would have been very different had they not been. Fascism, perhaps not irretrievably but yet at this point decisively, was defeated.

A famous Russian historian of classical antiquity has judged that Greece declined because men came to distrust reason and Rome fell because it tried to maintain an exclusively privileged society wherein the rich were enervated and the poor alienated. If these judgements on the ancestors of Europe's civilization have any bearing on its own fate, then the Fascism of the twentieth century begotten of anti-rational and anti-democratic authoritarianism was a malign cancer and its defeat in 1945 at least a reprieve.

The War in Asia

Part I
ASIAN CONFLICT

CHAPTER 1

China and Japan

THERE are two principal countries of the Far East with an ancient civilization, China and Japan: and the war in the Far East had its origin in the quarrel between them. This developed gradually out of events which began about a century earlier and set afoot historical processes which were seemingly uncheckable. With apparent fatalism inflammable materials were stacked.

Ultimately, the fire started and flames enfolded the two countries in a most bitter war of survival. This in turn caused a wider blaze in the Pacific; and the fire in the East coincided with Hitler's fire in Europe. The conflagrations merged, and the wars became one. Almost all the peoples of the Far East and South Asia were engaged.

The start of this great drama came with the different ways that China and Japan responded to the unfamiliar intrusion of the West into Asian affairs.

In East Asia China, even in its decadence, has always been a most absorbing topic. It has lain across the map of Asia, establishing standards and precedents, rather as the Roman Empire dominated the ancient western world. Traditionally, East Asia had no system of international relations in which independent countries coexist with one another, such as was known from the earliest times in Europe, but was a system in which all the lesser countries revolved like satellites around the great central structure, which was regarded by all men as central, necessary and almost unchanging. In the middle of the nineteenth century, this was still true, even though China was standing on the verge of one of the most calamitous periods of its history that was to cause its very name to be a reproach. It still dominated the political imagination, both of its inhabitants, and of visitors to the Far East. So much history had gone into its making, and so revered was Chinese civilization in Asia, that traces of mortal disease did not at first cause extreme alarm. Nevertheless China belonged to the ancient world, which, in 1850, was passing rapidly away.

What was threatening China was the impact of the western world. China was known as the Middle Kingdom for it seemed the centre round which all things revolved and it had flourished through so many ages because it was unique. Now, for the first time in its history, it was coming into contact with powers which had totally different traditions and which were totally ruthless. They came from the other side of the world, but, from the alarm they caused, and from the absence of normal human rapport, they might have come from Mars. These powers, well organized politically, were not inclined to concede to China a moral superiority.

The history of China and the West is chequered. The record of the foreign powers is not so black as it is painted, whether by Chinese communists or by liberal western historians, who are overwhelmed, often quite unreasonably, by guilt. In some ways China's suffering was inevitable. It was the necessary result of the unavoidable process of a withdrawn state being thrust upon the world. Many of its experiences can be seen today to have been renascent; they conferred new and valuable matter upon an ancient civilization. The version put about by the communists is exaggerated, perverted and untrue. But something like their view is held by most of the Chinese people. The myth has been agreed upon. It must be attended to in any account of what really happened.

China, according to this view, was, for nearly a hundred years, harried by several foreign powers which had projected themselves into the Far East by their navies and their fleets of merchantmen; and for most of the time it fought a losing battle against them.

The agony of China began in the middle of the last century. It was compelled by foreign governments to open itself for trade, which meant consenting to having its tariffs fixed by these agents; to accord to foreigners extra-territorial rights, which rendered them immune from Chinese law; and to permit them to set up in some of the choicest parts of the Empire small foreign communities which were thereafter protected from Chinese jurisdiction by warships and small bodies of troops. These were the famous Treaty Ports, now of dolorous memory. In addition, the same rights were exacted for Christian missionaries, who were let loose to subvert the ancient Confucian system. The Chinese government was powerless to resist. It had neither the technical means (in arms and warships), nor the political stamina, nor the control of its own people, nor the ability to organize them.

Externally nothing had changed except for the establishment of neat, well-ordered townships side by side with the sprawling cities of China. They were clean; they appeared innocent. In this innocuous guise, imperialism came to China and soon began its work without anybody recognizing that it was initiating a new age. The first trade treaty, the Treaty of Nanking of 1842, which opened the five ports to British trade and residence, contained crippling restraints on China's sovereignty, but at the time was regarded as relatively innocuous. The Treaty provided that foreigners should administer their own justice to aliens and so appeared to be relieving the Chinese of a vexatious duty and to be keeping the foreigner at arm's length, which was very much the Chinese desire.

Moreover, by specifying areas where foreigners could live, it appeared to have spared the Chinese demands for the sale of land elsewhere. The foreigner was generally prohibited from acquiring real estate in China – a kind of apartheid set-up. But the foreigner had been given the means to enforce his will, and used it ruthlessly. He partly got round the rule that he should not own land by inducing the Christian missionaries, specifically exempt from the prohibition which applied to foreign businessmen, to hold the land in their name.

At first the Chinese did not understand what was being done to them, or how serious was the damage done to them in the Treaty Ports. But the misdeeds of the imperialists slowly became clear to everyone, and gradually produced a mood of terrible baffled rage.

China had not only to fear imperialism when it was seaborne. Before the coming of the foreign ships, it had been conscious of the land threat from its neighbour, Russia. This threat endured without interruption and in varying degrees of intensity. By land or sea China was surrounded by adversaries. It was still the Middle Kingdom, but no longer the axis round which the world turned; rather it could boast the name because it was the centre against which the spoliative instincts of the world were directed.

China was, it is true, saved from conquest and annexation. This was because the foreign powers arrived not alone, but in multiplicity, because each was jealous of the other, because each realized that its trading rights depended on none achieving full political control of China. The Chinese Empire was thus permitted to continue.

It is important not to overstate the case. There were many personalities among the foreigners in China who bore nothing but goodwill to the country. There were institutions which were actively philanthropic. Foreign influence often brought about great changes, almost by accident. The Treaty Ports were often impressive for their neatness of construction and they disseminated new standards of public administration over a limited area. But the Chinese argued that this kind of imperialism did the maximum harm to China while ensuring that the imperialist powers conferred no countervailing benefits.

Thus, groups of foreigners – nearly all businessmen – lived in China, organized entirely according to the customs and conventions of their homeland and subject to their own laws, in juxtaposition to the Chinese who were still subject to their ancient form of government. Most of the foreigners had only one interest; to make money through trade. Inevitably, even if the foreign communities had had no intention to influence Chinese society, the free action of the foreign groups deeply modified the Chinese society all around them, especially because the Chinese government was unable to place limits on their activities. The operations of buying and selling, the freedom to conduct almost all forms of enterprise which private initiative could suggest, the freedom of money and its free use – all tended to erode the old Chinese civilization, which the Chinese, bound by treaty, were unable to safeguard.

The Chinese were in the position of a man bound hand and foot, watching the activities of an assailant who was openly plotting his ruin. As a result of the unwelcome guests, Chinese society was changing; but China could do nothing about it. Chinese anger mounted against the foreign communities, but China was impotent.

The Chinese feeling raged more strongly against the Chinese who collaborated with foreigners than against the foreigners themselves. The Chinese who showed himself unduly obliging to the foreigner, who set himself to make money by taking advantage of the conditions of foreign business, who was willing to act as the agent of the foreign business community and performed the indispensable role of interpreter and middleman, roused angry resentment. This class was called the compradors, from the Portuguese word meaning 'to provide': they were China's universal agents, at the disposal of the foreigner. Without the compradors, the pattern of the new type of imperialism would never have come into being.

The comprador class became extremely rich and prosperous. Eventually many of the Chinese nationalists came from this class. So did many people who contributed in various ways to the new China: in arts, in science, in medicine. For many decades the Chinese creative energies seemed to be located in this class. The fact that it was hated was never sufficiently appreciated by foreigners, whose needs had called it into being.

*

The principal state in the hostile group ringing China was Great Britain, but there was one foreign country which behaved in a way unlike the others, the United States of America, which had a different history and different traditions from those of the European nation-states like Great Britain.

The United States, which came into being as the result of rebellion against Britain, did not form a new national state of its own, but was, rather, a repository of the elements of the western world which showed, by emigrating to America, that they desired to have a new political civilization. The United States did not altogether escape the nineteenth-century trend of western countries to be aggressive and self-assertive, but was distinctly less predatory, less remorseless, than the others.

Thus in its relations with China the United States pursued a milder course than its western peers. True, it was drawn into the harrying. When the other states took the extra-territorial privileges, for the protection of their nationals, the United States joined in; and it took its share among the other powers in setting up the International Settlement at Shanghai. But its pursuit of China was not relentless, and it did not demand exclusive concessions of its own, which were the aim of other governments and which came to be dotted all over China like so many colonies. The United States' interest was in international trade – in contrast to Britain whose special concern was with the investment of capital in China – and in promoting it the United States was no more scrupulous than other states in forcing its activities upon China, which, officially, did not welcome them. But in this international trade the American concern was more with the attitude of other western powers than with that of China. The United States had always the fear that these would end in a policy of splitting up China into various spheres of interest, from which American interests would be excluded or discriminated against.

Hence the United States' aim of preserving the open door into China. On this principle American official policy turned. It sought to establish a system by which all the powers voluntarily restricted the use of political influence to secure for themselves an economic privilege such as was not enjoyed equally by other powers. The American activity on these lines culminated in securing in 1900 the assent of powers interested in the China trade to this 'Open Door doctrine' and in guaranteeing American support for China's territorial integrity. The United States regarded this as a pro-Chinese policy, anti-imperialist, and in fact it was more so than suited the habits and interests of the other powers. But it is understandable that later generations of Chinese should have pointed to the solid gains which it was the United States' intention to gain from it. They were not impressed by the advantages that this non-cooperation of the United States with the other powers undoubtedly brought to China, and regarded these as incidental and not philanthropic.

Nevertheless, the US was philanthropic. From the 1870s a section of the American public became aware of China as a great Asiatic people which might with justice call upon the United States for aid. This was the United States' first public response to the needs of a section of the world community; a response which has since become progressively wider, and embraced successively Japan, the states in Europe assisted by the Marshall Plan, and states of Latin America. They had no legal or other claim on the US; the US had no obligation to them. It responded in their cases to the simple fact that they had needs which the United States could fill, and the US did not pass them by on the other side. Often, of course, there was, mixed with the practical philanthropy, a great deal of hypocrisy, of unscrupulous dealing, of serving a concealed interest, of power hunger only a little better than Europe's because it was veiled; but, though these existed, it was a remarkable fact that there was a genuinely philanthropic policy in which these found a place.

The initiators of the wave of goodwill were the American missionaries. Thousands of these were active in China and, through them, links were forged between innumerable small towns in the United States and similar units in China. To a remarkable extent the American people actually took the Chinese people by the hand, and led them over the first stages of their modernization. Politically the organs of government in the United States impressed the Chinese people, many of whom recognized the remarkable behaviour of the US, even though their vast pride suffered from the American patronage. It was natural for the descendants of two thousand years of mandarins to feel disgust at becoming pupils of such a commercial people, lacking a long history, as the Americans. Relations were therefore not easy. But Chinese, in a more judicious mood, had to admit that this relationship was the most satisfactory that China had experienced in modern history.

This adventure in philanthropy was a part of the history of the American people, not the American government. It was not officially inspired. The thousands of American missionaries, the vast expenditure, the use of skill and manpower, were all of them privately directed. So also American businessmen for the most part took their own risks and reaped their return, and largely did not employ American organized public force. The interplay of the missionary and the businessman, the clash between disinterest and the long-term interest which American activity promoted, was of course one of the principal themes for the historian of the time to savour. And in the United States the widespread goodwill to China set up currents which, in a society as democratic as that of the US, were bound to influence the state and produce subtle changes in its policy towards China. So intertwined were most of the impulses of the United States.

*

Confronted with such acute danger, China made sporadic efforts to modernize itself and to generate a counteractive power; this should have been possible by reason of its size, its population and the reasonableness of its people. But for a long while its governing class was so set in conservative ways – as an essential part of their Confucian civilization – that the efforts failed. To reform and reorganize, China had to go through a shattering revolution, leave its ancient political civilization and venture out on ways new and untested. It had to experience a slow rebirth.

For a time the Chinese mandarins, the higher civil servants of the Confucian bureaucracy, had supposed that the secret of the terribly formidable strength of the West lay in some technical devices which had been added to the instruments of government. If they could discover what these were, the government of the ancient empire would be rejuvenated, and able to stand up for itself. Steam power, explosives, modern weapons were all of them the candidates for the shattering secret of western power. But the empire's attempt to purchase these devices from the West left it no better off. It was clear that the Chinese government lacked the talent to reorganize its society so that it might adapt itself to make proper use of these. It could not mobilize China. It remained inert, and a powerless victim to those who chose to victimize it.

Under constant strain, the old system of government was ceasing to act. The old régime had been based on the principle that a harmony had to be imposed on the disharmonious elements of which society consists. The policy was largely based on government by exhortation, and by displaying the example (at least in theory) of universal benevolence; and this proved workable because of the Confucian ideas which prevailed in all areas under Chinese rule. Confucianism, as much as the secular institutions of the old China, held the state together. But the old Confucian philosophy was being undermined as Chinese society, for the first time in two thousand years, began to change fundamentally. In the rough world which had developed, China had to discover new principles on which to base its government.

Some Chinese looked abroad at the new system of parliamentary democracy which was becoming so fashionable. Could this be the secret which made the West so strong, and could its institutions not be taken over by China? For a time there was enthusiasm and hope about these ideas. But it should have been clear that they were not likely to be a helpful model to China, which had its own powerful political traditions, built by more than two thousand years of history, and not readily set aside. Nor could a system of government be easily imported and acclimatized, which had been built up so painfully in Europe, which was the product of so many attitudes of action and habit, themselves born of wars, revolution, and the slow work of many centuries. China was too unlike Europe, and China was made a dangerous gift by its friends who intemperately supported this nostrum.

The course which China took was therefore quite unpredictable; it was empirical and, even today, with hindsight, it is hard to trace out what experiments it made, and how much China suffered.

One of the reforms which it made apparently without realizing the profound consequences which it had, was to abolish the civil service. This it did in 1905; the examinations by which it was recruited were suspended. Earlier, the existence of this college of administrators, chosen to serve the empire by competitive public examinations, had been regarded, with some justification, as one of the strong points of Chinese civilization. But in the first decade of this century, the Chinese civil service was held to be old-fashioned and conservative. It was selected from among the classes which were steeped in Confucianism, and this made it the enemy of reform. The classes in favour of modernization all combined their resentment against it as constricting the development of the country. It was supposed that by striking it away, China would release forces which would transform it. That the mandarinate preserved standards of government and maintained the unity of the country was totally ignored. A great blow was struck at public order by its abolition, but the country thought that it was a blow in the cause of progress and liberation.

The Manchu Empire survived the sacrifice of the mandarins by only six years. The empire and its outworn apparatus were discarded in 1911: it had stood in the way of reform; probably a revolution was the necessary prelude to recovery. But the first results of the fall were catastrophic. The power of the empire was divided between war-lords, who commanded their own provinces. This was the worst and most helpless period of Chinese history. Chinese politics seemed to be without rhyme or reason. Power drifted from one war-lord to another with no meaningful result. The rise or fall of one provincial satrap or another brought no lightening of the gloom. There was no change, no regeneration, no significance.

The dawn for which men hoped first became visible with the rule at

Canton, a city in the south of China, of the group called the Kuomintang, which had emerged from a revolutionary party of the last days of the Manchus. This group proclaimed itself the nationalist party of China and held its first National Congress in 1924. It was at first primitive, overlaid with the colour of circumambient war-lord governments, incompetent, corrupt, and very weak. But it was in certain aspects new, and had, at least in form, a modern party organization which was in part borrowed from western countries, though the methods of its operations were mainly drawn from China itself. It functioned in an authoritarian way, owing its power to its army and police, but it claimed that this method of government was a transitory one. After a period during which it held the nation in tutelage, it would transfer the basis of government, and would become liberal and democratic. In after years, the length of this period of tutelage, the holding of the Kuomintang to its promise of democratization, became one of the principal questions of Chinese politics.

The Kuomintang slowly widened its authority; and came to be looked on as the party of national regeneration. It was a focus which attracted the support of all Chinese everywhere, who longed for a sign that China was at last reasserting its national strength.

It was the turning of the tide. Nationalism, with all the social and political reorganization which that connoted, began to do its work upon the Chinese people. The leader of the Kuomintang, Dr Sun Yat-sen (1866–1925), had described the great weakness of China, in its enforced competition with the western powers, as the absence of any cohesive power which could hold the people together. China, he said, was like a tray of sand: shake it and it fell apart. But, in China as in other parts of the world, the power of nationalism was to introduce a new faculty of maintaining social unity. How and why is one of the *arcana imperii* of the time. But it was abundantly clear that, as the movement proceeded and gathered strength, China was behaving quite differently from the recent past. The tray of sand was shaken; and the grains now tended to cohere in patterns which promised well for the future.

A fact which should have recommended the Kuomintang of the 1920s to serious attention by the outside observer was that in its organization and spirit it was not a copy of the western parliamentary parties. It was something devised for China, produced by Chinese thought to meet specific Chinese needs. It owed something to Soviet practice – many of the features in the organization of the party being borrowed from Russia at a time when Sun Yat-sen was enthusiastic, but had little understanding of communism – and, with a rosy eye-wash, it professed to look forward to a time of universal democratic rights. But the Kuomintang – as it was to function in the 1930s – was a party of nationalist authoritarianism.

*

Cutting across the political vicissitudes of the times was a social crisis. In a sense China was doomed to experience disorders in any case. China has a long history, and has endured a time of acute crisis once in every three or four hundred years which is marked by troubles, the fall of a dynasty, civil commotion of a prolonged and hopeless kind. Various causes have been suggested for this clearly marked cyclical course of Chinese history, but the most probable is that it is caused by pressure of population.

In the time of prosperity – when a dynasty is at the peak of its fortunes – the population is within manageable limits. The prosperity continues; the population grows; it becomes too large; there is intense pressure on the land; there are rising rents, and a diminishing food surplus for the towns; there are social distress, outbreaks of civil war and banditry, reverses in the struggle to maintain the frontier; there are corruption and extraordinary administrative decadence. After a time there comes the near or total collapse of government. China enters on a nadir of its history, from which there comes eventual recovery as the population regulates itself. Malthusian checks come into play, the extreme pressures are relaxed, the natural Chinese civilization reasserts itself.

There can be no doubt that China had entered on one of those adverse phases in the latter part of the eighteenth century. The Manchu dynasty ended its golden age in the unnaturally long reign of the Emperor Chien Lung (who reigned from 1736–96), and the population increased ominously. In the nineteenth century it would have been due for its time of troubles, regardless of the troubles brought on it by its new problems of foreign relations. The middle years of the century saw the Taiping rebellion and the revolt of the Chinese Muslims against the government, both classic cases of a population explosion, both resulting in a very great slaughter. The two political maladies came together – the troubles from the cyclical character of Chinese history and the troubles from the totally new and exceptional strain of encountering its rivals in the world. Each set of troubles complicated the other; each intensified the other; recovery became ever more difficult.

The Kuomintang, and Chinese nationalism, promised to bring relief to the political problems of China in the 1930s. At the same time there were signs that the social causes which had brought political collapse were about to be ameliorated by process of time, and it seemed likely that the efforts of the Kuomintang at social and economic improvement would not continue to be dogged with adversity. These signs, however, were hard to read correctly, and may have been misconstrued.

For the relative slowness of China's regeneration there are a number of reasons. The rebirth of a nation – it was nothing less – takes time, which cannot be cut short beyond a certain measure. It is a natural process, not entirely controllable by political or human means. But China's peculiar and horrifying experience of the last century remains to some extent a mystery. China's progress in our day has been so rapid, so revolutionary, that it is hard to understand why in the fairly recent past it took so long to get off the ground. In the last resort one is left with the bare statement – that a crisis of population coincided with a crisis of foreign relations, that the results of both became merged, and that it took more than a century to work out the consequences.

*

The other country, Japan, had an altogether different experience and its past must also be studied if Japan's place in the world cataclysm is to be understood. Japan was a lesser country than China. Generally its population was only about one sixth of China's. But it was inhabited by a people, which, by vigour, by a genius for imitation, and by artistic and warlike qualities, had made itself unique in the history of Asia. Japan had built up a civilization in many respects peculiar and outstanding. It responded to the stimulus of the coming of the westerners in a way which transformed the history of the region.

Since the beginning of the seventeenth century Japan had been exercised by the problem of relations with the West. It read the writing on the wall in the shadow cast by the Portuguese and Spanish galleons which at this time used to visit Japanese ports. Should Japan encourage them or should it deter them? After a brief period of cultivating their friendship it withdrew itself into seclusion. It persecuted mercilessly, as possibly enemies of Japanese security, the missionaries about whom at first it had been enthusiastic. It cut all ties with the external world, diplomatic, cultural and, as far as this was possible, economic. It was the classic case of a hermit kingdom. This policy of exclusiveness preserved Japan intact until the United States, in the year 1853 and again in 1854, dispatched a naval squadron under the command of Commodore Perry and compelled it to resume normal intercourse and foreign trade.

Thereupon Japan was in danger of being reduced to a colony by the imperialist powers. For its escape it had to thank the diplomatic adroitness, the skilful reasonableness of a few leading Japanese statesmen during the first years of the 1870s while Japan was renewing its contacts with the world. Once they had lost their first instinctive anti-foreignness they exposed themselves with zeal to all western influences. Japan's survival beyond this critical interval it owed to the remarkable changes which were brought about in Japanese society as a result of contact with western countries. From a militarily weak country, with a contemptible technology, Japan in a few years became like a hedgehog, which the imperialist powers, even at the height of their aggressiveness, thought twice about mauling.

Japan's history, which made this national strength possible, has been one of social change – a marked contrast to the sluggish conservatism of China's official social history. Japan was able to accept change because the Japanese were born relatively free of an overpowering tradition. Its governing circles were able, in contrast to the Chinese, to produce men who were imaginative, forceful, and free of the deadening desire that life should be preserved exactly as it had been known in previous centuries. They were daring and iconoclastic. They were not bound by a thwarting public opinion, as was the mandarinate in China.

In China, the society, the civilization, took precedence over the government. It was a civilization not disposed for change. But in Japan the government was not held in invisible fetters by public opinion and by the past.

Furthermore a Japanese government which desired to make changes was more likely to be able to implement them. Society was more responsive to governmental direction: it was more at its mercy. For this the main reason was geography. Japan consisted of a chain of islands, all of them comparatively small, all of them accessible by sea. Thus a fairly good system of communication could be established. This alone made it very different from China: in China there were, by the standards of that day, majestic roads, but, even so, the population in the outer provinces was at three months distance from the seat of central government. In consequence the ability of the centre to regulate the affairs of a large part of China was much reduced. But in Japan, no such inhibition palsied the national administration. Its efforts did not peter out in vast distances which separated it from its subjects.

The progress of Japan was rapid and, to the western powers spreading their influence through the world, unprecedented. In 1868 occurred the so-called Meiji Restoration. This was a revolution, not a restoration, although this great political change in Japan was dressed up as a revival of things past. An old, vestigial system of an Emperor, long confined to a kind of museum existence, and preserved partly for religious reasons, was called into employment; the existing system of government, a highly traditional one presided over by hereditary prime ministers or Shoguns, was suppressed. The new system was organized by the Samurai, the ex-feudatories of Japan's feudal past which it was abandoning. Exercising their remarkable talent for mimesis, they copied from what their intelligence judged to be the essentials of the formidable western system. The Japanese surprised themselves by the ease with which they were able to reproduce in Japan most of what went into the making of western civilization. From Britain they copied the organization of the navy; from Germany the army, the educational system and some political institutions; from France an outline of the legal system. The degree of modernization was greater in appearance than in reality, for often the old, and essentially Japanese institutions and modes continued behind a façade of reform. Nevertheless, reform there was, and Japan began to operate with a revolutionary change in efficiency.

Soon the Japanese sensed that their basic aim – which was to attain a military power which would enable them to resist on level terms with the western powers – was slowly being realized. They felt strength beginning to pulse through the political system. From this time on, Japanese thought about the political miracle of their awakening was increasingly obsessed by considerations of power.

For the European onlooker, the spectacle of Japan at this time was of remarkable interest. For him it was a new experience to kick an ancient civilization, and to find that it did not crumble. It was bracing and fascinating. Enough of the old, graceful, picturesque, fragile civilization of old Japan still survived to make the process of the metamorphosis of Japan of almost incredible interest; and, in addition, of poignant pathos. American, British and French men of letters grasped the occasion of describing what was happening before their eyes, and the result was a series of books describing the topography, anthropology, ethics and aesthetics of Japan in transition. Among them Redesdale's *Tales of Ancient Japan* is especially valuable in the picture which it gives of the national ethos, and of the reaction to it of a civilized and imaginative westerner.

This was the elegiac tribute of the West to a country which showed spirit in resistance. It was quite different from the contemptuous tone and temper of the writings about India and China at the time. And for the foreigners who were blind to the more subtle qualities of a nation's progress, the rapid expansion of trade and of the whole economy were impressive and sobering.

*

By 1890 it was plain that the once real threat that Japan would fall a victim to western imperialism had spent itself. Instead, Japan shocked the western powers by joining with them in harrying and nibbling at China, whose disorders invited pressure.

In 1894 Japan became engaged in war with China, and won a spectacular victory. It was the first of the succession of Sino-Japanese wars. By the peace settlement Japan secured the off-shore Chinese island of Formosa. It also proposed to annex South Manchuria in full sovereignty. But this antagonized the West, which still regarded China as their destined prey, and they were unwilling that Japan should go hunting with them. Under intense pressure from Russia, France and Germany, Japan gave up this Manchurian conquest.

In this incident nearly all the ingredients of international politics in East Asia up to 1945 are already plain. Japan perceived that events were presenting it with an extraordinary opportunity: Japanese were to speak, until their final defeat in 1945, of 'Japan's hour of destiny', the fleeting opportunity of which they must take advantage. In East Asia, in the Japanese view, there must be a hegemony of either Japan or China: the concept of coexistence seemed to have no place.

In general, in the comparison between the two, Japan was the weaker power. The immense size of China, the antiquity and impressiveness of its civilization, its economic superiority when this could be mobilized, must in the end prove decisive. All the warlike qualities of the Japanese people and the advantages of geographic position could not prevail against this opposition. But over the short period, in a time of instability and of unnatural weakness of China, Japan would have the advantage of stealing a march on China, of becoming, despite the historical position of the two, the stronger partner; and then, if Japan was willing to rely on its will and on the use of force, it could count on maintaining for an indefinite period the advantage which it had. Japan would stake all upon its ability to repress by force the natural event of a revival of Chinese power.

*

From that determination came the events which led Japan to its fateful participation in the Second World War. Japan's resolution to stake all its future upon the employment of force came to determine most things in the life and domestic achievements of its gifted people.

It was an audacious resolution, and a rather horrifying one. It meant choosing to act against the progressive forces of the age, and allying with the darker tendencies, which were never far below the surface. It involved Japan in courses of action which gradually led to its having a reputation for cruelty and insensitivity and it coarsened the emotional life. Inevitably Japan turned away from the more delicate things in its civilization. Japan had chosen to follow *Bushido*, the way of the warrior, and to concentrate its interests on making itself feared as the ogre of the Far East. Japan was dazzled by its feudal past, and did not sufficiently take note of the fact that military effort in the new conditions of industrialism was quite unlike that of Japanese tradition. Bushido in the twentieth century was to be unlike that of the days of the Samurai and Daimyos. With fevered resolution Japan found itself impelled on the road of national brutality, and this was hard because in a part of their minds, the Japanese, like the Germans, desire to be loved, and find it difficult to understand that their actions make them monstrously unlovable.

*

The contrast between this alarming and determined imperialism, and the natural diffidence of a great many Japanese, perhaps the majority, has often been commented on. The Japanese have a tendency to be abnormally apologetic for themselves and unassertive. As a people, they reprobate individualism. It strikes the Japanese as selfish. This trait is one of the most pronounced in the Japanese character, and is at the root of much that is peculiar in politics, in ethics, in Japanese tradition. It explains why they have rarely produced great assertive figures to take charge of the affairs of the nation individually.

But the very modesty of individual Japanese explains much of what was horrible in recent Japanese history. When the fashion for national aggressiveness set in, few people had the decisiveness, the resolution and the courage to oppose it. What was the individual Japanese doing in taking it on himself to resist the rush of the whole people, even if their direction was to the Gadarene lake? This artistic people, when its emotions were touched, was capable of a national behaviour which was arrogant, demanding, fierce and sinister in the extreme. A naturally diffident people became ready to sweep aside all the restraints which stood in its way. But the fact that there was another side to Japan, another aspect to the machine of conquest, needs to be kept constantly in mind if Japanese action is not to be a continuous puzzle.

It was some time before this hardening of the Japanese attitude towards China became plain. This is often forgotten: it is wrongly assumed that the Japanese hostility became rigid much earlier than in fact it did. For a long while Chinese and Japanese had viewed each other with natural affection. Japan remained, in a peculiar way, tied to China by linguistic, cultural and religious connections. The two languages were distinct from one another, but the Japanese had borrowed the Chinese characters, and could write Japanese in these. This proved a powerful bond of attachment. In the modern period many of the leaders of Chinese nationalism had been inspired by modern ideas by residence as students in Japan. They looked back on that period with nostalgia. Japan, where the conditions of life were not so very different from China's, was for these young men the convenient forcing house and museum of western attitudes, the place where western institutions were on show but had not become too uncomfortable, and where life was not a leap in the dark. Moreover in Japan there still survived, by habit if not as the result of conviction, the consoling sense that China was a land with a magnificent past.

A belief that Japan could be the natural protector of Chinese nationalism, and that together the Chinese and Japanese peoples might discomfort the western world; the fascination of the Chinese at discerning the Japanese methods of surviving in the dangerous world and getting level terms with its horrific visitors: these facts tended to postpone an inexorable break between China and Japan. The Chinese and Japanese still preserved a special feeling for each other, even when the Japanese were behaving most brutally and insensitively. For a long while the Chinese had the instinct that they should be patient, and that the day might come when the temporary clouds between the two countries would disappear and that Japan would become useful to them. They cherished Japan's successes, as, for example, its victory in 1905 in the Russo-Japanese war, as a matter for the common pride of Asians.

In the end, the relations between China and Japan took a turn for the worse, and became cooler. Events on both sides contributed to this. Chinese nationalism became more unrestrained and irresponsible: it revealed more clearly its ultimate goal. Japan set itself with more determination to thwart reviving Chinese ambition; and the internal events in Japan had rendered inactive the groups which fostered understanding and indulgence. Relations became colder; but only disastrously so during the 1930s. When this happened, much of the warm regard of each country for the other, especially among the more traditional classes, still continued in latent form. It was suppressed, but it was always there just below the surface, an imponderable factor in the situation of the Far East.

*

While this national resolution was slowly forming as the response to the circumstances of the time, it should be remembered that the circumstances were different from those of today. Japan made a disastrous choice, which was to lead to untold retribution and havoc, but at the time of its first moves toward empire building its decisions did not appear so eccentric. In the later part of the nineteenth century, force was still the final tool in the conduct of international relations; all countries accepted this, and Japan was not peculiar. Britain's conquest of India still stood out as the brazen example of what imperialism might succeed in doing. The only deterrent was in the calculation of consequences, and these were at that time clear of such devastating things as the atom bombs, or even, for the most part, of the horrors of wars of attrition.

For all its apparent modernization, many features of the Japanese state continued to be very different from those of the West. In contrast with the western powers, Japan, though it wore the trappings of a modern state, continued to be at least mentally attached to the Middle Ages. This accounted for its often bewildering reaction to the situation in which it found itself. It explains the frequently surprising recourse to the methods of the past. They did not represent an abrupt move to reaction by the Japanese, as they were apt to be interpreted by the West. Rather they were the intrusion into modern ways of the instinct of an earlier day, which had never died completely in Japan. Japan, though suitably made up for the part of a contemporary power, never was quite at home in the modern world; it was wearing a kind of fancy dress, and the West dimly recognized the fact. The West was never entirely at home with Japan, for it sensed a certain eerie mystery, as of a survivor from a past civilization.

The psychological drama behind Japan's attempt to prevail by force, and especially behind the attempt to prevail over China, is exceedingly interesting.

Throughout their history the Japanese have always exhibited symptoms of schizophrenia, exemplified in their attitude towards China. Japan admired China, and simultaneously it despised it; it was tied to China and yet yearned to be free. Its attitude combined the pious reverence of a child towards a grandparent with the disrespect which eventually led to war with its cultural ancestor. For the civilization of Japan, though ultimately it was due to the Japanese spirit playing upon the various influences which went into its making, was, in its remote origin, derived from China. From China came the initial impulse, and the Japanese could never put this out of their minds. On one hand they accepted, in an excess of self-abasement, the traditional Chinese view of the Japanese as being a race of 'deformed dwarfs'; on the other, they felt themselves superior, and proclaimed themselves with neurotic insistence to be the children of the Sun Goddess – 'the race of Yamato' – and destined to rule the entire world, even a world as powerful, rich and wide as their extended knowledge of the nineteenth and twentieth centuries proved it to be. This ambivalence and the unreality behind so much of Japanese action – together with the extremes of violence alternating with extremes of self-control – are the key to understanding a great deal of Far-Eastern history.

The relations with China always preoccupied the Japanese. Even when Japan was led, via China, into war (which few people in Japan really desired) with the United States, Britain and finally Russia, it was essentially a by-product of this great absorbing interest. When Japan went to war with the US and Britain, it was because the West intervened between Japan and its victim China. In a sense, Japan was perfectly sincere in claiming that it wished to protect China: it was protecting it from the western aggressors so that it could be preserved intact for Japan.

However, it must not be supposed from this description that Japan acted monolithically. For a country as regimented as was Japan, there were always surprising divergencies from the norm. From time to time there rose movements which altered the policy of the government, and even at times seemed to offer the prospect of a reversal of policy. But, seen in perspective, Japan's drive on China continued with little interruption throughout the period.

CHAPTER 2

The Anglo-Japanese Alliance

JAPAN followed this resolute policy of maintaining its ascendancy over China for half a century down to 1945. It was hampered in its execution by the jealousy of the western powers, which believed that they had a monopoly in exploiting China. In asserting itself in China and the Pacific Ocean, Japan ran the risk of increasing opposition from these powers. It had discovered early that they would not willingly leave it in peace to bully China: not because they were sympathetic with China, but because they objected to Japan's rise.

In pursuit of its purpose, Japan had to resort to one of the oldest devices of diplomacy. Ringed by a group of unsympathetic powers, Japan set itself to split their united front, to woo one of them as its ally and advertise its useful role in return for patronage. If it could enlist the friendship of one of the larger powers, for which it was prepared to pay a price, it reckoned on being able to hold in check the others, and to avoid being compelled by them to forgo advantages at China's expense (as had happened in 1895).

Where could it find the friendly patronage? Which great powers could it woo away from the conventional attitude of suspicion of Japan as an upstart? Above all, how could Japan supply a great power with an inducement to take certain risks to gain its friendship? These problems exercised Japanese statesmen at the turn of the century.

Opinion was divided. It was generally agreed that the extreme enemy of Japan, the frustrator of all its schemes of advance, was its immediate neighbour, Russia. Nevertheless one school favoured an apparently direct appeasement of Russia, and, when it had the upper hand, began negotiations which might have found a way for Japan and Russia to coexist. Another school wanted an alliance with Germany. Already Japan felt the attraction of Germany; in its programme of modernization it had borrowed from Germany the outline of its constitution, and also it had copied much in the organization of its army. In the formative years of Japan's foreign policy Japan had soundings with Germany which looked towards a much closer link.

But eventually another school prevailed. It was the group which was inclined to rely on the Japanese navy. Japan was a group of islands; it was a maritime power; it felt that it was obeying its predestined fate in accepting a maritime solution of its problems. It did so by throwing in its lot with Britain. Japan, perched off-shore of the land mass of Asia, was aware that its conditions of life were very much the same as those of Britain, which was similarly an island off-shore of the land mass of Europe. The geopolitical attractions of an alliance with Britain were reinforced by a strong emotional reaction in Japan. The political attitudes of the western powers since the enforced opening up of Japan to foreign trade in the middle of the nineteenth century had been marked by galling restraints on its mainland explorations, for instance, in the restriction of its spoliation in China in the war of 1894–5, and in some quarters by a cultural insensitivity, of which the term 'yellow peril' was an example. The British readiness to come to an understanding not only promised a political alliance of real value but also wiped out a sense of previous humiliations and produced a response of warm friendship in Japan. Thus in 1902, there was concluded the Anglo-Japanese Alliance, which gave Japan the partner which it sought.

The alliance was an event of fundamental importance in Japanese history. The complicated diplomacy which preceded and followed it are a clue to all that happened in the Far East. History had taken hold of Japan, and placed it eventually in the position from which it drove on, blindly, but with a certain exhilaration, to its fated part in the Second World War, and to its doom. Too much attention cannot be given to these events by anybody wishing to find out what really happened. With one eye turned towards Pearl Harbor, and, what lay beyond, to Hiroshima, the complexities of the years which followed on the alliance must be unravelled.

The alliance was in effect a neutralizing arrangement so far as Japan was concerned. It provided that if either of the two partners became engaged in war with a Great Power, the other partner should give notice that it would come in on the side of its ally if it were attacked by another of the Great Powers. The effect of this upon Japan was that probably it would be relieved of the prospect of a war with more than one adversary. Thereby the neutrality of the other powers was likely to be assured. For example, under the protection of the treaty, Japan could safely make war on Russia, being reasonably assured that it would not be assailed by any power which otherwise might be inclined to come to the aid of Russia. The British power, promising war against any ally of Russia, or any combatant of Japan, was enough to secure the neutrality of all other powers. So, by a minimum use of actual force, the danger of war involving several countries was very much reduced.

The alliance worked as it was intended. It produced the results which were foreseen. In 1904 Japan did fight Russia as a result of the unappeasable rivalry between the two countries: rivalry for the control of north China as Japan uncovered its ambitions. The watching world was surprised at Japan's temerity at challenging such a mighty antagonist, and was astonished at Japan's survival. Its victory was less complete than popular legend might suggest. Japan was exhausted and grasped at peace after eighteen months of successful but gruelling hostilities. It was in no position to demand to annex Manchuria, though it might seem to have gained the right to do so. But by the treaty which restored peace, Japan was given the right to safeguard the South Manchurian Railway which was built with Japanese capital. This was fateful. From this military base, the power of Japan was to spread over and to menace all of China.

This first of Japan's great wars also set a precedent of undiplomatic conduct. Japan began it by a surprise attack on the Russian navy: it dispensed with a declaration of war. But in this war, at least, Japan's treatment of its prisoners and its observance of international conventions on clemency were exemplary.

In the same way that the alliance served Japan, it also served Britain. In effect, it provided that the British interest in the Far East would be protected in case Britain became involved in war in Europe. If that happened, Britain would rely on Japan to keep its empire and interests intact in the Pacific. And so it happened when Britain had to fight the first European war. The treaty was not quite perfectly observed, at least in spirit. Some Japanese, influential ones, could not help speculating on what Japan must do if Britain should lose the war, a possibility which they did not seem to see with regret; and the positive aid Japan gave was less than might have been expected of an honourable ally. It felt that it had done everything which could be asked of it when it had liquidated the German colonies in China. But concerning the effect of the treaty as a whole, Britain was content.

Throughout the two decades which it lasted the alliance was the corner-stone of Japanese policy. Under its umbrella Japan safely took the first steps to the establishment of its empire. The irony was that the extension of this empire was to lead Japan into the most disastrous war of the 1940s, and war with its former ally. It pressed ahead with its imperial enterprises when jangled events had deprived it of the British alliance, and had transformed Britain into an enemy, or a wished-for victim. It is no wonder that the Anglo-Japanese Alliance was, by old-fashioned and conservative Japanese, looked back on with melancholy regret. It represented the time of safety. It was the instrument which had brought Japan respect, growing power, and no doubts or perplexities. It was a tower of strength to Japan psychologically. It had been the dependable way, felt the solider elements in Japanese society, amid other kalaeidoscopic attractions, and Japan had been wise not to forsake it.

*

The alliance was allowed to die at the Washington Conference in 1921. The issues in the Far East had grown more complex and divided. In 1915, when the balance of forces in the East was disturbed by the western powers being engaged in war in Europe – which for the eastern countries was a kind of European civil war – Japan seized its opportunity and presented the government at Peking with a virtual ultimatum which has been called the Twenty-One Demands. Acceptance of these would have ended even the circumscribed independence of Northern China: it would have transformed it into a Japanese protectorate. The pattern of probable events had been made clear in Korea, which Japan had taken over as a protectorate and later annexed. China was saved by the diplomatic intervention of the United States.

Instead of obtaining the surrender of China, Japan in 1917 became entangled in negotiations with the United States which seemed to give a recognition of its claims on mainland China, though in vague form; and then, on peace being restored, it had the mortifying experience of coming to the Washington Conference, convened by the United States in 1921, and of being compelled to join with the remaining powers interested in the Pacific in pledging itself to respect China's integrity and independence.

The Washington Conference contemplated a period in which Treaty Ports and extraterritoriality in China would be no more. The powers were willing that China should eventually be admitted to the comity of states as an equal, and welcomed the signs of modernization. The instrument embodying these agreements, called the Nine Power Treaty, was to be for twenty years a memorial of the limitations put upon Japan from having a free hand to decide the shape of the Far East. In Japan itself the change of mood in the powers who were party to the treaty was received with consternation, which would have been greater if most Japanese had not regarded it as hypocrisy. In Japan the fires of imperialism had still to become at their most incandescent.

That such a high-minded document could be produced, and seriously debated, was a sign that great changes were coming over the whole world. The instincts of imperialism had begun to subside in all the

countries involved, Japan excepted; the climate of opinion was changing, and there was a reconsideration in many countries of their long-
term objectives. In all lands, the doubts of the liberal intelligentsia were
undermining the former certainties. It was even asked whether it was
certain that imperialism in certain countries really paid; whether the
profit from the economic rampage over China was equal to the costs
and dangers of keeping China down. There was an unfamiliar readiness
to receive politely the advances of Chinese nationalism. Above all, the
instinctive resort to force showed signs of waning; there was more
readiness to treat China as other countries were treated.

In these new circumstances the British decided to terminate their
Japanese alliance; and thereby struck a heavy blow at Japan's sentiment
and security. On balance Britain considered that the treaty had come to
have disadvantages which outweighed its attractions. The immediate
motive for not renewing it was pressure from the Canadian government,
which in turn reflected opinion in the United States, which had begun to
feel the naval rivalry with Japan. The first phase of American tension
with Japan happened as the result of American armament and exertion
during the first European war; the American navy felt its strength, and
the United States was less inclined than formerly to share the seas with
other powers. The chief reason for Britain's acquiescence in the American pressure to break the Anglo-Japanese Alliance was the belief that,
if Britain was faced with a choice between American goodwill and that
of Japan, the decision must go in favour of Anglo-Saxon solidarity.
Yet perhaps few such fateful decisions have been made so casually, with
so little national debate, and with such small realization of what had
been done, and what it meant for the future.

The ending of the treaty confirmed that the world was to divide upon
racial lines. By rebuffing Japan, this event compelled Japan to recognize
itself as being on the Asian side. It confirmed the tendency of some
Japanese – and some westerners – to see the tensions of this part of the
world as consisting in the white versus the yellow race. Japan, cast out
again from the inner ring of powers which had the last word in world
affairs, would in the end seek to overthrow this same inner ring. It
would do so in the name of the equality of races. In its manoeuvres it
could no longer be assured of the neutralization of most of the western
powers; and undoubtedly it would make a commotion in seeking to forward its interest in a world grown more hostile to it.

As a compensation for the old Anglo-Japanese Alliance, Japan had
to content itself with an agreement for limitation of naval power, in
which Japan's status as one of the greatest naval powers in the world

was recognized. Japan was accorded a ratio of three compared with that of five which was taken by the United States and Britain. But this was a poor substitute. It did nothing to give Japan a friend in the harsh world of competitive politics. On the contrary, it underlined the opposition of interests between it and greater powers. Whereas it had been able to count on the British navy as a possible ally while the United States pursued its policy guided only by American interests, after the naval agreement both the United States and Britain were lumped together as potentially unfriendly powers.

A further step in embittering relations took place in 1924, when the American Congress, alarmed by a sudden influx of Japanese, passed an Exclusion Act which barred Asiatics, including Japanese, from any hope of being accepted as immigrants. About the same time Australia became notorious for a White Australia Policy. These steps, more than any other, convinced the Japanese that, whether they wished it or not, the great world of contemporary history insisted that they were to be Asian; and Japan would take them at their word, and would seize the Asian leadership.

Japan, having been disowned by its partner among the great powers, was thereafter forever in a restless search for an ally which would offer it the same security as Britain had done. For a long while it did not find it, and as it cast around, its neuroses of alarm and resentment were deepened and became always more dangerous.

The Japanese efforts to thwart by force the recovery of China had been checked by diplomacy and by the intervention of other powers. Japan was induced to retreat. It was still lacking in self-confidence. It had not yet developed the willingness to outrage the rest of the world. But the stage was being set for the more determined confrontation from which Japan would not back down so easily; the Chinese would be goaded to stubborn effort to defend their revolution and the recovery of their vital power; Japan would be lured by the attractions of a danger-ous new ally in the West which it would calculate would give it the security it had sought; and all the powers concerned would in the end drift into a war in the complications arising out of this fatal competi-tion.

CHAPTER 3

The Japan which struck

AT the start of hostilities between two countries it is customary to take stock of their rival strength. Japan, both in its own eyes and in the eyes of the rest of the world, began the conflict, of which the first phase opened in 1931, with overwhelming advantages. Most eye-witnesses to the initial clash would have been astonished if they had had a glimpse of what it would eventually grow into. It was expected that Japan would settle the quarrel in a small-scale colonial war, such as the world had been accustomed to in the recent past.

Japan had reason for its confidence. It was a modern state, recognizably like the states of the western world. It had a formal constitution like a western country. It was indeed a copy of these, and it included such institutions as a constitutional monarchy, a cabinet, a civil service, and two houses of parliament with rather more than consultative powers. It had, moreover, a modern industrial structure. Its achievements in making a success of a western-style economic system is one of the wonders of Far-Eastern history, the more remarkable because the traditions of Japan had appeared to tell against commercial success. The ethos of Japan remained unbusinesslike. There was, fairly widespread, a deep contempt for money. But this had not prevented the Japanese from setting money to do its work.

The state machinery was strong. Its administration, even if there was much corruption, was reasonably well organized. Though Japanese institutions were apt to strike the westerner as being odd and haphazard in the way they were run, they produced the result intended: they had the secret of effectiveness.

The national unity, which had been so conspicuous in the war with Russia nearly three decades earlier, had not been undermined as Japan entered on a more sophisticated life in the 1930s. Its people, in spite of an increase in wealth, continued to be easily regimented. The success of the government in doing this was due to the extraordinary competence and ubiquitousness of the police, which was one of the traditional features of administration in Japan. For centuries the police had been harrying the Japanese people. One of the victims of modern extremism was the curious, nonconformist cults of Japanese Buddhism. The police seemed to be infuriated by their existence, and persecuted them severely.

Though there were the beginnings of social unrest and of a communist party, this was as yet scarcely reflected in Japan's political life. Dangerous ways of thought were appearing among students – in themselves a surprisingly large class – and there was a dedicated, but very small and ineffective left-wing movement: but though this was enough to give nightmares to the police, and to the army which played a special part in keeping the morale of the nation untainted, they could console themselves that they were dealing with an eccentricity rather than a serious threat.

Though Japanese is an exceptionally difficult language to learn, the population was almost entirely literate. Knowledge, especially technical knowledge, was advanced. The newly literate populace, which was so different from other populaces in Asia, did not band against the government. Indeed, the Japanese people, though hardy and enterprising, remained extraordinarily docile to govern. They had an ancient tradition of turbulence, upheaval, and a readiness to make civil war: but these had become only a distant memory. Their martial quality had been mobilized, exclusively and entirely, in the national interest, and was embodied in the Japanese army.

*

For the result of the war, much would naturally depend on the capability of the army. The Japanese army had had a various history, and had passed through changes since the days of the Meiji Restoration, at which it was organized. In the 1930s it was a national army, the product of universal military service. But though this was its origin, it stood apart from the nation in a rather sinister way.

The young men of the army, when called to the colours, were trained in a manner which was calculated to ensure their obedience, to brutalize them, to make them unlikely to act like the rest of the Japanese people. They became docile instruments of the officer corps. Extraordinary stories leaked out of the barbarity of the system of military training. The Japanese army was not the nation in arms – since it rejected much in Japanese life which might have made it more capable of self-control in the aftermath of battle – but it was the Japanese peasantry in arms. Such a force was dangerous because it was liable to be swayed by terrible spasms of inane and savage barbarism. The rigid discipline under which it was kept in Japan was suddenly set aside when it found itself under foreign skies and in different surroundings. The woes of the Asian continent wherever the Japanese soldier was to tread were to be proof of this.

The corps of professional officers, the centre of this military system, was drawn from the entire nation and, at least in theory, was not limited to certain parts of the country or certain social classes. Boys who chose the army as their career were withdrawn at the age of sixteen from ordinary education, and were trained in the numerous military academies. Later, with factionalism playing its peculiar part in Japanese affairs, their careers depended on the faction in the army to which they attached themselves. They followed a certain conventional pattern in their lives, with different aims, interests, ethics from those of the majority of the Japanese people. They were less liable to be swayed by ordinarily changing ideas because their education had been distorted.

Japan, as its army had grown larger and more free of political control, became like one of the great military empires with which the West had long been familiar in Europe. The army was largely autonomous: its isolation and self-regard led it to think that it had a divine right to be the custodian of the national soul. In a great crisis the country was more likely to follow the hectic counsels of the army rather than the sober ones of civilian government.

This was particularly obnoxious because of the peculiar quality of Japanese militarism. This derived from the fact that, in traditional Japan, the use of arms had been a monopoly of a military caste called the Samurai. Officially the Samurai had been brought to an end soon after the Meiji Restoration. Nevertheless, the tradition which animated these professional soldiers continued to prevail in the modern army, and became dominant in the period of national assertiveness which prevailed in the thirties. By and large, the Japanese army officers of the professional, thorough-going kind, guided themselves by the code called Bushido, the way of the warrior. Bushido prescribed the life of the soldier at all points. It proclaimed that his ultimate fate was to be killed: to kill others first, but in the end to be slain. Bushido laid down everything that was possible in the relation of one Samurai with another, but was silent about, because it was contemptuous of, the rest of humanity. Harshness, endurance, the carrying out ruthlessly of impossible orders, the savage treatment of the underdog, the duty in circumstances of disgrace to commit *hara-kiri* – self-slaughter in a peculiarly painful manner – were its subject. Leadership was to be enforced by fear, by iron discipline, and was not to be exercised by any reserves of human magnetism.

It was a deeply pessimistic cult. Its parallels are perhaps only to be found in old German sagas; its horror and its hopelessness. It is significant that the revival of the typical Bushido outlook was associated with a type of politics such as that which prevailed amid the Nazis. The gloom and grimness of this tradition of Japanese militarism was symbolized in the deliberate drabness of the Japanese uniform. The army was without glitter. Alone among military powers, Japan exhibited no military panache. Bushido painted the heroic life as one which excluded compassion and which was directed only to success.

Perhaps because Japanese militarism was so outwardly unattractive, it was curiously anonymous. It did not carry any 'cult of personality', as did most European brands of militarism. A consequence was that Japanese generals, interesting personalities though they might be, were seldom popular. The national heart did not warm in contemplating them. It might feel pride or respect, but never affection.

The tragedy of Japan happened in such dangerous ideas becoming so influential when, in the twentieth century, Japan possessed the power to make itself so formidable internationally. Japan's modern army machine was administered by men who took as serious guides of conduct a tradition quite out of date and barbaric. Of course, not all the officer corps lived by this repulsive code. Some were as civilized as the most progressive civilians, and by most of the country the ideas of the Samurai were regarded as absurd, medieval, deeply irrational, frightening and frightful. It was common to regard the cult as a plague centre in Japanese civilization which must be eradicated. But the fact that it was really an eccentricity in Japan made Japanese militarism the more difficult to keep under control, and it attached itself easily to wild and irresponsible aims. It escaped the censorship of commonsense of the whole of society. Little by little, this insane part of Japan succeeded in becoming dominant. Military, archaic Japan took captive twentieth century, ingenious, civilian Japan, and swept it along towards the challenge to the civilization of the world, which was the principal history of Japan in this time.

*

Japan was strengthened for war by a peculiar psychology of its people: so strange and well-marked that the study of its evolution has become one of the standard exercises of Far-East history. This psychology proceeded from certain moral conflicts which the Japanese, almost to a man, accepted as axiomatic. A Japanese longs, before all other things, for a world organized on the principles of harmony. Harmony is only to be achieved when everyone fills his predestined place, and asks for himself neither too much honour, dignities and awards, nor too little. It is an outlook curiously like that of the Middle Ages, at least in its theory. It is worship of 'degree, priority and place'. Above all it is an outlook which detests anarchy. The simple fact which the Anglo-American democracies found it hard to understand was the horror which the Japanese felt at an individual or group which had a clear conception of its own interests, as distinct and separate from those of the community, and which set out to realize them.

The Japanese also had a sense of being under an immense obligation, which any amount of altruistic behaviour could never requite, to their family predecessors, to the Japanese Emperor as embodying the Japanese state, and to the government of the day for making life tolerable. It was possible for a Japanese government to make extreme drafts upon this sense of obligation, and a diffused sense of responsibility in general among its people, and do so almost without limit. In war the Japanese government could only lose the support of the populace when it was evidently and completely beaten in the field: it would not be beaten because it had forfeited this support beforehand.

In organization for war, the Japanese system was the stronger because of the Emperor-system with which the whole was covered. Though in actual fact the Emperor had, or at least exercised, little political power, as a figure-head he was of the utmost possible importance. The Emperor, as an institution, has now undergone change, probably permanent. It is true that the Emperor survived the war; but he was to lose, by contact with the realities of the modern world, so much of the mystique which at this period continued to surround the office that today some careful inquiry is necessary to recapture it. He is no longer regarded as a divine person. But in the 1930s it was widely accepted as axiomatic that he was of different stuff from ordinary humanity.

Immensely awe-inspiring, extremely sacred, the incarnation of all that was meant by the Japanese national spirit, remote, mysterious, never criticized in press or parliament – the Japanese Emperor obviously possessed the qualities which made him the ideal mascot for war. What did it matter if all the actual deeds of government were the acts of common or garden Ministers? In fact the role of the Japanese Emperor, at least in its remoter origin, was as much sacerdotal and magical as it was governmental. It is significant that the Japanese word meaning to observe a religious rite is radically connected with the word meaning government. Simply to dwell in the same country as the Emperor conferred felicity, and laid on his subjects a readiness to endure sacrifice which recognized no limit.

The court of the Japanese Emperor was not notably military in its atmosphere. He existed as a man, as well as an idea, and it was hard for him to live up to the position required of him by the theorists of the

Japanese state. It was strange to find that the Emperor Hirohito was a mild-mannered, courteous prince, and that he lived in a court which was a museum of venerated or picturesque objects. It was rather like the entourage of a British monarch. It was decorous and somewhat dull: but it was colourful – and was much more strongly marked by fragile aestheticism than is ordinary life in Japan. This was not really surprising, because, in the long history of the Japanese monarchy, it had seldom been associated with military leadership. Though in theory the Japanese monarch was the supreme commander, in military matters as in civilian, only the Emperor Meiji had taken this at all seriously. His successors, including Hirohito, reverted easily to the more ancient attitude. The Emperor Hirohito was head of the state, he received reports from ministers, and advised but played a strictly constitutional part. He did not sully the office with politics. The court class clearly did not want war.

*

A basic cause of all the misfortunes in Far-Eastern politics was the fundamentally precarious state of the Japanese economy. Japan had built up, especially during this century, an impressive industry, but was at bottom a poor country. It lacked raw materials. Its chief asset was its manpower, and it owed its economic advance to the organization of this. Its people were strenuous, punctual, persevering, disciplined, adaptable: out of these talents, combined with a leadership capable of putting these to use, there was constructed one of the most thriving economies of the world. Japan threw itself with zest into imitating the western countries.

Starting in the early days of the Meiji Restoration, Japan built up its industry, and the rest of its economy, systematically. Its constant impediment was that it had to build bricks without straw. But it succeeded. The result was that the Japanese economy followed a particular pattern. It imported almost all the raw materials for industrial use: iron, the rare metals, coal, oil, and, in the early days, machinery; it exported many of the products of industry. The raw materials were sent to Japan, and the Japanese people, organized in a great productive machine, processed these and marketed the product. It lived thus upon the proceeds of being the workshop of the East, but one to which the raw materials were delivered from abroad, and one which was kept going by orders from abroad. This was the basic pattern which shone through, although of course much in the economy was exceptional to the system.

The broad lines of the Japanese economy were thus very similar to those of the British economy in Europe. There were differences; Japan never allowed its agriculture to become so small a part of the economy as did Britain when Britain concentrated on being the workshop of the world. Japan, unlike Britain, never took the decisive steps towards *laissez-faire*, and never abandoned the direction of its economic destinies to blind economic laws. It never, to the same extent, was confident, as Britain was at the time, that the economic machine, if left to itself, would automatically right itself, whatever the predicaments to which it was exposed by adverse political circumstance. The Japanese government had constantly in mind that Japan's prosperity was at the mercy of other countries allowing it unimpeded access to raw materials, and unimpeded access to markets for the sale of its products; and it sought, by countless means, to remedy this. Japan, like Britain at the present time, had a continual anxiety from its balance of payments. It lived dangerously. It knew that it must export or die.

Its great industrial machine, and along with this, the remarkable nexus of mercantile institutions which it built up, all depended on the inward flow of raw materials, and on being able to find a foreign market for the finished products. If ever this process was interrupted, or seriously dislocated, Japan would be halted, its national talents would be wasted, its prosperity disappear, its nakedness be exposed.

Such a restless, dynamic society, explosive and always ready to seek new opportunities, uneasily aware of the narrow conditions for its survival, was not easy to fit into the world around it. It was constantly producing new situations: its nature, and its indispensable quality, was to be at home in constant vicissitudes. Though, as a military empire, Japan stood for a certain stability, it was really, though it would have denied this, the force making for constant instability in the Far East.

*

As the twentieth century proceeded, it became a fixed idea in Japan that the country was in great peril, as the Japanese felt their economy to be ever more insecure. They had had experience of entrusting themselves to be carried forwards by the great expansion of world trade, and had been taught by successive trade cycles, to fear disaster. The grave effect of the world depression on Japan in 1930 strengthened the case of the army for finding a military solution to the economic dangers. World trade barriers which arose as a result of the depression caused desperate poverty in Japan. The army, with its intimate connection with the Japanese peasantry, was greatly concerned about the sensational collapse, in 1930, of silk purchases by the United States. This deprived the agricultural class of its second main source of income and caused widespread distress in the countryside. The younger army officers were frequently drawn from the class of small landowners, and viewed affairs with a countryman's eyes. It was significant that ideas of expansion through foreign conquest came, not from the generals in the first place, but primarily from the young officers.

If Japan were able to conquer the adjacent territory from which raw materials could be produced – such as Manchuria – and if it should obtain military control of some of the markets for buying Japanese exports, it could breathe at peace. It could have the assurance of maintaining its industrial greatness, of safeguarding the livelihood of the countryside and of solving problems of over-population. The peace, prosperity and progress of all Asia, as well as Japan itself, depended on this consummation. The Japanese military were able to argue that they supported not only a narrow national cause, but that they were crusaders for the whole of Asia. The well-being of the entire continent depended on the safeguarding of the Japanese economy. Only the western countries could think it an advantage that the Japanese talent should be thwarted.

This was the frame of mind behind the Japanese attempt to gain absolute control of China, and, later, of South-East Asia. The Japanese believed themselves to be economically propelled. This does not mean that the war was an economic necessity, or that the Japanese soldiers who made it were economic puppets. But they made Japan's economic problems the justification of their military action, and, not insincerely, supposed themselves driven on by economic forces which compelled them to act as they did.

The developing views on economics of the army became a matter of concern to the large mercantile institutions which dominated the economy of the country. These institutions, with plenty of money to spare, found that, in the condition of Japanese politics of the day, it was prudent to buy support wherever it was possible – not only from politicians in the Diet, but from soldiers and from the cliques involved in canvassing the plans of the army. Undoubtedly the degree of this corruption can easily be exaggerated: there were many honest army officers, just as there were many incorruptible Diet members. But the links between the army, with its economic fixation, and the opportunist commercial interests, were well established, widely ramified, and liable to influence Japan's politics in an irregular manner.

The gathering popular discontent, which is inevitable in a difficult economic situation, expressed itself in growing criticism of the established organs of government, and of the regular methods of doing public business. There were a few dramatic assassinations, which should have been seen as ominous. Brash, resolute, prepared for violence, the new men who were in power in Japan inclined to radical measures when faced by a Chinese challenge. The new western attitude of appeasement, of spinning out for as long as possible their period of privilege but of eventually coming to terms with the changed world, seemed to them hardly comprehensible. The harsh facts of the economic depression supplied them with arguments for expansionism. They were set on reducing China, or at least north China, to a satellite of Japan.

*

In the late twenties, a document called the Tanaka Memorial was in fairly wide circulation in Tokyo. This document, which has always been described by the Japanese government as a forgery, was a memorandum to the throne by the Japanese War Minister, and outlined a plan to take military possession of all north China. Always it was the northern part of the country which interested Japan. Though the nationalist ferment was happening in the south, and from south China came the impulses which were making China a revived power in world politics and a danger to such countries as Japan, even the forward bloc of Japanese imperialists was at first content that this should be left alone if Japan could obtain control of the vast resources of manpower and potential economic wealth in the north. All the while, Japanese diplomacy, and semi-secret organizations, were busy spreading Japanese influence in China, softening up the Governors of the Chinese provinces which had been marked down as potential victims, and making propaganda to counter the effects of the nationalist ideas spreading from south China.

Many political groups in Japan, even those which declared themselves activated by generally liberal principles, found themselves in sympathy with the policy of containing Chinese nationalism. At least, few strongly resisted it; many, however, were inclined to regard a decisive counter-move by Japan as being more of a dream than practical politics. But, as the country moved towards what was to be its great expansionist adventure in Asia, there began to appear sharp differences between the different sections of opinion. These were over the extent to which Japan should press China; over tactics, methods and timetable; over whether Japan should aim at direct conquest of Chinese territory, or some form of indirect control. As the critical period came nearer, the danger of collision with other powers grew increasingly plain, and there was disagreement about how they should be confronted. In particular the army and the navy came into conflict. The navy had favoured the old plan of advance behind the umbrella of good relations with the Anglo-Saxon naval powers, and for long was lukewarm towards Asiatic adventures. But the navy fiercely resented what seemed to be the pusillanimity of the civilian cabinets in tamely agreeing with the US and Britain to Japanese naval limitation. It supported conspiratorial sorties which resorted to assassinations as a protest; and in this set the army a fatal example to follow. The right wing in politics was also divided. There were differences between cautious conservatives and wild visionaries: between those who were carried away by a mythical view of Japanese history and those who interpreted the realities of the day with cool realism.

These differences became increasingly expressed in struggles between organized factions. In these, there took place the real conflict over the path which Japanese affairs were to take. In Japanese politics during these years the great decisions were not fought out in the formal seat of national debate, in the Japanese parliament, but were made as the result of fierce factional dispute. There were factions within the army, factions within the different sections of business, factions of the navy.

Political life of this kind – a tussle between factions fought in a jungle fashion – proved very congenial to Japan. It was more comfortably Japanese than was the contest between political parties carried on according to rules in the Japanese Diet. It was natural for a Japanese to look to a faction and its fortunes for forwarding his interests. The faction was organized in such a way as to give free play to Japanese paternalism. In Japan there is a disposition to see all problems in terms of personal relationships rather than as great political principles. This was more compatible with the breakdown of society into competing factions than it was with the struggle of political parties.

*

In 1931, Japan's conviction of its manifest destiny, its need for economic recovery, the restlessness and ambition of its new political leaders, especially of the army, converged. The year seemed to be the predestined time for action. The place for action was Manchuria.

Manchuria consisted of three provinces which were an integral part of China, but were not part of old China. It lay to the north of the Great Wall which had been built to shelter China from barbarian raids. It was the home of the Manchus, which had been the barbarian tribe which in 1664 had penetrated the defences, overthrown the Ming dynasty, and substituted for it the Manchu dynasty which had continued until 1911. Towards the end of its life, this dynasty nearly lost its original homeland to tzarist Russia. It had the mortification of proving powerless to protect it, and of seeing Japan wage the Russo-Japanese war to put an end to Russia's penetration of Manchuria instead of protecting it itself. As the result of that war, Japan did not annex Manchuria, but China did not recover its full and unconditional control of it, and Japan enjoyed special privileges.

The South Manchurian Railway Company, a corporation owned by the Japanese, had much authority and excessive control in the region. The railway company was operated by the Japanese in an expansive mood, and was used by them to build Japanese political power. It grew from being simply a railroad undertaking, operating the line which ran from north to south as the spine which held Manchuria together, into a general trading organization with vast interests in the development of the country: and it took on political functions which in turn led to Japan having to maintain a force for the defence of its employees.

In the civil war in China which followed the fall of the Manchu Empire in 1911, Manchuria suffered rather less than the rest of the country. A bandit named Chang Tso-lin was able to build up power with which he took over the territories. He recognized that in these provinces he could survive only if he had the protection of the Japanese, or, at least, that he could not flourish against Japanese wishes. He chafed at Japanese interference, but he submitted, and governed Manchuria, in all that was essential, as a Japanese puppet. In his old age, and perhaps in response to stirrings in China, he became restive.

He also had held a part of China south of the Great Wall. From there, in 1927, he was driven out by the expansion of the Kuomintang. The Chinese nationalist challenge had come in that part of China where Japan had become supreme. In Manchuria, Japanese capital was making very substantial profits, and it had become the lodestar for Japanese economic expansion. Japan was faced with the decision whether it would acquiesce in China's re-establishment of its control – in which case the Chinese pronouncements and record had left no reasonable doubt that they would terminate Japan's privileged position, at once or after a few years – or would stand and fight.

Chang Tso-lin himself did not try to resist. He could not do so. He bowed before the Kuomintang military success. In the course of his evacuation of his southern territory in 1928, the train in which he was travelling was blown up, and Chang Tso-lin perished. It was said that the Japanese had found him unsatisfactory as the Japanese agent for resisting the Kuomintang, and had murdered him. There was some evidence to support this. If he died in this way, it marked the passage of the Japanese army into conspiracies in which they acted without the knowledge of civilians in the Japanese government, or with the knowledge only of those civilians of whose willingness to conspire with them they felt secure: conspiracies which were designed to force the hand of the government and to present it with a *fait accompli*.

Chang Tso-lin was succeeded by his son, Chang Hsueh-liang. He was much closer in touch with the mood of China south of the Wall. To what extent was not realized: the surprise was general when he formally accepted the sovereignty of the Kuomintang over Manchuria. It was a recognition of the power of the national idea. Chang Hsueh-liang admitted that the day of the war-lord was over. Chinese nationalism had coerced him into accepting its claims to dispose of Manchuria as Chinese soil, and of himself as a Chinese subject. But this claim, even though Chang himself submitted to it, could not be recognized by the Japanese. It was a challenge to Japan, which was obliged to resist it.

In September 1931, while the West was dealing with a British financial crisis, which drove Britain from gold and forced the devaluation of the pound – and which led among other things to the British naval mutiny at Invergordon – Japan struck. There was an incident on the South Manchuria railway at Mukden in which the line was tampered with. The Japanese army stood forward as the undisguised makers of its policy towards China and sent units throughout southern and central Manchuria. The Japanese government, with obvious misgivings by some of its members, was dragged along in its wake.

The war was begun light-heartedly. The Japanese, conscious of the strength of modern armaments, and for a long time inclined by the experience of their early victories to underrate China's power of resistance, put their complete confidence in the use of force. Their levity recalls the comment in *Coriolanus* of the Volsces greeting war:

Let me have war, say I. It exceeds peace as far as day does night: it is sprightly, waking, audible, and full of event: peace is a very apoplexy, a lethargy, deaf, mulled, sleepy, insensible.

They would have been wiser to reflect on the comments of Thucydides at the beginning of the Peloponnesian war in ancient Greece. He makes a wise envoy argue that war is so full of accident and so difficult to control that one should always embark on it with deep anxiety, even if the results seem assured. Thucydides writes: 'Consider the vast influence of accident in war before you are engaged in it. As it continues it generally becomes an affair of chances, chances from which neither of us is exempt, and whose event we must risk in the dark.' But Thucydides was a Greek, not much read in Tokyo.

CHAPTER 4

The China which was struck at

THE notable advantage of Japan in the 1930s was that it was a relatively well-organized and modern state attacking, in China, a society which was still in the early stages of adopting modern institutions. At the time, Japan's resolve to subdue China did not seem absurd or incredible. It faced, it is true, a huge adversary. That China was immense, and had unlimited manpower, might well have daunted it. Japan had only one-fifth of China's population. But there were many factors which told against China's deployment of its potential strength, and which made Japan's ambition seem less absurd.

There was the economic position. China had a totally inadequate industry for making war. Except for coal, with which China was bursting, it was generally short of accessible raw materials. Initially it had a pitifully small steel industry. Its equipment for generating power was completely insufficient. Its railway system had great gaps. Its roads, for modern needs, were, for the most part, terrible. It had no system for enlisting its scientists, who were produced in some quantity in the gifted Chinese race, in its war effort. Its population contained far too many illiterate peasants, far too small a middle class, for its economy to be properly organized. Such was the technical side of China's capacity for war-making. The facts encouraged aggressors against it.

In China the state did not have the same reality as it had come to have in Japan. China, in spite of chaos, held together as a society, but this was because of the natural cohesiveness of families and clans. The principles of its unity were of very ancient origin. The family, and not the state, was the centre of loyalty. In a day when the Japanese were becoming, in form at least, more and more like the typical nation-states of the West, the Chinese continued to be rather archaic, to breathe the air of the ancient world, to be sceptical of the overriding claims of the state upon the individual. It is true that, from these very qualities, China drew on a massive strength – something primeval – with which it could confront Japan. But, equally, it was at a deep disadvantage.

In an effort to redress this weakness China put its faith in nationalism. In doing this, it followed the pattern of all the peoples of Asia. Nationalism was their support. Peoples responded to it, and it gave them an impetus which propelled them past crises which would otherwise have overthrown them.

Nationalism was an astonishingly simple force. For all its surprising lack of intellectual content, it produced in country after country, the same result. Nationalism brought in new considerations, and a man was given by it new motives by which to govern his conduct. It burst the narrow confines in which men had been content to see the affairs of the world. It made a man feel that he belonged to and had objectives in common with the whole community, and not simply his own family. The majority of the Chinese people espoused nationalism with passion. Few were untouched by it. Its wings beat strongly in all recent history. It was the central, compelling force of the times. It was the root of the war, just as religion was the base of events in the Thirty Years War in Europe.

Of course it happened that nationalism, great as was the stir which it made, loudly as it raised its voice, had often to compromise. Too often it came off second best in China at this time in a struggle with the quiet voice of family obligation. It was seldom that the claims of nation would totally prevail over the more ancient social ties. Throughout the period, this was true of China, as it was also of most other agrarian societies. All men, or nearly all men, acted in ways which proved that the family was still the centre of their interest. Society was simply a federation of families. To keep this in mind is to understand many things about the modern history of Asia. Yet, by and large, nationalism prevailed in China in the 1930s. It was the force which animated politicians, and gave them the power to make China perform tasks which would otherwise have seemed impossible.

*

At the start of the war with Japan, China was governed by the quintessential national party, the Kuomintang. The Kuomintang had its origin in a number of societies, more or less secret, which had worked to overthrow the Manchus. As a single party it dates from 1912. When the old régime fell, the Kuomintang was not yet strong enough to claim the succession. It came, however, to power in Canton, and raised an army. With this, and with the support of the relics of the old system of government, it had made good its authority, subduing the war-lords who had divided up the inheritance from the Manchus. It gradually became the dominant power throughout the country. But in doing so, it compromised, abandoned large parts of its revolutionary programme, and took care to make itself acceptable to the social classes which had great traditional authority in Chinese society. It took in tens of thousands of members who would have been shocked at the modernizing radical programme of the original founders. By the time Japan struck, it would have been hard to say exactly what the Kuomintang stood for. It was a purely national party. It was dedicated to advancing China's interests, and to protecting these against the foreigner, Japan included, and in this it was ferocious. But beyond that, it was hard to see any principles which it followed, except feathering the nests of its many members. Its government had to rule over a hotch-potch of interests, and for this a succession of compromises was necessary.

The party brought together the rural gentry and urban bankers and merchants, bosses of secret societies and trade unionists, brokers, soldiers and bandit leaders. Its attitude to the particular questions it faced was determined by expediency. Some classes, for example land-lords and bankers, were more powerful socially than others, and the party mirrored, instead of trying to modify, the existing social system. The Kuomintang was a comprehensive party, never a party of genuine revolutionaries. In general the party had become more conservative the older and larger it grew, because each group that it included strove, be-fore all else, for its own survival.

The Kuomintang liked to represent itself as a progressive, avant-garde party. The westernized and sophisticated classes, which made one of its influential parts, advertised it as being democratic. Certainly it was, in the intention of this wing, to be aligned with the progressive forces of mankind. But the enlightened part of the party leadership was all too aware that it sat with colleagues who were anything but liberal and democratic. They had also to reconcile their claim with the blatant fact that the Kuomintang operated a single-party system of govern-ment, that (with one temporary exception to be described later) it did not tolerate the existence of rival parties, and that it carried on govern-ment – if only as a temporary measure – as a Kuomintang dictatorship. It announced that it would become democratic in future but it fixed no date for this transition. The dictatorship aspect of the Kuomintang was to give many of its leaders a sense of unity with the Axis countries of Europe. It embarrassed greatly the pro-American and pro-British circles, which were very powerful among the Shanghai businessmen who formed the support of the Kuomintang with which westerners came most readily in touch. But they did not count in the party for as much as was supposed.

*

The Kuomintang, from its earliest days, owed its strength to the army. In fact the Kuomintang was the army. Its being, ethos, performance, all depended on the military. This was the outstanding fact about it, and the paradox is that this fact was never grasped by western observers. The westerners in China, in dealing with the rise of nationalism, commonly met and negotiated with the middle-class and civilian members of the party. Chinese militarism had a bad name, and the middle class, who struggled against it, were ready to assure the foreigner that their party – the Kuomintang – stood for the complete supremacy of the civilian element, which was what the West desired to hear. The westerner, in this and other matters in which the Kuomintang was interested in misleading him, too easily accepted the Chinese version of reality. After all, the civilians were often highly articulate and convincing. By contrast, the generals were for the most part ill-educated, and even the best of them trained in very poor military academies. The westerner seldom understood how the decisions as to power were taken in the Kuomintang; he did not understand how the mind of the generals moved. And yet for a true appreciation of Chinese history of the time, the politics of the generals were the essential study.

By Japan the peculiarly military nature of the Kuomintang was perceived, and Japan had a lively appreciation that, in dealing with the Kuomintang, its problem was to overthrow its army. The Japanese observer saw correctly that the struggle was one between the Japanese army, which claimed to control the development of Japanese society, and its rival, the Chinese military machine, which claimed the loyalty of the Chinese nation.

How, then, was the Kuomintang army made up?

*

The Kuomintang army was a painful thing to contemplate, especially in the early days of the Chinese revolution. Later, in the 1930s, it hired German military advisers, who made a part of it quite presentable. But the few smart, well-drilled regiments which they brought into being scarcely concealed that their work had essentially been window-dressing. Organization of the whole army continued to be dreadfully poor. The Kuomintang army appeared as much a rabble as did the army of the revolution in France in the years which followed 1793. But for a time these incarnated the spirit of the Revolution. In the same way, in an oriental and haphazard fashion, these soldiers were the life spirit of the Chinese revolution.

The Chinese army was an army of mercenaries. The leaders of the Kuomintang were content, unlike the Japanese, with raising an army by payment, as China always had done. This was peculiar for an army which was the instrument of revolution: a political force is more usually raised by making service compulsory. But China could raise a force of millions, at incredibly little expense, so overcrowded was the land. There were far more men than there was equipment. There was a rudimentary general staff. The financial administration of the army opened the door to corruption: the pay for whole regiments was made to colonels, who were left to fix the pay scales and conditions of service with their men. They were divided in their allegiance between the central and the provincial authorities, and between the centre and local generals, who were little more than respectable bandits. A Japanese, taking note of their indiscipline, had little cause to be anxious about them.

The weakness of the Chinese army reflected the essential backwardness of the social system. It was an army which was raised from the peasantry. This peasantry had so many just causes of grievance against the holders of power in China that it could not be relied upon to fight with any tenacity. Here is the key to the life of the country, here the explanation of all the events which have since followed.

The Kuomintang could not trust the rank and file of the army, and this lay at the core of the frustration of Chinese nationalism. The party, which claimed essentially to be the party of the nation, evolved a policy for which it could not expect the support of a sufficient part of the Chinese nation.

*

This was the most important fact about China in 1931. It leads to an examination of the realities of Chinese society.

The trouble of China at this period was that it was virtually without an effective administration. From this proceeded many of the peculiarities of Chinese society.

The government issued enlightened decrees – hence the good reputation internationally of the Kuomintang. But there was no civil service to give effect to them; no government with an effective will; almost anarchy. The apparatus of the Chinese administration was adequate when it was worked by educated and dedicated men; but the spirit of the times had forced these into retreat. A rapid and appalling worsening took place. The machinery of government fell into decay. There was an abundance of officials, but these were not bound together in any articulated system. They stood out, but each acted on his own, without giving the impression of orderly administration. Most offices became objects for purchase. The magistrates and assistant magistrates, having bought their posts, set themselves to exploit their office to recoup themselves.

They taxed remorselessly, and they sold justice. They were venal and incompetent in the performance of their principal functions which should have been to protect the people against those who always appeared to prey on them in the times of decay of government. In the atmosphere of general decline, the elements of society which felt themselves naturally strong organized themselves and usurped the functions of government. Usually this meant groups of landlords: in many areas they raised an unofficial militia, which terrorized the countryside and ran the locality: it seized grain from the peasants at low prices, intervened to back up the money-lender in exploiting the farmer, carried out a forced loan on the people to meet the government's demand for troops, put down forcibly the resistance of the bolder spirits, supported all kinds of obnoxious practices, such as protecting the opium trade, and gave more or less open protection to bandits. Sometimes the local bosses found themselves on different sides in support of different claimants on governmental power; and the pressures on the rank and file of society were thus doubled.

In spite of all this, it is important to remember that the Chinese peasant, if the whole circumstances of his life are considered, still probably enjoyed, at least at the start of this period, the best life of any peasant in any country in the world. China was in decay politically; it was in mortal danger from the powers around it; but for a long while the degree to which this affected the peasant, and the number of peasants whose lives felt the consequences, can be exaggerated. China had begun to fall to pieces, but this process had not yet reached a stage where, for the mass of the people, it discounted the other advantages of Chinese civilization. If the miseries over so large a part of the rest of the world are borne in mind, if the misfortunes and the quality of life caused by creeping industrialization are weighed up by the observer, the balance is tilted and the virtues of Chinese life appear very shining. The worst man-made calamities which the Chinese had to fear were famine and the insecurity of life due to there being no adequate rule of law. On the other side, he enjoyed the protection of the family, of public opinion, and the many things which are summed up in the term 'Chinese civilization'. At any rate, the peasant was not dissatisfied with his lot.

He would have been surprised to learn that he was pitied. The decay of China he regarded as a passing phenomenon: he must wait, be patient, and all would come well again. Misery was to break over him, but civil war, its root cause, did not become endemic until the middle of the second decade of this century. The checks and balances which limited arbitrary powers, the pressure of public opinion, still operated, and did not cease to do so until the break-up of society had proceeded a long way.

*

At the centre of life in China, there was, like a canker, the question of the ownership of the land. China had always been rent by a great schism. It was divided between the peasants who owned some land and the peasants who were landless. The schism was the fundamental one in Chinese life: from this division of the population, and all the facts incidental to it, there have followed, almost from the beginnings of Chinese history, many of the characteristic trends of its society and politics.

In 1931 five out of every six Chinese lived by agriculture: and the proportion had remained more or less constant throughout history. From his relation to the land depended most of what was significant to the status, to the life itself, of the typical inhabitant of the country. Land ownership gave a man the entitlement to a share in the good things of civilization. Without land he was virtually an outlaw. Education, which was the key to social advance and to status, was firmly in the hands of the landed. They controlled the village school. Without going to the school, there was no way of progressing upward on the educational ladder, and of taking advantage of the opening of careers to talent, which should otherwise have been a unique benefit of the Chinese social order.

A peculiarity of the Chinese agrarian system was that in spite of the social importance of land ownership, there was no rich landed class. There was nothing comparable to the Junkers, or to the landlords of eighteenth-century England or Ireland. There were a few excessively rich landlords, usually the product of families which had recently done extremely well in state service: but these were the exception, and were like fish out of water in the rural society. The landowners in China were very numerous, but each possessed land on a scale grotesquely small, and did nothing to make these privileges less painful to the landless labourers, and to the masses in the country districts who were totally unprivileged.

The division between the rural gentry and rural proletariat was exceedingly sharp and brutal. The landless were powerless: they were at the mercy of the landowners, who were also local officials, moneylenders, or merchants. (The only alleviation of their position was that if, by a miracle, they chanced to prosper economically, society put no obstacles in the way, legal or otherwise, of their acceptance.) The situation is now the constant theme of Chinese communist propaganda. Its contention is that in Chinese society one part has lived off and mercilessly exploited the other part. The classic film 'The White-headed Girl', represents very well the plight of the exploited class. Possibly their state of wretchedness is exaggerated, but not very much. In all China's long dynastic history, behind all the civilization and elegance of life, the reality was that it was the arena of a permanent class war. China has been permanently divided between two classes, one of whom has had nothing to lose but its chains, and has, through the centuries, sat down constantly with appalling insecurity. The Chinese landowners bled white the masses of the people. As it had been since the beginnings of time, so it was still in 1931.

This tension was reflected in the politics of the period. The Kuomintang, as it developed, came to be completely monopolized by the landowning class. Though it had originally had place for eccentrics, for deracinated Chinese, for émigrés who were the product of a different social system, it underwent a change as it spread widely throughout China, and was adapted for purposes of the class struggle. The landless were denied membership, or at least denied any office of power. The Kuomintang régime was essentially a landlord régime. The Kuomintang official or politician was bound together in a kind of freemasonry with most of the army officers. They all belonged to the exploiting class; they banded together against the landless. Any threat to the landed interest and the landlords closed their ranks, however much they might struggle and be divided over other matters; and as a result the landless mass had no escape, except to contract out of society, and take to a bandit life. Brigandage was thus endemic over every province of China; in China, alone among civilized countries, banditry was talked of as an everyday condition of life, to which the poor might resort from time to time as a matter of course. The provinces never had a police force which could cope with this stream of malcontents.

The nature of the Kuomintang had grave consequences in the organization of the army. Most of its rank and file were drawn from the landless class: on the other hand, all of the officers were from the landed. The officers were well enough contented with the policy of the party. The rank and file could not be. Thus there was always a sense of grievance in the army, and a sense of incipient revolt. The army might for a time be made loyal – by occasional bounties, by the popularity of some local commander. But over the long run the army remained sullen and of uncertain temper. It saw no reason to fight wars, or to incur danger, and found the lure of military life to lie in the plunder which was traditionally the reward of its exertions.

Here the contradiction at the centre of the Kuomintang – to use a Marxist phrase – became obvious. It was a party which, born out of revolutionary civil war, should have been carried forward by the army. But its leadership, after the early years, took fright, and did not countenance the army playing with revolutionary ideas such as the expropriation of the landlords. The army ceased to be revolutionary. Discipline was called in against radical sentiment. By this action, the Kuomintang ceased to be a genuine revolutionary force in Asia.

The social disruptiveness, which was the inevitable result of such a social system, was increased by a tendency which has always existed in Chinese society and which from time to time in Chinese history bursts out and determines the affairs of the country. This is a very deep sentiment among the Chinese people towards anarchy. This is found among all classes, landed and landless, and goes with Taoism and Buddhism, two religions which have always been popular in China. There is a deep distrust of government as such: the typical Chinese has an insuperable scepticism about its benefits, and a temperamental optimism about the chances of regulating life without the recourse to official paraphernalia. For the three decades after the fall of the Manchus, this instinctive trend in the country was powerful, especially among the landless. The rise of the Kuomintang happened essentially as a reaction to this, and was marked by a revival of Confucian ideas and the notions of the more realist figures of Chinese civilization. But at this time, the natural and amiable inclination of the Chinese towards anarchy was not yet passed. It weakened considerably the reformist aims of the Kuomintang.

*

The inclination of the Kuomintang rank and file to mutiny, and the dissent of much of the country from a social order dominated by the rural gentry, were expressed in the rise of a rival nationalist party and government, that of the Chinese communists. From the early 1920s, China had seen both the nationalist Kuomintang, and, though it was at first very weak, a Communist Party which also appealed to nationalism, though it claimed to be internationalist. The Chinese Communist Party was founded in 1922 by members of the intelligentsia. In its first months it had been a study centre for fostering the readings of Marxist writings. These had had a great boom in interest due to the revolution in Russia; before that, Marxism had been practically unknown. The achievements of communist government in Russia gave Communism a great prestige in China: and Communism in China also began to receive direct aid from Russia: Moscow began to direct its disciples. The doctrine spread widely, and the Communist Party began to be of some consequence. At this time the Kuomintang still retained some of the radicalism of its early days, and a section of the party was not averse from some of the communist ideas. It looked with envy upon the support which Communism was gaining, and was prepared to collaborate with the communists in return for the accession of strength which this might bring to a coalition. In the mid-twenties, the two parties collaborated in advancing their common cause against the war-lords. Together they established the Kuomintang power, sketchily it is true, throughout China.

But the communists, with their Marxist beliefs, were not a safe ally for such a party as the Kuomintang. The communists were real revolutionaries, determined that one branch of political thought alone should prevail. The Kuomintang was a comprehensive party. Though it was itself a dictatorship, it was in reality much more a federation of parties, and it attempted nothing like the rigid thought control of Communism. Gradually it became clear to the Kuomintang that, by the understanding with the communists, it was nursing a viper in its bosom. It drove them out of the alliance.

The breach occurred in 1927, at the moment when the great port of Shanghai fell to the Kuomintang. This brought the vast accession of the economic backing of bankers and great commercial interests. The Kuomintang judged that its strength from this was worth much more than the strength which an alliance with Communism could bring it. It was willing to sacrifice the former association, which brought it a certain mass backing, to the new partnership, which brought it the immediate, tangible economic strength. It seized, shot and arrested as many of the communist leaders as it could lay hands upon. In Shanghai it used the secret societies, which were its habitual allies, for rounding up the known organizers of the communist party. It included in this purge a number of radical Kuomintang members of whose sympathies it felt unsure. Radicalism withdrew from the Kuomintang. From the time of the coup in Shanghai, the Kuomintang was definitely a conservative and right-wing party.

In retrospect it is obvious that these events in Shanghai were of great importance for Chinese history. But at the time they were not appreciated fully. The western observers, in particular, saw them as a blood-letting which strengthened the Kuomintang. The Kuomintang was, at this period, in the ascendant, and there was no comparison between it, and its sudden great prestige – its recognition as the legitimate government of China, and the millions of dollars with which it was watered by Shanghai business – and the communists, who led a hunted life, and who only appeared in the news as the comrades of China's notorious bandits.

The communist party took years to recover from this blow. In the interval the Kuomintang appeared supreme. But the communists survived, and reorganized. Their earliest actions, on recovering the zest for a campaign, had been frittered away in trying to organize secret anti-Kuomintang centres in the towns. They were under the influence of the Russians, and the Russians, from the experience of the October revolution, considered that the only way of making revolution was by inducing the industrial proletariat to take action. But such a tactic was entirely impossible in China: the towns did not dominate political life, industry was too small, the powerful armies could move in to suppress them. From the futility of these tactics, they were saved by the genius of the rising young figure, Mao Tse-tung. He was the discoverer of the way to make Communism an effective power in China. From 1928 he had shifted the effort to the rural areas. He discovered the power of the peasantry. He used the slogans of land reform to raise revolutionary armies. Through Mao Tse-tung the communists became again a power in China, however modest was their strength at first in comparison with that of the Kuomintang.

The communists, by making alliance with local bandit chiefs, managed to organize a small opposition government in the heart of the Chinese countryside. This was the famous Kiangsi Soviet, the first communist government in China. It owed its being and its survival to the general disorder sweeping China. But their ability to create a government was to have vast consequences in the direction of Chinese affairs. It meant that the radicalism which was endemic in China was being provided with a practical programme. It is true that in the past there had often been a ferment of desperation in the country, but it had remained always without an effective organization and effective ideas to attach itself to. The masses were ripe for revolution, but their emotions were never attached to some cause worthy of them. For example, the Taiping rebellion, in the middle of the last century, was a far more significant revolt than is today in general understood, and came near to overthrowing the Manchu government: but the Taiping acted under an ideology which was unworthy of their rebellion. It was a half-crazy messianic movement, which borrowed most of its ideas from the corrupted teaching of Christian missions. The movement failed because the Taiping did not offer a régime which, in the country's judgement, was comparable to that of the imperial régime.

It was now different. In Kiangsi, the communists had set up an actual government. It had teachings, organization, slogans, all of which attracted the classes which were deeply hostile to the Kuomintang. It provided the standard round which they could rally. They had been able to set up on Chinese soil a Soviet government which had become the centre of revolutionary action.

At first the Kiangsi Soviet had simply the sympathy of the dispossessed and alienated masses elsewhere in rural China. It was conscious of waves of sympathy which washed round it, but it was unable to bear any effective support to its well-wishers. Over vast areas of the country, the Kuomintang was still unchallenged. Nevertheless, by founding the Kiangsi Soviet, and keeping it alive, the communists had kept open the possibility that one day they would eclipse the Kuomintang, and that, one day, the support of the country, still given to the Kuomintang, would be transferred in bulk to them.

At first, the significance of these events was overlooked by the outside world. Very little was known about them; the communists were underrated as a danger to the Kuomintang. The Japanese had a livelier appreciation than the westerners, but it was supposed that they were so much interested in blackening the face of the Kuomintang, as a disorderly, untrustworthy government, that their concern could be regarded as routine propaganda. Chiang Kai-shek, the military leader of the Kuomintang, judged however – rightly as events were to make clear – that the danger was acute and deadly. He threw a cordon round the communist district, and kept up a constant pressure upon it. He proclaimed that, if the communists were not extirpated, they might grow into a force which would eventually overwhelm the Kuomintang. They might transform all the existing politics in the Far East.

All this was eventually to prove a correct forecast. Chiang Kai-shek, who had received a very limited education, who was the product of rural China and who was obviously outshone in intellect by the *haute bourgeoisie* of the Kuomintang to which he had been linked, was found to have perceived the realities of China more correctly than did his more sophisticated colleagues, trained in the universities and banking houses.

Chiang not only judged events. He set himself to try to influence how these would move. It was his will which determined that at first the threat from Japan should be given less weight than the threat from the Chinese communists. As a result, the head-on clash between Japan and China was delayed for some years. He had a civil war on his hands, whose issue would be of greater consequence than that of any war between China and Japan. Therefore the civil war loomed far larger in his mind than a national war. The civil war came first.

Chiang Kai-shek was therefore in the unpopular position of demanding that Chinese should concentrate on fighting Chinese. He neglected to take account of the fact that Chinese national feeling demanded that Chinese should fight Japanese. Even though there were plenty of wealthy and propertied Chinese, who saw that Communism was a real threat to their interests, they were held back and checked by nationalism from whole-heartedly acting upon calculation. The majority were ashamed to do what calculation directed.

CHAPTER 5

Manchuria 1931

In September 1931, the Japanese army began a full-scale attack on the Chinese troops in Manchuria, taking as their pretext the bomb explosion on the railway line at Mukden. This section of the Japanese armed forces, known as the Kwantung army, had been stationed in Manchuria by the Sino-Japanese agreement of 1905, to protect the South Manchurian Railway. Its movements after the bomb incident (which the Chinese accused them of contriving) were so systematic, orderly and comprehensive that they had obviously been considered long in advance. The army was openly flouting normal civilian controls, and the Japanese government was uneasily following its lead and waiting for events to unfold.

The Japanese quickly overran Manchuria. Chang Hsueh-liang evacuated it. In the fighting, only one Chinese general resisted seriously. He showed, by his field tactics, that he had studied the teaching of the old Chinese military texts on how to feign and double-cross. He won momentarily a great deal of popularity in the national press of China by the successful action which he fought on the Nonni River. But he received no support, either from the other generals or from the central government, which did not use its forces to support him. Early in 1932 the conquest of Manchuria was complete.

The Chinese government, in distant Nanking, played the card which it hoped would relieve it of danger without its being driven to resolute action. It appealed to the League of Nations. The League's prestige as a peace-keeping machine had been growing in Europe; in minor European disputes in the previous dozen years, the Council of the League had at times intervened when peace was threatened; and China was led to think that it might do so over Manchuria. The League had never yet been engaged upon restraining a Great Power, and this was the task it was now set. Undoubtedly the Kuomintang leaders, though realist· enough in home affairs, showed themselves surprisingly ingenuous in supposing that text-book methods of collective security could be followed, with effective results, in checking Japan.

Possibly the Kuomintang politicians were misled by a number of western enthusiasts who abounded in Nanking and Shanghai, and who were later to be joined by refugees from the rising storm in Europe. It had become a matter of prestige to the Chinese to become the patrons of expatriate dilettantes. A great banker like T.V. Soong derived face from their permanent employment on his staff. This was reminiscent of a classical period of Chinese history; in the days before the establishment of the stable military empire, when China consisted of a group of warring feudal kingdoms, roving scholars offered themselves to the Chinese kings, who gladly employed them. Now as then, the scholars, though cosmopolitan, had more influence on policy-making than most of the regular politicians. They were dangerous advisers. Disillusioned by the western record, many of them made a cult of the Kuomintang because it was an apparently revolutionary power which was willing to experiment with new methods. They urged China to attach its fortunes to League procedures.

The League was embarrassed by the confidence shown in it. The skies were darkening over the world: the economic crisis had set in, and the Great Powers looked with alarm at being called upon to do anything which could further unsettle the world's economy. They were faced with awkward problems from the rise of Germany, and many of them were more concerned with what they could do to take the danger out of these problems than they were ready to risk much on a hazardous experiment in a course so doubtful as that of protecting China. The foreign ministers who composed the League Council felt that the situation was far too dangerous for them to gamble over the means of concerting action against one of the Great Powers. They used the customary expedient. They appointed an international commission of inquiry, which was presided over by an Englishman, Lord Lytton, who had been governor of Bengal, and was the grandson of the Victorian historical novelist, Bulwer Lytton.

While the Commission was preparing its report, the crisis took a new turn. The shock to China had been deeper, spread quicker and produced more results than Japan had expected. Events passed out of control. A commotion amongst the Chinese people, not any action by the Chinese government, was the unexpected factor. A boycott of Japanese goods took place, which was partly spontaneous and partly organized by Chinese secret societies. Violence broke out at Shanghai as a result of the boycott, and this provoked Japan to land troops there on 28 January 1932. They met with something like the resistance of a Popular Front, and soon they had to deploy four divisions. The defence, improvised on the spur of the moment, was impressive. This was one of the first demonstrations in modern times of which the world took effective notice, that the Chinese, or some of them, were a martial people.

Hitherto the Chinese had fought their wars by incompetent professional armies, operating from books of rules which, though they might give occasional apt counsel as they had done on the Nonni river, were hopelessly out-of-date. The people, who were sceptics by tradition, expressed their contempt for all things military. But in this, as in everything else, China was changing, and the powers in contact with it had to take notice of the fact.

The resistance was at first hampered by the ambivalent, cautious, lukewarm attitude of the Chinese government. But by accident, there happened to be garrisoned, on the outskirts of Shanghai, the unit of the Chinese army known as the Nineteenth Route Army. This force was commanded by Tsai Ting-kan, an ingenuous, simple-minded man who had breathed in the simple slogans of the nationalists (and also, it appeared, of the communists). This officer, whose military training had been elementary, and who had received no indoctrination politically, and his troops, simple peasants with the most ordinary equipment, stiffened the resistance of the rest of the Chinese. The fighting lasted until 3 March when the Japanese at last broke through to the open country beyond the city. The confidence of the Japanese military received a set-back from the unexpected resistance, and from the international stir which Japan's action was making. Finally, mediation from the United States, Britain, France and Italy managed to effect an armistice.

For a time the Nationalist Government of China, and even a realistic and cynical politician like Chiang Kai-shek, continued to put their faith in the League of Nations. The Lytton Commission paid a visit to Manchuria in the summer of 1932, and it reported at the end of the year. It made a fair-minded, rational assessment, which was written with the dispassionate voice of history. It stated, with a good deal of sympathy, the Japanese case, emphasizing how large was the investment which Japan had made in Manchuria, the Japanese right to have this protected, the natural Japanese resentment at the Chinese xenophobia, and Japan's suspicion, which it thought not unreasonable, of an alliance between communist Russia and Nationalist China. It agreed that Japan could in fairness regard itself as having a special position in Manchuria, and argued that lasting peace required that this should be recognized in an international treaty, which should contain safeguards for Japan which were genuine.

The Lytton Commission, however, did not scruple to say that Japan had been an aggressor, though in polite and reasoned language, and though it held that China had itself been provocative, and was therefore in part guilty. The report was accepted by the League Council, and it was too much for Japan to swallow. Japan objected to China, the parvenu, being treated as equal with Japan, which thought of itself as one of the established imperialist powers of the world. Its reply was to resign from the League of Nations in March 1933.

No attempt was made by the League Council to organize sanctions against Japan, although Japan's action did not technically relieve it of the threat: but it is obvious that the powers snatched at the excuse eagerly. Also, by withdrawing from the comity of nations, Japan relieved the League of the effort to regulate internationally the privileged position of Japan in Manchuria, which the Lytton Commission had agreed that it should have.

The final scene at Geneva was described as follows in *The Times*:

Mr Matsuoka announced immediately after the vote that his government found themselves compelled to conclude that Japan and the other members of the League entertained different views of the manner to achieve peace in the Far East, and were obliged to feel that they had now reached the limit of their endeavours to cooperate with the League with regard to Sino-Japanese differences. The Japanese then walked out in a body. They maintained the self-possession of their race to the last, but many of them are known to have been cleft in their emotions.

Their departure was seen with ruffled feelings by some of the officials of the League of Nations, who, while they recognized that Japan was aggressive, felt themselves obliged to state that, on the various international committees and agencies which the League promoted, Japan had been a most valuable member. The hearts of some of them were heavy at what they felt had been the driving out of Japan from associating with enlightened governments, and at the increased opportunity which this gave to all the darker forces at work in Japan. Some of them recognized that it was a water-shed, and were melancholy that a greater effort had not been made to control the future direction of the tides.

There followed a very brief and humiliating campaign in which Japan conquered the province of Jehol, which was part of Inner Mongolia, and incorporated it into China. This was a mopping-up operation and, once again, the central government made no serious attempt to frustrate it. Jehol was historically of interest as it had been a vast hunting-preserve of the Manchu princes when these ruled in Mukden. After this came a long truce. It was to continue, uneasily, until July 1937.

CHAPTER 6

Lull

IN spite of its apparently easy defeats, and in spite of its disappointments at Geneva, China did not lose face. In this Japan was disappointed. It had counted on its action being regarded in the public opinion of the world as an old-fashioned colonial operation, which, in the atmosphere of 1931, was still condonable. China, a manifestly unequal power, was to be put in its place. But the world, to Japan's surprise, was not inclined to revise its previous impression that China was genuinely in revival, and to write it off as now discredited.

As soon as the fighting in China was checked by a truce, China resumed its continuous, painful steps towards recovery as a power in world affairs. The Japanese became conscious, though at first they could scarcely credit it, that this Chinese ambition was now fostered by the former imperialists who had once treated it with so much contempt. In fact, Japan's determination to rise had now become so evident, and was seen with so much misgiving by other powers, that it was natural for its rivals to switch their interest benevolently to Japan's enemy. This slow, but lasting change was more evident in governments than in the sentiments of western businessmen, who, by the old habit of consorting with the Japanese, had for a long while found the change in their governments nearly as puzzling as did the Japanese.

In the next six years, from 1931–7, this progress continued. Domestically, for China, they were dominated by one man, Chiang Kai-shek. He drew ahead of his civilian colleagues in the government and came to hold in the public mind of China a position very much like that of the emperors of old. By foreigners he was equated with Chinese nationalism, its embodiment and its principal agent. Chiang was the dominant figure in China until the end of the Second World War. In this war, remarkable personalities were few in Asia. In Japan, for example, the whole melancholy conflict threw up no single figure who catches the imagination. Many people forwarded the drama but their personalities remain shrouded. In China, however, it is possible to tell what sort of man was Chiang Kai-shek. An attempt to analyse and assess his personality is necessary, for, in understanding what qualities he had and why they established his supremacy in Chinese government, many of the obscure facts about China's régime may be made plain.

Chiang was the successful general of the Kuomintang. He had mounted on the shoulders of the party and come to dominate it. His special characteristic was will-power. He knew just what he wanted, and was never idle in his pursuit of it. This gave him an advantage over most of his rivals and competitors in Nanking. He was gifted with a great self-confidence, which probably meant that he despised most of the other leaders of the party.

Devious, subtle, resourceful – these he had to be if he was to hold his position among the shifting sands of Nanking. His outstanding quality was an exceptional tenacity: he got his way through single-minded persistence. His mind being made up, he would never change. In this, but not in other ways, he was like Shakespeare's Julius Caesar:

> But I am constant as the northern star
> Of whose true-fixed and resting quality
> There is no fellow in the firmament.
> The skies are painted with unnumbered sparks,
> They are all fire, and every one doth shine,
> But there's but one in all doth hold his place.
> So in the world: 'tis furnished well with men
> And men are flesh and blood, and apprehensive,
> Yet in the number I do know but one,
> That unassailable holds on his rank
> Unshaked of motion: and that I am he.

He had a rather chilling attitude to the issues of life and death. If an object could be obtained with comparatively little sacrifice, so much the better. But if its purchase should cost 100,000 lives, he was willing, with scarcely any hesitation, to pay the price. He would have regarded this attitude as realist.

He was not especially clever, inspiring, good, proficient at public speaking or public appearance. He was the product of a provincial military college in China, and of a rather inferior Japanese education. With this background he was neither so well educated as to have eccentric views, nor so badly as to appear scandalously ignorant. Accordingly the middle ranks, the mediocre, served him well as the medium out of which he rose to fame. He had a poor imagination, but, as against this, an exceptionally good memory. He dissimulated, and always held back his real thoughts. His suspiciousness was boundless. But if he did not check this, he could point to it having served him well. He was habitually surrounded by so much deceit that only a carefully nurtured suspicion kept him aware of the plots of remarkable complexity which were the stuff of Chinese politics.

He had a flair for political manoeuvre, and was excellent at manipulating his colleagues. He knew, and was at home in, the labyrinth of Chinese affairs – in the secret societies, in knowing how to use money to build a personal empire, in knowing how to operate a front in politics, and what to say in public through that front. He had the political talent, which comes near political mysticism, for nearly always foreseeing how things would fall out, and for knowing what needed to be done in particular circumstances. This flair, which included judging a situation correctly – and not with the distraction of moral considerations – was perhaps the key to his success in politics.

He preferred to rule through the ubiquitous secret societies which were always one of the chief characteristics of China. Some of these societies were of ancient origin, had existed originally for respectable purposes, but had degenerated. Chiang took steps to bind the societies to himself. They secured discipline among their members by strong-arm methods, always secret. Chiang, being fundamentally uninterested in ideas, jumped at the opportunity of gaining China by means of authority in this twilight world, twitching a string here, a string there. The extent to which China, before the communist revolution, was a rabbit warren of secret societies, ramifying with weird ceremonies and tied up at distant removes to Confucianism, cannot be exaggerated. They caught in their net all who mattered in the government – bureaucrats, soldiers, businessmen. Because of these societies, Chinese public life was always shrouded in a certain mystery. Nothing happened in a quite straightforward way. In any transaction the trail at some stage went underground. Things could not be done without recourse to the secret society. And, more probably than not, Chiang would be involved.

If he never pursued lofty or exceptional aims, that meant he would be set on nothing he could not achieve. He kept his nose to the ground, and pursued ends which were strictly practical. He was cautious and did not expose himself recklessly to danger: but when danger found him, he could call forth the stoic courage of the better type of army officer to sustain him in it. Science and all the arts did not interest him. He became a Christian, and he used to read, and read again, familiar books: but he had no taste for new books. He was not speculative. He had no particular ideas about the way the world was changing, and probably was never in a position to understand this. When he did not understand a point, he was unwilling to speak, and became inscrutable.

He had the natural xenophobia of the uneducated man; but he had the wit to conceal this in his necessary dealings with foreigners. These found him puzzling, and they never established complete rapport with him. But some of them were very much impressed by the man, and agreed that he was dignified, not garrulous, and reserved. He had a cynical view of human nature. But by natural instinct he tended to consort with the type of man who was foreign to exceptional virtue. His cynical views thus proved correct, as far as those with whom he came into contact were concerned. His rancour and vindictiveness against his enemies were constantly spoken of. But probably this rancour proceeded from considerations of prudence, which taught him that a man who was once his enemy was likely to remain so, and that generosity had few conquests, rather than from bitterness of mind.

In private life he was rather dull, faithful by routine to his intimates, determinedly egotistical. In the wider circles of life, he had no friends. Those who knew him well agreed that he was neither particularly wicked nor noticeably squeamish. A study of the countless crises he survived, and his way of dealing with them, might be added as an appendix to Machiavelli's book.

He was not magnetic and not lovable, though he was sometimes loyal to his colleagues and was admired for this. To outer show, he appeared ascetic, and if, as his enemies alleged, this was a pose, it did not appear so to the mass of the people. He felt the pull of the past and he played round with Confucian ideas, and the somewhat austere and chilly teaching of Chinese conservatives which ceased to be revolutionary and swung to the Right, was his guiding thought.

Yet that Chiang was in many respects a remarkable man cannot be denied; otherwise he could not have battled on, receiving countless checks, seldom achieving total success. Only his will and obstinacy were indomitable.

*

The interest of the nation was in reconstruction. The prime concern of Chiang Kai-shek was in fighting the communists.

Chiang was obsessed with the civil war. At first the communists occupied, and maintained a Soviet government in, part of the Kiangsi province and neighbouring territory. They hurled back five successive so-called bandit-suppression expeditions, each of them more elaborate than the last. In 1934 they decided that they could not withstand another, and that the time had come for a move in a way which has become classic in Chinese communist strategy: one step back in order to prepare for two steps forward. They broke through Chiang's encircling armies and made an astonishing march, in which they again and again repelled the forces sent to block their way, to the Tibetan borderlands in the far west of China, and up to the remote and mountainous province of Shensi. Ninety thousand men began this long march and the number which reached relative safety in the north-west was 20,000.

By this fantastic march the communists associated themselves with all that was remarkable in Chinese military history. They captured the imagination of the country in a way that was quite disproportionate to their size and their real importance. Arrived in Shensi, they set themselves to build a new Soviet government, as they had had before in Kiangsi, one which was milder than the Kiangsi model and which did not automatically frighten off all the propertied class of peasants. It made more appeal than had the Kiangsi model to rational feeling, less to class warfare. Moreover, it was hallowed by the record of the patriotic deeds of communists in the transit force from Kiangsi to the new home. When they took up the cry for war with Japan, they were heard with increased respect in China.

Chiang Kai-shek, however, did not consider that he had suffered a setback. He was still growing in strength, and was building up an élite section of the Chinese army, which was under his personal control and on which his authority ultimately rested. This was the section which was trained by German military advisers in the 1930s by an agreement which Chiang had negotiated with the German government. These officers, who succeeded in adapting themselves to the manners of the more military Chinese, spoke significantly about their warlike qualities when they were properly led. In startling contrast with the hordes of ragged Chinese troops, in their tattered uniforms which were all too familiar in China, the occasional khaki-clad regiment was now to be seen, very smart, alert, marching with precision: the élite of the Kuomintang.

In everything, things began to go well for China. Its great weakness had been disunity, and the lack of a modern political structure. Now, very slowly, and largely by means of the tortuous, devious policies of Chiang Kai-shek, which he pursued with resolution, China's political unification made progress. The Kuomintang prevailed in new provinces: the war-lords who survived had their powers reduced: the central government of Nanking found new ways of undermining them, and of making new contact with the people by new institutions. Chiang Kai-shek, alert, like the Japanese of the earlier generation, to take advantage of borrowing what seemed to him relevant from abroad, took over various devices from the contemporary example of Hitler for reinforcing his personal ascendancy. The country began to be studded by a secret organization called the Blue Shirts, whose members were pledged to advance his interest: this included thugs, but also highly respected professors from Peking university, who felt that the desperate needs of the country required that Chiang should be supreme. During this period there was only one retrograde moment when a nationwide unrest among Chiang's opponents led to an outbreak of civil war on the old pattern: but this was soon prevented by diplomacy.

In 1935 the Kuomintang, advised and assisted by experts lent to it by the Bank of England, greatly enhanced its prestige when it introduced a new currency throughout the whole country: and held it stable. The new system replaced the silver standard which had been made unworkable by the financial policy of the US. The American government, under pressure from senators advancing the interests of silver producers, had raised the price of silver, and drove China to seek another basis for its currency. The success of the Kuomintang in bringing a fiat currency into areas which it had previously occupied by military means alone was the best sign of the consolidation of its authority. It gave both the Kuomintang and China a fillip: and braced it to face the approaching war. Britain, by giving aid in this reform, had shown that it considered the new China worth taking risks for, and that it was willing to develop its Far East policy on the hypothesis that China was becoming stable.

*

In these years an additional person of the drama was beginning to play an interesting and much publicized part. This was Madame Chiang, whom Chiang had married, as his second wife, in 1927. She was one of three ambitious and remarkable sisters, one of whom was the widow of Sun Yat Sen, the leading spirit among the founders of the Kuomintang, who had died in 1924 and was revered as a national hero. Her brother was T. V. Soong, the banker and Kuomintang politician. Madame Chiang supplied the female influence, which recalled to Chinese, who are extremely historically minded, many parallels in the dynastic histories of the past. In a way this increased their tendency to see Chiang as being like one of the founders of past dynasties. But, though her influence on Chiang was considerable, it must be seen for what it was, and not misinterpreted. She was not responsible for developing any new qualities in him: the stubborn will, which had made his place initially in the Kuomintang, was all his own. Madame Chiang, who was American-educated, and in temperament had become more American than Chinese, was his window on the United States. Through her, the relations of China and the US became closer than they would have been without her. Madame Chiang gave her husband a glamour, an interest, which he could not have hoped for himself in American eyes. She was a forceful personality, wilful and dogmatic, and, though she lacked great political wisdom, she had an intelligence which made her a useful intermediary with foreigners. Chiang's use of his wife was skilful.

In 1934, Chiang Kai-shek, assisted by his wife, launched what was called a 'new life movement'. This was not very popular: it was the subject of mirth among foreigners and the sophisticated classes of urban China. It was an attempt to revive the ancient Confucian virtues as the spiritual basis of the new state. Confucianism had been repudiated soon after the revolution which overthrew the Manchus; but a void had been left, and the Kuomintang lacked a spiritual basis on which to build the new order. Confucianism was not really a religion; it was a code of ethics which from earliest times had been accepted as the ideal of the Chinese people: it served throughout history as the powerful pillar of the state, and the fact that in China this role was performed by ethics, which in other states was performed by the great organized religions, has throughout been one of the characteristics and fateful elements of Chinese civilization. Confucianism performed the unlikely part of presenting in a fossilized form the ethical outlook and views of the feudal society which was the state of China two thousand years ago. Attitudes which would have been appropriate in a good Chinese feudatory continued to be advocated, though the society which gave rise to them had long since changed. Confucianism urges submissiveness, demands reverence to the old, deplores a headstrong attitude in individuals, prizes the rites of courtesy, assumes that the business of women is to obey in all things. The task which the Chinese set themselves was to reinstate Confucianism, without allowing a too evident Confucian control of all the institutions of public life.

The new life was to be puritanical. A gloom settled over Chinese society. Nevertheless, by dint of propaganda, by the use of all the government machinery for indoctrination, by the use of various army bureaux for its propagation, and by manipulation of all the government powers of patronage, a not unimpressive Confucian revival began to make headway in China. The change in the intellectual climate of China, with the substitution of a rather narrow Confucian dogma for bland scepticism, was one of the notable features of the time.

*

In the middle thirties the sense that China was recovering, which increased Chinese self-confidence at home as well as affecting the policies of all the powers concerned in the region, caused the Chinese to feel an increasing resentment at Japan's constant pressure upon them. In 1934 Japan, its ambitions enlarging after the conquest of Manchuria, was demanding that an area, carved out of China's northern provinces, should be declared autonomous, and that the writ of the government of Nanking should cease to run there. Obviously the calculation was that in a short time it would pass under the control of Japan. The activities of Japanese agents caused a wave of indignation, and this was particularly strong among the students of Peking. Peking was always the seat of three or four universities, and their pupils, partly because of the regard which China traditionally paid to scholarship and to the learned life, enjoyed peculiar prestige. They were buoyed up by memory of the great demonstration which they had made fifteen years earlier against a particularly corrupt government because of its craven acceptance of foreign demands; this had never been forgotten by the government or by the students themselves; they had come to think of themselves as the custodian of the nation's conscience; they felt themselves morally obliged to be the nation's barometer. The Japanese overstepped the limit. Pressed too hard, the students erupted, in December 1935, in a great demonstration against the Chinese officials who were subservient towards the Japanese.

Those who had the good fortune to be present on this occasion felt, even if obscurely, that they were taking part in a historic action. The beauty of Peking in the freezing mid-winter, the sense of great issues happening which could only be dimly seen, the foreboding and the excitement, the sense of returning power and rising might in the Chinese people – of a people long oppressed feeling strength to quell the brute and boisterous force of the oppressor – all this made a memorable event in the history of China's ancient imperial city. Even though Peking at this time was demoted, and had temporarily ceased to be the capital city, the students must have sensed the drama of its being the setting for this great demonstration that marked China's national resurgence.

The growing nationalist temper was directed in part against Japan: in part against Chiang Kai-shek, because, though he was the military leader of China, he declined to act as its champion. Instead of calling China to arms he continued to sit in central China, and called for the national attention to be riveted there, to wars for the eradication of communism. In doing this, Chiang began to be regarded as almost a traitor to the Chinese nation. China, or at least its intelligentsia, was ready to go to war, but it felt that one hand was tied behind its back by the Generalissimo of its own armies, or at least was engaged in keeping down the peasantry – an action which the younger, generous section of the nation did not desire at all, and was only necessitated because the landed interests of the Kuomintang required it. How long would these interests continue to control Chiang? When would he become responsive to the will of the younger and more virile section of the nation?

The tension came to a head in December 1936. Chiang went to inspect the Manchurian troops who had been driven out of their homeland by the Japanese five years previously: their quality and their record as fighting men were both rather poor, and their employment had been a problem. They had declared themselves loyal to the Kuomintang: and had been used for blockading the communist forces, who were now in Shensi. Blockading is a tedious duty: the soldiers and officers felt themselves in a strange land: they desired only to be led back to their homes. So disgruntled were they that they fell easy victims to propaganda by the communists, whom they were supposed to be cutting off from all communications with the outside world. Rumour of this had reached Chiang, but he did not realize how deeply the rot went. It is very strange that he ventured himself among such disaffected troops with no proper bodyguard. Not for the first or last time in his career, the secret police, and Intelligence services, who were a major factor in his government, failed him. He visited Chang Hsueh-liang twice, at his headquarters in Sian, and on his second visit, on the first night, he was surprised, while in a bungalow, by a rising of the Manchurian officers. He managed to escape in the darkness, and crawl up the garden, but he had hurt his back in getting away, and after a few hours he was discovered.

Chang Hsueh-liang sent telegrams to Nanking. A period of suspense followed. The mutineers tried to barter Chiang's release against an undertaking that he would declare war on Japan. So powerful was the national spirit that it impelled the officers to make this unrealistic demand, for it was plain that the war would be premature. Chiang refused absolutely to enter into negotiations with them, and tried, though power was all on their side and he was alone and defenceless, to overawe them and compel them, by superior strength of will, to set him free. He succeeded with Chang Hsueh-liang, who had been at the head of the conspiracy, but who wilted under Chiang's rebukes, and who, in consequence, became his protector against some of the more extreme officers, who would have shot him on the spot. Whatever may have been felt later about Chiang, his bearing among his captors compels admiration.

In the outer world, the government in Nanking was extremely bewildered. There were signs of a break-up, and some of the key personalities began to prepare for a struggle for the post which Chiang seemed to be about to vacate. In Tokyo too, the government had no plans for such an unexpected contingency. Britain and America likewise waited.

The people with resolution were on the one side Chiang's dynamic and opinionated wife and his brother-in-law, T. V. Soong: and on the other side the leaders of the communists, who were only a few miles away. After Chiang's captors had drawn blank in their efforts at compelling him to negotiate, they sent for Chou En-lai and the political officers of the communists. It has never been cleared up whether the communists had known beforehand of the plot. One view is that, immediately after the kidnapping, Moscow had taken a hand in the direction of events. There was radio communication between them and Yenan, the capital of the communists in Shensi province; and the policy of Moscow, which was itself under menace from Japan, had been to preserve, at whatever sacrifice this might be to ideological sense, Chiang Kai-shek alive as the most useful and strongest ally against Japan. The kidnapping threatened this policy, and the interests of the USSR. Simultaneously, Madame Chiang and her brother flew to Sian. By acting whilst others talked, they had intervened to prevent the Nanking government from using its planes to bomb the mutineers. Such an action might have seemed justified: but it would probably have resulted in Chiang's immediate execution. His death might have suited the ambitions of some of the higher officers of the Nanking régime.

There were confused and secret deliberations at Sian. In the end the communists returned home, apparently convinced that Chiang would call off another large-scale offensive against their position in Shensi, which had been planned for the immediate future: and they seem to have been given some assurance that he would in future carry on a more lively defence against the Japanese. The communists were to be autonomous in the areas, not very extensive, which they actively held, and an attempt was to be made at associating a few communist dignitaries in the central government of the Kuomintang. Chiang flew back to Nanking, a free man, and accompanying him was Chang Hsueh-liang, who said that he repented of his mutiny and desired to make retribution. Certainly Chang had neglected to obtain reliable guarantees of his treatment, for on arrival at Nanking he was promptly tried and imprisoned for an indefinite term.

The incident had been dramatic: and was also fateful. It might as easily have ended in an opposite way. Chiang Kai-shek might have been executed by the communists or his captors: the history of Sino-Japanese relations would in that case certainly have developed in a different way. It throws light on the intelligent and subtle mind of the communists, whose roughness of manner had hidden their talent for diplomacy. They must have calculated that Chiang alone could lead China into war: and they were content to use him, and the huge and growing armies of the Kuomintang, for this purpose. Ostensibly Chiang agreed to this; he accepted that it was allegedly the national decision to respond to Japanese aggression by making war.

In reality he fought still to temporize, to procrastinate, to trip up the persons who were relentlessly pressing him forward, to complicate the issues, to drag new considerations to the front. In any case time was needed to make dispositions for war. He was the Reluctant Dragon – dragon because all Chinese emperors (and Chiang was virtually an emperor) are thought of as dragons – reluctant because he was warned by his sure political instinct that his position – and much else besides – would not survive the war.

But in July 1937 the Japanese attacked, and Chiang had to accept their challenge. The assessment which he made, and which forced his hand, was probably as follows.

The students, and the university professors, so vastly influential in the China of that day, so exaggeratedly more important than their numbers or physical power made credible, were, with few exceptions, for resisting. They compelled the country as a whole to take a stiff line, beyond what it would otherwise have thought possible. Also, for an end to patience – though it was hard to speak of a solid voice of such a disparate class, and one not used to having its views considered – were the army officers as a whole, underneath the top commanders. They were variously derived: many were corrupt; but the national spirit was apparent, in varying degrees, in most of them. The same was less true, as Chiang knew well, of some of the senior commanders, who were exposed to the blandishments of the Japanese, whose attitude changed from time to time according to the inducements offered to them, and who did not constitute an inspiring leadership. However, in 1937, most were willing to fight. The landed gentry, while not exactly enthusiasts for resistance, reflected the mood of China: their patience was strained beyond endurance.

Of the true middle class – the native bankers and money-lenders, the petty manufacturers, the craftsmen, the minor civil servants – the disposition was fairly solidly nationalist, and ready to oppose Japan. Some sections were less forward than others; there was always the contradiction between defence of their commercial or other advantage, and the gratification of feeling: none of them could have felt that war would bring them benefits. But they also felt, obscurely perhaps, that they were instruments in a conflict, and it was not in their power to stand aside. They may have deplored their fate, but most of them, while privately desiring to be left in peace, were ready to follow the national path. The merchant guilds, which played a considerable part in the organization of the economic life, had been very prominent in the organization of the resistance in Shanghai in 1931. It was indicative of the part which national sentiment was to play in the organization of the people in the Chinese war effort.

More individualist and more cynical was the attitude of the great bankers and financial magnates of the Treaty Ports. Some of them, indeed were with the war party: many had greater political regard for the security of their possessions.

The masses of people – the poor peasantry, the unskilled workers of the towns – the people who were to bear the main burden of the war in hardship and toll of life – were not consulted, and their opinions would have been taken as being of little weight. But among these, so far as they were informed, the temper was apt to be nationalist, and strongly nationalist. In the Asia of the past generation, it was always remarkable how news circulated, and how accurate the reports tended to be which circulated in the back streets and urban slums. The temper of the vast anonymous mass could not be overlooked.

*

These years, 1931–6, had been, for Japan also, a period of relentless pressure towards a formal war with China, which had come to be regarded as inevitable.

The first experience of Japan's adventure in the conquest of mainland China had not been impressive. Much of the outside world was disappointed and surprised. What the Japanese would do in Manchuria had been awaited with some curiosity. Some countries had been ready to be tolerant. The record of China's rule had been dreary, and it would not have needed any exceptional skill in administration for the Japanese to do better.

Japan decided to govern indirectly through friendly Chinese rather than to establish direct administration. Thus far the choice was wise. Already, as early as 1931, direct imperialism had acquired a bad name, and Japan could not hope to overcome this unless it succeeded in wrapping up reality in some more acceptable political form. Therefore, in 1932, they created a state which was designed to give comfort to the Chinese of the old days of the Empire. It was called Manchukuo, the state of the Manchus. To administer it, there were invited a number of families of the old régime, especially those who had been noticed as friendly to Japan. At their head was Aisin-Gioro Pu-yi, who had been the boy who was deposed in 1911 as the Manchu Emperor of China, and who made his services available to the Japanese for Manchukuo.

Pu-yi, who was to survive many vicissitudes, died only in 1968, and wrote a book *From Emperor to Citizen*, in which he describes at first hand what it was like to be a puppet emperor in the hands of Japan. He explains, for example, how the government of Manchukuo was appointed and changed. He describes how, on one occasion, the commander of the Kwantung army – the Japanese general who supervised the state – came to see him and informed him that his Prime Minister wanted to retire:

He advised me to grant his request, and replace him with a new Prime Minister. I had already learned that Japan was dissatisfied with the existing incumbent, and I immediately agreed and proposed who should be appointed as his successor. I thought that the general, who had heard my views on Japan–Manchukuo friendship twice in recent days, would be bound to comply with my request. But to my surprise I ran straight into a brick wall. 'No,' he replied shaking his head. 'The Kwantung army has already considered the question and chosen a suitable man. Your Majesty need not worry about a thing.'*

The role of Pu-yi was purely token: he was to attract the attention, and ultimately perhaps the allegiance, of the Manchus, Mongols, and other border people who might play a part if there was war between Japan and Russia. But the Japanese did not propose to proceed very far with this indirect method of government. They soon dropped the pretence that they recognized Manchukuo as independent, and that it was only tied to Japan by a voluntary military alliance.

The Japanese military and the Japanese civil service were supreme in the country. The Japanese, though they had little racial feeling, were very arrogant: peoples who were subject to them saw their follies, feared their excesses, but secretly tended to despise them. The Japanese showed their worst qualities in their empire. In Japan itself there were people of intellectual and moral distinction: but the empire had proved a catalyst, sorting out the men of coarser fibre from the finer spirits. The dross was drafted as the agents of Japan's foreign venture. Soon they began to make a reputation which was to be a lasting impediment to the further spread of their rule. There were complaints of arbitrary actions, arrests, executions. The machinery of government was used diplomatically to

* Pu-yi: *From Emperor to Citizen: the Autobiography of Aisin-Gioro Pu-yi*, Foreign Language Press, Peking, 1965.

promote the interests of the South Manchuria Railway Company and to foster the multitude of subordinate economic enterprises. The camp-followers became worse exploiters.

Yet, little by little, the army's Manchurian adventure proved disappointing, and, as the Japanese because of their excesses had to abandon the hope of any sincere or large-scale cooperation from the Chinese, the Japanese army, far from meditating ending it and cutting their losses, became increasingly interested in the provinces in China itself south of the Wall, at least in the provinces of the northern half of the country. The grass seemed greener in that valley than it had turned out to be north of the Wall. It became the fashion in Japan for ambitious young officers to seek service in the Kwantung army, and from that vantage point to smell out the situation in Peking, and in the northern provinces of China. Their hopes grew, and they were not deterred by the ill end which some of their colleagues came to because the Chinese had naturally become anxious about the Japanese Secret Service.

*

Japan's economic measures in Manchukuo, and its discouragement of the presence of western businessmen, began to be unfavourably commented on internationally. In north China its pre-invasion action was more spectacular and more sinister. It used its political prestige to further all kinds of economic activity, some very detrimental to China. In particular it fostered the opium trade.

Opium had first become an issue in China at the beginning of the previous century. The British, in forcing the trade upon China, had sought to counter the fact that China bought too little from the West, and thereby caused an adverse balance of trade, by creating a new Chinese want, opium. It was grown in great quantities in India, and could easily be shipped to Canton. The Chinese government protested, and pointed to its duty to protect the Chinese people from the effects of the drug. Two wars had to be fought to overcome its moral protest.

The subsequent history of opium contains a number of unexplained matters. Why did the country as a whole take to opium smoking? What were the effects of the drug upon people's efficiency? Why was the habit, which had been so widespread a few years earlier, checked so completely and with such ease when China eventually had its communist revolution? In the 1930s this ultimate solution of the problem was still far off. Opium had long ceased to be an article of western import: it had become instead a major Chinese product, and though it was not legalized, it was consumed everywhere. The Kuomintang régime drew from its trade a revenue which was outside the ordinary state budget, which was unpublished, but which was the most important item in the financing of its army. Opium, as it is usually taken in China, is a comparatively mild drug, and the Chinese addiction to it probably did them no great harm. A quite different effect, however, was produced by the derivatives of opium: heroin and morphine.

The Japanese set themselves to flood the provinces of north China with heroin and morphine. Partly they did so because of the very high profits obtainable; partly they had in mind the destructive effects of these two drugs. Their use would corrupt the population, and cause them to become apathetic, and weaken their will to resist. They protected rings of Korean drug peddlers. For a time the press was full of stories of these traders, of the protection illegally given them by the Japanese army and navy, and of the unfortunate inhabitants reduced to fawning submission to the bowls in which the morphine was wrapped.

Scenes such as these were confined to only a minute percentage of the map of China, and only a small proportion of the population was affected. But it was symbolic of the new imperialism and the lengths to which it might go. Japan made no effort at hiding it away; it showed its face unashamedly to the world, and the world, startled by Japanese cynicism, reacted more deeply against it than Japan perhaps foresaw. The West, which had the opium wars on its conscience, was more scandalized by the Japanese re-enacting the events of the buried past, than prepared to hail them as brothers in crime.

*

Japan's descent into Avernus, during these six brief years, and the corruption of its political system were rapid. Most of what happened prepared Japan for the later part it was to play. In this time Japan took, with great speed, a series of plunges, which ensured that, when the Pacific war came, it fought this in a spirit that surprised the world by its barbarity.

A rapid deterioration set in among most of the national institutions. Many of these had the obvious effect of easing the path to war: and they harmed the spirit of the country profoundly. When there was a lull in the development of external events, the crisis deepened internally.

The process can be traced from point to point. In Manchuria, in 1931, the decision to act had been made by the Japanese army. It dragged the civilian government in the wake of its *fait accompli*. The precedent was alarming, and was regularly acted on by the army in the years which followed, and accepted by the nation. No revolution took place, and no change of institutions was necessary: the civil service continued to operate, and remained comparatively unpurged. But in the government of the day, with a constitution not too precise, it was enough that one of the controlling forces should shift the balance of power in the administration: and the whole nature of government changed. The civil authority ceased to intervene in matters which were properly its concern, and left these to the army. It was a species of anarchy.

The development was aided by a peculiar feature of the constitution. It was laid down by law that the Ministers of the navy and army must be serving officers holding a certain rank. The implications became apparent. Through this provision the army and navy gained a veto over all the dealings of the cabinet whenever they chose to express it. It was only necessary that they should withdraw their nominees from the cabinet, and forbid other serving officers to join it, and a situation would come about in which the civilian Ministers, even of high prestige, were forced to supplicate the army for terms which would make it possible for the cabinet to continue its work.

A curious development, which struck all historians of Japan as reviving historical precedents, was that, in the army, the readiness to exploit these full powers was found among the younger officers. Situations were constantly developing in which the more senior officers hesitated and prevaricated: sometimes they did not know what to do, or were frankly appalled at finding themselves called on to take the responsibility in unfamiliar civilian affairs. The junior officers could exercise this without nervousness or scruple. This explains why so much army initiative originated at quite a low level.

Under army protection a large number of so-called patriotic parties began to operate. These, made up chiefly of thugs, led in part by retired army officers and held together by histrionics and cash, drove out of public life the moderate or old-fashioned men who wanted to preserve the more dignified ways of the past. These irrational, violent forces were a feature of the politics of the period. A civilian Minister, or a sober, responsible service officer, had to be ready at all times to be struck at by these gangs: and knew that they were often employed by their apparently respectable rivals. Their method represented the violent way of doing politics which had come in, and no moral slur attached to the use of gangs for assassination, nor could public opinion be rallied against them.

The patriotic societies were active in everything. Within months of the Mukden incident a serious wave of unrest, violence and assassination began. The most important incidents were the murder of the

Finance Minister, Inouye Junnosuke, and the Prime Minister, Inukai Tsuyoshi. The societies sensed that the atmosphere had become suddenly propitious for their activities, and offered themselves to one faction or another. They interested themselves in all branches of government. But foreign affairs were their most dangerous concern. The Black Dragon Society – which took its name from the Japanese word for the Amur river which was the border between Manchuria and the USSR – was particularly obnoxious. It organized the assassination of Prime Ministers: it tried to dictate to the Foreign Office: it sought to win members among the bureaucracy: by terror it dictated much of the ideological guidance which the Japanese government was accustomed to give to the people. The murderers of Premier Inukai declared at their trial that their motive had been to protest against the Japanese ratification of the London naval agreement which the Japanese government had incurred much displeasure by accepting. It was to be the last constructive agreement for peace that a Japanese government was to be allowed by public opinion to make.

The investigation of these plots showed that there was a deep malaise among the services. These wanted a radical change in the form of government, though in precisely what form it was hard to specify. The talk was of national renewal, and a general new birth of institutions. The young officers were divided. Some were primarily interested in bringing about a domestic revolution: others wanted it because it seemed the best way of promoting a more ruthless foreign policy. But in the end the two trends were united: a sterner foreign policy went with the renewal of institutions at home.

In February 1936 the turbulence of the new army reached its peak. There took place then an incident which embodied all the trends to violence of the time, and all the flouting of established political conduct. A plot was made by the younger officers in some of the most respected regiments. Plots, it will be gathered, were nothing new: it was the scope and audacity of this particular one which were original. The conspiracy was to murder the leaders of the cabinet and the most respected elder statesmen who advised the throne: and then, as an act of unheard-of impiety, to give an ultimatum to the Emperor for the appointment of a particular kind of Ministry. They failed because their plot was prepared inadequately, and because some of the leading figures escaped their would-be assassins. But for some days the politics of Tokyo, which at the time was snow-covered, was divided between a barracks which housed the rebellious officers who were waiting for high personages to throw in their lot with them, and the rest of the town, stunned by the enormity of what had been done, and with police and the loyal section of the army gradually mustering the resolution to step in with repressive action. Finally they moved in, there were trials, and after a considerable delay, some exemplary executions.

Japan had been saved from the dictation of a ruthless and flamboyant figure only because no such figure had the ability to seize the government. The tradition of Japan was against individual action. Even in times of great crisis it required that revolutionaries should act in committees. But the spectacle of the administration of a great empire ceasing altogether for a few days, and great offices of state being hawked round by captains and majors, caused all lookers-on to marvel and to shudder.

This abortive revolution, by its radicalism, led to a realization that the Japanese army, or a part of it, was ceasing to be right-wing. One of its causes was said to be the unfamiliar outbreak of political discussion among junior officers. This was partly the result of their becoming affected by Japan's economic problems. They were seeking solutions; they did not mind if they were radical. Hitherto the army, to the comfort of the better-off classes of the Japanese, had seemed to connote safety, conservatism, stability. But they had to recast their thoughts rather rapidly when they saw at least a section of the officers playing with what in Japan had been regarded as dangerous thoughts. Some reflective onlookers noticed that, if the army should turn towards Communism in its new adventurousness it would have a good chance of putting the whole country on a communist footing. Japan, with its heavy industry, with its huge industrial population which was accustomed to strict discipline, and its underlying taste for violence, would be admirable material for a communist dictatorship to work on.

This uneasiness, vague but pervasive, increased the danger of war. Many Japanese, fearful that the army, which already they felt was beyond control, might now move towards the acceptance of all kinds of radicalism in Japanese internal affairs, felt that its giddy mind would best be occupied by foreign quarrels.

The national temper began to be touched with hysteria. Thought control, imposed by the government, meant the virtual interruption of all forms of rational thinking. An official version of Japanese history, made up of fairy stories and full of absurdity, was made to prevail: it became dangerous to publish more serious matter. A much respected Japanese professor, Minobe Tatsukichi, was hounded from his job because it was found that he had stated in a book on political science that the Japanese Emperor was an organ of the constitution. He was too sacred to be defined. The deification of the Emperor, which formerly had been inherited from the Japanese past, grew now to absurd proportions, and was especially ironical because it was known to be distasteful to the Emperor himself.

In these years, there also took place a distinct shift in the religious life of the country. Attention was less on the compassionate, often intellectually subtle religion of Buddhism; more emphasis was given to the religion which had coexisted with Buddhism for many centuries – Shinto, a rather simple form of animism and worship of the symbols of state. It had no intellectual corpus attached to it.

It became dangerous for a Japanese to diverge by however little from the norm in behaviour, sentiment, or thought. Japan had never been kind to the pronounced individual: and Japanese society had eyed any departure from conformity with uneasiness. (Only those cases where experimentalism had been backed up by a reputation of extreme religiosity were exempted.) The increasing tension in political life made the Japanese dislike eccentricity even more severely. In the years preceding the end of the Japanese military venture, there was an increasing sterility in Japanese literature and in all departments of creative life. Of true individualism, of the man with the social courage to stand up and denounce what society was doing, or the innovator who worked under the pressure of his *daimon* and ignored the praise or censure of the world, there was strikingly little.

CHAPTER 7

The War resumed

THE second phase of the war began in an obscure skirmish between the Japanese and Chinese troops at a place not far from Peking called the Marco Polo Bridge. This encounter happened on the night of 7 July 1937. In the next few weeks, at first sporadic, later general fighting spread through all north China, and reached Shanghai. As far as can be discovered, none of the main Japanese generals, and certainly not Chiang Kai-shek, wanted war at this particular moment: and peace efforts were made constantly. But the situation was out of hand. The Chinese communists, who were now formally reconciled with the Kuomintang, used every opportunity to drive their allies on to war. The decision was forced by relatively junior officers in command in the field. Compulsively the fighting spread. The top commanders on both sides saw this and made unavailing efforts to check it, and excused themselves from responsibility.

The two years which followed were the chief phase of slaughter in the war between China and Japan: then came a renewed period of lull. The conflict was still separate from the Armageddon which was being prepared in the West, and at first remained a separate war, when the explosion occurred in Europe. Naturally both sides followed with care the events in Europe, and at times they adjusted their policies accordingly. But the two wars were not to merge until December 1941. There were four years to go before that.

The history of these first years of fighting is fairly simple. As was expected, Japan quickly overcame the organized resistance in the north, and occupied the railway lines and the cities. It sent a powerful force to Shanghai, and the history of the landing there after the Mukden incident was repeated. The Chinese resisted for seven weeks, and there was jubilation in China. Improvising a guerrilla warfare, the Chinese discovered in some theatres the military prowess which has since been taken for granted. But at Shanghai, on breaking through in the end to open country, the Japanese this time crossed rapidly the 200 miles to Nanking, and occupied it without difficulty.

Chiang Kai-shek and his government had withdrawn to Hankow. In December 1937 they had lost Nanking, their capital; the slaughter and atrocities were far worse than in 1931. It was the history of an earlier time, of the Mongol ravages of Asia, of Timur and the cold terror he spread – a horror which his name can even now evoke in Central Asia. There are lurid tales of Timur sacking a city. If an army dared to oppose him Timur built up a pyramid of skulls of those he slaughtered. He camped in a tent of scarlet canvas outside the towns he besieged, thus symbolizing the massacres he intended to make. The ferocity of the Japanese at Nanking amazed the world. The massacre was done for the most part by Japanese conscripts, unfamiliar with war, perhaps neurotically working out of their system the extreme repressions in which they had passed so much of their lives. Some Japanese officers in other centres wept with shame and indignation when they heard the details of the ravage.

The effect was profound in other countries of the world. At first the news of the outrage was censored, but ultimately it got into the world press. Anxious though they were to avert their gaze from Asia, because of the preoccupations in Europe, the countries of the West turned their attention to Nanking, and were appalled by seeing a foretaste of what might soon be everywhere. From then on, the Japanese army was held to be uncivilized, savage and terrible.

In 1938 there was much fighting in north and central China. In the spring, in an effort to halt the Japanese advance, Chiang ordered the breaching of the Yellow River dykes. This failed to halt them; but it was estimated that over a million peasants were drowned in the flood which resulted. It began to be clear what torment had been let loose on the world. In October, the Japanese, in the south, took Canton and its hinterland. Canton was the original base of the Kuomintang. Its capture was significant, as it seemed to symbolize striking at the root of the Kuomintang. In the same month the Japanese, advancing up the Yangtse, had taken Hankow. This was not an easy victory, as many successes had been. There was heavy fighting: the Chinese engaged in positional warfare, and did not use guerrilla tactics. Some divisions showed the result of their having received German training from Chiang Kai-shek's German advisers. In the battle of Hsuchow the Chinese won triumphantly.

In spite of this, in October 1938, Hankow fell. Chiang Kai-shek's government withdrew to Chungking, the principal town (though not the capital) of the remote province of Szechuan, which bordered on Tibet, and which since 1935 had been prepared by Chiang as the national capital in an emergency. Chiang was now following what proved to be his masterplan for the war: to trade space for time; to care little for loss of territory provided the centre of resistance remained intact, to put faith in the huge distances in China, and to hang on in spite of defeats.

Gradually the truth about the Chinese armies became known in the outer world, which had at first been inclined to credit that China had become better organized than it was in fact. The organization went to pieces. Soldiers went into battle as part of a modern military formation, but this usually broke under strain, and they became pockets of fighting men. Hence came much of the nightmare quality which made this one of the most awful periods of China's recent black record. Administration was primitive: corruption was extreme. Army medical services and hospitals scarcely existed, and soldiers who were only slightly wounded usually perished. Volunteer medical aid began to appear from the sympathetic countries of the West, but all its doctors could do was to add to the swelling chorus of lamentation.

Chungking was well beyond the gorges in the Yangtse, which are one of the beauty spots of China. To attack Chungking was to involve the Japanese in such problems of logistics that Chiang was safe there. The Japanese did not follow him farther. A very long pause set in. There was no more large-scale fighting for six years. It might have been supposed that the war had petered out.

*

Japan took stock of what it had gained. Superficially it had conquered territory which contained 170 million people. China had lost its principal sea ports. It depended henceforward for foreign supplies on two routes, one an earth road from Russia through Turkestan, the other a road from Chungking to the south which ended in Burma: both were very long, poorly constructed, and liable to traffic blocks. For a time it had been able to use Hanoi, in Indo-China, but the bridges which carried the railway line which linked this port with Yunnan (in south-west China) were destroyed.

Such heavy fighting was not to happen again, even when this war was eventually swallowed up in the Second World War, and when China's weapons were much strengthened by aid from its allies.

Japan estimated the number of Chinese who had been killed during this period as at least 800,000: its own dead numbered only 50,000. Probably this is an over-estimate of the one, and an under-estimate of the other. Yet there was a great gap between the losses on both sides. Japan suffered its first reverses in the occupied districts in the north. Its control of the railways and towns did not give it control of the rural areas. It began to feel severely the effects of communist guerrilla action.

At first it had supposed that it had the measures for repressing the communists, and, for a time, little was heard about the communist armies. This was to the dismay of the friends of China who had built up extravagant hopes on the reconciliation between Chiang and the communists. Eventually, though, the stubborn resistance of the communists began to take a toll. To have overcome it, to have attempted a stricter control which would have eliminated this, would have cost many millions of troops, which the Japanese could not afford. China had begun to draw the advantages from one of its assets, size. Because the Japanese could not pacify the vast areas of Hopei, Shantung, and Shensi provinces, which they had overrun, they constituted themselves as a target for guerrilla action.

Chiang Kai-shek sat in his fortress at Chungking and waited. The city, though not beautiful as is Chengtu, the capital of Szechuan, was fitted for its purpose. Rainfall was heavy, and the clouds which overhung it for weeks on end, together with surrounding mountains which made it difficult to approach, prevented it from being an easy target of attacks from the air. It was bombed heavily for a time, but later was left in peace. The city was large, and had once been affluent. Chiang's task was to keep his government in existence, to survive the plots against him, to plot against others – to continue to be regarded as the symbol of nationalism. Alas, though wartime propaganda made the reputation of Chungking as a heroic centre of resistance, a long, slow demoralization set in among the Kuomintang establishment, the inevitable result among an army and bureaucracy condemned to too much idleness, and this proved in the long run too much for Chiang Kai-shek to combat. The Chinese of the Kuomintang and the army staff were a different people from the particularist Szechuanese, who resented their impact on their ancient provincial culture. Relations between them and the local people deteriorated steadily. 'Down-river gangsters' was the term used for Kuomintang officials by the Szechuanese people. Internal rot was the price the Kuomintang paid for the tactics of masterly inactivity.

Chiang Kai-shek was resting his hopes, not in the Kuomintang army, but chiefly in foreign aid, principally in American aid, which his diplomats in the United States tirelessly sought. Certainly there was abundant American goodwill to China, based chiefly on the vast American missionary enterprise in China. It seemed that China, before the war, had been willing to reconstruct its society according to American ideas, and this seemed to impose on the United States the obligation of protecting it internationally.

As far as China was concerned, Japan now turned its back on battles and daring campaigns, and engaged in political warfare and in political intrigue. The only military action was a single attempt in June 1940 to force the Yangtse gorges, which ended at Ichang. Japan decided that to carry on the war was to bring complication after complication, and, from now on, explored ways to end it. From this time, 1939–40, the Japanese army sought peace in China as constantly and assiduously (though maladroitly) as it had previously sought war. It was out of the question to arrange to annex the vast territory it had overrun, and to rule it directly as the British used to rule India. The need for civil servants would be immense, beyond anything which Japan could supply. It turned in consequence to indirect rule, to organizing north China as a puppet state (similar in general shape to Manchukuo), which would be under the rule of a single man or body of men upon whose loyalty they could rely, because it would be clear that, with Japanese aid removed, they would collapse.

Their first thought was to use Chiang Kai-shek himself. If they could have detached him from his nationalism, and made it worth his while, Chiang would have proved an excellent puppet. He would have had a full and apparently contented life hunting down communists. Realizing how greatly an alliance with Chiang would serve them, understanding that this was indeed the crisis of the war, the Japanese used the utmost finesse to bring it about. But neither the secret emissaries whom they sent tirelessly to visit him, nor the German Ambassador who proposed mediation, brought the Japanese any hopeful news. Chiang had little room to manoeuvre in. He had made his way to the top of the Kuomintang, but he had become a prisoner of the national movement, which would have broken him if he had sought to betray it. Chiang, who knew the dark corners of China's political life, and availed himself of the services of its inhabitants, knew well what agents it would employ.

Reluctantly the Japanese decided on an alternative plan. They set themselves to persuade respected nationalists, who were opposed to Chiang Kai-shek, to form a government which had all the outward shape of the Kuomintang, and which the Japanese could substitute for the official Kuomintang. They had resort to one of the most distinguished members of the Kuomintang, who had been almost a founding father of the party.

This man, Wang Ching-wei, one-time Vice-President of the Kuomintang republic, had previously built a career on the leadership of the left wing. He had never exhausted the fame which he had gained by being involved in a plot in the days of the Empire to murder a Manchu grandee. In private, his views were anything but radical and he had married a very wealthy wife, who came from a family of Singapore millionaires. But his political talents had been acceptable to the revolutionary branch of the Kuomintang. After the fall of Canton and Hankow he seems to have accepted the Japanese argument that further resistance was useless, and to have argued that China, by recasting its foreign policy, could still come to terms with Japan which would be mutually advantageous. At Chungking, he conferred at length with Chiang Kai-shek. Though no record exists of their conversation, it is known that the two men debated in full the Japanese peace offer.

In December 1939 he recognized his failure, and left the capital. The Japanese were willing to see in him the best substitute head of a cooperative Chinese government. He had the aura of a major politician. He had the record of being a persistent rival of Chiang Kai-shek. Mostly Chiang had succeeded in keeping him out of office, and, when Wang Ching-wei had manoeuvred so that he compelled Chiang to share power with him, Chiang was suspected of a hand in the mysterious shooting which had removed him from office. The Japanese acted with resolution. Wang's name, the prestige of Nanking city, the attraction of the Kuomintang – renamed by Wang the Reformed Kuomintang – all these were used to give the new government such prestige as it could have in a Nanking which remembered vividly what it had been made to suffer.

The government came into being in 1940. A fairly long list of land-holders, industrialists, former officials, diplomats out of employment, politicians who had ruined their prospects with the official Kuomintang, came to see if the vistas opened up under the new administration appeared brighter for them. Many were recruited for the régime. Many of the more or less respectable Chinese nationalists had begun to find the régime of the Reformed Kuomintang very beguiling, especially since it reconciled nationalism with the prospect of opting out of the war. Wang Ching-wei's government was a copy of the genuine Kuomintang. Its constitution was much the same; it contained the complications and intricacies which had puzzled all those who tried to follow Chinese politics. Its methods of administration were much the same.

In administration the régime was slightly less corrupt than had been expected. It did little that was outwardly disgraceful. As the head of a puppet government, camouflaged for the general public in the colours of nationalism, Wang Ching-wei did neither more nor less than was expected of him: he fought for China's interests while being ready in the last resort to yield to Japan's superior strength. In China he played the same part as Marshal Pétain in France. But Wang's government never succeeded in living down the sense of national shame in which it was born; never managed to take independent life; it remained a creature of the Japanese; it never became a serious body internationally.

*

Meanwhile the pretence that the war was a joint one, of the Kuomintang and the communists against Japan, was wearing thin. The Chinese communists, in the regions which they had overrun in the north, maintained a lively propaganda against the Japanese. Guerrilla warfare was their special art. There was also activity by guerrilla bands who fought in the name of the Kuomintang. But the pretence, which had been built up immediately after the Sian incident, that the armies of the communists were to be fused with the armies of the Kuomintang under some kind of common command, never became a reality. The communists had no intention of surrendering the sole command of their army. That was their most effective instrument in Chinese politics, and they would hold on to it. The communists relied on their army to win them new territory, and to retain what they had got; and they could scarcely trust their old enemy, the Kuomintang, with any recognized power to dispose of this force.

A subtle, concealed, very bitter struggle was resumed between the Kuomintang and the communists. Everybody who was interested in Chinese politics saw the danger of revived civil war taking shape. The Kuomintang, without entirely dropping the mask of the common front, was alert to the spread of communist power, and tried to guard against it by maintaining, as far as it could, an inner blockade of the regions which the communists ruled, including an embargo on all medical supplies. The most competent and orderly section of the Kuomintang army was in fact left permanently at Sian, where its sole duty was to watch and over-awe the communists. The communists directed their fire equally against the Kuomintang and the Japanese.

Sometimes the struggle became too obvious for decency between apparent allies. Each side had its own territory. Sometimes the communists would move into a Kuomintang region: the Kuomintang would drive them out by force. At such times the hollowness of the partnership became plain. There was a particularly flagrant example of this in 1941 when the communist Fourth Route Army was ambushed by patent treachery, and fighting flared up on a large scale. The communists lost several generals in the course of this affair. But even at such times both the communists and the Kuomintang tried to put limits to hostilities. An important part in keeping peace at least formally was played by the communist representative at Chungking, who was Chou En-lai, destined in the next decade to become the prime minister of China. A competition was being fought out between the two governments, to determine which of them, in the harsh conditions of war, had the better spirit to endure. The war was proving a hothouse, and had brought on the decision which otherwise might have taken half a century to deliver. All the data were to the discomfiture of the Kuomintang. The communists, which began as very much the weaker, became a steadily greater force.

Meanwhile a part of the horrors which had overtaken the Chinese people became known to the West – to a West which was bracing itself to face its own agony. The full terrors of war broke over the Chinese towns and countryside. They had gradually become accustomed to civil war during the thirty years of breakdown of ordered government. In much of the country, the old magistrates had left. The armies of the warlords had harried the villages, seized their grain, and sometimes carried off the young men and women. But all this was very little compared with what befell in the years after 1936. One estimate puts the number uprooted from their homes by the war as 50 million. The Chinese are as a rule greatly attached to their villages, and will not forsake a home which contains the graves of their ancestors. Many of the cherished customs of the village – the sweeping of the family graves, ceremonial meals eaten over the tombs – are connected with tomb-rites. Now a great wrench had loosened the population from its hold. China dissolved from people living in orderly, extremely conservative patterns of life, into a maze of people wandering aimlessly from village to village. They sought food, protection, shelter. All China seemed to be restlessly on the move. Any representation of its people at this time shows them trudging from place to place, carrying their belongings with them. (A similar nightmare befell persons who were compelled to see the sights in post-war Germany.) How many perished in this time will never be known. Their plight made them powerless to escape the scourge of famine and the scourge of the other terror of the Chinese countryside, flood. One by one, the very ancient annual ceremonies in the villages, which gave Chinese life its admirable quality and its deep sense of continuity, were given up. Life became especially hard for the old, the class which Chinese civilization was notorious for revering.

Colour, richness and elegance disappeared from China. Everywhere people went dressed in simple cotton clothes, either because they had been impoverished, or because the slightest display of luxury was an invitation to plunder. The pleasantness and decorum of the life of the Chinese upper classes, which had already been much shaken for a hundred years due to the impact of the West, descended to a new calamitous level, as society gradually disintegrated. Only in such protected centres as Chungking was the attempt made to live in accustomed Chinese style.

A similar break-up of society had taken place in France at the end of the Hundred Years War, and in Germany during the Thirty Years War.

*

Early during this period there had taken place one of the most unlooked-for emigrations in history. As we have seen, the universities of China had a precocious development. In wealth, in their standing in society, by the personal eminence of their staff, both Chinese and also the core of expatriate foreigners, they were ahead of the standards which universities might have been expected to reach in the country, and were suited for a society such as China might have evolved two or three generations later. In consequence of this, much of the most advanced, the purest, and certainly the most disinterested nationalism of the day was nursed to life within their walls.

Most of the universities were on the seaboard in the path of the Japanese invasion. They were one of its special targets, because the Japanese, being themselves Far-Eastern people, understood (though Japan did not share in this peculiarity) the extraordinary influence which the Chinese intelligentsia had over the rulers of the nation. The Chinese student was alone among the student class of the world in not feeling, or feeling much less, an acute sense of frustration. Why should he? The nation hung on his moods, was willing to follow him in his attitudes to Ministers and public affairs. Since he was so influential, the student buoyed himself up: and the conditions he put up with in the student life, the squalid poverty, were felt to be the necessary price of privilege. Besides it was spread equally over the whole student body. Let them reduce the pride and aspiration of the intelligentsia, the Japanese told themselves, and they would have gone a long way in subduing Chinese nationalism. Under Japanese domination, the universities knew that they would face a purge, and the conditions of the new life would be quite intolerable to them. Rather than suffer it, many of the university communities moved off by spontaneous resolution, and trekked from the coasts to new sites far in the interior.

Chinese learning was pulling up its stakes and was seeking out a territory where it might exist in freedom; and, as the price to be paid for this, live a life less gilded than before. The professors and their assistants, the student body, and university servants, all sought a home where they could continue their life with less harassment. Previously, Chinese scholars had not taken kindly to manual work; now they voluntarily undertook the hardship of the journey, the uncertainties of what awaited them, and a life of toil. It was the more surprising because these learned societies had to leave palatial premises, which had been given them by millionaires and foreign philanthropists, and had to fit their academic life into camps which had been made available to them as exiles. Throughout their vicissitudes they had safeguarded their libraries and the equipment of their scientific laboratories. Many of them transported these across the rivers and mountains of inland China.

During the war years the Chinese intelligentsia continued their studies diligently. In view of the way in which learning was regarded this turned out to be the most useful thing which they could contribute to China's war effort. They had firmly aligned themselves with China's decision to resist Japan, and by their action in seeking voluntary exile they increased their prestige in the eyes of the people. The scholars and the mass of common people came closer together.

The universities, in deciding on their odysseys, were influenced by the example of the Chinese communists on the Long March. From this time there began to grow up the great sympathy of the Chinese scholar class for the communists. The scholars felt themselves being blown along by the same hurricane which had swept together the communist insurgents throughout China: and as the leadership of the Kuomintang began to falter, they began to look to the communists for an alternative. They did so with more eagerness because when they had migrated in the cause of freedom, they found that, when they eventually reached the security of the interior, they were regarded with suspicion by the Kuomintang, and that their freedom was interfered with by an irksome secret police. The campus was invaded by an army of spies.

The reliance on the secret police by Chiang Kai-shek to maintain his exaggerated political role was a departure from Chinese tradition. Before Chiang, China had known periods of despotism; but the despot had, to a remarkable degree, avoided the organization of a secret police as the instrument of tyranny. Even in the last years of the Manchus the government, though repressive, had avoided the creation of an organ specially for intelligence and coercion. Therefore the collisions which now became frequent between the literati and the secret police offered the more provocation because the Chinese had not been accustomed in the past to think of the police as a necessary evil.

The writings of Chinese academics became full of woe; they had exchanged the persecution of the Japanese for the supervision of the police. It was less efficient, less rigorous, but it was deeply offensive.

The grievances thus sown were to bear fruit at the end of the war. Without the moral approval of the scholar class, the Chinese communists would never have been able to impose themselves so successfully on the Chinese nation.

*

The setting in of the war in earnest brought a decisive change in the attitude of the westerners. Sentiment, which among some classes in Britain, for example, had for some time been anti-Japanese, hardened; and it spread throughout most sections of the people, at least of those, admittedly a minority, who thought it necessary to take a view about such a distant part of the world.

The change was marked in the early period of the Japanese adventure. Westerners with foreign contacts, especially the businessmen resident in the Far East, had on the whole been well disposed to Japan. Japan professed to be the champion of foreign business interests. It claimed to be taking steps – in putting down bandits, in removing the Chinese officials who were the bane of traders – which the other countries would have followed if they had had the resolution to stand up for their interests. Chinese xenophobia was the enemy of all who had to do with China. And, for a long while, Japanese action received a great deal of sympathy from certain sections of westerners.

This view continued to be held, at least until the war became merged with the Second World War. A section of businessmen, progressively smaller in number but still powerful in influence, maintained their regard for Japan. They thought that no comparison was possible between the Japanese, clever, energetic, industrious, above all disciplined and punctual, and the Chinese, who, if they were clever, had all the faults which went with political impotence; who were corruptible, were voluble in justifying the inexcusable, were argumentative without being convincing to the not very admirable representatives of the West. These liked the Japanese way of life, Japanese discipline and Japanese customs: though it should be noted that most of the things they admired were regarded by educated Japanese, who had kept some standards from the past, as vulgar. They liked the solidity of the buildings in western style which the Japanese had put up. Some of the westerners felt that the Japanese had very sensible ideas about the status of women. The comic side to this is that very few of its would-be admirers understood correctly the genius of Japan, which is aesthetic, non-intellectual, and not acquisitive, is swept by temporary enthusiasms, and taking the culture as a whole, does not admire the use of force.

But this view was not unchallenged. A rival section of western residents in Treaty Ports had backed the rise of the new China. From among these, there was, it is true, not at first a strong condemnation of Japan. Most of these people felt, secretly if not openly, that China had been moving too fast and too far, and that chastisement by Japan would bring it to reason. A series of murders and outrages had occurred in previous years: and Nanking did its cause no good by obvious deception and the pretence that it could not unravel the circumstances.

Western businessmen were less far-sighted, less impersonal than their governments. They had also a sense of racial superiority, which they had abandoned in the case of Japan, which had demonstrated that it could not be pushed around. Business was conscious of the great advantage of living in concessions under an extra-territorial régime. It lamented the fact that negotiation had begun for their abolition, and that many concessions had already been surrendered: it saw itself vitally threatened. There were some men of vision among them, who looked ahead and saw the future; but these men were rare. Americans, in spite of their general liberalism and of the pro-Chinese sentiment of many of their countrymen, were of the same temper as the others.

However, as the great offensive of the Japanese began to take shape and its direction passed from the Japanese civilian, whom the western businessmen used to know, into the hands of arrogant generals, with whom they did not feel at home, they began more and more to change their minds. The fear grew up that it was the Japanese, not the Chinese, who would chase them out of the concessions. Japan was spending its blood and treasure to make China into a place fit for a man to live in; but it was to be a Japanese businessman, an agent of the Mitsui and the Mitsubishi, not the foreigner whom the Japanese regarded as more undesirable than the Chinese. The western traders or industrialists saw that if they lost the protection under which they were living, they would not have a very long tenure of life. By controls, by subsidies, by taxation, by withholding permits to move their capital and profits out of the country, Japan would be able to drive them away in a brief time, and in less than ten years' time the concessions would be no more.

Thus the change of attitude had become almost universal, and the businessmen were as anxious as the Chinese when in July 1937 the fighting began in earnest. At least they could console themselves that there was an end for the time being to the negotiation for the return of the concessions. The Chinese defence of Shanghai happened before their eyes, and the rape of Nanking was near enough to cause acute discomfort, however cynical the businessman might be.

The Chinese did not lose hope of entangling foreign powers, including Britain, in the war at various of its stages. In 1937 the Japanese, perhaps unaware of who was their prey, had machine-gunned from the air a motorcar on the way from Shanghai to Nanking. In it was Sir Hughe Knatchbull Hugessen, the then British representative in China. He was seriously wounded, and for a few days this nearly fatal accident caused an electric tension. But the British could do little more than protest, and the incident was closed by an exchange of notes that were meant to save everybody's face. (Sir Hughe thus goes down in history as a diplomat who was nearly murdered and started a war. He is remembered also as the Ambassador in Turkey who had the plans of the Second Front filched by his valet who gave them to the Germans. The incident is described in the book *Operation Cicero*. Fortunately the Germans could not credit their good fortune, and assumed that false information was being planted on them.) Though feeling was shifting among even local business men from being pro-Japanese to being pro-Chinese, the British were resolved to go to great lengths to preserve their neutrality. All eyes in Britain were on the European continent; from 1938 there was almost constant crisis in Europe; Britain was not ready to allow any of its armed strength to be engaged in the Far East when every ounce of it was required in Europe.

There was a certain comedy as the British Ambassador in Tokyo, Sir Robert Craigie, fought out the battle on what should be British policy towards the war with Sir Archibald Clark-Kerr, the successor to Knatchbull Hugessen in China. Clark-Kerr had pronounced left-wing views, which were in favour of Britain supporting China on grounds of plain international morality. China was weak, was being bullied, and, he thought, should be protected. Craigie, in Tokyo, was fully convinced of the benefits which Britain had derived from the Anglo-Japanese alliance as long as this had existed. He saw the best hope in working for its revival. The pro-Japanese views of the British Embassy were reinforced by the peculiarly romantic view of Japanese history held by the British Military Attaché, General Piggott. The divergent views of the two representatives, at Chungking and at Tokyo, clashed with vigour in their telegrams and reports. Those who took part in this conflict were convinced that the issue was of first importance. They failed to recognize that the attention of London was otherwise engaged, and their respective views were not treated very seriously.

Similarly, the Americans in the area were divided about their policy. There were incidents between them and the Japanese, which stirred up American hopes, but nothing came of these. The war was fought at

Shanghai in a vastly overcrowded space, and inevitably the bystanders were hit. The USS *Panay*, an American gunboat in the Yangtse, was bombed and sunk. Whether some of the Japanese commanders desired to frighten the United States away, or the bombing was a mistake, was not known. The United States was in the heyday of its neutrality, took no action and patched up an agreement. But privately, the Americans were strengthened in an anti-Japanese frame of mind. The tide was running in support of the China lobby which was made up of businessmen, scholars, philanthropists, former missionaries, and other specialists on Asia. The China lobby was to become one of the powers of the land.

By 1939, when the European war began, many businessmen in the Far East recognized that their bright day was over: and that, once the Treaty Port system was disbanded, it would not be set up again. In this year there was the humiliation of the businessmen of Tientsin. A Chinese collaborator had been murdered in the British concession, and the Japanese demanded that two suspects, who had been arrested by the police of the British concession, should be surrendered to them. Pressed to accept this radical demand the British refused: and in consequence the Japanese blockaded the British concession. People still went in and out but at the cost of an exhausting wait and a humiliating bodily search. A smile of appreciation went through Asia, even among countries which approved of China and were against Japanese militarism. The Japanese, it seemed, were effectively putting down the mighty from their seats, and scattering the proud in the imagination of their hearts.

The Taipans, as the heads of firms were called, saw the clouds darken steadily, and could not see their way ahead. The European war was beginning. The British government was preoccupied with that, and there was little hope that they would do much for their countrymen at Shanghai or Tientsin.

Meanwhile Japan had been making itself conspicuously disliked by the classes which had no interest at all in residing in the Far East, but made their living at home in trade. For them, Japan mattered simply because of its commercial policy. In the thirties this became increasingly competitive. Japan felt an increasing need to increase its exports or to starve; and, under this compulsion, it became notorious as the country hunting for markets, successfully snapping up the old markets of older countries, ruthlessly underbidding, successfully dumping.

Japan, in short, was feared and disliked by everybody in an established position in world trade, who saw its activities with dread. This dislike of Japan for commercial reasons was carried over into an irrational anti-Japanese prejudice. Feeling tilted over and became pro-China and anti-Japan; it was reinforced by a modish fashion amongst the intelligentsia for all Chinese things. Nevertheless, commercial competition was at the root of the sentiment.

CHAPTER 8

India and the Conflict

AT the time of the clash between China and Japan, the surprising fact in the rest of Asia was that most of it was under western government. Much of India, for example, had been under British rule for 150 years. Nearly all the rest of the region had also passed into the empires, or spheres of interest, of one European power or another. Two ancient, but comparatively small, countries, Persia and Thailand, were the only exceptions. They owed their preservation to uncommon adroitness, aided by the fact that in each case two foreign powers were competing for dominance over their territories.

From the beginning of the 1920s India, the heart and core of this series of subject countries, had made a resolute and persevering effort to throw off western rule. It was a fair deduction that, if it succeeded, an end would be put to the lesser imperialisms of Europe in Asia. Their circumstances were in some respects dissimilar: their end would be the same. All Asia would be free. Moreover India had so central a position in Asia, was a country with such prestige and resources, that the way in which it reacted to the issues of the time would have the deepest consequences for its neighbours. An account of the war requires therefore that the affairs of India should be followed, that its quarrel with Britain should be recorded, that the degree at different times of its pro-Japanese sentiment should be remarked, and its role in Japanese strategy examined. It demands also an inquiry into the different quality of British imperialism from Japanese which made the British Empire, even in its decay, by contrast so durable.

*

The major part of India was conquered by Britain between 1757 and 1820. The form of conquest was straightforward military annexation, but of a somewhat unusual kind. The conquest was not premeditated by Britain. A British trading company, the Honourable East India Company, had begun to trade peaceably in India. It was sucked into intervening in the management of Indian affairs by the anarchy which followed the downfall in the eighteenth century of the Moghul empire. Out of its activities, the British government, which had gradually assumed control of the political responsibilities of the company, eventually found itself the master of a great military empire.

The British Raj was unique in having been set up by a people which used no large standing army of its own countrymen for the purpose. Alone among governments which pursued an active imperialist role Britain operated with such a small army of its own that its aims seemed derisory. It was much too small for Britain to have played any notable part on the continent of Europe, and it might have seemed too small to undertake operations on other continents. The empire was won, not by British forces in the main, but by dexterous political manoeuvre, and by the Indian forces who chose to fight on the British side in a situation where there were several claimants for their arms. The East India Company, which was in India for trade, became, to all intents and purposes, one of the native powers between which India was divided; and from being one of these native powers it became gradually the paramount native state. It raised and paid for native armies which won for it territories for which it had to provide an administration: and this, though informed by British concepts, continued in many respects the traditional administration. The predominance of the company was due primarily to the coherent political organization which it imported into India. It was also due, initially, to superior military technique, but when other native powers through foreign advisers imported the technology, it was due to superior discipline and organization.

Those statesmen of the company who had conceived the policy, and saw where it tended, had usually to draw along their reluctant colleagues, who were always saying that a trading company had no right to be considering policies which would thrust upon it unwelcome political responsibilities. Nevertheless the bolder spirits prevailed, and they succeeded in their manoeuvres with startling ease. Thus Britain, which was five thousand miles away, found itself with an empire which it had never, in its deliberate moments, set itself to acquire. It had gained it with the minimum military force; and it held it by the stiffening effect of a garrison of British troops which, in normal circumstances, amounted to no more than 60,000 men. It would have been impossible with such a puny force to have held down a genuine national movement, and to have ruled India by the sword. British government thus rested, in the deepest meaning, upon the consent of the people to be governed. Its continuance depended on the tacit ballot that this government afforded benefits which the majority of the people accepted, either from apathy or from general appreciation of it.

The reason why the British had made such an easy conquest of the country was that for the most part a stubborn defence was never encountered. The country changed hands while the peasantry, from which a popular army would have to be recruited, looked on. This followed an old tradition of India. Observers of the country from earliest historical times had often exclaimed with wonder at the detached attitude of the peasantry, who went on with their agricultural tasks, ignoring a pitched battle of their betters which might be taking place a few hundred yards from them, and on which their destiny depended. Not all the conquests were as easy as this. The East India Company had to fight hard, for instance, against the Marathas and Sikhs, who both had organized military kingdoms of a formidable nature. But even with them, the kingdoms were the armies: once these were defeated the East India Company had no more to do: there was no great popular resistance to wear down. Popular feeling against the foreigner interfering in the political affairs of the country is mainly a product of the twentieth century.

*

In this take-over of India there was no intention on the part of the British to produce a social transformation. As regards forms of society, the British were willing to leave things put. This was in some part due to the fascination and esteem which Indian life, in all its astonishing variety, exercises over the spirits of those who encounter it. It was also due to the realization that any interference with existing customs was likely to cause trouble. For example, the British were at first reluctant to give any countenance to Christian missionaries. Later, with the growth of evangelism in the nineteenth century in England the resistance to missionaries was partly eroded; but the mutiny of 1857, which stemmed from the mistaken belief of Indian soldiers that the British intended to force Christianity upon them, demonstrated the wisdom of non-interference. Thereafter social change was on the whole carefully refrained from. Profound social changes did, in fact, take place, but these were the inevitable result of the impact of a modern, highly industrialized society, such as Britain became, on an archaic, predominantly agrarian one. They were part of a world-wide trend, and not peculiar to the relations of Britain and India.

It was in the sphere of politics and administration that the struggle for sovereignty developed in India, and it was here that interesting forms were evolved. Nearly all the strains of thought in political philosophy in Britain during a century and a half found at one time or another reflection in the institutions of India. At the end of the eighteenth century the main preoccupation was to protect the individual citizen against arbitrary power, and to put government in the shackles of regular procedure controlled by courts. Then for a while the dominant interest was the philosophy of utilitarianism. One Governor General, Lord William Bentinck, was a close disciple of Bentham, and for forty years James Mill, and his son John Stuart Mill, held key positions in the office of the East India Company. Certain questions were endlessly discussed, for instance, the case for direct administration by the British and the case for indirect administration; the duty of the government to promote change, and its duty to shield people against too rapid change; the virtues of control from above and the virtues of self-government; and the discussion resulted in action, or in some cases inaction – for instance, after the mutiny of 1857 there was no extension of direct British rule. Some of the shrewdest minds in Britain, from Victorian times to the late 1930s, found the Indian government more malleable to ideas than society in the West. A philosophically inclined visitor to India towards the end of the nineteenth century said that a trip there was like re-living his life as a student of politics at Oxford.

The civil service in British India became remarkable for its quality. In the kingdoms and empires of the sub-continent in the past, the central governments found it traditionally very hard to get anything done. Their acts might be sporadically vigorous and imaginative, but the sum total of their deeds was slight: it disappeared quickly in sand. The Indian Civil Service, first instituted by the British, and then increasingly operated by both British and Indians, gave India for the first time an instrument by whose means government could carry out reforms which were pushed through to the end. Such was the prestige, the intelligence, and the standard of service to the community of this body of men that, even when the freedom struggle was at its height, distinguished Indian families, including the Nehrus, sent some of their sons into government service while others were operating in the opposition movement. The ideal of the Indian Civil Service was to gain willing acceptance of the policies and actions of the government. To be compelled to use force at all was, therefore, regarded as a mark of failure; and its excessive use was rarely forgiven. This was a reflection of the fact that from the beginning of the Raj the number of Englishmen in India was far too small for them to govern the country arbitrarily and with incessant use of force. In the last years of British rule the British members of the administrative class of the civil service numbered less than a thousand, and in the subordinate services they hardly existed, whereas the population of India by the beginning of the war had swollen to three hundred and fifty million, or one sixth of the population of the world.

Although, through the British period, government was carried on chiefly by the civil service, India was also by stages equipped with free institutions. Because Britain, in the grip of nineteenth-century liberal ideas, knew only one way of being politically constructive, it instinctively introduced into India representative councils and assemblies and the whole apparatus of liberal democracy. At the beginning these councils were largely consultative, but they contained seeds which grew, and which decided that the struggle for freedom in India would take the form of a demand for parliamentary rule.

Constitutional reforms in India were partly a response to, and partly they stimulated the Indian national movement. That the transition from subjection to independence in India came in the end with such remarkable ease and restraint on both sides was due chiefly to three things: the liberal institutions set up in India by the British: the genius of Mahatma Gandhi, for many years the leader of the national freedom movement: and the quickening of a new age in Asia, and new ideas and a new type of British personality in India, as a direct result of the Japanese war.

*

On the Indian side, a vital factor in the struggle for independence was the emergence of a new Indian middle class. This class adopted English as its language, and owed its existence to the mass of institutions which the Raj fostered. Some members of it adapted themselves so phenomenally well to English culture that they became, to all intents and purposes, Englishmen. They lived in English style. They spoke English in their homes. Perhaps there is no comparable case in modern history of a class taking over so completely and with such ease the culture and language of another people: the parallel in the past is the assimilation of Latin culture by the provincials of the Roman Empire. Not that these families lost all touch with India; the women especially carried on the old Indian tradition, and in the deeper layers of the mind, the Indian structure persisted. But in practical action most of the men thought, felt, acted like Englishmen, and made very much the same value judgements. This victory of an alien personality was seen at times as a doubtful advantage to India; its psychological effects were frequently lamented by the social group in which it took place; but in the long run such fusions of culture are prized by the countries in which they occur, provided the assimilation is complete. The most surprising instance of this deep westernization is usually masked. Gandhi, the man under whose leadership the independence of India was achieved, a man who always stressed that he was a Hindu, the heir of the Hindu tradition; who wore Indian clothes, or very few clothes at all in the manner of Indian holy men, was nevertheless profoundly influenced by ideas from Britain. Equality of citizens, non-doctrinaire socialism, his apotheosis of the individual conscience, his social experimentation, prohibition, feminism, nationalism itself – this was the British tradition, not perhaps of government, but of radical non-conformism. Here, it might be said, was an example rare in history, of Rome making Greece its captive, not vice versa.

This westernized Indian middle class, though numerically very small, became immensely important, and in the eyes of the rest of the world, it *was* Indian, spoke for India, represented India. As it matured, it inevitably took to nationalism, and the Indian patriot became the most typical example of the nationalist in his time. He was the most eloquent in denouncing imperialism – often in admirable English prose. He demanded the most fiercely to be liberated. He was the most confident, and with reason, of being able to operate by himself the institutions amongst which he had passed his life. Some years before the First World War, Indian nationalism was already vigorous. At first the nationalists had been divided between revolutionaries and constitutionalists. The revolutionaries, who carried on old Indian traditions of romantic protest, wanted root and branch overthrow of British rule, and terrorism seemed to be their best instrument. By contrast, the constitutionalists did not expect to end British rule by a lightning stroke; but by forming political parties, by entering the representative assemblies, by propaganda, and by accepting and operating the political systems which Britain was setting up, they expected to be able to bring enough pressure on the government to make their voice felt in its decisions. They were buoyed up and encouraged by the support which they received throughout from radicals in Britain. This active lobby in Britain for Indian independence was an important factor in convincing Indian nationalism that constitutionalism would give results. After a time, terrorism lost its glamour, and the majority of nationalists opted for constitutional action, or only mildly unconstitutional action; and, with aberrations at times when crises came to a head, they remained faithful to this course.

On the British side there were, at times, explosive strains. There were, occasionally, violent men in the civil service and in the army, and until the end the danger existed below the surface that in an emergency they might react brutally. Once violence had started it would have grown by its own momentum and both sides might have drifted into open war.

An outrage occurred shortly after the First World War in the massacre at Amritsar. This town in the Punjab was the scene of demonstrations in which mobs got control of the city and martial law was proclaimed in the area. An Indian assembly convened in defiance of an order, was caught in a walled space, with inadequate exits, and a British general, General Dyer, ordered troops to open fire. As a result, nearly four hundred unarmed people were killed. That this atrocity should have taken place, and even been approved by a section of British opinion, was a shock to Indian leaders. But there were denunciations in London; those in parliament were led with much force by Winston Churchill. The repudiation by the British government of General Dyer was one of the factors which strengthened Indian nationalism in its belief that it could win freedom by relatively restrained means.

The chief organ of the freedom movement, the Indian National Congress, was led during the crucial years by one of the most extraordinary figures of history, Mahatma Gandhi. Gandhi's outstanding qualities were a combination of a peculiar gentleness with inflexible determination: his religious temperament, natural in an Indian, was allied with a practical ability, unusual in seers, to shape events to some extent in the light of his understanding. Gandhi made Indian nationalism self-confident: he fed it with imaginative ideas and moral fire. Avoiding the dreary tactics of terrorism and guerrilla warfare, he perfected the weapons of civil disobedience and non-violent resistance. Some of his methods, at first, struck his lieutenants in Congress as too ingenuous; for instance, Gandhi proposed a famous march to the sea, to defy the law and make salt, on which there was a very light tax. Congress regarded it as a useless demonstration and agreed to it only in order to humour him. But it set India alight, and demonstrated a method of inducing popular uprisings which was to be of first importance to Congress in their later campaigns. He pursued his ends undeviatingly, but discriminated about means: thus, in the greatest of human traditions, he made politics a branch of ethics. The moral reason for all his major decisions was clearly laid in view, and even if a sophisticated onlooker might sometimes think that he deceived himself, and that the moral judgements on which he based himself were sometimes the flexible handmaids of political experimentation, his concern with principle was authentic, never hypocritical, and it affected those who dealt with him. An English judge, sentencing him on one occasion to a prison term 'for sedition', addressed Gandhi, as he stood before him in the dock, in words which illustrate the effect he had on his political opponents:

It would be impossible to ignore the fact that in the eyes of millions of your countrymen you are a great patriot and a great leader. Even those who differ from you in politics look on you as a man of high ideals and of noble and even saintly life . . .*

The whole character of Indian history in this period is the collusion, unspoken and hardly admitted, between the British power and Gandhi. For thirty years they fought each other, but cooperated tacitly in preventing the fight from getting out of hand. Both acted as if guided by the maxim of Machiavelli that you should treat your enemy as if he may one day become your friend. Because of the phenomenon of Gandhi's personality, a momentous struggle for freedom was fought, resolutely on both sides, but with an almost cheerful cordiality on both sides, and in a way which enabled both sides to be reconciled and to cooperate when it was over.

The climax of the struggle before the war was the civil disobedience campaign of Congress of 1930. Civil disobedience covered a variety of activities aimed at bringing government to a standstill – strikes, boycotts of British goods and services, and especially of foreign cloth, non-payment of taxes, and massive demonstrations, which were remarkably non-violent in the main, but on a scale large enough to alarm the authorities. The police arrested prisoners on a large scale: the prisons were overflowing, and special camps had to be organized. By these means the British government in India felt that it had been able to prevent revolution and to maintain its power. But the years 1931–2 marked a watershed. The government realized that although a rebellion had been broken, it could not repeat the operation, and that, if it tried to do so, it would strain too far the allegiance of the Indians among the civil service and the police. The issue from this period was over the timing of the programme for self-government. While some of the diehards among the British were holding back on grounds of prestige, in other quarters in England and in British India there was anxiety on the more reasonable grounds that India was full of centrifugal and communal strains, and too hasty a withdrawal might lead to breakdown of government.

Congress, on the other hand, regarded the Government of India Act of 1935 as insufficient, although they were about to give it a trial. This Act had been thrashed out in a series of monumental deliberations in London, in which Mahatma Gandhi had taken part as the representative of Congress. It provided for parliamentary government and democratically elected Indian Ministers both in the central government at

*B. R. Nanda: *Mahatma Gandi*, Allen & Unwin, 1958.

Delhi, and in the provinces. It retained, however, a British authoritarian element in two vital subjects: foreign affairs and defence. The demand of Congress at this time was for full Dominion status.

*

On 3 September 1939 the war began between Britain and Germany, and India was declared by the British government to be also at war. It had no adequate cause of dispute with Germany to justify this declaration, and the Indian leaders said so forcibly. Nehru, it was true, and the more liberal leaders of Congress, shared the sense of outrage at Nazi misdeeds which was experienced by similar leaders in Europe. Nehru, while visiting England in the previous year, had written in the *Manchester Guardian* criticizing the policy of appeasement towards Germany. Gandhi, writing in his own newspaper, *Harijan*, after war broke out, expressed condemnation of Hitler and moral support for Britain and France, although as a pacifist he also condemned the fighting. The more reactionary Indian leaders were indifferent: not that they would have condoned Germany's brutalities had they credited them: they wrote them off as inventions of British propaganda. But since no attempt had been made to consult Indian opinion through any representative institutions, how, asked the Indians, could there be any sincere talk of a war for democracy when the war was begun in such an undemocratic way? As a result, the Congress Party resigned from the government, withdrew from the eight provincial Ministries which it held, and recorded its extreme disapproval of all the acts of British officialdom.

Yet India did not protest very effectively against the German war. Several divisions of its army fought in the Middle East, gaining battle honours at which even Indian nationalists were, paradoxically, rather proud. In one province of India the war was genuinely popular. This was in the Punjab, which was traditionally the chief recruiting ground for soldiers, and where the provincial government had not considered resigning. The Punjab actively demonstrated in favour of the war, and regarded as enemies those who were lukewarm in its service. Surprisingly accurate knowledge of the ups and downs of war strategy began to circulate in Punjab villages. Elsewhere the war, simply as war, began to appeal to the so-called martial classes. Anything to do with it – news about it, the social and economic changes consequent on it – interested them as trenching on their monopoly in life.

But by the rest of India the war was treated with indifference: with neither the excitement caused by the sense of genuine change in the air, nor with the alarm caused by the knowledge that India was compassed about by real dangers, some of which might soon hit India very hard. The fact that the war was to be enlarged, that a new enemy was at hand by means of whom the war would be transformed, that through no initiative of its own India was to be placed in its vanguard, and that invasion was to be a very near possibility, would jerk it out of its previous apathy. It would go to bed at night and get up in the morning with war at its elbow, instead of viewing it academically at a safe remove. The extension of the war would be the signal for a new phase of the freedom struggle to begin.

Part II

OCEAN CLASH

CHAPTER 9

The War changes its Character

THUS far the war had chiefly concerned China and Japan. Japan was aggressive towards China; considerations of how far this affected Japan's relations with other countries were peripheral. But from this time onwards, Japan's relations with the Great Powers became the prime concern of its government. The war between China and Japan became increasingly difficult to limit to a private war; Japan was faced with problems, rising out of this war, each one of which caused it to consider afresh its policy towards other powers. Sometimes it experimentally remoulded its policies towards them, only to change them again, with all the repercussions which such instability led to. Japan's policies became very uncertain. No settled principles guided its action.

Actually, since the days of the Anglo-Japanese Alliance, Japan had pursued a wavering foreign policy, spreading everywhere a diffuse suspicion. It had no sure base in a firm agreement with a Great Power. But until a late period, it seemed that its special, inexorable opponent was Russia. Suspicion of and hostility towards Russia governed its designs. One product of this attitude of mind had been the signing by Japan of the Anti-Comintern Pact with Germany in 1936. This was an alliance which somewhat nebulously pledged the partners to resist the infiltrations of Communism, and, in a secret clause, bound them to withhold aid from Russia should either party be involved in hostilities with the USSR.

Since even before Commodore Perry's expedition in 1853, which marked the opening of Japan's modern period of history, there was special meaning in Japan regarding Russia as its hereditary enemy. Russia, as the perpetual threat, had penetrated into the folklore of the people. Ever since the end of the last century, it had regarded Russia as the Great Power against which it was destined to fight for survival. In 1904–5 it had fought the first round; it was convinced that it would have to fight again. When Russia was stricken by the Revolution, Japan seized the chance and took part in the allied intervention against it. For a time it occupied a large part of eastern Siberia. Its army was persuaded finally to withdraw, but as a result relations between the army and the civil government became seriously strained. It was an example of the situation that was often to develop in the future, but this time the civilian government, using one of the anti-imperialist swings in public opinion which at the time alternated with moods of aggressive nationalism, had prevailed in restraint of the military. The army felt that it had been ordered to drop its prey when it had been certain of it, and the sense that the civilian government could not be trusted continued to weigh with it.

After Manchukuo came into being in 1932, Japan stationed there a large part of the Japanese army. This did not disguise the fact that its eyes were on war with Russia; all its training and manoeuvres were made with Russia as the certain adversary. Exchanges between the two countries became increasingly explosive.

In July 1938 Japan deliberately picked a quarrel with Russia in the Far East and systematically set out on the task of trying out the Russian defences to see whether Russia could be made to vacate its forward positions on the frontiers of Manchuria by a show of force. It selected a spot where the frontiers of Korea, the USSR and China meet. It demanded that Russia should withdraw it forces from the area. In spite of a convincing Russian argument, from a treaty map of 1886, that it was in the region by right, the Japanese attacked with a division and took the hill called Cheng Ku Feng.

The next week Russia replied. The area disputed was visited by General Zhukov, later to be covered with many laurels. He moved up heavy formations and overwhelmed the Japanese in a prolonged pitched battle: and the Japanese for a few months were quiet.

It is an interesting fact, showing in what a desert the war was fought, that this incident, which involved tanks, artillery and aviation, was reported in the British press in a quite inadequate way. Very few people heard that there had been large-scale fighting. All eyes were on Europe: Asia was licensed to be in upheaval, and not to be noticed. Nevertheless, it is surprising that with the probable conduct of the Red Army in war still an enigma, more regard was not paid to its striking success against the Japanese. Russia fought this action under the handicap that its army, especially the officer corps, was under the strain of being visited by Stalin's purge. The Russian commander in the Far East, the celebrated and experienced Marshal Blucher, was one of the victims during this time.

Next year, there was a repetition of these incidents. Japan considered that it was progressing. It was satisfied in part with its exploration of whether Germany was fated to be its sure and certain ally – the successor to Britain. In preparation for this it allowed it to become known that it relied on the Germans to handle Russia. This time the place was Nomonhan, on the Outer Mongolian frontier. In the middle of May the Japanese attacked unexpectedly and drove away the Mongol frontier guards. The Russians issued an official warning that, by virtue of its defence treaty with Mongolia, it would treat any further incidents on the Mongolian frontier as if it were aggression against the Soviet Union.

Japan decided to test whether Russian deeds would match Russian words. In July it sent an expedition of 30,000 men to Nomonhan: artillery, tanks and planes. The Russians replied resolutely. There was fierce fighting for well over a month; a whole division of the Japanese force was annihilated. While the fighting lasted, the Russo-German non-aggression pact, the pact which surprised Europe and was the signal for European war, was announced. This shocked Japan. It was regarded by Japan as a betrayal of its experimental advances with the tighter links with Germany, the more audacious disregard of Britain and the United States. Its immediate effect was to bring back to positions of influence in Japan the representatives of the more old-fashioned groups which looked back with nostalgia to the old days of the Anglo-Japanese Alliance, and who felt that no confidence was to be placed in new friends. There was a tendency to walk more cautiously for a period. Partly because of this, Japan was willing to wind up the Nomonhan incident, even though it was by an agreement which was interpreted by all concerned as a Japanese concession of a reverse. Moreover, it became known that Japan was feeling shock and anger at the lack of reliance it could place on its new friend, Germany.

There was no more fighting. The frontier gradually fell quiet. Even the small-scale incidents, the constant shooting and skirmishes, the espionage and incitements, which had from the start seemed natural to the relationship between these two powers, dwindled. There was plenty of rumour, and the outbreak of war on the frontier was still regarded as a very natural possibility by the Japanese. The psychology had not changed: Japan remained malevolent towards Russia. Russia was still regarded, with deadly cold hostility, as a national enemy, in a way in which China, even at the height of the war between the two governments, was not. But it became clear that in one way Japan had changed its behaviour. Unless it was attacked in Manchuria, it was content to do no attacking.

An unnatural peace slowly spread throughout the border. In this region not a shot was fired, while, in other parts of the world, fighting broke out with great savageness.

*

The key to Japan's policy was still the Sino-Japanese war. With this overwhelmingly in mind, it approached the matter of its relations with the western countries in the war which was beginning in Europe.

When the Japanese found that Chungking would not make peace with them, they became convinced that it was enabled to continue fighting, and was encouraged to keep up a hopeless resistance, because of the aid given to it by the western powers. In fact, China was complaining desperately because of the shortage of war supplies. The aid that it received was a trickle, which the Japanese greatly exaggerated. They became convinced, however, that only the severance of the link with outside powers would bring an end to the China adventure. The war was telling upon the Japanese, and most groups were anxious to be free of it. Some of them had begun to think that it had been too lightly embarked on.

The outbreak of the war in Europe in 1939 seemed to give Japan its opportunity to bring pressure to bear upon the countries which persisted in maintaining relations with China. Japan, on the world stage, found itself in much the same position as it had been in the war of 1914–18. The direction which it might take had suddenly magnified its value very greatly. For Britain especially, whether it remained strictly neutral or sided with the Axis powers was a life or death matter. Japan saw that a new bargaining opportunity had opened up. There was an unfamiliar flexibility in its international relations. Out of the international situation, by blackmail or cajolery, Japan could expect to bend the attitude of other powers in such a way as to tilt the whole of the Far East under firm Japanese hegemony.

Already from 1938 Japan, partly under the impetus of patriotic parties which increasingly dictated its policies, partly because of the weakening position of its rivals in the Far East, drifted into a steady widening of its powers in the region. The stage was being set for its collision with the US. It became convinced that it was practicable to clear the Far East of American influences. The United States, while avoiding aggressiveness, had no intention of vacating.

First, however, Japan sought to apply its growing power to complete the isolation of China, and thus to compel it to bring the Sino-Japanese war to an end. Japan's force had, as immediate object, the task of cutting off the links which enabled China, though beaten in the field, to refuse peace.

Chiang Kai-shek, in his retreat to Szechuan, had two life-lines to the West. There was a road through north-west China, occupied by the Chinese communists, down which there filtered a little oil from Russia, and some Soviet personnel. But it was clear to anyone who was at Chungking at this time that the channels of communication which were most valued were those with the Anglo-Saxon powers. It was on these – first on a railway through Indo-China which had its outlet at Hanoi, and later after it was wrecked by bombing, on an earth road through Burma, and still later on an air lift from Calcutta direct to Chungking – that Kuomintang eyes were riveted. The Japanese were right in supposing that as long as these remained open China would feel that it was not cut off from support from the West. However little was flowing at the moment, as long as the communication remained open, the hope endured that more might be made to flow. Especially if they put their trust in a turn in events making it appear more a matter of material interest to the West that they should put out aid to China. But always the hinge of China's fate depended on these communications remaining open. Always Japan saw the most immediate way to force an end to the war lay in interrupting these tenuous lines of communication.

The outbreak of war in Europe in 1939 gave Japan its opportunity. In the middle of 1940, after the fall of France, when Britain was in its most desperate condition, it demanded that Britain should close the Burma road. Britain was in no condition to refuse. Churchill demurred but in the end gave way. But he agreed only for a three months period, at the end of which the aid again flowed, though in minute quantity. It was enough to give China hope.

*

Japan came increasingly to collide with the other Anglo-Saxon power, the United States. The clash with the United States, which at first had seemed a passing incident of its China policy, swelled up until it came to dominate all Japan's foreign relations. The need to free itself from American pressure in its plans for the future of the Far East became an obsession with Japan.

Japanese relations with the United States had been worsening for years. They had taken a steady decline from the days of the Russo-Japanese war, at which time the United States had been very sympathetic towards Japan, and relations had been cordial. In those distant days the United States had the characteristic of not basing its sentiments in foreign relations so solidly on self-interest as did the other Great Powers. It gave more play to national feelings in favouring and disfavouring countries. America was temperamentally drawn to the underdog; Japan seemed to be a small Goliath.

Afterwards the relations became less good as Japan became a great naval power and a threat to the American domination of the Pacific. Simultaneously, the American policy in 1924, forbidding emigration to the United States, which it pursued with the maximum resolution and the minimum regard to sparing Japan's feelings, made Japan reconsider its sentiments towards the US. To Japan the United States was the insensitive Great Power, blocking Japan's progress, and exhibiting a dynamism which propelled them both towards an inevitable collision.

When the Manchurian affair happened, the United States quickly disclosed a policy which it was to follow with remarkable consistency. It would have nothing to do with the League of Nations or with collective attempts at restraining Japan as an aggressor. That was ruled out by the overwhelming strength of American isolationism. American opinion was behind isolation as the only way of preserving the United States from involvement in war: and it recognized that in isolating itself, it was cutting itself off from the possibility of influencing the course of world affairs. Many enlightened Americans chafed at this. But it was accepted by most realist Americans that the United States had no alternative in the state to which it had been brought by the many-sided propaganda to which it was subjected.

The United States was unwilling to draw the conclusion from its inactivity that it would acquiesce in the map of the world being redrawn by force. It declared that it would never recognize changes which were brought about by aggression. There was, it must be admitted, something slightly ridiculous in the spectacle of the United States refusing to recognize the facts brought about by war, but declining to do anything to prevent these changes. It was living in a fool's paradise. But the policy was calculated to bear fruit in the future: as in fact it did. By persistently refusing to recognize Japan's coups in defiance of international law, by obstinately declining to regard Japan as ever succeeding in closing a door, by leaving open every issue for regulation in the future, the United States managed to undermine, with surprising success, Japan's various steps at building its empire.

The United States, however, was peculiarly self-distrustful. It had had, in the First World War, the experience of being drawn into the fighting partly, as it decided afterwards, against its better judgement. Probably, when the war was over, a majority of the people, if their opinion had been tested in a plebiscite, would have opined that the war was a mistake. If they had had a second chance, they would have kept out. They believed that America had been over-persuaded by subtle propaganda. They were intent on warning their fellow countrymen to beware of all plots to make them go further than they meant.

So, when the second war broke out, most Americans, though their sympathies were for the most part engaged against Hitler and his supporters, were firmly against American participation in the war. They were bent on saving the United States from itself. Just because they wished for Hitler's defeat, they were suspicious that the United States would come under pressure to depart from its neutrality: they therefore sought to provide against American force being employed in his overthrow, and that the United States should not be officially engaged in war. They went to extraordinary lengths in devising laws which would tie up the American executive, and prevent it from drifting into war. Of the fetters by which the United States bound itself, the most remarkable was the Neutrality Act: a law which aimed at prohibiting the United States from engaging in commerce with either of the belligerents which might involve the country in warlike attitudes. The Neutrality Act had been passed by the US Congress in the teeth of opposition by the administration. It was made possible by the American constitution, which sharply divides the legislature from the executive.

Because of this resolution to maintain the peace, because of the peculiar institutions by which the American resolve was enforced, Japan was to a large extent protected from the consequences of its actions. The Neutrality Act was a product of the fear of war with Germany, but Japan derived the benefit of it. There had never before in world history been such a peculiar case of a Great Power deliberately tying itself up, and ensuring that in no circumstances should it act as it would have been natural for it to do. The consequences, the way that the United States responded to pressure from Japan, were curious. True, it was possible for the American government to thwart in various ways the intentions of the American Congress, but the laws were rigid, and there were limits to the degree to which they could be transgressed.

All the time, some powerful American personalities and groups were warning the country that Japan on the march was a threat to the security of the United States. Each Japanese thrust – the rape of Manchuria, the rupture with the League of Nations, the war with China which had set in in earnest in 1937, the blowing of the wind in Japan of a revolutionary assertiveness – caused the warning to be louder. American opinion became troubled. It had reacted with little force to the beginning of the crisis in 1931 when Japan had seized Manchuria; ten years later, Japan's moves were followed with tense interest by many people in the United States. At first the concern over Japan was largely regional, being found especially on the West coast, which had trading connections with Asia. Gradually it became more widespread.

Fortifying this group of people who would have liked the United States to take an active role in Asia was the China lobby. This became for some years an influential pressure group in American politics. The active and practical minded found themselves in an open conspiracy for bringing pressure to bear in Congress upon all matters in which Chinese interests were engaged. The curious thing was that in the United States this group was so intent, and generated so much emotion. Other countries, Britain for example, had had sectional groups which, by the accident of their history, had been equally exposed to the lure of Chinese civilization, a force which habitually proved attractive to minds of a certain type. But a Chinese lobby, in the sense in which it was known in the United States, never operated in British politics.

Japan probably failed to give due weight to the importance of the China lobby in the United States. It always mistook American politics: that was one of its features. Japan had, it is true, some experts on the US who were well-informed: but they were not attended to. The Japanese, especially those who made Japanese policies, believed, and acted on the principle, that the United States, whose soul was given up to commerce, could not prevail over a nation of Samurai warriors, whatever material advantages it seemed to possess. They misread American history. They took no account of the fact that, after the compromises and the prevarication of the democratic system, the United States had shown itself able to go to war, and to wage it with an obsessive stubbornness until its objects were achieved.

*

From September 1940 to July 1941 Matsuoka Yosuke was the Foreign Minister of Japan. It was a critical period in Japan's foreign relations; and he was a new and unusual man to handle them. He came from a different background from those who were normally appointed to that office. He had made his reputation as a business executive, working for the South Manchuria Railway. By temperament he was rather like the type of man who, in an earlier generation, had made the Meiji Restoration. He was abrupt, conceited, gauche, and impatient of the respect for old men which Japanese civilization, being partly Confucian, has usually shown. He was exaggeratedly westernized, or at least he had adopted wholeheartedly the characteristics which he thought to be the essence of western culture. At the same time, he was exaggeratedly xenophobic, and opposed the United States and Britain to the limit.

He began by negotiating Japan's adhesion to a Triple Alliance with Germany and Italy. The treaty, which was signed in September 1940, was subtly conceived. It was primarily directed against the United States: it was intended chiefly to immobilize the United States and to deter it from too active intervention in the Far East and in Germany's wars in Europe. It stipulated that if any power – and the United States was particularly intended – attacked one of the three signatories, or should, by giving economic aid, threaten to affect adversely to them the conflict then taking place, the other two should come to its aid. The United States rightly interpreted this as an attempt to put fetters upon its freedom of action, and a Japanese withdrawal from the pact became one of its demands upon Japan. The pact was aggressive: but on the whole, it could be regarded as operating to prevent the spread of war.

Matsuoka conducted his foreign policy on the principle of *sacro egoismo*. In the spring of 1941, filled with this spirit, he made a tour of Russia and Germany. Before he went he had been in favour of committing Japan up to the hilt for Germany, giving it his warm support and leading it to suppose that it would have Japan's military backing if it attacked Russia. He was convinced that Germany was the winning power, and that only by being among Germany's associates would Japan gain in the eventual share-out of the world at a peace settlement. He was restlessly aware that Japan could pluck great profit from the disorders of the world, and he feared that if it sat still it might fail to gain them. The world would have shaken itself to pieces – to no avail, if Japan did not set itself to win advantage from the outcome.

In his travels, however, his natural cynicism found the cynicism of Stalin irresistibly congenial. Conversation with him left Matsuoka convinced that Stalin was the wily man who would sit by Hitler's grave, and was the statesman whose combinations of policy were the most impressive to be met. The meetings of Matsuoka and Stalin were especially fateful. They resulted in a genuine change in policy by Japan, one of the Great Powers of the world. Matsuoka, behind his front of self-assurance, proved more volatile than is usually the case with Foreign Ministers; and he was able to communicate his erratic intentions to the Japanese state. So impressed was Matsuoka with what he deemed to be Stalin's superior power that he proposed that Japan and Russia should sign a Non-Aggression Treaty. Stalin, who was already alarmed over the German intentions towards himself, and would in the coming days find Japanese neutrality a pearl beyond price, was much gratified, and closed with the offer at once.

Stalin played on the rather crude imagination of this brash man. When Matsuoka left Moscow, he surprised everyone by coming to the railway station to take farewell of him. Stalin hugged him, and used a phrase about their both being Asian which was taken to mean that, as a result of the western countries' suicide in the war, the future hegemony, at least in Asia, belonged to Japan and Russia.

The non-aggression pact of Japan and Russia caused surprise. It was one of the sensational events of the war. The Japanese government, confronted with this astonishing decision of its Foreign Minister, had to take stock of the new position. Events – the dying down of tension on the Russo-Japanese border – had, it is true, been running in this direction; but it was a different matter for the Japanese government to recognize that its antagonism to Russia, the most cherished and traditional part of its foreign policy, should be formally suspended.

There are in existence the minutes of the Liaison Conferences and the Imperial Conferences held during 1941, at which the new situation was exhaustively debated. These conferences were a unique feature of the Japanese constitution. The Japanese government had been so much split up, particularly the Service Ministries which had been freed from civilian control, that special conferences were needed to achieve any kind of unity. The Liaison Conference became the centre at which the vital decisions of policy were made: there were present the Prime Minister, the Foreign Minister, the Service Ministers and the Chief of Staff. The Imperial Conference, which was held more rarely, was a meeting of the Liaison Conference together with the Emperor and the President of the Privy Council who acted as a spokesman: it was held when especially momentous decisions were being placed on record.

The notes of these meetings during 1941 are fascinating to read. They show the bewilderment of high Japanese officials at Matsuoka's radical new policy – which was the virtual designation of Japan's hereditary enemy, Russia, as the successor of Britain as the traditional friend of Japan. They show their constant bewilderment in the kaleidoscope of the contemporary world, always casting round for a dependable ally, always disappointed in their search. They reveal their experimentalism, which is very Japanese. The discussions took place under the urgent sense that at the time the world map was being re-made, and that a golden opportunity had arisen for Japan to share in the general loot – an opportunity which Japan, by its ineptitude, might lose.

The sense is conveyed that the Japanese have got out of their depth. Here are generals, admirals and high diplomats ruthlessly planning how to further Japan's interests at the expense of the rest of the world: and, though later it was to be found that this ruthlessness could bear heavy consequences, their deliberations seem oddly light-weight.

For the immediate period, the main preoccupation of the Japanese government was to get rid of Matsuoka. Clearly they felt an embarrassment in this colleague, who spoke with such an unaccustomed and uncomfortable directness, not taking advantage of the ambiguities and vagueness of the Japanese language. The Japanese are accustomed to convey their meaning by indirect hints and innuendoes, and the whole of life is in consequence strangely inexact, as if the Japanese did not dare to face the truth. In the case of Matsuoka, the Japanese dignitaries, already thinking of an enterprise which was so audacious that they hardly dared acknowledge it, were constantly embarrassed by a Foreign Minister who called a spade a spade. In the end, to get rid of him, the Prime Minister Prince Konoye, and the whole cabinet, had to resign; and it was thus reformed without him, but with a Foreign Minister who spoke the diplomatic language, and rescued his colleagues from contemplating too directly the stark realities of the world as it was being made by their policy.

*

By the summer of 1941, opinion in Japan had veered round to the view that Japan should strike south. To the south lay the vastly rich resources of oil, tin, rubber, and other valuable commodities. This was the area of colonies: British, Dutch, French and American. If it seized them, Japan could hope for three results. First, it would make itself free from the economic pressure of the western countries, which had the temerity to threaten it with economic sanctions in an effort to control Japanese expansion. Second, by making deadly war on these powers, it would finally crush the hopes of Chungking and make it sue for peace. And lastly, out of the defeat of these western adversaries, it would build up a great Japanese empire overseas, which would be the principal monument of the war. It would not have to take account of the feeling of its allies in Europe.

The birth of these new conceptions was guided by the plan being presented, not as a military operation or crude imperialist activity, but as being a beneficent, world-regenerating liberating empire in the East which was to be called 'The Greater East Asia Co-Prosperity Sphere'. It was to be a great enterprise, summoning under the Japanese flag the people of South-East Asia and of China, in which justice would reign and the needs of each would be promoted by what was done for the whole. The pride of Japan, the welfare of the world, would be satisfied in equal measure. The mixture of moral ideas reinforced by a popular Confucianism, with a dash of Buddhism and of hard-headed military strategy, made a powerful appeal to the Japanese mood of the hour.

These ideas had been for some time in parturition. As early as 1938 Prince Konoye had proclaimed solemnly that the aim of the Sino–Japanese war was not to conquer China but to win its cooperation. Looking at East Asia, seeing it threatened by communism, he said that Japan hankered after a 'new era' in the territory: an order marked by harmony, universal cooperation, and, it was taken for granted, by the benevolent, orderly presence of Japan. Individualism, materialism, the power struggle, everything to do with Communism, were to be ruled out.

The ideas fructified in the next years: and came to apply to a steadily widening territory. The 'New Order' was enlarged into the 'Greater East Asia Co-Prosperity Sphere'. In this the countries of Asia should be governed by what were thought of as essentially the ideas of Eastern civilization. This meant an end to the long night in Asia during which western ideas had prevailed. It meant that an end would be put especially to everything which favoured American ideas and the American business presence. East Asia would in future be under Japanese hegemony; and everyone who accepted the New Order accepted this. It was marked by a recognition of the arrangements which Japan had organized, such as the state of Manchukuo, and the special zone of close Sino-Japanese collaboration.

One of the fascinating things learnt about the war by inquiries afterwards is the butterfly-mindedness of many of the imperialists in Tokyo. They were not dogged, implacable men, tied down to a single idea. They were resilient and receptive. Contrary to the general opinion, they did not make their plans far ahead, and they were not unwilling to shift their enterprises and to change the details. So, in 1941, there took place the great movement which determined the course of the war: the shift of mental concentration from a land campaign against Russia, with armies locked together to see which would prevail, to a sea strategy, a joint operation of army and navy, which should have as its object the putting of western imperialism to its death, and which would be directed against the Anglo-Saxon powers, not against Russia.

In 1941 the decision was not taken: what had happened was that the willingness had appeared to take a decision when a great crisis should happen. A great mental revolution was lived through. New possibilities were envisaged and welcomed. For the present, Japan would press on as before.

The Japanese people responded to this policy. Quite honestly and sincerely, they saw themselves, in opposing western activity in Asia, as fighting a battle against imperialism. Sincerely they believed the Japanese government was altruistic, and that the Asian people, who objected to being saved by Japan, were simply misguided. There was little need for propaganda to prepare Japan for the war which Japan was risking with the United States. If ever a people has gone to war thinking it a just war, if ever a war has been thoroughly popular, so it was to be in 1941. There was little trace of an elaborate misleading of the people.

The first territory which Japan was tempted to bring in to the Co-Prosperity Sphere was Indo-China. Its government had been left helpless by the collapse of France. The only power to which it could have looked for aid was Britain, but Britain, especially since Dakar, had become the enemy of France. Thailand was incited to present ultimatums. Throughout 1940 and 1941 Japan was able to extract larger and larger concessions for not swallowing it up entirely. In 1941 it had reduced the northern part of Indo-China to a protectorate; Japanese garrisons were admitted to the key areas; they occupied the centres from which they could strike at Malaya and the Philippines.

*

Japan pressed on with this new policy regardless of the fact that on 22 June 1941 the war started between Russia and Germany. The German attack on Russia certainly did not take Japan completely by surprise; but Germany, in this as in several other matters of great consequence to Japan, acted without any consultation with the country which, since it had signed the German-Japanese anti-Communism pact in 1936 and the Tripartite pact of September 1940, was formally its ally. Seldom had an alliance been operated by a country with quite such painful, humiliating lack of confidential deliberation.

Germany now began to press Japan to throw in its forces against Russia. It had previously indicated to Japanese diplomats, in boastful language, that should it at any time attack the USSR, the campaign would be largely a police operation since Russian resistance would be swiftly overcome. The Japanese government was inclined now to wait and see. The Kwantung Army, bogged down in China, was not in a mood to venture further afield without the prospect of specific advantage in the overriding aim of bringing China to its knees. Moreover, the pull of the Asian Co-Prosperity Sphere was now being strongly felt. Japan the imperialist, among the other imperialist nations of the world, had suffered mortifying checks. In south Asia now seemed to lie its opportunity and its natural sphere.

CHAPTER 10

The Negotiation preceding War

IN December 1940, the American government, disturbed by the increasingly belligerent tone of the Japanese, had imposed an embargo on the sale of scrap iron and war materials to Japan. Hitherto it had put no hindrance in the way of trade with Japan, and China was able to argue, with reason, that Japan's operations, in the first three years of its warfare, had been made possible economically because of United States' policy. The American government took advantage of the rising temper of the US to act resolutely, but it still had to move cautiously. Its action was an attempt to halt Japan's military activity against China.

A new way of conducting diplomacy was being tried out: the method of using economic pressure to effect political ends. Ever since the covenant of the League of Nations was drafted, the efficiency of economic sanctions had been in dispute. They were tried out against Italy, unsuccessfully, and deliberately with so many imperfections that they were bound to fail (because that was the intention of some of the Great Powers which had been coerced by pressure of their electorates into taking part in the operation) at the Abyssinian crisis. But, as enforced against Japan, in the peculiar conditions of the time, they had an indisputable effect. They suggested to President Roosevelt the line of government action which, because of the caution of public opinion, he would not have dared to propose that America should take by more political means.

In July 1941 the Japanese extended their political control of Indo-China from the north to the south. Their motive was plain: the places Japan had demanded to occupy were those which the military experts regarded as essential for an operation to reduce South-East Asia. Japan had seized the opportunity of the desperate situation of the French in Indo-China, and of the inability of France, following its collapse, to give the local French government any decisive aid. The American press digested the facts, debated them, and had seen that the damage, which might or must result, to the security of the United States, was put before the American public. Even now the American will to peace, and the concern over its neutrality sentiment, remained strong. Its propagandists continued to warn that the United States was being led along the path to war by appeal to fear and sympathy. Many of them feared that the United States was being led by the back door of war with Japan into the war which they feared and opposed: war with Germany. In spite of the alarm which they expressed, President Roosevelt responded firmly in the crisis over Indo-China. He tightened very greatly the economic war which he had begun against Japan. He froze Japanese assets. He proclaimed what amounted to an embargo on Japanese trade in oil and steel.

This was a vital stage in the development of the crisis. The American government had suddenly stiffened its policy. It did so to the surprise of many of the parties concerned, including the Japanese. It had moved somewhat in advance of the change in the mood of the country. It had taken steps which it knew to be desperately inimical to Japan.

The effects on Japan were immediate. It was especially susceptible to pressure from the oil sanctions. Japan had stored enough oil for two years of war. Denied the opportunity of replenishing it from the US, it had to recognize in the circumstances of the time that it could not gain oil from alternative sources of supply. The US was immediately followed in its embargo by the British Empire and the Dutch in Indonesia: and Japan discovered that there was no possibility of driving a wedge between them. Each month brought the prospect of the exhaustion of its supplies that much nearer. It knew that its aggressive policies, Japan itself, must wither away when the time limit arrived – because the vital fluid which sustained them would no longer flow.

The United States during these months was in an extraordinary state. Roosevelt steered it resolutely on a course which must result in war. But he did not make the decision publicly: and the majority of the American public, though more deeply stirred by Japan than in previous years, still wanted peace, not war. A certain amount of the exchange of view with Japan was behind the scenes: but much of it leaked to the public. In the last period before the final catastrophe American feeling had moved towards greater caution, so that an impartial observer, if he believed that the great decisions followed the popular will, would have said that the chances of the United States going to war were lessening, not increasing. But the country had the sense that it was in the grip of uncontrollable necessity. Like a sleep-walker, it moved towards war.

The President, though he believed that war was inevitable, was willing to test the possibility of curbing Japanese expansion without fighting: he would have abandoned larger projects if he could have gained acceptable guarantees of a reversal of Japan's policies in China and Asia generally. The outcome of American economic pressure was not certain. The United States might indeed have forced Japan into belligerent action, but war against the British in Malaya and the Dutch in the Netherlands East Indies, and not against the United States itself. The American administration could have been helpless before the Neutrality Act, and have had to stand by while its allies in South-East Asia went down before Japanese attack.

When Japan proposed a final exertion to come to terms which would make war unnecessary, Roosevelt, and his closest advisers, entered with some hopefulness on negotiations. They did so with the more readiness because they knew (and nobody else knew) that they had the great advantage of seeing into the mind of their adversary. The United States had got possession of the Japanese cipher (one of the most notable feats of code-breaking in history), and during these weeks no communication passed between the Japanese Embassy in Washington and its home base in Tokyo, but the US government was aware of it. The putting of the Japanese war machine into readiness, its dispatch into action, all took place under the eyes of the American government, which knew that it was provoking Japan unendurably.

Unhappily, so highly did the Americans value this means of over-hearing the conversation of its adversaries, so resolute was it to defend the secrecy of its knowledge, that the circulation of this intelligence was rigidly circumscribed. Extremely few men were privy to it – President Roosevelt, the Secretary of State, the Secretary for War, and General Marshall – and these, to guard the secrecy, read the messages and des-troyed them on the spot within sight of the bearer. Whether full advant-age was taken of this unique knowledge is questionable. Possibly the intense precautions to guard security prevented it from being properly digested, and opportunities may have been missed.

In these negotiations, the United States rightly perceived that the interests of friendly powers with Far-Eastern involvements were en-gaged. It informed Britain in particular step by step of their progress. Churchill, for his part, offered no resistance. Churchill, indeed, was less than clear-sighted about Japan. He tended to discount the conviction at Washington that war was imminent. Down to the last he believed that Japan would probably back down. It must be said that the war sur-prised him.

*

The vital negotiations were started through the initiative of some gifted amateurs of diplomacy, the clerics of the Catholic mission in the Far East known as the Maryknoll Fathers. Their intervention is an interest-ing story. On the one side they misunderstood and immensely over-simplified the complexity of the issues dividing Japan and the US. They viewed the imminence of war with horror, and were convinced that, by taking diplomacy out of its accustomed rut, they could give men of goodwill on both sides the opportunity to turn their natural benevolence to useful account. In their opinion, in the new atmosphere which they tried to generate, matters which had appeared as great obstacles, matters which had in them the seed of war, would be found unexpectedly tractable and would shrivel away.

On the other side, their over-simplification of the issues, which they minimized for lack of adequate appreciation of them, led in the long run to increased confusion, and had the effect of making agreement harder to reach. They roused hopes in both sides by representing the exact nature of the demands to be other than what they were. Thus they roused the hopes, and stirred up the expectations of a settlement which was found impossible when the exact terms of the other side were clarified. The possibility of an accord receded. It left disillusionment, and made the situation seem more hopeless than before.

The contribution which amateurs can make in complicated dealings between Great Powers is always apt to run into this difficulty. The work of experts is written off, and it is assumed that the fresh approach by fresh minds is likely to succeed: in the end it is found that the expert has a dreary and hard truth on his side. In the present case, the Maryknoll Fathers undoubtedly for a time raised hope in certain quarters in the US, and in Japan also, of being able to draft a kind of Monroe Doctrine for the Far East which would be acceptable to those circles in the United States which were anxious before all to secure peace. Determined men in Japan seized on this, and translated it into a draft agreement between the two powers, which they sought constantly to put forward as the basis of negotiation. But their draft treaty revealed the insubstantial basis on which they proceeded. They would have been better advised to realize that in seeking an agreement of this kind they were bashing their heads against a stone wall.

The enterprise of the Maryknoll Fathers was a little like that of Swedish philanthropic interlopers who tried to come between Germany and the West in the years before the European war. They were prompted by goodwill: but their initiative did not achieve much.

*

The Maryknoll negotiations led on to official negotiations which began in July 1941. By November they reached their climax.

Japan had begun them out of desperation, but it hoped little from them. The sanctions were pressing hard. It is true that there were powerful influences in Japanese government circles which dreaded war, which were opposed to all the tendencies which Japanese foreign policy had given rise to, and which snatched at Japan's peril to recommend that safety lay in retreat: these men were quite sincere in wanting a rapprochement with the United States. But Japanese foreign policy was made now chiefly by generals and admirals, many of whom had come to the conclusion that war was the only policy which offered hope. They were being egged on by their exchanges of view with Germany, which in these months was urgent that they should embarrass Britain by attacking Singapore, and which supplied all kinds of information about how easy they might find this adventure to be. They judged that sooner or later war would be inevitable, and that Japan stood a better chance by having the war then rather than later.

By November, the United States was satisfied that general talks were fruitless. The negotiations had been interrupted by a government crisis in Tokyo: the resignation of the essentially moderate Prince Konoye, the Prime Minister, and his replacement by General Tojo Hideki. He was a military man, not in the highest position of control of the army, but a product of fashion. He had no special political ideas or standing, but represented in general the military ideas: contempt for the United States, willingness to take extreme risks, ignorance of the politics of the world. The government was negotiating, but had decided on war in principle; it was, however, ready to see whether anything would be offered by the United States which would make war unnecessary. Twice a deadline for a breakdown of the negotiations had been fixed, and later postponed. The absolute decision had been made, but, until the end, the fleet, which was to deliver the first blow, had been ordered to leave room for calling off its operations, so that it could return to Japan with peace preserved.

The government of the United States, though prepared for war, still manoeuvring for peace, decided to offer Japan a final bargain. The oil and steel embargoes, which threatened to cut its freedom of action, were to be lifted: in return, Japan would need to give territorial guarantees. But what? Over this there was a great deal of debate: and the United States consulted its friends abroad.

The first attitude was to let Japan down lightly. Withdrawal from Indo-China would suffice. It was hoped that this would lead on to a general withdrawal from the Asian mainland: but this was not to be rushed, and was not to be included in the immediate terms.

But here came in the China lobby. Chiang Kai-shek had been informed of what was to be offered. He was indignant: he reported it as unlikely that China would be able to continue to fight Japan. He telegraphed London, and, as unlikely partner, he enlisted Churchill in representations. All the China lobby was turned on to the President and Cordell Hull, the Secretary of State. In the result they stiffened the terms, and called on the Japanese to evacuate not only Indo-China, but all China as well, including Manchuria. In return for this the United States would rescind its oil embargo.

In the negotiations Cordell Hull took a stiffer line than Roosevelt. The President had been willing to accept an invitation from the Japanese Prime Minister, Prince Konoye, while he was still in power, to negotiate personally: Cordell Hull intervened, and stopped this. Konoye had gone so far as to propose that the two leaders should make a preliminary temporary pact under which Japan would agree not to make war on the US even if American activities led to war with Germany in the Atlantic Ocean. This meant that Japan would repudiate its Tripartite Alliance with Germany and Italy. The gist of that was to deter the United States from intervention in the German war by the threat of collision with Japan. Apparently Cordell Hull felt that Konoye had been offering an engagement which he would not be permitted to fulfil.

President Roosevelt made a final attempt at peace by appealing over the heads of politicians to the Japanese Emperor, But this action, though it was seriously meant, was misunderstood and resented in Japan.

On 7 December Japan sent a note which recognized that the negotiations had failed. By the time it was delivered, the consequences of the recognition were also clear: the Japanese were bombarding Pearl Harbor, which they had decided to do if the negotiations ended in deadlock. It is interesting to find that General Marshall, when the reports of the bombardment were first given to him, said incredulously that they must be mistaken: Japan would have bombarded Singapore, not American territory. This is perhaps a measure of the failure of the Japanese to wring final advantage out of the United States' preoccupation with remaining neutral.

CHAPTER 11

The Bombardment of Pearl Harbor

JAPAN, goaded into decisive action, was unleashing against the world its other major force, its navy. Hitherto Japan's army had been the agent of Japan's dynamism: it was the army which Japan's neighbours feared, and it was the influence of the army upon the Japanese government that kept the world in anxiety. The navy, which by tradition was preponderantly officered by men whose Samurai origin lay in clans different from those which were powerful in the army, was highly conspiratorial: it had tended to deplore the rashness of the army, and to favour much more cautious policies. It was conservative: it did not feel the same desire to intervene over the whole range of government: it had less connection, though it had some, with patriotic societies. In the navy, the old feeling in favour of the Anglo-Japanese Alliance lingered on, and there was a nostalgic sentiment in favour of the older basis of Japan's foreign policy.

But the navy, like all other institutions in Japan, was divided by factions. One faction had been captivated by the vision of the economic adventure in the South Seas, and by the empire which it felt lay open for Japan, open to the touch of the Japanese fleet. This section began to think of the war with the British Empire, which it would have to overthrow, as inevitable. It thought, too, that a collision with the United States was certain, for the US also was likely to block Japanese expansion in this direction. The navy, or this section of it, gradually came to regard the Anglo-Saxon powers as the inevitable enemy, against whom war was to be prepared.

This faction identified itself in the vital years with the 'Go South' movement. It naturally saw in this an opportunity to reinstate itself with the army in the public esteem, and to clip the army's wings as the instrument of expansion *par excellence*. The prevailing war, an army-inspired war, between Japan and China, would be transformed and eclipsed by being converted into a predominantly naval war, fought by different instruments, by the navy chiefly instead of the land forces, and with the adversary changed. The war would be in a different terrain, would involve huge distances, vast oceans, distant islands – in all of which, the navy, and not the army, would shine.

In calling into action the second of the great weapons of Imperial

Japan, the Japanese government was employing an instrument which had been untested for thirty-five years. The Japanese navy had won its greatest triumph as long ago as 1905, and had, since then, not fought a serious action. As long as the Washington Naval Limitation Treaty had been in force, the West had been able to inform itself of Japanese naval construction: and Britain, making use of old ties, had kept abreast of Japanese naval thinking. But the link had been severed in 1935: the American and British navies felt themselves incompetent at assembling information about interesting new developments in Japanese naval construction: in 1941, it was a matter of speculation how the Japanese navy would fare if pitted against those of the other Great Powers. A great spurt in construction of big ships had taken place at the end of the 1930s.

In the twenties and early thirties, while contact lasted, the Japanese navy had maintained a large battle fleet. It possessed ten large battle-ships: it was known to have built four more subsequently, though the West was without knowledge of their details. In addition the navy, from the beginning of the 1920s, had been interested in the air, and had built aircraft carriers. This was the speciality, not of the navy as a whole, but of a clique in it, whose most forceful member was a Japanese naval officer, Yamamoto Isoroku, who early on had been attracted by theories of air power. He was openly sceptical about the usefulness of battleships: he thought their value was chiefly prestige, and he compared them to the ancestral scrolls which were hung upon the wall of Japanese houses, proving the piety of their upkeep but not able to guarantee much to the present prosperity of the family.

Yamamoto had, however, a very difficult time in propagating his views. Most Japanese admirals regarded his insistence on air power much as British military officers regarded the use of the machine gun before the First World War. Some made it a point of honour never to fly in an aeroplane themselves, and to discourage flying by their officers. Yamamoto got his way, largely by becoming commandant of a naval school, which trained a considerable number of naval pilots: they were to be the heroes of the coming war. By a characteristically Japanese compromise Yamamoto secured, not the replacement of the existing Japanese navy by one which was governed by his ideas, but the organiza-tion of a separate fleet, which was geared to the air, in addition to the orthodox battle fleet. Apparently there was no stringent testing of naval construction in Japan by commissions from the Diet, which might have subjected this settlement to criticism on grounds of economy.

The air development of the Japanese navy was one of the things overlooked by the Intelligence of the Anglo-Saxon countries. In 1938 aeroplanes which had bombed Shanghai had flown direct from Kyushu in southern Japan and had returned without refuelling. In spite of the stir which this made at the time, the official judgement in England and the United States continued to be that Japan had made little progress in turning out skilled naval pilots.

Yamamoto had risen high in the navy, by great industry fortified by originality of ideas. In the middle of 1939 he was made Commander-in-Chief of the Combined Fleet, which made him one of the three or four men who were responsible for planning naval operations. As relations with the US worsened, he became convinced that, in the event of Japan being forced into war by the United States – as the Japanese thought – Japan should begin operations with a surprise attack on the US Asian fleet, which was stationed at Pearl Harbor. By doing so, the navy would be repeating its attack, before the outbreak of war, on the Russian fleet at Port Arthur in 1904. Yamamoto had himself been present at that famous action, and had lost two fingers. The American plans for war were known to be that, upon its declaration, the Pearl Harbor fleet should advance westwards, and that the war would take the form of great naval engagements with the Japanese fleet in the western Pacific. Yamamoto's plan was to make this impossible by destroying the American fleet, by surprise, before it could sail. As a professional sailor charged with advising his government on great matters, he recommended it to borrow from Japan's mode of action in the past, and to deal a lightning blow.

Admiral Yamamoto, it should be noted, was not a firebrand. For many years he had been associated with the moderate group, and he had risked assassination in consequence. His advocacy of his bold plan was conditional upon the Japanese government concluding that no means other than war was open to it. It was to be the desperate means when the situation was desperate.

For the attack on Pearl Harbor, Yamamoto proposed to use his aircraft-carriers, and to carry out the destruction from the air. No coup of such magnitude had as yet been carried out: it was its boldness which surprised the world. A relatively small operation of the kind had been executed by the British when they had bombed Taranto with twenty-three planes: their success undoubtedly persuaded Yamamoto to proceed. He had the operation studied minutely, and torpedoes were manufactured on the British model which were suitable for attacking in shallow waters: the depth of water at Pearl Harbor was little deeper than it had been at Taranto. The planning of the action to be taken at Pearl Harbor began in June 1941. Yamamoto had the greatest difficulty in getting the consent of the very few naval colleagues whom he had to consult, but whose number was rigidly limited by the need for entire secrecy. An appreciation by the naval General Staff was that success would depend on surprise, and that the chances of sailing a task force within reach of Pearl Harbor undetected were negligible.

Yamamoto, however, was finally permitted to proceed. His skill in advocacy must have been great, and it was one of the qualities which made him so conspicuous in the war. He assembled a task force of twenty-three surface ships (which included six carriers and two battle-ships) and twenty-seven submarines. In the middle of November, one month before the actual bombardment, this force sailed from Japan to Tankan Bay in the Kurile Islands; from there they approached Hawaii from the north, arriving within 220 miles of it on the night of 6–7 December. Though Yamamoto had supervised in detail the planning and rehearsal of the expedition, he did not accompany it, but remained, wisely, at his post of command near Tokyo.

It was understood that the issue of success and of disgraceful and humiliating failure turned upon secrecy. The United States had been warned many times that the Japanese did not exclude an attack on Pearl Harbor. It was not supposed that the Americans were likely to be as extraordinarily negligent as proved in fact to be the case. Japan took a formidable risk in relying on the friendless and empty seas of the north Pacific in protecting its fleet from discovery. In other ways it had taken security devices which had in some measure deceived the Americans, and were an essential part of the operation. When its fleet sailed from Japan, the fact had been camouflaged by setting up a system of fake radio messages which stilled any American suspicions that ships were on the move. After some time, however, the American monitors realized that calls to and from the aircraft carriers, specifically, had unaccountably ceased. They accepted that the carriers had been moved, but made the wrong deduction that they had been sent to the south. The Americans were already aware, from their interception of the code messages between Tokyo and the Japanese Embassy in Washington, that the Japanese were preparing for war in case the vital negotiations with the United States ended in deadlock; and they assumed that the operations would, in the first case, be directed against Malaya, the Netherlands East Indies, or the Philippines. With this inference, the assumption that the disappearance of the aircraft carriers meant a concentration of force in the South Seas fitted excellently. That the concentration was at the moment against Pearl Harbor never seems to have crossed the mind of anyone in authority.

So the evidence, and plenty was at hand, of a coming coup at Pearl Harbor was allowed to pile up, and no counter-measures were taken. The American monitors intercepted wireless messages between some source in Japan and a Japanese in Honolulu which were mysterious, and should have put them on their guard. After the attack it became clear that these conversations gave minute particulars of the American ships likely to be in port on 7 December. But they were thinly veiled, in a code which was subsequently seen to have been quite plain. All that was done with the messages at this time was to refer them to a language unit for a report on them, without any indication of emergency. The American Intelligence had knowledge of a key phrase which would be used in the Japanese radio programme a few hours before hostilities: it was to be a semi-secret way of conveying information to Japanese agents abroad, Japanese shipping and so on. It was used and remarked on: but the machinery for transmitting this information was tied up with red tape. What was necessary was that Admiral Kimmel, who was in command at Pearl Harbor, should have instituted air reconnaissance of all the seas around him: but this, after weighing the advice, and with the assent of his staff, he neglected to do. He believed that it was unnecessary, even though he had been warned, from the intercepted cipher messages of the Japanese, that Japan was seriously preparing for war.

The American blindness to their danger continued until the very morning of the attack. An outlying radar unit, whose business it was to track aircraft, picked up clearly the traces of two Japanese planes which had been sent out just before the attack, to search for all American carriers. They came on the radar screen at seven o'clock, one hour before the start of the attack, and, if this alert had been acted upon, it would, late though it was, have enabled the battleships to be put in some state of readiness, and the American planes to be in the air. The attack would quite possibly have failed, or the main havoc been averted. But this radar station, which was manned by an inexperienced but enthusiastic trainee, informed Honolulu of what had been observed, and was told not to be alarmed. It was assumed that it must have detected an American flight which was due from the mainland.

Similarly one of the Japanese submarines entered through the harbour gates at 4.50 in the morning. It was reported and hunted: but a general alarm was not given; the significance of the news, the fact that it heralded a full naval assault, was not appreciated.

The United States was amply served by an acute intelligence force. But what is the use of intelligence if there is sheer negligence over its use and interpretation? A dispatch rider, carrying a detailed warning from General Marshall in Washington to Headquarters Command – a warning that had taken an unaccountable time to transmit on the telegraph – was forced to take shelter in a ditch while the raid, which was accurately forecast in the document which he carried, was taking place round him. The warning never reached the authorities who, had it been forced to their attention twelve hours earlier, could have taken effective action.

Thus secrecy was maintained: the Japanese triumph was assured. To do Yamamoto justice, he had doubts about the propriety of what he was doing, and stipulated that the attack should not be made until thirty minutes after Japan had informed the United States that it considered that the peace negotiations were at an end. Thereby correctness would be observed, even though by a hair's breadth. Actually the attack, when it came, preceded the notification, and it appeared as perfidious as Admiral Togo's assault on the Russians had been in 1904. But the Japanese had in fact tried to observe the usages of war. The notification was in a bulky message which it took the Embassy much longer to decipher than had been foreseen in Tokyo. It was in a way symbolical of how often the actions of the Japanese authorities were to ruined by slovenly or incompetent work in their execution. When the note was delivered, the blow had already been struck.

In the early hours of Sunday 7 December, a last radio instruction came from Tokyo. By a quarter past six, the first wave of aircraft left the carriers. The flagship hoisted the flag which Admiral Togo had carried thirty-six years before in his victory over the Tsars. The operation was the more hazardous because the Japanese possessed very sketchy information about the forces they were about to assail. It is a legend that they were well supplied by their Intelligence organizations, and knew their way about the American defences. They were uncertain to the end, for example, about whether the Americans had torpedo nets to protect their ships. They only had information, which they themselves mistrusted, about exactly what ships they were to encounter. One of their agents in Honolulu had warned them that the four aircraft-carriers which were normally with the Pacific Fleet were away from port that week-end. To catch the carriers was a vital objective. They had had in consequence serious thoughts of calling off the entire adventure at the last moment, or of postponing it indefinitely. Many of the decisions were made by guesswork.

The bombing fleet which the Japanese let loose was divided into squadrons of fighter planes, high-level torpedo-bombers and dive-bombers. The leader of one squadron of torpedo-bombers has put on record the sight which met him. It is quoted in John Deane Potter's book, *Admiral of the Pacific*:

Below me lay the whole US Pacific Fleet in a formation I would not have dared to dream of in my most optimistic dreams. I have seen all the German ships assembled in Kiel Harbour. I have also seen the French battleships in Brest. And finally I have frequently seen our warships assembled for review before the Emperor, but I have never seen ships, even in the deepest deep, anchored at a distance of 500–1,000 yards from each other. A war fleet must always be on the alert, since surprise attacks can never be fully ruled out. But this picture down there was hard to comprehend. Had these Americans never heard of Port Arthur?*

Actually the mooring of the ships was culpably unsafe. It was odd that their radar protection, though it was in existence, did not afford more effective safety.

The attack lasted two hours. In this short time the Americans had suffered loss or damage to eighteen battleships and auxiliaries, the destruction or damage of 349 aircraft, and had 3,581 sailors, soldiers and marines and 103 civilians killed or wounded. By mid-morning the vast and impressive naval base, which had filled the United States with such confidence, was transformed into a vast ruin with flaming ships, a decimated garrison, and with a monumental disorganization. The base from which the US had counted on directing the war was a chaos enveloped in smoke.

To effect this massacre, the Japanese had used 353 planes. Of these they lost fifteen dive-bombers, nine fighter planes, and five torpedo-planes. Their total loss in personnel was fifty-five officers and men. It was the most spectacular triumph of the war. The Americans remained unaware throughout of the source of their attack, and the entire fleet sailed back in safety to Japan.

*

Impressive as were the results of the raid, humiliating as it proved to be for the American navy, Japan fell just short of making it the crushing success it was meant to be. The Japanese, inexplicably, did not destroy the vast oil stocks on Hawaii, or, as far as is known, consider whether it could seize them. America began the war with oil reserves which were

*John Deane Potter: *Admiral of the Pacific*, Heinemann, 1965.

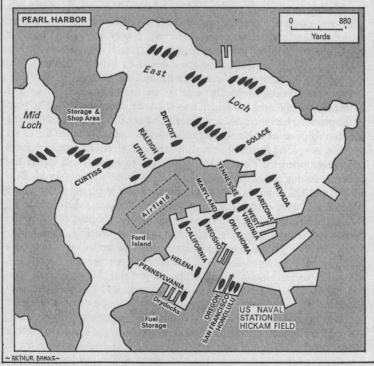

THE JAPANESE ATTACK ON PEARL HARBOR 7 DECEMBER 1941

ADMIRAL NAGUMO'S ROUTE

U S S R

Hittokapu
Bay

JAPAN

2/12   3/12   5/12

6/12
7/12 Oahu

PACIFIC   OCEAN

Hawaiian
Islands

International date line

0   500
Miles

THE ATTACK

0   10
Miles

FIRST WAVE
183 PLANES

SECOND WAVE
180 PLANES

O A H U

Pearl
Harbor

Honolulu

PEARL HARBOR

0   880
Yards

East

Loch

Mid
Loch

Storage &
Shop Area

DETROIT

RALEIGH

UTAH

SOLACE

CURTISS

NEVADA

Airfield

TENNESSEE

MARYLAND

ARIZONA

WEST
VIRGINIA

Ford
Island

CALIFORNIA

NEOSHO

OKLAHOMA

HELENA

PENNSYLVANIA

Drydocks

OREGON
SAN FRANCISCO
HONOLULU

US NAVAL
STATION
HICKAM FIELD

Fuel
Storage

~ ARTHUR BANKS ~

almost equal to the entire supplies of Japan. Japan had them at its mercy: why they neglected to fire them remains unexplained. At one stage it had, it is true, been the Japanese intention to try to seize Oahu, the Hawaiian island which contains Pearl Harbor, and in that case the oil would have passed into Japan's hands. But this part of the plan had been quickly given up as, among other reasons, it would have demanded troop transports and landing craft which were needed for the operation beginning at the same time in the South Seas. To have made the operation one which would really have altered the fundamental position of both sides, the Japanese would have needed, not only to destroy ships, but to have seized territory in the middle of the Pacific Ocean.

Japan did not include among its victims any one of the four major American aircraft-carriers which were attached to the Pacific Fleet. These were to prove the decisive weapon in the subsequent struggle in the Pacific, as was well understood by Admiral Yamamoto. Fortunate accidents led to one aircraft carrier being away delivering some planes to Midway Island; to another delivering planes to Guam: another being under repair on the American Pacific coast. The fourth was, as was found out later, trailed for some hours by a large Japanese submarine, but, in the eventual contest with this, the submarine was sunk.

Pearl Harbor contained also one failure of the Japanese which was little noted at the time but which was to have a decisive effect. The plan of Yamamoto had included a submarine attack as well as one from the air: but this was as uniformly a failure as the attack from the air was a success. A special Japanese invention, the midget submarine, a minute submarine operated by a crew of two, was to be let loose inside the harbour among the battleships, and to work what havoc it could. Five of these submarines, which were transported by large, ocean-going submarines, were inserted through the harbour gates: this was, to all intents and purposes, a suicide mission, for the chances of the crews being picked up again were, though it was just possible, exceedingly slight. In fact all the five submarines were destroyed and only one member of the crews survived, falling prisoner to the Americans. (Contrary to Japanese convention, he proved singularly talkative, and he disclosed useful information to the Americans.) In the subsequent share-out of the honours for the raid, the submarine commanders felt themselves neglected, and all the credit fell to the airmen. Subsequently, the submarine service was at a discount in Japanese eyes. No further plans were drawn up which devolved any great responsibility on it. Though attention had previously been given to the production of the midget, Japanese inventiveness swung away from the submarine and concentrated on other matters. Japan had begun the war with several very large and technically efficient submarines; they were subsequently engaged on colourful, hazardous action on the American coast and in the fighting at Guadalcanal; but they failed to keep their hold on the imagination of the public, which was fixed upon its navy pilots. So, in war, the issues can be decided by the irrational judgement of the public. An inference was that the Japanese navy, though it possessed one incontestable genius in Yamamoto, did not have the staff officers who were capable of recognizing that Japan possessed an asset which it was wasting: who were capable of evolving a strategy which would make use of this instrument; and who simultaneously had the ability to force their views on the attention of the rigid Japanese High Command. What Yamamoto had done for naval aircraft, nobody seemed able to do for the submarine.

Was Pearl Harbor therefore really a success for the Japanese? Taking into account the whole course of the war, this has been doubted. The American naval historian, S. E. Morison, doubts this. He sums up the situation by saying that Pearl Harbor, for all the destruction which it achieved, was really an empty triumph. He looks towards the careful Japanese plan which had been evolved for dealing with the United States' expected offensive by the United States Asian Fleet advancing in the Pacific: and thinks that Japan would have done more wisely if it had waited for the attack, and contained it somewhere in the Marshall or Caroline Islands. By fleet action on these lines, Japan would have gained the best chance of surviving. But such a view is hard to credit. Putting it at its most down-to-earth estimate, Yamamoto had gained eighteen months', or two years' respite for Japan, and, though the long-term prospects remained exceedingly black, he had insured that the typhoon should rage over Japan in two years' time, not rage at once. He gave the opportunity to his own warlike schemes, and to any others which Japan might produce, or, better still, to her diplomats and statesmen in their ability to work out a peaceable solution, to find a way of averting ultimate catastrophe.

One peculiar circumstance aided Japan at Pearl Harbor. It was to continue in some form throughout the war, and was to handicap American arrangements repeatedly. This was that the High Commands of the US navy and army at home were scarcely on speaking terms. The degree of discord varied from place to place, and depended in part on the accident of personalities engaged. But the tension was often an important fact of the situation: as it had been at Pearl Harbor, where there was the minimum cooperation between the air force, which in the

United States was part of the army, and the navy. Most of the responsibility for friction lay with the navy. The American navy existed in peculiar isolation from American society. It was self-sufficient and self-contained. It had its own politics, outlook, ethos. In a war it was apt to think that its chief enemy was at home, in the rival services which entrenched upon its own liberty of action. The result was peculiarly catastrophic. It was due to this self-imposed remoteness that the defence machinery creaked so badly.

There were other defects in the American defence machine. All these stood out clearly at Pearl Harbour. The extension of peacetime bureaucratic controls went so far that the anti-aircraft batteries were obliged to indent for every shell which was fired. As the American wartime machine swung slowly into action, a great many blunders were discovered which had their source in this over-meticulousness of civilian control. It was the natural consequence of a long period of peace.

If the sights are lifted beyond this war, it must be recorded that, by the shrewd blow delivered to the United States (which was so much larger than Japan) and by the superb secrecy which had been preserved in organizing such a complex operation, Yamamoto had given an increase to Japanese self-esteem, which would bear the people up in future periods of national calamity. One day the Japanese triumph at Pearl Harbor will be regarded in a different light from that in which it was inevitably seen by the opposite side at the time; the memory of treachery will fade: it will stand out as a most memorable feat of arms.

CHAPTER 12

The War after Pearl Harbor

AN imperial rescript – the manifesto which is issued at great decisions of the government – accompanied Japan's declaration of war, and read as follows:

We hereby declare war on the United States of America and the British Empire... It has been truly unavoidable... More than four years have passed since China, failing to understand the true intentions of our empire, disturbed the peace of Asia. Although there has been re-established the National Government of China with which Japan has effected neighbourly intercourse and cooperation, the régime which has survived at Chungking, relying upon American and British protection, still continues its fratricidal opposition. Eager for the realization of their inordinate ambition to dominate the Orient, both America and Britain, giving support to the Chungking régime, have aggravated the disturbances of East Asia. Moreover these two powers, inducing other countries to follow suit, have increased military preparations on all sides of our empire to challenge us. They have obstructed by every means our peaceful commerce and finally have resorted to a direct severance of economic relations thereby gravely menacing the existence of our empire... This trend of affairs would, if left unchecked, endanger the very existence of our nation. The situation being such as it is, our empire, for its existence and self-defence, has no other recourse but to appeal to arms and to crush every obstacle on its path.*

Except for the blame it casts on China for the convulsion, this is an accurate statement of why Japan went to war. Japan states that it enlarged the war because it believed that only by doing so was it possible to wind up a smaller war with China. Its intervention in Indo-China, to which America had reacted so stiffly, had been undertaken for the same reasons.

War on such a scale as Japan now determined had come out of the inability of the Japanese government to find any other means of dealing with a situation which had passed out of its control. It was due in the last resort to a failure of ingenuity. The war was not preceded by elaborate planning. There was no systematic scheme of operations against the United States and Britain, which laid down a timetable for

* Quoted by Jones, Borton and Pearn: *The Far East 1942–46*, Royal Institute of International Affairs, O.U.P., 1955.

successive undertakings. All the evidence which was to become available to the western allies at the end of the hostilities confirms that the war was a desperate venture, hastily decided on: that it was conducted by a series of improvisations, however brilliant some of these were: that no elaborate plans were made of the assets, military and economic, of the western allies, and that no intelligent scheme existed of how to erode them: that Japan was, quite literally, taking a great leap in the dark, and casting its faith into the keeping of a veiled providence, which it had no reason to think would be kind.

Admiral Yamamoto, the architect of Pearl Harbor, summed up the attitude of those who took the decision to go into the war:

> What a strange position I find myself in now – having to make a decision diametrically opposed to my own personal opinion, with no choice but to push full-speed in pursuance of that decision. Is that, too, fate?*

To his sister, he wrote, 'Well, war has begun at last. But in spite of all the clamour that is going on, we could lose it. I can only do my best.'†
And to a fellow admiral he wrote:

> This war will give us much trouble in the future. The fact that we have had a small success at Pearl Harbor is nothing. The fact that we have succeeded so easily has pleased people. Personally I do not think it is a good thing to whip up propaganda to encourage the nation. People should think things over and realize how serious the situation is.‡

He had, at Pearl Harbor, fought a successful holding operation, which had bought time. But he knew, as well as anybody, that this time would pass, and that, if at the end of it, Japan – and its ally Germany – had not found a way to peace, Japan would be ruined. He had said repeatedly that it was easier to start a war than finish one. However much territory the Japanese took, however many American battleships they sunk, final victory might elude them.

One way only seemed to offer hope. Japanese strategy should be to win, by the impetus of surprise, as much as it possibly could in the first six months of the war. The only chance of a satisfactory peace would be to follow up Pearl Harbor by sinking the American aircraft carriers: and then, from the triumphal height of that moment, to persuade the United States to negotiate peace. It might hope that it would seem to be in such a commanding position that its Anglo-Saxon enemies would be cast down by the difficulty of dislodging it. Though they had potentially

---

*John Deane Potter: *Admiral of the Pacific,* op. cit.
†ibid.
‡ibid.

invincible power, they would be unwilling to make the exertion of mobilizing it, the more so since they would have been worn out by the war effort they were making against Germany. Japan, it should be remembered, occupied a naval position of great strength strategically. After the war of 1914–18, it had inherited from Germany the Caroline and Marshall Islands in the Pacific which, by being thoroughly (and illegally) fortified, interposed a screen which hampered the Americans in defending the Philippines. The vast depths of the Pacific Ocean were in themselves a very strong defence. Japan could argue that the United States, confronted with the possibility of either a prolonged, arduous counter-assault, or with a generous peace offer by Japan – generous in the sense that it would not be against the United States' interest in any part of the world except East Asia – would choose the path of peace.

Of the chances of their ally Germany – who was little more, either then or later, than their nominal ally – they took a rather similar view: its long-term prospects were black, but it might find salvation in the war-weariness of the western allies. In this titanic world contest, one of the most curious things was the failure of Japan and Germany to co-operate. Their relations throughout were scarcely more than the conventional ones of peacetime association. Their relations were conducted by Ambassadors. The joint planning which essentially made up Anglo-American cooperation was almost totally absent in the war-time partnership of their rivals. When diligent spying failed to discover any joint war plans by Germany and Japan, at first it was assumed that an unusually opaque veil had been woven to hide them. Not until much later did the real and simple truth become credible. No such plans had been brought into being.

Japan, unlike Germany, had no well-considered long-term war aims. In contrast to what Germany planned for Europe, Japan invested little effort in its projects for the Greater East Asia Co-Prosperity Sphere. The direction of the war on the Japanese side was too widely diffused among different hands for a clear national policy to become plain. Japan, even though it had hopes of limiting the war, was easily diverted away from the idea of a defensive war. By Pearl Harbor and Japan's initial victories, the situation had been created which made prudence difficult, and lured the Japanese on. It was as impossible to restrain its generals and admirals from further adventures as it is to prevent bulls from charging in a bull-ring.

In general, Japan followed a strategy remarkably close to that by which Mr Micawber governed his life. It was to take violent action, and then to hope that something or other would turn up, enabling it to escape disaster and to re-establish peace.

*

Japan had committed the error of all military powers in dealing with the United States. It underrated grossly the willingness of the US to bear the adversities of war. It despised it; and continued to do so throughout the war. Because in the course of every war the United States armies began badly, because the democratic institutions encouraged crude criticism and loose talk, because its people were not ashamed to harp upon considerations of material interest, the Japanese, like Hohenzollern Germany before them, too easily expected the US to give up. They scoffed at the American commercial instinct, and they predicted that, in the grim struggle of war, this could never survive against the Samurai tradition.

But the nature of Anglo-Saxon democracy is its tenacity. This the Americans, and the British, have demonstrated clearly in passages of their history. Confront them with a desperate situation, give them disastrous leaders, let their economic policies have been deplorable, saddle their public life with a rising rate of casualties; and they become more stubborn. They are implacable, and seemingly their pocket is limitless. They become pitiless and merciless, alike to their enemies and to the civilian minorities among themselves which protest against the transfiguration of the values of life by the stubborn resolve to continue war. Passchendaele and the battlefields of the American Civil War are a terrible warning, which naturally militant people, but those untouched by the traditions of Anglo-Saxon democracy, have never taken to heart. Once it has taken up arms, and has suffered the blood-letting which warms its temper, the democracy ceases to understand the virtues of a peace which is negotiated, and is satisfied only with the barren conclusion spreading bitterness everywhere, of absolute victory. It sets aside all rules, and, with a mood created by the tempest of the hour, works simply and mechanically, grinding its way to victory. This was the tempest which Japan was bringing down upon itself: more awful than any of its feared typhoons.

It was to discover later that, terrible as a victorious democracy may be, it has at least the virtue of quickly changing its temper when the goad of war is removed. The resolution and implacability, while they thrive during war, are dissolved after a year or so of peace. Hence Japan, if it had dwelt on past history, need not have been so miserably cast down by its total defeat.

If the Japanese despised the United States, Americans no less misunderstood the Japanese. The mutual incomprehension is one of the facts, tragic and at times comic, of the war. Throughout its course, anyone visiting the US was at once made conscious of the passionate contempt, which was originally based on resentment, for the Japanese. All the discreditable facts about them were remembered. All that made Japanese civilization interesting was, as by system, forgotten. All Japanese were lumped together as a misshapen, ugly, stupid, dwarf people. They were like nothing so much as Mr Tolkien's orcs in the *Lord of the Rings*, creations of a people of sheer malevolence and hideousness.

The British reacted in a less extreme way. On going to war, Churchill wrote quite a sentimental letter to the Japanese Ambassador. The stream of American feeling did not sweep the British along with it; the British had their emotions concentrated on the Nazis, and, except where they had powerful reasons for hatred from personal experience of Japanese camps or other atrocities, regarded the Japanese as a provoking irrelevance.

*

By its fateful decision Japan altogether changed the character of the war.

China, which until then had preserved the fiction that its war was no war but merely an incident, declared war on Japan on 9 December. It rejoiced in the United States being committed and saw the prospect of its operation being enlarged by vast American aid. But the declaration was a voluntary act by China. Events might have taken a different course if China had not thus regularized its American alliance. Similarly, on the same day that it declared war on Japan it declared war on Germany.

Why it did so is not clear. As Germany was under no obligation to declare war on the United States, and did so against its interests, so China was under no obligation to declare war on Germany. Apparently it did so out of a kind of contagion. It might be assumed that the countries were beset by madness.

From this time onwards, the direst, and chiefly decisive part of the war was waged on sea and in the air. In fact the Japanese sea and air operations were probably the most spectacular in human history. It is true that the war with China continued desultorily, but the problems which compelled the attention of the Japanese government had very little relation to those of the earlier period. Pearl Harbor meant a huge increase in Japan's enemies. It had against it the British Empire, in those days still a major power, as well as the United States. It had defied a great part of the world, and though it had at first won prodigious successes, the precariousness of its position was always plain.

In the whole of the latter part of the war, in the struggle of Japan with the western powers, Japan was compelled by circumstance to appear as the liberator of the orient against occidental control. The role of the emancipator, which nationalists everywhere had first hopefully seen Japan as fulfilling in its victory against Russia in 1905, was now firmly wished upon it by the exigencies of the time. In India, in Indo-China, in Indonesia, in Burma, a tide was started which, if the Japanese had rightly worked with it, might have proved irresistible. In this new illumination the presence of the white man in Asia seemed a ghastly insult to the rights of the Asian peoples. Even the classes of people which had formerly been contented to work with the West hailed the new prospect of building the future of Asia upon Asian foundations.

The history of the war is the chronicle of Japan's lost opportunities; of a crusade which never got started: of a Japan which was so hampered by inner contradictions that it was astonishingly unsuccessful in rising to the occasion. As the war went on, Japan allowed it to become plain that it was bent on a simple predatory enterprise of the kind which had been supposed to have passed out of fashion with the passing away of the nineteenth century. It failed to disguise in a plausible way that its interest was no higher than the transfer to itself of the benefits enjoyed by western countries in the South Seas and in Asia. The gloss which it sought to put on this – the ideology of the Greater East Asia Co-Prosperity Sphere, with its picture of an eastern world finding harmony under the protection of the Japanese armies – was too perfunctory to carry conviction.

In three years, Japan, by a series of blunders, disappointed the hopes of Asia that it was the liberator. By extraordinarily insensitive action it convinced Asian nationalists that Japan offered little or nothing to the peoples struggling to be free; and satisfied the national leaders that more was to be had from western imperialists than from the victory of Japan. For this result, a part of the responsibility was due to the conduct, the repeated blunders, the arrogance and stupidity, of the Japanese army. Japan's imperial adventure was always associated with the Japanese army: Japanese diplomats, civilians, and captains of industry were of secondary importance. The opportunities for a genuine new era in the region, which were at first made available by the daring and glittering achievements of Japanese arms, were flung away because the Japanese army went in the teeth of the inhabitants of the region, and came to be odious throughout Asia. It was defeated by Anglo-Saxon powers in military combat, but when this came about, few tears were shed by Asian nationalism because of the result.

After Pearl Harbor, the war, or the Far-Eastern war and the European war, broadened out, and became a world war, in which nearly every country was engaged. It was more universal than the First World War had been. The greater part of the civilized world was drawn in.

There is a distinction, of kind as well as of degree, between a local war and a universal one. In a local war, there are boundaries to the general savagery. In general men can opt out of it: they, or at least some, can go to neutral territory. In a universal explosion, war is everywhere. The shortage of neutrals leaves man without refuge.

Ruskin, in a passage from *Praeterita*, describes the difference between a local war and war which had got out of hand and swept the world: that of Napoleon. Of this war, Ruskin says that it was marked by:

> Life trampled out in the slime of the street, crushed to dust amidst the roaring of the wheel, tossed countlessly away into howling winter wind along five hundred leagues of rock-fanged shore.

He continues:

> The death was of another range and power; more terrible a thousand-fold in its merely physical grasp and grief; more terrible, incalculably, in its mystery and shame. What were the robber's casual pang, or the range of the flying skirmish, compared to the work of the axe, and the sword, and the famine, which was done at this time in all the hills and plains of the Christian earth, from Moscow to Gibraltar. . . . Look on the map of Europe, and count the bloodstains on it, between Arcola and Waterloo.

So with this later convulsion; only the scientific progress with weapons of destruction made the havoc worse. What, in other ages, armies could bring about in a dozen years, they had now the capacity to do in a dozen days, or even hours.

The greater part of the civilized world was at war: little by little, in every country of the world, in all the great cities, and in most of the accessible villages, the sights and sounds of war were to become the commonplace of the age. In North America, in the Asian countries, in Australia, and in North Africa, the progress of the war became a grand preoccupation. In all too many centres of ordered life, centres which for more than a century had been famous for commerce or culture, the distant hum of conflict turned abruptly into the clash and commotion of sudden battle, to be followed often by the long tedium and horror of military occupation by an alien power. In all the world, only central Africa and South America were relatively undisturbed.

*

The whole world moved senselessly in one direction or another, suffered and died in great swaths. Peasants and citizens of the huge Asian towns were caught alike. Many more perished from famine and disease than were killed by the armies.

This huge populace was informed about what was happening chiefly by local newspapers. Other media of communication scarcely touched it. Only the rare Asian village was, at the time, equipped with radio. For the townsmen, the radio set poured out propaganda, but in the towns the people largely discounted this, and put their faith in the printed word. From the newspapers, and from human contacts by mouth to mouth, word was spread, without which the Asian people would have supposed that there was no rhyme or reason in the convulsion of the world. It is hard enough to see how these instruments were sufficient for their purpose. Even though newspapers made their way into most of the villages, into the very remote ones in China and India, the number of people who could read them was very restricted. The war which had engulfed the governments had drawn in a mass of illiterate peasants. Those who could read found their talent even more highly regarded than in the past. They read in the newspaper and told the rest of the people what it contained. They were the agents of the increasing self-awareness of the peoples of Asia during this time. But it is unlikely that many of them came to any conclusion about the events they contemplated more perceptive than that of little Peterkin on the battle of Blenheim two and a half centuries earlier:

> But what they fought each other for
> I could not well make out.

Part III

THE HIGH TIDE OF WAR

CHAPTER 13

Japan's Hundred Days

HONG KONG

JAPAN, following the brilliant start in the new theatres of its war, had the limelight in the times which succeeded. For the next three months it held the initiative in many different sectors. It concentrated on dealing with its new enemies, especially the United States and Britain, and it enjoyed a dashing period of cheaply won triumphs, rolling up the long established positions and colonial territories of the western powers in Asia. Its record was of almost unbroken success in the first hundred days of this war. This was to be a bitter recollection in Japan when its record ceased to be one of uninterrupted conquests, and the country faced the experience of endless decline.

Its first conquest was Hong Kong. That fell almost immediately. A very small off-shore island of China, useful for trade and for political action, Hong Kong had never been seriously prepared by the British for standing a prolonged siege, even in the recent years while the situation had looked threatening. It was ringed by Japan's armies and its fleet; it was without a hinterland of more than a few miles; its water supply was easily vulnerable; it was too far from a British base for there to be any possibility of reinforcing it. It never had a chance to survive, and it was surprising that it held out for as long as thirteen days.

The main feature of its siege was the confusion among the population, which was overwhelmingly Chinese. Many, though loyal inhabitants of the colony, had dual nationality with China, or else were moved by strong Chinese sentiments. These had for the most part been loyal to the Chungking government, and its most active and enterprising members, who in consequence had become marked men to Japan, succeeded in escaping to mainland China; as also did the Chinese politicians who, because they found it safer to operate beyond reach of the Kuomintang, resided in Hong Kong. Many civilians in Hong Kong responded to the call for at least a token resistance. The Japanese, in the use of their political warfare techniques, attempted to set off the Scots in the garrison against the English. Pamphlets were dropped which were full of Scottish sentiment, invoked the memories of Loch Lomond, and inquired whether the Scots were willing to be sacrificed in an English quarrel.

The siege was ended on 19 December when the guns were silenced. There was heartening drama at the finish when some of the spirited young men of the colony, together with a Chinese one-legged admiral who gave a foretaste of the astonishing toughness which the Chinese today display, but did so seldom at that period, got clean through the blockading Japanese, and escaped up country to Chungking. Politically the forfeiture of Hong Kong was a blow to the British; but strategically it was inevitable. It had been foreseen and meant little.

A serious loss at Hong Kong was of several of the Far-Eastern experts which the British army possessed at the start of the war. The number of these was appallingly scanty: the army authorities had caused surprisingly few of its officers to learn Chinese and Japanese at a time when trouble was evidently preparing in this part of the world. Of Chinese-speaking officers, many had been posted in Hong Kong, since naturally it was desired to employ them where their talents could be most immediately used. Apparently nobody foresaw that they would pass, after a few days, into captivity. The army, for example in India, would be crying out bitterly against the famine of China experts, for the interrogation of prisoners, the reading of documents, or for the countless ways in which expertise in language is required in warfare.

THE PHILIPPINES

On the same day that they attacked Pearl Harbor, Japan had made a similar raid on Clark airfield, the key to the defences of the Philippine Islands. This was an American possession which linked the United States with the imperial systems maintained by the European powers. The United States was expected to defend it tenaciously. It was not, like Hong Kong, regarded as expendable. With this attack, Japan launched upon the serious task of driving the white invader from the soil of Asia.

The Philippines are an island group off South-East Asia which had formerly been the empire of Spain in this part of the world. They had passed into American possession when the United States had defeated Spain in the Spanish-American war of 1898. It was a war which it was hard to justify: at first it seemed to show that the United States had given up its traditional stand against imperialism and was about to start on the acquisition of colonies. Its heart, however, was never in empire: it produced no specialist imperial class of dedicated administrators. No American literature had grown up around the Philippines; no class of Americans (except a small group of West Point army officers) could claim to have the Philippines in their bones.

Thus it had been easy for Americans to compromise when they found that, among their new subject peoples, the Europeanized middle class of Manila was becoming inspired by the nationalism of the day. Americans had engendered no professional imperialists, in their adventure with ruling subject peoples. They could therefore readily conceive a constitution, which was a replica of the United States one, and could foresee that the Filipinos would make a success of this, and of governing their country without disaster.

By the time that Japan attacked, the United States was already well-ahead with grooming the Philippines for liberation. Japan did not find in it a representative of imperialism at its most stubborn. When it struck, the United States had already passed a law which set a time-table for Filipino emancipation. This envisaged, however, that there would be a treaty between itself and the Philippines, regulating their defence.

By this treaty, the United States was to keep a moderately powerful air force, stationed at Clark Field. The rather sketchy chain of airfields throughout the islands was to be at its disposal. The United States also maintained a weak garrison of soldiers. When the war began, the defences were out of date. The communications between the islands were especially poor. The native Filipino army, which was being trained by the United States, was only half ready.

The Japanese bombed Clark Field some hours after they attacked Pearl Harbor. Reports of what was happening there had reached the Philippines by radio. On receipt of the news, the air force – thirty-five bombers and seventy-two fighters – was alerted and had taken to the air. But the Japanese attack was delayed by the dense morning fog. At lunch-time nearly all the American planes were grounded. While they were being serviced, while the pilots were being fed, the Japanese struck. Nearly a hundred American aircraft were destroyed in the air or on the ground.

Thus the war in the Philippines began with recrimination over an unnecessary loss. The American habit of concentrating its aeroplanes in formations which made the perfect targets had before this caused anxiety. Duff Cooper, who had been appointed a few weeks before as Resident Minister in the British administration of Singapore was horrified at seeing them parked wing by wing at Clark Field and had pointed out to the Americans what a temptation they might be to the Japanese. The loss was nowhere near as fatal as that at Pearl Harbor. Obviously the disaster had no deep influence on what followed. But the disgrace and the material damage had a very discouraging effect.

The raid was followed up by a landing of the Japanese army. It came from Formosa, and the troops had been embarked some days previously. At first there was doubt as to whether the Filipinos, under American command, would resist the Japanese armies, which proclaimed they were bringing freedom. But this doubt was quickly dispelled.

The command in the Philippines was in the hands of General MacArthur. He was thenceforward to play the most conspicuous part of any commander in the Pacific war. A rather older man than most of his contemporaries, a general with an outstanding record in the First World War, a former Chief of Staff of the American army, he had been loaned by the United States government to the Filipino Service to organize the future armies of the free Philippines. He entered with enthusiasm on this task. His father had been the first military governor in the American rule of the island. The relation of trust between him as generous patron of the Filipinos, and the Filipinos as loyal and grateful clients, caught his imagination. He believed that he had the knack and principle to do what other western soldiers and administrators had failed to do: to win the attachment of an oriental people. He was enabled to stand to his own government in the position of a semi-independent power rather than a subordinate servant, a relation which suited him much better than a more regular one.

At the time when the Japanese struck, he had completed six years of a planned ten-year period on this task, and the Filipino army had been brought to a stage of fair competency. Its worst impediment had been the multitude of languages and dialects which were spoken by the soldiers, which made it difficult for them to be organized under a single command. In the months preceding the war, it was, as part of the American preparation against the Japanese threat, reincorporated in the US army. But when the invasion came, the plans, such as there were, about the defence of the Philippines were sketchy and completely shattered by the events of Pearl Harbor. The American intentions had proceeded from the axiom that the Asian fleet would be intact, and would, at least within months, be able to come to the rescue.

MacArthur quickly appreciated that he could not check the Japanese landings. He met them with a scheme which had something of surprise. He gathered together his force, and withdrew into the historic fortress of Corregidor, on an island in Manila Bay, and into the peninsula of Bataan, on the northern side of the bay. Corregidor was one of the famous strong points in the East. It had first been built by Spaniards in the early years of their rule in the seventeenth century, and was heavy with history. But, though extremely picturesque – like Cyprus in the wars against the Turks or like a Crusader's castle – it had nothing done to it in modern times to make it suitable for modern war. On the other hand Bataan was more serviceable. It was a strip of country covered by jungle and had been prepared by MacArthur for its role by the installation of concealed factories, supply depots and hospitals. In these two centres MacArthur had more than 50,000 troops (of whom only 6,000 men were of the regular American army). He planned to withstand a siege by a Japanese army which numbered about 200,000.

MacArthur was at first optimistic that he would be relieved. Apparently, for a senior officer of the US army, he was singularly out of touch with the ways in which the US General Staff thought in time of emergency. He reckoned in terms of a six months' siege, for which he had stored ammunition, though his supplies of food were far less satisfactory. He refused to admit that the United States had been robbed by Pearl Harbor of all powers to relieve and reinforce its protégé. The United States might have lost its battleship fleet, but a great deal could be contrived with cruisers, destroyers and submarines. These ships remained in existence: they might have been used in relation to the Philippines. Actually the American navy fought actively for the next few years in the Pacific without receiving any large new ships. But the will and dash had departed temporarily from the navy. MacArthur, isolated in beleaguered Corregidor, did not grasp this fact. He adapted the tactics of strategic defence when they were in fact pointless because the defence, however resolute, could look for no eventual reward in the early restoration of communications with the United States.

When MacArthur in the end faced the facts as they were, he seriously planned that the entire Bataan garrison should attempt a break-out, and should then filter away to southern Luzon, where they should wage guerrilla warfare. But the scheme, transmitted to Washington, was coolly regarded, and was never sanctioned.

The Japanese began their serious offensive against MacArthur on 29 December, when they let loose their aeroplanes against Corregidor. Surprisingly, both Corregidor and Bataan held out. The Japanese met their first check of the war. The resistance, unexpectedly prolonged, began to upset the larger Japanese plan. They had calculated that their forces would be quickly disengaged from the Philippines, and would be free to move on to the belt of coral islands which lay along the northern coast of Australia. From these they would be able to prepare for the invasion of Australia, and the cutting-off of its communications with the United States.

Their delay continued. At one time the Japanese were so badly placed – stricken with dysentery, beri-beri, and other tropical diseases – that the Americans and the Filipinos, had they been able to launch an offensive, could have re-taken Manila. But this did not put hope into the Philippine President, Manuel Quezon. On 8 February he sent a telegram to Washington saying that the Filipinos were nearly exhausted, and proposing that, as the United States had been unable to fulfil its pledges of protection, it should immediately declare the Philippines independent, the islands neutralized, and the American and Filipino armies disbanded. Quezon, though personally loyal to the United States, judged it thus possible for the Philippines to take refuge in neutrality.

At the end of January the Japanese troops were heavily reinforced. Two extra divisions were moved in, together with heavy artillery groups. The Japanese offensive continued. It was marked by none of the brilliant improvisation which the Japanese were showing in Malaya.

On 22 February, the President of the United States sent a telegram to MacArthur, ordering him to leave the Philippines and to go to Australia to organize the war from there. He went unwillingly, half under the delusion, as is plain from the documents of the time, that he would be put in command of a mighty army with which he would return to the Philippines. From this time onwards he developed a monomania about return. 'I will return' were his last words on transferring his Filipino command to General Wainwright.

The American navy had kept four speedboats intact. MacArthur had sent Quezon, the Filipino President, to Australia in a submarine, but preferred to travel in a motor torpedo boat. On the night of 11 March this little flotilla ran the Japanese blockade. The sea is vast; it is surprising how many times a blockade has been successfully broken. The speedboat in which MacArthur sat found itself at one stage in the shadow of a Japanese battleship, but in the darkness it failed to be aware of its prize. Certainly Japan would have done well to have intercepted this general, who, once away, responded, as if to a magnet, to the powerful drawing force of Japan. But when he returned it would be with an army.

With MacArthur gone, the Filipinos carried on their resistance for a month longer, but the spirit passed out of it. It was one thing to resist under MacArthur's command, and another under General Wainwright, though Wainright was a valiant soldier. On 9 April Bataan surrendered; on 6 May Corregidor. The defenders, the majority of them of the Filipino army, had been still a large force, and, as Japan was in future to show, a Japanese garrison would have been disinclined to surrender.

But resistance seemed pointless when the Filipinos heard on the American radio that the United States was putting its energies first into the German war; and that, for the time being, it had written off the Philippines. The Filipino army had fought when there was still reason for fighting and, with that reason gone, was entitled by all the conventions of war to surrender.

The garrison of Bataan and Corregidor met with a terrible fate for having been the first to throw the Japanese timetable out of date. They were shepherded into captivity in a march which earned the grim name of 'the Death March'. Most of the victims passed into the hands of the Japanese military police, the Kempeitai.

The other American island possessions in the Pacific had been able to offer very much less resistance. Guam was taken on 10 December after a spirited defence. Wake Island held out gallantly, but succumbed on 23 December.

MALAYA

On the same day that Japan was attacking Pearl Harbor it began its assault on Malaya. This was to be one of the principal theatres of the war, the scene of what was probably its most brilliant campaign, and of disaster and disgrace for Britain which was to bring about the twilight of the British in Asia.

Malaya was a peninsula inhabited by Malay sultanates. Great Britain had extended its colonial rule over them in the nineteenth century while leaving formally intact the machinery of the sultanates; and the territory, with the great importance of its rubber, had become a major part of the British colonial empire. The rich and peaceful country had attracted the Chinese, who became a very large minority.

Malaya had a special significance for all the western powers with territorial possessions in the East. At the southern-most tip of the peninsula is the island of Singapore, as large as the Isle of Wight. In the early 1920s, with the ending of the Anglo-Japanese Alliance, Britain had determined to build up Singapore into a great naval fortress, and to make Malaya the vital centre of British power in the Far East. Singapore was to be a dockyard, a naval base, barracks and communications centre. It was to safeguard the communications with Australia and was the base from which the British navy could operate to ensure that the Indian Ocean continued to be a British lake. The British, having decided to rely in the Far East on steel and reinforced concrete instead of on diplomacy, spent £60 million, which at that time was a very large sum, on the fortification of the base. When finished, it was regarded as one of the four greatest sea-fortresses in the world (the others being Pearl Harbor, Malta and Gibraltar).

It would have such obvious military might that, while it stood, it would provide a guarantee of the continuity of British power and thus it would be looked to by all other British territories in Asia; nor was it without significance for France and Holland for the security of their empires in South-East Asia.

The plan was carried through. Singapore was completed. It seemed to double-lock the gateway of the empire so that it was useless for an unfriendly rival power, such as Japan, to dream of forcing an entrance. Japan might have been expected to be daunted by such prestige, and to avoid a direct attack on such an invincible place. It was to prove, however, that the complacency and false security which were generated about Singapore told against drawing up plans for a modernized, flexible defence of the system in case it should ever be challenged.

Almost unbelievably, a totally false estimate of its strength became general. It proceeded from an erroneous view of military reality, which was to prove so eminently disastrous that it is inconceivable how it could ever have been formed, or that, once it had come to determine the fixed lines of policy, it was allowed to continue for nearly twenty years unchallenged. There were two delusions. The first was that, as Singapore lay at the southern extension of 200 miles of jungle, it was militarily impregnable to land attack. Without any serious tests having been made, and as it turned out without any basis of reason, this fortress was given the certificate of virtual invulnerability. It was taken for granted that no enemy could carry on tank warfare in the hinterland of rubber plantations, and it was thought to be impassable, a region exempt from the manoeuvres of modern armies. The actual arrangements for the defence of Singapore were made from this misreading of fact. The rubber jungle was left undefended by human arts. From over-confidence, the garrison of Singapore was lamentably inadequate; the roads were poor; no network of airfields was made which would have been adequate for a great air force; no great air force had ever operated from the Malayan peninsula.

The second fatal miscalculation was that, as Singapore was to be a naval base, it would be threatened only in a great naval war. Singapore was envisaged as the centre of a titanic naval struggle, with a large fleet occupying her to capacity. The eyes of the world would always be on her, and those eyes would always look seawards. All the guns of Singapore would point seawards also. It was prepared with the most modern artillery which money could buy; but the guns were never in a position to fire at an adversary who came by land.

Alas, it was never to play its part in a great war of the seas; its guns necessarily remained silent, for they were not the mobile things of a hundred years before. They were built in concrete and could not in a matter of days or weeks be re-adapted to a new kind of war. Money spent on Singapore was largely useless, for the same reason as was the treasure of France which had been squandered on the Maginot line.

*

In the two years of the war – before Japan suddenly made its nature real and alarming – British people living in Singapore had had time to digest how deadly was their peril. Most of them did not do so. The old myths bore them up. They were cheered by the belief that the British navy, though it was away in other waters, had power to neutralize the Japanese. They could still see the apparent strength of Singapore, which they thought would house its navy, and did not grasp its essential weakness.

Only one British soldier during this time saw the ominous cracks appearing. Colonel Stewart, the commanding officer of a battalion of the Argyll and Sutherland Highlanders, refused to accept the conventions which govern the training of garrison troops. Day after day the soldiers under his command spent their time in jungle training. The Argylls were considered eccentric; but at the end, Colonel Stewart formed the view that Singapore was not in fact surrounded on the north and east by a vast and easily defensible belt of jungle. It was possible for an invading army to use tanks in the jungle; and in a short time the Japanese army, made formidable by all the instruments of modern war, would be at its doors. This was the uncomfortable message which he preached, but nobody attended to him.

It happens that one of the Japanese officers concerned with preparing the Japanese offensive has left a full account of the processes involved. (*Singapore – the Japanese Version*, by Colonel Tsuji). It was conceived as a rescue operation to free the inhabitants from British imperialism. It was not planned from years ahead, and in great detail, as was wrongly supposed by the British government. The expedition was improvised, and planned on a shoestring. The serious preparation and advance studies began only eleven months before the actual attack, in January 1941, and had started with a monthly budget of no more than 20,000 yen (or less than £2,000). The initial planning was carried out in Formosa, which was then a firm part of the Japanese empire, and it was rehearsed on

Hainan Island, which had passed under Japanese control in 1938. The Japanese forces were able to use a mass of photographs and other data which its enthusiastic agents had been busy gathering, partly as a matter of habit and by voluntary initiative. Every town and village had had its Japanese businessmen, Japanese doctors, and Japanese dentists, and these were now revealed as the advance guard of the invasion that was being launched; but it is surprising how sketchy was much of the information. It was discovered that for their coastal operation the Japanese had to rely upon the data furnished by a single master mariner, who had collected the facts for years in case they should come in useful.

*

The invasion did not begin with a surprise massive Japanese attack from the air, similar to that on Pearl Harbor and the Philippines. The war started with the transport of two divisions of Japanese soldiers from Indo-China; the overcoming of the weak coastal defences in northern Malaya. At first, the Japanese were too distant from Singapore to make effective use of the air; today it is overlooked how comparatively limited the range of massive air operations still was. The Japanese landing in the north did not take the British by surprise. It had clearly been a possibility ever since the Japanese took Indo-China, and plans had been worked out, which were in fact forestalled by the Japanese, for a possible seizure of a part of southern Thailand, as a defensive move. The British were, however, out-manoeuvred by the speed and resiliency of the Japanese in moving from their bridgeheads to a lightning drive on the south.

In the first days of the war the British commanders at Singapore disposed of two major warships, the *Prince of Wales* and the *Repulse*, which the government at home, as the skies blackened in the days before Pearl Harbor, had been persuaded to detach from other operations and to spare for the East. These were a powerful reinforcement: with them, Singapore appeared to be about to play the part intended for it by British planning. In theory, at least, they would restore mobility to British arms. They were meant to insure the safety of Malaya, in case the Japanese struck out during the negotiations at Washington. The battleship and battle-cruiser would enable Britain to strike at great distances. With sea power, Britain could exercise what Bacon had described as its natural advantage in all its wars: to take as much or as little of the war as it desired.

Yet the voyage of these two ships was a perilous excursion into the unknown, and should surely have filled those who ordered it with great alarm. Moreover, they were moving against forces which they could not compute. The Japanese had a history of waiting for, and dealing with, naval units sent out from European waters to alter the balance of force in the East. Admiral Rozhdestvensky had sailed a fleet half-way round the world in 1905 to be destroyed at the battle of the Japan Sea. In like manner, the *Prince of Wales* and the *Repulse* were to be the victims, not it is true of a waiting Japanese navy, but of the new Japanese fleet air arm by which the two warships were sunk on the fourth day of the war.

*

With these warships swept from the chess board, the Japanese advance down the peninsula to Singapore could go forward unimpeded. Troops came in by transport from Indo-China, and nothing availed to stop them; more alarmingly, they were accompanied by tanks, which against forecasts, overcame the natural barriers of the jungle. They advanced south with surprising speed. A clear picture of the Japanese strategy began to show itself. The British army, heavily burdened with its impedimenta, untrained for jungle warfare, resisted as hard as it could by throwing up positions across the roads. Meeting their challenge, the Japanese forsook the main road, advanced through the allegedly impenetrable jungle, and took the British in the rear. The jungle betrayed the British; the jungle which had been in their possession for eighty years and whose possibilities for war they had never learned. By these means, repeated so often that they became monotonous, the Japanese came on, and within six weeks were within sight of Singapore.

The achievement of the Japanese has been glossed over. It was remarkable. The Japanese army had until now acquired its battle experience in China, a terrain vastly different from Malaya: and its battle training had been almost exclusively the steppe country of Manchuria. Its performance in the tropics showed an adaptability and resourcefulness in the Japanese officers, and endurance by the Japanese soldiers which had been insufficiently recognized. Though the imaginative qualities of the Japanese army were not afterwards apparent, they shone in this campaign.

The manner of fighting by the Japanese surprised their antagonists. They showed none of the preference for long-range combat, such as most of the other civilized combatants exhibited. They seemed to exult in struggle body to body. They produced gestures of defiance and glee and also of fear which, by most other soldiers, were regarded as childish. A skirmish was accompanied by grunts, gasps and blood-curdling yells. Later, when the Japanese film became popular in the West, it was seen that the Japanese soldier had fought very much as Japanese actors traditionally represented him as doing. It made him a surprising and alarming adversary.

As the Japanese assault on Malaya intensified, it was noticed that the Japanese had a string of successes in air raids upon British aircraft. Time and again the British were caught on the ground. Japan's planes appeared in great force just when the British were getting ready to take to the air. Finally the reason for this striking good fortune of the Japanese came to light. An officer in the RAF, a citizen of southern Ireland, was pursuing his country's feud of twenty years back with the British government, and was detected signalling to the Japanese. This affair was kept secret. It had accounted for an unfortunate part of the air losses in the early stages of the campaign.

*

In the confused ill-temper of the retreat – and it was always retreat, without one solid success to restore self-respect – there was recrimination between the British commanders, and the commander of the large force of Australians, which had been a part of the allied garrison and who had shared in the defence. It was reflected in the lower ranks. Many of the Australians had been stationed in the Middle East before they fought the Japanese. As this was largely a time of defeat before the days of Montgomery, they had formed a disgruntled view of British competence. Their transfer back to the defence of the region where Australian interests were more vitally at stake had been agreed to with a rather ill grace by Churchill; this put the Australians in the mood to be touchy partners. By ill fortune they were under a general, Gordon Bennett, who, though a rather dashing soldier, had in addition the qualities which hardly endeared him to the usual type of British officers. He was not of a modest nature, he did not minimize any affronts shown to him, he did not agree with those people who saw virtue in silence.

To the necessary disgraces which afflicted the beaten army, there was thus added the scandal of a dangerous difference of opinion between England and one of the Dominions, which at bottom had always been so loyal to it, and whose feelings were the more ruffled because they had been so warm. The quarrel threatened to widen out into a dispute which uncovered a diversity in war aims. Australia was left with the feeling that it had been betrayed. Its interests were treated as of slight concern. It seemed that England would unfeelingly sacrifice Australian soldiers for its own advantage. It was the type of ill-feeling which sooner or later was bound to cloud the cooperation of England and the Dominions. A considerable effort was needed to overcome the bitterness: Britain was too occupied for the diplomacy needed. Singapore, which was becoming a curse to the empire which it had been called into being to serve, merely added to its demerits that, in the turmoil of this period, it caused London and Canberra to be for some weeks estranged.

In the long retreat through Malaya, the British had suffered much more than a great military reverse. For the first time their administrative system in oriental countries had been exposed, and went down in ridicule. They, the masters of political craft for conciliating the oriental, found that they had used up all their reserves of prestige, and had no comfort anywhere. In Penang, in Kuala Lumpur, in all the centres of administration, the events were disastrous. The institutions built up over decades, the loyalties so laboriously produced, the habits which the British had so complacently regarded as fixed and permanent – all were swept away. The British were not regarded with fear or hatred: had that been so, they would not have been so quickly written off. Their day was regarded as closed. The local Malay population (not the Chinese), giving a lead to other colonial communities of the empire, regarded it as politic to transfer their loyalties as quickly as possible to the Japanese.

When the backward movement of the British began, it was supposed by home public opinion that, with the example of a scorched earth policy in Russia before them, arrangements would be made for the Japanese to meet with a similar bleak reception. But in almost all cases, the government lacked the nerve to demand the sacrifice from the local people, or, more rarely, the demand was made and the people refused to cooperate. The British efforts to build up a resistance behind the rear of the Japanese army, and to create an adequate spying and Intelligence system were at first unsuccessful. Later on in the war, when the Japanese had made themselves detested, the organizations were to begin to function: but this was to be in the future.

It must not be supposed that the psychological atmosphere changed abruptly to contempt or hostility towards the British. There were many warm and compassionate acts of loyalty and friendship by the Malays and the very mixed population of this cosmopolitan peninsula. The British, in defeat and disillusion, often found unexpected shelter.

How news of great and dramatic events transmits itself in Asia, by what means it travels to remote valleys and distant villages, is not clear. At this time there were very few radio sets outside the larger towns. But in these months a great sensation was felt throughout Asia. The British

Empire was dying. It had been pushed over in Malaya, and it was found to have rotten roots. Soon it would be treated in the same way in the other countries, and in all parts of Asia where the union flag still flew. Britain never recovered from the deplorable events of these few weeks. The happenings in one small section of its empire were enough to destroy its prestige everywhere: and the life and soul of the British Empire had consisted of prestige.

*

While Singapore was in its death pangs, the British committed one more egregious mistake. Large reinforcements of British troops, complete with equipment, had been spared from the war in Europe and ordered to Malaya. These arrived off Singapore when the siege of the fortress was about to begin. With remarkable folly, and with the idea still prevailing that there would be a final effort to redeem the fortress by undergoing a siege, they were disembarked instead of sailing away to India where they were urgently needed, as quickly as they could. These troops, with all their artillery and stores, were put ashore, never to fire a shot, and were to enter on the long martyrdom of Japanese imprisonment.

On 31 January 1942, the army, defeated, bewildered and demoralized, re-entered Singapore. Their rear-guard was led across the causeway which connected Singapore with Johore by the remnants of the pipe band of the Argylls.

The final defence lasted fifteen days. Singapore surrendered on 15 February. It gave in because its defences crumbled; because its water supply passed out of its control; because the Japanese, again falsifying expectation, managed to infiltrate the island's defences at all points, and, within a week of crossing, were seen to be everywhere; because the troops were disorganized, and no pattern of defence established itself; because it was clear that the civilian population in the city had been paralysed and most of it did not desire that it should be defended; because the enemy, which had penned them up in the fortress, had swollen in their imagination to such a size by a unique series of triumphs that further resistance was not really thinkable. He had sunk two battleships which the English had naïvely supposed would have over-awed him: at Pearl Harbor he had struck away the navy that would have made the Americans an effective ally: he had demonstrated that the jungle, that was feared by all other armies, could be treated as the home of the Japanese, from which Japan could draw strength. When this Japanese army began to follow the British into Singapore, and to infiltrate over the island, the British recognized that the battle for South-East Asia had gone against them. By a local decision the fact was recognized: and Singapore was Japan's.

Yet it remained true that the army in Singapore was twice as large as the besieging force, and, in theory at least, a prolonged resistance would have been possible. Even the fact of the non-existence of prepared defences did not cancel out the fact of the great British superiority in manpower. There have been famous sieges in history that have been carried on long enough to embarrass the besiegers and which have been begun in circumstances as disastrous as those in Singapore. Exactly a year later, Singapore was to be followed in the news interest of the world by Stalingrad, and its defenders were not moved by the civilized sentiments of those who had to make the decision at Singapore. It is true that the defenders, unlike those of Stalingrad, could not have cut their way out to safety: but, in theory at least, they could have put up a notable resistance. The defeat was not gilded by any valiant enterprise, such as the rescue of the British troops at Dunkirk, which in after days made Dunkirk a stirring myth, instead of one of the worst reverses to British arms on the continent. In fact it became known later that General Yamashita, the rather eccentric commander of the Japanese, had outrun his supplies. He would have been in no position to support the troops which he had filtered through to the island; they must have fallen back if the garrison had been determined to make the counter-attack of which it was capable. Thus, to other humiliations, the British added that of being bluffed.

To one man, the decision was particularly unwelcome, to the British Prime Minister. It is a little hard to say how at any one moment the events of the war in the Far East affected him. On the whole they were always secondary to the affairs of Europe. It seems that through all this time of the brilliant hundred days of Japan he never succeeded in getting a grip of what was happening. Before the Japanese attack, he had continually underrated the chances of Japanese intervention. He did not equal the grasp which he had on the war in the Middle East. His speeches and his writings about it have a faint note of unreality, of a theatre of war where his views are not translated into action. The impression is dreamlike, of playing with vast conceptions which are fatally unrelated to fact: there is the occasional tumble into an abyss, which he must have foreseen but could not be reconciled to. General Percival's decision to surrender at Singapore had been approved by Wavell. He took the view that the soldiers had done all that could be expected of them, and that a resistance prolonged further would have been a pointless waste of life. In Churchill's distrust of Wavell, which was to become so painfully obvious, perhaps there was an element of resentment for his part in the capitulation.

Churchill's speeches at this juncture are very curious. They are the comment of a detached observer rather than of a committed politician who had to explain the disaster which had befallen one of his projects. The British had surrendered Singapore: that was the bare fact, which people in Britain must stomach, and which they could not be expected to dwell on with satisfaction.

There departed into Japanese captivity a large British force and most of the civilian staff which had passed their lifetime in the administration of Malaya. They had little further part to play in the war, though the suffering of the prisoners was very great, and was periodically used by the British Ministry of Information to stir up public effort, and to keep the people resolute on their liberation. Given the chance to resist, these same prisoners, many of whom died before they could be released, might have preferred to be sacrificed in making the end of Singapore a little more creditable than it was.

The Japanese rejoiced, and not without cause. They looked almost incredulously at the facts of the size of their forces, and what they had achieved against much larger British forces. Usually the attacking force has to be considerably greater than the defenders if it is to have any chance of success; in the Malaya campaign this was reversed. The Japanese losses had been extravagantly small. From the time of their first landing to their occupying the Johore causeway and beginning the assault on Singapore their casualties were, according to Japanese official information which need not in this case be disbelieved, 1,793 killed and 2,772 wounded. They had deployed a force not greater than 35,000 men, and from information they afterwards obtained, found that the defending force numbered 80,000. In the actual assault on Singapore they lost a further 1,714 men killed, and 3,378 wounded. The Japanese claim that not a single man was captured. The myth has grown up that the Japanese troops were helped by having a corps of men trained in Malayan affairs. This is quite false. The number of Malayan experts was less than ten.

During 1940 and 1941 Germany had discussed with the Japanese from time to time the possibility of an attack on Singapore. But the German estimate was that the initial campaign would last one and a half years and would need five and a half divisions. Actually Japan required fifty-five days; and only two divisions.

Japanese publications since the war have shown a high, rather theatrical morale among Japanese troops. The telegrams are still extant which Japanese generals sent to one another; their style is extremely patriotic, conventionally moralistic, reasonably free of the rivalries between officers and between services which were so common later in the war. One of the ceremonial acts which the Japanese performed after their victory was to build a tower which was dedicated to holding Buddhist requiem masses for the British killed in the campaign.

The Japanese, perhaps because they had taken Singapore with such an inadequate force, established there an occupation régime which governed it with extreme strictness, and rather purposeless brutality. They felt uneasy. Soon reports began to circulate of extraordinary Japanese measures against any suspected organization. Singapore was principally inhabited by Chinese, and the Kuomintang had used its citizens to extract funds for the Chinese government. They were determined to stop this. The Chinese, in general, were irreconcilable; some had the reputation of being extremely radical in politics, which Japan also feared. The existence, in a peculiarly ramifying form, of the Chinese secret society, was another thing which provoked them. So, from the earliest days of their triumph, ugly tales of police terror and torture were mingled with a great victory. In the first few days of the occupation of the city, they compiled a list of hundreds of the Chinese and arrested them *en masse*. The beaches near the centre of the city became execution grounds by night where the Kempeitai – the Japanese military police – took their preventive action.

BURMA

In Burma, the history of the Malayan campaign repeated itself. The Japanese army invaded it on 11 December from Thailand.

Burma, one of the smaller countries of the British Empire, had had, in the half century of its membership, a comparatively uneventful history. Now it became lurid in the extreme. In the minds of most English people, Burma became known, no longer as an oriental paradise inhabited by a merry, picturesque people, but a fated, evil country, the arena – from no fault of its own, it is true – for some of the most horrible fighting of the war. It was not simply to flare into prominence by the brief experience of being overrun, but was to remain a contested land until the end of the war.

Burma had formerly been attached to India. It had been annexed to it as the result of three wars in the nineteenth century. It was an act of convenience for Britain; by no shadow of claims could it be regarded as an Indian land. Its majority people, the Burmese, were one of the Asian peoples with the clearest national consciousness; their economy was not inevitably linked with the Indian; their language and script had only a distant connection with Sanskrit; their religion, to which they were peculiarly devoted, was the Hinayana form of Buddhism, which ultimately derived from India, but which had practically died out there. Hinduism, which Buddhism had once rivalled in India, had revived powerfully, and had overgrown Buddhism. But in Burma, Buddhism had no competitors, and flourished mightily. This rendered Burmese culture different from Indian.

The unnatural union of Burma with India was resented by the Burmese. Their desire for freedom was two-fold, freedom from Britain and freedom from India. This second freedom they won at the time of the great political recasting, at the time of the Government of India Act of 1935. It was perceived that to continue to enforce the unity of the two countries would impose an unnecessary strain on the problematical machinery of government devised for India. Burma was allowed to settle its own destiny, and the Burmese legislature voted to go on its own way. It had a constitution which half met Burma's growing demand for complete freedom. Its government had the same liberties as a provincial government in India under the Act of 1935. But what in India were to be the federal powers of government were in Burma controlled by the British.

In the days of the union between India and Burma, the British had neglected to build up communications between the two countries. A railway was planned, chiefly for military reasons, but was never made. Its absence was to have a powerful effect on the shape of the fighting now to break out. Shipping interests, powerful with the government, saw in it a threat to their monopoly of traffic with Rangoon, and successfully opposed the scheme.

In the years just before the war, political life developed rapidly. The professional and commercial classes were organized in orthodox political parties, which were willing to pursue their national aims through non-revolutionary means and within the framework of the institutions already conceded. But the desire for independence was greater, perhaps, than it was in India, though it was not taken as seriously. Moreover there were revolutionary parties, notably the Thakins, which meant the party of the 'masters' or 'gentlemen', which were ready to seek any aid, and do anything, which would bring about the end of British rule. These parties, which stirred up political consciousness in Burma, had a growing clientèle among students, and among people who had no limiting restrictions placed on their political activity by economic considerations.

Japan found the political situation in Burma more suited to its intervention than in any other country. Moreover Burma, through the existence of the Burma road, had become a major preoccupation of Japanese strategic plans.

Japan had prepared its action in Burma for several years, and more carefully than in most other centres. It had sent there a naval officer who, disguised as a trader, had made the first contact with Burmese politicians. The results were so promising that a Japanese consul was instructed to build up a pro-Japanese network. This, however, had brought the Japanese Ministry of Foreign Affairs into the picture. This, fearful of angering the British unnecessarily, demanded extreme caution.

Progress came, not from persons engaged in this part of the enterprise, but from the coming to Burma of a Japanese army officer, Colonel Suzuki, who was a natural genius at all kinds of espionage and subversion. He modelled himself on Lawrence of Arabia. Until 1939 he had had a career as a regular combat officer; it ended with Suzuki under a somewhat mysterious cloud, brought about by an incident in 1939 in the war with China. Thenceforward he was a spy. He chose Burma as his field of activity, and he was as little subjected to control in what he did there as was Doihara, a much more celebrated agent and planner of subversive action in Manchuria and China. Officers like him were given much latitude by Japan. They might create a situation which the Japanese army would be free, when the time came, to manipulate or to ignore, as circumstances decided.

Suzuki decided that the Thakins offered promising material with which to work. He was a curious man; he was genuinely interested in promoting the movements of Asian peoples to be free; he took seriously the claims of Japanese propaganda that Japan supported all movements for independence; he was regarded with suspicion and as a nuisance by the more orthodox Japanese, who had no intention of conquering large parts of Asia, and simply transferring them to native hands. In Japanese service, he was advancing views and actions which were not at all favoured. He has been described as a rebel by temperament, a conformist by upbringing. His conversation fascinated the Burmese with whom he came into contact. He would tell them to insist on being independent. If, after the Japanese conquered their country, they refused to grant independence, the Burmese ought to shoot back.

Suzuki set himself to form the nucleus of a Burmese independent army, which could be extended as soon as a Japanese army crossed the borders. He calculated that a Burmese force would prove a valuable auxiliary for bringing about the discomfiture of the British, whether in

harrying them politically, in forming a link with the Burmese population, or in straightforward military operations. In 1940 he began to
select likely young revolutionaries from the class of political adventurers
and arranged for thirty of them to be sent over to Formosa for military
training in Japanese schools. The thirty Thakins received this education
partly in Formosa, partly in Hainan Island; Suzuki had them well
grounded, by strict Japanese discipline, in combat tactics, in methods of
civilian cooperation with the Japanese army, and in all ancillary methods. It is clear that he had some difficulty in getting these young men
accepted in the various training camps, for he acted as a lone wolf, and
he had not fully emerged from the disaster which had temporarily
blocked his military career. The Thakins, for their part, objected to the
strenuous quality of their training, and contemplated desertion. They
had actually got control of a small sailing ship with which they proposed
to sail for home. On their fate depended much of the modern history of
Burma. The accident of who was chosen among the thirty Thakins, the
founder members of the Burma Independence Army, governed the
course of Burmese politics down to the present day. Because of personality difficulties, the Thakins tended to fall into factional groups, which
were reflected for long after, quite irrationally, in Burmese politics.

Suzuki, together with a staff of adventurous Japanese who were
looked at rather askance by the Japanese army, transported his thirty
Thakins to join the two divisions of Japanese troops waiting to invade
Burma. By a shrewd move to catch the Burmese imagination, he gave
each of the Thakins a new name from Burmese folklore, which was
peculiarly rich in such things. He devised ceremonial oaths to link them
together. And he revived the old Burmese legend that they had discovered ancient charms which brought them invulnerability. This,
which was traditionally affected by Burmese insurrectionists, and had
been the sustaining weapon of the peasant leader, Saya Sen, in a rebellion in 1930, was obstinately believed by the Burmese populace. It was
to support the Thakins handsomely. The atmosphere in their camp was
that of a boy scout jamboree, the same vague high-mindedness, the
same enjoyment in devising ruses, rather the same kind of humour. The
Thakins, half in terrified awe of Suzuki, half in naïve enthusiasm for
him, admired the way he genuinely fought for their interests with his
orthodox Japanese colleagues.

*

This Japanese dealing with Burmese politicians was to have interesting
consequences later as the history of Burma unfolded. But, in the actual

conquest, the principal agent was the Japanese army. This fought the battles, and defeated the British. The British were embarrassed by the Burma Independence Army, but it only contributed marginally to their downfall. They complained of the treachery of the population, the clamour against them by the Pongyis (Burmese monks), the betrayal of their movements to the Japanese, and the false intelligence often given to the army by the villagers. For all these things, the Burma Independence Army, playing the part of aide to the Japanese, was partly responsible. Their experience permanently soured the British troops, and gave Burma a bad reputation as a country to be fought in. Anything to do with Burma was thought to be unlucky, and the country filled the army with great apprehension.

However, for their rout, the British had to blame the Japanese directly. They had invaded at the start with two divisions with which they overran the south and took Rangoon, the capital. As in Malaya, the British had placed their confidence in the natural obstacles to troop movements in the rugged, jungle country of the border. Again it had become axiomatic that tanks could not penetrate this, and again the fact had not been tested. They quickly found out that they had deceived themselves. Unlike Malaya, the country was held by too few troops, badly trained, with a defective air force. From the start, the British were too unevenly matched to have any chance of holding the Japanese advance. After Singapore fell, the Japanese were reinforced by another two divisions, which had been campaigning there, and they advanced to the north, pushing back the British before them.

The British accepted the offer of Chiang Kai-shek to send a Chinese army to assist in the defence. They did so reluctantly because, through awareness of maps which were being published in Chungking, they had reason to suspect that Chiang had designs on the Burma frontier, and that, once they were in, the Chinese troops would be hard to evict. Japan, however, prevented this danger by driving them back into China. On the borderland some of the Chinese were broken up, and also suffered a great defeat.

By the end of April, the British were expelled from the country. They were pushed right out of Burma. Eventually the greater part of their forces escaped into India, marching out through the trackless jungle land which intervened between Burma and India. Only a part of the far north remained out of Japanese hands. It was inhabited by Chins and Kachins with whom British rule was unfamiliarly popular, being, like all British administration of the jungle fringes of their empire, so light as hardly to be noticed. This territory was held by a body of irregular troops, re-

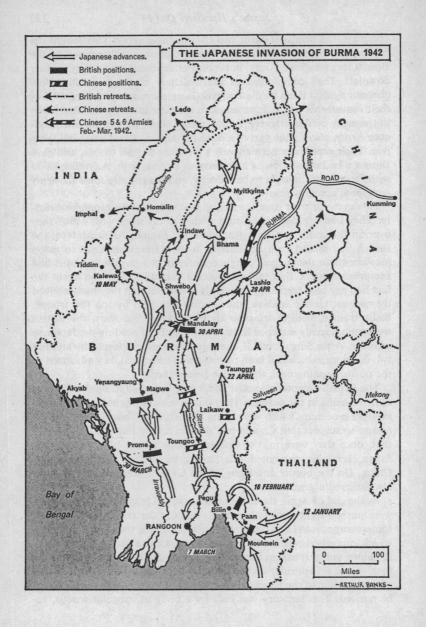

THE JAPANESE INVASION OF BURMA 1942

Japanese advances.
British positions.
Chinese positions.
British retreats.
Chinese retreats.
Chinese 5 & 6 Armies
Feb.- Mar. 1942.

INDIA

CHINA

Ledo

Chindwin

BURMA ROAD

Imphal

Homalin

Myitkyina

Kunming

Indaw

Tiddim

Bhama

Kalewa
10 MAY

Shwebo

Lashio
29 APR

Mandalay
30 APRIL

B U R M A

Akyab

Yenangyaung

Magwe

Taunggyi
22 APRIL

Salween

Mekong

Laikaw

Sittang

Prome

Toungoo

THAILAND

30 MARCH

Irrawaddy

16 FEBRUARY

Bay of
Bengal

Pegu

Bilin

Paan

12 JANUARY

RANGOON

Moulmein

7 MARCH

0   100
Miles

~ARTHUR BANKS~

cruited chiefly from the Chins, which was raised by British anthropologists. The exploits of this force, the intelligence and devotion of the Chin people, are one of the subjects which has escaped narration.

The same incidents marked the Japanese advance as had happened in Malaya. The civil government collapsed. It showed itself again and again to be extremely incompetent, its officers were lazy, its resolution was contemptible, its planning was certain to be based on faulty information, its complacency was unlimited. Its poor showing did not come altogether as a surprise. Before the war, the British administration in Burma had been notorious for delays and muddle. When it was put to the test, it perished with the same sense of scandal as the administration in Malaya. The machine of government had been allowed to rust, and its levers broke in the hand when pulled. It was unfortunate because it could not rely upon any machine of popular government to provide a link with the people, or to rouse any enthusiasm on the government side for the war. Shortly before the start of the war, the Prime Minister of Burma, U Saw, who had been on a visit to London, was detected while returning home in making contacts with the Japanese. He was arrested and interned in the Seychelles, but although U Saw was made harmless, the episode did little good to the British sense of security, and brought little change among the politicians who replaced him. (U Saw, a turbulent figure, was the powerful opposition leader in post-war Burma. He came to world notoriety in 1947, when he organized the assassination of U Aung San and half the Burmese cabinet. For this he was hanged.)

The growth of the Burma Independence Army took place as Suzuki had foreseen. By the time that they were able to parade in liberated Rangoon, they numbered 5,000 men, and claimed to number 10,000. Their appeal had been great. But their methods of recruitment were deplorable. The Burmese villages, partly because of the peculiarly rapid tendency of the Burmese to resort to violence, had always had a higher proportion of criminal types than was usual in the East. As the Burma Independence Army advanced through the country it proved to be irresistibly attractive to this sort of recruit. An armed force, with licence to rob and pillage, provided the ideal shelter behind which it was possible to hold the whole country to ransom. The army spread a reign of terror behind the Japanese advance. Its original Thakin leaders found that the control of their troops was passing out of their hands. For seventy-five years Burma had experienced deep and unfamiliar peace in its rural life. The exploits of the Burma Independence Army abruptly destroyed this peace, and, to Burma's cost, it was to prove impossible to restore peace in this generation.

The population of Burma consisted of a Burmese majority, and many non-Burmese people, organized with different customs and religions. Under the long British peace, these had relaxed their suspicions; the different peoples had mellowed, and their government had seemed easy. But the exploits of the Burma Independence Army stirred up the feeling of the Burmese that they ought by right to be dominant, and raised a consequent feeling among the minorities of great insecurity. In panic, the minorities organized for self-protection: where a minority possessed the remains of tribal life, its institutions were rapidly brought into play. In no time, civil war was provoked and was spreading, especially between the Burmese and the Karens, the Burmese and the very large Indian minority, and the Burmese and the hill people, the Kachins. As a result, there took place a terrified mass migration to India, and it is estimated that India, in the midst of war, had to receive half a million refugees. For every refugee to cross the Indian frontier, there were several others who starved and died on the way.

The Japanese became aware of the chaos which was being provoked. Having driven out the British from the whole country, except for a comparatively small corner which was inhabited by Chins, they were looked to by the law-abiding part of the population as the only power able to secure basic order in the country. They had been manoeuvred by Suzuki into giving countenance to Burmese revolution, but it had served its term, and they had really no sympathy with its explosive purposes. Japan, whatever its propaganda might declare, was never a revolutionary power, and generally was on the side of property and privilege. In the middle of June it applied itself to the problem of providing a government for the country. It was not willing to proclaim Burma's independence, but established a provisional government, made up of politicians of the orthodox parties. The Burmese cabinet could only rule the country through the civil service structure of the British, and this the Japanese sought to preserve. Burmese civil servants were promoted to take the part of British officials.

Stability, however, could not be expected as long as the Burma Independence Army was allowed to roam the country, doing its will by sheer force. The decision was therefore arrived at to suppress the army. Colonel Suzuki was to return home to Japan. He sought to stay, claiming that he held a commission for what he had done from Prince Kanin, and therefore came directly under the imperial house, of which Prince Kanin was a member; he asserted that this freed him from control by the Japanese army. But he argued in vain. In place of the Burma Independence Army, a new force was raised, much more regular in its structure, more firmly placed under the control of the new government.

This was a natural, merely prudent step of the Japanese government. It was a decision which any responsible government was bound to take: the Burma Independence Army had stirred up so much feeling that any orderly administration was really impossible so long as it persisted. But the apparent repudiation of Burmese revolutionary nationalism by the Japanese was held by nationalists all over Asia to be difficult to square with Japanese propaganda claims; the more so since the Japanese were at first unwilling to satisfy the Burmese with any talk of independence. In Burma it caused the start of a long-drawn-out quarrel between the Japanese and Burmese nationalism, which was to play a part in the Japanese downfall at the end of the war.

THE DUTCH EAST INDIES

The fate of the Dutch empire was the same. Because of oil, the territory was especially attractive to Japan. The first Japanese landing in Indonesia had taken place on 6 January. On 6 March, Batavia, its capital, fell. A large-scale naval battle had been fought between 27 and 29 February and resulted in the destruction of five Dutch cruisers, and of the few British cruisers which still were afloat in these waters. By April the fighting was at an end.

The experience of the Dutch was generally similar to that of the British. They had a considerable army in Indonesia; 98,000 men surrendered, almost without fighting, and were interned. Apparently the Dutch could not rely sufficiently on their Indonesian troops to risk combat. A feature of Dutch colonialism was the far greater number of Dutch residents in their colonial territories. The number of internees was therefore greater.

The impressions formed by the Dutch of the victorious Japanese army were interesting, since they come from people who formerly had less to do with the Japanese than the British or Chinese. Their first feeling was one of unwilling admiration. The Japanese marched in, in perfect discipline. For whatever reasons, the disorders of the Japanese occupation, which had been reported in the Philippines, Malaya and Burma, were avoided. There was no deliberate relaxing of discipline while the troops ran wild. Plundering and unlawful high-handedness by the soldiers were prevented. Before long, these first impressions were found to have been much too favourable; but in the early days were unquestionably widespread.

The Dutch noticed that the Japanese carried very little impedimenta, and went without demur, wherever their officers ordered them. It is usually reckoned that, in modern armies of the West, for every fighting man there are eight supporting soldiers; among the Japanese the ratio was said to be as low as one to one. The Japanese continually demonstrated before the eyes of the Dutch that no obstacle could deter them. And there was no sign that the Japanese private soldier, or junior officer, murmured against the savage discipline which was used against them.

*

With these conquests, there came to an end the extraordinary hundred days of Japan. The army and navy had raced ahead, and, after a period of rattling and shaking down the empires of Britain, Holland and the United States, they needed time to rest, and to make new plans. The extent of the territory which had fallen into their hands bewildered, while it exulted them. They had to provide for its administration. They had also to fill out the contents of the extremely vague and propagandist plans for the 'Greater East Asia Co-Prosperity Sphere', which had come into being long before it was planned as a reality.

Meanwhile the Japanese population would have been more than human if it had not given itself up for the time to the spectacle which was fed to it by all the propaganda machines of the modern state and was meant to generate a profound mood of self-wonder. The streak of exhilaration came after a long and anxious period which preceded Pearl Harbor, a period of grave economic anxiety, of regrets over the interminable war with China, of fears that it was getting out of its depth in international relations, and of perplexity over the disorders in its political life.

The great outburst of Japanese victories had lifted the reputation of the Japanese soldier to unexampled heights. He was suddenly regarded as superhuman and invincible: his military virtues were so stupendous that it struck wonder that they had not been noticed adequately before. It seemed to be useless to struggle against them: they had eclipsed the virtues of the white man, until then incontestably the most formidable in the imagination of the Orient. As the Japanese army went to war in 1941 it sang a song called 'Umi Yukaba'. One of its verses, in translation, is as follows:

> Across the sea,
> Corpses in the water;
> Across the mountain,

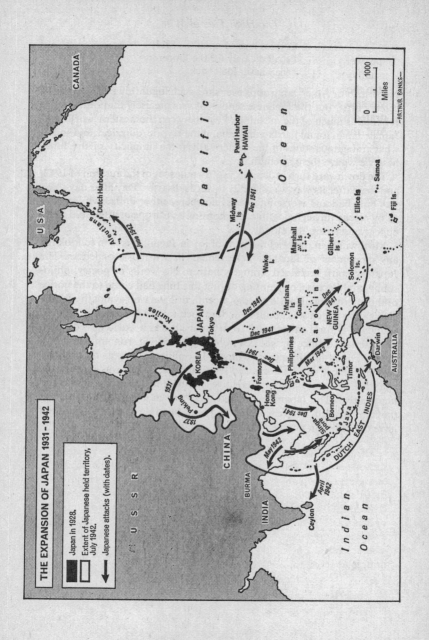

THE EXPANSION OF JAPAN 1931 – 1942

■ Japan in 1928,

☐ Extent of Japanese held territory, July 1942,

↓ Japanese attacks (with dates),

—ARTHUR BANKS—

0 ____ 1000

Miles

CANADA

U S A

Pacific Ocean

Dutch Harbour

Aleutians June 1942

Kuriles

U S S R

JAPAN

Tokyo

KOREA

CHINA

Peking 1937

1931

1937

Midway Is Dec 1941

Pearl Harbor HAWAII

Dec 1941

Wake I.

Marshall Is

Gilbert Is

Ellice Is

Samoa

Fiji Is

Dec 1941

Mariana Is Guam

Dec 1941

Caro lines

Dec 1941

NEW GUINEA

Solomon Is

Dec 1941

Philippines

Formosa

Hong Kong

Dec 1941

Borneo

Java

DUTCH EAST INDIES

Timor

Darwin

AUSTRALIA

Mar 1942

Singa pore Mar1942

BURMA

May1942

INDIA

Ceylon April 1942

Indian Ocean

> Corpses heaped upon the field;
> I shall die only for the Emperor,
> I shall never look back.

No British or American troops ever sang such lugubrious or unsophisti-
cated words. But the Japanese sentiment was precisely that of the song.
It contains much of the meaning of war between the western world and
Japan; Japan found hard to understand the cryptic, quizzical, and somewhat ambiguous songs of the western allies: the simplicity of the Japanese view gave them strength.

The downward turn in Japan's war fortunes set in the autumn of 1942,
and thereafter its way was steadily towards disaster. Day after day there
was only bad and worsening news; nowhere, either in its own fortunes
or by rescue through possible triumphs of its European allies, did there
appear any rift in the clouds.

Meanwhile, in the brief moment of joy in Japan, it is vain to look for
any monument of Japanese achievement in art, music or letters. The
Japanese spirit remained strangely barren. No works of poetry, philosophy, architecture, or painting during this time had come to the notice
of the international world of cognoscenti, or have won sympathy for the
civilization which was about to endure such ravage and destruction. No
sounds of natural gaiety came from Japan: it was a world now devoted
to material advance: it was devoid of lightness, wit, romantic lyricism,
the cultivated intelligence of women. In politics there was no originality: in science, having borrowed from abroad, Japan was ingeniously
adaptive, but was without a creative impulse; in sociology, it was unimaginative. The Japanese pursued their war in a grey atmosphere of
the human spirit. Victory, if that had been possible to them, would not
have conduced in any way to human enlightenment.

CHAPTER 14

The Storm in India

WITH Singapore and Burma lost, the storm was breaking on the edge of India. There the consequence was not at first military action, but an intensification of the political crisis which had lasted thirty years and which was compendiously called the freedom struggle.

A great excitement swept India. The British in India had the mortification of being made to realize that the military crisis did not signify for most people there a time of mortal danger, but was a time of opportunity and interesting uncertainty. The news of the rout in South-East Asia had the inevitable effect. Britain imposed only a very slight censorship on news, and it was in consequence possible to form a clear idea of Japan's military prowess. Under the influence of this situation the Indian political situation changed rapidly. The war, and its consequences, was suddenly at its gates: India was no longer to be the distant spectator of events: they were at hand.

By the time of the outbreak of war, it had been obvious, to all who chose to look, that India was nearing a period of deep change. Delhi, its capital, at this time was a place of unusual interest. The last days of the old order were bathed in a rather unreal light. They were touched by a sunset. This revealed possibilities and beauties of the scene which had never been noticed before. The British, who were about to put up the shutters on their period in India, suddenly discovered, as they were on the edge of terminating their role, the enchantment of the country, which most of them had ignored as long as they were in secure occupation. India was in the condition typical of countries which are approaching revolution. Only the first rustling of the storm could be heard. It was not yet disturbing because the politics were still interesting and had not yet become lethal.

New Delhi, built chiefly by Lutyens, was then at the height of its brief but real beauty. It had matured and had been sufficiently lived in to have the atmosphere of a city rather than a camp, as it had been only a short time before; but it had not been sufficiently encroached upon by planless building to be spoilt as it is today. Unlike most capitals which have played a part in this chronicle, it had remained outwardly at peace. It was full of talk, and uniforms, and war; but it remained unravaged. The war had brought a flood of new men to the city for the first time, especially young Englishmen of the citizen army of the war years: these were often intelligently attentive to the qualities of Indian life, and they refused to be bound by the restrictions of the colour bar – that fatal barrier which had done so much harm to race relations in the past, and also cut across the natural enjoyment of the country by British visitors. Though there was more political controversy than ever, there was a distinct thaw in the relations of the British and Indians. The old barriers were falling one by one. Life, in the capital though not in the back-woods, became more normal, relations more relaxed. Even while they were engaged in hot dispute, Indians and British alike began insensibly to sun themselves in the climate of emotional debate, which they en-joyed as the most engaging pastime in the world.

In the political arena war speeded up the struggle of Indian national-ism against the British. But the war had the effect of inflaming even more intensely the divisions within Indian nationalism: between Hindu nationalism, which stood for a united India, and Moslem nationalism, which envisaged a British withdrawal from the continent leaving the predominantly Moslem part to become the independent state of Paki-stan. The Hindu–Moslem crisis was the heart of political India. In the critical war years, politics turned chiefly on this, and it was the key to almost everything which happened.

*

The issue between Hindus and Moslems was relatively simple. Over a part of north India, the Moslems, chiefly as a result of past invasions, were in a majority. This was limited to certain regions: over the country as a whole, the Hindus were in a substantial majority. They were, more-over, the more advanced community in political activity.

When Hindus raised the cry of Indian independence, they had assumed that the Moslems would support them, as following the most advanced political leadership, and, at the start of the national move-ment, most Moslems had done so. At this period, those Moslems who were politically interested, had been attracted by the parties, which, though predominantly Hindu, claimed to be national, transcending both Hindu and Moslem. But, as politics set light to ever-widening circles of people, the Moslems began to draw apart, and to question whether they would have any benefit from independence, if it were won by Hindus.

The issues thus opened up were plain. Could Hindus and Moslems, by a compact between them, still agree on a common plan? Or, when independence came, should there not more properly be an independence for a Hindu India, and another independence, involving the creation of a new state, for a Moslem India? It took time for this conception to spread among the Moslems, but when it had taken root, it was plain that from the Moslems would come a fierce demand for secession. The Congress claims for independence, which the Moslems represented as a plan for transferring British sovereignty over India into Hindu sovereignty over Moslems, lost its shine and became a matter for controversy.

The Moslem community was at first widely regarded as more backward than the Hindus. At first the Moslems had not taken the same advantage as the Hindus of the opportunities of adopting modern style institutions. This was partly because the collapse of the Moghul power at the time when the British first arrived in India was a psychological blow from which it took the Moslem upper classes a long time to recover. Initially they had stood stubbornly aside from innovations and educational opportunities offered by the new Raj which, they felt, had displaced them. There was also the fact that Islam half a century ago was opposed to modern education: Moslems were more shackled by their faith at this time than were Hindus. The simplicity of the Moslem outlook commended itself to some temperaments among the British, who were mystified and repelled by the more subtle and exotic Hindu character: but some people sensed in the Moslem mind a greater confusion in the response to the modern world than was to be found among Hindus. The Moslem who fell back on Moslem traditions for guidance in the maze of the modern world often found himself afraid. The Islamic institutions were inadequate; they could not be brought up to date. Moslems tended to live in a world of the past, and, being called on to live in the present, were left with ways uncharted and with reactions for which there was no precedent. The Moslem response to the new life was often unpredictable, unreasonable, and, too often, violent.

The question turned on whether the Moslems were right in declaring themselves to be a separate nation from the Hindus, or whether both were fundamentally Indian, divided only by religion. Both Hindus and Moslems had shared a common Indian state for many centuries: at times the Hindus were dominant, at times the Moslems. Was religion alone sufficient to turn them into irreconcilables?

The Moslems argued that it was emphatically so. No common life for the two people was really possible; to hold them together was too artificial. Each community, though they had been joined under foreign rule, lived in isolation from the other. Each had a separate law, its own customs, wore its own clothes, had its own literature, preserved its own way of eating. Sometimes, after prolonged periods of ordered government, they would somewhat unbend and lower their guards. The natural affinities of neighbourliness would prevail to a limited degree over the divisiveness of religion. The common language would inevitably bear some influence in mingling the two peoples. But of a genuine merger of the two societies, there was no sign. Cases of intermarriage between the two communities were very rare, and free intermarriage is the best sign of the fraternization of communities.

The Hindus replied that this was a gross misrepresentation of the position. They could argue that in previous generations the Hindus and the Moslems had felt no such separateness, and automatically regarded themselves as forming a single people. Most Hindus were willing to concede that in recent years the relationship of Hindus and Moslems had often been bad, but this they attributed to the deliberate attempt of the government to play off one community against the other. To divide and rule was, they held, the first principle of the administration. They argued too that the difference between the communities was largely one of economics, and that, if the economic processes were given free play, these would be enough to break down the communal differences and mould the peoples into a single great society.

*

As the political situation became more fluid, with signs from the British that they would contemplate withdrawal, there was deadlock between the two sides. The arguments of both appeared to be conclusive. Attempts at mediation proved always in vain.

The coming of wartime tension gave a great impetus to the deterioration. The Moslems, in the fevered atmosphere of the times, set themselves, under the lead of their principal nationalist party, the Moslem League, to mobilize their forces. In all the provinces of north India they agitated formidably, concentrating on drawing back all the Moslems who still supported the nationalist Congress party. With an ever-increasing show of force, they intimated that they would resort to civil war if any attempt were made to surrender British power to Hindu hands.

The achievements of the Moslem League at this time are due chiefly to a single man, Muhammad Ali Jinnah. He had two distinct careers. Before 1930 he was an all-India leader of the Congress. The interest of Indian nationalism possessed him and the interest of the Moslem community seemed to be reconcilable with the ascendancy of Congress. In other words, he, though personally a Moslem, was very much like Motilal Nehru, the father of Jawaharlal Nehru, who, though a Hindu, assumed that Hindu interests would always be subordinate to Indian nationalism. In the beginning of the thirties, he had retired to England for some years, where he had a flourishing legal practice. During this time he reflected, brooded, thought about his previous career and meditated on the ways that his willingness to subordinate specific Moslem interests to national interests had not been met by a similar disposition in Hindu leaders. He returned to India, broke entirely with the old all-India ideas, and ceased to be in any sense a co-worker with the Congress leaders. Instead he challenged them, and on the whole outwitted and out-manoeuvred them. He denied their right to speak at all to the Moslems; his first major enterprise was to dislodge the Hindus from the foothold they had obtained in the Moslem community. Next he built up the Moslems as a formidable striking force which demanded a state for its expression and existence.

His achievement was to inform it with something like the questing assertive feeling of the Poles when for more than a century they had been deprived of a state. Eventually, in 1919, they succeeded in breaking through, and forced themselves on the map of Europe. In the same way the Jews, deprived of a state for many centuries, at last completed its reconstitution. Similarly the Indian Moslems had the will, at the time still partly subconscious, to carve out for themselves an independent state in the Indian sub-continent. Jinnah's contribution to history was to recognize the will in advance of anyone else, and to place himself in its service.

All his successes Jinnah won by the force of his character, by his iron will, and by his clearly marked intellectual superiority. He came to his ascendancy late in life. He had been obscurely born – he was a dentist's son in Karachi – and had had the handicap that he was hardly a true Moslem at all, but, according to local gossip, was the grandson of a converted Hindu. Gradually he made his career, and owed very little to any help which he received from any quarter. The unemotional single-mindedness of his character did not go with any of the amiable qualities which make a man the darling of the crowd. Nevertheless, his way forward was made in full view of the world. There were no secrets in his career: it could be discussed, analysed, appraised, and judiciously respected.

It was characteristic of the Moslem community that his worldly success won him solid esteem; as much as did Gandhi's unworldly conduct prevail with the Hindus.

At the beginning of the second chapter of his life history, his phase as leader of the Moslems, he began by taking over the leadership of a weak party, with a very vague ideology, representing every section of a deeply riven society. He hammered it together to be an exceedingly effective political instrument, to which he then, relying for persuasion on intellectual power, dictated policy. He was the new force of Islam incarnate. As such he was indisputably one of the great actors of the time in the war years. He was one of the few individual architects of the great changes which were coming about.

*

With the Japanese at the gates of India the British government felt that something must be done to rally the country to its own defence. The Labour party had at this time increasing influence on the policy of the British government towards India, and they succeeded in persuading the cabinet that the wisest course was to renew its attempt at conciliating Congress. The principal author of this policy was Sir Stafford Cripps. He was a peculiarly able lawyer, a masterly advocate, and firmly convinced of the benefits of democracy, which, he believed, was a suitable government for any territory, whatever might be its circumstances. He had devoted himself to the study of Indian problems. He was convinced that, if Congress demands were satisfied, it would be ready to take its share in the conduct of the war, and that, by a kind of political miracle, the Indian scene would be transformed.

Cripps was mistrusted by the more conservative influences in London. They believed that, in spite of the evidently superior quality of his mind, his judgement of reality was less than shrewd. They were convinced that his appreciation of India was wrong. The situation in India could not be transformed by eloquent appeal to Congress leaders; Congress support, they knew, might be bought at a price, but at a price which would worsen the situation, since it would bring about a revolt by the Moslem population, and would cause such chaos in India that it would be useless for the prosecution of the war and would drain off large forces of troops from elsewhere for internal pacification. At the same time Congress, if it were won round, could make no difference to the military circumstances. If Congress were given a free hand in war administration, it would, argued these critics, mismanage it. By its participation it would alienate a large part of India which, as the result of various appeals, was showing wartime zeal. There was a strong likelihood that Congress, having made a deal, would take the first opportunity of leading India out of the war altogether.

In spite of these doubts, Cripps was personally trusted with the mission to conciliate Congress. The situation for Britain was at the time so bleak, and the cabinet was so preoccupied with other matters, that his confidence that he could reason with the Indian leaders was contagious, and his offer to go out to see what he could do was welcomed. On 11 March 1942 he arrived and spent three weeks in the country, as a kind of ambassador from Britain.

Cripps, as the chief motive of his tour, carried with him a specific offer to Congress from the British cabinet. It proposed as the long-term part of the scheme, that at the end of the war a constituent assembly should draft a constitution for India, and no limitation should be put upon its work. Though it was hoped that India would stay inside the Commonwealth, it would be free to secede from it.

To most people in London, it had seemed that Congress could scarcely have asked for anything more complete or more explicit. Next, as a short-term measure, as something on account, Congress was offered immediate admission to the Indian central government, but on terms. The government would be a diarchy, partly British controlled, partly Indian nationalist in composition. It would continue to be under the chairmanship of the Viceroy. On its side Congress was to approve the war effort.

Bargaining on these terms had been what Congress had had in mind, when, in advance of the Cripps mission, it let it be known that the Labour party pressure for a new initiative was welcome to it. But politics had moved a long way since the world had been at peace in 1939. In India they had become purely communal: the conflict between Hindu and Moslem, Congress and the League, had put all else, even the conflict between nationalist India and the British, in the shade. The Cripps offer, being drafted in part by civil servants in London, had included matter to conciliate the Moslem League as well as Congress. A sense of realism dictated this. It would have been folly to win over the Hindus at the cost of causing inflexible hostility from the Moslems. In the midst of war, the British government could do nothing which would provoke a civil war in India. Nor could it overlook the fact that a high percentage of the Indian army was Moslem, and, in event of a Moslem rebellion, would have dissolved in its hands.

This explains why Cripps was equipped with a fatal document that came to be known as the 'Cripps Offer'. In the eyes of the Hindus, the proposals had the mortal defect that they were conciliatory to the Moslem League demand for Pakistan. The Cripps Offer included a provision that, if the Moslem parts of India declared their firm intention to be separate – by a plebiscite in the areas concerned – they should be permitted to secede and to form their own constituent assembly. This was a permissive clause; it was not a definite award; what was to be decided in fact was to remain open until the war was over. But though the plan was hedged round with limitations, and was only to looked on as one among several possibilities, the putting of it forward was a bitter shock to the Indian nationalists, who had not yet been taught by frustration, disappointed hopes, and blows of fate, to adjust themselves to realism.

This was the point of major controversy. It was the reason why the Hindus felt they had nothing to gain from the offer. They could not bring themselves to complicate a negotiation with the British over what they considered the national demands of India by introducing into it a solution, though only a possible one, of the Moslem problems; the more so because of their suspicion that the problem had been distorted by the British as a device to counter the national movement.

This was the reason for the breakdown of the negotiation for the long-term settlement. No less completely did Congress reject the short-term offer by which this was accompanied; this was the invitation to join the central government at once. Congress could argue, with some reason, that its Ministers, if it had supplied them, would have been installed in a subordinate position in the central government, from which they might have been again ejected; and, for this, they were asked, for the first time in history, for a solemn undertaking that, if the Moslems persisted in this demand, Pakistan would be conceded. Congress was quite sure that the Moslems would persist if they were encouraged to do so by the attitude taken up by Britain.

The Congress decision was not so unreasonable as it appeared at the time in London. The negotiations were not entirely straightforward. For tactical reasons, Congress preferred that the break with Cripps should come about over the powers which were to be offered to Congress Ministers if India threw in its lot with the war effort. These were to be limited in the army itself to various matters of administration and supply, which the government felt it would be safe to delegate; and it was made woundingly clear that from matters of the higher direction of the war, allied strategy and the organization of intelligence, the Indian leaders would continue to be excluded. Nehru, after an exploratory session with Cripps, said that the offer boiled down to Indian Ministers being given control of the army stationery and of canteens. In spite of exaggeration, there was some truth in this.

An American attempt to mediate in the negotiations was unsuccessful. The United States had become deeply disturbed at the situation. It saw a real danger that national India would secede from the war, and, for military reasons, greatly feared the loss of Indian territory as a base. It feared also the effects upon its ally, China. Few Americans understood the complexity of Indian problems, or the reasons which prompted the British government. For them the situation in India was simplified in terms of a repetition of the American War of Independence, and naturally their sympathies were strongly on the Indian side. The United States was embarrassed that, in a war which it increasingly advertised as a war for democracy and freedom, it should be tied in alliance with Britain, whose past role in India ran so counter to the principles of the Atlantic Charter. It therefore regarded itself as vitally interested in the outcome of Cripps's negotiations. But its endeavours to help them on, and to ease out difficulty, did not achieve their purpose.

*

Yet it was Gandhi who was ultimately responsible for Congress rejecting the British offer. Gandhi was still in effective command of Congress when Cripps came to India. Nominally he had for a long while stood aside from holding office in Congress. But in fact he, as Congress adviser, had the overriding influence – though it was never quite an uncontested influence – on Congress decisions.

This was understood by the British. Cripps knew that he must convince Gandhi before anyone else. He had long interviews with him. At the end of one of them, it happened that Sardar K. M. Panikkar, an extremely able politician of the Indian princely states, was seen to be going from the sweepers' colony, where Gandhi was staying, on his way to report to his masters, some of the Indian princes whom the excitement of the times had brought to Delhi. He was asked what view Gandhi took of the Cripps Offer. Actually, Panikkar did not know: his visit had not been directly to Gandhi. But from a knowledge of Gandhi's mind, he was certain, and he expressed the opinion in an epigram which has the accent of the Mahatma. It was, he said, a post-dated cheque on a failing bank.

Gandhi later repudiated the latter part of the epigram; he said that he in no wise wished to impute failure to Britain in the war, or success to Britain's enemies. On the other hand, it was clear that his attitude towards the waging of war differed from that of the belligerents. He proposed that resistance to the Japanese on Indian soil should be non-violent. In a letter written to one of his followers in 1942 (quoted by Shri B. R. Nanda in his book on Mahatma Gandhi) he said:

Remember that our attitude is that of complete non-cooperation with the Japanese army. . . . If the people have not the courage to resist (non-violently) the Japanese unto death and not the courage or the capacity to evacuate the portion invaded by the Japanese, they will do the best they can. One thing they should never do – to yield willing submission to the Japanese.*

However, Gandhi realized that the British in India, and a large element in Congress, could it have been brought to cooperate with the British by the ironing-out of their political differences, would not employ non-violent tactics in resisting Japan. He had, therefore, no wish to see a compromise between Britain and the Congress which involved the issue of waging war. He was, furthermore, possessed by the idea that if the British left India, Japan would then leave India alone, and it would be spared the fate of Burma and Malaya. Accordingly, his influence was thrown against the Cripps Offer, and, in the circumstances of the time, was strong enough to kill it.

*

In April, soon after Cripps had failed, Gandhi, by one of the daring simplifications of issues which were a part of his strength, began to use the slogan 'Quit India'. The precipitating cause of his decision was his foreboding of a coming crisis, should the government take steps to compel the peasantry to adopt a scorched earth policy in the case of an invasion. Gandhi said that it was one thing for the Russians to adopt this policy voluntarily; it was another for a government to impose it on a confused people, too poor to endure it.

The British protested that, as politically responsible beings, they could not, in the middle of war, walk out of India, without making arrangements for the orderly transfer of British power. The suggestion that they should go seemed self-evidently absurd, and the fact that it was made seemed to the local administration either to reflect on the political sense of the opposition, or to proclaim that the demand was made for objects of whipping up national feeling, and it was not expected that it would be considered seriously. The British had been willing to promise, in a series of policy statements, which gradually eroded their position, that British power should eventually be wound up. Most of these were sincere. They felt injured when Congress doubted their word. They argued that they must have time: essentially it was impossible to set about the hazardous political experiment in wartime. The British side, although under pressure of the social radicalism which was mounting at home – increasingly liberal in statements and assurances about long-term intentions – remained adamant against immediate radical changes until they judged that the war should have been won. The day-by-day pres-

*B. R. Nanda: op. cit.

sure of the events of war at home was too great to allow the liberal forces in the Westminster parliament to give very much consecutive attention to events in India. It was upon the constant distraction of the British government in London that British bureaucrats in India chiefly relied; it saved them from having their hands tied.

*

Congress, in facing a renewed rebellion, had the experience of its two major collisions with the British to work upon. It had learned much in these. In 1942 Congress was better organized than it had been ten years earlier.

The traditional Congress method in working against the government was to use the method of 'open conspiracy'. That it conspired could not be doubted: but it avoided anything in the nature of a secret plot, since by doing so it strengthened its moral force. Politicians who plotted secretly drew on themselves some of the odium that terrorists are never entirely free from, even when the government, as in India, was unpopular. Congress seldom made any secret of its plans; it carried them out in daylight.

Thus, when Gandhi turned from patient agitation and persuasion to direct action, he openly proclaimed it. Success in what he intended would depend on the willing cooperation of masses of the people. Therefore, after giving his ultimatum in late May, all through June and July he worked up the feeling of the country by explaining in every possible way what Congress, under Gandhi's direction, meant to do. He hoped, by summoning the people, to induce so many men at all levels to withdraw their support from the government – while taking care to be non-violent – that the business of carrying on the government would become impossible, and the British would evacuate. The army would have a large number of deserters; so would the police; the workers in the towns, by going on strike, would halt the production of war materials; chaos would set in in the civil administration. And all would be done without violence. Gandhi, even at a great crisis was enough of a lawyer to frame his own statements, and to persuade most of his colleagues to do the same, in such a way as to ensure that this point was clearly made.

Gandhi was waging a war of nerves. The British were bent on giving no provocation. Their interest was to prevent matters going to extremity. Though by the mid-summer, Japan had passed the peak of its war, though the battle of Midway Island was recognized by experts as having been a decisive test of strength, though Japan's *élan* was slightly drooping, the British government had still only a very slight margin of safety to play with. The danger of invasion was still very real, and a Congress rebellion would be found to add to the emergency of the war; it would threaten the Allied use of India, which, geographically, seemed likely at this stage, before subsequent successes of the United States in the Pacific, to play a major part. To contain the outbreak of national feeling, which Gandhi knew he could command, required great coolness and discrimination on the part of the government in deciding the precise moment for contending it.

The man who had to combat Gandhi, and who at this stage flared into prominence, was Lord Linlithgow. He had been Viceroy for five years. On the whole he had not had an impressive term of office. He had arrived with the reputation of being an expert on agriculture, having been chairman of a commission which was expected to do something about this flagging but vital Indian industry; but he had totally disappointed the country by taking no initiative. By the time of the war he had shown that he entirely lacked the common touch, the ability to communicate with the masses, and, if he was sympathetic with anybody, it was with the bureaucrats. He may have been unlucky in this; but though there were men who affected to find human feeling in him, few if any of the politicians ever established rapport with him. He had neither an evident enjoyment in the discharge of his great office nor a knack of handling the politicians of varying and often irreconcilable opinions who were his necessary acquaintances. He seemed totally to want imagination, and could not fire others with a vision of the importance of what he had to do. He had great industry without a capacity to turn this to account in ways which caught the imagination, considerable public spirit without it being able to gild any of his actions. Politically his main task had been to preside over the constitutional reforms which were meant to convert India into a Federation and to bring the Government of India Act of 1935 into operation; but in this also he failed to achieve anything. The Federation never got off the ground, and it was widely believed that its failure was partly due to Lord Linlithgow's willingness to let matters drift. He had allowed himself to be weighed down by the Indian realities and concluded, on seeing them at close quarters, that the proposed constitution was not really prudent.

There is no need to see Lord Linlithgow as an essentially fascist type, as was apt to be supposed by some Congressmen. In calmer times he would have been perfectly happy in presiding over a democratic and constitutional India; he was not a permanent adversary of liberalism. But in the conditions of war, he judged it clearly crazy to hand over political responsibility even in part, to politicians who were untested, and whose statements had aroused a strong suspicion that they were opposed to the war. Lord Linlithgow's view was that of British common sense at the time. He had the strength of seeing the situation in the same light as Churchill and the majority of the British cabinet, and therefore was given their confidence in taking the steps which he proposed. One needed to be a man of exceptional political vision to see that Indian national feeling might still be enlisted for the war, and that political boldness might still achieve what it set out to do.

Linlithgow's lack of imagination had allowed the initiative to pass to Gandhi. The government only prevaricated and played for time; Gandhi promised action. Now Gandhi was about to use his opportunity, to take the steps which many men feared to tread but which their mood would support, and to commit Congress to the greatest gamble of its career. The expectation of action set in strongly among the people, so that Congress, though the organizers of the mood, found themselves finally swept along by it. Linlithgow had cool nerves. That which made him incapable of giving creative leadership and made him dull to the distressed conditions of all around him, served him well in this crisis.

In the first week of August, Gandhi summoned the Working Committee of Congress to Bombay. He made no secret of the fact that his intention was to speak the words which would set in motion a new civil disobedience movement on a grand scale.

Late at night the police pounced and arrested Gandhi and all the Congress leaders. They were transported to carefully arranged and not uncomfortable prisons. Gandhi himself was interned in a requisitioned palace of the Aga Khan. The operation had been carefully planned, and, unlike most actions of the Indian government at that time, had been kept carefully secret. The success with which it was executed helped to restore the self-respect of the government.

*

For the rest of the war, Congress was inactive. Most of its leaders continued to be in prison. The government, which had been anxious about the extent of their popular support, discovered that this had been exaggerated; but exercised a perhaps understandable prudence in keeping in the leaders until Hitler was defeated.

The continuing incarceration of the Congress leaders left the way clear for Moslem agitation. By the time that Congress orators were once again free, they found that the Moslem leaders had organized the Moslem community fairly solidly, and that Congress opposition counted for little. One of the unforeseen consequences of Gandhi's 'open revolt' had been to let in Pakistan.

The British authorities were relieved at the passing of a crisis. But, though they might have been expected to revise their general attitudes in the light of a proved weakness of Congress, they did not do so. Their policy followed very closely the official and unofficial statements of it. This was that time was nearly up for the British in India, and that at the end of the war Britain would do exactly what it had said it would do: make a sincere attempt to set up a government, or governments, in India and leave the sub-continent. Most of the politicians in England, even the less enlightened ones, and most civil servants in India, even the more elderly ones, were in agreement about this. For the present India's war-effort was still needed, and nothing would be done to rock the boat. But as the war went on, the government gradually ceased to have the feel of certainty and stability, and took on the style and temper of a provisional government. From London a strong breath of discouragement was blown at anyone who played with other concepts of the future.

Gandhi, the man of peace, who had been obliged by political circumstance to play such a large part in wartime politics, ceased to be a determining figure of the war. Indeed, never again was he to have the personal dictatorship which he had had of the opinion and actions of Congress. His decisions in 1942 marked his passage from supreme authority. After the war, though he had great influence, and though for a time a great deference was used towards him by all who sought to mould events in India, new forces had appeared, and he had to bend before these.

Gandhi's eclipse for the rest of the war, and the eclipse of Congress, removed from India the feature of its politics which had made India fascinating for so many. In a world given up to the contest for brute power, and, worse still, for military power, the claim of Congress that it was striving for higher things was refreshing. Congress politics were intensely histrionic; drama was the essence of them. They were also steeped in arguments over political and secular morality. It was breathtaking to find Congress, in the middle of the war, calmly demanding on moral grounds concessions which no government could have made, least of all a government which possessed a still unbeaten army; yet it had the authority to compel the rational discussion of its demands. All this was now given up. The politics of India were deflated; they followed more practical, limited, lesser ends; greater vision had been dispersed by contact with reality. Yet never again were Indian affairs to be felt as touching the heart of humanity generally as they were when the arch prophet of them had moved around with his strange entourage which recalled, in manners and circumstances, that of St Francis of Assisi and the other compelling figures of the past and perhaps the future.

*

Gandhi's adversary, Lord Linlithgow, also stalked out of the picture. Immensely tall, gaunt, awkward, he had been out of place in Hindu India, which liked to discuss with passion those ideas which seemed to mean little to Linlithgow. His final actions were not much to his credit. In the summer of 1943 there took place a frightful famine in Bengal. For the first time for thirty-five years this dreaded event had recurred in India. It was an ugly fact that this spectre, to exorcise which had been one of the claims made for British rule, had again appeared. This particular famine was man-made. Throughout the episode there was no actual shortage of food supplies in India. But these were allowed to remain hoarded because the railways, under pressure of wartime operation, had broken down, because the civil servants, also under wartime pressure, realized too late what was happening. It did not adapt the famine code, which kept the country from starving in normal times, to the changed circumstances of war. It was too much harried by urgent and unfamiliar problems of administration.

In Bengal a great exodus took place from the countryside to the town, the opposite to the direction of population flow in the previous year when the panic set in that India was to be bombed. More and more frightful tales began to circulate of a population driven by hunger to roam until they fell dead from emaciation. The streets of the great modern city of Calcutta were strewn with corpses, and such sights began to appear there of the juxtaposition of extreme wealth and of stark hunger as had before the war been notorious of eastern metropolises such as Shanghai. Another blow had been dealt to the credit of the British government in Asia.

As reports of what was happening began to come out of Bengal people expected that the Viceroy would tour the famine area, to bring what help was possible, to be seen communing with the people, and to inquire into what was evidently a failure of administration. To visit the scene of disaster was a tradition of the Viceroy. But, inexplicably, Linlithgow on this occasion departed from tradition. Week after week went by, and he spent the last days of his term of office in Delhi and Simla.

His successor, the new Viceroy, promptly reversed this behaviour. The solid benefit which by his immediate visit he was able to do the administration struck the country as a rebuke to his predecessor. It was evident that more could have been done by energy, imagination and improvisation. Wavell called in the army to relieve the miseries of the people, and for a period this enjoyed a very real and unusual popularity.

Yet Lord Linlithgow, reluctantly though he may be praised, played a great part in guiding Indian affairs so that events took one shape and not another. He was given much latitude by the home government. After the failure of Cripps, his judgement prevailed on most matters. He handled the open rebellion of Congress almost under the eyes of the would-be invader. That so few lives were lost, and that India continued belligerent, was due to his calm and to his sense of proper timing.

CHAPTER 15

Midway Island's Battle

THOUGH the attention of the western allies was fixed uneasily upon the territorial gains of the Japanese, that of the most influential Japanese strategists continued to concentrate upon the war at sea. It was to be the greatest naval war in history. The great prize of war would be the mastery of the Pacific Ocean, and this would go to whichever navy proved to be the stronger. The Japanese war planners, in the months after Pearl Harbor, had kept a very flexible outlook. Some favoured a blow in the Indian Ocean, which would open the way to military operations in the region. There was even talk of a naval sweep of the Indian Ocean, which would end with the Japanese making contact at Suez with the victorious German armies. Others wanted an attack in the southern Pacific which would isolate Australia; others a renewal of the attack on Hawaii which Pearl Harbor had begun.

Nearly all sections agreed that Japan must continue to be aggressive. Only by exploiting the impetus gained by Pearl Harbor could Japan even seem to prosper. The long-term odds against Japan were so desperate that the conversion of the war into a defensive one would have been half to admit defeat. The best course lay in a constant series of surprises, which should divert attention from the sombre reality of Japan's true position.

During all this period, the Japanese army showed little willingness to embark on joint plans with the navy. At this time the situation and prospects of Germany were very uncertain: it was in the middle of its great adventures against Russia, which, if they had been successful, would have altered the complexion of the war: the Japanese army was therefore anxious to keep its hands free, so that it could be ready to strike whenever this might, by the unfolding of events, become desirable. Although, by its southward move, Japan had turned its back upon Russia, and was genuinely anxious to make its non-aggression pact with Russia a reality, it could not ignore the fact that Russia was reeling. If it were to be defeated, or to be in obvious danger of defeat, a new situation would come into being, and Japan would be driven to interfere in Siberia. Its divided attention during these months probably accounts for the salvation of India, and perhaps of Australia, from invasion.

The centre of initiative in the months between Pearl Harbor and June 1942 was the brain of Admiral Yamamoto. It is true that, as Commander-in-Chief, he was still technically subordinate to the naval General Staff. But he was regarded by everyone as the author of the victory at Pearl Harbour; and he used the prestige which this gave him to impose his concepts upon the more conservative Japanese admirals. In Yamamoto, Japan had produced its only undisputed genius of the war: a man whose ideas gave a new turn to naval strategy, and who had the capacity to translate the ideas into action.

As a next move, Japan sent a fleet of five aircraft carriers and three battleships, six cruisers and twenty destroyers, into the Indian Ocean in the direction of Ceylon. It was in the command of Admiral Nagumo, who had had the operational command at Pearl Harbor. It was a task force very similar to that which had raided Pearl Harbor, and its objective was to bomb Colombo and a naval base at Trincomalee in the same manner, though of course it could not hope for the same element of complete surprise. It was seeking out the eastern fleet of the British navy, and would try to put it out of action in the Far East by dealing it the same crippling blow that had been inflicted on the American Asiatic fleet.

On 1 April 1942 the British Admiral, Sir James Somerville, was alerted to the presence of Nagumo's fleet, and concentrated his available force to meet him. Somerville had a fairly large fleet, five battleships, seven cruisers, and three aircraft carriers and sixteen destroyers; but the battleships were chiefly obsolete. He had the enormous advantage that he held the Japanese naval cipher; and the Japanese did not suspect this. No major shift took place in the Japanese disposition but he was aware of it as soon as it happened. The eyes which this gave him were probably the decisive thing in the action which followed.

On 4 April the Japanese made what was intended to be a major air strike at Colombo. They found the British alert to the attack; no warship was in harbour; the air force was already in the air, and gave the Japanese a fair fight. The Japanese, denied the advantage of surprise, broke off the attack to bomb, and sink, two British heavy cruisers, which had approached dangerously near to the Japanese aircraft carriers from which the bombing planes had come.

Somerville had in the meanwhile discovered that Nagumo's force was larger than he had at first supposed. He recognized that he was hopelessly outclassed; his old and very slow battleships were no match for the enemy. He was therefore forced to take evasive action by day, and attempt to engage the Japanese at night, although in fact no naval engagement took place. On 9 April Nagumo made an air strike at Trincomalee, the British naval base, but again failed to take it by surprise. The anti-aircraft and fighter defences were formidable: nevertheless the Japanese bombers did more harm than they had done at Colombo. They ended the raid by locating and sinking one of the British aircraft carriers.

With that, the Japanese raid into the Indian Ocean came to an end. Their total loss had been five bombers and six fighters. They had sunk an aircraft-carrier and two heavy cruisers, with naval auxiliaries and a quantity of merchant shipping, and they had destroyed thirty-nine British aircraft. In conjunction with the Japanese casualties at Pearl Harbor, their losses were absurdly low from this initial combat with the American and the British navies. In ships traded, Somerville came off decidedly the worse. But he had saved the bulk of his fleet from the destruction that might have overtaken it from the Japanese aircraft carriers, and for this he had to thank the decipherers of the Japanese code.

The Japanese were planning the capture of Port Moresby. This was in New Guinea: from its occupation Japan counted on being able to menace Australian ports and airfields. Its capture, as some optimistic Japanese appreciation asserted, might even force Australia out of the war. The military force needed for this operation appeared to be so small that, for once, the navy had the ready cooperation of the army; and was to convoy a Japanese landing force. The Americans and the British agreed with the Japanese appreciation, and decided that, though still far from ready to offer serious opposition to the Japanese, the operation must be resisted. They mustered the forces available to them: these were built round the American aircraft carriers, the *Yorktown* and the *Lexington*, together with an Australian cruiser squadron, a British battleship and smaller craft. To deal with this concentration, Nagumo's fleet, on its way back from its operations in the Indian Ocean, was ordered to detach two of its aircraft carriers, which reached the Japanese base in the Coral Sea late in April, and joined the light carrier and six cruisers supporting the Japanese transports.

For the first time in the war a battle was fought between Japanese and American aircraft carriers. This action, the Battle of the Coral Sea, lasted from 6 to 8 May. It was a drawn action. The rival forces were never in sight of one another, and the battle resolved itself into a hunt for one another by their planes. One of the American carriers, the *Lexington*, was sunk, and the second so severely damaged that it was put out of action. But for the first time in the war, the apparent Japanese invincibility was checked: both Japanese carriers were crippled, and the light carrier was sunk. The heavy aircraft carriers were able to return to Japan, but in a condition which put them out of use for several months; their absence in the impending engagements was probably of decisive consequence. In the air combat, the Japanese airmen, among whom the losses had at last been severe, had shown faults in tactics and intelligence which surprised naval observers generally. They were unused to night operations, and out of their element in making night landings on their carriers. It became plain that the high standards of precision which had made Pearl Harbor possible had been gained by a very few fliers, and the majority of them were far below these. As the result of the operation, the aircraft carriers lost three quarters of their bombing planes and their pilots. Yamamoto, it began to be plain, had allowed his methods of warfare to outstrip the personnel which would have made these decisive. As a result of this first naval reverse, the attack on Port Moresby was called off, and this was to prove of great significance for the future development of the war.

. The Americans, though they were concerned about their losses in carriers, were not entirely displeased at the result of the battle. They had brought to an end the run of easy and almost insolent successes by the Japanese. As the result of the air battles, they drew various tactical conclusions, and strengthened the force of fighter planes on their carriers.

These two operations strengthened Yamamoto in his belief that the further acquisition of territory was not of consequence, and that any action which frittered away the Japanese power from its main preoccupations was dangerous. Under his insistent pressure, it was decided that Japan must concentrate its efforts on the destruction of what was left of the sea power of the western allies, especially of the American Pacific Fleet. He, who had designed the raid on Pearl Harbor, was in no illusion about Japan's hopeless position if the war was prolonged, or until Japan had gained the full advantage which had been hoped for in that bombardment. At the moment when Japan at home was still exulting in the mastery of the lands in the South Seas, he saw only the danger preparing for it in the American dockyards. If the United States had the time to bring its economic strength into play, and to translate this into warships, the United States would be irresistible. Japan could find safety only by striking again, and at once.

Yamamoto therefore urged, and after some dissent from the naval General Staff got it accepted, that Japan's next move should be a conquest of Midway Island. This island is 1,100 miles north-west of Pearl

Harbor. If it fell into Japan's hands, it would be ideal for mounting a Japanese offensive against the Pacific coast of America. Yamamoto counted on the United States accepting that its defence was of vital interest, and that it would bring out what was left of the American navy in its defence. In the battle which would result, he reckoned on sinking the American carriers; and this was the main objective of the expedition. The force which chance had put beyond Japan's reach at Pearl Harbor he would now succeed in driving into action.

Another motive which also weighed with him was to deprive America of the possible use of Midway Island as the airfield for the bombardment of Japan. Japan had been warned of the danger of bombardment because in April President Roosevelt had authorized a spectacular raid upon Tokyo, primarily for the effect of morale building in America. The raid, under the command of Lieutenant-Colonel James H. Doolittle, had been from land bombers released from American aircraft carriers which, after their attack, had flown on to land in China. Though Midway Island had played no part in this actual operation, it was clear that in fact it might do so in the future; Midway was only 2,500 miles from Tokyo. Yamamoto felt himself heavily burdened by the duty of protecting the capital of his master the Emperor from the indignity of bombardment. Everything pointed to Midway Island as the target at which he should strike. If he succeeded there, he planned to press on Tojo, the Prime Minister, the need to seek a negotiated peace with the United States, even to the extent of proposing terms which seemed plainly disadvantageous to Japan.

The United States had been in occupation of Midway Island since as long ago as 1867; but it was only in 1938 that it recognized its importance. It began to spend large sums of money in fortifying it as a kind of outpost of Pearl Harbor. It was to prove one of the chief theatres of the Pacific war. It was a small coral island; the colours, in the dazzling sunshine, were so bright and assertive that they wearied the eye. In the years just before the war the Americans had built a small but very up-to-date hotel. Its public rooms had, uncannily, the feeling of mountain hotels in, say, Austria; it was strange because the nearest mountains were thousands of miles away; the illusion was heightened because the views from the hotel rooms might have been alpine. The vivid white of the ubiquitous coral might have been from snow. The strangest phenomenon of the island was its prehistoric appearance. On all sides were small, gnarled, dried-up, gaunt trees, of stilted and incredible shape, looking like fossils. The whole place was unnaturally silent. There were noises of traffic and motor cars; but behind this a great hush prevailed.

The impression was unreal and nightmarish. This was now to be the scenery for one of the very great battles of the war.

The Japanese assembled a huge fleet. It consisted of eight aircraft carriers, of which four were very large, eleven battleships, twenty-two cruisers and sixty-five destroyers and twenty-one submarines; it was the greatest fleet concentration which had been known in the history of the Pacific. The fleet was divided into three parts. The main striking unit, in which were the aircraft carriers, was to make for Midway. Following this, three hundred miles in the rear, were the battleships. Very oddly, Yamamoto, who this time did not confine himself to making the general plan of action and supervising it from his headquarters in Japan, placed himself in command of this section. It was held in reserve to take whatever action was required after the aircraft-carriers had attacked at Midway. As Yamamoto imposed a radio silence throughout the battle, he was virtually a spectator of the action which was imminent. Thus Yamamoto condemned himself to impotence in the type of battle which he had for so long preached as the typical one in the stage which naval strategy had reached at the time. There was a convoy of eleven transports with the necessary landing party from the army. The third section of the fleet, grouped round two carriers, was to detach itself from the main body and to move up to the Aleutian Islands, attacking and landing on some selected places. This was included in the general plan as the complication and the feint which nearly all Japanese plans contained. The concept was that the United States would divide whatever forces were available to it, and one force would sail for the North Pacific in search of this decoy.

From the start there were grave doubts about the expedition among the Japanese naval staff. There was anxiety about the deficient preparation of officers, about their inadequate briefing, about the speed with which the expedition was launched, about the lack of time for adequate digestion of the lessons of the Battle of the Coral Sea, about the wisdom of the tactics which had been used in that, about the security which had been observed, even about the morale of some of the fleet. The senior officers were despondent at the boasting and indiscipline of some of the younger men. The navy pilots, whom Yamamoto had trained, were held in suspicion by the rest of the navy, and this was not relieved by their tendency to regard themselves as a race apart. Especially by the more responsible officers, Yamamoto was criticized for the speed which he demanded. This required that the two powerful aircraft carriers, which had been badly damaged in the Battle of the Coral Sea, could not take part; they had to be in dock under repair for several months. Their absence was severely felt. But Yamamoto felt that the political situation required immediate action, and everything was subordinated to this.

The sailing of the fleet from Hashira on 21 May was one of the most spectacular sights seen in any country during the war years. There were cheers and enthusiasm from the considerable crowd who witnessed it. The Japanese, though they lived with extreme frugality on all their expeditions, contrasting spectacularly in this with the standards of well-being required by British and American forces, observed ritual and ceremony for commemorating the start of such a major operation. On this occasion, the sailing of a fleet, which was intended to complete the work of Pearl Harbor, and sink the remainder of the American Asiatic navy, was blessed by all the forms of Shinto, the Japanese state religion, and also, though less wholeheartedly, by Buddhism. Cups of saki were drunk which were a present from the Japanese Emperor. Western scholars, reading of these scenes, may find their memory jogged to remember the account by Thucydides of the sailing of another fleet on what was meant to be the culminating operation in a war 2,300 years before.

The ships being now manned, and everything with which they meant to sail being put on board, the trumpet commanded silence, and the prayers customary before putting out to sea were offered, not in each ship by itself, but by all together to the voice of the herald; and bowls of wine were mixed through all the armament, and libations made by the soldiers and their officers in gold and silver goblets. In their prayers joined also the crowds on shore, the citizens and all others that wished them well. The hymns sung and the libations finished, they put out to sea, and sang. The first ships then raced each other in columns as far as Aegina.

The battle came on 4 June 1942. The Americans had been better informed than the Japanese Intelligence allowed for, and had again been admirably served by what they were able to learn from cracking the Japanese naval code. They were aware of what Japan had gone to ingenious lengths to hide: that their main objective was Midway, and that the assult on the Aleutians was a diversion. Yamamoto was right in supposing that the Americans would fight, even though their navy had not yet recovered from Pearl Harbor, and was manifestly not ready; he was wrong in thinking that they would divide their inadequate fleet, and would send a part to hunt for the raiders in the Aleutians. The Americans could assemble on the spot three aircraft carriers: in the whole American navy at this time there were seven. One of these carriers was the *Yorktown*, which had been so heavily damaged in the Coral Sea that the Japanese believed it sunk, and had accredited themselves with a groundless victory. In fact it escaped to Hawaii, and, while the Japanese ships in a similar plight had entered the Japanese shipyards for thorough repairs, and were out of action for some months, the Hawaiian shipyards, under pressure of the news from Midway, made the *Yorktown* fit for fighting again in three days, though their first estimate had been that it would take a matter of weeks. The Americans also assembled eight cruisers and fifteen destroyers. The Japanese had therefore a more formidable resistance to overcome than they had thought it possible for the United States to assemble, especially as they also underestimated the American strength in planes and troops on Midway.

The Japanese navy had no radar. That Japan, and that Admiral Yamamoto, who had espoused everything to do with the air, had neglected to acquaint himself with this invention, is astonishing. The fact must detract something from Yamamoto's reputation for alertness. Radar had already been widely used in Britain for more than two years, and a form of it was also known in Germany. The Germans sent the Japanese two radar sets by submarine, but either they did not send technicians with the apparatus, or these lacked the quality to make themselves attended to. This incident shows how slight and ineffective was the technical cooperation of the two powers. In the present case the deficiencies of Intelligence, working without adequate equipment, was to exact a price.

The first that the Japanese admiral commanding the aircraft carrier, who was again Nagumo, knew of the proximity of the Americans was when, about 9 o'clock on the morning of 4 June, he was surprised by an American raid when he had his aircraft assembled on deck for a raid on Midway, but when they had not yet taken off. As it appeared afterwards, the fate of the mighty armada, of the Midway expedition, and of the possibility of a future descent on the American coast, was decided in five minutes. Nagumo's carrier was torpedoed at this time, and three of the four carriers were mortally struck. The battle continued all that day, very similar to the Coral Sea, with the two navies out of sight of each other; this time the Japanese pilots, in contrast to the Americans, proved definitely inferior. The action was a confused affair of planes from each side which savagely attacked the others, and then pounced on each other's carriers when they were inadequately guarded.

The Japanese had more than their share of mischance. Radio messages were received five minutes too late; cloud movements happened in such a way as just to obscure the movements of the enemy. But in all the confusion, it stands out that on this occasion the high commanders, and the Japanese navy as a whole, did not display the professionalism, the power of rapid adaptation, the coolness amid the horrors of an air combat at sea, which were necessary to bring victory in this kind of action.

Except in the apparatus to facilitate information about what was happening, the defects in the Japanese fleet were personal rather than mechanical. Japan did not lose the battle because of the engineering superiority of the United States. In the actual fighting, the Japanese aeroplane, the Zeke, an improvement on the Zero fighter, which was first tried out in this encounter, was the best plane on either side.

The American fleet, as it appeared later, did not realize for some time how complete and profound their victory had been. In the confusion of the conflict, they assumed for some time that two of the carriers, which had in fact been sunk, had escaped and were on their way back to Japan. Ultimately the facts were established and they were these. Japan had lost all four of its largest aircraft carriers (the fourth was lost later in the day) and a heavy cruiser. It had lost 322 aeroplanes, and 3,500 sailors. The American losses were the *Yorktown*, which was finally sunk, and a destroyer; 150 aeroplanes; and 307 lives.

Admiral Yamamoto, with the main force of battleships, made some effort at retrieving the disaster. He recalled the aircraft carriers which had been sent to the Aleutians, and resumed the hunt for the American carriers, which had destroyed his own fleet. But, in the end, he broke off the battle, partly, it seems because he felt he could no longer rely on the Japanese Intelligence, and because he decided not to risk his battleships further.

The subordinate operation, the one against the Aleutian Islands, had petered out in aimless sailings. There were no serious Japanese losses. But there were no successes either to set against the losses at Midway.

The Japanese government, very prudently, did not risk the shock of the defeat and the collapse of hopes becoming public. Its first aim was to hush up the defeat. One of the Japanese admirals (quoted by John Deane Potter in his book, *Admiral of the Pacific*) said: 'Our forces suffered a reverse so decisive and so grave that details of it were kept as a secret to all but a limited circle, even within the Japanese navy. Even after the war, few among high ranking officers were familiar with the details of the Midway operation.'* A Japanese naval captain complained of the way that the returning sailors were held incommunicado. The wounded were brought ashore after dark, and taken to hospital through the rear entrances. He was himself among those who suffered.

*John Deane Potter: op. cit.

THE BATTLE OF MIDWAY 1942

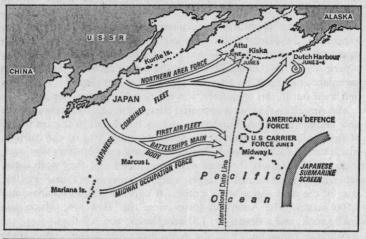

CHINA

U.S.S.R.

ALASKA

Kurile Is.

Attu
JUNE 6

Kiska
JUNE 6

Dutch Harbour
JUNE 3-4

NORTHERN AREA FORCE

JAPAN

COMBINED FLEET

FIRST AIR FLEET

AMERICAN DEFENCE
FORCE

BATTLESHIPS MAIN
BODY

U.S CARRIER
FORCE JUNE 3

JAPANESE

Marcus I.

Midway I.

JAPANESE
SUBMARINE
SCREEN

Mariana Is.

MIDWAY OCCUPATION FORCE

Pacific

International Date Line

Ocean

---

❶	June 4 - *0700*	❹	June 5 - *0100*	❼	June 6 - *1750*
❷	June 4 - *1000*	❺	June 5 - *1200*	⬅—	American air attacks.
❸	June 4 - *1500*	❻	June 6 - *0700*	⇢	Japanese air attacks.

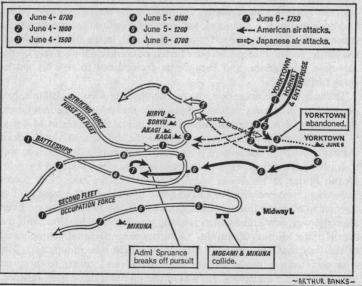

STRIKING FORCE
FIRST AIR FLEET

YORKTOWN
HORNET &
ENTERPRISE

HIRYU
SORYU
AKAGI
KAGA

YORKTOWN
abandoned.

BATTLESHIPS

YORKTOWN
JUNE 6

SECOND FLEET
OCCUPATION FORCE

Midway I.

MIKUNA

Adml Spruance
breaks off pursuit

MOGAMI & MIKUNA
collide.

~ARTHUR BANKS~

The experience is described in *Midway: the Battle that Doomed Japan* by Fuchida and Okumiya.* 'My room was in complete isolation,' he says. 'No nurses or medical attendants were allowed in, and I could not communicate with the world outside. All the wounded from Midway were treated like this. It was like being a prisoner of war among your own people.' After the Japanese surrender in 1945, all the papers about the defeat, classified as top secret, were burned. The extent and the gravity of the disaster which Japan had suffered did not become plain to the Japanese public until publication by the survivors in the course of the 1950s.

The long run of sensational Japanese victories, bought at such little cost, had come finally to an end. The crippling of the US Pacific Fleet at Pearl Harbor, and the blows at the Royal Navy, had all been made at the ridiculously small expense of the loss of four destroyers. This time was over. At Midway a technically smaller American fleet had challenged the passage of the Japanese Imperial Navy, had defeated it, had turned it back. It had lost prestige hopelessly, it had lost the *élan* of victory, and the margin of its losses turned decisively against it. It had forfeited its ability to strike where it chose, and to govern the course of the war. Having lost this initiative, it had condemned Japan to convert the war into a holding operation – this, as Admiral Yamamoto had warned, condemned Japan to be overwhelmed by the United States as soon as the American economic mobilization was complete.

* Fuchida and Okumiya: *Midway: the Battle that Doomed Japan*, U.S. Naval Institute, Hutchinson, 1957.

CHAPTER 16

MacArthur in the Pacific

THE naval war between Japan and the United States was to be waged henceforward with the utmost ferocity in the crucial theatre of the south-west Pacific. Japan had not foreseen that its action there would become so critical for its fate: but it had lost the freedom of action at the Battle of Midway Island. The United States set itself to wrest the south-west Pacific from its hold, and Japan, which had committed itself heavily in the region, set itself doggedly to oppose it, first of all trying to enlarge its position, and later selling its territory inch by inch, and with such grimness that it hoped that the United States would become tired of its enterprise.

As the fighting grew in intensity, it gradually became plain that, in this Pacific theatre, the war against Japan could be won. The Pacific offered the path to Tokyo. Interest fell away from the other theatres and other activities, from India and from China, and was concentrated on two American commanders, General Douglas MacArthur and Admiral Chester Nimitz, who shared the direction of events in this region.

General MacArthur, in whom burned most clearly the determination to restore the United States' position, and whose skill, confidence and military genius made him the most effective commander for the purpose, had in March 1942 been ordered to withdraw from the fighting in the Philippines. He began his duel with Japan under something of a cloud. His withdrawal from the Philippines, though it had been ordered by Roosevelt, and though it was common sense, had, in the hectic atmosphere of the time, been criticized by the American army, especially by the troops he had left behind. MacArthur was a general who in the ways of behaviour often did not conform to the conventions of his day, but flaunted them rather positively. In the Philippines he had won disapproval by insisting that his wife and family should remain with him: he was able to do so because he had been under Filipino regulations and was free of American army discipline. This singular man was to impose himself on the American and Australian armies, who were almost fanatical in their dislike of privilege, and to make himself respected by virtue of his superiority.

On his escape from Manila in a speedboat, he had had an adventurous voyage to the southern tip of the Philippines. When he got there, he found difficulty in going further. Rivalry between the American services made the American admiral in command in the region unwilling to spare any aeroplane for his rescue. Application had to be made over his head through Washington to transport MacArthur to Australia.

It had been agreed between President Roosevelt and Churchill that operations in Australia should be under an American command, and to this post MacArthur was designated. The forces of Australia many of them battle-trained in the Middle East, passed under his control. On taking over, MacArthur found the Australians thinking in terms of defence. Their morale had been shattered by the events in Singapore: they had been accustomed to thinking of this as a sure guarantee of Australian security, and they did not quickly adapt themselves to its overthrow. Psychologically they were in the position of France after the loss of the Maginot line. The Japanese appeared to be unstoppable, and were heading for Sydney and Melbourne; and the Australians looked round in despondency for a remedy. They aimed at holding the southern part of the continent on a line which passed through Brisbane. All to the north of this they had virtually reconciled themselves to losing when the Japanese invasion, which was expected in a matter of weeks, should begin.

MacArthur's initial success was in changing this attitude. He infused the Australians with confidence, and with the offensive spirit. His command was extremely short in manpower: it was poorly equipped, and air power was deficient. But within three months the counter-offensive started.

The area which was the scene of the fighting was the chain of coral islands which lies to the north of Australia and curls around to the north-east. The pressure of the original Japanese offensive had nearly carried them to this region. But it had begun to flag before Japan had occupied the whole system. If Japan had overrun the islands, it would have been able to set up bases there from which it could have interrupted communications between Australian ports. The chain of islands was half-held by the Japanese, but their firm occupation came to an end in the Solomon Islands, and did not extend to the New Hebrides or New Caledonia. The objective of their next offensive, with a dangerously extended line of communication, was the Australian outpost of Port Moresby in the south of Papua, which was the Australian extension of New Guinea. This lay just to the south of the islands occupied by Japan.

MacArthur's first move was to scatter the Japanese forces, which were preparing to take Port Moresby. The initial event was the drawn naval battle between American and Japanese aircraft carriers off the coast of Papua: the battle of the Coral Sea. It was drawn because the losses on both sides had been roughly equal; but the Japanese had been convoying troops, which were intended for land operations against Port Moresby, and these were turned back and never came again. Thus the issue of the battle was really in America's favour.

The Japanese were, however, favourably placed. From their bases they bombed Port Darwin, on the Australian coast, and severely damaged it. MacArthur moved to the attack, inadequate though his force was. He sent his troops to wrest Papua from the Japanese, and, in a painful struggle which took up a whole year, they prevailed. The backbone of the force was an Australian division which had won distinction at the battle of Alamein, and had been among the Australian forces in the Middle East which were shifted to defend Australia. The fighting was largely a series of savage hand-to-hand conflicts, and there was less skill in manoeuvre than was to be usual in the campaigns designed by MacArthur. It was notable for the endurance of the troops; for their overcoming the vast difficulties of nature; for the skilful use of aircraft, themselves largely improvised for supplying troops. An example was given of the maniacal tenacity of the Japanese which was to be a feature of the entire campaign: of 13,000 Japanese losses in action in the final stage, only thirty-eight men were taken prisoner.

This operation in eastern New Guinea was quite a small one, and, with so much happening in the rest of the world, not very much noticed. But in the record of the whole war, it was significant. It marked the end of the Japanese being on the offensive. It was the start of expeditions, which were desperately hard-fought, but in the end universally successful, to force Japan back across the sea on which it had sailed out to dominate so spectacularly. But MacArthur, surveying the tasks which still lay before him, was painfully aware of all the difficulties which lay ahead.

He was fighting over a vast area, large parts of which were still unmapped. This was a handicap which has been little recognized, but was very grave indeed. For an American general to plan a troop landing in Europe with maps and charts showing the tidal movements was one thing: to plan the same operation for coral islands, where all that was available was guess-work by natives, was quite another. He was short of ships; he was given only medium-range bombing planes, when he needed essentially long-range bombers; everywhere he went, airfields had to be constructed, often hacked out of the jungle by indigenous labour. For his supplies he had to compete with seven or eight rival theatres of war, and, as it seemed to him, invariably came out worst. Disease, especially malaria, was a still more deadly enemy than the Japanese, and the means of overcoming it could only be found by experimenting – and by exposing his armies at first to its ravages.

Nevertheless, from Port Moresby and the operations which he conducted for its relief in the encircling Owen Stanley Mountains, he was led on to the steps which, laborious operation after perilous initiative, in the end resulted in the reconquest of all New Guinea from the Japanese. From this position, he prepared to leap ahead, and he made havoc among the forces guarding the Japanese Empire.

In retrospect, it is plain that the Japanese, from the point of view of their long-term interests, would have done well to limit their offensive; to avoid overlong lines of communication; to have declined combat when this could be avoided; above all, not to have been lured into a contest for the possession of islands, which could only be of use to them marginally. This was the view of many of the Japanese generals, and if it had prevailed in shaping the strategy would have greatly increased the difficulty of the Americans in coming to grips with the Japanese Empire. But the Japanese navy, still determined to conduct the Pacific War as a naval war, still over-confident in spite of the Battle of Midway, still with an abundance of battleships and cruisers which it could safely risk, overruled the Japanese armies. Little by little the scope of the war enlarged, and eventually spread through all the intricate chain of coral islands in the Pacific. There was little rational planning behind the operations.

*

From the start the Americans had had a second headquarters command in the Pacific Ocean. In March 1942 the Pacific, by a decision of President Roosevelt, was divided formally between General MacArthur and Admiral Nimitz. MacArthur's command included Australia, the Philippines, the Solomons, and most of the Dutch East Indies. The rest of the Pacific fell to Nimitz. But it was not a clear-cut geographical division of responsibility. Each of these officers was entrusted formally with the command of all armed forces in his area, whether on land, sea or in the air; but, by the instrument providing for the division between the commands, it was provided that Admiral Nimitz should have general control of all amphibious operations, whether these took place in his own zone or MacArthur's.

This rather peculiar division caused trouble about the demarcation.

It was against logic, and ran counter to the teaching of experience in other theatres of war. MacArthur wrote:

Of all the faulty decisions of the war, perhaps the most inexpressible one was the failure to unify the command in the Pacific. ... It resulted in divided effort, the waste of diffusion and duplication of force, and undue extension of war with added casualties and cost.*

The division was difficult to stand by. For example, MacArthur's operations in clearing the menacing Japanese from Port Moresby were on various occasions more amphibious than military, but he succeeded in keeping the campaign to himself. MacArthur wrote with a personal interest about the danger of divided aims. It galled him that it was freely suggested that he, though he was celebrated for his caution, could not be trusted with the safety of the navy's precious ships. A further limitation on him was that the charter setting up the respective commands laid down that Nimitz was from the start to be offensive in his operations; MacArthur, by contrast, was to fight defensively. This grudging attitude was to run, as a discordant thread, throughout the early years of the American counter-attack.

In this issue, MacArthur set himself, not for the only time in his career, to oppose the general political plan of Washington, on which the plan of campaign eventually depended. The navy had for long looked forward to a war with Japan. War in the Pacific must essentially be a naval one: the principal interest with which it was fought must be the aircraft carriers and battleships and the commander of these must be an admiral. The plans according to which it was fought had for two or three generations been the basic manuals for American naval training. This was the prevailing conception among the service chiefs in Washington; MacArthur was a general, and that was fatal to him. American naval officers form a curious, exclusive caste in American society; the war was an opportunity for this caste which must not be neglected. It is true that in the European war the navy took second place; circumstances had taken charge and had directed a land strategy. It seemed only compensating justice that in the Far East, where geography restored primacy to the sea, the navy and its traditional ancillary arm, the marines, should be the main protagonists.

The arrangement of the two commands had further consequences. It had been agreed between Roosevelt and Churchill that the United States should have a large measure of independent initiative in the

* Charles Willoughby and John Chamberlain: *MacArthur 1941–51*, McGraw-Hill, New York, 1954.

organization of military affairs in the Pacific. As Britain had the lion's share of the initiative in the Middle East and in the Indian Ocean, so did the United States rule the Pacific war. The convention there was in contrast to that of Europe and the Atlantic; there the planning would be a matter of joint British and American responsibility; in the Pacific, any British initiative came to be headed off. Through this tendency, the United States to some extent evaded the main political directive, which had been laid down very soon after Pearl Harbor, that the war in the Pacific was to take second place to the war in Europe. In 1942 the Americans systematically built up their war-making capacity in the Pacific through the sympathetic connivance of the Chiefs of Staff in Washington. MacArthur might groan that he still had ridiculously inadequate supplies, but they were very much larger than had been envisaged by the directive. Twice as many supplies were sent across the Pacific in the first six months of March 1942 as were sent to the European theatre of war. By the end of 1942, the United States had reinforced its stations in the Pacific by more than 15,000 troops in excess of what was originally intended.

In August 1942 the navy had its first chance to take charge of amphibious operations on a large scale. These were in Guadalcanal, a tiny island in the Solomons: it was in MacArthur's command area, but the campaign there was directed by the naval Chiefs of Staff and played little part in his biography. Once more, the area of combat was in the disputed coral islands which ringed Australia. Guadalcanal was very little known or explored; before its conquest by Japan, it had been a British colony; the local people were extremely primitive; a few traders were like characters from a novel by Joseph Conrad. The colony, which is only ninety miles long and twenty-five miles broad, is the essential idea of a tropical island. Along its sandy beaches are coconut palms; abruptly behind them there rise jungly mountains and extinct volcanoes to a height of seven thousand feet. The flat ground is dark, steamy, rotting jungle, the perfect terrain for breeding the malaria mosquito.

The Japanese nearly forestalled the Americans in gaining possession of it. They had occupied it with a skeleton force, and American air reconnaissance showed that they were building an airfield on it. They were interrupted by a counter-invasion: the Americans landed a force of 11,000 men. At first, both sides supposed that the fate of Guadalcanal would be settled within a week. Actually a savage and terrible struggle developed there which lasted until February 1943, when the Japanese decided to release their grip. The Americans had discovered what war in the Pacific amounted to, and had done so at horrendous account.

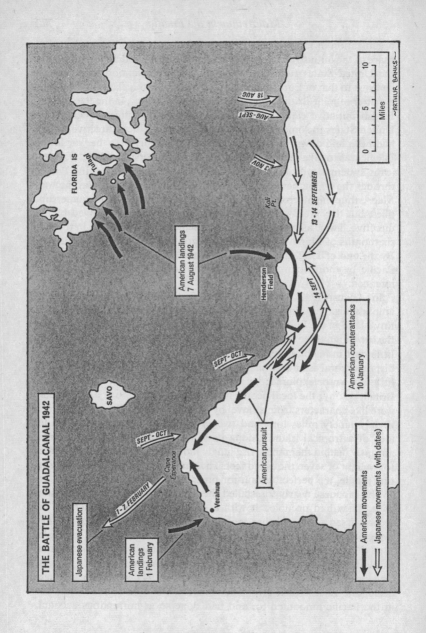

THE BATTLE OF GUADALCANAL 1942

Japanese evacuation

American landings 1 February

1 - 7 FEBRUARY

Cape Esperance

Verahue

SEPT - OCT

SEPT - OCT

SAVO

American pursuit

American counterattacks 10 January

14 SEPT

13 - 14 SEPTEMBER

Henderson Field

American landings 7 August 1942

FLORIDA IS

Tulagi

Koli Pt.

18 AUG

AUG - SEPT

3 NOV

American movements

Japanese movements (with dates)

Miles

0   5   10

~ARTHUR BANKS~

There had been no such gruelling campaigns before in the history of the war.

The battle cost the Americans six major naval engagements, and a heavy toll of shipping. Both sides lost an equal number of warships (twenty-four of all classes), though Japanese losses in supporting ships, such as transports, were much heavier. The Japanese dead among the ground troops numbered 24,000: American losses were lighter, but by a remarkable feint the Japanese managed to rescue 12,000 of their soldiers. The Japanese troop commander killed himself as the final troops were withdrawn.

This savage battle marked out the pattern of operations which were to be repeated again and again in the Pacific during the next few years. Careful and skilful preparation by the American staff had been the main factor in giving the Americans a victory; and so it was to be at Tarawa, in the Gilbert Islands, at Kwajalein and Eniwetok and Bougainville Island. The navy concentrated upon the islands and pushed the Japanese relentlessly back. This strategy was a head-on assault. It was effective, and remorseless; but it was not very imaginative.

As the Nimitz campaign developed, General MacArthur was simultaneously attacking in his corner of the Pacific and the strategy of the two campaigns inevitably invited comparisons. Both showed undoubted successes. From September 1942 down to the middle of 1944, MacArthur was employed in re-occupying New Guinea. It was not the extent of the land occupied which was significant; MacArthur had overcome the arts of the Japanese in defensive warfare, in territory very favourable to them, and he had inflicted enormous losses of manpower on them.

Nimitz's war machine had rolled over the Gilbert Islands and the Marshalls. Little by little the Japanese gave way at the edges of the vast empire they had seized; but Nimitz gained his successes by weight of assault and as a result of the endurance of his troops. His casualties were usually considerable. The American troops who were flung into action were for the most part a civilian army. Many of them had, however, been harshly prepared in the rather barbaric circumstances of the training grounds of the American Marines in the Carolinas. Stories which seeped out of these during the war seemed to have been well founded. Some troops had been less well prepared, and this accounted for some of the reverses which the Americans suffered in this campaign, which was the most sanguinary of any which were fought during the war. The American advance proceeded atoll by atoll. It was a war fought among tropical islands, with the same unreal beauty as a background, the same madness of non-surrender affecting the Japanese, the same monotony of desperate attack and desperate defence. It became taken for granted that the Japanese did not surrender, but were killed. Often those places which occasioned the worst slaughter were incredibly small. MacArthur, on the other hand, won his battles by sheer artistry. No other captain of the war had based his strategy so consistently on principles. He commanded with style. He was conscious of history, and of the examples of other generals. The ghosts of all the battles of the world walked in the combats for which he was responsible. In the map rooms of his headquarters there was an atmosphere of erudition which was unfamiliar in the war. The bloody patterns of assault on these remote coral reefs were studiously compared with Napoleon's famous victories, and even on one occasion with the victory of Hannibal at Canae in 204 B.C.

MacArthur despised brute strength. He sought, in a way which was rather like the principle on which the Japanese system of judo is based, to bring his force to bear on the enemy in places and at times that would find his opponent off balance. In this way he could hope to succeed with weaker strength, as was usually the position in which he found himself, and to succeed with the minimum loss. In this island warfare he eschewed the practice of Admiral Nimitz of reducing the Japanese strong-points one by one. Nimitz modified these tactics as time went on, and employed a limited plan of by-passing small islands which would have made an inconvenient defence. MacArthur, on the other hand, practised a strategy of envelopment. He refused to assail the Japanese head-on in one of their prepared fortresses, and thought out ways of isolating it by operating upon its exposed linear communication. The by-passed stronghold proved in the end to be his victim, but it had been left to 'die upon the vine'. General MacArthur then shifted his base forwards by some hundreds of miles, when the process was repeated with care never to expose his forces beyond the reach of protective air cover. He described as follows the system which he pursued:

The system is as old as war itself. It is merely a new name dictated by new conditions given to the ancient principle of envelopment. It was the first time that the area of combat embraced land and water in such relative proportions. Heretofore, either the one or the other was predominant in the campaign. But in this area the presence of transportation of ground troops by ships as well as land transport seemed to conceal the fact that the system was merely that of envelopment applied to a new type of battle area. It has always proved the ideal method for success by inferior in number but faster-moving forces. Immediately upon my arrival in Australia and learning the resources at my command, I determined that such a plan of action was the sole chance of fulfilling my mission.*

The concept that success lay with a commander who best cooperated with nature was ever-present to him. One of his maxims was: 'Nature is neutral in war, but if you beat it and the enemy does not, it becomes a powerful ally.' A part of his success was due to the American army becoming more at home in the coral islands than the Japanese: which reversed the experience of the Japanese and of the British army in the Malayan jungle at the start of the war.

In his campaigns, MacArthur relied to an exceptional extent on spying. He was fortunate enough to discover an Australian, Commander Long, with a great gift for attracting information and for sifting it. This was a new art in Australia, and Long organized a service which was free of the traits – the elaborate games and the affectation of policy making – which proved so constricting in other countries. The most valuable information was given by a force called the 'coast watchers of the islands'. These were a fifth column which had been left behind in the islands when they were overrun by the Japanese. They consisted of British and Australian civil servants, anthropologists, telegraph operators, traders: and they were admirably served by bands of local natives. They were able to communicate by wireless with MacArthur's headquarters. In war of unorthodox character of this kind information about Japanese strong-points and the distribution of Japanese manpower was often worth a whole division of troops. The exploits of these men are one of the most exciting chapters of war history; and it is very extraordinary that they have not become part of the folklore of the war.

To MacArthur's military tasks were added the military and diplomatic ones of welding Australia and the United States in a close alliance. The Australians, in spite of all their positive qualities, were at this period surprisingly hard to deal with: they were touchy, quick to take offence where none was intended, hypercritical as a kind of self-defence. In spite of a grotesque side to his character – which was self-assertive and boastful and which went with genuine confidence and did not mask self-distrust – MacArthur actually made himself liked, and won the confidence of Australia. He esteemed and got along well with Curtin, the Australian Prime Minister, and the two of them often collaborated in opposing Washington or London. He took an interest in preparing the reorganization of the Australian supplies so that by re-orienting Austra-

* Willoughby and Chamberlain, op. cit.

lian industry his armies in Australia actually received from Australia itself a much larger proportion of its needs than had been supposed possible.

In playing this role, MacArthur was much helped by accidents in his previous career which had detached him from the ordinary life of an American soldier. In his service as military adviser to the Philippine government, he had come to conduct himself with an unusual detachment from the American military machine. This, combined with a natural tendency to a certain Caesarism in politics, had brought it about that in his Pacific command he was often handled by the American government as if he were an independent political power and not a subordinate officer. His relation to the American authorities was very like that of a much-prized condottiere to an Italian city state. The legend of MacArthur as the great American pro-consul was added to by the fact that when the war began he had not been back in American for years, nor was he to return until 1951. Though MacArthur undoubtedly gained from this position, he had as a rule to forgo the ability to influence the military planners by personal knowledge of the officers concerned. A remoteness from understanding American politics complicated his career. Piercing political insight into fundamentals was combined with a pathetic political incompetence in day-to-day matters.

*

In all this fatal combat in which Americans were locked together with Japanese in a contest from which neither side could free itself, one single fact stood out. The war was waged with the utmost ferocity, but it was under the eyes of relatively idle armies which were spectators of what was going on. Of the vast number of men who were mobilized for the war, the greater part were destined never to come into combat. Japan had an army of fifty-one divisions: until the very end of the war, forty of these divisions were either occupied in China, which for most of this period had a totally inactive front, or were employed in guarding the frontier with Russia. And on the American side the number of troops employed in the actual offensive by MacArthur, and later in the reduction of the Pacific islands, was very small indeed in comparison with the vast army which the United States had concentrated for war in the Far East. (Similarly in this Far Eastern war the British troops who had actual combat experience were limited to the four or five divisions in Burma.) The western allies could not make use of a larger force. They had chosen to fight the Japanese on narrow fronts – in New Guinea and in the Pacific islands – and the circumstances of the war were such that there was no room for a great concourse of troops. Thus the war came to resemble the war at Troy. The serried ranks stood and watched the combat fought between the heroes. Their fate was decided in battle in which they had no part.

In this desperate fighting in the Pacific, Admiral Yamamoto, the one imaginative genius at war whom the Japanese, with their great military gifts, contributed to the conflict, was taken out of the picture. His death was plotted in Washington. It was brought about by arranging an ambush by American aeroplanes which fell on him in great strength as he was flying on a tour of inspection to one of the Pacific bases held by Japan. This was in April 1943, soon after the Japanese withdrawal from Guadalcanal. The details of his flight, the precise time of arrival, were all obtained by intercepting cipher messages which could be read. Yamamoto was always punctual to the moment: the surprise depended on the ambushing planes being able to count to the moment upon his presence at the destined place of the encounter with him. Yamamoto went to his death with a punctuality that was a rare virtue among orientals, even among commanding officers. His end was like the death of Hector who was similarly taken at a disadvantage by a force of Achilles' myrmidons:

> Look Hector how the sun begins to set
> How ugly night comes breathing at his heels
> Even with the veil and darkling of the sun
> To close the day up, Hector's life is done.

The American Admiral, having worked this overthrow, could find no more fitting words to announce it than the following telegram to the exterminators: 'Congratulations Major Mitchell and his hunters; sounds as though one of the ducks in their bag was a peacock.' Democracies have curious lapses of taste when they go to war. At the press conference to celebrate the success of the plan, the same Admiral observed: 'I had hoped to lead that scoundrel up Pennsylvania Avenue in chains with the rest of you kicking him where it would do the most good.' It is said that the audience whooped and applauded.

*

By July 1943 the American planners were already satisfied that they had chosen the right road. They lifted their sights, and began to consider what they should do when they drew near to Japan. Could intense air bombardment, which should be possible from Chinese airfields and from their great aircraft carriers, and unremitting submarine warfare, really reduce this proud people, or would the unemployed army of over a million be ready to dispute their way? Would an invasion be necessary; and, if so, would the history of the fanatical defence of small atolls be lived through once again, this time in the island centre of the terrible and warlike race?

MacArthur and Nimitz were the two American personalities who dominated the Pacific. They had taken up the initiative when it had been dashed from the Japanese by the battle of Midway Island. They had begun to attack, and had succeeded in their campaigns ever since. To halt them began to appear as being beyond Japan's capacity: the only doubt was how long they would take to cross over the Pacific, and to make war on Japan at its gateway.

Part IV

THE DEFEAT OF JAPAN

CHAPTER 17

Mid-1943

IN the middle of 1943 the war had resolved itself into a defensive struggle by the Japanese to hold the vast territory which they had over-run, for such little loss, in the hectic days early in 1942. With the crippling loss of their navy at Midway Island, their drive outwards had lost its impetus; it had failed in its purpose of gaining for them a rapid peace. But the Japanese were left in possession of a vast territory, economically very rich; and the operations of MacArthur and of Nimitz had only begun to win this back.

They held, and preparations had hardly begun to expel them from, a line behind which were included Burma, Thailand, Malaya, and the Dutch East Indies; and it extended far out across the Pacific. Behind this line they had obtained 80 per cent of the world's rubber, 54 per cent of its tin, 19 per cent of its tungsten, the oil wells of the Dutch East Indies with a huge reserve, and large supplies of manganese and iron ore. The map and economic intelligence suggested that Japan, if it showed the administrative competence to organize these assets, could, with some equanimity, face a prolonged war. It need have no panic, at least for the time being, before the very heavy counter-attack which America, now at last fully mobilizing for war, was mounting against it.

By 1943, however, it began to become plain that Japan, as an adversary of the United States, was outdated by two or three generations. In the organization for war, the contest was between the Americans, a nation of businessmen, amateurs in war but bringing to it all the skill learned in a century and a half of fierce capitalist struggle, in which lack of imagination and foresight exacted disaster and retirement, and the Japanese, who still regarded American business as vulgar, and who sought to combat it by an economy held together on a basis of command. Japan still thought of war in strictly military terms. Its eyes were fixed on territory which had to be held, on the battles which were taking place, and on the tactics to be used. The fact that the war was to be won or lost in the nation's factories and workshops had never clearly established itself in the mind of the Japanese Supreme Command. Japan had, it is true, passed a law even before Pearl Harbor, which gave the government totalitarian powers to regulate the economy; but the economy, under war conditions, exhibited nothing like the transformation which the United States and Britain underwent in similar circumstances.

Even after it had staked everything on the action at Pearl Harbor, Japan failed to give top economic priority to building aircraft, warships and submarines upon which the defence of the empire it had won must eventually depend. The Japanese had the initial advantage that they began the war with aircraft which surprised their antagonists in their performance. But the Japanese unaccountably failed to exploit this superiority. Japanese aircraft production in 1943, though it had tripled since 1941, was very much less than it might have been. In 1943 it was in fact only one fifth of the total American output. And, even for the use of its restricted air force, Japan failed to mobilize anything approaching the manpower which was needed. The skill and audacity of the pilots at Pearl Harbor, and the extreme popularity which the flying service enjoyed, showed that Japan was not wanting in resource to organize its air force adequately. Moreover, until the end of the war, the Japanese aircraft designers went on improving the standard fighters and bombers. But there was a failure of liaison: the army and navy were unwilling to make their wants clear, and to transmit these to the planners of the Japanese war effort. And even more than aircraft, a territory such as the Japanese had to defend, required warships and submarines. Here, also, the Japanese record is hardly comprehensible. In the months when America was turning out a prodigious number of aircraft carriers – twenty-two were under construction in 1943 – Japan, which by the action of Pearl Harbor had shown itself to be a pioneer of naval air strength, was content to build only three new carriers. The disparity was greater still in cruisers and destroyers. The Japanese naval staff had apparently reverted to an older view, recoiled from reading the lessons which they had themselves demonstrated, and put their faith in battleship construction. They did not seem to realize, for example, how fatal it was to be outrun in submarine production. They had begun the war with high-quality submarines, but this arm never played the defensive role which might have been expected in a campaign fought among countless islands.

For Japan to realize the advantages of the economic riches of its empire, a vast, flexible merchant navy was necessary. In scarcely any other department of war was Japanese planning so inefficient. It began the war without a realistic or adequate appreciation of the demands which were likely to be made upon its merchant shipping. In 1941, it possessed 5.3 million tons of shipping; about 35 per cent of Japanese trade had been carried in foreign vessels. The greater part of this fleet was at once requisitioned for service use, 1.2 million tons for the army and 1.4 millions tons for the navy; and a large part of this was squandered by the wasteful operations in the Solomon Islands. In 1942 the Japanese lost over a million tons of shipping, and by 1943, the shortage had become acute, and the estimates and forecasts of the Japanese Planning Board had been exposed. The losses, by submarine warfare, by mines, and by air attack, were such as to make ridiculous the attempt to weld together the Japanese territories in a single viable empire. Before this challenge, Japan made no adequate response: there were no interesting tactics, no system of convoys, no asdic, no radar. By 1943 they were forced to replace their dwindling merchant fleet with wooden ships, but these boats were terribly slow, and also vulnerable. Worse, they had neglected their shipyards, which were ill equipped and antiquated, and these were clogged, in the middle of 1943, by a fifth of the entire merchant marine undergoing repair.

These weaknesses must in the first place be put down to unimaginative planning by the Japanese Command, and the fact that civilian Ministries were instinctively held in contempt by service Ministries. At joint conferences the requests of civilians for allocations of manpower and materials tended to be overruled, even though the end product might be one of which the services were badly in need. For such reasons as these Japan was never able to utilize its huge economic assets. Japan had risked war for the sake of obtaining raw materials under its flag; but, when this was brought about, it could not transport them. It had the intense mortification of being in possession in the South Seas of one of the richest economic units in the world, but of being unable to enjoy its usufruct. The iron, the coal, the bauxite, nickel, tin, manganese, lead, salt, graphite, potash, all the vital materials for war, were all of them technically Japanese, guarded by Japanese troops, but they lay as useless to Japan as though they were in the hands of the enemy, because they could not be transported. They were a kind of fairy gold. Japan's plight is vividly shown by one figure. In 1940, before the war, it bought and imported three million tons of iron ore from the Philippines and Malaya. By 1942, though its troops had absolute control over the iron mines, it managed to carry just over 100,000 tons of iron ore from these territories to Japan.

The most acute famine was in oil. This had been foreseen, and the need for oil was the basic reason for Japan's going to war. But the oil had remained elusive. The wells of the Dutch East Indies produced an abundant supply, but it could only be transported in tankers, which were an easy target for the aeroplanes of the western allies and for their submarines. The shutting down of one economic activity after another in Japan was the consequence of this very real blockade. First civilian transportation was hit: then production in one industry after another. Already, by 1943, the oil shortages hampered the operations of the navy and grounded many of Japan's aircraft.

The weakness of the Japanese defensive structure was, then, economic. The Japanese waged a war against the most effective economic organization of history, and waged it with totally inadequate resources. In vain they put their trust in reeking tube and iron shard, when even their ability to manufacture tubes and shards was being limited. But, though the nemesis worked itself out in an economic form, the weakness was not really economic, but was one of intelligence. The Japanese civil service, Japanese planners, the Supreme Command, failed their country. The economic resources had been there, and they could not be used, because the Japanese Empire failed to remain linked together. Given flexibility and foresight, this weakness might have been overcome. A different organization of their supplies, more local initiative, more skilful prevention of submarine warfare, more adequate use of the submarine and the aeroplane in solving the economic problems – any of these might have availed to prevent the end, which already, in mid-1943, was becoming certain to those who possessed the economic intelligence to see where war was leading Japan.

The desperate reality was, however, still unclear to most people. It was to be found only in economic statistics, which were a military secret. One of the undeniable successes of the Japanese military was in concealing the badness of its Intelligence alike from the enemy, from its colleagues in the government of Japan, and from its own people. It was the consequence of the rigid drill in security which had been practised at least since 1930. Let nobody decry the effects of such a very tight anti-espionage system. The consequence was that, in 1943, Japan, though it was already toppling on its feet of clay, was able to deny this knowledge to a large part of the world, including the Intelligence services of the western allies. They saw the advantages which Japan possessed, its still formidable army, only a small part of which had been so far engaged in battle, and its tremendous morale. They were impressed by the fact that no rumours of mutiny ever reached them, and that there were no strikes or signs of civilian unrest in Japan. They were conscious too of the very great disadvantages under which they had to carry on the offensive against Japan. Japan held the inner lines, and could transport a stiffening of the defence forces wherever these were threatened. The Japanese themselves were conscious of the immense handicap of enormous distance: the handicap that weapons, fuel, ammunition, cement and road materials, were being shot out in an unending flow, and vanishing across the Pacific Ocean. It needed a calm judgement in their adversaries to realize that this would avail against them, and that, sooner or later, the inherent deficiencies of the Japanese would force them to the huge convulsion of surrender.

Many of the lands taken over by the Japanese, and included in their fortress area, were the homes of nationalist movements which had come near erupting against their former white imperialist rulers. Japan, in letting loose its campaign against the western powers had expressed its natural sympathies with Asian aspiration. The pricking of the balloon of western prestige, and the surprising ease with which the West was put to rout, had had a profound effect on everybody's mind; though the Japanese sympathy had largely a propagandist incentive, in fact many Japanese were sincerely committed. The campaigns thus had had the effect of intensifying the nationalist resolve. In some cases, Japanese propaganda had led the people of these South-East Asian countries to believe that Japanese conquests would automatically bring them independence. But time was lost by the Japanese in fulfilling the hopes. Had the peoples of South-East Asia merely exchanged white imperialism to pass under the rule of a Japanese Empire?

The territories, which had been occupied by Japan, were at different stages of political development. In most of them, the British or American influence was strong. They had accepted the way of parliamentary democracy as holding out the best prospects of obtaining their independence, and, since both the United States and Britain could apparently not envisage any other course of progress, they had accepted constitutions of a more or less truncated form of Westminster or Washington democracy. That the Asian nationalists had allowed themselves to be directed along these lines is one of the astonishing facts of Asia at this time. It is a sign of the political vitality in Asia of western ideas, which remained very vigorous in spite of the inefficiency which had been revealed by the western systems administratively. Japan, as was natural, was more open-minded about the forms of government which should ultimately prevail; it was inclined to be suspicious of all forms of democracy, as being intrusions by the West into the East, and favoured instead the forms which emerged from Fascism (though these were as much of western origin), but it recognized that, in the storm of war, it was in no position to apply itself to political experiment in South-East Asia. It preferred to leave this for the peace years which it hoped would follow, and for the time being to make do with provisional, make-shift forms of government. The régimes which Japan set up in the areas under its control usually took the form of a committee of the existing political parties, relieved of control by parliaments, which it declared abolished. The governments themselves used most of the institutions with which they were already familiar.

In Burma the new government was set up by a brief decree. In the Philippines, a Philippine Executive Commission, consisting of seven well-known politicians, took over the government. In Malaya, which was more backward politically, the Japanese were content to preserve the forms of government through the sultanates. It is illuminating to see how, in the more developed countries – Burma and the Philippines – the tracks which they had been following before the war still governed their minds and set the tone to their political life.

The fate of Burma in these years is especially worth study. U Ba Maw, a lawyer, a party leader, and former Prime Minister under the British, was designated by the Japanese as national leader in 1942. He later published a book, *Breakthrough in Burma*, from which a picture of Burma under the Japanese stands out. At first there was confusion. Japan raised the Burmese army, which has already been described, to harry the British, but this, which attracted the elements normally associated with banditry, grew out of hand; it was liable, from the first, to turn upon the Japanese. Ba Maw, once he had been appointed by the Japanese, had, it is clear, the mission of restoring order in Burma, in which he worked closely with the Japanese.

There was a period of euphoria, a festival of feeling Asian. Ba Maw describes in his book how

... on both sides we believed in an ultimate Axis victory, which would wipe out the western empires in Asia for ever. This lasted for several months, during which the leaders of the various political and communal groups went out to the districts in mixed teams on a 'trust Japan' campaign. The Japanese on their part reciprocated by giving the central government as much independence as their notion of independence would allow, and also by supplying us with most of the essential commodities and services we lacked and needed. This was the Asian relationship between the two sides in the first months of our administration.*

Ba Maw recognized that tension rose because of the different aims and interests of the Japanese and the Burmese.

*Ba Maw: *Breakthrough in Burma*, Yale University Press, New Haven and London, 1968.

The Japanese wanted the Burmese to put victory in the larger world war before their own limited political objectives in Burma, whereas the Burmese wanted to gain those objectives first and at once. Thus a basic contradiction which already existed when our administration was formed now began to harden and divide the two peoples. My view about this matter is that the blame lay with both sides, but more with the Japanese. They were a far more immature people, in that they proved to be so devoid of judgment in their dealings with others, so domineering and blinded by delusions of their own racial grandeur and Asian destiny when it was most clearly in their interests to move with history by getting rid of all such racial nonsense. They could have achieved so much more if they could only have shown a spirit of true Asian fellowship and equality with the other peoples in Asia instead of claiming, in defiance of the clear world trends, to be 'more equal' than the others. This happened not only in Burma but all over South-East Asia.*

In spite of this, Ba Maw's relations with many Japanese continued to be personally good. It is true that he had continual difficulty with the more brutal type of officer, and claims that he was constantly in conflict with them for the protection of the Burmese people. He condemns utterly the soldiers brought in from China, who had been hardened by long experience of occupying that country of hostile people. He gives details of the Japanese mania for slapping people, and of their insensitiveness to Burmese custom and convention. But the Japanese at the top make a very different impression. Of General Iida Shojiro, the Commander-in-Chief in Burma, he says:

I found him to be the best type of Japanese soldier, human, fatherly, and very understanding, a militarist on the surface, but not altogether so deeper down; at least he always tried to see things your way too, which was what made him different from the other militarists. It gave him a good deal of inner perception, particularly of the fact that a war can be won or lost in many ways and for many reasons, one of the surest ways to lose it being to rouse the hostility and resistance of a whole people.†

And of General Terauchi Hisaichi, who was the Supreme Commander of all the Japanese forces in South-East Asia, he says:

As a person I found him to be really remarkable, a handsome, princely figure, out of a long and mellow feudal past, and yet belonging very much to the present in Japan. I had thought that as the chief of the conquering Japanese army he would most incarnate the dizzy reflexes of the conquest, but I was completely wrong. It may have been because I had least expected to find it in him, but the quality which struck me particularly was his essential

* ibid.
† ibid.

humanity. Unlike most other militarists, this consummate war-lord was not afraid to show that he was also human, and precisely because of this he understood us better than many around him.*

Even General Tojo, the Japanese Prime Minister who had begun the war, gets a good report from Ba Maw.

National relations, as distinct from personal ones, however, continued to be bad. The Japanese army continued to insist that the Burmese puppet government was ultimately responsible to it. It continued to make demands on the Burmese civil servants which outraged them; and continued to produce a type of myopic and over-confident officer who angered the Burmese by racial arrogance. They were notorious for seizing the crops and carts of the peasantry; for insisting on forced labour, for intervening everywhere.

Relations became so strained that ultimately the government in Tokyo felt that it must make a great effort at their improvement. Early in 1943 General Tojo announced in the Japanese Diet that Burma would be declared to be independent within a year. Japan had grasped that independence was the deep longing in the soul of the peoples of South-East Asia, and that, if this were granted, Japan could continue in fact to direct their policies. There followed some hard bargaining over the exact form of their future relationship, in which the Japanese army endeavoured to stipulate that it should have the legal right to intervene if the Burmese government departed from agreed principles. In the face of Burmese opposition, it accepted instead a treaty of alliance between the two countries, in which they simply pledged their cooperation for the self-determined development of all the countries of South-East Asia. These negotiations were completed by August 1943, and the declaration of Burma's complete freedom was made in conditions of apparent reconciliation and confidence. Japan had certainly made an effort at overcoming hostility. But Ba Maw concludes on a disillusioned note:

On the Japanese side, many militarists went back to their old ways again. They could never remember for long that the Burmese were now a free people. I have already mentioned their charge against me that I took our independence too seriously. The cause of the mischief was that they wanted it both ways; they wanted the Burmese to fight the war as people defending their own independence and yet in other matters they were to behave as if they were not independent. The militarists merely changed their argument; previously they had tried to impose their will upon us in the name of military administration, and now it was in the name of military necessity without bothering to convince

* ibid.

us that there was really any such necessity at all; and as the pressures increased they refused even to argue about the necessities, but treated them as Japanese imperatives which ruled out all argument. Knowing how critical the situation had become we tried to go along some of the way with them, but they wanted us to go the whole way, which was clearly impossible unless we were convinced of the need for doing so. Thereupon these little war-lords accused me of trying to subvert their war effort; and so we drifted further apart.*

At the end of the same year, 1943, Japan made a further effort at demonstrating that it was really in earnest in seeking, by the gift of independence, to gain the friendship of Asia. It convened a conference in Tokyo between Japan and five governments, those of Burma, the Philippines, Thailand, Manchukuo, and of the anti-Chiang segments of China. It also invited the Indian refugee leader, Subhas Chandra Bose. The conference met for two days at the beginning of November. Opportunity was given for the oratory of several eloquent statesmen; their speeches were widely reported; some of them took the chance of ingratiating themselves with the Japanese. Most of those who took part, and the Japanese, felt that the conference had been helpful to them. At its end a joint declaration was issued, which pledged everybody concerned to work for Asian independence – which had become the fixed idea of all the lesser countries of Asia – and to support each other in the cause.

More than this was hardly to be expected of a political conference which had been called to demonstrate happiness and unity, not to discuss differences. The final resolution spoke, it is true, of economic cooperation. Japan had been pressing the idea of the economic interdependence of the region, and of the benefit, for all the countries of the area, of economic connection with Japan. The concept was of a kind of Asian Common Market. The odd thing was that Japan did not make more rapid progress with economic planning. It had set up in 1942 a Greater East Asian Ministry, and designated to it the task of preparing schemes; but no programme was published, and there were no elaborate accompanying sets of statistics. There was considerable conflict in Tokyo about this Ministry. By some civilians, especially those in the Foreign Ministry, it was feared that it would be regarded as provocative in South-East Asia: it would unmask Japan's determination to plan the life of the region, and would be counter to the policy of granting independence. Tojo, the Prime Minister, was adamant in its favour. The decision, however, cost him the resignation of his Foreign Minister in protest at the setting-up of such a Ministry.

* ibid.

The Dutch East Indies had been omitted from the countries invited to take part. It was barred from this celebration of regional independence. The Japanese attitude towards this territory was always peculiar. The nationalist movement there was as strong as, or stronger than, that in Burma; and the national parties had made it plain that they should receive the same coveted gift of independence. Japan, however, was not so understanding in their case. The Supreme Command firmly refused that Japan should commit itself on its post-war status, either because it was so rich economically that it was unwilling that Japan should forgo the possibility of annexing it and retaining it as a prize of war, or because it wished to keep it as something to bargain over with the western allies at the eventual peace settlement. In the meanwhile, the Dutch East Indies were governed by the Japanese military, tempered by local councils. Some of the Japanese Ministers thought that this was a mistake, and would have been very willing to buy amity at the price of eventual independence; but, at an imperial conference in May 1943, the views of the Supreme Command had prevailed. They had not changed by the time of the East Asia Conference in November.

The real purpose of that conference had apparently been to embarrass the western allies and, by demonstrating that total independence had become the political currency in Japanese Asia, to deter them from pressing on with plans for its reconquest. A rather more subtle aim may have been to cause dissension between Great Britain and the US. Japan was aware of the American criticism of Great Britain in being behindhand in meeting the demands of nationalism, and it counted on causing further disputes between the allies if it stirred up the nationalist claims still further. The difference in outlook towards nationalism between Britain and America was, in this and many other matters, the chink in their armour which Japan tried to exploit.

Yet the general feeling about the conference was cynicism, disbelief, and amusement. Japan had attempted to convince the people of South-East Asia that it was the sincere friend of the independence of their national units. At the same time Japan, by its action, demonstrated that it was establishing a new empire in place of the one which had been overthrown.

*

Similar experiences to those of Ba Maw with the Japanese were repeated again and again by other people in South-East Asia. Everywhere at first their expectations had been favourably aroused; the Japanese came in through general acclamation; their victories gave them glory; they strode over the vanishing West with pleasure. The *mise en scène* was admirably contrived for Japanese achievement. Restraint, moderation, modesty would have paid them huge dividends. But instead of even pretending to live up to their propaganda about the new age of Asian brotherliness, with which they flooded the countries taken over, most Japanese, and especially the army, made no secret of the fact that they considered that they had won an empire, and were determined to enjoy it. Nearly all instruments of the Japanese state were under the firm control of the Supreme Command, and this was determined not to release any prize which Japanese arms had gained. Those people in South-East Asia with a sophisticated understanding of the ways of government could reckon the callous, and more or less disguised, ways in which the Japanese economic and political instruments set about exploiting them; those who relied upon their eyes for information saw the Japanese, with a naïve disregard of consequence, humiliating the people, insulting their customs, not bothering to learn their languages, and enjoying their disarray.

There were certainly many Japanese, even many Japanese generals and high officers, who, with traditional civilization, understood the sensibilities of subject peoples. The Japanese Foreign Ministry, some Japanese politicians, and some businessmen, struggled hard to get official sanction for more generous policies. They were not blind to the writing on the wall in South-East Asia, and understood the strength of national feeling. That Japan was as receptive as it was, and that, at the top level, it was willing to meet Ba Maw and the other nationalists half way, says much for the quiet pertinacity with which they struggled. This (and the worsening position of Japan in the war) brought independence for the Philippines in September 1943 in the same way that it had come in Burma. But it bore the same sense of sham and unreality as long as the Japanese army and the much more dreaded military police were there and took the law into their hands. The milder Japanese were terrorized into acquiescence by the general will of the Japanese army which was to plunder and oppress. In face of the mass descent on to South-East Asia of the military machine, in face of the reality of Japanese extortion, brutality and incompetence, Japanese good intentions were advertised in vain. In a very short time, their empire had exhausted its credit, and the Japanese uniform had made itself detested.

*

In mid-1943 the British reorganized their command system in Asia. They recognized that Delhi was no longer the ideal centre for the headquarters of the military. It was too heavy with history, and had too many historic distractions. Essentially it was the base of the Indian army; and this was not suited for a war such as this had become, involving amphibious operations and Far East diplomacy. The eyes of a General Staff in India were apt to become fixed upon India's north-west frontier, and on the Middle East. Only by constant effort could they be prevailed upon to study the Burma frontier, and to give due weight to new allies and friends, the hard-pressed Chinese and peoples of South-East Asia. It appeared best to wrench the command away from its old associations, and to locate it at some centre where it could achieve a more correct view of the war. New men were to be brought in, and they would operate from a new place. It would be one in which more attention was paid to voices which went unheeded in Delhi. The command was in fact divided: Delhi continued to be responsible for the Indian army in its home organization; the new command was to be responsible for mobilizing and directing all the forces in the attack against Japan in the East. It would include all three services, army, navy and air force.

At the Quebec conference of the allied powers in 1944, it was decided that the new command should be located at Colombo. It was to be under Vice-Admiral Lord Louis Mountbatten. He was a cousin of King George VI, and it was felt that royal status would give him additional prestige in dealing with Britain's allies, and discharging the political duties which it was clear the post would involve. It was to be international; Mountbatten was to be equally responsible to the British Prime Minister and to the American President. Undoubtedly the arrangement was well conceived; it gave a new tone to the British war effort in the Indian Ocean: it created a new race of military planners who were free from traditional concerns.

A further ingenious tie-up of the command was made by appointing General Stilwell as the deputy of the Supreme Commander. He was the American general who was simultaneously acting as a ranking general of the Chinese army. His aims and objects had diverged greatly from those of the British, of whose military achievements he thought meanly. By this provision, he, and the Chinese, secured a share in the command; at the same time it proved easier to control him.

Mountbatten proved a heavy-weight figure, an ample complement to General MacArthur and to Admiral Nimitz as a member of the triumvirate by which the rest of the war was directed. He was a scientifically minded commander, and many first-rate scientists from England appeared on his staff at Colombo: a happening which in Delhi would have been thought eccentric. He had a gift for the use of public relations, and used this, among other ends, for establishing a rapport with the troops, many of whom had been in a dangerous depression when Mountbatten was appointed. He had in fact something of the personal glamour of the film star, which the public, as the war progressed, increasingly demanded of troop commanders.

With these developments, there faded out one of the most impressive commanders of the war, Lord Wavell. It is true that he continued for a time as Commander-in-Chief in India, and that in the summer of 1943 he was made Viceroy of India; as such he enjoyed political power. But as a maker of war strategy his role was finished. He had played an original, if an inadequately appreciated, part. As Commander in the Middle East in the early part of the war he had borne the brunt of the early attacks by the Italians. He had been starved of resources, and, by bluff and intellectual ability, he had won successes against immense odds. At the beginning of the Japanese war, he had been appointed to the Supreme Command of the troops in Malaya and in the Dutch East Indies, in addition to India, in the hope that, with his quite inadequate force, he might work the same miracle that he had done in the Middle East. The task was a hopeless one; Wavell, also, was by this time a tired man, and had lost a part of his cunning. By temperament an intellectual who combined reflection, and a strange kind of mysticism, with a life of action, a natural scholar whose career had been among soldiers, he failed to achieve recognition among the politicians who mattered because of an inability – or rather an unwillingness – to communicate his personality to his colleagues.

*

The creation of the Colombo Command put new energy into the conduct of British propaganda. It began to be classed as one of the major instruments of war.

Propaganda work had begun before Pearl Harbor. It had been centred in Singapore in an office called the Bureau of the British Ministry of Information, and had operated through the information sections of different British missions in the Far East, such as the British consulate in Shanghai. The early network, which thus came into existence, was disrupted when the Japanese captured most of these places, including Singapore. They were especially severe on prisoners who had any connection with this organization. This was not because they realized the latent power of propaganda, but because they assumed that a Bureau of Information must be concerned with espionage, of which they were particularly afraid. The officer who was Director

General of the Bureau, Robert Scott, formerly in the consular service in China, had a very grim experience during the years of captivity. The Japanese had a curious respect for legality, and were unwilling to execute their victims unless they had made a confession. Time and again, in an effort to extort this confession, they imposed savage tortures on him. He refused to confess, and therefore survived: but when he came out of prison he weighed only five stone.

With Singapore lost, an organization had to be built afresh. It was centred on Delhi; and soon a staff with a highly international flavour was put together – Chinese, Indonesians, Dutch, Frenchmen, Greeks, Hungarians – all the cosmopolitan elements which had escaped from Shanghai and Hong Kong and had taken refuge in India. Some of them were journalists or writers, some were businessmen, a few had been politicians. Their collective knowledge of the Far East was variegated and extensive. The predominant personality was the gifted and imaginative Director of Broadcasting, John Galvin. He was an Irish Australian who, in a crowded life, had seemed to have prepared himself for the role he now had to play. He had a vision of Asia as a force to be reckoned with in the world of the future, when the Japanese should have been thrown back to their own shores. He could appeal to intelligent nationalist sentiment in the occupied territories because of the genuinely democratic quality of his own outlook: upon the organization of propaganda he brought to bear original talents, and extraordinary energy and resourcefulness.

By all the regular methods of propaganda, by broadcasts from a radio station set up by Galvin in New Delhi, by pamphlets and books, by the organization of a news reporting service which was accurate about defeat and could be trusted in accounts of victory, little by little the British version of the war was radiated out. The propagandists in New Delhi exposed the falseness of the Japanese claim for a Greater East Asia Co-Prosperity Sphere. They stripped Japan of the claim to be anything but an old-fashioned imperialist. They gave to the Asian world the lively sense that western power still existed, was preparing for a riposte, and had good hope of a future in which men could live at liberty and in peace. They transformed the image of India from being a country in collapse to being a power house in which returning armies were girding on invincible force.

Of the powerful effect of this invisible arm of the British army there can be little doubt. Ba Maw speaks in his memoirs of the disquieting effect in Burma of British propaganda and the British agent on the minds of a rather mercurial population. The sense that the British were gone was undermined by the awareness that British eyes were still upon them, and that the slightest and most intimate details of the Burmese districts were being discussed in London and Delhi.

*

The propaganda had more effect on the peoples who were subordinate, and rather unruly, allies of Japan than on Japan itself. Showers of propaganda burst unavailingly on the granite of Japanese civilian morale, and the Japanese army was never known to have lost a battle, to have flagged in any way, or to have been at all diverted from its purposes by any of the wiles of psychological warfare.

It was proof against American propaganda no less than against British. A most effective instrument at the United States' disposal was the broadcasting station at San Francisco. Propaganda was backed up by the useful research done in numerous centres. On the whole, however, American arms gained little support from the labour of American propagandists against the monolithic Japanese.

On the other side, only perfunctory use of propaganda was made by the Japanese. Indeed, both Japanese and Chinese seemed to ignore the possibilities of propaganda until the very end of the war. No Japanese figure rose to play anything like the same part as Dr Goebbels, Minister of Enlightenment in Nazi Germany. Japanese propaganda was directed chiefly towards the people of the countries that it had occupied, or planned to attack. The media which it used were the same as those employed by its adversary, predominantly the wireless and the printed word. But there is little to be said of this side of Japan's war effort. On the whole it was parched for lack of imagination.

Thus all the eastern world resounded, both with explosives and with the monotonous exchange of propaganda. *Inter arma silent leges*: but the media of mass communications were busier than ever. Every nation talked with every other; to argue with it, to inform or mislead about the direction of hostilities. America spoke to Japan. Japan spoke to South-East Asia. Britain spoke through numerous languages on the Delhi wireless. In this general post there was one notable exception. Britain did not speak to India. The British political warfare executives operated from Indian soil, and used Indian facilities, but in return for this the British government had given an undertaking that radio propaganda would be directed outwardly, and that it would not use these instruments for arguing with Indian public opinion.

The Indian government had its own propaganda organization. This, though partly operated by British staff, conceived its task rather differently from the outward-directed political warfare. Its task was limited to explaining to the people of India the motives of the government of India in fighting the war, and to demonstrating the progress it was making. It was not to debate with Indians the rights and wrongs of their differences with the British. From this use of the radio, the British barred themselves. They accepted the limitation formally; and investigation shows that on the whole they stuck by this agreement. The British never, for example, put over to Indian opinion its own case on Indian constitutional developments, as it stated this in broadcasts to America. The motive was that the British feared to aggravate India the more by supplying its own commentary on events. As was usual, it put its confidence in bland silence; which of course in the end was the more provoking.

*

The allies announced, at the Cairo Conference of the US, Britain and China, in November 1943, the severe peace terms which they proposed to exact from Japan. They were not put forward as opening the way to peace, as a bait to negotiation: the allies intended them as declaring their programme of action, and as an encouragement to China, and persuasion of it to remain in the war. Japan's overseas empire was to be forfeit; it must surrender unconditionally. At first, this declaration did not have the deflationary effect on Japanese morale which had been hoped for. Japan, which privately had already begun to envisage the possibility of defeat, was, however, optimistic that it could avoid the worst consequences. It knew the very great defensive strength of its position, due to geography. It was confident that the United States and Britain would not risk the vast losses in manpower which they would have to incur in the last stages of the war when it came to a struggle to land in Japan itself. The United States and Britain would, it was sure, snatch at the possibility of a reasonable negotiation, in which much of what Japan judged to be indispensable could be preserved.

Therefore Japan interpreted the menacing words from Cairo as being a good deal less than their face value. They were reassured also by the absence of a Russian signature to them. Russia, though it was allied to the US and Britain, was active only in the German war, and had not committed itself to the eastern conflict. The conference at Cairo had been designed to take place without the USSR being represented, since Russia was unwilling to compromise its neutrality in the Pacific. Japan saw this and was deeply relieved. If Russia was firmly attached to neutrality in 1943, what might be its position in a year or two, when its experience with its western allies had further frayed its nerves? Besides, was it in the real interests of any of the great powers to destroy Japan as an organized force, and open the way to another power to occupy the vacuum? Did the United States or Britain desire to make a ruin there in which Communism would sprout? Japan still had sufficient reason for not regarding the Cairo Declaration as the accurate forecast of history.

Moreover Japan was to nurse, until the very end, false comfort from its long immunity from occupation. Japan, alone of Asian countries, had never known the tramp of invading armies. It had come to believe that it was especially protected by the gods from the hand of war. For a warlike people, the Japanese had been singularly little affected by threats from abroad. Only twice, in the thirteenth century, had Japan itself been in danger from invasion by foreign soldiers. In the time of Kubla Khan, in 1274 and again in 1281, great Mongol armadas set sail to conquer the small island empire, and annex it as a tributary. They were seemingly irresistible; Japan seemed done for; it quaked with terror, while it began to defend every inch of the way against those troops who had managed to land. But on each occasion great storms scattered and wrecked the mighty fleets, and the invaders stood no chance. This history became a part of the national memory. The 'kamikaze' or 'divine wind' which had saved Japan in the thirteenth century was expected, until the very end, to blow again, or the divine protection would manifest itself in some other guise.

The wind was not to blow. Russia entered the war, America put its trust in an army of occupation to avert Communism. The eventual peace was very nearly on the identical terms of Cairo. But no American or British life was lost storming the beaches of Honshu.

CHAPTER 18

Subhas Chandra Bose

THE Japanese, after overrunning Burma, had been content for two years to stand on the defensive. They had repelled the attack organized by General Wavell from India in the autumn of 1942, against Arakan. The operation, which was encouraged from London in the hopes that it would repair British prestige, was premature and was made with inadequate force and troops insufficiently trained; the Japanese were never embarrassed by it – except that it restricted a move which they had been intending to make at the same time into north India – and, by outmanoeuvring and outflanking the British, they compelled the British to retreat.

The country between India and Burma was peculiarly difficult; communications almost did not exist; the disease-infestation required that armies, if they were to operate with any degree of efficiency, should be remarkably well organized with medical services, which they were not until 1944. These facts, as much as any other, kept the British and Japanese apart, though great pressure was brought on British troops by Churchill to go on the offensive. In fact, the Japanese had acted on the principle that geography had contrived to give Burma the perfect scientific frontier, and calculated that they would do enough if they posted troops to guard the few practicable approaches from India.

In 1943 took place the adventure of General Wingate in Burma. This man, who had formed his ideas in Palestine and Abyssinia, and who took T. E. Lawrence and the Arab revolt in the First World War as his model, was confident that Burma could make an ideal field for guerrilla war. If it was hard for armies to make contact, he suggested that guerrillas should do their work for them; and that, once these had made a long-range penetration behind the Japanese lines, they could, by superior mobility and surprise, produce as much havoc as would be caused by a successful army invasion.

Wingate convinced the Indian army with great difficulty, and made an expedition with just over three thousand men. The higher Japanese officers regarded him without anxiety, and said that he must starve in the jungle; the more junior officers were shocked by the boldness of his strategy, and by their inability to hunt him down. The advance of Wingate upon T. E. Lawrence was in the use of wireless and of aircraft.

Wingate lost a thousand men, one third of his force, and had put a Burmese railway temporarily out of action. Whether his guerrilla successes came near justifying his theory was an open question; a much larger operation, employing aircraft, was planned for the next year, but it met with disaster at the outset, Wingate being killed on taking off. He is a hard man to assess. England, for prestige reasons, urgently needed a success, and it possessed at this time a propaganda machine, which could create heroes overnight. Wingate's personality and achievement were written up and blazed across the world. It may be that Wingate demonstrated, not the success of his own guerrilla strategy, but the success of British propaganda. He supplied to the waiting and idle troops of the British army, in the tedious interval of training and before they were offensively engaged, the spectacle of exciting warfare and of individual performance. Wingate believed himself to be a man of destiny and that the situation was also one of destiny.

A far more orthodox, and forceful, attack was intended by the British in the spring of 1944. The Fourth Army Corps was preparing it, using the small town of Imphal in north-east India as its base. The Japanese, who had two divisions in the region, had intelligence that it was coming, and resolved to strike first.

The campaign inside the borders of India which resulted was interesting partly because, in it, Japan again put to the test its claim that it was fighting, not simply for itself, but for the freedom of the Asian peoples. It is true that the organized forces of allegedly 'free India', which it had among its troops, played only a minor part; the campaign was so interesting, so stubborn, so terrible, and the 'free Indians' played such a small role in it, that the history of it, and its narration by the Japanese, might well overlook their presence. Yet, symbolically, the event is important, and was certainly seen to be so by the people of India and South-East Asia. Japan had announced that it had opted out of the circle of imperial predatory powers, and could rightly claim to be the patron of free Asia. It had not, until this time, done anything very striking to show that it was living up to this claim. In Japan, all attention was given to the gallantry of the Japanese forces; and the average man scarcely thought of their army as fighting Asian battles, or that their Asian allies could be of much worth to them. The opportunity had come to show that this was a mistaken view.

Chance presented itself in the shape of the Indian leader Subhas Chandra Bose. He played at this stage an extraordinarily decisive part. By accident, and by seizing an exceptional opportunity, he was able to cut a figure which made him outstanding among the comparatively small number of men who influenced the course of the war by their individual qualities. He chanced to be available to the Japanese to lead a movement to free India, and, in retrospect, it appears that this was the last chance of saving itself with which Japan was presented.

*

Bose was a Bengali, the son of a comparatively high civil servant who became a judge. Bengal had a special place in the history of Indian nationalism. It stood by itself culturally, and bred a type which was peculiar in being the exponent of a classical strain of regional loyalty. Bengali patriotism was deeply devotional: it was less associated than in other parts of India with day-by-day economic interests: the Bengali really believed the singularly powerful oratory which surged over the province especially after 1905. The passionate quality of Bengali nationalism, monomaniac, hot, somnambulist, is rather like that of the Sinn Fein patriot who is heard, off-stage, as a repeated theme in Sean O'Casey's play, *Red Roses for You*, repeating his hypnotic oratory. This nationalism expressed itself, to a degree quite unknown in other parts of India, in a fascination with violence and in a cult of terrorism. The typical Bengali nationalist was quite carried away, renounced his home and the ties of ordinary business, and plunged into secret conspiratorial activity in a way which horrified the rest of India as being extravagant and an affront to domestic obligation.

Bengal differed so much in temperament from the other parts of India that political cooperation with it was not easy. Bose became a leader of Bengali nationalism, and was so powerful a personality that his shadow fell over the rest of India. He was in the recognizable succession to the Bengal leaders of his youth who used to be carried away by the poetical implications of 'mother India', Hinduism, and Indian uniqueness. Always, Bose saw himself, and conducted himself, as a man of destiny. He had a great appeal to youth, frustrated, very poor but very proud, liking rhetorical leadership, always responding enthusiastically to the idea of a solution through some act of violence. He sought to turn Indian nationalism into the kind of movement which grew in Bengal.

As a young man, Bose, who was born in 1897, had been sent by his family to England, where he studied so diligently at Cambridge that he passed the entrance examination into the Indian Civil Service. This still enjoyed so much prestige in India that a lifetime spent in it, or a resignation from it, produced equal *réclame*. Bose chose the latter course. By resigning even before he had been posted to any particular duty, he gained a flying start in the Bengal Congress Party. Two decades of serious attachment to Congress, and a spell of office as Mayor of Calcutta, brought him, after a term of imprisonment which he spent in Mandalay Fort in Burma, to the presidency of the All-India Congress in 1938. Though the inner springs of his being may have been poetical, he developed, during his time as Mayor, a business-like aptitude, which won recognition from British officers.

This proved to be a parting of the ways with his non-Bengali Congress colleagues. In his struggle with them, and partly because of his temperament, he moved sharply to the Left, though for him there was no special attraction in socialism, and he was not moved by the conflict between this and free enterprise. The Left meant simply extremism, more determined personalities – a more congenial emotional atmosphere. He advocated ever more extreme Congress policies: and in particular he opposed Gandhi's stubbornly held non-violence. In this contest, Gandhi faced the blind emotional forces of Bengali nationalism, which repudiated Gandhi's homespun philosophy of the spinning wheel and of the virtues of simple peasant life. A religious preoccupation such as Gandhi's – a religion which dwelt on the virtues of the Sermon on the Mount which Gandhi had taken over in his version of Hinduism – was alien to him. Bose's passion was summed up in his favourite slogan: 'Give me blood and I promise you freedom.'

The year of his final breach with Gandhi was also the year of the outbreak of the war in Europe. Bose was not inclined to sit still among such events. For the attitude of Gandhi and Vallabhai Patel, the men he was opposing, it is possible to feel much admiration. They were realists. They were as intransigently opposed to the British as he was himself. But they accepted that military action was not the way to strike at them. They were organizing a vast, poor, ignorant, apathetic nation in the only way it could be mobilized. A military adventure *was* the kind of thing the British would expect and would know how to deal with. They were helpless against this unspeakable groundswell. Subhas Bose was simply too impatient for this Himalayan wisdom.

Bose thought otherwise. The world was being changed by armies, and he was impatient to have an Indian army. His agitation was impatient of bounds. He was arrested, rather oddly for a seditious speech in connection with the agitation for the removal of a memorial to the victims of the Black Hole of Calcutta, which was thought to be hurtful to national sentiment. In prison he meditated upon the progress of the war, on the might of Germany, on the great opportunities for Indian freedom which he felt that Gandhi, with a senile attachment to non-violence (as it appeared to Bose) was at this time allowing to pass by. He was distracted when he thought of what he might be able to effect if he was at liberty. He procured his temporary release by beginning a hunger strike, and assured that he would not thereafter be restored to jail by absconding from his home in Calcutta early on a January morning of 1941, disguised as an elderly Moslem mullah.

By a daring journey he made his way across India, through Afghanistan and through the Soviet Union, into Germany. There he found his spiritual home, and probably would have done better if he had stayed there instead of answering the call of Japan. He had always been attracted by Germany. His temperament was Wagnerian: the Nazi grandees proved attractive personally. The colourful side of Nazism appealed to him profoundly. The heroics, the constant legends, the dangerous and insidious concepts, the affected contempt for weakness and pity, the invocation of history, all seemed congenial to him. Bengali culture is strongly patriarchal, and the Nazi concept of the place of women in the warrior's life appealed to one who, till he went to Germany and married a German, had apparently been indifferent to women. In the Siegfried cult and the heroic life, he saw a model which he found admirable. He was deficient in the sense of humour that was the best preservative against Nazi fantasy; and his Hindu education had given him a natural tendency towards a narrow concentration on whatever happened to appeal to him for intellectual reasons. Even the Nazi brutality he found brisk, salubrious, and invigorating.

In politics he found the Nazi form of state entirely congenial. The rule by the Nazi party, and the authoritarian role of the party by a small caucus of leaders, seemed to him to provide India with a model form of government. Discipline, before all else, was what India seemed to need for overcoming its problems of the division into separate castes and communities, and for dealing with its great economic problem of poverty. The democratic type of government which it might imitate from Great Britain had the fatal weakness of permitting so much liberty that the state might fall in pieces. New vistas opened for an Indian government which would be equipped with a Gestapo, concentration camps and an SS. On the precise details of the policy he would pursue if the war should bring him to power, he was vague. It was enough that he should proclaim the bracing virtues of authoritarianism.

Bose therefore found the situation promising. He was satisfied with his personal reception. The Germans invited him to take charge of organizing the rebellious Indians in their hands into a body which might be useful for war purposes. He was given access to the Indian prisoners captured by the Germans in North Africa. He broadcast to India over the German radio; and he took part in the controversy over the Cripps mission to India. Volunteers began to come forward to form an Indian Legion, and about two thousand men were enlisted for training. There was much ceremonial feasting and mutual compliment.

Spiritually this was probably the happiest part of Bose's somewhat neurotic life. But after some months Bose had to recognize that his German friends had not acknowledged him as the head of an Indian government in exile. Perhaps this was due, as was explained to him, to the fact that they could as yet, while Russia remained undefeated, have brought no effective aid to an Indian rebel government; perhaps it was because Hitler could not bring himself to recognize that Indians would be equal citizens in the post-war world which he was planning. Hitler, if Germany won the war, intended to dispose of India by a diplomacy in which Indians would not play a part.

Whatever was the reason, the Germans put no obstacles in Bose's way when an invitation reached him from the Indians in South-East Asia to transfer himself to this new sphere, and to take charge of the free India movement which was being organized by the Japanese. His imagination, the dramatic part he might play, the appeal of the idea of pan-Asianism, his calculation of how India, or at least Bengal, would respond to new situations, all impelled him to accept.

*

Bose sailed from Kiel in a German U-boat in February 1943. He left behind some lieutenants to continue the work of organizing the available Indians, though he had failed to come to an agreement with the Nazis on precisely how they were to be used. The U-boat sailed to Madagascar, and there, off shore, it made a rendezvous with a Japanese submarine which carried him for the last half of his journey. He reached Tokyo on 13 June, after a voyage of thirteen weeks. That he was permitted to be so slow suggests that the Japanese, at least at this time, did not found great hopes on the plan for which he had been imported.

Indeed they had been making half-hearted bids at raising the Indians in revolt against the British ever since the first days of the war; and they had suffered a series of disappointments. At first the project had been entrusted to a man named Major Fujiwara Iwaichi, of the Army General Staff, who appears to have been of some amiability, with an understanding of what would appeal to Indians. He was fortunate in lighting, in the first days of the war, on a sick prisoner, Captain Mohan Singh. This was a man of character; he was a cousin of the Maharaja of Patiala, a great prince of the Punjab; he was a capable professional soldier, and had become, apparently without the knowledge of the Indian army, a convinced nationalist. With the backing of Fujiwara, and with the financial aid of some of the leaders of the 800,000 resident Indians in Malaya, he undertook to raise from the Indian prisoners of war a force which might prove useful to the Japanese.

Of the total of 115,000 men who surrendered during the whole of the Malayan campaign, Indians made up a very large number. Though at first a rather blind confidence was put in their loyalty by the Indian government, this had a rather unenviable, if amiable, record, of being deceived. In the Indian Mutiny of 1857, the inquiries held afterwards had shown that an almost insane trust had been placed in troops which had given every sign that they were preparing for rebellion.

Certainly the experience of some of the troops, in the months immediately before the surrender of Singapore, had not been such as to ensure their fidelity. Malaya was in many ways the weakest link in the British imperial chain. Among other disservices, it brought about the demoralization of the Indian army. The culture and atmosphere of Malaya has been described very exactly in the stories of Somerset Maugham, and this society did not seem to most Indians as one worth dying for. Near Singapore there was a very luxurious country club with a much sought-after swimming pool. In the six months before the war, it became known in Singapore that the wives of the planters and of local white businessmen had objected to the swimming pool being used by Indian officers. British officers from the same regiments were eagerly invited, solicitously treated, and competed for assiduously. The Indians were dismayed when this action of the club was officially condoned: at least no protest against it was made from the government or from the military command. This insult, casually offered by the Tanglin Club, did more than many other light-hearted steps to undermine the British Empire in Asia. A dispassionate observer, surveying what was done, must have decided that the English, and especially their wives, were mad. It is not politic to insult a man mortally who is about to defend you.

The Japanese attempts at subverting the loyalty of the prisoners had as their background this resentment at the arrogance of the white society of Malaya. In spite of this preparation of the soil, the first attempts of Fujiwara and of Mohan Singh to set up the Indian National

Army, which was inaugurated at Singapore on 12 February 1942, had only limited success. True, they had much to offer the Indian captives – immediate freedom, good wages, the resumption of their military careers, an apparently bright political prospect, exemption from the dreadful forced labour squads, for which Japanese prison camps soon became notorious. Yet the response was poor and Mohan Singh proved anything but an obedient tool. He laid down conditions that the Japanese were unwilling to accept; he stated plainly that if the Japanese aimed at replacing the British in India, they would, after a short time, have to face the aroused opposition of Indian nationalism. In December 1942 Mohan Singh resigned from his position and was arrested by the Japanese, and the first stage of the Japanese experiment at collaboration with Indian nationalism was over.

The Japanese had been handicapped in their efforts because of a deep-seated contempt which they had for prisoners of war, and, still more, for prisoners who were willing to be untrue to their oath of service. Nothing struck them as so contemptible as disloyalty, and they were unable to hide this. Simple-mindedly they judged their prisoners by the same exacting standards which they would have applied to their own people. This made them maladroit in the project of raising an army out of defaulters and deserters.

The decision was, however, taken to persevere in this venture. It was resolved to see whether better results could be obtained from enlisting a politician of standing to head the movement, instead of working exclusively through military men. Subhas Bose, whose mission in Germany had been favourably reported on by the Japanese military attaché there, seemed to be well qualified for this role.

Bose, on returning to Asia, threw himself energetically into organizing the Indian movement, and, in a short time, gave it a life of its own, irrespective of the intentions of its Japanese sponsors. Bose was a different type from the sycophants and commercial adventurers who were usually available to support the Japanese enterprises. The qualities of action he had once displayed as Mayor of Calcutta were now directed to the preparation of a government in exile, which should be ready to replace the existing government of India. On 23 October 1943 the provisional government of Free India (Azad Hind) was set up in Singapore, with Bose at its head. He bled the Indian businessmen white for funds for his enterprise, being given by the Japanese the power to levy taxes on them, and having acquired in the service of Congress the right combination of contempt for millionaires and of business-like respect for money. Bose worked under the great handicap that adequate human material for forming a provisional administration was absent. In spite of this, the sketchy organization of Azad Hind was set up.

Though Bose, between June and October, had transformed the position of the Indians in South-East Asia, and had built them into one of the forces which had to be taken account of, yet he had not succeeded in getting Japan to the point of recognizing a full-fledged government-in-exile. The most that he gained was an invitation to take part as an observer, along with the puppet governments of the Japanese system, in the Greater East Asia Conference in November 1943, although his status was certainly inflated by the oratory of those present; Japan also declared its readiness to hand over the Andaman and Nicobar Islands in the Indian Ocean, to Bose's administration. But as his organization grew in effective power, the relation with local Japanese officials deteriorated. All the vexations which Ba Maw had had to endure, also faced Subhas Bose. The Japanese army was aware of the nuisance which an opinionated exiled government could make, and, deeply suspicious, was anxious to thwart it. However, the Japanese commanders agreed to test out what effect the Indians could bring upon a battle; and Bose glowed at the opportunity.

*

In the meanwhile the Japanese had made their plans for an offensive from Burma which was to be directed against India. Their position was gradually growing dangerous. Large forces were being prepared against them – potentially fourteen divisions from China in the north, three or possibly six divisions from India in the west. In the spring the Japanese in Burma were reinforced, and the decision was made. Basically, the Japanese attack on India was intended to forestall an ultimate offensive against themselves by striking at once and dispersing the gathering British force. The conception was sound, if somewhat optimistic. The Japanese threw into disorder the aggressive plans on the British side.

First the Japanese hoped to overrun the British in Arakan, and then to advance into India, taking in the Assamese towns of Imphal and Kohima. From there they would move into Bengal, though probably they intended no larger action which would have taken them beyond that province. They affected, however, to fall in with Bose's plans for the general invasion of India, as they made stirring material for propaganda. In March 1944 they began their attack and crossed the Indian frontier. The Japanese army employed three divisions.

Bose was determined that they should be accompanied by regiments of the Indian National Army. His provisional government had been transferred to Burma in January 1944. He is described by Ba Maw at the time as a 'bold, khaki-clad figure, carrying with him everywhere the aura of his vast, fabulous country'. In what followed, Bose's sense of reality, his strong point compared with the Indian leaders on the British side of the dividing line, deserted him. He proclaimed the slogan 'Chalo Dehli'. 'On to Delhi.' Its Red Fort, the ancient citadel built by Shah Jahan, hypnotized him, and its occupation became an obsession. In his elation, he foresaw himself sweeping on, made master of the country by a popular upsurge; able, with the strength which this would bring him, to dictate terms to the surrendering British, and to ensure that the Japanese did not misuse their victory, or ride roughshod over the country. He calculated that a Japanese invasion of India would create a very divided feeling among Indians, and might even, the reputation of Japan being what it was, bring a mass of them to the side of the British; but the appearance on Indian soil of an Indian army of liberation would have the most rousing effect all over the country. The world would hear for the first time of the Indian National Army, and thousands of Indians would surge to it. It is strange to find a politician so practical as Bose nursing such illusions. The conversations at this time between Bose and his captains in the Indian National Army, the records of which have survived, are the proofs of his misconception.

The Japanese took a cooler view of his prospects. They wanted to divide the INA (Indian National Army) up into units of 250 men, who would act as liaison troops, guides and spies, and who would each be attached to a Japanese force. In the end a compromise was arrived at. The INA had three organized divisions in the expedition, each of two thousand men. The remainder moved as auxiliaries. It became known that the Japanese army had reserved for itself the right of gaining the first victory on Indian soil, and looked forward to offering Imphal as a birthday present to the Emperor, which would be the more welcome because the war was going badly on other fronts.

*

The army against which it moved, the Fourteenth Army, was, like the armies in the Middle East, a joint Anglo-Indian one. Battalions were either British, Indian or Gurkha, but the battalions were mixed up, and the brigade, and still more the division, were heterogeneous. Throughout the war, there was general good feeling and cooperation between the British and Indians. Whatever the grievances, they did not show themselves on the battlefield. This army, by the reorganization of command which took place in 1943, had passed under the supreme direction of Lord Louis Mountbatten, Commander-in-Chief in South-East Asia, with the ultimate command post at Colombo.

The army, which was about to receive its first campaigning experience, represented, at least in part, a new kind of India in arms. Its old pre-war armies had been drawn from a relatively few districts and, among Hindus, from a few chosen castes. Now, under wartime necessity, the army had very much widened its intake of recruits: and with surprising results. For example, Madrasis, who had formed an important part of the armies of Lord Wellesley at the Battle of Assaye, had not been recruited for many years. Now they were offered employment, and the Madrasis celebrated their readmission by supplying the most decorated air force pilots that came from any region of India.

The army undoubtedly gained from opening its ranks; and in so doing the government met a long-standing grievance of the people. The economic benefits of supplying troops were very considerable, and these accounted in part for the prosperity of such regions as the Punjab. It had seemed unjust to favour some parts of the country and to withhold benefits from the others. The lot was cast by a theory, largely arbitrary and false, that some of the people were naturally martial, others not; in fact the distinction dated from the Indian Mutiny, and went on the principle chiefly of rewarding the classes which had not joined the Mutiny, and of discriminating against those which had. At last the army shook itself free from baleful memories, and recruited itself on a more national basis.

This new army began to reflect the new interests of India. Whereas the old army had been entirely non-political, the new entries inevitably brought in with them something of their political interests. The attempt to bar out contacts with political leaders had to be given up: the brightest of the recruits, especially for the officer corps, were the most political: the pride in being above politics had to give way. These new recruits thought it unnatural and absurd to volunteer their lives for use in a war in which they had no say. The mess rooms became forums where every aspect of the world and of government action was under constant scrutiny. This was reflected in the concern of the government in seeing that the reading rooms of the army were well stocked with propaganda. The older generation of professional army officers, and of Indian NCOs looked on disapprovingly, but they could do nothing to stem this constant debate. Increasingly the government was compelled to open the barrack-room gates, so the army became less cloistered. In these months of the war, the old life of India was talked away in the heroic and mock bravura of undergraduate politics conducted by an army of civilians in uniform.

In the campaign which was about to begin, many of the regular Indian officers, whose admission to the army had been the great event in its history during the 1930s, were to be for the first time in action. Soldiers who afterwards became well-known, such as Ayub Khan, later to become President of Pakistan, were tested in this fighting.

About the British soldiers in this army, the main fact was that they began the campaign by being war-weary. They had many of them been on duty for a long time, in an unhealthy climate. They were unsettled by the separation from their families. They were bored by inactivity. They complained that they were the 'forgotten army': an army which had lain in preparation too long and had not the bracing experience of coming into action. It did not take to the atmosphere of the country it was to fight in, to the jungles and the eerie silences, to the leeches and snakes: its medical services were inadequate, and, before the introduction of mepacrin, it was always decimated by malaria.

*

The Japanese advance became bogged down in the siege of Imphal. For over eight weeks, beginning on 8 March 1944, a terrible contest, perhaps the most primitive of the war with the exception of the struggle for the Pacific atolls, took place for the possession of the city: there was resolute hand-to-hand fighting.

At the beginning of the siege, the Japanese, at the start of their offensive, looked very likely to succeed. But the expedition was doomed when the Japanese found it impossible, because of the nature of the country and the blockage of supply routes from the air, to reinforce it with men and materials to overcome the defence. For days the Japanese were convinced that a final effort by them would deliver the city into their hands: but always they were disappointed. They beat off British and Indian sorties, but their own attacks were repulsed. There was great carnage. The fighting was so intense because the Japanese had to be killed at their posts, in the bunkers and wherever they had found cover. A similar struggle took place a little to the north of Imphal for Kohima, where a gigantic battle was waged over the possession of a tennis-court in the garden of the Commissioner's house.

A tactical innovation which deprived the Japanese of one of their habitual means of securing advantage was made during the campaign. In their drive through Malaya and Burma two years before, they had, using their superior mobility, habitually surrounded British forces;

and, when this took place, the British habitually withdrew. This time the British did not retreat; and, though surrounded, relied on being supplied by air. An elaborate organization of the RAF flew in large amounts of food and ammunition. Without this airlift Imphal would have fallen. This change in tactics, which was due to the improved strength of the RAF in the area, changed the situation. The Japanese plans went awry when the troops, whom they thought they had trapped, stayed to fight it out instead of retiring in disorder. They misjudged profoundly the quality of the troops they opposed. They had formed so low an opinion of the British in the Malayan fighting that this betrayed them; the extent to which British troops under British command were underrated turned out to be one of their principal assets.

Another important, significant, hopeful change was that, for the first time in the war the Japanese began to surrender. Not in large numbers: the majority were still faithful to the idea that defeated Japanese are killed or commit suicide. But that some at least, when wounded, depressed, cut off, and cold, acted as other soldiers similarly placed were accustomed to do, was a cheering fact.

The action took place in the country of the Nagas. Some spectacular achievements brought the Naga tribesmen into the light of world publicity. Much more has happened since to these attractive people. Their activities in Intelligence, and as porters, played an unexpected part. A monument erected on the battlefield recalls how two Nagas, disguised as mess servants, stole the Japanese plans of their future lines of advance, passed these to the British, and enabled them to be frustrated.

One Japanese newspaper reporter wrote: 'These fierce battles are comparable with Verdun in the last war.' Finally, logistics were decisive. There was an utter failure of communications, and the Japanese air force was too weak to emulate the British in air transport. The Japanese could bring in neither rice, nor medical supplies, nor essential equipment. The Japanese, who always travelled light, had relied on capturing stores and living on stocks of rice which they might seize; but in this they had failed. The Japanese troop commander issued the following order: 'A decisive battle is the only battle known to a Japanese soldier, or fitting to the Japanese spirit, but now other methods may have to be adopted.' By this he meant a strategic withdrawal. On 4 July the Japanese lifted the siege, and, on their way back, their retreat became a disaster.

They began the campaign with an army of 85,000 men; in it they lost 53,000. British and Indian casualties amounted to 16,700. The result of the campaign was a terrible, wasteful, ignominious defeat. It was one of the worst disasters that the Japanese army suffered in the whole war; comparable in disgrace, if not in magnitude, to that of the Japanese navy at the Battle of Midway Island. Primarily, when all due allowance had been made for the performance of the Fourteenth Army, it had been due to ineffective staff work by an army which was not familiar with campaigning in the tropics. It must be remembered that the war in Malaya had been before this the only large-scale operation of this kind which the Japanese army had fought, and, on balance, its training was still for temperate climates. The higher officers would not cooperate with one another. Perhaps because of this, the Japanese GHQ demanded a rigid obedience to orders and thus checked initiative from the officers in the field, which could often have turned defeat into victory. Another cause of the rout was the numerical weakness of the Japanese air force.

But that the Japanese soldiers had fought like tigers cannot be denied. A quotation may be given from the book on the campaign by Colonel Barker entitled *The March on Delhi*:

Recruits in the Japanese army were subjected to an intense three-month course of indoctrination which changed them into fanatics, ready to die for their Emperor, their country and the honour of their regiments. The slogan 'Our highest hope is to die for the Emperor' was chanted until it became a positive obsession. The indoctrination of their families was not forgotten either; soon after the new recruit was called up, his relatives received a letter from his commanding officer asking them to be careful not to block his road to an honourable death. The effectiveness of the propaganda may be judged from the fact that there were cases of wives killing their children and committing suicide so that their husbands would not be reluctant to die. Many officers and men even had their funeral rites performed before leaving for the front to show their intention of dying for their country . . .*

Yet, impressive as their military behaviour was, it was undoubtedly an aberration. There was madness in it, as well as remarkable self-discipline. For, as the war dragged on to its close, and as the Japanese position grew steadily worse, so did the Japanese military behaviour become more ferocious. Its extreme cult of death was a new thing of this century, at least in the form which it took at the time. Early in this century, the Russo-Japanese war had not been particularly savage. And the new sternness was only to be found in the Japanese overseas. As long as they were in the homeland, they did not seem to be possessed, as were the troops in Burma, in the Philippines, and in China. It was as

*Colonel A. J. Barker: *The March on Delhi*, Faber, 1963.

if the Japanese army, once it had had battle experience, succeeded in passing its *furor Japonicus* to all the reinforcements which came to it from Japan. The madness came out in some of the battle orders which were captured:

> You men have got to be fully in the picture as to what the present position is. Regarding death as something lighter than a feather you men must tackle the task of capturing Imphal. You must accept that the division will be almost annihilated. I have confidence in your courage but should any delinquency occur, I shall take the necessary action. In order to keep the honour of his unit bright, a commander may have to use his sword as a weapon of punishment, shameful though it is to have to shed one's own soldiers' blood on the battlefield.*

Some of the men who were the victims of this military discipline, some of the officers who enforced it, are now living quietly in Japan, and they must look back on their wartime experience with surprise and almost with disbelief.

The news of the defeat on 4 July arrived in Tokyo at the same time as the news of the loss of Paris by Germany. It was hard to say which of them faced the blacker prospects, Germany or Japan. The disaster increased the bad relations between the army and the navy: this came, said the navy, of the army 'taking walks' in Asia, and entering on unnecessary adventures instead of concentrating on the problems of the defence of the homeland.

The adventures were nearly at an end. The army would be needed in the Japanese islands. This campaign was nearly the finish of the Japanese in Burma. For a time they were saved from effective pursuit by the monsoon, which put an end to all war. But when the monsoon ended, the Fourteenth Army moved forward; the offensive had already been joined by a bitterly fought advance of Americans and American-trained Chinese troops (who had fallen back on India in 1942) led by General Stilwell; a thrust from Arakan for which the prelude was the taking of Akyab from the sea; and by four Chinese divisions reluctantly introduced by Chiang Kai-shek from Yunnan. This time the offensive progressed. The allies had clear air supremacy, and this was decisive, particularly because it enabled them to keep their armies fully supplied. The Japanese had stirred up opposition from all corners of the world; they must however have felt somewhat surprised at finding among their pursuers divisions of West African and East African troops. They had been raised by the British, and the war in Burma in

* ibid.

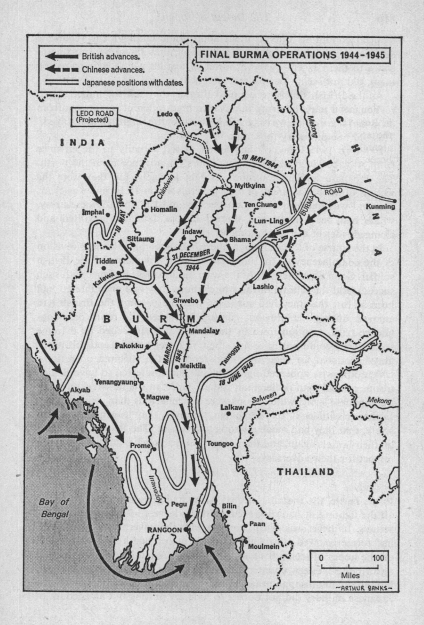

FINAL BURMA OPERATIONS 1944-1945

← British advances.
◄--- Chinese advances.
═══ Japanese positions with dates.

LEDO ROAD (Projected)

INDIA

Ledo

CHINA

10 MAY 1944

Myitkyina

BURMA ROAD

Ten Chung

Kunming

Imphal

Homalin

Lun-Ling

Chindwin

10 MAY 1944

Sittaung

Indaw

Bhamo

Tiddim

31 DECEMBER 1944

Kalewa

Lashio

Shwebo

B U R M A

Mandalay

Pakokku

MARCH 1945

Taunggyi

Meiktila

18 JUNE 1945

Yenangyaung

Magwe

Lalkaw

Salween

Mekong

Akyab

Prome

Irrawaddy

Toungoo

THAILAND

Bay of
Bengal

Pegu

Bilin

RANGOON

Paan

Moulmein

0   100
Miles

~ARTHUR BANKS~

tropical conditions offered them appropriate employment. That the African people had no quarrel with Japan, that Japan had no significance to them except as the exporter of textiles which were prized by them, did not seem to cause any comment.

As the British slowly reoccupied Burma, they felt the imperial itch reviving. An imperial army in advance bred different sentiments from an imperial army in retreat. 'By English bones the English flag is stayed.' This old line of poetry took on a new meaning.

By April 1945 Rangoon had fallen. It fell actually to the advance from Akyab, which beat by a few hours the advance from the north. The Japanese soldiers continued to fight savagely, but they were the victims of the bad strategy of their generals. Soon all Burma was clear. The end was made more certain because most of the Burmese army, which had been raised and trained by the Japanese, revolted and changed sides at a critical moment.

In the course of this campaign, there had taken place a sharp revision of the complacency of the Japanese about the demerits of the British soldier. Soon after the start of the war, the Japanese had met with such success, and the morale of the white troops they had encountered had been so low that they had supposed that the prestige the British had enjoyed during the previous century had been the result of a confidence trick. Caution towards the British was succeeded by extreme scorn. They could not have held them in lower esteem, and this probably accounted for their over-confidence in the Kohima operations, which otherwise appeared light-headed. They preferred to have British troops to deal with rather than Indian, since, in the new reckoning of the Japanese army, white troops were less tenacious than Asian troops. In the vicissitudes of this campaign, however, they learnt, very expensively, that they had made a wrong assessment. The British troops put on their laurels again, and their recent campaign gave the Japanese new respect for their adversary.

*

In the battle, the Indian National Army had proved useless. In nearly all the fighting, it had disgraced itself. Its largest losses were from desertion. Its heart was not in combat with the government to which it had formerly owed allegiance. Its performance had a depressing effect on the hopes of seeing the war turn into an Asian defensive operation against the western counter-attack. Subhas Chandra Bose sustained himself in his disappointment, and against the contempt which the Japanese military did not bother to hide, by putting out an account of near-treachery by the Japanese. Imphal, according to him, had been helpless before the Indo-Japanese force, but the Japanese had held back the Indian advance which would have taken it. They were unwilling that the Indians should have the great prize of the campaign; they wished to present Imphal as a Japanese conquest to the Emperor on his birthday. An Indian governor had been ready to take possession, but the Indian troops were forestalled from inducting him.

The tale was too inaccurate to be effective. Subhas Bose lost nearly all his magical appeal. In despair, he turned away from his concern with the Indian National Army to the political regimentation of the million Indians living in South-East Asia. But his fortunes sank with those of the Japanese. When these were finally overwhelmed, and had finally surrendered, he prevailed on a local officer to let him try to escape by air to Russia. It was a move consonant with his daring and his obstinate opportunism. He foresaw that relations between the West and Russia would be bad, and hoped that Moscow would see the opportunity of letting him set up in Russia his provisional government of India. But the aeroplane in which he was flying crashed on the way to Formosa, on 18 August 1945, and Bose ended his melodramatic life. In spite of his failure, he had, by his daring, so much caught the imagination of the Indians who had been in touch with him, that they refused to believe that he had really been killed. The rumour spread that he had gone underground and had become a Sadhu (there is some evidence that some of the defeated rebels did this in 1858 after the failure of the Indian Mutiny), and that he would emerge again to lead a triumphant rising against the British. The legend was firmly believed in by his brother, Sarat Chandra Bose, a leading, and apparently hard-headed, Congressman of Bengal.

Bose's idea of corrupting the Indian army, and of leading it back in triumph against the British in Delhi, though it turned out to be a fiasco, could have been a formidable threat to Britain. Its concept was sound: it was fortunate for Britain that the morale of the INA was such as to make the plan unworkable. For months the news of the INA caused very deep anxiety among the army staff and the informed civilians, in Delhi, and their failure in action was received with intense relief. The enterprise had been kept reasonably secret from the public in India. It was not entirely unknown, for the information about it was contained in the monitoring report which had a fairly wide circulation; moreover, Bose's radio was listened to fairly extensively. But the public was surprised when it learned later from the press how wide the conspiracy had been.

Of 70,000 Indians who had been captives, over half resisted all the lures to serve either Japan direct or else rebel India. They had nothing very much to induce them to remain loyal beyond their oath of service and their regimental pride. These ties held; and their strength was an important factor in determining the history of the war in Asia. For this the main credit goes to the regimental commanders of the previous two or three generations who, by and large, were trusted by their men to stand up for their interests, for fair treatment, and for an honourable status. These men built up the ties which between 1942 and 1945 bore the great strain.

This left the problem of what to do with the soldiers who had been less loyal. Most of these who had enlisted in the INA had passed into British hands, and for the second time had become prisoners of war. Technically they were all of them guilty of an internationally agreed crime of the darkest nature. For desertion, treason, rebellion, and levying war against the king, a harsh penalty was likely to be exacted. Actually, no drumhead court-martials were held on any of the prisoners upon capture. They were kept in captivity, and what to do about them became a political case which was hotly debated.

It was not decided until the war ended. The Congress leaders, on coming out of their own wartime captivity, saw in it an ideal means of attacking the government. The INA were presented as the true heroes of the Indian nation, and, if harshly dealt with, would become revered martyrs. The British were impressed by this danger. They were inclined to act in the spirit of Winston Churchill, who advising clemency on another occasion, had said: 'The grass grows quickly over the battle-field. Over the scaffold, never.' They decided to release the undistinguished mass of the prisoners. But they hesitated at the ring leaders, and those who, in the course of the campaign, had been guilty of war crimes, or had tortured their former comrades because these had stood firm against the allurements of the Japanese. They had to keep it in mind that those who felt most bitterly against the Indian National Army were the officers and men of the Indian army who had remained loyal. For the sake of the morale of this Army, it was scarcely possible to release without some punishment at least the more spectacular of the prisoners. Therefore, after much indecision, and much discussion which became involved with the renewed negotiations between the government and Congress, the decision was made to limit prosecution to a few cases, ultimately restricted to three.

The trials were held in the Red Fort of Delhi in 1946. A more peculiarly inept setting could not have been chosen. The Red Fort had become, in Indian national mythology, the shrine of Indian national hopes. It had been built as a citadel and palace by the Moghul Emperors, and symbolized the time before the British conquest, when all that Britain meant had been individual merchants coming to beg for patronage from the great ones of India. The trials gave so much publicity to the Congress lawyers, who were able to defend the prisoners, and to Jawaharhal Nehru who, having once been a barrister, could appear before the courts, that the government was glad to call them off quickly. It was content with the simple dismissal from further service of the great majority of officers and men. Such dismissal was punishment in itself, since service in the army brought with it economic privilege; and, by confiscating this advantage from the disaffected, it was thought that the loyal part of the Indian army would be at ease.

*

Burma had been freed as the result of a sustained thrust of the British and the Americans against the Japanese army, which had worn itself out by the offensive at Imphal and Kohima. From recovered Burma, the victors prepared to move afresh. Singapore and Malaya, were the next targets: and Japan had there, and elsewhere in South-East Asia, a very large army, as yet unscathed, its morale untouched by allied propaganda, with vast supplies of arms and ammunition. The prospect which this opened up, and the length of time which would be taken in ejecting Japan from one well-defended post to another, caused a great upsurge of criticism of British strategy. Had the drive on Burma, even though it was ultimately successful, really been justified? Were there not better ways of using British power than in following the withdrawal of Japan? Could Britain, using its recovered naval supremacy, not strike at some vital ports, less protected?

There is a notable passage in Tolstoy's *War and Peace* describing men's behaviour on the battlefield. When he is stricken on the field of Austerlitz, Prince Andrei sees two opposing men, French and Russian, both seizing hold of a ramrod, and struggling for its possession. Each would have done better to release his hold of it, and to free himself to use his musket. But they were too much hypnotized by the struggle to let go. So they continued to tussle. In the circumstances of the war in Asia, it was asked whether the British and Japanese really did any good for themselves, or brought the war nearer to an end, by remaining locked in conflict.

In fact, the decisive fighting was going on in the Pacific. Britain was denied a role in this: it could supply no adequate force, and the

American commanders were under pressure to distance themselves from allies who put their cause in such an imperialist colour. Keeping the British at arm's length was held to improve the American image with the national parties of south Asia. The future of that part of the world was held to lie with them.

CHAPTER 19

China 1942–4

BEFORE describing the end of Japan, and the breakthrough of the American ships from the Pacific, it is necessary to review the fate of China up to this point. After all, China had been the main cause of the war in the Far East. This conflict, which had spread so widely, had begun as the result of the refusal by Chiang Kai-shek to come to terms with Japan. China had not ceased to count. But, after the intervention of the United States, it had taken a relatively minor part in the military affairs of the nations.

Before the conflict was enlarged, Chiang had calculated that, if he held out, sooner or later Japan would come into collision with other powers. He had resolved, and it was more or less public knowledge, that, when this time came, China, which for four years had borne the fury of the Japanese offensive, would retire from the actual fighting, and would leave it to the fresher forces which should become engaged to complete the wearing down of Japan, of which China felt that it had done enough. Without fighting further, Chiang Kai-shek counted on being able to join in the eventual share-out of territory, and in the other benefits, when the world was rearranged at the general peace. In this, events had gone more or less as Chiang expected. Chiang, the simple and, in the eyes of the sophisticated statesmen of the West, rather primitive soldier, seemed at the time to have his judgement vindicated; his diplomacy confirmed.

China, poor in resources for making war, now held the best cards. The United States had chosen to take up the challenge of Japan. But it had handicapped itself by the decision to concentrate on fighting Germany first, Japan afterwards. In the interval before it could concentrate its whole attention on Japan, allies in the East were likely to be of greater moment to the United States than the United States was to them. It became a major preoccupation with it to keep China in the war, at the cost of offering it all possible inducement to stay. China could have all that it asked, in exchange for its willingness that the total commitment of American force in the Far East should be delayed. In the long run, the United States believed that the use of Chinese territory was indispensable for making it geographically possible for the allies to defeat Japan; it had no confidence that Russia, which also had a land army able to get to grips with Japan, would ever, in the way that events were shaping themselves, break its neutrality with Japan. For the United States, China represented the corridor along which their armies might eventually proceed, and get at Japan on level terms. In the meanwhile, China was to be the subject of a holding operation: to be kept in the war at all costs.

The impediment lay chiefly in geography. With the fall of Burma, the precarious link with Chungking along the Burma road was interrupted. China was cut off. Between it and the Americans there was the enormous barrier of the Himalayas. To keep China in the war, the Americans, with ingenuity, tried by every means to circumvent the obstacle. They organized an airlift to China over the mountain ranges from India; they sent American officers to re-train the Chinese army; they put continual pressure upon India to demonstrate that China might eventually find aid there. In immediate aid, China was given a large Anglo-American loan: America subscribed $500 million and Britain £50 million: this relieved its immediate financial problems.

This aid the allies intended for China as a whole. It was directed to whoever in China would fight Japan. Chiang Kai-shek's aim was to engross it all for himself. It was to ensure that his hold over the country was continuously and decisively strengthened; it was to deny aid to those who might threaten it. In his thinking at that time dollars counted for more than morale in the upkeep of government. He saw danger principally in one fact – that the communists, the party of revolution, might obtain the economic backing which would transform the situation, and put them on equal terms with the government. In a China, in which the ferment of revolution was working ever more actively, in which Communism had already mastered the circumstances of the war, it was essential that the communists should be denied their share of foreign aid, even at the cost of their military efficiency as allies against Japan. Technically, the Kuomintang and the communists were still allies; they were pledged together to fight Japan; the American aid, on a reading of the military situation, should have been divided between them. That it should not become the governing aim of Chiang's policy.

At first, the prospects appeared bright for Chiang. His more distant ambitions, of being the supreme force in Asia at the end of the war, buoyed him up when his government, as the result of the intensification of the blockade, suffered blow upon blow. Chiang was sanguine: this perhaps explains why he took phlegmatically even the worst of news. Both his enemies, Japan and Chinese Communism, were being trampled into ruin by the United States. His long-term prospects were heady. His standing in Washington mattered more to him than military realities in the Far East. In this he was served zealously, alike by plausible Chinese and by foreigners over whom China had cast its spell.

Chiang, in order apparently to gratify his sense of importance, struck out in directions which caused surprise, and ways which were unwelcome to his allies. He had insisted on visiting India, in February 1942, and seeing Indian affairs for himself. He could urge that India had suddenly become vitally important for China, both as a base, and as transit territory for American supplies. The bad relations between the government of India and Indian nationalists were a menace to China, because they could result in a situation which interrupted communication. Chiang insisted on studying matters for himself, and tried, by personal diplomacy with the Viceroy and Indian leaders, to bridge the gap between them.

The British were annoyed. They found Chiang extremely ill-informed, and privately judged that, in the guise of a mediator, he was prospecting the ground for Chinese intervention in case the military necessity in Europe should compel a British withdrawal from India. They objected to the need for providing Chiang and his wife with banquets at the moment when, too late in the judgement of many observers, they had become conscious of their desperate state. Especially, though, they demurred at the increased prestige which his interest brought to the Indian Congress in its duel with the Viceroy.

Chiang Kai-shek could not blame the Indian administration for a failure to back him. This somewhat lethargic government went out of its way to provide, with energy and great speed, the institutions which were needed to bind the two governments together in their war effort. On the Indian side, a China Relations Department was brought into being, to whose good offices a thousand things were owing: the Department did everything, from supply to strengthening military cooperation. It was efficient, it was prompt, it cut through delays. It was so much out of character for the government of India that it quite astonished the Chinese.

*

In spite of these inducements to be up and doing, China remained more or less militarily inactive. The performance of Chinese troops, in the rare action in which they were now engaged, was unmemorable. Nor was this surprising. Their armies were shockingly organized; relations between officers and men were deplorable; the officers were increasingly arrogant and corrupt; they embezzled the wages of the soldiers; they were often brutal and ignorant; the soldiers either were separated for many years from their families, or, if they had news of them, were rightly disturbed at the news of worsened conditions in the countryside. The rank and file had nothing to fight for.

Chiang Kai-shek chose, in March 1943, to publish under his name a highly controversial book. It was written in Chinese. The book was called *China's Destiny*. It contained the familiar story of the unjust dealings with China by the Great Powers, the unequal treaties, the shearing away from China of her dependencies. Thus it revealed that China still nursed her grievances when it would have been better policy to have concealed them. The powers which had done China its past wrongs had now shown a willingness to repair the damage, and the exposure of China's wound could only damage their cooperation. The effect of its publication was to cause mistrust, rouse suspicion, and generate bad blood. Madame Chiang Kai-shek shrewdly advised against an English translation: this did not appear therefore until 1947.

Chiang, in his relations with his allies, followed the tactics of 'threatening to fall'. He advertised that his position was calamitous. The weaker he was, the more anxious the Americans were for him, and the greater the efforts which they were willing to make on his behalf. Naturally he led them on; and he was helped by the chance that President Roosevelt revealed, from the United States' entry into the war until his death in 1945, an extraordinary partiality for China. The accidents of personality played here a fateful part. Roosevelt, active in Washington, had an even greater influence on events by the climate of opinion which he germinated, than by the measures he took as head of the American government. He dwelt much on the shape which the world must take as a result of the war; and he became convinced that, round a firm Sino-American axis, the Asian countries were destined to revolve. American aid would supply strength to China; China would revert to its traditional art of radiating its great civilizing influence out across its borders.

Roosevelt saw rightly that the crisis in the Far East was due ultimately to the collapse of the political power of China. The United States would restore it. This time there would be no imperialists to undermine it again; President Roosevelt was satisfied that the eastern role of Britain and other colonial powers was coming to an end. Asia would be safe again, except from its own dissension, and what power would thrive better in this atmosphere than China. He gained comfort from the signs that China's appetite for its historic greatness was beginning to recover. He became convinced that he was serving alike the interests of the United States, and also all the world, by throwing his mantle over China.

Roosevelt had an extraordinary power of communicating his vision to the public. In this case, however, he preached mostly to the converted. The United States' attitude towards China in the later stages of the war was rather unbalanced. If one nation can be said to adopt another, the United States adopted China. The United States has been liable to periodical phases of extreme partiality to certain foreign countries; in its fervent feeling towards China at this time, it outdid itself. The United States was hallucinated; like Titania by Bottom the Weaver. The reality was that the US became enthusiastic for the tyranny of the Kuomintang, which was passing increasingly into the most reactionary hands; the Americans saw it, not as it was, but as a democratic party full of vigour and promise. In place of a military rabble, the United States saw in the Chinese army an inspiring force, which was a mixture of a romanticized version of the American armies of the Revolution and the Civil War. Where there was evident, and apparently irreparable economic ruin, it saw lively economic promise. Its intellectual and artistic life, which, to the trained eye, was in the ruins of a great cultural past, appeared to the USA to be full of a fresh, imaginative view of the world. China appeared as nearly a new Utopia. The United States of course produced its realists, who protested against its romantic illusions, but they could scarcely make themselves heard against the newspapers and radio, which all of them followed the fashion.

Roosevelt's policies, the American hallucination, the realities of geography and of logistics in the East, produced, between them, a mood of accommodation of China which bewildered the rest of the world. China was pitied, but the United States postponed coming to its aid with immediate and effective military succour. It was encouraged by the United States to pass its time in discussing its growing ambition. American patronage ensured that China's claims were not regarded as simply ludicrous. Men like Winston Churchill took a sceptical view, but it was hardly worth their while to oppose the US over this. In war, naked strength is in the last resort the thing which counts; but prestige may be manufactured by the few statesmen who matter, and may, over the short run, pass for strength. China was in this condition, and advanced by several degrees in the world's esteem.

All the while that this was happening, the Chinese press, which was of course under strong government influence, had, as was natural in the relations between states, been biting the hand which fed it. The newspapers were full of articles which attacked the United States very bitterly. They made use of the stale propaganda methods of the Nazis early in the war in Europe. They claimed that the United States would fight until the last Chinaman; they envisaged that China, having made great sacrifices for democracy, would be a certain loser at the peace, and would itself be sacrificed. They painted a picture of the riotous life lived by Americans in luxurious camps in the midst of the poverty of China. This mood, when it became known in the United States, took a little of the glow out of the American feeling for China. But the work of the China lobby had been very far-reaching, and the suspicion that the Chinese were ungrateful was lightly borne by American philanthropy.

Although there was much criticism of Chiang Kai-shek by some Americans with a clearer vision, too much can be made of occasional Sino-American friction. In particular, the incompetence and bad morale of the Chinese were probably overrated by some American experts. There was no real likelihood of China making a separate peace. Chiang Kai-shek had steered China's policy since the earliest years of the conflict, but, by the latest years, China had probably steered itself. The muddle, constant criticism, and apathy misled the United States. China, though it detested war, was averse from surrender. It would have opposed Chiang if he had wished to make a dishonourable peace with nearly as much compulsive force as it had done when it suspected him in 1937. China's mood was frightening. It had not the least enthusiasm for the war; it was profoundly weary of it; but it was determined to continue to resist. If ever a war had in fact been a 'people's war', this was one, even though there were large and respectable elements of the population who were cooperating with the Japanese. The government was forbidden by the nation to make peace: by a nation which, by all reasonable arguments, yearned for peace. The war seemed likely to continue indefinitely.

*

It was the Americans who had to serve in China who were naturally less affected by the extreme American enthusiasm for all things Chinese. Their position was extremely difficult; they suffered much less from the delusions which were making American policy, but they were expected to act as if they did so. The attitude of the much-tried American General, Joseph Stilwell, deserves study. His mishaps are part of the misunderstandings of the time.

He was a naturally bilious man: he was nicknamed 'Vinegar Joe':

he was suspicious of everyone, especially of Americans who were fawning on Chinese, of all British, with whom he had to be in alliance but whom he suspected of outwitting the United States, and of the Chinese, above all of Chiang Kai-shek, whom he saw playing a gigantic confidence trick on the United States. The irony was that he, who had few illusions, was inclined to be grimly friendly towards China, and, in a professional manner, to defend its interests.

After Pearl Harbor, when American aid began to pour out on China, it was clearly desirable to appoint someone to be responsible on the spot for its distribution. A commander was needed for the American personnel who were militarily active in or near China. A military expert was also necessary to work out joint military plans with the Chinese. Stilwell, as a person of unquestionable experience, and available immediately, was appointed. He had served for many years in a quasi-diplomatic status in the American Embassy. At Roosevelt's instance, in his instinct to mix up American affairs with those of its allies, Stilwell was given by Chiang Kai-shek the Chinese rank of his Chief-of-Staff.

When, as described earlier, the British formed their South-East Asia command in 1943, Stilwell was appointed as the deputy of Mountbatten. From a comparatively minor position, he had accumulated appointments, all of which gave him authority. Few men in the war were in a position of such power.

The multitude of functions was a mistake. With such divergent pressures upon him, no man could have made a success of being a loyal servant of the United States and China. For a joint post to be workable, there must be coincidence of interests between the countries to which a man is jointly responsible. Stilwell, in serving Roosevelt and Chiang, had an impossible task. Much as Roosevelt respected the role that China was destined to play, the interests of the United States and China were different. Stilwell had decided that he would be through and through American: he would serve the United States and would correct Roosevelt's rather eccentric judgement.

The difficulty was increased because Stilwell's own judgement was defective. He did not see that, for the issue of the war, it really was unnecessary for Chiang to fight much more. Roosevelt himself had probably glimpsed this truth. But Roosevelt erred because he supposed that it was necessary for the United States to make strenuous efforts to keep China in the war. China would have remained belligerent in any circumstances, and its real interests, which Chiang saw very clearly, were all against making a separate peace. Having won credit with the western allies, China would have been suicidal to fling it away by becoming a renegade towards the end of the war, in which the difficult part had been the beginning. Nor would it have gained any advantage by doing so. The United States and Britain were satisfied as long as China remained formally at war, and turned a blind eye to the reality of much of China's wartime record.

Stilwell, however, did not perceive this. He had a mania to drive China back into war: both its bureaucrats living in comfort in Chungking, and its wretched conscripts herded to war by force. Chinese guile, Chinese pretence that it was doing much more than it was, he exposed with relish. Stilwell obtained Chinese agreement that thirty Chinese divisions should be allotted for cooperation with the British from India for the operations in Burma and to reconquer South-East Asia. To facilitate these operations, the road connecting Assam in India with Burma was constructed. It was one of the major engineering enterprises of the war. Stilwell, and his like-minded American staff, made no secret of the fact that they greatly desired that American and Chinese forces should get into many of these regions in advance of the British. They considered the British Empire obsolete and effete, and had no desire to see it re-established. They counted on a peace settlement which would create an Asia of self-determining nation-states, always the American ideal, as 1919 had shown in Europe. For this, they considered it of first-class importance that they should end the war in military possession of disputed territory. But the thirty Chinese divisions proved to be a paper force. Only a fraction was ever available. For Stilwell's aim, there was to be no Chinese manpower.

Stilwell, in his vigour for the war, could get little response from the Kuomintang officials, and from Chiang Kai-shek personally. He became increasingly obsessed with the fact that Chiang was employing 200,000 of his best troops for cordoning off the area that was occupied by the Red Army; and that this army, alone of China's military forces, had proved that it was anxious to fight, and had shown the value of its guerrilla strategy against the Japanese. But it was prevented by the Kuomintang from playing its part in the war. Chiang, in his fear that substantial economic aid would reach the communists, and would make them dangerous to him, blockaded them shamelessly.

Stilwell denounced him to the Americans as a bad ally: Chiang complained that he could have no confidence in such a Chief-of-Staff. To do him justice, he could say that Stilwell had not grasped the fact that the civil war in China was continuing. The merger of the armies, which was to have taken place by the pact which Chiang made with the communists at the time of the Sian kidnapping, had never been carried out. The communists had laid down their own strategy in their war with Japan, and, as by their guerrilla methods of war they penned Japan more and more to the towns, they continually occupied a larger and larger area of the country. All the while the communists were consolidating their hold. Was Chiang to assist them by removing his forces which kept them under surveillance?

The problem was difficult; Chiang was notable for his obstinacy, which had established him where he was; Stilwell was notorious for pertinacity and for courting disfavour. With Stilwell's agreement, a whitewashing of the communists took place in America. The news about them was surprising, and cheered an America which was hungry for hopeful news. It was said that they were not real communists at all; they were Jeffersonian democrats, simple rural reformers, who desired only to fight for their country, and they were held back by Chiang Kai-shek, the real nature of whose government had by this time become plain. They were a brand-new and unexpected ally, waiting to be used against the Japanese if the United States would sanction it. Chiang Kai-shek, treating this as a threat of American repudiation of him, fulminated, and put the blame on Stilwell. He supposed him responsible for the agitation in the press.

By the autumn of 1944 the breach between Chiang and Stilwell had become wider, beyond reconciliation. Chiang officially demanded that Roosevelt should dismiss Stilwell. Roosevelt, though his confidence in Chiang had been half-changed by Stilwell – but not his confidence in China – consented.

With the fall of Stilwell there vanished a plan which had been dear both to him and to Roosevelt. This was for the re-training and modernization by American officers of the entire Chinese army. The United States was characteristically ready to take responsibility for this gigantic task; but it required Chinese consent to the extent of being willing to make a reality of the appointment of Stilwell as Chief-of-Staff. Chiang would not trust such authority to any foreigner.

Admittedly it would have been difficult; there would have been storms, and, whilst Stilwell's attitude to the communists was at best ambiguous in the view of Chiang Kai-shek, it was clear that there were many fundamental principles on which the two men were divided in any reform. Stilwell would have certainly wanted to incorporate part of the Red Army, and much of its system of command and administration. Neither of them would compromise. But Chiang, in winning his point that there should be no foreign command in his army, sacrificed the possibility of ending the war with a re-born, reliable, modernized force.

*

The war was very depressing when seen in these years from Chungking. Air-raids, which had been plentiful, had died down, and had become rare. But with this there had come hunger and a dreadful boredom, with nothing to distract people from being conscious of their extreme discomfort. The city was overcrowded: it was full of refugees. The lives of most people had become a nightmare because of inflation; it was still under a semblance of control; it was to reach fantastic proportions, as in Germany during the period at the end of the First World War, only when the war was over; but already it cast very deep shadows, and was the main impediment in life.

The extent of the inflation was a novelty in human history. In Chungking, prices rose by two hundred and fifty times in the two years 1942–4. The price index of goods, quoted at 100 in 1937, was 125,000 by 1945. How to cope, how to find money, became the overriding concern of everyone, including all the army officers, and the events of the war sank a long way behind. Another stunning blow had been dealt at human society, and strong suspicions grew up as to whether life could ever be normal again, even if peace was restored. It was the classical effect of an uncontrolled inflation. 'If you wish to make a revolution,' said Lenin, 'first debauch the currency.'

In spite of this, many people were growing very rich, out of wartime enterprises and profiteering, but they hid themselves, and no bright plumage lit up the drab scene. Only the gossip and scandal circulated wildly. The inflation had the usual effects in disintegrating the society. The corruption became impudent. One day, when a general of the Indian army was paying a visit to the city, the cousin of the Chinese finance minister called on him by night, and outlined a plan of partnership by which the two could make a fortune. All that was necessary was the use of the general's means of transport, and of his prestige to keep official interference at arm's length.

To keep their armies in the field, the Chinese had to make more and more use of conscription. It was an ordinary sight to see in the country-side, even close to Chungking, squads of soldiers being deported to fighting areas; the soldiers were all chained together. Across the length of the huge country, there was constant, small-scale, sporadic action, which, though of little military consequence, did much material damage. The Japanese occupying the cities were harried, and in many parts of the country could not venture, except in great force, into the country-side; they raided and massacred sporadically. Insecurity was constant; the war had apparently ceased to have a reason and the possibility of an end.

In parts of the country, however, the war seemed to have run its course, to be exhausted, and to have fought itself out. It was succeeded by the armed forces on both sides following the age-old instincts for trade. The armies became trading organizations. Trading is a passion with the Chinese; with the Japanese it is familiar. As soon as the armies stood still, the Chinese put out their feelers, and the Japanese, who were not paid very highly and welcomed some supplement to their wages, responded. The metamorphosis of the barbaric Japanese con-querors into the scheming Japanese traders was curious to watch. The attempts by high Japanese officers to restrict the trade were in vain. The Japanese generals, even at the highest level of direction of the Japanese armies, were too deeply engaged. China, by the action not of its government or of its soldiers but by the private enterprise of its merchants, had woven a web of commerce, which within a month or so of conquest snared the Japanese and bound them in all sorts of ways to courses of action which aimed at the satisfaction of private wants rather than the advancement of Japan's public enterprise of subjugation. And so it was to continue until the end of the war. The spectacle is of exuberant trade springing up and flourishing wherever the two belli-gerents came in contact. Patrolling warships operated most. The Japanese navy was particularly notorious for doing traffic with the Chinese. This was very well attested by watchers in Hong Kong in the months before the island was invaded.

Stilwell's fall in 1944 coincided with the last great military effort in China by the Japanese. During 1943 and the first part of 1944, the Americans had built up a new war machine on Chinese soil with which they had at last succeeded in reaching the heart of the Japanese war effort, and which held out hopes of being deadly. This they did by expanding greatly the activities of General Claire Lee Chennault. This man had begun by recruiting a private air force, mercenaries, drawn from the staff of American airlines and college youths. They were known as Chennault's Flying Tigers. In the summer of 1941, while the United States was still neutral, this force, put at the service of the Kuo-mintang, proved itself indispensable for the air defence of Chungking. Later, when the United States entered the war, it was incorporated in the American army, and Chennault also returned to it. In the course of time he established airfields in Eastern China, and from there began the first systematic bombardments that the Japanese had had to endure. They were found so effective that the greater part of the material sent painfully to China by the airlift was used for constructing the airfields.

This finally prevailed on the Japanese to renew their military effort against China. They had halted large-scale military campaigning at the end of 1938, and, during the years since, it had seemed that they were best served by letting time work for them. They hoped that discomfort, and the upset from the perpetual strain of relations with the communists, would in the end induce Chiang to submit his stubborn neck to peace negotiations. They could place their trust in Chinese racial dislike of its western allies. During this period there were steady defections from the Kuomintang side to the Japanese and to the Wang Ching-wei government, which satisfied Japan. By 1942, the communists estimated, and published with smugness, that twenty-seven Kuomintang generals had gone over.

In 1944 Japan decided that it was necessary to renew the offensive. This was also in part prompted by the need to have land contact with its forces in South-East Asia, since its shipping had been so drastically reduced. It began a campaign with the purpose of capturing and dismantling the Chinese airfields. The revived Japanese onslaught burst like a thunderclap on China. Divisions were moved from Manchuria, where they had passed the war in idleness, watching Russia. The Japanese army found in a renewal of the Chinese war the opportunity to work out its feeling of frustration. The new divisions roared through the seaboard of China, and farther inland, destroying one airfield after another, not meeting any Chinese army able to stand up to them in pitched battles. Where there was a struggle, as in Hunan, the Chinese, when they were eventually broken, were set on by an enraged population, which blamed them for having disturbed the unofficial armistice. To such a squalid end had the aims of the Chinese army to defend the country been reduced.

The loss of General Chennault's airfields drew the world's attention once more to China's weakness. It settled a controversy which had been going on among strategists. One side had taken the view that Chennault had proved that land operations were unnecessary: it was enough to build airfields in distant places, lightly protected by guerrilla operations, and leave the air force to carry on the war. The other side argued that, without an army, airfields were entirely vulnerable. The latter view proved correct; it was found that the Chinese armies were inadequate to safeguard them.

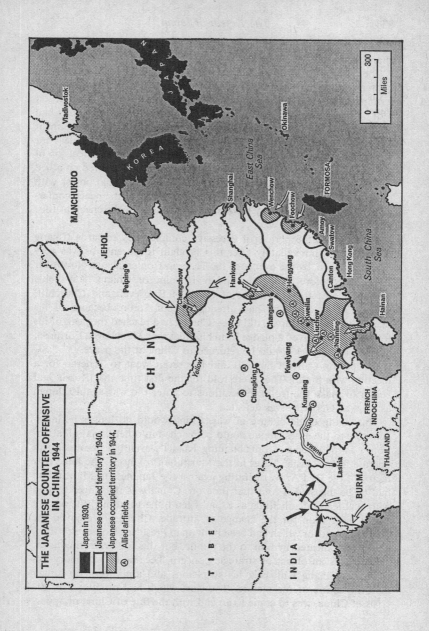

THE JAPANESE COUNTER-OFFENSIVE
IN CHINA 1944

■ Japan in 1930.
□ Japanese occupied territory in 1940.
▨ Japanese occupied territory in 1944.
Ⓐ Allied airfields.

MANCHUKUO

JEHOL

Peiping

CHINA

Yellow

Chengchow

Hankow

Yangtze

Changsha

Hengyang

Kweilin

Liuchow

Nanning

Kweiyang

Chungking

Kunming

BURMA ROAD

Lashia

TIBET

INDIA

BURMA

THAILAND

FRENCH INDOCHINA

Hainan

South China Sea

Hong Kong

Canton

Swatow

Amoy

FORMOSA

Foochow

Wenchow

Shanghai

East China Sea

Okinawa

KOREA

JAPAN

Vladivostok

300
Miles
0

But the usefulness and importance of China to the western allies had changed sharply.

The beginning of 1943 had seen the last great western incentive offered to the Chinese. In that year, the West had made the gesture of terminating their right to maintain Treaty Ports in China. The largest tool of imperialism was renounced. The negotiations, which they had pursued desultorily since the 1920s, were accelerated, and agreement was reached. If the war had ultimately grown out of China's endeavour to extirpate these foreign footholds in China, it had, by this decision of the allies, been won. Later in the year, Roosevelt had secured an allied statement of the intention to associate China as an equal power with themselves in remoulding the pattern of the world at the peace conferences. Other countries may have had their tongue in the cheek at this, but Roosevelt had his way.

Nevertheless the period of excessive complacency towards Chiang Kai-shek was immediately after this brought to an end, or was very much qualified, by the events of the Teheran Conference in November 1943. Just before had come the high point of Chiang Kai-shek's apotheosis. At the conference at Cairo of Roosevelt and Churchill, which Chiang Kai-shek had attended – but Stalin, because of his neutrality towards Japan, did not – Chiang had reached the peak of his fortunes. He received a pledge from his allies that Manchuria, Formosa, and the Pescadores would be returned to China at the peace.

On leaving Cairo, Churchill and Roosevelt went to Teheran for a meeting with Stalin. They were told for the first time that Russia had begun to make the troop dispositions to enter the war against Japan as soon as Germany was defeated.

This changed the picture of war. China would no longer be indispensable to the allies. Japan could be reached in other ways; all attention was now focused on obtaining Russia's eventual permission to operate from Russian bases in the Maritime Provinces. The huge new factor of the Red Army operating against the Japanese in Manchukuo had to be digested. From that time on, China was no longer treated with such careful solicitude as it had been hitherto, though it was not solely the reason for the change of attitude. China still enjoyed the delusive grandeur which had been built up in President Roosevelt's time, and communicated by him to the public, but this was a wasting asset.

China, as an object of strategic concern, became of secondary importance. Chiang Kai-shek, his suspicions and ambitions, no longer held the centre of the picture. The war, which had originated in the crisis of China, was to come to an end with the fate of China of appar-

ently of small concern to the Great Powers, which now pressed on towards the final kill.

*

In the course of the war, a profound change had, however, come over
the prestige of the Kuomintang and of the communists. They had both
of them engaged in warfare, which they had fought by different means
using different arms. They had been in competition with each other.
The upshot, though it was not yet definite, was that, in the judgement
of the various important groups of Chinese society, the communists
had shown themselves more durable than the Kuomintang. True, the
Kuomintang was, technically, to be one of the victor powers. But the
Kuomintang had lost face irrevocably.

It was not so much that the communists had shining victories to their
credit. They had latterly fought very little. But their government
survived the war with an infinitely better morale than the Kuomintang.

Soon after the war, the two governments would come into open
conflict. Support would vanish away from the Kuomintang. It would
transfer itself to the communists.

The Kuomintang had plenty of opportunity to see how unpopular
its régime was becoming, and plenty of opportunity to take up some
more popular course. But it kept obstinately on its disastrous career.
As it became clearer that China, thanks to its allies, was to be on the
winning side in the war, there grew up naturally a discussion about the
form that post-war politics was to take. Similarly the Kuomintang
could have met the public half way, and announced the approaching
end of its party dictatorship. But its reply, as the demand for this grew,
was to increase the size of the secret police. Its activities became intolerable. The Kuomintang gave every indication that it would continue unreformed.

CHAPTER 20

Twilight

THE attention now turns to the American offensive, far across the Pacific, and it turns away from all the other theatres of the Far-Eastern war. Fighting still continued in these, but it became obvious that it was irrelevant. The turmoil in the Pacific dwarfed all other, and this became increasingly so until the end.

In the middle of June 1944, the Americans invaded Saipan in the Mariana Islands. This island, 1,350 miles from Tokyo, was the most vital point in the outer defences of Japan. It had been strongly fortified, so strongly that even the naval experts believed it to be impregnable. Its strategic importance was appreciated; from Saipan, the Americans would be able to bomb Tokyo; they could also disrupt the communications of the remaining forward posts in the Pacific with Japan. Its loss would breach what was called in Japanese 'the absolute zone of national defences'.

The Americans had assembled huge forces. They had an escort fleet, for the troop transports for the invasion, of seven battleships, twelve escort carriers, eleven cruisers, and ninety-one destroyers. It took only half an hour for the assault forces to get ashore at Saipan, but it still remained to be captured. At once the Japanese assembled their still very formidable fleet, and sought a decisive battle. They had foreseen the American moves and were not taken by surprise; they had ample strength in Guam and in the islands of the Philippines. The battle which resulted was the fourth large-scale naval combat of the war. The sense of occasion was in the message of the Japanese admiral to the fleet before the action began: 'The fate of the empire rests on this one battle.'

The result was entirely disastrous to Japan. The successive strikes by Japanese aeroplanes were beaten off, and in the whole battle Japan lost nearly four hundred aircraft. The destruction of these, and the repelling of the Japanese attacks, were more spectacular than the loss of ships, though the operation cost the Japanese two battleships and an aircraft-carrier; two other carriers were disabled. This was far beyond the capacity of the Japanese shipyards, at this stage of the war, to make good. The American damage was very slight.

As was usual, the Japanese navy silenced the news of the defeat.

Even high officials of the Foreign Office remained without knowledge of what had been happening. They were especially confused because, after the defeat, they had been invited by naval officers to banquets to celebrate a great Japanese triumph.

The fall of Saipan could not, however, be hidden. The news began to circulate in the middle of July 1944. To most people it came as an entire shock, and for the first time the average Japanese, without any such information as had been weighing on the experts, began to surmise that Japan was in fact losing the war. Saipan had fallen with such ease, the Americans were ahead of their timetable. An evident *frisson* went through the nation, well disciplined though it continued to be.

A result was the resignation of General Tojo, the Prime Minister. He went, after a complicated intrigue of the politicians. This was the first sign of political malaise which had come from Japan during the war; and it was received with relief by those watching among its enemies. The procedures by which government changes were brought about in Japan were as a rule quite different from the official processes laid down in the Japanese constitution. In this instance, a group of high civilian and army officers, especially those who had formerly held official positions, began to agitate that General Tojo's cabinet should resign. Saipan had caused them to open their eyes, and to press their arguments as a matter of life or death. Their dissensions were heard at high level, and they arranged that they should be transmitted to the throne.

As a result, a great agitation was set afoot among a large circle of those holding the various offices of importance. Tojo, who, a week earlier had apparently been completely safe, suddenly found the ground trembling under his feet. He sought to appease his critics by yielding to one of their demands, and proposed that he should no longer combine the posts of Prime Minister, War Minister, and Chief of the Army Staff. The arrangements were made for General Umezu Yoshijiro to become Minister of War. But by this time, the opinion of the inner circle had moved on, and it could be satisfied with nothing less than the resignation of Tojo as Prime Minister. He demurred, and argued in vain. On the day of the announcement of the loss of Saipan, on 18 July 1944, his resignation was in the hands of the Emperor.

The choice of a successor fell to an informal group of seven elder statesmen. Their task was to find somebody able to carry on the war, but who would, in view of the bad prospects for its outcome, also seek earnestly to bring about peace. The Japanese had not abandoned all hope of fighting the war, at least to a drawn peace; they were intent on maintaining a warlike front; they were on their guard against exposing their irresolution and their anxiety; they desired the serious exploration of the possibilities of peace; but they felt that this must be completely concealed, or otherwise the quest would be hopeless.

Their deliberations about Tojo's replacement appear to have been unsubtle. All they could do was to agree on the nomination of General Koiso Kuniaki, an army officer who had a bad reputation from the days of terrorism in the thirties when the army was promoting a series of crises with the civilian Ministers in order to advance its claims of controlling the government. The Emperor, however, appointed him because he had been recommended.

It was a choice which was apparently made under the compulsion of avoiding events such as those which had happened a year earlier in Italy. The elder statesmen judged it necessary to avoid nominating a man who might play in Japan the same part as General Badoglio. The extent to which Badoglio had captured the mind of Japan is curious. It showed perhaps how much the Japanese desired a Badoglio, and for how long they found it imperative not to disclose this.

Toshikazu Kase, a senior Foreign Ministry official, has described these confused and rather dark transactions. He himself belonged to the 'pro-British, pro-American' circles. His book, *Eclipse of the Rising Sun*, is useful in showing how many of these men had continued throughout the war to hold high position in the Foreign Office, in certain Ministries, at the imperial court. They had been inactive from prudence: from the fall of Saipan, however, they began to work for peace. They had still to be very cautious, for they would have been rendered helpless if it had become known how specific, and actively specific, were their intentions. By their sympathies becoming known they would at best have made themselves ineffective: at the worst they would have been assassinated. And there were of course many who, when the war was over, claimed to have been pro-ally, but whose memory may have exaggerated its degree.

At the end of 1944, Toshikazu Kase wrote in his diary the following:

Defeat now stares us stark in the face. There is only one question left: how can we avert the chaos attendant upon a disastrous defeat? The preservation of my fatherland, that is a paramount task assigned to me by fate. The hostile attack is developing so surprisingly swiftly that it may be that diplomacy cannot intervene before it is too late. I must redouble my efforts to expedite the restoration of peace. For that purpose I shall secure friends in the army who will collaborate with me secretly, and enlighten public opinion through wider exchanges of view with politicians, publicists, and press representatives. The chances are that the re-orientation of our policy is yet feasible. If so the nation will escape annihilation. Even so, it will probably be accompanied by civil disturbances. Much blood will flow – and who knows that mine, too, will not be spilt? . . . This, in short, is my New Year's Day prayer.*

This sums up very well the feeling of the small class of clear-sighted, non-fanatical men. But a difficult task lay ahead for them. Toshikazu Kase and his friends had to convert a sufficient number of patriotic Japanese to enable them to shift the vital balance against the fanatical, the deluded, and the ignorant. They had to do this with the certain knowledge that charges of treason might well be brought against them, and would be paid for either with execution or else by the familiar old Japanese resort of private violence.

*

The American drive from the Pacific continued. After Saipan, the strongly fortified positions of Tinian and Guam were captured in August 1944. These were also considerable victories, made possible only by mobilization of resources, and their concentration upon tiny islands, which were possibly unique in military history. A feature of all these operations was the disparity of the losses. The Americans should in theory, being attackers, have suffered at least three to one more heavily than the Japanese. But, in all three operations, the American dead numbered just over 5,000, while the Japanese lost 42,000. On Guam, for the first time, there had been a dent in Japanese morale: over 12,000 prisoners were taken. Usually these island defences ended in a great *banzai* charge of the remaining garrison, who plunged to death, rather like the death charge of the chivalry among the Rajputs of medieval India, who vowed themselves thus to self-destruction. The generals on both Saipan and Guam committed ceremonial *hara-kiri*.

In October, General MacArthur, in the south-west Pacific, made his expected attack on the Philippines. He was still under the disadvantage of the somewhat complicated command arrangements which shared between him and Admiral Nimitz the control of operations in his area. He could count upon a powerful fleet detached from the central Pacific. Japan chose to regard his attack as a crisis of the war. Its generals recognized that, if the Philippines were occupied by the Americans, the supply lines of the Japanese Empire would be fatally obstructed. Therefore Japan stated that, on its ability to defend the Philippines, the issue of the war would depend.

Such repeated pronouncements were foolish, and, in making them,

* Toshikazu Kase: *Eclipse of the Rising Sun*, Jonathan Cape, 1951.

the Japanese generals should have had in mind their grave embarrassment if their defence proved ineffective. They would be in the position
of carrying on the war even while admitting that the war was a lost
cause. That they permitted themselves to talk so rashly was the best
proof that the morale of the Japanese General Staff was beginning to
fail even though the Japanese soldiers fought as tenaciously as before.

The Japanese lived up to the words of their military leaders. They
gathered their navy, which was still very powerful in surface ships –
only in the loss of the aircraft carriers had it been gravely weakened –
and sought, by putting all their effort into a single decisive blow, to
turn their great danger into a decisive victory. And circumstances
played into their hands. It had been calculated that the local airfields
would be operational for the landings, but the rainy season broke, and
they were flooded. The Japanese had a period of air superiority, flying
in from Samar. For a few days it was touch and go whether the American advance would be disastrously defeated.

MacArthur's invasion force, which landed on 20 October 1944 on
the shores of the Gulf of Leyte which is a central island of the Philippines, had the protection of very powerful warships. The Japanese
sought to lure this naval force away by sending a decoy fleet, and then,
with a much larger fleet, aimed to sink the American transports, and to
destroy MacArthur's army, which was to be taken at a disadvantage
while they were still engaged in disembarkation. The Japanese placed
their confidence in the battle upon the greater fire power of the Japanese
navy; the days of attacking by waves of aircraft from carriers was over,
since the Japanese naval air force had been virtually eliminated. The
navy was back to reliance upon its battleship fleet, and among this it
included the battleship, *Yamato*, which had been built free of the
former limitations on the size of battleships. It was the most formidable
ship in the world, mounting eighteen-inch guns.

If they had succeeded in their plan, the Japanese would have achieved
a second Pearl Harbor, this time destroying the American army in
Asia as formerly they had annihilated the American Asian fleet. Even
so, the United States, with its economic might only just beginning to
operate at its full strength, could, in all reasonable probability, have
regarded a defeat as a temporary setback, and the inevitable conclusion
of the war would have been merely postponed by a year or so. But,
though this possibility must have been clear to the Japanese admirals,
an interruption of the continuous American advance would have been
dear to them. They rejoiced in the likelihood of a pause in the war:
Japanese optimism would have taken on new life: a victory would have

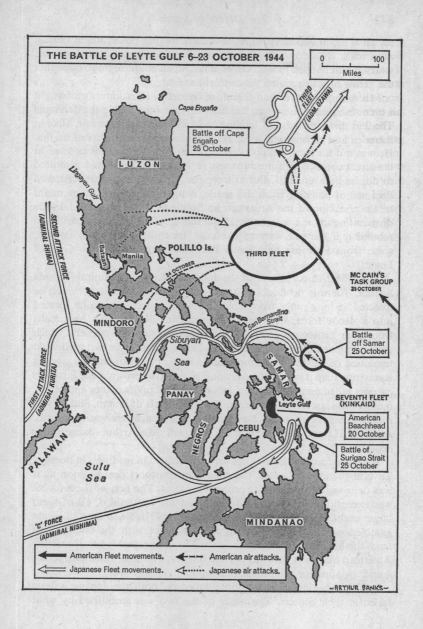

THE BATTLE OF LEYTE GULF 6–23 OCTOBER 1944

0   100
Miles

THIRD FLEET (ADM. OZAWA)

Cape Engaño

Battle off Cape Engaño 25 October

LUZON

Lingayen Gulf

Bataan

Manila

POLILLO Is.

THIRD FLEET

24 OCTOBER

SECOND ATTACK FORCE (ADMIRAL SHIMA)

MC CAIN'S TASK GROUP
25 OCTOBER

MINDORO

San Bernardino Strait

Sibuyan Sea

SAMAR

Battle off Samar 25 October

FIRST ATTACK FORCE (ADMIRAL KURITA)

PANAY

Leyte Gulf

SEVENTH FLEET (KINKAID)

NEGROS

CEBU

American Beachhead 20 October

PALAWAN

Sulu Sea

Battle of Surigao Strait 25 October

'C' FORCE (ADMIRAL NISHIMA)

MINDANAO

| ➤ | American Fleet movements. | ◄--- | American air attacks. |
| ➤ | Japanese Fleet movements. | ◄···· | Japanese air attacks. |

~ARTHUR BANKS~

set alive again Japanese hopes that their staying power might outlast America's. Nobody can foresee all the unexpected circumstances which might happen in war. Given time, Japan could begin to hope that the germs of a negotiated peace might sprout.

MacArthur's moves had therefore created a situation more fraught with consequence than even he, with his flair for reading the Japanese mind, at first realized. His landing had created a profound stir, alike in America and throughout Asia. He had chosen the elements of drama. He was not far from the point from which he had made his take-off in his direct contact with the Japanese in 1942, and, as he had promised to do, he had returned. But at once the Japanese navy pounced, and dreamed of plucking from this nettle, danger, the flower, which might be the checking of the American guillotine as it was about to fall, the dismantling of the instrument, and the creation of the necessity to rebuild it if the war were to continue. Its ships, some from Borneo, some from Formosa and Japan itself, converged upon the Gulf of Leyte.

The officer in command of the Japanese fleet was Admiral Toyoda Soemu. There is no doubt of the merit of his overall plan, which he directed at long range from Tokyo. The ships from Japan he formed into a decoy force, with which he aimed at dividing the Americans from their protective force of battleships and aircraft carriers, which were commanded by Admiral W. F. Halsey. This force included what remained of Japan's once formidable fleet of aircraft-carriers; it was less strong than it seemed for, as was discovered afterwards, the Japanese carriers sailed empty of planes. Japan had used up its planes and pilots, many of the last batch of these at the futile battle of Guam, and oil was running desperately short. Nevertheless, the manoeuvre was successful. Admiral Halsey went in pursuit, and left MacArthur dangerously exposed.

With two forces of battleships which were held in readiness in Borneo, Toyoda planned to attack the American transport fleet as soon as it was deprived of much of its protective escort. The first of these forces was exceptionally powerful; it contained five battleships, all of them larger and faster than any which they were still liable to meet. Toyoda gambled on these making unimpeded contact with the enemy, free from the diversion of air attack – which was reasonably certain, as the American transport fleet was beyond the range of land-based aeroplanes – and, by superior fire power, sinking it.

Against reasonable expectation, however, both the Japanese fleets failed in their objects. The lesser of the two was ambushed by what had been left behind of the American navy, which was rather larger than was foreseen by Japanese Intelligence, and was completely annihilated except for one destroyer. The Japanese had the mortification of seeing their ships sunk by ships which were technically inferior to their own. Ironically, in this action, the Americans employed battleships which were obsolete, had already been once sunk by the Japanese – at Pearl Harbor – and which had been dredged up from the mud of the sea bed. The larger Japanese fleet, though it was engaged and disorganized earlier on, got through the American defences, and for a time, if it had but known this, had the American transports at its mercy, but because of muddle, of being let down by other ships, and because of a deep misunderstanding of what was being done by the American ships, the Japanese Admiral did not bombard but sailed away inexplicably. His losses had been heavy; his actual gains were very slight; his potential gains, those which he had unaccountably let slip through his fingers, made this, their final battle of the war, very poignant to the Japanese navy.

Among the warships employed, the Japanese decoy force from the north alone avoided heavy losses. It retired in good order. Similarly Admiral Halsey's powerful battleships, which had been the main concern of the Japanese, were never in serious action throughout. They steamed 300 miles to the north, and when, as was afterwards discovered, they were within forty miles of the decoy force, they steamed 300 miles south. Upon their arrival, they found the battle of Leyte was over. Admiral Halsey was much criticized for having made so powerful a fleet ineffective in the action, but, given the system of communication prevailing among warships, he could hardly have done other than he did.

For the Japanese defeat, the same forces seemed to operate as before in the melancholy history of this navy. Bad Intelligence work, bad coordination between commanders, incompetent naval fliers, and inability of the Japanese commanders to retrieve disaster and to provide a new plan: these, which had dogged the navy since the battle of Midway, continued to do so until the death of the navy at Leyte.

The principal defect was in the quality of the command. The Japanese admirals and captains had been too old for their work. They were too fearful of risking their ships; they were certainly brave, and reasonably competent, but they creaked in manoeuvring a modern fleet, which was beyond their capacity. No common doctrine of strategy or tactics united them, and they were handicapped by the failure of Japanese engineers to provide for the navy some of the devices which had be-

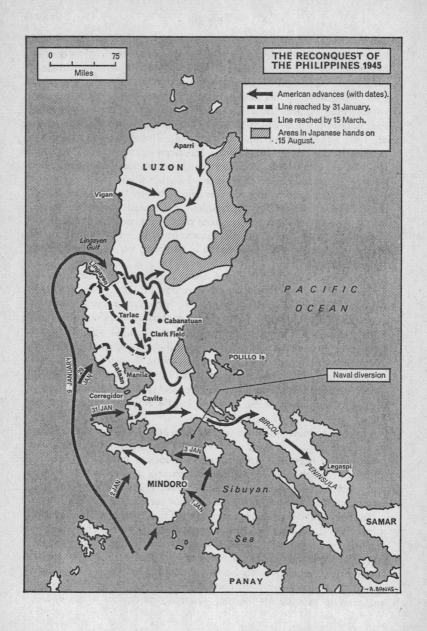

THE RECONQUEST OF
THE PHILIPPINES 1945

0 ———— 75
Miles

← American advances (with dates).
▬ ▬ ▬ Line reached by 31 January.
▬▬▬ Line reached by 15 March.
▨ Areas in Japanese hands on
15 August.

Aparri

LUZON

Vigan

Lingayen
Gulf

Lingayen

Tarlac

Cabanatuan
Clark Field

PACIFIC
OCEAN

POLILLO Is.

9 JANUARY

29 JAN

Bataan

Manila

Naval diversion

Corregidor

31 JAN

Cavite

3 JAN

BIRCOL

PENINSULA

Legaspi

2 JAN

MINDORO

Sibuyan

1 JAN

SAMAR

Sea

PANAY

~A.BANKS~

come common among other belligerents. Above all, it had turned out
that, where the Japanese had been forced to make an innovation in the
arts of naval warfare – in combining naval and air power – this advantage had not been sustained. Yamamoto, whose ideas had first prevailed, had not succeeded in training up a younger section of the navy
with ideas similar to his own, and Yamamoto's death at Bougainville
on 18 April 1943 ended the innovation. The pilots, who should have
become principal commanders, and who had had battle experience, had
all of them met their premature death in the Pacific Ocean, and the
direction of new recruits was left to men who had never been converts
to Yamamoto's ideas, and had seen his successes with a certain amount
of envy and scepticism. Especially, the tactics of Yamamoto required
an expert and highly trained personnel; he had begun the war with an
inadequate supply; it had continued lacking; nobody had come to
prominence as a gifted air trainer. The dash, the precision, and the
brilliance of his fliers at Pearl Harbor was seen to have been a performance out of character of the Japanese navy.

*

In January 1945 General MacArthur, thus surviving his most perilous
passage in the history of the war, overcame the Japanese resistance on
Luzon. From there he moved to Mindanao, the main island, and carried
through land operations, which followed the same pattern and had the
same results as the events in New Guinea. It turned out that the
Japanese army, in spite of its emphasizing that the fighting would be
decisive, had been unable to assemble a land force strong enough to
make the resistance as tenacious as that of the Pacific Islands.

This ended the war for MacArthur. He did no more fighting, though
after the war's end, another great historic role fell to him as Supreme
Commander for the Allied Powers, with chief responsibility for the
occupation of Japan. For the present, MacArthur wore the laurels of
having been the most spectacular commander of the allied side, in
both the Pacific and the European theatres of war. His victories, usually
gained with forces which were in the minority, were due to remarkable
imagination; and they were made possible by an extreme cult of
efficiency by his staff. For the time, MacArthur busied himself with the
preparation for the projected allied offensive against Japan itself,
which was to have begun with a landing on Kyushu island; not expected, however, before 1 December. For this projected operation,
the command arrangements were changed. MacArthur was given
command of all the army throughout the Pacific (with important

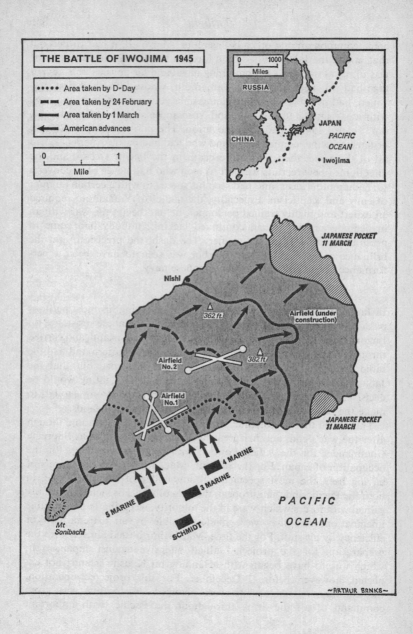

THE BATTLE OF IWOJIMA 1945

• • • • Area taken by D-Day

▬ ▬ Area taken by 24 February

▬▬▬ Area taken by 1 March

◄━━ American advances

0   1
Mile

0   1000
Miles

RUSSIA

CHINA

JAPAN

PACIFIC
OCEAN

• Iwojima

*JAPANESE POCKET
11 MARCH*

Nishi

△
362 ft.

Airfield (under
construction)

Airfield
No.2

△
382 ft.

Airfield
No.1

*JAPANESE POCKET
11 MARCH*

4 MARINE

3 MARINE

5 MARINE

*Mt
Sonibachi*

SCHMIDT

PACIFIC

OCEAN

~ARTHUR BANKS~

exceptions); but the American navy was still strong enough to oppose a unified command of all the sea forces.

For the first assault, 5 million men would have been employed. It is notable that they would for the most part have been American; though American allies begged a place in the operation, room was found for only a token force of three divisions from the Commonwealth. The war was coming to an end in a very different way from the war in Europe. The invasion of Normandy and the campaigns in France and Germany had been genuinely joint enterprises: there was not even the pretence of such in Japan. In the war in the Pacific in the later stages America had become very conscious that the United States was first, the allies nowhere. In the conquest of Japan the fact was to be rubbed in. The United States welcomed this sign that European imperialism had little part to play in the new Asia.

*

The way to final assault had been opened by the success of the United States' other campaign which advanced from the central Pacific to the entrances of Tokyo Bay. The fall of Saipan had been an important stage in this advance; it marked a change in Japanese defensive tactics. Hitherto the Japanese had sought to repel American invaders by making mass charges on them as they landed. But at Iwojima, the next island to be attacked after Saipan, the Japanese fought in prepared positions, inflicting great damage on the Americans before they were overwhelmed in March 1945. The island had to be wrenched from them, trench by trench. The Japanese losses were 20,000: the American marines lost 26,000 killed, and the US navy nearly 900 killed or missing and about 2,000 wounded.

From Iwojima, Nimitz had first intended to make his main target Formosa. He changed his plan, and launched his attack on Okinawa, a heavily fortified island, forty miles long, in the Ryukyu Islands, 500 miles from Japan proper. On 1 April 1945 the Americans landed, and at first met with almost no opposition. But they were in an enormous ambush: they realized suddenly that the northern part of the island was alive with troops, all of them skilfully hidden. A feature of the resistance was their use of light artillery, among the most effective of the war. While the Americans were meeting deadly resistance from the north, their plans were disordered by the Japanese use of Kamikaze planes. These were manned by volunteer squads of suicide pilots, who flew their planes to crash on the decks of ships and there explode. The Kamikaze ,who were first used by the Japanese in the battle of Leyte, had by now been incorporated in the general plan for the defence of Japan. The Kamikaze were genuinely volunteers; the Americans were unwilling to believe that such a corps could be formed on a free-will basis, but their efforts to find that they had been conscripted were in vain. By the ferocity of their action, by the unreason of their suicidal intentions, they struck the Americans with peculiar horror. The Kamikaze fought with a peculiar exaltation, they appeared insanely exhilarated, and they went to their death as though to a fascinating ceremony. It was the eschatology of war. In the battle for Iwojima they did very great damage. On one day they sank twenty-four ships. But they could not alter the fact that the number of aeroplanes, as also the number of pilots, was shrinking fast, and would presently be used up.

The battle for Okinawa changed rapidly into nightmare. It progressed like a surrealist film. On the sixth day, on 6 April, the Japanese dispatched from the Inland Sea their huge battleship, the *Yamato*. It was a huge Kamikaze. Its mission was to wreak as much havoc as possible: it carried only enough oil for a one-way trip, and was meant for destruction. In fact it was engaged by American aircraft, and was sunk before it could do much damage. But the madness of the sacrifice in such a way of the world's largest battleship convinced Japan's antagonists that the Japanese staff was near the end of its judgement.

The battle lasted until 21 June. It ended in scenes of horror. The Japanese commander and his deputy both committed ceremonial *hara-kiri*. Over a hundred thousand Japanese were dead. A very small number survived as prisoners.

The Americans were satisfied that a weighty section of the Japanese command, both in the navy and the army, now saw no chance of success in war, and no opportunity of gaining even a temporary respite, and would be glad to make peace. The war might have ended then. But how were these high officers to terminate it? They were afraid of being assassinated if they made any move: the mass of the army and navy was still able to fight, and there was still a minority of the more senior officers who were willing to fight on to the end. No mutinies or outbreaks of any kind took place among the forces.

The difficulty for the United States was that it lacked the means of making contact with the politically reasonable sections in Japanese life. The attempt to signal to the East that the United States would respond favourably to any bid for surrender was made again and again, usually by cryptic speech on the American broadcasting stations; but they met with no reply from any who could speak responsibly in Japan. Still the war went on, and no peace was yet possible, though the majority of all classes of Japan desired it greatly. The civil servants, the industrialists and bankers, the trade union leaders, the considerable classes of the intelligentsia – all despaired of war, and regarded with frenzy the piece by piece destruction worked on them by the American aeroplanes. But the intransigent section of the military, who had gained control of the direction of Japan ten years before, could not be set aside. A dramatic and novel development in the art of war was necessary for this.

*

A picture of the Japanese Empire in twilight, and approaching dissolution, is given by the puppet Prime Minister, Ba Maw. Ba Maw, as has been seen, had had his quarrels with the Japanese, and, though he had made his position tolerable, he had hardly cause to love them. The more remarkable is his sober account of the way in which they faced defeat and international disgrace. He was invited to Japan in November 1944, just as the systematic bombing of Japan's home islands was beginning, in an endeavour to organize Asian support for the tottering Japanese imperial structure. Ba Maw owed his eminence to the Japanese, and knew that he must fall with them. This is the general impression which he describes:

Tokyo and its people had changed since I had seen them a year ago, visibly subdued and disillusioned by events, but most of them as determined and defiant as ever. They were now a people in the grip of the biggest crisis in all their history and grimly waiting for the worst. But they were facing the situation wonderfully and revealing their latent racial qualities, their almost inexhaustible capacity to take whatever should come, to endure and survive and wait and even hope. They were more or less the same outwardly, but in the course of a long quiet talk they could not help but betray their true thoughts and fears. Unlike before, they now spoke mainly of the Kamikazes, thus showing that they were placing most of their hopes on something which was really an act of desperation. The people were living with a new terror, the threat of American mass air bombing; they knew that they had no real way to protect their millions of paper and bamboo houses; not even, as it turned out, the Imperial Palace.*

The topic of chief concern was the air bombardment, and the damage which that was able to do, especially on the morale of the population. This is what Ba Maw says of this:

One of the worst incendiary bombings of Tokyo occurred when I was there near the end of November 1944. The result was quite literally a holocaust, a mass burning of one of the densest areas of the city. I saw the ghastly devasta-

* Ba Maw: *Breakthrough in Burma*, op. cit.

tion the next morning. But there was no panic or self-pity or even audible complaint among the huge mass of victims. In fact some of them were able to express their happiness that the Imperial Palace had escaped. It was a heartbreaking sight but it also lifted one's heart immensely to see so much human endurance and strength of character displayed in so dark an hour.*

Ba Maw was taken round the headquarters of the Japanese army. The Kamikaze were exhibited to him as a kind of Japanese secret weapon. He met Koiso, the Japanese Prime Minister, and General Sugiyama, the Minister for Defence, who was soon to play a decisive part. He took every opportunity of discussing with the Japanese commanders their defence tactics, and represented that a scorched earth policy would be intolerable to the Burmese as was also the plan of using the Burmese forces to fight the rear-guard action against the British. Ba Maw had the satisfaction of saving the Shwe Dagon Pagoda from being incorporated in the Japanese defence perimeter. At least he gives himself the credit of having achieved it by the negotiations of his visit.

* ibid.

CHAPTER 21

The End

THE war had entered its final stage. Japan still battled on, but its position was hopeless. The United States, still arming, poured out its fleet and aircraft across the Pacific, and was preparing the great offensive against the sacred Japanese homeland. The expectation was that the American war machine, which had swallowed up so many Pacific islands, would in the long run devour Japan proper. The economic might of the United States must finally prevail. The war machine moved on, and the only uncertainty was the length of time it would take to complete the process. Japan, as Germany before it, was given no time to summon up its resources and to organize them for the optimum defence of its own country.

Japan, in its final phase, was like Macbeth cooped up in Dunsinane, without any rational hope of a happy issue from his adversities, mechanically wound up to continue to shout defiances at the armies investing him.

> Some say he's mad: others that lesser hate him
> Do call it valiant fury: but, for certain,
> He cannot buckle his distemper'd cause
> Within the belt of rule.
> ANGUS: Now does he feel
> His secret murders sticking on his hands;...
> Those he commands move only in command,
> Nothing in love; now does he feel his title
> Hang loose about him, like a giant's robe
> Upon a dwarfish thief.

One hope alone sustained Japan. The Soviet Union had not denounced the Non-Aggression Treaty which Matsuoka, Japan's Foreign Minister, had been able to negotiate with it in 1941. In spite of the bad blood between them five years earlier, this treaty, to the surprise of onlookers, had kept the peace between the apparently predestined enemies, though war had raged universally elsewhere. Japan could reckon that peace in Europe would bring to a head the issues between Russia and the United States. Was it too much to expect that Russia, threatened and thwarted by the United States, might see that its true interest lay in accepting the partnership of Japan? Japan could claim that it had already shown, by refraining from striking at Russia when Hitler was at the doors of Moscow in 1941, that no insuperable cause of conflict lay between it and the Soviet Union. It could represent that, in spite of the severe destruction which it had suffered, it still possessed an army which was one of the key pieces on the board internationally. The Japanese army still had fighting spirit, still had ammunition, and could hope to take an immense toll from a threatened invasion. It boasted that to overrun Japan, when all its natural advantages of defence were taken into review, the United States would need a force of 10 million men, a force which it could not hope to transport. If the United States came to be at loggerheads with Russia, it was unlikely that it would willingly force through the attack on Japan to its conclusion, which would be frightful carnage.

In 1945, as the Japanese position grew evidently more desperate, Russia began to unmask its intentions. In April, at the time of the attack on Okinawa, the Soviet government announced that it would not renew the non-aggression pact which was due to expire one year hence. When the Japanese made proposals about the possibilities of a new agreement, the Russian Ambassador was ominously evasive. Russia gave every sign that it was preparing for war with Japan. Thus its final hope was nearly extinguished. 'Despair thy charm' seemed to cry out the omens for Japan.

It seems probable that the Japanese Intelligence had not heard of Stalin's information to Churchill and Roosevelt at the Teheran Conference. Russia was preparing for war with Japan as soon as Germany was defeated. Confirmation of this should have come easily to Japanese spies; but there is no record of Japan having been well served by espionage. There were no figures in its employment comparable to Richard Sorge, the Russian agent, who, in the critical phase before Pearl Harbor, had spied on Japan for the USSR; he had been able to reassure Russia that Japan had decided not to hasten to the aid of Germany, and refused to attack Russia as Germany wished. Japan was of course under the handicap that, if it employed men of its own nation as agents, they were more conspicuous than others. Japanese could hardly wear the appearance of blank anonymity which is essential to espionage. The same is broadly true of western spies in an eastern country. They may succeed, by exceptional audacity, in exceptional circumstances, as Sorge was able to do. But in a war between East and West, espionage is likely to play less part than in a war in which the contestants share a similar racial background.

Espionage, therefore, paid the Americans only very mean dividends.

It is remarkable how little was the knowledge which reached them in this way from Tokyo. Japanese counter-espionage was very capable, but the United States had succeeded in developing the eyes and ears which pried on Japanese moves, though this was done at a distance by code-breaking, and not by means of spies. Its advantage in this has already been noted, for example at the time of the negotiations before Pearl Harbor, and in naval battles; it had continued to read the Japanese codes throughout the war, and never betrayed to the Japanese that it was in fact doing so. It required great restraint by the Americans to take no step by which it should become obvious to the Japanese that they possessed the secret. It is, in fact, recorded in Japan that a few men doubted from time to time the degree of security of Japanese communications, but they were not attended to.

*

Meanwhile the American air-raids on Japan went on relentlessly. Until June 1944 American planes, except for those in Lieutenant-Colonel Doolittle's adventure in 1942, had not been over Japan. Thereafter the Japanese homeland was subjected to a bombardment which was utterly destructive. The officer in charge of American bombardment was General Curtis H. Le May. He was a skilled technician, with experience of the air war against Germany. He had at first concentrated on organizing bombing expeditions from Chengtu, in Szechuan, but later decided that this base was unsuitable since he could not organize from there the massive squadrons by means of which America hoped to bring the war to an end. In February 1945 he shifted his base to the Marianas.

On 10 March he sent in waves of bombers which flew abnormally low: this was a protection against anti-aircraft guns, which were abundant in Tokyo. The Japanese, even as late as this, did not have their guns adjusted to radar; they were operated manually, and they were made largely ineffective by Le May's strategy. Flying so low the aeroplanes did not even have to carry guns. On this one raid the Americans distributed 2,000 tons of bombs. In this savage assault they used a device of air attack which had been perfected over Germany. The explosions which they employed raised intense heat on a large scale. As a result they caused violent storms of air currents, which were utterly beyond control, and proved one of the most lethal factors in this kind of attack. This one raid is estimated to have caused 125,000 casualties. It was estimated that 40 per cent of the city was destroyed in under three hours. Over a million people were made homeless.

These grim tactics, operated with the thoroughness of General Le May, were new, and marked a change in air warfare. Le May followed this first raid with others through May and June, at the end of which the Americans could see, by air reconnaissance, that they had destroyed half Tokyo and many provincial cities, many of them essential for the war effort. The destruction of civilian life was greater than it had been in Hamburg or Berlin. Much more damage could be done on Japanese cities by fire bombs, because of the light structure of most buildings; the same weight of explosives led to much more widespread destruction. A contemporary Home Ministry report described as follows the behaviour of the populace: 'The consequences of the air raids had caused the people to evacuate the area. In certain areas they neglected to keep the water tanks filled. The people lack a fighting spirit towards the incendiary bombing.' After May the Minister of Home Affairs admitted that civil-defence measures in Tokyo were futile.

The economic consequences were devastating. At first the destruction, as was the case in Germany, had less effect on industrial production than might have been supposed, but, as it became more wholesale, and surpassed the war damage in Europe, so its effects became harder to circumvent. The Japanese government took more sweeping powers to direct the economy of the country; but where was the economy left to direct? The food supplies began to fall dangerously, and could not be distributed because of the destruction of the railways and the breakdown of commercial organization. The description of the life of the Japanese worker at this stage of the war, underfed, harried to inhuman extremes by the government, lacking the elementary comforts of a safe home, must touch even the reader who knows something of the terrors endured by the German population. A great flight began from the towns to the countryside.

For the first time the civilian part of the nation began to turn against the military. In parts of the country it became positively dangerous to wear uniform. Such aberration shook deeply the Army General Staff.

Japanese experts at the time said that the Japanese standard of nutrition in the towns in the last year was below that of Germans in the fateful winter of hunger after the end of the first European war. Even the army, which was the last to be affected, was put on short supplies. The soldiers were found to be bartering military equipment for the scanty food supplies which filtered through to private hands. In spite of all this, both the civilian and military morale remained astonishingly high. There were no rice riots in the Japanese towns, such as were already causing great concern in Germany in the First World War as early as 1916. It may be that the Japanese were less shocked by this adversity than were European populations, because they had been inured to it. Twenty years before, the people of Tokyo had experienced similar devastation in their capital city; that time from the horrors of the Tokyo earthquake.

*

In April 1945 the Prime Minister, Koiso, fell from office. He had engaged in negotiations with Chinese emissaries, by which he had intended to split the Chinese and the western allies. They were of course secret, but they leaked out, and when they failed he was dismissed. Baron Suzuki Kantaro, an aged admiral, succeeded. It was remarked that he was sworn in on the day after the loss of Japan's prize battleship, the *Yamato*: Japan had turned to the navy for its Prime Minister just at the time that it had lost its fleet. He had a good record, having been a target of the army conspiracy of 1936, in which he was badly wounded. He was a hero of the Russo-Japanese war. He had a likeable, rather enigmatic, personality. He was almost universally popular, which is a rare thing in Japan. From experience, he believed that the scope for personal intervention in public affairs was limited, and he was apt to preside benignly over them, and to feel philosophically that nobody could have altered what had in fact come to pass. In fact, there was, in Suzuki, a touch of Tolstoy's Kutuzov: the much respected figure, clothed with glory from the past, who is wise enough to collaborate with events, rather than to attempt to withstand them – or even to understand them.

But he was eighty years old: too venerable to be effective, even by roundabout means. He had not the decisiveness, the single-mindedness which were essential qualities in a Prime Minister in such a crisis. The choice of Suzuki, however, was a sign that the peace party was gradually prevailing. He was not a born leader, he did not incarnate the Japanese desire to go down fighting. Intellectually he needed no conviction that Japan had lost the war; he was himself more than ready for peace. But he moved too slowly to be able to save Japan. The peace party was looking for a totem, was ready to be rallied, and to assert itself, but this was beyond Suzuki.

In the next month, May, Japan lost its ally, Germany. The Supreme War Council met and approved the decision to carry on the war notwithstanding. It declared, however, that Japan was released from the provisions of the Tripartite Pact. Japan had now to face the switch of the allied forces engaged in the European war, and their addition to the force already employed against Japan in the East; it had also to meet the possible use against it of the Russian army, now disengaged.

*

An outside chance for Japan lay in the complications set up by the death of Roosevelt on 12 April, and his succession by Vice-President Truman. But to have used these to advantage, to have extricated itself from the net which was closing on it, would have required a very flexible diplomacy. Flexibility was never a strong point with the Japanese and the number of neutral centres where Japan could operate, and from which it could obtain its intelligence, had, to the advantage of the United States, become very small.

At the Yalta Conference, in February 1945, Roosevelt had offered Russia a larger bait to enter the war against Japan. He unilaterally raised the stakes. Confident of Churchill's support, he promised Russia the southern part of Sakhalin and the Kurile Islands. He added the recognition of unspecified Soviet interests in the commercial port of Dairen and the reissue of the Russian lease of Port Arthur as a naval base; and he proposed that there should be Russian participation in the control of the Chinese Eastern Railway and the South Manchurian Railway. Roosevelt, by negotiating on these lines, had cancelled out the effect of the Russo–Japanese war of 1904–5, and had taken upon himself to re-make history. Furthermore, Roosevelt, with Churchill's unspoken assent, had behaved in a very cavalier fashion in disposing of huge Chinese assets and settling vast issues in disregard of wholly legitimate Chinese claims.

In spite of this agreement with the Russians, which had been so dearly purchased, the Americans, and to a large extent the British, continued to be profoundly distressed by the memory of the savage Japanese defence of the Coral Islands. The ferocity of their resistance in the homeland was expected to be as formidable. Nothing like the same internal collapse was foreseen as followed the death of Hitler in Germany. The war might continue for as much as a year, and with what was foreseen as the mounting strain of tension with Russia, in spite of the glitter of the terms of Yalta, the upshot was not clear.

In the meanwhile it became known that the Japanese General Staff was pressing on with plans for a fanatical defence of the Japanese islands. Rightly it was supposed that the principal American blow would be directed at Honshu. To deal with this it could assemble two and a half million troops in the home islands. Tales arrived to the effect that a vast underground headquarters was being dug out at Tokyo.

The Japanese army was said to be gambling on the blind determination which would halt the Americans on landing. Clearly the Americans had still much effort before them.

*

But very shortly after, a great change came over the situation. It was brought about by the completion of the atom bomb. Partly this was the result of German-Jewish genius, which, barred from Germany by racial madness, had been mobilized in the invention of this device of war, which had been meant in the first place for the overthrow of the Nazi system. Part of the early work was done in England: and, when it was concentrated in the United States, British scientists participated. The war against Germany had come to an end in May 1945, with the bomb still a project, and not realized in fact: but by June it was clear that it was about to become operational. The news that it was to be so, and would be available for use against Japan, had already been grasped by the very small circle in which, at this stage of the war, had been concentrated the making of American policy. Its immense, hardly credible, destructive power could quench the continuing flame of Japanese fanaticism. With its finality there could be no discussion.

By this trick of fate, the need to cajole and coax Russia, the need for Russian complicity and Russian power, were all removed.

By the summer of 1945 it was stated that American policy would be revised: Russian aid was now no longer so necessary for bringing to an end the war with Japan. The United States had initially perceived that through the possible intervention of Russia it could go ahead without perpetually needing to keep China contented, and now it saw that it would be able to discard Russia in its turn.

In fact America was by this time as zealous to deter Russia from entering the war as before it had been to bring Russia in. Truman had succeeded Roosevelt; his period was from the start different from the period of Roosevelt. Other considerations apart, Truman was less inclined to exert himself to maintain good relations with Russia. He was less of a historian. He was less inclined, especially at this point of his career, to look into the future, and to adjust his actions accordingly. Instinctively, Truman was thinking in terms of the containment of Russia, and was anxious that, in the Far East, Russia should make as little headway as possible. If Russia once went to war and invaded Manchuria, there would be little chance of keeping it out of Port Arthur and Dairen (which it had already been promised at Yalta). Even though Truman, who was new to these issues of foreign policy, did not himself stress all these points, he was more available than Roosevelt had been to advisers who suggested a frankly anti-Russian policy. None of the advisers knew, but Truman did, that the atom bomb would be available for putting Japan out of the war. For the time being he was satisfied that Russian demands would not be extravagant. If the effects of the bomb were to be as he was advised, a power without the bomb could not argue aggressively with the power which possessed it.

The condition of Japan continued to deteriorate. It was uncertain that the bomb would ever be required. General Le May was claiming that his air bombardment had totally paralysed life in sixty major cities. He claimed that Japan was being driven back to the stone age. The Joint Chiefs-of-Staff reported at the beginning of July: 'Japan will become a nation without cities, with her transportation disrupted, and will have tremendous difficulty in holding her people together for continued resistance.' By March 1945 Japan had lost 88 per cent of the merchant fleet with which it had begun the war, and it had become almost impossible to import any goods, even the most essential. The service departments of the government cried out for the punishment of those engaged in the economic administration; but this could do no good. American Intelligence was, however, rather less optimistic. It gave due allowance to the putting out of action of much of Japanese heavy industry through the blockade and through air bombardment. But it reported that the Japanese output of combat aeroplanes was still between 1,200 and 1,500 a month (as compared with a peak production of 2,300 reached late in 1944). The greatest shortage was of fuel oil, which was bringing orthodox air operations to a standstill. On the other hand Japan had little to worry about in its stock of ammunition. The Intelligence Committee still thought that the highly trained Japanese army, the greater part of which had as yet never been in action, was a formidable fighting force. It reckoned that it would probably take another twelve months to subdue it. It made its report, it must be noticed, without knowledge of the bomb.

At the Potsdam Conference in July, when the three masters of the world met face to face, Truman, with careful premeditation and calculated misdirection, told Stalin, apparently in passing, that the allies had in their hands a more powerful bomb than any previously used. No word was said about the bomb being nuclear, or about the transformation of the war by its invention. Churchill, who knew the true facts, and who watched Stalin carefully, agreed that he had not suspected the truth behind Truman's apparently routine information. He took it as an announcement that the United States had been able to charge its bomb with a heavier load of dynamite. There is drama in the spectacle of these two men, the pillars of the western world, systematically observing the demeanour of a man whom they both regarded as their potential enemy, while in public they played on him something which resembled a confidence trick. The drama is heightened because Stalin had in his pocket, in the communist offensive which he knew he could release in Europe, something like an atom bomb in politics.

A race, in which one of the partners, Stalin,was in darkness about the true facts and about their urgency, then took place between the Americans, who were about to explode the bomb, and the Russians, who were in the last stages of the preparation to attack in Manchuria. Russia had become aware of the change of attitude by the United States, of the desire that it should not participate, though it may have been partly puzzled about the reason. The United States rushed the preparations. At one time the bomb was to have been used on 1 August. Last-minute delays in completing its manufacture put this back a few days. Further delay came because the weather made it almost impossible to raid Japan accurately.

During the Potsdam Conference it was learnt that Japan had requested Swedish mediation in working out surrender terms. It was plain that peace could not be far off. The United States, however, showed surprisingly little zeal in developing this initiative.

The United States made at this time the decision to exclude Russians as members of an occupation force in Japan. The plans for occupying Japan were made surprisingly late. Their details were all improvised. For example, the decision to divide the occupation of Korea and to fix the boundary between the American zone and the Russian zone at the thirty-eighth parallel, was made between an American captain and a Russian major. Thus, casually, there came into being a frontier problem which subsequently divided the world. The Americans and the British were informed by Molotov about the repeated, almost frenzied, attempts by Japan to enlist the support of Russia as a mediator. They were being rebuffed by Russia. It was clear that Russia was not going to back Japan as a move in the war that had already begun between it and its allies.

At Potsdam, on 26 July 1945, the allies had issued a final and solemn summons to Japan to surrender. Its terms were broadcast over the wireless. They were that those Japanese who had been responsible for the policies which had led to war were to be forever eliminated; that Japan must renounce all its overseas empire; that war criminals must be punished; that Japan should be occupied. As had become the habit of the United States with beaten adversaries, Japan was required to surrender unconditionally. These demands, though exceedingly radical, were not entirely rejected by Japan, so desperate had its position become.

An answer was understood to have been given in a press conference on 30 July by the Japanese Prime Minister, Suzuki, at which he spoke in Japanese. It was, as might have been expected from an old man, doubtful, temporizing and ambiguous. Apparently he had meant to say that he withheld comment. The allies interpreted the Japanese word he used as meaning that Japan not only would not comment, but would treat the summons with contempt. This was taken by the handful of Americans who knew what was intended as the signal for dropping the bomb. Actually it has been since suggested that a word was mistranslated, and meant much less than was supposed, signifying merely that Japan's first reaction to the summons was not being published. The subsequent controversy about what really happened has been inconclusive. If the confusion in fact occurred, it is typical of the Japanese language, one of the most involved and muddled languages of the world, that it should have betrayed Japan towards its disaster.

The bomb was dropped on Hiroshima, the chosen target, on 6 August 1945. The attack was made from Tinian, not far from Guam, which had been taken in the previous year. The plane, a B 29 bomber, had been blessed for its mission by a Roman Catholic priest. The havoc made was as great as was forecast. It was clear that the war could not be pursued when America could drop bombs of this kind. Within three days a second bomb, of a different and even more deadly type, was dropped on the civilian port of Nagasaki. It did slightly less damage, because Nagasaki had better air-raid precautions and because the bomb did not set off what is technically known as a fire storm; but its blast was greater than that at Hiroshima. This time, to signalize the joint responsibility of the United States and Britain, the death plane was accompanied by a plane carrying British observers, Dr W. Penny, the physicist, and Wing Commander L. Cheshire, who, by one of the ironies of these events, was later to win celebrity in Britain as the leader of one of the most inspired missions of the day, that of bringing comfort and the opportunity of decent existence to the incurably disabled. With the bomb at Nagasaki, there was released a manifesto to the top Japanese physicist, addressed to him by his American colleagues and explaining some of the details of the bomb. It urged him to enlighten the Japanese government.

Ironically, Nagasaki was one of the parts of Japan which had the connections of longest duration with the West. It was founded in the sixteenth century by a feudal lord who was a Christian, and who wanted the trade between Japan and the Christian world to be based on it. For a time the port was actually ceded to the Jesuit missionaries, who organized its administration. It was subsequently the centre of persecution of Japanese Christians when the Japanese government became alarmed by their number.

The dropping of the atom bomb was so dramatic, the awed shock it provoked throughout the world was so final, and the sense that it was, in President Truman's phrase, 'the greatest thing in history', seemed so incontestable that there was a general instinct to think that it had brought to an end one phase of human affairs. From then onwards everything would be dwarfed by events. But the appalling news of the disaster produced by atomic radiation, the vaporizing and burning of human beings, the whole vast panorama of unutterable suffering, somehow failed to register with most people who lived through those days. Even the horrible details, published some months afterwards and set out with all the technical skill of American publicity, were too terrible for belief. The mind set up impediments to taking in such information. There was born at that time an uneasiness which has affected a whole age.

*

The Americans had thus won the race. They had set themselves against Russia; but it was virtually a dead heat because on the next day, before Japan had had time to surrender, the Russians crossed the frontier of Manchuria. By a two-pronged offensive, one prong from outer Mongolia, the other from the Soviet maritime provinces in Siberia, Russia overran the country as neatly as Germany had picked off countries earlier in the war. Though the fate of Hiroshima has stuck in the world's memory and though it has been regarded as the final cause of Japan's capitulation, it seems, in point of fact, that it was the Russian invasion that tilted the Japanese over to put an end to the war.

The effects of the atom bomb and the grim finality of its consequences were not immediately clear. Among most people outside Hiroshima itself, even among those in Tokyo, there was doubt about what had really happened. A great bomb had fallen; terrible destruction had been wrought; but Japan had become thoroughly used to such calamities. Actually the loss of life in the atomic phase, though it was rendered peculiarly horrible by atomic radiation, was less than that in the great B 29 raids, to which Japan had been subjected since March 1945. But all Japan knew the significance of the dreaded invasion of Manchuria, the advent of the Russian hordes, the coming into reality of that threat which had, as long as man could remember, been the governing fact in Japan's foreign policy. Japan could not face war with another Great Power. It was this which made it 'despair its charm', and accept the facts.

*

The history of the way Japan surrendered is dramatic, and even today, has probably been only partly told. At least, new accounts are constantly appearing in Japan with new details, which, true or false, require the narrative of events to be considered afresh.

A new personality in Japan played a large part at the conclusion. This was the most august person in the land. Hitherto he had been content to be a spectator of the great events, but now he entered the arena. This was the Japanese Emperor.

He was a virtuous prince. The irony is that such dark proceedings had been allowed to happen under his aegis. In the whole range of personalities who held positions of distinction in the war, whether of actual power or of decorativeness, he, and the English monarch, George VI, were the only ones without serious blemish. Like George VI he had a stammer; like him, he held in reality very little political power. It must have been discouraging for this young man, entering on his life's career, that he succeeded his father, who had been an idiot during almost the whole of his reign. Yet that fact had not compromised the monarchy, and this speaks highly of the reserves of credit which the institution enjoyed. In one respect the Emperor was ahead of George VI. He had strong intellectual interests, though these were concentrated on a single subject, marine biology. The corollary of the secure eminence of the Japanese Emperor was that ordinarily public opinion severely restricted the range of his activities; he was expected to do almost nothing because his role was almost deified. And Hirohito could not be said to have contributed anything remarkable to the political debates of his time. From the day he ascended his throne in 1926, to the day when he nearly lost it at the time of Japan's defeat, he did what was expected of him. He was reliable; he was thoroughly constitutional: he gave no trouble to the politicians by threatening to use the stored-up prestige of the Japanese monarchy to embarrass them. The inner circle of Japanese with knowledge of what went on behind the façade of public life knew that the course of Japan's affairs – the autonomy of the military, and a foreign policy which brought it into collision with the United States and Britain – was profoundly antipathetic to him. But beyond asking the occasional awkward question at imperial conferences, he gave no sign of his continual vexation.

However, at the crisis of Japan, he acted with much common sense. He borrowed from the Confucian philosophy of China the maxim by which he governed his actions. The Confucian wisdom was not to stand up like an oak tree before a raging tempest: in a storm, the oak tree is uprooted and perishes. The willow tree has the better chance of survival; it bends before the wind, but, when the hurricane is over, its root is unsnapped, and it stands up once again by its own resilience. Thus, before the storm of the Japanese military, which was to blow away many persons in its time, the Emperor bowed, and was inconspicuous. Now the storm was nearly blown out, and the opportunity came for the reassertion of the powers of the monarchy, which were real and legitimate even if they had been so long unused. He was guided, in the crucial days when he felt that his personal intervention was timely, that in fact the spirit of the Japanese constitution called for it, by a suave and subtle sense of correct timing. He was capable of choosing the right men to collaborate with – or he was very lucky in these being available, and in offering their services. His conduct at the time suggests that this marine biologist had developed a political instinct during the years of inoffensive constitutional practice.

Throughout July the conviction of defeat had been gripping one person after another and one institution after another. In the past year the fortunes of the civilian elements of government in their control of the military had begun to revive. In the complex balance of forces which made up Japanese politics, the centre of authority began to pass a little away from the soldiers and towards the civilians. A significant date had been the fall of the Tojo government (July 1944), which happened after the fall of Saipan. It was overthrown under pressure from the Jushin, the former Prime Ministers, who had formed a more or less informal council. This body was unknown to the written constitution; it had in consequence no rights, such as access to government papers; it came, however, to exercise great power. It had an influence like that of the Genro, or elder statesmen, though the power of the Genro had been openly recognized. The re-entry to Japanese politics of such an influence was important. It was the more so at this period because the Jushin had tended, with some exceptions, to work for peace. Most of them thought that the war was irrevocably lost, that the leaders knew this well, but that, floundering and indecisive, they saw no means of terminating it.

But the services, both the army and navy, were obdurate for continuing war: and the senior officers, even if compelled by reason to admit the hopelessness of their case, could point out that they were powerless to assent to peace. They would have been assassinated. The spirit of the nation had passed into the custody of the patriotic societies which would have employed the sanction of murder against anyone who dared to speak of surrender. Both the Jushin, and the more reasonable service officers, had to mask their intention, to carry on their intrigue behind walls of extreme secrecy, and had to say one thing while in fact strenuously doing another. As a result, Japan's resolution to fight on appeared undented. It had become as good as impossible for it to capitulate. Japan, having made a cult of the principle that no Japanese ever surrendered to the enemy, now found it impossible to accept the findings of common sense.

Behind the scenes, however, and with every secrecy, Japan had been sounding the possibilities of an honourable peace; and peace, with honour that would satisfy Japan meant, in effect, a peace on the simple condition that Japan was allowed to keep its Emperor. In every other respect Japan was ready, except for the irreconcilables in the army, to surrender unconditionally; with the Emperor's position guaranteed, the Japanese would sigh with relief and cease their hopeless resistance. There is undeniable pathos about these last days of Japanese agony. Japan was willing to trade the entire substance of capitulation for this one concession to a principle which, to its western conquerors, appeared perverted and of no worth. To the West, attachment to an Emperor was sentimental; a defeated Japan must eventually have a chief executive, and the title he would use of himself was no matter. But to the Japanese it was beyond price. Even so, some of the Jushin were frankly disposed to sacrifice the Emperor, if peace could be gained by this.

President Truman had to take account of the fact that feeling against the monarchy was strong in the United States. Those in favour of tolerating it were accused of being appeasers. Truman himself, backed by Henry L. Stimson, the Secretary for War, was in favour of accepting the Japanese terms on this point. They were influenced by the argument that the American occupying force would find it much simpler to do its work if it had the Japanese Emperor on its side. His prestige was so immense that he would, as it were, legitimize the occupation in Japan's eyes. Also, an American commander, able to speak through him, would be able to gain control of the surrendering Japanese armies; which, otherwise, would have presented a problem. Truman did not directly meet the Japanese condition. But he drafted the American reply in terms that, while avoiding all mention of the Emperor problem, conveyed the general sense that the Emperor would be kept.

These exchanges came between two vital meetings in Tokyo, the first on 13 August, between the Japanese Emperor and the Supreme Command, the committee of which directed the war; the second on the next day, a conference of the Emperor with the Japanese Cabinet. The meetings were held in a dug-out in the imperial palace. In spite of the belligerent circumstances, a certain formality was observed. All those taking part wore full dress uniform, or morning dress; the long table at which they sat was covered with a precious gold brocade. But the Emperor himself, appearing unshaven, increased the general sense of gloom. At the first meeting, no decision was reached: the case for further resistance, the case for immediate capitulation, were fully argued. But the Prime Minister Admiral Suzuki succeeded in getting agreement that the Emperor should be asked to decide personally what should be done. To follow such a procedure was revolutionary in Japan: the convention was that he should never be embarrassed by having to give instructions to his Ministers. At the second meeting, after those present had again expressed their views, and the American attitude towards the Emperor had been weighed up, the decision was taken by the Emperor. 'The unendurable must be endured', was the imperial pronouncement which terminated the war.

With the last military hope gone, with the Red Army pouring into Manchuria, and with further air attacks expected, which nobody had the remotest idea of how to resist, the Japanese Emperor, in form using the procedure with which he had committed Japan to the calamity of Pearl Harbor, but in fact having taken on himself the personal responsibility for what was now done, gave instructions that hostilities were to cease and, on 14 August Japan replied, accepting the Potsdam declaration.

Until the last moment, it continued to be uncertain if even the intervention of the Emperor would succeed. The military, which had made the war, would not lightly abdicate. It was one thing for the Emperor to forbid further war; it was another for him, great though the Imperial prestige was, to be obeyed. Moreover the United States, in refusing all bargaining, had not satisfied the army that it stood to gain nothing by forcing American troops to fight their way ashore in Japan. Action was precipitated because a fairly accurate account of the peace negotiations had leaked to the army. On the night after the decision to end the war was taken, a melodrama took place in Tokyo which was equal to any of the sensational passages in the history of conspiracy. It recalls Hitler's night of the long knives, in which there culminated the feud between him and the SA leaders; St Bartholomew's Eve in Paris four centuries earlier; the fight, again at Paris, on the night of Robespierre's fall, between the moderate politicians and those who wanted the terror to continue. A group of young, well-connected, passionately unappeasable officers tried to halt the negotiations, make a coup, and seize the sacred person of the Emperor.

To succeed, they needed the support of three or four generals, who were in key positions in Tokyo. Their plot began in the office of the general commanding the First Guards division, which was garrisoning the imperial palace. For hours they pleaded with him: then, their tempers breaking, and pressed for time, they abruptly murdered him. In these bloody proceedings, there is an odd atmosphere of a family quarrel which had passed out of control and become terribly serious. Many of the officers were related to the generals with whom they were pleading. One of them was the son-in-law of General Tojo, the former Prime Minister. Another was the brother-in-law of General Anami, the War Minister.

The officers went to the part of the palace where the Emperor was. Comedy then took over. On the evening before, the Emperor was known to have recorded a wireless address, which would be broadcast to the people of Japan on the next morning, 15 August, and in which he had declared the Japanese decision to surrender. When it was once played on the air, the act would be irrevocable; it was therefore vital to the officers to seize the record and destroy it. It was known to be present in the palace until it was needed for broadcasting, and the soldiers in the plot spent some hours searching for it in vain. Some of those taking part, with the curious detached Japanese aestheticism, remarked on the great beauty of the night, the uncanny and eerie moonlight which provided a backcloth of deep peace for these disordered events. The Emperor, the occasion of this wild conspiracy, was sleeping peacefully, a few yards away, and when it came to the point nobody would commit the impiety of waking him. In a cellar, directly underneath, the Lord Keeper of the Privy Seal, Marquis Kido, who was deeply committed to the peace negotiations, was quaking for his life, for, if the officers had discovered him, they would certainly have slaughtered him. Some radio officials, who had played a part in manufacturing the record, were rounded up and kept prisoner for a while. Their lives were also in danger.

The conspiracy ended because, with the passage of time, the officers began to ask themselves whether they were not going too far. *Sake* flowed; but this did not avail to stifle doubt. The failure to find the gramophone record put a lesion on the unfolding of the plot. Resolution drained away, and the band dispersed. Fake orders, which they had issued to the Guards division to rise and seize the palace, were intercepted. They did not dispose of a sufficient body of rank and file troops.

As a result of this sacrilege of army officers in seizing the imperial palace, the War Minister committed *hara-kiri*. He had been on the verge of this supreme act as a gesture of atonement for the behaviour of the Japanese army in losing the war; the night's doings probably overcame his natural hesitancy, and made death the way out of a situation which had become unbearable to him. In the ministerial debates of the previous days he was one of those whose opinion was most consulted, and had been the most vacillating. He had readily agreed that the military situation was hopeless; but he had been withheld from advising surrender as the only rational course by doubts over what the Americans intended to do about the Emperor. Now he was for capitulation, now he veered towards those who suggested that Japan should try again to save itself by force. His attitude, even towards those who attempted the military coup, was ambiguous. He was not taken by surprise; for days he had known that something was afoot. He had said to those around him that a coup would be impious and impossible; but, at the same time, he had shown marked favour to the more irresponsible officers. He summed up in himself the weakness that was general in the higher ranks of Japanese officer, considered from the point of view of their reliability to the state. He took it as axiomatic that a general need not in all cases obey instructions which reached him, but should be free to connive at gangsterism when the situation required. It was clear that his heart yearned for a coup: and his head only partially restrained him from siding with the young officers. Very distressingly, and rather characteristically, he bungled his suicide, and lived in great agony until the following day.

In the anti-climax which followed these exciting events, the rumours of which began to get about, Hirohito's speech was played over to the Japanese people. It was still touch and go how the speech would be received. In fact, the speech was not generally or at least clearly understood, and that for a very curious reason. The Japanese Emperor spoke the language of the court, very flowery, with a strange lilt, which it was hard for modern Japanese to grasp, at least auditorily. This, combined with sentiments so unexpected – to the uninformed – coming from such a source, produced at first a general bewilderment.

Meetings of colonels and majors were taking place the whole time in all parts of Japan. The plan for a final national effort by air force pilots who had sworn themselves to act as suicide squads was nearly put into effect. The proposal was to bomb the United States warship, the *Missouri*, which was steaming into Tokyo Bay, to accept the Japanese surrender. This was narrowly averted. Hirohito's speech contained a notable sentence, probably inserted on the Emperor's own responsibility, which may have irritated American and British listeners, but which represented the Emperor's own, perhaps naïve, views. He said:

We declared war on America and Britain out of our sincere desire to ensure Japan's self-preservation and the stabilization of South-East Asia, it being far from our thought either to infringe upon the sovereignty of other nations or to embark upon territorial aggrandizement.

He continued with a statement of the incontrovertible fact of Japan's utter helplessness, and the lunacy of continuing the war. He was aware of the danger of seeming to break faith with those who had been killed, but the plight of those still alive required peace absolutely.

The Japanese people wept tears of disbelief and shame, but also of relief, when the imperial message at last sank home. The long nightmare of hypnosis under which they had been held by the military at last was shaken off. With the disciplined self-control of their race, which usually succeeded in clamping down upon their very volcanic emotion – which always so surprised the onlookers – they switched their behaviour overnight, and became the welcoming hosts to the advancing wave of American occupiers. By one of the psychological swings, irrational and extraordinary, which are evident among people under severe strain, the Japanese passed abruptly from regarding the Americans as barbarians, who were contemptible and to be treated with unappeasable hostility, to accepting them as a people who had incontestably proved their superiority by victory, and who had earned their consequent respect. Peace had come partly because of the effort, at the risk of their lives, of the peace party, and, when they had succeeded, it was plain that it had the support of the majority of the people. But this mass had, to the very end, remained completely unorganized. Peace was brought about with the Japanese public still as spectators of the event. They contributed nothing to it.

*

Everywhere the Japanese Empire surrendered, or crashed. In Burma it was already a memory, and the Japanese were gone. In Indonesia

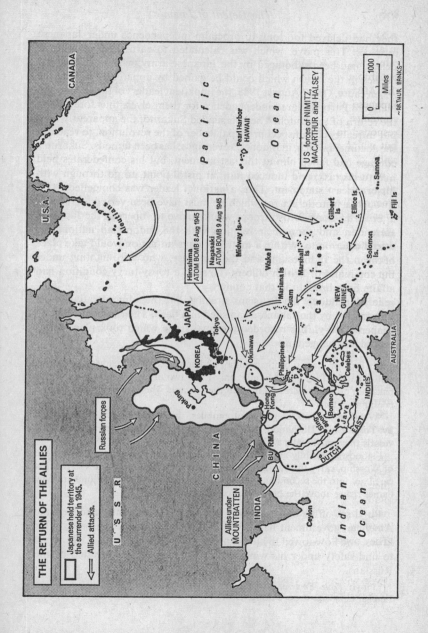

THE RETURN OF THE ALLIES

☐ Japanese held territory at the surrender in 1945.

⟹ Allied attacks.

Russian forces

Allies under MOUNTBATTEN

~ARTHUR BANKS~

0   1000
Miles

CANADA

U.S.A.

Aleutians

Pacific Ocean

Pearl Harbor HAWAII

Samoa

Fiji Is

Ellice Is

Gilbert Is

Solomon Is.

US forces of NIMITZ, MACARTHUR and HALSEY

Midway Is

Wake I

Marshall Is

Carolines

NEW GUINEA

AUSTRALIA

Hiroshima ATOM BOMB 8 Aug 1945

Nagasaki ATOM BOMB 9 Aug 1945

JAPAN

Tokyo

KOREA

Okinawa

Marianas

Guam

Philippines

Celebes

Borneo

Java

EAST INDIES

Dutch

Peking

Hong Kong

BURMA

Singapore

CHINA

U · S · S · R

INDIA

Ceylon

Indian Ocean

they had delayed too long to proclaim independence under Japanese auspices. This move, which was calculated to earn them plaudits in defeat, had been sabotaged by the Japanese army, which had no confidence in the return which could be gained by apparently serving the Asian cause. On 17 August 1945, the impatient leaders of the Indonesian National Party declared independence for themselves, thus forestalling the return of the Dutch. They persuaded Sukarno, the apparently fiery but in reality circumspect principal leader of the revolution, to read out the document which, in Indonesia ever since, has been famous. Sukarno's courage had failed him at the last moment, but his confederates held him to his task, and induced him, at pistol point, to go through with his broadcast statement. Thus a national leader was compelled to go through a historic act for which he must have been very grateful ever afterwards. Soon British troops would arrive to supervise the Japanese surrender, and soon their relation with the Indonesian nationalists would deteriorate. Within a matter of days an action would take place between the Indonesians and the Japanese, who were fighting under the command of British officers. To such a topsy-turvy condition had affairs been brought in that country.

In Manchukuo the Russians streamed in; the administrative structure erected by the Japanese vanished in a flash. Their puppet Manchu Emperor, Pu-yi, has recorded the final scene which took place at his capital at Changchun:

My brother, sisters, brothers-in-law and nephews were already at the railway station, and, of my entire family, only I and two of my wives were left in the palace. Yoshioka addressed me and the servants who were still with me in a peremptory tone:

'Whether we walk or go in automobiles, the sacred objects to be carried by Toranosuke Hashimoto will go in front. If anyone passes the sacred vessels they must make a ninety-degree bow.'

I stood respectfully and watched Hashimoto, the President of the Bureau of Worship, carry the bundle containing the sacred Shinto objects to the first car. I got into the second and, as we left the palace, I looked around and saw flames rising above the National Foundation Shrine.*

Pu-yi set off to make his way to Japan. He was informed that the American government had left Hirohito on his throne. He sank to his knees, and kow-towed to him, expressing his relief at the news. He hoped to find safety under his wing. But at Mukden he was arrested by the Russians.

* Pu-yi: *From Emperor to Citizen: the Autobiography of Aisin-Gioro Pu-yi*, Foreign Language Press, Peking, 1965.

The airfield reverberated to the sound of aircraft engines as Soviet planes landed. Soviet troops holding sub-machine guns poured out of the planes and immediately disarmed all the Japanese soldiers on the airfield, which was soon covered with Soviet troops.*

Pu-yi remained for five years the captive of the Russians. He was then handed over to the Chinese communists for 'brainwashing'. It took time, but eventually the Chinese were satisfied that he was in a desirable state of mind. From 1959, until his death in 1967, he was in Peking, employed as a gardener in the former imperial gardens of the city, and was a striking national monument.

*

Power was everywhere passing away from those who had held it; and a new world was being created. It was the same in those parts of Asia which were, at least formally, on the victors' side. In India the negotiations were beginning which resulted in its complete emancipation within two years.

The war was at an end, and no attempt will be made to trace the history of the countries further, or to examine the effects of the rewards and penalties which they incurred. It is arbitrary to mark a step anywhere in history, and the new age in Asia which began in 1945 is really the pendant of Asia at war, and is inseparably connected with that. It would take decades to work out the consequences of the great struggle. But the history of the world must be arbitrarily chopped into lengths. For the purpose of this book the dropping of the bomb is the terminus.

By dropping the atom bomb the Americans had done much more than put an end to the war with Japan. They had put an end to a chapter of human history, and had transformed the nature of war. In the future neither governments nor people would enter on a war as lightheartedly as the Japanese had done. The interest of the historian lies in the question of what induced Americans to take the responsibility of dropping it.

Why did the Americans, who had it in their power to terminate the war by simply notifying Japan of the terrible effectiveness of the new weapon which had come into their hands, go to the lengths of actually dropping it? Why did they not content themselves with one bomb, but in a matter of hours, and without waiting to see the consequences of Hiroshima, drop the second bomb on Nagasaki?

The answer to these questions is, and is likely to remain, the greatest single matter of controversy of the war. The documents do not clarify

* ibid.

the reasons. Churchill, for instance, is hardly enlightening. In his memoirs, he says, quite simply:

The historic fact remained, and must be judged in the after time, that the decision whether or not to use the atomic bomb to compel the surrender of Japan was never even an issue. There was unanimous, automatic, unquestioning agreement around our [Council] table.

The United States was nearly as well aware as Japan of the desperation of the Japanese. Virtually they had conceded defeat at the end of July, and had put out peace feelers, first asking the Russians to act as mediators, and, on finding them unobliging, had approached the Swedish government. Anyone with experience of diplomacy could perceive that the upshot, after a few days' natural hesitation, must be the surrender so much desired. In the days of decision during the Potsdam Conference anything like a sustained Japanese defence, from strong defensive positions, had clearly become impossible. By ending the war in a ghastly and fearful massacre, the Americans cast over their triumph a dark shadow, and one which may, as is the way in great historical transactions, return to plague the doers in the future.

After the bomb had been exploded, Russian policy became, for the time being, very conciliatory. It was in this period that Truman announced his recent decision that the occupation of Japan should fall exclusively to the Americans. The details of the occupation of Germany had been discussed inexhaustibly, and continued to be a major issue among the allies: by contrast, the occupation of Japan seemed to have been arranged at very short notice, and by the United States alone. Great Britain made no demur at the American decision. Russia limited its protests to a proposal that the surrender on the battleship, the *Missouri*, should have its counterpart on Hokkaido with a ceremony of the surrender of the Kwantung army to Russia. This was rejected. Probably the existence of the bomb frustrated Russian plans for insisting on a joint occupation of Japan, and the consequences of this were incalculable. It avoided endless intrigue, and conflict of puppet parties: probably it saved Japan from a great deal of hardship: it made the return to normal life in Japan much quicker: by taking out Japan as a major question of dispute, it probably made the relations of Russia and the United States by that much easier to handle. It may even have kept them from war. It was perhaps the only good thing which came out of the dropping of the bomb.

The fateful decision to drop the bomb was made within a matter of days. Most of the men who were responsible for Japan's policy had not known a fortnight before that the atom bomb was in existence. Even General MacArthur, who, more than any other man, was responsible for the overthrow of Japan, was given the information only a very brief time before the bomb was due. He had said that he deplored it, but he had no time to make his protest effective. Admiral William D. Leahy, the Chief-of-Staff of the President, was consulted in advance and said, bluntly, that he thought that the use of the bomb was brutal, and served no rational end. It is possible that President Truman, whose subsequent decisions about the bomb were on the whole sober and responsible as, for example, during the later Korean war, may have acted in these days very much in the dark; and it is at least charitable to suppose that he did so. Churchill remarked that, as soon as the news of successful tests arrived, the President seemed to be determined to use it. Churchill judged it useless to press for discussion. All these statesmen suddenly found the bomb at their disposal, and they had no reasonable opportunity to think out the implications of atomic warfare, nor, it seemed, was the phenomenon of fall-out clear in their minds. The real essential difference between an atom bomb and a larger conventional weapon had not been grasped. Most Americans supposed, like Stalin, that it was simply a bigger and more lethal weapon. The discovery of atomic power required that men of exceptional vision and judgement should have been in power, who could see the consequences of the action they took then upon the politics of the next half century or longer. Those men were hardly likely to have been thrown up by the circumstances of directing the war.

Epilogue

IT may have been useful to recapitulate the facts of this conflict. There can seldom have been fought a war which engaged so much of the attention of so many powers, the details of which have so rapidly been allowed to become vague. Within a generation the dramatic events of Japan's surrender, the particulars of the relations between Japan and China, the great struggle at Imphal, the island-hopping across the Pacific by the United States, the great naval battles, have all begun to be touched by the waters of Lethe. Even Pearl Harbor, which has naturally entered into the folk-lore of the USA, today appears far-off, and what happened there is vaguely understood.

The eastern war was inevitably overshadowed by Hitler's war in Europe. It was interdependent with it, and its events criss-crossed with those of the western conflict. But, in retrospect, they have assumed a subordinate part. The events of the European war stand out clearly; they are remembered sharply; the events of the war in the East are, by contrast, hazy in the public memory, and are heaped together in a certain confusion. Ask any young man born at or after the dropping of the bomb at Hiroshima, be he of Asian or European origin, to outline the events which led up to the fearsome drama, and you will be surprised to find what lacunae lie in his narrative.

And yet the events which had to be settled by arms, and by the atom bomb, were as great as the issues in Europe, the suffering was as widespread, the events spread over as many continents, involved more civilizations, and left as large a dent in the history of world culture. For this reason, it has seemed to be worthwhile seeking to protest a little at the progress of the waters sweeping away the recollection of those years – even if the waters are fundamentally healthful, doing the saving work of washing away the memories of brutality and the hatred of nations for one another, and other things which are best forgotten. The famous feats of endurance of the peoples, the daring projects of the national leaders, may, with justice, be offered up as alms to oblivion; yet no people can afford to neglect the history which has made them what they are.

The war, for all the damage it had done, was not, by the standards of past wars, a particularly long one. Three wars, which were needed to settle the opposition of deep conflicting forces, and which turned upside down the affairs of all the participants, took much longer. One was the Thirty Years War between Protestant and Catholic Europe. Another, the Peloponnesian War, which checked finally the Athenian attempt at imperialism, lasted nineteen years. The war which rose out of the French Revolution ran a course which ended at the Battle of Waterloo, and covered twenty-three years. The present war, from the time that the fighting set in in earnest on the Chinese mainland in 1937, and excluding the opening skirmishes between China and Japan, was over in eight years.

The comparatively shorter duration of the great modern wars reflects the deadly nature of modern armaments. The causes nevertheless have been weighty and complex. The issue of the strife in Asia settled a number of conflicts which, but for the war, might have dragged on for years, causing constant unrest, and keeping the region in continual uncertainty. It had been decided which of various trends were to continue, and which, among those which had seemed strong and flourishing a few years before, were either to stop abruptly or else to fade away.

The decision was sharpest for Japan. The attempt to maintain Japan's unnatural pre-eminence in the Far East, and to spread it over the lands to the south, had failed. Japan's empire was dissolved. Japan's efforts had been astonishing. A relatively small country, whose principal assets were the ardent will of its citizens and their regimentation, had had the temerity to challenge the three corners of the world to come against it in arms; and had withstood their reply for more than three years.

The Japanese of that generation had passed through a strange phase of their national history. In the past there had been little to single them out for peculiar reprobation. They were always very vigorous, usually artistic, always somewhat muddled intellectually, which was apparently due to the imprecision of their language. They were also perhaps outstanding for an exaggerated conformism, though they also had the tradition of lifting the tyranny of society over the older members of the community, and giving them a licence to do and say what they pleased. And always, as with any generalization about an entire people, one is conscious at once of many eccentric members of the community, for whom the general rule did not apply.

The main fact in the twentieth century is the acute military phase that the Japanese lived through. It was an aberration. It was not really traditional. It may be that Japanese society has a Samurai streak, and a prolonged feudal period had left it too ready to respond to the call of arms. Many of its ways of thought were military in origin. But, if one looks back on Japanese history, the Japanese do not appear to have been an unduly military people. At one period they were predominantly artists, and would not allow matters of soldierly concern to interfere with the artistic life. In the great Heian period, which is perhaps the outstanding example in history of a leisured class giving up all its time to artistic living, there was once a complaint that the imperial body-guard could not be properly sustained. The soldiers could not ride horses: they constantly fell off them. The detailed history of the society of this time is full of anecdotes of the extreme lengths to which Japanese aestheticism would go. The men of the Heian period are strange ancestors of the Japanese who took Singapore.

The Japanese who were born in the most recent generations were conditioned by the institutions of their society to offer themselves in the bid to establish a Japanese imperialism. These institutions, most of them borrowed from the West though given a peculiar slant in their development, are the monument of the Meiji Restoration. Gradually they induced in the mass of the people the willingness to support a more and more aggressive national policy. The institutions took on a life of their own. In the end, they carried the Japanese people into a great war, and brought down half a continent.

The prime evil of Japan was certainly the ascendancy of the military. This led, in time of war, to the Supreme Command conducting the war as a state secret from the civilian parts of the Japanese administration. Whatever else may be said of such a system, it proved to be most incompetent militarily. Thus Japanese militarism held within it the seeds of its own defeat. It was unable to organize Japanese society so that in modern warfare it could compete with the powers which were organized to be more flexible.

The same militarism, as far as it was able to prevail in making Japanese foreign policy, was responsible for the basic error which brought about Japan's downfall. This was to found Japan's policy on fear of the outside world, and to meet this by seeking to spread a counter-fear of Japan. Because Japan was in a difficult position internationally, because it was vulnerable, because its economic position required that it should have unimpeded access to imports and a constantly growing market overseas for its exports, and because it feared that these might be interrupted by force by an unfriendly power, it counted that prudence required it to be ever on its guard, to arm and show its teeth in a way that would fend off dangerous intentions in its rivals.

There were Japanese voices which protested at such a policy, and pointed, rightly, to the inevitable end; but they were not attended to. The result was a long period of tension, culminating in a war in which Japan lost everything, a war which could not possibly have safeguarded the things which Japan had armed itself to save.

The contradictions of Japan's foreign policy are stated compendiously by the Foreign Ministry official, Toshikazu Kase, who played such a useful part as intermediary of the court circles in bringing the war to an end. 'For a poor country like Japan,' he said,

the construction of costly warships meant a crushing burden upon the national treasury. And yet we built a good number of them. We also maintained a vast Army and an ever expanding Air Force. In the end we became like the mammoth whose tusks, growing ever bigger, finally unbalanced its bodily structure. As everything went to support the huge tusks, very little was left to sustain the rest of the body. The mammoth finally became extinct.

Why did the mammoth arm itself with weapons such as ultimately to bring about its own destruction? Because it was apprehensive. In its desire to defend itself against external enemies the poor creature forgot the very fact that its tusks were its own mortal enemy! Why did Japan arm herself to the teeth? Because she was apprehensive? Why was she apprehensive? Because she had enemies. Why were there enemies? Because her aggressive policy excited suspicion in others. Rather than abandon that objectionable policy she augmented her armaments. But armaments are a relative affair. There is no end to an armament race.*

The men who served ruthless, imperialist Japan were not by nature particularly ruthless or imperialist. They bore no signs of predestination, and there was nothing about them which marked them as enemies of the human race. The Japanese generals, though superficially they might seem to conform to a rather brutal and disgusting pattern, were often men of singular eccentricity. In other circumstances, they might have appeared as rather engaging. Many of them had a vivid and vigorous interior life, and the most varied traits of personality. Some of them practised Japanese archery and fencing each day, not for athletic reasons but for the self-control which these disciplines induced, and for greater proficiency in the art of meditation. They were an interesting contrast to the British army, much more emotional, much more given to adjusting their philosophy and their actions. The contrast between them and the commanders of the Anglo-Saxon forces was often richly comical. Rigid behaviour patterns in their native environment made them what they were and, uprooted from this en-

* Toshikazu Kase: *Eclipse of the Rising Sun,* op. cit.

vironment, their behaviour was unpredictable. It could of course, be terrible; occasionally, however, it was the reverse.

The behaviour of the Japanese soldiers, and their cult of non-surrender, may have seemed to those fighting them to mark them out as an especially desperate, unreformable species of military man. Here too, is only an example of the lengths to which institutions may go in marking their victims. Biologically similar young men, transported to another society and brought up under other institutions, turned out to be enthusiastic liberals or democrats, and found most reprehensible the Japanese cult of military national aggrandizement and the pursuit of death.

The Japanese, in the last war, were shocked at finding a most rigid refusal to respond to the call of their country and race on the part of the Nisei, the children of the Japanese emigrants to America, who had most of them continued to marry with Japanese. In this they were much disappointed: they had counted on being able to convert this class, and if they had succeeded, would have disposed a valuable ally for their war-making. The Nisei had some reason to attend to their call, for the United States was less than generous in its treatment of them, and did not hide its suspicion. The deportation or preventive confinement of the large masses of Americans of Japanese origin, who had given no reason for doubting their loyalty, was one of the blots on wartime American government. But the Nisei, almost without exception, refused the appeal of their blood relations, and were almost fanatical in their devotion to the new institutions among which they had been brought up.

The Nisei show that there is no such thing as a militarist through and through, made such by his physical make-up, and a stranger to civilization because of the military activities of his ancestors.

Most significant of all, the Japanese, since their surrender, have undergone a thorough change of heart. In no country in the world is militarism so thoroughly reprobated. All Japan's energies are now concentrated on remaining a friendly civilian state. Possibly the very completeness of the emotional swing is suspicious. What is today so violently renounced may tomorrow be once more violently espoused. But all the signs are that the world has, as the result of the war, gained a new Japan.

At the end of the war an international tribunal was set up by the allies in order to put on trial a large number of those who had allegedly been responsible for war crimes. The Japanese had wished to reserve a trial of war prisoners to themselves as a condition of Japanese surrender, but they had been overruled. At the major War Crimes Tribunal in Tokyo, twenty-five Japanese leaders were sentenced, seven of them to death, others to life imprisonment: among these were General Tojo, the Prime Minister; General Koiso, his successor; the wily court chamberlain, Marquis Kido, who played so large a part in bringing about Japan's surrender; Shigenori Togo, the Foreign Minister who had showed a most un-Japanese independence of judgement; and Koki Hirota, another former Prime Minister. The conveners even proposed trying Prince Konoye, but he evaded arrest by poisoning himself. These doubtful proceedings went like a swath through all those who had been in any way prominent in Japanese politics of the period. The biographical footnotes of a book on Japanese history at this time make heavy reading because of the end of most of the characters. The major good that came out of these proceedings at Tokyo was that they are the most complete, exhaustive account of Japanese politics in the militarist period.

Other war crimes trials were held in Hong Kong, Singapore, Borneo and elsewhere in the recent Japanese Empire. Detainees were arraigned for cruelty towards local populations and prisoners of war, and over 900 were executed. The thought of these melancholy figures, and the deeds which in many cases preceded this toll of life, leads to the reflection that had the war had a different result, the subsequent years might have been the age of Japanese imperialism. Asia has been spared that. The war, with all its horrors, had achieved this positive good. A reluctant admiration for Japan's military feats must not block out the consciousness of the sinister shadow which for a time hung over the eastern world.

Search the record how one will, it is almost impossible to find anything good to say of the Japanese Empire. Its liquidation was an unqualified benefit to the world. In the years before the conflict, Japan had had its opportunity to develop its empire in miniature – in Korea, in Formosa, and in the parts of China which it came to dominate – and in this exhibition of the Japanese spirit it failed to show any virtues. An empire, which by its definition is a political structure housing peoples of different cultures and languages, is different from the nation-state, which is the most approved political form in the twentieth century. Nations object to being included in an empire. Empires are out-of-date. But some empires are more tolerable than others. They may have qualities which actively catch the imagination of their people. In the case of a very few, their peoples will actually be willing to die in their defence, though instances of this have become increasingly rare. The classic case, in comparison with which other empires may be judged, was Rome of antiquity. That empire seems to have offered a wider life, richer opportunities, a larger destiny, than could be looked for within the confines of small states.

The Japanese Empire, if it is judged from its beginnings, was not at all likely to develop into one of these rarer structures. In its origin it was essentially primitive and of petty conception. It was put together by conquest, and its prime aim was to plunder the subjected peoples for the benefit of the Japanese. The empire offered hardly anything to its citizens which led them to take pride in membership of it beyond a pride in being Asian. This should not be neglected. The Japanese made considerable play with pan-Asianism. The contemporary writing is all about the joy of being Asian. It was the outstanding fact of the time. But it was not long before the contrast between Japanese idealism and Japanese practice took away this enthusiasm.

The Japanese system was founded on no great code of law. In its organization it embodied no exhilarating concepts such as have led men elsewhere into giving their loyalty, even if divided – concepts such as liberty, equality and fraternity; the career open to talents; the greatest good of the greatest number or restraint of the evil of exploitation. The Japanese Empire signified no large cult of reason, no vision, no distinctive habits of thought or behaviour, no corpus of books which set the tone of people's thought, no pattern of individual behaviour which might have given people a liberating vision. It was the starting-place of no system of philosophy which was likely to appeal to men of all races and different cultures: in other words, it lacked the universalist appeal. The most to which it invited its citizens was to the enjoyment of Japanese culture, and there the difficulty was that, though this culture is not inferior, it is one which most Asians find uncongenial and it is at best provincial and not a universal civilization. In particular, the Japanese language was unsuited as a medium of communication for holding the political machinery together. Nobody talked Japanese as a form of intellectual pleasure, as the subjects of the French Empire often spoke French: nobody preened himself upon its use: the language was thought to be muzzy and imprecise.

Japanese culture is especially strong on the inculcation of the correct attitudes for aesthetic appreciation: but aesthetics has never been strong enough to hold an empire together. Besides, this quality of mind was already considered out-of-date in Japan itself.

Calling on the people of its empire to share Japanese culture was summoning them to a Barmecide feast. Responding to the call, the

Chinese felt themselves sitting with more primitive people than themselves. They found that Japanese culture was a tiresome and constricting limitation on their minds.

A peculiarly evil feature of the system was that it had within itself no ability to evolve, to change, to end itself, and to merge with other forces in Asia. It would endure only as long as Japanese military power lasted: it was sustained by that and by that alone: it invited head-on collision with all the emerging forces of Asia, and if it had not been destroyed in war, it would sooner or later have led to bloody wars of liberation.

When the war was over, when Japan had given up the pretence at founding a new political order, and gave free play to its natural talents, the Japanese surprised the world, and themselves, by solving their problems by simple hard work, and without any use of force or creation of grandiose political structures. They recovered economically in the minimum of time; they rapidly became a beacon-light in Asia, they proved that an Asian people could save itself by its own exertions. And all this without even the dream of empire. Energy, skill in planning, imagination in enterprise, ability in the application of techniques to the economic processes proved enough to get Japan over all its obstacles; and Japan has discovered the political advantages in having a foreign policy which is audacious by reason of its modesty.

*

The war also precipitated everywhere the downfall of western power in Asia. The western powers withdrew from China. Treaty Ports were at an end: also the rights of extra-territoriality. Within two years Britain withdrew from India. This was a change which plainly doomed the French Empire in Indo-China, and the Dutch in Indonesia. Within ten years, they had each of them passed away. They did not go voluntarily, as did the British Empire in India; they attempted to stay, and they were willing to go to war against the national parties which rose up to extrude them. But they were too weak to prevail. Moreover they were too much concerned with their problems in Europe to be able to give the war their whole-hearted attention.

The Japanese Empire having been destroyed and the western empires put down, a power vacuum existed which only the nationalist organizations could fill. These were left to organize most of Asia in the pattern they desired. The West, including the United States, tried to influence them in one way or another, using their economic power to make their will effective, and in the case of the US, their armaments when the

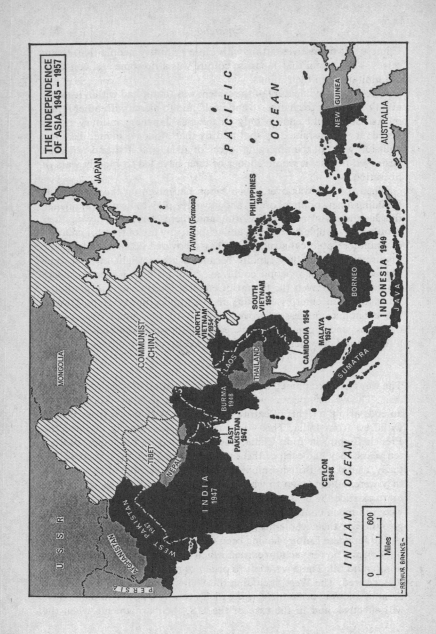

THE INDEPENDENCE
OF ASIA 1945 – 1957

U S S R

MONGOLIA

COMMUNIST CHINA

JAPAN

TAIWAN (Formosa)

TIBET

NEPAL

WEST PAKISTAN 1947

AFGHANISTAN

PERSIA

INDIA 1947

EAST PAKISTAN 1947

BURMA 1948

CEYLON 1948

LAOS

THAILAND

NORTH VIETNAM 1954

SOUTH VIETNAM 1954

CAMBODIA 1954

MALAYA 1957

PHILIPPINES 1946

BORNEO

SUMATRA

JAVA

INDONESIA 1949

NEW GUINEA

AUSTRALIA

PACIFIC OCEAN

INDIAN OCEAN

0   600
Miles

~ ARTHUR BANKS ~

situation did not respond to economic manipulation. By indirect means they hoped to prevail as effectively as in the days when they sat with political power in Delhi and in the eastern capitals. This was the phase of neo-colonialism, and the emancipated countries of Asia have been on their guard against it and have sought to render themselves really free.

*

China, released from the incubus of an imperial Japan, has been free to develop as the inward forces in the country directed. Within four years of the ending of the war China became communist. The excessive corruption, the paralysis of will and venal incompetence of the later years of the Kuomintang were increased by its unnatural isolation from the rest of the country. Once this was removed its downfall was inevitable.

The prolonged agony which had been suffered by the Chinese people as the twentieth century wore on, opened the way to a violent remedy. The chief leaders of the Kuomintang escaped the vengeance of the opposing party by retiring, with vast fortunes, to the island of Formosa whence they kept up, under an American umbrella, a somewhat ludicrous show of still exercising an influence in world affairs. In the first flood of revenge, many of the landlords, who had lived for so long in the sun of prosperity in China, were violently put down, with sufferings as cruel as any which they had, by past insensibility and negligence, occasioned among the poor. Later, 're-education' was the term used to describe the method by which the bourgeoisie were broken in. The mass of the people were liberated into a new life of undreamed-of sufficiency in living standards and educational opportunity: as against this, freedom for the individual – of thought or self-direction – was largely absent. In foreign relations, communist China's extreme isolationism, and the mutual suspicions between it and the United States, have kept the world on edge, but from time to time have shown signs of relaxing. There is no doubt of the greatly recovered prestige of China since the war, and its natural re-emergence as a major power in Asia.

*

What had been the effects in India? Great though the upheaval had been in India's domestic life, the war simply affected the pace of the development of its history, and accelerated the divorce of India and Britain: it did not give events an essentially new turn. Its chief effect was to bring to a head the emancipation of the country, and to accelerate the industrialization. Though these two occurrences were undoubtedly

CHINESE COMMUNISM 1934-1950

USSR

MONGOLIA

Under Soviet Control
1945-1948

Vladivostok

Mukden

PEKING

Port
Arthur

NORTH
KOREA
Occupied by USSR
1945-1948
Cease fire line
1953

Yenan

SOUTH
KOREA
Occupied
by US
1945-1949

Seoul

Nanking

JAPAN
Occupied by US
1945-1952

OKINAWA
U.S. military
Government since
1951

DAITO Is.
U.S. Administered
since 1945

MATSU

QUEMOY

TAIWAN
(FORMOSA)
Main Nationalist Stronghold under
Chiang Kai-Shek

Hong Kong
British since
1842

Macao
Portugese
since 1557

FRENCH

HAINAN

INDO

SOUTH

THAILAND

Cease fire line
1954

CHINA

CHINA

SEA

Saigon

★ Communists active in these areas 1934.
◄━━ Mao Tse-tung's `Long March' 1934-1936.
◄┅┅ Soviet attacks against Japanese-
occupied China 1945.
◄━━ Retreat of Chinese Nationalist forces 1949.
▦ Chinese Nationalist-held areas following
expulsion from mainland 1949.

THE GROWTH OF CHINESE COMMUNISM
▦ Areas held by communists 1936-1949.
▦ Communist acquisitions April 1947.
▦ Communist acquisitions July 1948.
▦ Communist acquisitions December 1949.
▦ Communist acquisitions 1950 onwards.

0   300
Miles

a consequence of the war, one of them, the withdrawal of the British, had been bound to happen in any case. Probably all that the war did was to advance this by a year or two. Everybody who looked with the eye of history on India at any time from 1930 onwards must have foreseen that the end of the British Raj was approaching. The precise steps by which it would come about were the only thing doubtful.

Yet in one fateful respect the war gave an unexpected twist to the long process of the freedom struggle by the Indian Congress. In the circumstances of wartime politics, a sudden and accelerated growth took place in the Moslem League. It had been provoked by the Congress success; it was already apparent before the war; but the war acted like a hot-house in compressing into a few years the development which might otherwise have been spread over decades. The Moslem League, which increased in strength so radically, was emboldened to press for the creation of the Moslem state of Pakistan.

Today this state has come into being. It is an exceptional creation which reminds us of the continuing force of religion in politics. Religion was the driving force in making for the existence of this state. As such, the creation of Pakistan seems to be a digression from the ideas of the Enlightenment, and a return to the Middle Ages. Its establishment was accompanied by forebodings and very great reluctance on the part of the British government. If independence had come in 1937, instead of 1947, it would undoubtedly have been given to a united India. The intensity of the divisions did not appear until later: they only manifested themselves in their full significance during the war years. But an undivided India would not have held together. The Hindu–Moslem cleavage would have declared itself under the strain of self-government. Sooner or later, unified government would have been made impossible: communal tension, and eventually communal civil war, would have brought it to a standstill. The same process would have taken place which later placed obstacles in the path of Nigeria, which, when it became independent, had appeared so gigantic and stable.*

It is easy to forget how at the end of the war the decision to partition the sub-continent was on a knife edge. Without the war, the British would hardly have considered the creation of Pakistan as a necessary act.

---

* This was written in 1968. Since then serious divisions have arisen between East and West Pakistan which have made an end of their conjunction in a single state. One of the fundamental factors which have produced this break has been the immense obstacle of geography, which a look at the map on page 882 makes clear. In addition, the populations of the two wings differed in race, language and character, and had little to combine them, except religion.

The state of Pakistan is therefore one of the monuments to the war with Japan. It is an unlikely one: nobody today sees any special connection between its history and that of Japan: yet the two are linked causally.

*

For the US the war was an incident in its rise to be one of the two greatest powers in the world. It received its baptism of fire. For many years before 1941, America had distorted the natural play of international affairs by utterly refusing to act the part of a Great Power. Its people, in general and except at certain conjunctures, appeared to be without the political instincts of the citizens of a major state. Because of their unique behaviour, and of the influence of this upon the official conduct of the American government, the United States, at a time when fate and its economic power called upon it to exert tremendous influence, limited its voice in world affairs to be hardly of more account than that of a third-class European state. Doubtless the reasons for this lay far back in American history, and touch on George Washington, the fear of 'entangling Alliances' and the belief that foreign governments were very wily and would inevitably bamboozle an American government which was rash enough to negotiate with them. But the United States had been in the First World War; its reaction from this experience and withdrawal into isolation, had been a setback to normal growth. When Pearl Harbor happened, the United States, in a world at war, still had an army of about the same size as Sweden's; it still made the gestures, to which it had accustomed itself before its entry in 1917 into the First World War, of being 'too proud to fight'. It is true that American ideas and American business influence were very prevalent, as also was the uncontrollable propulsive power of American culture. But the American state did not set itself to propagate them.

In the course of the war, the United States developed amazingly. It grew with the alarming speed of Alice when she swallowed the potion in the bottle marked 'Drink me'. It began the war with organs and Ministries for taking part in foreign affairs which seem like toys. But, with the creative wind of improvisation which swept through the US, the institutions developed rapidly. Simultaneously its public opinion, and the institutions by which this was made effective, grew in self-confidence. By the end of the war, the United States was moving in international affairs with professionalism and boldness.

American democracy was to show that while it was surprisingly persevering as long as the war lasted, it was, once peace was restored, capable of a rapid, revolutionary change of mood. The fires died as swiftly as they had blazed fiercely. Within seven years America had come to feel towards Japan as towards its protégé: and had transferred to Japan some of the abnormally cordial feeling which it had held towards China, until China became communist.

Finally, this was probably the last war which Great Britain took part in as a world power, certainly an Asian power. For the last time Britain manoeuvred as a government with interest and concern in every part of the world, especially in Asia. It ended its Asian history with panache. It was nevertheless an end. Within two years of the dropping of the bomb on Hiroshima, Britain ended its responsibility for India. By this one act it terminated its empire everywhere in Asia; for a British Empire in Asia which excluded India was not really a possibility.

Great Britain, at that time, was more than a small country, with a restricted part to play, as seemed to befit one of a cluster of west European islands. By the accident of history, by the energy of its peoples it had, for the previous two centuries, been shot out of its natural sphere. It had risen to a height of power and prestige which obviously it could not retain but to which people in Britain had become accustomed. The leaders of institutional life had risen to their opportunity, and for some decades this had been reflected in politics. These seemed to have an influence totally out of the proportion which would naturally be expected of such a numerically small people. Living in Britain at this time had a magnifying effect, so that what was done seemed to be done with a deep sense of responsibility. The proceedings of the parliament at Westminster were gazed at by so many people that those who took part in it had the uneasy sense of acting on a great stage of the world, and being the cynosure of the world's eyes. This sense was often embarrassing. It often invested relatively trivial affairs with a false glamour. It would have been healthier if they had been dealt with without these overtones. Even so, thought in Britain was still apt to be large; small conceptions were still at a discount. It was this quality which perhaps most separates the Britain of those days from what it has become.

Within ten years of Indian independence, Britain had liquidated practically all that was left of its Asian empire. Ceylon, Malaya, Burma – let them go all. It was not a matter of no longer discouraging their instinct to break away from the empire which had once been thought of as a supra-national organization, a house where all the rising nationalisms of the empire might, of their own free will, find asylum. They were positively conducted to the door. They were given a golden handshake – financially a rather mean one – and were sped into independence with expressions of goodwill.

Britain, which had enjoyed in Asia the great romantic period of its history, turned back, as a result of the war, and after an interval for readjustment, to the more sober task of discovering the contrast between being a world power and being a small country off the north-east corner coast of Europe. It became preoccupied with the total revolution which should adapt Britain for its new role; with anxious debate as to whether it should think once more to become a European power as it had been under its Angevin monarchs, or whether it could exist as a small island alone.

It is irony that, at the end, Britain finds itself in very similar circumstances to those which worried Japan at the start of this history. Transpose the islands off the north coast of Asia to the islands off the northwest of Europe, and the parallel is strangely apt. Its history, as Dean Acheson rightly diagnosed – only to be the object of bitter vituperation by people in Britain – was that it had lost an empire and not found a new part to play. The British may count themselves fortunate that the public opinion of the world has moved on, and it is unlikely that Britain will be tempted to try and solve its problems in a similar way to Japan.

*

And the human side? What of the war for the Little Peterkins of Asia?

The conflict had a recognizable pattern, though there were so many confusing cross-currents. One purpose of this book has been to trace it out. It settled the influences which were to be dominant in the lives of people for the next generation or so – until new pressures meet new obstacles, and all is again in the melting pot, the issue having again to be settled by conflict. For this last great cataclysm, the price paid in human life and suffering was truly prodigious. The numbers of those killed in the war on all fronts have been analysed in the earlier Epilogue. Of two of the great Asian families of people engaged, the Chinese casualties, difficult to estimate, have been given by Chiang Kai-shek in his book, *A Summing-Up at Seventy*, as over 3 million. 'These figures,' he says, 'do not include the heavy losses in life and property sustained by the people in general.'* Japanese losses in battle and air-attack have been estimated at around 2 million. Of the people elsewhere in Asia, by far the largest proportion had no wish to take part in the quarrel. They

* Chiang Kai-shek: *A Summing-Up at Seventy*, Harrap, 1957.

neither understood, nor cared for, nor were consulted about, the objects of conflict. From first to last they viewed the war as a fact of destructive nature, which everyone in his senses sought to evade, but which was fated to make enormous waves. Those who voluntarily went to war, or felt passionately about the issues to the extent of being genuinely willing to die for them, were very few. Submitting to the economic inducements because of poverty and destitution was the nearest that most combatants came to acting by a reasonable decision. The only Asian people of whom this was not really true were the fatally indoctrinated Japanese.

It is, however, economic pressure alone which interests nine tenths of the population of Asia. It is idle to think that people living in conditions of Asian poverty, and with so much mass illiteracy, can be capable of acting in any other way. Any system of government which offers them the prospects of seeing a barely tolerable life, barely tolerable though it be, for six months ahead, will be more than welcome. Frills of government, freedom, choice, are suspect to them. Those combatants who came from a society in which the compulsion of hunger was less present were swept together by conscription, and had even less say in their destiny.

The war was probably the last major conflict which will be fought in Asia in which all the Asian antagonists except Japan were predominantly agrarian. This gave the war its peculiar, and rather antiquarian flavour. Time will ensure that, before another great contest can happen, large segments of society will have become heavily industrialized, and, with industrialization, will have come the special type of social organization which renders society so different in behaviour from that which was traditional.

Even the very few of the educated classes – the Chinese university professors, the Japanese, the Indian leisured upper classes – who had the inclination and the ability to trace out the pattern of events behind the confusion, to understand the whys and wherefors, derived little consolation when they were compelled to live among a collapsing economy and the dangers of loot and arson from the fact that to them was vouchsafed the understanding of what the war was all about.

It is clear that, to the many millions who fought and suffered unvocally, to the ignorant armies clashing by night, unselfconsciously, those who survived owe an inexpiable debt. It seems, at some points in history, that only through a convulsion involving millions is understanding painfully acquired. 'The cut worm forgives the plough', said the poet Blake. By invoking this kind of charity, there can perhaps be forgiveness for the ungovernable fury of the instruments by which history is made.

Chronological Skeleton

1937		July 7	Japanese attack Chinese at Marco Polo Bridge
		Dec 14	Fall of Nanking to the Japanese
1938		July 11	Japanese-Soviet battle of Changkufeng
		Oct	Chiang Kai-Shek's Government withdraws to Chungking
		Oct 21	Fall of Canton to the Japanese
		Oct 25	Fall of Hankow to the Japanese
		Nov 5	Prince Konoye declares 'New Order' in Asia
		May–Sept	Battle of Nomonhan between Japan and USSR
1939		Sept 1	Germans invade Poland
	Sept 3 Great Britain and France declare war	Sept 17	USSR invades Poland

1939

Oct — USSR exacts mutual assistance treaties from Estonia, Latvia and Lithuania

Nov 30 — USSR invades Finland

Dec 17 — *Graf Spee* scuttled

1940

Mar 12 — Finland capitulates

Mar 30 — Setting up of Wang Ching-wei's puppet government at Nanking

Apr 9 — Germans invade Denmark and Norway

May — British occupy Iceland

May 10 — Germans invade Low Countries and France. Churchill Prime Minister

May 15 — Dutch lay down arms

May 20 — Germans reach English Channel

May 28 — Belgium capitulates

May 27–June 4 — Dunkirk

June 10 — Italy declares war

June 10 — Italy declares war

June 14   Germans enter Paris
June 22   France signs armistice
July   3   British action against French fleet at Mers-el-Kebir
July 10–   Battle of Britain
Sept 15

July–   Closing of the Burma
Oct   Road

Aug   4   Italians invade British and French Somaliland

Sept   3   Anglo-US bases destroyers deal

Sept 14   Italians invade Egypt

Sept 27   Tripartite Pact between Japan, Germany and Italy

Oct   Hitler confers with Mussolini (4), Franco (23), Pétain (24)
Oct 28   Italians invade Greece

Nov   5   Roosevelt re-elected President

Nov 11   British attack Italian fleet at Taranto

Nov   Hungary, Rumania and Slovakia brought into Tripartite Pact

1940			
	Dec	British Offensive in North Africa captures Tobruk (Jan 22) and Benghazi (Feb 7)	Dec — American embargo on sales of scrap iron and war material to Japan

1941		
Mar 11 Lend-Lease Act signed	Mar 1	Bulgaria joins Tripartite Pact
	Mar 27	Simovic coup: Yugoslavia refuses to join Tripartite Pact
	Mar 28	Battle of Cape Matapan
	Mar 31	First German offensive in North Africa: takes Benghazi and invests Tobruk
Apr US occupies Greenland	Apr 6	Germans invade Yugoslavia and Greece	Apr 13 Non-aggression pact signed between Japan and Russia
	May 2	British invade Iraq
	May 20–June 2	Germans take Crete
May 27 *Bismarck* sunk		

June 8 British defeat Vichy French in Syria and Lebanon

June 22 Germans invade USSR

July 2 Japan decides on extensive moves into Indo-China

July US joins occupation of Iceland

July 12 Anglo-Soviet Treaty of Mutual Assistance

July 28 & 29 US, British and Dutch East Indies impose embargoes on the sale of oil and steel to Japan

Aug 14 Roosevelt-Churchill conference, Placentia Bay: Atlantic Charter

Aug 17 Fall of Kiev

Aug 25 Anglo-Russian occupation of Iran

Sept 8 Leningrad invested

Sept US 'shoot at sight' order

1941

Oct 17 General Tojo replaces Konoye as Prime Minister of Japan

Dec 7 Japan sends a declaration of war to the US

Dec 7 Japan attacks Pearl Harbor, the Philippines, Hong Kong and Malaya

Dec 8 US and Great Britain declare war on Japan

Dec 9 China officially declares war on Japan and Germany

Dec 10 Japanese sink the *Prince of Wales* and the *Repulse*

Dec 10 Japan captures Guam

Dec 11 Japan attacks Burma

Dec 23 Fall of Wake Island

Oct 30 Sebastopol invested. German thrust for Moscow

Dec 1 Russian counter-attack

Dec 11 Germany and Italy declare war on US

Dec 24 British re-capture Benghazi

1942 June	Destruction of PQ 17
June 4	Battle of Midway Island
June 4	Japanese attack on the Aleutian Islands
July	Regular raids on Ruhr and Hamburg begin
July 3	Fall of Sebastopol
Aug 7	US landings on the Solomon Islands
Aug 9	Civil Disobedience campaign announced in India
Aug 12–15	Stalin–Churchill meeting in Moscow
Aug 17	First US raid on Germany
Aug 19	Dieppe raid
Aug 31	Battle of Alam el Halfa: German-Italian advance stayed
Sept 13	Battles for Stalingrad begin
Sept 21	Opening of the Arakan offensive under Wavell
Sept 21	Opening of US offensive in New Guinea

Nov   Record months for sinking by U-boats

Nov   Regular raids on Berlin begin

Oct 23 Battle of Alamein

Nov 8   Allied landings in Morocco and Algeria

Nov 11 Germans occupy southern France and Tunisia

1943

Jan 14–24 Casablanca conference

Jan German retreat from Caucasus

Jan 11 Treaty relinquishing extraterritorial rights between the US, Britain and China

Feb 2 German surrender at Stalingrad. Russians recover Kursk (8) and Rostov (14)

Feb 8 Wingate's expedition into Burma

Mar 2 Battle of the Bismarck Sea

Mar 29 Battle of the Mareth

Apr 18 Death of Admiral Yamamoto, at Bougainville

Apr 19–May 16 Rising and extinction of Warsaw Ghetto

1943

May 11   US begin to liberate Aleutian Islands

May 12   German-Italian surrender in Tunisia

May 17   Attack on Ruhr dams

May 26   Discovery of Katyn massacre and severance of Russo-Polish relations

June 29   US landings in New Guinea

July 5–Aug 6   Battles in the Kursk salient and Russian recovery of Orel and Belgorod

July 10   Invasion of Sicily

July 25   Dismissal of Mussolini

Aug 17   US daylight raids on Regensburg and Schweinfurt

Aug 17   Quebec Conference: setting up of South-East Asia Command, under Mountbatten

Aug 23   Russians recover Kharkov

Sept   Russians recover Novorossisk and Smolensk (25)

Sept 3   Invasion of Calabria and signing of Italian surrender

Sept 9   Landings at Salerno

Sept 12   Rescue of Mussolini

1944

Oct 13	Italy declares war on Germany
Oct	Russians recover Zaporozhe (14) and Dnepropetrovsk (25)
Nov 6	Russians recover Kiev
Nov 5–6	Greater East Asia Conference held in Tokyo
Nov	US landings in the Gilbert Islands
Nov 22–26	Cairo Conference: unconditional surrender demanded of Japan
Nov 28–Dec 1	Teheran Conference
Dec	Opening of the assault on the Marshall Islands

1944

Jan 12	Landings at Anzio
Jan 27	Leningrad relieved
Feb 15	Bombing of Monte Cassino
Feb–Mar	Beginning of Japanese offensive on borders of India, siege of Imphal and Kohima
Apr 2	Russians enter Rumania
Apr 17	Renewed Japanese offensive in China
Apr–July	US advances through Dutch New Guinea

1944

Western Front	Italy	Eastern Front	Pacific / Asia
June 6 Invasion of Normandy	May 17 Germans evacuate Monte Cassino	May Russians recover Sebastopol and Crimea	June 15 Americans invade Saipan
June 12 First V 1 s hit London	June 4 Americans enter Rome	June 23–July 3 Russians recover Belorussia	June 15 First B-29 raid on Japan
July 20 Attempt on Hitler's life		July 23 Russians take Lublin and establish Polish Committee of National Liberation	July 4 Japanese defeated at Imphal
			July 9 Fall of Saipan
			July 18 Resignation of General Tojo

Western Front	Italy	Eastern Front / Balkans	Pacific / Asia
Aug 15 Allied landings in southern France	Aug Kesselring mans the Gothic Line	Aug 1–Oct 2 Warsaw rising against the Germans	Aug US recovery of Tinian and Guam
Aug 17 Final victories in Normandy. Paris rises			Sept Allied counter-offensive in Burma, under Mountbatten
Aug 24 Leclercq enters Paris			
Sept 3 Brussels liberated		Sept 5 USSR declares war on Bulgaria	
Sept 8 First V 2s hit London		Sept 12 Rumania signs armistice	
Sept 17–30 Arnhem operations fail		Sept 19 Finland signs armistice	
		Oct 20 Partisans and Russians enter Belgrade	Oct 20 US landings in the Phillippines
			Oct 25 Battle of Leyte Gulf
			Nov Beginning of systematic US bombing of Japan
Dec 16 German offensive in the Ardennes			

1945

Jan 12	General Russian offensive begins
Jan 17	Russians enter Warsaw
Feb 4–12	Yalta Conference
Feb 13	Surrender of Budapest
Feb 13–14	Dresden raids
Mar 7	Americans cross the Rhine at Remagen
Apr 12	Death of Roosevelt
Apr 13	Russians enter Vienna
Apr 16	Last Russian offensive begins
Apr 28	Death of Mussolini
Apr 30	Death of Hitler
May 2	Berlin in Russian hands. Germans in Italy capitulate
May 5	Prague rises
May 7	Germans surrender at Rheims
May 9	Russians enter Prague
July 17	Potsdam Conference

Jan 9	US landings on Luzon
Apr 1	US landings on Okinawa
Apr 4	Japanese Prime Minister Koiso resigns and is replaced by Suzuki
Apr	Russia refuses to renew her non-aggression pact with Japan
May 3	Japanese surrender Rangoon
July 26	Allies at Potsdam call on Japan to surrender
Aug 6	Hiroshima
Aug 8	Russia declares war on Japan
Aug 9	Nagasaki
Aug 14	Japan capitulates
Sept 2	Japanese surrender signed

Books: the Western Hemisphere and General Bibliography

The bibliography of the Second World War is not only enormous but is growing so rapidly that any list of recommendations becomes quickly outdated. Nevertheless some attempt is made here to guide those who want to read more. By and large only books available in English are cited; but this is not a hard and fast rule and some exceptionally interesting works, not as yet translated, have been included.

ORIGINS

The best short introduction to the immediate prelude in Europe is C. Thorne, *The Approach of War* (London, 1967). For remoter roots A. J. P. Taylor *The Origins of the Second World War* (London, 1961, reprinted with new introduction 1963), A. Bullock *Hitler and the Origins of the War, 1939–45* (Raleigh Lectures, Proceedings of the British Academy, vol. 55, 1967), E. Wiskemann *Europe of the Dictators* (London, 1966) and *Czechs and Germans* (Oxford, 1938), J. Wheeler-Bennett *The Nemesis of Power* (London, 1953), M. Baumont *Les origines de la deuxième guerre mondiale* (Paris, 1969), E. Robertson *Hitler's Pre-war Policy and Military Plans, 1933–39* (London, 1963). On Munich K. Eubank *Munich* (Norman, Okla., 1963), and J. Wheeler-Bennett *Munich: Prologue to Tragedy* (London, 1964). On appeasement W. R. Rock *Appeasement on Trial* (Hamden, Conn., 1966), and M. Gilbert *The Roots of Appeasement* (London, 1966).

HITLER, NAZISM, FASCISM

The basic books on Hitler are A. Hitler *Mein Kampf* (London, 1939) and A. Bullock *Hitler: A Study in Tyranny* (London, 1952, rev. 1965; Pelican). For further reading A. Kubizek *Young Hitler* (London, 1954), F. Jetzinger *Hitlers Jugend* (Vienna, 1956), W. A. Jenks *Vienna and the Young Hitler* (New York, 1960), E. Calic *Unmasked* (London, 1971), H, Rauschning *Hitler Speaks* (London, 1939). On the Nazi party and Nazi State K. D. Bracher *The German Dictatorship* (London, 1971), H. Krausnick (et. al.) *Anatomy of the SS State* (London, 1968), M.

Broszat *German National Socialism* (New York, 1966), G. H. Stein *The Waffen SS* (London, 1966), F. Neumann *Behemoth: The Structure and Practice of National Socialism* (London, 1942), J. Nyomarkay *Charisma and Functionalism in the Nazi Party* (Minneapolis, 1967), W. S. Allen *The Nazi Seizure of Power, The Experience of a Single German Town 1930–1935* (London, 1966), B. Granzow *A Mirror of Nazism* (London, 1964), D. Schoenbaum *Hitler's Social Revolution* (London, 1967). For further background on Nazism and fascism E. Nolte *Three Faces of Fascism* (London, 1965), G. L. Mosse *The Crisis of German Ideology* (London, 1966), and *Nazi Culture* (London, 1966), H. Kohn *The Mind of Germany* (London, 1961), A. Hamilton *The Appeal of Fascism 1919– 1945* (London, 1971), D. Gasman *The Scientific Origins of National Socialism* (London, 1971), R. Butler *The Roots of National Socialism* (London, 1941), F. Meinecke *The German Catastrophe* (Cambridge, Mass., 1950), P. Gay *Weimar Culture* (London, 1969), A. J. Nicholls *Weimar and the Rise of Hitler* (London, 1968), S. J. Woolf, ed. *European Fascism* (London, 1968), J. Weiss *The Fascist Tradition* (New York, 1967), B. Moore *The Social Origins of Dictatorship and Democracy* (London, 1967), J. L. Talmon *The Origins of Totalitarian Democracy* (London, 1952), H. Arendt *The Origins of Totalitarianism* (London, 1958). On Nazi relations with the German army and churches the best books to begin with are R. J. O'Neill *The German Army and the Nazi Party, 1923–39* (London, 1966), T. Taylor *Sword and Swastika* (London, 1952), F. L. Carsten *Reichswehr and Politics, 1918–1933* (Oxford, 1956), J. S. Conway *The Nazi Persecution of the Churches, 1939–45* (London, 1958). On Italian fascism and the German-Italian alliance F. Chabod *A History of Italian Fascism* (London, 1963), F. W. Deakin *The Brutal Friendship* (London, 1962), E. Wiskemann *Fascism in Italy: Its Development and Influence* (London, 1969), C. Seton-Watson *Italy from Liberalism to Fascism* (London, 1967), I. Kirkpatrick *Mussolini* (London, 1964). Finally, and against complacency, M. Picard *Hitler in uns selbst* (Zurich, 1946).

ANTI-SEMITISM

The roots of anti-semitism are still being uncovered by psychologists, sociologists and historians. Besides general studies of fascism see M. A. Meyer *The Origins of the Modern Jew* (New York, 1967), G. Reitlinger *The Final Solution* (London, 1953), L. Poliakoff *Harvest of Hate* (London, 1956), N. Cohn *Warrant for Genocide* (New York, 1967), A. D. Morse *Why Six Million Died* (London, 1968). On the papacy and the

Jews, S. Friedländer *Pius XII and the Third Reich* (London, 1968), P. E. Lapide *The last three Popes and the Jews* (London, 1967), C. Falconi *The Silence of Pius XII* (London, 1970) and the series of Records and Documents of the Holy See relating to the Second World War now in the course of publication.

MILITARY HISTORY AND STRATEGY

All aspects are or are being covered by the many, massive and often excellent volumes of the official American and British war histories. Overall views are given in B. H. Liddell Hart *History of the Second World War* (London, 1970), J. F. C. Fuller *The Second World War* (London, 1948), G. Wright *The Ordeal of Total War, 1939–45* (New York, 1968), M. P. Gallagher *The Soviet History of World War II* (New York, 1968), H. Michel *La seconde guerre mondiale* (2 vols., Paris, 1968–9). On strategy see in particular K. R. Greenfield *American Strategy in World War II* (Baltimore, Md., 1963), S. E. Morison *American Contributions to the Strategy of World War II* (London, 1958), M. Howard *The Mediterranean Strategy in the Second World War* (London, 1968), A. Bryant, ed. *The Turn of the Tide* (London. 1957) and *Triumph in the West* (extracts from and a commentary upon Lord Alanbrooke's papers) (London, 1958), K. R. Greenfield, ed. *Command Decisions* (London, 1960), F. Halder *Hitler as War Lord* (London, 1950), F. Gilbert *Hitler Directs the War* (New York, 1950), F. H. Hinsley *Hitler's Strategy* (Cambridge, 1951), C. Bekker *The Luftwaffe War Diaries* (London, 1967), and the official British volumes entitled *Grand Strategy* (Official Series, q.v.).

On particular campaigns or battles H.-A. Jacobsen and J. Rohwer *Decisive Battles of World War II* (London, 1965), V. Tanner *The Winter War* (in Finland) (Stanford, Calif., 1957), D. Clark *Three Days to Catastrophe* (ditto) (New York, 1966), J. L. Moulton *The Norwegian Campaign 1940* (New York, 1966), T. Taylor *The March of Conquest* (Hitler's victories in the west) (London, 1958) and *The Breaking Wave* (the Battle of Britain) (London, 1967), D. Wood and D. Dempster *The Narrow Margin* (London, 1961), B. Collier *The Battle of Britain* (London, 1962), A. Lee *Blitz on Britain* (London, 1960), R. Wheatley *Operation Sea Lion* (London, 1958), V. Goure *The Siege of Leningrad* (Stanford, Calif., 1962), H. E. Salisbury *The Siege of Leningrad* (London, 1969), P. Carell *Hitler's Wars on Russia* (London, 1964). A. Clark *Barbarossa* (New York, 1964), V. I. Chuikov *The Beginning of the Road* (London, 1963) and *The End of the Third Reich* (London, 1967),

I. S. Konev *L'invasion du III Reich* (Paris, 1968), A. Seaton *The Russo-German War 1941–45* (London, 1971), C. Ryan *The Last Battle* (London, 1966), C. Malaparte *The Volga rises in Europe* (London, 1959), I. M. G. Stewart *The Struggle for Crete* (London, 1966), C. Buckley *Greece and Crete 1941* (London, 1952), J. Strawson *The Battle for North Africa* (London, 1969), P. Guedalla *Middle East 1940–42: a study in air power* (London, 1944), C. Barnett *The Desert Generals* (London, 1960), F. Majdalany *The Battle of El Alamein* (London, 1965), D. Macintyre *The Battle for the Mediterranean* (London, 1964), W. G. F. Jackson *The War in Italy* (London, 1967), G. A. Shepperd *The Italian Campaign, 1943–1945* (London, 1968), D. W. Orgill *The Gothic Line* (London, 1967), S. E. Morison *The Battle of the Atlantic* (History of the United States Naval Operations in World War II, vol. 7–15, London, 1952–62), P. K. Kemp *Victory at Sea, 1939–45* (London, 1957), S. W. Roskill *The Navy at War* (London, 1967), B. B. Schofield *The Russian Convoys* (London, 1964), C. Bauer *The Battle of Arnhem* (London, 1966), C. Hibbert *The Battle of Arnhem* (London, 1962), J. Nobécourt *Hitler's Last Gamble: The Battle of the Ardennes* (London, 1967), J. Toland *Battle: the Story of the Bulge* (London, 1960), H. Essame *The Battle for Germany* (London, 1969), S. Westphal *The German Army in the West* (London, 1951), M. Schulman *The German Defeat in the West* (rev. edn New York, 1968), A. Verrier *Bomber Offensive* (London, 1968), C. K. Webster and N. Frankland *The Strategic Air Offensive* (London, 1961), N. Frankland *The Bombing Offensive against Germany* (London, 1965), H. Rumpf *The Bombing of Germany* (London, 1963), US Strategic Bombing Survey *The Effects of Strategic Bombing in the German War Economy*, British Bombing Survey Unit *The Strategic Air War against Germany 1939–45*, B. Klein *Germany's Economic Preparations for War* (Cambridge, Mass., 1959), A. S. Milward *The German Economy at War* (London, 1965), M. Kaldor *The German War Economy* in *Essays in Economic Policy*, vol. 2 (London, 1964).

On the workings of the Grand Alliance, H. Feis *Churchill, Roosevelt, Stalin* (Princeton, N.J., 1967), W. H. MacNeill *America, Britain and Russia: their Co-operation and Conflict, 1941–46* (Survey of International Affairs, Royal Institute of International Affairs, London, 1963), S. E. Morison *Strategy and Compromise* (Boston, 1968), G. Hentsch *Staline négotiateur* (Neuchâtel, 1967), J. R. Deane *The Strange Alliance* (New York, 1947), General Sikorski Historical Institute *Documents on Polish-Soviet Relations, 1939–45* (2 vols) (London, 1968), J. A. Wilson *The First Summit* (Argentia).

OCCUPATION AND RESISTANCE

A. M. Meerloo *Total War and the Human Mind* (London, 1944), A. Roberts, ed. *The Strategy of Civilian Defence* (London, 1967), H. Michel, *Les courants de la pensée dans la Résistance* (Paris, 1962) and *Histoire de la Résistance* (3rd ed. Paris, 1962), P. Arnoult *La France sous l'occupation* (Paris, 1959), Vercors *The Battle of the Silence* (London, 1968), B. Ehrlich *Resistance: France 1939–40* (Boston, 1965), C. Bellanger *Presse Clandestine 1940–44* (Paris, 1961), J. Kruuse *Madness at Oradour* (London, 1969), W. Warmbrunn *The Dutch under German Occupation* (Stanford, Calif., 1963), W. B. Maass *The Netherlands at War 1940–45* (London, 1970), J. Bennett *British Broadcasting and the Danish Resistance Movement, 1940–45* (Cambridge, 1966), K. Haukelid *Skis against the Atom* (London, 1954), J. Gorlinski *Poland, S.O.E. and the Allies* (London, 1969), T. Bor-Komorowski *The Secret Army* (London, 1950), F. W. Deakin *The Embattled Mountain* (Yugoslavia) (London, 1971), V. Dedijer *Tito Speaks* (London, 1953), C. M. Woodhouse *Apple of Discord* (Greece) (London, 1948), G. Chandler *The Divided Land* (London, 1959), E. C. W. Myers *Greek Entanglement* (London, 1955), D. G. Kousoulas *Revolution and Defeat* (London, 1965), A. Kédros *La Résistance Grecque 1940–44* (Paris, 1966), E. Schramm von Thadden *Griechenland und die Grossmächte im zweiten Weltkreig* (Wiesbaden, 1955), R. Battaglia *Risorgimento e Resistenza* (Rome, 1964) and *Storia della Resistenza Italiana* (trs. London, 1957), G. Bocca *Storia dell'Italia partigiana* (Bari, 1964), C. Amè *La guerra segreta in Italia, 1940–43* (Rome, 1954), C. F. Dalzell *Mussolini's Enemies: the anti-fascist Resistance* (Princeton, 1961), A. Dallin *German Rule in Russia, 1941–45* (London, 1957), J. A. Armstrong ed. *Soviet Partisans in World War II* (Madison, 1964), W. Strik-Strikfeldt *Against Stalin and Hitler* (London, 1970), A. Oras *Baltic Eclipse* (London, 1948), M. R. D. Foot *S.O.E. in France* (History of the Second World War, UK Civil Series, London, 1966), E. H. Cookridge *Inside S.O.E.* (London, 1966). Also *European Resistance Movements, 1939–45* (Proceedings of the International Conferences on the History of Resistance Movements, Milan 1961 and Oxford 1962) and the periodicals *Revue d'histoire de la deuxième guerre mondiale* and *Esprit de la Résistance*.

ANTI-NAZI GERMANS

H. Rothfels *The Secret Opposition to Hitler* (New York, 1962), G. Ritter *The German Resistance* (London, 1938), F. von Schlabrendorff *The*

Secret War against Hitler (London, 1966), C. Sykes *Troubled Loyalty* (London, 1968), C. Fitzgibbon *The Shirt of Nessus* (London, 1956), W. Hoettl *The Secret Front* (London, 1954), M. Mourin *Les complots contre Hitler* (Paris, 1948), A. Dulles *Germany's Underground* (New York, 1947), T. Prittie *Germans against Hitler* (London, 1964), R. Pechel *Deutscher Widerstand* (Erlenbach, 1947), G. C. Zahn *German Catholics and Hitler's War* (London and New York, 1963) and *In Solitary Witness* (New York, 1964), G. Lewy *The Catholic Church and Nazi Germany* (New York), 1964, A. Leber *Das Gewissen steht auf* (Frankfurt a. M., 1954), E. Zeller *Geist der Freiheit* (Munich, 1952).

PSYCHOLOGICAL WARFARE

The best book so far is E. K. Bramstedt *Goebbels and National Socialist Propaganda 1925–1945* (East Lansing, 1965). See also L. Fraser *Propaganda* (London, 1957), Z. A. B. Zeman *Nazi Propaganda* (London, 1964), D. Lerner ed. *Sykewar: Psychological War against Germany* (New York, 1949), M. Mégret *La guerre psychologique* (Paris, 1963).

FRANCE

G. Warner *Pierre Laval and the Eclipse of France* (London, 1968,) H. Cole *Laval: A Biography* (London, 1963), C. M. de la Gorce *La république et son armée* (Paris, 1963), G. Chapman *Why France Collapsed* (London, 1968), M. Bloch *L'étrange défaite* (Paris, 1946), A. Beaufre *1940: the Fall of France* (London, 1967), P. Stehlin *Témoignage pour l'histoire* (Paris, 1964), N. Jucker *Curfew in Paris* (London, 1960), A. Werth *France 1940–45* (London, 1956), A. D. Hytier *Two Years of French Foreign Policy, Vichy: 1940–42* (Geneva, 1958), F. Mauriac *Cahiers Noirs* (London, 1944), P. Novick *The Resistance versus Vichy* (London, 1968), E. d'Astier *De la Chute à la libération de Paris, 24 août 1944* (Paris, 1965), D. G. Anglin *The St Pierre and Miquelon Affair of 1941* (Toronto, 1966), R. Aron *De Gaulle before Paris* (London, 1962), A. W. De Porte *De Gaulle's Foreign Policy, 1944–46* (Cambridge, Mass., 1962). And see under Occupation and Resistance.

GREAT BRITAIN

R. M. Titmuss *Problems of Social Policy* (History of the Second World War, UK Civil Series, 1950) and *Essays on The Welfare State*

(London, 1958), A. Bullock *The Life and Times of Ernest Bevin*, vol. 2 (London, 1967), D. N. Chester, ed. *Lessons of the British War Economy* (London, 1951), W. K. Hancock and M. Gowing *The British War Economy* (History of the Second World War, UK Civil Series, 1948), T. H. O'Brien *Civil Defence* (History of the Second World War, UK Civil Series, 1955), H. M. D. Parker *Manpower* (History of the Second World War, UK Civil Series, 1957), C. B. A. Behrens *The Merchant Navy and the Demands of War* (History of the Second World War, UK Civil Series, 1955), A. J. Youngson *The British Economy, 1920–1957* (London, 1960), H. D. Henderson *The Inter-war Years and Other Papers* (Oxford, 1955), M. Bruce *The Coming of the Welfare State* (London, 1968), S. Ferguson and H. Fitzgerald *Studies in the Social Services* (History of the Second World War, UK Civil Series, 1954), A. Marwick *Britain in the Century of Total War* (London, 1968), L. Woodward *British Foreign Policy during the Second World War* (History of the Second World War, UK Civil Series, 1962).

USA

W. L. Langer and S. E. Gleason *The Challenge to Isolation* and *The Undeclared War* (Council for Foreign Relations, London, and New York, 1952–3), W. A. Williams *The Tragedy of American Diplomacy* (New York, 1966), C. A. Beard *President Roosevelt and the Coming of War* (New Haven, 1946) and *American Foreign Policy in the Making, 1932–40* (New Haven, 1948), E. E. Robinson *The Roosevelt Leadership 1933–45* (New York, 1955), A. A. Offner *American Appeasement* (Cambridge, Mass., 1969), C. C. Tansill *Back Door to War: The Roosevelt Foreign Policy 1933–41* (Chicago, 1952), J. M. Burns *Roosevelt: The Soldier of Fortune 1940–1945* (London, 1971), P. Schroeder *The Axis Alliance and American-Japanese Relations* (Ithaca, N.Y., 1958), S. Friedländer *Prelude to Disaster: Hitler and the United States, 1939–41* (London, 1967), R. A. Divine *The Reluctant Belligerent* (New York, 1965) and *Roosevelt and World War II* (Baltimore, 1970), D. Drummond *The Passing of American Neutrality* (Ann Arbor, 1955), G. C. Smith *American Diplomacy during World War II* (New York, 1965), G. Kolko *The Politics of War: Allied Diplomacy and the World Crisis of 1943–45* (London, 1969), W. L. Langer *Our Vichy Gamble* (New York, 1966), R. W. Leopold *The Growth of American Foreign Policy* (New York, 1962), K. S. Davis *The American Experience of War* (London, 1970), essays in B. J. Bernstein, ed. *Towards a New Past* (London, 1970).

USSR

N. Jasny *Soviet Industrialization, 1928–52* (Chicago, 1961), M. Dobb *Soviet Economic Development since 1917* (London, 1966), A. G. Mazour *Soviet Economic Development* (New York, 1968), G. Nutter *Growth of Industrial Production in the Soviet Union* (Princeton, 1962), S. N. Prokopovich *Histoire économique de l'URSS* (Paris, 1961), V. Conolly *Beyond the Urals* (London, 1967), N. A. Voznesensky *The Economy of the USSR in the Period of the Patriotic War* (Moscow, 1948), C. E. Black, ed. *The Transformation of Russian Society* (Cambridge, Mass., 1960), M. Fainsod *Smolensk Under Soviet Rule* (London, 1959), E. H. Carr *German-Soviet Relations between the two World Wars* (London, 1952), D. J. Dallin *Soviet Foreign Policy, 1939–42* (New Haven, 1945), A. Werth *Russia at War, 1941–45* (London, 1964), G. Fischer *Soviet Opposition to Stalin* (Cambridge, Mass., 1952), M. Djilas *Conversations with Stalin* (New York, 1962), R. Kolkowicz *The Soviet Military and the Communist Party* (Princeton, 1967), J. Erickson *The Soviet High Command: a Military-Political History 1918–1941* (London, 1962), M. Mackintosh *Juggernaut: a History of the Soviet Armed Forces*.

AUTOBIOGRAPHY

Winston Churchill *The History of the Second World War* (6 vols.) (London, 1951–4) is an idiosyncratic blend of the personal and the cosmic, of military and diplomatic history and autobiography. Charles de Gaulle *War Memoirs* (3 vols., with separate documents, London, 1955), is uniquely interesting as well as being among the greatest literary memorials of the war. Next to these in interest are R. Sherwood *The White House Papers of Harry Hopkins* (London, 1948), Henry L. Stimson and McGeorge Bundy *On Active Service in Peace and War* (New York, 1947), C. Hull *The Memoirs of Cordell Hull* (New York, 1948), E. Kordt *Nicht aus den Akten* (Stuttgart, 1950), U. von Hassell *The von Hassell Diaries* (London, 1948), P. Schmidt *Hitler's Interpreter* (London, 1951), R. G. Vansittart *The Mist Procession* (London, 1958). But this is a category of even more boundless proliferation than any other. The eminent have with few exceptions, but varying success, laboured to retrace events or justify their parts in them. The catalogue is too long to be useful here.

Books: the Eastern Hemisphere

This section compiled by D. E. T. Luard

It is one of the joys of Guy Wint's superbly spare style of writing that his texts are never cluttered with innumerable footnotes giving references to doubtfully relevant learned sources for every statement made. His own reading in this field was, none the less, very wide and it may be that, if he had not tragically died before this book was completed, he would have added a short booklist at the end, or possibly even separate lists for each chapter. In any case, for the sake of those readers who may be inspired by the book to explore in greater detail some of the subjects it has opened up, these notes on further reading may prove useful.

PART 1

On the background of the differing responses of China and Japan to the incursions of the West, described in the first chapters of this book, a good deal has been written. So far as China is concerned, the longest and most complete account, still very readable, is contained in H. B. Morse's *The International Relations of the Chinese Empire* (London, 1910–18), which is in three volumes and covers Chinese relations with the outside world until the fall of the empire in 1911. A more succinct account of the same period, including more analysis of events within China itself, is given in E. R. Hughes's *The Invasion of China by the Western World* (London, 1937). A superb, first-hand picture of the reaction of Chinese officials and others to the problems created by the West, and their image of the western world, is given in *China's Response to the West* edited by J. K. Fairbank, and S. Y. Teng (Cambridge, 1954). A somewhat similar book, covering a longer period, also containing original texts, is that edited by R. Pelissier, *Awakening of China, 1783–1949* (New York, 1967).

Japan's response to a similar stimulus is described in a number of books on modern Japan. Richard Storry's admirable *A History of Modern Japan* (London, 1960) contains a highly readable account of the dynamic reaction of Japan to its first contacts with the West in the middle of the last century. A longer perspective is given in I. Nish's *The Story of Japan* (London, 1968), an elegant and scholarly account of Japan's history; and in M. Hurlimann and F. King's *Japan* (London, 1970).

On the international political developments in the Far East from the middle of the nineteenth century to the 1930's, the best account is still Geoffrey Hudson's brilliantly written *The Far East in World Politics* (London, 1945). Other books, covering roughly the same period, less readable but giving rather more detail is N. Peffer's *The Far East: A Modern History* (Ann Arbor, 1958) and *Far Eastern International Relations* (Boston, 1931) by H. B. Morse and F. H. McNair.

China's history in the years before the Sino-Japanese War began is only rather patchily covered in works in English. There have been a spate of excellent books about the growth of the Chinese Communist Party and its early struggles, of which B. Schwarz's *Chinese Communism and the Rise of Mao* (Harvard, 1952) and Conrad Brandt's *Stalin's Failure in China, 1924–27* (Oxford, 1958) are among the best. A vivid, if highly partisan (that is, Trotskyist), view of this period is given in A. Isaac's *The Tragedy of the Chinese Revolution* of which the first edition appeared in 1938, full of revolutionary fire, and a second, somewhat watered-down version in 1951 (Stanford, Calif.). Another work of considerable historic interest is that of M. N. Roy, who was the Comintern representative in China at this time, *Revolution in China* (Calcutta, 1951). The best accounts of life in the communist-controlled areas of China at the time, are given in Edgar Snow's *Red Star Over China* (London, 1937) and Simone de Beauvoir's *The Long March* (London, 1958).

There are, so far as I know, no other books in English describing the general situation in China at the period covered by Guy Wint's chapter 4. A good general work is O. E. Chubb's *Twentieth Century China* (New York, 1966) which gives some account of China under the Nationalist Government, including both debits and credits. A fascinating picture of Japanese rule in Manchuria is given in the book by Pu-Hi, the last Chinese Emperor, later placed on the throne of Manchuria by Japan, quoted several times by Guy Wint: *From Emperor to Citizen* (Peking, 1965). Life in Peking in this period is described in G. N. Kates's *The Years that were Fat: Peking 1933–40* (New York, 1952). Finally, a readable, somewhat journalistic general picture of Far Eastern politics in the late 1930s is given in John Gunther's *Inside Asia* (New York, 1939).

On the Manchurian 'incident', and the West's response to it, two books giving very different view-points are W. W. Willoughby's *The Sino-Japanese Controversy and the League of Nations* (Baltimore, 1935), which exposes convincingly the weakness and ambiguity of the western reaction to Japan's encroachment and the total ineffectualness of the measures taken by the League. A far more lenient view of western actions, and especially British action, is taken in R. Basset's *Democracy and Foreign Policy* (London, 1952), which is something like an apologia for the passivity of western governments in the face of the Japanese attack. An account of US policy during this period is contained in Dorothy Borg's two books *American Policy and the Chinese Revolution, 1925–28* (New York, 1947) and *The US and the Far Eastern Crisis of 1933–38* (Cambridge, 1964). J. W. Christopher's *Conflict in the Far East, American Diplomacy of China 1928–33* (Liden, 1950) fills the gap between these two books. US policy at a somewhat later stage is covered in T. A. Brisson's *American Policy in the Far East, 1931–40* (New York, 1941) and in C. A. Beard's classic *President Roosevelt and the Coming of the War, 1941: a Study of Appearances and Realities* (Yale, 1945).

On Japan's policy at this time, and especially the growth of Japanese militarism, there are a number of books: Y. C. Maxon's *Control of Japan's Foreign Policy, a Study of Civil-Military Rivalry, 1930–45* gives a brilliant account of the factional fights within the Japanese government, and especially the struggle between the Ministry of Foreign Affairs and the military for the control of Japanese foreign policy during this period, showing very clearly the responsibility of the armed forces for expanding and intensifying Japan's ambitions in the outside world, and often, as in Manchuria and North China, pursuing virtually a foreign policy of their own. R. Butow's *Tojo and the Coming of the War* (Princeton, 1961) looks at the same period, examining especially the sinister role of Marshal Tojo in these events. Other books on Japanese militarism are R. Storry's *The Double Patriots* (London, 1957), H. Lory's *Japan's Military Masters* (New York, 1943) and J. M. Maki's *Japanese Militarism: its Cause and Cure* (New York, 1945).

PART 2

On Japanese actions in China after 1931 T. A. Brisson's *Japan in China* (New York, 1938) is valuable. D. J. Lu's *From the Marco Polo Bridge to Pearl Harbor* (Washington, 1961) describes Japanese policy and actions during the period between the outbreak of full-scale war in China in 1937 to the attack on Pearl Harbor in 1941; and some of the same ground is covered in more journalistic style in H. S. Quigley's *Far Eastern War 1937–41* (Boston, 1942). A. N. Young's *China and the Helping Hand* (Harvard, 1963) gives a detailed account of US policy in assisting China during this period. An account of the Burma Road and the diplomatic and military discussions which surrounded it, is given in *Behind the Burma Road* by W. R. Peers and D. Brelis.

There are a number of books which describe the diplomatic man-oeuverings preceeding the Japanese attack on Pearl Harbor. Among the best of these are P. W. Schroeder's *The Axis Alliance and Japanese-American Relations* (New York, 1958) and F. W. Ikle's *German-Japanese Relations, 1936–40* (New York, 1956). For those who are prepared to delve into more voluminous official records there are *The US Department of State Papers Relating to the Foreign Relations of the US: Japan 1931–41* (Washington, 1943); *The Archives of the Japanese Ministry of Foreign Affairs, 1868–1945*, which were published in Washington in 1954; and the relevant volume of the British Official Documents. (The British Official Documents are in any case now open until 1941).

On Pearl Harbor, its approach and its aftermath there are a number of books. Of special interest is a work by Joseph C. Grew, US Ambassador in Japan at the time of Pearl Harbor and later Under Secretary of State, *Ten Years in Japan* (New York, 1944) and that of Sir Robert Craigie, British Ambassador at the same time, *Behind the Japanese March* (London, 1946). A straight-forward account of the diplomatic history preceding Pearl Harbor is given in H. Feis's book *The Road to Pearl Harbor* the first of a series of books by this author on diplomatic history in the period from the late 1930s to the late 1940s.

PART 3

A basic source book for the war itself is of course Churchill's *History of the Second World War*. All the volumes contain some material regarding to the Far East, but perhaps the most relevant are volume III *The Grand Alliance* and volume VI, *Triumph and Tragedy*. Even larger in scale is *The Official British History of the Second World War* of which the five volumes on *The War against Japan* (London, 1957–69) are by S. W. Kirby. There is also J. Ehrman's *Grand Strategy, October 1944–August 1945* (London, 1956) which is volume VI of the British official history and deals with the discussion and diplomatic dealings concerning the war strategy to be adopted in the Far East. Other military histories are the volume produced by C. Romanus and R. Sunderland, for the US Department of the Army, which gives a detailed account of US Army activities in China, Burma and India (the titles of the volumes are *Stilwell's Mission to China, Stilwell's Command Problems* and *Time runs out in CBI*); and the corresponding volumes on the Army and

Air Forces in World War II by W. L. Craven and J. L. Cate (Chicago, 1958). On the British side of the war an interesting account is contained in Field Marshal Slim's *Defeat into Victory* (New York, 1961). Finally the official British diplomatic history of the period is contained in L. Woodward's *British Foreign Policy in the Second World War* (London, 1962).

For those who want something rather more condensed, a good general military history is given in B. Collier's *The War in the Far East, 1941–45* (London, 1969). There are a considerable number of books on individual campaigns and battles. Among the best and most famous is Spencer Chapman's *The Jungle is Neutral* (London, 1949) about the campaign in Malaya. The battle for Singapore is described in an English version *Singapore: The Battle that Changed the World* (London, 1965). and in a Japanese version by the Chief of Operations and Planning Staff of the Japanese 25th Army who designed the Japanese operation, M. Tsuji's *Singapore, the Japanese Version* (London, 1968). The American campaign in Guadalcanal is vividly depicted in a book by Sam Griffith, a Brigadier in the US Marine Corps, *The Battle for Gaudalcanal* (New York, 1963).

Of the struggle in other parts of S. E. Asia, A. W. H. Harterdorp's *Japanese Occupation of the Philippines* (Manila, 1967) based on personal experiences in a Japanese prisoners-of-war camp and many personal interviews, describes Japanese conduct in that country. *Japanese Military Administration in Indonesia* (Yale, 1965) gives an account from Japanese documents of the way that country was administered. On the battles in Burma and China the *Stilwell Papers* (New York, 1948), which were published by his widow after his death, presents General Stilwell's own justification of his activities in the Far East sector. M. Collis's *Last and First in Burma, 1941–48* (London, 1956) is more concerned with political and social developments in that country during and after the war. On the attitude of many educated Burmese to the Japanese conquest, BaMaw's *Breakthrough in Burma,* quoted a number of times by Guy Wint in this book, is especially enlightening; as is the book written by U Nu *Burma under the Japanese* (New York, 1954). A. Gilchrist's *Bangkok, Top Secret* (London, 1970) provides an exciting account by a British Army officer of S.O.E. activities in Japanese-occupied Siam. The struggle for India, and the real threat that developed to that country for a time, is described in A. J. Barker's *The March on Delhi* (London, 1963). Two first-class books presenting the Indian picture, are B. R. Nanda's *Mahatma Gandhi* (London, 1958) quoted by Guy Wint, and Penderel Morn's *Gandhi and Modern India* (London,

1968), both of which include accounts of the attitude of Gandhi and other Indian leaders to the war.

The naval war in the Pacific is described in two excellent books by S. E. Morison, the great American historian, *Two-Ocean War* and *The Rising Sun in the Pacific* (Boston, 1948). There are also two interesting books by Japanese writers on the naval war: M. Ito's *The End of the Imperial Japanese Navy* (London, 1962) and M. Fuchida and M. Okumiya's *Midway: The Battle that Doomed Japan*. Two other interesting books presenting the war through their eyes, are: T. Kase's *Eclipse of the Rising Sun* (London, 1951) filling a diary of the reactions of a Japanese to his war-time experiences and increasing disillusion with his government, and J. D. Potter's *Admiral of the Pacific* (London, 1965), a biography of Admiral Yamamoto.

The diplomatic history of the war period, including relations between Japan and Germany and between Japan and the Soviet Union (in the curious situation when Germany and Japan were allies, though one was linked in deadly combat with the Soviet Union, while the other remained in diplomatic relations with her) has been the subject of several works. One of the best is E. L. Presseisen's *Germany and Japan, A Study in Totalitarian Diplomacy* (The Hague, 1958). The same theme is studied over a much shorter period (1941–2) in J. M. Meskill's *Hitler and Japan: The Hollow Alliance* (New York, 1966). H. von Dirksen's *Moscow, Tokyo, London* (Oklahoma, 1952) includes an account of some of the diplomatic complexities of this period. Also of some interest is *Stalin's Correspondence with Churchill, Attlee, Roosevelt and Truman* published in Moscow in 1957.

Accounts of Japan's Empire in the Far East and the way she governed it are contained in F. C. Jones's *Japan's New Order in East Asia, 1937–45* (London, 1954). And a good general account of developments in the Far East throughout the whole of this period is contained in a book by the same author, together with H. Burton and B. R. Pearn, produced by Chatham House, *The Far East, 1942–46* (London, 1955).

PART 4

On the diplomatic to-ings and fro-ings in the year or two before the defeat of Japan there is now an enormous volume of material. There are first a large assembly of the memoirs and papers of those who were involved. These include *The Memoirs of Cordell Hull* (New York, 1948); D. W. Leahy's *I Was There, A Personal Story of the Chief of Staff to Presidents Roosevelt and Truman* (New York, 1950); James Forrestal's

The Forrestal Diaries (New York, 1951); Roosevelt's *Victory and the Threshold of Peace; The Collected Papers of FDR, 1944–45* (New York, 1950); R. E. Sherwood's *Roosevelt and Hopkins* (New York, 1948); McArthur's *Reminiscences* (New York, 1964) and Truman's *Memoirs* – volume I (which includes his account of the decision to use the atomic bomb).

On the British side, besides the books of Churchill and Slim already mentioned, there is the second volume of Eden's autobiography *Memoirs* (London, 1960–65).

Among Chinese books Chiang Kai-shek *China's Destiny* (London, 1947) is in a sense the official bible of KMT policy towards the end of the war (it was written in 1942–3) and his *Summing up at 70* is a more personal review of his life and political aims. There are also two interesting memoirs by Japanese statesmen of this period, both (inevitably) among the doves within the Japanese government, describing their effort to secure peace: *The Case of Japan* (New York, 1956) by Shigenori Togo, who was the Japanese Foreign Minister towards the end of the war; and *Japan and Her Destiny: My Struggle for Peace* (New York, 1958) by M. Shigemitsu.

On the closing period of the war, and especially on the thinking behind the decision to use the atomic bomb, two differing views are put forward in H. Feis's *Japan Subdued, The Atomic Bomb and the End of the War in the Pacific* (Princeton, 1961), which stresses that the bomb was used for a strictly military purpose and with the minimum loss of life which it was thought was necessary to bring about a Japanese surrender; and G. Alperovitz's *American Diplomacy: Hiroshima and Potsdam* (London, 1966) which seeks to show that an important motive in the use of the bomb was to improve US bargaining power in dealing with the Russians in Europe and elsewhere. *Behind Japan's Surrender* by L. Brooks (New York, 1968) looks at the same events from the Japanese side, describing the deliberations in the Japanese capital after the bomb had been dropped and its effect in bringing about the decision to surrender.

Maps

LIMITS OF GERMAN, JAPANESE AND ITALIAN
DOMINANCE 1934 - 1944

GREENLAND

ICELAND

Murmansk

SWEDEN

Leningrad
●Moscow

USSR

Stalingrad

ANADA

Montreal

UNITED
KINGDOM

UNITED
STATES

New York
Washington

Casablanca

IRAN
Basra

MEXICO

Atlantic

Cairo

WEST
INDIES

FRENCH
W. AFRICA

VEN.

GUIANAS

NIG.

COL.

SUDAN

FR. EQ. AFRIC.

Accra

BELG.
CONG.

KENYA
TANGANYIKA

EQUADOR

PERU

BRAZIL

Natal

BOL.

Ocean

ANGOLA

Madagascar

Rio de Janeiro

S.W.
AFRICA

CHILE

ARGENTINA

Cape
Town

SOUTH
AFRICA

Buenos
Aires

~ARTHUR BANKS~

WORLD POWER 1949

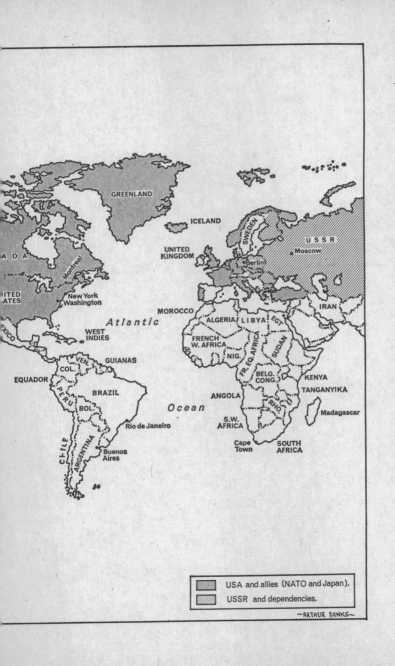

GREENLAND

ICELAND

SWEDEN

U S S R

Moscow

UNITED
KINGDOM

Berlin

A D A

Montreal

ITED
ATES

New York
Washington

IRAN

Atlantic

MOROCCO

ALGERIA LIBYA EGY.

XICO

WEST
INDIES

FRENCH
W. AFRICA

FR. EQ. AFRICA

SUDAN

VEN.

GUIANAS

COL.

NIG.

EQUADOR

PERU

BRAZIL

BOL.

Ocean

BELG.
CONG.

KENYA

ANGOLA

TANGANYIKA

RHO.

Madagascar

Rio de Janeiro

S.W.
AFRICA

CHILE

ARGENTINA

Buenos
Aires

Cape
Town

SOUTH
AFRICA

| | USA and allies (NATO and Japan). |
| | USSR and dependencies. |

~ARTHUR BANKS~

Index

Sub-entries are in chronological order. Italic numbers refer to the main entry.

Index

MORE ABOUT PENGUINS
AND PELICANS

Penguinews, which appears every month, contains details of all the new books issued by Penguins as they are published. From time to time it is supplemented by the *Penguin Stock List*, which contains around 5,000 titles.

A specimen copy of *Penguinews* will be sent to you free on request. Please write to Dept EP, Penguin Books Ltd, Harmondsworth, Middlesex, for your copy.

In the U.S.A.: For a complete list of books available from Penguins in the United States write to Dept CS, Penguin Books, 625 Madison Avenue, New York, New York 10022.

In Canada: For a complete list of books available from Penguins in Canada write to Penguin Books Canada Ltd, 2801 John Street, Markham, Ontario L3R 1B4.

A. J. P. Taylor

THE FIRST WORLD WAR

AN ILLUSTRATED HISTORY

For four years, while statesmen and generals blundered, the massed armies of Europe writhed in a festival of mud and blood. All the madness, massacres and mutinies of the foulest war in history are brought home here by action pictures of the day and the text of an uncompromising historian.

THE WAR LORDS

The Second World War was remarkable in that it produced five great war leaders who dominated their countries' political and military affairs. Most modern wars have been run by committees and rival authorities: the Second World War was uniquely different. Once the British and French governments had declared war on Germany, virtually every decision of the war was made by one of these five men, except when Japan's chaotic anarchy intervened.

Five of the lectures in this book are biographical studies of the five War Lords: the sixth explains why there was no such man in Japan.

Alistair Horne

THE PRICE OF GLORY
Verdun 1916

Verdun was the battle which lasted ten months; the battle in which at least 700,000 men fell, along a front of fifteen miles; the battle whose aim was less to defeat the enemy than to bleed him to death; the battle whose once fertile terrain is even now 'the nearest thing to desert in Europe'. This profoundly moving study shows it to be also the key to an understanding of the First World War.

'It has almost every merit . . . Mr Horne sorts out complicated issues with the greatest clarity. He has a splendid gift for depicting individuals'—A. J. P. Taylor in the *Observer* (London)

TO LOSE A BATTLE
France 1940

'One last battle' Hitler demanded in *Mein Kampf* 'with France'. And in 1940 he fought and won it in six weeks of lightning warfare, using combined operations techniques that sent the French armies reeling. Alistair Horne tells the blow-by-blow story of the battle with all the subtlety and compulsion of a novel and 'all the formal excellences of a work of art'.

A SAVAGE WAR OF PEACE
Algeria 1954-1962

'Occasionally an epic subject encounters a fine historian. This is the case with the Algerian war and Mr Horne. The result is a book of compelling power, written with compassion and understanding . . . It has the poetic sense of place without which no great work of history can be written' – Raymond Carr

'Mr Alistair Horne is one of the best writers of history in the English-speaking world' – C. P. Snow